PORTRAIT OF A PARTY

Portrait of a Party

The Conservative Party in Britain 1918–1945

STUART BALL

OXFORD
UNIVERSITY PRESS

OXFORD
UNIVERSITY PRESS

Great Clarendon Street, Oxford, OX2 6DP,
United Kingdom

Oxford University Press is a department of the University of Oxford.
It furthers the University's objective of excellence in research, scholarship,
and education by publishing worldwide. Oxford is a registered trade mark of
Oxford University Press in the UK and in certain other countries

© Stuart Ball 2013

The moral rights of the author have been asserted

First Edition published in 2013

Impression: 1

All rights reserved. No part of this publication may be reproduced, stored in
a retrieval system, or transmitted, in any form or by any means, without the
prior permission in writing of Oxford University Press, or as expressly permitted
by law, by licence, or under terms agreed with the appropriate reprographics
rights organization. Enquiries concerning reproduction outside the scope of the
above should be sent to the Rights Department, Oxford University Press, at the
address above

You must not circulate this work in any other form
and you must impose this same condition on any acquirer

British Library Cataloguing in Publication Data

Data available

ISBN 978–0–19–966798–7

Printed in Great Britain by the
MPG Printgroup, UK

Links to third party websites are provided by Oxford in good faith and
for information only. Oxford disclaims any responsibility for the materials
contained in any third party website referenced in this work

For my wonderful wife, Gilly, without whom this book could never have been written

Preface and acknowledgements

This project has been under way for many years; indeed, I first conceived it in the early 1980s, before completing my doctoral thesis. The research materials have been gathered since then, and much of the constituency research in particular was undertaken in the 1980s; for this reason, a number of the primary sources are no longer at the locations where they were originally seen. In the course of this long journey, I have incurred many debts, and it is a great pleasure to be able to acknowledge them here. I am most grateful to Alistair Cooke (now Lord Lexden), who for many years has been the first port of call for all historians of the Conservative Party, originally at the Research Department at Central Office and latterly as advisor to the Conservative Party Archive Trust. The Conservative Party Archive itself is a remarkable collection of the richest resources, and is of inestimable importance to any political history of modern Britain; the Trustees who voluntarily support it, under the chairmanship of Dr Philip Brown, are deserving of all our thanks and appreciation. The many visits that I have made to the Archive have been made easy and pleasurable by its fortunate series of excellent archivists. The project began, and much of the initial work was done, during the tenure of Sarah Street; since then, it has been facilitated by her successors, Martin Maw, Jill Spellman, Emily Tarrant, and particularly the present archivist, Jeremy McIlwaine.

I am glad to have this opportunity to thank Colin Harris and Godfrey Waller (now retired), who have presided over the modern manuscript reading rooms at the Bodleian Library and Cambridge University Library respectively for most of my working life, and whose unfailing courtesy and helpfulness has made researching there a pleasure; I am also grateful to Helen Langley of the Bodleian Library for help and guidance on many occasions. To the staff of these institutions, and of Churchill College Archives Centre, the Parliamentary Archives, the British Library, Birmingham University Library, and the many other libraries and record offices which I have visited over the years, I express my sincere thanks for their assistance and high level of professionalism. The research into the constituency records would have been impossible without the generous welcome afforded by local Conservative Party agents (sadly, now much fewer in number than when I began visiting association offices in the early 1980s), officers and members. I particularly appreciate their kindness on a number of occasions in allowing me to borrow the minute books to work on in Leicester. Priscilla Baines of the History of Parliament most generously gave me a copy of her transcripts of Josiah Wedgwood's original questionnaires to MPs in the 1930s, and Peter Catterall kindly provided information on Nonconformist MPs.

It is a matter of great sadness to me that John Ramsden, the pre-eminent historian of the twentieth-century Conservative Party, died tragically early, so that I am unable to show him the finished book and express my thanks for the friendship and encouragement so generously given over many years. Although I did not know him as well, like all of those who work in this field, I also greatly miss the lively presence of Ewen Green. I am grateful to Edward Baldwin (Earl Baldwin of Bewdley), Nick Crowson, Mark Garnett, Peter Hennessy, Christine Jesman and Philip Williamson for their comments and assistance. Parts of Chapter 1 have been given as papers at the 'British History 1815–1945' seminar at the Institute of Historical Research in November 2008, the 'Conservatism Today and Yesterday' conference at Churchill College, University of Cambridge, in November 2010, the Political Studies Association conference in April 2011, and the Modern History Research Seminar at the University of Bradford in November 2011, and has benefited from the ensuing discussion on these occasions. I have also had stimulating discussions on various points with my past and present research students who have been working in related areas: Harry Bennett, Ian Cawood, Matthew Coutts, Gavin Freeman, Robert Walsha, and Alun Wyburn-Powell.

I am grateful to my colleagues in the School of Historical Studies (and previously in the Department of History) at the University of Leicester for their goodwill and the maintenance of a pleasant collegial spirit, and in particular to Norman Housley, Keith Snell, and Roey Sweet for their encouragement and support. I would like to express my appreciation to the University of Leicester for the benefit of regular periods of study leave, and for some assistance in the last few years from the School of Historical Studies staff travel fund. The project has also benefited from the award of an additional semester under the AHRC research leave scheme, and from small grants in aid of research travel expenses from the British Academy on two occasions in the 1980s and again in 2005, and I record my thanks to both institutions. I am also grateful to Christopher Wheeler, and previously Seth Cayley and Rupert Cousens, of Oxford University Press for their interest in, and encouragement of, this project; to Emma Barber and Cathryn Steele for overseeing production, Elizabeth Stone for copy-editing, and Francis Eaves for proof-checking.

I gratefully acknowledge the permission of the Conservative Party, the Scottish Conservative and Unionist Party, the 1922 Committee, and the many constituency Conservative associations, to quote from unpublished documents in their copyright. I am grateful to the following for their kind permission to make quotations from documents in their care or ownership: Atholl Estates, Blair Castle; Berkshire Record Office; Bodleian Library; British Library; Cadbury Research Library, Special Collections, University of Birmingham; Cambridge University Library; Carmarthenshire Archive Service; the Master and Fellows of Churchill College, Cambridge; Durham County Record Office; East Sussex Record Office; Edinburgh City Archives; Kent History & Library Centre; Liverpool Record Office; London School of Economics & Political Science Library; Modern Records Centre, University of Warwick; National Library of Australia; the Trustees of the National Library of Scotland; National Library of Wales/Llyfrgell Genedlaethol Cymru; Parliamentary Archives; Shropshire Archives; Southwark Local History Library; the Master and Fellows of Trinity College, Cambridge; University of Southampton Library; University of Dundee Archives. I also wish to acknowledge and thank the document and copyright owners for permission to make quotations from the following collections: Edward Anderson (Templewood MSS); Lady Avon (Avon MSS); Dickson Middleton C.A. (Steel-Maitland MSS); Sir John Gilmour (Gilmour MSS); David Greenslade (Ward MSS); the Earl of Halifax (Halifax MSS); Viscount Hanworth (Hanworth MSS); Jeremy Hogg (Gwynne MSS); Knebworth Estates (Lytton MSS); the Marquis of Londonderry (Londonderry MSS); Sarah Morrison (Long MSS); the Countess Mountbatten of Burma (Brabourne MSS); Jonathan Peto (Peto MSS); the Earl of Ronaldshay (Zetland MSS); the Marquis of Salisbury (Salisbury MSS); the Earl of Selborne (Selborne and Wolmer MSS); Edward York (York MSS). I have sought to contact the copyright owners of the other quotations made, but it has either not been possible to trace the current owner, or no response was received to letters and emails sent, and I apologise here to any copyright owner whom it has not been possible to consult.

The electoral analysis in Chapter 2 has made use of two databases of census statistics, funded by the Economic & Social Research Council and the Leverhulme Trust, and deposited at the UK Data Archive, with grateful acknowledgement to the funding bodies, the UK Data Archive, and the copyright holders: Study Number 4559 (occupation statistics), H. R. Southall (University of Portsmouth), D. Dorling, E. M. Garrett (University of Sheffield), P. Ell (Queen's University of Belfast), D. A. Gatley (University of Staffordshire), D.R. Gilbert (University of London), C. Lee (University of Aberdeen), A. Reid (University of Cambridge), and M. Woollard (University of Essex); Study Number 4560 (parish-level population statistics), H. R. Southall, I. Gregory (University of Portsmouth), P. Ell (Queen's University of Belfast), and D.A. Gatley (University of Staffordshire). The original data creators, depositors, copyright holders, the funders of the data collections and the UK Data Archive bear no responsibility for their further analysis or interpretation. I have also benefited from drawing on the statistical analysis of Conservative MPs in J. M. McEwen's doctoral thesis of 1959, which provided the data for some of the tables in Chapter 5.

My greatest debts I have left to last, for they stand above all others. My former colleague, Graham Smith, has with the greatest generosity given much time to the electoral analysis in Chapter 2, which could not have been accomplished without his programming expertise and, most of all, undertaking of the complex and laborious linkage of the census and electoral data. I am grateful to my sons, Alastair and Duncan, for the interest they have taken in this project, which is even older than they are. I owe by far the most to the most important person in my life—my wife, Gilly, whose love, unstinting support and constant encouragement has made this project possible, and without whom it would never have been completed. To dedicate this book to her with all of my love and thanks is only the smallest token of my heartfelt gratitude and appreciation.

Stuart Ball

Contents

List of Tables	xii
Abbreviations	xiv
Introduction: The Portrait of a Party	1
1. Conservatism: Principles and Temperament	9
2. The Public: Appeal and Support	82
3. The Constituency Associations: Members and Activities	146
4. The National Union and the Central Office: Representation and Organization	241
5. The Parliamentary Party: Composition and Dissent	307
6. Ministers: Juniors and Cabinet	391
7. Leaders: Authority and Crises	450
Conclusion: Effectiveness and Nature	507
Appendix 1: Conservative Party Office-Holders 1918–1945	523
Appendix 2: The Economic and Social Analysis of Conservative Electoral Support	526
Appendix 3: The Regional Analysis of Conservative Electoral Support	533
Appendix 4: Conservative Party National Expenditure 1925–1945	535
Bibliography	541
Index	571

List of Tables

2.1	Conservative Party overall performance in general elections 1918–1945	103
2.2	Constituencies not contested by the Conservative Party 1918–1945	103
2.3	The representation of the university seats 1918–1945	105
2.4	Plural voters and Conservative electoral support	105
2.5	The middle class and Conservative electoral support: (i) an overview of England and Wales	109
2.6	The middle class and Conservative electoral support: (ii) a detailed analysis of London and the large cities in England	110
2.7	The economic and social profile of Conservative electoral support	112
2.8	The economic and social profile of the larger English cities	115
2.9	The working class and Conservative electoral support	117
2.10	The gender gap and Conservative electoral support	118
2.11	The regional pattern of Conservative electoral support	122
2.12	Conservative safe constituencies	123
2.13	Unopposed returns of Conservative MPs 1918–1935	124
2.14	Conservative marginal constituencies 1922–1935	126
2.15	Three-way and two-way 'major party' contests 1922–1931	127
2.16	Patterns of Conservative contests in the 1918 general election	128
2.17	The economic and social profile of the Conservative gains and losses in the general election of 1922	129
2.18	The challengers in the Conservative-held constituencies 1922–1929	131
2.19	Nonconformity and Conservative electoral support	132
2.20	The economic and social profile of the Conservative gains and losses in the general election of 1923	134
2.21	The regional pattern of Conservative gains in the general election of 1924	135
2.22	The economic and social profile of Conservative gains in the general election of 1924	135
2.23	The regional pattern of Conservative gains in the general election of 1929	137
2.24	The economic and social profile of Conservative losses in the general election of 1929	138
2.25	Conservative gains in the general election of 1931	140
2.26	The economic and social profile of Conservative gains in the general election of 1931	140
2.27	The economic and social profile of Conservative losses in the general election of 1935	143
2.28	Conservative performance in the 1945 general election	144

List of Tables

3.1	Estimate of Conservative Party membership 1919–1939	166
3.2	Constituency 'round-robin' resolutions sent to all other constituencies	220
3.3	Political resolutions passed by the sample of constituency associations 1919–1939	224
4.1	Political resolutions debated at the Central Council 1919–1939	251
4.2	Executive Committee: composition and attendance 1919–1939	266
4.3	Number of Central Office and Area Office staff	283
4.4	Summary of Conservative Party national income and expenditure	299
5.1	Occupational background of Conservative MPs	310
5.2	Conservative MPs closely related to the peerage (by blood or marriage)	312
5.3	Public school education of Conservative MPs	313
5.4	University education of Conservative MPs	313
5.5	Religion of Conservative MPs in England	315
5.6	Age profile of Conservative MPs	316
5.7	Departure and retirement of Conservative MPs	317
5.8	Continuity and political experience of Conservative MPs	318
5.9	Length of service and honours of Conservative MPs	320
5.10	Conservative women candidates and MPs	323
5.11	The Conservative whips in the House of Commons 1919–1945	372
6.1	The career pattern of Conservative junior ministers in the House of Commons 1919–1945	394
6.2	The career pattern of Conservative Law Officers in the House of Commons 1919–1945	397
6.3	Conservative Party share of Cabinet offices in coalition governments	406
6.4	The career pattern of Conservative Cabinet ministers in the House of Commons 1919–1945	409
6.5	The educational background of Conservative junior and Cabinet ministers	410

Abbreviations

The following abbreviations and short-title forms have been used in the footnotes:

AC	Austen Chamberlain MSS
ACDL	R. Self (ed.), *The Austen Chamberlain Diary Letters* (Cambridge, 1995)
AGM	Annual General Meeting
Amery diary	J. Barnes and D. Nicholson (eds.), *The Leo Amery Diaries*, vol. 1: *1899–1929* (1980), and *The Empire at Bay—The Leo Amery Diaries*, vol. 2: *1929–1945* (1988)
AR	Annual Report
Bayford diary	J. Ramsden (ed.), *Real Old Tory Politics: The Political Diaries of Sir Robert Sanders, Lord Bayford: 1910–1935* (1984)
Bernays diary	N. Smart (ed.), *The Diaries and Letters of Robert Bernays 1932–1939* (Lampeter, 1996)
BL	British Library
BP	P. Williamson and E. Baldwin (eds.), *Baldwin Papers: A Conservative Statesman 1908–1947* (Cambridge, 2004)
Bridgeman diary	P. Williamson (ed.), *The Modernisation of Conservative Politics: The Diaries and Letters of William Bridgeman 1904–1935* (1988)
CA	Conservative Association
CAC	Churchill Archives Centre, Churchill College, Cambridge
CAJ	*Conservative Agents' Journal*
Cazalet diary	R. R. James, *Victor Cazalet* (1976)
Channon diary	R. R. James (ed.), *Chips: The Diaries of Sir Henry Channon* (1967)
COA	Central Office Agent
Conf.	Conference
CPA	Conservative Party Archive
Crookshank diary	Crookshank MSS, MSS.Eng.hist.d.359–361
Crawford diary	J. Vincent (ed.), *The Crawford Papers* (Manchester, 1984)
CRD	Conservative Research Department
Ctte.	Committee
Derby diary	Diary file (with letters), 1921–24, Derby MSS, DER(17)/29/1
Duff Cooper diary	J. J. Norwich (ed.), *The Duff Cooper Diaries 1915–1951* (2005)
EDC	Eastern Divisional Council
EIA	Empire Industries Association
Exec.	Executive Committee
F&GP	Finance and General Purposes Committee
Fin.	Finance Committee
GP	General Purposes Committee
Headlam diary	S. Ball (ed.), *Parliament and Politics in the Age of Baldwin and MacDonald: The Headlam Diaries 1923–1935* (1992), and *Parliament and Politics in the Age of Churchill and Attlee: The Headlam Diaries 1935–1951* (Cambridge, 1999)

JCCD	R. R. James (ed.), *Memoirs of a Conservative: J.C.C. Davidson's Memoirs and Papers 1910–1937* (1969)
JIL	Junior Imperial League
LAC	Labour Advisory Committee
Lady Peto diary	Peto MSS
MSS	Manuscripts
NC	Neville Chamberlain MSS
NCDL	R. Self (ed.), *The Neville Chamberlain Diary Letters* (4 vols, Aldershot, 2000–05)
Nicolson diary	N. Nicolson (ed.), *Harold Nicolson: Diaries and Letters 1930–1939* (1966), and *Harold Nicolson: Diaries and Letters 1939–1945* (1967)
NU	National Union of Conservative and Unionist Associations
PD	Provincial Division
RO	Record Office
SACC	Standing Advisory Committee on Candidates
SUA	Scottish Unionist Association
WDC	Western Divisional Council
WSC	M. Gilbert (ed.), *Winston S. Churchill*, vol. 5: *Companion Documents* (3 parts: 1979–82)
York diary	York MSS

Introduction
The Portrait of a Party

A political party is the voluntary combination of many people whose interests, values, and aspirations overlap to a greater or lesser extent. It is characterized by a particular spectrum of attitudes and opinions, and entails different forms of commitment and participation. This creates a complex political, social, and cultural organism, which both touches upon and is influenced by the other elements in national life and the human environment of the age. This book is an attempt to explore the most significant such body in Britain, in all of its many aspects, in the period in which it is most richly documented, and at a time of fundamental change in the party and electoral systems. It is a paradox that in the two decades following the introduction of near-universal adult suffrage in 1918, the Conservative Party was dominant electorally and in government, and yet also fearful of its future and almost constantly troubled by internal conflict.

The phenomenon of Conservative success is the most distinctive feature of British politics in the last 150 years. Since the widening of the franchise in the second half of the nineteenth century, the Conservative Party has had four periods of dominance: 1886–1905, 1918–45, 1951–64, and 1979–97. The second of these, which is examined here, had several distinctive features: it followed the economic and social stresses of a war on an unparalleled scale, it began with the advent of a democratic franchise and a massive increase in the electorate, and it saw the rise of new political ideologies (Socialism, Communism, and Fascism) and a major change in the party system (the decline of the Liberal Party and the rise of Labour). Any explanation of why the Conservative Party was the dominant force in the first era of democracy in Britain is dependent upon an understanding of its ethos, structures, and modes of operation, and that is the purpose of this study.

It takes advantage of a unique opportunity, for the interwar Conservatives have the richest archival record of any British political party in any historical period. It is perhaps not surprising that both party and personal records have survived more extensively than is the case for any of the parties in any earlier era. This has been due partly to the simple fact that more tends to survive from more recent times; partly to the stability, continuity, and wealth of the Conservative Party specifically, and partly to the social class from which its leaders were drawn, as they generally had private secretaries to archive their papers and the household space in which to retain them. For these reasons, much more material exists for the Conservatives in the interwar years than for either the troubled Liberal or emerging Labour parties, which have thinner archives of their leading figures, much less by way of backbench papers, and fewer and less representatively varied local party records (particularly so in the case of the Liberal Party). What is less obvious is that the documentary sources for the Conservative Party between the wars are richer in quality than is the case for either the Conservatives or Labour since 1945, even if, in some respects, the quantity of the postwar material is greater. This is because the interwar records tend to be more revealing, at every level.

There is a substantial documentary coverage of the interwar Conservative leadership, including extensive archives of personal papers for all five Leaders of the Party and collections, some of them substantial, for forty-nine other Cabinet ministers. Amongst these are several diaries, journals, and series of 'diary letters' (regular personal accounts written to a close relative);[1] the only other Cabinets as well served are the Labour administrations of 1964–70 and 1974–79. Much of this material is very frank and direct in expression, and its coverage of key events is fuller because letter-writing was still the normal method of communication when people were not in face-to-face contact (and was also a means of record-keeping even when they were). It was a period in which the role of the switchboard operator made confidential discussion by telephone impossible,[2] even if such a method of transacting business had been considered acceptable behaviour, and it long predated the development of the equally ephemeral electronic message, few of which are likely to survive and form the archives of the future. The interwar Conservatives also have more backbench diaries and, although the quality is variable, more collections of junior ministers' and MPs' papers than for any other party or period. To supplement this, there is a considerable range of published memoirs by backbench MPs, although there are fewer Cabinet-level memoirs than in recent decades, partly due to stricter conventions of Cabinet secrecy and partly to ministers retiring at a greater age and in poorer health than was general in the late twentieth century.

For the interwar period, there are extensive records of the representative side of the Conservative Party (the National Union), including for its most important national bodies, for ten of the twelve regions of England and Wales, and for Scotland (both centrally and regionally).[3] However, there is a major gap in the sources for the professional party machine at the national level: due to the destruction of most of Central Office's files in the paper salvage drives of the Second World War, little of its everyday organizational correspondence has survived, especially in comparison with the postwar period. In fact, this is less serious than it might seem, for the reports of all of the internal inquiries into the organization survive, as do examples of some other files, and there are many significant Central Office reports and memoranda in the personal papers of the Party Leaders and of J. C. C. Davidson (who was Party Chairman in the late 1920s and also, as, effectively,

---

[1] The weekly letters of Austen and Neville Chamberlain to their sisters are well-known, and have been edited for publication by Robert Self; less well-known are R. A. Butler's letters to his parents in the Butler MSS, Trinity College Library, Cambridge.
[2] Rathbone to Duchess of Atholl, 23 December 1938, Atholl MSS, 18/1.
[3] There are only limited records for the London and Wales & Monmouthshire regions.

Baldwin's chief of staff, closely involved with the party machine over a much longer period).[4]

The source material for the Conservative Party at the local level is far richer and more extensive than for any other party in this period or earlier. Although it is probable that more local records exist for the period since 1945, as the decades advance these are generally thinner, blander, and more uniform in content, as they became more professional and standardized. Whilst the majority of interwar constituency minutes are brief and consist mostly of formal business, their language can be more revealing and there are often full accounts of discussions at times of crisis or disagreement. In many cases, the surviving records include extensive or complete sets of the minutes of the executive body and of Annual General Meetings; in others, the span of these is limited, or there remain only the records of the women's association or of some district branches.[5] This study has sought to investigate all of the significant collections of local records which could be traced in England, Scotland, and Wales, resulting in material from a total of 215 constituencies.[6]

Although there are broad similarities in the structure and activities of local associations, which could be identified from a more restricted or targeted sample, investigating so many constituencies has several significant benefits. Most obviously, it provides a very wide geographical coverage and an extensive economic and social range, although two types of constituency are under-represented in the surviving records. The first of these is hardly surprising: there are comparatively fewer sets of minute books for districts where the Conservative Party was at its weakest, especially in coal-mining and heavy industrial constituencies—although there are some.[7] Paradoxically, the second lack concerns some areas where the Conservative Party was at its strongest: the series of substantial changes of constituency boundaries in the large cities and their suburbs since 1945, and the consequent relocations of association offices, which often caused the purging of old records in the process, has resulted in the loss of records not only for inner city areas but also for the prosperous outlying suburbs—Middlesex and Surrey are particularly lacking in material, in view of their number of constituencies and the strength of the Conservative Party's support.

A full survey of constituency sources is also essential for the analysis of grass-roots opinion on political issues and the relationship which the local voluntary

---

[4] Amongst other things, the Davidson MSS includes the only surviving copies of the annual Balance Sheets and Schedules for 1925–29, complementing the series for 1930 onwards at the Conservative Party Archive. There are also a number of Central Office reports and memos for 1930–31 in the Templewood MSS, which do not appear to survive elsewhere.

[5] Much of this research was undertaken between 1980 and 1995, in many cases by visits to Conservative association offices; a considerable number of these records have since been deposited in local record offices, although, sadly, in some other cases they may no longer exist. For a discussion of the nature of the local material, see S. Ball, 'National politics and local history: the regional and local archives of the Conservative Party 1867–1945', *Archives*, 22/94 (1996), 27–59.

[6] A number of constituencies for which there are only limited district branch records have not been investigated.

[7] For example, Ayrshire South CA, Cannock CA, Forest of Dean CA, Ilkeston CA, Keighley CA, Kirkcaldy Burghs CA, Rother Valley CA.

membership had with their leaders. The reason for this is that although the more accessible national sources, in particular the minutes of the National Union's Executive Committee, contain a number of resolutions sent in by local associations, this practice was only followed by a small minority of constituencies and with considerable regional variations, and so they cannot be regarded as either complete or fully representative (see Chapter 4). Whilst the resolutions which appear in the minutes of national and regional bodies are indicative of the topics about which the rank and file were concerned, because there is generally only one example (at the most, two or three) on a particular point, this does not give a measure of how extensively such views were held or whether they were particularly expressed in certain types of constituency—considerations which are important in crises such as the fall of the Coalition in 1922, the Empire Crusade in 1930, and India in 1933–35. Furthermore, although the final texts of resolutions are important, still more is revealed by the debate which surrounded them—including those resolutions which were withdrawn, defeated, or amended, and the balance of voting—and the only source for this is the constituency minute books. Where matters were not controversial, the account is generally brief (often simply stating that a discussion occurred), but where there were strong feelings or differences of view—which was more frequently the case with the more important matters—the local minutes can be much fuller, and researching the widest range produces a rich seam of evidence.

The final benefit of such an extensive investigation is that some revealing and significant points occur infrequently: in a smaller sample, they would either be missed altogether or be too few upon which to rest any reliable conclusions. These matters include not only some political issues (such as responses to the inquiry after the 1929 defeat, constituency relations with the small band of anti-appeasement MPs in 1938–39, and de-selections of MPs more generally), but also the thinly scattered figures on local membership and such matters of ethos as the consideration of women as parliamentary candidates, the instances of agents embezzling the funds, and the responses to MPs involved in divorce proceedings. There were also matters which were so basic and well-understood at the time that there was normally no need to record them, but upon which the occasional comment shines a revealing light. A limited sample would inevitably miss many of these, as well as lacking the appreciation of nuance and milieu that results from any extensive investigation of a particular type of source.

Two other types of primary material have been used in this study, both of which are rich in detail and illuminate key aspects of the party. Conservative values and attitudes must be the starting point of any investigation, as a discussion that is limited to leaders, organization, and events overlooks a vital part of the equation.[8] Because policies change most visibly—even more frequently than leadership or organization—they are often given considerable attention, especially in chronological histories and in analyses of particular elections. However, if the spotlight is

---

[8] This is the main weakness of most of the chronological histories, and in particular of the Longman 'History of the Conservative Party' series.

shone upon them too exclusively, it can be forgotten that the stage upon which they make their bow is constructed from a party's broader values and image, without which they have no context or credibility. In order to understand three key aspects of the twentieth-century Conservative Party—its aims and purpose, its cohesion and resilience, and its electoral appeal—the principles and temperament which underlie these must first be explored. This is possible due to the substantial contemporary literature about Conservatism published in book and pamphlet form, much of it written by active Conservative politicians, which is further supplemented by the numerous party publications and propaganda leaflets. The latter are a bridge to the second area: an analysis of the basis of Conservative electoral support. Due to its scale and complexities, this is an undertaking which has not previously been attempted in any systematic way.[9] However, it has been possible here to explore the patterns of Conservative voting by means of a unique database, which links the constituency electoral results with the economic and social data derived from the occupation tables of the 1931 census (see Appendix 2).

The range and depth of the available primary sources enables us to explore interwar Conservative politics with a fullness and complexity that will remain unrivalled. Of course, despite the intimidating scale of the archives, what remains to us is but a tithe of what originally existed, and there are many doors that will remain forever closed. First and most extensively, there is everything that was conducted orally rather than on paper. So much of British government and parliamentary politics occurs in meetings of small groups and in the conversations and rumours that pervade the Palace of Westminster; the same occurs in miniature in party bodies, nationally and locally. However, the surviving diaries and the notes made of some key conversations give us enough to be confident that the archives, although far from capturing all that was said and done, nonetheless are representative of it. Secondly, there are important lacunae in the written records, such as the Central Office papers already mentioned.[10] A particularly regrettable gap is the records of the Whips' Office and of individual whips, for whom there is a marked lack of personal papers.[11] The financial records for this period held at the Conservative Party Archive have recently been opened to research and are valuable on expenditure and the level of funds, but contain little on the sources and methods of national fund-raising.[12] Almost no day-to-day papers and correspondence

---

[9] The only information previously available has been for a limited number of constituencies and only for agricultural workers, miners, and a selected 'middle class', using the 1921 census. It was originally published in 1968: M. Kinnear, *The British Voter: An Atlas and Survey since 1885* (2nd edn, 1981).

[10] A particularly regrettable loss is the minute book of the 1922 Committee for 1943–50; this disappeared at some point after the writing of the fiftieth anniversary history: P. Goodhart and U. Branston, *The 1922: The Story of the Conservative Backbenchers' Parliamentary Committee* (1973), which fortunately quotes extracts from it.

[11] Margesson left only a handful of unimportant papers, and it appears that no archive exists for any other interwar Chief Whip. It is a similar desert for the ordinary whips; regrettably, the extensive Southby diary only starts in 1941, several years after his service as a whip.

[12] The Davidson MSS are more revealing in this respect; see also R. R. James (ed.), *Memoirs of a Conservative: J.C.C. Davidson's Memoirs and Papers 1910–1937* (1969), 283–8.

survive at the constituency level; as with the representative side of the organization nationally, what has been kept are the minute books—irreplaceably valuable, but still only a distillation of what was said (and, still more, felt) during the meetings, never mind the chat before and after, and in the everyday encounters in the association office, the club, and the street. Finally, we lack personal papers for local figures: constituency chairmen, committee members, agents, and the men and women of the rank and file.[13] This means that certainly no claim to an impossible 'completeness' is being made, and the light which our sources cast is still limited and leaves important areas in impenetrable shadow. Nevertheless, the claim made above remains valid: that more can be known and understood for this party in this time than for any other party in this or any other time.

Whilst contemporary primary sources are the foundation throughout this work, no historical investigation takes place in a vacuum. However, for many years the history of the Conservative Party was the poor relation in British political historiography, to be acknowledged only occasionally and with some reluctance. It is natural that explaining the upheaval involved in the decline of the Liberal Party and rise of Labour would attract the greatest interest, and the salience and significance of this change was all the more evident in the 1960s and 1970s—a period during which the Conservative Party struggled, and for a while lost its customary advantage of appearing to be the 'natural party of government'. This comparative neglect began to change with the ambitious multi-volume Longman History of the Conservative Party, and systematic investigation of the twentieth-century party can be said to have begun with the publication of John Ramsden's volume on 1902–40, *The Age of Balfour and Baldwin*, in 1978.[14] One of its several strengths was the pioneering research utilizing the records of local constituency Conservative associations, seventy-six of which were used to investigate the development of the party organization between 1910 and 1930.[15]

The success of the Conservative Party under Mrs Thatcher in the 1980s fostered academic interest in its history and nature, and against this background a number of other works appeared, mainly focused on the late Victorian and Edwardian era.[16] The present author's investigation of the internal party crisis of 1929–31 used a more extensive range of constituency party sources to explore their political role and the relationship between leaders and followers, a pattern followed by Nicholas

---

[13] Such records may exist here and there amongst personal deposits in local record offices, but these are unindexed and there seems to be no practicable way of finding them.

[14] The most important work before this had focused on the fall of the Coalition and the crises of the early 1920s: M. Cowling, *The Impact of Labour 1920–24* (Cambridge, 1971), and M. Kinnear, *The Fall of Lloyd George* (1973). The other important work, N. Thompson, *The Anti-Appeasers: Conservative Opposition to Appeasement in the 1930s* (Oxford, 1971), was based mainly on published sources.

[15] This part of the book was based upon Ramsden's thesis: J.A. Ramsden, 'The Organisation of the Conservative and Unionist Party in Britain 1910–1930', DPhil thesis, University of Oxford, 1975, which focused more on organizational development than political opinion.

[16] The most important were M. Pugh's study of the Primrose League, *The Tories and the People 1880–1935* (Oxford, 1985); A. Sykes, *Tariff Reform in British Politics 1903–1913* (Oxford, 1979); D. Dutton, *Austen Chamberlain* (Bolton, 1985); and, on the interwar period, R. Self, *Tories and Tariffs: The Conservative Party and the Politics of Tariff Reform 1922–1932* (New York and London, 1986).

Crowson's study of the late 1930s.[17] In the 1990s, issues relating to the party's interwar success were explored in an influential essay by Ross McKibbin,[18] in several articles by David Jarvis focusing upon the role of class and gender,[19] in a study of the development of the local party organization for women, youth, and trade unionists during the 1920s by Neal McCrillis,[20] and in an examination of Baldwin's values and mode of politics by Philip Williamson.[21] During the same decade, aspects of the Conservative Party between the wars were assessed in the substantial archive-based collaborative history of its fortunes since 1900, the title of which coined the description of this as the 'Conservative century',[22] and in some other general surveys.[23] The 1990s also saw, after long delay, the completion of the Longman series, and John Ramsden's subsequent overview of the history of the party since 1830.[24] However, since the late 1990s, perhaps in reflection of the slump in the party's contemporaneous fortunes, its interwar history appears to have entered a new phase of neglect,[25] especially in comparison with the Labour Party.[26] No monograph on the interwar Conservatives has yet been published in this millennium, although there has been a recent clutch of doctoral theses.

---

[17] S. Ball, *Baldwin and the Conservative Party: The Crisis of 1929–1931* (New Haven and London, 1988); N. Crowson, *Facing Fascism: The Conservative Party and the European Dictators 1935–1940* (1997).
[18] R. McKibbin, 'Class and conventional wisdom: the Conservative Party and the "public" in interwar Britain', in R. McKibbin, *The Ideologies of Class* (Oxford, 1990), 259–93.
[19] The most important of which are D. Jarvis, 'British Conservatism and class politics in the 1920s', *English Historical Review*, 111/440 (1996), 59–84; D. Jarvis, 'The shaping of the Conservative electoral hegemony 1918–1939', in J. Lawrence and M. Taylor (eds.), *Party, State and Society: Electoral Behaviour in Britain since 1820* (Aldershot, 1997), 131–52.
[20] N. R. McCrillis, *The British Conservative Party in the Age of Universal Suffrage: Popular Conservatism 1918–1929* (Columbus, 1998); however, this was based on a limited selection of twelve constituencies.
[21] P. Williamson, *Stanley Baldwin: Conservative Leadership and National Values* (Cambridge, 1999).
[22] A. Seldon and S. Ball (eds.), *Conservative Century: The Conservative Party since 1900* (Oxford, 1994).
[23] S. Ball, *The Conservative Party and British Politics 1902–1951* (Harlow, 1995); A. Seldon (ed.), *How Tory Governments Fall: The Tory Party in Power since 1783* (1996); J. Charmley, *A History of Conservative Politics 1900–1996* (Basingstoke, 1996); A. J. Davies, *We, the Nation: The Conservative Party and the Pursuit of Power* (1995); A. Clark, *The Tories: Conservatives and the Nation State 1922–1997* (1998).
[24] J. Ramsden, *The Age of Churchill and Eden 1940–1957* (1995); J. Ramsden, *The Winds of Change: Macmillan to Heath, 1957–1975* (1996); J. Ramsden, *An Appetite for Power: A History of the Conservative Party since 1830* (1998).
[25] The most important works have been biographical, in particular: R. J. Q. Adams, *Bonar Law* (1999); R. Self, *Neville Chamberlain* (Aldershot, 2006); G. Stewart, *Burying Caesar: Churchill, Chamberlain and the Battle for the Tory Party* (1999); S. [Simon] Ball, *The Guardsmen: Harold Macmillan, Three Friends and the World They Made* (2004).
[26] Amongst recent important works are: N. Riddell, *Labour in Crisis: The Second Labour Government 1929–1931* (Manchester, 1999); J. Swift, *Labour in Crisis: Clement Attlee and the Labour Party in Opposition 1931–1940* (Basingstoke, 2001); D. Howell, *MacDonald's Party: Labour Identities and Crisis 1922–1931* (Oxford, 2002); M. Worley, *Labour Inside the Gate: A History of the British Labour Party between the Wars* (2005); D. McHugh, *Labour in the City: The Development of the Labour Party in Manchester 1918–1931* (Manchester, 2006); C. Griffiths, *Labour and the Countryside: The Politics of Rural Britain Between the Wars* (Oxford, 2007).

As a result, the historiography is still surprisingly limited, and it remains the case that many facets of the interwar Conservative Party have been little explored. There is a need to investigate these areas in depth, and to draw the various themes together and establish an integrated picture. It is the aim of this study to explore the interwar Conservative Party in all of its aspects, by assessing the party's ideology and outlook, its sources of public support, the ways in which these were mobilized, the relationships within its constituent parts, its modes of operation, its social composition and political opinions—in the constituencies and in parliament—and the role of its leaders. This has led to the adoption of a thematic structure, in order to examine the Conservative Party from its foundations of belief, electoral support, and constituency grass roots, upwards through the regional and national machine and the parliamentary ranks, to the apex of Cabinet ministers and Party Leaders. However, it should be understood that this is an examination of the Conservative Party as such, and not a history of Conservative governments.

Whilst a 'total history' of anything is unattainable by human endeavour, still it is worth seeking to travel as far along that road as it is possible to go. I have sought to combine the strengths of the 'traditional' British political history of the 1960s to the 1990s—in particular, the examination of high political manoeuvre, of the development of party structures, and of the psephology of past elections—with the insights provided by the 'new' political history and its concerns with culture, identity, and language. I have also sought to combine political, social, and economic history, and to investigate the Conservative Party as a human organism. The intention has been to bring all of these aspects together into an integrated whole; the result, I know, is a long book, and yet I am still conscious of how much more could be said, and how many more sources cited, on almost any aspect of what follows hereafter.[27]

---

[27] The work is based upon contemporary primary sources wherever possible; for reasons of space, the citation of secondary works has been kept to a minimum, and there is a full list of these in the Bibliography.

1

Conservatism
Principles and Temperament

The Conservative Party in this era was not ideological in ethos or practice, but there was a recognized and understood Conservatism which gave its adherents common ground and mutual empathy. This was rarely analysed in depth, and could seem to lack definition—but references to 'Conservative principles' were not empty phrases, and the term was shorthand for a range of views which had a motivating force. Of course, Conservatives who enjoyed the benefits of wealth and status were open to the charge that their principles were no more than superficial justifications for a determination to hold on to what they had. In many cases, self-interest and opinion must have reinforced each other, whether consciously or unconsciously. However, even if they were convenient ideals, they were ideals nonetheless. Whatever their origins, the values which Conservatives endorsed established the context within which Conservative politics operated. There was more to Conservatism than just pragmatism or the seeking of power— the principle of being in rather than out. The Conservatives certainly wanted to be in office, but the record shows that their flexibility in pursuit of this goal had definite limits. There were boundaries that were crossed, if at all, only in times of peril and with great reluctance. There were beliefs and values, and deviation from these caused serious strains. There were also instincts, anxieties, and prejudices, and all of these have to be acknowledged before the nature of Conservative politics and the party's role in history can be understood: 'there are conservative principles, and there is a conservative mind'.[1]

The ideas and attitudes analysed in this chapter were not all held by all Conservatives, but most would have agreed with most of them and directly dissented from almost none. It is on the basis of such an overlapping outlook that mutual action becomes possible and congenial, and it acts as the foundation upon which the existence of any political movement rests.[2] Conservative principles were always broadly defined, and were rationalizations which codified the already-established but inchoate elements of temperament, assumptions, fears, and hopes. In this period, there was certainly a diversity of views within the Conservative Party, and individual Conservatives varied in the weight they accorded to particular aspects, which in turn produced a range of responses to any specific issue. This spectrum had outer parameters which could overlap with some views held in other parties, most often of centrist-inclined Liberals or Labour rather than of radical-right or Fascist groups. Nevertheless, it was a clearly Conservative set of attitudes which

[1] K. Feiling, *What Is Conservatism?* (1930), 9.
[2] SUA, Reconstruction Ctte., *Unionist Party Organisation in Scotland* (Edinburgh, 1944), 1–2.

had sufficient tensile strength to hold the party's supporters together. There was an underlying commonality of outlook and a consensus about long-term objectives, and these offset the sometimes sharp and certainly more visible disagreements over short-term issues, so that these eruptions did not cause the Conservative ranks to split apart or to splinter with secessions. Indeed, an acceptance of the individual variations within Conservatism was an important factor which promoted tolerance of the diversity of opinion within the party (which could be substantial), which in turn was the basis of the elasticity that enabled the Conservative Party to stretch—sometimes in surprising ways—without breaking.

Conservatives made the basic assumption that Conservatism 'starts from temperament rather than logic', and so was arrived at individually.[3] This was a process which did not happen immediately, and any such swift conversions were intrinsically suspect. Conservative views were expected to take form slowly, honed by maturity and experience of life; in this way, Conservatism 'begins as a mood and a point of view—it ends as a political system and an abiding faith'.[4] Conservatives believed that their outlook was based upon a 'subconscious, intuitive' disposition, and was therefore different in nature from an ideology.[5] They were uncomfortable with the latter term, which spoke to them of doctrinaire inhumanity and impractical rigidity. However, their adoption of the position of being non-ideological was not—as they assumed—natural and neutral, but was a constructed self-image which shaped their perspective; affirming that their beliefs were instinctive was in itself a political choice. Its corollary was acceptance that Conservatives did not hold a single set of views; 'my party have no political bible', declared Stanley Baldwin, the Party Leader from 1923 to 1937.[6] Nor was Conservatism defined by the working of an institution or the wisdom of a leader, for it was 'a code of principles which is above parties or personalities'.[7]

Almost all would have agreed as a starting point that Conservatism 'exists to oppose revolutionary change'.[8] Beyond this were principles and attitudes which were often implicit or assumed. Most Conservatives arrived at and understood these emotionally rather than intellectually, as 'a faith within himself'.[9] They did not feel a need to analyse their principles, and so could appear 'silent, lethargic, confused, incoherent, inarticulate, unimpressive'.[10] A disinclination for introspection and disinterest in abstract debate often gave an impression of almost circular thinking, or a lack of thought altogether: 'many Conservatives are Conservatives because they are Conservatives'.[11] Certainly, there were many who had no doubt

[3] K. Pickthorn, *Principles and Prejudices* (1943), 5.
[4] Duff Cooper speech notes, 'Toryism', n.d., Duff Cooper MSS, CAC, DUFC/8/1/17
[5] N. Skelton, *Constructive Conservatism* (1924), 8.
[6] S. Baldwin, *On England* (1926), 205.
[7] Hertford CA, AR, 1936, 'Conservatism'.
[8] Lord H. Cecil, *Conservative Ideals*, NU leaflet 2184 (1923), 2.
[9] B. Braine, *Conservatism and Youth: As a Young Man Sees It* (1939), 2.
[10] F. J. C. Hearnshaw, *Conservatism in England* (1933), 6; the book was based on lectures given at the Conservative Party's educational centre at Ashridge.
[11] Report of an unnamed Central Office organiser, enclosed in Gower to Ball, 9 November 1934, CPA, CRD/1/7/17; *CAJ*, July 1938, 164.

that Conservatism was the term for their views, but 'for the life of him could not put into words what he meant'.[12] For most of the time, this was not seen as a problem, as the absence of precise or confining definitions permitted the flexibility which both supporters and opponents considered to be one of the Conservative Party's enduring strengths. Even so, there was an underlying coherence in the views that made up Conservatism. It was much more than just an instinctive objection to change, which was formed by what it resisted, as if it were only a shadow or reflection. Conservatism was 'a distinct way of thinking' with its own rationale,[13] from which it derived substance and relevance: it was 'a philosophy of life and of society'.[14]

Conservatives reached positions more quickly and easily through instinct than reason and, as one observer noted, generally 'seem to share in a distaste for intellectual effort, and almost in a disbelief in its relevance to practical politics'.[15] Despite this, during the interwar period Conservative principles were the subject of a range of short books and pamphlets. These were aimed at a general readership, and in many cases written by practising politicians; they sought to express a Conservative 'spirit', 'faith', 'tradition', or 'outlook', and to enunciate principles which were of enduring value.[16] Whilst many had some form of official approval (a preface from a leading figure, or inclusion in the series of party leaflets), they were not commissioned or directed by the party authorities but were the result of individual initiatives. They were stimulated by the rise of the Labour Party and the challenge of Socialism, in response to which Conservatism needed to be established as a distinct alternative with its own strengths and merits.

This neglected seam of material is revealing, but it has two limitations. Firstly, most of the works on Conservatism were written as personal statements and did not engage with each other. There was no tradition of internal debate: only the historic founders of British Conservatism, Edmund Burke and Benjamin Disraeli, tended to be mentioned, usually for purposes of validation rather than analysis.[17] Secondly, the majority of the works came from two particular sectors along the spectrum of Conservative opinion: MPs on the youthful left (such as Harold Macmillan, Noel Skelton, Duff Cooper, and Walter Elliot) and an academically inclined governing mentality generally located in the moderate right (such as Lord Hugh Cecil, Keith Feiling, Leo Amery, and Lord Eustace Percy). These are generalizations, but it is noticeable that two other areas were under-represented: the mainstream centre (which was the largest parliamentary group) and the right wing, known as the 'diehards'. However, even with this clustering, the contemporary

---

[12] D. Stelling, *Why I Am a Conservative* (1943), 1; R. V. Jenner, *Will Conservatism Survive?* (1944), 9.
[13] Braine, *Conservatism and Youth*, 3.
[14] J. Buchan, preface in A. Bryant, *The Spirit of Conservatism* (1929), viii; Sir A. Wilson at Hitchin CA, AGM, 26 May 1933; York diary, 17 January 1945.
[15] Feiling, *What Is Conservatism?*, 8.
[16] The terms are taken from the titles of various works; see also J. D. Fair and J. A. Hutcheson, 'British Conservatism in the twentieth century: an emerging ideological tradition', *Albion*, 19/4 (1987), 549.
[17] S. Baldwin, foreword in Sir R. M. Banks, *The Conservative Outlook* (1929); W. H. Greenleaf, *The British Political Tradition*, vol. 2: *The Ideological Heritage* (1983), 216.

publications reveal what Conservatives believed in and considered significant, and wished to inculcate in their supporters. Although presented in published form with the intention of either justifying Conservatism or broadening its support, these are the words of Conservatives themselves about themselves, and unfold their politics as they understood and perceived them. Together with further more scattered statements in public speeches and private documents, they are the basis of the analysis which follows.

PRINCIPLES

Conservative ideas are best understood as a series of connected and mutually supporting themes. Lord Hugh Cecil's influential study *Conservatism*, published in 1912, described it as 'an amalgam', and used the metaphor of a river, 'the waters of which come from many converging streams'.[18] Of all these sources, the one that came first and fed into many that followed was a view of human nature which accepted that 'man is shot through with evil'.[19] This was founded upon the religious concept of original sin, that man had fallen from a state of grace and was an impure being prone to temptation and wickedness. Many of those who attempted to define the basis of Conservatism had a strong personal Christian belief, which shaped their ideas, whilst those who accepted the evolutionary origins of humanity started from the position that man had descended from the beasts, and civilization was but a veneer overlaid on the law of the jungle. There had been no noticeable change in human nature since the dawn of civilization, and so 'within us are instincts and powers unbroken in descent from early man'.[20] Whether biblical in inspiration or not, Conservatives were agreed upon the innate imperfection of human nature and its tendency to evil rather than good. This was reinforced by the experience of the two world wars, which undermined any expectation that improvement was a natural state, and demonstrated that 'the crust which separates us from chaos and collapse into barbarism is far thinner than we had ever guessed'.[21] Whilst the record of human history had its share of heroism and virtue, it was even more clearly evidence of fallibility and weakness, and proof that 'men are guided by self-interest'.[22]

The deduction which followed was that human social and political structures were incapable of rising above their own nature: 'the mechanism of human society will only express human character; it will not regenerate it'.[23] For this reason, idealistic schemes based upon appeals to the better nature of people in the mass were bound to fail; the only sound method was to take account of human venality as a given fact and make provision accordingly in any institution or legislation.[24] This

---

[18] Lord H. Cecil, *Conservatism* (1912), 23.   [19] A. Jones, *Right and Left* (1944), 6, 3.
[20] Feiling, *What is Conservatism?*, 11; P. Loftus, *The Creed of a Tory* (1926), 78–9, 87; L. S. Amery, 'Conservatism and the future (part 1)', *Ashridge Journal*, 72 (April 1943), 2.
[21] C. Hollis, *Quality or Equality?* (1944), 4.
[22] Cecil, *Conservatism*, 91.   [23] Cecil, *Conservatism*, 91.
[24] A. M. Ludovici, *A Defence of Conservatism* (1926), 60.

was even truer of positions of authority, for their holders, 'being men, must have their share of human faults and even vices, which are only intensified by power'.[25] The reality was that 'all human instincts are corrupted, and require discipline and restraint'.[26] A further consequence of the Conservative view of human nature was a distrust of dealing with people as collectives, for this assumed that all would act in the same way. However, it was 'the contention of Conservatism that the average man does not exist'.[27] Instead, Conservatives accepted that humanity encompassed 'sinners, drunkards, horse-copers, saints, bankrupts, congenital idiots, genius', and that policies had to allow for all of these.[28] They were 'resigned to the mysteries and the muddles of human nature', and recognized 'that most of the light and shade of life depends on them'.[29] From this perspective, 'the first duty of a humane government is to accept the facts of human nature as they actually are'.[30] This was the reason for the centrality of the individual in the Conservative view of economic life, complemented by the role of the family as 'the basic unit of national life'.[31] Whilst Conservatives certainly preferred the conventional to the experimental, they expected variety rather than uniformity and instinctively approached issues on an ad hoc basis.

The second formative element in the Conservative outlook, following directly from the acknowledgement of human fallibility, was scepticism of the power of reason. It was considered self-evident that human faculties did not have the capacity to comprehend the vastness and complexity of all creation, and therefore men were mistaken in believing that they could acquire the knowledge and skill needed to determine the shape and direction of society.[32] Abstract reason was a device invented by humans and so had human defects; it could not provide absolute truths, and thus systems of thought founded upon the seductiveness of its logic did not have a reliable basis. They sought to impose an artificial order on a chaotic and unpredictable reality, and attempted 'to make straight that which God created crooked'.[33] Those who acted on such a basis were mistaken, and misled into an illusory and dangerous self-confidence; 'the Conservative deplores the idealism that assumes the goal to be attainable because it is desirable'.[34] From this followed a distrust of intellectuals and experts, and the rejection of the notion that state authorities could give direction due to their superior knowledge or supposed disinterest.

---

[25] Lord Cranborne, *Our Political Future*, NU leaflet 43/5 (1943).
[26] Cecil, *Conservative Ideals*, 8.
[27] Feiling, *What Is Conservatism?*, 23; Tory Reform Committee, *What is a Tory?* (1945).
[28] Feiling, *What Is Conservatism?*, 15.
[29] A. R. Parker, R. G. Cooke, and F. Green (eds.), *A Declaration of Tory Principles* (Cambridge, 1929), 7.
[30] D. M. Crichton (ed.), *Tory Oxford: Essays in University Conservatism* (1935), 39.
[31] SUA Conf., 30 October 1942; H. Sellon, 'The river of Conservatism', *Ashridge Journal*, 7 (August 1931), 15–16.
[32] Parker et al., *Declaration of Tory Principles*, 28, 30–1.
[33] Bryant, *Spirit of Conservatism*, 32.
[34] Stelling, *Why I Am a Conservative*, 11.

The essence of the Conservative view was that reason was a weak and flawed process, not a strong and certain one upon which human society could be built, for the reality was that rationality was not powerful enough to contain unaided the forces of envy, greed, ignorance, and fear.[35] However, Conservatives did not reject the utility of reason, provided that its limitations were understood and adhered to; they did not retreat into irrationality or incline to mysticism (which had aspects of fanaticism and dogma),[36] and were not attracted by nihilism—a fact which placed an important philosophical and temperamental gulf between British Conservatism and continental Fascism. Instead, they accepted reason as a tool which provided only partial understanding, for 'the more important part is generally played by semi-conscious or sub-conscious sentiments and instincts'.[37] This view drew upon the developing theories of Freudian psychoanalysis, which were understood to show that 'the subconscious is the supreme directing force of the individual and the nation'.[38] Man was thus animal in nature, and moved by sentiment and desire rather than rationality.

The civilizing process, developed over many centuries, placed restraints upon the innately bestial nature of mankind, but it was a fragile construct whose effectiveness was neither universal in extent or absolute in effect: 'civilisation is a compromise'.[39] For that reason, it needed to be buttressed by 'the factors of order and authority, externally imposed'.[40] Conservatives were therefore not in sympathy with the concept of 'natural' rights of man founded upon rational inference, as this was 'an abstract idea which may have no correspondence with any actual experience'.[41] Instead, they regarded such entitlements as existed to be privileges, which had been earned and established by custom. The vote was a civic duty; it was not a free gift to be used capriciously or carelessly, but 'a great trust', which carried with it weighty obligations of sober deliberation.[42] There were no universal panaceas to be found, and Conservatives had no belief in the power of politics to remedy the problems of the world: 'cut-and-dried political schemes will fail, and will be bound to fail'.[43] This led to their reliance upon the experience of what already existed, rather than seeking something yet to be created, which might turn out to be very different from the intentions and hopes of those who devised it. Conservatives feared the 'cold certitudes' that resulted from a purely rational approach,[44] having

---

[35] Feiling, *What Is Conservatism?*, 10.

[36] An exception was Lord Lymington MP's involvement in the English Mistery movement, and later the English Array, which were based upon a semi-mystical ruralist feudalism; see also Viscount Lymington, *Ich Dien: The Tory Path* (1931).

[37] E. Wood, *Conservative Beliefs*, NU pamphlet 2311 (1924), 3.

[38] Loftus, *Creed of a Tory*, 52.

[39] J. Buchan, introduction in D. Crisp (ed.), *The Rebirth of Conservatism* (1931), ix.

[40] E. Wood, 'Thoughts on some of the present discontents of the Conservative Party', not dated but marked 'early summer 1922', Halifax MSS (Borthwick), A4/410/9/1–13.

[41] Banks, *Conservative Outlook*, 7.

[42] *To Women Voters*, NU leaflet 1836 (1918).

[43] W. Elliot, *Toryism and the Twentieth Century* (1927), 96; *Conservatism in a Nutshell*, NU leaflet 3773 (1945).

[44] Loftus, *Creed of a Tory*, 53.

'a horror of uniformity of institutions and of economic formulas'.[45] On the contrary, the weakness of human character and the fallibility of reason enjoined caution in the making of any changes, for 'reason must walk humbly and take second place to instinct'.[46] Conservatism favoured inductive rather than deductive methods, and its approach was empirical and practical rather than logical and theoretical. George Younger, Chairman of the Party from 1916 to 1922, considered that its fundamental principle could be summed up 'in a single word—common-sense'.[47]

The third fundamental aspect of Conservative thought was the belief that society was organic in nature—that it was a living organism which must be considered as a whole, and not treated as a mechanism which could be redesigned at will. It was too complex to be understood from the human perspective, and so closely interwoven that removal of, or drastic change to, any of its constituent parts could not take place in isolation and must have effects—most likely detrimental—upon the rest. Nor was it only the present that had to be considered, for society was 'composed not only of the living but of the dead and the yet unborn'.[48] Restructuring society was more likely to destroy than to improve it, and common prudence suggested that radical surgery and wishful experiment upon a living entity were dangerous to its continued existence. Any change must therefore be cautious, limited in scope, and manifestly necessary to the point that failure to act would be the more perilous course. At the same time, Conservatives were aware of the danger of ossification, and accepted that the continued health of society was not automatic and that some adjustments to circumstances had to be permitted.[49] However unwelcome, the 'ever-changing conditions in which we live' were a reality, to which the Conservative response was 'always that development rather than innovation is the true road to progress'.[50] Even so, care should be taken to limit the resulting interference to a minimum, as human action was likely to be crude and hasty. Society was held to be formed neither of pure individualists (a Liberal concept) nor of impersonal masses acting on a class basis (a Socialist concept), but rather to consist of many associational groupings of communal interests, which overlapped with each other and contained 'lives interpenetrated, interdependent, but yet each integral'.[51] Human beings were not manufactured automatons: it was recognized that each person's life consisted of many facets and that 'the whole of him goes into no one of them more than momentarily'.[52] Class was just one of these groupings, and not necessarily the cardinal one. National loyalties had a higher claim, and for Conservatives 'the working-class stream is but a large tributary of the main national river'.[53] Furthermore, to think in terms of just two or three class blocs was

---

[45] K. Feiling, *Toryism: A Political Dialogue* (1913), 96; Elliot, *Toryism*, 135.
[46] Elliot, *Toryism*, 6.
[47] *Sunday Times*, 12 June 1927, in Hearnshaw, *Conservatism in England*, 33.
[48] Braine, *Conservatism and Youth*, 4.
[49] Skelton, *Constructive Conservatism*, 21.
[50] A. D. Cooper, *The Conservative Point of View*, NU leaflet 2616 (1926), 24.
[51] Feiling, *What Is Conservatism?*, 14.
[52] Pickthorn, *Principles and Prejudices*, 8.
[53] R. Northam, *Conservatism: The Only Way* (1939), 82.

hopelessly simplistic, and failed to recognize 'the almost infinite variety of our social forms'.[54]

Society was considered to have evolved over time in a natural way, and to have developed checks and balances because 'nature decrees separate functions'.[55] Inequality was not a sign of social malfunction or a moral stain: 'diverse quality' was instead 'a conservative criterion of national well-being'.[56] People were born unequally gifted with ability, character, strength, and health, and no human agency could achieve material equality without reducing all to the lowest level, thereby oppressing the better-endowed and barring the road to creativity, progress, and prosperity. Egalitarianism was not an objective to be admired, as it was both unworkable and undesirable. The levelling of society would undermine authority, remove incentive, and impose a drab uniformity; inequality was preferable to such tyranny. The Conservative approach to equality had a moral basis: 'in the eyes of the Conservative all men are worthwhile', as 'they all possess something of infinite value—a soul'.[57] This belief enabled Conservatives to adjust relatively easily to universal suffrage, without considering that there was any connection between equal rights and equal wealth. On the contrary, Conservatism 'recognises the distinction between the classes as natural, fundamental and beneficial', as each had its particular role.[58] This was leavened by an emphasis on equality of opportunity, in the sense that 'each one should have the chance to fulfil the best that is in him'.[59] Conservatives were primarily concerned with justice, and their belief that rewards should be based upon merit was founded upon Protestant Christianity. Whilst it was understood that in this imperfect world good and evil often did not receive their proper deserts, justice was the means by which the weak could be protected from the strong and civilization prevail over the law of the jungle. The founding principle of human justice was that 'every man shall, so far as the transient and uncertain nature of life permits, have a reasonable chance of reaping where he has sown'. In this way, justice 'gives to each man some measure of certainty, enabling him to know where he stands and to plan for the future accordingly'.[60] This made the difference between anarchy and order, and was of fundamental importance as 'a stable condition of society is the main preoccupation of Conservatism'.[61]

The ownership of property was defended because it was the basis of this stability: it provided individuals with security and independence, and these, in turn, encouraged responsibility. Societies where rights of property were clearly defined and protected were peaceful and prosperous, as each member of the community understood their entitlements and could rely upon them. Attacks upon property would lead to loss of confidence, economic depression, and, ultimately, social disintegration. The maintenance of property rights was therefore not a matter of selfishness or greed, for they preserved the fabric of society and were an essential pillar of

---

[54] Q. Hogg, *The Times We Live In* (1944), 15.   [55] Feiling, *What Is Conservatism?*, 11.
[56] Feiling, *What Is Conservatism?*, 16; Cecil, *Conservative Ideals*, 10.
[57] Braine, *Conservatism and Youth*, 19.
[58] Hearnshaw, *Conservatism in England*, 24; Parker et al., *Declaration of Tory Principles*, 32.
[59] M. V. Allison, 'The goal of modern Conservatism', *Ashridge Journal*, 23 (September 1935), 38.
[60] Bryant, *Spirit of Conservatism*, 8.   [61] Skelton, *Constructive Conservatism*, 21.

freedom. Conservatism should not be 'the cause of rich people, but it ought to be the cause of the defence of property against unjust treatment'.[62] It was a legitimate expectation that 'men should be allowed to retain the fruits of their honest endeavour', and so 'Conservatism would safeguard the individual's savings'.[63] Whatever their means, all persons had the same rights to their private property and were similarly motivated by its care and protection. The desire to acquire property was seen as a natural human characteristic, which was beneficial to society. It involved fundamental instincts: the need to make a secure home for the family, the wish to protect children from the hardships in life and pass on an inheritance, the prudence of making provision for infirmity and old age, the desire for autonomy and security from others, the satisfaction of accomplishment in a career, and the recognition of that success by society. The quest for property encouraged men to strive with all their strength and talents to better their condition in ways that were not only of material worth but of moral value as well; it stimulated endeavour, efficiency, invention, foresight, and thrift, and so was 'the true basis for the development of individual character'.[64] The hereditary principle was an essential part of this as it provided a motivation and certainty of purpose that extended beyond each ephemeral life, for 'life is not an adventure of one generation'.[65] The property which was gained or created might be held by individuals, but the process had wider beneficial effects, 'to build up society and to contribute in countless ways to the onward march of social progress'.[66] The great wealth of a few might be envied by the many, but 'we shall not succeed in removing poverty by trying to destroy wealth'.[67] On the contrary, the real lesson of the previous century was 'that when many large incomes spring up small ones increase'.[68] It was desirable that the working class should be encouraged to save and to invest, 'so that, so far as possible, everyone may have a stake in the country'.[69] Noel Skelton pointed in 1924 to 'the greatest of all social truths—that the success and stability of a civilisation depend upon the widest possible extension amongst its citizens of the private ownership of property'; later in the same pamphlet he coined the phrase 'a property-owning democracy', which was taken up by following writers and by Anthony Eden (Party Leader 1955–57) in speeches after 1945.[70]

The defence of property had been an established Conservative theme since the French Revolution, but the rise of Socialism, with its doctrine of public ownership, put it in the political spotlight. This shone most strongly on the gap between rich and poor, in reply to which Conservatives argued that in a free society it was

---

[62] Cecil, *Conservatism*, 158.   [63] Northam, *Conservatism*, 69, 70.
[64] Hogg, *Times We Live In*, 23.
[65] Hollis, *Quality or Equality?*, 7–8; Braine, *Conservatism and Youth*, 12.
[66] Cecil, *Conservatism*, 119–20.
[67] Memo by Salisbury, 'Post War Conservative Policy at Home and in External Relations', first draft, 3 July 1941, Swinton MSS, CAC, SWIN/II(270)/5/1.
[68] Crisp, *Rebirth of Conservatism*, 27.   [69] Cranborne, *Our Political Future*.
[70] Skelton, *Constructive Conservatism*, 9, 23; the term is also used in R. Boothby, G. Loder, H. Macmillan, and O. Stanley, *Industry and the State: A Conservative View* (1927), 13; Crisp, *Rebirth of Conservatism*, 173; H. Sellon, *Whither, England? The Letters of a Conservative* (1932), 171, 157; Stelling, *Why I Am a Conservative*, 9–10.

possible for the talented and hard-working to prosper, however humble their birth. Nevertheless, not everyone could be equally successful in the acquisition of property and status. Conservatives regarded the existence of different levels in society as a natural consequence of the variation in human ability and character, and so saw no intrinsic reason for this to be a source of conflict, and certainly not for it to be a basis for political organization. It was 'the true genius of our people' that 'the political divisions in our country have been perpendicular and not horizontal'.[71] Although there would be disagreements on particular issues, Conservatives believed that, fundamentally, there should be a harmony of classes and interests, and recognition of the common bonds which cut across class distinctions. Conservatives held that 'the interests of what are called the different classes...are not different, but the same'.[72] It was therefore self-evident that 'no class can hope to benefit from a policy which injures the nation as a whole'.[73] All those who derived their livelihood from a business had an interest in its continuation and would gain in some way from its success, even if they did not own any part of it: 'the prosperity of any one class depends upon the prosperity of the rest'.[74] This was just as true of the genders; after the grant of female suffrage, it was necessary to point out that 'the interests of men and women are one and the same in the long run: as in married life, so in public life, the one should complement the other'.[75] More broadly, there were connections through shared social customs and, for men in particular, joining together in competition against other nations, whether in war or peace. As the Cabinet minister Edward Wood observed: 'there is not much difference between the millionaire and the pauper in the presence of a common fear, a common bereavement, or a common love of sport'.[76] Conservatives regarded it as natural that society would be hierarchical, ideally with each person having his or her own familiar place and being content with its duties and rewards. This implied the existence of a natural governing class, with authority and leadership flowing from those who were most capable of providing it. Thus, when recruiting 'the natural leaders of the people' to act as voluntary service chairmen in their districts during the General Strike of 1926, it was automatic to look to 'the local "big man" with a title or some distinction gained in the Army, in India, etc'.[77]

The Conservative emphasis upon authority and order was prevented from leading to a coercive and reactionary outlook by an underlying element of populism. This was not just pragmatic, although there was acceptance that a democratic franchise meant that 'the people can make any change they like by electing a Parliament that will carry out their wishes', and so 'they have the supreme power'.[78] The Conservative Party drew strength from sharing 'the prejudices of the common

---

[71] A. Chamberlain, *Keep Liberty through Unity*, NU leaflet 2017 (1921).
[72] A. D. Cooper, *Why Workers Should Be Tories*, NU leaflet 2659 (1926).
[73] A. R. M. Murray, 'The Conservative Party and the National Government', *Ashridge Journal*, 27 (September 1936), 7.
[74] Parker et al., *Declaration of Tory Principles*, 32.
[75] *To Women Voters*.   [76] Wood, *Conservative Beliefs*, 5.
[77] Winterton to Irwin, 3 June 1926, Halifax MSS, C152/17/1/48.
[78] *Direct Action: The Violence that Prevents Progress*, NU leaflet 1912 (1919).

Englishman' and rested upon 'his common sense and loyalty and public spirit'.[79] The record of history, and particularly the recent experience of the First World War, encouraged confidence that the British people could be trusted. A common heritage had shaped values which were shared across class boundaries, and thus Baldwin attributed the failure of the General Strike to 'the spirit of fair play and inborn common sense' of the people.[80] This powerful strand in Conservative thought was reinforced by the concept of 'Tory Democracy': the natural alliance of aristocratic leadership with the yeoman qualities of proud and independent working men. Promoted by Disraeli and Lord Randolph Churchill in the 1870s and 1880s, this had been an electoral stratagem with little real substance—but the attraction of the idea and the charisma of its inventors created a myth which later figures could call to their support. Disraeli became the icon and inspiration of post-Victorian Conservatism, and no other figure was referenced so frequently and uncritically. Thus the former MP and junior minister Lord Bledisloe could write with complete sincerity of 'the *idealism* which lent inspiration to Disraeli', whilst Baldwin considered that 'you might find our ideals best expressed in one of Disraeli's novels'.[81] Conservatives were proud of 'the Disraelian tradition' of 'real sympathy on social questions',[82] whilst it had been 'the Tory Lord Shaftesbury who led the fight for the workers' in promoting the early Victorian Factory Acts.[83] There was nothing insincere, or incongruous to his audience, in Baldwin's statement in his valedictory remarks in 1937 that 'the leaders of the Tory Party have always understood and been sympathetic to the working man'.[84] This was consistent with the 'new Conservatism' of the early part of his leadership in 1923–24, which emphasized social harmony and partnership, and trust and confidence in the people. Addressing the 1928 Annual Conference, four years after becoming an MP, the young Eden saw nothing unusual in stating that 'they, being Conservatives, were also democrats'.[85] By the 1940s, it could be declared as a truism that 'the tradition of the Conservative Party is to win the people's trust by putting its trust in the people'.[86] Honesty and openness were the best courses to follow on both moral and tactical grounds, as 'the English people are so extraordinarily quick to perceive what is taking place'.[87] Even in the dangerous atmosphere of 1919, grass-roots Conservatives were confident that 'the British working man was no fool, and...when he thoroughly understood the problem', he would vote for constitutionalism and not Socialism.[88]

---

[79] C. Dawson, 'Conservatism', *Ashridge Journal*, 11 (September 1932), 41; Accrington CA, Exec., 6 October 1936; SUA, WDC, 9 September 1931.
[80] Baldwin to the King, 13 May 1926, Baldwin MSS, 177/7.
[81] Bledisloe to Baldwin, 31 January 1924, Baldwin MSS, 159/183–4 (emphasis in original); Baldwin, *On England*, 205.
[82] Salisbury to Baldwin, 26 January 1924, Baldwin MSS, 159/258–61; H. Bentinck, *Tory Democracy* (1918), 8, 16–22.
[83] G. Beyfus, 'Conservatism', *Ashridge Journal*, 105 (July 1944), 3.
[84] Memo by Dugdale, 'Mr Baldwin's testament', 28 April 1937, BP, 433.
[85] NU Conf., 1928.   [86] Stelling, *Why I Am a Conservative*, 12.
[87] R. Cecil to Irwin, 22 June 1926, Halifax MSS, C152/17/1/58.
[88] Wood Green CA, Palmers Green branch, Exec., 8 October 1919.

It must be acknowledged that there was also a fear of class politics which ran counter to this sentiment, and this was the reason why many Conservatives expected the 1918 enfranchisement to be disastrous for their party.[89] Conservatives did not always act or think in accordance with their professed faith in cross-class harmony and national unity, and sometimes appeared almost Marxist in their assumption of economic and environmental determinism; thus Austen Chamberlain (Party Leader 1921–22) could not understand why anyone living in the slums of his West Birmingham constituency did not become a revolutionary.[90] Certainly, some of the people were considered to be more trustworthy than others. When Conservatives spoke of 'the public', they had in mind the middle-aged and older: those with some experience of life and a stake in society, such as parents and householders, who knew how the world worked and would not be carried away by impulse or illusion. The overwhelming support of the voters for the responsible and stable choice of the National Government in 1931, and its renewal in 1935, did much to ease concerns about the instincts of the people.[91] By the later 1930s, Conservatives had become accustomed to the new landscape, and could take pride in contrasting its merits with the parlous state of affairs in continental Europe. Democracy was now a guarantor of freedom to be defended, and the sentiments of Baldwin's final speeches were echoed in the rhetoric of the 'people's war' of 1939–45.[92] By the end of the war, younger Conservatives could describe democracy as 'the only form of government consistent with the freedom of the human spirit'.[93] However, Conservatism retained a resistance to legitimation on the basis of simple numbers, as there was a predisposition to value quality over quantity, and a recognition that 'there can be no permanency without quality'.[94] The essence, and the residual ambivalence, of the Conservative view was captured in Baldwin's valedictory remarks: 'The heart of the country is sound, but it wants watching.'[95]

Religion was considered by Conservatives to be 'an eternal necessity of human nature', which interpreted the world and acted as a binding force in society.[96] This did not mean that all Conservatives had a personal faith: some did (and it was a motivating force for several leading figures, including Baldwin), but for many it played little or no part in their lives beyond conformity to conventional attitudes and participation in expected activities such as church attendance, saying the Lord's Prayer and carol singing. However, those who lacked any religious conviction could still share the view that human nature was essentially sinful, irrational, untrustworthy, and unruly, and the recognition of the impermanence of human

---

[89] D. Jarvis, 'British Conservatism and class politics in the 1920s', *English Historical Review*, 111/440 (1996), 69–70.
[90] A. to I. Chamberlain, 18 November 1922, *ACDL*; for a similar sentiment, Birmingham CA, Management Ctte., Deritend division report, 12 March 1926.
[91] SUA, EDC, 4 November 1931.
[92] S. Baldwin, *This Torch of Freedom* (1935), 39, 51; S. Baldwin, *An Interpreter of England* (1939), 45; Edinburgh North CA, AGM, 19 April 1938.
[93] Stelling, *Why I Am a Conservative*, 3; Braine, *Conservatism and Youth*, 9.
[94] F. Lee, 'Quality and Conservatism', *Ashridge Journal*, 17 (March 1934), 34–5.
[95] 'Mr Baldwin's testament', *BP*, 433.
[96] Bryant, *Spirit of Conservatism*, 61.

life and the small scale of human endeavours. Furthermore, 'the constraining influence...of religious ideals' shaped 'the personal integrity of the people', which in turn was the foundation of social stability.[97] It was not necessary to be a believer to regard religion as 'the keystone of the arch upon which the whole fabric rests', with the corollary that 'the championship of religion is therefore the most important of the functions of Conservatism'.[98] This generally translated into recognition of the historic role and value of the Church of England as 'the repository of tradition; in its voice alone rings some tone of authority'.[99] As always, it was better to retain any pillars of stability that had worked in the past, especially when the alternatives were so unattractive. Materialism was shallow and unsustaining, if not corrupting, whilst the example of Nazism suggested that 'there appears to be no national alternative to religion except devil-worship'.[100]

Conservatives believed strongly in the value of the lessons of the past, and 'that history is a better guide to policy than theory'.[101] Conservatism did not need to be propounded in ponderous philosophical treatises because its essence was discernible from the events of the past, and it therefore had the greater merit of being based upon fact (or supposed and accepted 'fact') rather than speculation. The later popular historian Arthur Bryant, then a young lecturer at the Conservative Party's Stott and Ashridge educational centres, wrote his summary of *The Spirit of Conservatism* in 1929 'in the belief that history...bears out the wisdom of Conservatism as a practical creed for men'.[102] Indeed, much of the content of many of the contemporary works on Conservatism was taken up by a historical survey. The Conservative view was that wisdom was found not in the pronouncements of individual geniuses, but in the slow historical accumulation of experience by society as a whole: 'we work within limits ruled by the past'.[103] There was security and confidence in relying upon the cumulative wisdom of previous generations, 'on what time has tried and tradition has cemented'.[104] Precedent was the basis of the common law and of the constitution, which was 'the result of centuries of evolution and native in its growth'.[105] The future was shaped by the past, which must be known in order to understand what is developing (although prediction was not possible—human affairs were an art and mystery, not a science). 'We go to history in order to learn,' Feiling argued in 1930, 'the last thing that we shall find is a fixed programme and the first thing is a continuing spirit.'[106] Walter Elliot defined two of the core beliefs of Toryism as 'a humility of the intellect and therefore a trust in

---

[97] Memo by Salisbury, 'Post War Conservative Policy at Home and in External Relations', second draft, 10 October 1941, Swinton MSS, CAC, SWIN/II(270)/5/1.
[98] Cecil, *Conservatism*, 116; Sir G. Lloyd and E. Wood, *The Great Opportunity* (1918), 11, 99; Jenner, *Will Conservatism Survive?*, 7.
[99] Banks, *Conservative Outlook*, 13.
[100] Stelling, *Why I Am a Conservative*, 5.
[101] Stelling, *Why I Am a Conservative*, 25.
[102] Bryant, *Spirit of Conservatism*, x.
[103] Feiling, *What Is Conservatism?*, 11; Hearnshaw, *Conservatism in England*, 14.
[104] Cecil, *Conservatism*, 246; *Looking Ahead*, NU leaflet 3751 (1941).
[105] Baldwin, *Interpreter of England*, 35; Beyfus, 'Conservatism', 3.
[106] Feiling, *What Is Conservatism?*, 8.

continuity', together with 'a conviction that whatever has worked once may work again'.[107] No generation had sufficient virtue to claim a monopoly of wisdom, or was entitled to cast aside the accumulated achievements of its predecessors: 'a generation of men is no more than trustee in the name of the past for the sake of the future'.[108] For these reasons, Conservatives should 'hold on to what has proved to be good' and 'hold in suspicion new things until they are tested'.[109]

The purpose of Conservatism was not to prevent all change, in part because such an endeavour was no more likely to succeed than King Canute's command to hold back the tide. Furthermore, the result would be undesirable even if it could be achieved, for it would create a fossilized rigidity whose brittleness would pose a greater danger of collapse: 'the policy of leaving things alone is the policy of decay', and to prevent this 'you must ever be at work renewing, altering, repairing, replacing'.[110] This was the basis of the Conservative doctrine of adaptation, accepting 'change in order to preserve' when it was clear that continued resistance was more likely to endanger order and stability than to defend them. However, caution had always to be the watchword, for 'there is no benefit conceivable that can compensate for the destruction of order'.[111] Instead, by the careful management of pace, scope, and consequences, 'we shall reform without devastating experiment and render justice without mangling the national quality'.[112] The pot of gold at the end of this particular rainbow was the ideal of a stable, ordered, and united society; evolution rather than revolution was the path to harmony and happiness. It was therefore essential not to ignore where change had become necessary, and 'a sincere respect for facts' should take precedence over any dogma.[113] By the end of the Second World War, this had assumed a more active mode, with the Cabinet minister Oliver Lyttelton declaring that 'Conservatives believe in marching forward', and the 1945 leaflet *Conservatism in a Nutshell* offering the novel definition that 'we are called Conservatives because we believe in taking what already exists and improving and perfecting it'; the latter concept at least would have raised eyebrows twenty or even ten years earlier.[114]

The role of Conservatism was to provide the prudence which was an essential component in any successful change, to be a brake acting in the vehicle rather than a wall built across the road. 'Progress depends on conservatism to make it intelligent, efficient and appropriate to circumstance', and without it progress would be 'if not destructive at least futile'.[115] The problem was how to mix the elements of prudence and progress in the correct proportion, and herein lay the whole field of

---

[107] Elliot, *Toryism*, 4; Banks, *Conservative Outlook*, 1.
[108] Elliot, *Toryism*, 19; Crisp, *Rebirth of Conservatism*, 15; Loftus, *Creed of a Tory*, 36.
[109] Gwynne to Baldwin, 1 February 1931, Gwynne MSS, 15; Ludovici, *Defence of Conservatism*, 17.
[110] Duff Cooper speech notes, 'Toryism', n.d.
[111] Duff Cooper speech notes, 'Toryism', n.d.
[112] Feiling, *What Is Conservatism?*, 32–3.
[113] Buchan, in Crisp, *Rebirth of Conservatism*, ix; Crichton, *Tory Oxford*, 42.
[114] *Seven Points of Conservative Policy*, speech by Lyttelton to Birmingham CA, 6 November 1944, NU leaflet 3757 (1944); *Conservatism in a Nutshell*.
[115] Cecil, *Conservatism*, 14; Cecil used the uncapitalized term to distinguish the general conservative outlook from specifically party aspects.

political debate both within the Conservative Party and outside. It followed from this that there was no single answer which met every case, and that a different balance had to be struck not only on each issue but also from one day to another on the same issue, as circumstances altered. There also had to be a selection of priorities, as tackling too many issues at the same time dissipated energy whilst maximizing strain and disruption. This was the error of the left, whilst 'the Conservative Party takes the saner view that to concentrate upon one urgent need is wiser than to attempt the reconstruction of everything'.[116] By such means something of lasting value might be accomplished, with each generation making incremental improvements upon its inheritance. In this sense, 'Conservatism is a progressive creed', although one which understood that 'ordered progress alone can ensure an advance of a permanent nature'.[117]

Conservatism has been defined as 'positional', in that it responds to situations and challenges as they are encountered rather than on the basis of a prior body of doctrine.[118] This allows for the incorporation of past changes (even though they were strenuously resisted at the time) as part of the existing settlement which is now being defended. This could produce an appearance of inconsistency, and it encouraged a focus on immediate strategy rather than long-term aims. It could also suggest that the Conservatives accepted the terms of debate established by their opponents and defined their position in response, that they lacked a power of initiation and were stimulated only in reaction to others. In this respect, it could seem that they subscribed to their own version of 'gradualism', in which progress, although slower, was still inevitable.[119] At times this led the rank and file to suspect leaders who emphasized moderation and caution of being 'pink' and implementing a watered-down Socialism rather than a genuinely Conservative approach— this was the substance behind some of the antagonism to the Lloyd George Coalition, and was explicitly charged against Baldwin's second government of 1924–29.[120] However, such methods were equally in the Conservative spirit of working with what was rather than what might be wished for; of the practicality encapsulated in the famous title of the long-serving cabinet minister R. A. Butler's memoirs, that politics was *The Art of the Possible*; and of acceptance that the only reliable route to change was 'one developing continuously out of present practice'.[121]

---

[116] Banks, *Conservative Outlook*, 270; Salisbury to Ormsby-Gore, 25 January 1942, Ormsby-Gore MSS, PEC/11/2/29.

[117] Braine, *Conservatism and Youth*, 4; Davidson, 'Notes on Conservatism', n.d. but c.June 1937, Davidson MSS, DAV/233.

[118] H. Glickman, 'The Toryness of English Conservatism', *Journal of British Studies*, 1/1 (1961), 114–15.

[119] Allison, 'The goal of modern Conservatism', 36.

[120] Salisbury to Selborne, 18 March 1929, Selborne MSS, MS.Selborne/7; Campbell to Bowyer, 15 September 1930, Baldwin MSS, 51/13–15. For two examples a decade apart from the same constituency, see Blaze to Irvin (Chairman, Louth CA), 28 January 1927, Goulton to Heneage, 8 June 1937, Heneage MSS, HNC/4/40, HNC/1/G.

[121] Elliot, *Toryism*, 96.

Nowhere was this more strongly held than with the constitution, the legitimacy of which was derived from its gradual evolution by custom and precedent as 'the natural outcome, through long centuries, of the common sense and good nature of the English people'.[122] It had accumulated the experience and wisdom of many centuries, and its continuance was in itself proof of its validity: 'our curious medley of law and tradition works'.[123] A key feature was a balance between its component parts, so that there would be no 'sole and absolute depository of power'.[124] The growth of the constitution and the common law were not the product of rational calculation but of 'the cases as they have actually occurred'.[125] This store of experience was not to be discarded in favour of the untried, however superficially attractive it might appear. The loss would outweigh any possible gain, as 'institutions to which a country is accustomed derive great strength merely from their familiarity'.[126] The faith of Conservatives in the merits of the constitution was the principal cause of their rejection of authoritarianism, and particularly distanced them from the doctrines of Fascism. Baldwin argued that to even think of having a dictatorship would be 'an act of consummate cowardice, an act of surrender, of throwing in our hands, a confession that we were unable to govern ourselves'.[127] Totalitarianism was 'fundamentally repugnant' and alien to the principles of Conservatism,[128] and there was equally vigorous rejection of the conduct of the British Union of Fascists in the 1930s as outraging the traditions exemplified in British history and enshrined in the constitutional protection of civil liberty. It was believed that 'our people regard a democratic constitution as the pre-condition of all other values'.[129] A pamphlet written by a young serving army officer in 1943 affirmed that 'there is nothing which Conservatism is so jealous to conserve and extend as the personal rights that are the Englishman's most precious heritage and the human dignity that goes with them'.[130] The evolution of these rights through history meant that even 'the poorest Englishman has much to conserve'.[131]

The preservation of individual liberty was 'one of the important parts of the Conservative creed'.[132] Freedom was founded upon political and legal rights, and was linked in the Conservative mind not with economic equality but with the ideal of 'personal freedom through service'.[133] The Conservative conception of freedom embraced inequality, rather than (as with Socialism) seeing the latter as its antithesis. It was the freedom to act differently, to select varying paths and priorities, and so inevitably to arrive at a diversity of outcomes. As it was founded upon choice, any imposition of uniformity or artificial levelling of circumstances was the enemy of

---

[122] Baldwin, *Torch of Freedom*, 5; Baldwin, *Interpreter of England*, 35; NU Conf., 1927, speech by Lord Londonderry.
[123] Beyfus, 'Conservatism', 3.   [124] Bryant, *Spirit of Conservatism*, 46–7.
[125] Banks, *Conservative Outlook*, 8.   [126] Cecil, *Conservatism*, 17.
[127] *Our Heritage of Freedom: The Menace of Dictatorships*, broadcast by Baldwin, 6 March 1934, NU leaflet 3411 (1934).
[128] Lord Eustace Percy, in E. T. Cook (ed.), *Conservatism and the Future* (1935), 21.
[129] Murray, 'Conservative Party and the National Government', 10; SUA Conf., 18 November 1936.
[130] Stelling, *Why I Am a Conservative*, 7.   [131] Braine, *Conservatism and Youth*, 15.
[132] Cecil, *Conservative Ideals*, 12.   [133] Northam, *Conservatism*, 54, 115.

freedom. The aim was 'the utmost freedom of expression', restrained only where it would interfere with the freedom of others.[134] However, it was recognized that society could not be left entirely unsupervised, for 'it is impossible to have liberty without order',[135] and 'without authority liberty becomes licence'.[136] 'English liberty' was therefore defined as 'freedom limited by legality'.[137] In order to avoid chaos, there was a need for some form of government, by means of the recognized hierarchy of leadership.[138] Such authority therefore took a paternalist form, and the relationship between leaders and followers which this exemplified—mutually dependent and sympathetic, with supplication flowing upwards and direction downwards—was mirrored in the structures of the Conservative Party itself. Leadership must have consent and government could not be by force alone; if such was the case, it would have shown itself unworthy of its position and would lack legitimacy, which was one of the reasons why Conservatives disliked the concept of dictatorship.[139] However, there was an obligation on government to carry out its functions; in Lord Hugh Cecil's view, 'nothing is a right except good government'.[140]

The constitution provided the assurance of stability, as the guarantor of the existing order and methods. It was therefore at the centre of the Conservative view of society and politics, and shielded everything else which they sought to conserve. The aim of Conservatism 'must be to preserve national institutions, for on these the benefits of organised society depend'.[141] The monarchy was the legal fount of authority even if its role had become ceremonial and its powers were exercised by ministers, and Conservatives had 'a constant and deep attachment to the Crown'.[142] The historic position of the Tory Party from the seventeenth to the nineteenth centuries was as the Crown party, and due to this it was less identified with the maintenance of aristocratic privilege.[143] By the Second World War, the Crown had 'become the personal expression of the nation's will, the national symbol and the chief unifying link of the British Empire'.[144] Lord Eustace Percy summarized 'the essence of the constitution' as 'the balance between a strong executive and effective popular criticism'.[145] The working core of the constitution was parliament, which was venerated for its age and customs, and validated by its ability to absorb the forces of economic and social change and to contain the expressions of grievance and dissent. With rare exceptions, such as the organizing of the volunteer forces in Ireland in 1912–14 and the General Strike of 1926, political confrontations did not spill over into ordinary life. As early as 1920, Conservatives presented the new concept of democracy as integral to the constitution, for 'it was a constitution

---

[134] Sellon, 'River of Conservatism', 13.   [135] Cooper, *Conservative Point of View*, 16.
[136] Northam, *Conservatism*, 89; S. Baldwin, *Our Inheritance* (1928), 12.
[137] Hearnshaw, *Conservatism in England*, 306; Tory Reform Committee, *What is a Tory?*.
[138] Crisp, *Rebirth of Conservatism*, 94.   [139] Northam, *Conservatism*, 118–19, 121–2.
[140] H. Cecil to Irwin, 31 July 1930, Halifax MSS, C152/19/1/104a.
[141] Bryant, *Spirit of Conservatism*, 37.   [142] Feiling, *Toryism*, 96; Cecil, *Conservatism*, 223.
[143] Banks, *Conservative Outlook*, 9.
[144] Stelling, *Why I Am a Conservative*, 6; Jenner, *Will Conservatism Survive?*, 7; Mrs Hudson Lyall, *The Vote and How to Use it*, NU leaflet 2035 (1922); Stonehaven to Baldwin, 1 November 1933, Baldwin MSS, 59/262–4.
[145] Cook, *Conservatism and the Future*, 37.

which said that majorities must rule'.[146] Public acceptance of the legitimacy of parliamentary government was recognized by Conservatives to be one of the most significant factors in the cohesion and stability of British society. When economic crisis led to the formation of the National Government in August 1931, one beneficial consequence was that 'the importance of Parliament as the governing body had once more been asserted'.[147]

The established Church of England was also an important part of the constitution, but for much of the century before 1914 its position had been contested between the Liberal and Conservative parties. The challenge of Nonconformity to its status and endowments meant that during the Victorian and Edwardian eras the defence of the established Church had been 'an essential part of the work of Conservatism',[148] but with the decline of denominational issues and hostilities after the First World War this ceased to be an important issue. The final pillar of the constitution was the law, which both united and protected people: as Baldwin declared during the General Strike, 'the laws of England are the people's birthright'.[149] The principle of equality before the law defended liberty, by protecting the weak against the strong. The rule of law prevented abuse by the powerful, held institutions to their responsibilities, provided a means for redress, and thus secured a stable political community. This rested upon 'a system of incorruptible justice that accepts no dictation from the State or any interest within the State'.[150]

The most important functions of the state were to restrain conflict within society and to marshal its strength so that it was defended from assault by other societies around it.[151] The first of these required maintaining order, administering the statutes, and acting as arbiter between competing groups and claims. The government alone was able to survey the whole scene, and was required by its duty to act as 'trustee of the interests of the whole community'.[152] For that reason, 'economic forces which would have an anti-social effect must be checked by the authority of the state'.[153] As the expression of a collective will and wisdom, the state had some rights of precedence over individual choice and conscience, and so prevented anarchy.[154] However, the state was just a mechanism, and as such it did not have 'any exceptional or accumulated morality beyond that of the men who compose it'.[155] The basis of the Conservative approach was that 'the state was made for man, not man for the state'.[156] The proper purpose of the state was 'to permit the individual to expand his personality, develop his potentialities and thus contribute to the advancement of the community'.[157] Conservatives therefore located the

---

[146] NU Labour Ctte. report of Conf., 6 March 1920, NU leaflet 1976 (1920).
[147] SUA, WDC, 9 September 1931.   [148] Cecil, *Conservatism*, 100.
[149] Baldwin's statement, *British Gazette*, 6 May 1926.
[150] Stelling, *Why I Am a Conservative*, 5; Bryant, *Spirit of Conservatism*, 27–8.
[151] Scottish Unionist Whip's Office, *The Choice: Unionist Principles versus Socialism* (Edinburgh, 1936), 5; Sir H. Williams, 'Against nationalisation', *Ashridge Journal*, 108 (October 1944), 3.
[152] Cecil, *Conservatism*, 165, 168–9, 195.   [153] Northam, *Conservatism*, 105.
[154] Pickthorn, *Principles and Prejudices*, 16–17.   [155] Feiling, *What Is Conservatism?*, 15.
[156] *Who's for Revolution?*, NU leaflet 3463 (1935); *The Conservative Approach to World and Domestic Affairs*, speech by Eden to Bristol CA, 7 October 1944, NU leaflet 3754 (1944).
[157] Braine, *Conservatism and Youth*, 7; L. S. Amery, *The Forward View* (1935), 417.

freedom of the individual within a communal framework, which was, in turn, based upon the family.[158] This led them to the essential basis of a democratic society: 'the dual principle of co-operation and individual self-government'.[159]

The Conservative ideal was a limited state whose role was focused upon protecting the liberty of the individual from abuse by others, rather than eroding it itself. There was no desire for a vacuum of authority, as 'we believe in being governed, but not in being spoon-fed, and kicked, and patted, and praised, and cursed, and directed, and fined, and licensed'.[160] Conservatives understood that liberties were not derived from the state, but, on the contrary, had to be upheld against it. Powers for the compulsory acquisition of property were always a sensitive matter, and aspects of the housing measures of the 1930s and Coal Bill of 1937 aroused much grass-roots hostility, with the latter condemned as 'too arbitrary and not in keeping with English constitutional practice'.[161] An over-mighty state posed grave dangers to the individualism and enterprise upon which a healthy society depended, for 'the state is a hard master'.[162] This was particularly the case with a Socialist state that would be based on regulation, intervention, and perhaps outright confiscation, but it was also the case in the existing system at the point where the state most regularly impacted upon the owners of property: the levels and forms of taxation. Cecil argued that 'it is impossible for the State equitably to distinguish between one kind of property and another', and that it was wrong to place heavier burdens on a particular group or trade: 'to tax a class specially is to punish them; to punish except for crime is unjust'. In that respect, 'taxation is distinguished from confiscation only in degree'.[163]

Conservative views about the proper role of the state were the product of two strands of thought, which have been described as 'paternalist' and 'libertarian'.[164] However, individual Conservatives cannot be neatly pigeonholed into one or other of these categories, as their views on different issues often varied between the two. These positions were neither absolute nor mutually exclusive, for state action 'should be freely used to defend individual liberty and dignity'.[165] Conservative responses were issue-related rather than the product of an overarching theory; the determining factor was not the abstract concept of the state in itself, but immediate perceptions of the working of 'the agencies of civil society'.[166] No state intervention was desirable where these voluntary and independent economic and social organizations were effective, but where they were not working properly then action by the state had become necessary—although time should be allowed before it was certain that steps should be taken, and these should be the minimum to render

---

[158] Crisp, *Rebirth of Conservatism*, 24–6; Loftus, *Creed of a Tory*, 37.
[159] Braine, *Conservatism and Youth*, 9.   [160] *Seven Points of Conservative Policy*.
[161] Middleton & Prestwich CA, F&GP, 3 February 1938; Harborough CA, Exec., 17 April 1939.
[162] Scottish Unionist Whip's Office, *The Choice*, 35.
[163] Cecil, *Conservatism*, 150, 153.   [164] Greenleaf, *British Political Tradition*, vol. 2, 192–3.
[165] Salisbury, 'Post War Conservative Policy at Home and in External Relations', first draft, 3 July 1941.
[166] E. H. H. Green, *Ideologies of Conservatism: Conservative Political Ideas in the Twentieth Century* (Oxford, 2002), 241, 261.

them effective again. The variation as to which agencies were seen at any time to be functioning inadequately explains the differing judgements as to where and how the state should act. One example of this in the interwar period was in housing, for Conservatives were often appalled by the ugly spread of private and speculative 'ribbon' development along the main roads, whilst public provision on a large scale was pioneered by Conservative local authorities in cities such as Birmingham, Glasgow, Sheffield, and Leeds. In addition, in the rural areas, which were almost always under Conservative control, smaller-scale municipal housing projects tackled the problem of decrepit cottages and lifted a burden from the estate owners, many of whom were in financial difficulties.

Conservatives started from 'a healthy prejudice' in favour of private enterprise, but 'when something different is needed they are prepared to accept whatever method is preferable'.[167] On the surface, this could seem inconsistent or to be no more than a form of 'patch the leaks' pragmatism. However, it was founded upon the view that society had to be regulated and supported in certain ways, and that it was the duty of government to see this carried out by means which were consistent, economical, and balanced the need for efficiency and cohesion with the liberties of the individual. Informing this was the underlying sceptical current in Conservatism, which produced the predisposition against state action and the feeling that it should be employed only where clearly necessary—of which wartime was the best example. Even then, restrictions upon individual liberty 'can only be justified by the greater need of the community in every instance'.[168] In general, Conservatives were doubtful of the wisdom or practicality of intervention by the state in customary relationships, as it was likely to take the form of crude and simplistic regulation of what had evolved in complex and subtle ways. However, this did not entail an absolute proscription against state intervention, and there was regular emphasis that any such inflexible position was descended from 'Cobdenite' Liberalism and the claim that state action was contrary to Conservative principles 'has no foundation'.[169] Instead, Conservative attitudes were governed by the understanding that 'the State is not simple but complex, not uniform but a harmony of opposites'.[170]

The widespread oversimplification that Conservatism was opposed in principle to action by the state was largely a by-product of the defence of the existing economic system against Socialism. This became a central political issue in the interwar period due to the rise of the Labour Party and its specific attacks on the deficiencies of capitalism. Conservatives defended capitalism as a system which had proven itself through the rise in living standards from which all classes had benefited since the Industrial Revolution, which was responsive to public demands, and which required much less in the way of regulation and bureaucracy than any

---

[167] Northam, *Conservatism*, 106–7.
[168] NU Conf., 1943, Brighton & Hove CA resolution.
[169] Conservative Research Department memo, 'The relations between the state and industry', December 1934, CPA, CRD/1/64/5.
[170] Feiling, *What Is Conservatism?*, 14.

alternative.[171] It had the advantages of enterprise, invention, openness, and efficiency, and its benefits came with comparatively little financial cost in terms of the burden of taxation. Making a profit was not immoral, and 'the hope of reward is one of the great motives for energy, and in itself a perfectly honourable motive'.[172] Conservatives were rather more uneasy about some of the social costs which might be involved, and for that reason they never favoured the unrestrained operation of market forces, or what they regarded as the Liberal policy of pure laissez-faire.[173] This would have a dissolving effect upon the social bonds to which they attached greater importance, and this explains the hostile reaction of many Conservatives to the endorsement of competition and ambition in the Earl of Birkenhead's famous Rectoral Address of 1924; this was seen as 'the gospel of sordid, self-assertive greed (and contempt for the underdog)',[174] which was 'the very point of view which the war has rendered definitely hateful'.[175] Instead, 'it must be the duty of anything calling itself a society to keep the balance between its members',[176] and the role of government was to protect those unable to look after themselves, as in the much-celebrated Tory tradition of the early Victorian Factory Acts. The most significant equivalent in the first decades of the twentieth century was the Conservative policy of tariff protection, as this gave the state the role of moderating economic activity with the aim of sheltering industries that were in difficulty and maintaining their workers' standard of living. However, there was general acceptance that it was not the function of the state to ignore economic realities: as Sir Isidore Salmon MP, head of the Lyons food consortium, told the 1934 annual conference, 'let the State govern, but not bolster up industry that could not be kept going'.[177] The Conservative approach was summed up by Sir John Gilmour, the Home Secretary, in 1932: 'it was the duty of Government not to run businesses but to oil the machinery and to give opportunities for industries to run their businesses upon proper and sound lines'.[178] However, it was Macmillan's view that industry, left to its own devices, was failing to respond to changed world economic conditions, and so the state must 'step in and insist' on reorganization.[179]

Conservatives were always reluctant to resort to economic intervention in peacetime, and their underlying view was 'that government intervention should be invited by industry, not forced upon it'.[180] Two other more general considerations held back the Conservatives from enlarging the scope of government: first, that they had no desire to establish precedents which their opponents could exploit and might dangerously extend; second, that the effects of intervention were difficult to predict and control, for 'the State is a clumsy, rigid instrument, difficult to handle and operating heavily and unexpectedly'.[181] The Conservatives were always restrained by the belief

---

[171] *Progress under Capitalism*, NU leaflet 3478 (1935); Crisp, *Rebirth of Conservatism*, 44–7; Bryant, *Spirit of Conservatism*, 84.
[172] Hollis, *Quality or Equality?*, 6.
[173] Boothby et al., *Industry and the State*, 18–19; *Conservatism in a Nutshell*.
[174] Bledisloe to Baldwin, 31 January 1924, Baldwin MSS, 159/183–4.
[175] R. Cecil to Baldwin, 1 February 1924, Baldwin MSS, 35/203–7.
[176] Feiling, *What Is Conservatism?*, 16.   [177] NU Conf., 1934.
[178] SUA Conf., 30 November 1932.   [179] H. Macmillan, *The Middle Way* (1938), 127.
[180] Banks, *Conservative Outlook*, 265.   [181] Cecil, *Conservatism*, 189–90.

that too active a role for the state would require intrusive powers and a large bureaucracy, which would be ruinously expensive, unaccountable, and dictatorial; hence the infamous claim by Winston Churchill (Party Leader 1940–55) in an election broadcast on 4 June 1945, that a future Socialist government would need 'some form of Gestapo' to impose its edicts. The latter was not an isolated or maverick remark: the left-wing Tory Reform Committee also thought 'it is a short step from the present Socialist worship of the State to a form of National-Socialism'.[182]

Conservative attitudes were not static during this period, and it was observed in the 1940s that the party mainstream now espoused views 'which would have made Conservatives of twenty years ago do more than sit up and rub their eyes in surprise'.[183] It was accepted that since the beginning of the century, Britain had become 'a far more closely integrated community', in which people recognized 'a moral responsibility for the welfare of our fellow citizens'. As Lord Cranborne, the Leader of the Party in the House of Lords, told Conservative MPs in 1943: 'we have indeed already become...a social democracy, if by those words is meant a democracy with a social sense and a social conscience', whilst the growth of a 'community sense' which had resulted 'inevitably involves some interference by the state in the life of the individual'.[184] Primarily due to the experiences of the two world wars, together with the state-promoted marketing and rationalization schemes of the 1930s, the permissible areas of government activity were pragmatically extended. In the mid-1930s, even such an orthodox figure as Neville Chamberlain (Party Leader 1937–40) could state as an incontrovertible and uncontroversial fact 'that laissez-faire was completely dead'.[185] By the end of the Second World War, younger Conservatives believed that 'public works, public control of monopolies, public utilities, all have their part to play in the orderly development of a modern nation's resources'.[186] The widespread acceptance that there was a place for both a public and private sector made the adjustment to Labour's reforms after 1945 that much easier, although Conservatives held that state intervention should be restricted to 'practical expedients to supplement private enterprise'.[187]

The Conservative approach to social issues was founded upon the Victorian legacy of Shaftesbury, Disraeli, and the 3rd Marquess of Salisbury: practical and undogmatic reforms in areas such as factory legislation, sanitation, housing reform, local government, the establishment of some trade union rights, and so on. This was cited as proof that Conservatism had never been hostile to the working class, and was contrasted with the moralistic, rigid, and interfering nature of radical measures. Conservative policy also reflected the party's tendency after a time to accept reform measures, which it had resisted, once they had become part of the established system, and so to operate them without carping or seeking to under-

---

[182] Tory Reform Committee, *What is a Tory?*.
[183] Arran to Scott, 21 December 1943, Scott MSS, MSS.119/3/P/AR/3.
[184] Cranborne, *Our Political Future*.
[185] Conservative Research Department, minutes of meeting, 2 March 1934, CPA, CRD/1/64/5.
[186] Stelling, *Why I Am a Conservative*, 13; Jenner, *Will Conservatism Survive?*, 31.
[187] Stelling, *Why I Am a Conservative*, 13; SUA Conf., 17 November 1933; *Looking Ahead* (1941).

mine them. This was the case with the Liberal welfare reforms of 1906–14, which in some cases had been objected to only on matters of detail. If anything, these were extended and codified by the measures of the 1924–29 government, especially the introduction of pensions for widows and orphans in 1925. However, the comprehensive nature of the integrated welfare state proposed in the Beveridge Report of 1942 raised important issues of principle. It was referred by Churchill to the party body considering plans for reconstruction, the Post-War Problems Central Committee, where it was examined by a small sub-committee chaired by Ralph Assheton (Party Chairman 1944–46). Their report noted the logical implications of the scheme: 'provision by the state of complete Social Security can only be achieved at the expense of personal freedom and by sacrificing the right of an individual to choose what life he wishes to lead and what occupation he should follow'.[188] Their concern about the costs was shared by the Conservative Chancellor of the Exchequer, Kingsley Wood, who doubted the affordability of the scheme in the likely postwar economic situation. These reservations, and concerns about the financial costs, shaped the Conservative response in the debate on Beveridge in the Commons in February 1943, and this in turn affected public attitudes to the party, as many people embraced the report as the blueprint for a better, fairer, and more classless society. However, although the Conservative Party sought, as always, to adapt to the temper of the times and to use new methods and tools, the fundamental purpose of its social policy had not changed: 'It should be our aim, as Conservatives, to build up a brave, healthy, industrious and independent population devoted to the cause of freedom and alive to the responsibilities which such a cause demands, and brought up to put duty and service before rights and privileges.'[189]

National security in the wider world was a high priority for all Conservatives, as 'we rank the security of this country and the Empire as the first duty of the Government'.[190] This depended upon having both adequate armed forces and resolution of purpose, although by the late 1930s it was being emphasized that 'British foreign policy can never be aggressive'.[191] Conservatives were always dubious of the robustness of international law and institutions such as the League of Nations, which were founded in Liberalism and its optimism about human intentions. Their instincts of realism and self-reliance suggested that the nation must look to its own resources to survive. These were not only its evident outer defences (the armed services and the support given by the empire) and the economic strength that underpinned them, but also its inner health—both moral and physical, and hence the interest in encouraging physical fitness amongst the young. However,

---

[188] Post-War Problems Central Ctte., report of ctte. on the Beveridge Report, 19 January 1943, CPA, CRD/2/28/6; Eastern Area, Council AGM, 24 March 1943.
[189] Post-War Problems Central Ctte., report of ctte. on the Beveridge Report, 19 January 1943, CPA, CRD/2/28/6.
[190] *Conservatism in a Nutshell*; security against external aggression and of the seaborne trade came first in the 'seven main precepts of Conservative policy' defined by one local association: Hertford CA, AR, 1936, 'Conservatism'.
[191] Northam, *Conservatism*, 148; Braine, *Conservatism and Youth*, 20.

the stridency of Victorian and Edwardian patriotism had been moderated by the impact of the Great War. This left a significant legacy in Conservative attitudes to Britain's world role: as a satisfied power with no desire for more territory, the aim was to retain what was held in a defensive and non-provocative posture. The priority was for peaceful resolution through reasonable compromise, or 'appeasement', and the avoidance of sabre-rattling and jingoism. A discussion of Conservatism published in 1939 was clear that 'a wise foreign policy must aim at making necessary readjustments', 'in accordance with facts as they are and not as we would like them to be'.[192] There was both advantage and reassurance to be obtained from Britain's position as one of the greatest powers, and a wish to maintain its former (possibly romanticized) prestige and reputation. Thus Baldwin considered that Austen Chamberlain was 'an admirable Foreign Secretary' because 'our word goes once more and our prestige abroad stands where it ought to'.[193] Although there was a traditional hankering for isolationism, it was recognized that being a great power carried with it moral responsibilities which could not be shrugged off. Britain had a duty as well as an interest in the maintenance of peace, and this combination led to the acceptance of multilateral naval disarmament in the 1920s, to the awkward dichotomy of the Hoare-Laval Plan in 1935, and to Neville Chamberlain's flights to Germany in 1938. There was no desire to interfere in the internal affairs of other powers, but it was always understood that no British government could permit the continent of Europe to fall under the dominion of a single aggressive power, and so this danger had to be resisted by force in 1939 as it had been in 1914.

The empire had been central in Conservative thoughts as a focus of pride and patriotism since Disraeli enshrined its preservation as the second of his three principles; for Baldwin, this was 'his fundamental creed'.[194] Its existence was the great success of recent history, and captured the imagination with its tales of heroism and the romance of exotic places and the remote frontier. The story of the empire exemplified Britain's finest traditions: 'the spirit of adventure, independence of character, individual effort, courage and fortitude'.[195] However, in the 1920s there was 'nothing in the nature of flag-wagging or boasting of painting the map red'.[196] Instead, the empire was seen 'as a responsibility and an opportunity'.[197] Many Conservatives were either personally or through their family directly connected with the fortunes of the empire by trade, service in the colonies or India, and settlement in Africa and the Dominions. The outlook of most party members and many MPs on imperial issues was fairly simplistic, and usually based upon the conceptions current at the time when they reached adulthood—thus Churchill's views of India did not greatly develop from those formed when serving there as a young army officer in the 1890s. Attitudes to non-Europeans were rooted in the

---

[192] Northam, *Conservatism*, 148, 152.
[193] Baldwin to Irwin, 15 September 1927, Halifax MSS, C152/17/1/253f.
[194] Statement to the Cabinet, 10 March 1933, *BP*, 306; E. S. Riley, *Our Cause: A Handbook of Conservatism* (Derby and London, 1939), 13.
[195] *Empire Day*, NU leaflet 2559 (1925).
[196] Baldwin, *Our Inheritance*, 68.
[197] 'A Gentleman with a duster' [H. Begbie, pseud.], *The Conservative Mind* (1925), 53.

unquestioned racism which, in this era, pervaded all classes of British society, generating 'an innate and strong feeling of racial difference and superiority'.[198] In the 1920s, even young MPs on the party's left wing had no hesitation in asserting that 'we can govern many races better than they can govern themselves', and should therefore ignore 'any whines or whimpers about self-determination'.[199] There was an assumption that native populations were like children, who needed—and indeed would appreciate—firm paternalist government.[200] In this, it was essential to avoid the sentimentalism that characterized Liberal and Labour approaches, which were 'simply the old tale of sparing the rod and spoiling the child'.[201] Alongside this, the belief that democracy was 'essentially an English institution, utterly unsuited to foreigners and orientals' underlay right-wing doubts about any rapid political developments in India or the colonial empire.[202]

Conservatives took pride in the empire's diversity and in the continued association within it of the self-governing and now almost autonomous Dominions, and especially their support in wartime. There was faith in its future, based upon the belief that 'each country in the Empire finds its completest expression as part of it'.[203] As an empire which was also a democracy, it was 'unique in the history of man' in being 'founded, not upon the sword, not upon might, but upon moral principles'.[204] However, this did not entail a dilution or diminution of the British role of leadership, because 'the Conservative has faith in his own race and believes that the gifts which have been bestowed upon that race carry with them obligations'.[205] The development of the empire was seen by Conservatives as a 'spiritual inheritance which we hold in trust', whether or not it produced measurable economic gains.[206] The late Victorian concept of the empire as 'the white man's burden' was upheld with certainty and pride: 'its final justification exists in the cultural mission that it fulfils'.[207] The colonial empire was presented not as a resource for exploitation to the material benefit of the home population, but as a Christian duty to which the mother country would send forth its finest sons: 'Conservatives regard the work that we are doing for the Colonies as a mission that is essential to the welfare of the world.'[208] The size and unity of the empire meant 'we can be such a great influence in bringing peace and prosperity to the world'.[209] However, for this to happen, the empire had to be sustained against its tendency to drift apart

---

[198] Beamish memo, 'Notes on a speech given by Gandhi', 23 September 1931, Beamish MSS, CAC, BEAM/3/3.
[199] Cooper, *Conservative Point of View*, 40.
[200] Salisbury to Balfour, 16 October 1918, Balfour MSS, Add.49758/319–20; Winchester CA, Council, 23 July 1934.
[201] Banks, *Conservative Outlook*, 44.
[202] Gwynne to Baldwin, 5 April 1929, Baldwin MSS, 36/111–15.
[203] Northam, *Conservatism*, 125.
[204] Braine, *Conservatism and Youth*, 22; Baldwin, *On England*, 222.
[205] Cooper, *Conservative Point of View*, 40.
[206] Richmond & Barnes CA to Baldwin, 27 July 1935, Baldwin MSS, 141/136; U. Norris, *Under One Flag: A Short Empire Sketch for Children*, NU leaflet 2560 (1925).
[207] Dawson, 'Conservatism', 46.
[208] Stelling, *Why I Am a Conservative*, 10–11; Baldwin, *On England*, 71–2.
[209] 'First Principles', *Young Britons' Organisers Manual* (c.1937), copy at Bolton CA.

and the feebleness of the Liberal and Labour parties, and so it was incumbent upon the Conservative Party to 'constitute the core' of imperial sentiment.[210]

The interwoven ideas which have been discussed in this opening section were collectively recognizable as 'Conservative principles', although there was 'certainly no explicit philosophy consistently put forward and consciously defended'.[211] Even so, although it was not exhibited as a visible process, a philosophy of Conservatism did permeate the fabric of the party, perhaps unconsciously more than consciously, so that there were strong connections between the political conceptions of the leadership and their followers, and between the minority of active local workers and the passive wider membership. Although articulated by the rank and file in explicit forms much less frequently and more briefly, those expressions which did occur were complementary in ideas and attitudes to those presented in print by the MPs and political academics. The grass-roots opinions discussed in Chapter 3 and the factions of the parliamentary party outlined in Chapter 5 were all nourished by the waters of Cecil's river of converging streams, which was why references to 'Conservative principles' invoked a tangle of meanings that were shared by those using the term and the audiences to whom they were communicating.

At a basic level, this could be defined even more accessibly in terms of objectives, as in the classic Disraelian triptych. If the Conservative Party ever had a single accepted statement of its creed, it was the three-point definition which he gave at the Crystal Palace in 1872: the maintenance of the constitution, the preservation of the empire, and the improvement of the condition of the people. This summation's lack of specific objectives gave it universality and adaptability; it was constantly referred back to, and became a form of touchstone.[212] In 1945, the Chairman of the Party had no doubt that 'the principles laid down by Disraeli still hold good'.[213] By the close of our period, the practical meaning of each part could be translated as the preservation of order, the defence of national interests, and the responsibility to govern in ways that maintained social cohesion. This was put with equal brevity, but in slightly different order, in the resolution passed by the party's Central Council in March 1937, which defined 'the fundamental and inseparable principles of the Conservative Party' as 'empire unity, social progress and constitutional democracy'.[214] A three-point definition was almost *de rigeur*, and thus for the young army officer David Stelling in 1943, it was the preservation of institutions and traditions, the maintenance of social stability, and 'the progressive development of conditions under which every individual may be enabled to enjoy the fullest life of which he is capable, rendering due service to the community in return'.[215]

---

[210] Churchill to Irwin, 1 January 1930, *WSC*; Winterton to Lytton, 8 November 1923, Lytton MSS, F160/26/25–33.

[211] Elliot, *Toryism*, 98.

[212] W. Smithers, *Conservative Principles* (Sidcup, 1933), 1–2; *Looking Ahead*, speech by Baldwin, 5 October 1934, NU leaflet 3434 (1934); 'First Principles', *Young Britons' Organisers Manual*; Riley, *Our Cause*, 8, 62; Jenner, *Will Conservatism Survive?*, 5; Uxbridge CA, Council, 12 July 1938.

[213] R. Assheton, *Facing the Future*, NU leaflet 45/2 (1945).

[214] NU Central Council, 23 March 1937.

[215] Stelling, *Why I Am a Conservative*, 4; Amery, 'Conservatism and the future (part 1)', 1.

The common ground of all the definitions, however they were phrased, was that Conservative principles were of universal application: Conservatism was 'an imperishable, practical ideal, which is applicable to all modern political problems, however new or complicated they may appear'.[216] Conservative principles were held to be constant truths that were not limited to time and place, and so they provided consistency in the party's responses to the ephemeral issues of the day. However, as Baldwin declared during the party's participation in the National Government, 'there does not exist any gospel of Tory principles which can tell you what principles to apply...in a changing world'.[217] Specific problems of government were therefore approached in terms of their current context and with the aim of identifying immediate and relevant remedies, and were considered individually rather than in relation to any overall pattern or theory. This could easily be mistaken for no more than pragmatism, or a purpose no more profound than providing efficient and economic administration. In fact, although they were not normally matters of debate, the concepts and values which were wrapped up in the term 'Conservative principles' shaped their adherents' policies in government, building on assumptions and marking out boundaries, although to a different extent from one issue to another.

TEMPERAMENT

Conservatism was defined by the author and politician John Buchan as 'above all things a spirit', and this living element was the product of the outlook and values which underlay the ideas discussed above.[218] Conservatism was 'an attitude to our national life', based 'on certain established principles but developed in each man according to his own temperament'.[219] The foundation of its ethos was 'natural conservatism', which Cecil defined as 'a tendency of the human mind' deriving from two elements: 'distrust of the unknown' and 'liking for the familiar'.[220] Although they often reinforce each other, these are not the same thing; even when there is no danger or difficulty in something new, people will often prefer to stay with what exists simply because it is familiar. Many people feel most comfortable in their accustomed environment, and prefer security to adventure or experiment. What is known may not be perfect, but its imperfections are understood. Challenges to custom are upsetting, unwelcome, and raise fears more than hopes, whilst conformity is the path of least resistance. At the least, change involves a readjustment which entails varying degrees of 'perplexity, effort, confusion of mind, weariness'. No such strains are imposed by remaining with what already exists, and if it has proven 'to be at least safe and endurable' then the balance of doubt lies in its favour.[221] As the 'natural conservative' frame of mind made the least demands, it

---

[216] Hertford CA, AR, 1936, 'Conservatism'. [217] *Looking Ahead* (1934).
[218] Buchan, preface in Bryant, *Spirit of Conservatism*, vii; York diary, 17 January 1945.
[219] Stelling, *Why I Am a Conservative*, 3.
[220] Cecil, *Conservatism*, 9, 14; Ludovici, *Defence of Conservatism*, 2.
[221] Cecil, *Conservatism*, 10.

could be adopted without conscious recognition and appear to be the consequence of laziness or apathy. Inaction is always easier than action, and the avoidance of disturbance has an appeal in a world where there is already too much uncertainty. In the aftermath of the unprecedented strains of the Great War, the fear of unsettling and unpredictable change—as a general anxiety rather than in any specific form—was a particularly powerful force in 'natural conservatism'. This 'small c' conservatism could be the product of personal temperament or of social and economic position; it was the consequence of outlook, age, and experience as much as of the possession of property or the fear of descent into a lower class. It may have been a particular impulse amongst the less confident and less educated, and those in respectable but modest circumstances. It was fostered by insecurity, and the dangers of change were likely to seem greater to those least able to be resilient, either by their character or their material resources. However, preference for the status quo did not necessarily have a negative basis, for such conservatism also 'springs from contentment; it tends to tranquillity and to a desire to be left alone'.[222]

The Conservative temperament was also inclined to pessimism. This was a natural consequence of the recognition that humanity existed in a disorderly world which had no innate tendency to goodness: 'all our lives are "thwarted" and "security" is unobtainable in our precarious existence'.[223] As human beings could not control or predict the future, change was at least as likely to produce bad results as good; hence the presumption expressed in the proverb 'if it isn't broken, don't mend it'. There were two other strands that reinforced this basic pessimism, of which the first was the view held by every generation that standards had fallen since its youth: 'in every walk of life they found people saying that things were not as they used to be'.[224] Changing times are always unsettling, as is the sense of being left behind, and these give impetus to the second and equally perennial strand: anti-modernism, provoked by dislike of recent developments in fashion, leisure, art, personal behaviour, and so on, even more than in political affairs. These elements of pessimism were most likely to strike a chord with those of a more fatalist or passive frame of mind, who might grumble but in practice accepted that 'what will be, will be'. This could easily elide into torpor, and hence Conservatives often felt themselves struggling to get apathetic voters to go to the poll, even when it was clearly in their self-interest to do so.

This sentiment of pessimism was often combined with its close relation of scepticism, and together these informed the Conservative suspicion of grand plans and universal panaceas: 'we are not perfectionists'.[225] Buchan ascribed to the 'Tory' element in the party's heritage the duty 'to maintain honesty and candour of mind, to examine all things, and to give the lie to folly'.[226] It was considered that reformers

---

[222] Hearnshaw, *Conservatism in England*, 8.
[223] Emrys-Evans to Bartlett, 23 January 1941, Emrys-Evans MSS, Add.58248/117–19.
[224] Rochdale CA, AR, AGM, 3 March 1938.
[225] Hogg, *Times We Live In*, 4.
[226] J. Buchan, *A Message...to the Junior Imperial & Constitutional League*, NU leaflet 2804 (1928).

were too hasty and glib in their assumptions of what was possible, and 'Conservatives instinctively mistrust the "clever chaps"'.[227] The rejection of idealism could lead to cynicism, but generally did not do so because the Conservative temperament was almost never one-dimensional; as Feiling wrote in 1930, 'in such a creed there are elements both of scepticism and of faith'.[228] Conservative pessimism was not bitter or antagonistic, but rather derived from experience of the world and human understanding; 'Toryism is based upon good nature,' declared Duff Cooper, and so it was shaped by a 'kindly humour' and a 'genial acceptance of people and conditions'.[229] Furthermore, there was a countervailing—if diffuse and underlying—strand of optimism, in the simple conviction that 'love is more natural than hate, and co-operation more natural than strife'.[230] Thus Conservatives were sustained by 'faith in this people', although it was 'not devoid of fears'.[231]

For most people, the world turns upon each day. Their views are formed by the matters which directly affect their own lives, and not by prospects on the far horizon. Conservatism was 'based on the observation of life',[232] and took as its starting point the world as it was: Conservatives 'claim to be ordinary human beings concerned with the actual conditions of life'.[233] When Conservative MPs were asked which books had influenced them, some predictably cited Burke, Disraeli, and Macaulay, but far more declared simply 'none', and would have agreed with Aylmer Hunter-Weston MP, who cited 'the great Book of "Life"', and Basil Peto MP, who responded: 'my political views shaped themselves on the events of the times'.[234] The Conservative outlook placed strong emphasis upon 'realism', which was seen as a virtue and not a limitation: it derived from the 'preference for experience over theory'[235] and 'determination to know the world and mankind as it is and not as one would like it to be'.[236] Its essence was distilled in the 'conventional wisdoms' which many people found supportive rather than confining. These were so customary and habitual that they acted at the level of assumption rather than being subject to analysis: 'look before you leap', 'a bird in the hand is worth two in the bush', 'let sleeping dogs lie', 'better the devil you know than the devil you don't', 'don't rush your fences', and so on. Such sentiments were often summarized by proverbs; for example, that you could not expect 'something for nothing'—a simple caution that could be used to undercut Socialist promises of a rosy future. These values were instilled by traditional homilies and children's stories, such as the tale of the girl who played with matches and died in the resulting conflagration. Many of these stories dramatically conveyed the dangers of rashness and the imprudence of trusting the glib promises of strangers, and carried an underlying conservative message. They also had contemporary resonance, and thus Socialist agitators could be seen as a

---

[227] Northam, *Conservatism*, 39.   [228] Feiling, *What Is Conservatism?*, 12.
[229] Duff Cooper speech notes, 'Toryism', n.d.   [230] Northam, *Conservatism*, 87.
[231] Loftus, *Creed of a Tory*, 41.   [232] Elliot, *Toryism*, 4.
[233] Cambridge CA, Adoption Meeting, 20 November 1923, speech of Sir D. Newton MP.
[234] Replies to question 3 of Wedgwood's survey for the History of Parliament, Wedgwood Questionnaire MSS.
[235] Cecil, *Conservatism*, 9; *Conservatism in a Nutshell*.
[236] O. Stanley, conclusion in Crisp, *The Rebirth of Conservatism*, 198.

new and sinister form of the Pied Piper, especially as Conservatives feared that younger working-class voters would most easily fall under their spell. Conservatives believed in working with the grain, employing settled methods and customary practices; however, this could easily become the assurance (and reassurance) that this was the only way in which things should be done. In part, this was a matter of low expectations, often based upon personal experience of the hard knocks received in the 'school of life'. This outlook could be expressed in the view that 'the facts of life are Tory', and contributed to the widely recognized tendency of people of both sexes to become more resistant to change as they became older, and for personal and social conservatism to become mirrored by political Conservatism. Similarly, attitudes to economic issues were based upon a 'common sense' extrapolation that national policy should be modelled on conduct that would be advisable for an individual or family: not living beyond your means, honouring debts and paying them off before borrowing more, and so on.[237]

In all of these ways, 'Conservative thought is a true counterpart of life'.[238] However, although it saw itself as grounded in realism, the Conservative approach consisted of much more than pragmatism and expediency: there were higher aims in politics which resulted from attitudes that were deeply and sincerely held. Conservatism 'stands for the universal and permanent things of life',[239] and so 'to turn things transient into things enduring, this is the task of the Tory'.[240] There was a need for 'living political principles', which should be based 'on the national as against both the international and the class outlook; on the historic, conservative and constructive as against the theoretical and destructive point of view'.[241] It was also aspirational: in the words of Dorothy Crisp, the editor of a volume of essays by younger Conservatives published in 1931, 'Conservatism is a quest'.[242] Its essence was to be found not in codified principles but in values which in turn shaped 'standards of conduct'.[243] These were more important than wealth or status, for 'service not profit' should be 'the motive of all conduct'.[244] The party regretted the decline in public respect for those engaged in politics, for 'politician' should be not a term of denigration but 'a person who is devoting his time and talents to the service of his country'.[245] Much of Conservative idealism was based upon an ethic of service which influenced many of those from aristocratic and upper-class backgrounds to play a part in public life and to undertake offices that might be onerous and unrewarding (particularly posts in the empire), as 'only service can justify privilege'.[246] Neville Chamberlain explained his wish to go to

[237] R. McKibbin, 'Class and conventional wisdom: the Conservative Party and the "public" in inter-war Britain', in R. McKibbin, *The Ideologies of Class* (Oxford, 1990), 274–5.
[238] Wood, *Conservative Beliefs*, 12.
[239] Hearnshaw, *Conservatism in England*, 23.
[240] Bryant, *Spirit of Conservatism*, 4.
[241] Amery to Baldwin, 28 January 1924, Baldwin MSS, 42/166–73.
[242] Crisp, *Rebirth of Conservatism*, 57.
[243] Northam, *Conservatism*, 40, 115.
[244] Salisbury, 'Post War Conservative Policy at Home and in External Relations', first draft, 3 July 1941.
[245] *To Women Voters*.   [246] Stelling, *Why I Am a Conservative*, 9.

the Ministry of Health rather than the much more prestigious Treasury in 1924 in similar terms: 'I believe I may do something to improve the conditions for the less fortunate classes—and that's after all what one is in politics for.'[247] His leader approved, for to Baldwin 'the political career properly viewed is really a kind of Ministry'.[248]

One of the most powerful of Conservative values was duty, a term which was frequently employed.[249] The foremost claim upon the individual was his or her duty, and it was the discharge of these responsibilities which justified the privilege of a stake in society and a voice in its counsels, for 'when a privilege is allowed, a duty is also demanded'.[250] There was no doubt which was more important: as Baldwin stated, 'put your duty first, and think about your rights afterwards'.[251] The highest of all duties was that owed to God, but this was a matter of private conscience which the state no longer governed. The greatest public duty was to the nation, for 'we can best perform our duty to the world by discharging adequately our duty towards our own people first'.[252] This entailed obligations to act in ways which made the nation healthier and more secure, and to obey the law—if necessary, to the extent of military service at the risk of life. The beneficiary of such duty might be the state, but it was usually expressed symbolically by the Crown—hence the impact of the Oxford Union resolution of 1933 not to fight 'for King and country'. It was also understood that there was a duty to act morally and with responsibility to others, and this held society together, preventing self-indulgence and irresponsibility. One danger of Socialism was its claim that the upper class would only follow its own material self-interest, for such a neglect of the duties that were integral to its privileges would dissolve the bonds of social unity and release the lower classes from any obligation to accept the existing order. This charge had to be shown to be false, and hence the disapproval of misconduct in the upper class, or displays of wealth that were so conspicuous that they would widen class divisions—such vulgarity was looked down on by the social elite, in part because it would provoke contempt from below and undermine the legitimacy of all wealth.[253] The Conservative view that property 'has its duties as well as its rights' originated in the feudal obligations of landowners to those above them and those below.[254] The country gentleman George Courthope MP was not unusual in having been taught 'from early youth' by his father 'that it was the duty of everyone to take an interest in national politics'.[255] However, the poor were not without their duty

---

[247] N. Chamberlain to Baldwin, 7 November 1924, Baldwin MSS, 42/256–7.

[248] Baldwin, *On England*, 197.

[249] Service and duty were prominent themes in Baldwin's speeches, e.g. *On England*, vii, 19, 21, 61–3, 73–4, 200; *Our Inheritance*, 201–3; *Service of Our Lives* (1937), 157.

[250] Hollis, *Quality or Equality?*, 20; Wessex Area, Exec., 24 February 1943.

[251] Baldwin, *Service of Our Lives*, 157; Riley, *Our Cause*, 15; *Conservatism in a Nutshell*; Post-War Problems Central Ctte., report of ctte. on the Beveridge Report, 19 January 1943, CPA, CRS/2/28/6.

[252] Lloyd and Wood, *The Great Opportunity*, 7.

[253] Parker et al., *Declaration of Tory Principles*, 31–2; Gilmour to Macdonald (organiser of the Fife Hunt Ball), 16 November 1931, Gilmour MSS, GD383/39/1.

[254] Banks, *Conservative Outlook*, 15.

[255] Reply to question 1 of Wedgwood's survey for the History of Parliament, Wedgwood Questionnaire MSS.

also, especially of patriotism and observance of the law. For this reason, it was 'the acceptance of those principles of mutual service which are the condition of all ordered liberty'.[256] It was understood that the path of duty might—perhaps even should—be a thorny one and require an element of sacrifice or self-abnegation, and for this reason the easiest or most comfortable course might not be the right one. The corollary of duty was obedience, by which was meant not unthinking subservience to authority but recognition of obligations within the nation and under the law, and, on a more personal level, of servant to master and of child to parent. In the same spirit, a talk for children in the party's 'Young Britons' organization made it clear that 'the right kind of freedom is unselfish'.[257]

The ethical code within which Conservatism operated was derived from a long-established national tradition of Christian principles. These were concerned with the salvation of the individual, and thus 'it is ultimately on his respect for the dignity of the human soul that the Conservative bases his political faith'.[258] The teachings of the New Testament provided the moral foundation of society, elevating concepts of truth and charity, denying legitimacy to the imposition of brute force, and offering ideals higher than the acquisition of worldly goods. However, the Bible did not prescribe material equality; whilst it stated that the rich man would have great difficulty in entering heaven, it did not say that there should be no rich men. In the parable of the talents, it was those who had worked and used their skills to double their wealth who were commended; what mattered was not wealth as such, but how it was regarded and used.[259] The succour of the poor should be through actions of individual charity, which bettered the soul of the donor, and not the compulsory redistribution of wealth by the state, which bypassed the sense of responsibility and was in that manner corrupting. Moral conduct was the responsibility of the individual, for 'man cannot be made good by Act of Parliament'.[260] An essential element in Conservative morality was an expectation of justice, which was not dependent upon economic or social uniformity: 'what matters…is not where a man starts but the amount of ground he covers'. Progress and attainment were intrinsic, personal, and relative, as 'every man should endeavour to raise himself by his own efforts to the highest point to which his nature can attain'.[261] In the Conservative view, the true morality was 'that justice shall be done to the man who makes the effort'.[262]

'Fairness' was a fundamental value which was embedded in the culture not only of Conservatism but of the British people as a whole, as 'Fair Play is a *finer jewel* to any Englishman than any political creed.'[263] This was also often expressed as 'the British spirit of sportsmanship', and sporting analogies and metaphors were commonplace in Conservative discourse.[264] The concept of 'fair play' was considered to

---

[256] Lloyd and Wood, *The Great Opportunity*, 10.
[257] 'First Principles', *Young Britons' Organisers Manual*.
[258] Stelling, *Why I Am a Conservative*, 25; Cecil, *Conservatism*, 164.
[259] Wood, *Conservative Beliefs*, 7.   [260] Northam, *Conservatism*, 61.
[261] Bryant, *Spirit of Conservatism*, 10.   [262] Crisp, *Rebirth of Conservatism*, 38.
[263] Mann to Baldwin, 5 November 1930, Baldwin MSS, 165/224–5, emphasis in original; Lloyd and Wood, *The Great Opportunity*, 17–18.
[264] *CAJ*, September 1924, 212.

merge elements of justice and equality in a uniquely British way, and Conservatives saw no hyperbole in declaring that 'English Justice' was 'perhaps the greatest thing man has ever achieved'.[265] It was expected that all persons would receive similar treatment before the law and by public administration; other than being able to employ a better barrister, wealth would have no precedence in the eyes of justice, and the vote of the millionaire and the workman would have 'the same weight in the ballot box'.[266] More generally, this ethic entailed open conduct and equivalence in the opportunity to achieve a successful outcome. Conservatives should protect the public from abuse of their position by the rich and powerful, 'operating through rings, monopolies or trusts'.[267] Government had to act even-handedly: hence the view of Lord Irwin (formerly Edward Wood) during the coal strike of 1926, that it was 'of the first importance that we should jump at every offer we can of coercing masters not less than men'.[268] There was a long-standing view that the public tended to favour the underdog, especially if there was any element of bullying or unjustified coercion; 'anything like unfairness always appeals unfavourably to the Englishman'.[269] This was the basis for the sympathy with the plight of the Jews in Germany that Amery noticed at the annual meeting of the Birmingham Association in 1933, which was all the more notable (and perhaps all the more possible) because there were few Jews living in the city.[270] The concerns expressed by the cabinet ministers who were doubtful about calling an election in late 1923 (as to how fairly it would be perceived) were not just a stalling tactic. Edward Wood's opinion that 'we should be acting both unwisely and wrongly...if we were to attempt to "snatch a verdict"', was echoed by the Cabinet minister Lord Novar's view that it would be 'almost unfair to the country to rush an election'.[271] Similarly, the proposal in 1928 to disenfranchise those receiving Poor Relief was dropped, despite being 'right in principle', because 'the man in the street would consider it unfair' and 'the Government would lose the confidence of the people, because it could be represented that we were making a purely Party move for Party advantage'.[272] In 1929–31, the effectiveness of the press magnates' attack upon Baldwin was considerably reduced by revulsion at their 'unfairness and un-English methods'.[273] All of these moral values were treated as timeless and immutable constants, although in fact social attitudes constantly evolve.

Respect for tradition was a pervasive element in Conservatism, as it acknowledged the value of the customs which had developed through experience. Conservatives aimed 'to make progress continuous with the past, so that there shall be

---

[265] Bryant, *Spirit of Conservatism*, 9.
[266] *Council of Action: Its Challenge to the Constitution*, NU leaflet 1987 (1920); to some extent, this ignored the limited forms of plural voting, in the business property and university franchises, but the point was that all votes when cast were equal, regardless of the person casting them.
[267] Wood, *Conservative Beliefs*, 9.
[268] Irwin to N. Chamberlain, 15 September 1926, Halifax MSS, C152/17/2/108.
[269] Lane-Fox to Irwin, 13 April 1927, Halifax MSS, C152/17/1/208; Amery diary, 7 April 1933.
[270] Amery diary, 7 April 1933.
[271] Wood to Baldwin, Novar to Baldwin, 8 November 1923, Baldwin MSS, 35/77–80.
[272] Davidson to Baldwin, 14 February 1928, Davidson MSS, DAV/182.
[273] Smithers to Salisbury, 19 August 1930, Salisbury MSS, S(4)136/148.

no violent dislocation, no rupture'.[274] Precedent was a guide that could be relied upon in the law and in constitutional practice; as the latter was not codified, it was tradition and convention which were the bulwarks of the established freedoms of worship, speech, and assembly. Traditional practice was identified particularly with the pastoral environment, and the roots of Conservatism were to be found in an idealized pre-industrial England of rural villages, where community was paramount and each person worked contentedly in 'an easily accepted structure', in which 'no one was wasted' and 'everyone counted'.[275] In this agrarian society, contact with the land taught the lessons of prudence and patience; in the present day, the farmer still knew 'the necessity of moving slowly, of acting with circumspection and in conformity with the facts of nature, of relying on experience rather than theoretical reasoning'.[276] Evoking tradition called upon the images and language of this partly mythical 'England', which was powerful through being the inherited cultural talisman of the whole population, although only a small minority still lived a country life. When considering the need for the 'regeneration of the Party, and through it, the Nation' shortly after the outbreak of war in 1939, Butler was certain that 'a return to the traditions of the countryside is urgently needed by a nation too accustomed to great cities'.[277] Topography and polity could become melded together; for Stelling, 'the first article of my Conservative political faith' was 'love of my country and its institutions, love of the physical beauty of the country which those institutions have helped to shape, love of my countrymen and their characteristics, born of their age-long environment'.[278] The effect was that 'this love of English earth spreads to what England has made of herself and others'.[279]

National identity was crucially important in the shaping of the Conservative mentality. It was based upon an assurance of British exceptionalism which was long-established and deeply rooted in all social classes. This fostered an insular outlook and Conservatives felt no kinship with other European parties of the right,[280] disliking the close links which most of these had to industry and the Roman Catholic Church. There was an unquestioned assumption that the British people (usually referred to as 'the Englishman') had 'distinctive characteristics' which were superior to those of other nations.[281] These had developed partly from their island location and partly from the contributions of the various races who had combined to form a nation that was greater than the sum of its parts. The Conservative sense of nation was not primarily territorial, apart from the vague conception of a 'mother country', which provided an emotional bond for those who were serving in, or had emigrated to, the empire. 'England' was in part a moral concept, and there was both certainty and pride in its 'God-sent gifts of enterprise, honesty, compassion—and geography'.[282] The essence of national identity was the unifying heritage of institutions,

---

[274] Cecil, *Conservative Ideals*, 4. [275] Northam, *Conservatism*, 55.
[276] Bryant, *Spirit of Conservatism*, 3–4.
[277] Butler to Dugdale, 22 November 1939, NC 7/11/33/33.
[278] Stelling, *Why I Am a Conservative*, 7. [279] Feiling, *What is Conservatism?*, 20.
[280] Cook, *Conservatism and the Future*, 4–5.
[281] Lloyd and Wood, *The Great Opportunity*, 16, 20.
[282] Fremantle to Baldwin, 1 January 1932, Baldwin MSS, 167/54.

law, culture, and customs, which rested upon the firm foundations of British history and the English language. The strong sense of separateness and the feeling that Britain had nothing to learn from other nations was a factor in the considerable element of self-congratulation in the Conservative vision of the nation and its past. Thus, the British constitution was 'a system which has reconciled order and liberty more perfectly than any other in the world's history'.[283] Even a setback could be viewed as evidence of merit, with the evacuation of the British concession at Hankow in 1927 demonstrating 'a patience which no other country could ever have emulated'.[284] Such sentiments could easily become chauvinism, and even take the playground form of making fun of foreign names and accents. Nevertheless, the predominant Conservative sensibility of the interwar era was a 'tolerant and receptive nationality', which frowned upon aggression and bombast.[285]

The Conservative view of the national character emphasized qualities which were comfortable and unthreatening, in a stereotype which mixed pride and complacency. 'The best Englishman', Bryant wrote, was 'a stolid, tolerant, good-humoured, reliable kind of person', who because he was at peace with himself could be both strong and gentle.[286] At the end of a career particularly identified with being 'an interpreter of England', Baldwin summed up the 'common stuff' of the people as 'fundamentally a stout individualism, yet with the power of co-operation, a broad and tolerant humanity, and humour'.[287] This was consistent with a national spirit which celebrated independence, initiative, and competition, for the British were 'people to whom friendly rivalry was the very essence of their being'.[288] The result was 'a passionate love of variety', which found expression in the enjoyment of sports, the 'worship of personal independence', and the acceptance of the eccentric.[289] It was also considered that 'as a race we have some curious instinct for preserving the old'.[290] The national character had been moulded by the twin traditions of the land and the sea, both of which fostered a sturdy self-reliance. From agriculture came the yeoman farmer, certain and capable within his own domain, who, in the emblematic figure of John Bull, was still resonant as a national icon. The role of the sea was of fundamental importance, not just as a defensive barrier but as a gateway to the world which encouraged boldness and enterprise.[291] Explorers, seafarers, and fishermen were admired for being brave, resourceful, and independent. However, they also shared the 'love of home', which was 'one of the strongest features of our race'.[292] British identity was located in the pastoral past, evoked not so much for the sake of nostalgia or a wish to turn back the clock but

---

[283] Murray, 'Conservative Party and the National Government', 9.
[284] Crawford to Irwin, 12 January 1927, Halifax MSS, C152/17/1/173b.
[285] Pickthorn, *Principles and Prejudices*, 11; Baldwin, *Our Inheritance*, 51–2.
[286] A. Bryant, *The National Character* (1934), 18–19; Loftus, *Creed of a Tory*, 49, 63; Parker et al., *Declaration of Tory Principles*, 10.
[287] Baldwin, *Interpreter of England*, 18.
[288] Winchester CA, North Stoneham & Bassett Women's branch, 28 June 1923, Southampton RO.
[289] Loftus, *Creed of a Tory*, 64.
[290] Beyfus, 'Conservatism', 3.
[291] 'A modern Conservative' [C. Alport, pseud.], *A National Faith* (1938), 32–3.
[292] Baldwin, *On England*, 8; Bryant, *National Character*, 18, 131.

as a reminder of a common heritage and a source of values which, because the people were 'rustic in their souls',[293] were still just as relevant in the modern urban and industrial society. When Baldwin gave a radio broadcast on the national character in 1933, he emphasized virtues of resilience in the face of adversity: 'the more difficult times are, the more cheerful we become.... We have staying power, we are not rattled'.[294] A parallel aspect was 'the English genius for compromise', which had led to political stability and commercial success, 'for business capacity is chiefly a power of adaptability'.[295] From this stemmed the 'singular power of working institutions of whatever character to suit the political ideas of the time'.[296] There seemed little doubt about the conclusion that 'our native English character' was founded upon 'stolid conservatism' and a wisdom that was instinctive rather than rational.[297] The reciprocal effect was that the Conservative Party was trusted by the people because it was 'instinctively British in its ideas and its ideals'.[298]

The Conservative concept of the nation was not defined in ethnic terms, partly because the physical geography of being an island rendered it unnecessary to delineate in any other way who was inside the nation and who was outside. Conservatives were aware that the British people had been formed by waves of incoming settlement and, together with pride in the more recent tolerance of British society, which allowed it to offer a refuge for the persecuted, this militated against any interest in racially based definitions: Conservatives were 'completely opposed to any idolatry of race or blood'.[299] Instead, the Conservative outlook was based upon 'the old Christian principle that in his moral character the common man is very much alike regardless of race, nationality or colour'.[300] British political culture deprecated hostility against groups within the national borders and promoted absorption, and since the Aliens Act of 1905 the Conservative Party had felt little need or desire to identify itself with any ethnic 'Englishness' or even 'Britishness'. Only where there was a large and distinctive concentration of an immigrant group which appeared to have predominant ties outside the country or in conflict with national unity, such as Irish Catholics in Merseyside and Clydeside or European Jews in London's East End, did it develop into a matter for disapproval. For Conservatives, there was an 'essential unity of the British nation'[301] which was focused upon its institutions, the celebration of its history, and the common values shared by its people, so that 'we are all one family in this Isle'.[302]

Conservatives wished 'to preserve Britain's glory and greatness'.[303] They took pride in the nation's past as a story of endeavour, discovery, and achievement,

---

[293] Bryant, *National Character*, 31.
[294] 'Our national character', broadcast by Baldwin, 25 September 1933, in *Torch of Freedom*, 7–14; see previous similar sentiments in *On England*, 3–4.
[295] Bryant, *Spirit of Conservatism*, 25.   [296] Cecil, *Conservatism*, 221.
[297] Bryant, *National Character*, 154–5.   [298] Beyfus, 'Conservatism', 3.
[299] Northam, *Conservatism*, 58; NU Central Council, 23 March 1937; for a rare example of different emphasis, see Loftus, *Creed of a Tory*, 56–9.
[300] P. F. Drucker, *The Future of Industrial Man: A Conservative Approach* (1943), 8.
[301] Buchan preface in Bryant, *Spirit of Conservatism*, vii; P. Lynch, *The Politics of Nationhood: Sovereignty, Britishness and Conservative Politics* (Basingstoke, 1999), 5.
[302] Lord Croft, *The Past, the Present, the Future*, pamphlet of speech delivered at Bournemouth, 10 August 1943, copy in Emrys-Evans MSS, Add.58248/153–4.
[303] Northam, *Conservatism*, 247.

which explained Britain's accomplishments and eminence during the period of living memory, the previous five or six decades. They did not regard this as faultless or untroubled, especially since the dislocation of the Great War, but in the 1920s there were still few signs of decline that impinged directly on the general public, especially in comparison with the fortunes of other powers. The Conservative view of British history had absorbed a Whiggish perspective which attributed its stability and progress to the avoidance of extremes and the strife and upheaval that flow from them. Interwoven with this was the Conservative ideal of social unity and a belief that moderation and reasonableness, often defined as 'common sense', would engender a reciprocal response. Conservatives believed that historical developments were due to more than just impersonal economic forces, and 'that only through individual insight or genius can progress be secured and maintained'.[304] In the Conservative pantheon, the heroes of British history were the monarchs and military leaders (particularly those who overcame adversity or inspired by personal example), the innovators and explorers (including reformers such as Florence Nightingale), and the literary icons such as Chaucer, Shakespeare, Milton, Bunyan, and Walter Scott—especially those who wrote in the vernacular.[305] Their merits were to be 'valiant, gentle, unshakeable', and they were admired 'not so much for what they won as for what they dared and were'.[306] The greatest sense of pride was focused upon the empire, and its founding figures were widely celebrated. There was a compelling mystique of empire, which appealed to the romantic imagination, and featured in boys' stories, novels by writers such as H. Rider Haggard, and the books and poetry of Rudyard Kipling. However, the theme most prominent in accounts of the empire was not battle and conquest, but the moral rightness of Britain's civilizing role and the benefits which enlightened, stable, and fair government had brought to the native populations under its care.[307]

Patriotism, which 'in its truest sense arises from an affection for the known and familiar', was perhaps the most powerful of all the Conservative values.[308] For many, it was 'those principles of National Patriotism which we call Conservatism' that had shaped their political outlook, rather than the other way round.[309] The community feeling of Conservatives was not founded upon the social abstract of class identity, but rooted in the geographical facts of locality, county, and country. These could be visibly called to memory and vividly evoked, and, whether it was conventional pastoral images such as 'the scent of our native downs' or 'the gaunt power of our great industrial centres', it was understood that 'these things are part of us'.[310] Patriotism was the element which bound individuals together in a greater whole, not any common economic circumstance. Doctrines of class feeling were regarded with suspicion and hostility for the very reason that they seemed incom-

---

[304] Crisp, *The Rebirth of Conservatism*, 164.
[305] *Young Britons' Organisers Manual.*
[306] Bryant, *National Character*, 129, 4.
[307] *Something to be Proud of*, NU leaflet 2568 (1925).
[308] 'Modern Conservative', *A National Faith*, 23.
[309] Derbyshire South CA, Exec., 13 April 1923, Gascoyne (chairman) to Hunt (agent), 9 April 1923.
[310] Braine, *Conservatism and Youth*, 19–20.

patible with patriotism, for by dividing classes they cut across its higher claims and duties. This was the reason why specifically middle-class political bodies never attracted any wide support, and were regarded as alien in nature.[311] It was also for this reason that Conservatives viewed their opponents to the left as unpatriotic—sowing seeds of disunity from within, and thereby aiding the cause of the nation's jealous enemies. Fighting against such opponents was a defence of the national interest, and therefore work for the party was an honourable and patriotic endeavour; 'without it the country will perish'.[312] This feeling led logically to the adoption of patriotic symbols as party emblems, such as the use of the national flag to drape its platforms, and to the validity of conferring honours upon those engaged in this political but patriotic work. Such sentiment was also a powerful force for unity: those who split the party did not merely damage it, but were 'guilty of imperilling their country and their Empire'.[313] Patriotism was an attitude rather than a programme and was at its most useful when it was unspecific; when it became linked to particular policies, it became more problematic. All Conservatives would have agreed on the need for 'strong' defence forces and a 'firm' foreign and imperial policy, whatever these might exactly mean—but beyond that, differences of resources and priorities were likely to emerge. The language of patriotism had been, to some extent, discounted by the experiences of the First World War, and any element of 'jingoism'—an assertive patriotism of competition and conquest—had become unattractive.[314] Although pride was still an important element, the patriotic spirit which was now evoked was more sober and shaped by the need to honour the sacrifice made by the fallen in the war. It looked inwards as much as outwards, and was defined by one writer as 'a recognition of the obligations and duties of citizenship'.[315]

Closely linked to patriotism was the veneration of national unity. Conservatives had been concerned about the division of society into 'two nations' ever since Disraeli drew attention to this in the mid-nineteenth century. As Duff Cooper wrote in 1926, Toryism 'hates the division of Englishmen into classes'.[316] However, the reforging of one nation could not be achieved by imposition from above, and had to develop from 'a spontaneous faith in a common ideal'.[317] This was based on the understanding that the whole was greater than the parts, and so the 'essential unity of all classes and interests' was 'the essence of Conservatism'.[318] It was in this context that the prewar party name of 'Unionist' continued to have vitality and relevance, as its meaning changed from the specific defence of the Act of Union with Ireland to a broader appeal to social harmony, and thus 'the meaning of the

---

[311] Torquay CA, Exec., 29 July 1919.
[312] Davidson to Nall-Cain, 8 December 1929, Davidson MSS, DAV/188; Clapham CA, Clapham South Park branch, AGM, 20 February 1931.
[313] Bridgeman to Croft, 11 October 1930, Croft MSS, CAC, CRFT/1/5/Br5.
[314] Lloyd and Wood, *The Great Opportunity*, 6–7.
[315] 'Modern Conservative', *A National Faith*, 89; Watford CA, Rickmansworth Women's branch, AGM, 22 February 1927.
[316] Cooper, *Why Workers should be Tories*.
[317] Northam, *Conservatism*, 76.
[318] 'Gentleman with a duster', *The Conservative Mind*, 55, 145–6.

word had become more comprehensive'.[319] All ranks in society were drawn together by the symbolic representations of the nation: the monarch, the flag, and the anthem. On a smaller scale, there were constant evocations of team spirit, of putting the communal effort first rather than seeking individual advantage.[320] Related to this was the convention of individual modesty and the view that no one was indispensable. Patriotism was the cement that held the classes together, even in conditions of stress and upheaval such as the General Strike or the Blitz. Indeed, such occasions could be as much a source of relief and reassurance: as the Solicitor-General, Sir Thomas Inskip, wrote in 1926: 'the great mass of working people have behaved quite admirably. I really feel that it has been worth while having a General Strike to really appreciate what the British nation is'.[321] Significantly, in defeating the General Strike it was not party or government but 'the country had triumphed'.[322] By the late 1930s (and only partly in consequence of the continuing existence of the National Government), Conservatism was being presented as 'essentially a *national* faith', maintaining national traditions and institutions, and 'striving to produce a harmony between the various interests in Britain, and so build up a national unity upon a basis of fairness and justice'.[323]

National patriotism was founded upon a bedrock of local pride, and confidence in national unity was so strong that regional identities were regarded as contributory rather than subversive. The Conservative preference for variety led to acceptance that people were from, and of, many different places, and regional and local connections were cherished as products of history and tradition. For most people, 'England' was represented by their own particular experience, and the heart was wherever the home was.[324] Yet, although this was often a very different environment, it was seen as complementary to—rather than in conflict with—the general image of Englishness which evoked the countryside of the south and Midlands. Conservative visualizations of the idealized past pictured a network of small communities, largely self-sufficient and existing in good neighbourliness with each other. This celebrated a tradition of authority vested in local government which understood and was sympathetic to its subjects, and which acted as a counterweight to the centralizing tendencies and remoteness of national power. Local loyalty therefore fostered independence and self-reliance, whilst maintaining social bonds. Relationships were defined within a scale that was comprehensible, and with consequences for good or ill which were visible and immediate. Community necessarily entailed obligations, and so 'we insist that we all depend upon one another, that we live in a coherent society'.[325]

---

[319] Penryn & Falmouth CA, Council, 16 November 1918; NU Conf., 1924, comments of the Principal Agent; Baldwin, *On England*, 73.
[320] Brittain to Baldwin, 12 April 1929, Baldwin MSS, 36/128–9.
[321] Inskip to Irwin, 9 May 1926, Halifax MSS, C152/17/1/28. Some similar sentiments were expressed after the Abdication crisis: Zetland to Linlithgow, 9 December 1936, Zetland MSS, D609/7.
[322] Lewisham West CA, Council, 18 June 1926.
[323] 'Modern Conservative', *A National Faith*, 89, emphasis in original.
[324] Lloyd and Wood, *The Great Opportunity*, 9–10.
[325] Cecil, *Conservative Ideals*, 15.

The Conservative desire for social order was usually accompanied by a recognition of 'the natural hierarchy of life'.[326] There was comfort and security in knowing one's 'place' in society, and thereby acknowledging the relative status of those in a higher position—a relationship which has been termed 'deference', and which in Victorian times often involved acceptance of the political leadership and party affiliation of the local elite. Class was a reality that was rarely addressed directly, but not because it was not recognized—on the contrary, it ran through everything. This was particularly the case in a period where class distinctions in speech, dress, work, and leisure were much clearer than later in the twentieth century. However, the more that class permeated the political environment, the less it was—or needed to be—talked about. At both a conscious and a subconscious level, for Conservatives, class was bound up with quality—indeed, a common popular term for the upper classes was 'the quality'. Those who were in higher stations were considered more refined in character as well as by education, and were tacitly assumed to be of superior nature.[327] This did not mean that they were all of admirable character or ability, but rather that they could draw upon their background for the strength and guidance to do the right thing: in the words of another piece of conventional wisdom, 'quality will out'.

This quality was found in its purest form in the historic aristocratic families, and especially in their connection with the land; even their favoured sport of fox-hunting had merit as 'a school of hardiness and decision'.[328] The Conservative 'naturally inclines to a belief in good lineage, heredity and in sound and pure stock'.[329] Leadership was 'based on an inherited instinct' and 'the possession of character and industry and ability'.[330] However, wealth had to conduct itself according to expected, moderate, and respectable standards, and there was criticism of snobbery, arrogance, and conspicuous consumption. Deference was given less automatically than in Victorian times, and operated conditionally; it was earned by the involvement and conduct of members of the traditional governing class—such as Lady Dorothy Macmillan in depression-struck Stockton or Lady Diana Cooper in the socially mixed Westminster St George's division, both of them the daughters of dukes; or the apogee of the regional grandee, the Earl of Derby, nicknamed 'king of Lancashire'. In their turn, the aristocracy retained a clear sense of their own position and proper role, especially in the historic great political families such as the Cecils, Stanleys, and Cavendishes. Their outlook often combined approbation of the decent working class with a disdain for middle-class values and culture; Lady Irwin labelled this element of her husband's colleagues in the 1924–29 Cabinet as 'middle-class monsters'.[331] Frequently this was paralleled by a dislike of industry and businessmen, especially 'money-grubbing' financiers and the 'plutocracy'.[332] Thus a Cabinet minister from the Cecil family could write

---

[326] Ludovici, *Defence of Conservatism*, 55.   [327] Crisp, *Rebirth of Conservatism*, 68–9.
[328] Lymington, *Ich Dien*, 75.   [329] Ludovici, *Defence of Conservatism*, 55.
[330] Northam, *Conservatism*, 92.
[331] R. Cecil to Irwin, 16 December 1926, Halifax MSS, C152/17/1/155f.
[332] Bentinck, *Tory Democracy*, 2–3, 61–2.

to the Viceroy of India and next Earl of Halifax: 'My gracious, how I hate employers! Their stupidity is only equalled by their arrogance'.[333] Similarly, the Duke of Atholl considered the middle classes to be 'more particular about their skins, and personal safety means more to them than it does to others who have been more accustomed to soldiering, etc'.[334]

An important consequence of the Conservative belief in social hierarchy and its links and responsibilities was the ethos of paternalism which infused all aspects of the party's organization, activities, and policies. This was an inheritance from the feudal relationships of earlier centuries, and was supported by the view that rightful authority should exercise its functions and not shirk from its duties: 'Toryism means leadership in national service.'[335] Thus one element in the Conservative frame of mind was always the demand for 'strong' or 'firm' government. This meant not just the preservation of order, but also that government should be conducted upon clear and consistent lines. Conservatives expected to be shown a definite direction by those who had the vantage and duty of leading, rather than seeking their own course through a process of internal debate and negotiation—this was one reason why they were comfortable with the structure in which the party conference and other representative bodies expressed opinions but did not determine policy. This does not mean that they wanted an absolute and unquestionable authority, and there was no attraction in continental-style dictatorship or the forms of a quasi-military discipline.[336] Good leadership treated its supporters with respect and understood that there were obligations of communication and of conduct—most of all, in keeping the party united. The terms in which leadership were described were those which would give inspiration, confidence, and purpose to their followers: 'clear', 'vigorous', 'courageous', 'resolute', 'bold', and so on.[337]

The foundation of almost all Conservative values was character, which was both the source of a principled, moral, and dutiful outlook and its active expression.[338] Character was the basis of the trust which was essential for a stable society; for that reason, 'character in itself constitutes a programme',[339] and 'everything that weakens individual character and lessens individual effort and initiative is anathema to the Conservative'.[340] The basis of the trust and confidence in Andrew Bonar Law (Party Leader 1911–21 and 1922–23) was not brilliance, or even effectiveness in debate, but quite simply 'character, character, character, which was the greatest gift of all'.[341] The importance of personal character in political conduct was underlined by the view of Inskip that the General Strike 'is going to be broken as much by the

---

[333] R. Cecil to Irwin, 22 June 1926, Halifax MSS, C152/17/1/58.
[334] Duke of Atholl to Lloyd, 14 June 1933, Atholl MSS, 9/1; Boothby to Duff, 2 December 1938, Cilcennin MSS, 42.
[335] Lymington, *Ich Dien*, 11.
[336] Northam, *Conservatism*, 63–5; Braine, *Conservatism and Youth*, 9–10.
[337] Amery to Baldwin, 12 January 1924, Baldwin MSS, 42/162–5.
[338] Lymington, *Ich Dien*, 123; Hearnshaw, *Conservatism in England*, 30–1; L. S. Amery, 'Conservatism and the future (part 2)', *Ashridge Journal*, 73 (May 1943), 1–2; Northwich CA, Chairman's Advisory Ctte., 29 October 1937.
[339] Feiling, *What Is Conservatism?*, 7–8.   [340] Skelton, *Constructive Conservatism*, 22.
[341] Speech of Pretyman at the party meeting of 28 May 1923, *The Times*, 29 May 1923.

really great impression which the Prime Minister has made on the Labour leaders as by the steadiness with which the country has organised the essential services'.[342] This was no accident, for character was one of themes which Baldwin both exemplified and placed at the heart of his political style. In this conception, sincerity was much more important than brains; indeed, there was a positive suspicion of wits that moved too quickly or tactics that were too dexterous, summed up in the damning popular expression of being 'too clever by half'. This was not a manifesto for stupidity, and ability was highly valued when it was exerted in support of something more than personal ambition. It was rather an expression of the need to avoid the pitfalls of manoeuvre and inconsistency, and see a larger picture: it was a rejection of exhibitionism, and an affirmation of discipline and purpose. It is significant that when Baldwin, in 1927, considered Douglas Hogg, the Attorney-General, to be his most suitable and likely successor, he described him as 'stuffed with character'.[343] This was in keeping with the long-standing Tory tradition of the importance of men rather than measures.

Character was linked to being straightforward, and simple in the sense of honesty and openness, for 'affectation cannot live in the presence of truth'.[344] As one MP, concerned about the protectionist policy in 1923, told his local executive committee: 'it was always his endeavour to do the straight thing'.[345] The best guide to this was common sense; as something possessed by all rather than being the preserve of a few, it was also in tune with the democratic principle. One consequence of the Conservative rejection of being ideological was the embracing of what was seen as its opposite, and hence celebration of 'the practical character of the Tory'.[346] This in turn promoted an idealization of practical men: the explorers, inventors, and military heroes who populated British history and, in the present, the businessman and business virtues—the latter were a constant motif in the recommendation of persons and policies in this period. At the same time, there was still much admiration for the amateur ideal—it was more human, and represented service and voluntary effort; gentlemen were preferred over players.[347] The aspects of character most lauded were the traditional 'manly virtues': courage (moral as well as physical) in the face of difficulty; effort and perseverance in a task to be done; dignity in both success and adversity, and the avoidance of vituperation; giving aid to those weaker and taking care of dependents. Steadiness and steadfastness were admired, for 'only he who can govern himself is fit to share in the governing of others'.[348] Character was often described in sporting metaphors, and it was believed to be demonstrated and strengthened in sporting activity, particularly in team games. Thus the Conservative candidate in a by-election in an industrial Scottish constituency had a much wider popular appeal because he 'combined

[342] Inskip to Irwin, 9 May 1926, Halifax MSS, C152/17/1/28.
[343] Baldwin to Irwin, 15 September 1927, Halifax MSS, C152/17/253f.
[344] F. Lee, 'This is England', *Ashridge Journal*, 112 (February 1945), 4.
[345] Dorset West CA, Exec., 19 November 1923.
[346] Sir R. Horne, introduction in Skelton, *Constructive Conservatism*, 5; Cooper, *Why Workers should be Tories*.
[347] Peterborough CA, AGM, 17 March 1925.   [348] Braine, *Conservatism and Youth*, 8.

being a Marquis and a well-known boxer'.[349] The virtues of individuals were accumulated in the collective whole, so that the greatest strength was derived from 'the character of the people...the genius of the British nation'.[350]

Another aspect of character admired by Conservatives was breadth of outlook and avoidance of dogmatism. Human imperfection meant that no person, group, or doctrine could claim absolute moral authority, and this encouraged 'tolerance, moderation and a reality of consent'.[351] Baldwin's view was 'that no party on the whole is better than another; that no creed does more than shadow imperfectly forth some one side of truth'.[352] It was from this standpoint that he counselled a friendly tone in debating with Labour MPs in the Commons and was willing to acknowledge the sincerity of their motivation; their methods and programme might be misguided, but they were not to be depicted as wicked. This attitude was the basis of the repugnance felt for intolerance and extremism, as castes of mind which learnt nothing and forgot nothing; most would have agreed with the Duke of Atholl's view that 'every true Conservative must I think dislike extremists of both the right and the left'.[353] Toleration was seen as one of the great contributions made by the British nation to the sum of happiness of the human race, and any regression from it was to be deplored; this was an important factor in Conservative distaste for the outlook and methods of Fascism in Britain and abroad. Conservatism embraced the variety of the individual, and its followers responded to those who displayed warmth and humanity. In the midst of the Second World War, Stelling wrote that 'the independence and decency and laughter of Englishmen and Englishwomen, form the basis of my politics and the touchstone of my principles'.[354] This was linked to the recognition that there was a life outside politics, and that other things—especially sport, literature, art, and participation in communal activity—were equally or more important. An exclusive focus on politics was unnatural and raised doubts about a person's sense of balance as well as their motives; it was close to being a 'crank'. In this respect it was not surprising that Conservative supporters did not match the supposedly tireless evangelism of the Labour grass roots, for to do so would run counter to their values and conception of life.

Conservatism was 'the creed and policy of the moderate, sensible, pious and patriotic middle portion of the nation'.[355] This was its most expected and 'natural' core of support, and the values summed up as the 'moral economy' of the middle class permeated the party's outlook. This encompassed more than political attitudes, and included matters of acceptable and proper conduct. The middle- and upper-class Conservatives who ran the party at local level and filled the benches of the House of Commons had been brought up in a polite society in which the conventions regulating behaviour placed emphasis upon consideration, obligation,

---

[349] Lane-Fox to Irwin, 3 December 1930, Halifax MSS, C152/19/1/180.
[350] Stelling, *Why I Am a Conservative*, 5.   [351] Pickthorn, *Principles and Prejudices*, 9.
[352] A. W. Baldwin, *My Father: The True Story* (1955), 128.
[353] Duke of Atholl to Dawson, 20 December 1937, Atholl MSS, 22/6; Tory Reform Committee, *What is a Tory?*.
[354] Stelling, *Why I Am a Conservative*, 3; on laughter, see also Baldwin, *On England*, 5.
[355] Hearnshaw, *Conservatism in England*, 38.

modesty, and service. There was a concern with the maintenance of 'standards', which were 'the sole lasting justification of class'.[356] They were also the means by which position and status were signalled and recognized, and so made class identity distinctive and apparent. Another aspect of the middle-class values which permeated the Conservative outlook was that success was individually achieved; it was a product of personal skills and endeavour, and did not depend upon a collectivity. The role of professional associations was to maintain standards and status, but they were not—or not ostensibly—direct economic agents. The middle class were the most determined and concerned for social stability, believing that 'in the wake of the ordered blessings of good government follows prosperity'.[357] This was certainly important for the middle-class practice of investing in monetary savings and the acquisition of professional skills, in particular through educating their children. At the intangible level, middle-class values were almost synonymous with Conservative sentiments. For Sir Waldron Smithers, who was perhaps typical of MPs from the professional upper-middle class and sat for a Home Counties suburban constituency, the essence of Conservatism was 'truth, patriotism, honour, credit, and that elusive something we call national character'.[358]

FEARS

In politics, as in life, by your demons you are known—and thus the Conservative mind cannot be understood without an analysis of its fears about the threats and enemies which it believed that it faced. What Conservatives dreaded is as illuminating as what they desired—perhaps even more so, as there was often greater agreement about what they were against than what they were for.[359] The effects of the First World War and the rise of Socialism led Conservatives to believe that they were facing greater dangers then ever before, and in consequence they often portrayed the politics of the previous two centuries as having been just a game, with no fundamental differences between political leaders or parties.[360] Conservatism was 'primarily a defensive creed', and its outlook was always tinged with pessimism.[361] At the most fundamental level, Conservatives feared national decline from both without and within. The external peril was the erosion of the empire, upon which Britain's place in the world depended. There were two aspects to this: the drifting away of the Dominions (especially of Canada into the American orbit), and a loss of authority in the colonies to native agitators and conspiracies. At the very start of the interwar period, attention was focused upon the armed resistance in Ireland, but from the mid-1920s the main concern was India, which was of vital economic and strategic importance. There was also a pervasive belief that Soviet Communist (usually referred to as 'Bolshevik') agents were actively seeking to

---

[356] Feiling, *What Is Conservatism?*, 24. [357] Bryant, *Spirit of Conservatism*, 167.
[358] Smithers, *Conservative Principles*, 9. [359] Braine, *Conservatism and Youth*, 2.
[360] Cooper, *Conservative Point of View*, 9–12; Sellon, 'River of Conservatism', 11.
[361] Hearnshaw, *Conservatism in England*, 7.

undermine the empire, stoking the flames of unrest with adroit propaganda and pulling strings behind the scenes whenever trouble occurred; the fear of this was even greater than of subversion at home, especially by the 1930s.

The internal danger was degeneracy, a loss of character and willpower; this was particularly linked to the effects of the war, with its shock to previous certainties and the belief that the best of the younger generation had been lost. This added fuel to the anti-modernism and dislike of change which has been common to the conservative outlook in all generations, with its recurring sequence of alarm over youthful delinquency, loss of respect for elders, decline in moral standards, and cultural decay. The 1920s in particular were marked by a conservative-minded dislike of new social mores, leisure activities, and artistic movements, ranging from the 'flapper' fashions adopted by young women to Cubism, jazz, and the non-rhyming poetry dismissed by one Conservative minister as 'the soliloquies of the padded cell'.[362] Cinemas were 'harmful every day of the week and break up the home life'.[363] There was renewed criticism of the 'cosmopolitanism' associated with metropolitan society, especially in the financial sector, which corroded patriotism and led to a shallow and selfish outlook. The most evident political effect of this sapping of the national backbone was the neglect of personal duty on the part of the natural leaders of society, and the turn to reliance on the state on the part of the working class, through lack of confidence in their own capacity for self-reliance and enterprise.

This contributed to the fears about the new democracy, which greatly worried Conservative opinion in the decade after its introduction in the Reform Act of 1918. The new electorate was an unknown factor, volatile and unpredictable. The male additions were believed to be of the poorest class, which would increase the element of vulgarity. Particularly disliked was the removal of the disqualification from voting of those in receipt of Poor Law assistance:[364] these 'pauper voters' were considered akin to vagrants—rootless and corruptible, if not individually then by the self-interest of voting for whoever promised higher doles, which inevitably would be 'soak the rich' Socialists. There were equally widespread doubts about the inclusion of women, especially on such a large scale. Three years after the first general election with female suffrage, the Principal Agent considered that it was 'having a narrowing effect on politics, making them more parochial and...reducing them to bread and butter politics'.[365] Echoing this conclusion, one leading opponent of appeasement in the 1930s considered that the influence of women had prevented any strong foreign or defence policy, and thus had 'brought nothing but degradation and dishonour to politics'.[366] There was particular concern over the lowering of the age limit for women from thirty to twenty-one in 1928—pejoratively labelled the 'flapper vote'—and many of the young voters of both sexes were assumed to lack experience and responsibilities, and expected to be sentimental

---

[362] Banks, *Conservative Outlook*, 51. [363] Lady Peto diary, 6 October 1931.
[364] Sheffield Ecclesall CA, Exec., 23 January 1928.
[365] Fraser's report to A. Chamberlain, 30 December 1921, AC 32/4/1b.
[366] Law to Emrys-Evans, 30 December 1939, Emrys-Evans MSS, Add.58239/4–6.

and impulsive in the casting of their ballot. As a whole, the new electors were thought likely to be 'wholly ignorant and entirely uninterested in politics', prey to demagogues and credulous of charlatans, swayed by emotional appeals and easily misled.[367]

Conservatives feared that the new polity existed in a dangerous imbalance between rights and responsibilities, and was in need of education. Until it could mature, there would be a need to simplify all issues and to sloganize—methods which were considered antithetical to the nature of Conservatism, and at which the Socialists were much more adept. The feeling of peril was crystallized in Baldwin's comment of 1927: 'Democracy has arrived at a gallop in England, and I feel all the time that it is a race for life: can we educate them before the crash comes?'[368] This was Baldwin's most constant theme; the following year, he told a rally of the party's youth movement that the real issue was not to 'make the world safe for democracy', but 'a much more difficult task'—to 'make democracy safe for the world'.[369] Broadcasting to schools in 1934, Baldwin told his young audience that 'democracy is a most difficult form of government', which 'wants constant guarding, lest democracy should slip over in the one direction into licence, and licence means chaos'.[370] In his final term as Prime Minister, Baldwin still saw his task as being 'to try and educate a new democracy in a new world and to try and make them realise their responsibilities in their possession of power, and to keep the eternal verities before them'.[371] As Walter Elliot declared, 'democracy if it means anything must mean understanding by the people as well as rule'.[372] This was still a concern during the Second World War, for if democracy was to survive 'it must be told the truth and asked to give, not taught to beg'.[373]

Much of this anxiety was based upon the middle-class alarm which resulted from working-class militancy and assertiveness in the early 1920s. There was fear of social upheaval and the collapse of accepted morality and status in general, and an individual dread of descent into a lower class and the loss of independence and autonomy. The Conservative outlook was shaped by middle-class attitudes; from lack of familiarity with working-class life, these were largely founded upon stereotypes which, as usual in such cases, were distorted due to being hostile, mistaken, and out of date. The working class was a foreign country, where people lived, thought, spoke, and behaved by different standards; they were assumed to be uneducated and motivated by short-term gratifications—to be profligate, self-indulgent, vulgar, and careless. The middle class feared being overwhelmed by the weight of working-class numbers, both economically and—due to the extended

---

[367] Lady Peto diary, 29 January 1930; Allan to Derby, 31 May 1929, Derby MSS, 6/3.
[368] Baldwin to Irwin, 26 June 1927 (letter misplaced and not sent until 14 January 1938), Halifax MSS (Borthwick), A4/410/14/2; for a similar sentiment, see Hogg to Smithers, 27 September 1927, Smithers MSS.
[369] Baldwin at JIL rally, 10 March 1928, *Democracy, Youth and Patriotism*, NU leaflet 2768 (1928).
[370] *Our Heritage of Freedom*.
[371] Baldwin to Monica Baldwin, 22 December 1935, *BP*, 365.
[372] Notes for speech to constituency association, *c.* October 1938, Elliot MSS, 6/3.
[373] Emrys-Evans to Bartlett, 23 January 1941, Emrys-Evans MSS, Add.58248/117–19.

franchise—politically and socially. There was also a fear of being found superfluous, for Socialism had no place for a property-owning middle class; if all is vested in the state, the best that could be hoped for was to be clerks in its bureaucracy, losing both autonomy and status. Finally, there was a fear of dependency: the demands of the war had demonstrated the vital importance of the working class, and no major steps could be taken which did not have their acceptance—as the governments of the 1930s were very aware when formulating their foreign and defence policies. These fears were partly eased by the orderliness—even more than the defeat—of the General Strike in 1926: the Conservative junior minister George Lane-Fox hailed it as 'a perfectly splendid example of what a great nation can do; not a real sign of revolution'.[374] However, anxiety about the possible actions of an untrammelled Socialist government gave force to the constant pressure from the Conservative grass roots for constitutional protection by means of strengthening the powers of the House of Lords.

In the wake of the First World War, Conservatives feared organized labour in its different manifestations of 'Socialism' and a much more powerful trade union movement. Many Conservatives had little direct experience of either, and their anxieties were stoked by ignorance and distance. Even so, Conservative attitudes to trade unionism were not intrinsically hostile, and there was frequent and genuinely proud citation of the part played by Conservative governments in the nineteenth century in establishing trade union rights. The causes of tension were partly the labour movement's enhanced scale and confidence, after a decade of expansion between 1910 and 1920, and most directly the involvement of the trade unions outside what Conservatives considered to be their proper industrial sphere, through their promotion of the Labour Party as the vehicle for securing their objects and in the General Strike of 1926, which Conservatives regarded as an attempt to use industrial power to coerce an elected government. The symbol of this inappropriate mode of trade union activity became their political funds, and in particular the form of the levy which sustained this, under which a worker had publicly to dissent by 'contracting-out' if he did not wish to fund a party for which, after all, very many workers did not vote. There was considerable pressure from the Conservative rank and file to alter the system to 'contracting-in', whereby those who wished to make a payment would have to volunteer to do so; of course, as under either scheme most trade union members were apathetic and took no action, the latter method was vigorously resisted by the unions and the Labour Party. In the early 1920s, this partly symbolic issue became emblematic of containing the threat of organized labour. The failure of the postwar Coalition to address the matter (together with its similar inaction over the House of Lords) was one of the main diehard and grass-roots grievances of 1921–22. The question of the political levy returned to the fore after the first Labour government and the Conservative victory in the 1924 election; it led to the private members' bill proposed by the diehard MP F. A. Macquisten in March 1925, and in the consequent debate to Baldwin's

---

[374] Lane-Fox to Irwin, 11 May 1926, Halifax MSS, C152/17/1/31.

eloquent and successful appeal to take no action, in the hope that the gesture of restraint would improve the atmosphere of industrial relations. However, the General Strike made legislation unavoidable; although the resulting Trade Disputes Act of 1927 was far from punitive, it made general strikes illegal, restricted picketing, and changed the levy to 'contracting-in'.

Fear breeds anger and contempt, and there were elements of both in the Conservative view of the Labour Party, especially in the early and mid-1920s. Disdain for the ideology of Socialism and the woolly impracticalities of its intellectual and parliamentary advocates was typified by the dismissive impatience of Neville Chamberlain in the House of Commons. However, even if the Labour leaders were unimpressive paper tigers, no Conservative could forget the overthrow of Kerensky's moderate regime in Russia by the conspiratorial coup of the Bolsheviks, and so the prospect of Labour forming a government was seen in many quarters as 'a serious danger'.[375] At the time of the first Labour government's treaty negotiations with the Soviets, it was not beyond credibility to suggest that 'there are many Communists today in our so-called "Labour Party"; and so strong are they even now that our Socialist Government must do their bidding'.[376] The threat to property was clear, and not just from the proposed capital levy; Labour's first budget 'would be ruinous' and 'destroy everybody in this country who had got anything to lose'.[377] This certainly included the working class, for, as Duff Cooper pointed out, 'revolutions may rob the rich of superfluities, but they deprive the poor of necessities'.[378] Even after the moderation of the minority first Labour government, the commonly held Conservative view was that if Labour should obtain an overall majority in the House of Commons, 'this would mark the end of the country and the Empire'.[379] The rise of the Labour Party, which would make this possible, was attributed not to any abilities of its leaders but to its popular identification with working-class interests and the untiring work of its supporters at local level.[380] Although the latter was considerably overrated, between the wars, most Conservatives believed in the constant commitment and missionary zeal of Labour activists, and contrasted this with the passivity and ignorance of their own members.[381] A large proportion of Conservatives believed that behind the Labour Party's apparently constitutional façade there lurked the hidden and greater threat of the extreme left, waiting for its moment of opportunity to seize power.[382] These shadowy forces, and their few visible personifications, were assumed to have deeply laid plans and the cunning and skill to implement them: they would either be the puppet-masters of the constitutional Labourites or sweep them easily aside.

[375] Horne to Baldwin, reporting Balfour's views, 10 December 1923, Baldwin MSS, 35/183–5; *Oil and Vinegar: What Does the 'Labour' Party Stand for?*, NU leaflet 1970 (1920).
[376] *To Women: Communism Destroys Marriage*, NU leaflet 2409 (1924).
[377] Memo by Derby to the Cabinet, 10 December 1923, Derby MSS, 29/1.
[378] Cooper, *Why Workers Should Be Tories*.
[379] Holt to Herbert, 11 October 1925, Baldwin MSS, 160/90–3.
[380] Cook, *Conservatism and the Future*, 312; Birmingham CA, Management Ctte., 29 December 1922.
[381] Keighley CA, AR, 1924.   [382] Clapham CA, AR, 1923, AGM, 7 April 1924.

The overestimation of Communist support and capabilities was because 'this horrible phantom' was 'always lurking in the background, and all the more alarming because it is tireless and unseen'.[383] More than property was being defended, as 'the Communist Party, as a section of the Third International, preached not only sedition and atheism, but the sexual corruption which was one of the Russian revolution's most horrible results'.[384] Apocalyptic aims were attributed to revolutionary extremism: not just to tear down the throne and flag, but to destroy 'all the old fine qualities of loyalty and kindliness... and all things revered and dignified and beautiful', in fact 'even civilisation itself'.[385] There was no doubt that Communism was 'a creed of hate and destruction'.[386] It was believed that a constant flow of Russian gold was fostering revolutionary agitation within Britain and the empire, and that at home and abroad 'we are fighting against plots laid in Moscow'.[387] This was not least because British Communists 'take their orders from Moscow', so that 'They are British only in name. In their aims and objects, they are Russian all the time.'[388]

Bolshevism was pictured as an octopus whose tentacles reached everywhere, and the frightening degrees of effectiveness which were often ascribed to these tireless enemies could lead, amongst the diehard right-wing at least, to paranoid suspicion and conspiracy theories. It was held that these demonic figures—largely faceless, with few examples known and named—were well aware of what they were doing, and cynically sought to arouse passions and mislead the masses for their own ulterior agendas. In the case of the General Strike, a former Cabinet minister believed that 'sedulous and adroit propaganda had obfuscated the minds of the strikers', whilst a constituency chairman was equally definite 'that it was a carefully organised attempt on the part of revolutionaries to starve and ruin the nation'.[389] As a Central Office speaker told a local women's branch, Socialism 'was being spread largely by aliens, whose one object was the destruction of this country'.[390] In most cases, it was assumed that these agitators worked in the interests—and perhaps the pay—of foreign states; Fascism was equally vulnerable to the suspicion of treasonable tendencies, and its ideology was thought to be partly derived from similarly foreign origins in the philosophy of Hegel. Fascism and Communism were alike in key respects: they both sought to exalt the state and make the individual its servant—under both, people were 'trained to be either Bolshevik robots or Nazi robots'.[391] They both utilized violence to achieve their ends, they both crushed all

---

[383] Crawford to Irwin, 11 March 1927, Halifax MSS, C152/17/1/196b.
[384] NU Conf., 1926, speech by Kindersley.
[385] Loftus, *Creed of a Tory*, 86; *Communism Unmasked* and *Communism: What it Is and What It Wants*, NU leaflets 2339–40 (1924).
[386] *A Gospel of Hate*, NU leaflet 3630 (1936); *A Policy of Destruction: The Aims and Methods of the Communist Party*, NU leaflet 3674 (1937).
[387] *Communism: A World Force*, NU leaflet 2402 (1924).
[388] S. Molton, *The Truth about Communism*, NU leaflet 3746 (1940).
[389] Crawford to Irwin, 15 May 1926, Halifax MSS, C152/17/1/35a; Lewisham West CA, Council, 18 June 1926.
[390] Winchester CA, North Stoneham & Bassett Women's branch, 22 February 1923, Southampton RO.
[391] *In Defence of Freedom*, speech by Baldwin at Ashridge, 1 December 1934, NU leaflet 3447 (1934); B. Baxter, *Why Go Left?*, NU leaflet 3696 (1938).

voices of opposition, and they both were 'alien plants—for they neither have their roots in England'.[392]

There was no doubt in Conservative minds that Socialism and Communism were 'dogmas subversive and destructive of our ancient free institutions'.[393] All of the familiar reference points of existing society would be swept away, and there would be 'no God, no religion, no King, no money, no property, no commerce, no happiness and no safety'.[394] They viewed as anathema the underlying assumption of Marxism and Socialism that everything in human affairs was reducible to economic forces. Conservatives regarded Socialism as based upon envy and greed, and seeking to obtain by false means what had not been earned—nothing less than offering loot to the mob.[395] Its proponents were deliberately fomenting class hatred, a course which would end in revolution and anarchy.[396] Communism, or 'Bolshevism' as it was usually called, was simply Socialism taken to its logical extent, and indeed its supporters at least had the honesty to proclaim their violent and revolutionary intentions.[397] It was unarguable that 'Bolshevism is the name given to the Socialist form of government in Russia', and therefore it was perfectly reasonable for Conservatives to hold up the situation in Russia as evidence of the future under Socialism and proof of where Labour's policies ultimately would lead.[398] The foreign origins of both doctrines provided an easy target, both triggering and reflecting elements of xenophobia; in one pungent metaphor, 'modern Socialism is a mushroom forced by Russian atheism on the dunghill of German economics'.[399] Not only did Socialism's alien nature make it by definition unsuitable and inferior, but it was also damned as 'the child of Radicalism, and the grandchild of Liberalism, and shows hereditary characteristics'.[400]

The Conservative critique of Socialism consisted of two parallel elements, the first of which was denial that any positive case had been made for it, and insistence that there was no evidence from any other society of it working beneficially.[401] It was therefore a highly risky exercise in experimentation and foolish wishful thinking, and, moreover, was riddled with inconsistencies. Of course, given the wide spectrum of left-wing opinion, and the liberality with which Conservatives included examples from overseas when it suited their purpose, it was easy to find

---

[392] *Our Heritage of Freedom*; *Mr Baldwin on Fascism: Danger of Class War*, NU leaflet 3417 (1934).
[393] Horne, in Skelton, *Constructive Conservatism*, 5.
[394] *What Socialism Means to Women*, NU leaflet 2036 (1922).
[395] Banks, *Conservative Outlook*, 41.
[396] 'Gentleman with a duster', *Conservative Mind*, 152.
[397] Crisp, *Rebirth of Conservatism*, 54–5; Gretton to Baldwin, 12 February 1925, Baldwin MSS, 11/101–2.
[398] *What Bolshevism Means to Women*, NU leaflet 1980 (1920); *What Bolshevist Socialism Has Done for Russia It Would Like to Do for You*, NU leaflet 1846 (1918); *The Frozen Breath of Bolshevism*, NU leaflet 1934 (1919); *The Bolshevist War against Christianity*, NU leaflet 1947 (1920); *Socialism Has Reduced Russia to the Depths of Despair*, NU leaflet 2126 (1922); Wirral CA, AR, 1936–37.
[399] 'Gentleman with a duster', *Conservative Mind*, 9.
[400] Banks, *Conservative Outlook*, 43.
[401] H. G. Williams, *What Is Socialism?*, NU leaflet 2012 (1921); G. C. Tryon, *Socialist Policy Exposed*, NU leaflet 3473 (1935).

disagreements amongst the advocates of Socialism on even quite fundamental points. Labour politicians and intellectuals were 'a chorus of hideously discordant voices, giving irreconcilable replies, and abusing one another'.[402] With the Socialists not agreed amongst themselves about how to proceed, Conservatives argued that it would be folly to give them power without knowing what would happen. The Conservative rejection of Marxism was on firmer ground in contending that the motor of Karl Marx's theory—that the deprivation and alienation of the poor would worsen to breaking point—was not happening. The justification for Socialism was therefore based on an economic fallacy: whilst capitalism was not perfect and had not provided assured employment for all, over the previous 150 years it had increased the standard of living, reduced the hours and much of the labour of work, and financed an extensive welfare system, all for a vastly larger population; the trend was for improvement and not the increased misery forecast by Marx. The reality was that 'we shall not destroy poverty by destroying capital and the right to save and invest'.[403] On the contrary, 'the capital must be there or the job won't be there'.[404] The functioning of the existing system was a fact, whilst Socialism was mere hypothesis; there was no evidence that it would work better than capitalism, or even work at all. The conclusion from limited experiments, such as in Australia, was that Socialism 'has failed wherever it has been tried', whilst the only major example of a Socialist society was Soviet Russia, a brutal dictatorship with a starving population.[405] The arguments of the Socialists were based on precisely the kind of abstract principles and chain of logic that Conservatives distrusted as unrealistic and inflexible. Socialist theorists had constructed 'an imaginary world in which all the facts of existence and the characteristics of humanity were disregarded'.[406] The Socialist utopia was a delusory dream, because it was predicated upon a naïve misreading of human nature which was 'not applicable to men as they are'.[407] Self-interest was an innate human characteristic which Socialism would not abolish; competition would therefore continue, but in the form of pressure exerted on the state to gain a more advantageous position.[408]

The second element in the critique was even easier: to expose the negative aspects of Socialism. Within this, there were four strands: the nature of a Socialist state, its demoralizing effects, its inevitable economic failure, and its divisiveness and lack of patriotism. Despite its cloak of idealism, the basis of Socialism was an outlook of 'gross materialism', in which the only motives were economic.[409] It was argued that Socialism was 'entirely centred round the State',[410] and therefore was bound to lead to ever-closer regulation and loss of freedom: it was 'merely another name for State

---

[402] Banks, *Conservative Outlook*, 33.   [403] Jenner, *Will Conservatism Survive?*, 28.
[404] *Socialism and Your Boy's Job*, NU leaflet 2623 (1926).
[405] *Bogey Socialism and Real Socialism*, NU leaflet 2071 (1922); W. W. Paine, *Why You Should Not Be a Socialist*, NU leaflet 3694 (1938).
[406] Cooper, *Conservative Point of View*, 27.
[407] Lee, 'Quality and Conservatism', 36; *Answered! A Reply to Philip Snowden's Case for Socialism*, NU leaflet 2144 (1923).
[408] Cecil, *Conservatism*, 93–4.
[409] Crisp, *Rebirth of Conservatism*, 41; NU Conf., 1922, speech by Bardsley.
[410] Cecil, *Conservatism*, 82.

Slavery'.[411] Whatever reformist good intentions might be present at the outset, 'the more absolute the Socialist state becomes, the more it tends to assume the character of a dictatorship'.[412] A particular feature would be the need for a swollen bureaucracy of officials and inspectors, unscrutinized and over-powerful. This would be inefficient and unresponsive: 'Socialism operates through bureaucracy, which means long-distance control', a system 'bound by its very nature, to play for safety and to stifle individuality and initiative'.[413] The suffocating blanket of 'cradle to grave' regimentation and control would have a demoralizing impact on the individual, as well as removing his existing freedoms—including choosing his line of work, the place that he lived, and so on.[414] As a result, 'once self-reliant men and women would become twisted into mere cogs in a machine'.[415] Socialism would enfeeble natural self-reliance and remove personal and moral responsibility; it was 'a policy of State restraint upon the enterprise of individual citizens'.[416] This was self-defeating and unrealistic, for 'the competitive instinct' had been 'the means of all progress' in the past.[417] Furthermore, no one would either invest or work if they feared that the fruits would be confiscated and enjoyed by the feckless and lazy. The redistribution of wealth would result in little material benefit for each recipient, and at the cost of 'quality everywhere in chains'.[418] In any case, a nationalized institution did not attract people's loyalty: 'what everyone owns, nobody owns...communal ownership, when obtained, neither interests nor influences a single human being'.[419]

Socialism would thus be the quickest route to national bankruptcy; one telling point was that if Britain became a Socialist society, no consideration had been given as to how the export trade upon which the country depended to feed its population would deal with competition from non-Socialist economies.[420] Rising costs due to nationalization would render British goods uncompetitive abroad, whilst 'the spirit of adventure and enterprise would cease to be characteristics of British business men'.[421] Socialism would lead inevitably to economic decline, in a descending cycle of depression, overtaxation, and waste. Its economic and moral effects were summarized by Skelton: 'the omnipotent State, the kept citizen, responsibility checked, initiative crippled, character in cold-storage, wealth squandered'.[422] Even the tempting prospects of generous doles funded by despoiling the rich would soon prove illusory, as nationalized industries would run at a loss and the national budget would be unbalanced: 'benefits cannot be paid out of deficits', as the 1931 crisis had shown.[423] Ultimately, whilst there might in theory be equal

---

[411] Williams, *What Is Socialism?*.   [412] Cranborne, *Our Political Future*.
[413] Stelling, *Why I Am a Conservative*, 13.
[414] *Cards and Coupons*, NU leaflet 1838 (1918). This was also a concern about the integrated welfare system proposed in the Beveridge Report: Post-War Problems Central Ctte., report of ctte. on the Beveridge Report, 19 January 1943, CPA, CRS/2/28/6.
[415] Northam, *Conservatism*, 107.
[416] Horne, in Skelton, *Constructive Conservatism*, 5; H. M. Adam, *The Fallacies of Socialism* (1926), 11.
[417] Parker et al., *Declaration of Tory Principles*, 34.   [418] Feiling, *What Is Conservatism?*, 25.
[419] Skelton, *Constructive Conservatism*, 19.   [420] Tryon, *Socialist Policy Exposed*.
[421] Scottish Unionist Whip's Office, *The Choice*, 36.
[422] Skelton, *Constructive Conservatism*, 7.   [423] Tryon, *Socialist Policy Exposed*.

shares for all, the outcome would be 'a share of nothing, which is NOTHING'.[424] These themes were the reason why many Conservatives, including Churchill, were receptive to Friedrich Hayek's arguments in *The Road to Serfdom* when it appeared in 1944—not as a new gospel, but because it added chapter and verse to their established critique of Socialism.[425]

The final strand in the negative critique aroused some of the strongest Conservative emotions: the divisiveness and unpatriotic nature of Socialism, due to its putting class loyalty before national unity: 'the extreme Socialist behaves as if there were no such thing as England'.[426] Conservatives were antagonistic to any doctrines based upon class differences, which they sought to relegate to the background as far as possible. Talk of 'class war' was deeply alarming, especially when the Socialists claimed that the big battalions of the working class were on their side (or inevitably soon would be), and when the capture by Socialists of the leadership of important trade unions seemed to be evidence of this. Conservatives were adamant in denying that the 'Labour' Party had any special right to speak for the workers, and their propaganda consistently sought to uncouple this popular notion and expose the Labour Party as a narrow sect of intellectual Socialist dogmatists.[427] Class consciousness was exclusivist, and therefore nothing more than an inverted form of snobbery.[428] Its corrosive effect upon national unity meant that it was inconsistent with patriotism, and this licensed Conservatives to any and all attacks upon the loyalty of Socialists. This was facilitated by the latter's belief in the international brotherhood of the working class, and the institutionalization of this by Labour's links to European Socialism and the Second International, and still more by Communism's subordination to the orders of Moscow transmitted by the Third International. Little difference was seen between the two cases, and thus the chairman of a constituency in the industrial north in 1919 simply referred to 'the Bolsheviks of the Labour Party'.[429] Conservatives were acting in accordance with their view of the realities when a letter, purportedly sent by Grigory Zinoviev, the head of the Communist International, to British Communists, was used in the 1924 general election campaign to cast doubts upon the motives and aims of the Labour Party, for it was a patriotic duty 'to tear the mask of moderation from the Bolshevik features of Labour'.[430] Some of this was genuine fear of 'reds under the bed', and some was contempt for what were at best the naïve dupes of foreign enemies of Britain. This was linked to the decades-old criticism of Liberalism as always inclined uncritically to take the side of the foreigner: 'they will ostracize half their fellow countrymen but fawn on murderous savages'.[431] This aspect of Socialism had visi-

---

[424] *Russia's Object-Lesson in Socialism*, NU leaflet 2054 (1922); emphasis in the original.
[425] Smithers to Churchill, 8 June 1944, Churchill MSS, CAC, CHAR/20/146b/155; W. Smithers, *Socialism Offers Slavery* (1945).
[426] Feiling, *What Is Conservatism?*, 28.
[427] *Is the 'Labour' Party Labour?*, NU leaflet 2079 (1922).
[428] Davidson to Irwin, 14 June 1926, Halifax MSS, C152/17/1/53a.
[429] Rotherham CA, Quarterly Meeting, 3 January 1919; South East Area, Council, 20 July 1938.
[430] 'Gentleman with a duster', *Conservative Mind*, 9.
[431] Feiling, *What is Conservatism?*, 28.

ble symbols in the honouring of the Red Flag over the Union Jack (the subject of one striking Conservative poster) and the singing of the 'Internationale' (with emphasis in the pronunciation on its foreign origin) rather than the national anthem at Labour conferences. Finally, the strong connections between Socialism and Pacifism (which most Conservatives viewed as a threadbare cloak for cowardice) damned it further; it might be red, but it was far from red-blooded.

Socialism therefore had negative aspects which were both masculine and feminine: it was aggressive, rowdy, and linked to violence and mob rule, but also weak, sentimental, and naïve.[432] However much they loathed it, Conservatives were only too well aware that it might attract the poor and the weak-minded, and that simply presenting a negative critique would not be enough to forestall this. Amery was emphatic, and far from alone, in believing that 'if we have no better policy than "anti-Socialism" and so-called Social Reforms which are a pale imitation of our opponents' schemes, the rot in the working class will go on faster than ever'.[433] It was understood that it was 'the apparent hopelessness of their environment' which encouraged the aspirational working class to embrace Socialism.[434] Many Conservatives recognized that Socialism appeared, at least superficially, to be 'comprehensive, challenging, alluring' and appealed to idealism: 'It is presenting a "view of life" to the nation in a method admirably suited to the mood and atmosphere of the new era.'[435] Their response must therefore include two elements, the first of which was the traditional Tory approach of good government: 'In the long run the best way to defeat Socialism is to remove the distress, the unemployment, and the discontent which Socialists foster and exploit.'[436] This was a slow, difficult, and sometimes dull endeavour, and so the second element was vital: the presentation of a positive alternative to capture the hearts and minds of the working class for the patriotic cause. It was easier to see this need than to answer it, and the suggested remedies were sometimes divisive within Conservative ranks, but for many the solution was to raise the standard of the empire as the rallying point of national sentiment, and therefore to prioritize the policy of imperial preference and tariff protection, from which the British worker might gain more and better-paid employment.

Fear and loathing were potent ingredients in the composition of Conservatism, and its 'demonology' is a revealing aspect of its outlook. This took two forms: a focus upon certain individuals amongst the leading ranks of the opposition parties, and a denunciation of groups or elements of their support. The individuals were those whose opinions, personalities, or past conduct were particularly objectionable: one such bogeyman was the radical Liberal politician David Lloyd George (before 1914 and after 1922), and others were the left-wing Labour figures of Sir Stafford Cripps in the 1930s and Aneurin Bevan in the 1940s. Trade union leaders

---

[432] D. Jarvis, 'Mrs Maggs and Betty: the Conservative appeal to women voters in the 1920s', *20th-Century British History*, 5/2 (1994), 144–5.
[433] Amery to Baldwin, 28 January 1924, Baldwin MSS, 42/166–73.
[434] Parker et al., *Declaration of Tory Principles*, 14–15.
[435] Skelton, *Constructive Conservatism*, 13.
[436] Tryon to Baldwin, 11 December 1923, Baldwin MSS, 35/188.

could also fill such a role: A. J. Cook, a leader of the miners in the coal strike of 1926 and a Communist, was a gift from heaven in this respect. However, hostility was not usually directed at the leader of the main opposition party, and there was no personal antagonism towards Ramsay MacDonald (Leader of the Labour Party 1922–31) and H. H. Asquith (Leader of the Liberal Party 1908–26) in the 1920s, or afterwards to Clement Attlee (Leader of the Labour Party 1935–55). The identification of groups was inevitably vaguer, but several were consistently targeted for obloquy and blame. As a whole, the Labour Party was seen as a combination of 'crazy idealists working with acquisitive, embittered and destructive elements'.[437]

A particularly derided group were the 'intellectuals'—a term which normally denoted the political theorists and writers of the left, rather than including novelists and artists as well.[438] For Conservatives, 'ideology' and 'intellectual' were unattractive terms with connotations of the dry, rigid, and remote, whilst Socialists and Communists 'are very fond of long words'[439] and had the type of mind which 'revels in committees'.[440] There was distrust of those who put politics before all other interests in life, as lacking in balance and humanity. They were dismissed as too clever for their own good, pontificating without either understanding or experience of the real world: 'even if the economic theory were right, the people who profess it are so wrong that they could not work it'.[441] The Socialist was regarded as being in a separate category from 'the normal man'; inadequate, an 'oddity', and deliberately perverse in his views.[442] The left-wing activist was 'commonly a gloomy fanatic, filled with envy...a raging Philistine wholly devoid of both sweetness and light'.[443] Such people were easily dismissed as 'cranks', especially where they held other unconventional ideas, such as Pacifism or vegetarianism. The Conservative suspicion of theory was the basis of a wider anti-intellectualism, which could become small-minded and parochial in spirit. This was given voice by Harold Macmillan, who presumably did not have his own economic theories of the 1930s in mind when he declared in a speech in 1946: 'The clever people in a nation at any given moment are nearly always wrong. Distrust the clever man.'[444] However, this was not a repudiation of ability where it was combined with steadiness in judgement and a sense of responsibility, but rather of self-advertising and arrogant brilliance. A former Chief Whip observed that 'the very word "genius" carries with it something derogatory. It connotes unconventional clothes and doubtful morals'.[445]

Most Conservatives held fairly simple views about their opponents; there were few incentives for them to do otherwise, and little need to see the world from any

---

[437] Beamish speech notes, 22 April 1932, Beamish MSS, CAC, BEAM/3/3.
[438] *In Defence of Freedom*, speech by Baldwin.   [439] Molton, *The Truth about Communism*.
[440] Adam, *Fallacies of Socialism*, 11.   [441] Banks, *Conservative Outlook*, 56.
[442] Banks, *Conservative Outlook*, 50–1.
[443] Hearnshaw, *Conservatism in England*, 25–6; Loftus, *Creed of a Tory*, 85–6.
[444] *The Conservative Approach to Modern Politics* (Central Office, 1946), speech of 7 May 1946, quoted in Glickman, 'The Toryness of English Conservatism', 122.
[445] Memoir by Margesson, 'Chamberlain—A Candid Portrait', n.d., Margesson MSS, CAC, MRGN/1/5/1–5.

other perspective. This is true of most political groups, and is a cause of the rifts which can open between followers and their leaders—who by necessity are more receptive to other positions in debate, in government, or for electoral gain. The more insulated followers who face little of a local challenge are naturally the most assertive, hold the least sophisticated views, and have the least developed understanding of the motives and impulses behind support for their opponents. Ironically, the greatest levels of fear and mistrust were often to be found amongst those furthest from the fray, whilst in the areas where Conservatism was the weaker force a broader and more phlegmatic outlook was likely to be engendered. The 'Plays for Patriots' series of short dramas, which local party branches re-enacted for propaganda and entertainment, depicted Socialist agitators and Communist trade union officials as aggressive, bullying, underhand, and mean-spirited; at the decisive point they were also unveiled as cowards and hypocrites.[446] However, the working class as a whole were generally viewed favourably as the 'salt of the earth' and possessed of a true 'John Bull' spirit of independence and patriotism. During the General Strike, as well as approval (tinged with relief) of the steadiness of the people, it was noted that many strikers were primarily motivated by loyalty to their trade union—a value with which Conservatives had empathy—and that 'the vast majority...are not only good citizens but very patriotic'.[447] This particularly applied to 'the respectable working class, who were really some of the best citizens in the country'.[448]

The middle- or upper-class supporters of Socialism were another matter; they were open to parody and ridicule, and the image fostered was unattractive. In the case of the middle-class Socialist male, it was one of ineffectuality: pale and anxious young men, physically weak and bespectacled, and with the personal cowardice that most Conservatives instinctively felt lay at the root of Pacifism. In the case of the middle-class Socialist woman, the dominant image was not that of an alluring siren, but of an arid and aggressive spinster, 'with Eton crop and horn-rimmed glasses'.[449] Taken together, the expectation was of priggish, boring, ineffectual, and quirky personalities with an unspoken question mark over their sexuality. Thus, a Conservative junior minister in the mid-1920s noted 'disquieting rumours of the effeminacy and perverted political views of Oxford undergraduates'.[450] Another MP drew a picture of the 'emotional creatures with the fanatical eyes, the enlarged thyroids, the narrow chests and the hydrocephalous foreheads who may be seen wherever the Socialist intelligentsia congregates, from the London School of Economics to the latest queer theatre for the production of the dreary drama'.[451]

---

[446] *Plays for Patriots*, NU leaflets 2611, 2612, 2614 (1925), 2630 (1926), 2738 (1927); E. M. Gell, *Look Before You Leap! A Sketch for the Times*, NU leaflet 2386 (1924); *Love and Mr Smith*, NU leaflet 3359 (1932).
[447] Davidson to Irwin, 14 June 1926, Halifax MSS, C152/17/1/53a.
[448] NU Conf., 1923, speech by Lady Selborne.
[449] Description of a Socialist woman in the stage directions of the play *Lady Monica Waffle's Debut*, NU leaflet 2630 (1926).
[450] Winterton to Irwin, 3 June 1926, Halifax MSS, C152/17/1/48.
[451] Banks, *Conservative Outlook*, 46, 48–52.

Of course, these were no more than caricatures, but it is upon such images that people act and it is from them that they reinforce their own certainties and superiority. When such stereotypes are widely absorbed into the general consciousness it is they, and not the reality, which provide the basis of opinions and actions.

This was also true of another area which has become much more sensitive since 1945: attitudes towards the Jews. These partly derived from broader concerns about the influence of 'the alien' and the foreigner, and the need 'to preserve the identity of our nation and its culture';[452] in some instances, it was linked to the nebulous bogey of 'international finance'.[453] However, there was certainly an undercurrent of anti-Semitism in Conservative circles, although this was the product of the social prejudices of the upper class rather than of any political ideology. Conservatives disliked, even despised, the openly paraded anti-Semitism of Fascism, and neither sympathized with it nor really understood its racial basis. The unfolding stages of Nazi persecution were widely regarded by Conservatives with disgusted incomprehension; after the 'Kristallnacht' pogrom of November 1938, even those who had been inclined to sympathetic views in the mid-1930s, such as Henry Channon MP, considered the German regime had lost all reason and sense of civilized values.[454] Most of the Conservatives who were the strongest opponents of Soviet Communism, such as Churchill, saw nothing in Nazi Germany with which they would make common cause. Indeed, the virulently anti-Communist MP Oliver Locker-Lampson declared at the 1933 Annual Conference, the first held after Hitler had come to power, that 'it was wicked to bully a man because of the blood in his veins or faith in his heart'.[455] He also took pride in the protection given to Jewish academics and scientists, naming Albert Einstein as an example, although—also like most Conservatives—he was against allowing any mass influx of refugees, not least because of the cover this might give for the entry of hostile agents. Expressions of overt anti-Semitism were more likely to draw criticism than to rally support, as was demonstrated by the fate of Edward Doran: elected unexpectedly at Tottenham North in the landslide of 1931, his crude attacks on the character of German Jewish refugees led to his deselection as the association's candidate in August 1933.

Anti-Semitism was certainly not universal in the Conservative ranks, and several of the leading figures were favourable to Zionism, including Arthur Balfour (Party Leader 1902–11), Amery, and Churchill. However, whilst anti-Semitism was generally mild in tone—virulence in this, as in other areas, being unattractive to most Conservatives—Jewishness was nevertheless a matter of comment.[456] This was particularly the case with the Jewish figures in opposing parties, especially the Liberals—and thus a junior minister would write that Herbert Samuel was 'meeting Mond and Reading and other Hebrews'.[457] The same MP attributed defeat in the

---

[452] Ludovici, *Defence of Conservatism*, 116, 149–55.
[453] Bath CA, AGM, 10 July 1922, speech by Foxcroft.
[454] Channon diary, 15 and 21 November 1938.   [455] NU Conf., 1933.
[456] Channon diary, 27 January 1935, 27 April 1937
[457] Lane-Fox to Irwin, 11 May 1926, Halifax MSS, C152/17/1/31.

North Hammersmith by-election in 1926 to the selection as candidate of 'a horrible Jew, who could pay his expenses...The slogan of "Vote for Gluckstein and save the Empire" was not convincing.'[458] The difficulties of Herbert Jessel in the wealthy Westminster St George's constituency in 1921–22 were due partly to personal frictions, but mainly to his being Jewish, and the rumour in January 1923 that he might be appointed Party Chairman was regarded by such mainstream figures as William Bridgeman, the Home Secretary, and his wife, as 'calamitous'.[459] Of course, there had been a few Jews in the parliamentary ranks for several decades and there was always the famous example of Disraeli, for whom there was genuine reverence. However, there was an awareness of who was Jewish and this coloured all interactions, at the least adding a certain extra distance.[460] There was an unconscious expectation that Jews would incline to the behaviour that prejudice attributed to their race, and therefore a latent mistrust, which was most likely to come to mind where the person's physical appearance was similar to the imagined stereotype.

In many ways, the most venomous Conservative hostility was focused not upon the new rivals of Labour but on the old enemy—the Liberals.[461] The basis of this was, of course, the negative views formed during the decades of party competition up to 1914, which rapidly re-emerged after their temporary suppression during the wartime truce and postwar Coalition. This emphasized the priggish dominance of the 'Nonconformist conscience', and the twin themes attributed to the influence of the 'Manchester School': blinkered adherence to unrestricted free trade and the abdication of Britain's world role—the worst aspects of being 'little Englanders'. The postwar Liberal Party seemed to have little to say beyond a stubborn adherence to these (in Conservative eyes) outmoded doctrines, and therefore they could see no justification for the Liberal Party's continued role.[462] Whilst Socialism and Conservatism both stood 'for something real and living for which people can work and fight', the Liberal Party 'stands today for nothing more than an organised hypocrisy and not for any real political faith'.[463] The problem was that it seemed 'neither fish nor fowl'; the Liberal Party had sustained the first and second Labour governments in office, whilst in many areas, at local government level, the Liberals had negotiated an anti-Labour pact with the Conservatives.

The desire to eliminate the Liberal Party had a sound tactical base as it was a potential rival for the role of providing the 'constitutional' defence against Socialism, even though Liberal ideas and policy seemed to be 'hardly distinguishable from Socialism, except in its lack of courage and conviction'.[464] A bi-polar party

---

[458] Lane-Fox to Irwin, 8 June 1926, Halifax MSS, C152/17/1/49.
[459] Bridgeman to Law, 12 January 1923, Bonar Law MSS, BL/118/8/28.
[460] Beamish diary notes, 6 May 1941, Beamish MSS, CAC, BEAM/3/4.
[461] Amery to Baldwin, 8 December 1923, Baldwin MSS, 35/169–72; H. Balfour, *Wings Over Westminster* (1973), 70–1.
[462] Skelton, *Constructive Conservatism*, 11; Hearnshaw, *Conservatism in England*, 4.
[463] Amery to Baldwin, 21 December 1923, Baldwin MSS, 42/150–5.
[464] Banks, *Conservative Outlook*, 62; Hoare to A. Chamberlain, 25 January 1924, Templewood MSS, V/1.

system was clearer, easier to operate, more stable, and even more 'traditional' or 'natural'; it was believed that a two-party Conservative–Labour dichotomy would work to the Conservative advantage, as well as pulling Labour towards the centre. Amery acknowledged that the Labour Party 'are equally interested with us in the break up of the Liberals' and 'it is to the interest of both of us to clear the ground of the Liberal Party... We may each hope to get the larger share of the carcase, but meanwhile the great thing is to get the beast killed and on that we can be agreed.'[465] Another element in this was the return after 1922, on the part of most Conservatives, to hostility towards Lloyd George, in which there was some element of fear. He was seen as unprincipled, having 'no definite line of policy beyond trying to create as much mischief as possible'.[466] There was also the continuing controversy over Lloyd George's fund and the sale of honours during his premiership, and even one of the Conservative cabinet ministers who had supported his continuance in 1922 commented a few years later: 'The little man is not straight and everybody knows it.'[467] Until January 1924, when the Liberals voted the Labour Party into its first term in office, a significant minority of Conservatives still believed that the two 'constitutional' parties could work together in an anti-Socialist alliance; after this turning point, there was near unanimity that the Liberal Party was a dangerous hindrance that should be swept aside. For many Conservatives, there was a personal element in this antagonism, as the intervention of Liberal candidates cost many MPs their seats in 1923 and 1929. The presence of a Liberal was especially resented when it was clear that they had no chance of winning the seat, and so would have a purely spoiling effect which could only help the Labour Party; the consequence was Conservatives 'hating them more for their unpatriotic attitude than a good honest Socialist'.[468] The silver lining to the cloud of the Conservative defeat in 1929 was the failure of Lloyd George's effort to revive the Liberals, and one mainstream backbench MP expressed the general view: 'let us hope this may have been the last death struggle of the Liberal Party'.[469] This was not to be, but again in 1945 there was some consolation, mixing relief and pleasure, in 'the Liberal debacle' as final confirmation of that party's marginalization.[470]

IDENTITY

The elements discussed above shaped the Conservative outlook, forging a clear sense of identity and a loyalty to the Conservative Party as its continuing embodiment and defender. Whilst specific policies came and went, the underlying attitudes provided continuity and unity. Conservative principles were 'sufficiently

---

[465] Amery to Baldwin, 21 December 1923, Baldwin MSS, 42/150–5.
[466] Lane-Fox to Irwin, 4 July 1926, Halifax MSS, C152/17/1/61.
[467] Crawford to Irwin, 13 May 1929, Halifax MSS, C152/18/1/260.
[468] Memo of conversation with Berry, 5 May 1928, Davidson MSS, DAV/182; Headlam diary, 7 May 1929, 15 November 1935; Crichton-Stuart to Baldwin, 3 June 1929, Baldwin MSS, 37/67.
[469] Colfox to Baldwin, 1 June 1929, Baldwin MSS, 37/60.
[470] Parker Leighton to Emrys-Evans, 30 July 1945, Emrys-Evans MSS, Add.58254/38.

rigid and sufficiently flexible to serve the needs of every generation'.[471] This 'elasticity' was the basis of the party's resilience and longevity,[472] and its ability to shed issues without eroding its core support: 'all that is lasting is the intellectual approach and the emotional appeal'.[473] The latter also explains the reluctance to alter the name of the party, despite the suggestions periodically put forward to drop 'Conservative' as outdated and a handicap in recruiting young people or new sources of support. These proposals particularly arose during periods in coalition, when the success of a cross-party appeal led some individuals and constituencies to propose alternative titles such as 'Constitutional' or 'National', often from a mixture of patriotic idealism and electoral pragmatism.[474] However, as one Chairman of the Party pointed out, any such reorientation entailed changing more than just a name: 'the whole character and composition of the Party will have to undergo fundamental alteration as well'.[475] There was a danger that such a change might alienate traditional Conservative supporters, and yet not secure the long-term adhesion of any large number of former opponents.[476]

Not surprisingly, whilst the various alternatives had an attractive ring, after reflection it was always decided to stay with 'Conservative'. In the debate on this issue at the 1932 Annual Conference, the first held after the formation of the National Government, one delegate opposing any change revealingly argued that it was as futile to 'ask Englishmen to call themselves Europeans as expect Conservatives to call themselves by any other name'.[477] In fact, the label 'Conservative' had only recently returned to general use, during the period between the Anglo-Irish Treaty of 1921 and the first Labour government in 1924. For over three decades prior to 1924, the party had used the term 'Unionist', due to the primacy of the Irish Home Rule issue and the alliance with the Liberal Unionists. Even after the union with Ireland was dissolved, in many areas—significantly, Scotland and Wales in particular—the name Unionist continued to be used, folding the inertia of old loyalties into a new resonance as the antithesis of Socialist class-war ideology.[478] The Conservative Party had no hesitation about taking up the role of shield and sword against the Socialist menace, for it had always considered itself first and

---

[471] Parker et al., *Declaration of Tory Principles*, 5.
[472] Riley, *Our Cause*, 17.
[473] Boothby et al., *Industry and the State*, 8.
[474] Eastern Area, AGM, 24 March 1923; West Midlands Area, Exec., 18 September 1931, GP, 14 October 1932; Northern Area, AGM, 27 February 1932; Cambridgeshire CA, Exec., 16 April 1932; James to Duchess of Atholl, 26 September 1934, Atholl MSS, 90/8; Guildford CA, Exec., 21 February 1936; Bedford CA, Council, 9 March 1938.
[475] Stonehaven to Baldwin, 15 November 1931, Central Office staff conference minutes, 27 November 1931, Baldwin MSS, 166/299–300, 46/33–5; Winchester CA, AGM, 24 March 1934.
[476] Ponsonby to Baldwin, 22 November 1935, Baldwin MSS, 41/159; Headlam diary, 11 June 1934.
[477] NU Conf., 1932, speech by Holland; Yorkshire Area, AGM, 23 January 1932.
[478] In the late 1930s, of the constituency associations in England and Wales, twenty used the title 'Conservative and Constitutional', twenty-one used 'Constitutional' only, sixty-seven had retained 'Unionist' only, 109 used 'Conservative' only, and 303 used 'Conservative and Unionist': 'England and Wales: Titles of Associations', n.d., Essex & Middlesex Area, misc. correspondence file, 1937–38, CPA, ARE/8/26/1.

foremost to be the constitutional party. This was part of the founding title of the National Union in 1867, as the federation of 'Conservative and Constitutional Associations', and was still used in some constituencies in the interwar era; it was also the label used by Winston Churchill when migrating back from the Liberal Party in 1924.

The assumptions that underlay the Conservative identity were revealed in the language which Conservatives chose to use, particularly in the public forms of speeches and resolutions. There was a desire for unmistakeable and uncomplicated action, based upon a distinctive programme, and thus 'it would be better to lose the next election on a straight issue rather than fight it on a "policy of wobble"'.[479] On matters that were causing concern, constituency resolutions repeatedly urged the leadership to take steps that were 'strong', 'bold', 'vigorous', and 'positive'; after the 1929 defeat, one association complained of 'the want of a distinctive courageous live Conservative policy'.[480] Whilst on specific issues such terms could be euphemisms for the adoption of hard-line or right-wing positions (such as 'rigid' and 'drastic' economy, and the 'utmost caution' over India), at a fundamental level they showed a belief in the intrinsic merit of a simple remedy applied with determination and consistency. The rank and file wanted policies that were 'firm', 'practical', 'definite', and 'clear', and not open to disputation over fine shades of meaning. As one local businessman told his MP at the height of the party crisis in September 1930: 'what we want is guts and commonsense'.[481] Similarly, the Party Chairman advised his Leader, as the crisis over the Lloyd George Coalition broke in September 1922, that 'frankness and pluck were necessary', and that 'a straightforward statement' from the leaders 'might have a considerable effect'.[482] Such attitudes were founded upon the view—or the hope—that issues did not need to be complicated, and that measures which could be understood easily, implemented in a direct manner, and produce visible effects were most likely to be successful. For this reason, such language offered reassurance and confidence, even if the specific proposal being supported was actually divisive and controversial. The measures being urged were often described as 'common sense', 'straight forward', or 'plain', for anything which was not readily comprehensible by the average person raised suspicions that it was at best impracticable and at worst involved some element of trickery. Proposed reforms were 'constructive', which meant that they addressed an issue that was agreed to be a problem in ways which would attain a defined result through specific and limited action. Another key validatory adjective was 'sound', which for a policy conveyed that it was consistent with Conservative values and interests, and when applied to a person indicated probity, reliability, and subscription to the conventional ethos.[483] The belief that the party approached problems 'without unnecessary fuss' underscored its gentlemanly nature; if this should seem

---

[479] St Albans CA, Exec., 30 June 1930.
[480] Rochester & Chatham CA, report of Special Ctte., 30 September 1929, Salisbury MSS, S(4)131/103–5.
[481] Dixon to Heneage, 30 September 1930, Heneage MSS, HNC/4/40.
[482] Younger's memo of interview with Chamberlain, 26 September 1922, Bayford diary.
[483] NU Conf., 1922, speech by Fremantle.

dull, it was the consequence of the virtues of humility, practicality, steadiness, honesty, and sincerity.[484] As Baldwin declared when opening the 1929 general election campaign: 'our first duty is not to be popular, but to run straight'.[485]

The language of interwar Conservatism was universalist in mode, and ostensibly applicable in all contexts and to all genders and classes. In reality, its derivation and orientation was both masculine and elitist, reflecting the values and upbringing of the privileged social strata who provided its MPs and leaders. The clichés of Conservatism were expressed in the code words and shorthand which were in common usage in this upper- and upper-middle-class milieu, drawing particularly upon two aspects: agriculture and sport. Metaphors from farming—such as 'ploughing a straight furrow' and 'separating the wheat from the chaff'—were frequently employed, and such expressions were used just as much by those who had no personal involvement in agriculture. The use of sporting images was even more common, mainly drawn from the team games familiar from public school and Oxbridge (cricket and rowing) and from the landed gentry's favourite recreation of fox-hunting. Thus, anyone who acted in a collective or co-operative manner was described as 'playing straight', and an effective member of the Cabinet would be 'pulling his weight in the boat'.[486] Similarly, at a difficult point in 1930, Baldwin appealed to his followers 'for a long pull, and a strong pull, and a pull together'.[487] Newly elected MPs understood perfectly the values and conduct expected of them, and were unsurprised when given an introductory lecture by the whips on the importance of 'playing the game'.[488] Most famously, Churchill's dismissal of Bonar Law's Cabinet in 1922 as the 'second eleven' spoke directly to Conservative MPs who had been educated at cricket-playing schools. Although Conservatism in general was often described as a 'faith', religious language was otherwise comparatively rare. The one instance where religion was frequently evoked was the description of the programme of tariff reform, or protectionism, as a 'gospel' by its more fervent supporters—a metaphor which explains much of the passion and rigidity that were features of its advocates.[489] There were expressions with which Conservatives were uncomfortable, especially those linked to changes of which they disapproved or to foreign connections. At various times, Baldwin publicly denounced the words 'intellectual' and 'propaganda' as alien and unpleasant to English ears, whilst he led into the peroration of one of his most famous speeches by way of a sideswipe at 'that pentasyllabic French derivative, "proletariat"'.[490] National identity was virtuously contrasted with the 'vague and watery cosmopolitanism' which made

---

[484] Northam, *Conservatism*, 38; Beyfus, 'Conservatism', 4.
[485] *Our First Duty is to Run Straight*, speech at Bristol, 25 April 1929, NU leaflet 2950 (1929).
[486] Derby to Rawlinson, 28 May 1923, Derby MSS, 33; Davidson to Joynson-Hicks, 19 July 1928, Baldwin MSS, 163/94–5; N. Chamberlain to Irwin, 25 December 1927, Halifax MSS, C152/17/1/277a; SUA, EDC, Exec., 22 June 1932; NU Conf., 1923, speech by Nield.
[487] Baldwin's remarks at the private dinner to MPs and candidates at the 1900 Club, recounted by Peto to his wife: Lady Peto diary, 5 February 1930.
[488] J. R. J. Macnamara, *The Whistle Blows* (1938), 144.
[489] Amery to Baldwin, 29 December 1923, Baldwin MSS, 42/159–61.
[490] Baldwin, *On England*, 60. The word 'stunt' was similarly pilloried as un-English during his conflict with the press lords: notes for speech in the House of Commons, 7 November 1929, Baldwin MSS, 103/170–3.

men 'turn into a sort of political eunuch'.[491] Conservatives were ambivalent about the term 'working class', and preferred expressions which de-emphasized the sense of class division, such as 'working men', 'wage-earners', or the simple unspecific of 'the man in the street'.

The language used could help to rally Conservative support around particular standards and totems. Issues such as the 'contracting-in' system for the trade union political levy were linked to liberty and the freedom of the individual, and were thus matters of constitutional principle and not merely of industrial relations. Although the agricultural sector was comparatively minor as a proportion of the population and in its contribution to national wealth, the connection with the land was emotive in the historic identity of both nation and party, and was still valued as fundamental. Walter Elliot, later a successful Minister of Agriculture in the 1930s, commented in 1927 that 'the Tories of today feel a certain responsibility for the countryside even though they neglect it'.[492] In broader context, one expression which had particular significance and meaning was 'the public'. This could appear to be comprehensive and class-neutral, but it was also used as the term for the rest of the nation, as distinguished from the organized working class.[493] Thus, the party was 'proud to represent the man-in-the-street as well as...the trade unionist in the workshop'.[494] In reality, 'the public' represented the middle-class outlook and values, against which other perspectives and claims were tested and rejected. It was therefore both exclusive in that it placed the labour movement and left-wing politics outside and in conflict with a more legitimate and virtuous majority, and inclusive in that it consolidated and validated all those groups who subscribed to the dominant political culture. The middle class was also the core of what was termed 'the constitutional classes', which similarly meant those who opposed any significant changes in the role of institutions or the distribution of wealth. This was the 'public' to which appeals were made for order, resolution, and calm in facing challenges from sectional groups or hostile powers, and for patriotism and sacrifice in time of crisis or war. Much of Conservative policy, especially in economic aspects, was conducted consciously or unconsciously with the interests of this class-specific 'public' in mind, and hence references to 'the public interest' were focused more upon the minority who paid income tax than the majority who did not.

The role of party was another aspect of Conservative identity which contained elements of paradox. There was recognition that parties were at the very least a necessary evil, and that they had become integral to the working of the constitution: it was 'impossible...to govern a nation without some kind of party or group system'.[495] Furthermore, the only alternative was separation into 'groups, sections, interests

---

[491] Baldwin, *Our Inheritance*, 51.   [492] Elliot, *Toryism*, 11.
[493] McKibbin, 'Class and conventional wisdom', 284, 292–3.
[494] G. Lloyd, 'A modern Conservative's attitude to post-war problems', *Ashridge Journal*, 67 (November 1942), 4.
[495] Bryant, *Spirit of Conservatism*, 49; Baldwin's speech at the party meeting of 11 February 1924, *The Times*, 12 February 1924; Hogg, foreword in Jenner, *Will Conservatism Survive?*; Skipton CA, AR, 1932.

and classes', and so 'the broad allegiance to the party of one's choice keeps those smaller, narrower and baser motives in check'.[496] However, whilst 'party is an essential element in free parliamentary life', it must operate within the constitution and in sympathy with its traditions, and not seek to dictate to parliament from outside.[497] In this respect, the structure of the Conservative Party, in which the representative organizations did not determine policy, was more 'constitutional' than that of the Labour Party. It was accepted that party was the most effective form of political combination, and Conservative MPs were realists in this respect. They believed more would be lost than would be gained by shifting to another existing party, and that to found a new one was either rather ridiculous (as in Henry Page Croft's National Party of 1917–22) or positively dangerous (as in the United Empire Party of 1930). There were powerful pragmatic reasons for remaining within the fold, especially as the Liberal Party collapsed into backbiting futility from the mid-1920s. Crossing the floor of the House of Commons to join the Socialists was a distance of political leagues and not feet; anything else was a walk to the exit of the chamber with little prospect of return. Most Conservatives in the House of Commons, and most of the leading figures at local level, had grown up between the 1870s and the early 1900s, an era of intense two-party competition. There was thus an understandable momentum to the presumption that a two-party system was the most natural form of politics, in which one group emphasized order and the other progress.[498] Indeed, at least in theory, 'a strong and capable Opposition is almost as important as a strong Government'.[499] Conservatives were clear that a party must be more than a socio-economic bloc acting, either offensively or defensively, in material self-interest; this was one of their strongest criticisms of the Labour Party, and especially of occasions when the Trades Union Congress pulled on its leash. As Baldwin declared, the mechanism of party was a useful device, but 'mechanism is nothing without that animating spirit that gives it its impulse'.[500]

A foundation of mutually accepted principles was essential, for 'a permanent party can only rest upon a permanent scale of human values'.[501] Whatever elasticity there might be in methods or details, there was an inner core which was immutable; as the leading diehard MP, John Gretton, asked at the Annual Conference in 1921: 'What was a party worth unless it had principles to which it was attached and for which it was prepared to make sacrifices?' If a party was not based upon principles, it turned from being a pillar of constitutional government into a force for dissolution. David Margesson articulated this view in the early 1920s, when it was held particularly strongly, telling the selection panel at Rugby Conservative Association that he 'hated coalitions because they always led to a sacrifice of principles'; ironically, his term as Chief Whip from 1931 to 1941 was spent in making coalitions work.[502] The clearer the distinctions between parties the better, and problems arose when the boundaries were blurred (as in coalitions) or a party lacked a definite identity and purpose (as

---

[496] Chamberlain, *Keep Liberty through Unity*.
[497] Amery, 'Conservatism and the future (part 1)', 3.
[498] Hearnshaw, *Conservatism in England*, 13–16; *CAJ*, December 1932, 350.
[499] *To Women Voters*. [500] Baldwin, *Democracy, Youth and Patriotism*.
[501] Crichton, *Tory Oxford*, 30. [502] Rugby CA, Exec., 2 February 1924.

with the Liberals in the 1920s). From this perspective, party conflict was natural and healthy, and so there was a proper place for partisan feelings and party spirit. The latter was reinforced by the longevity of the Conservative Party, which fostered a form of tribalism; thus the MP for Weston-super-Mare declared in 1930 that his family 'from father to son' had been Tories since the English Civil War, and that he would 'be a traitor to all that I hold most dear were I even to think of changing my allegiance'.[503] This was a powerful cohesive force, not lightly to be set aside. Breaching these boundaries of loyalty had its cost, and thus it was seen as a damaging transgression that, before launching his charge of a breach of privileges in 1934, Churchill had approached the Labour Leader 'against a member of his own party'.[504]

Although 'in essence the party system is team work', it was also founded upon conflict and was intrinsically sectional.[505] It institutionalized and amplified the divisions within the nation, leading to 'unreasonable and unpatriotic extremes of thought' and 'an exaggeration of our differences and to the minimising of the great mass of agreement'.[506] There was a constant undercurrent of ambivalence, even antipathy, in Conservative attitudes towards the concept of party, because party loyalty could run counter to the powerful pull of patriotism.[507] This particularly applied to foreign policy, where 'the Conservative Party prided itself that it alone amongst political parties had the caution and the discretion to treat foreign affairs…with a greater regard to the national interests'.[508] Especially in times of national difficulty, party identity could seem a petty affair, and Conservatives were drawn to the noble self-image of 'being patriots before politicians, placing country before party'.[509] At the end of the First World War, there was a strong feeling that the challenges facing the nation 'were far too great to be treated as party questions, they were too big for that'.[510] The tireless Conservative campaigner Page Croft was quite sincere in declaring in 1942: 'I hate politics in this perilous time.'[511] Subordinating party feeling during the wartime coalitions was thus working with the grain of the Conservative mentality, as was the abandonment of a strong tactical position by accepting office under Ramsay MacDonald in the emergency National Government of August 1931. Lord Burghley, prospective candidate for Peterborough, summed up the position to his constituency executive: 'all present want to fight as Conservatives—but we must think of the Nation'.[512] Such sacrifice synchronized with the party's self-image of its role and duty; in the words of the Chief Agent in Manchester, 'we, the Conservative Party, have, as

---

[503] Erskine to Beaverbrook, 24 February 1930, Beaverbrook MSS, BBK/B145.
[504] Butler to Brabourne, 19 April 1934, Brabourne MSS, F.97/20c/197–203.
[505] SUA, *Unionist Party Organisation in Scotland*, 1.
[506] Chamberlain, *Keep Liberty through Unity*.
[507] Ripon CA, statement to the Exec. by Hills MP, 26 March 1938.
[508] NU Conf., 1923, speech by McNeill (junior minister at the Foreign Office).
[509] Halifax CA, General Meeting, 20 November 1918; Stirling & Falkirk Burghs CA, Falkirk Council, 15 October 1924; Waterloo CA, Council, 4 September 1931; Harwich CA, Extraordinary General Meeting, 24 October 1935; SUA, WDC, 7 January 1942.
[510] Stirlingshire West CA, Special General Meeting, 21 November 1918.
[511] Croft to Stuart, 13 April 1942, Croft MSS, CAC, CRFT/1/19/St7; Winchester CA, Special General Meeting, 27 April 1940.
[512] Peterborough CA, Exec., 3 October 1931.

usual, got to get the country out of the mess that it is in'.[513] On the other hand, when the Chamberlain government seemed to hesitate over declaring war on 2 September 1939, senior Conservatives called across the floor of the House of Commons to the Labour opposition to 'speak for England'—a telling sign of the conflict they were feeling between party loyalty and national honour.[514] Conservatives found a virtuous attraction in sacrificing 'narrow' party interests at the altar of the greater national need; it was this sentiment which made Churchill's later charge that Baldwin had put party interest over rearmament in the early 1930s such a damning indictment. Many Conservatives thought in terms of aims and loyalties which engaged at a more profound level than any party purposes, and which had claims that overrode those of party; as the Vice-Chairman of the women's organization in Birmingham declared, 'the women's political efforts were for God, King and Country, and the benefit of all humanity'.[515]

The Conservative Party used both its own and the national past selectively, according to the needs of the moment; it created, and was in turn shaped by, its own myths. As with any individual or group, the party's perception of itself was an amalgam of reality and wishful thinking.[516] Conservatives always placed themselves in the political mainstream, and it was acknowledged that the party 'likes to walk in the middle of the road'.[517] Thus, after defeat on the radical tariff programme in 1923, one Cabinet minister felt 'we should with as little delay as possible re-establish our position as the party of stability'.[518] Conservatives believed their policies to be reasonable and centrist, never confrontational or extreme. They always saw themselves as aligned with—indeed, as embracing—the majority, categorized as the 'public', the 'common man', 'ordinary decent people', and so on. Thus, despite the dominance within the party of the social elite and its permeation by middle-class values, it could sincerely be asserted that 'Conservatism has never identified itself with a class.'[519] Instead, Conservatives regarded their party as a unifying force which sought to 'give its best for all classes'.[520] It was thus 'a party broad-based upon the nation's will, blending different classes in its composition'.[521] From this flowed the assumption that the ethos of Conservatism and of the 'national character' were synonymous, a merger of identity from which Conservatives derived much of their confidence and their sense of ownership of national values and destiny. Baldwin affirmed in 1928 that 'amongst us we feel that we are indeed a National Party, and representative of the whole Nation in a way that no other party can claim to be'.[522] This made it quite natural to sing patriotic songs

---

[513] Carter to Derby, 1 October 1931, Derby MSS, 16/3; Thirsk & Malton CA, AGM, 23 May 1932.
[514] Amery diary, 2 September 1939; Crookshank diary, 2 September 1939.
[515] Birmingham CA, Women's Central Advisory Council, 21 February 1924.
[516] *Why You Should Be Unionist*, NU leaflet 2059 (1922).
[517] Beyfus, 'Conservatism', 4; Crichton, *Tory Oxford*, 8.
[518] Hoare to A. Chamberlain, 25 January 1924, Templewood MSS, V/1.
[519] Dawson, 'Conservatism', 41; Cardiff Central CA, Exec., 12 May 1930.
[520] Jenner, *Will Conservatism Survive?*, 30; Berkshire South CA, Exec., 21 August 1920; SUA, WDC, 1 May 1935, 'Report on Glasgow Municipal Elections', Propaganda Ctte., 31 January 1934.
[521] Bentinck, *Tory Democracy*, 138.
[522] Baldwin, *Democracy, Youth and Patriotism*.

(including the national anthem)[523] at party events, and to drape the platform with the Union Jack; when the party's own recently designed 'house flag' was used instead at the 1935 conference, complaints led to an immediate decision to return to the previous practice.[524] The Conservative Party's members had no doubt that it was the 'natural guardian' of the national tradition.[525] Its long history was important in establishing its claims to understand and uphold that tradition, as were its origins and continuing outlook of being 'in essence the country party'.[526]

The independence of the party was greatly prized, even over the next most important qualities of unity and loyalty; the tension between these was the cause of the strains that mounted during 1922, and of the lasting impact of the revolt from below against continuing the existing coalition arrangement. The Party Chairman warned 'that the Conservative Party have never been accustomed to be dragooned or ordered about and that they won't have it'.[527] It became the view of the victorious anti-Coalitionists that in 1922 'it was the rank and file of the Party who stood pat against their own leaders who would have sold them into bondage permanently to Lloyd George'.[528] Whether that was fair to the pro-coalition viewpoint hardly matters—it was how it was perceived by the majority of the grass roots at the time and, with the benefit of hindsight, even more strongly afterwards. This concern over the heart and soul of the party overrode other considerations, and obligations of personal loyalty to the Leader were subordinated by duty to the greater whole,[529] particularly in the case of key figures in the party machine—the Chief Whip and the Party Chairman, Deputy Chairman, and Principal Agent at the Central Office. Even more crucially, this was the fundamental force that brought Bonar Law out of retirement to attend the Carlton Club meeting in October 1922. It was also an important factor in sustaining Baldwin after the defeat of 1923, for he had become both symbol and guarantor of the party's recovery of a distinctive sense of self. Thus Noel Skelton could write: 'defeat has been no unmixed evil. 1922 preserved Conservatism; 1923 consolidated it.'[530]

In a similar way, as the emergency which had led to the National Government eased, its continuation caused 'many Conservatives grave anxiety regarding the independence and integrity of their political faith'.[531] In the mid-1930s, concern focused upon the particularly sensitive spot of the role of the National Government's three-party 'Co-ordinating Committee', and the leadership had to make clear the strict limits upon its role. However, neither Baldwin as Party Leader nor Lord Stonehaven, the Party Chairman from 1931 to 1936, seemed likely to sell the pass, and the

---

[523] *Songs for Conservative and Unionist Meetings*, NU leaflet 2653 (1926); the 1924 Annual Conference was typical in opening with the mass singing of 'Land of Hope and Glory'.
[524] NU Exec., 11 December 1935.
[525] Northam, *Conservatism*, 53.
[526] Boothby et al., *Industry and the State*, 9.
[527] Younger to Long, 27 March 1922, Long MSS, Add.62427/31–2.
[528] Davidson to Irwin, 6 March 1931, Halifax MSS, C152/19/1/254.
[529] Memo by Griffith-Boscawen, 'The Break Up of the Coalition', n.d., Griffith-Boscawen MSS, c.396/120–1.
[530] Skelton, *Constructive Conservatism*, preface (dated September 1924).
[531] Murray, 'Conservative Party and the National Government', 6.

latter was unequivocal in assuring the Executive Committee of the National Union that 'under no circumstances will an organisation be created that will boss us in any way'.[532] In fact, the multi-party nature of the National Government was a key factor in its identity and appeal; this was a crucial difference from the Lloyd George Coalition, which always had the potential for merger and in which 'fusion' was the objective of some of its leaders. The Conservatives had their own myths and suspicions of being sold out by the Westminster leadership, either for the sake of the fruits of office or through lack of assertiveness and too ready an acceptance of compromise; it was not only the Labour Party which believed that its true spirit was to be found away from the corrupting centre of power and at the grass roots, though for the Conservatives this was located not in a foundry or down a mine shaft, but in the green shires that Baldwin so eloquently evoked in speeches and broadcasts.

An important aspect of the Conservative self-image was the emphasis on loyalty, the dependability of which was later famously described by the Cabinet Minister David Maxwell-Fyfe (Lord Kilmuir) as the party's 'secret weapon'.[533] 'A cornerstone of the principles of Conservatism was founded upon the spirit of loyalty towards its leader', declared a delegate at the 1927 Annual Conference.[534] This ideal involved an appealing element of self-abnegation for the sake of the group, which was balanced by the comforting consolation of conformity to both the norm and an ideal. The Conservative suppressed the 'inclinations of his baser self' in the loyalties given to family, friends, school, profession, and causes.[535] Addressing the 1922 Annual Conference, Bonar Law turned back one of the jibes of the ousted Coalitionists by observing that his administration might not have all of the first-class brains, but 'they are a Government of first-class loyalty', a statement greeted by cheers from his audience.[536] As one constituency chairman declared: 'what we had to think of was the Cause, not the individual who represented it'.[537] The party was thus the beneficiary of a wider outlook, and the emotional cost of breaching this was much higher than simply stopping a subscription. This goes far to explain why amongst MPs or local members there was often grumbling but few departures, and amongst voters an inclination when disgruntled to stay at home but not to vote for another party. There was both a satisfaction and a sense of support in solidarity, especially when advantageously compared to the other parties. In a typical fox-hunting metaphor, the MP and junior minister Earl Winterton observed: 'The Tory pack are essentially a hunting pack; they do not cast themselves over half a Parish in search of new ideas, like the Socialist and Radical packs.'[538] Cohesion depended upon an allowance of latitude and an understanding of limits, factors that might seem contradictory but which in fact were mutually dependent. One leading figure considered that 'we have never been an intolerant party and never has one section in the Party tried to drive out another section', although the latter part ignored the Edwardian pogrom of the Conservative free traders.[539] It was

---

[532] NU Exec., 13 February 1935.
[533] A. Sampson, *The Anatomy of Britain* (1962), 89.
[534] NU Conf., 1927, speech by Morgan.
[535] Hearnshaw, *Conservatism in England*, 25–6.
[536] NU Conf., 1922.
[537] Bath CA, General Ctte., 29 June 1928.
[538] Winterton to Irwin, 6 February 1930, Halifax MSS, C152/19/1/15.
[539] Hoare's speech at Chelsea CA, AGM, 22 March 1935, Templewood MSS, VII/3.

considered that because Conservatism was 'not...a fixed quantity, it does not lend itself to fanaticism'.[540] However, there were always doubts about any erosion of party identity, even in working with cross-party or ostensibly neutral bodies; if these leaned at all to the left of centre, this undermined the credibility of the Conservatives associated with them.[541]

There was a great deal of flexibility in Conservative attitudes, and the leadership had considerable scope within which to operate. Together with the tradition of loyalty and the habit of deference to superiors, this could give rise to at least the appearance that Conservatism was simply whatever Conservative governments said or did, with the sole proviso that it be effective. Conservatives certainly wanted their governments to be successful, and were willing to accept a good deal of pragmatism if it was necessary to that end; it was not a criticism of the National Government that 'it will adopt any sound method that genuinely serves this purpose'.[542] However, the party was 'opportunist only in the sense that it is not doctrinaire'.[543] Rigid adherence to any particular theory or policy was never seen as advisable—it flew in the face of reality, and had undercurrents of hubris. Unlike their opponents on the left, Conservatives 'have no fixed or unalterable picture of what human society always ought to be like'.[544] The knowledge that both society and humanity were neither simple nor uniform propelled Conservatives towards navigating by 'rule of thumb about what is practical and tolerable'.[545] A satisfactory solution was always more important than the purity of its methods, and what did not work or was an obstacle could be discarded with little regret. Nevertheless, Conservatives wanted something more than a purely pragmatic government, and abandoning core principles in order to win office would be a worthless victory.[546] The safeguard against opportunism was not an ideology, but the 'code of honour which was the greatest possession and value in English statesmen'.[547] Captain Shipwright was not the only MP to lose his seat in 1923 on the protectionist programme and yet affirm that he 'would rather fall fighting for the truth than get returned on a misrepresentation',[548] whilst after the 1929 defeat many Conservatives took consolation from having eschewed populist promises for a principled if dull campaign: 'we lost the election because we told the truth'.[549] Conduct based upon expediency alone made Conservatives uncomfortable, even during the dangers of wartime. The most pragmatic peacetime ministry of modern times, the Lloyd George Coalition of

---

[540] Crichton, *Tory Oxford*, 7.
[541] Hills to Duchess of Atholl, 4 October 1937, Mickel to Duchess of Atholl, 24 May 1938, Atholl MSS, 45/2, 22/24.
[542] *Shall We Socialise?*, NU leaflet 3460 (1935).
[543] Parker et al., *Declaration of Tory Principles*, 5.
[544] Hogg, *Times We Live In*, 4.   [545] Pickthorn, *Principles and Prejudices*, 7.
[546] Memo by Lloyd of conversation with Baldwin, 4 March 1931, Lloyd of Dolobran MSS, CAC, GLLD/19/5.
[547] NU Conf., 1924, comments by Lord Selborne, referring to the death of Walter Long.
[548] Penryn & Falmouth CA, Council, 7 February 1924; speech of Pretyman at the party meeting of 11 February 1924, *The Times*, 12 February 1924.
[549] Stockton CA, meeting to open the Constitutional Hall, 3 December 1929; SUA, Exec., 11 September 1929.

1918–22, alienated most Conservative MPs and was brought down because its conduct deeply offended Conservative sensibilities. On the other hand, the multi-party National Government of 1931–40 retained Conservative support not just because its policies were more successful but also because its style and agenda made a positive appeal to Conservative aspirations.

Conservatism was not marked by any sense of guilt about the nature of society, and Conservatives were not inclined to introspection. They were always more comfortable looking outwards and attacking the enemy rather than engaging upon inward contemplation, too much of which produced 'a feverish condition'.[550] Their natural tendency was to affirm their basic principles rather than to analyse them; all the more so in times of crisis, when they were clung to with tenacity. Setbacks often failed to dent the underlying complacency; one Cabinet minister's explanation for the 1929 defeat was that 'we fell because we were too good' and had not pandered to press and public sensationalism.[551] When the party appeared to be unpopular, the tendency was to blame the leadership for failing to be sufficiently clear or firm in the Conservatism of the party's platform. Conservatives derived a basic self-confidence from their certainty of the merits and appropriateness of Conservatism. The fundamentals were not questioned, and so debate could occur upon specific topics with great vigour without raising fears for the existence of the party in the long term, even if there was damage to its more immediate prospects. For the same reasons, Conservatives did not incline to the kind of sustained or general disagreement that could lead to the fragmenting of the party. There was disappointment when governments did not take the sweeping measures which their supporters were sure would bring swift benefits, and of course there was grumbling from individuals who did not feel adequately recognized, or interest groups which were not handled with the solicitude that they desired. If these negative aspects were widespread or went on for too long, they could lead to apathy and eventually to alienation, but, in general, criticism was focused upon specific measures, policies, persons, or events, and so was short-term in nature. There was sometimes disharmony between the idealized vision of Conservatism and the strategies used by Conservatives to maintain their political or social position. The most serious dissension during periods in office occurred when the leadership set a course which was contrary to the currents of Conservative values or instincts, as occurred in the final months of the Lloyd George Coalition in 1922 and over India in 1933–35.

For most of the period from 1918 to 1945, Conservatives were generally agreed on what was important and what outcome was desired. However, this does not mean that they agreed about the details or the methods of achieving this. The simplest and most direct expression of any viewpoint will always strike a chord with those who broadly share it, and thus at his constituency association's annual meeting a diehard MP's 'vigorous outspoken remarks greatly impressed his audience'.[552]

---

[550] Davidson to Baldwin, 8 October 1929, Davidson MSS, DAV/188.
[551] Worthington-Evans to Birdwood, 24 June 1929, Worthington-Evans MSS, MSS.Eng. hist.c.896/203–4.
[552] Aldershot CA, AGM, 29 July 1922.

Purity of principle and lack of equivocation are attractive, and command respect even when they cannot be put into effect. For interwar Conservatives, this 'pure milk' was embodied by the diehards of the party's right wing. There was a feeling that they represented something fundamental which the party could not afford to dispense with; they expressed the impulses of its heart, even if the head decided to face another way. Whilst their apocalyptic prophecies tended to be discounted and their specific proposals were regarded by the mainstream as impracticable and even counterproductive, they acted as a necessary element of conscience—sounding a warning if the leaders allowed too much distance to open up between principles and practice. As one constituency chairman observed, 'every true Conservative man or woman had something of the diehard in his or her constitution'.[553] The tug of the diehards was a counterweight to the tendency to move towards the centre and accept compromise.[554] It was important for keeping the party in contact with its core support, and for denying any competing political force further to the right the space in which to grow.

Disputes and factionalism took place within the party, and almost never led to secession. This was principally because most of the disagreements were about methods and strategies (sometimes just of degree and of timing), and were not differences at the fundamental level of either principles or overall objectives. Indeed, common ground here was important in holding the party together during the disagreements, and was a major part of the reason why the disputes were contained within the party and did not lead to splits or secessions. Of course, there was also the pragmatic consideration that there was no credible alternative party to move to, whilst at the same time concern about the danger of Socialism discouraged any lapse into apathy. Upper-class restiveness over the moderate course of Baldwinian policy was constrained because, as one Duke observed, 'they have an instinctive idea against upsetting constituted authority and are sincerely anxious not to split the Party'.[555] Similarly, despite their almost constant tension with the leadership, the diehards never considered leaving the Conservative ranks. This was not just electoral pragmatism; it was more their certainty that their position was the true Conservative lodestone, and therefore to leave the Conservative Party was a contradiction in terms which was emotionally incomprehensible.[556] As was demonstrated on several occasions, this was also the view of those who leaned to the left; Christopher York MP, a founder of the Tory Reform Committee, noted in his diary: 'I am I know a Tory and as such a man without a party is in difficulties.'[557]

Such attitudes held the Conservative Party together even during the bitter rift between pro- and anti-Coalitionists in the period after the fall of Lloyd George in 1922–23. On the day after his rejection at the Carlton Club meeting in 1922, Austen Chamberlain unequivocally told a sympathizer: 'I have no intention of

---

[553] Lewisham West CA, AGM, 12 May 1922.
[554] Derby to A. Chamberlain, 1 September 1922, AC 33/2/12; Glickman, 'The Toryness of English Conservatism', 118.
[555] Duke of Atholl to Lloyd, 14 June 1933, Atholl MSS, 9/1.
[556] Thorp to Duchess of Atholl, 7 June 1935, Atholl MSS, 23/3.
[557] York diary, 16 December 1942.

leaving our Party or of joining any new combination.'[558] This was the general pattern with those who resigned or were disaffected, whether they were Cabinet ministers or local party members. In the immediate wake of the Irish settlement of 1921, the leader of the Conservative Party in Manchester noted that many active workers had resigned in disgust; he was concerned at the loss of their assistance at an election, but 'as they have no other party they could possibly join, I am not anxious about their votes'.[559] Furthermore, as a leading opponent of the India policy affirmed, once the specific matter over which there was disagreement was settled, 'the Party would stand united again'.[560] The existence of a consensus on fundamentals was not inconsistent with differences over policy and even quite severe internal party disputes—the key point is not that these took place, but that they took place *within* the party, and (notwithstanding Conservative dislike of the term) it was an ideological consensus just as much as the reality of the party system which kept such apparently diverse figures as Harold Macmillan of the youthful left wing and Frederick Banbury, the archetypical diehard, under the same umbrella.

During the interwar period, the few defections which did occur were of individuals rather than groups, were idiosyncratic in nature, and were towards the left. There was nowhere for dissident Conservatives to go in a rightwards direction, because there was nothing there that felt or looked like Conservatism: not the narrowly defensive class-based pressure groups such as the Middle Class Union, and certainly not the Fascism of Sir Oswald Mosley in the 1930s—a foreign-born ideology derived from Socialism which advocated control by the state and the direction of affairs by a party bureaucracy.[561] The British Union of Fascists was never regarded as a significant rival, and was viewed with a combination of ridicule and distaste: it attracted marginal individuals, was based on 'low passions', and its leader was 'an unbalanced egomaniac with no sense of responsibility'.[562] The bemusement that anyone should wish to 'be dressing themselves up as Italians and adopting foreign gestures' was matched by disapproval of the Fascists' intention 'apparently to fight...their own countrymen'.[563] Even at its strongest in 1933–34, the Fascist movement caused little concern either in the constituencies or amongst MPs; the diehard rebel MP Lord Wolmer thought that little would come of it, on the telling grounds that 'it is not really English in conception'.[564] Some of the Con-

[558] A. Chamberlain to Newman, 20 October 1922, AC 33/2/116.
[559] Notes by Woodhouse, enclosed with Fraser to A. Chamberlain, 31 December 1921, AC 32/4/10.
[560] Sir Nairne Stewart-Sandeman MP, Middleton & Prestwich CA, AGM, 16 March 1935; SUA, EDC, 9 October 1935.
[561] Northam, *Conservatism*, 118–19, 230–3, 238–9; S. [Simon] Ball, 'Mosley and the Tories in 1930: the problem of generations', *Contemporary British History*, 23/4 (2009), 445–59.
[562] Somervell journal, 17 June 1934, Somervell MSS, MSS.Eng.c.6565/50. Sir Thomas Moore MP's suggestion of possible co-operation with Mosley's movement was a rare exception, and was in the period before it was discredited by the violence at the Olympia rally in June 1934: *Daily Mail*, 25 April 1934.
[563] *Home & Empire*, June 1934.
[564] Wolmer to Mackie, 11 December 1933, Wolmer MSS, MSS.Eng.hist.c.1013/123–5; Liverpool CA, Central Council, Chairman's Report, 11 April 1934.

servative Party's grass-roots membership were attracted to the Empire Crusade movement in 1929–30, but generally due to regarding it as a pressure group within the Conservative spectrum; when it was transmuted into the United Empire Party in February 1930, and then promoted its own candidates in by-elections, there was a widespread negative reaction that this divisive step could only help the Labour government.[565] The only apparent attempt to form a separate organization founded on Tory diehard positions, Page Croft's 'National Party' of 1917–22, was in reality more of a protest and ginger group, and never strayed completely outside the Conservative fold. Its members were too few and too lightweight for it to pose any real threat, although there was much sympathy with its manifesto; after the fall of the Coalition, its members were seamlessly absorbed back into the ranks. The diehard right shared the Conservative dislike of gesture politics, and whatever their grumbles 'your "diehard" is never very willing to go out into the wilderness'.[566] They were treated with basic respect, but not accorded special weight; one minister considered it a 'great merit…that we are not afraid of our extremists within the Party'.[567] The resulting cohesion was seen as one of the Conservative Party's great virtues and strengths—similar in ethos to the trade union tradition of 'united we stand, divided we fall', although from very different social origins.[568] The cumulative effect of 'common memories, sentiments, aversions, hopes and principles' not only kept the Conservative Party together, but also gave it direction and purpose.[569]

---

[565] Thirsk & Malton CA, Exec., 28 February 1930; Elibank, 'Empire Free Trade' diary, November 1929–May 1930, Elibank MSS, GD32/25/74 f.8.
[566] Dawson to Irwin, 13 March 1931, Halifax MSS, C152/19/1/268.
[567] Somervell journal, 15 July 1934, Somervell MSS, MSS.Eng.c.6565/53.
[568] This was a repeated theme, and often explicit: see Grattan-Doyle's appeal for the withdrawal of the diehard resolution on Ireland, NU Conf., 1921.
[569] Pickthorn, *Principles and Prejudices*, 6.

2

The Public
Appeal and Support

THE NATURE OF THE APPEAL

There are only two reasons for voting: to support something, or to oppose something. The rise of Socialism gave the Conservatives an easy target in the latter respect, but they were aware that a purely negative stance was not enough: 'we cannot go on forever relying upon the demerits of our opponents'.[1] There had to be 'something to offer to the people, and particularly to the women, beyond a mere appeal to the rights of property and the fear of Socialism'.[2] Nor was the alternative 'a colourless programme which will unite Conservatives and Liberals because there is nothing in it to which either will take serious objection. You must have a more definite policy.'[3] At the surface level, this focused upon the particular issues of the day, but these would always be ephemeral and below them were deeper currents that moved people in the Conservative direction. This chapter considers how the themes discussed previously shaped the party's public appeal, how this was communicated and projected, and the nature and extent of the electoral support which the Conservatives received.

The most basic and widespread connection between the party and the public was the 'natural conservatism' identified by Lord Hugh Cecil (see Chapter 1). As he observed, it was 'found in almost every human mind', and support for the Conservative Party was 'largely recruited from and dependent' upon it.[4] Its needs were responded to through the party's identification with continuity and custom, and presentation of itself as the bulwark against unsettling or threatening change and the consequent probable danger to status and property.[5] This was achieved by defending the institutions crucial to the latter's protection, such as the monarchy and parliament, from being overthrown by revolution or more gradually diminished by the loss of authority to uncontrollable elements such as the trade unions or the maverick demands of the popular press. The core appeal was thus to 'the prudent, moderate man who believed in stable government'.[6] 'Natural conservatism' was

---

[1] Robb to Gretton, 20 February 1930, Beaverbrook MSS, BBK/C71; NU Central Council report to Conference, 1923–24; *The Conservative Past and the Conservative Future*, NU leaflet 2606 (1925); Cranborne, *Our Political Future*.
[2] R. Cecil to Baldwin, 1 February 1924, Baldwin MSS, 35/203–7.
[3] Cunliffe-Lister to Davidson, 3 January 1930, Davidson MSS, DAV/190.
[4] Cecil, *Conservatism*, 8.
[5] On stability, and particularly the appeal to the 'black-coated worker', see Stelling, *Why I Am A Conservative*, 9.
[6] Cambridge CA, Exec., 24 February 1922.

found in all social classes, but in the interwar period it had a particular resonance with a middle class concerned about the effects of mass democracy and the rise of the Labour Party, and nostalgic for its more secure position and the certainties of the supposed prewar 'golden age'. The appeal of 'tranquillity' should not be underestimated, and it played the main part in three Conservative election victories, each of which shaped an era: 1874, 1922, and 1951. The Conservatives were automatically identifiable as the party to uphold the constitution and social order, and this hardly needed to be clarified or demonstrated. One Leader of the Party summed it up: 'it is our business to try to rally all the conservative elements of the country'.[7] The problem with this was that the party had 'the prosaic and unexciting duty of displaying the merits of things as they have been and are', which could easily lapse into simple negativism.[8]

The second connection was the identification of the Conservative Party with the established social and political culture, which brought considerable benefits. As the historian Ross McKibbin has argued, the party was 'associated with the predominant value order', and only those who felt themselves to be outside of, or hostile to, that order would be drawn to other parties.[9] The attraction of inclusion was a powerful force, offering reassurance, respectability, and the comfort of conformity. Its consequences were a presumption in favour of the status quo, a respect for existing institutions, and an acceptance of social gradations, which entailed at least unconscious deference to leadership from the traditional governing elite. In the case of the working class, the appeal was to consider themselves part of a national community that was more attractive and legitimate than a purely class identity. Conformity to the dominant values in society was not a one-way street; it shaped the Conservative frame of mind discussed in Chapter 1, which in turn placed invisible but powerful restraints upon the way in which the party operated. One of the most important of these was the imperative to govern in the interests of whole nation, and promote community rather than conflict. For this reason, any 'hard-shelled defence of the Haves against the Have-Nots' had to be avoided as it would be divisive, dangerous, and counterproductive.[10] Instead, there was a much broader emphasis on what were regarded as universal values: the rule of law, the rights of property, and individual autonomy in thought, economic action, and domestic life. If the Labour Party, through its trade union identity, was the party of the workplace (but mainly for men, working in the larger units and the old-established industries), the Conservatives could be the party of the home, with values to appeal to both genders and all occupations and classes. The Conservative Party was attuned to their most fundamental needs: 'there's such a comfortable feeling in knowing that the little world in which you live is safe; that you can pay your way and perhaps save a bit'.[11] Furthermore, there was confidence that women 'were

---

[7] A. Chamberlain to Parker Smith, 11 October 1922, AC, 33/2/38.
[8] Hearnshaw, *Conservatism in England*, 7.
[9] McKibbin, 'Class and conventional wisdom', 262.
[10] Salisbury to Baldwin, 26 January 1924, Baldwin MSS, 159/258–61.
[11] *A Word to Every Woman by Jane Bull*, NU leaflet 3535 (1935).

essentially patriotic and full of love for home life and the true welfare of their country'.[12] From such assumptions, the Conservatives developed a broader, more pervasive and inclusive appeal than Labour's, and one less masculine and confrontational in ethos. Not surprisingly, women responded across class barriers to the tone as well as the content of the Conservative appeal, and the result was a gender gap in voting which benefited the party from 1918 until the 1980s. In 1928 the Party Chairman, J. C. C. Davidson, noted the analysis of 'our shrewdest observers' that in the marginal seats 'the women's vote will inure to our advantage by at least 10 per cent on balance'.[13]

Another attractive element of inclusion which the Conservatives presented and represented was pride in the nation and its achievements and history. The Conservative Party's identification with patriotism gave it a cross-class appeal, for this sentiment was as strong in the poorest classes as the wealthiest, and sometimes even more so. It has been suggested that the First World War had an effect in all of the combatant states of strengthening the 'sense of national character', which then contributed to the postwar success of conservative appeals in many countries.[14] In the case of Britain, this was aided by the continuity of established institutions, which provided a focus for Conservative sentiment and public confidence. However, the form of patriotism which the Conservatives espoused tended to be English rather than British in tone, and this reduced its effectiveness in Wales. Scotland was rather different, as its brand of Conservatism was institutionally separate—notably retaining the name Unionist throughout this period—and linked to a distinctly Scottish social elite, which had an acknowledged role in its native history and culture. The strongest card to play was the empire, which could be presented as the achievement of the whole nation and held up as an example of Britain at its best as well as its most powerful. Popular views of national strength were based more upon the visible evidence of the amount of the world coloured red in the school atlas than complex matters of trade statistics. In 1919 the British empire reached its greatest-ever extent, although concerns about overstretched resources were rarely apparent to the general public—at least, not until the combined effects of disarmament and the triple challenge from Japan, Italy, and Germany became evident after 1935.

The deteriorating international situation in the later 1930s focused public interest, to an unusual extent, on issues of foreign and defence policy. The response of the Conservative-led National Government, summarized by the term 'appeasement', secured strong support not just because of the deep reluctance to risk another war and the fear of the horrors that it would bring, but because it combined to a remarkable degree both realism and idealism—two elements which Conservatives were generally inclined to regard as polar opposites. It was realist in the sense

---

[12] Wood Green CA, Southgate branch, Ctte., 13 April 1921; McCrillis, *Conservative Party in the Age of Universal Suffrage*, 69–73.

[13] Davidson to Irwin, 3 December 1928, Halifax MSS, C152/18/1/173.

[14] A. Reimann, 'Popular culture and the reconstruction of British identity', in H. Berghoff and R. von Friedeburg (eds.), *Change and Inertia: Britain under the Impact of the Great War* (Bodenheim, 1998), 99–120, quote at 119–20.

of taking the most pragmatic and least dangerous course, however unpalatable; of directly addressing the causes of tension and the key personalities, whatever the unattractiveness of their regimes and diplomatic methods; and of recognizing Britain's lack of allies and military resources, and the state of the economy, defence forces, and public opinion. It was also idealist, in its belief in the possibility of rational discussion and the self-evident fact that war could be in no one's interests; in its willingness to accept a share of responsibility for current problems and to offer concession and compromise; and in its aim of avoiding what were thought to be the causes of the last war: jingoism, arms races, and secret alliances. Appeasement was a Christian and compassionate policy, and so had extensive support from all of the churches and from Liberal opinion, which was so important electorally to the National Government. It was an amalgam of both masculine and feminine elements, and, not surprisingly, had a powerful appeal across both gender and class divisions.

During the interwar era as a whole, a crucial aspect of the Conservative Party's positive appeal was an image of openness and moderation, which was most easily communicated by the Party Leader. 'The personality of the leader was even more important than policy,' declared one backbench MP, 'because at election times people voted for a trusted leader.'[15] It was essential that this should reach across class distinctions; it had to be national and unifying in tone, and avoid any impression of the sectional defence of middle-class interests. There must be no appearance of class warfare and confrontation, or of hostility to the working class and the labour movement in general. Baldwin was particularly effective at this, and his style of reconciliation and empathy with the values of labour was a great electoral asset. Conservatism was 'in its essence a tolerant creed',[16] and its past record of protecting the leisure activities of the male working class from puritanical interference by middle-class Liberalism gave it credibility when warning of the dangers of Socialist state control in the 1920s. Conveying a sense of openness rather than elitism was self-evidently sensible with a democratic franchise, and as part of their alternative to Socialism the Conservatives emphasized opportunity and attracted many of those with aspirations. Even before the post-1945 emphasis on the 'property-owning democracy', it was clear that the Conservatives were the party of upward mobility. The working class lived in rented accommodation; home ownership was generally restricted to the middle class, but was an ideal that was universally aspired to—the Englishman's home was more truly his castle if it was freehold.[17] It was the Conservative Party which dominated the political landscape of suburbia, and the 'ribbon developments' along the main roads of southern England only further entrenched its hold upon these constituencies. Conservative values were evoked by the traditionalism of the mock-Tudor style used in many of the new estates, whilst 'Dunroamin' was not just a popular choice of house name—

---

[15] Sowerby CA, AGM, 12 April 1937.
[16] Braine, *Conservatism and Youth*, 5.
[17] *The Landless People*, NU leaflet 2077 (1922); *Yours! But Not under Socialism*, NU leaflet 2334 (1924); *Socialism and Your Home*, NU leaflet 2622 (1926).

its evocation of repose and security had a political dimension as well. As one Conservative MP wrote in 1942: 'to give security and a comfortable and healthy home life to all must be our ideal'.[18]

Whilst the Conservative Party had a definite position in the political spectrum, this was still broad and diffuse. The ground which it occupied spanned from the traditional right to the empirical centre, and in some cases and policies to the centre-left. It could thus be the party of both the diehards and those with no strong views; indeed, its appeal to those who were disinterested in politics, who saw them as unattractive or irrelevant to their own lives, was an important factor in the composition of its electoral support. There was much to be gained by being the party of 'the sleepy, congenitally complacent ordinary man', and it was not surprising that at local level in many districts it was almost the non-political party.[19] At the most basic level, the Conservative Party could be little more than a vehicle for stability and tranquillity, given form by its outer substance of middle-class good manners; when members of a women's branch were unexpectedly asked to define their Conservatism, some replied that it was because Conservatives were 'such nice people'.[20] The final positive factor in the party's appeal was also a matter of unspecific expectations: the prospect of more prosperous times under a Conservative administration. The habit of scepticism and the desire to avoid a competitive auction with its rivals, which the Conservative Party, by the nature of its support, could not win, meant that there was caution about making precise promises—even the long-trumpeted merits of tariff reform were not shackled to any exact quantification of the gains that would result. It was rather that the Conservatives represented competence in government, restraint in state intervention, and 'economy' in expenditure, so that their being in office would foster business confidence and thus lead to a greater volume of trade and employment.

Over the long term, a party becomes identified with particular broad stances on policy and with recognized styles and methods. The road to electoral victory lies through promoting these aspects into salience, by deploying the weapons in a party's arsenal which most effectively target the fears or desires of the electorate. In this arena, the parties do not compete by arguing directly with each other, as if they were debating in the House of Commons. Their audience is the public, and they try to make their own priorities and agenda more prominent and meaningful than those of their rivals. There is an element of who can shout the loudest (and therefore also whose purse is the deepest), but effectiveness is achieved less by indiscriminate outpourings than by relevance and shrewd understanding. Thus, what the Conservative Party stood for needed to resonate with its constituency, to be heard by them, and to be in tune with their views and concerns. The response which this sought to evoke in most cases would be no more than the passive act of casting a vote, with a sufficient minority being drawn into active involvement. Material self-interest might provide an initial motivation, but the construction of

---

[18] Lloyd, 'A modern Conservative's attitude to post-war problems'.
[19] Parker et al., *Declaration of Tory Principles*, 5. [20] *CAJ*, July 1938, 164.

a cross-class majority required something more than 'the uninspiring character of a society for the defence of property or for the reduction of the income-tax'.[21] Instead, 'the ultimate appeal is made to the whole character of the man, of the nation', and was most effective when it combined rational argument and factual evidence with deeper instincts and accustomed traditions.[22] The party's values and outlook were integral and essential parts of this appeal, which then had to be given effect in form and delivery—the subjects of the next two sections.

THE LANGUAGE OF THE APPEAL

The Conservative appeal was directed to reason, emotion, and instinct, and thus tone and language were inseparable from content. The imagery that was employed used forms which would attract the sympathy of a cross-section of society. There was frequent use of metaphors from agriculture and rural life, which were readily understood, despite the fact that most Britons now lived in an urban environment. For women, there were settings and similes from domestic life; thus, one parallel given for free trade equated it with allowing strangers to steal the flowers from your garden.[23] The series of *Over the Garden Wall* leaflets depicted conversations between two married women who were neighbours,[24] and a regular feature in the party's journal for women members, the revealingly titled *Home and Politics*, took the form of the older and more sensible cook, Mrs Maggs, giving good advice to her flighty junior, Betty the maid.[25] A validatory reference often employed, which must have had most resonance with middle-class men, was of 'business virtues', which was a shorthand term for directness, robustness, and effectiveness, linked with practicality and common sense. On a broader canvas, Baldwin was adept at deploying the concept and imagery of 'Englishness' to foster an atmosphere of community and social harmony, but he was far from unusual in using the national identity as a touchstone. It was the avatar for a mental map rather than a geographical one, and thus 'English' was an adjective which Conservatives regarded as unproblematically positive, and wherever it was applied it was used to commend or emphasize the attributes of an inherent straightforwardness, fairness, common sense, self-reliance, practicality, or decency.

Conservative politicians and propaganda shunned making appeals which were class-specific, and focused instead upon the generic individual. They would talk in terms of 'the man in the street', and, revealingly, this term and 'the popular view' were titles chosen for two of the party's regular publications. The former paralleled the contemporary cliché of 'the man on the Clapham omnibus', and it is worth remembering that such an archetypal commuter would have been a white-collar

---

[21] Wood, *Conservative Beliefs*, 3.   [22] Parker et al., *Declaration of Tory Principles*, 7.
[23] *Home and Politics*, 95 (1929), 8.
[24] *Over the Garden Wall*, NU leaflets 2227–32 (1923); *Over the Tea-Cups: A One-Act Sketch*, NU leaflet 3724 (1938).
[25] Jarvis, 'Mrs Maggs and Betty', 133, 141.

worker, probably lower-middle class. Although there would always be tactical reasons for producing leaflets aimed at particular groups, it was to the image of this citizen that the Conservative appeal was normally directed. As middle-class values had permeated much of the class below since the mid-nineteenth century, this came close to being of universal appeal; its general application is underlined by the probability that a shipyard worker in Tyneside or Clydeside would probably have considered himself to be included rather than excluded by a reference to 'the man on the Clapham omnibus'. The expression 'working class' was rarely used, and the party instead employed the definition 'wage earner' in the organizations which were designed for workers and trade unionists.

This does not mean that Conservative publicity did not employ stereotypes; indeed, as David Jarvis has observed, it was 'shot through with class'.[26] Stock figures of working-class men and women regularly appeared in the party's leaflets and journals; as is the nature of such things, they lacked subtlety. They were tools for immediate and concise communication, and projections of what Conservatives considered to be the essential reality—for a stereotype that is unrecognizable to its audience is useless. These ordinary members of the working class might be depicted as foolish and ignorant or misguided and mistaken in their priorities, but they were not evil. They had an essentially decent nature and could be won for the communal good over sectional class interest; after all, the woman depicted as thinking that Californian raisins counted as empire produce had only erred whilst trying to do the patriotic thing.[27] In these respects they stood for what Conservatives hoped rather than what they feared, and party publicity avoided scaremongering about the British working class or employing tactics which would exacerbate class hostility, whether upwards or downwards. Of course, this propaganda was produced by middle-class party officials for predominantly middle-class constituency associations, and naturally it reflected the outlook of its creators and users. It was shaped by their external perspective: it was paternalist and patronizing, assumed that a lack of education meant a lack of knowledge, and treated working-class life and culture simplistically.

All propaganda tends to be shaped by the lowest common denominator, and the images and methods used by the Conservatives reveals what they considered this audience to be: in the words of one local agent in 1927, 'thick skulls filled (more or less) with primitive and sluggish brains'.[28] Those at Central Office responsible for producing the leaflets and posters were aware of, and followed the precepts of, the advertising industry of the period, requiring no reminding of 'the need of the use of clear and simple language'.[29] Posters and cartoons constantly used the emblems of national unity, such as the flag and the figures of Britannia and the plain yeoman farmer John Bull, whilst idealized images of the honest working man and his family were contrasted with fanatical demagogues and scruffy Bolsheviks with

---

[26] Jarvis, 'British Conservatism and class politics', 78.
[27] *A Family Affair*, NU leaflet 3225 (1930). [28] *CAJ*, May 1927, 125.
[29] NU Conf., 1929, amendment by Alderman Julyan to resolution on propaganda.

revolvers stuck in their belts.[30] Strikers were either selfish in their outlook, or decent men led astray as the dupes of devious agitators, who pursued a sinister and disloyal agenda of their own and cared nothing for the workers' real interests.[31] Virtue was to be found in plain speaking, in recognizing the obligations of position and place (on the part of the upper as well as the lower classes), and in working together on that basis. The emphasis was on community and order, in which all could respect and be respected for the part that they should play.

Despite their belief that this should not be the case, Conservatives assumed that class was a key factor in determining votes. They also, perhaps surprisingly given their practical knowledge of the prewar electoral system, had a fairly simplistic view of the new electorate created by the 1918 Reform Act as composed predominantly of the lower levels of the working class. It was taken for granted that the new male voters were likely to favour the Labour Party, or at least be easily seduced by its message; there was more uncertainty about how the women might vote, but the general expectation was that Labour would benefit much more from the extension of the franchise than any other party.[32] A particular reason for expecting this was the increased membership and assertiveness of the trade unions since 1910, as it was believed that the links between the Labour Party and the trade unions made the latters' members regard Labour as their automatic choice, due to the combined pull of class sentiment and union solidarity. Conservatives further thought that the trade union leaders were able to control and direct their members' political allegiance with machine-like precision, a perception based mainly upon the highly visible—but atypical—example of the coal miners. They therefore expected an uphill struggle in a difficult electoral environment after 1918, in which new methods and styles would be needed.

The appeal to women addressed them more as individuals, as they were visualized as being primarily located in, and concerned with, their separate home environments.[33] Communication to working-class men treated them more as a group with common interests, even when party leaflets targeted particular trades and industries. However, Conservative awareness of the disproportionate influence exerted by the minority of trade union activists at local level meant that they sought to develop a counterbalancing element of their own sympathizers who could engage effectively with their opponents and strive to capture the hearts and minds of the unthinking majority. Fostering this was the aim of the organizational initiatives into which the party put much effort and funds, especially in the 1920s.[34] The short cut to economic and political stability was to reach what Conservative leaders

---

[30] *So This Is Socialism!*, NU leaflet (1924); *The Bolshevik Yoke*, NU leaflet 2448 (1924); *The Danger of the Class War*, NU leaflet 2066 (1922); *Don't Back his Horse or Socialism*, NU leaflet 2116 (1922); for examples of posters from the 1929, 1931, and 1935 elections, see S. Ball, *Dole Queues and Demons: British Election Posters from the Conservative Party Archive* (Oxford, 2011), 29–66.

[31] Gell, *Look before You Leap!*.

[32] Jarvis, 'British Conservatism and class politics', 69–71.

[33] *Why Women Should Vote Conservative*, NU leaflet 2735 (1927); *To Women: Your Home—And You!*, NU leaflet 3326 (1931).

[34] These are discussed at constituency level in Chapter 3 and at national level in Chapter 4.

habitually referred to as the 'best element' of the working class, or 'the leaders of thought in the democracy', who were believed to be 'panting after ideals which they are afraid may be slipping away from them'.[35] This required a positive appeal, which took the form of emphasizing the immutable national values and traditions which Conservatism upheld, and citing the party's tradition of social reform. The latter was the connecting thread running through the Factory Acts and trade union legislation of the nineteenth century, the domestic record of Baldwin's second government, and the reforms promoted by the National Government in the 1930s, such as slum clearance and paid holidays.

However, a negative message is always easier to communicate than a positive one; as Amery presciently warned on the eve of the 1923 election, 'criticism can become much more effective in three weeks than a constructive policy can be explained'.[36] On that occasion this was to the Conservatives' disadvantage, but in no other election did they try to present either new or substantial departures in policy, and it was their opponents who had the task of making the case for change. Conservative attacks on the Liberals developed two main themes, the first of which was that they were outmoded and irrelevant, as the reforms they sought had either been achieved (such as franchise extension and Irish Home Rule) or were no longer the issues that mattered most (such as disestablishment, temperance, and land reform), and they had nothing new to offer. The second theme was that a vote for the Liberals was not a third choice, but an indirect vote for Labour—that the Liberal Party sided with Labour in parliament, and its support maintained the Labour governments in office. A typical example of this line of attack was the 1929 election poster, showing Lloyd George helping Ramsay MacDonald attain the power which would otherwise have been beyond his reach, with the slogan 'Another Leg-up from the Liberals!'[37]

The Labour Party was always the greater concern and focus, even in 1918. During the interwar period, Socialism was mentioned much more often in the election addresses of Conservative candidates than of Labour ones. The Conservatives followed a deliberate strategy of always referring to the Labour Party as 'the Socialists', identifying them as an ideological sect rather than a broad constituent in the community.[38] Labour's claim to represent the whole of the working class, and consequently to have a right to their support, had to be refuted.[39] Conservative propaganda emphasized that there was no betrayal of the interests of labour in not voting for the 'Labour' Party, and that large numbers of good trade unionists did not do so.[40] Conservative speeches and propaganda never attacked the working class as such, but instead aimed to free the fundamentally decent and patriotic working man from those who were manipulating him by exploiting his sense of

---

[35] Salisbury to Baldwin, 26 January 1924, Baldwin MSS, 159/258–61.
[36] Amery to Baldwin, 8 November 1923, Baldwin MSS, 35/71–4.
[37] Ball, *Dole Queues and Demons*, 42.
[38] *Oil and Vinegar; Call a Spade a Spade and the 'Labour' Party also by its Proper Name: Socialist*, NU leaflet 2075 (1922); *Calling a Spade a Spade*, NU leaflet 2888 (1929).
[39] *Labour and the 'Labour' Party*; NU leaflet 1955 (1920).
[40] *Is the 'Labour' Party Labour?*.

solidarity and loyalty to his trade union. The Labour leaders were depicted as men without practical experience beyond a narrowly industrial trade union sphere—if even that. The Conservative Party's publicity eagerly exploited the opportunities frequently given by the extreme, unwise, or contradictory statements of trade union leaders and Labour politicians.[41] In particular, it highlighted the impractical theorists and the middle-class intellectuals, Pacifists, and ex-Liberals who had gravitated to Labour since 1918. The aim was to isolate these figures from the mass of the public, to challenge their legitimacy to represent it, and to expose them as bereft of any true understanding of either the worker or the nation.[42] The Labour Party was portrayed as divided beneath its misleading surface façade, with left and right wings having little in common.

To drive these points home, Conservative speeches and publicity naturally seized upon the most extreme statements of Labour Party and trade union figures. There were sufficient bold or incautious comments to provide a constant stream of such material which, as Neville Chamberlain observed in 1925, 'is helping us by frightening the respectable public'.[43] The use made of the 'Zinoviev letter' in the 1924 election was the most famous example of 'red scare' tactics, although this was a case of exploiting a golden opportunity rather than a planned attack. Some examples of the synonymity that was taken for granted between Soviet Communism and the Labour Party were simple to the point of crudity: during one campaign, Oliver Locker-Lampson MP toured his constituency of Birmingham Handsworth with a figure labelled 'Bolshie' hanging from a gibbet in his car.[44] Even the Labour Party's membership of the gradualist Second International was vulnerable to attack, with Conservative propaganda suggesting that its minority position on the organization's executive committee meant that Labour was 'forced to consider the interests of foreign workers before our own', with the alarming consequence that 'England would really be governed by *German* and *foreign* Socialists'.[45] However, by 1929, Labour's careful moderation meant 'that the country was not seriously frightened of anything the Socialists might do'.[46] After 1931, Conservative anti-Socialism became less strident in tone, as well as less extensive in the number of leaflets produced and copies distributed. The reason for this was partly the reassurance provided by the mass support for the National Government in the 1931 crisis, and partly the evidence provided by Labour's failure in office in 1929–31. Before this, Conservative propaganda had been rolling the stone uphill, issuing warnings of a

---

[41] *Hurrah for the Red Republic by Comrade Bob Williams*, NU leaflet 1991 (1920); *Real Socialism: Authenticated Extracts from Socialist Leaders' Speeches and Writings*, NU leaflet 2175 (1923); *Under Which Flag?*, NU leaflet 2798 (1928); *Truth Will Out! Candid Confessions of Socialist MPs*, NU leaflet 3264 (1931); *A Socialist Dictatorship: An Outline of Socialist Policy*, NU leaflet 3381 (1933).

[42] *What Do 'Labour Leaders' Know About Farm Workers?*, NU leaflet 1887 (1919); *A Word to Farm Workers*, NU leaflet 2131 (1922); *Why Do Socialists Call Themselves 'Labour'?*, NU leaflet 2153 (1923).

[43] N. Chamberlain to Baldwin, 30 August 1925, Baldwin MSS, 43/48–51.

[44] Green, *Ideologies of Conservatism*, 126 n.51.

[45] *Over the Garden Wall: Mrs Brown Tells Why Socialists Want Free Trade*, *Over the Garden Wall: Mrs Brown on the Socialist 'Paradise'*, NU leaflets 2232, 2229 (1923), emphasis in original.

[46] Hartington to Salisbury, 11 July 1929, Salisbury MSS, S(4)130/124–6.

hypothetical danger to an unconvinced electorate. After 1931, less effort was required, as the second Labour government could be cited as irrefutable proof of Labour's unfitness to govern (which was further underlined by its apparent shift to the left in 1931–35). With slump and crisis fresh in the mind, there was less need for red scares, less sense of urgency, and less fear that the ground was slipping away from under the Conservatives' feet.

To be most effective, the degree of alarmism had to sow doubts in the minds of opposition supporters and simultaneously motivate Conservative activists and voters. Fear of the confiscation of property did not just alarm the middle class, for Conservative propaganda emphasized that Socialism posed an equal—or even greater—threat to working-class living standards, possessions, and savings.[47] The classic instance of this, though the hare was not set running by a Conservative politician, was the scare in the 1931 general election over Labour's supposed threat to the Post Office Savings Bank, the most popular depository for the working class.[48] Another resonant theme, to which Conservative propaganda regularly returned, was the intrusive powers which Socialism would confer upon officialdom—depicted as unsympathetic, rigid, and remote—to intrude into every aspect of personal life with regulations and proscriptions.[49] Prospects of the removal of freedom of choice and the loss of liberty, especially over where to work and live, were just as unappealing to working-class voters as to those higher in the social scale.[50] There were even more frightening spectres, such the claims made repeatedly in leaflets in the early 1920s that the Soviets had instituted 'a decree of nationalisation of women' and were removing children from their parents to be raised in state orphanages.[51] As their actions were based on the same concept of state authority that the Labour Party endorsed, the imputation was that Labour's programme would also lead to the end of normal family life. Extreme Socialism would go even further, undermining morality and rejecting religion, and was at its most insidious in its attempts to indoctrinate children through movements such as the Socialist Sunday Schools.[52] Even such an unalarming figure as Clement Attlee, the Labour Leader, was depicted in 1935 as intending 'to introduce an Act of Parliament which will abolish patriotism and national allegiance'.[53] The Conservative critique was neatly summarized in a single-sheet leaflet in 1922, which offered this definition for each letter in the word Socialism: 'State Ownership Confiscated Incomes All Liberty Imperilled Security Menaced'.[54]

[47] *Nothing for 15/6: Your Savings under Socialism*, NU leaflet 1890 (1919); *What You Have the 'Labour' Party Wants: They'll Search Your Pockets*, NU leaflet 2068 (1922); *Nationalisation Takes Your Money*, NU leaflet 2449 (1924); *Your House to Go! Your Building Society Too! If Socialism Comes*, NU leaflet 3555 (1935).
[48] This theme was returned to at the next election: *Guard Your Savings!*, NU leaflet 3506 (1935).
[49] *Cards and Coupons*; *Are You a Tradesman? Nationalisation Would Hurt You*, NU leaflet 1957 (1920).
[50] *Over the Garden Wall: Mrs Brown and Labour Party Promises*, NU leaflet 2227 (1923).
[51] *Frozen Breath of Bolshevism*; *Save Those You Love from Bolshevism*, NU leaflet 1944 (1920); *What Bolshevism Means to Women*; *Bolshevik Torture of Women*, NU leaflet 2481 (1924); NU Conf., 1920, speech by Mrs Hoard.
[52] *Stop Socialist Blasphemy*, NU leaflet 2096 (1922).
[53] *An End to Patriotism!*, NU leaflet 3475 (1935).
[54] *Socialism*, NU leaflet 2111 (1922); for another variation: *What Socialism Spells*, NU leaflet 2885 (1929).

However, Conservative attacks had to observe some restraints in order to remain credible and because of the danger that a hysterical atmosphere would lead to reactionary policies—which would alienate the working class, and thus make a spiral of extremism and revolution more likely. In the early 1920s, the party's anti-Socialist propaganda sometimes had more than a tinge of paranoia, as when women were warned to 'look out for the Communist spies who are now working among you', as these 'specially trained agitators...may come disguised as nurses and health visitors'.[55] An excess of pessimism would also be counterproductive, for if lack of confidence in the future became too pronounced it could lead to apathy or loss of nerve, especially amongst the party's middle- and upper-class supporters. It was therefore necessary for the leadership to avoid any general doomsaying, and instead to project confidence and a sense of positive and attainable goals. This was almost always the underlying tone of the Conservative appeal, and this encouraged the vigour and fundamental self-assurance which were characteristic features of the party rank and file. Despite their doubts about the composition and capacity of the democratic electorate, Conservatives drew sustenance from an unshakeable belief in the intrinsic merits of their principles and policies, certain that they had 'the best of wares to offer'.[56] Baldwin's idealistic agenda and his ability to evoke the 'higher plane' were greatly valued, and his rhetoric should not be seen as being in conflict with the strand of anti-Socialism. Rather, they were complementary and gave breadth to the Conservative appeal: it contained both a positive call to endeavour and a negative warning of peril.

THE PROJECTION OF THE APPEAL

Having a message was only part of what was needed; in the age of the mass electorate and the mass media, the Conservatives were aware that it had to be communicated—and, with so many other things competing for public attention, that it was essential to invest time, trouble, and money in doing so. It was recognized that there was a need for constant efforts between elections, partly because the complex party balances made it even more unpredictable when these would occur (there were three in the two years from November 1922 to October 1924), and partly because it was understood that opinions were shaped between elections and that the campaign was too brief to make a large impact on this. There was some uncertainty about how to detect and respond to public opinion; as one Cabinet minister remarked: 'The difficulty is how to know whether we are in touch or not. Each of us in one way or another has to do with a certain number of people from outside, though these are mostly on more or less special subjects' of departmental responsibility.[57] There were also doubts about the capacity and interest of voters—especially the younger ones, who were expected to be uninformed, unreliable, impulsive, and too easily swayed by the 'sob stuff' of emotional appeals.[58] This public had to be

---

[55] *To Women: Communism Destroys Marriage.*   [56] *CAJ*, October 1935, 239–41.
[57] Steel-Maitland to Baldwin, 4 May 1925, Baldwin MSS, 160/160–2.
[58] Headlam diary, 1 May 1927.

reached, and to do so effectively required a co-ordinated effort and the use of methods old, adapted, and new.

The traditional method of public meetings was the most visible form of communication. Since the 'rise of the platform' in the 1880s, it had become customary for the most prominent politicians to deliver speeches on a regular basis to big audiences in the major regional centres. These rallies were normally limited to party supporters through admission by ticket, and were usually peaceful affairs; the development of electric amplification made these large gatherings more effective, as well as enabling the speaker to override any interruption. However, whilst these events gave further stimulus to those who were already politically engaged, one long-serving MP noted that 'very little that is said at these meetings ever gets down amongst the masses'.[59] Public meetings were also the mainstay at local level, and it had become customary for the MP or candidate to address them periodically between elections; if he did not live in the constituency, this was sometimes formalized as an annual speaking campaign, usually held towards the end of the summer parliamentary recess. Some of the local speeches were given at constituency association functions, but it was essential that most of them—and all during an election campaign—were open to the public, if they were to have any credibility or value. One development in the 1920s was that the greater use of motor cars enabled candidates to move rapidly between meetings and address several in an evening, resulting in a schedule which made the three weeks or so of an election campaign an exhausting test of physical stamina. The pre-1914 practice of hiring the larger local venues was replaced by the holding of many more small meetings; this was mainly due to the lower limit on expenses introduced in the 1918 Reform Act, together with its provision for the free use of schoolrooms.[60]

The problem of public meetings was that they drew the committed (both for and against), together with a handful of the curious.[61] In country districts, the lack of other excitements might bring in rather more people, but still only a minority of the mass electorate would attend them, and 'they only touched the same people each time'.[62] In the late 1930s, a conference of local agents in Scotland estimated that 'a candidate can only now expect to establish contact with about 15 per cent of his constituency'.[63] There was a change in attitudes after 1918 towards conduct at public meetings. Being the target of disruption was no longer seen as evidence of unpopularity and weakness, but of the unfair and illegitimate tactics of the opposition; disorder would now rebound to their discredit, and so became something to complain of and even exaggerate.[64] This development was partly a consequence of

[59] Sir P. Richardson, 'The political truce', *Ashridge Journal*, 62 (June 1942), 4.
[60] J. Lawrence, 'The transformation of British public politics after the First World War', *Past & Present*, 190 (2006), 196.
[61] *CAJ*, April 1935, 84.
[62] Birmingham CA, Management Ctte., 14 November 1924; Chelmsford CA, Report of Propaganda Sub-ctte, Exec., 28 October 1927; Glasgow CA, General Ctte., 25 November 1935.
[63] Inverness CA, Exec., 12 October 1937.
[64] Headlam diary, 28 October 1924; Lawrence, 'Transformation of British public politics', 196–8.

including women in the franchise, and still more of the view of Labour as a brute force against which free speech, law and order, and civilized middle-class values had to be defended. There was a decline in rowdy behaviour, although organized disruption of meetings remained a feature of the 1920s, and Conservative candidates could still expect—and be expected to handle—vigorous heckling when speaking in working-class districts, particularly in the coalfields.[65] Speeches at local meetings mainly communicated fairly simple messages, following the line given by the party leaders. Even when not actually given by a paid speaker from Central Office, these speeches generally drew on the briefings which the party issued in publications such as *Hints for Speakers* and the weightier selection of facts and press-cuttings, *Gleanings and Memoranda*. The value of these meetings lay mainly in enthusing the existing supporters; as the party's senior official in Scotland noted in 1929, 'even if any particular meeting makes no converts it at least has "shown the Flag"'.[66]

The medium of the press enabled speeches delivered at both local and national level to reach a much larger audience than could be present in the hall. Local newspapers generally gave considerable space to the speeches of local candidates, and very often every word was reproduced. Their reporting was factual and descriptive, with a limited editorial commentary, which was normally either neutral or favourable to the Conservative cause. It was rare for the party or its candidate to have a poor relationship with the local press, most of which was owned by Conservative supporters, while the links were sometimes strengthened by payments for advertising and general printing.[67] The most important provincial newspapers were almost all reliably and orthodoxically Conservative, such as the *Yorkshire Post* (edited by Arthur Mann, a friend of Baldwin),[68] the *Birmingham Post* (which was under strong Chamberlain influence), *The Scotsman*, and the *Glasgow Herald*—the principal exception being the Liberal *Manchester Guardian*. In the 1920s, Central Office provided political notes and articles to the local and regional press through its Lobby Press Service, which in 1930 was being sent out to 230 newspapers.[69]

The national press was more varied in nature, and the Conservative Party's relationship with it was more complex. It was least problematic with the four most respected titles, whose more restricted circulation than the popular press was balanced in the scales of influence by its concentration in the higher social classes. The

---

[65] *CAJ*, April 1923, 84, October 1923, 221–5, January 1927, 11–12; Headlam diary, 10 September, 21 November 1925; Birmingham CA, Council, 15 March 1929; Sir G. Gaunt, *The Yield of the Years* (1940), 277–8.

[66] Memo by Blair for SUA, 'Impressions of the General Election', 12 July 1929, Gilmour MSS, GD383/29/32–5; Berkshire South CA, AR, 1920.

[67] Rye CA, agreement with the *Sussex Express*, Exec., 5 April 1924; Kincardine & West Aberdeenshire CA, Special Sub-ctte, 19 September 1924.

[68] Mann to Baldwin, 29 October 1930, Baldwin MSS, 165/222–3. The *Yorkshire Post* demonstrated its 'customary staunchness' on India in 1933–35, but was more critical of appeasement in 1938–39, after Eden's resignation: Davidson to Hoare, 2 October 1933, Davidson MSS (Bodleian), MSS.Eng.hist.c.560/102–3; Hoare to Dawson, 28 February 1939, Templewood MSS, X/4.

[69] 'Conservative Central Office Publicity Department', memo 'no. 1', 7 July 1930, Templewood MSS, VI/3.

most authoritative voice in the British press was that of *The Times*, which, after the death of Lord Northcliffe in 1922, resumed a moderate centrist position in conventional Conservative opinion. Under the editorship of Geoffrey Dawson, it gave consistent support to Baldwin—a personal friend—and afterwards to Neville Chamberlain, closely identifying itself with the policy of appeasement. The next most established Conservative newspaper was the *Morning Post*; this regarded itself as 'the organ of the Conservative Party',[70] and generally supported diehard opinion. It was bitterly hostile to the Coalition in 1920–22 and opposed the India policy in 1931–35; between those times it generally supported the party leadership, even when it expressed unhappiness with its moderate direction. Its editor from 1911 to 1937, H. A. Gwynne, was on visiting terms with Baldwin, though not as close to him personally as Dawson. In 1937, dwindling circulation led to the *Morning Post* being absorbed by the *Daily Telegraph*, which was the least heavyweight of the three respectable Conservative national papers, but had the largest circulation, reaching 737,000 by 1939. It had developed under the Berry brothers, who owned a range of newspapers; they were both strong supporters of Baldwin, regular contributors to party funds, and were raised to the peerage as Lord Camrose (in 1929) and Lord Kemsley (in 1936). All three of these more elite-oriented newspapers would print the speeches of major political figures in full—especially *The Times*, which was recognized as the authoritative newspaper of record. Thus, addresses delivered by the Party Leader could communicate directly with many of the party's members and particularly the key figures of the local constituency associations, who were very likely to be readers of one of these newspapers. The last of the quartet was the *Observer*, which published only on Sunday; its editor from 1908 to 1942, J. L. Garvin, was widely read and was on personal terms with many leading Conservatives.

The majority of ordinary members in the local branches, and certainly of Conservative voters, if they read a national newspaper regularly—which was not necessarily the case—would have contributed to the huge circulation of the popular press. This reached unprecedented levels in the interwar period: the *Daily Mail* had a circulation of 1.53 million in both 1921 and 1939, peaking at 1.84 million in 1930, but was overtaken by the *Daily Express*, which rose from 850,000 in 1925 to 2.54 million in 1939. However, although these newspapers had a national coverage, it was well known that the greatest concentration of their readers—and thus of their influence—was the middle class of London and the Home Counties.[71] The role of the mass circulation press was most important in general elections, and especially so in the 1920s, following the creation of a vast and largely unknown electorate. In fact, people choose to read the newspaper which they find most congenial, and so it reinforces their views rather than changing them. Nevertheless, following the decline of the Liberal press in the 1920s, almost every popular newspaper was oriented towards the Conservative Party, and this must have had at least a general effect upon the outlook of their readers. It may have been no more than

---

[70] Heild (deputy editor, *Morning Post*) to Baldwin, 20 May 1923, Baldwin MSS, 159/64.
[71] Hartington to Salisbury, 11 July 1929, Salisbury MSS, S(4)130/124–6; Incorporated Society of British Advertisers, *The Readership of Newspapers and Periodicals in Great Britain 1936* (1937), 1a.

that because both the *Daily Mail* (owned by Lord Rothermere) and the *Daily Express* (owned by Lord Beaverbrook) were regularly critical of the Conservative Party during Baldwin's leadership—to the point, in 1930–31, of trying to force him out by launching a pressure group campaign and running unofficial candidates in by-elections. The failure of this assault was held to have exposed the limits of their power, and certainly they were regarded less fearfully in the 1930s. During that decade the balance in the popular press also changed to some extent, with the development of the *Daily Herald* as a pro-Labour mass circulation title, whilst, during the Second World War, the *Daily Mirror* was transformed into a popular working-class anti-Conservative paper, with sales rising from 1.75 million in 1939 to 3 million in 1946, and *The Times* and the *Observer* moved towards the political centre and centre-left respectively.

The power of the press was accepted as a fact of life, but not accorded legitimacy or respect. Many Conservatives resented the pretensions of the press lords as perversions of constitutional propriety, and the latter's exploitation of the position conferred by their ownership of a particular type of business was seen as irresponsible, selfish, and capricious—even as a form of blackmail. There were also sufficiently frequent instances of 'their dirty political tricks' to alienate most mainstream MPs.[72] These factors made Baldwin's repeated stands against 'press dictation' effective, and were the reason why his most famous attack—the denunciation that the press lords sought 'power without responsibility—the prerogative of the harlot throughout the ages'—struck a lasting chord.[73] However, for pragmatic reasons some Conservatives sought a less antagonistic relationship with the owners of the mass circulation press, in order to secure the benefits of their support at general elections.[74] Anxiety about the possible electoral consequences of the press barons' hostility to Baldwin particularly concerned those who had a fairly mechanistic view of the relationship between a newspaper's circulation and its power, and of the extent to which newspaper owners and editors could control their readers like puppets. This difference in outlook followed broadly the same pattern as the pro- and anti-Coalition divide, with the leading Coalitionists inclined—like Lloyd George—to be more fearful of the press and to urge concessions upon Baldwin. The latter, when telling Churchill that he overrated the importance of Rothermere, noted that the press baron's influence 'is suburban mainly, in a wide sense, but the provincial press is very strong and it is working well for us'.[75] However, with the mass circulation *Daily Mail* and *Daily Express* frequently hostile during Baldwin's leadership, and the trio of heavyweight elite newspapers inclined at times to adopt 'the role of "candid friend"', the party leaders never felt that they could absolutely rely upon the ostensibly Conservative press.[76] This was a view also shared by many in the constituencies, especially after

---

[72] Hogg to Wolmer, 31 January 1924, Wolmer MSS, MSS.Eng.hist.c.1012/143.
[73] *The Times*, 18 March 1931.
[74] N. Chamberlain diary, 4 November 1929, NC, 2/22; even Davidson advocated a minor concession to Rothermere before the 1929 election: Davidson to Baldwin, 13 September 1928, Davidson MSS, DAV/185.
[75] Baldwin to Churchill, 15 May 1928, *WSC*.
[76] Ball to N. Chamberlain, 1 June 1938, NC, 8/21/8.

the unhelpful role of the Beaverbrook and Rothermere press in the 1929 defeat, and there were frequent calls for the establishment of a popular daily newspaper which would compete with them whilst being politically reliable; however, such a venture was far beyond the party's financial resources.[77]

The most direct way of reaching the voters, especially the uncommitted and disinterested, was the personal contact of the door-to-door canvass, as 'our only method of reaching the people is to get in touch with them in their own homes'.[78] 'A call made in a friendly spirit was the ideal to be aimed at', armed with effective and appropriate supporting leaflets.[79] Canvassing was an important campaigning method during a general election, as the 'electorate like to feel that they have been called upon'.[80] However, although canvassing was 'the real work that does most good', after 1918 the comprehensive coverage of a constituency required the sustained efforts of a large force of volunteers, and so a more selective approach was often adopted.[81] The traditional canvass was an exercise undertaken in the period between elections with the aim of identifying a party's own supporters—so that they could be encouraged to turn out—as much as of making converts.[82] In the early 1920s, some constituencies sought to carry on with prewar methods of scrutinizing the electoral register, but the scale of the task made it almost impossible, especially in the marginal seats where it might have been worthwhile. During the interwar period, the task of canvassing increasingly devolved upon the female membership, mainly due to their larger numbers and greater amount of leisure, but also because they might be more persuasive—especially of other women—and would at least receive a politer hearing. Even so, in the urban areas, party workers were often reluctant to go into hostile districts, so that canvassing was a more practicable proposition in the villages and suburbs than in the towns and cities. A partial substitute was the use of paid staff, usually known as missioners, but here the canvassing aspect was usually secondary to the principal aim of recruiting more members for the constituency association. Time and cost meant that such campaigns could only be undertaken occasionally, whilst the legal limits on candidates' expenses meant that paid workers could not be used in this way in a by-election or general election. For all of these reasons, the delivery of leaflets came to replace the personal canvass as the main outdoor work of constituency members, and this, together with the expanded electorate, explains the great increase in this activity. The peak was reached in 1929, when 16.5 million leaflets were distributed in the four months before the dissolution of parliament and a further 85.2 million during the election campaign.[83]

---

[77] NU Conf., 1924, resolution of Thornbury CA and comments of the Party Chairman.
[78] Kinross & West Perthshire CA, Exec., 17 October 1929; Central Office, *Political Education* (1934).
[79] SUA, EDC, 12 June 1935; Chelmsford CA, report of Propaganda Sub-ctte, Exec., 28 October 1927; Birmingham CA, Central Council, 15 March 1929: Cornwall South-East CA, Agent's Report, 7 February 1930; Edinburgh West CA, agent's report on by-election, 1935.
[80] *CAJ*, September 1920, 15–17; Western Area, Women's Advisory Ctte., 2 July 1929.
[81] Worcester CA, Exec., 13 June 1945.   [82] Ealing CA, Exec., 20 April 1928.
[83] NU Central Council report to Conference, 1928–29.

Propaganda had played a significant role during the First World War, and its techniques were further developed in the interwar era. The Conservatives were successful yet reluctant innovators; their ambivalence was shown in their dislike of the term 'propaganda', and they constantly preferred the more respectable sound of 'publicity' and 'political education'. On the day after the dissolution of parliament was announced in November 1923, Amery commented to Baldwin that 'our leaflets etc. matter much more than platform oratory'.[84] This was partly because they could reach a much larger audience, and partly because they could focus on specific issues in a concise and accessible way. The leaflets came in many forms; some were more substantial pamphlets which were intended for existing party members, dealing with organizational aspects such as the establishment of local trade unionists' groups. The items intended for the general public were much briefer than these, although they appear wordy and densely laid out in comparison with their late twentieth-century equivalents. The minority of such leaflets explained or extolled Conservative policies, usually focusing on the record of the government rather than its future promises, whilst the majority were attacks on the opposition parties. By far the larger proportion of these were anti-Labour, and here the main themes were the intention of Socialism to turn all private property into public ownership, the extent of the interfering bureaucracy that would be needed to administer this, the differences of view within the Labour Party, and the state of affairs under Bolshevism in Russia. Over this period, Conservative leaflets become more sophisticated at targeting different groups, rather than seeing the working class as a monolithic entity.[85] A common method of reaching women voters was a leaflet containing an appeal from the candidate's wife, something which was all the more effective when she was a glamorous or aristocratic figure such as Lady Diana Cooper or Lady Dorothy Macmillan (both the daughters of dukes). This was carried out on a national scale in 1929, with an appeal issued to women voters by Mrs Baldwin.[86] The limitation of leafleting was that its distribution depended upon the constituency associations, and because these varied considerably in resources and efficiency, and inevitably were weakest where the need for propaganda was the greatest, the coverage of the electorate was 'hopelessly sporadic'.[87] As one local executive committee observed: 'money is the main prop in propaganda'.[88]

As well as using a selection of the leaflets prepared by Central Office, each candidate issued their own election address. These were modelled on the address of the Party Leader to his constituents, which in this period was the form in which the official party manifesto was published. Each candidate was entitled under electoral law to one free postal delivery to every voter on the register, and this was used to circulate the election address. A major task undertaken by the local party member-

---

[84] Amery to Baldwin, 14 November 1923, Baldwin MSS, 42/125.
[85] Jarvis, 'British Conservatism and class politics', 80, 83–4.
[86] *Making History: A Message from Mrs Stanley Baldwin*, NU leaflet 3022 (1929).
[87] 'Conservative Central Office Publicity Department', memo 'no. 2', n.d. [7 July 1930], Templewood MSS, VI/3.
[88] Norwich CA, report of Exec. to Council, 27 January 1926.

ship was addressing the thousands of envelopes necessary for this; the aim was to have these prepared before parliament was dissolved, and then quickly filled and despatched as soon as the candidate's address arrived from the printers. There was some advantage, at least of confidence and prestige, in getting the address issued before opposition candidates did so, and this added a further point of competitiveness and drama to the contest. Whereas leaflets were produced on a regular basis, with 5.3 million circulated in 1925 and 9.7 million in 1928, posters were mainly used in general election campaigns; at other times, 'it is doubtful if the results obtained justify the heavy expense involved'.[89] A wide range of posters were used in election campaigns, varying considerably in topic and design; whilst there might be a slogan which became emblematic, such as 'Safety First' in 1929, this was featured on a single poster and not repeated as a tag-line on others.[90] Nor was there a particular colour which identified the Conservative Party in this period, for due to local traditions thirty-four different combinations were in use across the country.[91] With the time available to prepare for the 1929 general election, Central Office considerably expanded its own Publicity Department and consulted a leading advertising agency of the day, S. H. Benson. The result was an extensive selection of colourful and striking posters, some warning of the dangers of Socialism and others extolling the social record of the Conservative government, 464,614 of which were used in the campaign.[92] These were displayed on rented street hoardings and on constituency association offices, but not usually on private property; as one London constituency noted, 'there was considerable reluctance on the part of even members of the Executive Committee to display posters in or on their houses'.[93]

The Conservative Party was consistently receptive to exploiting new methods of publicity which were made possible by technological advances, such as the fitting of gramophone loudspeakers to cars for election campaigning.[94] However, some of these ideas were impracticable or too expensive, such as the use of sky-writing by aeroplanes. There was an experiment involving issuing the speeches of leading figures as gramophone recordings, but these were intended more for playing at branch meetings in rural areas than for home listening. Much more important in reaching the public was the new medium of broadcasting, which was controlled by the British Broadcasting Corporation from the early 1920s. However, during most of the interwar period, it interpreted the requirements of its charter to be politically neutral with such rigour that very little was aired of a partisan nature. The main exception was the institution of general election broadcasts for each party, the number of which were proportional to its vote in the previous election. At first, Labour and Liberal politicians broadcast from a public mass meeting that they were addressing, but these did not project very well to the radio audience. Baldwin consulted the

[89] East Midlands Area, Exec., 20 September 1934.
[90] Ball, *Dole Queues and Demons*, 29–43.
[91] NU Central Council, 24 February 1925; Hampshire East CA, AGM, 21 April 1933; J. Ramsden, *The Age of Balfour and Baldwin 1902–1940* (1978), 259–60.
[92] NU Central Council report to Conference, 1928–29.
[93] Ilford CA, Exec., 27 June 1934.   [94] Bewdley CA, Secretary's Report, 1939.

Director-General of the BBC, John Reith, about how people normally listened to broadcasts and, on being informed that the majority did so at home with their family gathered around the hearthside, tailored his style and tone accordingly.[95] Just over one-quarter of households owned a radio by 1929 and the proportion continued to rise steadily during the 1930s, embracing the middle class and much of the skilled working class, and it was into these homes that Baldwin reached when he spoke. His mode of 'fireside chats', delivered as if he was sitting in the living room with his listeners, was notably effective and added to his established image of being an honest and sincere figure without artifice or trickery. In the 1930s, a view developed within the party that there was a deliberate left-wing bias in BBC programmes,[96] and this became a source of vehement complaint during the Second World War, especially over the broadcasts of the novelist and playwright J. B. Priestley.[97]

The other rapidly growing new medium of the early twentieth century was cinema; this did not have the statutory restraints that governed the BBC, but for commercial reasons did not wish to antagonize its mass audience with the kind of political partiality found in the press. Cinema newsreels concentrated on factual depiction and often proclaimed that they were unbiased, although this was not entirely true. The owners of the newsreel companies and cinema chains were sympathetic to the Conservatives, though often discreetly, and the content of the newsreels was, to some extent, manipulated in their favour. This was partly because factual reporting tended to include the work of the government—the Prime Minister attending an international meeting, for example—but exclude the more clearly partisan activities of the opposition, and for nearly all of this period the Conservatives were in office. However, at election times the bias was rather more apparent, with Labour, particularly, getting fairly scant attention.[98] In the 1931 election, a short news film supporting the National Government, featuring Ramsay MacDonald, Baldwin, and Sir John Simon, a leading Liberal, was shown for three nights at every cinema in England, and was estimated to have been seen by 25 million people.[99] The combined effect of radio and newsreel was that Baldwin became the first Prime Minister whose appearance and voice was personally familiar to most of the population.

Finally, cinema was also used directly by the Conservative Party, with considerable effect; indeed, it was 'the best form of propaganda the Party has'.[100] From the mid-1920s onwards the party produced its own films; these were not for screening in the ordinary cinemas, but were taken around the country by a number of specially constructed cinema vans. The equipment which these carried could be used to show the films indoors by hiring village halls and similar venues, or at any outdoor

---

[95] Reith diary, 17 October 1924, in C. Stuart (ed.), *The Reith Diaries* (1975), 90.
[96] Stonehaven to Baldwin, 6 December 1932, Baldwin MSS, 59/210–11.
[97] Ball to N. Chamberlain, 1 June 1938, NC, 8/21/8.
[98] J. Ramsden, 'Baldwin and film', in N. Pronay and D. W. Spring (eds.), *Politics, Propaganda and Film 1918–1945* (Basingstoke, 1982), 126–43.
[99] NU Exec. report to Central Council, 8 March 1932.
[100] East Midlands Area, Exec., 20 September 1934.

location, using the van itself as projection platform and screen.[101] The latter was more dependent upon good weather, but it had become the main form of reaching small communities by the late 1920s. In this period, the novelty of the cinema vans could attract large numbers, and they were particularly popular with rural constituencies; accompanying the van for a week in August 1928, the MP for Hertford 'was able to address between six and seven thousand electors'.[102] The films drew 'an entirely different audience than the ordinary political meeting', reaching people who were usually disinterested or uninvolved in politics.[103] The Conservative Party was always eager to adopt the most wide-ranging and innovative approaches to propaganda, as outlined in Party Chairman J. C. C. Davidson's ambitious plan to reach voters not just at home but also at work, whilst travelling, and during their leisure pursuits.[104]

THE ECONOMIC AND SOCIAL BASIS OF CONSERVATIVE ELECTORAL SUPPORT

The interwar era was the second of four periods of notable success for the Conservative Party in modern times, the others being 1886–1906, 1951–64, and 1979–97. The Conservatives were the largest party in the House of Commons for 90 per cent of the twenty-seven years from 1918 to 1945, the sole exception being the parliament of 1929–31. The party won governing majorities on its own in 1922 and 1924 (the latter very substantially), and was the main element in the coalitions which triumphed in 1918, 1931, and 1935. There were three defeats: in 1923, when it still remained the largest party; in 1929, when the Labour Party came first but lacked an overall majority, and in 1945, which, although a Labour landslide, was not as severe a defeat for the Conservative Party as either 1906 (156 MPs) or 1997 (165 MPs). Moreover, in 1923 and 1929 the Conservatives polled more votes than any other party; only in 1945 were they unmistakably beaten at the ballot box.

The coalition arrangement with Lloyd George reduced the number of Conservative candidates in 1918 and also affected the election which immediately followed its fall in 1922; in both cases this was reflected in a lower share of the vote, despite winning more than half of the seats in the House of Commons. In 1931 and 1935 the Conservatives stood aside in a smaller number of constituencies for the Labour and Liberal supporters of the National Government, but even so the

---

[101] *CAJ*, August 1931, 199–200; February 1933, 42–4; May 1934, 91–2.
[102] Hertford CA, AR, 1928; Dorset East CA, Exec., 11 February 1929; Warwick & Leamington CA, 'Cinema Van Report', Exec., 22 March 1938; Merionethshire CA, Exec., 5 April 1937, 3 April 1939; they were also effective in industrial areas: Wolverhampton Bilston CA, Management Ctte., 28 June 1935. They were used less frequently in Scotland, but a tour of seven constituencies drew an estimated total audience of 25,000 adults: SUA, WDC, Propaganda Ctte., 3 October 1934.
[103] Wells CA, Agent's Report, Finance Ctte., 30 September 1927; memo by Party Chairman, 'Cinema Propaganda', 11 January 1937, CPA, CCO/4/1/37.
[104] Notes by Davidson, 'The Campaign', n.d. but *c*.March 1927, Davidson MSS, DAV/180.

Conservative Party alone still secured its two highest shares of the vote during the period. This fell significantly in 1945 and, in what was effectively a two-party battle, the total 39.6 per cent share of the poll gained by the Conservatives and their Liberal National and 'National' allies resulted in a major defeat.

Table 2.1. Conservative Party overall performance in general elections 1918–1945

The House of Commons consisted of 615 MPs at the elections of 1922–35, but was increased to 640 MPs before the general election of 1945. The figures are for the Conservative Party alone, and do not include any coalition allies (in this table, the figures for 1922, 1923, and 1924 do not include the 'Constitutionalist' candidates). The university seats are included and Northern Ireland is included, as in this period Ulster Unionist MPs took the Conservative whip and were counted as part of the Conservative Party.

Date of election	Candidates nominated	Unopposed returns	MPs elected	Total votes received	% share of vote
14 December 1918	445	41	382	4,144,192	38.6
15 November 1922	482	42	344	5,502,298	38.5
6 December 1923	536	35	258	5,514,541	38.0
29 October 1924	534	16	412	7,854,523	46.8
30 May 1929	590	4	260	8,656,225	38.1
27 October 1931	518	49	470	11,905,925	55.0
14 November 1935	515	23	387	10,496,300	47.8
5 July 1945	559	1	197	9,101,099	36.2

Table 2.2. Constituencies not contested by the Conservative Party 1918–1945

The university seats and Northern Ireland are not included; for definitions of the regions, see Appendix 3.

Region	1918	1922	1923	1924	1929	1931	1935	1945
London	9	10	7	6	–	9	9	6
Home Counties N	6	3	–	2	–	2	2	1
Home Counties S	1	–	–	–	–	–	–	–
South Central	7	4	2	3	3	2	3	3
South-West	3	2	1	–	–	2	2	3
East	6	3	–	–	–	6	6	5
Midlands East	13	8	2	3	–	6	5	3
Midlands West	9	7	2	–	1	3	5	4
Yorkshire	25	15	8	6	3	9	9	8
Tyneside	13	6	6	3	1	7	7	7
North-West	12	6	4	2	4	3	4	3
Wales Industrial	9	6	9	3	–	11	5	6
Wales Rural	7	7	2	7	–	4	5	7
Scotland South	17	19	12	9	1	7	7	5
Scotland North	9	12	2	2	4	2	5	3
TOTAL	146	108	57	46	17	73	74	64

The seats which the Conservative Party did not contest in the general elections from 1918 to 1945 were mostly the result of coalition pacts or, in the case of 1922, their legacy. In 1918, in 100 cases the uncontested seats were won by another Coalition candidate, and in two further instances by nominees of the 'National Party' (a temporary grouping of a few right-wing Conservative MPs); in 1922, National Liberal followers of Lloyd George won thirty-eight of the uncontested seats and came second in a further forty-eight. Local agreements with the Liberal Party—mainly with former Coalition Liberal MPs—continued in some areas during the two general elections which rapidly followed in 1923 and 1924, and so the lowest number of uncontested seats occurred in 1929, the one election which took place both at the end of the expected life of a parliament and without any preceding coalition. In this election, nine Labour, seven Liberal, and one Independent MP were returned without Conservative opposition. The regions where the Conservatives stood aside in larger numbers between 1918 and 1924 were those where the Liberal Party had been strongest in the Victorian and Edwardian eras: inner London, the East Midlands (proportionately compared to the West Midlands, where there were more seats), Yorkshire, and the north-east (notably in comparison to Lancashire), Wales, and Scotland.

The pattern was broadly similar in the elections under the National Government in 1931 and 1935, as these were the regions where the declining Liberal Party still retained some strength. In 1931, sixty-one of the seventy-three uncontested seats were won by another party in the National Government (twenty-five Liberal National followers of Sir John Simon; twenty adherents of the official Liberal Leader, Sir Herbert Samuel; twelve members of Ramsay MacDonald's tiny National Labour group, and four non-party supporters of the National Government). This strategy continued to be effective in 1935: twenty-five Liberal National MPs, seven National Labour, and one National were elected in the seats where the Conservatives stood aside. Even more crucially, the Labour Party candidate was defeated in forty of the uncontested seats, and elected in only thirty-two of them. The cardinal feature of the Conservative Party between the wars was that it had a presence in all regions and in all types of constituencies, to a greater and more effective extent than either of its rivals—for whilst the Liberal Party withered in the industrial areas, the Labour Party was barely able to make an impression in the suburbs, small towns, and rural shires. The following discussion explores the economic and social foundations that underlay this, and which explain the patterns of Conservative electoral strength and weakness.

The Conservative Party drew its local leadership and parliamentary candidates from the upper class and the upper-middle class. It had possessed the support of the majority in these social categories before the First World War, and the ensuing decline of the Liberal Party made this overwhelming. The retention of two forms of plural franchise in the 1918 Reform Act gave this support an extra electoral advantage, as most of those who were entitled to an additional vote were middle class at least. University graduates (in England, an almost wholly upper-middle- and upper-class group) were entitled to a vote in one of the seven university constituencies, which cumulatively elected twelve MPs. The elections for these seats were conducted by postal ballot, and in the three double-Member and one triple-Member seats the single transferable vote system was used. Campaigning for the university seats was conducted in a very different way, according to their particular conventions of discretion and integrity, and candidates did not themselves overtly compete or canvass. However, although the university seats had a certain tradition of independence, they were in practice dominated by the Conservative Party between 1918 and their abolition by the Labour government in the Representation of the People Act 1948.

Table 2.3. The representation of the university seats 1918–1945

This table analyses the twelve university seats in England, Scotland, Wales, and Northern Ireland; it does not include the three southern Irish university seats, which ceased to exist in 1921.

Party	1918	1922	1923	1924	1929	1931	1935	1945
Conservative	9	8	9	8	8	8	7	3
Liberal	3	4	2	3	2	2	2	1
Independent	–	–	1	1	2	2	3	8*

* This includes three National candidates, two of whom were ministers in Churchill's 'caretaker' government.

The other additional franchise was spread throughout the territorial constituencies of the United Kingdom, but not evenly. This was the possession of a second vote due to occupying business premises of an annual rental value of at least £10; nationally, this was estimated to amount to 370,000 votes in 1929. By its nature, this was also generally an upper-middle- and upper-class group, as the small shopkeepers who made up an important element of lower-middle-class Conservative support often lived in the same building as their shop and therefore did not qualify for the business vote. However, the 1918 Reform Act placed a limit on plural voting so that no person was allowed to cast more than two votes in total; in consequence, those who had more than one business premises, or who qualified for both a university and a business vote, had to decide which to use.

Table 2.4. Plural voters and Conservative electoral support

This table analyses the 373 constituencies in England and Wales which can be exactly matched to the geographical units used in the occupation tables of the 1931 census, and which were contested by all three main parties in the 1929 general election (for the methodology, see Appendix 2). For the constituencies in each band of the Conservative share of the vote, it shows the proportion of electors per thousand electors who had other franchise qualifications in addition to the basic residential franchise, according to the 1931 census.

	up to 14.9	15.0–19.9	20.0–24.9	25.0–29.9	30.0–34.9	35.0–39.9	40.0–44.9	45.0–49.9	50.0–54.9	55.0 & above
Plural voters	5.4	14.7	8.6	11.3	11.5	10.3	6.4	5.7	5.8	21.4

% Conservative share of the vote in 1929

Whilst there is not a uniform correlation between the incidence of plural voters and the Conservative share of the poll, the figures are certainly suggestive of a link. This is especially the case when it is considered that the dip in the 40.0–54.9 per cent range is due to the high proportion of county divisions (115 of 147 constituencies) in these bands: many of these covered a large rural area, and contained fewer industrial and commercial properties. The business vote was of unusual importance in the double-Member City of London constituency, due to the concentration of office premises and the comparatively small number of persons who were actually domiciled there: in 1931, 839 per thousand of its electors had a qualification other than residence.[105] This was one of the safest of Conservative seats, and only twice during this period was it even contested by any other candidates: in 1929 a Liberal recorded 12.4 per cent of the vote, and in 1945 a Liberal gained 11.0 per cent and an Independent 10.2 per cent.

However, Conservative success in the other eleven double-Member and 567 single-Member constituencies in England, Scotland, and Wales depended upon a broader social basis. The upper and upper-middle classes were powerful but numerically few, and the large majority of those who voted Conservative were either lower-middle or working class. In numerical terms, an authoritative contemporary survey used by advertising agencies graded 0.9 per cent of households as 'upper class', with an income above £1,000 per annum; 3.4 per cent as 'upper middle class', with incomes of £500 to £1,000; and 14.3 per cent as 'lower middle class', with incomes of £250 to £500 a year; this left 81.5 per cent as working class.[106] As a whole, the middle class comprised three elements: business (owners or managers of factories, shops, and other enterprises), professional (working for themselves or employed by others), and white-collar (office and other non-manual workers). There was a range of wealth and status in the first two elements and these included members of the upper and lower-middle classes, whilst the white-collar element—numerically by far the largest—was entirely lower-middle class. Although the secret ballot makes it impossible to determine an exact breakdown, the pattern of the electoral results and contemporary observations strongly suggest that a very large part of the lower-middle class consistently voted Conservative. Of the rest, only a small portion supported Labour and most remained Liberals; when there was no Liberal candidate standing, the majority of the latter could often be persuaded to vote Conservative. During the interwar period, the middle class increasingly found the Liberal Party to be an unsatisfactory defender of its interests. This was both a consequence and a cause of Liberal decline: it was due to its divisions, its organizational decay, and the discrediting of its leaders, and also to the gap between middle-class concerns and the left-leaning inclinations of many of the Liberal leaders and MPs, which was highlighted by their

---

[105] The other constituencies which had more than 100 per thousand of electors with a qualification other than residence were (with proportion): Manchester Exchange (316), Holborn (305), Westminster Abbey (278), Liverpool Exchange (242), Leeds Central (120), Finsbury (118), and Sheffield Central (112).

[106] Incorporated Society of British Advertisers, *Readership of Newspapers*, 1a.

support in office of the first and second Labour governments. This tension further fragmented the Liberal Party, firstly in the summer of 1931, when a group of MPs led by Simon were already negotiating an electoral pact with the Conservatives before the collapse of the Labour government in August, and secondly in September 1932, when the Simonite wing remained in the National Government despite the withdrawal of the other Liberals over fiscal policy. Following this, middle-class support for the Conservative Party and its allies was even more extensive and deeply entrenched in the 1930s than it had been in the 1920s, with corresponding electoral and organizational advantages.

Lower-middle class support was the backbone of the Conservative Party, both electorally and organizationally. It provided most of the ordinary members of constituency associations, especially at branch level and particularly in the women's and youth sections, and gave the party a living presence which upper-class wealth alone could never provide. As a result, Conservatism was closely identified with the values and concerns of this class, with clear effects in its ethos and practice. It was not only the rich who feared disorder: owners of small property as much as large were threatened by social upheaval, loss of status, and dispossession.[107] Indeed, the lower-middle class may have been the most anxious, for they had less surplus income and financial resources, and they often lived in closer proximity to working-class districts and were more aware of the advance of the labour movement. The Party Chairman noted in 1928 that 'from no class of the community has the Conservative Party received more consistent support than from the small shopkeeper'.[108] Respectability was still a powerful force amongst the middle classes, especially in the smaller communities of country towns and villages. It was also essential in the new and rootless suburban developments, where homogeneity of class and the absence of a pre-existing network led to greater dangers of exclusion, especially for the women, who were solely dependent upon their locality for social interaction. As the Liberal politician and journalist C. F. G. Masterman commented in 1922, the suburban middle-class outlook was 'modest in demand, indeed, in face of life's possibilities, but very tenacious in its maintenance of its home and garden'.[109] In this atmosphere, conformity to the assumed norm was by far the easiest route to take; in political terms, that meant holding Conservative views and voting for (and in many cases joining) the Conservative Party. This was not necessarily due to having any great interest in politics or strong party feeling; as one local agent observed, 'an appreciable number of people will support us at the polls for no other reason than that the people with whom they are accustomed to foregather at our social events do likewise'.[110]

Conservative fortunes were certainly assisted by the expansion in number of the middle class, and the general prosperity which they enjoyed in this period. Conservative and Conservative-dominated governments delivered a deflationary

---

[107] *Shopkeepers and Traders!*, NU leaflet 2968 (1929).
[108] Davidson to Joynson-Hicks, 25 January 1928, Baldwin MSS, 48/134–6.
[109] C. F. G. Masterman, *England after the War* (1922), 54.
[110] Ipswich CA, AR, AGM, 2 March 1928.

economy in which the value of incomes and savings remained stable, the banking system was secure, there was a low level of middle-class unemployment, and there were improving and affordable consumer luxuries. For much of the middle class, it was the 1930s rather than the 1950s which saw the advent of affluence and a rise in material living standards, including widespread car-ownership. Over 2 million houses were built for private ownership during the 1930s, and their comparative cheapness and the easy mortgage terms resulted in many being purchased by the lower-middle class, who acquired a new stake in property. Where there were economic concerns, they impelled the middle class towards the Conservatives—and, of crucial importance, away from the Liberals. As a Central Office organizer noted of the 'middle and semi-middle class electors' in Leicester in 1934: 'the one thing these people worship is economic security'.[111] The extension of taxation was in some ways more important than the extension of the franchise in establishing the Conservative dominance of the interwar era. Many more voters came into the income tax bracket after the war, with the number of taxpayers more than trebling from 1.13 million in 1913 to 3.9 million in 1919. In addition, the amount levied had vastly increased, with the standard rate of income tax rising by 500 per cent, from one shilling and twopence to six shillings in the pound (the equivalents in decimal currency are six pence and thirty pence). The incidence of local taxation—which was paid by a much wider social spectrum—also rose due to the increased responsibilities of local government. These factors greatly aided Conservative appeals for limiting the role—and therefore cost—of national and municipal government. Socialism was now a direct danger to the pockets of many more people than it had been before the war, and the prospect would also worry those who were not far below the tax threshold. Those dependent upon savings and pensions were particularly prone to such anxieties, and even in the late 1930s there were '*so* many retired people who think they will lose their money if Socialism got into power'.[112] Finally, this was also a period of social stability during which the middle class felt personally secure: levels of crime were low, and they had confidence in a police service that was deferential in conduct and effective at containing unruly behaviour.

The tables which follow are derived from the occupation data in the published reports of the 1931 census; the methodology of the analysis is explained in Appendix 2. In most of the tables, this is compared to the Conservative vote in the general election of 1929, which has been chosen as the best measure of the party's support for an accumulation of reasons. Most obviously, it was central in the interwar period and proximate in time to the census of 1931 (the peculiar circumstances of the 1931 general election, a Coalition landslide in which many persons who had previously voted Liberal or Labour supported Conservative candidates, render it unsuitable for identifying the party's core support). More valuably, 1929 was the most 'normal' election of the interwar era: there were no coalitions between parties, there was no crisis or potentially distorting issue (such as the 'Zinoviev

---

[111] Report of an unamed Central Office organizer, enclosed in Gower to Ball, 9 November 1934, CPA, CRD/1/7/17.
[112] Kelley to Duchess of Atholl, 27 December 1938, Atholl MSS, 22/31, emphasis in original.

letter' of 1924), and it was the only contest to take place at the expected time, at the natural end of a parliament. It is also the most suitable of all the elections for statistical analysis, for two reasons. Firstly, it was held after the franchise reform of 1928 had equalized the voting age for both sexes at twenty-one, creating the most broadly based electorate. Secondly, it had the highest incidence of seats which were contested on the same basis and thus can validly be compared: with all three parties putting forward the largest number of candidates of any interwar election, 453 single-Member constituencies in England, Scotland, and Wales saw a three-way fight between Conservative, Labour, and Liberal nominees. Finally, and not of least importance, as a Conservative defeat it reveals the party's foundations of support more clearly than would a victory, for presumably the large majority of those who voted Conservative in 1929 were persons who did so in other elections and who would have considered themselves to be Conservative supporters. Even if we do not go quite so far as Beaverbrook's caustic judgement that the party obtained 'the votes that would have been given to brass monkeys if they had been put up as Conservative candidates', it is nonetheless reasonable to take the Conservative vote in 1929 as a base level.[113]

Table 2.5. The middle class and Conservative electoral support: (i) an overview of England and Wales

This table analyses the 373 constituencies in England and Wales, which can be exactly matched to the geographical units used in the occupation tables of the 1931 census, and which were contested by all three main parties in the 1929 general election (for the methodology and definitions of the categories, see Appendix 2). For the constituencies in each band of the Conservative share of the vote, the columns show the percentage of the total 'occupied' in each category in 1931.

Occupation	% Conservative share of the vote in 1929

Occupation	up to 14.9	15.0– 19.9	20.0– 24.9	25.0– 29.9	30.0– 34.9	35.0– 39.9	40.0– 44.9	45.0– 49.9	50.0– 54.9	55.0 & above
Shopkeepers	2.8	2.5	2.8	2.9	3.0	3.1	3.1	3.3	3.3	3.1
Clerical	2.6	4.5	5.2	4.9	8.2	7.0	6.8	8.9	9.3	7.1
Professional	3.3	2.6	2.7	2.9	3.2	3.6	4.1	5.1	6.0	6.7
TOTAL	8.7	9.6	10.7	10.7	14.4	13.7	14.0	17.3	18.6	16.9

Table 2.5 clearly demonstrates the correlation between the proportion of the occupied population in the 'core' categories of the middle class and the Conservative vote. It is possible to take this analysis further in the case of London and the larger cities, due to the more detailed data provided in the census for areas with a population of over 50,000. This makes it possible in these places to identify a narrower range of occupations which might be defined as 'upper-middle' class

---

[113] Beaverbrook to Birkenhead, 7 June 1929, Beaverbrook MSS, BBK/C41. The 1929 vote was so considered in a Conservative Research Department analysis in 1933: memo by Brooke, 'Note on the six recent By-elections', 30 November 1933, CPA, CRD/1/7/16.

(see Appendix 2). Domestic servants are also separately categorized here, and a higher level of these would indicate a wealthier area. However, a problem with analysing this census data is that figures are only given for the borough or city as a single unit, and it is not possible to relate them to the individual parliamentary divisions within it. For this reason, the census profile for the larger boroughs and cities can only be compared to a percentage share of the poll, which is calculated from the total number of votes cast for all the Conservative candidates. There are two further difficulties in doing so: firstly, some of the city constituencies were not contested by all three main parties in 1929, and so it is necessary to combine the results of three-way and two-way contests; secondly, the Conservative Party did not contest one seat in Bradford, Newcastle, and Liverpool respectively, and three seats in Bristol, which affects their share of the vote in these cases—although only to a significant degree in Bristol. Nevertheless, the total Conservative vote is the best available measure of Conservative support, and it is more accurate than taking the mean of their percentage share in each of the divisions, as the size of their electorates could vary substantially.

Table 2.6. The middle class and Conservative electoral support: (ii) a detailed analysis of London and the large cities in England

This table analyses the London boroughs and the eleven larger cities in England (defined as those consisting of four or more parliamentary divisions), in relation to the Conservative vote in the 1929 general election. The occupational data are drawn from the 1931 census; for the methodology and definitions of the categories, see Appendix 2. The Conservative share of the vote in 1929 is derived from the sum of the votes cast for all of the Conservative candidates in the city or London borough, including both two-way and three-way contests, calculated as a percentage of the total number of votes cast in the city or London borough as a whole. Cities and London boroughs have been ranked in descending order of the Conservative share of the vote.

	No. of seats	% Upper-middle class	% Core middle class	% Domestic servants	% Con. vote 1929
Birmingham	12	2.4	15.6	3.8	48.2
Liverpool	11	1.6	14.9	5.4	45.1
Manchester	10	1.9	15.4	3.8	38.0
Leeds	6	2.6	13.6	4.3	37.7
Sheffield	7	2.5	13.3	5.5	37.4
Hull	4	1.9	13.8	6.1	35.4
Nottingham	4	2.1	12.9	4.5	33.9
Newcastle	4	2.0	14.9	6.7	33.7
Bradford	4	2.4	12.5	3.4	25.9
West Ham	4	1.0	13.5	3.4	24.5
Bristol	5	2.4	16.4	6.8	20.8
London Boroughs					
City of London	2	3.4	19.6	11.4	87.6
Westminster	2	4.3	16.7	29.4	76.2
St Marylebone	1	5.3	18.6	25.9	61.4
Chelsea	1	3.4	17.2	28.8	58.4

	No. of seats	% Upper-middle class	% Core middle class	% Domestic servants	% Con. vote 1929
Hampstead	1	6.3	26.7	24.2	58.3
Holborn	1	4.8	19.8	14.2	56.8
Kensington	2	4.6	19.2	25.7	52.7
Wandsworth	5	3.5	27.8	8.3	49.7
Lewisham	2	3.3	28.2	6.7	45.3
Hammersmith	2	1.7	17.2	6.4	43.1
Fulham	2	1.9	19.4	7.4	41.5
Woolwich	2	1.9	19.5	4.6	41.3
Paddington	2	3.5	19.2	17.5	40.9
Lambeth	4	1.8	19.4	6.6	40.2
St Pancras	3	2.2	16.8	8.7	39.1
Greenwich	1	2.2	17.3	6.6	38.1
Stoke Newington	1	4.0	21.7	7.2	38.1
Battersea	2	1.7	18.8	5.4	37.3
Camberwell	4	1.9	19.1	5.1	35.6
Islington	4	1.7	15.7	5.1	32.7
Hackney	3	3.5	16.4	5.2	31.7
Deptford	1	1.5	17.2	4.2	30.5
Finsbury	1	0.9	9.1	4.4	28.3
Stepney	3	2.8	10.0	3.3	24.6
Poplar	2	0.8	9.5	3.0	20.9
Bermondsey	2	0.7	10.2	3.0	18.5
Southwark	3	0.7	10.2	4.7	18.2
Shoreditch	1	0.9	6.0	2.6	15.9
Bethnal Green	2	1.6	7.6	2.3	7.7

Whilst the middle class were a core element of Conservative support, their votes were not numerous enough on their own to bring electoral success: a survey of national income levels in 1924 found that of the occupied male population, 4.9 per cent were employers, professionals, or farmers, 11.9 per cent were salary (rather than wage) earners, and 6.3 per cent were self-employed. Indeed, this total of 23.1 per cent was certainly larger than the actual middle classes, as a considerable number of the self-employed were craftsmen and tradesmen, and some of the smallest farms provided only a basic subsistence.[114] The basis of Conservative electoral success was the combination of most of the middle class with a sizeable proportion of the working class, probably one-third at its least and rising to around half at its peak.[115]

---

[114] R. Bowley and J. Stamp, *The National Income, 1924* (1927), 12.
[115] The level of one-third was found in the 1950s and 1960s, and there is little reason to suggest that it would have been radically different in the interwar period: D. Butler and D. Stokes, *Political Change in Britain* (1969), 104–5; J. Blondel, *Voters, Parties and Leaders: The Social Fabric of British Politics* (1963), 54–7; R. T. McKenzie and A. Silver, *Angels in Marble: Working Class Conservatives in Urban England* (1968), 243.

The factors which created this working-class support were several, and it must be remembered that class is a complex matter, with many subtle distinctions and relationships of subordination or antagonism within each broad category. No one can be looked down upon more thoroughly than those who are just one small step below, for this is the gap that must be emphasized and maintained. The differentials which matter are those with the adjacent street or neighbourhood, rather than with the stately home some miles away. Class is also only one element in shaping identity and opinion; other powerful influences are occupation, age, religion, family tradition, and regional culture.[116] Not everything is structural: generational change, social aspirations, deferential attitudes, and personal experience play their part. Dislike of change is a function of temperament rather than of class, and the general tendency to increasing 'natural conservatism' with advancing years has long been recognized. However, the latter effect was mitigated by the age structure of the population: the census of 1931 found that only 28 per cent of the male population was aged forty-five or older, although they formed a higher proportion in the rural districts than the urban areas. Finally, the Conservative Party was often effective in appealing to a significant proportion of those in all classes who did not have a habitual voting pattern, and who therefore might be open to persuasion on the issues of the moment and the appeal that a party or its Leader could project.

Table 2.7. The economic and social profile of Conservative electoral support

This table analyses the 373 constituencies in England and Wales which can be exactly matched to the geographical units used in the occupation tables of the 1931 census, and which were contested by all three main parties in the 1929 general election (for the methodology and definitions of the categories, see Appendix 2). For the constituencies in each band of the Conservative share of the vote, the columns show the percentage of the total 'occupied' in each category in 1931.

Occupation	% Conservative share of the vote in 1929								
	up to 14.9	15.0–19.9	20.0–24.9	25.0–29.9	30.0–34.9	35.0–39.9	40.0–44.9	45.0–49.9	50.0–54.9	55.0 & above
Agriculture	3.1	2.2	2.4	4.4	3.2	6.8	12.1	10.8	9.6	10.5
Mining	39.0	19.3	13.7	6.5	3.8	2.0	1.7	1.0	0.7	0.4
Metal Industries	6.6	6.8	7.5	11.2	9.3	9.2	6.5	5.3	4.6	3.4
Construction	4.4	4.8	4.4	5.3	5.6	5.5	5.9	6.3	6.0	5.9
Light Industries	3.8	5.8	5.5	4.8	7.4	6.4	6.1	6.8	6.6	4.9
Textiles & Clothing	3.1	8.0	17.7	18.7	13.1	7.8	10.3	5.1	2.9	2.9
Service & Leisure	7.5	10.1	8.5	8.6	10.2	12.6	12.8	16.8	20.2	25.4
Commerce & Finance	8.5	9.0	9.7	8.8	10.8	11.0	10.6	12.4	13.1	12.3
Clerical	2.6	4.5	5.2	4.9	8.2	7.0	6.8	8.9	9.3	7.1
Professional	3.3	2.6	2.7	2.9	3.2	3.6	4.1	5.1	6.0	6.7
No. of constituencies	18	21	20	21	53	71	57	63	27	22

[116] This is demonstrated in studies of the early postwar era: Blondel, *Voters, Parties and Leaders*, 57–67; Butler and Stokes, *Political Change in Britain*, 90–213; McKenzie and Silver, *Angels in Marble*, 82–104.

Certain relationships are clearly apparent in the above analysis of the nature of Conservative support. Firstly, the party polled better as the proportion of those in middle-class, 'white collar', and service occupations increased. Secondly, the Conservative vote was also higher in occupations with a lower density of trade unionization and where workplaces were often smaller in scale, with employers working alongside their employees (such as agriculture and much of the construction sector), or where skill and educational levels were higher and working conditions better (as in many of the newer light industries, such as electrical goods, and in some more established trades, such as furniture-making and printing). In reverse, industries with a high proportion of manual labourers, substantial and long-established trade unions, and often poor industrial relations (such as steel-making, heavy engineering, and—above all—mining) were inimical environments for Conservative support. Textiles had many similarities with the latter groups, and its unusual and non-linear profile, with its highest levels in the mid-range of Conservative voting, is most probably accounted for by its significant proportion of women workers. Geographically, the greatest Conservative strength was in the south: of the forty-nine constituencies in the above sample where the party's vote in a three-way contest in 1929 was 50 per cent or more, twenty-six were in London or the Home Counties, fifteen in other parts of southern England, four in the Midlands and east, and four in the north. However, the drift of population to the south-east was a mixed blessing, as the electorate in some suburban London and Home Counties constituencies, such as Epsom, grew rapidly during the 1930s. This had two disadvantages: firstly, that the numbers were unmanageable for canvassing and campaigning, and secondly, that the party's vote piled up wastefully in large surpluses whilst returning fewer MPs than elsewhere.[117]

The Conservatives had particular electoral success in two types of constituency, the first of which was the districts containing the main bases of the armed services. In the 1931 census, sixteen constituencies had more than 10 per cent of the total 'occupied' in the category of government and defence (census order XXIV), and the Conservative Party won these seats on eighty-six occasions out of a possible maximum of ninety-six in the six general elections from 1922 to 1935. The second group was those linked to the leisure sector (hotels and boarding houses, restaurants and catering, and all forms of entertainment), which included districts of central London as well as the coastal holiday resorts. Of the nineteen parliamentary seats in the seventeen constituencies with more than 7 per cent employed in this sector in 1931,[118] the Conservatives won on ninety-nine occasions out of a possible 114 in the 1922–35 general elections; in the same period, the party won fifty-three times out of a possible sixty in the ten parliamentary seats outside London which had more than 5 per cent occupied in this sector. A further factor

---

[117] Channon diary, 12 July 1937.
[118] Defined as order XXVI plus groups 861–2, 864–9 and 871 of order XXVII, *Census of England and Wales, 1931: Occupation Tables* (1934). This data were only published for the urban areas with populations exceeding 50,000 (Table 16, pp. 154–425), and therefore does not include a number of major resorts located in county divisions. In the six most important of these (Isle of Thanet, Lancaster, Rye, Scarborough, Torquay and Weston-super-Mare), the Conservative candidate won forty-five times out of forty-eight in the eight general elections from 1918 to 1945; the three defeats were all in 1923.

contributing to this success was that the highest level of shopkeepers (groups 670–85 of order XXIII) were found in the holiday resorts and coastal towns. Conservative candidates also scored well in the three constituencies which had more than 5 per cent engaged in fishing (Grimsby, Lowestoft, and St Ives), winning these on fourteen of the possible eighteen opportunities in the 1922–35 general elections. Finally, the party did better than might have been expected in the places with larger numbers of railway workers (sub-order 1 of order XXII): of the nine constituencies with more than 4 per cent employed in this industry, the Conservatives won on forty-one of the fifty-four possible occasions in the 1922–35 general elections.

By the end of the nineteenth century, Britain had become a predominantly urban society; in 1931, 80 per cent of the population of England and Wales lived in urban districts of some sort, and 50.7 per cent lived in the 113 large towns with a population of over 50,000; in consequence, 'a small house in a large town, only too often ugly and smoke laden, is now the typical home of the Englishman'.[119] Whilst Conservative support was generally strong in the rural areas, it was more variable in the urban districts. The more detailed census data provided for the towns with a population above 50,000 makes it possible to identify certain economic sectors more precisely, and a larger number of occupational categories have been used in Table 2.8. However, agriculture and mining have been eliminated, as these activities had a negligible presence in the cities.

As well as having by far the lowest level of success for the Conservatives, West Ham had a different occupational profile from elsewhere, as its two largest groups were in categories which were not sufficiently salient to be included in Table 2.8 for the other cities: 15.6 per cent of those occupied were engaged in transport, and 16.8 per cent were in the census category for 'other and undefined workers', which primarily consisted of general labourers and unskilled workers. In addition, although they had subsequently declined, this area had been a birthplace of the 'new' trade unionism for unskilled workers in the late 1880s, and it had a long tradition of support for the Labour Party. Birmingham and Liverpool, the two large cities where the Conservative Party did consistently well across the period, were not cities with large-scale manufacturing; whilst Birmingham had a high proportion of workers engaged in metal-based industries, many of these were in small and medium-sized businesses. However, there is nothing particularly distinctive about their pattern in other key respects (such as the proportion engaged in retail, wholesale, and finance, domestic service, clerical, and professional), and other cities where the party fared less well had higher or nearly as high figures in these categories. It is clear that other factors entered into the equation here, of past history and associations, of religion and popular culture, and also of the effectiveness and prestige of Conservative organization in these two cities since the 1880s.

---

[119] A. M. Carr-Saunders and D. Caradog Jones, *A Survey of the Social Structure of England and Wales as Illustrated by Statistics* (2nd edn, Oxford, 1937), 26.

Table 2.8. The economic and social profile of the larger English cities

This table analyses the larger cities in England (defined as consisting of four or more parliamentary divisions), excluding London. The columns show the percentage of the total 'occupied' in fifteen categories in 1931, drawing on the more detailed census data that are provided for towns with a population of over 50,000 (for the methodology and definitions of the categories, see Appendix 2). The percentage of seats won is the total number of Conservative wins in the six general elections of 1922–35 as a proportion of the maximum possible number of wins during that period (by-elections are not included).

	Bir	Brd	Bri	Hul	Lds	Liv	Man	New	Not	Shf	WH
No. of seats	12	4	5	4	6	11	10	4	4	7	4
Con % seats won 1922–35	90.3	33.3	40.0	58.3	50.0	74.2	55.0	41.7	50.0	54.8	12.5
Docks & Shipping	0.1	0.0	2.8	11.8	0.1	9.2	0.4	1.8	0.1	0.0	6.1
Railways	1.2	1.3	1.8	2.5	1.4	1.6	1.5	1.4	1.7	1.5	1.5
Metal Industries	22.7	5.5	6.4	7.4	9.2	5.2	8.6	13.8	6.8	22.4	7.1
Construction	6.2	4.0	6.1	4.5	4.9	5.0	4.0	4.0	5.2	5.4	5.4
Chemicals	0.2	0.2	0.3	0.6	0.2	0.3	0.3	0.2	0.2	0.1	0.6
Electrical	2.2	0.9	0.9	0.8	0.9	1.2	1.4	1.5	0.9	0.9	1.2
Textiles & Clothing	3.1	32.6	5.2	2.9	22.4	4.1	15.4	2.6	20.4	2.0	6.0
Paper & Printing	1.8	1.6	4.0	1.6	2.4	1.7	2.8	1.4	2.8	0.9	2.4
Food, Drink & Tobacco	1.2	1.0	4.0	2.4	1.2	2.2	1.3	1.4	2.4	1.2	2.2
Retail	6.5	6.9	8.1	8.4	6.8	8.6	7.3	8.8	7.3	7.4	6.2
Wholesale & Finance	4.1	4.3	5.2	4.0	5.1	4.1	5.7	4.8	4.1	3.8	3.3
Entertainment & Catering	3.0	2.6	3.4	3.0	3.1	4.3	3.8	3.8	2.9	2.4	3.7
Domestic Service	3.8	3.4	6.8	6.1	4.3	5.4	3.8	6.7	4.5	5.5	3.4
Government & Defence	0.5	0.5	0.9	0.8	0.5	0.9	0.5	1.1	0.5	0.5	0.7
Clerical	9.3	6.5	8.8	7.2	7.1	8.5	9.1	8.4	6.3	6.9	9.0
Professional	3.2	2.7	4.2	3.1	3.2	3.5	3.0	3.8	2.9	3.3	2.2

City codes: Bir = Birmingham; Brd = Bradford; Bri = Bristol; Hul = Hull; Lds = Leeds; Liv = Liverpool; Man = Manchester; New = Newcastle; Not = Nottingham; Shf = Sheffield; WH = West Ham.

Working-class Conservatism was not particularly related to having a higher level of income or skills than other workers, and indeed was perhaps more prevalent amongst the unskilled than the skilled.[120] It was more a function of the place and type of work, and of relationships within the workplace and the industry more generally. The larger concerns were less fertile soil, because in their more stratified environment the employer or manager was often a distant, alien, and unsympathetic figure, and workers here were more likely to be members of trade unions and to feel their class identity to be an emblem of self respect. Conservative supporters were more likely to work for smaller and non-unionized businesses, and less likely to be involved actively in trade unionism or the other institutions which promoted a strong sense of class solidarity.[121] It was also the case that Conservative policies might be of material benefit: shorn of the 'food tax' liability, defensive protectionism could be just as attractive to the workers in a particular industry as it was to the owners. It is a mistake to assume that the norm of working-class attitudes was hostility to capitalism and the existing basis of economic activity, simply because the Labour Party asserted that this was the case. In fact, grievances were usually specific and local rather than concerning the system, whilst increased living standards would 'make every worker, in some degree, a capitalist' and increase Conservative support as well.[122] There were, therefore, a variety of factors which encouraged some of the working class to vote Conservative, in some cases occasionally and in others regularly, and this provided a crucial element in the party's electoral support. Even so, and particularly with the rise of the Labour Party after 1918 and its assertion that it had a natural claim upon the loyalty of the working class, it is certainly the case that the majority of that class voted for the other main parties. From 1924 onwards, this was less for the Liberals, but with increasing solidity for the Labour Party, which gave the latter the resilience to retain nearly one-third of the votes cast in 1931, despite losing so many of its seats. The correlation between higher proportions of the working class and lower levels of Conservative support is demonstrated by Table 2.9; this uses the census information on unemployment and two other categories, which relate to the lower quality of housing that was a feature of working-class districts in towns and cities: the overall population density (the average number of persons per acre), and overcrowding within houses (the average number of persons per room).

In the first half of the twentieth century there was a real cultural divide between the lower-middle class and the working class.[123] This was a barrier over which the Conservative Party found it much easier to reach down than the Labour Party to

---

[120] This was found in studies of the immediate post-Second World War period, which it is reasonable to assume was generally similar: R. S. Milne and H. C. Mackenzie, *Straight Fight: A Study of Voting Behaviour in the Constituency of Bristol North-East at the General Election of 1951* (1954), 44; M. Stacey, *Tradition and Change: A Study of Banbury* (1960), 43; McKenzie and Silver, *Angels in Marble*, 84.

[121] Sir G. B. Hurst, *Closed Chapters* (Manchester, 1942), 90.

[122] Feiling, *What is Conservatism?*, 19, 30; *Are You a Capitalist?*, NU leaflet 2080 (1922); McCrillis, *Conservative Party in the Age of Universal Suffrage*, 136–44.

[123] Essex & Middlesex Area, LAC, 5 February 1938.

Table 2.9. The working class and Conservative electoral support

This table analyses the 373 constituencies in England and Wales which can be exactly matched to the geographical units used in the occupation tables of the 1931 census, and which were contested by all three main parties in the 1929 general election (for the methodology, see Appendix 2). The level of unemployment is the number of persons aged fourteen and over who were classified as 'out of work' as a percentage of the number classified as 'occupied' in the 1931 census.

	% Conservative share of the vote in 1929									
	up to 14.9	15.0–19.9	20.0–24.9	25.0–29.9	30.0–34.9	35.0–39.9	40.0–44.9	45.0–49.9	50.0–54.9	55.0 & above
Persons per acre	1.44	1.99	2.92	1.33	1.77	1.01	0.56	0.62	0.91	0.74
Persons per room	0.94	1.04	0.96	0.92	0.89	0.89	0.79	0.77	0.76	0.79
% unemployed	18.85	15.26	15.18	12.81	11.72	12.64	9.60	7.30	6.55	6.17

climb above. The cause of this was that many elements of the Conservative appeal were attractive to the working class, extending beyond the late Victorian combination of 'beer and Britannia'—pride in the nation and the defence of working-class pleasures from Liberal prudery—whilst much about the labour movement repelled the middle classes: its social origins and identification with trade unionism, its policies (nationalization, the capital levy), its advocates (bohemian intellectuals, pacifists, freethinkers, atheists), and its links with extremism (Bolshevism, disorder). These vulnerable points were exploited by Conservative rhetoric and propaganda, which had an impact not only on the middle class but also upon receptive sections of the working class.

It is often suggested that the most significant category of the latter was women, and certainly the pattern of gender support was another distinctive feature of Conservative electoral performance. Vivian Henderson's experience of contesting poor districts of Glasgow and Liverpool in the 1920s was not unusual: 'I have found working-class women far more Conservative than their husbands or brothers.'[124] This was an advantage on its own, and a still greater benefit in the constituencies where (after the equalization of the franchise in 1928) there were significantly more female voters than male. Of course, these generally correlated with the more prosperous areas, as a major category of employment for women was as domestic servants, of whom there would be more where there was more wealth.[125] Nevertheless, it is clear that the Conservatives polled better where women were more numerous, which suggests that the party had some success in projecting an appeal to them across class boundaries.

There was some concern in the immediate postwar years that women might establish a new party of their own or seek to promote a feminist agenda, and doubts remained as to whether the female electorate was a threat or an oppor-

---

[124] *Home and Politics*, 98 (1929), 7–8.
[125] J. Turner, *British Politics and the Great War: Coalition and Conflict 1915–1918* (New Haven and London, 1992), 414.

Table 2.10. The gender gap and Conservative electoral support

This table analyses the 373 constituencies in England and Wales which can be exactly matched to the geographical units used in the occupation tables of the 1931 census, and which were contested by all three main parties in the 1929 general election (for the methodology, see Appendix 2). For the constituencies in each band of the Conservative share of the vote, the table shows the average percentage of male and female electors in 1931. The gender gap is calculated by subtracting the percentage of male electors from the percentage of female electors.

	% Conservative share of the vote in 1929									
	up to 14.9	15.0–19.9	20.0–24.9	25.0–29.9	30.0–34.9	35.0–39.9	40.0–44.9	45.0–49.9	50.0–54.9	55.0 & above
% male electors	51.4	49.3	48.6	47.5	47.2	47.7	47.1	45.6	44.6	43.5
% female electors	48.6	50.7	51.4	52.5	52.8	52.3	52.9	54.4	55.4	56.5
% gender gap	–2.8	+1.4	+2.8	+5.0	+5.6	+4.6	+5.8	+8.8	+10.8	+13.0

tunity.[126] The fear was a reflection of prewar masculine doubts about the fitness of women for the suffrage, that they would vote 'without knowledge or thought and actuated solely by some temporary sentiment or impulse'.[127] This shaped the franchise of the 1918 Act, which limited the female vote to those aged over thirty and who, either themselves or through their husbands, qualified as a ratepayer for the local government franchise; in other words, to older women who had the steadying responsibilities of property or a family. It was expected that the latter, and domestic issues more generally, would be the focus of women's political horizons.[128] There were encouraging signs from the beginning that these new voters were a source of support: after the 1918 election, the leader of the party in Manchester reported 'The women worked very well for us especially in the suburbs and they voted in large numbers and materially helped our majority.'[129]

By the mid-1920s it was clear that women voters were content to make their choices between the existing parliamentary parties, and that the Conservatives had gained more from this than their rivals. However, the equalization of the franchise in 1928, with the inclusion of all women over twenty-one on the same basis as men, revived Conservative anxieties in an acute form. In fact, around one-third of those whom the measure brought onto the electoral roll were aged over thirty, but had not previously qualified through being neither a ratepayer nor the wife of a ratepayer. However, Conservative apprehension focused entirely on the women aged between twenty-one and thirty, who were widely expected to be particularly fickle, foolish, and easily swayed by sentimental Socialist propaganda, as they were 'for the most part composed of girls who take not the slightest interest in

---

[126] *To Women Voters.*
[127] *Women and the Election*, NU leaflet 2498 (1924).
[128] *Women in Public Life: Conservative and Unionist Aims*, NU leaflet 2352 (1924).
[129] Woodhouse to Derby, 1 January 1919, Derby MSS, 20/1.

politics'.[130] This fear was summed up by the label given to the new voters, the term 'flapper' stigmatizing them as vapid young hedonists, concerned only with frivolity and self-indulgence. This image was powerful but misleading, as in this era most women were wives and mothers by their mid-twenties,[131] especially in the working class, whilst the younger element of the new voters were likely to be in employment and still living with their parents: the 1921 census showed that 48 per cent of the women who worked outside the home were younger than twenty-five. Their principal occupations were domestic service, the textile industry, and clerical work, of which the first and last were—in their different ways—conducive of identification with the middle classes. The economic stagnation of the 1920s increased the number of women in domestic service from 1.1 million in 1921 to 1.3 million in 1931, of whom about 60 per cent lived in their employers' homes. Furthermore, despite the depression of the 1930s, job opportunities were expanding for younger women in shops, offices, and in transport; all of these were at a distance from the world of the factory, and had low levels of trade unionization. However, the largest group of adult women were the 8.6 million recorded as married in the 1931 census, nearly all of whom were not in paid work but occupied with their own household and family.

Although many Conservatives blamed the defeat in 1929 on the 'flapper vote', this did not seriously undermine their growing confidence that, as one candidate commented, 'we always thought women were of a conservative nature'.[132] Several factors were believed to contribute to this, in particular that Conservatism's basis upon instinct would appeal to women as they were considered to 'have always relied upon intuition rather than reason' and so 'are by nature Tories'.[133] More materially, it was thought women's loyalties would be focused on the more intimate level of the family rather than a broad class identity, and that as consumers they would be 'interested above all in stability'.[134] Of course, the failings of the Labour Party to secure women's support were as much a part of this as any power of attraction exerted by the Conservatives.[135] Organized working-class life was heavily masculine in focus, excluded women from power and often from employment, and placed the husband and father even more authoritatively in the centre of the picture than did the middle or upper classes. Trade union and Labour politics at local level were often tinged with misogyny and could seem aggressive and confrontational. Women were unattracted to this and tended to identify instead with the broader 'public', whilst if their family was their first concern it was by no means self-evident that its position was made more secure by class separatism and antagonism.

---

[130] Derby to Baldwin (not sent), 28 October 1930, Derby MSS, 33.
[131] NU Conf., 1927, speeches by Morgan and Fraser.
[132] Keymer to Baldwin, 11 December 1923, Baldwin MSS, 35/122–123.
[133] Loftus, *Creed of a Tory*, 67, 75.
[134] Elliot, *Toryism*, 83.
[135] Data on generational groups of voters collected in the 1960s showed that working-class women who reached the age of twenty-one between the wars were much less likely to be Labour voters than men of the same age: Butler and Stokes, *Political Change in Britain*, 59–61.

A further factor affecting the political affiliation of both genders was the pattern of generational change. Most people form their views shortly before or during their young adult years, between the ages of around fifteen and twenty-five, and thereafter do not greatly vary their fundamentals. It follows that the influences of the period in which they passed through this emergent process have a formative effect, and in particular that this might be crystallized by the first general election in which they were entitled to vote. The difference in the nature of the environments in which particular groups of voters come to maturity, together with the lasting impress of this upon each cohort as it ages, produces the variation in outlook between different generations.

There were three occasions in this period when an unusually large group of first-time voters participated in a general election: 1918, 1929, and 1945. The number in 1918 was enormous, and of course many of these voters were above the age of thirty and had formed their political opinions in the late Victorian and Edwardian eras. The Conservatives had dominated much of this period (especially from 1886 to 1906) and their popular organizations of the Primrose League and the Conservative Working Men's Clubs had socialized a large membership, whilst the Liberals, up to 1910, had often appeared divided and ineffectual; on balance, it was probable that the Conservatives would draw more support from those who became adults at least up to 1906. The impact of the new voters, and especially of young men in the armed forces, was to some extent mitigated in 1918 by the low turnout of 57 per cent, but even with this the new voters hugely outnumbered the old. The fact that they cast their first vote—whether this was in 1918 or 1922—in a period when the Liberal Party was divided, weak, and largely discredited, and whilst the Labour Party was not yet contesting many constituencies, must have been to the Conservatives' advantage.

In 1929 the new voters were mainly young women aged twenty-one to thirty, together with women over thirty who had not qualified under the local government franchise and who were likely to be in the poorer classes—in particular, domestic servants, those residing in lodgings, and the elderly living with their children. The addition to the electorate was considerable: there were 21.7 million electors in 1924 and 28.9 million in 1929, an increase of one-third. As the turnout remained very similar, it can be presumed that the new voters participated in a more or less similar proportion to the existing ones. The Conservative Party expected to be the losers by the addition of so many inexperienced and probably ill-informed voters who would be susceptible to their opponents' simplistic and sentimental appeals. Certainly the party grass roots had been hostile to the 'flapper vote', hankering after the politically unworkable idea of depriving younger men of the vote and equalizing the franchise for both sexes at the age of twenty-five. The third election with a high number of new voters was 1945, due to the passage of a decade since the previous election. The new voters included everyone aged between twenty-one and thirty-one, and it has been estimated that only about 58 per cent of the 1945 electorate had voted previously. The greatest impact upon these young voters was the experience of the war, and in political terms the revulsion of popular feeling against the Conservative-dominated governments of the 1930s, which were retrospectively blamed for their selfish economic policy and disastrous foreign and defence policies.

Whilst no statistical data on generational attitudes were collected between the wars, the investigations of psephologists in the 1960s—when many interwar voters were still alive—demonstrate some distinctive features.[136] The Conservatives were found to have a higher level of working-class support amongst both those who reached the age of twenty-one before 1918 and those who did so between 1918 and 1939, but to have noticeably less amongst those reaching adulthood after this.[137] Additionally, Conservative support in the interwar cohort was at a markedly higher level amongst women than men, but it was similar in both genders in the pre-1918 group. Another study found that working-class men and women who reached the age of twenty-one before 1935 were almost twice as likely to be Conservative voters in the late 1950s as those who became adults after 1935.[138] The pre-1935 age group were those whose socialization was in the period when the Labour Party was either marginal, untried, and possibly alarming (before 1923), or when it was a more significant force but not yet an established or successful party of government (1924–35). Of the three main parties, only the Conservatives were credible contenders for power throughout the interwar era, a position which has always paid dividends for the party in attracting support from all social classes.

THE POLITICAL BASIS OF CONSERVATIVE ELECTORAL SUPPORT

The Conservative Party prided itself on being 'a truly national party', transcending the divisions of class and region, and extending into all walks of life and every corner of the country.[139] This was a powerful ideal and self-image, and not so far from the reality as to be difficult to sustain. There were more problematic regions (primarily Tyneside and Wales) and some weak seats in all areas, but the party had a genuinely broad base, both socially and geographically.

The Conservatives certainly were not equally strong in all regions, and there were significant areas where it was very much an uphill and dispiriting struggle; one woman organizer in Wales commented that her work had frequently seemed 'like flogging a dead horse, and often she had gone home and wept with disappointment'.[140] The party polled notably better in industrial Lancashire (where many women worked in the cotton mills) than it did in Yorkshire, although this was partly a legacy of religious denominationalism, as the influence of Nonconformity was stronger east of the Pennines. However, there was also a link with rising female unemployment as the slump took effect in 1930–31: eleven constituencies

---

[136] Butler and Stokes, *Political Change in Britain*, 59–61.
[137] Butler and Stokes, *Political Change in Britain*, 105–15.
[138] McKenzie and Silver, *Angels in Marble*, 88–91.
[139] *Why You Should Support the Conservative Party*, NU leaflet 2839 (1928).
[140] Wales & Monmouthshire Area Women Organisers, meeting, 17 September 1931.

Table 2.11. The regional pattern of Conservative electoral support

This table shows the percentage of seats in each region won by the Conservative Party; the university seats and Northern Ireland are not included (for definitions of the regions, see Appendix 3).

Region	1918	1922	1923	1924	1929	1931	1935	1945
London	71.0	69.4	46.8	62.9	38.7	79.0	61.3	17.7
Home Counties N	80.0	77.8	48.9	82.2	57.8	86.7	71.1	21.7
Home Counties S	97.2	97.2	88.9	100.0	91.7	100.0	100.0	73.2
South Central	69.4	77.8	52.8	88.9	72.2	88.9	86.1	55.6
South-West	77.8	70.4	29.6	96.3	59.3	81.5	81.5	59.3
East	56.7	63.3	43.3	90.0	53.3	73.3	70.0	26.7
Midlands East	41.9	45.2	35.5	67.7	29.0	71.0	61.3	12.9
Midlands West	66.0	70.2	61.7	74.5	42.6	89.4	72.3	30.0
Yorkshire	43.9	42.1	35.1	47.4	26.3	71.9	43.9	21.1
Tyneside	35.7	25.0	25.0	39.3	17.9	67.9	39.3	10.7
North-West	67.4	59.3	36.1	73.3	36.1	86.1	69.8	30.7
Wales Industrial	18.2	27.3	18.2	27.3	4.6	22.7	22.7	4.6
Wales Rural	–	–	–	23.1	–	7.7	7.7	15.4
Scotland South	51.9	21.2	19.2	50.0	23.1	71.2	44.2	23.1
Scotland North	15.8	10.5	21.1	52.6	42.1	57.9	63.2	63.2

(ten of which were in Lancashire, and the other in Cheshire), comprising fourteen parliamentary seats, had more than 20 per cent of the number of 'occupied' women classified as 'out of work' in the 1931 census, and whilst the Conservatives won only two of these seats in 1929, they swept to victory in twelve of them in 1931.

The combination of the social, economic, and regional factors created a considerable number of safe seats, mainly in the Midlands and southern England, and particularly in the country districts, the non-industrial towns, and the suburbs. In the interwar period, the Conservatives benefited from having a larger core of safe seats than either of their rivals. This meant that they had to win fewer of the marginals to gain an overall majority, and this was the solid foundation upon which their larger victories were built (see Table 2.12). The regional pattern is not surprising, but it is striking in its scale. Sixty-one seats in the south-east (London and the Home Counties) were won in every interwar election (1918–35). Together with those in the two other key regions of the West Midlands (sixteen seats) and northwest (fourteen seats), these account for ninety-one MPs, which is more than one-third of the parliamentary party after the 1923 and 1929 defeats, and not much less than a quarter of the landslide gained in 1924. On the other hand, in the regions which might loosely be termed the 'Celtic fringe' (Scotland, Wales, and the south-west), the Conservatives had few strongholds, especially outside Edinburgh. Both patterns are mirrored in the distribution of the unopposed returns of Conservative MPs (see Table 2.13).

Although still greater than in the second half of the twentieth century, in the interwar period it was noticeable that party identity was less ingrained and

Table 2.12. Conservative safe constituencies

Double-Member constituencies, the university seats, and Northern Ireland are not included (for definitions of the regions, see Appendix 3). Thirteen constituencies with large electorates were abolished and divided into two or more newly created constituencies before the 1945 election; in these cases, the 1918–35 constituency has been linked to the most appropriate of the successor seats in 1945 (see Appendix 2). The constituencies in the column 'Won in 1922–35 but lost in 1945' are mainly seats which in 1918 were not contested by the Conservative Party due to the Coalition arrangement.

Region	Won in all elections 1918–45	Won in 1918–35 but lost in 1945	Won in 1922–35 but lost in 1945	Regional total
London	9	9	9	27
Home Counties N	6	10	10	26
Home Counties S	20	7	7	34
South Central	9	4	4	17
South-West	4	1	1	6
East	3	2	5	10
Midlands East	4	1	1	6
Midlands West	11	5	5	21
Yorkshire	9	2	3	14
Tyneside	1	1	1	3
North-West	10	4	5	19
Wales Industrial	1	–	–	1
Wales Rural	–	–	–	–
Scotland South	6	1	1	8
Scotland North	1	–	–	1
TOTAL	94	47	52	193

dependable than had been the case in late Victorian and Edwardian times, especially among the younger population. Whilst the habitual Conservative voters provided a substantial foundation, on their own they were not sufficient to guarantee electoral success. The party was aware of this, and as a result was often more conscious of its weaknesses than its strengths—of a lack of funds rather than their plenitude, of the apathy of its members rather than their number, and of the particular appeal that the Labour Party could make to working-class sentiment. The position was put bluntly by Neville Chamberlain in 1928: 'We are not strong enough to win alone. In fact, we are a minority of the country.'[141] If victory was to be achieved, the core of regular Conservative support had to be augmented and extended. For this reason, the Conservative appeal could not be pitched for Conservative ears alone, as that would isolate the party in perpetual minority status—an experience which it had endured in 1846–74 and to a lesser extent in 1906–14, and did not wish to repeat.

[141] N. Chamberlain to Irwin, 12 August 1928, Halifax MSS, C152/18/1/114a.

Table 2.13. Unopposed returns of Conservative MPs 1918–1935

Double-Member constituencies are included, but the university seats and Northern Ireland are not included (for definitions of the regions, see Appendix 3). There was no unopposed return in England, Scotland, and Wales in 1945.

Region	1918	1922	1923	1924	1929	1931	1935	Total
London	7	3	6	5	1	5	2	29
Home Counties N	4	1	–	–	–	–	–	5
Home Counties S	2	4	4	–	–	3	2	15
South Central	5	1	1	–	–	6	3	16
South-West	2	–	–	–	–	1	1	4
East	1	1	1	–	–	1	1	5
Midlands East	3	–	–	–	1	2	1	7
Midlands West	6	6	4	3	–	2	2	23
Yorkshire	3	6	3	3	–	5	1	21
Tyneside	–	–	–	–	–	1	–	1
North-West	7	7	5	2	–	5	1	27
Wales Industrial	–	1	–	–	–	–	–	1
Wales Rural	–	–	–	–	–	–	–	0
Scotland South	1	–	–	–	–	1	1	3
Scotland North	–	–	–	–	–	2	–	2
TOTAL	41	30	24	13	2	34	15	159

In practice, this required the attraction of voters who did not have a partisan outlook or a regular pattern of voting, and, in particular, of the most loosely attached bloc in the interwar electorate—the remaining and former Liberals. On three occasions—1918, 1931, and 1935—this was attained through a coalition pact with a large part of the Liberal Party, and the resulting elimination of competing candidatures was greatly to the Conservatives' advantage. In the four elections from 1922 to 1929 which were fought on a party basis and with Liberal opposition, a broadening of support was sought by persuading Liberal voters that their needs and concerns could be better met by rallying to the constitutional standard as borne aloft by the Conservative candidate. This was least effective in 1923 and 1929 when the Liberal Party was at its strongest and most united, and more so in 1922 and 1924 when there were fewer Liberal nominations and the advance of Labour made anti-Socialism a stronger card to play. However, in all these cases it was recognized that pure negativism lacked sufficient magnetism, and that there must be a positive aspect to the attraction as well. This element was mainly found in the appeal of Baldwin's public image and style, and his ability to attract 'the middle unattached vote' was recognized as a great electoral asset.[142] One former Liberal MP commented shortly before the 1929 election: 'what is best in Liberalism is expressed in Baldwin's attitude to affairs', and the latter's broadcasts in 1935

---

[142] Davidson to Irwin, 6 March 1931, Halifax MSS, C152/19/1/254.

had a similar appeal.[143] The most effective combination was to energize the Conservatives without alienating middle opinion, to present the issues in a way which widened the ground between Labour and the Liberals whilst minimizing the distance between the latter and the Conservative Party, and to have a lesser number of three-way contests in constituencies.

Another factor to impact upon electoral success was which party had been in office and with what degree of fortune, for there is much truth in the adage that 'oppositions do not win elections—governments lose them'. In fact, the Conservatives only entered one campaign as the opposition party, in 1924; in 1931 they had taken office a few weeks before the election as part of the emergency National Government, and attacks on the former Labour government's record had to be finessed around the continuance in the new ministry of the former Prime Minister (Ramsay MacDonald) and Chancellor of the Exchequer (Philip Snowden). On the other hand, by overthrowing Lloyd George and their own leaders in 1922, in the immediately following election the anti-Coalition ministry of Bonar Law reaped the advantages of both incumbency and opposition. Apart from 1922 and 1924, on every occasion that a Conservative government or a predominantly Conservative coalition appealed for a continuation in office, it did so under its existing Prime Minister: Lloyd George in 1918; Baldwin in 1923, 1929, and 1935; MacDonald in 1931; and Churchill in 1945. This meant that the record and general image of the government was of particular importance, as it affected both the opinions of voters and the morale and enthusiasm of party members. Governments inevitably disappoint some of their supporters, in part because their expectations may be unrealistic, but an unsuccessful tenure of office—or even a period of dull routine—will cause a greater erosion of support. Thus, as early as the summer of 1920—before the impact of the economic downturn and many of the difficulties and policy failures of the Lloyd George Coalition—the Deputy Party Chairman, Robert Sanders, noted that 'the government is getting more and more unpopular among Conservatives'.[144] Similarly, only a year after the landslide victory of 1924, an MP for a working-class constituency in east London wrote of 'a deep-seated dissatisfaction with the delays and procrastinations which are producing a feeling of helplessness and alarm', and forecast a Labour majority at the next election.[145]

These ebbs and flows of opinion were crucial, as the outcome of a general election hinged upon the variation in a comparatively small proportion of votes in the marginal seats. In 1922, Bonar Law's governing majority depended upon the thirty-seven seats which had been won by fewer than 1,000 votes (half of which were held by fewer than 400 votes), whilst in 1923 if the fifty seats that were lost by fewer than 1,000 votes had been retained, Baldwin would have had an overall majority of one. In 1929, if the thirty seats lost by fewer than 1,000 votes had returned Conservative MPs, then the Conservatives rather than Labour would

---

[143] Shaw to Bridgeman, 23 March 1929, Moore to Baldwin, 17 November 1935, Baldwin MSS, 175/52, 39/287.
[144] Bayford diary, 23 June 1920.
[145] Holt to Herbert, 11 October 1925, Baldwin MSS, 160/90–3.

have been the largest single party in the House of Commons, although still losing their overall majority. The larger victories of 1924, 1931, and 1935 were less dependent upon the marginals, and there were notably fewer close results on these three occasions, as shown in Table 2.14. However, even after two successive substantial victories, in the late 1930s Conservative Party strategists were still very conscious 'that only a small turnover of votes would defeat the government'.[146]

Table 2.14. Conservative marginal constituencies 1922–1935

This table analyses all of the single-Member constituencies in England, Scotland, and Wales which were contested by Conservative candidates in each general election during the main period of interwar party competition. Two-way and three-way contests are treated on the same basis, as this is a measure of how many seats had close results in terms of the number of votes, rather than the share of the poll.

Constituency results	1922	1923	1924	1929	1931	1935
Con win by 801–1000 votes	3	8	6	5	–	8
Con win by 601–800 votes	10	3	9	6	4	4
Con win by 401–600 votes	6	13	2	8	2	6
Con win by 201–400 votes	6	13	5	5	1	5
Con win by 1–200 votes	12	11	3	7	3	1
Con lose by 1–200 votes	4	13	5	4	1	5
Con lose by 201–400 votes	5	6	3	5	1	3
Con lose by 401–600 votes	6	9	5	8	2	2
Con lose by 601–800 votes	8	12	5	6	3	2
Con lose by 801–1000 votes	7	10	5	7	2	6
Total no. of marginal seats	67	98	48	61	19	42

Between the two world wars, the Conservative Party gained its best results in the general elections with a high proportion of 'two-way' contests, where it faced only one candidate from another major party. It did less well when there were more 'three-way' contests, where both a Liberal and a Labour candidate stood against the Conservative. In some constituencies, there were also candidacies from minor parties or independents, but these were almost always electorally negligible and are not counted in this analysis—it was the presence or absence of the three main parties of Conservatives, Liberals, and Labour, in different combinations, which was significant. In particular, the Conservative Party benefited from 'two-way' contests with Labour, especially on occasions when an emphasis upon anti-Socialism would attract support from voters who were not customarily Conservatives: there were 219 such 'straight fights' in 1924, but only seventy-seven in 1929. Coalition arrangements with all or part of the Liberal Party maximized this effect in 1918, 1931, and 1935; the peak of 341 'two-way' contests with Labour in 1931 contributed substantially to the scale of the Conservative landslide. There was some legacy from

---

[146] Clarke to Director of CRD, 'By-election results', 28 November 1938, CPA, CRD/1/7/35.

the 1918 Coalition pact in 1922, when the high level of 'two-way' fights included eighty-six constituencies which the Conservatives did not contest; this was mostly where they were weak and the Liberal was thought to have the best chance of defeating Labour.

'Three-way' contests were a particular feature of the period between the coalitions in 1922–29. The incidence of such contests was a symptom of the health of the Liberal Party: when it was weak or divided, the number of Liberal candidates fell, but when it was united and had a sense of purpose—as in 1923 and 1929—then three-way fights reached their peaks. For the most part, this was a disadvantage to the Conservatives: they tended to gain more than Labour from the absence of a Liberal candidate, and so to lose more support when a Liberal was nominated. In many cases, when combined with a strong Labour campaign, this tipped the balance and ousted the Conservative MP. The experience of Cuthbert Headlam in the highly marginal seat of Barnard Castle was typical: combining part of the Durham coalfield with Pennine valleys in which Nonconformity remained strong, it was winnable in straight fights with Labour when the latter were on the defensive in 1924 and 1931, but was lost when a Liberal intervened in 1929 and 1935. Where a constituency was contested by all three of the main parties, very often the winner secured less than 50 per cent of the poll. Whilst a margin of one vote over the second-placed candidate was all that was required for victory, holding a seat on the basis of a minority of the votes cast was always an insecure position.

Table 2.15. Three-way and two-way 'major party' contests 1922–1931

This table analyses all of the single-Member constituencies in England, Scotland, and Wales. A three-way contest has candidates from the Conservative, Labour, and Liberal parties, and a two-way contest has candidates from any two of these; minor parties and independents are not counted. A minority of the vote is less than a 50 per cent share of the votes cast.

	1922	1923	1924	1929	1931
Three-way contests	184	245	219	453	54
No. Con seats won on a minority	84	88	81	151	13
% Con seats won on a minority	24.4	34.1	19.7	58.1	2.8
No. Con second places	52	100	38	186	4
Two-way contests	310	280	318	109	429
of Con & Lab only	120	105	219	77	341
of Con & Lib only	104	122	53	16	34
of Lab & Lib only	86	53	46	16	54

The general election of December 1918 was a confused and hurried affair, being called immediately after the armistice in November and with polling set for mid-December. It was a leap in the dark in many ways, with the hugely increased electorate—including women over the age of thirty—created by the 1918 Reform Act; it was also the first occasion on which all constituencies polled on the same day. The campaign was dominated by the issues of the war and the personality of

Lloyd George, and the outcome was marked by the low turnout of only 57.2 per cent. Uncertain of the domestic political and economic environment, and facing the challenges of peacemaking and reconstruction in Europe, the Conservative leadership considered that continuing the Coalition with Lloyd George was the safest and wisest course to follow. The result was an agreement on seats, with 145 Liberal supporters of Lloyd George given the Coalition's endorsement—derisorily termed the 'coupon' by Asquith. In eighteen other constituencies, mainly in working-class industrial districts, candidates of the National Democratic Party were recognized as the Coalition standard-bearers. However, as a united and major force within the Coalition, it was the Conservative Party which received the lion's share of the 'coupons', some 362 in all. The deal on seats was sanctioned by the Conservative leaders and supported by Central Office as far as its influence ran, although with residual reluctance. This was similarly reflected by the Conservative associations, who nominated a total of forty-three 'uncouponed' candidates, mainly against sitting Liberals whose pre war or wartime attitude had left a legacy of friction and lack of confidence. The strength of the Conservative appeal is underlined by the fact that twenty-five of these unsanctioned candidates were victorious, including Alexander Sprot, who defeated Asquith in the modified East Fife constituency (where no coupon had been issued).

Table 2.16. Patterns of Conservative contests in the 1918 general election

The university seats and Northern Ireland are not included (for definitions of the regions, see Appendix 3). The party abbreviations are CoL (Lloyd George or couponed Liberal), L (Asquithian or uncouponed Liberal), and Lab (Labour). Unopposed returns of Conservative candidates are not included.

Region	'Couponed' Conservatives			'Uncouponed' Conservatives			
	won	lost to L	lost to Lab	won	lost to CoL	lost to L	lost to Lab
London	35	2	–	2	4	–	1
Home Counties N	31	–	–	1	1	–	–
Home Counties S	32	–	–	1	–	–	–
South Central	20	1	–	–	1	–	–
South-West	19	1	–	–	–	1	–
East	16	1	1	–	1	–	–
Midlands East	9	2	–	1	–	–	–
Midlands West	25	–	3	–	–	–	1
Yorkshire	20	1	3	2	–	–	–
Tyneside	8	–	1	2	–	–	1
North-West	40	–	6	11	–	–	2
Wales Industrial	1	–	1	3	2	1	–
Wales Rural	–	–	–	–	–	–	–
Scotland South	25	1	4	1	–	1	–
Scotland North	2	1	–	1	–	–	–
TOTAL	283	10	19	25	9	3	5

Table 2.17. The economic and social profile of Conservative gains and losses in the general election of 1922

This table analyses the boroughs (including double-Member boroughs) and county divisions in England which can be exactly matched to the geographical units used in the occupation tables of the 1931 census. For the seats in this sample which the Conservative Party gained or lost in 1922, it shows the percentage of the total 'occupied' in each category in 1931 (for the methodology and definitions of the categories, see Appendix 2). Gains and losses are assessed in comparison to the previous general election result, and do not take account of intervening by-elections. The regional columns are: Southern England (South), Midland and East England (Midland), and Northern England (North); for definitions of the regions, see Appendix 3. Wales is not included as there was only one gain that matches exactly to the census units, which is too small a sample.

Occupation	Gains from all parties			Losses to all parties		
	South	Midland	North	South	Midland	North
Agriculture	10.3	15.4	4.8	11.6	15.5	3.1
Mining	0.7	3.6	3.3	0.6	0.4	5.9
Metal Industries	6.5	9.4	7.6	5.3	8.9	8.5
Construction	6.2	6.2	4.4	6.6	5.9	4.0
Light Industries	6.9	5.2	4.6	7.4	5.6	4.7
Textiles & Clothing	4.1	12.7	26.4	4.0	6.9	24.4
Service & Leisure	16.1	10.1	9.2	16.9	13.4	8.2
Commerce & Finance	11.8	8.9	10.2	11.9	10.5	9.4
Clerical	6.8	4.6	4.7	9.1	5.4	4.9
Professional	4.6	3.3	3.1	5.4	3.7	2.8
No. of constituencies	10	12	10	12	7	18

Although the Coalition was brought to an end as an agreed national partnership in October 1922, the sudden shift to Conservative independence and the local electoral landscape led to the continuance of some pacts with the Liberals, particularly in the double-Member constituencies.[147] These were mostly with sitting Coalition Liberal MPs who were regarded as having fulfilled their pledges of 1918, and were a particular feature in Scotland and industrial areas in Yorkshire.[148] In other cases, local Conservative associations were unable to find a candidate in time and did not contest the seat for that reason rather than any reluctance to do so. The party entered the election defending the gains of 1918 and did well in scoring a net loss of only thirty-eight seats. However, there was more electoral turbulence than this outcome might suggest, as a number of gains (mainly from Lloyd George Liberals) offset some of the sixty-five actual losses in England, Scotland, and Wales. This gave Bonar Law's administration a secure working majority, but one resting on somewhat precarious foundations: eighty-four seats were won on a minority of

---

[147] This continued in Dundee to 1931, in Blackburn to 1929, and in Derby to 1923; it also operated in Norwich in 1922, 1924, and 1929.
[148] Renfrewshire West CA, Exec., 26 October 1922.

the vote in three-way contests with both Liberals and Labour, and 10 per cent of Conservative MPs had a majority of under 800 votes. The losses were particularly heavy in Scotland, where the thirty seats won in 1918 were reduced to just thirteen; it is not surprising that support for continuing the Coalition had been strong there, and that the Scottish Whip (who was in charge of the party headquarters in Edinburgh) had taken a pro-Coalition line, in contrast to his colleagues at the Central Office in London.

In the early 1920s, the Labour Party advanced to become the dominant force in the working-class constituencies of the cities and larger towns; this absorbed some seats which had been Conservative before 1914, particularly in London and parts of Lancashire, but was much more at the expense of the Liberal Party. As early as the 1922 general election, Labour had become the leading challenger in two of the Conservatives' key regions of support, the south-east and the West Midlands, and had almost done so in the north-west; in addition, Labour won more seats than the Liberals in these regions. However, the latter's larger number of second places in 1923 and 1929 should not be seen as a sign of strength, for the Labour Party was winning significantly more first places—especially in 1929, when the Liberal performance was, in fact, testimony to the failure of Lloyd George's attempt at revival, and confirmation of third-party status. The 1924 general election was critical in this process, with the Liberal Party remaining the leading challenger in only three of its former stronghold regions: the south-west, eastern England, and rural Wales. Even so, a Liberal came second in 138 cases in 1924, and this underlines the continuing threat which they posed to Conservative fortunes, especially in the areas outside the large industrial conurbations: between 1918 and 1929 the Liberals won at least once in a total of 281 seats—only slightly fewer than Labour's figure of 304.[149] However, most of the Liberal victories occurred in 1918 (as Coalitionists), 1922, and—particularly—1923, when they won over half of the rural seats (including some which they had not even gained in 1906). The 1924 general election was a major setback for the Liberals, and Lloyd George's unsuccessful attempt at revival in 1929 showed that they were now definitely the minor party of the main three, with all the problems and pressures which that position entailed.

During the 1920s, the disappearance of denominational issues from the political spotlight and the Christian ethic and moral tone of Baldwin's moderate appeal encouraged the drift of middle-class Nonconformity towards Conservatism. This particularly advantaged the Conservative Party in 1924 in the constituencies where no Liberal candidate was nominated: as Table 2.19 shows, the Conservatives polled significantly ahead of Labour in the seats where Nonconformists had comprised 2.5–14.9 per cent of the voters in 1922, and were still slightly ahead even in the highest category (the low figure for the 15.0–17.4 per cent category is derived from only one constituency); a similar pattern was apparent in 1931, when the levels of Conservative support were even higher. By the end of the 1920s, a higher proportion of Nonconformists in a constituency no longer automatically produced a

[149] Kinnear, *The British Voter*, 84.

Table 2.18. The challengers in the Conservative-held constituencies 1922–1929

This table shows the second-placed party in the seats which the Conservative Party won in each election; in the case of the double-Member constituencies where the Conservatives won one or both seats, the highest-placed non-Conservative candidate is counted. The leading challenging party in each region is shown in bold. Liberal followers of Asquith and Lloyd George have been treated as one party. 'Independent Liberal' and 'Independent Labour' candidates are not counted. The university seats and Northern Ireland are not included (for definitions of the regions, see Appendix 3).

Region	1922 Labour	1922 Liberal	1923 Labour	1923 Liberal	1924 Labour	1924 Liberal	1929 Labour	1929 Liberal
London	20	16	14	9	31	3	18	4
Home Counties N	21	12	12	10	25	12	13	13
Home Counties S	17	11	11	16	25	10	14	18
South Central	10	16	10	7	16	15	5	21
South-West	5	14	4	4	6	20	1	15
East	9	9	5	7	11	16	6	10
Midlands East	9	4	3	7	15	6	4	4
Midlands West	17	9	12	13	22	9	13	7
Yorkshire	5	12	7	10	15	8	8	7
Tyneside	2	4	2	4	6	4	1	4
North-West	20	22	9	16	39	20	16	15
Wales Industrial	3	2	2	2	6	–	–	1
Wales Rural	–	–	–	–	–	3	–	–
Scotland South	6	5	6	2	21	5	10	2
Scotland North	–	2	1	3	3	7	3	5
TOTAL	144	138	98	110	241	138	112	126

lower Conservative share of the poll. As the analysis in Table 2.19 of the 'three-way' contests in 1929 demonstrates, in that election the Conservative vote was slightly higher in the seats where Nonconformists had comprised 12.5–17.4 per cent of the electorate in 1922 than it was where they had been 0–4.9 per cent; only in the handful of seats with more than 17.5 per cent Nonconformists did it tail off, and that was as much due to regional economic and cultural factors as it was to religious denomination. However, Liberal candidates still had a residual appeal to Nonconformity; when they stood, they were likely to draw away support, and the data for the 'three-way' contests in 1929 demonstrate a clearer relationship between Nonconformity and Liberal voting than it does with Conservative support.

The general election of December 1923 was called unexpectedly as a result of Baldwin's adoption of a protectionist programme. The campaign was dominated by the Edwardian controversy between tariff reform and free trade; defending the latter reunited and re-energized the Liberal Party, and presented it with the opportunity of fighting an election on the historic issue upon which its identity was most closely based, eclipsing even the pro-free-trade Labour Party. The

Table 2.19. Nonconformity and Conservative electoral support[150]

For the constituencies in England (excluding London, cities of five or more parliamentary divisions, Salford, and the county divisions of Middlesex), the number of Nonconformists in 1922 has been calculated as a proportion of the electorate in 1922. The top section shows the average Conservative vote in the 1924 general election in the constituencies in each band which were contested by the Conservative and Labour parties but where no Liberal candidate stood. The middle section shows the average Conservative and Liberal vote in the 1929 general election in the constituencies in each band which were contested by all three of the major parties. The lower section shows the average Conservative vote in the 1931 general election in the constituencies in each band which were contested by the Conservative and Labour parties but where no Liberal candidate stood. In all sections, for the towns of two to four divisions, the per cent vote is calculated from only the constituencies which match the particular pattern of contest.

Nonconformists as a % of the electorate in 1922	0– 2.4	2.5– 4.9	5.0– 7.4	7.5– 9.9	10.0– 12.4	12.5– 14.9	15.0– 17.4	17.5 & above
1924 Con & Lab contests:								
no. of constituencies	11	24	35	24	19	5	1	4
Con. % vote	47.6	58.9	57.7	54.4	55.4	64.2	37.0	51.3
1929 'three-way' contests:								
no. of constituencies	6	44	74	74	61	19	13	9
Con. % vote	36.3	40.8	41.8	38.7	36.4	41.3	36.5	33.3
Liberal % vote	17.6	23.9	25.2	28.0	25.4	33.2	35.0	30.5
1931 Con & Lab contests:								
no. of constituencies	11	32	54	50	43	10	5	5
Con. % vote	56.3	68.9	67.5	65.8	65.6	70.6	62.2	58.2

Conservative campaign was marked by confusion as to which categories of imports (especially food and raw materials) would be taxed and how, and by individual candidates giving conflicting pledges on this according to the particular pressures in their constituencies.[151] The overall result was an unmistakeable defeat, with the net loss of eighty-eight seats eliminating the government's overall majority, although the Conservatives still remained the largest party in the House of Commons. Of the 108 defeats, only forty-one were to Labour—the remaining sixty-seven were to the Liberals. The losses to Labour were part of the process of that party's increasing dominance in the iron, steel, and engineering industrial areas, although some of Labour's gains in southern England had a noticeably higher middle-class profile. The Conservative Party generally performed well in the rural seats, but lost ground to the Liberals in some agricultural districts in the

---

[150] From data in Kinnear, *British Voter*, 125–8: Salford is excluded because it is not shown separately, but combined with Manchester; for reasons which are not given, there is no information for the county divisions of Middlesex.

[151] C. Cook, *The Age of Alignment: Electoral Politics in Britain 1922–1929* (1975), 142–3.

south and the Midlands, in textile towns in the Midlands and especially the north, and in the middle-class constituencies generally. The latter trend was largely attributed to the loss of women's votes due to concern about dearer food; as one London candidate noted, 'we knew women were "Conservative", and in this case they voted true to type'—against a radical change.[152] However, many of the Liberal gains had only small majorities in three-cornered fights, and would be easily recoverable when the Conservatives had a less controversial policy and a better-prepared organization. Indeed, it was a sign of the vulnerability of many Liberal constituencies that even in this defeat, the Conservatives gained fifteen seats from sitting Liberal MPs—but only three seats were won from Labour. Table 2.20 provides a comparative analysis of the fifty-one constituencies lost to the Liberals and the nineteen lost to Labour which can be matched exactly to the census units. These seats account for 76 per cent of the total Conservative losses to Liberals and 46 per cent of the losses to Labour, the latter figure being lower because more of these losses were in divided boroughs, where the separate constituencies cannot be exactly matched with the census data. The table also includes fourteen of the fifteen gains from the Liberals, but omits the gains from Labour as being too few to be statistically meaningful.

The general election of October 1924, which followed the short-lived first Labour government, was a major victory for the Conservatives, and was the only single-party landslide victory in the interwar period. The role in this of the famous 'Zinoviev letter', a document published in the Conservative press which apparently revealed instructions from the Bolshevik 'Third International' in Moscow that British Communists should seek to subvert the trade unions and the Labour Party, should not be overrated. It appeared late in the campaign, and the party which suffered heavily at the poll was not Labour but the Liberals. The key factor was Liberal division and lowering of morale since the decision in January 1924 to support Labour taking office, which caused organizational decline and a sharp fall in the number of Liberal candidates, from 457 in 1923 to 359 less than a year later. The reduction in the number of three-cornered contests greatly benefited the Conservative Party, as there were 219 straight fights with Labour compared with only 105 in 1923. When this was combined with the alarm of many non-Labour voters regarding the advent of a Socialist government, the dropping by the Conservatives of the unpopular protectionist programme of 1923, and the increasing prominence of Baldwin as a moderate and attractive Conservative Leader, it produced a landslide victory. The number of Conservative MPs elected was 412, together with seven anti-Socialist 'Constitutionalists' who had the support of the local Conservative associations in their constituencies; one of these was Churchill, who took the Conservative whip immediately after the election, on being appointed Chancellor of the Exchequer. Taken together, this amounted to a net increase of 161 seats; in fact, as seven seats had been lost to Labour and one of the university seats to an independent, there were 169 actual

---

[152] Sir Daniel Keymer in Metropolitan Area report on the general election, Jessel (London Whip) to Jackson, 17 December 1923, CPA, ARE/1/29/1.

Table 2.20. The economic and social profile of the Conservative gains and losses in the general election of 1923

This table analyses the boroughs (including double-Member boroughs) and county divisions in England which can be exactly matched to the geographical units in the occupation tables of the 1931 census. For the seats in this sample which the Conservative Party gained or lost in 1922, it shows the percentage of the total 'occupied' in each category in 1931 (for the methodology and definitions of the categories, see Appendix 2). Gains and losses are assessed in comparison to the previous general election result, and do not take account of intervening by-elections. Gains from Labour are not included as there was only one of these that matched exactly to the census units, which is too small a sample; Wales is not included as the two losses (in divisions of Cardiff) do not match exactly to census units. The regional columns are: Southern England (South), Midland and East England (Midland), and Northern England (North); for definitions of the regions, see Appendix 3.

Occupation	Gains from Lib	Losses to Liberals			Losses to Labour		
		South	Midland	North	South	Midland	North
Agriculture	9.8	14.8	18.3	4.7	6.5	10.0	1.8
Mining	2.7	1.2	5.2	2.0	1.3	1.8	7.6
Metal Industries	6.2	4.3	7.3	6.1	7.6	15.3	12.0
Construction	5.1	6.9	5.7	4.5	6.1	6.1	4.8
Light Industries	5.0	7.2	4.9	4.9	8.9	7.3	4.6
Textiles & Clothing	18.6	3.9	13.3	21.4	3.4	10.1	17.9
Service & Leisure	9.9	18.2	10.3	13.0	12.5	10.5	8.4
Commerce & Finance	10.1	10.9	8.7	11.9	10.5	9.7	9.4
Clerical	6.0	5.9	4.4	5.8	8.5	6.3	4.8
Professional	3.4	5.2	3.3	3.7	4.1	3.3	2.9
No. of constituencies	14	25	12	14	9	5	5

gains by Conservative and Constitutionalist candidates. Two of these were from Irish Nationalists in Ulster and one of the mainland gains was from an independent; of the remainder, two-thirds (111) were from the Liberals and one-third (fifty-five) from Labour, with forty of the latter resulting from straight fights. The geographical pattern of the 166 gains from the two main opposition parties is assessed in Table 2.21, and the economic and social composition of those constituencies which can be precisely matched to the census data is explored in Table 2.22.

Gains from the Labour Party were only made on a significant scale in north-west England, southern Scotland, and the Home Counties, although in some of the more agricultural regions of southern and eastern England this was largely because at this time Labour had few seats to defend in these areas. More noticeable is the resilience of Labour strength in three key regions: Wales, north-east England (which includes Yorkshire), and the West Midlands. In contrast, the Liberal Party collapsed in every region apart from Wales, and was left with only ten seats in England south of the Cheshire–Yorkshire border: seven in the whole of southern England, and one seat in each of

Table 2.21. The regional pattern of Conservative gains in the general election of 1924

This table examines the 166 Conservative and Constitutionalist gains from the Labour and Liberal parties in England, Scotland, and Wales; gains are assessed in comparison to the previous general election result, and do not take account of intervening by-elections. The regional columns are: London (Lon), Home Counties (HC), South Central England (SC), South-West England (SW), East England (East), East Midlands (EM), West Midlands (WM), North-East England (NE), North-West England (NW), Wales (Wal), Scotland South (ScS), and Scotland North (ScN); for definitions of the regions, see Appendix 3.

Gained from	Regions											
	Lon	HC	SC	SW	East	EM	WM	NE	NW	Wal	ScS	ScN
Labour	5	9	1	1	4	4	3	4	11	1	12	–
Liberal	6	9	12	17	11	6	5	7	23	4	5	6
TOTAL	11	18	13	18	15	10	8	11	34	5	17	6

Table 2.22. The economic and social profile of Conservative gains in the general election of 1924

This table analyses the boroughs (including double-Member boroughs) and county divisions in England and Wales which can be exactly matched to the geographical units used in the occupation tables of the 1931 census. For the seats in this sample gained by Conservative and Constitutionalist candidates in 1924, it shows the percentage of the total 'occupied' in each category in 1931 (for the methodology and definitions of the categories, see Appendix 2). Gains are assessed in comparison to the previous general election result, and do not take account of intervening by-elections. The regional columns are: London (Lon), Home Counties (HC), South Central England (SC), South-West England (SW), East England (East), East Midlands (EM), West Midlands (WM), North-East England (NE), North-West England (NW), and Wales (Wal); for definitions of the regions, see Appendix 3.

Occupation	Regions									
	Lon	HC	SC	SW	East	EMid	WMid	NE	NW	Wal
Agriculture	0.4	9.8	14.9	19.2	23.4	5.3	6.5	5.9	3.1	20.1
Mining	–	0.3	0.6	3.3	0.3	4.7	8.2	9.6	1.8	8.5
Metal Industries	7.7	5.9	5.7	3.7	5.4	8.0	16.6	10.7	7.9	5.1
Construction	5.0	6.8	6.8	6.7	5.8	5.4	6.0	5.1	4.2	5.5
Light Industries	9.6	9.1	6.4	5.4	5.4	5.7	7.1	4.3	5.3	3.5
Textiles & Clothing	6.4	2.3	4.5	3.9	8.3	26.2	6.3	9.0	21.6	3.4
Service & Leisure	13.0	15.2	16.9	18.3	12.5	8.4	9.6	10.6	10.8	13.5
Commerce & Finance	11.1	11.7	9.9	10.9	10.5	8.8	8.7	9.4	11.2	9.7
Clerical	11.9	9.8	5.1	3.8	4.5	5.9	6.1	4.5	6.2	2.8
Professional	4.6	5.2	4.8	4.9	3.5	3.1	3.3	3.5	3.3	4.6
Persons per acre	32.2	1.0	0.5	0.3	0.4	1.1	1.0	0.6	2.3	0.2
Persons per room	1.0	0.8	0.8	0.7	0.7	0.8	0.9	1.0	0.8	0.8
No. of constituencies	2	14	12	18	15	6	7	8	22	3

eastern England, the East Midlands, and the West Midlands. The general election of 1924 left the Liberals isolated and dependent primarily on three regions, two of which were at the periphery: Wales (ten seats), northern Scotland (six seats), and north-east England (seven seats). This was the crucial blow in the Liberal decline, and its effects were rendered more damaging by the fact that, in contrast to the turmoil of the previous two years, there was not to be another election for four and a half years.

After three general elections in just under two years, there was a much longer gap until the next contest, in May 1929. As noted earlier, this took place at an expected time, near the end of the parliament and without any overshadowing crisis, and the campaign was uneventful. With Lloyd George as its dynamic if controversial Leader, with an infusion of money from his political fund, with new interventionist policies to tackle unemployment and a radical land programme, it was the re-energized Liberal Party which was the more directly dangerous competitor to the Conservatives in 1929.[153] It is therefore not surprising that Conservative strategy was focused more on attacking Lloyd George than Ramsay MacDonald; this was not misconceived paranoia over Coalitionism, but a clear recognition of how the Conservative majority might be undermined—as indeed occurred. A total of 513 Liberal candidates were nominated—the highest number for that party in any election between 1906 and 1974—and, combined with the further growth of the Labour Party, this resulted in the peak of 453 three-party contests, and only seventy-seven Conservatives enjoying a straight fight with Labour. Many Conservative MPs lost their seats, as a significant number of 'old Liberals' who had then supported them were drawn back to their former allegiance by the presence of a Liberal standard-bearer.[154] As a result, many Conservatives bitterly blamed 'the unnecessary and futile intervention' of Liberal candidates for the party's defeat,[155] although there was also a strong undercurrent of dissatisfaction, particularly at local level, with Baldwin's moderate manifesto and a perceived lack of consultation with the rank and file, which emerged in the post-election inquest and fed into the internal crisis of 1929–31.[156]

Although the 1929 election was a defeat for the Conservatives in the short term, the danger of a Liberal revival had been contained. The Liberals secured only 23.6 per cent of the national vote; despite winning thirty-four Conservative seats, they lost fifteen to Labour and came out of the contest with a mere nineteen net gains and the election of only fifty-nine Liberal MPs. However, the party which benefited immediately from this was Labour, which for the first time became the largest single party in the House of Commons, with 287 MPs to the 260 Conservatives, and thus formed its second—but again minority—administration; as in 1923, the Liberals held the parliamentary balance, and they were again to find it an uncomfortable, unpopular, and divisive role. The Conservative

---

[153] Joynson-Hicks to Ashley, 31 May 1929, Ashley MSS, BR/77.
[154] Stigant (chairman, Rochester & Chatham CA) to Salisbury, October 1929, Salisbury MSS, S(4)131/95–98.
[155] Deputy Director of Publicity to Party Chairman, 11 June 1929, Baldwin MSS, 37/2; Bridgeman to his son, 1 June 1929, Bridgeman diary.
[156] Ball, *Baldwin and the Conservative Party*, 31–3, 220–1.

Party made one gain from Labour in 1929, but lost 160 of the 419 seats that had been won by the 412 Conservative MPs and the seven Constitutionalists in 1924. Two of the losses were to Irish Nationalists in Ulster, and two were to independents in England; of the remainder, thirty-four seats (21.8 per cent) were lost to the Liberals and 122 (78.2 per cent) to Labour. In addition, due to the large number of three-way contests, many of those which the Conservatives had held were retained on a minority vote (see Table 2.15). However, a two-way contest did not necessarily mean that a seat was safe: of the fourteen constituencies in England and Wales where the absence of a Labour candidate resulted in a straight fight between Conservatives and Liberals, the Liberals won two of the English dozen (Eddisbury and Harwich, where the vote was partly split by an Independent Conservative candidate) and both of the Welsh pair (Cardiganshire and Denbighshire). During this period of three-party rivalry, the pattern in many marginal seats was for them to be held by the Conservatives in 1922, lost to a Liberal in 1923, recovered in the 1924 landslide, and lost to Labour in 1929—in the latter instance, this affected both rural, mixed urban/rural, and the smaller industrial towns of northern England. Even so, the Liberal danger could not be dismissed, for in 1929 in many constituencies the Liberal was the challenger in second place to the Conservative MP (see Table 2.18).

Table 2.23. The regional pattern of Conservative losses in the general election of 1929

This table examines the 156 losses to the Labour and Liberal parties in England, Scotland, and Wales; losses are assessed in comparison to the previous general election result, and do not take account of intervening by-elections. The regional columns are: London (Lon), Home Counties (HC), South Central England (SC), South-West England (SW), East England (East), East Midlands (EM), West Midlands (WM), North-East England (NE), North-West England (NW), Wales (Wal), Scotland South (ScS), and Scotland North (ScN); for definitions of the regions, see Appendix 3.

Lost to	Regions											
	Lon	HC	SC	SW	East	EM	WM	NE	NW	Wal	ScS	ScN
Labour	15	12	6	2	3	10	15	18	24	6	11	–
Liberal	–	2	–	7	8	2	1	–	7	2	3	2
TOTAL	15	14	6	9	11	12	16	18	31	8	14	2

The Liberal revival was a particular failure in southern England and the Midlands: apart from the success of winning all five seats in Cornwall and three others in the south-west, they emerged from the campaign with only four seats in the rest of the south, and four in the East and West Midlands. In addition to the south-west, the Liberals made their largest advances in eastern England, where they had strong roots in some agricultural areas, and in the north-west, which was again the most volatile region. However, the nearly complete absence of Liberal MPs from large swathes of the country undermined any credibility in their future as a major party and challenger for government. The opposite was the case for Labour, as they became, for the first time, the largest single party in the House of Commons, following significant gains in the south-east, the Midlands, and in the urban and industrial regions of northern England and southern Scotland. The Labour Party formed its second minority government, and was on the crest of a wave during the six months after the election; it was only twenty-one seats short of a bare overall majority, and during this period the Conservatives were nervous that Labour might call a sudden election and achieve power without the safety of any parliamentary restraint. However, the onset of the depression and steep rise in unemployment during 1930 eroded Labour's standing, and the 1929 result was to prove its high-water mark in the interwar era.

Table 2.24. The economic and social profile of Conservative losses in the general election of 1929

This table analyses the boroughs (including double-Member boroughs) and county divisions in England and Wales which can be exactly matched to the geographical units used in the occupation tables of the 1931 census. For the seats in this sample which the Conservative Party lost in 1929, it shows the percentage of the total 'occupied' in each category in 1931 (for the methodology and definitions of the categories, see Appendix 2). The level of unemployment is the number of persons aged fourteen and over who were classified as 'out of work' as a percentage of the number classified as 'occupied' in the 1931 census. Losses are assessed in comparison to the previous general election result, and do not take account of intervening by-elections. The regional columns are: London (Lon), Home Counties (HC), South Central England (SC), South-West England (SW), East England (East), East Midlands (EM), West Midlands (WM), North-East England (NE), North-West England (NW), and Wales (Wal); for definitions of the regions, see Appendix 3.

Occupation	Regions									
	Lon	HC	SC	SW	East	EM	WM	NE	NW	Wal
Agriculture	0.5	7.0	1.8	17.5	23.4	6.7	4.9	3.4	3.0	12.7
Mining	–	0.2	0.1	5.2	0.4	9.2	7.4	8.3	2.2	5.3
Metal Industries	9.9	7.1	10.0	4.4	5.8	8.2	19.2	13.0	8.2	6.8
Construction	5.3	6.9	5.8	6.6	5.8	5.8	6.4	5.6	3.9	5.4
Light Industries	8.6	8.5	7.8	5.4	5.1	5.1	6.6	5.7	5.0	4.0
Textiles & Clothing	3.4	2.4	2.6	3.0	9.2	18.9	6.2	6.2	27.2	2.8
Service & Leisure	12.4	12.5	13.3	16.3	11.5	9.0	8.7	11.2	7.7	13.6
Commerce & Finance	8.7	11.3	13.1	11.6	10.1	8.7	8.8	10.5	9.6	11.3
Clerical	10.3	10.5	8.6	4.1	4.3	5.7	5.9	5.1	5.4	4.8
Professional	4.9	4.2	3.8	4.6	3.5	3.2	3.0	3.6	2.8	4.7
Persons per acre	26.1	1.4	8.2	0.4	0.4	0.9	1.4	1.6	2.7	0.3
Persons per room	1.0	0.9	0.8	0.7	0.7	0.8	0.9	1.0	0.9	0.8
% unemployed in 1931	9.9	7.6	10.1	8.2	8.9	9.1	12.4	20.5	17.5	14.4
No. of constituencies	1	7	3	9	11	9	8	10	21	5

Between the autumn of 1929 and the spring of 1931, the preoccupation of the Conservative Party with its internal divisions prevented it from making much capital from the increasing difficulties and ineffectiveness of the second Labour government. The improvement in Conservative fortunes was mainly due to the impact of the world depression and the rapid increase in unemployment, which rose from 1.5 million in January 1930 to 2.7 million a year later. From the autumn of 1930, there were signs of a shift of public opinion in the urban and industrial constituencies, especially in the Midlands and the north of England.[157] These were the seats which had been lost in 1929 that the Conservatives needed to regain in order to secure a majority in the House of Commons, and for the first time it seemed that the party's favoured policies of a full protectionist programme and cutting back on government spending were proving attractive to the beleaguered and bewildered urban working class. By-election results from April to June 1931 in a number of northern urban constituencies showed a significant increase in the Conservative share of the vote, pointing to a probable election victory on a similar scale to 1924. As parliament rose for the summer recess, negotiations were in progress with a breakaway section of Liberal MPs led by Sir John Simon, which gave a good prospect of defeating the government in the House of Commons when it reassembled.

Instead, the financial crisis of August 1931 changed the political landscape: it caused the collapse of the Labour government, but brought the Conservatives into office in a subordinate role in an emergency 'National' government of leading figures from all three parties, with Ramsay MacDonald remaining in office as Prime Minister. Largely at Conservative insistence, its role was intended to be limited and for the emergency period only, but during September 1931 further setbacks forced the abandonment of the gold standard and made it increasingly necessary for the government to demonstrate to the world that it had popular support. After some manoeuvring, mainly over the position of the Liberal Party and the Conservative determination to permit no encroachment upon their freedom to put forward their tariff policy, the government called a general election for 27 October. This was fought as a coalition under the National banner, albeit with separate party programmes under the vague overall proposal of securing a 'doctor's mandate' to take whatever steps were necessary.

The general election of October 1931 was entirely shaped and dominated by the financial crisis which preceded it. The overriding aim for the Conservatives was to ensure the defeat of the Labour Party, almost all of whom had rejected MacDonald as a traitor and had gone into opposition, vehemently denouncing the National Government. In order to achieve this, the Conservative Party did not contest ten of the eleven constituencies held by MacDonald's handful of National Labour MPs (the local association insisted upon fighting Liverpool Everton, and won by a majority of 4,400 against both the National Labour former MP and a Labour candidate), or thirty-seven of the fifty-six constituencies still held by the Liberal Party. In return, the Liberals withdrew in many of the other constituencies; only forty-one Liberal National members of Simon's group (most of whom were sitting MPs) were nominated, together with 111 candidates who followed Samuel, the acting-Leader of the Liberal Party, and six Independent Liberals (four of whom were members of Lloyd George's family group, who opposed the National Government). The result was a sharp fall in the number of three-way contests, and it was

---

[157] Sowerby CA, Exec., 26 September, 28 November 1930.

Portrait of a Party

Table 2.25. Conservative gains in the general election of 1931

This table gives the overall pattern of the 210 gains in England, Scotland, and Wales; gains are assessed in comparison to the previous general election result, and do not take account of intervening by-elections. The regional columns are: London (Lon), Home Counties (HC), South Central England (SC), South-West England (SW), East England (East), East Midlands (EM), West Midlands (WM), North-East England (NE), North-West England (NW), Wales (Wal), Scotland South (ScS), and Scotland North (ScN); for definitions of the regions, see Appendix 3.

Gained from	Regions										
	Lon	HC	SC	SW	East	EM	WM	NE	NW	Wal	ScS	ScN
Labour	25	15	6	2	5	12	21	40	38	5	24	2
Liberal	–	1	–	3	1	1	1	–	4	–	1	1
Independent	–	–	–	1	–	–	–	–	1	–	–	–
TOTAL	25	16	6	6	6	13	22	40	43	5	25	3

Table 2.26. The economic and social profile of Conservative gains in the general election of 1931

This table analyses the boroughs in England and Wales (including double-Member boroughs), and county divisions which can be exactly matched to the geographical units used in the occupation tables of the 1931 census. For the seats in this sample which the Conservative Party gained in 1931, it shows the percentage of the total 'occupied' in each category in 1931 (for the methodology and definitions of the categories, see Appendix 2). The level of unemployment is the number of persons aged fourteen and over who were classified as 'out of work' as a percentage of the number classified as 'occupied' in the 1931 census. Gains are assessed in comparison to the previous general election result, and do not take account of intervening by-elections. The regional columns are: London (Lon), Home Counties (HC), South Central England (SC), South-West England (SW), East England (East), East Midlands (EM), West Midlands (WM), North-East England (NE), North-West England (NW), and Wales (Wal); for definitions of the regions, see Appendix 3.

Occupation	Regions								
	Lon	HC	SC	SW	East	EM	WM	NE	NW	Wal
Agriculture	0.3	4.3	2.1	10.7	16.5	5.7	3.9	3.4	1.8	9.3
Mining	–	0.1	0.1	6.2	0.7	9.7	7.4	14.5	3.4	5.5
Metal Industries	6.1	7.2	11.0	5.3	8.2	8.9	21.8	10.6	8.6	7.4
Construction	6.1	6.9	5.9	6.7	6.2	5.7	7.1	4.8	4.3	5.3
Light Industries	9.4	9.5	7.9	6.2	5.6	5.5	6.1	4.7	5.8	4.2
Textiles & Clothing	6.1	4.0	2.9	3.2	8.3	18.1	5.9	12.0	23.6	2.0
Service & Leisure	16.3	10.9	12.9	16.5	12.6	8.8	7.8	9.4	7.8	13.8
Commerce & Finance	11.2	11.7	12.9	12.8	10.6	8.9	8.4	9.5	9.6	12.1
Clerical	11.2	12.6	8.5	5.2	5.2	5.8	5.9	5.0	5.9	6.1
Professional	3.4	3.7	3.8	4.8	3.8	3.2	2.7	3.3	2.8	4.8
Persons per acre	65.3	2.3	6.4	0.8	0.5	0.5	1.8	1.7	4.0	0.3
Persons per room	1.1	0.9	0.8	0.7	0.7	0.8	0.8	1.0	0.9	0.8
% unemployed in 1931	10.5	8.0	9.1	9.4	10.2	9.9	12.6	15.3	15.8	14.5
No. of constituencies	13	11	3	5	6	10	12	23	24	3

this, as well as the issues and the crisis atmosphere of the election, which led to the unprecedented landslide victory of the National Government, which as a whole received 67.7 per cent of the overall vote and returned 558 MPs to Labour's remnant of only fifty-two. The Conservative Party was by far the greatest beneficiary of the coalition arrangement, winning a total of 470 seats with a 55 per cent share of the votes cast. Thirty-four of the 452 MPs from England, Scotland, and Wales were returned unopposed; as far as the presence of candidates of the main parties were concerned, 328 of the Conservative victories were in straight fights with Labour (in four of the double-Member seats, running jointly with a Liberal or National Labour candidate), thirty were in straight fights with a Liberal, twelve were in straight fights with an Independent Labour Party or Independent Labour candidate, and only forty-eight were in three-cornered contests (forty-seven against both Liberal and Labour candidates, and one against both an Independent Labour and a National Labour candidate).

Thirty-five of the forty-one Liberal National candidates were elected, mainly because only four of them had faced a Conservative opponent; in three cases, these were sitting MPs, two of whom were ousted by their Conservative challenger. The remainder of the Liberal Party had nothing like so easy a ride, despite Samuel (and not Simon) being one of the founders of the National Government and a member of its initial emergency Cabinet of ten. Although the Central Office made some efforts to persuade local Conservative associations and candidates to stand down in the wider 'national interest' in seats held by Samuelite Liberal MPs, in many places party feeling and hostility to the Liberal incumbent was too strong. Sixteen Conservative candidates ran against sitting Liberal MPs who were followers of Samuel or Lloyd George, and in nine cases they gained the seat; one of those opposed was Samuel himself at Darwen, although he held his ground. In total, eighty-four of the 109 Samuel and six Independent Liberal candidates in the English, Scottish, and Welsh constituencies were opposed by Conservatives, and in consequence only nine were successful. Thus, despite the advantages of being in the coalition, only thirty-two followers of Samuel were elected (including two in university seats), leaving them slightly behind the Simonites; there was also Lloyd George's group of four MPs, who stood aloof from both of the main Liberal sections. The Conservatives also won two seats that had elected a Liberal MP in 1929 but which that party did not contest in 1931, making an overall gain of thirteen, but this was a drop in the ocean compared to the 195 gains from the Labour Party. There was no change in the university seats or in Northern Ireland, but the Conservatives also gained two seats in England from MPs who had been sitting as Independents.

The Samuelite wing of the Liberal Party withdrew from the National Government when it adopted a full protectionist policy in September 1932, but the continuing participation of the Simonite 'Liberal Nationals' (who, together with 'National Labour', had a disproportionately large share of Cabinet places) meant that the government retained credibility as a cross-party alliance. The presence of MacDonald as Prime Minister until June 1935 and the moderate and centrist course of the government's policies at home and overseas gave the government a broader public appeal than any purely Conservative ministry could have had, and nearly all Conservative

MPs and the vast majority of the local membership were happy with—indeed, were reassured by—the continuance of this increasingly comfortable alliance. By 1935 the economic picture was definitely improving, although concentrations of unemployment remained in some areas most dependent on the traditional 'smokestack' industries, particularly shipbuilding. Baldwin exchanged offices with MacDonald and became Prime Minister after the Royal Jubilee in June 1935, and in October he took advantage of some disarray within the Labour Party and called an election for mid-November. Although Baldwin sought, in carefully unalarming terms, a mandate for some rearmament and the international situation played a larger part than in any election since 1918, nevertheless it was the domestic economic situation which had most impact. The National Government had little difficulty in showing evidence of steady improvement since it took office, whilst Labour's credibility still suffered from its failure in 1929–31. The core Labour vote had remained substantial in 1931 at 6.6 million votes, and it now recovered to 8.3 million votes and 38.0 per cent of the poll. This was almost the same number and share of the votes as in 1929, but whereas then the three-way fights in many seats had led to 287 Labour victories, in 1935 only 154 Labour MPs were elected. A significant factor in this was the falling away of the opposition Samuelite Liberals, who ran only 161 candidates, securing a mere 6.7 per cent of the vote and twenty-one MPs. The National Government cruised to a comfortable victory and retained a substantial majority: the Conservative Party obtained 47.8 per cent of the votes and won 387 seats, and its partners returned a further forty-two MPs to give a total of 429. A notable feature was the retention of support in southern England and the Midlands, where the economic recovery was more apparent. Despite the unprecedented scale of the 1931 victory, the Conservative Party lost only twenty seats in the south (eleven of which were in London) and only thirteen in the Midlands and eastern counties, and it was in these regions that any Labour revival was decisively blocked (see Table 2.27).

In the later 1930s, the indications from by-elections, local elections, and opinion polling (which began in 1937) all pointed towards another victory for the National Government, if there had been a peacetime election in 1940. In May 1939, the Home Secretary, Sir Samuel Hoare, believed that 'if there was an election, it looks as if the majority would not be much altered'.[158] It was the impact of the war which changed everything, and in the two years after the Dunkirk evacuation in 1940 an increasingly critical view was formed of not only the foreign and defence policies of the National Government but its domestic social and economic record. The unofficial polling organization Mass-Observation estimated that by December 1942 about 40 per cent of the population had changed their political outlook since the start of the war, and almost all of this movement was away from the Conservatives.[159] In February 1939, the Gallup opinion poll had recorded 50 per cent support for the National Government, but by February 1944 the proportion intending to vote Conservative at the next general election had declined to 23 per cent, and was still at 24 per cent a year later.

[158] Hoare to Sassoon, 13 May 1939, Templewood MSS, X/4.
[159] P. Addison, *The Road to 1945: British Politics and the Second World War* (1975), 127.

Table 2.27. The economic and social profile of Conservative losses in the general election of 1935

This table analyses the boroughs in England and Wales (including double-Member boroughs), and county divisions which can be exactly matched to the geographical units used in the occupation tables of the 1931 census. For the seats in this sample which the Conservative Party lost in 1935, it shows the percentage of the total 'occupied' in each category in 1931 (for the methodology and definitions of the categories, see Appendix 2). The level of unemployment is the number of persons aged fourteen and over who were classified as 'out of work' as a percentage of the number classified as 'occupied' in the 1931 census. Losses are assessed in comparison to the previous general election result, and do not take account of intervening by-elections. The regional columns are: London (Lon), Home Counties (HC), South Central England (SC), South-West England (SW), East England (East), East Midlands (EM), West Midlands (WM), North East England (NE), North-West England (NW), and Wales (Wal); for definitions of the regions, see Appendix 3.

Occupation	Regions									
	Lon	HC	SC	SW	East	EM	WM	NE	NW	Wal
Agriculture	0.2	2.4	–	18.2	15.7	2.6	3.0	4.2	3.6	26.4
Mining	–	0.1	–	0.3	1.9	16.4	12.0	17.6	7.6	17.3
Metal Industries	9.0	6.9	–	3.0	13.4	13.4	19.9	10.5	7.6	3.0
Construction	5.4	8.4	–	7.3	6.7	5.2	7.5	5.1	4.7	5.4
Light Industries	7.6	10.7	–	5.9	3.7	5.9	5.1	4.7	4.0	2.9
Textiles & Clothing	5.0	4.4	–	4.3	1.4	6.7	7.7	9.4	28.9	1.6
Service & Leisure	11.2	8.6	–	22.0	9.7	9.2	6.7	9.4	6.9	14.2
Commerce & Finance	11.1	11.0	–	11.9	9.0	9.3	7.5	9.3	8.4	8.3
Clerical	12.1	12.0	–	3.5	3.8	6.4	4.8	4.3	4.1	2.3
Professional	2.9	3.3	–	4.8	3.6	3.4	2.4	3.2	2.6	5.0
Persons per acre	68.3	6.9	–	0.3	0.5	3.0	2.2	1.1	1.1	0.1
Persons per room	1.0	1.0	–	0.7	0.8	0.8	0.7	1.0	0.9	0.8
% unemployed in 1931	11.4	7.5	–	8.1	12.3	12.5	12.6	17.1	17.5	10.7
Total number of losses	11	7	1	1	1	4	8	24	15	1
No. of losses in sample	1	2	0	1	1	3	6	16	9	1

Despite such indicators, Labour's landslide victory came as a shock to many, for they had assumed that Churchill's wartime prestige and popularity would translate into a victory similar to that of Lloyd George in 1918. This had been the belief of the Prime Minister himself, partly based on his reception by applauding crowds as he toured the country during the campaign, and his disappointment was bitter. However, a few Conservatives had sensed that the tide was running against them before the dissolution, and to some experienced local agents during the campaign 'it became obvious at an early stage that there was a definite swing to the left'.[160] The long delay since the previous election in 1935 resulted in an unprecedented number of new voters, and 21 per cent of those entitled to cast a ballot would be doing so for the first time. Unlike 1918, turnout was quite high: at 72.8 per cent being above

---

[160] Berkshire South CA, agent's report on the 1945 general election; Headlam diary, 14 March, 12 and 27 April, 21 May 1945.

the 71.1 per cent of 1935. The huge size of the armed forces by the end of the European war meant that the service qualification accounted for 3.1 million of the 33.2 million voters, and collecting their votes from around the world was the cause of the delay between polling day on 5 July and the announcement of the results on 26 July. This revealed that Labour had won 393 seats, whilst the supporters of Churchill were reduced to 210 (consisting of 197 Conservative, eleven Liberal National, and two 'National' MPs).[161] It was a bruising defeat, although not as severe as those of 1906 or 1997, despite the more adverse circumstance of popular blame for policies which had led to war, and nearly to national disaster.

Table 2.28. Conservative performance in the 1945 general election

This table analyses the outcome for the 544 Conservative candidates in England, Scotland, and Wales. As the election result was a severe defeat, a wider banding has been given for the seats which were not won. For definitions of the regions, see Appendix 3.

Region	Margin of victory in seats won			Margin of defeat in seats not won				
	2,000 & above	1,000–1,999	1–999	1–999	1,000–1,999	2,000–3,999	4,000–5,999	6,000 & above
London	9	1	1	1	–	5	9	29
Home Counties N	12	1	–	4	2	9	4	27
Home Counties S	27	2	1	–	3	3	–	5
South Central	18	1	1	1	1	3	1	6
South-West	12	2	2	–	1	5	2	–
East	6	2	–	6	1	2	2	5
Midlands East	2	2	–	4	1	1	1	17
Midlands West	11	1	3	1	2	1	7	20
Yorkshire	9	1	2	1	–	3	3	30
Tyneside	2	1	–	1	–	2	1	13
North-West	21	3	3	4	1	9	14	28
Wales Industrial	–	1	–	–	–	–	2	12
Wales Rural	–	1	1	–	–	1	2	1
Scotland South	6	4	2	3	3	2	7	20
Scotland North	8	1	3	–	–	1	–	2
TOTAL	143	24	19	26	15	47	55	215

The interplay of the various economic, social, and political elements, which were discussed earlier in this chapter, determined the outcomes of the eight general elections from 1918 to 1945. However, on each occasion, the particular contingent factors of events, issues, and personalities had the effect of varying the scale and strength of the underlying structural forces. It is essential to avoid a deterministic connection between social class and party support; in its crudest form, this depicts the various strata in society as if they possessed the cohesion of the Guards'

---

[161] As a very small consolation, the Conservatives gained four seats from the Liberal Party: Berwick, Caernarvon Boroughs, Caithness and Sunderland, and Isle of Ely.

battalions at the Trooping of the Colour, wheeling first to the left and then to the right. As always, the truth is more messy, unpredictable, and difficult to pin down. Although human beings can be categorized in groups, each remains an individual with a capacity for self-determination. In the privacy of the polling booth, voting is a personal decision. Tribal and kinship (in modern terms, class and community) connections will always be important influences, but they are neither automatic nor absolute in their effect. Each individual's political opinion is an amalgam of their background, temperament, circumstances, and experience, and the way in which this engages with the broad image of a party or a particular leader.

Whatever underlying trends and structural forces can be detected with hindsight, at the time the situation seemed unpredictable from moment to moment. The 1920s in particular were marked by the volatility of the electorate, so that a landslide victory was as much a cause for concern as of confidence—as 1929 demonstrated, support could ebb as easily as it had previously flowed. Another destabilizing factor was the apathy and unreliability even of customary Conservative supporters amongst the middle class, who constantly had to be cajoled into protecting their own interests: 'only too frequently has this "sleepy" attitude cost our Party a seat', complained one local chairman.[162] The effect was that victories soon turned to ashes, whilst defeats only confirmed the precariousness of the Conservative position. The party found reassurance in the steadiness of the people at times of real danger, as in 1914–18, 1931, and 1940–45, but in more normal times it feared that the public was easily distracted or misled; hence the defeat following the dull campaign of 1929. However, one conclusion is incontestable from the electoral statistics: in the interwar period, as for much of the rest of the twentieth century, the Conservative appeal had more resonance for more people most of the time than did any of the alternatives.

[162] Putney CA, F&GP Report, 28 February 1939.

3
The Constituency Associations
Members and Activities

Parliament and government were the preserve of an elite few, and involvement in politics for most people was confined to the affairs of their locality. Where there was engagement at all, it was through membership of the constituency association, and it was here that the ebb and flow of everyday Conservative politics took place. The combination of strict limits on election expenses and the widening of the franchise meant that by 1918 voluntary involvement had become essential to the existence and functioning of the party. It was necessary to maintain enthusiasm and organization between general elections, and increasingly elaborate structures evolved for this purpose. The focal point was the central association for each parliamentary constituency; this had both a subordinate network of local and specialist branches, and, through affiliation to the National Union of Conservative and Unionist Associations, was connected outwards to the regional and national tiers of the party organization, which are discussed in Chapter 4.

The principle of local autonomy was fundamental to the operation of the constituency associations, and of profound importance to the structure and ethos of the Conservative Party as a whole. It was acknowledged and accepted by the leadership and the national organization, and jealously defended from below against any suspicion of encroachment.[1] Local autonomy was the most significant limitation on the power of the Leader and party officials—for whilst they had much influence over their voluntary followers, they could not command them in anything. The only direct limitation upon a constituency association was the ultimate sanction of disaffiliation, and this was solely in the power of the rank and file's representative body, the National Union; it was only used exceptionally, when a constituency was already in disarray, and usually after it had split into rival associations. In all other respects, the local association was sovereign within its boundaries, and all activity that occurred there was subject to its permission and pleasure—a sensitivity that party officials and leaders ignored at their peril.[2] Baldwin did not exaggerate when

---

[1] NU Conf., 1923, comments by the Principal Agent; Topping to N. Chamberlain, 'Reorganisation', 23 October 1930, Templewood MSS, VI/3; Middleton & Prestwich CA, FGP, 30 May 1935; letter from the Chief Whip quoted in Cheltenham CA, Joint Meeting of Men's Exec. & Women's Management Ctte., 19 July 1937.

[2] Special Finance Ctte. Report, 16 March 1944, 2, CPA, CCO/500/3/1; SUA, EDC, 15 January 1936. For a rare example of Central Office intervening to persuade a candidate to stand down against the wishes of the constituency association, and the following reaction, see: Wrexham CA, Exec., 3 November, 8 December 1924, 2 February 1925, Special Meeting, 20 July 1925.

he declared 'democracy is a reality in the Conservative Party and each constituency is a law unto itself'.[3]

For this reason, coalition alliances or electoral deals negotiated by the leaders or Central Office could not be made binding upon individual constituencies and would be disregarded if unpopular—hence the fraying of support for the Lloyd George Coalition in 1922. If a constituency decided to ignore any national compact, the most that could happen was that their candidate would not receive the customary message of endorsement from the Party Leader and there would be no direct assistance from the Central Office, but in many places the lack of these would hardly matter.[4] Thus, despite its importance in the larger scale of imperial policy, Baldwin could only request that the Spen Valley association withdraw its candidate when the sitting Liberal MP, Sir John Simon, agreed to chair the statutory commission on India in 1928; when so doing, the Party Leader was careful to acknowledge the 'inalienable right of a constituency Association to pursue its own course of action either in the selection of a candidate or the contesting of a parliamentary election'.[5] In many cases, an appeal by the Leader to a higher 'national' interest could be effective, especially in a crisis or wartime, but such pressure could only be applied sparingly and was not always successful.[6] However, although the leadership were sometimes inconvenienced, they did not seek to undermine the autonomy of local associations, for they were aware that it was a vital factor in maintaining the self-respect and morale of party members, and that 'local initiative and local opinion are a very considerable asset to the Party'.[7] As the Area Agent for London observed in 1920: 'no organisation is alive, unless it runs its own show'.[8]

THE OFFICERS AND CENTRAL COMMITTEES

The two leading positions in a constituency association were the president and the chairman. A significant number of presidents were titled (in England and Wales in 1937, 30 per cent were peers and 21.3 per cent baronets or knights),[9] and some

---

[3] Baldwin to Simon (public letter), 26 October 1932, Baldwin MSS 167/254–5.
[4] West Midlands Area, GP, 'Report on 1922 Election', 19 January 1923; Norfolk East CA, AGM, 9 May 1936.
[5] Baldwin to Smith (Chairman, Spen Valley CA), draft, 19 January 1928, Baldwin MSS, 53/265–8. In this case, the direct appeal from the Party Leader was successful despite considerable local reluctance: Wicks to Duff, 6 January 1928, Maxwell-Fyfe to Baldwin, 21 January 1928 [misdated 1927] Baldwin MSS, 53/261–2, 256.
[6] Cardiff Central CA, Exec., 7 and 12 October 1931; corres. on Southwark Central, February–April 1935, Baldwin MSS 47/15–31; Stonehaven to Croft, 3 May 1935, Croft MSS, CAC, CRFT/1/19; Aldershot CA, Adoption Meeting, 16 November 1940.
[7] Comments of Lady Bridgeman, in papers circulated to members of the NU Sub-committee on Rules & Organisation, 27 September 1929, Steel-Maitland MSS, GD193/121/5/36–51; Birmingham CA, Management Ctte., 12 September 1924.
[8] Lewisham West CA, special meeting, 20 February 1920.
[9] The only extensive data on local office-holders is provided by the resolutions presented by the National Union to Baldwin on his retirement in June 1937, Baldwin MSS (Worcs RO), BA 14208. Almost every active local association sent in a resolution for inclusion, nearly all of which were on headed notepaper. In Scotland, unfortunately, this frequently did not list the office-holders, but for

were current or former MPs for the seat, but the majority were local 'territorial leaders',[10] drawn from the gentry in rural areas and substantial business or professional men in the towns. A few great aristocrats who were actively engaged in politics acted in this capacity for several places, but most presidents held office in a single constituency or town.[11] They gave their patronage to fundraising appeals and hosted events in the grounds of their estates, but otherwise had only ceremonial functions—the most important of which was to take the chair at the Annual General Meeting. The association was actually run by its chairman, which was always the crucial position. The chairman's authority was rarely questioned, especially when it was supported by the other officers. However, although the function was that of leader, the tone and method could not be dictatorial. The chairman was restricted by the need to maintain consensus, and the foremost priority was always to keep the association intact.[12]

The chairmanship was almost invariably a male preserve: in 1937, only three associations in England and Wales were led by a woman (the term 'chairman' still being used).[13] In all cases, the chairman was someone of local eminence who would be expected to be a generous subscriber; one claimed to have spent £100 a year on his association in a weak seat.[14] On a purely practical basis, 'he must have a certain amount of leisure', and in a rural seat would need to own a car in order to get around and visit the branches.[15] To secure a person of suitable standing, it was not unusual to invite someone to take up the post who was not an existing

---

England and Wales there is information for 442 constituency associations (excluding overall city organizations). Forty-three of these listed a Chairman but not a president, and the figures given are based upon the 399 associations for which a president is named. Of these, the president was also listed as being the chairman in nine cases (2.3%), but elsewhere the offices were separate. Only eleven associations (2.8%) had a woman president. In thirty-one constituencies (7.8%), a sitting MP was also the association president, of whom twenty were the Member for that seat and four had previously represented it but now sat elsewhere; for local discussions on the appropriateness of this, see Lewisham West CA, Council, 18 June and 1 September 1926, Advisory Ctte., 28 October 1944.

[10] Assheton to Martin, 5 January 1945, Churchill MSS, CAC, CHAR/2/545/8; Loyd to Glyn, 14 February 1944, Glyn MSS, D/EGL/C37/9; Bury CA, AGM, 4 February 1920.

[11] Lord Derby was president of the city organizations of Liverpool and Manchester, and of six other Lancashire constituencies; Lord Salisbury was president of five seats and also chairman of St Albans CA, which listed no president; the Duke of Devonshire was president of five Derbyshire divisions, and the Duke of Portland and the Earl of Plymouth were each president of four seats: NU presentation resolutions, June 1937, Baldwin MSS (Worcs RO), BA 14208.

[12] Paton (Chairman, Kinross & West Perthshire CA) to Duchess of Atholl, 27 June 1937, Atholl MSS, 22/6; Kinross & West Perthshire CA, Council, 22 April 1938.

[13] Oxford, West Ham Plaistow, and Willesden West are the only examples amongst the 442 English and Welsh associations which list a female chairman: NU presentation resolutions, June 1937, Baldwin MSS (Worcs RO), BA 14208. Plaistow also had a woman president, treasurer, secretary, and parliamentary candidate. In Scotland, Argyll had a woman chairman; one was elected at Devizes in the following year and Rutland & Stamford had a woman chairman from 1939 to 1945, due to the previous chairman being called up for military service: Devizes CA, Exec., 18 October 1938, Rutland & Stamford CA, AGM, 14 June 1945.

[14] Black to Bonar Law, 4 December 1918, Bonar Law MSS, BL/95/4. In 1937, 5.4% of chairmen were peers, 13.3% baronets or knights, and 12.7% an alderman or local councillor, of the 442 chairmen in England and Wales listed in the NU presentation resolutions, June 1937, Baldwin MSS (Worcs RO), BA 14208.

[15] Sevenoaks CA, General Purposes Ctte., 27 September 1924.

member of the executive committee.[16] The re-election of a chairman was almost automatic, and, as they could generally serve for as long as they were willing and able, there were instances of considerable continuity; the record may have been held by Sir Edward Brooksbank, who stood down in 1932 after forty-seven years as chairman in Barkston Ash.[17] Indeed, a respected or capable chairman was difficult to replace, and in many cases offers to step aside for someone younger were met with vigorous pleas to remain at the helm.[18] Contests and challenges were extremely rare; in one instance, when two associations were merging due to the boundary revisions of 1918, to avoid the taking of sides which a formal vote would entail, the chairmanship of the new constituency was decided upon the toss of a coin.[19] The chairman, together with the salaried agent and a few prominent supporters, normally 'exercise the real power, and the Association will usually follow their suggestions'.[20] The two crucial relationships at local level were those between the chairman and the agent, and the chairman and the MP or candidate. Local constituency chairmen tended to be loyal to the established party hierarchy and leadership, accepting their greater knowledge of affairs and seeking to avoid disputes and disunity.[21]

The other most important office was that of treasurer; this entailed a good deal of time and work, and involved wide-ranging responsibilities of oversight for both the income and expenditure of the association—with the former being critical to its continued operation.[22] A good treasurer was almost harder to replace than a good chairman, and, although there were some instances of service for several decades, there tended to be a more frequent turnover of this position. Associations also had an honorary secretary, but this was not onerous, as in most active constituencies there was some paid staff who dealt with clerical duties (the agent's position normally being described as 'secretary and agent'), whilst in the weaker ones there was little activity and fewer meetings. The officers were usually elected at the AGM, although in some associations they were chosen by the executive committee or council and merely confirmed by the larger assembly. The AGM also functioned as a local rally, usually closing with a political address by the candidate or Member. In some cases, the central committees were directly elected at the AGM, whilst in others only the association officers and the representatives to the regional and national bodies were chosen here. In those cases, the rest of the executive or council was formed on a federal basis, with specific numbers of representatives sent forward to sit upon it by the district branches and other sub-sections. Many associations

---

[16] Herefordshire North CA, Advisory Ctte., 9 April 1920; Stockton CA, Exec., 15 April 1930; Westminster St George's CA, Exec., 19 July 1932; Maidstone CA, Exec., 10 April 1933; Shrewsbury CA, Exec., 29 April 1936.
[17] Barkston Ash CA, AGM, 1925, 1932; Clitheroe CA, Exec., 8 February 1937; Rye CA, Exec., 4 February 1939; Salisbury CA, AGM, 22 April 1939; Louth CA, General Meeting, 21 September 1944.
[18] Newark CA, Exec., 20 May 1931, 24 April 1936; Oxfordshire North CA, Exec., 30 January 1938.
[19] Shrewsbury CA, Provisional Ctte., 16 March 1918.
[20] 'Memorandum on the working of our Party Organisation', 10 October 1930, Templewood MSS, VI/3.
[21] Butter (chairman, Kinross & West Perthshire CA) to Duke of Atholl, 19 April 1933, Paton (chairman, Kinross & West Perthshire CA) to Duchess of Atholl, 15 June 1938, Atholl MSS, 9/1, 22/18.
[22] *The Finances of a Constituency Association*, NU leaflet 3684 (1938).

had a considerable number of vice-chairmen or vice-presidents, but these were not elective or executive posts, and 'the duties in this office were nil'.[23] Such appointments were a recognition of local social status and of the larger donors to the constituency's central funds; Sevenoaks had fifty-nine vice-presidents who subscribed five pounds or more, seven of whom were peers, whilst in the more middle-class suburb of Acton, all those who gave over one guinea automatically became vice-presidents.[24]

Each association made its own rules (specimen rules were provided by Central Office but, as with all things, their adoption was entirely optional[25]), and so there were many variations in structure and nomenclature. The most typical arrangement was an executive committee or executive council, usually of between twenty and fifty members, but sometimes as large as eighty. In some cases this met quarterly, but a more common pattern was eight to ten meetings a year, on a monthly basis but with a gap during the summer.[26] Another structure was a variation on this, of a more formal council of a hundred or more, convening between two and four times a year, whilst the administrative affairs were handled by a smaller executive. Where the executive was on the larger scale and met less often, or in rural constituencies where calling it together involved members in some inconvenience, there was often a much smaller finance or finance and general purposes committee, frequently with an attendance in single figures. Whatever its title and exact composition, every association had a central committee which took the key decisions, considered resolutions, planned events, and authorized expenditure. Minutes were kept, usually by the agent, but the discussion was confidential and normally did not appear in the local press, except when a resolution was passed for public release. The Conservative Party was hardly unusual as an organization in preferring to keep its disagreements 'behind closed doors', this being 'much better than washing our dirty linen in public'.[27] In fact, disputes and debates on controversial subjects were a rarity, and the business which mostly occupied the agenda was the raising of funds, the programme of local social and political work, and—in urban areas—local government elections.

The membership of these committees was drawn primarily from the local elite of the gentry, retired military officers, professionals, businessmen, and their female relatives. In the Conservative Party, 'the secret at the bottom of all organisation is local leadership'; in districts where such leadership did not exist or held back from involvement, it was an uphill struggle to maintain an effective organization.[28] The class, age, and gender bias was reinforced by unstated reservations about the

---

[23] Dundee CA, AGM, 25 November 1926.
[24] Sevenoaks CA, AR, 1930–31; Acton CA, rules, 1923, Brittain MSS, 14.
[25] Central Office, *Model Rules for Associations, Branches and Sections* (1933); Central Office, *Procedure* (1935); Winchester CA, Rules Ctte., 6 May 1936.
[26] Memo by Blair, 'Impressions of the General Election', 12 July 1929, Gilmour MSS, GD383/29/32–5.
[27] Zetland to Bower, 23 February 1939, Zetland MSS, D609/29; Herefordshire North CA, Advisory Ctte., 17 May 1921; Pembrokeshire CA, Exec., 15 October 1935.
[28] Inverness CA, Organiser's Report, AGM, 17 October 1928; SUA, *Unionist Party Organisation in Scotland*, 3; Headlam to Baldwin, 16 January 1925, Baldwin MSS, 11/94–6; Headlam diary, 3 October 1926, 24 January 1927, 19 December 1930.

capacity for mature judgement of women and youth, and the restricted outlook and experience of working-class men. Although women became a presence on executive committees in increasing numbers after 1918, they tended to concentrate upon their own 'separate sphere' of work in the women's committee and branches. In the central committee of the association, it was usually the men who took the initiative in decision-making and the proposing of resolutions, and in this respect 'politics is still essentially the business of men'.[29] Thus, despite the female preponderance in the membership, effective control lay in the hands of a small circle of males who were at least upper-middle class and generally over middle age. This pattern was reinforced by the considerable continuity in the composition of committees; as with other voluntary organizations, it was only a minority of the membership which chose to take an active part, and the problem was more usually one of filling posts than of any competition for them.[30]

There was a parallel organizational structure in the towns and cities which consisted of two or more constituencies. In most cases, an overall association was dominant and the individual divisions acted more as its branches; this was particularly the pattern in the largest cities such as Birmingham, Liverpool, Manchester, and Glasgow, where there were strong central bodies dominated by a cohesive business and social oligarchy.[31] The organization in the larger cities usually operated from a single office, headed by a chief City Agent on a salary rivalling that of the Central Office Area Agents, with whom there was often an ambivalent relationship. The exceptions were the Aston division in Birmingham and Withington in Manchester, both of which organized themselves individually at a separate location from the main city office; the reasons for this appear to lie in the Victorian era, and were not due to any recent rift. In Sheffield, the Hillsborough and Park divisions were worked from the city headquarters, but the other divisions had separate offices, as did all four of the Hull constituencies. The pooling of the financial resources of the whole city enabled coverage of the weaker seats in the working-class districts, which otherwise could not sustain an organization of their own. In some cities, this provided a full-time agent for each constituency,[32] and in others adjacent divisions were grouped together. Liverpool had a particularly strong central structure based on the popular Toryism of the nineteenth century and the legacy of the Irish Home Rule issue, and here and in Glasgow there was a notable element of Protestant sectarianism in the local Conservative identity. In Liverpool the MPs were kept in an unusually subordinate role, which caused some frictions, although this system declined after the sudden death in 1928 of the 'city boss', Sir Archibald Salvidge, 'left everything in absolute chaos'.[33] However, even here the

---

[29] *CAJ*, April 1934, 76; Wolverhampton Bilston CA, Management Ctte., 29 May 1934.
[30] Norfolk North CA, AGM, 6 June 1927.
[31] Birmingham CA, Management Ctte., 20 November 1918; Special Finance Ctte., 20 May 1943, memo on organization in Birmingham, CPA, CCO/500/3/1.
[32] Manchester CA circular, Beattie (Chief Agent) to Derby, 11 October 1939, Derby MSS, 16/3.
[33] Derby to Sandeman Allan, 2 January 1929, Derby to Baldwin, 30 May 1927, Derby MSS, 6/4, 33; Liverpool CA, Board of Management, 3 October 1929; P. Waller, 'Sir Archibald Salvidge', in *Oxford Dictionary of National Biography*.

city leaders could not dictate to a constituency association in such matters as candidate selection.[34] Tensions could develop between the interests of the divisional and the city leaders, particularly in the smaller cities and large towns. Nevertheless, the divided boroughs generally worked in effective co-operation, and Salford was unusual in its three seats operating independently without any central link.[35]

BRANCHES AND SECTIONS

Below the central committee, and usually with representation upon it, was a foundation of branches and sections. It was to these that most of the membership actually belonged, and in many cases only a few of the relatively wealthy gave a subscription direct to the main association. The branches were territorial: in constituencies which were entirely urban they were based upon local government wards, and in the mixed and rural seats upon either the electoral polling districts or the individual small towns and villages. Large county divisions could have many branches, with most activity taking place at district level and correspondingly infrequent meetings of the central executive; in 1924, Derbyshire West had eighty-six 'Township Leagues', whilst in the later 1930s, the Harborough division of Leicestershire had nineteen men's, thirty-four women's, and nineteen joint branches, and Ashford in Kent had fifty-three branches in a similar pattern.[36] The question which attracted a lot of attention in the decade after the enfranchisement of women was whether in each district there should be a single branch with both male and female membership or separate bodies for men and women.[37] Both approaches had their advantages, and in 1925 the Deputy Party Chairman commented 'we are still passing through the formative period'.[38] However, where the genders were organized separately, the women's committees tended to be more inward-looking and had the reputation of being more prone to personal frictions: one exasperated constituency chairman complained that 'when women get together they are petty and mean and jealous'.[39] By the late 1920s, a consensus was emerging that joint branches were more effective, and this became the prevalent pattern.[40]

The branches elected their own officers and committees, and were responsible within their area for recruitment, canvassing, and campaigning, but had no

---

[34] Liverpool CA, Board of Management, 25 November 1918, 29 December 1922; Derby to Churchill, 14 October 1935, Derby MSS, 33.
[35] Woodhouse to Derby, 3 April 1924, Derby MSS, 20/2.
[36] Derbyshire West CA, Fin., 30 September 1924; Harborough CA, AR, 1937–38; Ashford CA, Agent's Report, Joint Standing Ctte., 22 February 1935.
[37] *CAJ*, June 1920, 6–8; August 1920, 7–10; September 1920, 6–10; June 1922, 4; June 1924, 138–9; Ripon CA, Joint Meeting of Chairmen and Secretaries, 21 March 1921.
[38] Linlithgow to Baldwin, 9 March 1925, Baldwin MSS, 160/101–2.
[39] Dillon (chairman, Seaham Harbour CA) to Ross, 21 May 1925, Londonderry MSS, D/LO/ C277; Lady Peto diary, 20 April 1927; Northampton CA, Women's Advisory Ctte., 19 November 1928, Consultative Ctte., 22 March 1929; recollections of Lady Larcom, *CAJ*, summer 1984, 42.
[40] *CAJ*, November 1927, 301–3; November 1933, 321–6; Putney CA, Exec., 20 December 1929.

authority to take executive decisions or pass resolutions on policy. Except in the most compact and centralized urban constituencies, the branches ran their own programmes of minor social and fundraising events; from this income, they often paid a quota to the central funds.[41] The relationship of the geographical branches to the central body depended upon the size and type of the constituency, and they were most important and autonomous in the rural seats. Local particularism could be a sensitive issue here, and care often had to be taken that one district did not appear predominant and provoke resentment; this was generally avoided by having direct branch representation on the central bodies, and sometimes by a rotation of meeting place or of officers between different towns and districts.[42] As one chairman observed, 'hard and fast rules were impossible', as 'different districts found different methods applicable to the needs of the particular area'.[43]

The most important of the sectional organizations was that for women. This had its own officers, and normally control of its own separate funds.[44] Even where the branches were organized on a joint basis, it was normal for there still to be a central women's committee for the constituency. This was elected separately from, but was subordinate to, the association's overall executive or council, on which the women's committee normally had direct representation.[45] There had been a role for women in politics before 1918, but it was always limited in effect and importance because it was at one remove from the ballot box, consisting of campaigning, fundraising, and influencing the male voters in their families. Before their enfranchisement there was no need to consider women as autonomous political agents, to shape presentation or policy to their needs, or to develop an official organization to secure their adherence. This had been left to bodies which were linked to the party but outside it, such as the Women's Tariff Reform League. The oldest and most important of these was the Primrose League, which was founded in the 1880s and rapidly gained a large membership, of which it has been estimated that 48 per cent was female.[46] The result was that many women had already been involved in political work long before they acquired the vote, and their experience of organization made it comparatively easy for them to establish the new constituency committees and branches. In many districts, the Primrose League had faded into the background during the wartime truce, and its female members joined the new constituency women's organizations which were established in the early 1920s; by 1926, these were functioning in 408 constituencies in England and Wales.[47] For a while,

---

[41] Aylesbury CA, Fin., 28 September 1929; Ealing CA, Manor Ward Branch Ctte., 5 March 1936; Norfolk North CA, Exec., 12 March 1937; *CAJ*, June 1932, 170.

[42] Devizes CA, Central Ctte., 25 January 1919; Sevenoaks CA, Emergency Ctte., 23 January 1920; Dumfriesshire CA, Council, 15 December 1926; Merionethshire CA, F&GP, 4 January 1937. This also applied at the regional level: Eastern Area, Council AGM, 2 May 1924.

[43] Knutsford CA, Exec., 9 August 1933.

[44] *CAJ*, November 1933, 321–6; January 1934, 5–9; Reigate CA, Exec., 28 April 1920; Herefordshire North CA, Fin., 8 February 1932.

[45] *Handbook for Women Organisers and Workers* (1928), 3; Derby CA, Exec., 16 March 1925; Worcester CA, Exec., 3 February 1932; Kinross & West Perthshire CA, Exec., 13 January 1933; SUA, EDC, 27 July 1923.

[46] Pugh, *Tories and the People*, 49.   [47] NU Central Council Report to Conference, 1925–26.

the Primrose League remained a significant and active body in some areas where it had previously been strong, which sometimes led to rivalries and frictions, but even in these places it had dwindled into irrelevance by the late 1930s.[48]

The combination of their greater activity with the view that social events were more in the female domestic sphere resulted in the women doing most of the fundraising. However, whilst the men were happy to relinquish the more tedious organizational tasks to women, this did not give the women a commensurate role in the direction of associations. As a male member of a branch in Manchester observed, 'it's the hen that delivers the goods', but 'it's the cock that does the crowing'.[49] Up to the 1940s, this division of gender roles was generally accepted by Conservative women as the natural order, with occasional grumbles as the men spent the money which the women had raised. However, in a few cases it led to more serious disputes over the relationship with the constituency executive, the employment of staff, and the control of funds.[50]

The party organization for youth was originally separate, but during the interwar period it progressively became integrated into the party structure at every level. The Junior Imperial League had been founded in 1906 by Henry Imbert-Terry MP for young men aged eighteen to thirty, most of whom were not voters in the pre-1918 ratepayer franchise. It remained very much under his influence, and was still a comparatively small body when it revived from wartime dormancy, with just sixty local branches in January 1920.[51] In the new electoral system, membership was opened to young women, and proved to be popular with both sexes, primarily drawing on shop and office workers and the lower-middle class; Headlam described the branch in South Shields as composed of 'shop boys and girls', and observed that 'the small bourgeoisie will not mix with the proletariat'.[52] During the 1920s, there was a move to the different age range of fourteen to twenty-five, but some branches allowed members to stay on to the previous limit of thirty, and a few had no effective maximum.[53] At local level, the League's activities revolved around a calendar of popular social events: tennis parties, cricket tournaments, treasure hunts, campfire suppers, rambles, debates, amateur dramatics, and, most of all, dances.[54] Its last Chairman, Lord Dunglass MP, observed that it employed 'every entertainment which can be included under the head of

---

[48] Bolton CA, Council, 13 October 1919, GP, 29 March 1920; Wood Green CA, Women's Exec., 14 September 1926; Gloucester CA, Exec., 21 March 1930.

[49] Hurst, *Closed Chapters*, 89–90.

[50] *CAJ*, November 1933, 324; Winchester CA, Council, 27 April 1927; Worcester CA, Exec., 1 May, 22 June, AGM, 23 June 1933; Harborough CA, Special Council Meeting, 12 October 1935; Walsall CA, Officers' Meeting, 1 April, 7 July, 7 and 19 October 1936.

[51] JIL, AR, 1921; *CAJ*, March 1921, 11–15; *Handbook for Organisers and Workers* (n.d. but c.1933), CPA, CCO/506/5/5.

[52] Headlam diary, 9 February 1931.

[53] JIL, Exec., 11 March 1925. Some branches in Yorkshire 'took people up to 60 years': Yorkshire Area, Council, 18 December 1924.

[54] *How to Sustain a Branch of the Junior Imperial and Constitutional League*, NU leaflet 2749 (1927); Tamworth CA, JIL Divisional Council, minutes & correspondence files, 1928–39; *CAJ*, December 1927, 347–9. For examples of local activities, see McCrillis, *Conservative Party in the Age of Universal Suffrage*, 95–102.

"Social" where all the various evening pleasures are carried on under respectable Conservative auspices'.[55] The attraction was similar to that more familiarly linked with its successor, the Young Conservatives, from the 1940s to the 1960s, as a congenial and socially acceptable way to meet like-minded young people, especially of the opposite sex. The immediate benefit was that in many districts—and not just the shires and suburbs—the League provided a lively cadre of energetic helpers, although it was only 'the few who were really politically interested'.[56] Dunglass estimated the latter as 'at most 15 per cent' (which was much in line with constituency membership as a whole), and was quite content with this, for 'a nation of politically-minded youths would be one of prigs and truly fearful'. In his experience, what drew the rest was '(a) waving a flag for King, Country and Empire, (b) airing their views which are always immature and in nine cases out of ten the most arrant nonsense, (c) enjoying themselves with their fellows and having a good time'.[57] However, a perennial weakness of the League was that many of its members ceased active involvement in politics either on marriage or on reaching the upper age limit. Comparatively few, perhaps around 40 per cent, moved on to join the senior association, where even fewer took an active part; the problem of a dip in activism amongst the 'young marrieds' age range of twenty-five to forty was a common post-1945 pattern also, and understandable in view of the demands of establishing both a family and a career.[58]

Encouragement of the junior movement was a priority of J. C. C. Davidson when Chairman of the Party from 1926 to 1930, and one part of this was its reorganization on a constituency basis in 1928.[59] The branches in each seat were now linked together and placed below a Divisional Council, which was usually given some direct representation on the association's central committee; by 1930, there were such councils in 473 of the 507 constituencies in England and Wales.[60] The closest link with Central Office was during this period, when in 1927 the Deputy Party Chairman, Lord Stanley, also became Chairman of the Junior Imperial League (with Imbert-Terry, after twenty-one years in that office, becoming a Vice-President). Stanley gave up his Central Office role after the 1929 election but remained the League's Chairman until 1932, after which he retained a connection as President until his sudden death in 1938. His successors as Chairman were other youthful aristocratic MPs: Lord Burghley (who was also an Olympic gold-medallist) in 1932–36, and then Dunglass, who held the post when war broke out.

The Junior Imperial League grew rapidly from the mid-1920s, with 45,000 membership badges being sold in 1927, and in the following year a recruiting campaign in which 552 local branches participated, added over 16,000 new members.[61]

---

[55] Memo by Dunglass, 29 January 1943, CPA, CCO/506/4/4; *Make New Friends: For Comradeship and Service, Join the Junior Imperial League*, NU leaflet 3718 (1938).
[56] Accrington CA, AGM, 14 May 1935; Denbighshire CA, F&GP, 28 October 1938.
[57] Memo by Dunglass, 29 January 1943, Dunglass to Dugdale, 23 January 1943, CPA, CCO/506/4/4.
[58] Fraser Ctte. Report, 19 July 1937, CPA, CCO/506/4/2.
[59] JIL, Central Council, 10 November 1928.
[60] JIL, AR, 1929, 1930.
[61] Maclachlan, 'Summarised Report on Conservative Organisation at Central Office and in the Constituencies during 1927', 30 December 1927, Baldwin MSS, 53/118–49; JIL, Exec., 16 January 1929; JIL, AR, 1924, 1925.

The membership peaked in 1930, when it was claimed to be 'upwards of 250,000'; whilst almost certainly an overestimate, it probably exceeded 150,000 and may have approached 200,000.[62] The specific data for the period 1925–39 which survive in the local records often give a constituency figure around the 500 mark, and in some cases several hundred more, and so a total in the same region as Young Conservative membership in its 1950s heyday is quite possible. However, the existence of the local branches could be ephemeral, due to their rapid turnover of membership and their dependence—even more than other parts of the local organization—on the commitment of their more transitory officers.[63] There was certainly a decline in the depression years of the early 1930s, and a private and more specific calculation, based upon regional returns, gave a total of 118,868 in December 1934.[64] After this there was some recovery, and by the end of the decade the Western Area alone had 112 branches in its twenty-eight constituencies.[65] However, development was still patchy, and Scotland in particular lagged behind; the youth wing was also weaker in London in the late 1930s, which may reflect the greater variety and choice of leisure activities available in the capital. After weighing the evidence, the Fraser Committee of 1937 considered that 'at the moment the membership of the League may be placed at about 150,000', although this may still have erred on the generous side.[66] Basil Sheasby, the national Vice-Chairman at the outbreak of war in 1939, frankly told a confidential enquiry committee in 1943 that the JIL membership total had been '250,000 propaganda figure, actual figure 100,000'.[67] Looking back in 1943, Dunglass commented that the League 'had been through a bad time when organisation and numbers were weak but 1938–39 showed a marked improvement in both'.[68] The Junior Imperial League closed down abruptly, and perhaps with undue haste, when war broke out, and those of its members who did not put on a uniform were heavily involved in various forms of war work.[69] During the war, its future was considered by the Palmer Committee, which recommended an even closer integration into the party structure at every level, placing it more under the agents' control in the constituencies, and thus it re-emerged, renamed as the Young Conservatives, after 1945.[70]

---

[62] *Handbook for Organisers and Workers* (n.d. but *c.*1933), CPA, CCO/506/5/5.

[63] 'Branches formed or renewed during 1936', 'Branches formed or renewed during 1937 (to date)', n.d., CPA, CCO/506/5/8; *The Hendon Imp*, October 1936, CPA, CCO/506/5/6; Harborough CA, JIL Council, AR, 1932–38.

[64] 'Approximate membership 1934', 3 December 1934, CPA, CCO/506/5/8.

[65] Western Area, AR, 1938–39.

[66] Fraser Ctte. Report, 19 July 1937, para 5, CPA, CCO/506/4/2. A list with figures for branches in 154 constituencies in 1939 suggests a much lower total, but many safe seats are not included, especially in London and the Home Counties, and others seem to refer to a local branch rather than the constituency as a whole: 'Junior Imperial League membership, 1939', n.d., CPA, CCO/506/4/12. The Palmer Ctte. Report gave the figure of 'approximately 100,000' for 1939: 'Youth Report', 14 December 1943, 4, CPA, CCO/500/1/10.

[67] Youth Ctte., minutes, 12 July 1943, CPA, CCO/506/4/8.

[68] Memo by Dunglass, 29 January 1943, CPA, CCO/506/4/4; JIL, 'Reports from the Areas', AR, 1938–39.

[69] Palmer Ctte. Report, 14 December 1943, 6, CPA, CCO/500/1/10.

[70] Palmer Ctte. Report, 14 December 1943, 8, 14–15, CPA, CCO/500/1/10.

The youth movement was generally seen as an asset, even a necessity. It was not a source of friction or rebellion: its members did not take a different ideological line to the parent body, and were normally polite and deferential to their elders.[71] At the local level, it provided a significant proportion of those eager and energetic enough to work at election time and even to canvass, an activity from which many older party workers shied away. It was also regarded as a nursery of members and future officers of the senior association, despite the tendency for membership to lapse during the first period of married life, generally in the twenty-five to forty age range. In the interwar period, the Junior Imperial League had its own nursery, more literally, in the shape of the Young Britons. This body was for children aged from six to fourteen, and was founded in 1925 as a deliberate counter to the Socialist Sunday School movement.[72] Whilst it was a Conservative Party initiative, and throughout its existence was supported by paid organizers who were funded by Central Office, there was considerable ambivalence about bringing politics to such a young age group. It therefore disavowed any partisan intentions, whilst aiming at 'instilling into the minds of children good citizenship, love of country, love of Empire and realisation of simple Conservative principles'.[73] The tone and activities were very similar to Cubs and Brownies, and there was much emphasis upon the empire: in the larger local groups, the children were organized into sections that were named after each of the Dominions.[74] The normal pattern of the meetings was a 'non-political talk for ten or fifteen minutes', which usually focused on the empire, the constitution, or a heroic historical figure, 'followed by games and drill for the boys, and sewing and singing for the girls'.[75] The Young Britons' organization grew quite rapidly and had a membership of 33,000 by 1927; in July 1929, there were 471 branches and enrolment was nearly 50,000, and the number of branches had reached 559 in 1938.[76] However, activity was suspended at the outbreak of the war and, unlike the youth movement, it never really recovered afterwards.

The next section was rather different in that it tended to consist only of a central sub-committee in each constituency, without any branches of its own. This was the organization aimed at trade unionists and working men, which was actively promoted after the 1918 Reform Act.[77] The aim was the establishment in every

---

[71] This was evident during the crisis of 1930: JIL, Central Council, 8 February, 28 June and 8 November, Exec., 14 May 1930.

[72] *Handbook on Young Britons* (1931), 3–4; Memo, 'Young Britons', 11 October 1938, CPA, CCO/506/7/4; *The Citizens of Tomorrow*, NU leaflet 2759 (1927); *A Counter to Communism*, NU leaflet 3700 (1938); McCrillis, *Conservative Party in the Age of Universal Suffrage*, 102–9.

[73] *Handbook on Constituency Organisation* (1933), 15–16; Stockton CA, Exec., 2 February 1933.

[74] *Handbook for Young Britons: Officers and Helpers* (1936), 33–5; Ealing CA, Grosvenor Branch Young Britons, reports, 1932–33.

[75] Bute & North Ayrshire CA, AR, 1935; *Handbook on Young Britons*, 10, 20–5. For examples of talks: *Young Britons' Organisers Manual* (c.1937), Bolton CA; 'Linked Young Britons', February–April 1939, CPA, CCO/506/7/6; *Young Britons: Who Knows? The Empire*, NU leaflets 2650–1 (1925).

[76] Maclachlan, 'Summarised Report on Conservative Organisation at Central Office and in the Constituencies during 1927', 30 December 1927, Baldwin MSS, 53/118–49; NU Exec. Report to Council, 28 June 1927, 2 July 1929; Memo, 'Young Britons', 11 October 1938, CPA, CCO/506/7/4.

[77] *CAJ*, March 1920, 1–5; May 1920, 5–9; *The 'Wherefore and the Why' of Unionist Labour Committees*, NU leaflet 1982 (1920); McCrillis, *Conservative Party in the Age of Universal Suffrage*, 110–22.

constituency of a 'Labour Advisory Committee' (LAC); as with the women's and youth organizations, this was linked to its own regional bodies and central committee, and from 1930 had guaranteed representation on the Area Councils and the National Union Executive Committee. However, at local level there was often resistance to the creation of sections for trade unionists. This was partly because the concept of a group which was based upon its class identity ran counter to Conservative attitudes and aroused an instinctive suspicion; setting up such a body 'differentiated at once between the classes, which was…the one thing to avoid'.[78] Another element was social unease: a mixture of unfamiliarity, awkwardness, and snobbery on the part of the middle-class majority, which left the working men feeling unwelcome or disregarded. This was compounded by the reluctance of working-class Conservatives to stand up and be counted or to devote effort to political work, and the practical difficulties of the time and cost involved in attending meetings, especially in the large agricultural constituencies or at the regional level.[79] Many LACs struggled to keep enough attendance to remain in existence, and were far from being capable of strengthening the association or proselytizing in the workplace. In many cases, the result was a section with a small, often cliquish, membership, which required a lot of effort on the part of the local agent to sustain, and demonstrated little practical value in return. As the movement's national organizer admitted, many constituency agents were 'inclined to fight shy of Labour Committees'.[80]

The trade unionist organization tended to be limited to districts where it was clearly relevant, and these were mainly Labour strongholds where the Conservative Party was at its weakest—in particular, often lacking the full-time agent whose presence was critical in maintaining the labour movement. In the agricultural and residential seats, the need for an LAC was often not apparent; the concept might be endorsed in principle, but with the comforting thought that its relevance lay elsewhere.[81] Where LACs existed, they had the closed status of a sub-committee of the association council or executive, often with a limited size defined in the rules, rather than the open nature of a branch which could be joined by anyone. They were also often isolated from the local working-class and trade union world, and unable to claim the legitimacy and importance that would have flowed from a substantial membership.[82] Their membership frequently consisted mainly of the retired, housewives, or those in white-collar occupations; many LAC members were not 'wage-earners' in the real meaning of the term, and sometimes not even working-class.[83] The characteristics of most

[78] Oswestry CA, Exec., 3 February 1925; Guildford CA, Council, 1 May 1925; Canterbury CA, Council, 29 November 1924. In one case, its role was balanced by the formation of a 'Business Men's Committee': Gloucester CA, Exec., 2 September 1929.
[79] Yorkshire Area, F&GP, 19 September 1930, 12 February 1931.
[80] NU Labour Ctte., 16 March 1920, Organising Secretary's Report, CPA, NUA/6/1/3.
[81] Cambridgeshire CA, Exec., 20 February 1926; West Midlands Area, LAC, 9 March 1935.
[82] 'The Conservative Labour Movement', 7 June 1946, CPA, CCO/500/4/1.
[83] Lewisham West CA, LAC, 8 January 1926, gives the occupations of the eight members of the founding committee, of whom three were craftsmen, three were dealers and salesmen, and one an analytical chemist; see also J. R. Greenwood (1981). 'Central Control and Constituency Autonomy in the Conservative Party: The Organisation of "Labour" and Trade Unionist Support 1918–1970', PhD thesis, University of Reading.

LACs were infrequent meetings, poor attendance, low morale, and a feeling of irrelevance, all feeding upon each other in a depressing cycle.

There was an initial surge of development during the strained industrial situation of 1920–21, and the establishment of a number of local labour branches led the Party Chairman to assert that 'this movement is really very successful'.[84] In 1925, it was reported that there were LACs in 262 constituencies in England and Wales, which was just over half. However, by the end of the decade, apathy and economic depression had taken a toll: a return in 1930 gave a figure of only 172 constituencies with an 'effective' LAC, although forty-seven more were classed as 'in abeyance or pending'.[85] There are no definite figures for later in the 1930s, but it seems likely from the evidence of the constituency records that there was a gradual increase, mainly in the rural and suburban areas—especially in southern England—which had shunned the concept in the 1920s. Thus Guildford, having explicitly rejected forming an LAC in 1925, did so in 1933 in consequence of the decision of the Surrey Provincial Division to form a county Labour Committee and to ask each of its divisional associations to do likewise.[86] Even so, it is unlikely that more than two-thirds of constituencies had an LAC by 1939, and probably a considerable number of these had little more than a paper existence. From the outset, the strength of the movement was concentrated in a few industrial areas, principally Glamorgan, Lancashire, Durham, and Northumberland. Although the vigour with which Central Office and its Area Agents promoted the labour movement was essential in fostering its limited success, this also had its drawbacks. Constituencies disliked being pushed too much from the centre, and stubborn unresponsiveness was the instinctive and most effective reaction.

In a few areas, an ancillary working-class movement was established outside the formal organization: this was called the National Conservative League (NCL). As with other attempts to organize working men for the Conservative cause, its vitality and success were largely determined by the extent to which regional leaders and local agents were prepared to take an active part in fostering it. The relationship between parallel bodies such as the NCL and the official party structure tended to lack definition, and often rather than formal representation they were linked through individuals who happened to participate in both organizations. Apart from such overlapping membership, the League had no role in candidate selection and took little part in election campaigns; its function was more in the background, as an antidote to the hegemony of the Labour Party in the industrial areas and a support for working-class Conservatives. The NCL had its own structure, and its lodges looked to this rather than their local Conservative association. Their activities were not within the remit of the constituency agents, and this led to them being ignored or regarded as a distraction. The official trade unionist organization

---

[84] Younger to Waterhouse, 19 January 1921, Bonar Law MSS, BL/96/7; this mentions 200 local branches, but some constituencies had more than one branch and so this figure does not represent 200 constituencies.
[85] NU Labour Ctte., 8 June 1925, 13 October 1930.
[86] Guildford CA, report of Sub-ctte to Council, 1 May 1925, Exec., 31 March 1933; Bedford CA, Council, 6 March 1937; St Albans CA, Exec., 6 May 1938.

regarded its potential rival with some hostility: it dismissed the NCL as not 'in any real sense' national, Conservative, or a league, considered that they 'practice a ritual which has no meaning except to themselves', and concluded 'their utility is doubtful'.[87]

However, this was not the case everywhere and the NCL had a visible presence in certain regions, particularly in County Durham during the 1920s.[88] The Conservatives were on the defensive here: local politics were dominated by the miners' trade union, and it was the first county council to be captured by the Labour Party. In the mid-1920s the agent employed by the Durham county Conservative organization, Allan Hand, and the county's leading active MP, Headlam, were both keen to promote the NCL, with which Hand had close connections. Its lodge structure and mix of social and political functions mirrored both the Primrose League and the Durham Miners' Association itself. However, keeping the NCL going was always an uphill task, and whenever encouragement from the top lapsed the lodges tended to become apathetic and decline. Hand was energetic but impulsive and sometimes difficult, and he was eased out of the county agency in 1927. Headlam had been given a junior ministerial post at the end of 1926 and was less available for local work; he eventually tired of the unequal task, and the Durham NCL faded into the background in the 1930s. It was replaced by the party's official labour organization, but the momentum imparted by the NCL was a principal reason for the Northern Area in 1939 having, at 37.1 per cent, a higher proportion of constituencies with LACs than any other region.[89]

In the country as a whole, the concentration upon promoting the official party trade unionist organization marginalized alternative bodies during the 1920s, and only one other significant Conservative working-class movement remained. This was the Conservative Working Men's Clubs movement, which had emerged in the second half of the nineteenth century and remained widespread and popular. In 1937, there were 1,530 clubs in England, Wales, and Scotland affiliated to the Association of Conservative Clubs.[90] This was an independent organization, but it had representation in the National Union at national and regional level, and in many constituencies the local clubs nominated delegates to the executive or council. By the 1920s, the role of the Clubs had become almost entirely social, with beer and billiards their main attractions—for many of their members, these were the only reasons for joining, and they had little interest in politics and still less in political work.[91] Constituency associations frequently complained of the lethargy and lack of commitment of the Club membership, only a minority of whom provided any active support, whilst most were 'conspicuous by their absence when

---

[87] NU Labour Ctte., 21 June 1920, Organising Secretary's Report, CPA, NUA/6/1/3.
[88] *CAJ*, March 1925, 58–9; May 1925, 91–4; July 1925, 164–7; Headlam to Baldwin, 16 January 1925, Baldwin MSS, 11/94–6.
[89] Adamson memo, 'Labour Movement', 1946, in Greenwood, 'Central control and constituency autonomy', 88.
[90] Association of Conservative Clubs resolution in NU presentation resolutions, June 1937, Baldwin MSS (Worcs RO), BA 14208.
[91] *CAJ*, November 1929, 208; Berkshire South CA, agent's report on the 1945 general election.

there is work to be done'.[92] By 1943, the view from Central Office was that 'to a large extent Conservative Clubs can no longer be relied upon as rallying points', and their political value had become 'practically non-existent'.[93] However, one agent noted that 'whilst one does not see any obvious signs of political activity... the members are continually discussing among themselves political matters', and thus the Clubs were 'centres which are invaluable to the organisation as a whole'.[94] Their more practical roles were usually as a minor contributor to association funds and the provision of a venue to hold meetings; in some cases, the constituency office was located in a Club for a nominal rent.

THE LOCAL MEMBERSHIP

Local Conservative associations were voluntary organizations, and, like all such, their fortunes depended upon the calibre and commitment of those who chose to join them. Membership was open to all without exclusions,[95] and required no specific commitment to activity—in some cases, not even a small subscription.[96] The incentives for involvement were mainly personal and social; only for a very few could there be direct rewards, such as paid employment, a parliamentary career, or the conferment of an honour. Of those who gave their time or money at the constituency level, the large majority were motivated by their sympathy with the Conservative values, temperament, and appeal which have been discussed in Chapters 1 and 2, although they were unlikely to have spent much time thinking about them or to regard themselves as being particularly politically minded. A further incentive, which may have been the main attraction for some, was the social opportunities which membership provided, ranging from simply attending events for entertainment and companionship to the involvement and satisfaction of being amongst the inner group which arranged them.

Participation was generally regarded as a leisure pursuit, in which activity and responsibility were rewards in themselves. 'It affords an outlet to many whose lives would otherwise be dull and uninteresting,' noted a Central Office analysis of 'the attitude of mind of the average Party worker'; attending meetings was made worthwhile for them by the sense of purpose and importance which resulted from 'in so doing to have a say, however small, in the management of the country's affairs'.[97]

---

[92] Dunbartonshire CA, Secretary's Report, Exec., 26 June 1929; Oxfordshire South CA, Exec., 27 March 1926; Northwich CA, Exec., 14 October 1929.
[93] Staff Conference Report, 18–20 September 1943, CPA, CCO/500/1/11.
[94] Denbighshire CA, F&GP, 28 October 1938.
[95] The rare exceptions were Liverpool Workingmen's CA and Liverpool West Toxteth women's association, which had a religious test which excluded Roman Catholics: White to Derby, 12 April 1933, Derby MSS, 6/33.
[96] Dundee CA, Exec., 2 March 1922; Cannock CA, Fin., 25 September 1936. In at least one case, not even all of the members of the executive committee were subscribers: Edinburgh East CA, AGM, 24 April 1935.
[97] Memo by Selby, 'The Party Problem', in Gower to Lloyd, 23 May 1933, Baldwin MSS, 59/248–55.

There was certainly also an attraction in cutting a figure in local society, and this brought advantages in prestige and contacts. In many places, the Conservative association was entrenched in the local community and membership of it was as useful a social—and sometimes therefore an economic—network as the golf club, the Rotary Club, and the Freemasons. For all of these reasons, association activities were often apolitical in tone and even content, with the more partisan aspects deliberately de-emphasized; this particularly could be the case in the more middle-class and rural districts, where it was almost taken for granted that 'we are all Tories round here'. In the main, members were drawn in not by the prospect of partisan conflict, but of marking their place within the established order. As the Principal Agent observed: 'it must not be forgotten that local politics are means by which local people may advance in the social scale'.[98]

Leadership at constituency level came predominantly from the upper and upper-middle classes, who provided the central association's officers and most of its committees. In the county divisions in particular, there was often an aristocratic element: the Earl of Midleton, chairman of the Unionist Independent Peers, claimed that 'probably there are at least two hundred constituencies returning Conservatives in which peers and their families are the largest subscribers, the chief office holders, and the heartiest workers for the cause'.[99] This support from the upper strata of society gave the Conservative Party a range of valuable resources: not just money, but educated and socially self-confident candidates for parliamentary and local elections, traditions of leadership and public service, established roots in the community, social prestige and deference, grounds available for staging functions, and often ownership of the local press. Personal status was crucial, and the organization was at its most effective when 'it acts through "local leaders" who really influence their neighbours, and who are looked upon by the people with whom they come in contact with confidence and regard'.[100] The active participation of some figures of 'good social position' was a vital ingredient, especially in the women's organization.[101] In the opinion of one constituency agent, three-quarters of the active members 'are there because they like someone who is prominent in the Association...and not because of their love for political work'.[102] The officers at branch level varied from upper- to lower-middle class in different districts,[103] whilst the bulk of the general membership was lower-middle class: clerical workers, teachers, owners of small businesses, and tradesmen. Typical was the woman described by the wife of a constituency chairman as 'a great worker for the cause, very respectable sort of shopkeeper class'.[104]

A unique insight into the social profile of the grass roots is provided by a list from 1921 of the 384 shareholders in the company established to publish a

---

[98] Fraser's report to A. Chamberlain, 30 December 1921, AC, 32/4/1b.
[99] Midleton to Baldwin, 10 August 1928, Baldwin MSS, 59/211–16.
[100] Inverness CA, Organiser's Report, AGM, 17 October 1928.
[101] Wolverhampton West CA, Management Ctte., 29 November 1921.
[102] *CAJ*, October 1936, 241.
[103] Stone CA, agent's notes on local supporters, c.1934, D1289/11/1.
[104] Lady Peto diary, 7 October 1922.

Conservative-supporting newspaper in Cheltenham, as an occupation is given for nearly three-quarters of the males.[105] It is reasonable to assume that the persons listed were all members of the constituency association, and they probably accounted for most of the subscribers to its central funds. Having some stake in the company, however small and symbolic, seems to have been an important sign of support for the cause, and whilst the list leans towards the better-off (as, of course, did the subscribing party membership as a whole), there is still a wide social range, with many small stakes of between one and five shares, as well as some larger holdings of several hundreds. Of those named, 115 are women for whom no occupation is given (thirty-three are unspecified, twenty-six are given as 'married woman', twenty-seven as 'widow', and twenty-nine as 'spinster'), and seventy-three of the men have no declared occupation—although, from their addresses, at least thirteen of these were gentry. An occupation is stated for 196 persons, almost exclusively male, 31.6 per cent of whom can be categorized as upper class or professional upper-middle class, 14.3 per cent as lower-middle class in white-collar work, 26.5 per cent as shopkeepers, 13.3 per cent as skilled craftsmen, 8.7 per cent as farmers or market gardeners, and 5.6 per cent as unskilled and working class.

Working-class Conservative voters—especially men—were much less likely to join the constituency association in the first place, to retain membership over a lengthy period if they did so, or to take an active or prominent part.[106] This was partly because the atmosphere of local branches could seem alien and unwelcoming, and their activities were mainly middle class in nature. More practically, it reflected the different amounts of time and energy available for leisure, and differing concepts of the pleasurable spending of that time. As a delegate remarked at the 1934 annual conference, it was difficult to attract men to evening meetings 'after a hard day's work, especially in inclement weather'.[107] For working-class men, political activity of any colour had to compete with physical tiredness on the one hand, and on the other with the appeal of the pub, club, music hall, and cinema, and spectator involvement in popular sports such as football, racing, and boxing. Working-class women were occupied in the household chores of cooking, cleaning, and child-rearing, and in many cases were also in full- or part-time work; these commitments limited the scope of their participation, for 'women members generally like to meet in the afternoon...and conduct the routine business of their branches over a cup of tea'.[108] As well as having more leisure time, higher disposable income, and better access to transport, the middle class were culturally more inclined to devote leisure time to meetings and administration. They were, therefore, preponderant amongst the joiners of educational, charitable, or campaigning organizations, and provided those most able or willing to take a lead in these bodies.

This different social pattern explains the variations in the level of party membership across the country. It was not a constant proportion of the Conservative vote:

---

[105] List of shareholders in 'The Cheltenham Newspaper Company Limited', 22 March 1921, loosely inserted in the minute book of Cheltenham CA, Council, 1898–1938.
[106] Duchess of Atholl to Mickel, 26 May 1938, Atholl MSS, 22/24.
[107] NU Conf., 1934, comment of delegate from Islington West CA.
[108] Darlington CA, 'Agent's proposals with regard to re-organisation', Fin., 5 December 1938.

in the more middle-class areas party membership reached large numbers, whilst in the most working-class urban districts the organization was even weaker than the party's lower share of the poll might suggest. In the latter areas, particularly those dominated by heavy industry and coal mining, where trade unionism was at its strongest, it was an uphill struggle to obtain the involvement of what middle-class element there was, due to fears of hostility and possible economic reprisal, and to the apathy which resulted from isolation and alienation. This left those few who did provide the leadership in such depressing (and often depressed) localities heavily burdened and bitterly complaining of neglect both from those around them and—rather less justifiably—from the regional and national party machine. Headlam's attempt to encourage Conservative activity in the west Durham coalfield, and later in the county as a whole, was an example of both how much and how little could be achieved, and how frustrating was the endeavour.[109] These weakest constituencies were often without a candidate for most of the period between elections, which was both a financial disadvantage and a disincentive to political work, and were reliant upon subsidy from Central Office if they were to have any professional organizer. Without the latter, there was even less activity and little prospect of breaking out of the self-perpetuating cycle of minimal funds and few members. There were no nationally promoted recruiting drives of the kind which were adopted after 1945, and instead membership was based upon local networks and the vagaries of their differing levels of resources, competence, and enthusiasm for the task. However, Central Office could supply assistance in the form of missioners who would work to recruit supporters in a particular district, and it often subsidized their pay and expenses in the weaker constituencies.

Membership of the Conservative Party was entirely a local matter; there was no national register, and no obligation upon the local associations even to report a total.[110] The overall membership can only be estimated by extrapolating from the individual data which can occasionally be found in constituency records. Unfortunately, this is patchy and comparatively infrequent; information was discovered in only thirty-two of the 215 constituencies which have been researched, and in several cases this was only a figure for one or two years. Local associations were noticeably coy about giving a definite figure for their membership, especially in any public document such as their Annual Report.[111] The latter confine themselves to vague phrases, and, although they will more often refer generally to an increase in members (even giving a number for this), usually this is without saying what the past or present total actually amounts to. Information was given on some occasions for the membership of the women's branch only, presumably because this was often an impressive figure, whilst a cloak of silence covered the more problematic men's side, and therefore the overall total. Where figures were published in an Annual Report, it was often as a rounded total, and the more precise (and probably

---

[109] Headlam diary, 1924–35 *passim*.
[110] The information was not even requested, as can be seen from an example of the Central Office 'Constituency Records' form in the minute book of Warwick & Leamington CA, April 1934.
[111] Sowerby CA, Council, 1 April 1925.

more reliable) numbers were generally given in the private minutes of committee meetings. The latter are the most episodic, and in both cases there is rarely a consistent run of data over many years. However, the handful of constituencies for which there is an extensive series follow a similar trajectory, with variations which reflect the economic and the political circumstances of the time.[112] The general pattern was for low membership in 1918–22, followed by a swift rise in 1922–26, and a continuing increase in numbers up to a peak around 1929–30; after this there was a dip, especially in the mid-term of the 1931–35 parliament, and then a recovery in the later 1930s, but in most cases not to the peak of a decade earlier. Of course, local membership did not always neatly follow this pattern, as its level was also affected by local circumstances and particularly by organizational efforts and efficiency: a new agent, the use of new methods such as adoption of the 'book scheme', a recruitment drive, or the employment of a professional collector or missioner, could have a considerable impact, sometimes against the national trend.

Inevitably, the sample of data which could be found is doubly tilted towards the safer seats; first, because their records have survived to a greater extent, and second, because higher memberships were more likely to be trumpeted whereas weakness was better concealed. Geographically, there is an over-representation of the southeast in the sample, although curiously it also includes a high proportion of Scottish constituencies (with a mixture of city, suburban, and county divisions); this may to some extent counterbalance the bias to the stronger region, as membership in Scotland seems to have been generally below that of similar socio-economic constituencies in England. The surviving data have been used to calculate a projected national membership for each of the main phases of the period, as explained in Table 3.1. However, whilst this can only be founded upon such evidence as exists, the projection almost certainly overestimates the actual position. Understandably, any published figures tended to be rounded up rather than down, and numbers which were given as an exact thousand may therefore have been increased by several hundred. Branches and associations also tended to keep lapsed subscribers in their lists for quite some time, in the hope that they would eventually renew; such tardiness happened often enough to encourage this practice, together with a natural reluctance to strike names off the roll and diminish the total.[113] An analysis in the suburban constituency of Ilford in midsummer 1934 found that 45 per cent of the 2,812 members had not yet paid their subscription, although it is reasonable to assume that a substantial number of these did so in the second half of the year.[114]

---

[112] The most complete data is for Lewisham West CA, which gave a non-rounded specific figure in its Annual Reports, 1919–44; at Kinross & West Perth CA, the Agent's private reports in the Exec. minutes gives a specific figure, 1926–45 (except 1932); Dunbartonshire CA has an overall total 1924–37 (except 1931), mainly in the Exec. minutes but sometimes in the AR, and for 1926–37 also gives a breakdown of men, women, and juniors; Westminster St George's CA similarly gives a total and the male/female numbers for 1927–35 in its Annual Reports.

[113] *CAJ*, May 1931, 103–5; Edinburgh North CA received 1,050 subscriptions in 1936, but kept on its books 1,800 names of persons who had subscribed 'from time to time': Exec., 10 November 1936.

[114] Ilford CA, Report of Fin. to Exec., 27 June 1934; Worcester CA, JIL Ctte., 4 September 1931. At Kensington South CA in 1936, of the £963-worth of subscriptions received by November, only £575 had been paid by July: Fin., 24 July, 27 November 1936.

In constituencies which had no fixed minimum subscription, it could be difficult to define exactly who was a member, and some branches did not keep records; in one instance, a scrutiny of the returns that did exist indicated that the membership of the women's branch was only about half of the figure which had been given in their Annual Report.[115] It is impossible to know how much allowance should be made for these cumulative inflationary effects, but the actual membership is likely to have been between at least 25 per cent less than the totals projected below.[116]

Table 3.1. Estimate of Conservative Party membership 1919–1939

This table uses all of the data on total constituency membership found in local association records in England, Scotland, and Wales; however, these figures were usually of the men and women members of the senior association only, and (particularly in the 1920s) did not include the members of the Junior Imperial League. For each constituency, an average number of members has been calculated from all of the data found during the relevant period (in some cases, there is a figure for only one year). The constituency averages for the period have been added together and compared to the sum of the Conservative votes in those constituencies at the general election of 1929 (in double-Member constituencies, where there were two Conservative candidates in 1929, only the higher of the two votes has been counted). This has produced a percentage level for the period, which has been applied to the total Conservative vote in England, Scotland, and Wales in 1929, to generate the estimated number of the national party membership.

Period	Number of constituencies	Average local membership	% of 1929 Con vote	Estimated membership
1919–22	5	1,395	6.8	561,633
1923–27	15	2,559	14.8	1,222,377
1928–31	14	3,688	19.1	1,577,528
1932–35	18	3,581	18.5	1,527,972
1936–39	8	2,814	15.1	1,247,156

Due to the very small number of examples, the projection for 1919–22 should be treated with particular caution. However, it is apparent from many other contemporary comments that party membership was low during this period. This was partly because the existence of the Coalition limited activity and recruitment in some areas, and partly because it took some time for constituencies to adapt to the enlarged post-1918 electorate; in several cases, women's branches were not established until after 1923. Indeed, the relative lack of evidence for the immediate post-war years is in itself evidence of the lack of activity and growth. The slump of the early 1930s affected membership to some extent, but not as markedly as it affected association income, due to the fact that in many places there was no compulsory

---

[115] Cannock CA, Fin., 25 September 1936; Oswestry CA, Women's Ctte., 18 February 1933.
[116] One agent estimated the loss of members in a year due to deaths, removals, and lapses as about 12%: Kinross & West Perthshire CA, Organising Secretary's Report to Exec. Council, 15 October 1937, copy in Atholl MSS 22/6.

subscription or the minimum was only a few pennies.[117] Whilst the main factor here was the economic squeeze of the depression on supporters' incomes, it was also the case that a coalition—even one considered to be doing 'excellent work' and 'fully accepted', such as the National Government, diluted party feeling, 'with a resultant decrease of interest and practical support'.[118] The lower projection for the period 1936–39 is partly due to five of the eight constituencies for which there are data being in Scotland, where numbers were generally less. However, there was certainly a falling off in membership during the Second World War, with many constituencies ceasing activity and others making little effort to collect subscriptions.[119]

What is evident is that between the mid-1920s and the outbreak of war in 1939, Conservative Party membership reached high levels in some districts, especially the leafy suburbs and rural shires. One instance of a precise breakdown was at Ashford, which in February 1935 had 3,592 members, including 509 in its ten Junior Imperial League branches.[120] Other county divisions, especially in southern England, had even larger memberships, particularly at their peak in the late 1920s. Chichester has the highest figure of the examples found, with a total membership stated as 9,290 in 1931, and two other southern county divisions were not far behind, Epsom having 8,627 members in 1929 and Winchester some 8,500 in 1927; in Scotland, Dunbartonshire reached its highest point of 6,933 in 1930. Within the membership, there was often a striking variation in the gender balance, and it was commonly observed that it was difficult to get the men to take an active interest during the lull between general elections.[121] The pattern noted by the Bath Association was typical even of safe seats: 'they had a large number of lady members but their husbands were not members'.[122] In many places the female membership outnumbered the male by a factor of three, four, or even five to one. Thus the ratio at Ipswich in 1926 was 20.1 per cent males to 79.9 per cent females, and at Bute & North Ayrshire in 1936 it was 25.2 per cent males to 74.8 per cent females, whilst the membership at Putney in 1924 broke down into 30.6 per cent men, 59 per cent women, and 10.4 per cent in the junior branch. The balance was less tilted in some of the more urban seats in Scotland's central belt, with the division in Stirling & Falkirk Burghs in 1932 being 35.4 per cent male to 64.6 per cent female, and in Dunbartonshire in 1926 being 48.1 per cent male to 51.9 per cent female. Even so, after the very early 1920s, there was nowhere an example of a constituency with more men than women members, and the rising level of party membership during the 1920s made matters worse in this respect, as female recruitment expanded more rapidly than male. Thus, whilst the total number of members at Winchester more than doubled, from 3,100 in 1923 to 8,500 in 1927, the proportion of women became even more marked, increasing from 74.8 per cent to 81.2 per cent.

---

[117] Darlington CA, 'Agent's proposals with regard to re-organisation', Fin., 5 December 1938; Guildford CA, Exec., 30 January 1925.
[118] Glasgow Maryhill CA, AR, 1933, 1934.
[119] Camberwell North, Exec., 10 April 1945; Dundee CA, Exec., 22 September 1942; Argyll CA, AGM, 8 October 1942.
[120] Ashford CA, Agent's Report, Joint Standing Ctte., 22 February 1935.
[121] Monmouth CA, AR, 1927.   [122] Bath CA, General Ctte., 23 October 1936.

The women's membership expanded rapidly in the early 1920s in many places, especially in the period after the uncertainty and apathy of the postwar Coalition, and it was then maintained at a high level throughout the interwar period.[123] Thus, Berkshire South had 4,445 subscribing members of its women's association by 1921, Shrewsbury had over 5,000 women members in 1928, the Wirral had 4,990 in 1928–29, Warwick & Leamington had 4,308 in 1929, and Maidstone had nearly 6,000 women members in spring 1939.[124] These were safer county divisions, but the northern industrial constituency of Stockton had close to 3,000 women members in 1928 and the urban marginal seat of Newcastle West had 1,050 in the trough of the depression in 1933.[125] The strongest districts could reach high levels of penetration: in two of the twenty-seven branches of the Winchester women's association, the membership in 1933 exceeded 50 per cent of the district's female electorate; in another nine branches, it was over 20 per cent, and in only three branches was it less than 10 per cent.[126] The national women's membership was reported in 1927 to total 887,000, and it was later claimed to have reached 1 million by 1929 and to have remained at about this level during the 1930s.[127] As with other estimates, this will have erred on the generous side, but it may not have been exaggerated by much. In 1926, the South East Area women's committee collated quite specific information from its constituencies and arrived at a total of 104,681, and in 1927 the Eastern Area recorded 89,200 women members.[128] These figures were 9.08 per cent and 14.26 per cent respectively of the number of women voters in their regions in the 1931 census; if the lower figure is taken as a national average, 9 per cent of the 13,025,997 female electors in England (excluding Monmouthshire) amounts to 1,172,339. Even with allowance made for the exaggeration of membership figures discussed above, this suggests that a female membership of between 750,000 and 1 million was quite possible, together with a male membership of around 250,000 and between 100,000 and 150,000 members of the Junior Imperial League. Of course, as one local agent pointed out, 'membership alone was not necessarily an indication of efficiency. What was required was active membership', but in this respect the party's women members proved to be a particular asset.[129]

The participation of middle-class women was facilitated in many cases by their relief from household tasks due to having domestic servants (for the less well-off, a 'daily help') and, in the case of the upper-middle class, to educating their children at boarding schools. Most middle-class men worked some distance away from their

---

[123] *Home and Politics*, June 1923.
[124] *CAJ*, January 1921, 18; Shrewsbury CA, AR, 1928; Wirral CA, Women's AR, 1928–29; Warwick & Leamington CA, AGM, 26 March 1930; Maidstone CA, Exec., 27 March 1939.
[125] Stockton CA, Women's AR, 1928; Newcastle West CA, Women's AGM, 28 March 1933.
[126] Winchester CA, Women's AR, 1933.
[127] Maclachlan, 'Summarised Report on Conservative Organisation at Central Office and in the Constituencies during 1927', 30 December 1927, Baldwin MSS, 53/118–49; *Home and Politics*, May 1929; comment of Topping in *CAJ*, July 1934, 143.
[128] South East Area, Women's Parliamentary Ctte, AGM, 30 June 1926; Eastern Area, Women's Council, AGM, 29 June 1927; Petersfield CA, AGM, 2 April 1927.
[129] Hemel Hempstead CA, AGM, 30 April 1927.

home, and so their wives—particularly in the suburbs of the larger cities—were relieved of the necessity to provide a weekday lunch. When combined with the lack of respectable and available employment opportunities (including the operation of the marriage bar in teaching and the civil service), and the absence of such severe pressure on middle-class family budgets from either inflation or male unemployment as to force married women into the labour market, the effect was to channel this available time and energy into a range of voluntary associations. Activity in local Conservative branches was attractive in an era when acceptable behaviour was more circumscribed, conventions more rigidly adhered to, and choice in lifestyle and leisure more limited, localized, and repetitive than they became in the second half of the twentieth century, when party membership steadily declined. In the interwar period, political work offered greater social opportunities to middle-class women than it did to men, and this led to the frequently observed pattern of the women being the more enthusiastic and hard-working, in some cases to the point of being 'fatiguingly zealous'.[130] However, this was balanced by the recognition that many of the women members regarded their participation primarily as a social pastime.[131] This contributed to their tendency to keep their horizons at a parochial level, and perhaps explains the comparative lack of grievance over the male domination of the leading positions and the decision-making of the constituency associations.

Many of the more active Conservative women had a range of interests and commitments, and often were also involved in the overlapping networks of other organizations, such as the Women's Institute, the National Council for Women, the Townswomen's Guild, the Mothers' Union, the various societies for professional women, and the many bodies which supported local philanthropic, artistic, and recreational activities.[132] These specifically women-only or preponderantly female organizations continued the Victorian outlook of 'separate spheres' whilst avoiding any challenge to male roles, and fostered a culture of non-partisanship with a focus on sociability rather than political controversy. Conservative women at every level took pains to emphasize that they were not feminists, by which term they meant or understood an aggressive and controlling desire for dominance, the rejection of the traditional domestic roles of wife and mother, and the advocacy of alarming doctrines of social and familial dissolution, such as free love.[133] Even so, particularly during the 1920s, amongst the male members and officers of constituency associations there was sometimes 'an uneasy sense that the feminine tide may sweep everything before it'.[134] This trend continued to such an extent that during the 1930s

---

[130] The description is of a tiresome member of Barnstaple CA, but 'there is at least one in every constituency': Lady Peto diary, 22 November 1923; Hampshire East CA, Secretary's Report, AGM, 2 April 1927, *CAJ*, January 1934.

[131] Memo by Johnson (Deputy Area Agent, North West), 15 November 1930, Templewood MSS, VI/3.

[132] The scheduling of the national Women's Conference took account of the Women's Institute annual meeting, 'as many delegates attended both': NU Central Women's National Advisory Council, 10 July 1935. See also J. Hinton, *Women, Social Leadership and the Second World War* (Oxford, 2002), 55–6.

[133] *CAJ*, November 1927, 301. The regional women's committee in the Western Area changed its name from 'Women's Parliamentary Council' to 'Women's Advisory Council' in November 1926 because the original name had caused suspicion 'that it might be a feminist movement within the Party'.

[134] *CAJ*, November 1926, 343.

there was frequent concern about the lack of participation of men, and fears that the attitude was developing amongst male Conservatives that local organization had become a female activity, and to leave the women to it.[135] However, the counter to this view was the fact that men had always been cyclical rather than constant in their political involvement; that they were not indifferent, and when an election came they would step forward and provide their customary impetus and direction.[136]

Conservative associations were bodies of like-minded people who were generally comfortable in each other's company, where the conventions of behaviour were understood and adhered to.[137] As a whole, and particularly in the case of branch and association committees, they were both socially and temperamentally homogeneous. Conservatism was 'a spirit drawing men together into a sensible comradeship'; this did not mean the absence of frictions and rivalries, but rather that these took place within the parameters of an accepted consensus.[138] 'Team spirit' was regarded with approbation, and there was general understanding and acceptance that 'success depends on the goodwill and co-operation of all'.[139] The effects of this were that tensions were rarely given public display and powerful social conventions inhibited serious friction or confrontation. Thus, when the disagreement about the control of funds between the women's association and the constituency executive in Worcester reached an impasse, a male member of the latter was concerned lest the meeting should 'break up in a spirit of antagonism and appealed to the chairman to help create a more friendly feeling'; the outcome was an agreed statement 'that there was evidence of a sincere desire on all sides to settle any differences'.[140] Difficult issues were often simply avoided, or dropped if they threatened to cause a split. Where there were divisions, the sense of community and habit of restraint helped to limit their corrosive effects. After the potentially divisive strains of the end of the Lloyd George Coalition, one county congratulated itself 'that all the leaders in the county shewed a great spirit of tolerance and mutual forbearance, and did everything possible to maintain the general unity of the Party'.[141] Such patterns of behaviour also explain the comparative ease and equanimity with which reunions followed a rift; a local chairman observed that 'naturally they had their own opinions, but they did not sulk in their tents'.[142] As always, matters of personality were more likely to cause trouble and be more difficult to set aside than differences of political opinion.[143] There would always be the human failings—in

---

[135] *CAJ*, January 1934, 9–11; April 1934, 75–8; July 1934, 141–5; August 1934, 167–72; February 1935, 33–6; January 1936, 9.
[136] *CAJ*, May 1939, 121.
[137] Hertford CA, Council, 27 March 1935; there were, of course, isolated aberrations, such as the campaign of anonymous letters in one London branch: Hackney North CA, Stamford Hill Ward, Council, 13 January 1938.
[138] 'Gentleman with a Duster', *Conservative Mind*, 140; Chippenham CA, Exec., 2 November 1934.
[139] Harborough CA, AR, 1927.
[140] Worcester CA, Exec., 20 May 1932.
[141] Cornwall PD, AR, 1922, AGM, 28 February 1923.
[142] Denbighshire CA, Northern Area, AGM, 20 March 1930; Derbyshire South CA, Exec., 3 December 1930.
[143] Wimbledon CA, Finance & Organisation Ctte., 11 April 1927; Gloucester CA, Exec., 25 October 1928; Kennington CA, FGP and Exec., 23 November 1928; Perth CA, Exec., 20 November 1935.

particular, jealousy and rivalry, ambition and self-aggrandizement, snobbery and pomposity, procrastination and laziness. Social competitiveness and local territoriality could divide the membership within and between branches, but such tensions were normally storms in a teacup and rarely did much real or lasting damage.[144] In any case, some friction and drama added spice to local affairs and probably encouraged participation as much as discouraging it. The horizons could be limited: 'the members of the Association were parochial,' declared one committee stalwart without regret; 'their work was voluntary and they were keen on their own constituency'.[145] Even so, any negative elements were more than outweighed by the extent to which the constituency associations mobilized support, and provided 'the opportunity for local enthusiasm and the pride of competence'.[146]

THE PROFESSIONAL STAFF: AGENTS AND WOMEN ORGANIZERS

The vitality and efficiency of a constituency association depended largely upon having the services of a full-time professional agent, and the quality of that agent.[147] As one local officer acknowledged, 'most constituency officials recognised the Agents as the backbone of the Party'.[148] An agent provided continuity and consistency of organizational effort, and was both a stimulus and a focal point. They were the front-line infantry of political warfare, and without doubt the Conservative Party benefited greatly from having the big battalions; in 1927, every constituency in the Metropolitan Area had an agent.[149] The agents' work was subject to few rules and largely unsupervised, and so motivation and honesty were essential requirements. However, some agents became lazy and many more were stuck in a rut. The measurable indicators of achievement were relatively few and far between: the health of the annual balance sheet and the outcome of the occasional election, and for neither of these was the agent solely accountable. Local communities were much more discrete entities in this period, especially the rural districts and smaller towns which had restricted and interwoven professional and business circles. Connections were made and maintained by the lubricants of middle-class society: the Rotary movement, Freemasonry, clubs, charities, and churches. Inevitably, in such a milieu, there was a considerable element of back-scratching, of favours owed and received, and of understandings on a nod and a wink; this was at best a form of comfortable social inclusion, and at worst a cronyism which could degenerate into corruption. The agent had to live and work within his local context, and to be

---

[144] Birmingham CA, Agency Sub-ctte, 23 May 1927; Ayr Burghs CA, Organisation Ctte., 20 December 1928, Ayr Branch, special general meeting, 6 February 1923.
[145] Winchester CA, Rules Ctte., 6 May 1936.
[146] Lord Woolton, *The Memoirs of the Rt. Hon. the Earl of Woolton* (1959), 333.
[147] 'Memorandum on the working of our Party Organisation', 10 October 1930, Templewood MSS, VI/3; Headlam diary, 20 August 1930.
[148] Wessex Area agents, meeting, 16 July 1934.
[149] London Department Report, 30 December 1927, Baldwin MSS, 53/143.

successful had to be adept at manoeuvring within it. It was necessary to remain on good terms with all, and a pleasant personal manner was an agent's most valuable asset. He needed 'to keep fit, be always bright and approachable, have a pair of very broad shoulders…and be a hale fellow well met'.[150] The agent was expected to be politically neutral and thus 'friendly with all shades of politics' within the party, and not to voice opinions on questions of policy.[151]

The ideal agent was hard-working and efficient, but combined this with patience, tact, and charm, and so possessed 'the very desirable quality of being able to enthuse others'.[152] Such paragons were hard to find; some agents were highly competent but too fussy or assertive, whilst others became frustrated or harassed.[153] This created unwelcome tensions, and most executives preferred steadiness and pleasantness, even if accompanied by an over-reliance upon customary methods and a lack of initiative.[154] A bad agent could do a lot of damage to an association, especially in a small community, such as the incumbent at Barnstaple 'who has hardly a friend left among the Conservatives, has put *all* their backs up…and said to take too much to drink at times', and the woman organizer at Louth with unpaid bills to local tradesmen who were party subscribers.[155] In one case, the departing agent was paid £75 a year provided that he and his wife did not live in the constituency during the next three years.[156] As in any walk of life, there were moments of triumph and of tragedy; an example of the latter was the suicide of Albert Beale, part-time agent at Tottenham South, who jumped in front of an underground train at Piccadilly Circus after his association decided 'it would be better to have a younger and more energetic man'.[157] However, an effective and popular agent could amass a considerable fund of goodwill, which was often expressed in actual funds by a testimonial collection or grant on his departure; when the agent at Southport retired after twenty years' service in 1928, he was presented with a piece of silver plate and a cheque for the very handsome sum of £1,040, which was nearly three times the average annual salary.[158]

The crucial relationship in the constituency organization was that between the Chairman and the agent; committees met relatively infrequently, but these two would be in contact on an almost daily basis, and the effectiveness of the association depended very largely upon their harmonious co-operation. The dynamics of this relationship depended upon the interplay of five factors: social class (and its consequent patterns of deference and authority), age (and especially any generational difference), experience (of life as well as politics), competence (which would be capped by success in electoral contests), and character. Although the servant of the association, with certain combinations of the above factors the agent could

---

[150] *CAJ*, September 1924, 212.   [151] Chichester CA, F&GP, 20 January 1926.
[152] Blake (chairman, Wiltshire West CA) to Long, 15 December 1923, Long MSS (WSA), 947/885; *CAJ*, September 1919, 6–8; Reigate CA, Exec., 8 March 1921; Cheltenham CA, AR, 1925.
[153] Berwick & Alnwick CA, Council, 16 July 1929.
[154] Pembrokeshire CA, Special Exec., 17 July 1937.
[155] Lady Peto diary, 24 October 1922, 6 October 1928; Webb (agent, Louth CA) to Heneage, 18 June 1930, Heneage MSS, HNC/2/2.
[156] Northwich CA, Fin., 28 April 1923.
[157] *CAJ*, July 1925, 163.   [158] Southport CA, AR, 1928–29; Knutsford CA, Exec., 18 June 1927.

become the dominant figure and effectively be in control. This was particularly likely to happen in urban industrial areas, where the local social elite was non-existent (or at least non-resident, and devoting its attention to the more congenial suburbs) or was, for reasons of religion and political tradition, distanced from the Conservative Party. In such cases, the agent, who had usually served as an officer in the Great War and used his former military rank, and often had connections to an upper-middle-class milieu, could have the chairman and executive committee under his thumb. The officers of associations in these poorer constituencies were likely to be small businessmen and older shopkeepers, probably with no special record of war service and little experience of life outside their district, who had much on their minds from their own affairs. This could lead to the agent becoming lazy or even corrupt, and dependent upon the continuation of the present regime, thus perpetuating inactivity, defeatism, or complacency and discouraging the rise of younger and more energetic local leadership. Breakdowns in the relationship between agent and chairman were rare, but when it did happen, it was almost always the agent who had to go—even when he was very popular, as in the case at Stafford, where the agent had withdrawn a previous resignation after a petition was signed by around 1,500 local members.[159]

The nature of the agents' job required long and often unsocial hours. As well as working during the normal day, he was expected to be available for evening meetings and weekend events: 'an agent's work necessitated going out at night in all sorts of weather throughout the year'.[160] During 1925, the agent for Torquay attended over 300 meetings, in addition to his 'manifold duties' in the constituency office.[161] In the latter respect, another constituency estimated that 'the number of callers at the office averages over 250 per month, all of whom require attention, advice or help of some kind'.[162] There was constant engagement with a wide variety of people, and the ideal was that the agent should know personally every member of each local branch.[163] A long-serving agent acquired valuable expertise; one such was described as 'the living encyclopaedia' of his constituency.[164] The duties involved a combination of office work and getting out and about in the constituency; in that sense, whilst there was much that was routine, there was an attractive variety to the work.[165] Rural constituencies particularly entailed a considerable amount of travelling, with the agent in Norfolk North estimating that he had covered 9,000 miles in ten months.[166]

---

[159] Stafford CA, Exec., 12 February 1921, 20 May 1922; York CA, Management Ctte. emergency meeting, 24 March 1930.
[160] Knutsford CA, AGM, 18 June 1927; Middleton & Prestwich CA, F&GP, 26 April 1934; Oxfordshire South CA, Exec., 26 January 1938; *CAJ*, September 1924, 212.
[161] Torquay CA, Annual Report 1925, AGM, 10 April 1926. For humorous accounts of an agent's working day, see *CAJ*, July 1928, 208–11; December 1929, 241–2.
[162] Cambridge CA, Consultative Council, 23 April 1926; Wessex Area agents, meeting, 27 November 1934.
[163] *CAJ*, February 1923, 29; Canterbury CA, AR, 1937.
[164] Burton CA, AGM, 13 May 1944.
[165] Bute & North Ayrshire CA, 'Conditions of appointment of Organising Secretary', 28 May 1925.
[166] Norfolk North CA, Exec., 10 November 1928; Almond to Divisional Petroleum Officer, 2 September and 7 November 1939, Flyde CA, DDX/1202/3/7.

Before the First World War, the primary task had been the preparation of the electoral register (securing the inclusion of Conservative supporters and objecting wherever possible to those of other parties), and the need for knowledge of electoral law meant that many agents were local solicitors, working on a part-time basis. However, the 1918 Reform Act not only created an electorate too vast to manage in this way, but placed the compilation of the register in the neutral—and usually efficient—hands of local government officials. The result was a reorientation of the agents' functions, and the need for a broader expertise. Registration remained part of the work, but it was now focused more upon tracing those who had moved away and as a basis for canvassing.[167] Rather than determining exactly who was on the register, it was more important to know the politics of the electors, as 'the great need in these days was to concentrate on known supporters'.[168] The ideal was to have these marked up on the register, as a key element in success was ensuring that your own voters went to the polling stations, arranging transport for those in need of it, and—using the returns from the district committee rooms—in the final hours chasing up those who had not yet turned out. Most of the work between elections now revolved around arranging social and fundraising events, organizing meetings, and distributing propaganda.[169] The agent also had a valuable role in gathering intelligence on public opinion, for the benefit of both the MP and national headquarters.[170] In the towns and cities where the Labour Party had a presence, local government elections were now generally fought on party lines (although sometimes, in a pact with the Liberals, under a local umbrella label), and the agent and organization were engaged upon these more frequently than upon parliamentary elections.

In the interwar period, agents were drawn mainly from the middle and upper strata of the middle class. Although only some had a career background in the armed forces, very many of them had served in the First World War, and so captains, majors, and commanders abounded in the following two decades. They had the advantage of some experience of organizing people and of working within a clear hierarchy, and usually had a useful self-confidence and appropriate social status. Others turned to political work from less satisfying occupations in the commercial world, either in administrative roles or as salesmen.[171] From the 1920s, there was a start in recruitment from the ranks of the Junior Imperial League; one such example was E. S. Riley, formerly Secretary of the JIL in his home town of Derby, who trained as an agent in Bristol in 1926, secured his first agency at Gloucester in 1927–31, and then returned to Derby as agent for this double-Member borough until 1950, with a break for service in the RAF from 1939 to 1945. Some agents remained in the same constituency for the whole of their career, such as Mr Allday, who retired in 1944 after fifty-nine years' service to the party in

---

[167] *CAJ*, September 1927, 250–3; Northampton CA, Agent's Report, AGM, 30 March 1925.
[168] Wessex Area agents, meeting, 27 January 1933.
[169] *CAJ*, January 1923, 1–2; Ayr Burghs CA, AGM, 30 April 1924.
[170] Address by Thomson (Scottish Whip), Scottish Unionist Organising Secretaries' Association conference, 27–30 April 1928, copy at Edinburgh West CA.
[171] *CAJ*, November 1926, 342.

Bournemouth; H. A. Drudge, who started work as a lad in the office of the Isle of Wight association in 1908, became the agent in 1922, and served there until the late 1940s; and Elton Halliley, the editor of the *Conservative Agents' Journal* and a founder of the National Society and the pension fund, in Bury St Edmunds. The more usual career structure was one of migration from weaker to stronger seats, which brought with it not only a higher salary but also greater job security, a less challenging political task, and a pleasanter environment in which to live and work.[172] The effect, however, was that poorer seats were unable to retain the most capable agents for very long, and either suffered from discontinuity or were left with the second-rate. However, the fact that agents were employed by the local associations, who were autonomous in making appointments, meant that Central Office was powerless to direct the best and most experienced to where they were most needed, in the key marginals. A route which agents did not take was to enter parliament, and there were only two instances of an agent directly doing so. The first was from the prewar era of part-time agents: Thomas Davies had acted in that role in the Cirencester division from 1885 to 1918, before sitting as MP for Cirencester & Tewkesbury from 1918 to 1929; he was also a prominent member of Gloucestershire County Council from 1899. The second example was Colonel A. J. Todd, MP for Berwick in 1929–35; however, he had entered the agent's post by an unusual route, was of fairly high social standing, and was something of an independent figure in his own right.[173] He continued that style in the Commons, and was one of the five Members to decline the National Government whip in 1935; the resulting dissension in the constituency contributed to his defeat, although Berwick was at best a marginal prospect.

After the organizational stagnation of the Coalition period and the defeat of 1923, many constituencies began to reorganize and there was a greater demand for agents in the mid-1920s.[174] Together with the changing nature of the work and the need for more managerial skills, this led to the rise of professionalism and a demand that posts be reserved for those who had qualified for the official certificate.[175] This coincided with the desire of Central Office, under the impetus of Herbert Blain and then of Davidson, to increase the efficiency and the status of the agents. These already had a corporate body, the National Society of Conservative Agents, which had been founded on their own initiative in 1891.[176] This now assumed more formal and important roles, which was recognized by its representation in the restructuring of the National Union in 1924 and 1930. The crucial initiative was

---

[172] Special Finance Ctte. Report, 16 March 1944, CPA, CCO/500/3/1.
[173] Todd was originally appointed in 1924 as an election sub-agent, on the recommendation of Leigh Maclachlan (then deputy to the party's Principal Agent), after having assisted in the Area Office during the 1923 general election: Berwick & Alnwick CA, Sub-agent Selection Ctte., 4 April 1924, Exec., 28 November 1928; *CAJ*, November 1970, 16.
[174] Blain to Heneage, 24 April 1924, Heneage MSS, HNC/2/2.
[175] West Midlands Area, GP, 15 February 1924.
[176] Records of the National Society of Conservative Agents, Westminster City Library; of the Metropolitan Branch, BLPES; of the Wessex Branch, ARE/10/25; E. Halliley, *A Short History of the National Society of Conservative and Unionist Agents*, supplement to *CAJ*, December 1947; A. Fawcett, *Conservative Agent: A Study of the National Society of Conservative and Unionist Agents and its Members* (1967). There was a parallel Organising Secretaries Association in Scotland: SUA, Exec., 14 July 1926.

the establishment in 1925 of a Joint Examinations Board, administered by representatives of the agents' National Society and senior figures of the Organisation Department at Central Office (who were themselves mainly former agents). This Board oversaw the curriculum and assessment of the training courses; by the outbreak of war in 1939, 791 successful students had received certificates.[177] The next vital step was taken in 1933, when the National Union Central Council resolved that all future appointments in constituencies must be certificated. However, for some time afterwards this was not always observed, particularly where an association lacked funds and was seeking an agent on the cheap.[178] In other cases, it was due to the desire to appoint a particular local person, sometimes simply from nepotism but usually because he had already been working on a less formal basis; these were sometimes dealt with by insisting that the person undertake the training whilst in post. All such cases were greeted by protest from the National Society, and they were particularly exercised over the 'Liverpool affair' of 1936 (when an uncertificated man was appointed as the chief City Agent), due to the impact of such a large city breaking ranks.[179] The touchy question of professionalism also fuelled the outrage of the agents over the proposition in the revised rules of the National Union in 1930 to exclude them from attending the Central Council and Annual Conference. The reason was an attempt to make the size of these gatherings manageable, but the agents were deeply offended, lobbied the regional Areas, and successfully objected to this clause at the Central Council meeting of 4 March 1930. The other important reform of the agents' profession in this period was the regularization of pension arrangements with the introduction of a superannuation fund in 1926, described by the Deputy Party Chairman as 'probably the most fruitful of all reforms', with 325 members enrolled in its first year.[180] The National Society had its own tier of regional committees; like the parent body, these normally limited themselves to politically neutral organizational topics, but occasionally—'respectfully' and disavowing any intention of influencing policy—in times of tension they sounded a warning note.[181]

The income of associations in the Conservative strongholds was usually more than sufficient to offer a good salary to an agent. Many of the marginal seats could also finance this from their own resources, although here the pay was less generous and the continued viability of the agent was more dependent upon his own fund-raising work. In some of the marginals and in the weaker seats, the presence of an agent was made possible by subsidies from Central Office, particularly in the run-up to an election in the seats that might be holdable or winnable. In the interwar period there was no national pay scale; salaries were a matter of individual negotiation, and varied widely according to the funds of the employing association.

---

[177] *CAJ*, August 1939, 209–10; April 1932, 87–9.
[178] NU Exec., 'Status and Efficiency of Agents and Women Organisers', 10 July 1935.
[179] NU Exec., 15 July, 9 December 1936, 6 October 1937.
[180] Linlithgow to Baldwin, 9 March 1925, Baldwin MSS, 160/101–2; NU Central Council Report to Conference, 1926–27. Until this fully took effect, cases of hardship continued to be dealt with by a charitable fund, the Agents' Benevolent Association.
[181] Metropolitan Area Agents, Council, 8 August 1921, 3 August 1922.

The poorer seats could only offer between £250 and £350 per annum, whilst in the wealthier seats a new appointee would often start at £350 and an experienced agent receive between £400 and £500, with a handful of salaries rising to £600.[182] A house might also be part of the package, provided either free or at a reduced rent, especially where affordable housing in a suitable location was hard to find.[183] An agent's out-of-pocket expenses were often considerable and were usually paid in addition to the salary, although often up to a fixed maximum amount. Transport was an essential consideration in the county divisions, and from the mid-1920s it became the normal practice to provide a car, or at least to pay an allowance for the agent's use of his own vehicle.[184] Increases in salary sometimes came as automatic annual increments, especially to a younger agent in his first years in post. More usually, they had to be applied for, and were usually given as a reward for electoral success or improvement in the finances, or as a mark of long service.[185] In some cases, constituencies sought to retain a popular or efficient agent by matching the higher salary which they had been offered to move elsewhere.[186]

The most frequent causes of the end of an agent's employment were inadequate funds and electoral defeat, and quite often they went together. In the disappointment that followed an unsuccessful contest, the organization often took the brunt of the blame at local as well as national level; as one agent commented: 'The candidate wins the election, the Agent loses it.'[187] However, the impetus was usually less the demand for a scapegoat and more the need to economise, especially when the withdrawal of the defeated MP or candidate left a large hole in the balance sheet.[188] The pressure of the economic slump in the early 1930s also led to the termination of some posts, as local supporters tightened their belts and cut back on their subscriptions. In both such cases, agents often offered or accepted a reduction in salary in order to keep their position.[189] The other most common cause of dismissal was the personal failings of the agent, in particular for financial transgressions.[190] This was fundamentally a matter of the flaws in individual characters, combined with the pressure of circumstances and the opportunity provided by access to the funds. However, three contributory elements emerge from the cases in the Central Office files. The first of these was that salaries were sometimes

---

[182] Horncastle CA, Report of Sub-ctte on Finances, 19 January 1932; Norfolk North CA, Exec., 2 February 1934.

[183] Dunbartonshire CA, Exec., 20 October 1920; Cambridgeshire CA, Exec., 17 January 1925; Wells CA, Exec., 25 November 1937.

[184] Dorset West CA, Fin., 14 February 1936, 'Particulars of arrangements between Associations and Agents regarding their cars and transport in constituencies of Dorset, Devon, Somerset and Wilts'; Shrewsbury CA, Car Sub-ctte Report, Fin., 21 October 1933.

[185] Herefordshire North CA, Advisory Ctte, 17 December 1926, 13 September 1929; Reigate CA, Exec., 18 July 1929; Norfolk North CA, Exec., 24 January 1930.

[186] Dunbartonshire CA, Exec., 6 October 1926; Stafford CA, Fin., 26 September 1929; Devizes CA, Exec., 18 December 1930.

[187] *CAJ*, July 1928, 205; Walsall CA, Exec., 10 January, 11 June 1923, Emergency Ctte., 29 July, 16 September 1929.

[188] Camborne CA, F&GP, 24 July 1929; Stirling & Falkirk Burghs CA, Exec., 14 November 1929.

[189] Llandaff & Barry CA, Exec., 8 February 1933; Bury CA, Finance & Exec., 8 November 1933.

[190] Canterbury CA, Exec., 23 October 1930.

inadequate for maintaining a respectable position, either to do the job effectively or for the agent's family.[191] This was a feature of the type of constituency—not the poorest, but those which found it difficult to raise a mid-range budget—which was most frequent in these cases. The second factor was pressure during periods of financial stringency, and Marjorie Maxse, the Chief Organisation Officer at Central Office, noted the particular incidence of frauds in 1932.[192] The third factor was more general in both time and political geography: a lack of proper supervision by the officers of the association.[193] This was most likely in the case of an agent who had been in place for some time, or was a local person from a familiar family.

The work of the agent required constant operational access to the funds, and administering both the income and the expenditure gave plentiful scope for doctoring the books. This was even easier during wartime, as was discovered at Penryn & Falmouth when the agent retired in 1940.[194] These factors together created a situation in which it was not surprising that some agents succumbed to temptation. However, most of the frauds were hopeless affairs, in which the discrepancies were bound to be discovered sooner or later. They were acts of desperation, even of protest, and lacked ingenuity. Even the case in Battersea South in 1937—where a relatively sophisticated embezzlement had been conducted over several years by adding forged entries to the bank statements, using a typewriter with a matching typeface—could have been exposed at any point by a single enquiry to the bank from the Chairman or Treasurer.[195] These were cases of sad and pathetic ruin, of breakdown and humiliation, or of weakness and self-deception: there were the usual excuses of money only borrowed, or owed to the agent for unspecified expenses in the cause.[196]

The other principal causes of dismissal on personal grounds were alcohol and adultery. Sexual misconduct was rarer than financial, but exhibited some of the same features: the need to maintain a respectable façade and the sudden, often foolish, surrender to temptation and opportunity.[197] Sometimes there was a connection, such as the agent at Skipton who embezzled to cover the costs of maintaining two households and also to pay off a blackmailer, or the agent at Chelmsford in 1931, who vanished after being accused of 'immorality', after which an audit of the accounts found that a substantial sum was missing.[198] Finally, there were cases where there was no fraud as such, but the agent was in debt to the point of bankruptcy. One example of this was the unfortunate agent at Belper: after he was

---

[191] Thornton (West Midlands Area COA) to Maxse, 14 February 1936, CPA, CCO/4/1/29.
[192] Maxse to Little (East Midlands Area COA), 16 November 1932, CPA, CCO/4/1/33.
[193] Memo by Potts (North West Area COA) of interview with Chairman of Darwen CA, 31 January 1934, Potts to Maxse, 6 April 1934, CPA, CCO/4/1/4.
[194] Penryn & Falmouth CA, Exec., 20 May 1940.
[195] *Clapham Observer*, 17 December 1937.
[196] Barker to Topping, 9 December 1932, CPA, CCO/4/1/16; Bury CA, Exec. emergency meeting, 31 July 1936, Exec., 27 August 1936; Skipton CA, Exec., 11 August 1938.
[197] Report of Disciplinary Ctte. of the National Society of Conservative Agents, Halliley to Maxse, 19 June 1936, CPA, CCO/4/1/2.
[198] *Daily Mail*, 2 December 1938; Rawcliffe (Yorkshire Area COA) to Maxse, 16 August 1938, CPA, CCO/4/1/49; Chelmsford CA, Exec., 13 August and 25 September 1931.

ambushed at the gate of his house on a dark autumn evening by an unknown assailant who threw sulphuric acid in his face, the following police enquiries revealed the amount that he owed within the constituency, and his employment was ended for this reason.[199] The problem here was partly fouling one's own nest, as such debts were mostly to the class of shopkeepers and small businessmen who were association members. Furthermore, the middle-class culture of most supporters and committee members viewed debt with moral abhorrence, and an agent in this position could not command respect or enthusiasm. A response to these problems in the later 1930s was the 'fidelity bond', a form of insurance cover which the agent had to pay for; this was both a deterrent to defalcation, and a means by which an association could recoup its losses.[200]

Where fraud did occur, the most common response of association officers and executives was not to prosecute.[201] There were two reasons for this tendency to cover up. First, prosecution would not recover the money—in nearly every case it had been spent and the agent was destitute; often they were in poor health as well, and some were clearly suffering from nervous breakdowns.[202] Legal action would only add further costs, and bring the spotlight of public attention. Avoiding bad publicity was the second consideration, as a court case would be likely to damage the prestige of the association and its officers, who were often irreplaceable due to their status and the lack of willing alternatives.[203] The case for the defendant might at the least suggest incapacity on their part; if the association was shown to be badly run or careless with the money that had been donated, then local support would fall away and the deadly weapon of ridicule placed in the hands of the opposing parties.[204] Thus, the general response was that it was better that a rogue should get away than fools be exposed to the light of common day. Perhaps appropriately, the form of cover-up normally adopted was the replacement of the missing funds by personal donations from the officers and committee members, without the wider membership even being aware of the problem.[205] The agent was therefore generally allowed to resign, usually with immediate effect and accompanied by belated precautions such as changing the locks on the constituency office; in a few cases, they returned some of the money or made promises (usually later broken) to repay in instalments.[206] They were then placed on the Central Office 'black list', which was intended to prevent them from securing a post in another region.[207]

---

[199] Little (East Midlands Area COA) to Maxse, 11 October, 15 November 1932, CPA, CCO/4/1/33.

[200] NU GP, 20 May 1936; SUA, EDC, Exec., 14 July 1937; Bedford CA, Agent Sub-ctte, 27 July 1938; Skipton CA, Exec., 11 February 1939.

[201] Hampshire North-West CA, Special Joint Meeting of Exec. and Fin., 24 July 1933; Harborough CA, Exec., 29 July 1933; Epsom CA, General Ctte., 11 December 1931; Kensington South CA, Special Exec., 22 December 1927 (in the case of the subscription collector).

[202] Memo on Rotherhithe election, 1929, CPA, CCO/4/1/7.

[203] Maxse to Thornton (West Midlands Area COA), 17 November 1932, CPA, CCO/4/1/16.

[204] Selley to Armstrong (Metropolitan Area COA), 12 October 1937, CPA, CCO/4/1/48.

[205] Chelmsford CA, Exec., 25 September 1931.

[206] Penryn & Falmouth CA, Emergency Ctte., 6 November 1940, 23 April 1941, 29 April 1942; Kensington South CA, Fin., 22 March 1932.

[207] Maxse to Potts (North West Area COA), 9 April 1934, CPA, CCO/4/1/4.

Only in the most serious cases, where the agent's subsequent conduct or the scale of embezzlement made avoiding publicity impossible, was the full rigour of the law applied; one such was in Battersea South in 1937, described by the party's most senior official as the worst case in ten years, where the amount embezzled was estimated at £750 (i.e. twice the average agent's annual salary).[208]

With the enfranchisement of women in 1918 and the growth of the women's branches, there emerged in the 1920s a new adjunct to the agents' profession in the form of the 'Women Organisers'. At first some of these were volunteers, but as the amount of potential work expanded it became normally a paid part-time or full-time position.[209] In most cases, the woman organizer was additional to a full-time agent and was something only the wealthiest seats could afford, although the practice developed in some Scottish seats of employing the cheaper female where a man agent could not be afforded. It was often the case that the funding of the woman organizer came directly from the coffers of the women's branches, who usually initiated such employments, and this led to the fears of some executives—and particularly of some agents—of a divided command, with a battle of the sexes being conducted in the association's office.[210] The practical consequence was an insistence on a clear chain of command in which the woman organizer was subordinate to the agent; however, a sensible agent did not make such constant demands on her time that the officers of his women's committee became resentful. The salaries of the women organizers were on a level below that of the agents, with full-time positions generally in the range of £200 to £250 per annum.[211]

The woman organizer's post was less secure than the agent's, for she was always regarded—at least by the men on the executive—as a luxury, and the first to go if costs had to be cut, although this could lead to friction with the women who raised most of the funds.[212] The other cause of a frequent turnover of posts was that it was an occupation mainly for younger single women, and they normally resigned on marriage—there was not a formal bar, as in the civil service, but it was generally expected and very few continued to work afterwards. For much of the interwar period, the women organizers were regarded with a mixture of suspicion and alarm by the male agents, who were determined that they should neither encroach upon their own newly won professional status nor secure equality of pay. This hostility was particularly concentrated in the agents' National Society, and its grudging concession of an 'associate' status in 1927, which some of its regional branches refused to implement, led the women to form a separate organization with the aim of raising their status: the National Association of Conservative and Unionist

---

[208] Topping to Armstrong (Metropolitan Area COA), 25 October 1937, CPA, CCO/4/1/48; Gloucester CA, F&GP, 18 January 1937.
[209] Kensington South CA, Women's Fin., 17 January 1930.
[210] *CAJ*, November 1923, 249–52; Moray & Nairn CA, Sub-ctte, 24 November 1931; Edinburgh North CA, Council, 20 February 1933; for an example of the work, see recollections of Lady Larcom, *CAJ*, summer 1984, 42–3.
[211] St Albans CA, Exec., 11 March 1932; Guildford CA, Exec., 24 July 1936.
[212] Dorset West CA, Exec., 10 January, 18 July 1923, 21 January 1925.

Women Organisers.[213] However, there were never sufficient numbers to make this a really effective body, and at Area level its branches were only periodically active.[214] At the outbreak of war in 1939, there were 136 women organizers; by November, twenty-eight of these were still in their post full-time and three part-time, another thirty-one were in the armed forces, twenty-eight were doing 'other work', and twenty-nine had resigned, been dismissed, or given notice.[215] Generational and social change slowly eroded the resistance of the men, and after the Second World War women became eligible for the agents' certificate and admission on equal terms to their National Society; as a consequence, the women's organization was wound up in 1946.

All constituencies which had an agent needed an office for his use. Although a few agents worked from their own home, the normal practice was the renting of office premises, with a balance being struck between the cost of space in town centres and having a convenient location for callers. Less frequently, associations bought or even built their own property, sometimes in quite ambitious undertakings: the double-Member borough of Bolton spent £5,917 on the purchase and refitting of its headquarters, Derby Hall. These larger properties often contained meeting rooms which could be hired out, and thus earn additional income for the association.[216] Whatever their scale, all of the offices had running costs, and these were the other main items of expenditure: generally the everyday matters of heating, lighting, cleaning, stationery, printing, telephone, and postage, but from time to time more capital investment was necessary, such as in typewriters or—becoming more common in the 1930s—a duplicating machine.[217] Constituencies which were more securely funded often employed a clerk or typist as well, and some of the richest ran to a staff which included a second clerk to assist the woman organizer. Whereas the agents and women organizers spent some of their time out and about in the constituency and their commitments included evening and weekend meetings, the clerks worked only in the office and to fixed daytime hours. In the interwar period, these positions became generally filled by women. However, they were usually a significant step, socially and financially, below the women organizers; depending upon age and experience, they were normally paid a weekly wage of around one pound.

During the Second World War, many constituencies lost the services of their agent either completely or for most of his time, with inevitable consequences for the

---

[213] *CAJ*, June 1927, 154; Metropolitan Area Agents, Council, 14 July 1931, 25 April 1932; North West Area Women Organisers, 16 February 1926; East Midlands Area Women Organisers, meeting, 7 September 1927.

[214] National Association of Conservative and Unionist Women Organisers, minutes 1936–46, and East Midlands, North West, Wales, Wessex, and West Midlands Branches, CPA, CCO/170.

[215] CCO/170/2/1/1, National Society of Women Organisers, Officers Meeting, 10 November 1939. The first postwar minute refers to the membership of the society as having been 155 at the outbreak of war, but not all of these may have been in post: Exec., 27 November 1945.

[216] Bury CA, Fin., 14 July 1926, 18 July 1927 (but due to declining income it was later decided to sell this: Finance & Exec., 6 December 1933); Stockton CA, Exec., 25 October 1928; Ilford CA, AR, 1934; Maidstone CA, Exec., 6 February 1934; *CAJ*, January 1939, 12–15; February 1939, 38–40.

[217] Cambridge CA, office inventory, 1 September 1927.

efficiency and even existence of the organization. Many younger agents were reservists who were called up into the armed forces at the start of the war. They were usually stationed away from their previous Area; some fought in the front lines, and some were killed—the most famous being the former agent for High Wycombe, Captain Kennedy, who commanded the armed merchantman *Rawalpindi* in its heroic defence of a convoy against German warships in November 1939. The middle-aged and older agents tended to take up posts in the wartime bureaucracy; they were more often still in the district and sometimes could continue limited part-time work for the association; in a few cases, their wife acted in their place. Only the most elderly agents remained in place, and some constituencies covered the gap by using a retired former agent. In June 1940 there were 193 agents and sixty-nine women organizers in the armed forces and full-time national service combined, and by March 1941 this had increased to 156 agents and thirty-three women organizers in the uniformed services, and 119 and forty-three respectively in other posts.[218]

Some constituencies closed down for the duration, but others sought to remain in being through such expedients as sharing an agent's time with neighbouring seats or having some oversight from the Central Office Area Agent; financial help from Central Office or the Area was often conditional upon retaining an agent.[219] MPs were also actively pressing to keep agents in place: they needed them as eyes and ears in their constituencies, and because of their bigger wartime caseload, and they were also well aware that an election would immediately follow the end of hostilities.[220] The removal of the agent's salary considerably eased the pressure on constituency finances, which were depleted by the reduction of subscriptions and absence of any fundraising efforts. Most associations observed the principle of making up the shortfall in their agent's salary, as the pay in government service and the junior commissioned ranks was often significantly lower; this was a drain, but a reducing one when the former agent gained promotion. As well as recognition of the agent's patriotic work, this was a form of retainer on his services, although some former agents found their new work more interesting or financially rewarding, and gave notice of their intention not to return. However, most were keen or willing to do so at the end of the war, and the main difficulty was in securing their release from war service. The return of the agent was the key to reviving the organization, and this made the delays which many constituencies suffered particularly frustrating and damaging. Although the release of the agents of all political parties had been authorized at Cabinet level in 1944, in practice it seemed that unsympathetic authorities at lower levels put many impediments in the way, and those who did return often had little time to pick up the threads. In December 1944, there were 210 agents and eighty-three women organizers in the armed services and

---

[218] Memo, Topping to Hacking, 26 June 1940, NC, 8/21/19; NU Exec. Report to Central Council, 27 March 1941; list of agents on national service, *CAJ*, January 1940, 21–39; April 1940, 47–8.

[219] Flintshire CA, 11 September and 25 November 1939; Wessex Area, F&GP, 28 February 1940, 24 November 1943.

[220] Clitheroe CA, Exec., 21 September and 16 October 1939; Chichester CA, F&GP, 12 September 1939.

other government employments, of whom 164 agents and twenty-three women organizers obtained release for the 1945 general election campaign.[221] In consequence, as the war entered what was clearly its last few weeks, in the spring of 1945, some associations, in desperation, sought to secure whoever was available, even of very limited experience.

FINANCE AND ACTIVITIES

The income of an association came from subscriptions, donations, and the profits from fundraising events. Most subscriptions were made at the branch level, with a proportion then remitted to the central association, in some cases to meet a specific quota contribution. Payment of a subscription was not always a requirement of membership, particularly in the 1920s when a large membership was a valuable demonstration of democratic credibility. However, this pattern was viewed as outmoded by the 1930s, and instead the ideal was a large number of small subscribers.[222] Constituencies which were successful in fostering this were examples to be followed, and methods of collecting small amounts on a weekly basis, such as the 'book scheme' pioneered by the Tamworth association, were publicized in the *Conservative Agents' Journal* and promoted by Central Office.[223] Whilst this was generally found to be effective in broadening the funding base, most associations still drew much of their funding from a more limited range of larger subscriptions, which were paid directly to the central association by the upper-middle class and above. The experience of Liverpool was typical: 'the number of contributors is very small, and the same persons respond almost every time'.[224] This could result in a perilously narrow basis of funding, even in safe seats: the chairman of the Rushcliffe association pointed out 'that more than half of our total income is generously borne by five individuals—one of whom is our Member'.[225] In many places, central subscriptions above a certain amount were recognized and encouraged by making their donors honorary vice-presidents of the association; in 1923, Hemel Hempstead had forty-six vice-presidents who provided £392, and 108 members of the central association, most of whom also subscribed to one or more local branches, who gave directly a further £109.[226] The amounts given were normally between ten shillings and five pounds, with the most frequent amount being one pound or one guinea. Of the 359 subscribers to the central fund of the Canterbury association in

---

[221] Memo, 'Agents in the Forces', 22 December 1944, Watson to General Director, 'Release of agents for the general election', 10 August 1945, CPA, CCO/4/2/2.

[222] *Finances of a Constituency Association*; Special Finance Ctte. Report, 16 March 1944, 4, CPA, CCO/500/3/1.

[223] *CAJ*, November 1927, 303–5; February 1933, 48; *Constituency Finance*, text of an address by the Principal Agent, 18 December 1929; Wimbledon CA, Finance & Organisation Ctte., 22 February 1928; Cheltenham CA, Fin., 19 October 1923, 31 May 1932.

[224] Salvidge to Derby, 13 May 1924, Derby MSS, 8/6.

[225] Rushcliffe CA, AR, 1938; *CAJ*, May 1926, 162.

[226] List of subscriptions and donations, Hemel Hempstead CA, 1923, Davidson MSS, DAV/164; Epsom CA, Exec., 9 October 1923.

1926, only eleven gave five pounds or more, and one of these was the large subscription from the MP. Similarly, 119 of the 166 subscribers in Argyll in 1934–35 paid between one and four pounds, and most of these were at the bottom end of that range.[227]

Donations were a lesser and irregular proportion of the income; they came from the same upper-middle-class strata of local gentry, businessmen, and professionals, and were usually given for a specific purpose, such as the general election fund, a new car for the agent, the acquisition or improvement of office premises, and the attendance of wage-earners at the party's educational college. Not all support came in monetary form, and wealthier supporters sometimes gave additional subventions of goods and services.[228] As well as the use of grounds and premises, commercial and professional services were often provided free or at cost, in particular legal advice and auditing. In many places, especially in marginal and weaker seats, the support of a relatively small number of wealthier individuals was crucial, and an unfortunate congruence of deaths and removals could cause serious problems, as did the need of many such patrons to curtail their support during the depression of the early 1930s.[229]

In every constituency, the most important single contribution came from the parliamentary candidate or MP. As well as paying the expenses of their election campaigns, which were often around £1,000,[230] they were expected to give an annual subscription to the association. This was likely to be at least £100, and in the better prospects was frequently as much as the entire parliamentary salary of £400; Baldwin's contribution at Bewdley of £300 was average for a safe seat, whilst a few were as high as £600.[231] The largest amount was paid by Samuel Samuel, MP for Putney, who gave £1,000 annually from 1920 to 1924 (accounting for between 82 per cent and 68 per cent of the total income), although this reduced to £800 thereafter.[232] The MP would sometimes give further periodic assistance, such as paying off an overdraft, acting as a guarantor, or contributing to a special fund project.[233] The withdrawal of a candidate was a double blow for an association, simultaneously removing the focal point of its political work and a large part of its resources; in Horncastle, the retirement of the sitting MP and of the prospective candidate reduced the income from £1,181 in 1922 to £443 in 1923, even though the number of local subscribers had increased from ninety to 102.[234] One chairman

---

[227] Canterbury CA, AR, 1926; Argyll CA, AR, 1934–35.
[228] Hertford CA, AR, 1924; Hammersmith South CA, Chairman's Report, 1927, Bull MSS, CAC, BULL/5/20; Cardiff Central CA, Ways & Means Ctte., 28 May, Exec., 13 June 1930.
[229] Cardiff South CA, Exec., 4 September 1933; Melton CA, AGM, 15 May 1931; St Albans CA, Exec., 14 October 1932.
[230] Memo on cost of 1923 general election, n.d., Ashley MSS, BR/76.
[231] Bewdley CA, balance sheets, 1919–30; examples of MPs paying £500 include Wolverhampton West CA, Management Ctte., 19 June 1922; Thelma Cazalet initially paid £600, Islington East CA, Exec., 31 March 1931.
[232] Putney CA, balance sheets, 1919–27.
[233] Harborough CA, Exec., 10 April 1923; Walsall CA, Fin., 19 March 1919. Macmillan was particularly generous: Stockton CA, Fin., 27 April and 22 May 1928, F&GP, 3 May and 7 October 1935, 12 August 1938, and constituency corres., Macmillan MSS.
[234] Horncastle CA, balance sheets, 1922 and 1923; Kennington CA, Exec., 15 July 1939.

summed up the problem: 'without a candidate they could not raise funds, and without funds they could not have an effective organisation'.[235]

It was this imperative which, after an election defeat, made constituencies keen either to reaffirm their previous nominee or to find a replacement; being without a candidate for most of the duration of a parliament could lead to a lassitude that was difficult to overcome in the few weeks of an election campaign. The fact that without a candidate in the field 'it would be impossible to keep the Conservative organisation alive' was a major cause of problems during periods of coalition, for it was this practical consideration—much more than disagreements of principle—which led to associations in constituencies represented by the allied parties wanting to select a Conservative candidate for the next election, a problem which recurred in 1931–35 despite the grass-roots approval of the National Government and desire to maintain it.[236] It was notorious that the ability to pay, and the amount on offer, was frequently the most decisive—and sometimes the only—factor in the selecting of the candidate (see further below). Ironically, the safer the seat, the less it needed the income but the more it could demand, and the richest areas in the country were thus amongst the most exacting.[237] During the Second World War, some MPs applied to reduce their contribution, as constituency running costs were much lower due to the suspension of activities and absence of agents on war work. This caused some tensions, for local subscriptions had also diminished or were not being collected, and whilst this was agreed to in most cases, a number of associations took the view that the MP had made a contractual commitment and 'would be expected to honour this pledge'.[238]

In one sense, the payment by the candidate evened the scales of dependency with the association, whose endorsement was vital, and so helped to retain some vestiges of the concept of the 'independent' Member; this was taken even further on the occasions that the MP bailed out the organization in times of difficulty. On matters of organization, particularly where they touched directly on the MP's electoral prospects (such as retaining the services of an agent), there was a natural view that 'if the Member contributed such a large sum of money, surely he was entitled to have his views considered'.[239] However, from 1931 any assistance given by Central Office with election expenses was no longer paid to the candidate but to the association.[240] This had the effect of making MPs in weak and marginal seats more reliant upon their association, reducing their authority and prestige. Quite apart from the issue of the quality of candidates when chosen by their bank balance, depending too much on this income had unhealthy effects upon the associations. At the least, it led to a lack of local effort and a small membership and subscription list; one such case was Hampstead, which declared that it was 'a blot on the

---

[235] Inverness CA, AGM, 21 October 1926.
[236] Memo by Stonehaven, c.August 1932, Baldwin MSS, 46/49; the quoted comment is attributed to a deputation from Norfolk East CA, where the sitting MP was Viscount Elmley, a Liberal National whip.
[237] Special Finance Ctte. Report, 16 March 1944, 1, CPA, CCO/500/3/1.
[238] Fylde CA, Emergency Ctte., 20 October 1940.
[239] Harborough CA, Council, 8 December 1934.
[240] Dugdale, 'Memorandum on Party Finance', March 1943, CPA, CCO/500/3/2.

constituency's good name that some four-sevenths of the subscriptions and donations come out of the Member's own pocket'.[241] At the worst, it could turn a constituency into the 'pocket borough' of its MP, with the agent looking to the Member as the effective source of his salary, rather than owing his first loyalty to the association.[242] The effect in such cases was to keep the association small, partly because it did not need to make the effort to secure more involvement and partly to make it easier to maintain control; this was Headlam's particular criticism of Sir Nicholas Grattan-Doyle's methods as MP for Newcastle North, the safest seat in the north-east, and led to the clash and split associations of the 1940 by-election. Constituencies protected their financial territory as a vital part of their autonomy, and were always jealous and suspicious of any regional or national fundraising which might draw off resources from the locality.[243] However, whilst this fear was understandable, it was usually unfounded; those who were sufficiently wealthy and politically engaged to be approached by the Area or the national Treasurer nearly always made such donations in addition to their constituency support, and not at its expense.

The income of an association naturally derived from the strength of Conservative support in the constituency. The safer seats had the benefit of sitting MPs who were usually paying a substantial subscription, but they also generally had a number of wealthy local donors, a large membership, and regular fundraising activities. Even so, the central association could still struggle to secure sufficient funds; for example, Wirral in 1939 had 4,314 women members in twenty branches, but only 399 subscriptions were received by the association itself.[244] The levels of income tended to follow the same profile as that of membership, rising from the early 1920s to peak around 1930, dropping noticeably in the early 1930s, and then stabilizing—often with some improvement—in the later 1930s. However, the pattern was not uniform, and varied according to local initiatives and levels of efficiency, such as a change of agent or treasurer. Thus, Shrewsbury had an average income of £885 in 1925–31, but—despite the MP's annual subscription reducing from £250 to £200—a higher average of £1,068 in 1932–38. At Devizes, the subscriptions from members nearly doubled from £387 in 1928 to £734 in 1938, whilst the MP's contribution remained static at £200. Well-founded associations in beneficial environments could regularly raise over £1,000, and the very wealthiest even more: suburban Wimbledon raised £1,825 in 1931 and £1,674 in 1934, whilst Westminster St George's received £2,273 in subscriptions in 1928. The more usual income band in the period 1924–39 for seats which were generally won by the party was between £600 and £900, but weaker seats were often struggling on incomes of £250–450, and so caught in a vicious circle in which they were

---

[241] Hampstead CA, AR, 1935.
[242] *CAJ*, September 1924, 211; 'Memorandum on the working of our Party Organisation', 10 October 1930, Templewood MSS, VI/3.
[243] Wessex Area, Fin., 22 August 1927; Oxfordshire North CA, Exec., 22 March 1932; SUA, EDC, Meeting of Exec. with No. 3 Area Officials, 16 February 1934; Stroud CA, Fin., 31 July 1935; Berkshire South CA, Exec., 24 September 1936, 11 January 1938; Circular from Chairman, East Midlands Area, 19 January 1939, Heneage MSS, HNC/2/18.
[244] Wirral CA, AR, 1938–39.

unable to afford an agent or mount fundraising efforts. However, these levels left even the safer seats feeling constrained, as there was general agreement that an income of at least £1,000 was needed to work a constituency effectively, especially in the county divisions, where £750 was a minimum.[245] The more compact industrial, urban, and suburban constituencies could manage on less: in Yorkshire, Sowerby considered that 'at least £650 per year would be needed' and Sheffield Central estimated its costs at £500, whilst the more scattered Ayr Burghs thought that £800 was the minimum required.[246]

The consequence was that few associations were so comfortably placed that they did not need to make periodic efforts to maintain their subscription list. Appeals for new subscribers were pitched to the middle class as the persons most likely to be able to contribute, and emphasized the threat posed by the Socialist programme to their property and livelihood. Active Conservatives often felt strongly that the middle class should pay for their own defence, and subscribing to party funds was sometimes directly presented as a form of insurance, as with the slogan of the party journal *Home and Politics*: 'A penny a day keeps Socialism at bay.'[247] However, it was a frequent complaint, particularly in the safer seats, that 'there were numerous affluent Conservatives who were not doing their financial duty to the Party', for 'we were working for their interests and they must play their part'.[248] Given the conventions of upper-middle-class behaviour, the best method of securing the more substantial subscriptions was by a personal approach, either to someone already known or through an introduction from an intermediary.[249] This was one reason for the need for association chairmen and treasurers to belong at least to the same class as those they were contacting, and higher status was an asset. However, reliance upon a few larger donors left an association vulnerable to the chance effects of removals and deaths, and the healthier approach encouraged by Central Office was to widen the base of the financial pyramid.[250] This had the benefit of energizing party workers to higher level of activity, but the time and effort involved was difficult to maintain and there was a tendency to flag after the initial spurt of enthusiasm.

The alternative was the employment of paid canvassers, known as either collectors or missioners. The former were generally recruited and employed directly by the association, on a part-salary/part-commission basis or entirely on commission.[251]

[245] Hitchin CA, Secretary's Report, 7 October 1918; Newark CA, Fin., 11 June 1919; Dorset West CA, Fin., 28 July 1921; Bewdley CA, AGM, 31 May 1924; Thirsk & Malton CA, Exec., 26 November 1924; Cannock CA, Fin., 13 April 1934.

[246] Sowerby CA, Exec., 23 November 1924; Sheffield Central CA, Fin., 13 July 1931; Ayr Burghs CA, Fin., 5 July 1929; Uxbridge CA, Exec., 1 July 1919.

[247] *Home and Politics*, February 1928; Rugby CA, Exec., 7 July 1923; Blake (chairman, West Wiltshire CA) to Long, 15 December 1923, Long MSS (WSA), 947/885; Birmingham CA, Management Ctte., 14 November 1924; Rushcliffe CA, AR, 1934, 1938.

[248] Lancaster CA, General Purposes Ctte., 14 July 1923.

[249] Ripon CA, Exec., 18 June 1919; Birmingham CA, Management Ctte., 5 February 1920; Edinburgh West CA, Exec., 6 May 1931.

[250] Peterborough CA, AGM, Treasurer's Report, 2 April 1927; Memo by Blair, 'Impressions of the General Election', 12 July 1929, Gilmour MSS, GD383/29/32–5.

[251] Torquay CA, Fin., 23 June 1919. Similarly to the agents, their independent role led to some cases of fraud: Kensington South CA, Special Exec., 22 December 1927; Wood Green CA, Palmers Green Branch, Exec., 11 March 1929.

These fundraisers approached the upper-middle-class figures in the constituency who were not subscribers or whose contribution had lapsed, and needed to have an equivalent or higher social status. If not locally connected themselves, they would use letters of introduction from leading members of the association, and worked from a list supplied by the agent or chairman. The missioners were usually trained by Central Office, which often partly or wholly subsidized their employment by the local association for a fixed period. This was the only way in which the marginal and weak seats—who needed it most—could receive a shot in the arm, and in their case the initiative often came from the Area Agent. The aim was to set an association on its feet, so that it could then build up its strength on its own. Such campaigns were labour-intensive, slow, and expensive; they often had a specific purpose, such as the revival of a moribund branch or restoring the financial health of an association which had too few subscribers. A missioner worked through a specific area on a house-by-house basis, usually in lower-middle-class or skilled working-class residential neighbourhoods. This form of activity was most feasible in the suburban, rural, and mixed urban/rural constituencies, and could be effective—in 1936, a canvasser at Clapham doubled the size of the association's membership.[252] As well as the benefit in recruitment and funds, the missioners' work provided much valuable information about voters' affiliations and public opinion generally.[253] Providing such assistance was considered by Central Office to be more constructive than direct financial grants; the latter had to be finely judged, as too much support eroded the incentive to collect funds locally and thus was counterproductive.[254]

The other source of local funds was social events in the constituency; this had the advantage that to a large extent the more effort that was made, the better was the result not only financially but politically. The functions organized by Conservative associations were still a significant contributor of entertainment to local society in this period, particularly in the rural areas, the small towns, and the suburbs—which were also the places where the party was strongest.[255] Much of this was conducted at branch level, and mainly by the women; one constituency agent estimated that 90 per cent of the social activities were organized by the women's branches, that 75 per cent of these were held at the times of day that suited women (mainly in the afternoon or early evening), and that they had almost no political content.[256] This was especially true of the most frequent and popular event of the period: the whist drive. This competitive but not excessively demanding card game was hugely popular with middle-class women and the retired; there would be a small payment at the door, refreshments available at a modest charge, and prizes for the tournament winners—often donated by the MP and prominent local figures.[257]

---

[252] Clapham CA, AR 1936.
[253] A rare example of weekly missioner's reports for 1 April to 26 August 1939 survives for Edinburgh West CA.
[254] Hall to Derby, 27 June 1923, Derby MSS, 31/3.
[255] Central Office, *Some Suggestions for Raising Funds* (1936); Norfolk East CA, Fin., 15 May 1934.
[256] *CAJ*, January 1936, 9.
[257] *CAJ*, February 1925, 37–40; March 1932, 53–5; Clapham CA, Clapham Park South branch, whist drive accounts, 11 March 1926.

It was an activity which could engage large numbers over a long period: Berkshire South held more than fifty whist drives in its 1934–35 season, with 'well over 5,000 competitors taking part'.[258] Dances and balls were more occasional events, and activities linked to entertainment and sport were also common; thus Argyll had a dramatic society; Reigate, a tennis club; Gloucester, a Conservative angling association; and Putney, a Conservative choir.[259] In general, activities which were attended by both genders and of a more genteel nature became more popular between the wars, and there was a decline of the Victorian and Edwardian masculine staple of the smoking concert. Women's branches organized luncheon clubs and 'at homes', for 'tea, talk and women go very well together',[260] and on a larger scale they engaged in fashion parades, tableaux, and amateur theatricals.[261] During the Second World War, these gatherings were replaced by knitting parties to make comforts for the troops, the preparing of Red Cross parcels, and the promotion of the war loans.

Larger undertakings were the responsibility of the central women's committee or the association executive, although the detailed planning was often delegated to a sub-committee.[262] These included outings of various kinds, some over long distances by train or charabanc; in 1926, the women's branch at Newport in Wales chartered three special trains for a day outing to Brighton, a journey of five hours each way, whilst in more sombre spirit 900 members of Nottingham Central visited the Flanders battlefields in July 1928.[263] More usual were the sales of work, fetes, and bazaars. Some of the latter were on a grand scale and involved a major effort which could only be mounted once in every three or four years, but these could raise large sums: in 1929, the city of Leeds held one lasting four days which raised £15,259.[264] In a number of constituencies, a large annual or biennial fete was a substantial source of regular income, usually producing profits of several hundred pounds.[265] The most ambitious of such ventures involved much planning and would run for several days; in November 1932, in the depths of the depression, the Blackpool association ran a three-day bazaar at the Winter Gardens which raised £2,369. Many events drew enough of a crowd that they provided an opportunity for propaganda as well, with the local MP or his wife opening the smaller fetes and the biggest affairs rating a junior, or even a Cabinet, minister.[266] Some of

---

[258] Berkshire South CA, AR, 1935; *CAJ*, April 1926, 112–14; April 1932, 102–3.
[259] Argyll CA, AGM, 12 October 1933; Gloucester CA, Exec., 16 April 1928; Putney CA, AR, 1927–28.
[260] *CAJ*, June 1928, 169.
[261] Headlam diary, 20 November 1932.
[262] *CAJ*, February 1930, 47–50; Cambridge CA, Fete Management Ctte., May–July 1924; Gloucester CA, Fete Ctte., April–July 1927.
[263] Newport CA, Women's Section officers meeting, 20 April 1926; for Nottingham Central, see *CAJ*, September 1928, 285–9; Horncastle CA, F&GP, 12 June 1933; Howdenshire CA, F&GP, 29 November 1937.
[264] Leeds CA, AR, 1928–29.
[265] *CAJ*, March 1924, 62–7; May 1931, 100–3; July 1932, 187–98; Lewisham West CA, Council, 7 February 1928; Moray & Nairn CA, balance sheets, 1931, 1934; Bedford CA, Fin., 20 July 1938.
[266] Kincardine & West Aberdeenshire CA, Bazaar Ctte., 5 November 1926; Birmingham CA, Council, 19 December 1924.

most ambitious ventures were similar in scale to the major regional rallies that were addressed by the Party Leader, although in those cases the primary purpose was political and fundraising was secondary. An estimated 40,000 persons attended the gathering addressed by Baldwin at Bramham Park, Yorkshire, in July 1928, where 'there was a forest of huge marquees', and the ancillary attractions included 'pony shows, horse jumping, motor bicycle races, athletic sports, merry-go-rounds, etc'.[267]

The main headings of local association expenditure were first and foremost the salaries of the agent and any other staff (normally accounting for between half and two-thirds of the costs), secondly, the running of the constituency office, and thirdly, the expenses of campaigning, such as the hire of halls and the purchase of propaganda produced by Central Office.[268] A typical breakdown, from the safe seat of Dorset West, was: salaries, £642 (55 per cent); general working and office expenses, £217 (18 per cent); 'fixed charges: rent, rates, taxes and pensions', £104 (9 per cent); propaganda, meetings, and literature, £155 (13 per cent), and repairs and renewals, £37 (3 per cent).[269] The constituency was only unusual in having a small credit balance of £26 (2 per cent), whereas a deficit, often of considerably more, was more frequently the case, even in the Conservative strongholds. Transport was an increasingly important expense in the interwar era, as the agent had many calls to make and mobility was essential, especially in the county divisions.[270] This sometimes took the form of a motorcycle, but from the mid-1920s was usually a saloon car, with the association either paying a mileage allowance and running costs, or purchasing the vehicle itself; the latter was a substantial expenditure, and one ideally needing periodic renewal.[271] Social events rarely appeared as a charge on the annual balance sheet, as they were expected to more than cover their costs. It was still rare for an association to make a contribution from its own funds to the candidate's election expenses, but one unusual and early example of the practice was Chippenham in Wiltshire. This was a safe seat which certainly had no need to do so, as it could easily have secured a paying candidate, but it took pride in not asking its Member to pay for himself. However, whilst this obviously enlarged their choice in selection, and their MPs were effective figures (including W. S. Morrison, a rising star of the 1930s), it did not lead to any desire to venture outside the usual social bracket from which MPs were drawn. A few of the wealthier associations gave financial assistance to a weaker constituency in their region, but the continuation of such help could not be relied upon.[272] This was an entirely voluntary local initiative, although it was particularly encouraged in London, where there were great differences in circumstances and a concentration of very poor constituencies; it foreshadowed the more extensive postwar 'mutual aid' scheme.

---

[267] Lane-Fox to Irwin, 26 July 1928, Halifax MSS, C152/18/1/102.
[268] Dorset West CA, Fin., 23 July 1921, 'Analysis of 1924 and 1925 expenditure', 12 December 1925.
[269] Dorset West CA, 'Analysis of 1924 and 1925 expenditure', Fin., 12 December 1925.
[270] Cirencester & Tewkesbury CA, Fin., 18 February 1921.
[271] Oswestry CA, Exec., 26 March 1921; Denbighshire CA, F&GP, 30 October 1925; Wells CA, Exec., 25 November 1937; Newark CA, Fin., 27 January 1926, 20 May 1931, 4 July 1934, 17 June 1938.
[272] Wessex Area, Exec., 3 March 1930.

For the most part, there was a circular relationship between constituency expenditure and income, by which an association tended only to raise the amount needed to pay the salaries, maintain the office, and keep the organization in being. Furthermore, most of the activity of the voluntary membership and paid staff was devoted to raising this money.[273] With associations treading water at their various levels of financial and electoral strength, the question remained as to what they were achieving in terms of winning new support.[274] The overall effect was something of a subsistence economy, and when savings were needed there was usually little or no operating margin or reserves. In fact, even safe seats tended to have an almost constant deficit at the bank: Chelmsford had a recurring annual deficit of £250 and its overdraft reached £517 before steps were taken to reduce it, whilst Rugby was £730 overdrawn in 1924, and Rye arranged a facility for up to £400 with its local bank in 1938.[275] The political sympathy of the branch manager must have played a part in allowing such substantial and extended overdraft facilities: although there was often a guarantee given by a number of prominent members, these were almost never called upon.[276]

The raison d'être of the local association was to win and hold the parliamentary seat. The vigour of party spirit was such that every constituency wanted to run a candidate, and it was sometimes a difficult matter for the national officials and leaders to persuade a local association to stand down as part of a coalition arrangement, even in the weaker seats. In 1929, when there was no coalition pact and the election was not sudden or early, only seventeen seats went uncontested; everywhere else, even in many hopeless Labour strongholds, a candidate was run. Doing so provided a focal point and encouraged further efforts: as the association in the coal-mining district of Ayrshire South was advised by the party's chief official in Scotland in 1929, 'it was necessary to have a candidate to keep our people's interest alive'. A decade later, after a succession of defeats, they were still being encouraged to run a candidate, because even though they could not hope for victory, this would tie down the sitting Labour MP and his supporters, and thus assist neighbouring associations in their campaigns.[277]

The traditional part of the political effort was registration and canvassing: knowing who the party's supporters were, and getting them to poll. In the 1920s personal canvassing in the old style was still highly regarded by the experienced agents and the senior figures at Central Office, such as Maclachlan, who had learned their trade before 1914. With the hugely expanded electorate, there was a need to recruit more volunteers to undertake canvassing, which was more effective than public meetings in reaching the uncommitted and disinterested: due to 'the wireless and

---

[273] Ball to N. Chamberlain, 1 June 1938, NC, 8/21/8; *CAJ*, February 1926, 46.
[274] Sevenoaks CA, 'Note on Finance', September 1925.
[275] Chelmsford CA, Council, 25 January 1922; Rugby CA, Exec., 2 February 1924; Rye CA, Fin., 2 November 1938.
[276] Rugby CA, Exec., 7 July 1923; King's Lynn CA, Fin., 31 July 1923; Oxfordshire North CA, Exec., 28 December 1927, 21 December 1928; Bosworth CA, Exec., 26 March 1938. At Stockton CA, the bank only became restive when the overdraft reached £1,900: Exec., 17 December 1935.
[277] Ayrshire South CA, Exec., 24 September 1929, Organisation Ctte., 9 May 1939.

the many counter-attractions now existing...if the electors will not leave their homes to attend meetings, political information must be given to them on their own doorsteps'.[278] However, there was continual concern that there were too few active and effective workers—'workers who can speak, who can canvas, and who can heckle'.[279] In particular, there were few men, even amongst the officers of branch committees, who were comfortable with talking 'serious politics' regularly with their neighbours.[280] The willingness of Conservative supporters to strive for the cause was often contrasted unfavourably with what was believed to be Labour's messianic zeal, and thus Austen Chamberlain was advised that a summer election would be better because Conservative workers were more likely to turn out in better weather.[281] Public meetings still had their value, and were the best way for a candidate or MP to become known and make a positive and active impression, although in other respects they were more a matter of showing the flag than a means of making converts. There was less rowdyism than before 1914, but in election meetings in particular a candidate had to be capable of handling interruption and heckling, and to be effective in answering more or less hostile questions.

The introduction in 1918 of polling on the same day for every constituency was one of the features which created a more uniformly national campaign, and another cause of the decline of local influences upon voting was the increasing dominance of a national media—the mass circulation newspapers of the press lords, cinema newsreels, and radio. The party leaders only had time during the campaign to speak at a few major centres of population, and so, paradoxically, the constituencies had to be more dependent upon their own resources. At the same time, the great increase in the electorate after 1918 shifted the tactical emphasis to propaganda, particularly by poster and leaflet. The pressure was greatest in the early 1920s due to the lower limits on candidates' expenses, but monetary deflation after meant that more could be afforded within the unchanged legal amount.[282] The peak of the agent's work was the organizing of an election campaign; his expertise, and his role as the candidate's agent for authorizing expenses under the terms of the law, made him more of a commander-in-chief than a chief of staff. A good deal of preparatory work could be done beforehand, most obviously in preparing the marked register, addressing the envelopes to be used for distributing the election address, and in planning the location of committee rooms, booking of halls, and availability of supporting speakers; in one instance, this enabled the venues and chairmen for fifty meetings to be arranged within twenty-four hours of the dissolution being announced.[283] The law provided for one free postal delivery of each candidate's election address, but this had to be made ready in suitable form, and as

---

[278] Central Office, *Politics on the Doorstep* (1935); Memo by Blair, 'Impressions of the General Election', 12 July 1929, Gilmour MSS, GD383/29/32–5.

[279] T. N. Graham, 'The constituencies and Ashridge', *Ashridge Journal*, 22 (June 1935), 21.

[280] Chelmsford CA, Report of Propaganda Sub-ctte, Exec., 28 October 1927.

[281] Notes by Jessel (London Whip), AC, 32/4/9, appended to Fraser's report to A. Chamberlain, 30 December 1921, AC, 32/4/1b; Adams to Harrisson, 10 June 1938, Adams MSS, 7.

[282] Lawrence, 'Transformation of British public politics', 206.

[283] Berwickshire & East Lothian CA, East Lothian AGM, 29 October 1938, comment on 1935 campaign.

early in the campaign as possible; in one rural Scottish constituency in 1929, this entailed '32,000 envelopes to address, something like 150,000 circulars to fold and enclose', work which was now 'largely carried out by the ladies'.[284] The candidate was expected to embark upon a gruelling campaign of public meetings, often speaking several times each night in a timetable as complicated as a military mobilization; there was nothing unusual, especially in a rural division, in a schedule involving eighty speeches during twenty days.[285] The candidate in the Hammersmith North by-election of 1934 claimed, probably accurately, to have worked fourteen hours a day during the several weeks of the contest, and to have addressed sixty-five public meetings and personally canvassed 3,500 people.[286] High levels of enthusiasm could be engendered by such whirlwind intensity; in the Handsworth division of Birmingham it was claimed that the final series of meetings on the eve of the 1929 poll drew a total attendance of 10,000.[287]

When polling day was reached, keeping track of who had voted and contacting supporters who had not yet done so was a task which in the marginals could make the difference between defeat and victory: 'many votes were secured in this way'.[288] Another crucial organizational contribution was arranging the use of supporters' cars for conveying the elderly or unwell to the polling station, and in rural areas this was often critical for poorer electors if they were to be able to vote at the end of a long working day. The number of cars which the Conservative Party's middle- and upper-class support could furnish was in such pointed contrast to Labour's position that the Electoral Reform Bill brought forward unsuccessfully by the second Labour government intended to restrict their use. Great importance—almost certainly, too much—was attached to the precision of all these electoral arrangements. At the end of the day, superior organization was probably worth a few hundred votes at the most; it could add to the scale of victory, but was unable to prevent the party's defeats. Whilst it could be argued that the worst setback in 1945 was also when the local organization was almost moribund, it was clearly the case that the Conservatives were more unpopular then than they had been in 1923 or 1929.

Enthusiasm and activity were not the natural states, and had to be fostered and encouraged. The large majority of Conservative voters took no part in politics beyond casting their ballot, and of the minority who joined their local branch, many had little or no further involvement.[289] Apathy was like gravity, ever present and all around, as inevitable as it was invisible. The concern was not so much that the bulk of the membership was passive, but the extent to which this submerged and absorbed the necessary minority of active local leaders. There were places and times when apathy was particularly pronounced and perceived as a problem, and

---

[284] Kinross & West Perthshire CA, Crieff branch, Secretary's Report, 1929.
[285] Oxfordshire North CA, Council, 11 May 1929; Hamilton to Davidson, 15 February 1928, Davidson MSS, 182.
[286] Davies to Baldwin, 27 April 1934, Baldwin MSS 51/43–4.
[287] Birmingham Handsworth CA, AR 1929, AGM, 21 March 1930.
[288] Edinburgh North CA, Exec., 11 November 1931.
[289] A similar pattern was found in the early 1990s, with less than 20% of the members even moderately active: P. Whiteley, P. Seyd, and J. Richardson, *True Blues: The Politics of Conservative Party Membership* (Oxford, 1994), 68.

this was the result of the additional effect of political or economic factors upon what might be considered the 'normal' level of apathy. This pattern was evident when Conservative supporters were unhappy with the policies of their leaders in government, and especially when there were economic pressures upon the business and professional middle class or a normally supportive sector such as agriculture. The effects could range from the grumbling over such perennial chestnuts as the reform of the House of Lords, through the more serious weary disillusion of the agricultural seats in the late 1920s, to the periods of stress in which assertive, simplistic, and populist campaigns such as Anti-Waste in 1920–21 or the Empire Crusade in 1929–31 could draw support away from the official associations. As one experienced local agent noted: 'we dread the apathy of our supporters much more than the activity of our opponents'.[290]

The recovery of the constituency organizations from inactivity during the First World War was slow and patchy. Although the effects of the boundary revisions and the enfranchisement of women in the 1918 Reform Act necessitated the formation of a large number of new associations and the revision of rules and structures everywhere, in many places very few meetings were held during the Coalition period. In February 1923 the Treasurer at Tynemouth stated 'that with very few exceptions no subscriptions had been paid for nine years', and this was not unusual.[291] There was a particular problem of inactivity and uncertainty in the constituencies held by Coalition Liberal MPs; whilst the associations in some of these from late 1921 onwards broke with the pact and selected a Conservative candidate, many others were too unprepared to contest the seat in 1922 or even in 1923.[292] The real revival of the Conservative Party in many localities followed from the fall of the Coalition, after which 'it has been much easier to get more work done and more enthusiasm aroused in the constituencies'.[293] This was given further stimulus by the occurrence of two more general elections in the next two years, and not only by success: the loss of a seat—sometimes unexpectedly—could lead to reappraisal and modernization, and invigorate the local organization.[294] The period from 1923 to 1930 saw an expansion of membership and activities in many constituencies, as such pre war auxiliary bodies as the Tariff Reform League and the Primrose League withered away or were greatly reduced in importance. There was an elaboration and diversification, with the growth of the women's associations and the Junior Imperial League, the founding of the Young Britons, and the fostering by Central Office of the Labour Advisory Committees and of opportunities for political education. One local agent commented that the effect

---

[290] *CAJ*, December 1927, 345.
[291] Tynemouth CA, Exec., 23 February 1923.
[292] Sanders to Younger, 2 December, Younger to Davidson, 4 December 1920, Bonar Law MSS, BL/99/8/4; Berwick CA, Agent's Report, AGM, 29 May 1920; Norwich CA, Exec., 23 October 1922; Kincardine & West Aberdeenshire CA, Exec., 6 July 1923; West Midlands Area, GP, 12 October 1923.
[293] Jessel (London Whip) to Jackson, 4 June 1923, CPA, ARE/1/29/1; West Midlands Area, GP, 19 January 1923.
[294] Hampshire North West CA, Fin., 2 March 1926; Ashford CA, Annual Report, 1929.

of these initiatives and the 'vitality' which they stimulated was such that 'the work of organisation during the past five years has more than trebled'.[295]

There was some stagnation in the wake of the disappointing defeat of 1929, and during the internal party crisis which caused enervating tensions for much of the following two years. The restoration of unity in the early part of 1931 led to a revival of activity, stimulated by the increasing urgency of replacing the ailing Labour government with a Conservative ministry which would, it was believed, restore business confidence and stabilize the economy. With the onset of the depression in 1930 and 1931, 'a tendency to lower subscriptions to political organisations' became apparent.[296] However, these difficulties were general rather than specific to the party, and there was some comfort in the knowledge that the problems 'were only similar to those of endless other concerns'.[297] Shortfalls in income led to some marginal seats having to dispense with a full-time agent, at least for a while, whilst elsewhere agents were either asked or offered to take a salary cut. Associations in the industrial north were the most affected, but in many places the decline in income due to the slump was less than might have been expected.[298] The national crisis of August 1931 led to heightened activity, and many constituencies were able to raise funds for the ensuing general election with relative ease. However, there was a lapse into quiescence during the next two years, especially in propaganda activity; this was 'almost negligible', with only 921,100 leaflets being distributed nationwide in 1933.[299]

From the mid-1930s, as the economic situation improved, particularly in the Midlands and south, and the political position stabilized under the comfortably secure National Government, the Conservative Party's constituency organization became a smoothly running machine, perhaps reaching a plateau of efficiency. Nearly all constituencies had an effective women's organization (even in the Labour Party's strongholds) and an active junior movement, even if the latter sometimes ebbed and flowed; most of the industrial seats also had a Labour Advisory Committee. Most associations were actively engaged in holding political as well as social meetings, organizing fundraising events, and distributing propaganda. Significantly, the grass roots were more financially self-supporting than had been the case in the 1920s, and this enabled both the constituency and the regional organizations to cope with the withdrawal of most of the direct subventions from Central Office after 1932, due to the economic slump.

The health of the grass roots is illustrated by the snapshot picture provided by the constituency resolutions submitted for the presentation to Baldwin in June 1937. This shows an active body in existence in 452 (88.8 per cent) of the 509 English and Welsh constituencies, and in sixty-seven (95.7 per cent) of the seventy

---

[295] Cambridge CA, Agent's Report, Council, 4 May 1927; Uxbridge CA, Council, 3 March 1928.
[296] Aldershot CA, Exec., 22 November 1930; SUA, EDC, Treasurer's Ctte., 12 February 1931; Canterbury CA, Finance & Emergency Ctte, 2 May 1931; Oxford CA, F&GP, 28 September 1931.
[297] St Albans CA, Exec., 14 October 1932.
[298] Wakefield CA, Fin., 10 December 1929; Wood Green CA, AR, 1929–31; Epsom, AR, 1929–32; Bute & North Ayrshire CA, AR, 1930–39; Bedford CA, AR, 1932–34.
[299] NU Exec., 'Memorandum on Publicity and Propaganda', 30 May 1934.

Scottish constituencies.[300] However, the picture in England and Wales was actually stronger than this, for although the eleven seats in Liverpool, the four in Bradford, and five out of the six in Leeds sent no individual resolutions, their overall city association did so. Setting aside these twenty, there remain thirty-seven associations (7.3 per cent) which did not respond to the invitation, of which seven were in London and eleven in Wales. However, twelve of these constituencies had sitting Conservative MPs (in one case, Stafford, a Cabinet minister), and can be presumed to have had some active organization.[301] This leaves only twenty-five seats (4.9 per cent) as possibly moribund, and, significantly, fifteen of these had not been contested by a Conservative candidate in 1935.[302] Taken as a whole, this demonstrates a breadth of national coverage far beyond the capacity of the Labour Party, and still more of the Samuelite Liberals. The presentation resolutions also provide another striking testimony to the strength and efficiency of the Conservative Party in the localities: of the 421 constituencies in England for which the resolution was sent in on their official notepaper, 344 (81.7 per cent) employed an agent.[303] This is in line with the analysis in 1938, which found that only 128 constituencies in England and Wales did not employ a full-time certificated agent; of these, twenty-one were in Wales, forty-four in the three northern Areas, and fifteen in London.[304]

The Conservatives were gearing up, in most places effectively, for the general election anticipated in 1940 when the Second World War began in September 1939.[305] For grass-roots Conservatives, the war effort became the overriding priority and politics were seen as irrelevant, distracting, and even dangerously divisive: 'it was impossible for Party political strife to exist during such a period'.[306] Although there was no change in the party composition of the National Government and the Labour Party remained in opposition, Conservatives were keen to avoid controversy and to both foster and demonstrate national unity.[307] For this reason, they tended to interpret the political truce between the main parties in a much broader spirit than its actual terms, which avoided contests in the inevitable by-election vacancies.[308]

---

[300] There were 449 actual resolutions from England and Wales, because in Birkenhead, Middlesbrough, and Swansea the two borough divisions were organized by a single Association: NU presentation resolutions, June 1937, Baldwin MSS (Worcs RO), BA 14208.

[301] Cheltenham was in some disarray following a divisive by-election, and Newcastle North was known to be small and inactive.

[302] Of these, minute books exist for Denbighshire CA, Ilkeston CA, and Pembrokeshire CA, which show that an organization was in being.

[303] This does not include those listing an 'Acting Agent' or 'Organising Secretary', who were usually women and sometimes only worked part-time. In addition, some constituencies which almost certainly employed an agent do not show this on the letterhead, possibly due to a recent change of incumbent: these include Eastbourne, Hitchin, Torquay, and Windsor.

[304] *CAJ*, January 1938, 7.

[305] Accrington CA, Agent's Report, AGM, 25 April 1939; Mid-Bedfordshire CA, Exec. Report for 1939, April 1940; Northampton CA, AR, 1939–40; Skipton CA, AGM, 2 March 1940.

[306] Hastings & St Leonards CA, Exec., 7 September 1939; Circular from Party Chairman, 6 February 1940, CPA, CCO/500/1/9.

[307] NU Central Council, 4 April 1940.

[308] See comments of Dugdale (Party Chairman 1942–44) at East Midlands Area, AGM, 20 November 1943; North West Area, Council, 20 March 1943; Chief Organisation Officer to Area Agents, 'Party Activities in Wartime', 14 June 1940, CPA, CCO/500/1/9.

The patriotic sentiments of Conservatives led them to regard all forms of party activity as out of bounds, in some places even the holding of social meetings, and in turn this led to complaints when their opponents were more active and continued with propaganda.[309] Many Conservative associations shut down completely, some immediately after the outbreak of war and others in 1940; Baldwin's former seat of Bewdley was not unusual in going into suspension for the entire duration.[310] This was widespread in the weaker seats: the Rother Valley association was not even able to get a quorum together to authorize its closure, and was then dormant until 1945, by which time 'none of the original officers remained', whilst in Cornwall North 'the Conservative Party had practically given up their organisation during the war'.[311] Other constituencies wound down to 'a skeleton organisation' to be 'kept going with the least possible expense',[312] and with infrequent, brief, and mainly formal meetings held 'merely to maintain a nucleus'.[313] It is revealing that Northampton, who recorded no meeting between March 1940 and March 1944, considered that their 'comparatively dormant state...compares more than favourably with many others'.[314]

Those constituencies which did try to maintain their organization faced almost insuperable difficulties. Apart from an elderly few, nearly all of the professional agents and women organizers volunteered or were called up for war service, and the same pattern applied to the officers of central committees and branches.[315] Due to its age group, the Junior Imperial League was especially affected, and at the start of the war it closed down both at national level and in almost every constituency. Many Conservative women were engaged in making comforts for the troops, promoting the war loans, and work for the Women's Voluntary Services and the Red Cross, whilst others took up employment (generally clerical) or joined the auxiliary armed services, so that 'almost every member was engaged in some kind of voluntary work in connection with the war effort'.[316] The blackout made it difficult for people to go out to evening meetings of committees; in the cities and industrial towns there was the further discouragement of the danger of air raids, whilst the limited petrol ration made work and meetings difficult in county seats.[317]

---

[309] Harborough CA, Special Exec., 23 September 1939; SUA Central Council, Notes on discussion, 28 February 1941.

[310] Bewdley CA, AGM, 11 April 1945; Denbigh CA, F&GP, 21 June 1945; Moray & Nairn CA, Special Meeting, 15 January 1946; Rothwell CA, F&GP, 11 September 1939; Memo, Topping to Hacking, 26 June 1940, NC, 8/21/19. For the effects of the war on local Conservatism, see A. Thorpe, *Parties at War: Political Organisation in Second World War Britain* (Oxford, 2009), 155–88.

[311] Rother Valley CA, 'Informal meeting', 4 September 1939, 'Meeting to re-form Association', 8 March 1945; Cornwall North CA, Exec., 15 September 1945; Renfrewshire West CA, Exec., 4 May 1944, 24 April 1946.

[312] Oswestry CA, Exec., 15 September 1939.

[313] Norwich CA, AR, 1941.

[314] Northampton CA, AR 1943–44, AGM, 16 March 1944.

[315] Bristol CA, Policy Sub-ctte, 31 August 1943.

[316] Cardiff South CA, Fin., 13 February 1940; Hinton, *Women, Social Leadership and the Second World War*, 56–9.

[317] Camberwell North CA, Exec., 19 October 1940, in the following year this Association's premises and records were destroyed by bombing: Exec., 4 June 1941; Argyll CA, Exec., 30 September 1941, AGM, 3 April 1945; North West Area, Council, 1 April 1944.

Whilst subscriptions fell away during the war years, often with little effort to collect them, the removal of the major cost of staff salaries and the closure of many offices meant that expenditure fell even further. The result was that associations were often accumulating a surplus of funds, and, ironically, ended the war with a healthy balance sheet, although in other respects they had crumbled away.[318] The decay of the local associations was a major factor in the series of spectacular by-election defeats in normally safe seats between 1942 and 1945; when the vacancy occurred at Grantham, the Area Agent found that 'the organisation and local officials had vanished into thin air'.[319] Even Churchill's own constituency was not immune from torpor and decay, with the chairman greeting the executive committee in June 1945 with the comment that it was 'the first meeting for six years'.[320]

SELECTING THE CANDIDATE

The single most important function and power of a Conservative association, especially in a winnable seat, was the selection of the candidate. This was the most jealously defended aspect of local autonomy, and it was the sole right of the constituency association to confer or withhold the party label. The latter had become essential for any chance of election to parliament, as most voters cast their ballot in support of a party and its Leader, rather than a particular local contestant. However, this did not diminish the care and importance attached to candidate selection. In many constituencies it was an infrequent event, and the safest seats might be held by the same MP for a generation. There was a strong preference for representation by a local person, and in almost every case this was considered first: 'they wanted a man... who was born amongst them, had lived amongst them, and knew the needs of the constituency'.[321] The general view was that 'a local man would do far better than a stranger', and 'would create more interest'.[322] Often the most prominent local figures would be encouraged to put their names forward, and in some places there was a particular dominant family, usually landed.[323] However, a local man (a woman was deliberately sought only in a few rare cases, where her husband had preceded her as MP) was not always forthcoming, or he was a divisive prospect who aroused local jealousies.[324] As a Vice-Chairman of the Party noted, 'a bad local man, without doubt, makes the worst possible candidate'.[325] Cases where the association's chairman sought the nomination were particularly problematic due to the conflict of interest, and the long-running disputes at Newcastle North

---

[318] Kinross & West Perthshire CA, AGM, 20 November 1942, Fin., 5 November 1943.
[319] Horncastle CA, AGM, 18 May 1942.
[320] Essex West CA, Exec, 11 June 1945.
[321] Dorset West CA, Council, 29 October 1919; Knutsford CA, Exec., 9 July 1921; Gurney (chairman, Hereford Borough CA) to Hewins, 27 November 1918, Hewins MSS, 72/171–3; Sir P. Richardson, *It Happened to Me* (1952), 178.
[322] Pembrokeshire CA, Exec., 26 March 1938.
[323] Younger to Ashley, 3 December 1919, Ashley MSS, BR/71.
[324] Derby to Hall, 27 April 1923, Derby MSS, 17/2; Northampton CA, Exec., 13 December 1927.
[325] Memo by Bowyer, 'Candidates', 19 July 1934, Baldwin MSS, 48/240–4.

from 1943 to 1951 originated from this.[326] Finding a candidate from outside the area could avoid or overtrump local rivalries, and some of the stronger constituencies particularly desired—and considered their importance merited—a future political star as their MP.

There was no customary route leading upwards from the general membership in the local branches to parliament and the party leadership. Instead, the Conservative Party operated similarly to the armed services, with almost no transition between the lower ranks and the officers—the MPs—who entered directly into that category, and then ascended their own ladder of promotion. Due to the need to possess social prestige and personal wealth, those who became MPs did so by one of two routes. The first might be termed 'local': due to his status as a landowner, employer, or respected professional in the constituency or in an adjacent one, a man would be seen as a desirable candidate—very often being approached to stand, rather than having sought nomination. Such persons might already be leading figures in the constituency association, but would have assumed that role—even entering directly as chairman—because of this same local standing. They often provided candidates for marginal and weak seats, if no one else would come forward; in the safe seats, the preference for a local man would frequently carry the day if there was someone sufficiently willing and well-established; this was Baldwin's route of entry, and perhaps contributed to his being regarded as solid backbench material rather than a future Leader. It was generally, though not necessarily correctly, considered that frontbenchers mainly entered by the second route, which might be termed 'national'. These were aspirant parliamentary candidates who were seeking a winnable seat, either anywhere in the country or over a very wide area. They tended to be more focused upon a parliamentary career, more interested in gaining ministerial office, and were often younger—although this category also included men who had made a success in another career (including the armed forces, imperial service, etc.) and were building on that. Energetic activism at the grass roots might lead to becoming a local councillor or a party agent, but generally not beyond; unlike the post-Second World War Young Conservatives, the Junior Imperial League was not a breeding ground for future Cabinet ministers.

The instinctive Conservative assumption that the training, experience, and qualities for political leadership were to be found in the highest social classes shaped the preference for candidates of this type. Public school and Oxbridge educations led to the possession of assurance, the accent associated with the exercise of authority and—usually—articulateness. A man of the aristocracy or gentry, especially from a family prominent in the area, would always be considered for a candidacy, and there was an inverse ratio between the high prestige of the name and the low age at which its bearer would be credible. In some constituencies, the representation was almost a dynastic monopoly, with each generation taking its turn. The asset of a recognized name and social prestige helped the potential candidate to leap over the first hurdles of acceptability with the association and with Conservative voters. Thus, the candidate selected at Abingdon in 1920, although 'at present a stranger

---

[326] Headlam diary, introduction, 30–7.

to most of them', was 'one of the largest landowners in the district' and from a family 'which had been good for generations all round his way'.[327] In many places, the local elite was restricted in number and intimately interwoven: in the neighbouring seat of Oxfordshire South, there would have been no great surprise when the two aspirants for the candidacy were introduced by the chairman as 'a very great personal friend of his and the other was his nephew'.[328] In the urban and suburban seats, the most usual type of candidate was either a local businessman or a lawyer; the latter was usually a barrister, and also often from outside the district. In the mixed urban/rural and rural seats the usual choices in addition to a businessman were a local solicitor or large farmer; demonstrable knowledge of agriculture was essential in a rural seat, especially in someone who was not a local resident.

The reluctance to select working-class candidates was partly based on prejudices about class hierarchy: working men could appear to the middle- and upper-class selectors as uneducated and alien in their accent and experiences. Pragmatic matters were often used to justify this reluctance: the first was doubt whether middle-class supporters would vote for such a candidate, and the second was concern that his appeal to working-class voters could be less rather than more, as he would lack social prestige and might arouse the jealousy of his peers.[329] The question of finance was in reality the lesser concern, although it was the easiest excuse. Central Office was keen to promote working-class candidates, but constituencies which were financially sound—which meant nearly all of the winnable seats—did not wish to go cap in hand to Central Office for the extra costs that choosing a working man would entail, nor did they wish to have an MP who was more beholden to the national authorities than to his local association. There was a general desire to show that the Conservatives were not a class-based or socially exclusive party (an important concern with the advent of democracy), and to counter the claims of Labour to be the natural and only repository of working-class loyalties and aspirations, and this explains the regular passage at the Central Council and Annual Conference of resolutions supporting the trade unionist organization and calling for working men to be selected as candidates.[330] However, whilst meant sincerely enough in this harmless verbal form, when it came to practice there were always good reasons why it was not suitable in the particular case. The 'not in my back yard' syndrome restricted the prospects of working-class and female candidates,[331] and also fostered the unwillingness to stand down in favour of allies in a coalition pact in 1918, 1931, and 1935. In reality, as an Area Chairman observed, 'no Conservative Association (if it could get anyone else) would dream of running a working man candidate'.[332]

In a similar way, there was an assumption that governance and political partisanship were the natural province of the male gender. The growth of the female party

---

[327] Abingdon CA, Council, 21 June 1920.
[328] Oxfordshire South CA, AGM, 30 July 1924.
[329] Memo by Proby, 'Note on Conservative working men candidates', April 1944, submitted to SACC, 11 May 1944; Wessex Area, Exec., 24 February 1944.
[330] NU Conf., 1928, speech by Green.
[331] Stirlingshire West CA, Exec., 22 July 1935; NU Conf., 1928, speech by Rowlands.
[332] Headlam diary, 23 April 1937.

membership and presence of the leading local women on constituency executives and selection panels did not bring with it any great desire for female MPs; indeed, the women members seemed often to share the view that becoming an MP was an unnatural and unfeminine role, and they lacked empathy with aspirants' ambitions.[333] Women could not normally compete with men for winnable prospects, partly due to fears that the electorate would not vote for them and the seat would be lost.[334] The rare cases of their selection were all due to special circumstances—in the case of all of the women MPs up to 1931, they were chosen in a constituency where their husband had been the MP, and where they already had an established public popularity (see Chapter 5).[335] Otherwise, women were sometimes selected for the poorer prospects, but usually only when no other choice was available; one industrial seat unable to find a candidate still ruled out a woman, unless 'a Lady of outstanding personality was forthcoming'.[336]

The combination of status, connection, money, and experience determined who was chosen, but within that framework, finance carried the greatest weight and was a crucial factor in reinforcing the preferences of class and gender. The experience of Central Office in the early 1930s was that 'in nine cases out of ten it is the wealth of the candidate, and his readiness to pay, that seems above all to commend him to the local Association'; the inevitable consequence was that 'the better the seat, the richer must be the candidate'.[337] Even in the safe seats, it was assumed that 'we must have somebody that can reasonably supply their own money for the constituency'.[338] A very substantial annual contribution to the association funds was the accepted norm; this was often linked to the parliamentary salary, for there was an assumption that a gentleman did not need it. Thus, Quintin Hogg was told in 1936 that a candidate was 'unlikely to get away with anything less than a guaranteed minimum subscription of £400 a year'.[339] As well as usually having to pay the expenses of their election campaigns, candidates needed to be able to patronize local charities and clubs, with such gestures as donating a cup for a tug-of-war competition or a case of oranges for a children's outing.[340] As one selection committee admitted, 'there would be many calls on his purse and...every kind of Club in the division would be anxious to have his support as a Patron'.[341] The Conservative view was that an MP should be a person of some standing and substance; a credible candidate should be self-supporting, and neither financially nor politically

---

[333] Sir H. P. Mitchell, *In My Stride* (1951), 229.   [334] Newcastle West CA, Exec., 7 April 1922.
[335] This was also the pattern with possible candidacies in other constituencies: Walsall CA, Emergency Ctte., 14 November 1921; Epsom CA, General Meeting, 9 June 1928.
[336] Wolverhampton Bilston CA, Management Ctte., 6 September 1934; Rothwell CA, F&GP, 22 December 1936; Ayrshire South CA, Candidate & Organisation Ctte., 16 and 23 November, 8 December 1936; T. Cazalet-Keir, *From the Wings: An Autobiography* (1967), 90.
[337] Memo by Bowyer, 'Candidates', 19 July 1934, Baldwin MSS, 48/240–4; Headlam diary, 21 January 1937; York diary, 6 November 1938.
[338] Woolwich West CA, Exec., 1 October 1943.
[339] Lord Hailsham, *A Sparrow's Flight* (1990), 112.
[340] These examples are from Steel-Maitland's correspondence with the agent of Birmingham Erdington CA, 18 May 1923 et al., Steel-Maitland MSS, GD193/95/2/17; see also Macmillan's correspondence with Stockton CA, Macmillan MSS.
[341] Bradford South CA, Exec., 24 June 1926.

tied to the apron-strings of the local association. A need for monetary assistance would create obligations running counter to the proper ones, complicate the psychology of the relationship, and, by involving Central Office, make it a marriage of three partners—never a healthy prospect. There was hostility to any potential nominee who appeared to be a 'Party Hack', for 'any candidate receiving help from the Party would of necessity be ruled by the Party'.[342] In order not to undermine the candidate's credibility and prestige, any subsidies other than grants for election expenses were kept confidential between Central Office and the recipient, as in the case of Reginald Clarry at Monmouth.[343]

The mechanics of candidate selection were informal and often secretive; there were rarely any rules governing the crucial initial steps, which usually operated on a basis of personal contact and recommendation. When local names were being considered, their ability and suitability was already well-known to the selectors, and there was usually no need for formal interview. The initial approaches, and sometimes the final decision, were generally handled by an inner group of association officers, and sometimes by the chairman alone.[344] Thus the chairman of the Gainsborough association, the head of a large engineering firm in the town, after a single meeting with Tufton Beamish 'made it clear that he was satisfied that I was the right man and that his word to that effect to the executive committee would ensure my being accepted as prospective candidate'.[345] However, in most cases a wider—though still restricted—circle was involved and a more formal procedure was followed, with possible names being discussed by a selection sub-committee or the whole executive, often over several sessions.[346] The only body outside the Conservative Party which was allowed any involvement was the local branch of the National Farmers' Union in certain agricultural seats, mainly in the south and the Midlands; this was a pragmatic acknowledgement that a nominee who was unacceptable to the farmers would not be electable, and a means of ensuring that they did not run their own independent candidate.[347]

After the initial search had produced some potential nominees, the next stage was normally for these to appear before a meeting of the selection sub-committee or the full executive. This could be a frustrating affair in more ways than one: Beamish was successful at Lewes after enduring 'a long wait...in the dismal surroundings of what turned out to be a Ladies cloak-room!'[348] In contrast to the practice since 1945, aspirants usually attended alone; where their wives accompanied them, this was generally at the applicant's initiative rather than the selection

---

[342] Chelmsford CA, Selection Sub-ctte, 2 October 1934; Staff Conference Report, 2–3 April 1944, CPA, CCO/500/1/12.
[343] Davidson to Evans, 2 February 1927, Davidson MSS, DAV/180.
[344] York diary, 2–5 November 1938; Stirlingshire West CA, Exec., 16 April 1937.
[345] Beamish memo, 'I enter Parliament', 10 May 1931, Beamish MSS, CAC, BEAM/3/3.
[346] Reigate CA, Exec., 14 March 1930; Lewisham West CA, Council, 24 October 1938.
[347] Sevenoaks CA, Sub-ctte, 5 April 1918; Oxfordshire South, Exec., 10 May 1919; Abingdon CA, Council, 21 June 1920; Stafford CA, Exec., 27 January 1928; Devizes CA, meeting of Selection Ctte. and NFU delegation, 21 October 1938.
[348] Beamish memo, 'I enter Parliament', 10 May 1931, Beamish MSS, CAC, BEAM/3/3; Duff Cooper diary, 31 July 1924; Macnamara, *The Whistle Blows*, 129–31.

panel's request.[349] Invited into the meeting in turn, each applicant gave a short address—usually of ten to fifteen minutes—and answered any questions. Sincerity and brevity were the most effective approaches, whilst grand or lengthy orations were often counterproductive.[350] In some cases, only one person was willing to stand or be put forward, but where there was a choice it was usually determined by a vote of the constituency executive or council. The expected outcome was that the successful candidate, however slim their margin, would then be approved unanimously and presented for adoption to a general meeting of the association without mention of any alternatives, but the importance of selection meant that it could become divisive and messy.

Of course, every constituency wanted 'a man of character' who was 'young, active, energetic, clever and able to speak'.[351] However, in reality, 'many local associations... ask little of their Member, except that he should pay'.[352] The next criteria were usually the possession of experience or knowledge that was relevant to the constituency, and being an active presence—preferably by residing in the locality.[353] The least important factor about aspirants was their place in the spectrum of Conservative political opinion; at the selection meeting, they would be expected to address the questions which directly affected the constituency, but were rarely asked about their stance on issues which were controversial within the party. The few instances of this occurred during periods of acute tension: the decline of the Coalition in 1922, the height of the Empire Crusade in 1930, and the divisions over India in 1933–35. They stand out because of their rarity, and were motivated by concerns to avoid disunity. On most occasions, applicants gave orthodox presentations of party policy and affirmed their support for the Leader, and that was quite sufficient.[354] What mattered was not so much what they said, but how they said it; as one MP advised a hopeful applicant, 'people instinctively judge by the eyes and the tone in the voice'.[355]

It was often difficult for weak seats to find a candidate, for few were willing to spend their own money on a hopeless prospect if there was a chance of something better elsewhere. Getting a candidate in the field early in a parliament and retaining them was the ideal but rarely the reality: a high turnover was not unusual. If there was constancy, it tended to come from a local stalwart who might not be very

---

[349] York diary, 10 November, 16 December 1938; *Hammer & Tongs*, monthly journal of Hammersmith South CA, February 1929, Bull MSS, CAC, BULL/5/22.

[350] C. Ponsonby, *Ponsonby Remembers* (Oxford, 1965), 61–2; Richardson, *It Happened to Me*, 177–8.

[351] Northwich CA, Chairman's Advisory Ctte., 29 October 1937; Berkshire South CA, Exec., 12 November 1938; for an ironic summary, see N. Chamberlain to Blain, 24 July 1926, NC, 5/10/68.

[352] Feiling, *What is Conservatism?*, 7; Derbyshire South CA, Emergency Ctte., 17 January and 26 June 1930; Blackpool CA, Selection Ctte., 7 February 1935; Sheffield Ecclesall CA, Exec., 1 July 1935; Oxford CA, F&GP, 15 August 1938; this was still the decisive factor at the end of the period, e.g. Bath CA, Special Exec., 14 April 1944,

[353] Pembrokeshire CA, Candidates Sub-ctte, 2 October 1937; Winchester CA, Council, 25 April 1931; Worcester CA, Report of Officers' Conference, 22 September 1944.

[354] Sowerby CA, Exec., 24 May 1928, transcript of adoption speech by Colegate, and following questions and answers.

[355] Heneage to Crossley, 6 January 1931, Heneage MSS, HNC/1/C; Cardiff South CA, Candidate Sub-ctte, 13 May 1924; York diary, 3 December 1938.

impressive, and whose repeated defeats—often by wide margins—meant that his campaign had little credibility with voters and so gave rise to little enthusiasm amongst party workers. In a few cases, the agent was nominated as a last resort or for special reasons, as in that of Allan Beaton, a charismatic and effective platform speaker, in the mining seat of Kirkcaldy Burghs in the 1920s. Otherwise, the difficult seats were seen as proving grounds in which a young man might gain valuable experience, but there was no definite expectation of progression. Central Office had a particular role in these constituencies, where a subsidy was often an essential for the candidate and sometimes for the association as well. Ensuring that there was a contest was important for two reasons: firstly, the organization was likely to crumble completely if it did not fight the seat, as it would lose all sense of purpose; secondly, although the chance of victory was extremely slim, forcing a contest dissipated the opposition's resources and could reduce the extent to which some of their leading figures were available to campaign in the marginals.[356]

In the better-founded constituencies, Central Office 'has no right to offer opinion' and could only have a role by the invitation of the association.[357] However, the difficulty of securing the right candidate meant that this happened more often than might be expected, and it was not uncommon for an association chairman to contact party headquarters and ask for names to be suggested; often this was by personal visit to Palace Chambers, and discussion with the Chairman, Vice-Chairman, or Principal Agent.[358] If the relationship with the Area Agent was working well, he could encourage the constituency chairman to enquire about outside possibilities, especially if he thought the local possibilities might be too weak or divisive. It often remained a delicate business, in which the centre and the locality danced around each other, and there was a constant suspicion of what was termed 'wirepulling' by the party managers.[359] Thus the chairman of Winchester CA 'did not want to go and ask Central Office for a list, being an independent Association'.[360]

Usually party headquarters was seeking to encourage candidacies, but in the coalition elections of 1918, 1931, and 1935 it had the much more difficult role of attempting to persuade—for it could not require—the local parties in some places to stand down. This was no light matter, for it involved severe damage to morale and motivation: it meant the abandonment of hopes and work, and the bitter pill of supporting an MP of another party—usually Liberal—who was often neither liked nor trusted.[361] The other influence which Central Office sought to exert was due to concern over the quality of the candidates chosen, and the overall image and representativeness of the parliamentary party. Acceptance that there were problems

---

[356] Hall to Derby, 23 November 1923, Derby MSS, 31/3.
[357] Memo by Topping, 'Principal Agent's Report to the Chairman of the Party Organisation', September 1929, Steel-Maitland MSS, GD193/121/5/54–7.
[358] 'Memorandum on selection of candidates', by Bowyer, 1 December 1930, Baldwin MSS 48/187–92.
[359] Central Office Report on Isle of Thanet CA, selection meeting, 23 October 1919, Bonar Law MSS, BL/96/1.
[360] Winchester CA, Exec., 20 March 1931.
[361] Wicks to Duff, 6 January 1928, Baldwin MSS, 53/261–2; Clitheroe CA, Exec., 13 and 21 November 1918.

led to the creation of the National Union's Standing Advisory Committee on Candidates (see Chapter 4), but this did not change the essential fact that making the selection was the autonomous preserve of the constituency association. The leadership had no powers or authority in this area; as Bonar Law found when seeking a seat for a Cabinet minister who had been defeated in the general election of 1922, even a popular and trusted Party Leader could not impose an unwanted candidate on the local executive—he could ask, but if the answer was negative, then it had to be accepted.[362]

Given its importance and infrequency, it is not surprising that selecting the candidate could become a major cause of conflict.[363] Indeed, all but one of the cases where an association split in two were due to disagreements about either selecting or deselecting a candidate; the exception was East Ham North in 1932, where the rift was ostensibly caused by a decision to drop the word 'Conservative' in the association's name, but was almost certainly rooted in personality clashes.[364] The splitting of an association over choosing the candidate occurred only six times between 1918 and 1945: at Ilford in 1922, at Kensington South (due to the controversy over the divorce of the MP, Sir William Davison) in 1929, at Newcastle North in 1940 (when Headlam stood as an Independent Conservative against the son of the former MP), at Norfolk South in 1945, and twice at St Marylebone in London, due to the divisive impact of Alec Cunningham-Reid (the candidate and later the MP, in 1932 and again in 1945. It was sometimes threatened elsewhere, as in the dispute over the candidate selection for the Wansbeck by-election of 1928, but in that case the danger was avoided by an adroit intervention from Central Office.[365] Where an association fractured, the product was two rival groups, each claiming to national headquarters that it was the properly constituted body and that the other faction had breached the rules. The usual response in such situations was an attempt at mediation and reconciliation, by regional leaders or by the officers of the National Union Executive, often on the basis of seeking the retirement of both of the nominees around whom entrenched positions had been formed, in favour of a new and unsullied candidate. Where these efforts failed—as they often did—and both candidates stood, the Party Leader normally kept out of the fray and did not send the standard letter of endorsement to either of them, a practice followed at St Marylebone in 1932 and Newcastle North in 1940.[366] Ultimately, as in the latter case, the national authorities had to recognize one of the rival associations and shun the other; the role of the local MP could be crucial in this decision, as at East Ham North in 1932.[367] Ironically, at St Marylebone in 1945 this involved disaffiliating the association which had been endorsed in 1932, and giving recognition instead to the anti-Cunningham-Reid faction who had been spurned then.

[362] Derby diary, 28–9 November 1922.
[363] Comments on Worcester in West Midlands Area, GP, 'Report on 1922 Election', 19 January 1923.
[364] NU Exec., 11 May, 15 June 1932.
[365] Topping to Derby, 3 January 1928, Derby MSS, 31/4.
[366] Gower to Lloyd, 25 April 1933, Baldwin MSS, 51/144–5; Headlam diary, 25 April, 8 May 1940.
[367] NU Exec., 15 June and 14 December 1932.

Whilst the disintegration of an association in this way was comparatively rare, there were a larger number of cases where disagreements over the candidacy were disruptive and led to the loss of some workers and voters. In some of these instances, the MP or candidate who was set aside had sufficient support or sympathy within the constituency, in addition to a personal sense of grievance, to threaten to stand as an Independent Conservative, in opposition to their successor.[368] This was not often carried through to the ballot box, but, when it was, it could be very damaging. Under whatever label they stood, a rival right-of-centre candidate would split the Conservative vote in a way likely to gift the seat to one of the opposition parties; this was the case despite the effect of the 'third party squeeze' factor in the first-past-the-post electoral system, for in many seats the defection of less than two thousand votes meant the loss of the Conservative majority. This explains the ripples of nervousness which ran through the party's ranks at the prospect of widespread rival candidacies, backed by the money and propaganda machine available to the newspaper owners, in the Anti-Waste campaign of 1920–22 and Empire Crusade of 1930–31, and the reaction to the anti-India Act nominees promoted by Winston Churchill's son, Randolph, at two by-elections in early 1935.

Victories for unofficial candidates were unusual, but not unknown: two Anti-Waste candidates were elected at by-elections in June 1921, and one Empire Crusader at the very nadir of Baldwin's stock in September 1930. In two cases, Sir Robert Newman at Exeter in 1929 and John McKie at Galloway in 1945, a rejected sitting MP was successful in retaining his seat as an Independent Conservative, despite the nomination of a new official candidate against him and the consequent splitting of the usual Conservative vote. However, Newman did not contest the seat again, whilst McKie's position was regularized by the restoration of the whip in March 1948, after which he remained the Member for another decade. The only other deselected MP to fight his seat as an Independent Conservative, J. H. Lockwood at Shipley in 1935, received only 13.5 per cent of the poll and came last, but with the effect of losing the seat to Labour. By-elections saw similar disunity on a few occasions, with a victory for the unofficial candidate, Daniel Lipson, the current mayor, at Cheltenham in 1937. In particularly peculiar circumstances, Headlam, who was at the time the Chairman of the Northern Area, stood successfully in the safe seat of Newcastle North in 1940; under the wartime truce, no other parties put up candidates, and he had the advantages of substantial local support and the tacit approval of the party authorities, to whom he had better access and connections—thus ensuring that his 'official' opponent did not receive any endorsement or assistance.[369] However, as the bitter saga of conflicts in Newcastle North during the following decade vividly demonstrated, such disputes could have damaging and lasting effects; as a protagonist in one of the most serious of previous breakdowns observed, in such a conflict 'there will be so many different cross-currents of thought and loyalties'.[370]

---

[368] *Leicester Mercury*, 22 March 1924; Harborough CA, special general meetings, 29 March, 21 June, 11 October 1924.
[369] Headlam diary, 26 October 1939, 25–26 April, 2 and 8 May 1940.
[370] Duke of Atholl to Wilson, 21 April 1938, Atholl MSS, 22/6.

THE RELATIONSHIP BETWEEN THE LOCAL ASSOCIATION AND THE MP

Conservative politics operated on the basis classically expounded by Edmund Burke, that MPs had a duty to exercise their own judgement and discretion.[371] Indeed, when in difficulties over his opposition to appeasement, Paul Emrys-Evans reminded his local executive of this by reading out to them Burke's 1774 address to the electors of Bristol: 'some of them didn't like it at all, but that could not be helped'.[372] As a senior party official acknowledged during one of the most serious breakdowns, the MP was 'not the delegate of the Association with a commission to act on its behalf, but...the representative in Parliament of the constituency'.[373] The frictions which arose were not conflicts over this principle, but practical disputes about the degree of latitude that was acceptable; understandably, dissident MPs and loyalist local chairmen and committees tended to have different perspectives on this. In a few rare instances, association executives used such terms as 'instructing' their MP how to vote, but this was almost always to do so in support of the government or Party Leader when they were under attack.[374] In the late 1930s, an MP who was sympathetic to the anti-appeasers, but not himself an open critic, considered that local associations had become less tolerant of MPs exercising their own judgement, and so, ironically, were 'undermining at the same time the independence of spirit that has kept Britain a free country for generations'.[375] In reality, MPs were not isolated from, or indifferent to, the views of the active supporters and voters upon whom their chances of re-election depended. On issues where there was much concern and (especially) press agitation, this could push MPs into action, either of complaint to the whips or of open dissent. This pattern was a widespread feature of the last ten months of the Lloyd George Coalition in 1922 and was repeated to a lesser extent during the Empire Crusade in 1930, although in both cases it had most effect upon those MPs who were already sympathetic to the critical view.[376] In most cases, there was a harmony of outlook between the local committee and the MP, and thus no need for any coercive pressure; during the Hoare–Laval Plan crisis in December 1936, the Maidstone executive decided not to ask their MP for an assurance that he would support Baldwin, with the chairman commenting 'that he felt sure [the MP] could be relied upon to take the right course'.[377]

It was understood that MPs' duties were at Westminster, rather than in their constituency. A good division record was an electoral asset, and there was

---

[371] Bryant, *Spirit of Conservatism*, 48: Leeds West CA, 25 February 1938.
[372] Emrys-Evans to Attlee, 24 April 1957, to Doncaster (chairman, Derbyshire South CA), n.d. but c.13 April 1938, 3 January 1939, Emrys-Evans MSS, Add.58247/43–4, Add.58249/8–11, 78–82.
[373] Blair to Duchess of Atholl, 27 May 1938, Atholl MSS, 22/18; Ealing CA, Exec., 21 November and 19 December 1921.
[374] Uxbridge CA, Council, 8 October 1927.
[375] Macnamara to Duchess of Atholl, 25 November 1938, Atholl MSS, 22/15.
[376] Hemel Hempstead CA, Council, 7 January, Exec., 30 September 1922; Terrell to Bonar Law, 18 September 1922, Bonar Law MSS, BL/107/2/60.
[377] Maidstone CA, Exec., 7 December 1936.

recognition that the workload had become considerably more demanding due to the extension of the franchise and the increased role of central government, especially in matters such as pensions.[378] A Member who regularly attended the House and was effective in dealing with constituents' cases was unlikely to encounter problems, even if he was somewhat aloof and not often in the constituency—especially if there was regular contact by letter and telephone with the chairman and agent.[379] The Member's or candidate's public meetings in the constituency were arranged by the association after consultation, and a common pattern was an annual campaign during the summer recess. Non-resident MPs whose seats were distant from London might visit only rarely at other times of the year, but a considerable number of MPs were either local in origin or maintained a residence in the constituency (this was sometimes a requirement of their association, and a source of friction if the candidate was dilatory in doing so).[380] However, even when the MP was handily available, some distance in the relationship was both inevitable and desirable, and the normal convention was that 'the Member or candidate is outside the organisation'.[381] Most constituencies preferred their candidate or Member to have a detached and advisory role, rather than participating directly in managing the association's affairs; the latter course would disturb the balance between them, tilting it too much to dominance by the MP. It was also an advantage for the MP to be above the inevitable personality frictions and to avoid being drawn into parochial disputes—especially on matters which were in the remit of local government.[382]

The nature and frequency of contact with the MP took place in this context. The Member or candidate would address the Annual General Meeting, which was normally a public event and open to the local press. However, the MP was not usually a regular attender at meetings of the executive, even when he lived in the constituency. There were some exceptions to this pattern, usually when the Member had previously been a leading figure in the association, such as Sir Philip Dawson at Lewisham West and Archibald Southby at Epsom, although few would have gone quite as far as the Member for Accrington, who 'regarded the Executive and himself as one large family'.[383] More usually, the MP might occasionally be present at the request of the committee; this would particularly occur if the Member's conduct was at issue, and a rebel position that was out of line with grass-roots feeling would need to be defended, either to the executive or a general meeting.[384]

---

[378] Cornwall South East CA, Exec., 17 July 1926.

[379] There were a few exceptions, such as the opposition which developed to Sir Keith Fraser's candidacy in 1922–23: Harbough CA, AR, 1920 and 1921, Exec., 28 October 1922, 21 November 1923, 15 March 1924. It appears this was due to his support of the Coalition (although he voted with the majority at the Carlton Club), and resulting hostility from local diehards: *Market Harborough Advertiser*, 31 October 1922; *Leicester Mercury*, 22 March 1924.

[380] Dorset East CA, Exec., 24 June 1929; Hastings & St Leonards CA, Exec., 3 July 1919.

[381] Wolmer to Robertson (chairman, Aldershot CA), 7 July 1922, Wolmer MSS, MSS.Eng. hist.c.1012/3.

[382] Blain to Derby, 23 June 1925, Derby MSS, 31/4; Ealing CA, Public & Social Services Ctte., 14 November 1930.

[383] Accrington CA, Exec., 6 October 1936.

[384] Wirral CA, F&GP, 14 December 1936; Ripon CA, Exec., 19 October 1935, 29 April 1944; Leeds West CA, Exec., 28 February 1938; York diary, 1, 22, and 29 April 1944.

However, the combination of the Burkean principle and recognition that the MP had access to more information fostered a degree of tolerance of independence and dissent, especially when this was explained.[385] There was reluctance to oppose the MP on a matter upon which he held strong views, and a pragmatic preference not to embarrass him or undermine his position by passing any resolution of censure, which was bound to leak out even from the privacy of a committee meeting.[386] In fact, cases of such tension were the rare minority, and usually the Member had been invited to attend because his guidance was desired on a particular matter (when it would usually be deferred to), or because of his own wish to consult the committee and ascertain local opinion.[387] On these occasions, influence operated in both directions: the MP's views would carry weight with the committee, whilst a clear expression of opinion from the latter would generally shape the Member's course of action.[388] In some instances, when an important vote in the House of Commons was imminent and the MP was unable to consult in person, he would ask for the local view to be telegraphed—especially if he intended to dissent from the official line.[389] Similarly, local executives would privately inform the MP of matters about which they, or constituency opinion more generally, were concerned.[390] Much business was dealt with by correspondence or discussion with the chairman, on both routine matters and more important points, such as the continuation of the candidacy, financial contributions, and—less often—political issues on which there was strong local feeling.[391]

The local associations could use their MP as a route of communication to the leadership, and the frequent informal contacts which the chairman and agent had with the Member were a quicker and more direct method than waiting for the next committee meeting. This was also a means by which views held strongly by a section of supporters could be transmitted, without the passage of a formal resolution; in one such instance, the MP was specifically asked 'to put its tenor forward in the appropriate quarter'.[392] In this way, the constituencies exerted a more general influence than is apparent just from their minute books. Baldwin once spoke of changes in parliamentary opinion occurring after a weekend, and surmised that

---

[385] Norwood CA, Council, 12 December 1928; Thirsk & Malton CA, Special Exec., 4 March 1938; Harborough CA, Council, 19 November 1938.
[386] This was the cause of Gates' criticism of his local chairman: Middleton & Prestwich CA, F&GP, 25 May 1944.
[387] Ealing CA, Special General Meeting, 21 September 1921; Hastings & St Leonards CA, Exec., 5 October 1922; Dorset East CA, Exec., 4 July 1927; Lewisham West CA, Special Exec., 27 February 1930; Gravesend CA, Exec., 7 April 1933; Stockton CA, Special Exec., 26 September 1935; Cambridgeshire CA, Fin., 8 October 1938; Essex West CA, Council, 4 November 1938.
[388] Stafford CA, Exec., 15 March 1933; Winchester CA, Council, 5 December 1924; Uxbridge CA, Council, 28 February 1925; Perth CA, Council, 18 February 1938; Devizes CA, Exec., 18 October 1938.
[389] Torquay CA, Fin., 3 April 1922.
[390] Norwood CA, Exec., 6 July 1921; Edinburgh South CA, Exec., 6 February 1924, 13 October 1926; Oxfordshire North CA, Exec., 2 April 1927; Chippenham CA, Exec., 28 April, 1 June 1928; Cirencester & Tewkesbury CA, Exec., 12 May 1934.
[391] Howcroft (chairman, Oldham CA) to Duff Cooper, 7 July 1924, 4 March 1925, Duff Cooper MSS, CAC, DUFC/2/3; St Albans CA, Exec., 26 February 1926; Worcester CA, Exec., 17 March 1937.
[392] Harborough CA, AGM, 21 April 1934; Gravesend CA, Exec., 5 May 1933; Horncastle CA, AGM, 29 July 1933.

MPs, when visiting their constituencies, had talked to the local stationmaster; whilst they may have done so, it is much more likely that they would speak to their association chairman and would have business with the agent, and that they would give the greatest weight to their opinions and reports.[393] In a similar way, although over a longer period, the dissatisfaction with the Coalition in 1922 swelled up from below; it was Edward Wood's informed assessment that the 'atmosphere from the constituencies' was being 'reflected in the House of Commons among Members'.[394]

The most important relationship was that between the association chairman and the MP. This revolved around the same factors as that between chairmen and agents: class, age, experience, character, and competence. However, here it normally had a different pattern, with the MP or candidate likely to be of at least the same, and sometimes higher, social class than the chairman, but—in the case of candidates particularly—also to be younger and less experienced; there was sometimes the feeling of a generation gap.[395] Maintaining a mutually respectful working relationship was essential, and if the support of the chairman was retained this was normally a sufficient shield against other local criticism. As the dissident MP Robert Boothby explained, 'without his support I should be helpless in my own constituency; whereas with it I can go to the point of *virtual* independence with at any rate a good chance of success'.[396] The vital bulwark of Churchill's position in Essex West during the 1930s was the support of his chairman since 1927, Sir James Hawkey, who shared his views on India and served on the executive committee of the India Defence League. Following Churchill's opposition to the Munich Agreement, his position came under some pressure in the winter of 1938–39, with a number of local branches talking of deselection and some former supporters turning against him, but with Hawkey's support the challenge was contained.[397] In fact, given the latitude which the Member was normally permitted, and often his articulate defence of his views, differences over policy were not the most frequent cause of a breakdown in relationships. A more serious concern, as it more immediately impinged upon and imperilled the seat, was a candidate or MP who was not adequately performing his duties, either locally or at Westminster. This placed his chairman in a difficult position, with a conflict of duty between his obligations to the association and its nominee, and the need for plain speaking, which could lead to a falling out.[398] The stresses were certainly not always caused by the MP; although

[393] G. M. Young, *Baldwin* (1952), 242.
[394] E. Wood, 'Thoughts on some of the present discontents of the Conservative Party', not dated but marked 'early summer 1922', Halifax MSS (Borthwick), A4/410/9/1–13.
[395] Middleton & Prestwich CA, F&GP, 3 February 1945.
[396] Boothby to Duchess of Atholl, 30 November 1938, Atholl MSS, 22/31, emphasis in the original; he had earlier been threatened with deselection after the Munich debate: Boothby to Churchill, 10 October 1938, *WSC*.
[397] Goschen to Hawkey, 20 October 1938, Essex West CA, Buckhurst Hill branch resolution, 26 October 1938, Illingworth (chairman, Harlow branch, Essex West CA) to Hawkey, October 1938, Churchill to Hawkey, 26 November 1938, *WSC*; C. Thornton-Kemsley, *Through Winds and Tides* (Montrose, 1974), 93–6.
[398] Gurney (chairman, Hereford Borough CA) to Hewins, 27 November 1918, Hewins MSS, 72/171–3.

it was comparatively rare, there were some instances where the chairman was the instigator of division, either through loss of confidence or antipathy to the Member, or—even more rarely—through wishing to displace him and become the MP. The latter was a major cause of the conflicts in Newcastle North during most of the 1940s, whilst Robert Bower claimed that his difficulties at Cleveland in 1939 were due to a personally hostile chairman who did not represent the real feeling in the branches, and who had 'for a long time... been a focus of disaffection in the constituency', and thereby undermined the MP's position; 'it is terrible to feel that one is being stabbed in the back'.[399]

The rare instances where a dissident MP survived a breach with his chairman were due to the latter adopting an intransigent position and forcing a confrontation which other members of the local executive sought to avoid. Both the India rebel Lord Lymington and the anti-appeaser Emrys-Evans were popular with their associations, and were accorded considerable personal latitude.[400] However, in both constituencies the chairman was a vigorous supporter of the official leadership, and took the votes of confidence which the MP requested and obtained to be a repudiation of their own position. In both cases, despite appeals to stay—including from the MP—the chairman insisted upon resigning, and in doing so became the promoter of disruption and conflict.[401] Emrys-Evans in particular remained moderate and conciliatory, assuring his chairman, Sir Robert Doncaster, that he had 'no desire to split the Party in the House or in the constituency' and 'you may rely upon me to be as discrete as possible'; he also maintained cordial relations with the agent.[402] Encouraged by Central Office, Emrys-Evans attempted to persuade Doncaster to resume his office, but their personal relations deteriorated, culminating in March 1939 in a blazing row during which the latter telephoned for the police to eject the MP from his office.[403] A few days later, Hitler's seizure of Bohemia undermined the Munich Agreement and vindicated its critics, and Emrys-Evans remained the MP for Derbyshire South until his defeat in 1945. However, in Hampshire North-West, a number of other prominent figures had also resigned, and continuing dissension led to Lymington's decision several months later to quit as MP.[404]

The position of a sitting MP was buttressed by a general presumption of continuity; the normal practice was one of unquestioned readoption,[405] and vacancies

---

[399] Bower to Zetland (president, Cleveland CA), 24 February 1939, Zetland MSS, D609/29/37–8.
[400] Derbyshire South CA, AR 1931–32, 1933–34, 1936–37, Exec., 18 March 1938.
[401] Hampshire North-West CA, Special Joint Meeting of Exec. and Fin., 23 June 1933; Doncaster to Harriss, 18 November 1938, Emrys-Evans MSS, Add.58249/43–4. Doncaster had once previously taken umbrage and resigned as chairman, following criticism by a member of the executive for 'dictatorial' conduct, and was only with difficulty persuaded to continue: Derbyshire South CA, Exec., 18 November, 3 and 10 December 1930.
[402] Emrys-Evans to Doncaster, n.d. but c.12 April, 13 October 1938, to Harriss (agent), 8 October 1938, Emrys-Evans MSS, Add.58249/8–11, 25, 17.
[403] Doncaster to Perks, 3 January, Derbyshire South CA, Report of the Emergency Ctte., n.d. but c.2 February, Emrys-Evans to Perks, 21 March 1939, Emrys-Evans MSS, Add.58249/65–6, 94–7, 117–18.
[404] Hampshire North-West CA, Exec., 14 February 1934.
[405] Blair to Duchess of Atholl, 27 May 1938, Atholl MSS, 22/18.

resulted almost entirely from the sitting Member's own decision to retire or his death. The few instances of refusal to readopt were mostly the result of inadequate performance of duties or scandal, and strains in the relationship were caused by personal matters far more often than political differences. Thus, the decision of the Herefordshire North association in 1921 that they would not renominate their present MP was due primarily to his general unpopularity in the constituency, which was causing a serious loss of subscribers, than to his loyal support of the Coalition government on financial votes in the House of Commons.[406] Even die-hards could have problems over their character and conduct, such as the abrasive Howard Gritten, and F. A. Macquisten, who drank and was the subject of complaints about absenteeism both in the constituency and at Westminster.[407] The stigma of divorce could be fatal to an MP's or candidate's position, even where good service had been given. Charles Rhys had to retire at Guildford in 1935 even though he was not the guilty party in the case, and his divorced status still counted against his being considered as a possible candidate a decade later.[408] In Shrewsbury, concerns about George Duckworth's divorce led to his offer to withdraw, which the local executive accepted with alacrity, despite the imminent general election.[409] In July 1931, John Grace informed the members of his executive committee that he was giving his wife a divorce due to her insanity, a condition which he not known about on their marriage in 1929; after further correspondence with the chairman, his decision to stand down in October was accepted with regret, but with no attempt at dissuasion.[410] However, divorce was not invariably terminal, and some MPs were able to continue or to return; although Arthur Evans was dropped at Cardiff South in January 1929 (despite an appeal from the wife who was divorcing him that he be retained as candidate), and another candidate was found for the general election in May, when that person subsequently retired, the problems of finding a successor led to the readoption of Evans in January 1931.[411] Nevertheless, divorce was always a problem, and Sir William Davison's continuation at Kensington South in 1929 was at the price of heated disputes and resignations in the branch committees, with strong opposition from the women's organizations.[412] Davison had the support of the association's influential President, the Duke of Northumberland, and—even more remarkably—of a confidential letter from the moralistic Home Secretary, Sir William Joynson-Hicks, but a crucial factor may well have been his blunt declaration that if a vote of no confidence

---

[406] Herefordshire North CA, Advisory Ctte., 14 January 1921.
[407] Malcolm to Baldwin, 26 November 1935, Baldwin MSS, 39/278; Argyll CA, Exec., 10 August 1936, 7 June 1937.
[408] Guildford CA, Exec., 1 February 1935; Bolton CA, Exec., 23 April 1945.
[409] Shrewsbury CA, Exec., 27 February, Special Exec., 10 April 1945.
[410] Wirral CA, Grace to Macdona (chairman), 16 July, Exec., 24 July and 2 October 1931.
[411] Cardiff South CA, Exec., 17 January, Special General Meeting, 18 January 1929, Special Exec., 2 January 1931, special general meeting, 16 January 1931.
[412] Kensington South CA, Exec., 15 November 1928; Women's Exec. special meeting, 30 November 1928; Holland Ward Ctte., 6 and 25 March 1929; Queens Gate Ward Ctte., 15 January, 26 March, 16 April 1929; Redcliffe Ward Ctte., 11 and 25 February 1929.

was passed, he would have no option 'but to resign his seat at once and to seek re-election, thereby causing a by-election'.[413]

The most frequent type of complaint against a Member was of lack of diligence, in either the constituency or the House of Commons.[414] In the case of Alan Chorlton at Bury, the relationship with the association broke down primarily due to his poor division record, and only secondarily to his reducing his subscription during the Second World War.[415] Advancing age was less crucial in the parliamentary arena and more of a concern for the electoral contest; Butler Lloyd was dropped by Shrewsbury because he was considered not strong enough to hold the seat, as 'he did not get about the constituency, and no one knew him'.[416] Similarly, Alan Graham's unpopularity with voters, rather than with his executive, led to the latter telling him 'that they felt he had no hope whatever of winning the next election', after which he stood down.[417] The problems of C. T. Culverwell in Bristol West originated from objections to a speech which he made in the House of Commons in the early stages of the Second World War that was considered defeatist, and which he complained had led to 'my political ostracism', but the main reasons for the decision to deselect him in 1944 were complaints of his neglect of the constituency and unpopularity as a candidate.[418] Crucially, the association chairman considered that Culverwell 'had lost touch with the electorate', and 'the workers would not work or subscribe if he continued'.[419]

It was easier to drop a Member or candidate after he had lost an election, when the presumption of continuation no longer applied, and this happened on a wider scale after the 1923 and 1929 election defeats. Often the former candidate was allowed to save face by announcing their retirement, as if it had been entirely voluntary.[420] Problems were often hidden from public view in this way, and thus George Hartland's announcement in 1933 that he would not stand again for Norwich due to 'business and financial reasons' in reality followed from the association's decision not to readopt him due to his drinking and embarrassing conduct.[421] However, some breaches were too blatant to be disguised in this way. The most remarkable example of cavalier disregard was shown by Charles Baillie-Hamilton, a younger son of the Earl of Haddington and a former private secretary to Baldwin, who was elected MP for Bath in March 1929. Within little more than a year, he capped a poor division record, neglect of his constituency, ignoring his

---

[413] Kensington South CA, Special Exec., 19 December 1928. Davison had also not long before agreed to guarantee the association's overdraft up to £1,000: Fin., 2 July 1928.
[414] York CA, Management Ctte., 22 January 1937.
[415] Bury CA, Exec., 8 January and 26 February 1941, 23 April 1945.
[416] Shrewsbury CA, AGM, 5 April 1921, Selection Ctte., 1920–22; the next MP also retired for similar reasons, Selection Ctte., 19 May 1928.
[417] Wirral CA, Finance & Exec., 2 June, 11 July, and 22 August 1944.
[418] Culverwell to Downes-Shaw (Chairman, Bristol CA), 9 June 1944, Bristol CA, Council, 16 June 1944; Bristol West CA, Exec., 15 December 1939. He was also in arrears with his annual subscription: Bristol West CA, Management & Fin., 3 April, AGM, 24 April 1944.
[419] Bristol West CA, Exec., 22 May 1944.
[420] Sevenoaks CA, Emergency Ctte., 4 and 19 January 1924.
[421] Norwich CA, Fin., 10 April, 26 June 1933; Headlam diary, 20 December 1934.

association chairman, and failing to answer letters, with giving as the explanation for cancelling a local speaking engagement that he was required by a three-line whip to attend the House—although this was during the Whitsun recess. Not surprisingly, 'such an obviously puerile excuse' and 'his contemptuous treatment of the association and its officers' led to his deselection as candidate and the end of his brief parliamentary career.[422]

The financial arrangements between the Member and the association were always a sensitive matter, and misunderstandings or disputes over these could be damaging.[423] Disagreements over the amount to be contributed affected even some senior figures and long-serving MPs, as in the dispute between the Cabinet minister Sir Laming Worthington-Evans and the Colchester association in 1928, which led to his withdrawal to contest Westminster St George's in the 1929 election.[424] In the slump of the early 1930s, and again during the Second World War, some MPs sought to reduce their payments, but associations were not always willing or able to accept this. Difficulties in an MP's personal finances could force their withdrawal, as in the case of the former Assistant Treasurer of the party, Sir Albert Bennett, who lost his fortune in the slump in 1930 and resigned his seat. It was often possible to hang on until the next general election and step down then, publicly giving ill health as the reason, and by-elections were avoided if possible.[425] Bankruptcy was comparatively rare and its public nature was more embarrassing, as in the case of the flight from his creditors to Paris of the MP for Hastings in 1920.[426]

In all cases, the attitude and conduct of the MP was the critical factor in either reducing or exacerbating the tensions. For this reason, the same issue could produce quite different outcomes in different places, as can be seen with the anti-appeasers Paul Emrys-Evans and the Duchess of Atholl, or the Tory Reformers Christopher York and Eric Gates. Adopting a non-confrontational approach similar to that of Emrys-Evans in 1938, York defended his vote against the government on the equal pay issue in March 1944 in a reasonable and conciliatory tone, telling the Annual General Meeting of his association in Ripon that 'I held to my opinion on equal pay but it might have been wise to have abstained', after which local criticism fizzled out.[427] However, both Atholl and Gates made a difficult situation much worse due to their personal style, and both combined inflexibility with a surprising degree of naïvety. Whilst the breach between Gates and his local committee originated from his vote against the government in the equal pay debate of 1944, the real problem was his insulting and belligerent conduct during the following months; indeed, a former supporter on the committee whom he alienated thought that 'the Member had had a brain storm'.[428] In fact, Gates' active,

---

[422] Bath CA, Exec., 13 and 27 January, AGM, 28 April 1931.
[423] Rochester & Chatham CA, Fin., 29 February and 11 March 1932.
[424] Correspondence with Sanders (chairman, Colchester CA), 16–21 December 1928, Worthington-Evans MSS, MSS.Eng.hist.c.893/83–8.
[425] Blackpool CA, Exec., 30 November 1934.
[426] Hastings & St Leonards CA, Exec., 9 July–17 December 1920.
[427] York diary, 29 April 1944.
[428] Middleton & Prestwich CA, F&GP, 25 May, 30 March, 29 April 1944, 3 February 1945.

indeed aggressive, promotion of the Tory Reform Committee's agenda was given considerable leeway by his local association, and it was the growing conviction that 'the Member had no intention of working in harmony' which led to a decision to drop him.[429] However, at the eleventh hour, Gates met the committee in February 1945 and made an abject apology, and in view of the approaching election they decided to let 'bygones be bygones' and readopt him as candidate.[430] In a similar way, the Waterloo association dropped their MP in 1923 not just because his free trade views conflicted with the official policy, but because of his inflexibility. Albert Buckley, who had resigned his junior ministerial post in opposition to tariffs, declared in answer to a question that he would vote against a Conservative government on the issue of protection even if his action caused its downfall, and he was later reported to have refused to meet the party leaders to discuss matters and to be willing only to stand as an Independent.[431] Tact and good tactics in the presentation of a case could help to calm a constituency storm, especially when accompanied by promises of future good behaviour or emphasis upon other aspects of official policy with which the MP did agree. Thus Sir William Wayland obtained a vote of confidence after explaining his conduct at the October 1930 party meeting and promising to 'bow to the decision of the majority', whilst following the more serious incident of the withdrawal of the whip in March 1931, he gave a forty-five-minute apologia, which was accepted mainly because he had promised to give loyal support to the party and its Leader.[432] The anti-appeaser Dick Briscoe's conciliatory line and focus on the need for rearmament in October 1938 satisfied his executive at that time, although his position became more difficult in the spring of 1939.[433]

In most cases, a considerable degree of respect and freedom was accorded to an MP who took an 'independent' line on a particular issue. A chord could always be struck by a Member who declared that 'he did not intend to be a "Yes Man"' to the leadership; after all, that was not what the grass roots wanted.[434] The boundaries of acceptable dissent depended upon the interplay of eight factors: the perceived importance of the issue, its specific relevance to the constituency, the particular expertise of the MP, his strengths as a candidate, the safety of the seat, the potential danger of a split in the party, the size of the government's majority, and the imminence of a general election. Rebellion on a minor matter, as in the case of Sir Basil Peto in 1927, caused little concern, and stepping out of line for a constituency interest was naturally popular.[435] Macmillan's command of economic theory impressed more in depressed industrial Stockton than as prospective nominee for rural Hitchin, whilst Emrys-Evans combined personal experience of diplomacy with popularity as a candidate; significantly, the key objection of the latter's

---

[429] Middleton & Prestwich CA, F&GP, 29 June, 27 July, 28 September, 13 October 1944.
[430] Middleton & Prestwich CA, F&GP, 9 February 1945; there were further problems, and in 1951 Gates stood down after criticism from the association.
[431] Waterloo CA, Council, 16 November, Exec., 21 November 1923.
[432] Canterbury CA, Council AGM, 15 November 1930, Finance & Emergency Ctte., and Council, 28 March 1931.
[433] Cambridgeshire CA, Exec., 29 October 1938, 25 March 1939.
[434] Harborough CA, Council, 19 November 1938.   [435] Chelmsford CA, Exec., 1 March 1933.

chairman was that dissent would result in the loss of the marginal seat. As the economic thunderclouds gathered in the summer of 1930, advocacy of protectionism was readily understood even though it went beyond the Leader's cautious policy, but there was much less tolerance of dissent when war loomed in 1938–39: the issues were too grave, and the imperative of showing national unity was too great. A well-established MP, particularly in a safe seat, was naturally in a stronger position, and thus—with crucial support from the incoming chairman—the anti-appeaser Wolmer rode out the storm after Munich in his Aldershot constituency.[436] On the other hand, only a few months after being elected for marginal Oldham, Duff Cooper was given a plain warning by his chairman not to vote against rank and file convictions on the issue of the trade union political levy—which would, of course, have been to deviate in a leftwards direction.[437]

Principled dissent on an isolated occasion was one thing, but repeated criticism was seen as harassing or damaging the government, and likely to produce a backlash.[438] However, dissidence in a rightwards direction would often receive unanimous local support.[439] It is striking that the repeated votes against the government over India in 1933–35 caused almost no constituency problems for the rebel MPs, except when there were concerns that their aim or effect was to bring down the National Government, as with the divisive by-election candidacies in the spring of 1935.[440] This contrasts with the considerable difficulties of the anti-appeasers in 1938–39, even though hardly any of them actually voted against the government, even once. Rebellion which was linked with opponents was much less tolerated, because this undermined the party as a whole and not just the present Leader or his policy. Thus, Henry Bentinck's opposition to the Trade Disputes Bill in 1927 led to him being 'promptly called to order and muzzled by his constituents', despite his aristocratic lineage and long service.[441] Churchill's most difficult period in Essex West came only after he had actually voted with the opposition, and during the period when a cross-party 'United Front' of anti-appeasers was being publicly urged by the leading figure of the Labour left, Sir Stafford Cripps. The more serious case of the Duchess of Atholl, who resigned the National Government whip on two separate occasions, and was considered by members of her constituency executive to have been allowed 'tolerance almost to breaking point', was similar.[442] The corrosion of her relationship with the Kinross & West Perthshire association

---

[436] Aldershot CA, Exec., 14 December 1938.
[437] Howcroft (Chairman, Oldham CA) to Duff Cooper, 4 March 1925, Duff Cooper MSS, CAC, DUFC/2/3.
[438] Doncaster (Chairman, Derbyshire South CA) to Emrys-Evans, 12 April 1938, Emrys-Evans MSS, Add.58249/6–7.
[439] Skipton CA, AR, 1920, Exec., 14 August 1922; Nield to Ashley, 13 October 1921, Ashley MSS, BR/71; Hitchin CA, Exec., 22 February 1927.
[440] The problems of the Duchess of Atholl and A. J. K. Todd resulted from their resignation of the National Government whip in the summer of 1935, rather than their previous dissent over India.
[441] Lane-Fox to Irwin, 22 June 1927, Halifax MSS, C152/17/1/232a.
[442] Mickel to Duchess of Atholl, 12 May 1938, Atholl MSS, 22/24. This important case is discussed in detail in S. Ball, 'The politics of appeasement: the fall of the Duchess of Atholl and the Kinross & West Perth by-election, December 1938', *Scottish Historical Review*, 69 (1990), 49–83, particularly 58–68.

was due primarily to her views on the Spanish Civil War, which had put her in the company of Liberals, Labour, and even Communists, and only later to her opposition to Chamberlain's appeasement of Germany and the Munich settlement. Whatever the Burkean theory, there were obligations entailed in being endorsed as the official candidate; as Wayland's local chairman at Canterbury pointed out, they were 'part of the great Conservative Party and as such must abide by its constitution'.[443] At the end of the day, local associations and their chairmen had their own duty to look to: 'loyalty to one's Member, however much he is admired and respected, cannot outweigh loyalty to one's party; and when these loyalties conflict, the latter must be paramount'.[444]

POLITICAL DEBATE AND THE INFLUENCE OF THE CONSTITUENCIES

The most characteristic feature of political discussion in the executives of constituency associations was its rarity, and it was clearly not regarded as being part of their normal duties. However, the fact that it arose only when real concern or strong feelings were engaged underlines the importance of those expressions of opinion which did take place. There was variation in the habits and culture of different associations: some were more frequently inclined to pass resolutions on political matters, whilst others almost never did so—for example, both Newark and Woolwich West went through the whole interwar period without doing so once.[445] Where a resolution was proposed, its terms and the decision taken upon it were recorded in the minute book; in some cases, especially with the less formalized style of minute-taking that was widespread in the 1920s, with a full account of the discussion. The passing of a vote of confidence in the MP or candidate, and often the Leader as well, was part of the formal business at the Annual General Meeting of many associations. These motions were usually brief and phrased in conventional terms, in some cases being identical every year; they are not really expressions of grass-roots political opinion, and they certainly do not mean that there were no private doubts and disagreements. However, the resolutions passed at other times, mainly by executives or councils, were clearly spontaneous and represented genuine sentiments. They tended to be more congratulatory than critical, and this was particularly true after a serious crisis: Baldwin received floods of appreciative resolutions in the wake of the General Strike and the Abdication, as did Neville Chamberlain after the Munich settlement.[446]

---

[443] Canterbury CA, emergency meeting of Finance & Emergency Ctte, emergency meeting of Council, 28 March 1931.
[444] Berwick & Alnwick CA, Milburn (Chairman) to Todd, 15 June 1935, loose enclosure in Alnwick Branch Exec. minute book.
[445] The closest that Newark came to doing so was a discussion of India, at which it was decided to leave the matter in the hands of the MP: Newark CA, Emergency Ctte., 9 May 1933.
[446] Resolutions after the General Strike, Baldwin MSS, 137/241–95, 138/2–251; after the Abdication, Baldwin MSS, 143/140–234, 144/2–183.

Resolutions which sought to highlight an issue often began by congratulating the leaders or government on what they had already done, before asking them to go further. Where anxiety and criticism was voiced, it was usually couched indirectly, with calls for 'stronger' and 'bolder' action or for 'more vigorous', 'clearer', and 'more definite' pronouncements of policy; a direct attack on a key policy or a statement of no confidence in the Leader was extremely rare.[447] When the Perth association passed a motion in 1927 strongly critical of the government's performance in several areas, it added a rider that it was 'not to be regarded as being of the nature of censure but is put forward with a sincere desire to warn... of the state of public opinion'.[448] In general, critical resolutions tended to meet resistance even if there was widespread sympathy for the view being expressed; they were often amended into something milder or replaced with an expression of confidence, at least on the basis of giving the leaders more time.[449] There was an awareness that those in positions of responsibility knew much more of 'the inner facts of the case',[450] and a reluctance to add to their burdens with uninformed objections—especially on external affairs, where 'we are not in a position to advise our leaders'.[451] Thus the Torquay association, which might be thought natural diehard territory, responded to Central Office's sounding of opinion in 1925 about the Macquisten Bill on the trade union political levy that, whilst in favour of its principle, they had 'entire confidence in the Leader of our Party in whatever attitude he may deem it fit to adopt'.[452] However, the customary deference, or allowing the leaders room in which to act, made the impact all the greater on the occasions when the constituencies did lose patience and become openly critical.[453]

Whilst any member of an executive was entitled to propose a motion—and in many places, no advance notice was required—the lead most often came from the chairman. Given the greater predisposition of loyalty to the leadership of local chairmen, and still more the latter's desire to maintain and affirm party unity, such resolutions were nearly always positive—albeit sometimes at the level of the blandest statement that would receive unanimous endorsement. If the MP or candidate had addressed the meeting, any motion afterwards was usually proposed by the chairman or another member of the executive. Committees were usually inclined to follow the lead which their chairman gave, but they were not sheep to be driven, and there were instances when an executive rejected even a united front of the chairman and MP. This tended to be when they were opposing the party leadership, and thus the council of the Liverpool Walton association in June 1933 refused, by forty-seven votes to eighteen, to pass a resolution moved by the chairman in support of the MP's diehard line on India—and this was a Lancashire seat, where there

---

[447] Chelmsford CA, Women's Exec., 23 September, Exec., 26 September 1930; Walsall CA, Emergency Ctte., 19 November 1929.
[448] Perth CA, Chairman's & Finance Ctte., 7 March 1927.
[449] Bath CA, Exec., 13 October and 10 November 1925; Hitchin CA, Exec., 18 September 1928; Peterborough CA, Exec., 21 July 1932.
[450] Accrington CA, Exec., 24 February 1920.
[451] Ealing CA, Exec., 19 June 1922; Epsom CA, General Ctte., 2 May 1927; Northampton CA, Council, 19 May 1927.
[452] Torquay CA, Exec., 4 March 1925. [453] Uxbridge CA, Central Council, 11 October 1930.

was much concern about the impact of the official policy on cotton exports.[454] Even when feelings were running high, debate normally followed conventions of middle-class politeness: before a lengthy discussion on India in December 1934, the chairman of the Bath association noted that 'everything had been conducted in a friendly way', and afterwards he closed the meeting with the hope that 'they had all now ventilated their various difficulties'.[455] A particular feature was the desire to avoid any splits, and motions which ran into resistance were often not pressed to a vote.[456] The chairman of the Rugby association went to the heart of the matter: 'it would mean a division in the Executive, and unity was our main strength'.[457] Movers of contentious resolutions were often persuaded to withdraw them, usually after an appeal from the chairman; in many cases, this was supplemented by an assurance that opinion would be conveyed informally to the MP or the party leaders.[458] If it came to a vote, defeat was generally accepted without further acrimony, and resignations from committees or the withdrawal of financial support from associations were not only unusual but regarded as unsporting and ungentlemanly conduct; spitefulness was conspicuously absent from most interactions amongst the comfortably interwoven cohort of the constituency elite.[459]

Direct attempts to influence constituency opinion from outside were few, and almost always disregarded; if anything, they were likely to be resented as an infringement of local autonomy.[460] This was the case even with the generally respected and respectable independent 'Conservative movement' of Lord Salisbury and John Gretton in 1922, despite the appeal of its diehard platform and rejection of the Coalition.[461] Central Office occasionally asked for views or for the passage of supportive resolutions as a publicity weapon in a major campaign, as on trade union legislation in 1927; whilst this was not considered inappropriate, it was, even so, often ignored. There were a number of occasions, particularly in the 1920s, when an individual constituency association sought to marshal rank and file opinion more generally by circulating a resolution to other associations, sometimes in its own region only, but often nationally. There was considerable ambivalence when these 'round-robin' resolutions were received elsewhere: they were usually on issues that the grass roots cared about, but there was also sometimes resentment of another association's presumption in seeking to take the lead and stepping outside the normal conventions. The result was that in many cases they were simply noted and let 'lie on the table'; when the Cirencester & Tewkesbury association sent

---

[454] White to Baldwin, 14 June 1933, Baldwin MSS, 106/94–5.
[455] Bath CA, Exec., 11 December 1934.
[456] Kinross & West Perthshire CA, Exec., special meeting, 2 June 1937.
[457] Rugby CA, Exec., 9 June 1923; Dorset West CA, Exec., 30 September 1922; Aberdeen South CA, Political Ctte., 4 October 1923, 31 October 1934; Torquay CA, Fin., 5 May 1930.
[458] Cambridgeshire CA, Exec., 27 May 1922; Rotherham CA, Exec., 6 April 1926; Wimbledon CA, AGM, 29 May 1933; Ealing CA, AGM, 23 March 1934; Ipswich CA, Exec., 1 May 1934.
[459] Knutsford CA, Exec., 31 October 1930; King's Lynn CA, Exec., 9 December 1930; Alston (Agent, Kinross & West Perthshire CA) to Dawson, 3 June 1937, Atholl MSS, 22/5.
[460] Sheffield Ecclesall CA, Exec., 26 September 1933; Chelmsford CA, Exec., 29 September 1933.
[461] Reigate CA, Exec., 31 July 1922; Cambridge CA, Consultative Ctte., 9 October 1922; Uxbridge CA, Exec., 10 October 1922; Cockerill to Long, 11 August 1922, Long MSS (WSA), 947/827.

Table 3.2. Constituency 'round-robin' resolutions sent to all other constituencies

This table shows the topics of circular resolutions or letters which were sent by a local association on its own initiative to all other constituencies in England and Wales. Resolutions which appear to have been circulated only within the originating association's region are not included.

Originating CA	Date	Topic
Peckham	1920	autonomy on candidate nomination in Coalition Liberal seats
Streatham	1922	pro-Coalition: urges support of leadership and to avoid a split
Liverpool	1924	opposes plans of the Labour Party to scrap the business vote
Burnley	1925	cost of education, need for economy in building programmes
Smethwick	1926	against government attitude on Coal Commissioners' Report
Smethwick	1926	Electricity Bill
Isle of Wight	1926	amendment of trade union laws
Carlisle	1927	urges abolition of the State Liquor scheme in Carlisle
West Bromwich	1927	need to fulfil promises for economy made at the last election
Taunton	1927	need for House of Lords reform, but disagrees with Cave plan
Camberwell North-West	1928	urges government to disenfranchise pauper voters
Bristol	1928	directors of companies should be given an additional vote
Hackney North	1929	criticizes poor attendance of MPs in economy debate
Chichester	1930	criticizes Central Office on lack of co-operation & literature
Fulham West	1930	opposed to a referendum before introduction of tariffs
Esher	1931	need for economy in government expenditure, to reduce taxes
Cirencester & Tewkesbury	1932	need for House of Lords reform
Cirencester & Tewkesbury	1933	India: caution, stick at Simon Report, give free vote to MPs
Bath	1934	asks Baldwin to confirm pledge to consult on India
Leeds	1934	compensation for property demolished in slum clearance
Bath	1934	India: calls for holding a special party conference
Twickenham	1938	criticizes features of the government's Coal Bill
Herefordshire North	1938	appeals for further government assistance for agriculture

a resolution about India to every constituency, it received only thirty-two replies.[462] In November 1934, a resolution from Bath calling for the convening of a special conference on the India question was noted by the National Union Executive to have produced only twelve similar requests from other constituencies, which was well below the number which the rules required in such a case.[463] By the mid-1930s, with the regional Areas developing a greater role as a channel of opinion, the National Union became positively hostile to the sending of 'round-robin' resolutions, and the practice dwindled away.[464]

The other forms of external pressure were part of the recognized mode of politics: resolutions, letters, or delegations from outside bodies, seeking an expression of support on a particular issue. There was a general unwillingness to be drawn by these, and the usual reaction was to ignore them if possible; however, in some cases a response had to be made to an approach from an important group within the constituency, if only to avoid giving needless offence. This sometimes took the form of requests to appoint delegates to the other body, such as the local League of Nations' Union branch, or send representatives to a meeting or debate—the latter sometimes with the other local parties. The campaigns of pro-Conservative parallel organizations were looked on more favourably, but still with a sense of reservation. These included the Ulster campaign over Home Rule in 1919–21, the Empire Industries Association's (EIA) promotion of protectionism in 1927–31, and the rival bodies of the India Defence League and the Union of Britain and India in 1933–35. Their contact with local associations was nearly always in the form of the offers of speakers and sometimes literature. Where the issue was not divisive, this might be taken up as a useful free supplement to the association's propaganda, which was quite often the case with the EIA, but on other occasions there was a fear that it would be damaging. In all cases, local associations would rather let political sleeping dogs lie than poke them with a stick to see what would happen.

There were a number of issues about which the grass roots cared strongly over a long period—the topics which could 'light a fire'.[465] These were most noticeable in the 1920s, when fears were greater due to the new democracy, the rise of Labour, economic dislocation, and the political turmoil after the Coalition. The largest number of resolutions (albeit with encouragement from Central Office) in the period 1919–27 concerned the political aspects of trade unionism: the political levy, the General Strike of 1926, and the passage of reforming legislation in 1927. After the advance of the Labour Party in the 1922 election, Younger told Bonar Law that the political levy 'has become a very burning question'.[466] It was of intense

---

[462] Cirencester & Tewkesbury CA, Fin., 8 July 1933.
[463] NU GP, 9 January 1935.
[464] NU GP, 8 November 1933; Wessex Area, Exec., 9 March 1937; Essex & Middlesex Area, Exec., 16 December 1938; Winchester CA, F&GP, 25 October 1938.
[465] Blair to Hoare, 5 December 1934, Templewood MSS, VII/3.
[466] Younger to Bonar Law, 29 December 1922, Bonar Law MSS, BL/111/34/162; the backbench MP Meysey-Thompson's unsuccessful bill of May 1922 resulted in himself and Central Office

interest to the local Labour Advisory Committees, whilst in February 1925 the National Union Central Council and Executive Committee passed resolutions in favour of Macquisten's Private Member's Bill to alter the levy system.[467] The next most constant issue was also closely related to the rise of Labour, as it was clear that only some restoration of powers to the House of Lords could protect the constitution, personal liberty, and private property against despoliation by a Socialist majority in the House of Commons.[468] The need for 'second chamber reform' was a regular topic of constituency resolutions and was frequently pressed by the National Union Central Council and Executive.[469] As Austen Chamberlain admitted in May 1922, the result was that 'the National Union stands deeply committed and a small but active body of opinion keeps reproaching me with our silence'.[470] The failure of the Coalition to deliver upon its repeated pledges to tackle House of Lords reform was a significant factor in the growing alienation of the Conservative grass roots, and was the key point made by Younger against an early dissolution in his famous circular to constituency chairmen in January 1922.[471] Despite the moderation of the Labour governments (albeit constrained by their minority status), the issue remained a staple for the remainder of the interwar period, partly stimulated by the various failed attempts to bring forward legislation.[472]

Three recurring issues were related to the economic defence of sectors of the economy closely linked with Conservatism. The first of these was the continuation of the Edwardian campaign for tariff reform, although after 1920 with more emphasis upon the protection of domestic industries than their wider agenda of imperial integration. This was a response to the difficulties of many long-established manufacturing sectors, which were struggling with stagnation and falling profits, and also to the consequent problem of unemployment—which was a heavy burden upon the ratepayer and taxpayer, and seen as the fuel driving the juggernaut of Labour's advance in the 1920s. The labour movement was also intimately bound up with the third concern: the privileged position enjoyed by the co-operative societies. The shopkeeping class was an important element amongst Conservative Party membership, and between the wars they felt most threatened not by the big department stores (which were only a feature of the largest town centres) but by the growth of the co-operative societies. This period was the latter's heyday: their enormous network of branches penetrated small towns and even villages, offering prices and rewards with which it was difficult to compete. Their advantageous tax

receiving 'over 800 resolutions from various sources, mostly official [i.e. Conservative Party]': Cabinet Political Levies Bill Committee, memo by Jones based on information from Central Office, 24 February 1925, Worthington-Evans MSS, MSS.Eng.hist.c.918/148–51.

[467] Younger to Birkenhead, 23 February 1925, Steel-Maitland to Baldwin, 27 January 1925, Wicks to Gower, 22 February 1927, Baldwin MSS, 11/113–15, 86–9, 237–8; Hall to Davidson, 23 July 1923, Davidson MSS, DAV/155. However, in Scotland constituency opinion was three to one against the government supporting the bill: SUA, WDC, 4 March 1925.

[468] Chelmsford CA, Council, 6 March 1925.

[469] NU Central Council, 20 May 1919, 23 February, 21 June 1921, 27 June 1922; Younger to Bonar Law, 3 January 1920, Bonar Law MSS, BL/96/2.

[470] A. Chamberlain to Curzon, 20 May 1922, Curzon MSS, F112/223.

[471] Bayford diary, Younger circular to CA chairmen, 9 January 1922; Wakefield CA, Council, 16 January 1922.

[472] NU Central Council, 24 February, 30 June 1925, 28 June 1927, 28 February 1928, 4 March 1930, 8 March 1932, 25 March 1936.

position was a matter of frequent complaint, with calls for co-operatives to be treated on a level playing field with other businesses.[473] The economic grievance was entangled with objections to their political support for the Labour Party, while the regular appeals to Conservative members of co-operatives to participate in their society's affairs echoed the similar exhortations to trade unionists.[474]

The second long-running issue was assistance for agriculture, and this remained a constant pressure throughout the interwar era due to the deep depression in that sector.[475] Most rural seats were represented by Conservative MPs, especially after the near elimination of the Liberals in the 1924 general election, and the sector had a vocal presence in both the House of Commons and the National Union. British agriculture had been in depression since the 1870s and then, after a brief revival due to wartime needs, fell into even deeper difficulties after 1920. Whilst not all sectors and regions were in similar straits, the issue was focused upon the iconic crop of wheat, and the severe problems of the cereal growers held centre stage. It was for this reason that the greatest pressure came from the arable districts, especially in eastern England and eastern Scotland.[476] By 1927, 'a terrible season for the British farmers', they were 'very much up against the Government'.[477] There was increasing friction with the National Farmers' Union, and the apathy and dissatisfaction in these rural seats was apparent in the 1929 defeat and the troubles which followed it.[478] In the spring and summer of 1930, Beaverbrook's Empire Crusade attracted its highest membership in some of the arable eastern counties, amongst people who were almost certainly Conservative voters and, in a lesser proportion, party members. Baldwin's adoption in October 1930 of a 'free hand' on protection that would include agriculture, although perhaps by quotas and subsidies rather than import duties, drew most of these supporters back into the Conservative ranks, but the depression in the industry only deepened. Agricultural policy took a new and more successful direction under the National Government in the early 1930s, with the setting of import limits and quotas for some types of produce, and for others a limited and practical form of state intervention through the creation of marketing boards. However, this was not a universal panacea, and during the 1930s cries for help continued to be heard from the constituencies, especially from the meat producers and the growers of crops that were not receiving such assistance, such as malting barley and oats.[479]

Finally, there was a perennial demand for 'economy' in government expenditure, prompted by the pressure of high taxation and local rates. As it was led at every level by those who paid taxes but received comparatively little in the way of

---

[473] Whittaker to Derby, 28 October 1934, Derby MSS, 16/3; Lewisham West CA, Council, 10 September 1928.
[474] Northwich CA, Exec., 19 and 28 March 1927; East Midlands Area, LAC, 29 July 1933; SUA, WDC, 3 March 1937.
[475] Eastern Area, Annual Conf., 23 March 1928, Exec., 12 September 1932.
[476] Eastern Area, Exec., 10 November 1927; SUA, EDC, 22 March and 5 July 1933.
[477] Ormsby-Gore to Irwin, 24 October 1927, Halifax MSS, C152/17/1/259d; Eden to Guinness, 14 November 1927, Avon MSS, AP/14/1/49.
[478] 'Agricultural Position', memo by backbench Agricultural Ctte., 7 March 1929, Baldwin MSS, 25/276–7; Stafford CA, Exec., 15 March 1929.
[479] Norfolk North CA, AGM, 8 February, Exec., 4 October 1932; East Midlands Area, Exec., 7 January 1939.

direct benefit from the expansion of state activity, it was hardly surprising that in times of economic depression the Conservative Party called for the reduction of expenditure, and thereby of taxation, more stridently than anything else. There was an underlying assumption that large reductions must be possible,[480] in view of the comparison with the prewar situation. This led to the feeling that governments were simply not trying hard enough, an attitude fostered by the mass circulation Conservative press, especially Rothermere's *Daily Mail* and his Anti-Waste League campaign of 1920–22. Economy was a recurrent theme, and was given renewed impetus in the 1930s, first by the slump in 1930–35 and later by the pressures of funding the rearmament programme; of course, Conservatives were disinclined to oppose the latter, but sought relief through cuts in other areas.[481] The priorities and pattern of grass-roots opinion can be seen in the following table.

Table 3.3. Political resolutions passed by the sample of constituency associations 1919–1939

This table shows the topics on which, between January 1919 and September 1939, five or more resolutions were passed by constituency associations for which surviving records of the executive or other central committee, council, or AGM have been located. Resolutions at AGMs of confidence in the Leader or approval of policy are included only where this was not a routine practice, and therefore represents a deliberate expression of opinion. Letters or telegrams sent by the association chairman are included if they were subsequently endorsed by a meeting. Resolutions which were defeated or withdrawn, and resolutions on local topics and organizational matters, are not included. The number of associations with surviving central records for at least half of each period is shown, but this is only indicative of the sample, as resolutions have been included from all surviving central association records, however short their timespan.

Topic of resolutions	*Number*
January 1919 to December 1924 (122 constituencies):	
Trade union law and the political levy*	37
House of Lords reform*	30
Support of Bonar Law and Baldwin as Party Leaders in 1922-24	17
Economy in government expenditure and reduction of the burden of taxation	11
Support for the continuation of the Coalition	10
Opposition to the continuation of the Coalition[482]	8
Party policy on tariffs and imperial unity (including the McKenna duties)	8
Opposition to a general election in January 1922	7

---

[480] E. Wood, 'Thoughts on some of the present discontents of the Conservative Party', not dated but marked 'early summer 1922', Halifax MSS (Borthwick), A4/410/9/1–13.
[481] SUA, Exec., 6 July 1938, Sub-ctte on Expenditure, 5 October 1938; South East Area, Council, 20 July 1938; Thirsk & Malton CA, Exec., 20 May 1938.
[482] Opposition to the Coalition, especially in 1921–22, was more widespread than support, but it often took the form of discussion about the label under which the candidate or MP would stand at the next election, and did not result in a formal resolution.

Support of Lloyd George and approval of the performance of his government	6
Ireland (including the 1921 agreement and the boundary issue in 1924)	6
Miscellaneous other topics	48

January 1925 to May 1929 (136 constituencies):

Trade union law and the political levy*	88
House of Lords reform	36
Economy in government expenditure and reduction of the burden of taxation	28
Communism, sedition, & Soviet Russia	23
Support and appreciation of Baldwin over the General Strike of 1926	23
Extension of the franchise to women aged under thirty	14
Extension of the Safeguarding (limited protectionist) legislation	12
Agriculture (including protectionist measures specifically to assist agriculture)	9
Support of the Party Leader	7
Disqualification from voting of persons in receipt of Poor Relief	7
Repeal of the State Liquor Scheme	6
Removal of restrictions imposed by the Defence of the Realm Act	5
Miscellaneous other topics	48

June 1929 to December 1931 (144 constituencies):

Confidence in Baldwin as Party Leader	57
Approval of the official policy on protection and imperial preference	33
Approval of the formation of the National Government (August–December 1931)	20
Condemnation of press attacks on Baldwin (including support for Duff Cooper in 1931)	12
Agriculture (including protectionist measures specifically to assist agriculture)	11
Criticism of the leadership, policy or Central Office	11
Calls for a stronger protectionist policy (including 'Empire Free Trade')	10
Economy in government expenditure and reduction of the burden of taxation	10
Criticism of the poor attendance of Conservative MPs in economy debates	9
Extension of the Safeguarding (limited protectionist) legislation	8
Opposition to the Labour government repealing the 1927 Trade Disputes Act	8
Miscellaneous other topics	24

January 1932 to December 1935 (147 constituencies):

India: concern and criticism about the government's policy	57
India: support for the government's policy	23
Agriculture (including protectionist measures specifically to assist agriculture)	17
House of Lords reform	14
Support of the National Government	11
Support for protectionist measures (including the Ottawa Agreement)	11
Criticism of legislation on lotteries and betting, and of the beer duty	10
Support for strengthening defence and beginning rearmament	10
Economy in government expenditure and reduction of the burden of taxation	6

(continued)

Table 3.3. Continued

Topic of resolutions	Number
Foreign policy issues	6
Housing and slum clearance	6
Tithes and land valuation duties	6
Miscellaneous other topics	40
January 1936 to September 1939 (150 constituencies):	
Support of Neville Chamberlain in the Czech crisis (September–November 1938)	36
Support of the policy of appeasement generally (before and after the Czech crisis)	27
Agriculture (including protectionist measures specifically to assist agriculture)	24
Support (in general terms) of the Party Leader and/or the National Government	21
Introduction of a National Register and/or implementation of National Service	19
Opposition to the Coal Mines Bill	11
Support for increased rearmament and air raid precautions	10
Thanks to Baldwin for handling the Abdication crisis of December 1936	8
Foreign policy issues (including possible return of the former German colonies)	7
Issues related to unemployment	7
Miscellaneous other topics	38

* The large number of resolutions on this topic at this time was partly due to a specific request from Central Office to send in resolutions on the issue.

Whilst the topics discussed above were the constant background noise of Conservative politics, other issues came to the forefront for shorter periods, as a result of particular economic and political crises. An example of this early in the postwar period was the controversy in 1920 over the action of General Dyer at Amritsar in northern India; many Conservatives believed that his use of force at a critical moment had saved India from descent into revolutionary chaos, and they bitterly resented the Coalition government's treatment of him.[483] Of greater significance was the return of the critical prewar issue of Irish Home Rule, in a new and more difficult form with the guerrilla war of 1919–21. After failing to suppress this, the government's U-turn to negotiate with the 'murder gang' of rebels was, at best, reluctantly accepted for lack of a viable alternative.[484] However, although the majority of the rank and file supported the united leadership, it was a strain on their loyalty: a leading member in one constituency declared in July 1922 that 'ever since "this cursed Treaty" had been in existence he had felt ashamed of being an Englishman'.[485] Ireland remained a source of tension after the treaty was signed, due to concern over Ulster's boundary and the descent of the Free State into civil

---

[483] Shrewsbury CA, Exec., 19 June 1920; Harborough CA, AGM, 10 July 1920; Sevenoaks CA, Exec., 7 October 1920.
[484] SUA Conf., 19 January 1922; SUA, WDC, 5 October 1921; Bradford CA, Management Ctte., 19 December 1921.
[485] Aldershot CA, AGM, 29 July 1922; Clapham CA, Council, 9 January 1922; Yorkshire Area, Council, 12 November 1921.

war, and it contributed to the most serious internal rift, over the continuation of the Coalition in 1921–22. Apart perhaps from the tidal wave of relief and gratitude which followed the unexpectedly rapid end of the Great War in 1918, and which was capitalized upon in the December election, the Coalition had never been popular with the activists at the grass roots. It was widely accepted as necessary during the strains of postwar readjustment in 1919–20, but decreasingly so as time passed, and as early as autumn 1919 Sanders noted: 'The Coalition is not running smoothly in the constituencies. Reports of ill-feeling are constant.'[486]

The departure of the trusted Bonar Law from the Leadership and Cabinet in early 1921 coincided with the impact of economic depression and the continuing failure and unpopularity of government policies, and anti-Coalition feeling grew at the local level.[487] This was a difficult period, with local associations facing the combination 'of industrial unrest, commercial depression and political indifference'.[488] An increasing concern for the constituencies was the loss of subscribers due to disapproval of the government, and one junior minister wrote of 'supporters lukewarm and aloof, with the natural consequence of local and central divisional organisation falling into dangerous disrepair'.[489] In some areas, the tensions were such that it was better not to hold committee meetings, or to keep only to anodyne subjects upon which all could agree, such as anti-Bolshevism, for on the record and future of the Coalition 'discussions were dangerous to our membership'.[490] The growing grass-roots alienation was visible first in stronger Conservative areas such as Devon, where by January 1922 'no one about here will have anything to do with a Coalition man' as a candidate.[491] There was more support for the Coalition in the industrial districts of the Midlands, northern England, and Scotland, and in peripheral agricultural regions such as Cornwall, Wales, eastern Scotland, and the Highlands, particularly in the marginal seats and those won unexpectedly in 1918.[492] However, by the summer of 1922, even this was waning, and Austen Chamberlain's claim to be receiving 'numberless resolutions from Associations in nearly all parts of the country' supporting the Coalition is not substantiated by an examination of the constituency records, as Table 3.3 demonstrates.[493] In reality, the general sentiment, especially in seats with Con-

---

[486] Bayford diary, 9 October 1919, 129.
[487] Younger to Bonar Law, 19 July 1920, Bonar Law MSS, BL/99/3/24; Putney CA, Agent's Report, Exec., 21 April 1921; Pilditch to A. Chamberlain, 31 October and 20 November 1921, 7 September 1922, AC, 33/1/14–15, 33/2/16; Long to A. Chamberlain, 27 March 1922, Long MSS, Add.62405/96–9.
[488] Wirral CA, AR, 1921.
[489] E. Wood, 'Thoughts on some of the present discontents of the Conservative Party', not dated but marked 'early summer 1922', Halifax MSS (Borthwick), A4/410/9/1–13; Rye CA, Fin., 22 April 1922; Dorset West CA, Exec., 5 July 1922.
[490] Kinross & West Perthshire CA, Agent's Report for 1922, Exec., 18 December 1922.
[491] Lady Peto diary, 7 January 1922; Salisbury to Bonar Law, 4 March 1922, Bonar Law MSS, BL/107/2/21.
[492] Yorkshire Area, AR, 1921, Council, 10 March 1922; Cornwall PD, AR, 1920, Exec., 26 April 1922; Skipton CA, Exec., 30 October 1920, 25 March 1922; Stockton CA, Exec., 17 February 1922; Dundee CA, Council, 6 March 1922; Rotherham CA, F&GP, 13 October 1922.
[493] A. Chamberlain to Long, 27 April 1922, Long MSS, Add.62405/100–1. If received, such resolutions were not preserved in Austen Chamberlain's papers, although correspondence from MPs and party officials has been retained. For the rejection of any future coalition, see Yorkshire Area, Council, 21 July 1922, AR, 1922.

servative MPs, could be summed up as: 'the more we disassociate ourselves from the Coalition the better'.[494]

Local resistance to standing down in favour of a sitting Liberal MP in 1918 had been overcome in many cases by persuasion from Central Office, which included an understanding that this was for one occasion only. As the next election became a closer prospect from late 1921, the local associations began to consider their position. Many that had withdrawn candidates in 1918 now decided to adopt them, whilst those with Conservative MPs were seeking undertakings that they would stand without any Coalition commitments, as Independent Conservatives if necessary.[495] This pressure had considerable effect, although in most cases it was pushing MPs in a direction they were inclined to go.[496] In September 1922, the Chief Whip acknowledged that 'the influence of their Associations' would be critical in the refusal of many MPs to follow the Party Leader's strategy of continuing the Coalition in its present form.[497] At the Carlton Club meeting, 'it was very evident that Members had been visiting their constituencies during the recess' and were fully aware of the state of feeling.[498] The rebel junior minister William Bridgeman had no doubt about where the impetus for the overthrow of the Coalition had originated: the revolt 'came up from below with great force from the constituencies'.[499]

The tariff issue was the focus of particular concern during the rest of the 1920s. Whilst Baldwin's protectionist policy in 1923 was popular in the Conservative southern strongholds and in rural seats, it was unwelcome in many industrial constituencies.[500] Furthermore, the manner of its adoption and the consequent election defeat caused some anger, and there were widespread objections to the lack of consultation.[501] In the immediate aftermath, the grass-roots response pulled in different directions, and the arable farming region of eastern England was not untypical in its contradictory wish to retain protection 'as an integral part' of party policy, provided that it did not involve any increase in the taxation of food.[502] Support for tariffs remained strong in agricultural and even some industrial areas despite the defeat: the Paisley association told Baldwin 'we all feel so keen on the P.M.'s policy' and hoped that he would not drop it.[503] To some extent, it was easier to blame the usual external targets of 'misrepresentation' and unfair tactics by the Liberal and

---

[494] Dorset West CA, Exec., 30 September 1922; Herefordshire North CA, Advisory Ctte., 16 October 1922; Lane-Fox to Bonar Law, 14 October 1922, Bonar Law MSS, BL/107/2/68.
[495] Reigate CA, Exec., 15 September 1922; Dorset West CA, Exec., 30 September 1922.
[496] Ormsby-Gore to Bonar Law, 17 October 1922, Bonar Law MSS, BL/111/19/92; Cirencester & Tewkesbury CA, Exec., 18 March 1922.
[497] Wilson to A. Chamberlain, c.14 September 1922, AC, 33/2/26.
[498] Account of the Carlton Club meeting by Curzon's private secretary, 19 October 1922, Curzon MSS, F112/319.
[499] Bridgeman diary, 'October 1922'; Derby diary, 21 October 1922.
[500] Renfrewshire West CA, AGM, 29 October 1923; Yorkshire Area, Council, special meeting, 20 November 1923.
[501] Norwich CA, Exec., 21 January 1924; Liverpool CA, Board of Management, 23 January 1924; Rye CA, Exec., 8 February 1924; NU Exec., 11 March 1924; SUA, WDC, 7 May 1924.
[502] Eastern Area, Exec., 8 January 1924.
[503] Shaw to Waterhouse, 14 December 1923, Baldwin MSS, 35/126–7; Lincoln CA, Exec., 26 September 1924.

Labour parties,[504] whilst awareness that the fall of Baldwin would bring about the rise of the Coalition phoenix from the ashes was as powerful a restraint upon constituency criticism as it was upon the MPs. Even so, many Conservative businessmen shared the fears expressed by the most business-dominated constituency of them all, the City of London, where the executive committee was 'greatly alarmed' at the prospect of a Labour government.[505]

The moderate policies of Baldwin's 1924–29 government were at first a source of relief but later became a focus of criticism. The actions of the government's first year in office were favourably received, particularly the introduction of pensions for widows and orphans, although the decision to give a subsidy to the coal industry in July 1925 looked too much like a concession to the industrial muscle of the miners' union.[506] However, both this and Baldwin's conciliatory approach to the political levy were seen to be vindicated by the defeat of the General Strike in May 1926, and the flood of congratulatory resolutions of relief and thanks which followed this was to be the high point of the ministry's popularity with its followers.[507] There was further satisfaction that the trade union issue was to some extent tackled in the act of 1927; this dealt with the political levy, which had been a frequent topic of constituency resolutions. A particular issue in the mid-1920s was the danger posed by 'Communist propaganda and sedition, which is striking at the heart of the British Empire and defiling the fair name of England'.[508] In the wake of the General Strike, there was a demand that something be done about the subversive activities of 'Bolshevik' agents, and criticism of government inactivity. This concern was eventually appeased by the police raid in May 1927 on the London office of ARCOS, the Russian trade delegation, and the resulting breach of diplomatic relations. However, in other areas the second half of the government's term was marked by frustrations which led to grass-roots disillusion and apathy. Proposals to reform the House of Lords foundered in the Commons, little was delivered by way of economy in expenditure, and the refusal to extend the safeguarding duties—especially to iron and steel—or to protect agriculture ran counter to the needs of party supporters in many areas.[509] The betting and petrol taxes were unpopular with the working and middle classes, respectively, and there was annoyance over the failure to repeal the restrictions of the wartime Defence of the Realm Act.

A particular grievance was the almost careless way in which the government had become committed to lowering the female franchise to the age of twenty-one. In 1927 Lane-Fox noted 'an amazing dislike of the flapper vote proposal among the organising, Association-frequenting Tories', and 'Conservative Associations all

---

[504] Darwen CA, Exec., 19 January 1924.
[505] Hundson (chairman, City of London CA) to Baldwin, 18 December 1923, Baldwin MSS, 35/131–3.
[506] Jackson to Baldwin, 24 December 1925, Baldwin MSS, 160/96.
[507] Typical of many examples are Northwich CA, Exec., 3 May 1926; St Albans CA, Exec., 4 June 1926; Blackpool CA, Exec., 14 June 1926.
[508] Uxbridge CA, Council, 17 October 1925, 5 March 1927.
[509] Yorkshire Area, Council, 10 December 1927; NU Central Council, 28 February 1928; Amery diary, 27 September 1928.

over the country are sending in frantic messages'.[510] Despite the growth of the women's branches, giving the vote to women aged twenty-one to thirty was assumed to benefit the party's opponents by adding thousands of ignorant and easily led voters to the electorate. Whilst a variety of views were held on this issue, especially by women members, the general consensus favoured an equalization of the franchise for both sexes at twenty-five, although the difficulty of withdrawing the vote from the men younger than this was a recognized problem.[511] In December 1926, the former Party Chairman, Younger, had warned of 'much grumbling' about the government's 'weakness and their Socialistic tendencies'.[512] During the remainder of the government's term, unpopular and unsettling measures reforming local government, the Poor Law, and a Factory Act led to 'great dissatisfaction' amongst both wealthy supporters and the constituency membership.[513] A local councillor in a northern industrial town spoke for many in complaining of 'the general tendency towards Socialism, instead of the greater development of private enterprise'.[514] London businessmen accused the government of 'pandering to their enemies' and 'paltering with every big issue', and it was charged that 'you have no nerve'.[515] After the election defeat in May, the National Union's inquiry into constituency opinion about its causes revealed extensive criticism of the government's policies, particularly the 'flapper vote' and the failure to protect the iron and steel industries.[516] The view was widespread that 'there appears to be a gap between the Leaders of the Party and the local Associations'.[517]

All this set the scene for the severe party crisis during the opposition period of 1929–31, in which constituency pressures played a crucial role—both for and against Baldwin. Following the election defeat, the lack of a clear economic policy caused increasing unrest in the safe southern seats and the arable counties of eastern England.[518] This feeling was given expression and further impetus by the 'Empire Crusade' campaign mounted by the press lords, Beaverbrook and Rothermere.[519] In January 1930 the Party Chairman admitted this had 'caught on and the Party is very unsettled through the lack of a lead'.[520] The real strength of the Empire Crusade was that it vocalized the grass-roots opinion in the safe seats, and it was

---

[510] Lane-Fox to Irwin, 28 April 1927, Halifax MSS, C152/17/1/212.
[511] Dorset East CA, Exec., 5 May 1927; Uxbridge CA, Council, 7 May 1927.
[512] Younger to Davidson, 27 December 1926, Baldwin MSS, 53/31–3.
[513] Bowden to Smithers, Glorney to Smithers, Artindale to Smithers, 18, 5, and 22 March 1929, Baldwin MSS, 55/35–48; Derbyshire South CA, Exec., 3 December 1927; Oxfordshire North CA, Exec., 28 December 1927.
[514] Halifax CA, Exec., 19 January 1927.
[515] Lorden to Smithers, Phillpotts to Smithers, 4 March and 25 February 1929, Baldwin MSS, 55/35–48; Robb to Gretton, 20 February 1930, Beaverbrook MSS, BBK/C71.
[516] For the results of this inquiry, see Ball, *Baldwin and the Conservative Party*, Appendix 1.
[517] Lewisham West, Council, 11 October 1929.
[518] Winchester CA, Exec., 22 July 1929; Lincoln CA, Exec., 27 February 1930; Lady Peto diary, 20 November 1929, 29 January 1930; Fremantle to Salisbury, 19 December 1929, Salisbury MSS, S(4)132/147.
[519] Norfolk North CA, AGM, 24 February 1930; Cirencester & Tewkesbury CA, Fin., 28 February 1930; Chichester CA, F&GP, 24 April 1930; Chelmsford CA, Exec., 13 June 1930.
[520] Davidson, 24 January 1930, Halifax MSS, C152/19/1/8; Bristol West CA, Exec., 15 January 1930; Somerset PD, Council AGM, 27 January 1930.

the former junior minister William Ormsby-Gore's view that the press lords 'took their chance and got it only because there is a very widespread feeling in the constituencies, and especially in the local associations, that Baldwin has been too timid, weak and pacifist'.[521] In a few constituencies, the chairmen 'dare not summon meetings of their executives, lest a majority should go over "bag and baggage" to Beaverbrook'.[522] However, adopting a policy which entailed a commitment to 'food taxes' was considered by many to be risky strategy, on which even adjacent constituencies held contrary views.[523] For much of 1930, opposition to protectionism remained strong in the industrial Midlands and north, and Baldwin remained popular here and in the marginals, although the Party Chairman admitted that 'the Party is in a bad position... in the south'.[524]

This was the basis of the compromise policy of a referendum before the introduction of any tariffs, which had been welcomed by the grass roots in the spring of 1930 but was becoming generally unpopular by the late summer. The crucial change was that, due to the impact of the slump, a movement of opinion towards protectionism had begun in the industrial areas, and by September the editor of *The Times* noted that 'the tariff agitation is coming from more and more constituencies'.[525] In the south and east, the pressure caused considerable strains and some political acrobatics: in July, the Dorset West executive committee resolved 'that all steps be taken to show why the official Party policy embraced the policy of Empire Free Trade as advocated by Lord Beaverbrook', which at this time it certainly did not.[526] The mounting anxiety and impatience in the safer seats was summed up by the chairman of the Whitstable association: Baldwin's attitude was 'absolutely beyond one's comprehension, and we are rapidly losing support and subscriptions owing to it'.[527] This period was the most serious phase of the crisis, as a dangerous gap was opening between the leaders and their followers, and a rupture as severe as that of 1922 was only averted by two factors. The first of these was that the methods, and still more the motivation, of the press lords' attacks upon Baldwin were regarded dubiously by the grass roots. Baldwin's counter-attacks on the question of press dictation rallied support behind him, as once again he seemed to be standing for 'the best traditions of British public life which are presently threatened by a

---

[521] Ormsby-Gore to Irwin, 3 July 1930, Halifax MSS, C152/19/1/91a; Oxfordshire South CA, AGM, 31 May 1930; St Albans CA, Exec., 30 June 1930.

[522] Memo by Bowyer on his work as Deputy Party Chairman since appointment in March 1930, 1 December 1930, Baldwin MSS, 48/187–92; Kennington CA, GP, emergency meeting, 21 June 1930.

[523] Chippenham CA, Exec., 10 October 1930, commenting on letter from Wiltshire West CA; NU Central Council, 4 March 1930 (debate on resolution from Mid-Bedfordshire CA).

[524] Davidson to Irwin, 27 May 1930, Halifax MSS, C152/19/1/66a; SUA, EDC, Exec., 25 June 1930; Tynemouth CA, Exec., 24 October 1930.

[525] Dawson to Irwin, 28 September 1930, Halifax MSS, C152/19/1/136.

[526] Dorset West CA, Exec., 25 July 1930; there was a similar and understandable desire to square this circle in the Norfolk North by-election: Norfolk North CA, Council, 17 June 1930.

[527] Chairman, Whitstable CA to Beaverbrook, 15 October 1930, Beaverbrook MSS, BBK/B171; Butler to his father, 11 July 1930, Butler MSS, D48/14/744–54; Spelthorne CA, central and branch resolutions, September–October 1930, Baldwin MSS, 165/275–9; Chelmsford CA, Women's Exec., 23 September, Exec., 26 September 1930.

certain section of the Press'.[528] There was an element of collective self-respect in the rank and file reaction: 'a great historic party could not be dictated to by Press Lords'.[529] The second development was that an opportunity was seized in October 1930 to advance policy to the unfettered protectionist stance of the 'free hand'; this was what the rank and file wanted, and it was followed by a rally of loyalty to the Leader.[530] Although the press lords continued their assault on Baldwin for several months more, from this point onwards their support at the grass roots almost vanished; by March 1931, they were considered to be engaged upon an 'insidious attempt to break up the Conservative Party'.[531]

As the threat of a rift receded, the normal relationships within the party were resumed. The driving force behind the desire for unity in the winter of 1930–31 was the impact of the world depression, and the need to concentrate upon getting the failing Labour government out of office.[532] From early 1931, the issue that Conservative opinion cared about most was 'economy', and the party leaders satisfied this by putting it at the front of their programme, ahead even of tariffs and help to agriculture. The primacy of this domestic concern was one reason for the lack of grass-roots concern or objection to the bipartisan policy on reform in India followed by Baldwin from the Irwin Declaration of October 1929 to the Irwin–Gandhi Pact of March 1931, and at this point there was rarely any mention of the issue in the local executives.[533] The economic crisis of August 1931 occurred with rapidity at a time of year when local committees did not normally meet, but the leadership's entry into the emergency National Government was accepted after the event as 'an absolute necessity'[534] due to the gravity of the crisis, as 'the whole country was at the present moment on the brink of a precipice'.[535] The concept of non-partisan 'national' government had considerable appeal to the Conservative temperament and, with reassurance given from the start that it involved no watering down of the tariff policy, the new coalition was greeted with relief. It became popular with Conservatives as a source of economic confidence and political stability, and there was little dispute that it should be maintained into the general election and in government beyond.[536]

The National Government did not provoke the hostility of the Conservative grass roots in the way in which the Lloyd George Coalition had done, for several

---

[528] SUA, EDC, Exec., 13 March 1931; Bristol West CA, Exec., 9 September 1930; Bradford Central CA, AGM, 12 March 1931; Ealing CA, AGM, 13 March 1931.
[529] Birmingham Handsworth CA, AGM, 6 March 1931; Northern Area, Council, 19 July 1930; Winchester CA, AGM, 14 March 1931.
[530] SUA, Exec., 10 September 1930; Ipswich CA, Exec., 16 October 1930; Chelmsford CA, Exec., 17 October 1930; Sowerby CA, Exec., 31 October 1930; Guildford CA, Council, 20 November 1930; Lincoln CA, Exec., 21 November 1930.
[531] Northampton CA, Advisory Ctte., 16 March 1931; Wolverhampton West CA, report of candidate's speech, 21 March 1931.
[532] SUA, EDC, 14 January, 25 March 1931.
[533] Winchester CA, AGM, 14 March 1931; Chichester CA, Exec., 13 April 1931.
[534] Bristol West CA, Exec., 15 September 1931; Sowerby CA, Exec., 25 September 1931.
[535] Inverness CA, Special General Meeting, 15 October 1931; Uxbridge CA, Central Council, 12 September 1931; North West Area, Exec., 5 September 1931.
[536] Halifax CA, AGM, 7 May 1934, 8 April 1935.

reasons. First, it delivered on the promise of introducing the tariff measures in 1932. Secondly, the blame for the economic problems lay with the previous Labour government, and, although things got worse before they got better, from 1933 it was nevertheless apparent that the picture was improving in many areas, especially in the Midlands and south; the National Government was given grateful credit for having stabilized the situation, and its continuation was seen as essential in maintaining this.[537] Thirdly, although it had a non-Conservative Prime Minister in Ramsay MacDonald, he was not as assertive as Lloyd George had been, mainly focused his attention on foreign affairs, and had no party of any significant size behind him. Finally, it was important that the National Government had no agenda for a fusion of parties, as the retention of their separate identities gave it credibility and the broadest electoral appeal. It is significant that the only initiative to arouse grass-roots concern about the overall operation of the National Government was the creation of the all-party Co-ordinating Committee and the National Publicity Bureau, which had the appearance of embryonic rivals to the Conservative organization.[538] With reassurance that the Conservative Party's autonomy and identity would not be diluted, the National combination became an acceptable and advantageous part of the landscape. There was little doubt about the value of continuing it in the 1935 general election, and by 1939 it had become an established permanency, with acceptance that 'the next election would without doubt be fought on a National basis'.[539] During the decade, several constituency associations discussed changing their name to include 'National', although fewer actually did so,[540] whilst in a handful of very weak seats the associations disbanded to fuse into a local 'National' organization.[541]

There were, of course, some criticisms of individual policies of the National Government. Whilst some reforms, which went further than a purely Conservative government might have ventured, were accepted from the cross-party combination, there remained hostility to measures which created dangerous precedents in extending the compulsory powers of the state, such as the amalgamation clauses proposed in the Coal Mines Bills of 1936 and late 1937.[542] The economic conditions of the 1930s ensured that there were continued and frequent calls for both economy in expenditure and assistance for agriculture. There was also a new concern which arose regularly during the 1930s: housing legislation, and, specifically, the operation of the slum clearance programmes. The problem was that many of

[537] Tynemouth CA, Exec., 30 September 1932; Argyll CA, AGM, 14 October 1932; Horncastle CA, AGM, 4 November 1932; Wirral CA, AR, 1933; SUA, EDC, Exec., 12 October 1933; Denbighshire CA, Northern Area, AGM, 19 July 1935.
[538] NU Central Council, 28 March 1934, 27 March 1935; Bradford East CA, AGM, 16 March 1934; NU Conf., 1934, speech by Burns-Lindow; Middleton & Prestwich CA, F&GP, 30 May 1935.
[539] Essex & Middlesex Area, Council AGM, 2 March 1938; NU Central Council, 24 June 1936, 30 March 1939.
[540] Islington East CA, Exec. 18 February 1936; Bedford CA, Council, 9 March 1938; Cambridgeshire CA, Exec., 16 April 1932; Guildford CA, Exec., 21 February 1936.
[541] Forest of Dean CA, General Meeting, 23 May 1936; a merged 'National Association' functioned briefly in Ilkeston in 1935–36.
[542] Penistone CA, Administrative Ctte., 22 May 1936, 21 January 1938; Rother Valley CA, Exec., 1 February 1938; Rothwell CA, F&GP, 28 January 1938; SUA, EDC, 28 March 1934.

the middle class who were not particularly well-off had invested their savings in the ownership of a few houses for rent, but they did not have sufficient income to maintain or improve them. When compulsorily purchased to make way for new housing, these properties were frequently condemned as unfit for habitation and demolished without compensation. This represented a serious loss to their owners, and led to 'a feeling of seething discontent and resentment at such confiscatory proposals'.[543] The result was a recurring flow of critical resolutions from the constituencies demanding revision of the 1934 Housing Act; this issue was particularly strong in the west of Scotland and some of the northern industrial areas.[544]

The only issue during the 1931–35 National Government to raise serious and widespread grass-roots unrest was the proposals for devolution in India, and here the key figures in the government were Conservatives: Baldwin and Hoare. At the most basic level, there was a fear of the eclipse of the empire and loss of Britain's position as a world power: Lane-Fox noted 'the sort of keen constituency politician who is saying "India is being given away—what are the Conservative Party and above all what is this wretched woolly Baldwin doing to save it?"'[545] However, grass-roots opinion only began to focus extensively on the India question after the publication of the White Paper in March 1933, and this was already too late to change the direction of policy: commitments had been made, conferences had been held, inquiries had reported, and the reform proposals had acquired considerable momentum. Between 1933 and 1935, the India question raised widespread concern in the local associations, and many critical resolutions were tabled for discussion.[546] Whilst these sometimes voiced fears of 'surrender' and of handing India over to unrepresentative and hostile extremists, generally they called for limited progress—resting upon the Simon Commission's report, and emphasizing the need for safeguards—rather than outright negation or repression.[547] Even so, it was usually only the vaguer and more moderate resolutions which were passed without amendment or dissent. Whilst there was considerable anxiety about the implications of the reform proposals, crucially any alternative to the government's policy lacked conviction with the 'considerable weight of middle opinion'.[548] In many cases, executive committees avoided or postponed discussion, and sought to follow a neutral line between the critics and the supporters of the government's policy; this occurred even in the constituency where the most senior opponent,

---

[543] Glasgow Maryhill CA, Exec., 18 February 1935; Stirling & Falkirk Burghs, Exec., 7 February 1935; East Midlands Area, AGM, 26 January 1935; SUA, Central Council, 21 May 1935; Stonehaven to Baldwin, 21 November 1934, Baldwin MSS, 25/29–42.

[544] Cental Office memo, 21 November 1934, Baldwin MSS 25/30–5; Yorkshire Area, Council, 24 September 1938; SUA, WDC, 6 February, 1 and 10 May 1935; SUA, Central Council, 21 May 1935; Whittaker (Secretary, Manchester Exchange Ward CA) to Derby, 28 October 1934, Derby MSS, 16/3.

[545] Lane-Fox to Irwin, 4 March 1931, Halifax MSS, C152/19/1/246.

[546] Wells CA, AGM, 5 May 1933; Devizes CA, Exec., 5 May 1933; Finchley CA, Council, 26 May 1933; Derby CA, Exec., 28 November 1934.

[547] Stone CA, Exec., 29 April 1933; Norfolk North CA, Exec., 2 June 1933; Ealing CA, Exec., 28 August 1933.

[548] Croom-Johnson to Davidson, 2 June 1933, Davidson MSS (Bodleian), MSS.Eng.hist.c.559/125; Ipswich CA, Exec., 1 May 1934.

Lord Salisbury, was also the chairman of the association.[549] The resolutions which were passed generally urged caution and restraint, especially on matters such as control of the police, and only a minority were explicit rejections of the official line.

One reason why the India issue produced more debate in constituency associations, and more critical resolutions than any other internal party crisis, was because the slow maturation of the legislative process gave many opportunities for it to be discussed between the White Paper and the passage of the Act over two years later. Within the overall anxiety, the India question was of greatest concern to the Conservative rank and file in two areas. The first of these was south Lancashire, due to fears about the future of cotton exports to the valuable Indian market. The other was the Home Counties and the retirement towns of the south coast, where considerable numbers of former Indian army and civil service officers were active figures on constituency executives.[550] It was particularly in such places that the 'flaming rhetoric' of Churchill and other critics had an impact, to 'stir up all the old men and old ladies'.[551] Furthermore, the diehard line was vigorously supported by Rothermere, and the influence of his newspapers was strongest here, with MPs being 'hustled by their constituents who read the Rothermere press'.[552] This contributed to the volume of constituency resolutions from these areas, to the rejection of the official line by the Essex & Middlesex Area in February 1934, and to the discretion given by their local associations to many of the diehard MPs who opposed the bill, such as Page Croft who represented Bournemouth and Churchill who sat for the West division of Essex. However, Baldwin considered that Churchill 'had no great following outside London and the Home Counties' and 'did not cut much ice in the north of England'.[553]

Despite the natural concern of the Conservative grass roots about the future of the 'jewel in the crown' of the empire, the India 'revolt' was unable to shake the leadership or achieve even the slightest amendment in their policy. Grass-roots critics were at a considerable disadvantage in claiming to have a better knowledge than the responsible ministers and imperial administrators on an issue of this type, and the balance of prestige was tilted against them even more steeply than on matters of domestic policy: 'such a complicated problem could only be dealt with by experts of many years' experience'.[554] Even where objections were raised by members who had had personal experience of India, it was difficult for them to claim more than a worm's-eye view. Most members of local executives did not feel qualified to deliver a verdict and consequently were reluctant to side with the dissidents, and in some cases there was annoyance with the latter for putting them on the

---

[549] St Albans CA, Exec., 28 April 1933; Reigate CA, Exec., 12 April, 10 August, 11 December 1933; Winchester CA, Exec., 28 July 1933; Stirlingshire West CA. Exec., 10 August 1933; Thirsk & Malton CA, Exec., 31 October 1933.

[550] Glyn to his mother, 14 April 1933, Glyn MSS, D/EGL/C9/2: Lewes CA, Seaford & District Men's branch ctte., 29 November 1933.

[551] Hoare to Stanley, 4 April 1933, Templewood (BL) MSS, E240/9/7–8.

[552] Lane-Fox to Irwin, 4 March 1931, Halifax MSS, C152/19/1/246.

[553] Notes by Crozier, interview with Baldwin, 12 June 1934, *BP*, 319–20.

[554] Sowerby CA, Exec., 27 March 1931; Kinross & West Perthshire CA, Exec., 20 April 1933; Thirsk & Malton CA, Exec., 25 April 1933.

spot.[555] The sense of exceeding their competence and caution in dealing with a divisive issue were features of those discussions recorded in detail in the local minute books, and it is likely that these were also significant factors in the many constituencies where no critical resolution was brought forward.[556] A further restraining element was that (apart perhaps from in Lancashire) there was no sense of public concern to act as a driving force behind constituency opinion, and no expectation that this would be a significant issue at the next general election—which would be fought on domestic social and economic issues.[557] Therefore, although the importance of the question to the future of the empire was undisputed, it was not seen as a valid reason for damaging party unity at the local level—especially as this would only benefit the opposition, who were committed to a more radical policy on India. Finally, there was one factor which underlay everything: the preservation of the National Government. This was the greatest priority, and something that Conservative opinion became more united and fixed upon as time progressed rather than, as in 1918–22, less so. As the Labour Party moved to the left in the early 1930s, the security and stability provided by the broader-based National combination became an even more essential asset. However, it was clear that repudiation of the India policy would entail bringing down Baldwin and almost certainly destroying the government. Not only did almost none of the Conservative rank and file want this, but they were also receptive to the charge that this was the real purpose of Churchill and his followers, and that they would not support.[558]

In a striking contrast with the previous internal struggles over the Coalition, tariffs, and India, the parliamentary critics of appeasement found almost no support at constituency level in 1935–39. This was not because local Conservatives did not concern themselves about issues of foreign policy in this period; if anything, it was because they thought them too important. The absence of grass-roots dissent was principally due to deference to the expertise of those in authority and the lack of a credible alternative policy. Memories of the Great War and dread of another such conflict were the powerful forces behind the hope that, if given a chance, appeasement would succeed in resolving international disputes peacefully, and the fear of the consequences if it did not. The question of expertise applied particularly to the conduct of diplomatic negotiations and the complexity of the issues involved in the various territorial disputes. Most Conservatives, in parliament as well as in the constituencies, were conscious that they lacked sufficient knowledge of the situation to take the considerable step not just of forming a different judgement but of seeking to press it on the government.[559] Several elements contributed to their reluctance, including the appreciation (perhaps overestimation) of the arcane skills of the diplomat, the understanding that negotiations in progress were often confidential and could be upset by premature public debate,

---

[555] Butter (chairman, Kinross & West Perthshire CA) to Duke of Atholl, 19 April 1933, Atholl MSS, 9/1.
[556] Waterloo CA, Council, 20 June 1933.
[557] Chelmsford CA, Exec., 15 January 1935.
[558] Headlam diary, 28 June 1934.   [559] SUA, EDC, 14 October 1936.

and the awareness that the decisions of government were based upon information and intelligence which could not be disclosed. Most of all, there was recognition that the 'men on the spot'—in this case, particularly the Cabinet—were best placed to take decisions, and that the burden of responsibility for the fate of the empire rested upon their shoulders. All this made it very difficult to dissent from the policy adopted by the government, and many Conservatives felt that they should be supported in the discharge of their duty. This question of expertise had not been a restraint in the crises over the Coalition in 1922 or protection in 1930, which concerned frequently debated issues of domestic politics upon which everyone could form an opinion. It was a factor in the India revolt, but to a much lesser extent, as a considerable number of the middle- and upper-class leadership of local associations had personal or family acquaintance with India. It was also the case that some figures in India and some retired officials supported the critics, whereas over appeasement there was barely a crack in the unanimity of the establishment.

The second factor in the absence of constituency dissent was the lack of viable alternatives. The Conservative anti-appeasers were much clearer on what was wrong with government policy than what should be done instead, some of which seemed to be scarcely different, some vague, some impracticable, and some positively dangerous. There was a presumption that any alternative policy could only mean war, and from that it was but a short step to accusations that the critics of appeasement positively desired war—a charge which put them, rather than the government, on the defensive. On the model of previous party disputes, it might be expected that the grass roots would favour the views of the more robustly Conservative, or 'right wing', section of the parliamentary party. The complications here were firstly that most of the diehards were strong supporters of Chamberlain, and secondly that the experience of the First World War and contemporary views of its causes made any confrontational strategy an unattractive proposition. However, variance in the opposite direction had little appeal: more concessions, further disarmament, and reliance upon the League of Nations were the policies of the opposition parties, and even if they were credible they would have been a difficult pill to swallow. For all these reasons, it genuinely seemed that there was no realistic alternative to the government's policy, with the consequence that even unpalatable events were accepted on the basis of being unavoidable and a lesser evil than war. The result was that constituency opinion barely commented upon foreign policy, except to express support for the government—in particular, extensively and fervently in the wake of the Czech crisis in autumn 1938. There was genuine admiration for Chamberlain's bold stroke of flying to Germany to negotiate face-to-face with Hitler, and heartfelt gratitude when war was averted; the widespread view was articulated by one local chairman, who praised the Prime Minister's 'wonderful achievement... and said we were proud to belong to a Party whose leader had accomplished so much towards a peaceful settlement of the serious European situation'.[560]

---

[560] Middleton & Prestwich CA, F&GP, 29 September 1938; Pembrokeshire CA, Exec., 1 October 1938; SUA, WDC, 5 October 1938.

However, there was one foreign policy question upon which the grass roots did express concern, and, significantly, this was the occasion when it seemed that appeasement might diminish Britain's imperial position. Rank and file opposition to the suggestion of returning any of the former German colonies was marked, and effectively ruled this out—but as the government had not actually proposed such a concession, this did not involve any direct criticism.[561] Apart from this, there were resolutions in favour of rearmament and other defence preparations, especially against attack from the air. These were generally intended to encourage the government rather than to criticize its progress, although there was a negative reaction in May 1937 to the imposition of an unexpectedly heavy tax in the National Defence Contribution.[562] As war loomed nearer in 1938–39, there were demands for greater urgency in rearmament and a widespread call for the reintroduction of conscription, firstly by the preparation of a national register and then, after Hitler's seizure of Bohemia in March 1939, for the immediate implementation of National Service.[563] Even so, such resolutions often indicated that the decision was one for the government to take when they should deem it necessary or expedient.

The winter months of 1938–39 saw many of the anti-appeasement MPs under severe pressure in their constituencies, with some on the brink of deselection. Even Churchill, with all his prestige and the loyal backing of his constituency chairman, came under threat in Epping, where the consideration of a possible replacement candidate became entangled with suspicions of Central Office intervention. In fact, there was little of this; partly because Hacking chose to follow a carefully neutral line, and partly because no such manipulation was needed—the fervour of grass-roots support was real and effective enough without an external encouragement which could easily be counterproductive (indeed, claims of Central Office manipulation were a frequent defensive tactic of MPs whose problems were, in fact, of their own making and on their own doorstep).[564] The most serious breach occurred in the Kinross & West Perthshire constituency, where there had already been considerable strains at the independent stance of the MP, the Duchess of Atholl, earlier in the decade. Especially damaging was her support for the Republican government in the Spanish Civil War, which appeared to align her with Socialists and Communists, and provoked much local criticism. She was eventually deselected as candidate and, perhaps unwisely in view of the crest of support for appeasement, resigned her seat and fought a by-election in December 1938.[565] However, even with the other parties standing aside, she was defeated in a straight fight with the official Conservative and National Government candidate, a local farmer. No other dissident MP was pushed this far, and the pressure eased after the German seizure of Bohemia in March 1939; in the following years, after the

---

[561] NU Central Council, 24 June 1936; SUA, EDC, 10 June 1936; NU Conf., 1936, resolution moved by Sandys; Cambridgeshire CA, Exec., 13 November 1937; Inverness CA, AGM, 20 October 1938; Harborough CA, Council, 19 November 1938.
[562] Hitchin CA, AGM, 26 May 1937; Winchester CA, Exec., 27 May 1937.
[563] Chippenham CA, AGM, 1 April 1938, 21 April 1939.
[564] Cambridgeshire CA, Exec., 29 October 1938.
[565] Ball, 'Politics of appeasement', 49–83.

evident failure of appeasement and the setbacks in the early stages of the war, the anti-appeasers were vindicated and became the new orthodoxy. Nevertheless, at the start of the war, and even after his downfall as Prime Minister in May 1940, grass-roots support for Chamberlain remained deeply entrenched.[566]

As in the First World War, the main focus and priority for Conservatives was the prosecution of the war. This led to their adoption of an absolutist interpretation of the political truce, which was in fact only an agreement not to contest by-elections and to postpone the general election. As a result, there were constant complaints about the failure of the Labour Party to observe the truce in the same scrupulous spirit. Labour was seen as exploiting its position in National Government to advance its political agenda, whilst continuing tirelessly at local level to 'spread their political views and propaganda wherever possible'.[567] This left-wing influence was permeating even further due to polemical anti-Tory tracts such as *Guilty Men* and *Your M.P.*, and later of left-wing influence in the army's education services. However, the finger of accusation was pointed most often at the broadcasts of the BBC, which were considered to be biased against the Conservatives and affording uncritical licence to avowed Socialists, such as the popular author J. B. Priestley.[568] In fact, although this was a matter of perennial complaint, when Central Office closely monitored the broadcasts for a period, the Party Chairman reported that 'he had come to the conclusion that there was no valid case for making representations to the BBC, as on the whole they had shown little "left" tendency'.[569] The Conservative grass roots shared the caution of the parliamentary ranks about the possible burdens involved in financing the Beveridge Report's plans for a welfare state, and were equally dubious about the grander visions of postwar reconstruction and of a brave new world to be tidily regulated by planning.[570]

The German invasion of Russia in June 1941 brought to an end the desperately dangerous year during which Britain had stood alone against a Nazi-dominated continent, following the collapse of France in June 1940. There was strong support, very much in tune with popular opinion, for 'giving all possible aid to that country in its fight against our common enemy'.[571] Grass-roots views of Russia underwent a significant—if temporary—shift during the war, primarily due to its 'splendid resistance to the Nazi blast' of invasion; at least one party official was explicit that the views previously held about the Soviet system might have to be revised, and, more generally, there were hopes of better relations after

---

[566] Merionethshire CA, AGM, 5 February 1940; Bury CA, AGM, 3 April 1940; Dundee CA, Council, 10 May 1940; Camberwell North CA, Exec., 19 October 1940; Eastern Area, Exec., 11 December 1940.

[567] Derbyshire West CA, Agent's Report, 19 July 1940; Camberwell North CA, AGM, 27 June 1941.

[568] Wessex Area, Council AGM, 27 May 1942; Shrewsbury CA, Exec., 9 January 1945; Sussex PD, AGM, 13 April 1945.

[569] NU Exec., 13 January 1944.

[570] SUA, WDC, Education & Propaganda Sub-ctte, 29 December 1942; Yorkshire Area, AGM, 20 February 1943.

[571] Northern Area, Council, 18 October 1941.

the war.[572] Understandably, there was determination that Germany must not only be completely defeated, but also receive 'full retribution for her terrible atrocities when victory has been attained'.[573] Even more understandably, the view from one central London division as it suffered heavily during the Blitz, was that 'the most effective way of preventing Germany again breaking the peace of the world would be to shoot all Nazis'.[574]

From the moment that he became Prime Minister in May 1940, Churchill received strong support from the grass roots, and this did not waver even in the setbacks of 1942.[575] However, whilst Churchill was lauded for his 'magnificent leadership' of the nation in war,[576] there was some concern at his neglect of the party, which 'had lost ground very considerably'.[577] The lack of a Conservative programme and uncertainty as to whether the coalition would continue into peacetime left local chairmen feeling 'that we were groping in the dark'.[578] Even so, there was more optimism than pessimism at the start of the 1945 general election campaign. Where the constituencies had anxieties, these were due to the moribund state of the local organization rather than any doubts about Churchill's appeal, and thus the party's landslide defeat came as a shock to many.

---

[572] Camberwell North CA, general meeting, 4 October 1941; East Midlands Area, AGM, 25 October 1941.
[573] Stafford CA, AGM, 4 July 1942.
[574] Camberwell North CA, general meeting, 31 August 1941.
[575] Rochdale CA, AGM, 19 February 1942; Stafford CA, AGM, 17 June 1944.
[576] Aberdeen South CA, Political Ctte., 25 October 1940.
[577] Wessex Area, Exec., 26 November 1941; Kincardine & West Aberdeenshire, Exec., 27 October 1944.
[578] Ealing CA, Exec., 13 January 1944; Holderness CA, AGM, 12 May 1945.

4
The National Union and the Central Office
Representation and Organization

Taken as a whole, the organization of the Conservative Party had nine important functions, all of which, in various ways, related to its principal purpose: the winning of parliamentary elections at the constituency level, by ensuring that the largest possible number of electors turned out to vote for the Conservative candidates. The first necessity was finding suitable persons to be such candidates, and ensuring that there was an electable Conservative standard-bearer in every possible constituency. The second function was recruiting supporters across the country who would be willing and able to assist the candidates, and the third was raising from these supporters the financial resources needed to maintain the organization locally and nationally. The fourth purpose followed from the second: securing the adherence of all like-minded supporters so that divisive candidatures, split votes, and rival groups were avoided; this led to the emphasis upon unity and loyalty, and the avoidance of controversial matters within the ranks. The fifth role was communicating the views of the membership upwards through regional and national structures, and this was mirrored by the sixth function: providing the leaders with a means of monitoring their followers' opinions, meeting with them, and, when necessary, convincing or appeasing them, and so defusing conflicts before they became serious. The seventh purpose was to obtain the maximum popular support for the party's programme by publicizing it attractively and effectively, and producing propaganda material for use in the constituencies. The two final functions were the most diffuse, but by no means the least important: maintaining a visible presence in the affairs of local communities and the nation, and presenting a favourable face to the general public, especially on formal occasions. Achieving these aims required goodwill, discipline, and efficient interaction between the various parts; in most places, at most levels, and for most of this period, the Conservatives were able to maintain these—even to take them for granted—and this contributed significantly to their cohesion and electoral success.

The National Union of Conservative and Constitutional Associations was founded at the time of the Second Reform Act in 1867 and, with some adjustments of title, has remained the representative organization of Conservative supporters ever since. It was originally a small and marginal body, but by the end of the nineteenth century there was an affiliated local association in every constituency in England and Wales, and in Scotland through a parallel body. In 1912 the formal absorption of the Liberal Unionist Party led to the adoption of the description 'Conservative and Unionist' by many local associations and the Central Office.[1] The latter had been established by Disraeli in 1870 with the primary purpose of finding suitable candidates for the marginal and more difficult constituencies. The tasks of the office expanded to some extent beyond this, but up to 1914 its role was limited and its staff few in number; at their head was the Principal Agent, who was the personal appointment of the Party Leader. A period of organizational success in the later nineteenth century was followed by defeats in the Edwardian era, and, after the general elections of 1910, the Unionist Organisation Committee was appointed to conduct an inquiry. The key recommendation of its report, accepted by Balfour shortly before he resigned the leadership in 1911, was the creation of a position to oversee and direct the work of the Central Office. The 'Chairman of the Party Organisation' would carry out the instructions of the Party Leader and be in authority over all of the paid staff of the Central Office; the Principal Agent would now function as his executive deputy. This chapter considers the development and roles of these two sides of the party organization—voluntary and professional—during the interwar era. It examines first the regional level, which provided a crucial link between the local constituencies and the central organizations, and then the various institutions of the Conservative Party at national level. This is more of a human story than an administrative history; as the Chairman of the Sub-committee drawing up new rules for the National Union in 1929–30 observed: 'dry bones can always be re-arranged, but the trouble is to clothe them and give the system life'.[2]

THE REGIONAL ORGANIZATION

Regional organizations in England and Wales were first established after the passage of the Third Reform Act in the mid-1880s. For the next two decades there were ten Provincial Divisions, but after the defeat of 1906 many of these fragmented into their separate counties, creating more than thirty units. In most cases this proved inefficient, for although the county was an important focus of identity, community, and pride, many of them were too small or lacking in resources to maintain an effective intermediate organization. During the 1920s some of the previous groupings began to reform, with Bedfordshire joining the Eastern Area in 1922 and Lancashire and Cheshire merging in 1925, while a new south-central grouping was established in 1926, which later adopted the name Wessex.[3] The revised rules adopted by the National Union in 1930 decided that its 'Provincial Areas' should be identical in territory with the regions covered by the twelve Central Office Area Agents, but that 'there should be no element or suspicion of

---

[1] The National Union used the title 'National Unionist Association' until 1924, when it became the 'National Union of Conservative and Unionist Associations': NU Rules, 1918, 1924.

[2] Memo by Ellis, 'Note on Policy and Organisation', 16 October 1929, Steel-Maitland MSS, GD193/121/5/22.

[3] Eastern Area, Exec., 24 April 1922; Cheshire PD, Exec., 2 December 1924, 10 January 1925; NU Exec., 9 February 1926, 12 June 1928; Ramsden, *Age of Balfour and Baldwin*, 260.

compulsion' upon the counties within them to merge into a unitary structure.[4] In fact, eight of these Areas either already existed or were formed by the following year, and the remaining four took shape by 1937. The greatest degree of county particularism was in southern England, where Essex and Middlesex rejected partnership in 1930 and 1932, before eventually combining in 1933; Kent, Surrey, and Sussex did not link up until 1936 (and in 1946 they sought to separate again[5]), and the south-western region was the last group to come together as the Western Area in 1937. In many of the Areas, a committee for each county was retained as a subordinate tier of regional organization, in some cases for practicality but in most as a reflection that the force of county loyalty was much stronger than that evoked by the wider region. However, in two cases they were synonymous, with Yorkshire and London (known as the Metropolitan Area up to 1939) containing so many constituencies that they were each an Area on their own.

The most important institution in each Area was its council, which had direct representation from each constituency and from all of the specialist sections, and which considered matters of policy and passed resolutions. These were large assemblies, and normally met three or four times each year. In-between, the administrative business of the Area was handled by an executive committee, and, in some cases, when this became too cumbersome, by a smaller finance and general purposes committee. The key figure presiding over all of these bodies was the Area Chairman; he needed to be a person of some substance and authority in the region, and to be able to give some time to the role if he was to be effective.[6] However, the Area Chairman had no power of command over individual constituencies; his influence depended entirely upon his prestige, personality, tact, and vigour, and his working relationship with the Central Office Area Agent. Some Chairmen were also MPs, such as Eugene Ramsden in Yorkshire and Nigel Colman in London. The Area Chairmen became increasingly important at the national level, and frequently provided the Chairmen of the Central Council and the Executive Committee. In the early 1930s, Stonehaven, the Party Chairman, began the practice of having regular meetings with the Area Chairmen.[7] This was taken logically further when the national General Purposes Committee was created, and they formed the core of the smaller group, which acted as a deputation to convey important resolutions to the Party Leader. The final step was the creation of the Standing Advisory Committee on Candidates, which was dominated by the Area Chairmen.

The post of President of the Area was usually occupied by a landed aristocrat, such as Lord Londonderry in the Northern Area. Such presidents were generally figureheads, but the 17th Earl of Derby kept in close touch with affairs in the North West Area and acted as regional spokesman to various Party Leaders.[8]

---

[4] NU Exec., Sub-ctte on Rules & Organisation, 27 May 1930.

[5] Maxse to General Director, 'Provincial Area Organisation', 12 July 1946, CPA, CCO/4/2/5.

[6] Draft memoirs, Williams MSS, c.1095; for the daily work of an Area Chairman, see Headlam diary, 1936–46.

[7] Memo by Stonehaven for meeting with Area Chairmen, 12 December 1933, Baldwin MSS, 46/96–100.

[8] Derby to Baldwin, 13 December 1934, Baldwin MSS, 169/79.

On three occasions, he exerted pressure by warning or threatening that the region might openly repudiate the Leader's policy. The most serious and effective of these was the 'Lancashire revolt' against food taxes in 1912–13; the second, after the 1923 defeat, was also hostile to protectionism but was pushing at an already open door—Baldwin dropped the tariff policy in February 1924 in response to the electoral result and a wide range of party opinion, in which Lancashire was one voice amongst many.[9] Similarly, in the summer of 1930, when ironically Derby used similar tactics to push Baldwin towards the 'free hand' tariff policy, this was in tune with the main current of party opinion. Whether chairman or president, the regional leaders expected a certain amount of deference and to be consulted over changes in the Central Office staff in their Area; the lack of such courtesy was the source of Lady Londonderry's complaints against Davidson as Party Chairman.[10]

The representative institutions at regional level were rarely assertive, but this does not mean that they lacked weight and influence. The culture of debate was on similar lines to that at constituency level, with the emphasis on unity leading to the withdrawal of resolutions that might be contentious.[11] In a similar but even more effective way, regional opinion could be transmitted privately and informally by the Area officers and the Central Office Area Agents: 'by doing so, the Leader could be equally informed of the committee's views as if they had formally passed a resolution'.[12] An Area was too large a unit for its opinions to be dismissed lightly, and, by definition, it spoke for a representative and substantial body of opinion.[13] The regional councils were also more autonomous than the committees at national level, as the Party Leader or a Cabinet minister would arouse jealousy by attending one or two particular Area meetings and it was not practicable to visit them all. They were therefore managed by the established regional elite, who usually had a mutually co-operative relationship with the national leadership and did not wish to go beyond the parameters of accepted party opinion and policy. For this reason, and because they were large enough not to be easily swayed by dissident opinion, the regional tier was a stabilizing and unifying element in the party structure. An exception which underlines the general rule was Churchill's securing of the passage of a negative resolution on India in the Essex & Middlesex Area in 1934, but this reflected his role as a leading MP in the region and it was couched in moderate language.[14] As the Areas developed a more authoritative role during the 1930s, it became expected that constituency resolutions would go to their Area first and only be forwarded to a higher level if they were endorsed there, with the result that the Areas provided an increasing proportion of the resolutions debated at the Central Council and Annual Conference. They could also be an important channel of

[9] R. Churchill, *Lord Derby, 'King of Lancashire'* (1959), 163–83, 560–6.
[10] Lady Londonderry to Davidson, 7 and 11 December 1929, Davidson MSS, DAV/188.
[11] Yorkshire Area, Council, 12 November 1921; Wessex Area, Council AGM, 2 May 1930; Eastern Area, Exec., 20 February 1930.
[12] SUA, EDC, Exec., 24 May 1933, 22 January 1930.
[13] Davidson to Baldwin, reporting Metropolitan Area discussion of the 'flapper vote', 20 June 1927, Baldwin MSS, 52/185.
[14] Essex & Middlesex Area, Council, 9 February 1934.

communication downwards, and in the uncertain period following the formation of the National Government, the Party Chairman and the women's Vice-Chairman, Lord Stonehaven and Lady Falmouth, toured the Areas to provide a confidential briefing.[15]

The regional tier was also a key component of the various specialized elements of the party organization, and all of the Advisory Committees at the national level were mirrored by similar committees as subordinate bodies to the Area Councils. The first of these were the women's and labour organizations, followed by youth, and then political education later in the 1930s. These were often one of the most active parts of the regional bodies, and they worked closely with the relevant specialist staff in the Area Office. The funds which they had available were not large but could be used effectively in encouraging constituencies to greater activity or co-operation. As at local level, the women's committees were often the most energetic and imaginative, and frequently organized day schools, conferences, or outings which were beyond the pocket of any single seat. In the south-east and south-west, these began in the early 1920s as meetings of the wives of MPs and then developed into more representative bodies, operating on a regional basis for many years before the separate counties linked up in other respects.[16] The Labour committees were less effective, and the factors which inhibited their functioning in the constituencies also affected them at regional level, as the representation was drawn from the local committees and reflected their outlook and composition. The days and times of Area Council and executive meetings were often difficult for wage-earners, and with limited funds at their disposal many Areas would not or could not pay travelling expenses or compensation for lost working hours.[17] However, the movement to larger and more effective regional groupings after 1930 helped the labour wing, and the Area Offices were able to give it more effective support.

The Area Offices in each of the twelve regions were answerable to Central Office in London, which provided their staff and finance; in 1930 Neville Chamberlain's committee of inquiry rejected the idea of any local contribution so that they would not have divided obligations.[18] However, although not under the direction of the Area Chairmen or Councils, in practice they worked in partnership with them; the Area Agent acted as Honorary Secretary to the Area Council, and his Deputy similarly served the Women's Committee. The Area Offices were a vital link in the chain, and were described by one Party Chairman as 'our normal channel of communication with the constituencies'.[19] Their primary means of influence was through personal

---

[15] North West Area, Exec, 5 September 1931; Wessex Area, Extraordinary Council, 10 September 1931; Eastern Area, Council, 17 September 1931, and similarly elsewhere.

[16] Western Area and South East Area, Women's Parliamentary Ctte., inaugural meetings, 13 May 1920. These meetings, and those for some other Areas, were summoned and initially chaired by the wife of the Chief Whip, Lady Edmund Talbot: Eastern Area, Women's Ctte., inaugural meeting, 21 June 1920.

[17] For refusal to pay expenses because the money was needed for more urgent matters, see Yorkshire Area, Council, 2 May 1924.

[18] General Director to Party Chairman, 'Office reconstruction and reduction of expenditure', 30 July 1931, CPA, CCO/500/1/5.

[19] Stonehaven to Baldwin, 9 December 1931, Baldwin MSS, 166/144–5.

contact with constituency chairmen and agents, but their role could only be one of tactful 'advice and suggestion, directly and indirectly applied', and they had to be careful of the ever-present sensitivity over local autonomy.[20] A Central Office commentary on their role noted that 'success can often be more readily obtained by flank movements than by frontal attacks', and that they should achieve their purpose 'by way of helpful suggestion rather than by that of criticism', crucially 'avoiding anything which might be construed as an attempt to dictate'.[21] During the interwar period, the Area Offices increasingly became the route for organizational support and financial assistance from the centre, and these carrots were much more effective than any stick.[22] Of course, the richest and safest seats could still go their own way if they wished, and the Area had no effective sanctions against them. Most of the work of the Area Office staff involved aiding and encouraging activity at the regional and local levels, organizing speakers, assisting in the placing of candidates and agents, and responding to unusual events such as by-elections.[23]

The Area Offices were also the eyes and ears of Central Office; the constituencies were well aware of this, and it caused the element of ambivalence in the relationship.[24] Part of the Area Offices' function was to gather information on opposition activity, the public mood, and electoral prospects, but they were also involved in monitoring opinion within the party.[25] There were instances when Central Office asked for reports on a particular issue, such as the equalization of the franchise in 1927, but it was generally a less formal transmission of sentiment.[26] Another method of keeping a finger on the pulse was the summoning of the Area Agents to a meeting at Central Office to report opinion and act as a sounding board; this was used when time was short in September 1931.[27] Each office was headed by an Area Agent, who was an experienced former constituency agent, and from 1919 there was a female Deputy Area Agent who took particular responsibility for the women's organizations.[28] The Area Agents' salaries were generally £800 in the 1930s, rising to £900 in the cases of the more senior and the larger regions; the female deputies were paid £400 or £450. In the later 1930s, the full integration of the youth wing into the party organization led to the appointment of a dedicated Junior Imperial League organizer in most regions. The Offices also had clerical staff (usually two), and were situated at a central point in their region's transport network; in most cases, this meant in the business district of a city, with the resulting costs of

---

[20] 'Memorandum on the working of our Party Organisation', 10 October 1930, Templewood MSS, VI/3; Thornton (COA South East Area), 'Central Office Agents and their work', n.d., c.October 1930, CPA, CCO/500/1/5.

[21] 'Memorandum upon the duties of District Agents', n.d., c.October 1930, CPA, CCO/500/1/5.

[22] Essex & Middlesex Area, Council, 19 October 1937, F&GP, 17 December 1937, 16 December 1938.

[23] Area Agents' reports in Maclachlan, 'Summarised Report on Conservative Organisation at Central Office and in the Constituencies during 1927', 30 December 1927, Baldwin MSS, 53/118–49.

[24] Winchester CA, Finance Ctte., 4 March 1932.

[25] Monsell Ctte., memo by Chief Organisation Officer, 14 October 1937, CPA, CCO/500/1/7.

[26] 'Summary of Replies from Central Office Agents to letter of 6 April 1927'; , Baldwin MSS, 52/138–42: Norfolk East CA, Finance Ctte., 15 May 1934.

[27] Gower to Baldwin, 16 September 1931, Baldwin MSS, 44/141–2.

[28] Memo by Johnson (Deputy COA North West Area), 15 November 1930, Templewood MSS, VI/3.

renting accommodation. The Metropolitan Area Office was located in Central Office itself, and during the 1920s the South East Area Agent also worked from there due to the easier rail access from London.[29] In 1932, the offices of the Essex & Middlesex Area and the South East Area were merged, and for the rest of the decade they operated under a single male agent and two female deputies.

The Metropolitan Area had some unique functions and its role was similar to the central associations of the provincial cities. It required closer co-ordination between its constituencies than other Areas, as large numbers of people moved home within London and there was a need to trace these removals. The size of the city and the extent of its social stratification posed major challenges: 'there is no civic spirit here, the place is too big', commented the long-serving local agent in Clapham; 'the great mass of voters come home only to sleep'.[30] If these dormitory suburbs were difficult to organize, within their outer circle lay 'vast districts in which it is almost impossible to raise any money from the supporters of the party, owing to the great poverty, and to the fact that there are no upper class residents in them'.[31] These constituencies needed outside support to maintain even a basic organization, but this was expensive and an uphill struggle, for when the assistance ended the ground gained was soon lost. The other factor in London was the particular focus on local government, as the whole Area came under the single authority of the high-profile London County Council. These matters were the main concern of the separate London Department, which was also housed at Palace Chambers; its staff was overseen by the specially appointed London Whip. From 1920 to 1927, this office was held by Lord Jessel, a former London MP; his successor was a sitting MP, Lord Curzon, who continued in the post after he succeeded to the peerage as Earl Howe in 1929. The costs of the London Department were high, running at between half and two-thirds of all twelve Area Offices combined in the late 1920s, and it was closed under the impact of the slump in 1933.[32] The setbacks of Labour winning control of the London County Council in 1934 and the loss of several seats in the 1935 election led to a review by the London Reorganisation Committee in 1938, but there was caution in applying its recommendations in case other Areas resented the special treatment, and also some opposition in the safer and better-organized metropolitan constituencies.[33]

Scotland was a separate matter and had its own national and regional organization, although—similarly to Northern Ireland—it also sent a small delegation to the National Union Central Council and conference.[34] The Scottish Unionist Association paralleled the form and functions of the National Union south of the

---

[29] 'Palace Chambers, First Floor: List of Rooms and Occcupants', c.November. 1926, Davidson MSS, DAV/179.
[30] *CAJ*, December 1927, 344–7.
[31] Jessel (London Whip) to Jackson, 1 January 1925, CPA, ARE/1/29/1.
[32] Principal Agent to Party Chairman, 23 October 1930, CPA, CCO/500/1/5.
[33] London Reorganisation Ctte., report, 15 June 1938, NC, 8/21/17, minority report, 15 June 1938, NC, 8/21/10; Headlam diary, 15 June 1938; Hacking to N. Chamberlain, 17 June 1938, NC, 8/21/12; Putney CA, F&GP Report, 28 February 1939.
[34] NU Exec., 9 December 1930. This arrangement was a compromise between those who wanted a complete merger and those who wanted no contact at all: SUA, EDC, 12 December 1934.

border, with its own officers, national committee structure, and representative gatherings, which included an annual party conference. Below this were two regional groupings: the Western Division was based in Glasgow and covered the south-west, the Clydeside industrial region, and part of the western Highlands. The Eastern Division covered the rest of the Highlands and the eastern half of the central and Border counties, and was centred upon Edinburgh. The role of these bodies was similar to that of the Areas in England and Wales, and reports on public and party attitudes were passed back to the Leader.[35] The two Divisional Councils were served by staff in the prewar mould with backgrounds as solicitors, especially Lewis Shedden in the west, whose long service was recognized by a knighthood. Scotland continued to organize and operate on prewar lines for much of the interwar period, and was slower to take up new organizational and campaigning initiatives; thus, even by 1929 there was no regional committee for the youth movement in the Eastern Division, and it only began to encourage constituencies to form Labour Advisory Committees in the early 1930s.[36] Contrary to the separation of roles in England and Wales, the reforms of the national party structure in 1911 placed the direction of the party organization in Scotland in the hands of the Scottish Whip, who effectively became Party Chairman for Scotland. This was a heavy load, and for much of the year the Scottish Whip had to attend parliament in London. Day-to-day matters were therefore largely in the hands of his chief official, who held the post of Political Secretary to the Scottish Whip. This post was filled not from the ranks of constituency agents but from a higher social class, and from 1922 to 1960 it was held by Colonel Patrick Blair, whose combination of efficiency, experience, and continuity made him a very effective party manger.

THE NATIONAL UNION: THE CENTRAL COUNCIL AND THE ANNUAL CONFERENCE

The Central Council of the National Union was the key representative institution of the Conservative Party, and those eligible to attend included delegates from the constituencies, representatives from the various ancillary organizations, Conservative peers and MPs, and the party leaders. As the party structure developed during the interwar period, each new element was given a share of representation on the Central Council, and its numbers significantly increased. The average attendance in the years before the First World War was 102, but the rules adopted in 1919 to reflect the expansion of the electorate—especially the inclusion of women—raised the number entitled to be present to 737.[37] In the 1919–24 period, the attendance averaged 280, but all previous records were broken when 'about 450' came to the

---

[35] Ford to Baldwin, 26 February, 11 September, 23 October 1930, Baldwin MSS, 31/49–52, 151–4, 178–81; SUA, EDC, 22 March 1933.
[36] Memo by Blair, 'Impressions of the General Election', 12 July 1929, Gilmour MSS, GD383/29/32–5; SUA, EDC, Exec., 22 June and 27 July 1932.
[37] NU Exec. report to Central Council, 11 March 1919.

meeting in February 1924, which followed an election defeat and the advent of the first Labour government.[38] The major revision of the rules in 1924 expanded the number of constituency delegates, and the theoretical size of Central Council grew to 1,762; after the amendments of 1930, which increased the direct representation of the Areas, the total entitled to be present reached 2,174, of which 1,584 were delegates directly nominated by the constituencies.[39] At the first meeting under the new rules in February 1925 the number present jumped to 790, and the average attendance between 1925 and 1939 was 681. There were two exceptions to the normal level of interest, when the concern over the India question resulted in turnouts of 1,238 in June 1933, after the publication of the White Paper, and of 1,474 at the special meeting in December 1934. However, in the 1936–39 period the attendance at some meetings was only around 400.

The most significant reform of the Central Council was that drawn up in 1924 by Herbert Blain, the Principal Agent, in which the local associations became 'the basis of representation'.[40] In the revised rules of 1930, this was set at three delegates from each constituency, two of whom had to be the association chairman and the chair of the women's branch, and one of the three had to be working-class: a 'wage-earner' or wage-earner's wife.[41] The Central Council had met quarterly before 1914, but from 1921 to 1939 the normal pattern was for two meetings a year, in late February and late June (the exception was 1930, when the special conference to approve the new rules met in the summer and a second Central Council meeting was held in November). The meeting was on a single day, and consisted of a morning session from 11.00 a.m. (11.30 a.m. from 1931) to 1.00 p.m., and an afternoon one from 2.00 p.m. to 5.00 p.m. However, due to delegates leaving to catch their trains, the discussion often ended earlier than this, as the continuation of debate depended upon a quorum of 200 being present. This pattern was acknowledged in 1935 with the recommendation that the closing time should be 4.00 p.m., but with a proviso that proceedings could continue beyond this if there was sufficient demand.[42] To get through the agenda as effectively as possible whilst also providing opportunities for delegates to speak, the procedural rules kept speeches deliberately short: the mover of a resolution was limited to ten minutes and all other speakers to five minutes, although this did not apply to the replies by ministers in response to a debate.[43] The Central Council was originally a private meeting, and in 1920 a leak of some proceedings to the press was condemned as 'a gross breach of confidence'.[44] In 1926, it was decided that although the proceedings would still be conducted in private, a full note would be taken and afterwards the Chairman of Council and the Party Chairman would release to the press what

---

[38] NU Central Council, 12 February 1924.
[39] NU Exec. report to Central Council, 24 February 1925; NU Central Council, 1 July 1924.
[40] NU Central Council, 1 July 1924.
[41] NU Exec., 25 February 1930; NU Rules, 1930.
[42] NU GP, 12 June 1935; NU Central Council, 25 March 1936, 29 June 1939.
[43] The special Central Council meeting on India in December 1934 followed a different procedure with longer speeches, as it was a debate on one issue only: NU Exec., 28 November 1934.
[44] NU Central Council, 17 February 1920.

they considered to be advisable.[45] This proved to be a halfway house, and in 1933 the press were admitted to those parts of the Council meeting in which motions 'on matters of policy or public interest' were discussed, although not to the 'business session', which considered organizational matters, such as the report of the Executive Committee.[46]

The Central Council had several important functions. Firstly, it was the constitutional body of the National Union and changes in the rules were normally proposed and approved here, although in 1930 a special party conference was called for the purpose. Secondly, it was the forum for the annual election of the officers of the National Union, the most important of which were the President and the Chairman. The former was an honorary post that was normally occupied by a prominent figure from the Area which was next hosting the Annual Conference; the duties of the latter were limited to chairing the meetings of Central Council and the Annual Conference during his or her year of office. There were also three Vice-Chairmen; normally the most senior of these automatically succeeded to the Chairmanship, creating one vacancy each year. The first woman Chairman (the term was not affected by the gender of its occupant) was Dame Caroline Bridgeman, the wife of a Cabinet minister, in 1926–27. By this time it had become customary that one of the Vice-Chairmen should be a woman, and so by rotation there was a woman Chairman every three years thereafter: Lady Iveagh MP in 1930–31, Dame Regina Evans in 1934–35, Mrs C. Fyfe in 1937–38, and Lady Hillingdon in 1940–41.

The Council also approved the appointment of the Secretary of the National Union, a salaried official who headed its small but autonomous office.[47] This was housed at Central Office, and arranged the meetings of the committees, Council, and Conference. The Secretary was recruited from the professional agents, and from 1921 to 1938 the post was held by George Godwin, who had previously been agent at Guildford in Surrey; he was succeeded by Horace Armstrong, who began his career as the agent at Horsham in 1919, and between 1928 and 1938 served as Area Agent in the Northern and then the Metropolitan Areas. Another of the Central Council's roles was that it received at each meeting a formal report from the Executive Committee, which described the work undertaken by the national party organization. This was normally circulated with the agenda, and then was often amplified at the meeting with comments from the Party Chairman and (when this became a separate post in 1930) the Chairman of the Executive; it also provided an opportunity for questions and discussion on the running of the party machine.

As well as these organizational functions, the Central Council had significant political roles. Most obviously, the main part of each meeting was devoted to the discussion of resolutions sent in by constituencies or Areas. The agenda was selected by the Chairman, with advice from the Secretary, but the need to reflect what the rank and file wished to debate—and the relatively few motions sent in—meant

---

[45] NU Exec. Report to Central Council, 23 June 1926.   [46] NU Exec., 10 May 1933.
[47] NU Central Council, 23 February 1921; Headlam diary, 8 December 1937.

that in practice the degree of managerial discretion was not that large. In the case of the Scottish Annual Conference, 'a feeling that there was too much exclusion of controversial matters' led to protests from some constituencies in 1936, but others defended the choices as fair and necessary to produce a manageable and balanced agenda.[48] In fact, any overt manipulation or attempt to exclude an issue from discussion would have been counterproductive, especially as the rules permitted the introduction of emergency motions from the floor if a sufficient number of members called for this. The resolutions selected for debate therefore reflected the concerns and priorities of the day, as can be seen from the table below; if they had not done so, there would have little incentive for delegates to take the trouble of attending.

Table 4.1. Political resolutions debated at the Central Council 1919–1939

The Table includes all of the resolutions on political topics which were debated, whether or not they were passed. It does not include resolutions on the agenda which were not reached, or resolutions on organizational topics. When several resolutions on the agenda were combined at a meeting into a composite resolution for debate, this is counted as one resolution, but resolutions on the same topic which were debated or voted upon separately are counted individually.

Topic of resolutions	Number
Protection (including safeguarding, tariffs, and imperial preference)	26
House of Lords reform	16
Agriculture (including protectionist measures specifically to assist agriculture)	15
Trade union law	13
Government regulations & restrictions (including DORA, shop closing hours, etc.)	13
Conservative principles, general programme, & relations with coalition parties	12
Economy in government expenditure and reduction of the burden of taxation	12
Industrial policy & unemployment	12
Defence (including civil defence and national service)	11
India (government, constitutional development, & law and order)	10
Pensions (including war pensions)	9
Social policy (including education, immigration, health, etc.)	9
Housing and slum clearance	8
Communism, sedition, & Soviet Russia	8
Criticism of opponents	5
Franchise & electoral system	4
Integrity of the empire (excluding imperial preference and economic unity)	3
Foreign policy	2
Resolutions on various other topics	7
TOTAL	195

The primary function of the Central Council was undisputed: together with the other gatherings of the National Union, it existed 'for the purpose of giving the rank and file of the Party, through their delegates, an opportunity to express freely their views on current political topics and the working of our Party Organisation

---

[48] SUA, Exec., 9 December 1936.

generally'.[49] On the latter, its impact was substantial and often decisive; on the former, it had to take its place as one voice amongst many, but it was still an influential one. In 1927, following some expressions of concern, the Central Council was reassured that 'great weight is attached by the Government to the criticisms and suggestions embodied in resolutions passed'.[50] However, this did not mean that it was possible either economically or politically to act upon them, and it was for reasons of pragmatism and practicality rather than any lack of sympathy or agreement that the gap existed between what the Conservative rank and file wanted and what Conservative (and, still more, coalition) governments delivered. The Central Council was, in some respects, an even more authoritative expression of grass-roots opinion than the Annual Conference: it met more frequently, its membership was nearly as large, and it included the most influential constituency leaders—the additional bodies at the conference being delegates of lesser weight. The Central Council was normally passive, in that it responded to resolutions submitted by the localities, but in February 1921 it actively sought to stimulate constituency opinion on the question of House of Lords reform: a resolution urging action was passed as 'a matter of urgent business' and sent to every constituency (with a request that they pass a similar one) and to every member of the council (which included many MPs and peers).[51] As feeling turned against the Coalition in 1922, the Chairman of the Council, Sir Alexander Leith, felt obliged to take a position increasingly divergent from that of the Party Leader, ending in almost open revolt.[52]

The Central Council also provided a valuable platform from which the leadership could seek to invigorate or soothe their followers. Bonar Law spoke at the first Central Council meeting after the 1918 election and Austen Chamberlain addressed the first meeting after he became Leader, 'upon the subject of the Coalition the continuance of which he said was still essential to the national welfare'.[53] In the turbulence that followed the January 1922 election scare, he found it advisable to speak again at the next meeting, when 'he insisted upon the foolishness of disputing with those who were ready and willing to cooperate with the Unionist Party'.[54] Talking directly to the key regional and local figures in this forum was the most effective way to reach them and retain their support; although Chamberlain's strategy was rejected later in the year, this does not mean that these addresses were ineffective when they were delivered. Baldwin spoke at the critical meeting in February 1924 which followed the 1923 election defeat; revealingly, he did not attend the Council again until immediately after the loss of the 1929 general election. In the following year, under pressure from the press lords' Empire Crusade campaign, he used the Central Council meeting of 4 March 1930 to unveil a limited policy advance which was sufficient to secure a short-lived truce with Beaverbrook. The Leader was present at the next gathering in November 1930,

---

[49] NU Exec., Sub-ctte on National Union Rules, 23 October 1929.
[50] NU Exec. Report to Central Council, 28 June 1927; NU Exec., 15 March 1927.
[51] NU Central Council, 23 February 1921.
[52] Leith to A. Chamberlain, 4 March 1922, Salvidge to A. Chamberlain, 17 March 1922, AC, 33/1/22, 29.
[53] NU Central Council, 21 June 1921.   [54] NU Central Council, 21 February 1922.

which followed the most acute stage of the party crisis, but he did not appear again until the meeting of 28 June 1933, after the publication of the India White Paper, when 'nothing could have exceeded the warmth of the reception he received'.[55]

In 1933–34 Baldwin was able to keep the Central Council behind the National Government's policy on India despite the widespread concern in the constituencies. After he spoke at the meeting in June 1933, a resolution critical of government policy was rejected by 838 to 356 votes. The latter figure may have overstated the support for the critics: Amery, who had delivered a short speech on the government side during the debate, considered that the show of hands before the vote had been 'at least four or five to one in favour' of the official policy, and he noted that there had been 'much confusion, as always' as to whether marking 'for' on the ballot paper signified a vote for the critical motion or for the pro-government amendment to it.[56] Baldwin had given a pledge to 'take counsel' with the party before legislation was passed by parliament, and revealingly chose to do so by summoning a special meeting of Central Council rather than a special conference. Held on 4 December 1934, after 'a fine appeal' from Baldwin,[57] a 'very poor' speech from Churchill,[58] and another lengthy debate, the assembly endorsed the government's proposals by 1,102 to 390, a majority of 712.[59] It is significant that the narrowest outcomes occurred when Baldwin was not present: on 28 February 1933, in the vacuum of uncertainty before the publication of the White Paper, the official line was approved by only 189 to 165 votes (with 151 abstentions), whilst on 28 March 1934 it was supported by the slightly more comfortable margin of 419 to 314. After December 1934, Baldwin did not return until the presentation made to him on his retirement in June 1937. Neville Chamberlain did not feel the need to attend the Council until April 1940, when his only appearance was the occasion of his ill-judged claim that Hitler had 'missed the bus'.[60] Although supposedly disinterested in party affairs, Churchill spoke at two of the five Central Council meetings that were held during his wartime Premiership, in March 1941 and March 1942, and sent a letter, which was read out at a third, in October 1942; it was not coincidental that these spanned the difficult middle period of the war.

The Annual Conference of the National Union was described by Page Croft at its 1934 meeting as the heart of the party, whilst a less flattering view was that it was where 'disgruntled Tories unloose their grievances and make the feathers fly'.[61] Both descriptions had elements of truth, although a more sober analysis was given by Davidson in 1930, that it was 'intended in the main as a clearing house for the

---

[55] White to Derby, 29 June 1933, Derby MSS, 6/33.
[56] Amery diary, 28 June 1933.
[57] Winterton diary, 4 December 1934, Winterton MSS.
[58] Cazalet diary, 4 December 1934.
[59] Amery diary, 4 December 1934; Headlam diary, 4 December 1934; NU Central Council, 4 December 1934.
[60] NU Central Council, 4 April 1940.
[61] S. Salvidge, *Salvidge of Liverpool: Behind the Political Scene 1890–1928* (1934), 200; *CAJ*, December 1929, 232.

views and opinions of the rank and file of the Party in the constituencies'.[62] It also had an important role in drawing the party together, promoting unity and enthusiasm, and thereby giving 'fresh direction and stimulus to the workers in every constituency'.[63] The conference was already a large assembly when Blain's reforms of the National Union in 1924 rationalized its composition, but also increased its numbers. Each single-Member constituency could send a total of six delegates, and there was also direct representation of the Areas and the various specific wings of the party. A considerable number of subscribers, peers, and MPs were also entitled to attend, but fortunately most of these did not do so. An analysis after the 1926 conference, which was described as 'a fair average of recent years', showed that 2,603 of the possible total of 7,371 were present, most of whom were constituency and Area representatives; only eight peers and sixty MPs attended of the 873 who might have done so.[64] However, a proposal to make numbers more manageable by reducing the categories of honorary members was reflected by a large majority at the conference of the following year. By the 1929 Conference, 492 constituencies were represented in a total attendance of 3,920, and it was felt that the numbers were 'excessive' and the size 'prevented the average delegate from a free expression of opinion'.[65] The revised rules of 1930 reduced the allowance for each constituency from six delegates to five, and dropped the honorary subscribers and the officers of county committees, whilst giving a greater role to representatives of the regional Areas. The aim was to reduce the Conference to 'about 3,000 delegates', of whom 'in practice not more than 70 per cent would be present'.[66] This target was more than met, for during the 1930s the number who intimated their intention to attend was generally around 1,900, of whom only between 59 per cent and 73 per cent actually did so.[67]

The Conference met for two days, although it was only from 1932 that it used the whole of the second day.[68] It was very difficult to hold it when parliament was sitting (unless it met in London), and the number of hotel rooms required meant that the only possible times were either before or after the main holiday season; from 1924 onwards, early October became the customary—though not invariable—time.[69] It had been decided in 1923 that the Conference should visit each of the Areas in rotation, and for propaganda reasons to hold it in a large industrial centre, but many of these lacked suitable meeting halls and sufficient accommodation.[70] The possible venues outside London were limited to a few cities, and many Areas made use of the larger seaside resorts, such as Brighton, Scarborough, Margate,

---

[62] Davidson to Baldwin, 15 April 1930, Davidson MSS, DAV/190.
[63] *Home and Politics*, November 1926.
[64] NU Exec, 10 May 1927, appendix.
[65] NU Exec., Sub-ctte on National Union Rules, 23 October 1929; for attendance, NU Exec., 10 December 1929.
[66] NU Exec., 25 February 1930; NU Exec., Sub-ctte on Rules & Organisation, 3 February 1930.
[67] NU Exec. reports to Central Council, 1933–38; NU Conf., 1933–35.
[68] NU Exec., Sub-ctte on National Union Rules, draft report, 20 November 1929.
[69] NU Exec., 8 June 1926; NU GP, 13 June 1934. There was considerable support, particularly from the Agents' Society, for holding it in May or June, but this did not gain a majority: NU Conf., 1924, 1926; 'Memorandum upon the subject of the Annual Conference', 13 May 1930, Steel-Maitland MSS, GD193/120/3/541–2.
[70] NU Exec., 10 May 1927, appendix; Birmingham CA, Management Ctte., 15 March 1920.

Blackpool, and Bournemouth. However, Wales & Monmouthshire were still unable to host the Conference when their turn came in 1939, and the Eastern Area stepped in with an offer to hold it at Great Yarmouth.[71] There was some financial cost to the host region, which was estimated in 1932 to be about £800.[72] Only in 1931 was the Conference cancelled due to it coinciding with a general election, although in 1938 it was called off because of the threat of war during the Czech crisis. The result was that 1937 was the last peacetime Conference, and there was a gap of five and a half years until the next Conference in May 1943, and then of nearly two years to the Conference of March 1945.

The Conference agenda was drawn up by the Executive Committee of the National Union until 1933, when it delegated the task to the new General Purposes Committee. There were always suspicions, especially from the diehards, that the party managers manipulated the Central Council and Conference agendas to exclude controversy and criticism, but in fact this was not really possible.[73] Ignoring burning issues would have been both obvious and counterproductive, and those responsible for shaping the agenda did not see their role as restricting debate. At the special conference on the revised National Union rules in 1930, Davidson explicitly stated that neither he nor previous chairmen of the executive had interpreted their power in such broad terms, and had regarded their role as being limited to arranging the order of business; 'it is not a question of veto'. In response to the ensuing question from a delegate whether this meant 'that any proposal sent to the conference is printed and put before the conference?', Lady Iveagh, the current Chairman of the Central Council, replied 'that has always been the practice'.[74] In fact, the objective of those preparing the agenda was an efficient Conference that got through its business, and they were more concerned with avoiding duplication of topics and matters which were outside the scope of the National Union. With the number of submitted resolutions increasing, in 1934 it was formally decided that they would only be admissible if they came from a constituency or an Area, or from the executive itself, but this was simply a procedural rationalization and had no relation to their content.[75] There was certainly a preference to avoid provocative resolutions, and thus the executive decided in 1928 to put Page Croft's motion for a wider application of the protectionist 'safeguarding' duties in the first place of those on that subject, provided that he agreed to drop the final few words which specifically mentioned iron and steel.[76] The rare case of a resolution being excluded, in this instance from the Scottish Central Council, was excused as due to the sensitivity of the international situation, required letters in explanation from the President and Secretary of the Council, and elicited vigorous protests from the originating constituency.[77] In any case, the omission of an issue from the agenda

---

[71] NU Exec., 6 April 1938; however, it had been held at Cardiff in 1927.
[72] North West Area, Fin., 14 January 1932.
[73] Lady Peto diary, 26 October 1930.
[74] NU Special Conf., 1 July 1930.
[75] NU Exec., 18 July 1934.
[76] NU Exec., 28 August 1928.
[77] Kinross & West Perthshire CA, Exec., 21 November 1936, 19 March 1937.

hardly restricted debate, as it was open to anyone at the Conference to move an emergency resolution or an amendment from the floor, and thus any wording could be changed if there was the desire to do so. Far from the Conference being 'muzzled', a substantial amount of time was given to the discussion of such issues as Ireland in 1921, safeguarding and tariffs in 1927–29, and India in 1933–34.[78]

The Conference was chaired by the Chairman of Central Council, and his or her skill in doing so was of considerable importance; 'tact, firmness and good humour' was the ideal combination, and it was noted that with good management the Conference should never cause trouble.[79] The main problem was that not all the resolutions were reached, which disappointed their promoters; in 1929, only thirty-three of the fifty-seven were discussed. This was attributed partly to unrealistic agendas and partly to too many persons speaking for too long. To remedy the latter, it was suggested that the Chairman should 'take the fullest advantage of the powers conferred upon him' and 'be on the alert to put the question at the earliest possible moment'.[80] One issue which frequently arose was the balance of time between speeches from MPs and ordinary delegates, with the latter sometimes feeling sidelined at their own show.[81] Replies to debates from ministers were another matter, and in 1936 the Chairman of the Executive noted: 'The conference wanted to hear ministers, but got somewhat restless if they were too long.'[82] Ministers generally sought to be responsive to the mood of Conference, whilst often having to introduce 'a little cold breath of reason coming in to mingle with the hot air'.[83] A necessary part of each Conference was its organization and business sessions, which were generally seen as a chore: 'everyone who has attended a conference realises how quickly it desires to slide over matters of routine and organisation and to pass on to the more exciting problems of Party policy'.[84] The other standard feature was one of the main attractions: the address given by the Leader of the Party. Technically, this was a separate event and not part of the Conference agenda; up to 1929, it was held on the evening of the first day, but when the Conference was extended to two full days it was moved to become the closing event of the final day.[85] The speech was an important event in the Party Leader's annual calendar, with care taken over the content and awareness of its effect.[86] In 1928, with a general election

[78] In 1934, the debate ended when an unnamed delegate from the floor of the hall moved that 'the question be now put' and this was carried; Page Croft, mover of the original hostile resolution, protested at 'the muzzling process', but the Conference Chairman (Regina Evans) pointed out that the normal standing orders required that discussion cease and the vote be taken immediately.
[79] *Home and Politics*, November 1926; Linlithgow to Baldwin, 4 November 1927, Baldwin MSS, 102/133–6; Bayford diary, 23 June 1920.
[80] NU GP, 11 March 1936, appendix, 'Criticisms affecting the Annual Conference at Bournemouth'.
[81] NU Exec., 8 December 1925; Hemel Hempstead CA, Exec., 29 November 1937.
[82] NU GP, 11 March 1936, appendix, 'Criticisms affecting the Annual Conference at Bournemouth'.
[83] Memo by Steel-Maitland on trade union policy, for guidance of Party Chairman at 1926 Conference, 29 September 1926, Baldwin MSS, 11/45–7.
[84] NU Exec., Sub-ctte on National Union Rules, draft report, 20 November 1929.
[85] Exceptionally in 1922, because there had been many mass meetings during the immediately preceding general election, a separate rally was not held and Bonar Law gave a short speech directly to the Conference before lunch on the first day: NU Central Council Report to Conference, 1922–23.
[86] Amery diary, 8 October 1925.

in prospect before its next meeting, Baldwin noted that the Conference was 'composed of delegates and agents, and he should try to hearten these up and make what is called a fighting speech'.[87] However, the rally was also open to many others; in 1932, as well as the 1,700 delegates, there was a further attendance 'of about 5,000 people'.[88] At the Cardiff Conference of 1927, Baldwin's speech was relayed by electric amplification to several indoor and outdoor meetings and heard by 'at least 15,000 people in all'.[89]

Party leaders were sometimes doubtful about the representativeness of those who attended the Central Council and Annual Conference. Inevitably, they were drawn from the narrow social range of the local elites, and one MP considered that 90 per cent of those at the 1927 Conference 'were of the old kind, and only there because they had money and leisure'.[90] As delegates attended at their own expense, the poorer constituencies, which were a long distance from the venue, were often under-represented, and sometimes, due to the cost and time involved, sent no representatives at all.[91] However, even at the lowest point in 1934, 419 (82.3 per cent) of the 509 constituencies in England and Wales intimated their intention to be represented. Walter Long thought that the delegates 'consist not of the real workers but of those who possess the gift of the gab, like the outing, and are pleased with the temporary importance of the position'.[92] The stalwarts who filled the hall were often assumed to favour strong but simplistic diehard views; writing on the closing day of the 1932 conference, Hoare categorized it as 'two thousand extreme partisans who want a brass band and drums and plenty of shouting'.[93] In fact, the Conference was much more than just a rally. Those attending did not think they were only participating in a social and celebratory event, and would not have been motivated to spend the time and money for that alone. Certainly, the sociable aspects were attractive and it was enjoyable to mix with like-minded people; one delegate reported that it had been an educative experience and 'the happiest time of her life'.[94] The atmosphere of such a large gathering was stimulating, and its value in renewing enthusiasm and raising morale was self-evident. In many ways, 'what was most important was the *spirit* of the conference'.[95] However, part of the interest derived from the feeling of involvement in larger affairs, and this reflected the roles of the Conference as a two-way transmission of influence.

The first of these functions was its use by the leadership to explain and defend their actions, although the Conference was 'not primarily an occasion for a declaration of policy'.[96] Whilst this was a form of top-down communication, the leaders'

---

[87] Dawson, memo of meeting with Baldwin, 26 September 1928, Dawson MSS, 73/97–100.
[88] NU Conf., 1932.
[89] NU Central Council Report to Conference, 1927–28.
[90] Crichton-Stuart to Davidson, 31 January 1928, Baldwin MSS, 59/185–6.
[91] Skipton CA, Exec., 15 September 1923; Newcastle West CA, Exec., 24 September 1923; Stockton CA, Exec., 12 August 1938; lack of offers to attend could be a problem even in a safe seat: Westminster St George's CA, Exec., 17 July 1935.
[92] Long to Younger, 11 September 1922, Long MSS (WSA), 947/859.
[93] Hoare to Macdonald, 7 October 1932, Templewood MSS, VII/1.
[94] Stockton CA, Women's Ctte, AGM, 28 May 1925.
[95] *Home and Politics*, November 1926 (emphasis in original), July 1927.
[96] Stonehaven to Baldwin, 27 September 1933, Baldwin MSS, 48/225–7.

need to do so and their awareness of the audience's reaction also made this a form of indirect consultation. Neville Chamberlain, a regular attender during his ministerial career, declared that the value in so doing was that 'it enabled him to gauge to some extent the feeling in the Party about any proposal with which he was concerned'.[97] Following from this, the second role of the Conference was to provide a forum for the marshalling of grass-roots opinion, thereby raising concerns and priorities which were expected to be taken into account by the leaders. As one member of the Executive observed: 'The receipt of a number of resolutions on one subject shows the importance attached to that subject.... The broader the range of resolutions, the better and truer the political effect.'[98] The purpose was general rather than particular, 'to give the leaders a broad indication of the directions in which it was desirous the Party should go'.[99] The tenor of the debate was also an important element in communicating with the leadership, and thus Amery attended the 1921 Conference in order 'to judge the real feeling of the party, not the mere voting'.[100] In fact, votes by ballot were rare: most resolutions were passed unanimously, and others decided by a show of hands. The Conference was more comfortable with general statements, and the feeling that it lacked detailed knowledge had much to do with its resistance to overly specific or directive resolutions. Lord Derby's effective speech immediately before the vote was taken on the Irish issue in 1921 significantly closed with appeals for unity and for the delegates 'not to make a decision on matters upon which they knew absolutely nothing'.[101]

Whilst 'any apparent criticism' was usually 'of the most good-natured kind', it is a misreading to view the Conference as entirely deferential to the leadership.[102] Thus, when a motion in 1928 criticized the government for 'slow progress' in extending safeguarding duties, an amendment to remove that phrase was overwhelmingly defeated. Agriculture was the subject of frequent resolutions calling for more vigorous action, and in 1934 the Conference passed several resolutions critical of the National Government's policies, including the important issue of housing. However, direct challenges were usually avoided, and thus a hostile resolution on the lack of legislation on the trade union issue at the 1926 Conference was withdrawn by its proposer after a 'very clever and conciliatory' appeal from the Party Chairman for trust in the leaders, although there was clearly such strong support that, had it been put to the vote, it would have been carried overwhelmingly.[103] The essential point is that such trust was given by consent and not under constraint. If there was an element of deference, it was no longer mainly social in basis, but rather an acknowledgement that those who led were shouldering heavy responsibilities and were much more fully informed than the rank and file, and that whilst doubt and criticism were quite legitimate, they should not be capricious or careless in either origin or expression. The party leadership is often simplistically summarized as controlling or dominating the Conference, a judgement

---

[97] NU Conf., 1928.   [98] NU Exec., 9 December 1936.
[99] NU Conf., 1929, speech by Williams; Gretton to Steel-Maitland, 28 November 1924, Baldwin MSS, 11/82–3.
[100] Amery diary, 16 November 1921.   [101] NU Conf., 1921.
[102] Salisbury CA, F&GP, 8 October 1936.   [103] Amery diary, 7 October 1926.

which justifies ignoring it or comparing it unfavourably with other parties. In fact, any such degree of command has been greatly overestimated. The leading lights of the National Union selected the agenda, and most of these were weighty regional figures who were at least as much concerned to represent those who looked up to them, and so retain their respect and loyalty, as they were to shield the leaders. The agenda had to reflect the issues of the day and the tenor of the resolutions submitted, and any leadership 'control' here was limited and at one remove.

The leaders had even less influence over who was to speak; the Chairmen of the Conference and of the Central Council were chosen by the National Union, and whilst of the social elite they were not normally from the party leadership group. In any case, the standing orders of both Conference and Central Council allowed amendments from the floor of the hall, emergency resolutions, and the right to insist upon a secret ballot. If enough delegates or constituencies demanded it, a special conference could be summoned by the grass roots without reference to the leadership—this was proposed but defeated in 1934, discussed seriously in 1930–31, and (on the initiative of the Executive) was set in motion in October 1922. The rules under which the Conservative Party conducted its meetings were not peculiar or arcane rituals, but rather clear and simple procedures not much different from other organizations of the day, including the other political parties, charities, societies, and clubs. Certainly, both Conference and Council were open to persuasion,[104] and most delegates had a free hand to decide how they would vote on any issue; their local associations only occasionally 'asked' or 'requested' them to support a particular resolution on the agenda, and very rarely gave definite instructions as to how they should act.[105] There was a reluctance to prejudge matters, not least because it devalued both the purpose of holding a debate and the status of those attending, and most constituencies considered that 'the delegates were quite competent to use their own discretion after hearing the pros and cons of the various resolutions'.[106]

There were several Conference debates of political significance, including a few at which the party leadership was potentially at risk. The most critical occasion was in 1921 during the Irish negotiations, as their disavowal by the party whose customary name had become 'Unionist' would have destabilized the situation and possibly brought down the government. Unusually, the motion—moved by the diehard leader, Gretton—was a direct challenge to the leadership's policy, but 'the speeches were not bitter, and all were most anxious to avoid a split'.[107] The critics dominated the first part of the debate, but there was then a break for lunch which was significant in reducing their impact and momentum. In the afternoon session,

---

[104] York CA, Exec., 10 July 1933; Walsall CA, Exec., 10 December 1934.

[105] Thirsk & Malton CA, Exec., 28 September 1926; Chippenham CA, Exec., 29 April 1927, 4 October 1929; Oxford CA, F&GP, 3 October 1927; Chichester CA, Exec., 24 July 1933; Melton CA, Exec., 29 September 1934. However, Norwood CA regularly 'instructed' its delegates how to vote: Exec., 23 September 1924.

[106] Aldershot CA, Fin., 20 September 1928; Cardiff Central CA, Exec., 9 June 1933; Rochester & Chatham CA, Special Meeting, 30 August 1933; Cambridge CA, Exec., 25 September 1934.

[107] Bayford diary, 27 November 1921; NU Conf., 1921; Salisbury to Bonar Law, 18 November 1921, Bonar Law MSS, BL/107/1/71.

the balance was turned in favour of the leadership by a series of key speakers. The first of these was the former Cabinet minister and long-serving leader of the southern Irish Unionists, the Earl of Midleton, who stated bluntly that 'they must face the facts of the situation', and then refuted earlier claims by stating that the commercial and landed classes in the south were in favour of a settlement.[108] He was followed by Archibald Salvidge, the populist leader of the party in the Conference's host city of Liverpool (an area where the Irish issue was felt strongly), who made the issue one of confidence in the party leaders. The final impetus was given by Derby, the prestigious leader of Lancashire Conservatism (and, because this was the host region, the current President of the National Union), who argued that Salvidge's amendment to the diehard motion still retained the points which the party considered essential: the preservation of allegiance to the Crown, the security of the empire, and no compulsion of Ulster. The combination of a strong appeal to loyalty and the evidence of united conviction on the part of the leadership carried the day, despite many delegates' unhappiness and their concern about Ulster's position.[109] However, the Party Leader, Austen Chamberlain, waiting nearby to deliver his Leader's address to the mass meeting scheduled for that evening, had taken nothing for granted and had prepared two alternative speeches depending upon the outcome.

There was increasing criticism of the Coalition at the 1920 and 1921 Conferences, with a delegate from Newport at the former describing its effects as 'committing party suicide', and the 'unrest' was acknowledged in Austen Chamberlain's address in 1921.[110] Whilst the leadership carried the day over Ireland, the 1921 Conference stimulated a revival of party spirit so that it 'was once more fully conscious of its own existence', and this contributed to the erosion of support for the Coalition over the following eleven months.[111] As the 1922 Conference approached, it was clear that it would 'completely upset the applecart' if the leaders did not change direction,[112] but instead Chamberlain decided to pre-empt the Conference by calling a meeting of MPs at the Carlton Club on 19 October. This transparent 'political trickery' infuriated the Executive of the National Union, and provoked alarming signs that it might mutiny and refuse to accept the decision of the MPs.[113] The Executive met on 18 October, and apparently accurate accounts leaked to the press revealed that 'many strong things were said about the unrepresentative character' of the meeting of MPs, including that, because many of them were not standing for re-election, they were 'not competent to decide a question affecting the whole policy of the Party'—a doctrine which implied a considerable change in the balance of power and authority between the parliamentary and representative sections of the party. Declaring that Austen Chamberlain was 'entirely out of touch

[108] NU Conf., 1921.
[109] Derby to Long, 21 November 1921, Long MSS, Add.62405/135–6; Younger to Bonar Law, 19 November 1921, Bonar Law MSS, BL/107/1/72.
[110] NU Conf., 1920, 1921; Bayford diary, 23 June 1920.
[111] Salisbury to Steel-Maitland, 28 November 1921, Steel-Maitland MSS, GD193/275/22–3; Derby to Lloyd George, 18 November 1921, Derby MSS, 33.
[112] Younger to Long, 29 August 1922, Long MSS (WSA), 947/859.
[113] Younger's memo of interview with Chamberlain, 26 September 1922, Bayford diary.

with the real wishes of the rank and file of the Party', the Executive further concluded that in trying to avoid the Annual Conference, the Leader was trying 'to burke their opinion and that it is necessary for them as a democratic body to assert themselves'.[114] They therefore resolved to issue an immediate summons for an emergency conference, which was to be held even if an election was called; however, when on the next day the Coalition fell, the need for this final defence evaporated and it was cancelled.

In the case of India, the diehards were aware that 'our main strength is in the Conservative conference', and the responding tactic of the leadership was to cool the atmosphere with soothing reassurance and generalities.[115] In the first significant debate at the 1932 Conference, the responsible minister, Hoare, 'had to make a very careful speech'. His aim was to 'be both patient and conciliatory to the many Conservatives who are genuinely anxious', in order to 'take them along quietly'.[116] In this he was broadly successful, and in 1933 and 1934 the doubts of the rank and file were overcome by a similar combination of more effective speeches and a much greater weight of relevant experience supporting the leadership, reinforced by calls for unity and loyalty. Winding up the debate for the government in 1933, Neville Chamberlain ruthlessly played the cards of the delegates' lack of knowledge of India, the need to suspend judgement whilst the Joint Select Committee was deliberating, and the support for the proposals of 'the overwhelming authority of those now holding the most responsible positions in India', capped by the blunt assertion that—whatever its wording—the critics' motion 'really amounts to this—a vote of want of confidence', and was thus 'a direct challenge to the Government'.[117] In 1934, the leadership used a tactic similar to that of 1921, in having the amendment to the hostile resolution moved by the respected local leader of the host city—in this case, Alderman Inskip of Bristol, the brother of the Attorney-General. On both occasions, ballots were held: in October 1933, the amendment approving the policy was passed by 737 to 344, but the depth of misgiving was evident a year later when the government's position was approved by only the narrow margin of 543 to 520. However, the latter was partly due to the Conference chairman, Regina Evans, acceding to calls from the floor for the vote to be taken, before the waiting government minister, Duff Cooper, could give his speech.[118]

Demands for action from the Conference on trade union reform in 1926 and rearmament in 1933–35 had an effect on government policy, although this was partly because the parliamentary party took a similar view. Where it did not, the Conference alone had much less impact, as was shown by its repeated pressure for

---

[114] These quotes from reports in the *Daily Express* and *Daily Mail* are from Younger's letter to members of the Executive of 24 October 1922 enquiring into the leaks, which would hardly have been necessary if they were incorrect: copy in Bonar Law MSS, BL/108/1/10. They are consistent with his briefer report to A. Chamberlain immediately after the meeting, written at 12.15 a.m., 18 October 1922, AC, 33/2/85; see also Derby to Bullock, 19 October 1922, Derby MSS, 42/1.

[115] Knox to Croft, 6 February 1934, Croft MSS, CAC, CRFT/1/15/Kn1.

[116] Hoare to Macdonald, 7 October 1932, Templewood MSS, VII/1.

[117] NU Conf., 1933; N. to H. Chamberlain, 7 October 1933, *NCDL*; Amery diary, 6 October 1933.

[118] Amery diary, 4 October 1934.

House of Lords reform through most of the interwar period. Nevertheless, the party leaders were always careful to give reasons why it was not possible or expedient to act, and did not simply ignore grass-roots opinion. Quite apart from the self-defeating problems that such conduct would bring, the delegates at the Conference could offer valuable guidance on the attitudes of the wider public. One Party Chairman commented: 'in the conference we have people talking from the constituencies on things which they know about and in which the constituencies are interested'.[119] As the largest and clearest articulation of Conservative opinion, the party Conference could never be treated as negligible and would always have an effect.[120] This was also the case, although to a lesser extent, with the Annual Conferences held by the women's and youth organizations; in 1935 the former was attended by 2,200 delegates and the latter by 400. The women's conferences in particular were popular gatherings, but the debates were rarely contentious and they had a more restricted impact. In the case of the Junior Imperial League, the age and inexperience of the participants meant that any criticism was easily discounted as poorly informed, naïve, and the product of the natural impatience of youth.

The role and functions of the Central Council, Annual Conference, and sectional gatherings were quite willingly assumed, and considered to be reasonable and valid by the participants. If there was an effort to avoid damaging public discord and to seek a unifying outcome—even if this entailed bland and formulaic resolutions—then this reflected the preferences of all levels in the party, and not just the needs of its leaders. There was no impediment to prevent the Annual Conference from demanding whatever it wanted, and therefore it must be the case that it did not wish to select the Party Leader, set policy imperatives, or debate the details of legislation. Even near the height of the internal crisis of 1930, a proposal that the National Union should have 'a large voice' in the selection of the Leader was overwhelmingly rejected by its Conference.[121] However, the rank and file rumblings of 1921–22, the late 1920s and 1930, and 1933–34, all show that the National Union had the potential to assert itself if the need to do so was felt strongly enough, especially in the safer seats. The leadership played a quite limited role in structuring the meetings of the Central Council and Annual Conference, and a rather more active one in their debates—but in the form of a respondent, after having listened to the rank and file. The truth has a simplicity which too often has been missed: at Conservative Party gatherings of all sorts—national, regional, and local—the normal course was that the designated leaders fulfilled their required function of leading, in a responsive relationship of 'harmonious discussion' and not of dictatorship.[122] This role was both expected and welcomed by their followers, whose complaints were nearly always about the lack of a clear lead and hardly ever of being provided with too much of one.

---

[119] James, *Memoirs of a Conservative*, 269.
[120] N. to I. Chamberlain, 28 September 1928, *NCDL*.
[121] NU Special Conf., 1 July 1930, speech by King.
[122] Epsom CA, General Ctte., report of delegates to party Conference, 11 October 1935.

THE NATIONAL UNION: THE EXECUTIVE COMMITTEE AND THE ADVISORY COMMITTEES

The Executive Committee had its own Chairman, and from 1912 to 1930 this post was held ex officio by the Chairman of the Party. The linking of the positions aided co-ordination and efficiency, but also created a potential conflict of interest. Younger disliked the dual role, and it led him into a difficult position in 1922 as he sought to straddle the widening gap between the Leader and the grass roots over continuing the Coalition. He was diligent in representing the concerns of the Executive and, after acting on these to oppose the rumours of an early election in January 1922 and being publicly attacked as a result, the National Union rallied behind him as the defender of its interests.[123] However, the link became more contentious during Davidson's Party Chairmanship in 1926–30. He had less experience and personal weight, was very closely identified with the Leader, and was sometimes tactless and clumsy in his manoeuvres, which included an attempt to prevent the leading diehard Gretton from following the normal succession from Vice-Chairman to Chairman of the Central Council in 1927.[124] The election defeat of 1929 opened up the question of the Party Chairman's role, and there was pressure from below and from the diehards for a change. In July 1929, the Executive established a sub-committee to revise the rules of the National Union, and the positions were separated in the new rules, which were ratified at a special party conference in June 1930; as it happened, Davidson had resigned the Party Chairmanship just a few days earlier. In fact, both the sub-committee redrafting the rules and the NU Executive had originally proposed to retain the status quo, and this was overturned when their interim proposals were considered at the 1929 Annual Conference. Here the mover of the amendment, Sir Charles Marston, a diehard stalwart of the Executive, criticized the dual role as 'a bottle-neck' and was cheered when he declared: 'They felt that all the time at the top they were being controlled and directed, whereas they ought to have a perfectly free hand.'[125]

From 1930 this became the case, with the Executive electing its own chairman and the Party Chairman being simply an ordinary member of the committee. The change had marked a desire for greater autonomy and was a cumulative reaction to Davidson's managerial methods, but it was not intended to erode the authority of the Leader and did not lead to any significant departure of role or tone. The first chairman elected by the Executive in October 1930 was Kingsley Wood, a respected moderate MP on the verge of Cabinet rank, who had a known record of service in the Metropolitan Area and who was personally close to the new Party Chairman, Neville Chamberlain, having been his junior minister in 1924–29. Wood's successors were similarly drawn from the loyal centre and the established regional leaders: George Herbert (of the Wiltshire family of the Earls of Pembroke) from 1932 to

---

[123] Bayford diary, 3 March 1922; NU Exec., 7 February, 16 March 1922.
[124] Gretton to Davidson, 15 and 19 February 1927, Davidson MSS, DAV/180.
[125] NU Conf., 1929; NU Exec., Sub-ctte on Rules & Organisation, 18 October 1929; NU Exec., 22 October 1929.

1937, George Stanley (a brother of the Earl of Derby, and formerly an MP, junior minister, and governor of an Indian province) in 1937–38, Eugene Ramsden (an MP and long-serving Chairman of the Yorkshire Area) in 1938–43, and Richard Proby (also an Area Chairman) from 1943 to 1946. If they wished to continue, the Chairmen were normally re-elected each year without opposition, but in 1938 Ramsden stood against the incumbent and defeated him. Ramsden was, in turn, challenged by several candidates in the following year and in 1942 by another of the Area Chairmen, Cuthbert Headlam, but although an unpopular Chairman with many, he was re-elected on both occasions, only finally being ousted in 1943.[126]

The trend during the interwar period was for the membership of the Executive to increase and the frequency of meetings to decrease. After the merger of the Liberal Unionists in 1912, the Executive was to be 'about 30 members elected by the Central Council'.[127] Some places were added for women in 1918, bringing the total eligible to attend to forty-eight, but the most significant expansion was in 1924 when the committee ceased to be chosen by the Central Council as a whole. This had led to some regions being marginalized and to undignified and potentially divisive canvassing for support, and under Blain's reforms this was replaced by the direct election of delegates from each Area in proportion to its number of constituencies.[128] These accounted for forty of the possible total membership of seventy-three; in the revised rules of 1930, the Area representatives were increased to fifty-one, and with some other changes the full membership of the Executive rose to eighty-one.[129] The actual attendance never reached this level, tending to be in the high forties and fifties on most occasions, but lower in January and the early autumn. It only exceeded sixty on four occasions: two of these were special addresses by Baldwin (in November 1931 before the general election, and in May 1933 on India), and the other two were in July 1936 and February 1937, the latter being attended by the Minister of Agriculture. The feeling that the Executive was becoming too cumbersome led to the creation of a General Purposes sub-committee in 1933.[130] This normally had an attendance of between fifteen and twenty-five, and its membership included all of the Area Chairmen. It had the effect of reducing the meetings of the full Executive from the nine or ten which had been customary in the 1920s to six.[131]

The membership of the Executive was mainly drawn from the elite of the regional leadership, and included a substantial number of MPs and peers; in 1934, twenty-four of the eighty-eight members were MPs, fifteen of whom had been elected as Area representatives.[132] The Executive was sometimes felt to be complacent and out of touch, especially with the circumstances in the weaker

---

[126] NU GP, 15 March 1939; NU Exec., 19 April 1939; Headlam diary, 13 and 26 May 1942.
[127] NU Exec., 15 March 1912.
[128] NU Exec., 17 June, 9 December 1924.
[129] NU Rules, 1924, 1930. In 1925, the Chairman of the Women's Advisory Ctte. was added, bringing the total to seventy-four.
[130] NU Exec., report of Sub-ctte 'appointed to consider the better organisation of National Union business', 15 March 1933; NU GP, 13 September 1933.
[131] NU Exec., 10 May 1933.
[132] NU memo, 'List of members of the Executive Committee showing their qualifications for membership', 17 May 1934, Steel-Maitland MSS, GD193/120/3/664–9.

constituencies and more difficult regions.[133] Austen Chamberlain considered that the diehard element was disproportionately represented, but this was more a reflection of the strains of 1922 than the normal situation.[134] In fact, the Executive was dominated by stalwarts of the centre and centre-right, and this was reflected by the MPs who served longest upon it. Fourteen of these were from the mainstream, and only two were diehards: Gretton (a member up to 1930 and in 1935) and Page Croft (a member for seven years in the 1930s). The longest-serving MP of the interwar period was Arthur Steel-Maitland, the first Party Chairman of 1911–16, whose membership continued from the war years until 1934. The longest-serving peer by far was the Marquess of Salisbury, who was a member throughout the period apart from the three years of 1919, 1925, and 1937; although he opposed the Coalition in 1920–21 and the India policy in 1933–35, he also served as Party Leader in the House of Lords from 1925 to 1931, and was much more of a loyalist than a rebel. The other long-serving peers were also generally in the mainstream: the Earl of Selborne was a member from 1919 to 1927, during which he constantly urged the case for second chamber reform; Lord Bayford (previously Robert Sanders) was a member for nine years as a peer, and had earlier been a member for ten years when an MP; and the Earl of Plymouth and Lord Kyslant were both members for eight years. The women members were disinclined to support dissident positions, and from 1921 they normally accounted for at least one-third of those present, and often 40–45 per cent. The Executive could co-opt up to twelve additional members, and up to 1930 there were also six men and three women nominated by the Party Leader. These unelected places were principally used to retain long-standing and respected figures whose qualification had for some reason lapsed, and to secure a greater element of working-class representation (see Table 4.2).

The two roles of the Executive were defined by Kingsley Wood, when taking office as its first elected Chairman in 1931, as being firstly 'to make suggestions regarding policy to the Leader of the Party', and secondly to deal with organizational matters, in co-operation with the Party Chairman and the Central Office.[135] The Executive was also the clearing house for the business of the National Union, and received regular reports from its various sub-committees. It had the power to pass its own resolutions, and did so at times of crisis.[136] More usually, it considered resolutions sent up from Provincial Areas, county organizations, and individual constituencies. However, whilst the latter category gives the flavour of grass-roots opinion, it does not provide a truly representative sample. Most constituencies sent their resolutions directly to the Leader, the Party Chairman, or the local MP, and so they did not come before the National

---

[133] Memo by Davidson, 1 July 1927, Baldwin MSS, 59/138–41; Headlam diary, 22 March 1932, 28 November 1934.
[134] A. Chamberlain to Salvidge, 10 March 1922, AC, 33/1/28; 'List of Members of the Executive Committee, 1929–30, with their attendances', Bull MSS, CAC, BULL/5/24.
[135] NU Exec., 16 June 1931.
[136] NU Exec., 7 February, 11 April 1922, 28 August 1931.

Table 4.2. Executive Committee: composition and attendance 1919–1939

The number of meetings was reduced following the establishment of the General Purposes subcommittee in September 1933. The figures for composition count any MP or peer who attended at least one meeting during that year. In the figures for attendance, women MPs are counted in both the number of MPs and the number of women who were present at the meeting.

	No. of meetings	Composition		Attendance total		Attendance of MPs		Attendance of women	
		No. of MPs	No. of peers	Most	Least	Most	Least	Most	Least
1919	9	13	9	32	21	9	2	10	1
1920	9	12	7	33	15	10	3	10	2
1921	9	11	6	29	21	8	4	10	6
1922	10	14	6	35	25	11	4	14	7
1923	9	11	5	31	21	8	4	14	6
1924	9	14	9	44	20	11	1	17	5
1925	9	15	7	54	23	10	3	21	8
1926	9	15	9	52	31	10	4	20	11
1927	10	15	9	52	31	9	5	21	11
1928	9	15	9	53	23	14	3	19	9
1929	8	15	5	50	41	10	5	21	16
1930	11	13	7	52	32	12	5	20	10
1931	10	20	10	63	35	15	6	21	9
1932	7	21	7	59	31	15	6	16	9
1933	8	18	10	67	33	17	6	21	12
1934	7	22	10	59	40	15	7	19	13
1935	5	20	5	58	42	17	7	20	15
1936	6	19	3	64	40	13	7	17	15
1937	6	19	4	63	43	15	8	22	13
1938	6	24	7	54	39	14	9	20	10
1939	5	25	8	55	34	21	10	17	9

Union Executive.[137] Only 104 (20.4 per cent) of the 509 constituencies in England and Wales submitted any resolution to it between January 1919 and September 1939. Furthermore, there were marked regional variations, with the Eastern Area accounting for 21.8 per cent of the 170 local resolutions submitted, and London, Middlesex, and Essex together providing a further 30.5 per cent.[138] On the other hand, there were very few resolutions from local associations in the north: the North West Area submitted only four during the entire interwar period, despite containing seventy-five constitu-

---

[137] Only thirty-seven (3.3%) of the 1,132 resolutions on political issues found in the constituency association records (see Table 3.3) were sent to the NU Exec. and also appear in its minutes.
[138] There was also a chronological imbalance: only thirty-eight resolutions (22.4% of the total) were submitted in 1919–29, of which over half were from London, Essex, and Middlesex; however, all but three of the thirty-seven resolutions from the Eastern Area were submitted in 1930–39.

encies in comparison to the twenty-five of the Eastern Area. Furthermore, from the early 1920s, most of the resolutions on the Executive's agenda came from regional organizations, where the expression of grass-roots opinion had been, to some extent, already filtered and diluted.

Discussion of the submitted resolutions occupied a considerable part of many meetings, and those which were considered important were endorsed by the Executive and forwarded to the Party Leader. In 1920, 1921, and 1922, concern over the House of Lords issue led to the Executive sending a deputation to interview the Party Leader; from December 1929, the transmission by such means of the resolutions passed by the Annual Conference and Central Council, and any others which the Executive particularly wished to emphasize, became a regular and formalized procedure, undertaken by a small deputations sub-committee, which included the Area Chairmen.[139] This developed partly due to frustrations in the later part of Davidson's Chairmanship, with a feeling that he was not representing opinion fully and frankly, and partly to Baldwin's reluctance to take action over two issues upon which the grass roots felt strongly: House of Lords reform and the extension of tariffs. The deputations were more a means of dialogue than of pressure: a typical response was that reported on the repeal of the land taxes in 1932, about which Baldwin said that 'he quite appreciated their point of view, but asked them to exercise patience and wished to assure them that his sympathy was entirely with them'.[140] On another occasion, Baldwin 'gave the deputation a most friendly and appreciative reception', and 'stated that he was impressed by the statements that had been made'.[141] Although the answers were generally this bland and emollient, the deputations were a useful device which gave the Executive a feeling of closer and more regular contact with the Leader, and so encouraged greater harmony. This was also facilitated by the developing practice of the Party Leader attending an Executive meeting about once a year for a general discussion. Baldwin was present for the first time in February 1927 and on a further eight occasions from 1930 to 1937; Neville Chamberlain attended three times, the last in June 1940 after he had ceased to be Prime Minister, but Churchill only did so once during the war, immediately after becoming Party Leader.

The bland form of the Executive's minutes can conceal the nature and temperature of the discussions which took place; however, even when there was 'a little heat', normally 'the atmosphere ended friendly'.[142] Although regarded as its champion in 1922, Younger described the Executive as 'a most meddlesome body', which on some occasions between 1916 and 1921 had been 'at daggers drawn' with Bonar Law.[143] In fact, with the exception of their resentment at the broken promises over

---

[139] NU Exec., 22 October 1929, interim report of Sub-ctte on Rules & Organisation; NU Exec., 14 January 1930, 23 February, 22 March 1932.
[140] NU Exec., 4 September 1932, report of delegation on 7 July 1932.
[141] NU Exec., 14 February 1934, 'Representation of Conservative wage-earners on Royal Commissions, etc. Report of Deputation to the Leader of the Party', 30 January 1934.
[142] York diary, 20 April 1944.
[143] Younger to Bonar Law, 12 April 1921, Bonar Law MSS, BL/107/1/14.

House of Lords reform in 1921–22 and outrage at Austen Chamberlain's blatant attempt to bypass the National Union in October 1922, the Executive sought to encourage the Leader but not to coerce him, for to do so would be exceeding their proper role of representation. Thus, even on the vexed second chamber issue in 1926, 'while concerned, they did not want to press the Prime Minister if not convenient to him'.[144] As with the grass roots as a whole, the Executive were inclined to suspect that the leaders might compromise too much, especially in a coalition situation, and they were rather more restive immediately after the election defeats of 1923 and 1929. Even so, this was very far from mutiny: when Leith proposed that the Executive should press for representation at the crucial party meeting in February 1924, others of its members demurred that 'it was hardly the province of the Committee to advise the Leader of the Party as to whom he should invite to the meeting', and he withdrew his resolution.[145] In July 1929, the Executive decided to set up a sub-committee 'to enquire into the relationship between the National Union, the Central Office, and the Leader of the Party', and this eventually led to the revised rules of the National Union in 1930. However, it was the Annual Conference which referred back the initial proposals and insisted upon the separation of the Party Chairmanship from the chairing of the Executive, and it was the Central Council which instigated the inquiry into the causes of the defeat—an investigation which the Executive allowed to wither on the vine, and eventually dropped.[146] Furthermore, after both election defeats, the Executive explicitly refused to endorse resolutions which called for greater influence over party policy and consultation on the timing of elections.[147] The Executive was also used by the leadership to communicate with the wider party. It was summoned immediately after the National Government was formed in August 1931, so that it 'should be informed at the earliest possible moment of the reasons for the decision arrived at by the leaders of the party'; one reason for this was so that its members could answer 'questions that might be raised in their Areas'.[148]

Each of the ancillary wings of the party organization had its own national Advisory Committee which reported to the Executive, where it also had representation. The first established and most important of these reflected the extension of the franchise in 1918, and were for women and trade unionists. The women's organization was a visible success from the outset, and, most importantly, it was a financial asset and not a drain. The women's committee was led at first by the wives of prominent party figures and members of the aristocracy, such as Lady Edmund Talbot, the Countess of Selborne, Lady Sanders, and Caroline Bridgeman; others involved later included Lady Iveagh, Lady Hillingdon, and Lady Falmouth. It was the apex of the party's extensive and active female membership, and convened the Annual Women's Conference; this was a popular event, generally attended by around 2,000 delegates. In 1928 the committee was reconstituted as the 'Central Women's National Advisory Council', with a

---

[144] Steel-Maitland to Baldwin, 17 April 1926, Baldwin MSS, 59/95–6.
[145] NU Exec., 29 January 1924.
[146] NU Central Council, 2 July, NU Exec., 16 July, 10 December 1929, 14 January 1930.
[147] NU Exec., 11 March 1924, 22 October 1929.
[148] NU Exec., 28 August 1931.

membership comprising the sixteen women members of the Executive elected by the Areas, the chairman of the Women's Advisory Committee in each Area (several of whom were likely to be included in the members of the Executive), and up to ten co-opted members. At the same meeting, Lady Iveagh explained that its role was mainly organizational and that 'with regard to questions of policy, the Committee had kept to their advisory capacity'. To this she added that it was 'a channel of communication by which they could ascertain and give the views of the women of the country', and that through the Area committees they 'were able to test the opinion of the women generally'.[149] It was in these ways that all of the advisory committees performed a useful function, by both monitoring and stimulating their particular wing of the party. They worked closely with the staff in the relevant section at Central Office, the head of whom normally acted as honorary secretary to the committee. The women's committee had strong support from the women's department, and together they enjoyed considerable autonomy in their affairs. However, one reason for this was that they caused few ripples, and it was noted that the general perception was that 'the Advisory Committee did not allow anything controversial to be brought forward'.[150]

This was rather less true of the other advisory committee founded in 1919, which oversaw the organization aimed at male working-class trade unionists. The initiative for the formation of the 'Unionist Labour Movement' (ULM) came from Lancashire, where a prewar trade union sub-committee was revived in February 1918. A resolution moved by the chairman of this body, Alderman John Whittaker, at the Central Council in May 1919, led to the creation of the Labour Sub-committee of the National Union. This held its inaugural meeting on 22 July 1919; its first chairman was Whittaker, and the official appointed as its secretary, Captain R. Mathams, had been Central Office Agent for the North West before the war.[151] These Lancashire influences combined with the other region where Conservative trade unionists were active, in south Wales. The driving force of the Glamorgan Unionist Labour Committee was Gwilym Rowlands, a former miner; he became chairman of the national Labour Sub-committee in 1925 and for most of the interwar era was the most visible representative of working-class Conservatism, serving as chairman of the Central Council in 1929–30 and finally securing a parliamentary seat at Flintshire in 1935. The ULM was launched in a flourish of publicity with six provincial conferences in 1920, but it failed to recruit large numbers of Conservative trade unionists and it was not apparent that it was helping to deliver working-class votes in the ballot box. The ULM never had the confidence, numbers, and, to a lesser extent, resources to compete with the Labour Party for influence in the trade unions and working-class votes. In such circumstances, it is hardly surprising that its national spearhead became a dull and blunt instrument, lacking in initiative and unlikely to innovate—and that these characteristics permeated the labour organization as a whole.

During the interwar period working-class representation in the party structures became increasingly formalized, partly to encourage participation and partly to

---

[149] NU Exec., 10 July 1928.
[150] Central Women's National Advisory Council, 29 June 1938, CPA, CCO/170/1/1/1.
[151] *CAJ*, May 1924, 110–11.

demonstrate that the party was not socially exclusive. In the early 1920s, the Labour Sub-committee was formed from members of the Executive and reflected its social composition, but the revised rules of 1930 established direct election from the Area Labour Advisory Committees. However, whilst this made its membership more representative of the wider movement, it did not address other problems. The national committee met in London in mid-week, on the day before the meetings of the Executive; this was intended to make things easier for those who were coming to both, but it still posed great difficulties for any genuine wage-earner.[152] Attendance at Labour Sub-committee meetings was poor, and delegates were sometimes fewer in number than the party officials and officers who were present ex officio. The meetings were often marked by a sense of frustration and futility, and in general the labour movement felt marginal and disregarded. The topics about which it held strong views were politically sensitive issues where the party leadership was often reluctant to take assertive action. However, its consistent pressure on the issue of the political levy did have some influence on the shape of the Trade Disputes Act of 1927.

The other subsidiary committees dealt with more routine organizational matters. The committee on propaganda worked closely with the Central Office Publicity Department which prepared the leaflets and posters, although formally they were published by the National Union. The position of the existing Education Sub-committee was regularized in 1933, a development which reflected the increasing importance attached to political education and the evolution of the party's initiatives in this area.[153] The most important part of this was the educational centre of the Bonar Law Memorial College, but another aspect was the organization of Conservative supporters in the teaching profession into Teachers' Circles. The latter had many of the same defects as the Labour committees, and, in addition, suffered from the drawback that many Conservatives felt that the intrusion of party politics into school education was inappropriate. In fact, the role of the Teachers' Circles was not to initiate propaganda but to detect and counter cases of Socialist indoctrination, which were assumed to be widespread.[154] In the later 1930s, an advisory committee was established for the Junior Imperial League, the latter being a consequence of fully integrating the youth movement into the party structure.[155]

The most significant development for the future was another new body, the Standing Advisory Committee on Candidates (SACC). This was a small but powerful group of the key figures in the party management, and included the Chairmen of the NU Central Council, Executive, Women's, and Labour Advisory Committees, the Area Chairmen, the Chairman of the Party, and the Chief Whip in the House of Commons, and had the General Director of Central Office as its secretary. The SACC was created in response to continuing concern over the methods and quality of selection, in which too often it seemed that the depth of the chosen nominee's pockets had been the determining factor. This practice had been the subject of frequent criticism at Central Council and conference meetings since the

---

[152] Derby to Woodhouse, 18 December 1924, Derby MSS, 20/4.
[153] NU Exec., report on 'Proposed New Sub-committees, c.10 May 1933.
[154] *CAJ*, April 1927, 95–8; Rye CA, Exec., 28 March 1925.
[155] NU GP, 26 May 1937.

early 1920s. The almost complete lack of any working-class Conservative MPs was an increasing embarrassment, symbolized by the failure of Gwilym Rowlands to secure a winnable seat—so much so that in 1930 the Central Council had passed a resolution specifying that he should be returned to parliament as 'an effective illustration of the democracy of the Conservative Party'.[156] However, as with women, working-class candidates were something that the safer constituencies considered to be a worthy aspiration which was better put into effect somewhere else, and nothing developed until further resolutions at the 1934 Annual Conference were referred to the General Purposes Committee for practical action.[157] Their report was careful to include reassurance that 'the unquestioned right of a constituency to select its own candidate is recognised', but nevertheless the SACC was an innovation and it aroused some suspicion.[158] There were fears of 'the danger that the Advisory Committee might control, and not advise', and that it might be used as a disciplinary sanction against dissident MPs; however, the 1935 Annual Conference was given emphatic reassurance on these points.[159]

Whilst the central party had no power of veto over local candidates, it did possess the sanctions of withholding any financial subsidy, the support services from Central Office, the assistance of MPs as speakers, and, ultimately, the official letter of endorsement from the Party Leader.[160] Few constituencies were so secure or so isolationist that they would willingly cut themselves off in this way, and thus an effective form of central approval was instituted—although generally after the constituency had made its choice. The procedure proposed was that before completing the selection of a candidate, the constituency chairman should consult the SACC 'in order to ensure that the proposed candidate shall receive the full support of the Party'.[161] Whilst local autonomy was maintained, this was the first significant restraint upon it; after 1945 it was followed by limitation to an approved list of qualified candidates, from which constituencies had to make their selection. This had also been developed by the SACC from its early meetings, when it began examining the existing list, supplied by the Party Vice-Chairman responsible for candidates, and deleting 'any of whom they do not approve'.[162] By June 1938 the list had been formalized into several categories, and there were 265 potential 'first-class candidates' suitable for anywhere, 133 'good candidates' who were 'not suitable for all constituencies', twenty-one 'young, inexperienced candidates', and eighty-six rejects 'against whom there is something definite as to character, loyalty, etc., and who may not be adopted anywhere'.[163] However, whilst this was certainly less haphazard, it

---

[156] NU Central Council, 4 March 1930.
[157] NU GP, 9 January 1935.
[158] NU Exec., 'Report of Special Sub-committe. appointed to consider the matter of Parliamentary candidates', 13 February 1935; NU Exec., 2 October 1935; Middleton & Prestwich CA, FGP, 30 May 1935; Rochdale CA, Exec., 28 April 1938; Thorp to Duchess of Atholl, 20 September 1935, Atholl MSS, 23/3.
[159] NU Conf., 1935, speech by Wise and response by the Conference Chairman.
[160] SACC, first meeting, 1 May 1935.
[161] Special Sub-ctte, report to Exec., 13 February 1935.
[162] SACC, 1 May, 4 and 26 June, 3 July 1935.
[163] SACC, 15 June 1938; for definition of the categories, SACC, 10 November 1937.

had made little difference to the social pool from which candidates were drawn: they were still almost entirely upper-middle class and above, and there were very few women.

CENTRAL OFFICE: THE PARTY CHAIRMAN AND THE PRINCIPAL AGENT

The report of the Unionist Organisation Committee in 1911 which led to the creation of the post of Chairman of the Party Organisation had recommended that its holder should be of Cabinet rank. However, Balfour deliberately ignored this and chose Arthur Steel-Maitland for the new position because his standing in the party was not senior enough to be a cause of division or jealousy.[164] The implication remained that the post would lead to Cabinet membership, and Steel-Maitland resigned in December 1916 when, for the second time, he was given only junior office. For the rest of the interwar period, there was no suggestion that the Party Chairmen were of Cabinet status;[165] whilst they attended meetings of the shadow cabinet when the party was in opposition, they did not—unlike the Chief Whip—attend when it was in office. Apart from one case in special circumstances (Neville Chamberlain in 1930–31), the Party Chairmen between 1916 and 1946 were drawn from the whips and junior ministers.[166] The feeling that the Chairman should be a person of some substance returned after the tenure of the relatively lightweight Davidson from 1926 to 1930, and was one reason for the exceptional appointment of Neville Chamberlain in 1930–31. Chamberlain had not only already been a Cabinet minister in 1923–24 and 1924–29, but was recognized as one of rising figures on the front bench and a likely future Leader. His appointment as Chairman was necessary to shore up Baldwin's crumbling position during the height of the party crisis in 1930; it was announced as temporary from the outset, and he served for just under ten months. Early in his tenure he chaired a committee of inquiry into the party organization, and this revived the recommendation that the Chairman should be of Cabinet rank.[167] Once again, this was not implemented: his successor, Stonehaven, was perhaps not far from this level, having been Minister of Transport in the 1922–24 government before taking a peerage and serving a five-year term as Governor-General of Australia. However, he had not been a member of the shadow cabinet before his appointment and, despite membership having been 'a

---

[164] Balfour to Long, 2 June 1911, Balfour MSS, Add.49777.
[165] However, it appears that a promise of future Cabinet status was made to persuade Assheton to undertake the Chairmanship in 1944, although 'he will not set too much store by [this]': Beaverbrook to Churchill, 13 October 1944, Churchill MSS, CAC, CHAR/2/507/155.
[166] It seems that Margesson, a former Chief Whip and Cabinet minister, was offered the post when Dugdale stepped down in 1944, but declined it: Churchill to Eden, 6 October 1944, Churchill MSS, CAC, CHAR/2/502/157.
[167] Chamberlain Ctte. Report, 9 March 1931, CPA, CCO/500/1/5.

sort of condition of his taking the office', Baldwin balked at including him.[168] When Stonehaven retired in 1936, he raised with Baldwin the 'loss of contact' which resulted from the Chairman not being in the Cabinet, with the consequence that the government was solely under the influence of the civil service, but arrangements remained unchanged until Lord Woolton became the first serving Party Chairman to sit in a Cabinet in 1951.[169]

The Party Chairmanship was not a prize which was sought after or a stepping stone to higher office; George Herbert, Chairman of the National Union Executive for five years, categorized it as 'all the blame and no thanks'.[170] Davidson observed that the post 'was regarded as a blind alley', and it was more often the culmination of a career than the start of one.[171] Five of the nine Chairmen appointed before 1945 held no further ministerial office (Younger, Stanley Jackson, Stonehaven, Douglas Hacking, and Assheton), although Jackson left Central Office for an Indian governorship. Davidson returned to office outside the Cabinet as Chancellor of the Duchy of Lancaster from 1931 to 1937, a post he had held in 1923–24, and he continued in the role of acting as Baldwin's principal aide. Only two of the regular holders of the Chairmanship later reached the Cabinet, and in both cases after a considerable interval. The only former Chairman to enter the Cabinet in the interwar period was the first incumbent, Steel-Maitland, but the link was tenuous at best, as there were eight years between his departure from Central Office in 1916 and his appointment as Minister of Labour in 1924. Thomas Dugdale, Chairman in 1942–44, became Minister of Agriculture in October 1951 and the post was brought into the Cabinet in September 1953; he was to enjoy this status for less than a year, resigning in July 1954 following a critical public inquiry into the actions of his department over the compulsorily purchased estate of Crichel Down. The final case was, of course, the exceptional appointment of Neville Chamberlain, who had already held high office before his temporary spell as Party Chairman, and who continued to do so as Chancellor of the Exchequer in 1931–37 and Prime Minister in 1937–40. Ironically, the only person to move directly from service at Central Office into the Cabinet was not a Chairman but his Deputy. In the unusual circumstances following the fall of the Coalition in 1922, Bonar Law had to appoint a considerable number of former junior ministers to his Cabinet and one of these was Robert Sanders, who became Minister of Agriculture. The Deputy Chairman of 1927–29, Lord Stanley, also later entered the Cabinet, but only in 1938 and after a succession of junior ministerial offices. Davidson drew no salary whilst serving as Party Chairman, which he considered 'has certainly cost me several thousands', whilst Younger, an independently wealthy businessman, estimated that his term of office had cost him at least £30,000.[172] It is unclear if Jackson or Stonehaven received any recompense, although payment of expenses

---

[168] N. to I. Chamberlain, 18 April 1931, *NCDL*.
[169] Stonehaven to Baldwin, 31 January 1936, Baldwin MSS, 171/284–7.
[170] Herbert to Stonehaven, 28 February 1936, Stonehaven MSS, 2127/4/3.
[171] Davidson to Hoare, 30 December 1929, Templewood MSS, VI/1.
[172] Memo by Davidson, n.d. but marked 'summer 1930', Davidson MSS, DAV/190.

was normal, but when Hacking became Chairman in 1936 Baldwin authorized a salary of £2,000, an arrangement which, significantly, was to be kept secret.[173]

The Party Chairman was chosen solely by the Leader of the Party, whose 'right to do this could not be challenged',[174] and they had a close working relationship, especially when the party was in opposition or during the approach of a general election. Indeed, it was no coincidence that three Chairmen (Davidson, Stonehaven, and Dugdale) had previously served as Parliamentary Private Secretary (PPS) to a Party Leader. Davidson was particularly seen as Baldwin's personal preference in 1926, although the position had been offered first to the Marquess of Linlithgow (who had recently served as Deputy Chairman) and then to George Tryon, the Minister of Pensions.[175] Previously, Younger had been very much Bonar Law's man, which was an additional tension in his relationship with Austen Chamberlain. Although the post was at their discretion, all of the incoming Party Leaders during this period retained the Chairman whom their predecessor had picked— Hacking was appointed by Baldwin in March 1936 and continued under both Chamberlain and Churchill, until he stood down in March 1942.[176] As a result, several had long spells in office: Hacking's was exceeded only by the six years and two months of Younger's tenure, and Stonehaven was in post for just under five years. Apart from Chamberlain's temporary appointment, the briefest terms were the final two of Dugdale (1942–44) and Assheton (1944–46). Stonehaven was unwell during his final year in office and Dugdale's period was cut short by illness, but two of the earlier Chairmen departed because of mounting problems with regard to their conduct.[177] In Jackson's case, it was becoming evident that he lacked the necessary ability and was 'making a terrible mess of the Central Office'.[178] Neville Chamberlain 'formed rather a poor opinion of his capacity, for he showed little backbone and less initiative', perhaps not the best qualifications for the Indian provincial governorship which he was given (although such posts were often filled from the middle-ranking who were unlikely to rise further).[179] Davidson was hardworking and energetic, and introduced several important changes in the course of his Chairmanship. However, his overly zealous defence of Baldwin's interests and maladroit handling of influential figures in the party undermined his position. Misjudgements in the year after the 1929 defeat made him an increasing liability, and in the spring of 1930 Neville Chamberlain, with increasing bluntness, pressed

---

[173] Baldwin to Davidson, 4 March 1936, Davidson MSS, DAV/212.
[174] Memo by Ball, c.10 May 1940, Ball MSS, MSS.Eng.c.6652/44–8.
[175] Birkenhead to Irwin (for Linlithgow), telegram, 19 October 1926, Baldwin MSS, 102/93; Tryon to Baldwin, 30 October 1926, Baldwin MSS, 161/228.
[176] Hacking had originally agreed to serve for five years, but, on becoming Leader, Churchill asked him to continue in post: Hacking to Churchill, 19 February 1942, Churchill MSS, CAC, CHAR/2/450/4. However, his retirement may also have been due to the 'growing feeling' amongst Conservative MPs that he was 'not nearly strong enough to deal with modern political problems' and that a change was needed, of which Churchill was informed by his PPS: report by Harvie-Watt, 24 October 1941, Harvie-Watt MSS, CAC, HARV/1/1.
[177] N. to H. Chamberlain, 10 June 1935, *NCDL*.
[178] Lane-Fox to Irwin, 15 September 1926, Halifax MSS, C152/17/1/102.
[179] N. Chamberlain to Irwin, 25 December 1927, Halifax MSS, C152/17/1/277a; Irwin to Cunliffe-Lister, 11 October 1926, Swinton MSS, CAC, SWIN/II(270)/3/22.

him to resign.[180] Davidson was sacrificed not to save Baldwin, but to avoid endangering him: as Hoare commented, his departure 'had become inevitable and, if he had delayed it, Stanley would have been dragged down with him'.[181] Davidson himself attributed his fall to an inevitable accumulation of criticism and grievances, and drew the consoling if self-serving conclusion that 'no Chairman who does his work can hope to survive'.[182]

The Chairmanship was seen as a backroom job: unglamorous, bureaucratic, and tedious. The position was clearly subordinate; in Bridgeman's view, 'it is not the business of the Party Chairman to argue policy with the Leader, but to act as a means of sounding the feeling in the country and report it, and carry out the organisation by which the Leader's policy may be brought before the country'.[183] Chamberlain was again the exception: due to his personal prominence, he was able to take more initiative—in particular in the various negotiations with Beaverbrook—and his position and authority continued to be that of a senior Cabinet colleague. However, the experience of the other interwar Chairmen was closer to Younger's categorization of 'the terrible drudgery and constant worries of this post'.[184] The main part of the Chairman's work was the daily management of Central Office in the placing of candidates, production of propaganda, and organization of campaigning, and he could inform and exhort the rank and file by issuing general circulars to constituencies. The Chairman also had a role in the resolution of local disputes, and in a coalition he dealt with the tricky details of the electoral arrangements with other parties. Through information collected by Central Office he could monitor the readiness and mood of the local associations; he also ex officio held the Chairmanship of the Executive Committee of the National Union up to 1930, and was an influential member of that body thereafter.[185] Until the same year, the Chairman was also the principal fundraiser for the costs of Central Office and the general election fund. Davidson was good at this, but the additional burden was too time-consuming, and in the reforms of 1930 a new office of Party Treasurer was created. The Chairman was not involved in ministerial appointments: Hacking declared he was 'never' consulted about this;[186] whilst Davidson may have been, this was rather in his personal capacity as Baldwin's long-standing aide and confidant. Although this was not part of their responsibilities, those Chairmen who were MPs were naturally aware of the mood in the Commons; as Jackson observed, 'I am in a position to hear the opinion in the House and in the country.'[187] A good

---

[180] Hoare to N. Chamberlain, 24 December 1929, NC, 7/11/22/9; N. Chamberlain to his wife, 2 April 1930, NC, 1/26/421; N. to H. Chamberlain, 25 May 1930, *NCDL*.
[181] Hoare to Irwin, 31 May 1930, Halifax MSS, C152/19/1/71; Ball, *Baldwin and the Conservative Party*, 83–4.
[182] Memo by Davidson reviewing his Chairmanship, n.d. but *c.*June 1930, Davidson MSS, DAV/190.
[183] Bridgeman to Irwin, 15 June 1930, Halifax MSS, C152/19/1/79.
[184] Younger to Bonar Law, 12 April 1921, Bonar Law MSS, BL/107/1/14.
[185] Younger to Bonar Law, 14 July, 12 October 1920, Bonar Law MSS, BL/96/2; Davidson to Baldwin, 27 February 1929, Baldwin MSS, 164/40–1.
[186] Hacking to Derby, 5 June 1936, Derby MSS, 31/6.
[187] Jackson to Baldwin, 24 December 1925, Baldwin MSS, 160/96.

relationship with the parliamentary party was essential, and 'much depends upon this whether a Chairman's life is tolerable or not'.[188] As a whole, as Stonehaven commented in the year before he was appointed, the Chairmanship was 'a thankless and most difficult task—but it is vitally important'.[189]

The Party Chairman was assisted during much of the 1920s by a Deputy, and after 1930 this was transmuted into a more formal division of labour amongst three Vice-Chairmen (the male term was used, regardless of the gender of the occupant). The first Deputy Chairman was Robert Sanders, a whip who was appointed in February 1918 to assist with the changes resulting from the Reform Act. He remained in the post until October 1922, and played a significant part in the fall of the Coalition. The office was then held by the Marquess of Linlithgow from May 1924 to January 1926, Lord Strathcona very briefly in October 1927, and Lord Stanley (an MP and the eldest son of the 17th Earl of Derby) from November 1927 to July 1929. Stanley's main task was to encourage the expansion of the Junior Imperial League, of which he was Chairman from 1928 to 1933. Although things started well, his personal relationship with Davidson deteriorated and he resigned as Deputy Party Chairman after the election defeat.[190] After a gap of several months, in March 1930 two Deputy Chairmen were appointed— the innovation being that one was female and given particular responsibility for the women's organization. It was intended that this post would be occupied by the Countess of Iveagh, one of the party's first female MPs, and a popular and capable figure. However, as she had just been elected Chairman of the Central Council for the coming year, Lady Falmouth was appointed in her place.[191] Although this began on an acting basis, Lady Falmouth continued to serve until the outbreak of war in 1939, and was succeeded by Lady Hester Bourne in 1940. The male Deputy Chairman appointed in March 1930 was George Bowyer, who continued also to serve as a whip during his tenure.

In the following year, during Neville Chamberlain's Chairmanship, the title of these posts was amended to Vice-Chairman; this was not formally announced, but the change can be traced in the headings of Central Office notepaper. Bowyer looked after a range of organizational matters until December 1931, when a third Vice-Chairman was added and given specific responsibility for candidates.[192] From this point onwards, there was always a Vice-Chairman for women and one for candidates, the latter during this period being Sir George Hennessy (created Baron Windlesham in 1937) from 1931 to 1941, and Harold Mitchell from 1942 to August 1945. In fact, it was the original position with the more general duties that

---

[188] Jackson to Irwin, 5 November 1926, Halifax MSS, C152/17/1/134.
[189] Stonehaven to Gilmour, 22 September 1930, Gilmour MSS, GD383/27/35–7; N. Chamberlain to Baldwin, 23 June 1930, Baldwin MSS, 165/53.
[190] Memo by Davidson, 13 March 1928, Davidson MSS, DAV/182; Baldwin to Stanley, draft reply, 10 July 1929, Baldwin MSS, 164/226–7.
[191] *The Times*, 6 March 1930.
[192] Chamberlain Ctte. Report, 9 March 1931, CPA, CCO/500/1/5; Stonehaven to Baldwin, 9 December 1931, Baldwin MSS, 166/144–5. However, Bowyer seems to have remained involved in candidate matters: see his memo, 'Candidates', 19 July 1934, Baldwin MSS, 48/240–4.

was not always filled. Bowyer served until December 1935 but was not replaced, and then in 1937–38 the position was occupied by the experienced and respected Sir Malcolm Fraser, who had previously been honorary Principal Agent in 1920–23. As with the Party Chairmen, the work was mostly routine and a matter of duty, but also had its compensations: Bowyer bitterly regretted standing down, having 'just loved' his time at Central Office and the fascination of being 'behind the scenes in everything'.[193]

The most senior of the professional staff at Central Office was the Principal Agent, who worked closely with the Party Chairman and oversaw the organizational work.[194] In the decade after the First World War, it remained a priority that the Principal Agent should be of sufficient social standing to interact with the upper-class figures in the regional and local leadership. Apart from this, a general executive capacity was felt to be sufficient qualification, and the three Principal Agents from 1920 to 1927 had no personal experience of elections at local level. However, the professional expertise that the latter provided became a more significant asset, and since 1927 all of the Principal Agents have followed a career path from constituency agent to the Areas and then to Central Office. The Principal Agent at the end of the war, William Jenkins, had risen from the agents' ranks but was not a success when he was promoted from the position of deputy in 1915. He was 'simply unequal to the responsibility' and suffered a nervous breakdown in July 1920, retiring a few months later.[195] His successor appeared to mark a return to the prewar model of the amateur rather than the professional. In reality, Sir Malcolm Fraser combined the best of both worlds, and was one of the most effective holders of the post. Already a baronet, he had the social status and also did not need to be paid, acting on an honorary basis which put him on an almost equal footing to the Chairman and Deputy Chairman, and he worked very closely with Younger and Sanders during the downfall of the Coalition. He was a former newspaper editor, and as the party's press adviser since 1910 was already familiar with the organization and many of the staff.

Fraser retired at the same time as Younger in March 1923, and the new Chairman, Jackson, appointed Sir Reginald Hall at a salary of £2,000 plus £1,000 in expenses.[196] A former admiral, he had been Director of Naval Intelligence from 1914 to 1919, when he became MP for a Liverpool constituency. Fraser's success had been due partly to his personality and partly to his expertise, but Hall was lacking in both respects. He did not have time to get his bearings, as the unexpected dissolution of 1923 occurred only seven months after he took office. It was held in particularly difficult circumstances, and Hall was further handicapped by the need to defend his own seat as well; in the event, both it and the election were lost. There was criticism when both the Party Chairman and Principal Agent were

---

[193] Bowyer to Davidson, 5 November 1936, Davidson MSS, DAV/226.
[194] See Maclachlan's description of his work in 'Summarised Report on Conservative Organisation at Central Office and in the Constituencies during 1927', 30 December 1927, Baldwin MSS, 53/118–49.
[195] Bayford diary, 10 July 1920; Younger to Fraser, 22 August 1920, Fraser MSS, MSS. Eng.c.4788/80–3.
[196] Bonar Law to Hall, 14 March 1923, Hall MSS, CAC, HALL/1/2.

away from Central Office during the campaign, with Younger reluctantly returning as caretaker.[197] After the defeat, the majority shared the opinion of the former Chief Whip, Leslie Wilson, who stated: 'I am quite sure it is not right for a Chief Agent to be in the House.'[198] In February 1924, having lost the confidence of the party leadership, Hall was effectively required to resign.[199] His replacement was from a completely different mould: Herbert Blain was one of the new breed of managers of public companies, and was brought in particularly due to his expertise in office administration (on which he had written a standard textbook), with a mandate to modernize and streamline the party organization.[200] He approached this with care and sensitivity, and his rationalization of the National Union was a particular success; he also sought to target central resources to assist the weakest seats. However, Blain found working with 'so uncertain and so untrustworthy a boss' as Jackson too frustrating,[201] and, with the essential restructuring accomplished, he indicated in the spring of 1926 that he wished to return to the business world.[202] On 25 November 1926, four days before Davidson took charge at Central Office, *The Times* announced that Blain's resignation had been 'tendered some time ago' and would take effect at the end of the year; this casts much doubt upon Davidson's accounts of sacking Blain for disloyalty to Baldwin.[203] However, it is clear that Davidson disliked Blain and was critical of his methods, distrusting 'supermen' who came in from outside to shake up the organization.[204]

Davidson was keen to revive the system of promotion from the agents, partly on grounds of efficiency and partly to raise the status and morale of the profession. His first step was intended as a temporary measure: the appointment of Leigh Maclachlan, who had held the second position since 1921, as Principal Agent. Maclachlan had worked for the party since 1887 and was aged sixty-two, and Davidson did not intend for him to fight the next election in two or three years' time.[205] However, Maclachlan was disinclined to go, and within a few months Davidson was complaining of 'his lack of courage and initiative and his ineradicable love of intrigue'.[206] He was also old-fashioned and set in his ways, and, crucially, was unsympathetic to the women's organization which Davidson particularly

---

[197] The former Chief Whip, David Margesson, performed a similar role in 1945: Sir H. P. Mitchell, *The Spice of Life* (1974), 70.
[198] Wilson to Baldwin, 30 December 1923, Baldwin MSS, 35/195–8.
[199] Hall to Baldwin, 17 March 1924, Baldwin MSS, 159/205; Headlam diary, 25 February 1924; Blain appears to have been suggested around 17 December 1923, initially 'temporarily until the ideal man could be found', by a committee of Hoare, Wood, and Worthington-Evans: memo of events of 22 October 1923 to 3 January 1924, Worthington-Evans MSS, MSS.Eng.hist.c.894/57–78.
[200] *CAJ*, April 1924, 82–3.
[201] Lane-Fox to Irwin, 15 September 1926, Halifax MSS, C152/17/1/102; Bayford diary, 9 June 1926.
[202] Blain to Baldwin, 25 March 1926, Baldwin MSS, 53/2; *The Times*, 3 June 1926.
[203] James (ed.), *Memoirs of a Conservative*, 265–6; Davidson also refers to 'the peremptory action which I was forced to take 12 months ago in dispensing with Blain, Jessel and Underhill': Davidson to Stanley, 17 January 1928, Davidson MSS, DAV/182. However, there is no suggestion in any other source of any disloyalty.
[204] Davidson to Caroline Bridgeman, 24 December 1926, Davidson MSS, DAV/179.
[205] Davidson to Steel-Maitland, 29 December 1926, Baldwin MSS, 53/34–9.
[206] Davidson to Stanley, 17 January 1928, Davidson MSS, DAV/182.

wished to encourage. Maclachlan did not impress MPs or the Executive of the National Union, and, after some resistance, Davidson was able to push him into retirement in February 1928.[207] One reason for doing so was that Davidson had now settled upon a long-term solution in the form of one of the most capable of the Area Agents, Robert Topping. Originally from Ulster, he had been an agent in Dublin, south Wales, and Cheshire, and was appointed North West Area Agent in 1924; he had been considered for the post of Deputy Principal Agent when it was vacated by Maclachlan in early 1927.[208] Davidson was very impressed with him, and resisted pressure from Younger and Neville Chamberlain to return to the concept of the gentleman amateur and appoint Major Joseph Ball, the former Military Intelligence officer who had become head of the Publicity Department at Central Office in 1927.[209] Even before the ink was dry on Maclachlan's resignation letter, Davidson appointed Topping at a salary of £1,400, rising in annual increments to £1,800.[210]

At the point when Topping took up the post, the role and status of the Principal Agent had been reduced in Davidson's recent restructuring of Central Office. This had created two main departments of equal status, one dealing with publicity and the other with organizational matters. The Principal Agent was now only the head of the latter, and not 'the "Managing Director" of the Party as he has been in the past';[211] this was the reason why Davidson wanted, and had been able to insist upon, a professional agent for the post. This structure meant that the task of overall co-ordination rested upon the Party Chairman, which did not prove entirely satisfactory during the 1929 election campaign. Topping established a close working relationship with Neville Chamberlain during the latter's tenure of the Party Chairmanship, and in the changes which were instituted in March 1931 the position of Principal Agent was restored to its former pre-eminence and, to underline this, retitled General Director. This position was held by Topping until after the general election of 1945, although he had intended to retire earlier and only remained in place because of the wartime emergency.[212] A capable figure, he was described by a colleague, Patrick Gower, as 'tough as an individual and tremendously efficient', and by the Chief Whip, James Stuart, as a 'forthright and determined' character with whom 'relations...were never unpleasant'.[213] Topping retained the confidence of successive Party Leaders, despite his role in drafting the memorandum in February 1931 which suggested that support for Baldwin had declined to a point which made his position untenable. He worked closely and harmoniously with

---

[207] Maclachlan to Baldwin, 6 February 1928, Baldwin MSS, 53/53–4.
[208] Hall to Derby, 18 January 1924, Maclachlan to Derby, 17 January 1927, Derby MSS, 31/3, 31/4.
[209] Davidson to Stanley, 25 and 26 January 1928, Davidson MSS, DAV/182.
[210] Davidson to Topping, Davidson to Stanley, 1 February 1928, Davidson MSS, DAV/182.
[211] Stanley to Davidson, 27 January 1928, Davidson MSS, DAV/182.
[212] Recollections of Armstrong (COA Northern Area), *CAJ*, December 1970, 24.
[213] Gower and Stuart, oral history interviews in Cohen, 'Disraeli's Child', unpublished typescript history of the Conservative Party organization, *c.*1964, 572, 581, Cohen MSS, CPA, CRD/731; *CAJ*, November 1932, 330.

Stonehaven and Hacking, and his experience was such that he was given fairly free rein by the latter.[214] Assheton, the last Party Chairman under whom Topping served, described him as 'a just man, utterly loyal and quite outspoken—sometimes, however, not without a slight streak of vanity', who, when a decision had been made, 'put his full energies into seeing it carried out'.[215] He was ably supported and complemented for many years by his deputy, Marjorie Maxse, a woman with 'a memorable face' and 'very unusual and attractive voice', who 'combined great executive ability with humanity, and firmness with wisdom', and possessed that organizational essential: 'solid common sense'.[216]

CENTRAL OFFICE: THE ORGANIZATIONAL ROLE

The authority of the Chairman of the Party consisted only of that delegated by the Leader, under whose authority the party headquarters operated and whose policies and strategy it was its duty to implement and promote; in Stonehaven's words, 'the Central Office was in the nature of a General Staff to the Leader'.[217] Its primary purpose was the winning of elections, and the means of doing so was through providing assistance and encouraging efficiency in the constituencies, where the battle was actually fought. During the campaigns and in the periods between elections, Central Office made important contributions in two main areas: organizational support and propaganda. In order to do this more efficiently, and in response to the evolving needs of the time, it passed through a series of internal reorganizations of its own, which will be described first. The organization had been 'allowed to get into a chaotic condition' during the war and, although he had been Party Chairman since January 1917, it was only in late 1920 that Younger felt 'I'm getting a grip now for the first time.'[218] As Fraser later commented, 'first the War, and then the Coalition, reduced the organisation to ashes', and in 1920–22 he and Younger strove to restore prewar efficiency and to respond to the new political environment.[219] The previous premises soon proved too cramped, and in December 1921 Central Office moved from 1 Sanctuary Buildings in Great Smith Street to Palace Chambers, Bridge Street, immediately opposite the Palace of Westminster, a 'gloomy labyrinth' where it remained for the rest of the interwar period.[220] However, although the location was convenient, the building was shared with other users and soon became overcrowded, and both Topping in 1930 and Stonehaven in 1936 urged the importance of moving from the 'present very inconvenient and ill-planned quarters to a modern office building'.[221]

[214] Topping to Stonehaven, 6 March 1936, Stonehaven MSS, 2127/4/16.
[215] Assheton, oral history interview in Cohen, 'Disraeli's Child', 566–7, Cohen MSS, CPA, CRD/731.
[216] Recollections of Lord Fraser of Kilmorack, *CAJ*, June 1975, 15; *Times*, 6 May 1975.
[217] Croft to Salisbury, 14 December 1933, Croft MSS, CAC, CRFT/1/18/Sa4.
[218] Younger to Long, 14 November 1920, Long MSS, Add.62425/58–61.
[219] Fraser to Steel-Maitland, 20 June 1930, Steel-Maitland MSS, GD193/120/3/428–9.
[220] Macnamara, *The Whistle Blows*, 127.
[221] Stonehaven to Baldwin, 31 January 1936, Baldwin MSS, 171/284–7; Principal Agent to Party Chairman, 23 October 1930, CPA, CCO/500/1/5.

Following the extension of the franchise in 1918, various new sections of Central Office were established, with Younger particularly devoting resources to the trade unionists.[222] However, 'as each new organisation became necessary, it was simply added to those already in existence'.[223] The result was a 'haphazard growth' of Central Office's activities and structure which 'resulted in general confusion and a lack of efficiency'.[224] When Davidson became Party Chairman in November 1926, he felt that Central Office was in need of rationalization; as an interim measure, he grouped its diverse sections under two headings, one of 'organisation' and the other of 'operations'.[225] In November 1927, he appointed a small committee of enquiry under the Deputy Chairman, Lord Stanley, which reported shortly before Christmas. It found that there was 'no complete co-ordinated organisation of the Office as a whole', that the Principal Agent was overloaded with day-to-day administration, and that there was 'insufficient financial control by senior officials'.[226] Its recommendations were put into effect at the start of 1928; the revised structure was clear and simple, with the multitude of activities grouped into three units. The Organisation Department dealt with candidates, speakers, constituency finance, the training of agents, the women's and trade unionists' wings, the youth organizations, and oversaw the Area Offices. It was headed by the Principal Agent, and Marjorie Maxse, head of the women's department since 1923, became his deputy with the title of Chief Organisation Officer.[227] The other main department contained all of the sections which dealt with publications and propaganda, and was the charge of the new post of Director of Publicity.[228] Supporting these departments was a third, comprising the accounting and clerical staff; this was the responsibility of the Office Controller, whose status was not quite equal with that of the other two chiefs. However, this plan was modified in 1929 when the Controller, Collingwood Hughes, transferred to oversee the establishment of the new educational college at Ashridge, after which his department was absorbed into the Principal Agent's.[229]

Neville Chamberlain made some modifications to this scheme during his Chairmanship in 1930–31. He found a lack of business methods and that financial control was still too loose, which were particular concerns with income shrinking due to the depression and the criticisms of Baldwin's leadership.[230] Lady Falmouth,

---

[222] Younger to Birkenhead, 23 February 1925, Baldwin MSS, 11/113–15.

[223] General Director to Party Chairman, 'Office reconstruction and reduction of expenditure', 30 July 1931, CPA, CCO/500/1/5.

[224] Chamberlain Ctte. Report, 9 March 1931, CPA, CCO/500/1/5.

[225] Ball to Strathcona, 17 May 1927, Davidson to Younger, 22 February 1928, Davidson to Nall-Cain, 8 December 1929, Davidson MSS, DAV/180, DAV/182, DAV/188.

[226] Central Office Reorganisation Ctte., report, 20 December 1927, CPA, CCO/500/1/4 and Davidson MSS, DAV/180.

[227] Monsell Ctte., memo by Chief Organisation Officer, 14 October 1937, CPA, CCO/500/1/7.

[228] The creation of such a position had been recommended by a report in 1924: McNeill to Baldwin, 21 May 1924, Baldwin MSS, 48/18–23. For the department's responsibilities, see Monsell Ctte., 'Publicity Department', 14 October 1937, CPA, CCO/500/1/7.

[229] Hicks to Davidson, covering letter to annual balance sheets, 3 June 1930, Davidson MSS, DAV/176; Hughes to Davidson, 28 June 1929, Baldwin MSS, 164/95–9.

[230] N. to I. Chamberlain, 10 August 1930, *NCDL*.

who worked with him as Vice-Chairman, later paid tribute to Chamberlain's contribution, which was 'not only in technical improvements, though these are great, but in a totally different spirit, and an altogether higher level of thought and atmosphere'.[231] Chamberlain set in motion several inquiries into the working of Central Office, and these fed into a final committee which he chaired himself.[232] Its most important conclusion was the need for a clearer chain of command, and, as a result, in 1931 the post of Principal Agent was renamed General Director and returned to its previous position of overall responsibility.[233] Initially, the new General Director's Department encompassed the finance and support staff as well, but this soon proved too unwieldy. In 1933 there was a final reshuffle which essentially restored Davidson's tripartite scheme, with the clerical and support sections grouped together as 'General Establishment' under the Chief Accountant, whilst the small National Union Secretary's office became autonomous.[234] This revision reduced the General Director's bureaucratic responsibilities but did not affect his overall authority; the Publicity Department continued as before, alongside a streamlined Organisation Department, which continued to be headed by Maxse. After five years' experience as Party Chairman, Stonehaven's view in 1936 was that further reform was unnecessary; similarly, in 1937 a committee chaired by the former Chief Whip, Bolton Eyres-Monsell (now Lord Monsell), examined the work of several departments and made only minor suggestions.[235] In fact, Davidson's basic structure was to remain in place for a further three decades after 1945.

Davidson was good at raising funds and had no reluctance about spending them, and during his Chairmanship the staff and activities of Central Office greatly expanded. In 1911 there had been only six men and a few female typists, but by 1928 there were 249 people working at Central Office and the Area Offices, with a further thirty-five staff speakers and organizers on retainers, making the unprecedented total of 284.[236] The cost of such a large establishment could not be sustained following the defeat of 1929 and the onset of the slump. Neville Chamberlain made a start during his Chairmanship in 1930–31, reducing expenditure and removing 'the tallest poppies'.[237] However, his successor, Lord Stonehaven, still found spending levels to be 'completely disproportionate to the scale of our income', and he was forced to make further substantial economies.[238] One part of this was the devolu-

---

[231] Falmouth to N. Chamberlain, 16 November 1931, Maxse to N. Chamberlain, 29 March 1931, NC, 7/11/24/8 & 21.

[232] Topping to N. Chamberlain, 'Re-organisation', 23 October 1930, CPA, CCO/500/1/5; report by Hill for the Chamberlain Ctte., 'Organisation of Conservative and Unionist Central Office', 15 December 1930, Templewood MSS, VI/3.

[233] Chamberlain Ctte. Report, 9 March 1931, CPA, CCO/500/1/5.

[234] Covering memo by Hicks, 12 April 1934, to annual balance sheets for 1933, CPA, FIN/5.

[235] Stonehaven to Baldwin, 31 January 1936, Baldwin MSS, 171/284–7; Monsell Ctte. reports, December 1937, CPA, CCO/500/1/8.

[236] Schedules to annual accounts, 1926, and 'Central Office Staff, Area Agents and Staff, Speakers and Organisers', c.February 1928, Davidson MSS, DAV/176, DAV/184.

[237] N. to H. Chamberlain, 14 February 1931, *NCDL*.

[238] Stonehaven to Steel-Maitland, 1 February 1932, Steel-Maitland MSS, GD193/120/3/138; there was a similar contraction of personnel in Scotland, SUA, WDC, 1 June 1932.

tion to the regional Areas, in 1932, of responsibility for funding the provision of speakers and grants of money and literature to the constituencies. However, as the largest part of the Central Office budget was personnel, the only way to reduce costs significantly was to shed staff; this included some long-serving and loyal officials, although the blow was usually softened by generous severance payments or pensions; in 1932, the latter reached nearly three times their 1925 level.[239] The substantial cuts of 1930–32 were unique during the period, and even here much of the reduction was achieved by natural wastage and voluntary departures.[240] After this, staff levels stabilized for the rest of the decade, and in 1936 a long-serving party accountant observed that 'generally speaking there are no dismissals'.[241]

Table 4.3. Number of Central Office and Area Office staff

This table shows the number of staff centrally employed in England and Wales who were in post on 31 December each year, as listed in the schedules to the audited accounts (for 1925–29, Davidson MSS, 175–6; for 1930–45, CPA, FIN/2–9 and Accn/2004/28). Before 1932, clerical staff in the Organisation (later Principal Agent's/General Director's) and Publicity Departments were included under those headings and cannot be differentiated; after 1932, all clerical and support staff were listed under the Establishment heading. Throughout the period, clerical staff in the Area Offices were not indicated as such, and were included in the general lists of shorthand and copy typists. However, a separate staff list from c.February 1928 indicates that there were three male and twenty-two female clerical staff in the Area Offices (Davidson MSS, 184); expenditure on the Area Offices was maintained during the 1930s, and a memo for the Monsell Ctte. in 1937 lists twenty-six clerical staff at the regional offices (Topping to Windlesham, 25 October 1937, CPA, CCO/500/1/7).

	1926	1928	1930	1932	1934	1936	1938	1940	1942	1944
Organization[a]	33	58	39	30	21	19	17	3	4	11
Publicity	35	50	47	27	23	25	23	3	5	8
Finance & Accounts	9	12	13	12	10	11	[b]18	1	3	6
Clerical	50	76	76	56	63	64	73	13	19	30
Support[c]	[d]–	17	15	14	15	13	14	5	3	5
TOTAL	127	213	190	139	132	132	145	25	34	60
Of which Male	61	91	78	61	47	50	47	10	8	18
Of which Female	66	122	112	78	85	82	98	15	26	42
Area Agents[e]	32	36	29	27	26	25	24	9	10	13

[a] Includes the Chairman's office, Labour section, youth sections, and National Union office.
[b] Includes seven staff of the new Treasurer's Department, working from separate premises.
[c] Sales & Supply section, warehouse, telephonists, tea kitchen, and maintenance.
[d] Staff are not identified in this way in the 1926 accounts schedules.
[e] Includes the London Department (to 1932) and three JIL regional organizers in 1928, but does not include the Scottish Whip's Office.

[239] See Appendix 4; for details, 'List of Central Office pensions and allowances', in Vice-Chairmen's Ctte. on the Publicity Department, report, June 1932, CPA, CCO/500/1/6.
[240] This was less the case with the speakers on retainers, where there were considerable cuts after the 1931 election: Edwards to Steel-Maitland, 1 July 1932, Steel-Maitland MSS, GD193/120/3/155.
[241] Bottome to Hicks, 'National Unionist Association: system as to payment of wages and salaries, engagement of staff, etc.', 29 June 1936, CPA, FIN/1.

The staff at Central Office handled a considerable volume of business: it was estimated that in 1925 some 370,000 letters and circulars had been despatched, together with 4,200 telegrams, and that around 11,000 callers had been received.[242] Gender roles followed the conventional pattern of the time: in 1934, all of the accounting department were male, as were the Enquiry Office (which dealt with MPs and local officials) and the warehouse staff; the head of Registry was male, but the rest of its staff and all of the General Office, the typists, the telephonists, and the tea kitchen were female. In the Publicity Department, nearly all of the literature and library personnel were male, but all of the press cuttings staff were female. However, principally due to the size and importance of the Conservative Party's female membership, nationally in the Women's Department at Central Office, regionally as Deputy Area Agents, and locally as salaried women organizers, there were more opportunities for women to attain senior and more autonomous positions than in other contemporary institutions or businesses. The Conservative Party was a good employment prospect for men and women: at all levels, it paid quite well; it offered work that was more interesting than that of other large offices (including a sense of being at the centre of affairs); and it gave considerable security of tenure.

The result was a notable continuity of staff, with many senior and middle-level employees serving for long periods. As well as Topping (Principal Agent and General Director 1928–45), there was Joseph Ball (head of the Publicity Department 1927–29 and Director of the Research Department 1929–45), Sir Patrick Gower (deputy head of Publicity 1928–29, and head from then until February 1939), and A. T. Rivers (Chief Accountant and Establishment Officer 1911–45). Below them were staff such as George Godwin, Secretary of the National Union from 1921 to 1938; G. E. M. Walker of the Labour and Speakers' sections from 1921 to 1939; Percy Cohen, who worked in the Library and Information sections from 1911 to 1960;[243] and A. G. Mitchell, national organizer of the Junior Imperial League from 1924 to 1939, who returned from war service to become Chief Accountant in 1945. Durability was not a male preserve: Miss M. Muirhead was in charge of the General Office from before 1925 until 1945; Dorothy Spencer was secretary to the national women's committee in 1927–39 and returned to work for the party after 1945, and Marjorie Maxse worked in the women's department and then as Deputy Principal Agent and Chief Organization Officer from 1923 until a wartime absence, after which she served as a Party Vice-Chairman in 1944–51. The consequent advantages of experience, camaraderie, and practised teamwork were significant contributors to the widespread reputation of the Conservative headquarters as a well-oiled machine. Even with the reductions of the early 1930s, the number of staff was still substantial, and the national and regional organization remained a formidable force. However, on the outbreak of the Second World War many staff left for military service or wartime administrative work. There were plans to evacuate to premises at 15 Gunnersby Avenue in Ealing, but the 'depleted staff' were 'exceedingly busy' in autumn 1939, and in the end only the Finance Department was relocated.[244]

[242] *CAJ*, February 1926, 40.
[243] *CAJ*, February 1960, 19; Gower to Fry, 5 April 1935, Baldwin MSS, 170/83–4.
[244] Hacking to Hicks, 9 October 1939, CPA, FIN/19.

Central Office had a range of functions, the most vital of which was the brief and intense period during which it was the headquarters of a general election campaign. Then, even more than at less crucial moments, it was the nexus at which efficiency, expertise, and resources made a difference. However, matters did not always run smoothly; a visitor to Central Office in November 1923 found a state of 'chaos and confusion', and concluded that 'the Conservatives were as unready for the fight as everyone else'.[245] Younger noted that 'the Office is very much inclined to lose its head at election times'; he had to come out of retirement and take charge during the 1923 campaign, when Jackson was preoccupied with fighting his own constituency.[246] This was less of an issue in 1929, as, with a Home Counties seat, Davidson was able to be at Central Office for seven or eight hours a day, whilst in 1931 and 1935 the Chairman was not an MP. The Party Chairman and his staff relieved the Leader from having to manage the details of the campaign, and made the arrangements for the speaking tours of the prominent figures. Central Office also gathered intelligence, monitored the campaign, and provided the constituencies with propaganda materials and guidance.[247] It had a similar supporting role in by-elections, arranging and financing the assistance of agents and workers from other seats, which Younger estimated at £600–700 per contest in 1919.[248] In the Norwood by-election of 1935, it undertook the first telephone canvass, calling every voter who was in the telephone directory—in this period, a fairly select middle-class group.[249]

The co-ordinating role of Central Office was particularly important during periods of coalition, and it handled the detail of the electoral pacts before the campaign, and of liaison during it; in both cases, the Office could take a tougher line in preserving the party's interests without involving the Leader directly and thereby complicating relationships in the Cabinet.[250] Ironically, it always had to deal with suspicions from the grass roots that it was being overgenerous, with accusations of 'selling the pass' to the Coalition Liberals in 1918.[251] The persistent feeling in 1918–22 that, despite Younger's best efforts, the Lloyd George Liberals had too much of the upper hand (although, of course, that was not their perspective) added to the strains upon the Coalition. There were difficulties over the Samuelite Liberals in the 1931 general election, although Samuel himself paid tribute to the efforts of Central Office to overcome local problems.[252] During the remainder of the National Government, matters were generally harmonious, despite a series of

[245] Headlam diary, 8 November 1923.
[246] Younger to Davidson, 18 February 1928, Davidson MSS, DAV/182.
[247] 'Synopsis of confidential reports by Unionist Central Office Agents on the progress of the Coalition campaign', 3 December 1918, Bonar Law MSS, BL/95/2; Younger circular to candidates, 8 November 1922, Davidson MSS, DAV/133.
[248] Younger to Bonar Law, 12 December 1919, Bonar Law MSS, BL/98/5/11.
[249] Topping to Lloyd, 8 April 1935, Baldwin MSS, 51/157–8.
[250] Younger to Derby, 6 November 1922, Derby MSS, 31/2.
[251] 'Coalition Arrangements re Seats', Younger to Bonar Law, 26 September 1918, Bonar Law MSS, BL/95/2; Clitheroe CA, Exec., 13 and 21 November 1918.
[252] Gower to Baldwin, 15 October 1931, Baldwin MSS, 45/44–6; Stonehaven to Baldwin, 23 October 1931, Baldwin MSS, 45/103–4; Samuel to Baldwin, 26 October 1931, Baldwin MSS, 45/123–4.

complaints from MacDonald to Baldwin about Central Office.[253] These frictions were fairly minor and from March 1933 relations were effectively managed by the National Co-ordinating Committee, a forum for the managers of the three parties which was dominated by Central Office. Of course, its creation led to a wave of concern and grumbling from the Conservative rank and file that the party's sovereignty was being eroded, but these fears proved misplaced; after the 1935 victory, the proposal to continue its existence was uncontroversial.

Between general elections, Central Office provided a range of services to the Leader and leadership. These ranged from the clerical (arranging meetings, press releases of ministerial speeches) to the strategic, as it was 'the best centre for collecting information'.[254] Some of this was obtained by clandestine means, especially during the anxieties of the 1920s over Labour's rapid rise and possible extremism. Much of this was masterminded by Ball, using his background and connections in counter-espionage; it included the placing of undercover agents, or perhaps the suborning of staff, at the printers who produced Labour's leaflets and even, possibly, in the Labour Party's headquarters, which gave the Conservatives advance notice of their opponents' plans.[255] Information on public opinion and electoral prospects was collected at Area level and by the heads of Central Office sections, and passed upwards by the Chairman.[256] Central Office provided estimates and forecasts of election results, and views on the best timing of a dissolution.[257] It had the expertise to advise on the effects of extending the franchise, on proposals for redistribution or proportional representation, and on lesser issues such as a back-bench bill for the relief of Roman Catholics.[258] It also monitored the mood of the grass roots and reported on this to the Leader, and in that respect Topping's memo to the Chairman in February 1931 was unusual only in its conclusion.[259] An important reciprocal element was the dissemination of guidance to the constituencies, informally and by circular letters from the Chairman. Younger's famous message in the January 1922 'election scare' was just one amongst many, most of

---

[253] MacDonald to Baldwin, 7 October 1931, Stonehaven to Baldwin, 8 January 1932, Stonehaven and De La Warr corres., July–August 1932, De La Warr to MacDonald, 15 November 1934, Baldwin MSS, 45/25, 51/128, 46/37–58, 46/110–13.

[254] Steel-Maitland to Baldwin, 4 May 1925, Baldwin MSS, 160/160–2.

[255] Reports to Ball, May 1928–June 1929, Ball MSS, MSS.Eng.c.6653/5–107; James, *Memoirs of a Conservative*, 272.

[256] Stonehaven to Baldwin, 18 September 1931, Baldwin MSS, 44/148–9.

[257] Fraser to A. Chamberlain, 31 December 1921, AC, 32/4/1a, 1b, 2; Central Office election forecast of 1923 result, Baldwin MSS, 35/136–7; Davidson to Baldwin, enclosing memo by Topping, 12 October 1928, Davidson MSS, DAV/185; Gower to Baldwin, 1 August 1935, Baldwin MSS, 47/103–8; 'Area Agents' forecasts, 1945 election', CPA, CCO/4/2/61.

[258] Central Office memo on redistribution, 5 March 1926, on the franchise, 6 April 1927, Baldwin MSS, 52/39–70, 138–42; Maclachlan to Wicks, 28 January 1926, Baldwin MSS, 52/23.

[259] Party opinion on Home Rule, 26 April 1918, Bonar Law MSS, BL/83/3/11; Blain, report of responses to a circular sent to local Labour Advisory Cttes., 16 July 1926, Baldwin MSS, 11/257–349; Uxbridge CA, Council, 23 October 1926; Deputy Director of Publicity to Party Chairman, 11 June 1929, Baldwin MSS, 37/2; Stonehaven to Baldwin, 'Slum clearance and compensation', 21 November, Stonehaven to Baldwin, 4 December 1934, Baldwin MSS, 25/30–5, 169/336. On the correctness of Topping's action, see the comments of Davidson and Cunliffe-Lister, oral history interviews in Cohen, 'Disraeli's Child', 564, 574, Cohen MSS, CPA, CRD/731.

which dealt with lesser but still awkward issues.[260] Central Office could also attempt to stimulate constituency opinion, especially for an active campaign such as over the Trade Disputes Act in 1927 or the 'Home and Empire' campaign of 1930. In the various internal party tensions over tariffs, India, and appeasement from 1927 to 1939, it was understood that it was the duty of the Central Office staff and Area Agents not to act as neutral figures, akin to civil servants, but actively 'to further the policy of the Leader and his colleagues, and to do all that lies in our power to secure support for that policy'.[261]

The other essential role of Central Office was to provide services to the constituencies.[262] These were many and varied, each of individual value and cumulatively contributing to the morale, efficiency, and electoral success of the party. As a long-serving official at the Central Office observed, these were 'all activities probably humdrum in themselves but very much the life and soul of intelligent political organisation'.[263] One of the original and most important of these functions was in helping constituencies to find suitable candidates, and vice versa. In this period, Conservative associations were under no obligation to choose from a central list and often selected candidates from their local aspirants (see Chapter 3). However, when these were not suitable or forthcoming, particularly in the marginal and weaker seats, an association would usually approach Central Office for suggestions. For this reason, Central Office kept details of applicants, and seeking an interview there became recognized as a first step to becoming an MP.[264] In the late 1930s, the practice began of seeking formal references for prospective candidates, and in 1942 of doing so also for their spouse.[265] There was an element of management, in that party officials would naturally seek to promote those whom they viewed as good candidates, the criteria for which included orthodoxy and loyalty as well as ability, experience, and (preferably) resources; they would also discourage the adoption of the troublesome.[266] A crucial part of helping the difficult and marginal seats to find strong candidates was the provision of funds, and many candidates received assistance with their election expenses in whole or in part. Up to 1929 this was paid directly to the candidate, 'usually without the knowledge of any of the constituency officials', but from 1931 the

---

[260] Younger circular to CAs, 14 October 1919, Bonar Law MSS, BL/96/1; Topping and Maxse to CO Agents, 20 December 1929, Baldwin MSS, 57/13; Stonehaven circular to CAs, 30 May 1931, circular to CAs, 23 July 1934, Baldwin MSS, 129/174, 133/229–30.

[261] Topping to Central Office Agents, 'India', 23 May 1933, CPA, CCO/4/1/80; Long to Bonar Law, 26 May 1917, Bonar Law MSS, BL/81/6/18.

[262] NU Conf., 1923, comments by the Principal Agent.

[263] Cohen, 'Disraeli's Child', 278, Cohen MSS, CPA, CRD/731.

[264] Corres. from Central Office, July–December 1938, Cheltenham CA; Headlam diary, 1923–24; H. K. Hales, *The Road to Westminster and My Impressions of Parliament* (n.d. but 1936), 29–32.

[265] See correspondence from Hacking to Derby, 1936–39, and for an early example of requesting information about the candidate's wife, Dugdale to Derby, 3 April 1942, Derby MSS, 31/6, 31/7; Dugdale to Churchill, 'Candidates forms', 29 February 1944, Churchill MSS, CAC, CHAR/2/507/63–4, with example copy, 68–9.

[266] Memo by Bowyer on his work as Deputy Party Chairman since appointment in March 1930, 1 December 1930, Baldwin MSS, 48/187–92; Hacking to Derby, 1 November 1939, Derby MSS, 31/6.

amounts were considerably reduced and given as a partial contribution to the local association's election fund.[267] The primary purpose of such subsidies was to mobilize the most effective force for the electoral battlefield; the recipient candidate or association might be grateful, but, as Topping acknowledged in 1930, this did not in practice give Central Office any effective power or control.[268]

The Organisation Department assisted the constituencies in other practical ways.[269] Another long-standing service was the provision of its paid speakers, who travelled into the regions to take many of the smaller meetings or support local speakers.[270] In 1927, an average year in the mid-term of a parliament, male staff speakers addressed 11,695 meetings and women spoke at 6,203.[271] There were also the missioners, whose skill was in door-to-door canvassing, and who could help an association increase its members and income. Through the Area Offices, the central organization gave advice to constituencies on the appointment of agents, and usually had some influence over the choice; there was also a 'black list' of former agents who had in some way defaulted and should not be employed. From the 1920s, Central Office sought to encourage associations to appoint only agents who had received certification; it arranged the training, often providing subsidies during this and some initial placements, and conducted the examination process in partnership with the agents' society. There were other initiatives in the 1930s, such as the subsidiary company National Tours, which provided travel services for constituencies undertaking excursions—some of which were on an ambitious scale.[272]

Throughout the interwar period, much organizing work was devoted to the women's, youth, and labour sections. The Women's Department was established in 1919 and grew extensively over the next decade into an effective and smooth-running machine.[273] Further effort was applied to promoting the Junior Imperial League: under Davidson, Central Office provided a full-time organizer and financed the national expenditure with a generous grant that was actually 'greatly in excess of its needs'.[274] In the late 1930s, following the report of the Fraser Committee, a pool of regional organizers were appointed; however, their work ceased when the League suspended activity at the start of the war.[275] There was a similar pattern with the Young Britons' movement: in 1938 Central Office was

---

[267] Financial schedules, 1929 election, Davidson MSS, DAV/187; Dugdale, 'Memorandum on Party Finance', March 1943, CPA, CCO/500/3/2.
[268] Principal Agent to Party Chairman, 23 October 1930, CPA, CCO/500/1/5.
[269] Monsell Ctte., memo by Chief Organisation Officer, 14 October 1937, report on Speakers', Education, and Labour Departments, December 1937, CPA, CCO/500/1/7–8.
[270] Report by Hill for the Chamberlain Ctte., 'Organisation of Conservative and Unionist Central Office', 15 December 1930, Templewood MSS, VI/3; N. Chamberlain, circular letter to MPs on the reorganization of the Speakers Dept., 9 March 1931, Kennet MSS, 16/5.
[271] Maclachlan, 'Summarised Report on Conservative Organisation at Central Office and in the Constituencies during 1927', 30 December 1927, Baldwin MSS, 53/118–49.
[272] National Tours, report of manager on 1937 season, CPA, CCO/4/1/83; Monsell Ctte., report on National Tours, November 1937, CPA, CCO/500/1/8.
[273] 'Central Office, Women's Branch: functions', c.October 1930, Templewood MSS, VI/3; Chamberlain Ctte. Report, 9 March 1931, CPA, CCO/500/1/5.
[274] JIL, Fin., 23 May 1928.
[275] Palmer Ctte. Report, 14 December 1943, 4–5, CPA, CCO/500/1/10.

funding nine female Area Organisers for this, at a total salary cost of £1,850.[276] In the mid-1920s, Linlithgow, as Deputy Chairman, began steps in 'the rather delicate task of establishing adequate touch with undergraduate life in all the English universities': this later became the party's student organization.[277]

A particular effort was devoted to reaching out to Conservative trade unionists. The establishment of the National Union's Labour Sub-committee in 1919 was supported by the creation of the Labour Department at Central Office. Although its staff was not large, the labour movement was the focus of much Central Office endeavour in the 1920s. Speakers and literature were often provided free or at subsidized rates, and frequent circulars exhorted the formation of Labour Advisory Committees in every constituency. However, this remained patchy, and outside the main industrial districts it ran into the sands of constituency resistance and apathy. The general failure of the trade unionist organization was a clear example of Central Office's lack of power to direct and control the constituencies. Despite the application of resources—and the frequent endorsement of the labour movement's importance in resolutions at every level—Central Office was unable to make things happen. In the early 1920s, few counties or regions had the resources or willingness to employ salaried organizers devoted to the labour movement, and only Glamorgan, Lancashire, and Northumberland are known to have done so.[278] Even these initiatives languished after a while, and for most of the interwar period the activities of the local and regional Labour Advisory Committees were supported by a single designated member of staff at Central Office, working-class paid speakers provided through the Speakers Department, and propaganda literature produced by the Publicity Department.

Relations between Central Office and the constituencies were always influenced by the sensitive issue of local autonomy, and were a complex web of connections and mutual dependencies.[279] As Lady Bridgeman commented, 'if the constituencies were thought to be too much "run" from Headquarters the loss to the Party would be greater than the gain'.[280] Central Office was always careful to acknowledge its lack of control, and in particular that it could 'only request' a constituency not to run a candidate, whatever the wider picture.[281] As Stonehaven declared in 1934: 'we have not any seats at all. They belong to the constituencies.'[282] However, local independence was, in practice, diluted to some extent by the need for co-operation and assistance.[283] Safe seats could and sometimes did stand aloof, and in the early 1930s the wealthy county of Sussex was unique in opting out of any wider finan-

---

[276] 'Young Britons Area Organisers and their salaries', 1938, CPA, CCO/506/7/4.
[277] Linlithgow (Deputy Party Chairman) to Baldwin, 9 March 1925, Baldwin MSS, 160/101–2.
[278] NU Labour Advisory Ctte., 13 July and 15 November 1920; Lancashire PD, Labour Ctte., 1918–20 passim.
[279] Younger to Derby, 3 November 1922, Derby MSS, 31/2.
[280] Papers circulated to members of the NU Exec., Sub-ctte on Rules & Organisation, 27 September 1929, Steel-Maitland MSS, GD193/121/5/36–51.
[281] 'Coalition Arrangements re Seats', Younger to Bonar Law, 26 September 1918, Bonar Law MSS, BL/95/2.
[282] NU Central Council, 28 March 1934.
[283] Accrington CA, Emergency Ctte., 22 May 1928.

cial and administrative links.[284] However, it was widely recognized that such isolationism was unhealthy and ultimately led to decay. Even the wealthiest seats used the Central Office services of speakers and literature, and agents increasingly relied upon national resources for the latter. The Area Agents were often advisors on the selection of agents and even candidates, and, if effective and tactful in their methods—as many of them were—they could acquire considerable influence in their region. The regional and national headquarters could mediate in the disputes which sometimes split associations, although they had to be invited to do so. In practice, nearly all of the time the party machine worked with local chairmen and agents in a considerable degree of harmony; there was, of course, a certain amount of grumbling, but this should not be overrated. Even during a period of great internal stress, an experienced Area Agent concluded that Central Office 'carries great weight, and is looked up to in the bulk of the constituencies throughout the country'.[285]

In normal circumstances, a local association had the right to expect support and this was not discretionary: up to 1935, Central Office was obliged to assist any officially adopted candidate, provided they adhered to party policy.[286] Thus, support was withdrawn from the candidate in the Twickenham by-election of 1929 but—despite strong pressure from Beaverbrook—not from the candidate at Nottingham Central in 1930, because the former departed from the official line and the latter sheltered behind it.[287] Even after the creation of the SACC in 1935, the Party Chairman's assumption was that 'the Leader must support a candidate adopted by a local association, never mind...how improperly the candidate and his association had behaved'.[288] It was also the case that assistance might be appreciated but it did not give control, and it was noted that Central Office support for the London region had not done so.[289] It is revealing that when the leadership sought to sway opinion in the party on India, an issue where there were deep divisions, Central Office could not be used overtly—instead, a separate body, the Union of Britain and India, had to be created as an ostensibly spontaneous development and kept at apparent arm's length.[290] The idea that Central Office was a disciplinary tool was almost entirely a myth, although it was a persistent and enduring one; in reality, its role and powers were strictly circumscribed. A candi-

---

[284] Comments by Topping at Essex & Middlesex Area, Joint Exec., 12 September 1932.

[285] Thornton (COA South East Area), 'Central Office Agents and their work', n.d., c.October 1930, CPA, CCO/500/1/5.

[286] When East Dorset CA decided to nominate a candidate in 1931 despite being urged not to, 'that settled the matter so far as this Office was concerned': Stonehaven to Croft, 20 October 1931, Croft MSS, CAC, CRFT/1/19/St2.

[287] N. Chamberlain to Ashley, 1 October 1930, Ashley MSS, BR/74; Bonar Law to Bayly, 5 November 1922, Bonar Law MSS, BL/110/3.

[288] Headlam diary, 25 April 1940.

[289] Topping to N. Chamberlain, 'Re-organisation', 23 October 1930, CPA, CCO/500/1/5.

[290] In fact, it had a close working relationship with both senior figures at Central Office and Ministers and their staff at the India Office: UBI correspondence 1933–35, Thompson MSS, F137/49; Morley to Tweedy, 15 October 1934, Butler MSS, F73/66–67; Davidson to Davis, 26 April 1933, Gower to Davidson, 25 May 1933, Tweedy to Davidson, 10 December 1934, Davidson MSS, DAV/201, DAV/220.

date or MP who pulled their weight was an asset not lightly to be discarded, and they rarely came under any deliberate pressure; if there was orthodoxy, it was largely voluntary. As the Party Vice-Chairman for candidates assured one local chairman: 'it was our duty to carry out as far as possible the wishes of the constituency association'.[291]

CENTRAL OFFICE: THE PROPAGANDA AND EDUCATION ROLE

The departmental structure established in 1928 was based upon a distinction between organization (which was concerned with existing supporters) and propaganda (which aimed to win converts to the cause).[292] The latter was acknowledged to be crucial in the new mass democracy; the old focus on electoral registration was no longer important, whilst the size and more educated nature of the electorate made communication the highest priority. To achieve this, the Publicity Department had two main functions: 'the collection of information', and 'the dissemination of policy through literature and the press'.[293] The first of these was the responsibility of the Library, which had both a substantial collection of books and extensive files collated by its press cuttings section. It was much more than an information repository: it monitored the parliamentary division lists and the activities of the opposition parties, it provided an enquiry service for MPs and constituencies, and it published several briefing and reference works. *Hints for Speakers* gave fortnightly practical guidance on topical issues, *Gleanings and Memoranda* was a bulky monthly compilation of public statements and press reports, and the *Constitutional Yearbook* was an annual bible of lists, statistics, and guidance on electoral law; each of these had circulations of between one and two thousand.[294] The second function had two aspects, one of which was relations with the press and the other was producing the party's own publications and propaganda. For the former, the Publicity Department fostered a close working relationship with the major newspapers' lobby correspondents, who were 'in almost constant telephonic communication' and were also provided with a daily written digest.[295] Of particular effectiveness was a practice begun by Neville Chamberlain when Party Chairman in 1930–31, of holding a weekly informal briefing meeting with

---

[291] Cheltenham CA, Windlesham to Pruen (chairman), 29 July 1938, and similar assurances were reported from the Party Chairman, Joint Meeting of Men's Exec. & Women's Management Ctte., 7 July 1937.
[292] Central Office Reorganisation Committee, report, 20 December 1927, Davidson MSS, DAV/180.
[293] Vice-Chairmen's Ctte. on the Publicity Department, report, June 1932, CPA, CCO/500/1/6.
[294] General Director to Party Chairman, 'Office reconstruction and reduction of expenditure', 30 July 1931, CPA, CCO/500/1/5; 'Publicity Department', report by Ball, in 'Summarised Report on Conservative Organisation at Central Office and in the Constituencies during 1927', 30 December 1927, Baldwin MSS, 53/108–17.
[295] Vice-Chairmen's Ctte. on the Publicity Department, report, June 1932, CPA, CCO/500/1/6.

the lobby journalists. The department also sent out draft articles and notes, which were used by around 160 provincial newspapers, partly through a front organization called Lobby Press Services.[296]

The Publicity Department was responsible 'almost entirely on its own resources' for producing posters, pamphlets, and leaflets, and a range of journals.[297] Posters were a keynote element in general elections, as with the famous 'Safety First' slogan in 1929. That campaign had the longest gestation period, and was marked with a range of striking and colourful posters.[298] The timing of the dissolutions of 1922, 1923, 1924, and 1931 was much less predictable, and in some cases there was little warning. The Publicity Department could respond quickly, changing captions to read 'Vote National' in 1931, producing new posters for the tariff policy in 1923, and attacking the Russian treaty in 1924. A total of 464,614 posters were produced in 1929 and, even with short notice, 326,000 were used in 1923 and 222,000 in 1931. However, the main form of publicity was leaflets, and enormous numbers of these were used during the general election campaigns: 18.5 million in 1922, 26 million in 1923, 36 million in 1924, and a staggering 85.1 million in 1929 (which followed 16.5 million in the four months prior to the dissolution).[299] Pamphlets and leaflets were also frequently issued between general elections, with the number circulated rising from 1,485,700 during 1923 to 9,748,153 in 1928. They were particularly employed in the 1920s, with 1,246 items published between the end of 1918 and the end of 1929; in the decade from then until the outbreak of the Second World War, there were a further 673 items.[300] Although the quantities circulated in the 1930s diminished to a level comparable to the earlier 1920s, with 23.5 million leaflets printed in 1931, this still represented a considerable output. The reduction was due partly to financial factors and partly to participation in the National Government—party propaganda was restrained by the need not to conflict with its non-partisan image, and from 1934 the government's propaganda effort was co-ordinated by the National Publicity Bureau. However, after the outbreak of war, the production and circulation of propaganda almost entirely ceased, with just a handful of leaflets in 1943–44 and a small number for the 1945 general election.

The Conservative Party's various journals were focused primarily upon its existing membership. The principal monthly magazine of the early 1920s, *The Popular View*, was reconstituted as *Man in the Street* in 1924. During the 1924–28 period, for which there are detailed monthly figures, its distribution was consistently in the range of 100,000 to 110,000 copies. The separate journal for women, *Home and*

---

[296] Vice-Chairmen's Ctte. on the Publicity Department, report, June 1932, CPA, CCO/500/1/6; Monsell Ctte. memo, 'Publicity Department', 14 October 1937, CPA, CCO/500/1/7.
[297] 'Conservative Central Office Publicity Department', memos 'no. 1', 'no. 2', and 'no. 3', 7 July 1930, Templewood MSS, VI/3; *CAJ*, February 1926, 40–2.
[298] Ball, *Dole Queues and Demons*, 29–43. 'Safety First' had previously been used effectively as a leaflet slogan: NU leaflets 2022 (1921), 2066 (1922), 2805 (1928).
[299] NU Exec. Report to Central Council, 24 February 1925; NU Central Council Report to Conference, 1928–29.
[300] These figures are calculated from the identifying number which each item was given; however, an effective leaflet could be reproduced on a later occasion, so the number of different titles was not actually as great as this.

Politics, began as a supplement of this but by December 1928 was considerably outselling it, with a circulation of 214,400.[301] However, financial stringency led to their amalgamation in 1930 into *Home and Empire*, a substitute which did not have as much appeal to women members. These and other publications were sold in bulk to the constituencies to distribute (in the less affluent cases, at subsidized rates or sometimes given free of charge); as recipients were encouraged to pass their copies on to non-members, they are likely to have reached an even larger audience. Some of the wealthier constituencies created 'localized' versions of these magazines by enclosing them within locally printed covers and outer pages, and distributing them under their own title. By 1927, there were fifty-two such editions of *Man in the Street* and seventy-three of *Home and Politics*.[302] The other monthly productions included a smaller propaganda sheet introduced in 1924 for 'the less educated class of voter', titled *The Elector* (in 1926–28 this had a circulation generally between 170,000 and 200,000), and the journals of the youth wings.[303] The Junior Imperial League's gazette *The Imp* (renamed *Torchbearer* in the late 1930s) increased its circulation from 11,860 in December 1925 to 30,000 three years later, whilst by 1928 sales of the *Young Briton* were around 16,000. In early 1939, *The Elector* was replaced by a monthly news-sheet entitled *The Onlooker*; perhaps appropriately, this was the only publication produced regularly during the Second World War.[304]

Under the direction of Joseph Ball (1927–29) and then Sir Patrick Gower (1929–39), the Publicity Department was particularly innovative in supplementing traditional forms of paper propaganda with new media and technology. This was at its most effective, and had the greatest impact, in the use of film. With the assistance offered by the film producer Albert Clavering,[305] the party made its own propaganda films to a high level of technical competence.[306] The delivery of these to large audiences was achieved by means of a fleet of specially constructed cinema vans, whose operation was subsidized by Central Office.[307] From 1927 onwards, these toured the country, accompanied by a staff speaker; in rural districts particularly they were a novelty and entertainment which could draw a large crowd of people who would not otherwise have been likely to attend a political meeting.[308] They were greatly valued by the constitu-

[301] NU Exec. reports to Central Council, 1924–28.
[302] NU Exec. Report to Central Council, 28 June 1927; *CAJ*, August 1931, 187–9; October 1938, 241–3. For surviving examples, see *Bedford Division Monthly Gazette* (1925–39), *Llanelly Division Man in the Street* (1925–28), *Uxbridge Division Review* (1927–39), *Wallasey Review* (1929–31), and *Wellingborough Division Monthly Magazine* (1926–31), all at British Library; *Northampton Conservative Journal* (1927–39), Northamptonshire RO; *The Torbay Standard* (1926–32), Torquay CA.
[303] NU Exec. Report to Central Council, 1 July 1924.
[304] NU Exec. Report to Central Council, 30 March 1939, 4 April 1940, 27 March 1941; Topping to Hacking, 26 June 1940, NC, 8/21/19.
[305] Gower to Fry, 5 April 1935, Baldwin MSS, 170/83–6.
[306] Draft script for film on Disraeli, *c.*November 1930, Gower to Fry, 10 September 1931, Baldwin MSS, 166/8–20; T. J. Hollins, 'The Conservative Party and film propaganda between the wars', *English Historical Review*, 96 (1981), 359–69; J. Ramsden, 'Baldwin and film', 126–43.
[307] Principal Agent to Party Chairman, 'Film Propaganda', 29 May 1930, CPA, CCO/4/1/37.
[308] 'Report on Tour of Daylight Cinema Van, April–November 1926', Baldwin MSS, 48/74–9; Wells CA, Finance Ctte., 30 September 1927.

encies, who considered them to be the most effective form of propaganda. From 1930 they were operated by the Conservative Films Association, which was run by Clavering on a block grant from Central Office.[309] In 1934 and 1935, working under the aegis of the National Publicity Bureau, the cinema vans conducted a series of 'very successful' campaigns in the approach to the general election, and they remained in constant demand by local associations up to the outbreak of war.[310] The party was also able to exert some influence on the content of the newsreels shown in conventional cinemas, and for the 1929 election had paid attention to the developing strategies of the advertising industry and employed one of its leading firms, S. H. Benson, to prepare posters and publicity.[311]

If propaganda was the key theme of the 1920s, that of the following decade was 'political education'.[312] This was something different: it was directed towards the party's own supporters, and aimed to raise their political awareness and equip them to refute Socialist arguments on the doorstep. As early as 1921, 'summer schools' were launched to foster the political awareness of party members.[313] More centralized efforts to promote political education began in the late 1920s, partly under the impetus of Davidson and partly through the efforts of the popular author and Conservative MP, John Buchan.[314] Formal organization began under the latter in January 1928, and the Education Department remained important until, like many other parts of Central Office, it went into hibernation at the outbreak of war. In the 1930s its work was supported by the establishment of education committees at Area level, and by the creation of a specialist advisory committee in the National Union. It became an elaborate—and expensive—structure through the development of the party's own national educational institutions. The first initiative was the Stott College, which was created to support the trade unionists' organization. To provide its members with the necessary training, Sir Phillip Stott, a wealthy businessman who was an early member of the National Union Labour Committee, offered the use of a country house at Overstone in Northamptonshire for a nominal rent.[315] The Stott College opened in April 1923 with a series of fortnightly courses running through to September. However, few wage-earners could afford to attend for such a long period, whilst the cost of subsidizing more than the occasional student was possible only for the wealthier constituencies—which were generally far removed from the industrial areas, and had the least incentive. The problem of

---

[309] NU Exec., 8 December 1931; Monsell Ctte., 'Publicity Department', 14 October 1937, CPA, CCO/500/1/7, f.5.
[310] Stonehaven to Derby, 9 October 1934, Derby MSS, 31/5; Memo by Party Chairman, 11 January 1937, CPA, CCO/4/1/37.
[311] Ball to N. Chamberlain, 'Some Notes and Suggestions about Propaganda', 14 April 1934, NC, 8/21/9; 'Publicity Department organisation, no. 1', 7 July 1930, Templewood MSS, VI/3.
[312] Central Office, *Political Education* (1934); Central Office, *Study Circles* (1934).
[313] *CAJ*, October 1921, 14–16.
[314] Buchan to Baldwin, 5 January 1928, Ball to Waterhouse, 10 January 1928, Baldwin MSS, 53/76–7, 97.
[315] NU Labour Ctte., 10 July 1922.

recruiting sufficient students resulted in the introduction of shorter courses and the widening of access to all sections of the party, and attendance rose to 1,186 in 1927. However, the college was too small to be effective as the educational centre for the party as a whole. The Party Chairman, Davidson, was a keen advocate of the educational work and at his most effective in raising large donations from business supporters. He conceived the idea of establishing a substantial facility as a permanent memorial to Bonar Law (to whom he had been close), and he carried the project through with enthusiasm and determination. Davidson raised £200,000 from several wealthy businessmen (half coming from a single donor, Urban Broughton), and the estate of Ashridge, which was in his own Hertfordshire constituency, was purchased in 1928. The building work required to make it suitable for its new role took longer than expected, but in July 1929 Baldwin formally opened the Bonar Law Memorial College.[316]

The college was an independent institution, owned and overseen by its own Trust and Board of Governors. The latter were drawn from senior party figures who were sympathetic to its aims and methods, and Baldwin took an active interest between his retirement from the leadership in 1937 and the outbreak of war. Ashridge operated under its own Director, Sir Reginald Hoskins, and employed younger academics and journalists as part-time lecturers; one of the keenest of these was the historian Arthur Bryant. Its endowment meant that it did not draw on national party funds, but, to meet the costs, a fee was charged for most courses.[317] These were usually of a week or a fortnight, and focused upon a specific topic. The approach was explicitly not partisan or propagandist; in the words of one attender, the college aimed 'at providing some grasp of the fundamentals and an appetite for further knowledge', an approach which was not always appreciated by more practically oriented party stalwarts.[318] Davidson's ambition was to equip the students intellectually, acknowledging 'the many-sidedness of truth', and to inculcate a spirit of service.[319] There were courses for particular groups such the Junior Imperial League, and, on one occasion, for the wives of MPs and parliamentary candidates. Ashridge also became the venue for the training courses for agents and women organizers, and these were an important feature of its work by the late 1930s. However, it was less effective in reaching the voluntary party membership, as the time and cost involved in taking residential courses at a national centre remained a barrier to enrolment, and from the start 'there were far too few weekly wage-earners'.[320] Constituencies which had some surplus income often subsidized

---

[316] J. C. C. Davidson, 'The foundation of Ashridge', *Ashridge Journal*, 8 (December 1931), 49–50.

[317] *Ashridge: The Bonar Law College: Session 1931*, NU leaflet 3244 (1931). The gardens were open to the public on certain days and some funds were raised from admission and providing teas; in 1938 over 9,000 people visited: Bonar Law Memorial College (Ashridge), Governing Body, 25 October 1938.

[318] Graham, 'The constituencies and Ashridge', 19–20; SUA, Exec., 21 February 1934.

[319] Davidson's speech notes, 'Ashridge: what it means', February 1937, Davidson MSS, DAV/229.

[320] Bonar Law Memorial College (Ashridge), Governing Body, 29 November 1929; Middleton & Prestwich CA, F&GP, 30 November 1933.

a deserving active member who could not otherwise afford it, but this did not provide very many students. By the late 1930s, the attendance at Ashridge was a mixture of the most politically committed and intellectually minded party members and those who had the necessary resources and leisure; from amongst the better-off, this was particularly the young, the retired, and women. Ashridge remained a rather exclusive experience for a minority, upon whom its combination of intense discussion and collegial sociability often made a lasting impression. The bond was perpetuated by the 'Ashridge circles' which were formed in some constituencies by its alumni.[321] These were debating groups with a social role, supporting and encouraging recruitment to the college; in some cases, they also acted as the local political education committee. They provided much of the readership for the *Ashridge Journal*, the most intellectual of the party's publications.

Whilst Ashridge remained an aspirational focus and a source of pride, the cost of running it was all too clear whilst the benefits were intangible.[322] It equipped some party workers with arguments, understanding, and greater confidence, but others who returned from it seemed more interested in talking to each other than in canvassing the difficult districts. Its financial position was never sound, and the decision to close it on the outbreak of war was not only an inevitable consequence of the suspension of normal politics, but also something of a relief. The college was used as a military and civilian hospital during the war, and the buildings were returned in a dilapidated condition. It reopened in 1946, but, despite the party's revival in the late 1940s, the deficits mounted to even higher levels; in 1954, by a private act of parliament, it was converted into an educational trust and ceased to have any direct link with the party. Much more visibly effective during the 1930s were the many regional educational activities, which included short conferences and schools, lectures, canvassers' classes, and speaking competitions.[323] In 1929, twenty-one constituencies in the Wessex Area took part in a short course of political lectures, which had a cumulative attendance of over 10,500 persons.[324] Organized on an Area or county basis and usually focused on a particular section of the membership, these events normally took place on a single day or weekend and were held at accessible times and attractive locations.[325] They were a much more practicable proposition for working-class or lower-middle-class supporters, especially women with family commitments, and proved to be well-attended and popular gatherings which fostered a co-operative spirit and had beneficial effects upon morale and commitment.

---

[321] F. Lee, 'Ashridge in Harborough', *Ashridge Journal*, 6 (May 1931), 56–7; *CAJ*, January 1938, 5–7.
[322] See figures on the operating deficit in C. Berthezène, 'Ashridge College, 1929–1954: A glimpse at the archive of a Conservative intellectual project', *Contemporary British History*, 19/1 (2005), 82.
[323] D. Boot, 'Some aspects of Conservative education', *Ashridge Journal*, 25 (March 1936), 34–8.
[324] Wessex Area, AR, 1929.
[325] Headlam diary, 29 November 1937.

PARTY FINANCE

A party machine on the scale into which Central Office had developed by 1929 was a very expensive affair.[326] Expenditure rose significantly in 1924–26 during Jackson's Chairmanship, for which he was unapologetic: 'What I am concerned with is the efficiency of the organisation, and if the expenditure has increased by twenty per cent and the efficiency has increased by fifty, the expenditure is probably not colossal.'[327] In fact, it was spending which rose by 50 per cent after 1923, whilst the gain in effectiveness was harder to quantify. Nevertheless, costs increased still further under Davidson in the late 1920s, due to his fostering of the women's and junior movements, an expansion of propaganda work, and the long run-up to the 1929 general election; it reached an interwar peak of £248,256 in 1928 (see Table 4.4 and the detailed breakdown in Appendix 4). During the 1920s, there was a roughly comparable level of expenditure in the three main areas of activity: organization, publicity, and the regional offices. The increases in the later part of the decade were mainly in grants to constituencies, by-election campaigns, the cinema vans, and a general increase in staff, particularly clerical. After Davidson's departure in June 1930 spending began to diminish, due partly to the internal party strife but mainly to the deepening depression. Neville Chamberlain considered there was lax financial administration and was concerned about liabilities he had inherited, particularly the cost of Ashridge and loans made to the Ladies' Carlton Club; at the end of 1930, he admitted that the Central Office was 'very short of funds'.[328] Although the concordat with Beaverbrook in March 1931 ended his campaign against Baldwin and restored unity, and in the following months the party was resurgent in by-elections against a visibly tottering Labour government, by July the financial situation had become 'very serious'.[329]

The problem had to be tackled more drastically by Chamberlain's successor as Party Chairman, Stonehaven, who was clear that 'we have simply got to cut our coat according to our cloth'.[330] Following the triumph of the National Government in the 1931 general election, expenditure was cut to its lowest point of £114,342 in 1933; even so, the operating account at Drummonds Bank was overdrawn by £35,954. However, despite a reduction of more than half from the peak of 1928–29, there was no significant loss of functions or efficiency. Spending on some key activities was maintained, such as the Area Offices and the youth organizations. Some aspects actually improved, with the receipts from publications being turned round from a loss of £12,667 in 1930 to a profit of £2,055 in 1934, after which they did not make a loss again until 1939. The more favourable political situation after 1931, with the Liberal

---

[326] General Director to Party Chairman, 'Office reconstruction and reduction of expenditure', 30 July 1931, CPA, CCO/500/1/5.
[327] Jackson to Hicks, 16 April 1925, CPA, FIN/1.
[328] N. to H. Chamberlain, 14 December, 18 October 1930, *NCDL*.
[329] Hannon to Beaverbrook, 7 July 1931, Hannon MSS, HNN/17/1; Headlam diary, 10 March 1931. The situation was even worse in Scotland: the annual running cost of the Eastern Division's office was about £5,000 per annum, and in early 1931 there was only £175 in the bank to meet the monthly salary bill of £377: SUA, EDC, Treasurer's Ctte., 12 February 1931; SUA, EDC, Meeting of Exec. with no. 3 Area Officials, 16 February 1934.
[330] Stonehaven to Steel-Maitland, 1 February 1932, Steel-Maitland MSS, GD193/120/3/138.

Party eliminated as a significant rival and the Labour Party at least temporarily marginalized by the National Government, enabled a scaling back of spending on the Organisation and—in particular—Publicity Departments, the latter being achieved by reorganization and redundancies in 1932.[331] Three-quarters of the reduction in spending from 1928 to 1933 came from four areas: the near elimination of grants to constituencies and spending on by-elections provided 27.6 per cent and 11.9 per cent respectively, the closure in 1933 of the London Department (which was a separate body from the Metropolitan Area Office) contributed 12.7 per cent, and the fall in overall spending of the Publicity Department accounted for 23.4 per cent. Remarkably, none of this caused even a ripple of complaint or concern at the local level. As by-election performances were no worse than in the 1920s and there is no evidence of the collapse of local organizations, the likely explanation is that constituency associations were now generally better founded within their locality than had been the case earlier, with support for the weaker seats coming to a greater extent from within their regional Areas.[332] Assistance from the national coffers was now mainly confined to general elections, where subsidizing candidates' expenses in the weak seats and some marginals still came to a substantial sum.

The central party expenditure remained in a constant band of £118–127,000 for the rest of 1930s. The lack of impact from the 1935 election or the approach of another campaign in 1938–39 was largely due to the money raised and spent by the National Publicity Bureau, who also took over the running of the effective but costly cinema vans. Between 1 January and the end of the campaign in November 1935, the Bureau disbursed £119,220, mainly on posters and the cinema vans.[333] However, financing this absorbed a considerable proportion of the subscriptions which would normally have come to Central Office, causing the Party Chairman to declare in October 1935 that 'we are desperately hard up'.[334] Matters stabilized after the election, and the next significant development was the suspension of most activity during the Second World War, with the organization 'now working on more or less skeleton lines'.[335] Spending was reduced by over half from 1939 to 1940, and reached its lowest-ever point, of £48,172, in 1943. Much of this was on irreducibles: the breakdown in 1942 was 14 per cent on administrative and clerical staff, postage, and stationery; 13.6 per cent on premises (rent and running costs), and 13.1 per cent on pensions, with only £5,395 (10.3 per cent) spent on political organization (including by-elections and grants to constituencies) and £4,891 (9.4 per cent) on publicity. The largest item, exactly 25 per cent, was the Area Offices and the Scottish Whip's Office; these were crucially important in maintaining coverage of the constituencies, as so many local agents were absent on military or national service. The approaching end of the war saw a restoration of staff and spending from late 1944, and the end-of-year figure for 1945 of £109,094 was comparable to the prewar level.

---

[331] Vice-Chairmen's Ctte. on the Publicity Department, report, June 1932, CPA, CCO/500/1/6.
[332] Dugdale, 'Memorandum on Party Finance', March 1943, CPA, CCO/500/3/2.
[333] National Publicity Bureau, balance sheet, November 1935, CPA, FIN/43.
[334] Stonehaven to Derby, 16 October 1935, Derby MSS, 31/6.
[335] Covering memo by Hicks, 29 April 1941, to annual balance sheets for 1940, CPA, Accn/2004/28.

Table 4.4. Summary of Conservative Party national income and expenditure

The figures in this table are from a one-page summary drawn up *c.*1952 (CPA, FIN/12). In this, the Central Office expenditure figures are rounded to the nearest fifty or hundred from the exact figures in the balance sheets (see Appendix 4). The figures are for the calendar year, except where indicated (1918–20). It is not clear what the heading 'Private' in the expenditure table refers to, but it is likely to be support for the Leader's Secretariat and/or the Policy and later Research Departments, which were in separate premises (the large sum in 1929 may relate to the purchase and refurbishment of Ashridge rather than to the election fund deficit, which is also separately listed).

	INCOME			EXPENDITURE		
	Subscriptions & donations	Income from investments	Election fund surplus	Central Office	Private	Election fund deficit
1918[a]	68,350	17,200		63,300	4,000	
1919[b]	144,600	18,000		86,400	2,100	1,300
1920[c]	205,150	28,350		127,400	4,400	5,950
1921	86,450	22,900		105,200	7,200	2,000
1922	36,550	22,100		105,550	5,550	
1923	700,000	22,000		120,200	10,650	54,300
1924	51,450	41,200		180,600	4,600	69,100
1925	108,800	37,700	1,850	186,800	4,850	
1926	87,050	37,600		180,100	11,550	
1927	329,500	37,900		215,450	23,800	
1928	250,800	37,000		238,400	45,050	
1929	215,900	30,200		234,900	140,650	140,050
1930	56,250	20,300		225,800	4,850	
1931	60,850	14,600	98,100	193,500	1,600	
1932	44,650	18,500	10,550	134,450	2,550	
1933	15,050	10,650		114,350	1,200	
1934	58,250	10,150		127,700	12,600	
1935	130,000	9,650	83,700	121,500	10,500	
1936	77,050	9,100		127,250	11,900	
1937	245,250	10,500		118,650	9,100	
1938	147,250	10,900		122,250	3,400	
1939	127,850	11,600		125,150	3,350	
1940	51,650	10,050		60,300	2,150	
1941	64,950	5,050		51,650	1,900	
1942	58,050	4,750		52,300	11,900	
1943	87,900	5,950		48,150	2,600	
1944	192,900	7,150		60,300	5,400	
1945	313,800	10,100		109,100	16,900	71,400

[a] For year from 1 October 1917 to 30 September 1918.
[b] For year from 1 October 1918 to 30 September 1919.
[c] For fifteen months, from 1 October 1919 to 31 December 1920.

In addition to the regular expenditure, there was the need to finance the general elections; when in 1922–24 there were three of these within two years, the demands on the party's coffers were considerable. At the time of the 1923 dissolution, Younger reported that the 1922 campaign had taken £120,000 from central funds, and he estimated that £150–160,000 would be needed for the next one, as 'many of our men who asked for no help last time will do so for this election, and all who got it last time will want increased grants now'.[336] At the same time, raising funds after such a short interval was difficult, and Younger admitted, when gratefully accepting an offer of help from Beaverbrook, that 'money is really very scarce, and subscriptions come in very badly'.[337] The reason was the economic situation rather than the political, as 'people are not so well off as they used to be', and in 1923 and—still more—in 1924, the gap had to be bridged by drawing upon the capital reserves.[338] The 1929 election had the longest preparatory period and marked the peak of expenditure: grants to 175 candidates in England and Wales amounted to £102,547, the special costs of the Organisation Department were £32,431, and of the Publicity Department £155,495: together with some small payments, this resulted in a total expenditure of £300,873—a massive sum for that era. The largest part of the Organisation Department costs was £20,566 for the fees and expenses of paid speakers, whilst the Publicity Department amount was almost entirely the costs of printing and distributing the vast numbers of posters, leaflets, and other election materials.[339] This was partly covered by £156,000 of special donations to the election fund, with the balance coming from the increase in general donations which the approaching contest stimulated.[340] Such a level of support could not be sustained, even without the exacerbating impact of the slump, and during the next two years Central Office pursued a policy of persuading constituencies to raise funds for the election expenses, or at least to provide one-third in a matching contribution with the candidate and the national funds. The circumstances of the 1931 election made it less expensive than its predecessor, but, even so, the fall in Central Office subventions of election expenses was dramatic, with only £33,584 being expended. After this, 'it was decided that no definite undertakings to provide money would be made before the date of an election was known, to encourage constituencies to set up election funds', and in 1935 the amount given declined further to £22,107.[341] The 1945 election was slightly more expensive, with the lack of time for preparation being balanced by the urgent need of many constituencies for assistance in reviving from wartime torpor: of the total expenditure of £71,427, grants to candidates and the Areas accounted for £25,153, and £23,273 was spent by the Publicity Department, with an additional £4,014 on the national poster campaign.[342]

[336] Younger to Baldwin, 7 November 1923, Baldwin MSS, 35/67–70.
[337] Younger to Beaverbrook, 27 November 1923, Beaverbrook MSS, BBK/C334.
[338] Younger to Derby, 30 November 1923, Derby MSS, 17/2; Younger to Beaverbrook, 20 October 1924, Beaverbrook MSS, BBK/C334.
[339] 1929 General election balance sheets, Davidson MSS, DAV/187.
[340] Hicks to Davidson, 14 January 1930, Davidson MSS, DAV/190.
[341] 'Election Expenses', General Director to Party Chairman, 5 July 1939, CPA, CCO/4/1/55; Pierssene (Yorkshire Area COA) to General Director, 'Election Grants', 30 November 1931, CPA, CCO/4/1/53; Area Agents' memoranda on 1935 election expenses, CPA, CCO/4/1/54.
[342] Annual balance sheets, 1945, CPA, Accn/2004/28.

There is a very clear pattern to the ebb and flow of party income. Most of the high points related to the general elections, when the evident need for funds and the prospect of a non-Conservative government encouraged more and larger donations. This explains the high figures for 1919 (which included the 1918 election), 1925 (the election being in late 1924, and much of the promised money coming in afterwards), 1928–29, 1935, and 1945, whilst the phenomenal £700,000 of 1923 relates to two general elections—one in late 1922, and the other in December 1923 (with the latter on the protectionist programme that so enthused many party supporters). It is unclear from the data in Table 4.4 where the money for the 1931 campaign came from; what is apparent, and hardly surprising, is that the national crisis stimulated so much concern, even in the depths of recession, that the party was left with a surplus of nearly £100,000 after the campaign (which, admittedly, was a relatively inexpensive one). The other peaks also correlate with points of national crisis: the industrial unrest of 1920 (the figure here is also for fifteen months), the aftermath of the General Strike of 1926 and the campaign over the Trade Disputes Act in 1927, and the Abdication crisis of December 1936, which was followed by Baldwin's retirement at the height of his popularity in 1937. The troughs are also not surprising: the severe unpopularity of the Coalition in 1922, the internal strife of 1930, and the impact of the slump from that year to 1934 (especially 1933, in the mid-term of the parliament),[343] and the early wartime years of 1940–42—although the latter was not an immediate problem, as expenditure had fallen still further. Indeed, a surplus built up, and £49,204 was transferred for investment in 1944.

It was one of the Conservative Party's greatest strengths that it could obtain the financial resources to support its extensive activities. As discussed in Chapter 3, much that was spent in the constituencies on a routine basis was also raised there, by subscriptions and by fundraising events. The national party funds came by another route, although they similarly depended upon the party's increasing predominance in the wealthiest social groups. During the nineteenth century, tensions between the three main elements in the wealthiest class had produced a divided and often contending political response. The traditional landed elite (based in the rural shires) was mainly Conservative; the newly assertive industrial elite (based in the urban north, Wales, and Scotland) was mainly Liberal, and the older-established mercantile, financial, and professional elite (based in London) was divided between the two parties but leant more to the Conservatives in the last quarter of the century. In the first decades of the twentieth century, and particularly during and after the First World War, these groups consolidated into a more homogeneous whole that overwhelmingly supported the Conservative Party.[344] This was mainly due to the advance of the Labour Party; many of the wealthy felt threatened by Socialism, and looked to the Conservatives as the only effective

---

[343] Davidson to Wilson, 11 October 1930, Templewood MSS, VI/3.
[344] W. D. Rubinstein, 'Britain's elites in the inter-war period', *Contemporary British History*, 12/1 (1998), 2–3.

barrier. As one City businessman commented when donating 2,000 guineas to the 1929 election fund: 'I regard it in the nature of insurance.'[345] Of course, some amongst both the landed and the business sectors continued in their loyalty to the Liberals, but they were a remnant whose numbers and commitment waned considerably after the early 1920s. Other individuals eschewed any party commitment for reasons of temperament, of being too busy with their own affairs, or of concern that it might harm their business or profession. Even so, it is clear that between the wars the Conservative Party could call upon the financial resources of a great many of the richest people in the country, and from them it obtained the large sums which financed the central party organization and the general election campaigns.[346]

The economic problems of the interwar era particularly affected those whose wealth depended upon land, and some—but not all—of the northern and Celtic industrial elite, weakening their influence. In general, however, many of the upper-middle and upper class prospered: whereas the number of people paying supertax had averaged 13,134 per annum in 1911–15, it rose to 28,359 in 1925–30, fell back to 22,572 in 1930–35, and partly recovered to 25,182 in 1935–40—considering that prices fell by around 10 per cent in the 1930s, the real dip was fairly shallow.[347] Wealth remained highly concentrated: in 1919, one-third of national wealth was held by just 36,000 people—less than one-thousandth of the total population.[348] However, despite its support from this elite, the Conservative Party never felt itself to be rich, especially in contrast with the 'vast resources' which it believed were available to the Labour Party from the trade unions' political levy and the grants from the profits of the co-operative societies.[349] By comparison, 'the financial resources of the Conservative Party are restricted' as it 'possesses no similar automatic source of income'.[350]

In this period, donations were given by individuals from their own wealth, as it was not considered legal for a company to make political disbursements. In most cases, these captains of industry, bankers, and entrepreneurs were the owner or majority shareholder of their business, and in that respect its profits came to them to be used as they wished.[351] There was a considerable shroud of secrecy over political fundraising; indeed, a committee investigating party finance in 1942–44 concluded that 'excessive secrecy…in the past has produced unfortunate results', with the 'unwholesome sense of mystery' giving opponents an easy target to attack.[352] However, the consequence is that only a handful of the largest and most public donations are known.

---

[345] Richmond to Smithers, 10 March 1929, Baldwin MSS, 55/35–48; Yorkshire Area, AR, 1921; Rye CA, Fin., 11 February 1933.
[346] Davidson to N. Chamberlain, 8 January 1929, Davidson MSS, DAV/186.
[347] Rubinstein, 'Britain's elites in the inter-war period', 4.
[348] Carr-Saunders and Caradog Jones, *Survey of the Social Structure of England and Wales*, 109.
[349] Special Finance Ctte. Report, 16 March 1944, 1–2, CPA, CCO/500/3/1.
[350] NU Exec. Report to Central Council, 14 March 1945.
[351] For a rare surviving example, see cheque for £30,000 from Basil Zaharoff to Fraser, 7 January 1920, Fraser MSS, MSS.Eng.c.4788/65.
[352] Special Finance Ctte. Report, 16 March 1944, 7, CPA, CCO/500/3/1; Marchwood to Churchill, 16 October 1940, Churchill MSS, CAC, CHAR/2/402/14.

It was generally easier to raise money for a specific purpose, such as the establishment of the party college at Ashridge or an approaching general election.[353] One such substantial donation financed the extensive propaganda campaign in 1934 of poster displays in 250 constituencies and a four-month campaign by the effective but costly cinema vans.[354] The Berry brothers, owners of the newspapers which were most supportive of the party leadership, regularly gave financial assistance—including, in Lord Camrose's case, helping Churchill to avoid losing Chartwell when he sustained stock exchange losses in the 1930s. The landed aristocracy were no longer the monetary resource that they had been, as they were sapped by death duties and the slump in agriculture, but there was still a role for the greatest grandees: in the 1923 general election the Earl of Derby personally funded the election expenses of five candidates in his bailiwick of Lancashire.[355] Derby expected no reward other than the reaffirmation of his standing in the inner counsels of the party, but other donors often had a mixture of motives.

Fundraising was bedevilled by the complex issue of the relationship between donations and the conferment of honours. The use of patronage had been linked with party finance long before Lloyd George's more naked need and methods had caused outrage during the postwar Coalition. The fall of the Coalition, and especially the accession of Baldwin as Conservative Leader in 1923, with his self-appointed task of cleaning up politics, led to the rejection of any direct link with honours. As Baldwin's right hand, Davidson's tenure of the Party Chairmanship was marked by efforts to make a distinction between money given with a request for an honour attached—which was refused or, when this became clear, returned—and money given by persons whose status and public activities made them suitable candidates for an honour in any case.[356] This was a fine line to walk, and every so often Davidson came close to falling flat on his face. However, he achieved one success, partly through that element of guile which made him less than popular with many outside the Baldwinian circle: the breaking of the honours tout 'Maundy' Gregory, a go-between who had flourished in the Coalition period.[357] The preservation of standards and respectability in the award of honours—which Lloyd George had dangerously ignored—meant that recipients had to appear worthy in terms of their eminence in their field, their philanthropic gifts or other voluntary contributions to public life, and their personal conduct. Support for the party could be part of this broader engagement, and as a proper and patriotic activity it was certainly not irrelevant. The party managers who dealt with honours were clear that a due share of patronage should go to 'our people', and one of their grievances during the Coalition had been the poaching of Conservative

---

[353] Davidson memo of interview with Brotherton, 9 May 1929, Davidson MSS, DAV/186; in another case, in 1920 the coal owners paid for a month's propaganda campaign: Younger to Fraser, 22 August 1920, Fraser MSS, MSS.Eng.c.4788/80–3.
[354] NU Exec., 'Memorandum on Publicity and Propaganda', 30 May 1934.
[355] Derby to Woodhouse, 21 November 1923, Derby MSS, 20/4.
[356] James, *Memoirs of a Conservative*, 283–8.
[357] Baldwin to Ball, 8 November 1930, memo by Ball, 8 February 1933, Ball MSS, MSS. Eng.c.6657/78, 82–4; James, *Memoirs of a Conservative*, 280–2, 288.

supporters by Lloyd George's machine.[358] Party recommendations for the honours lists originated partly from the Chief Whip's suggestions regarding MPs, and mainly from the Party Chairman, who 'ought to dispense patronage, as he alone can know the people on whom it should be bestowed and who are the most useful to himself and the Party'.[359] There was an element of a nod and a wink about the process of soliciting and granting honours, in which the essential point was that there must be no presumption of a link between financial support given and honours granted—it must not appear to be a commercial transaction. Maintaining the legitimacy not just of titles but of a ranked society required that honours be a reward for merit and service.[360]

It is difficult to establish the exact extent of the Conservative Party's financial resources, as there were both donations which were used for current purposes—especially the election campaigns—and funds which were deposited in long-term investments. Much of the latter had been built up before the First World War, and were 'of very old standing indeed'.[361] These were held in a series of trusts, not in the name of the party but by trustees drawn mainly from the network of former party managers. Steel-Maitland, Younger, and Davidson all served in this capacity for many years after they had ceased to be Party Chairman, whilst others included Leslie Wilson (a past Chief Whip), Lord Bayford (a former whip and Deputy Party Chairman), Sir John Gilmour (a previous Scottish Whip), and Malcolm Fraser (a former Principal Agent). Documents in their personal papers shed some light on the deposited funds, but cannot be taken as a complete picture, not least because the various accounts had different trustees. In 1924, the funds for which Steel-Maitland was a trustee had a face value of £464,527 (of which the largest item was £170,000 in War Loan stock bearing 5 per cent interest), but these presumably were not all of the party's holdings, as this was insufficient to generate the £41,200 income shown in Table 4.4. In the same year, Gilmour was trustee of funds valued at £265,137, which seem to have been separate.[362] However, taken together, perhaps with other undisclosed sums, these holdings are broadly consistent with the comment of the Party Treasurer in 1927 that 'the party fund is now less than a million'.[363] A memorandum to Davidson in 1929 listed four trust accounts with a total current value of £615,774, but again this does not seem to be a complete list.[364] The financial problems of

---

[358] Younger to Derby, 11 July 1921, Derby MSS, 17/2; Younger to Bonar Law, 2 January 1921, Bonar Law MSS, BL/100/1/2.

[359] Younger to Davidson, 21 May 1927, Davidson MSS, DAV/180; Younger was making the point that the Treasurer should not make recommendations.

[360] See the correspondence regarding honours in the Davidson MSS, not only for his tenure of the Party Chairmanship (1926–30) but also when acting as, effectively, Baldwin's chief of staff in 1935–37. For an example of party work influencing a legal promotion to a recordership, see Jackson to Joynson-Hicks, 26 July 1926, and reply, 27 July 1926, Joynson-Hicks MSS, 2/1.

[361] Steel-Maitland to Chilston, 3 August 1923, Steel-Maitland MSS, GD193/120/1/54.

[362] List of party funds, April 1924, Steel-Maitland MSS, GD193/120/1/6–7; Hicks to Gilmour, 30 June 1924, and annual returns, 1924–33, Gilmour MSS, GD383/19/6–40.

[363] Bayford diary, 20 February 1927.

[364] Hicks to Davidson, 11 January 1929, Davidson MSS, DAV/186. This document listed trusts designated 'A', 'C', 'D', and 'F'; there is no indication whether accounts still existed for the missing letters, but the only one of these funds for which Steel-Maitland was a trustee did not contain stock that matched the 1924 list in his papers.

1930–31 forced two sales of stocks, the second being £60,000 of the War Loan; faced with the plunge in subscription income, the Treasurer declared 'there is no other course for us to adopt'.[365] By the end of 1935, the investments, 'arranged under various trusts', were worth 'approximately £310,000', a sum which is fairly consistent with the return of £9,650 shown in Table 4.4.[366] Even so, there were either other trusts or (which is less likely) further investments, as a list in the party's financial files for 1941 gives a total market value of £453,379.[367] Throughout the period, there was also a separate fund at the direct disposal of the Party Chairman; this was not intended for the regular running costs of Central Office, but for special purposes, much of which had to remain confidential. This account stood at £1,250,000 when Younger handed it on in 1923, but by the autumn of 1927 it had been eroded to 'well under a million'.[368]

Most of the party's funds were held at Hoare's Bank and Drummonds Bank, whilst their administration—including the auditing of the annual accounts—was undertaken by the chartered accountancy firm of Maxwell Hicks & Co.[369] Before 1922, the administration of the party funds had been partly separate from Central Office. As the party did not have a corporate legal status, it did not have its own named accounts and its bankers 'have no official knowledge of the Unionist Party funds'.[370] Instead, these were administered by the Treasurer, and kept in accounts under his name and those of one or two other trustees. This led to a major problem in 1922: the holder of the accounts, Lord Farquhar, was both loyal to the Coalition and in declining mental health, and he refused to release any money for Bonar Law's campaign. Most of it was eventually recovered, but Younger had to work in 1922 from £90,000 'left over after the 1918 fight' and some quickly raised additional money, which together were just sufficient to cover the cost of £120,000.[371] When he retired from the Party Chairmanship in 1923, Younger agreed to take on the responsibility of looking after the party funds as Treasurer, but considered that his role was to raise the special funds for general elections and not to obtain the ordinary running costs of Central Office. This devolved largely upon his successors as Chairman, but Jackson 'did not do nearly enough in this particular direction' and the general fund became seriously depleted.[372] However, whilst his successor was more effective at fundraising, Davidson found that he did not have enough time to pursue this task effectively, and he became 'genuinely worried... that the number of annual subscribers to the

---

[365] Hoare to Gilmour, 20 April 1931, Gilmour MSS, GD383/19/27.
[366] Hicks to Greenwood, 15 January 1936, Davidson MSS, DAV/226.
[367] 'Schedule of Investments arranged under the various Trusts as at 31 December 1941', CPA, Accn/2004/28.
[368] Younger to Baldwin, 27 August 1927, Davidson MSS, DAV/180.
[369] Much of the surviving information comes from correspondence between Hicks and Davidson, in the Davidson MSS, and with various Party Chairmen, 1924–46, CPA, FIN/1, 19, 32, and 37.
[370] Hoare's Bank to Gilmour, 23 July 1923, Gilmour MSS, GD383/19/2.
[371] Younger to Baldwin, 7 November 1923, Baldwin MSS, 35/67–70; Bayford diary, 28 January 1923.
[372] Younger to Davidson, 21 May, Younger to Baldwin, 27 August 1927, Davidson MSS, DAV/180.

Party has been diminishing of recent years'.[373] This led to the initiative of appointing Albert Bennett, a wealthy businessman and MP, as Assistant Treasurer in September 1927; his efforts were rewarded with a baronetcy in 1929, but his own fortune foundered in the slump and he had to retire from politics in 1930. From January 1930 to July 1931 the post of Treasurer was held by Hoare, who worked closely with Neville Chamberlain during the latter's Party Chairmanship. After Hoare returned to the Cabinet in August 1931, the Treasurership was held during the remainder of the period by three peers who were former MPs: Lord Ebbisham to November 1933, Lord Greenwood from then until June 1938, and then Lord Marchwood until February 1947. Informal assistance was also given by others previously connected to the party machine, especially Malcolm Fraser.[374]

To support this work, a Treasurer's Department was established in June 1938, with a staff of seven housed separately at 24 Old Queen Street. However, this barely had time to become established; after the outbreak of war, all of its personnel left for other work, although by 1945 it had recovered to a staff of two. The war years encouraged a reappraisal of the party's financial methods, partly due to the decline in large individual donations, partly to increasing embarrassment and criticism of the role which wealth played in candidate selection, and partly to awareness of the growing financial strength of the trade unions. A 'Special Finance Committee' was appointed in November 1942, and its eventual report in March 1944 recommended the creation of a 'National Conservative Board of Finance'. This was to be chaired by the Treasurer of the Party, and to include members of both Houses, 'a number of representative party men from the provinces', and some 'outstanding business personalities with special contacts in the world of finance'; it would work in conjunction with a standing committee of the Area Treasurers.[375] The aim was to eliminate the past competition and friction between the national and Area fundraisers, and instead to utilize the knowledge and contacts of the regional officers 'to draw subscriptions for central funds from an enormously wider field than has been possible in the past'.[376] In return, the Areas would be remitted an agreed proportion of the money collected from their region, with the incentive that if the scheme worked this would be a larger amount than they had previously raised by their unaided efforts. However, the report did not encroach upon local autonomy by recommending any change of relationship at the constituency level, as 'local initiative and responsibility must be encouraged in every possible way'.[377]

---

[373] Davidson to Younger, 20 May 1927, Davidson MSS, DAV/180; Baldwin to Younger, 26 August 1927, Baldwin MSS, 162/22–3. Davidson later stated that he had raised £1 million between March 1927 and March 1929, in addition to the £200,000 endowment fund for Ashridge: memo on resigning the Chairmanship, n.d. but c.June 1930, Davidson MSS, DAV/190.
[374] Hacking to Fraser, 15 February 1938, Fraser MSS, MSS.Eng.c.4788/118–19.
[375] Special Finance Ctte. Report, 16 March 1944, 6–7, CPA, CCO/500/3/1.
[376] Summary of Special Finance Ctte. Report by Proby (Chairman), 'Conservative Party Finance', in Stuart to Churchill, 14 June 1944, Churchill MSS, CAC, CHAR/2/507/99–101.
[377] 'Conservative Party Finance', 14 June 1944, Churchill MSS, CAC, CHAR/2/507/99–101.

5

The Parliamentary Party
Composition and Dissent

COMPOSITION

The most famous comment on the parliamentary Conservative Party between the wars is Baldwin's description of the MPs elected in 1918 as 'a lot of hard-faced men who look as if they had done well out of the war'.[1] His categorization embraced the Coalition Liberals as well as the Conservatives, and was always an oversimplification: wealthy businessmen were a significant element, of course, but even here there was a wide variety of background, experience, occupation, and character. There were some who looked to their own interests first, and the Conservative Party was the natural home for those most concerned with defending the property that they had. In a period when the defects of capitalism had become a significant political battleground, this could take an obdurate and narrow-minded form. One of their own number, perhaps more fairly, considered Conservative MPs to be 'a fairly ordinary selection of people, though usually critical by nature, rigid in outlook, and imbued with varying degrees of determination'.[2] The parliamentary Conservative Party was drawn almost entirely from one gender and a restricted range of the higher social strata. Within those parameters, it was not a monolith but a mosaic, in which each tiny piece was separate and unique. The upper-middle and upper classes contained many subtle variations in status, circumstance, and experience, and the pattern which from afar seems so homogenous becomes more complex and distinctive on closer scrutiny.

Conservative MPs were a collection of individual characters, each with their own needs and concerns. Their lives ranged beyond the House of Commons and politics, and they were as much preoccupied as any other group of human beings with their health, their finances, their families, and their other occupational and recreational interests. Their time as an MP was a valued element in their life, but

---

[1] Originally quoted anonymously as a 'Conservative friend' in J. M. Keynes, *The Economic Consequences of the Peace* (1919), 91; see also Baldwin to Louisa Baldwin, February 1919, in Baldwin, *My Father*, 82. For a similar comments, see Winterton diary, 17 March 1919, Winterton MSS, and Lord Swinton, *I Remember* (n.d., c.1948), 15; for a more positive view, see Ormsby-Gore to his mother, 15 March 1919, Ormsby-Gore MSS, PEC/10/1/11/10.

[2] Beamish diary notes, 31 July 1942, Beamish MSS, CAC, BEAM/3/4.

for many it was not the most essential part of their livelihood or sense of identity.[3] Most had had a significant career before entering the House and, even if they did not continue activity at the same level, retained connections to their established business, professional, or social networks. Others had a local prestige which they wished to retain, and which absorbed time and energy—whether in landownership, business, or public affairs.[4] Beyond being male and possessing a level of income which included the wealthier parts of the middle class as well as the upper class, there was no such thing as the typical Conservative MP. The parliamentary party included its share of those with unusual experiences and distinctive expertise, as well as the maverick and the bore, the cultured and the shallow, and the ambitious and the indolent. A number of examples, while unable to stand as fully representative of such a diverse body, will serve to illustrate the range.

Some MPs were the founders or managers of large businesses, such as the car manufacturer Herbert Austin, George Balfour of the construction firm Balfour Beatty, Arthur Du Cros of the Dunlop rubber and tyre company, Frank Hornby (creator of the Meccano and Hornby toy and model brands), Charles Peat of accountants Peat, Marwick & Mitchell (the antecedent of KPMG), Cyril Entwistle of Decca Records, and Isidore Salmon of the Lyons food and restaurant chain. There were several shipowners, including Herbert Cayzer (Clan Line), R. M. Hudson (Tyne-Tees Shipping), and Thomas Royden, chairman of Cunard. Alfred Critchley, who was born on the Canadian prairie, made three notable impacts upon national life: he was co-founder of the giant Portland Cement (later Blue Circle) company, he established modern greyhound racing in Britain (he introduced the electric hare, and built White City and several other stadiums for this popular sport), and, as the director-general of the British Overseas Airways Corporation in 1943–46, he conceived and saw through to fruition the building of Heathrow airport; in addition, he was a talented amateur golfer who won the French and Belgian Opens in the 1930s.

As well as the entrepreneurs, there were MPs who were continuing a substantial family enterprise; this was particularly so with the well-established brewers, such as George Younger, Richard Wells, William Everard, and John Gretton (whose company, Bass, Ratcliff & Gretton, was a major employer in his Burton-on-Trent constituency), but it also applied to numerous others, including the publisher Harold Macmillan, Leonard Lyle of Tate & Lyle sugar, Gerald Palmer of the biscuit manufacturer Huntley & Palmer, Willard Weston of Fortnum & Mason, Robert Bird of the eponymous custard-makers, and Douglas Vickers of the armaments and shipbuilding consortium. Oswald Lewis, MP for Colchester in 1929–45, was the son of John and effectively the creator of the retail business of John Lewis & Company. Many MPs were active in the business world, at least at the level of holding some company directorships; these were often, but not always, a reflection of the usefulness of having a Member of Parliament's name on the company letterhead rather than the possession of any particular expertise in relation

---

[3] Sir C. Mott-Radclyffe, *Foreign Body in the Eye* (1975), discusses his diplomatic career at length but says little about his time as an MP.
[4] H. Balfour, *Wings over Westminster* (1973), 71–3.

to its activities.[5] Thus Cuthbert Headlam became a director of the company which provided electricity for the Tyneside area and was involved in the development of the Gateshead trading estate in the later 1930s, as well as becoming the director of a number of small companies in London, partly through his friendship with Oliver Lyttelton, who was then a prominent figure in the City. Other MPs, whilst not actively engaged themselves, came from prominent business families: two examples connected with prestigious banks were Angus Hambro and Samuel Hoare.

There was still a considerable group involved in agriculture, in which the manorial gentry were well-represented. They tended to be members of the Country Landowners' Association, and included such leading figures such as Gilbert Acland-Troyte and George Courthope (who was also chairman of the brewers Ind Coope), whilst Ernest Pretyman had links to the National Farmers' Union, which in this period was mainly a body of small farmers. This element also included some recognized agricultural 'experts', such as Percy Hurd (grandfather of the later Foreign Secretary, Douglas Hurd). Of course, there were many lawyers, of whom two typical examples were Basil Nield and Gervais Rentoul: the former became Chairman of Middlesex Quarter Sessions and Recorder of York, and the latter Recorder of Sandwich and then a stipendiary Metropolitan Magistrate. Not all were barristers, such as the leading London solicitor Sir William Bull, who was a friend and confidant of Walter Long. The law was the largest professional group, but there were MPs with medical backgrounds, such as Walter Elliot and Joseph Leech, or technical expertise, such as the mechanical engineer Herbert Williams and Edward Hopkinson, designer of the power plants for the electrification of the London Underground.

Another area of activity which fitted well with the demands of a parliamentary career was the media, which included famous names such as the author John Buchan, as well as journalists (such as the former editors of the *Daily Express*, Beverley Baxter, and *The Times of India*, Thomas Bennett) and members of press-owning families (such as Esmond Harmsworth, the heir of Lord Rothermere, and Sir John Findlay, proprietor of *The Scotsman*). There were also a number of MPs from academia, and not only from the university seats: the geographer Halford Mackinder represented a Glasgow division, and the historian Sir John Marriott sat for York, a centre for both the railway and confectionery industries. There were actors, such as William Hutchison, and impresarios, such as Alfred Butt, manager of five West End theatres, and Walter de Frece, founder of the Hippodromes, who at the age of nineteen had married the music hall star and male impersonator Vesta Tilley. Retirement from the armed forces was often at an age young enough for a second career in parliament, and this group included former generals such as Sir Aylmer Hunter-Weston (known as 'Hunter-Bunter') and Sir Newton Moore (commander of the Australian Imperial Force from 1915 to 1917), as well as admirals such as Tufton Beamish (captain of a battlecruiser at the battles of the Falklands and Jutland) and Roger Keyes, who commanded the raid on Zeebrugge in April 1918.

---

[5] Examples of directorships are detailed in the contemporary critique, 'S. Haxey' [pseud.], *Tory M.P.* (1939), 36–45.

There were many others with experience from the theatres of the First World War and of service in various parts of the empire, especially India. Of the younger generation who had served on the Western Front, Harold Balfour had been a noted 'ace' fighter pilot, whilst in the trenches below, two other Harolds, Macmillan and Crookshank, received life-threatening wounds that left permanent disabilities. However, not all of the former officers were distinguished: Thomas Adair had been captain of the battleship *Montagu* when it was wrecked on Lundy Island in 1906, and was severely reprimanded in the resulting court martial; he retired from the navy and, due to his expertise in gunnery, became manager of an ordnance factory in Glasgow from 1907 to 1918 and then one of the city's MPs in 1918–22.

In Table 5.1, the category of 'landowners' includes small as well as large estates, and the heirs to estates who had no other principal occupation. The second category are those who had retired from careers in the armed forces or the civil, diplomatic, and imperial services before entering the House of Commons; some of them had a small estate, took up directorships, or were authors and journalists. The category of 'lawyers' comprises barristers and solicitors, but a few of the barristers did not practise and were engaged in other occupations. The 'other professions' were mostly in the fields of writing, publishing, and education, together with smaller numbers from medicine, the churches, and the theatre. The 'commerce' category includes merchants, bankers, stockbrokers, accountants, and company directors, whilst 'industry' contains those involved in manufacturing. The latter were spread fairly evenly across all sectors, with the larger groups in shipping, textiles, engineering, and brewing; the very rare instances of MPs from working-class backgrounds are also included here.

Table 5.1. Occupational background of Conservative MPs[6]

The figures exclude women MPs, and a very few male MPs for whom no specific occupation can be identified.

Year of intake	% Landowners	% Military and service	% Lawyers	% Other professions	% Commerce	% Industry
1918	15.0	15.8	23.3	7.4	17.5	21.0
1922	13.8	15.9	25.9	8.9	13.0	22.5
1923	15.6	13.7	24.4	10.3	16.4	19.4
1924	12.1	18.1	26.0	10.5	16.4	16.9
1929	14.2	18.9	25.1	9.8	15.6	16.4
1931	11.1	17.4	26.0	9.8	18.9	16.9
1935	9.5	19.0	20.3	11.3	22.3	17.7

The most notable feature of these figures is how little the occupational structure changed. The lawyers were almost always the largest single group; within this, the proportion of barristers increased from 77 per cent in 1922 to 89 per cent in 1935.

[6] From data in J.M. McEwen, 'The Unionist and Conservative Members of Parliament 1914–1939', PhD thesis, University of London (1959).

The combined total of the MPs in the commerce and industry categories was only slightly higher after the 1935 election than it had been in 1918, although after 1931 the number from commerce exceeded that from industry. Landowners tended to become MPs in their own locality and these were often areas with stronger Conservative support; when the parliamentary ranks shrank in number they retained more of their seats, and thus were a higher proportion in 1923 and 1929 than in 1924, 1931, and 1935. However, there was an overall decline of the landowning element during the period, which was almost certainly a consequence of the economic difficulties of agriculture. It is significant that there was no reduction in the military and service group, who had similar backgrounds but usually did not depend upon land for their income. Indeed, this category increased after 1924, which was when the younger men who had seen active service in the First World War started to enter the House in significant numbers.

There is one occupational group which these data cannot measure, and that is the number of MPs who were effectively full-time politicians. This was clear enough for ministers when in office, and indeed the rules governing ministerial conduct required them to give up active work in business, relinquish directorships, and—rather less clearly—cease writing press articles for payment. Amongst the backbenchers, however, there were both the old-style 'gentlemen of means' and a younger group whose ambition for office led them to give most of their energies to politics, and who either had a nominal occupation in business or supported themselves as writers and journalists. Their number is impossible to determine; there was some contemporary feeling that the professional politicians were more numerous, but these observations tended to come from more traditionalist quarters whose disapproval may have caused exaggeration.

The very few instances of apparently working-class MPs were, in fact, not unambiguously so. Gwilym Rowlands, who finally secured a seat under the National Government umbrella at Flintshire in 1935, had begun work as a coal miner in 1895 but his family background was lower-middle class: his grandfather had been the first schoolmaster in Rhondda and his parents had owned a small mining company before going bankrupt. His own occupation is unclear after the colliery at which he worked closed in 1928; he may have been employed by the party as a speaker, and there is a suggestion that he was in business as a coal merchant.[7] A similar case was Robert Gee, an ordinary soldier who had served in the ranks for twenty-two years before being commissioned in 1915 and winning the Victoria Cross in 1917; after the war he studied law at Gray's Inn. He defeated Ramsay MacDonald in a bitter by-election at East Woolwich in 1921 but lost the seat in 1922, later becoming MP for Bosworth from 1924 to 1927. His career ended in scandal as he 'bolted with somebody else's wife' and 'then disappeared to Australia and was said to be ill', leaving the constituency without effective representation for two years; not surprisingly, the eventual by-election was a notable defeat.[8]

---

[7] See comment of Percy Cohen in Greenwood, 'Central Control and Constituency Autonomy in the Conservative Party', 113.
[8] Lane-Fox to Irwin, 9 June 1927, Halifax MSS, C152/17/1/229.

All of the remainder of the parliamentary party was drawn from the higher sectors of the professions, commerce, and industry, capped by the traditional governing class of landed gentry and aristocracy. It was derived from a small elite of the population, albeit a broader one than had been the case fifty or a hundred years before. The nature, and the considerable homogeneity, of this elite is apparent from analysis of the ancestry and education of Conservative MPs.[9] A considerable number were members of aristocratic families; they tended to sit for safer seats, and so became a larger proportion when the parliamentary party was fewer in number. Some of

Table 5.2. Conservative MPs closely related to the peerage (by blood or marriage)[12]

	1918	1922	1923	1924	1929	1931	1935
Number	59	56	59	75	59	79	76
%	15.4	16.3	22.9	18.2	22.7	16.8	19.6

these were continuing the political tradition of long-established and prestigious aristocratic families, with brothers and sons of the Earl of Derby, Marquesses of Salisbury and Londonderry, and Dukes of Devonshire and Buccleuch. Winston Churchill was the grandson of the Duke of Marlborough, whilst other MPs were related by marriage: Macmillan and James Stuart were sons-in-law of the Duke of Devonshire, and Duff Cooper (a nephew of the 1st Duke of Fife) was married to the charismatic celebrity figure Lady Diana Manners, daughter of the Duke of Rutland. However, it must be remembered that not all peerages were of such lofty or ancient status: many had been created since the 1850s, and were based on industrial or financial wealth rather than land. As well as the relatives of peers, there were county gentry families, which had produced MPs over several centuries, including such names as Blundell, Bridgeman, Courthope, Heneage, Long, and Pym. Although by 1939 Conservative candidates were being drawn from a broader spectrum of the middle and upper classes, at the outbreak of war there were still thirty-two MPs who had followed their fathers into the House.[10] A parental involvement in politics was an early influence upon the many who, like Evelyn Cecil, 'grew up in a political atmosphere'.[11]

The education of Conservative MPs further illustrates their upper-middle- and upper-class backgrounds. A very large proportion had travelled the conventional route of public school and Oxbridge; not only had they imbibed the ethos which this inculcated, but in many cases they were already known to one another. Of the remainder, around 18 per cent were from Scottish or Irish equivalents of public schools, around 16 per cent had been educated by private tutors, and about half

---

[9] This is strikingly displayed in the chart of the 'Cousinhood' in Haxey, *Tory M.P.*, 125.
[10] McEwen, 'Conservative MPs 1914–39', 408; the number in 1914 was fifty-three, a proportion of 18.4% compared with 8.6% in 1939.
[11] Replies of Cecil and others to question 1 of Wedgwood's survey for the History of Parliament, Wedgwood Questionnaire MSS.
[12] McEwen, 'Conservative MPs 1914–39', 294–5, 376.

had attended grammar schools or small academies; it is not known how the remainder were educated.[13]

Table 5.3. Public school education of Conservative MPs[14]

Year of intake	Eton No.	Eton %	Harrow No.	Harrow %	Rugby No.	Rugby %	Winchester No.	Winchester %	Others No.	Others %	TOTAL No.	TOTAL %
1918	72	18.8	30	7.9	15	3.9	8	2.1	77	20.2	202	52.9
1922	76	22.1	32	9.3	12	3.5	7	2.0	57	16.6	184	53.5
1923	65	25.2	26	10.1	12	4.7	6	2.3	40	15.5	149	57.8
1924	97	23.5	32	7.8	13	3.2	9	2.2	74	18.0	225	54.7
1929	71	27.3	22	8.5	11	4.2	8	3.1	41	15.8	153	58.9
1931	103	21.9	35	7.4	16	3.4	12	2.6	79	16.8	245	52.1
1935	98	25.3	26	6.7	14	3.6	10	2.6	66	17.1	214	55.3

Within the number educated at the recognized 'public schools', the predominance of Eton—the most aristocratic choice—above even Harrow was striking (although the contingent from the latter included several leading figures, such as Baldwin, Churchill, and Amery). There was a similar pattern with university education, not only in the dominance of Oxford and Cambridge (with the preponderance to the former), but also in the colleges within these. Christ Church alone furnished between a quarter and a third of the Oxford contingent, and four other colleges (Balliol, Magdalen, New, and University) together regularly provided almost half. The Cambridge cohort was dominated by Trinity, which accounted for between 52 per cent (1931) and 67 per cent (1923); the highest figure for any

Table 5.4. University education of Conservative MPs[15]

The figures in the overall 'attended university' column are less than the sum of the other columns, as some MPs attended more than one university.

Year of intake	Oxford No.	Oxford %	Cambridge No.	Cambridge %	London No.	London %	Other English No.	Other English %	Scottish, Irish, & overseas No.	Scottish, Irish, & overseas %	Attended university No.	Attended university %
1918	89	23.3	61	16.0	9	2.4	5	1.3	38	9.9	187	49.0
1922	82	23.8	59	17.2	9	2.6	8	2.3	22	6.4	168	48.8
1923	70	27.1	42	16.3	5	1.9	4	1.6	20	7.8	134	51.9
1924	100	24.2	74	18.0	6	1.5	10	2.4	43	10.4	213	51.7
1929	68	26.2	49	18.8	3	1.2	6	2.3	34	13.1	144	55.4
1931	121	25.7	85	18.1	12	2.6	15	3.2	43	9.1	257	54.7
1935	109	28.2	74	19.1	7	1.8	13	3.4	29	7.5	222	57.4

[13] Based on figures for the 1922 intake in McEwen, 'Conservative MPs 1914–39', 196.
[14] From data in McEwen, 'Conservative MPs 1914–39'.
[15] From data in McEwen, 'Conservative MPs 1914–39'.

other college was 12 per cent from King's in 1929. However, whilst the proportion who had a university education rose during the interwar period, it was similar to the public school element in being not much more than half of the MPs. Most of those who had followed a service career had instead attended Sandhurst (Churchill was one such example) or one of the naval colleges, whilst others had entered immediately into business.

There was some antagonism just below the surface in the social base of the parliamentary party, fuelled by the resentments and snobberies which traversed its finer social gradations. Certainly the aristocracy possessed, or exhibited, greater poise and self-assurance, and in some instances (most likely amongst the gilded youths whose early entry into the House of Commons, generally for safe seats, naturally provoked envy) this shaded into, or was perceived as, arrogance and elitism. At the same time, some of the provincial businessmen were inclined to have a chip on their shoulder; J. R. Remer, MP for Macclesfield, complained to his local chairman of the lack of men with business experience on the front bench, declaring 'unless a man has been at one of the universities or one of the public schools, he is regarded as utterly incapable of knowing anything about politics'.[16] There was an element of exclusivity, and one MP who represented an industrial seat in 1931–35 complained of the incompetence of 'the Old Tie Brigade', which was concealed from public view by 'the obscene and perverted sense of loyalty which urges them to hang together'.[17]

The large majority of Conservative MPs were adherents of the Church of England, at least nominally; the proportion who were so from social convention rather than any personal belief is, by its nature, impossible to quantify.[18] The minority who made clear their membership of another religious group were perhaps more likely to be committed participants in that faith, but here also family tradition and loyalty could be a determining factor. About one-sixth of the parliamentary party belonged to a Christian denomination other than the Church of England, but the largest group within this were members of the Church of Scotland—which was the established church north of the border, and thus the conventional choice.[19] Of the MPs representing English constituencies, only around one in ten was publicly identified with another church or faith. Several of the Roman Catholic MPs came from long-established recusant gentry and aristocratic families, such as the Blundells and Hennessys; Lord Edmund Talbot, Chief Whip 1913–21, was a son of the Duke of Norfolk, and the long-serving MP Lord Colum Crichton-Stuart was a son of the Earl of Bute. The Nonconformists were generally businessmen and sat for urban,

---

[16] Remer to Taylor, 31 October 1930, Baldwin MSS, 31/185–7; Headlam diary, 2 February 1932.
[17] Spencer to Adams, 29 June 1936, Adams MSS, box 6.
[18] Fifty-five interwar Conservative MPs answered question 4 on religion in Wedgwood's survey for the History of Parliament, Wedgwood Questionnaire MSS: thirty-six indicated Church of England in some form (including Church of Ireland and Scottish Episcopal); five were Nonconformists (including Church of Scotland); seven gave affirmative but vague responses, generally of 'Protestant'; two were Roman Catholic; two were Jews; and three indicated they had no personal belief. However, it should also be noted that nine MPs who had answered question 1 gave no reply on this question.
[19] McEwen, 'Conservative MPs 1914–39', 424.

often northern, seats, many of which were marginals, whilst several of the Jewish MPs represented constituencies in London and the south-east.

Table 5.5. Religion of Conservative MPs in England[20]

This table excludes Wales & Monmouthshire, Scotland, Northern Ireland, and the university seats. It is assumed that English MPs who did not otherwise identify themselves should be regarded at least nominally as members of the Church of England. However, it has not been possible to identify all of the Roman Catholic MPs in the period 1918–23, and therefore there is also no total for Church of England MPs for these elections. The percentage figures are the proportion of the Conservative MPs elected for constituencies in England at each general election.

Year of intake	Church of England No.	%	Nonconformist No.	%	Roman Catholic No.	%	Jewish No.	%
1918	?	–	13	4.1	?	–	7	2.2
1922	?	–	14	4.6	?	–	6	2.0
1923	?	–	9	4.1	?	–	5	2.3
1924	313	90.2	15	4.3	10	2.9	9	2.6
1929	202	91.4	8	3.6	5	2.3	6	2.7
1931	352	88.4	18	4.5	18	4.5	10	2.5
1935	295	89.7	14	4.3	11	3.3	9	2.7

The change in the number of MPs who had a personal connection with their constituency reflected the economic circumstances of the interwar era. A local link was always desired, but the straitened circumstances of the landed gentry and the problems of agriculture were the main cause of the proportion of MPs for English county divisions who resided or owned land in the same county declining, from 81 per cent in 1914 to 55 per cent in 1939. However, over the same period, the number of MPs for the English boroughs (excluding London) who lived or had a business interest in their borough rose from 43 per cent to 64 per cent.[21] This reflected the rise in status of the local businessman, and a greater tendency of borough associations to look within their own district rather than to a landed county family. Of course, aristocratic candidates were still elected in boroughs, such as Lord Apsley in Southampton and Bristol Central, Lord Henry Cavendish-Bentinck in Nottingham South, Viscount Ednam in Hornsey, and Roger Lumley (later Earl of Scarbrough) in Hull East and York. This was not simply a consequence of deferential attitudes, for despite

---

[20] I am grateful to Dr Peter Catterall for the numbers of Nonconformists, taken from the lists published after each election in *Baptist Times, British Weekly, Christian World, Methodist Times, Primitive Methodist Leader, The Friend*, and *The Inquirer*; numbers of Roman Catholics from the *Catholic Directory* (which did not list Catholic MPs before 1924); numbers of Jewish MPs from G. Alderman, *The Jewish Vote in Great Britain since 1945* (Glasgow, 1980), 31, and adjusted for 1931 and 1935 from M. Stenton and S. Lees (eds.), *Who's Who of British Members of Parliament*, vols 3 and 4 (Brighton, 1979 and 1981).

[21] McEwen, 'Conservative MPs 1914–39', 56, 404.

economic changes many such men still possessed the combination of wealth, education, and assurance that was needed to be a credible contender.

Table 5.6. Age profile of Conservative MPs[22]

Year of intake	% 21–9	% 30–9	% 40–9	% 50–9	% 60–9	% over 70	% unknown
1918	0.8	16.0	29.1	30.1	20.4	2.9	0.8
1922	3.5	12.8	27.0	35.5	16.0	4.4	0.9
1923	5.0	13.6	28.7	32.6	14.7	4.3	1.2
1924	7.8	14.3	28.4	33.5	12.9	2.4	0.7
1929	4.2	16.5	25.8	34.6	14.2	3.0	1.5
1931	8.1	23.2	21.9	30.0	12.8	2.6	1.5
1935	3.1	22.7	24.3	26.6	16.8	3.9	2.6

The introduction of the generation who had seen combat in the First World War began with just a few cases in 1918, and rather more in 1922. These were generally the slightly older men, such as Walter Elliot, although they included the Jewish MP, Jack Brunel Cohen, who had lost both legs at Ypres in 1917; a founder of the British Legion in 1921, he remained an MP until 1931. The main influx of those who had been in the front lines of the Western Front or in other theatres occurred in 1924, partly because they were now in their late twenties and early thirties and thus credible as candidates, and partly due to the scale of the Conservative victory. As well as Macmillan and Crookshank, this intake included Ian Fraser, blinded in the Battle of the Somme, and many others: nearly two-thirds of the new entrants in 1924 had served overseas in the war, and many of the later intakes—especially those in 1931—also had combat experience. The result was that the older generation of leading figures who felt keenly their inability to share in the physical dangers of the Great War, such as Baldwin, were surrounded every day of their working lives by the living remainders and reminders of the sacrificed youth, not a few of whom bore the visible scars and disabilities of their wounds; it was hardly surprising that the quest to avoid another such cataclysm was followed so determinedly in the 1930s. However, the 1924 intake also saw the first arrivals of another cohort: men born in the early 1900s who had been too young to serve, such as Lord Balniel, Sir Hugh Lucas-Tooth, and Robert Boothby; a few more followed in 1929 (such as R. A. Butler—yet another of the many gulfs of sympathy which separated him from Macmillan), and more still in the 1931 landslide, such as Vyvyan Adams and Lord Dunglass (who succeeded as the 14th Earl of Home, but later repudiated the title on becoming Prime Minister in 1963, and returned to the House of Commons as Sir Alec Douglas-Home).

[22] Data on male MPs from McEwen, 'Conservative MPs 1914–39', recalculated to include women MPs (their dates of birth from *Oxford Dictionary of National Biography*).

Table 5.7. Departure and retirement of Conservative MPs[23]

Peerage includes successions to an existing title and new creations. Appointed refers to official salaried posts which require resignation from the House: these are not ministerial, but mostly judicial and imperial offices.

Year of intake	No. elected	Departed during the parliament						Retired at end	
		Died	Resigned	Peerage	Appointed	Total	%	No.	%
1918	382	21	15	10	8	54	14.1	87	22.8
1922	344	5	3	2	1	11	3.2	27	7.8
1923	258	4	1	1	1	7	2.7	15	5.8
1924	412	23	5	13	9	50	12.1	63	15.3
1929	260	5	7	2	–	14	5.4	28	10.8
1931	470	17	8	12	10	47	10.0	57	12.1
1935	387	74	23	29	15	141	36.4	75	19.4

Throughout the period, there was considerable turnover in the parliamentary ranks. Nearly 37 per cent of the MPs elected in the 'coupon' election of 1918 and more than a quarter of those of 1924 did not stand at the next election, whilst just under 56 per cent either departed during the extended 1935 parliament or stood down at its dissolution. After the 1922 election, there were only eighty-seven Conservative MPs who had sat in the House before the First World War; after 1929 this was reduced to forty, many of whom were on the front bench.[24] In 1918 and 1945 there was something of the passing of a generation: in 1918 it was those elected during the period of Conservative success from 1886 to 1900, whilst by 1945 many of the entrants of 1918, 1922, and 1924 had become too old to continue. In 1945 the high turnover was exacerbated by heavy defeat: of the 171 MPs elected in 1935 who stood again, 101 were defeated and only seventy continued directly into the postwar House. That this was a mere 18 per cent of the 387 Members who had been returned in 1935 underlines the scale of the discontinuity.

Most departures from the House of Commons were involuntary: in addition to electoral defeat, the main causes were death, old age, illness, financial difficulties, or succession to a seat in the House of Lords. More choice was involved on the part of those who accepted the offer of elevation to the peerage or appointment to a post in government service (such as colonial and Indian provincial governorships). The level of retirements at the end of the short parliaments of 1922 and 1923 was proportionate with the longer ones, and so it does not seem that the cost of several elections in rapid succession was a significant factor. Issues may have been more influential: in the aftermath of the India controversy, it was noticeable that sixteen of the fifty-seven retirements in 1935 were from seats in Lancashire and Cheshire.

---

[23] 1918–31 parliaments from data in McEwen, 'Conservative MPs 1914–39' (with error in 1922 figures corrected); 1935 parliament calculated from F. W. S. Craig (ed.), *British Parliamentary Election Results 1918–1949* (2nd edn,1977).

[24] McEwen, 'Conservative MPs 1914–39', 184, 283.

Membership of parliament did not always come up to expectations: after being elected at his third attempt, Critchley stood down with little regret after only sixteen months as an MP. However, a more frequent reaction was to fall in love with the place and hold onto a seat with limpet-like tenacity despite advancing age and declining health. This contributed to the number of by-elections which resulted from the death of the sitting Member, although some of these were unexpected and even shocking, such the drowning of Henry King when his yacht was wrecked on the Cornish coast in August 1930, the flying accident at Hendon whilst preparing for an exhibition which killed the youthful Viscount Knebworth in May 1933, the car which ran over Sir Alfred Bird as he crossed Piccadilly in February 1922, and the fall from the London to Glasgow night express of Sir John Rees four months later.

The Second World War brought its share of fatalities, for the same reason as the First had done: many Conservative MPs were young enough to fight in combat, were often already army reservists, and were of the social class to be commissioned as an officer with the accompanying expectation that they would set the other ranks an example by leading them into battle—which was the most exposed position of all. Others were inspired by patriotism, such as the fifty-five-year-old Sir Arnold Wilson, accused in the late 1930s of being pro-Fascist, who volunteered for the ordinary ranks of the RAF and was the rear gunner of a bomber which was shot down in May 1940. Most of those killed were relatively junior officers, such as Richard Porritt in the German breakthrough at Sedan in May 1940 and Ronald Cartland a few weeks later at Dunkirk. However, Colonel Edward Kellett, who was killed in action near the end of the North African campaign in March 1943, had been a career officer prior to entering the House in May 1939. Not all of the deaths were in uniform or the result of enemy action: Victor Cazalet had been appointed liaison to the President of the Polish government-in-exile, General Sikorski, and died with him in a plane crash at Gibraltar in July 1943, together with John Whiteley, MP for Buckingham.

Table 5.8. Continuity and political experience of Conservative MPs[25]

Year of intake	No. of MPs continued from the previous parliament	No. of new MPs who had sat in an earlier parliament	No. of new MPs elected for the first time	% of new MPs elected for the first time	Total no. of MPs
1918	209	5	168	44.0	382
1922	229	4	111	32.3	344
1923	220	6	32	12.4	258
1924	235	65	112	27.2	412
1929	224	3	33	12.7	260
1931	236	51	183	38.9	470
1935	341	3	43	11.1	387

[25] From data in McEwen, 'Conservative MPs 1914–39'.

It is striking that the number who continued directly into the next parliament was remarkably similar in all of the elections from 1918 to 1931, remaining between 209 and 236, although the total number of Conservative MPs varied considerably. The number continuing in 1935 differed partly because the previous intake had exceptionally large, and partly because the electoral circumstances enabled many of the marginals to be held. In each intake, there were some MPs who had not been in the previous parliament but had served in an earlier one. In a few cases the interval was substantial, as with E. B. Fielden, who represented Middleton in the 1900–06 House and returned for another seat in 1924. The gap was usually one parliament, and the large number of former MPs in 1924 and 1931 consisted almost entirely of those who had lost their seats in 1923 and 1929. The newcomers were, in some cases, succeeding to vacancies in safe seats, and this accounts for the first timers in 1923 and 1929, and many of those in 1935. When the party was gaining marginals, the number of novice MPs was much higher, and was thus at its peak in 1931 and 1918.

Although some Members did not stay long in the House, there was a core of long-serving MPs who sat for the safer seats. Of the Conservative MPs of the period 1918–45, fifty-nine sat in the House for thirty years or longer, of whom nineteen attained the Cabinet at some point during their career, even if only briefly (such as Winterton, Tryon, and Dugdale). The biggest totals were accumulated by two Leaders of the Party: Churchill was by far the longest-serving at one month less than sixty-two years, and Balfour was his runner-up with forty-eight years and three months in the House. However, the majority of the longest sitting were either backbenchers or, at most, junior ministers. The record for this category was held by the diehard leader, Gretton, with forty-six years and seven months as an MP between his first election in 1895 and retirement in 1943. One of the most notable examples was Sir James Agg-Gardner, who contested his beloved home town of Cheltenham in almost every election from 1868 to 1924, winning more often than losing and sitting for a total of thirty-eight years and four months, until his death in 1928; at the other end of the period, Robin Turton was elected for Thirsk & Malton in 1929, and remained its MP until 1974. To some extent there was a two-tier parliamentary party, with a core of long-serving stalwarts around whom ebbed and flowed a larger group of more ephemeral Members. The latter can be divided into two types: those who sat for a single parliament only, and those who were in or out in relation to the party's fortunes, like political yo-yos; one such was Headlam, who won a marginal constituency in 1924 and 1931 but lost it in 1929 and 1935, before making the crucial transition to a safe seat in a wartime by-election and thus surviving the 1945 landslide.

The correlation between the length of parliamentary service and the conferment of honours is clearly demonstrated in Table 5.9, and there was indeed almost an unofficial queue for knighthoods.[26] This or a baronetcy was very likely for MPs who stayed the course, and a peerage was quite possible, as is shown by the figures for those who sat for more than fifteen years in the House of Commons. These honours were normally earned by steadiness and diligence, and by a standing in the House which depended more upon character and reputation than debating

---

[26] Headlam diary, 25 November 1936.

Table 5.9. Length of service and honours of Conservative MPs[27]

This table includes all Conservative MPs who were elected from the general election of 1918 to the last by-election prior to the 1945 general election. Lengths of service are for their whole career (taking account of any period out of the House of Commons), and have been calculated to the nearest month. The category 'courtesy title' comprises the sons of peers who were given the courtesy titles of lord, viscount, earl, or marquess (but not 'the Honourable'), the wives of peers, and the holders of Irish peerages. The category 'already knight or baronet' consists of those who possessed such a title before their first election to the House of Commons. The 'becomes' categories consist of those who acquired such a title during their parliamentary career or at any time afterwards, and includes creations of knights, baronets, and peers (including life peerages and law lords), and successions to baronetcies and peerages. Each person is counted only once in each category (e.g. an MP who became a knight and a baronet is counted as one in the category 'becomes knight or baronet'). However, if an individual had honours in more than one category, they will be counted once in each category (e.g. where a person with a knighthood or baronetcy became a peer, or a person with a courtesy title inherited a peerage). The final row indicates the proportion of each cohort with any title, and is not the sum of the rows above.

Total length of service (years and months)	Less than 2.0 years	2.0 to 4.11	5.0 to 9.11	10.0 to 14.11	15.0 to 19.11	20 years & above
Number in cohort	75	265	193	228	139	243
As % of all MPs	6.6	23.2	16.9	19.9	12.2	21.3
% courtesy title	4.0	2.6	3.1	3.9	5.0	4.1
% already knight or baronet	13.3	13.6	15.5	10.1	7.9	7.8
% becomes knight or baronet.[28]	10.7	13.2	26.9	51.3	55.4	58.4
% becomes peer (all ranks)	9.3	9.8	11.4	12.7	28.8	36.2
Number of cohort with any title	25	92	92	158	107	206
% of cohort with any title	33.3	34.7	47.7	69.3	77.0	84.8

skills. They were a customary reward for loyalty, which it was assumed would continue—hence the Chief Whip's angry remarks to Basil Peto (who had been made a baronet in the previous year) when his opposition to a minor bill caused an embarrassing defeat.[29] Baldwin decided upon all honours for MPs in consultation with the Chief Whip and would not override his advice, even at the behest of a senior colleague.[30] Knighthoods and baronetcies were also regularly given to junior ministers, in many cases at or near the end of their period in office. Indeed, this was so customary that Headlam was more insulted than gratified to be offered a baronetcy

---

[27] Calculated from the entries in Stenton and Lees, *Who's Who of British Members of Parliament*, vols 3 and 4.

[28] This includes J. W. Hills, who was to have been created a baronet in the New Year honours list of January 1939, but died a week before the announcement; the honour has been counted, as it was instead conferred upon his son.

[29] Peto to Eyres-Monsell, 1 August 1928, in Lady Peto diary, 2 August 1928.

[30] Baldwin to A. Chamberlain, 23 June 1929, AC, 38/3/74.

when he decided to relinquish junior office in 1934, regarding the honour as a tombstone publicly interring his political career.[31] In some cases, the honour came many years after leaving the House and was primarily earned for other reasons (most usually prominence in business or industry, as in the case of Clavering Fison, chairman of the eponymous chemical and fertilizer company, who was an MP in 1929–31 and knighted in 1957).

Peerages of the rank of baron were quite often given to the most senior backbench MPs of a suitable social background and wealth; there were also cases (as with knighthoods) where they were conferred after a relatively short period in the House, but this was due to the recipients' eminence in some field outside politics. It was customary for a former Cabinet minister to be entitled to a peerage, and the usual convention was that Cabinet rank merited a viscountcy and the Premiership an earldom;[32] examples of the former were Bridgeman and Joynson-Hicks in 1929, and of the latter Balfour in 1922 and Baldwin in 1937. The peerages were usually created immediately upon the person ceasing to be an MP, but if the minister was continuing in office whilst moving to the upper chamber, a barony was sometimes the initial rank, with a step to viscount later: this was the case with Lee, Birkenhead, and Hailsham. However, the most coveted honour for any politician was not inheritable: it was to become a Privy Councillor, with the prefix 'Right Honourable'. This gave precedence in debate in the Commons, and was usually recognition of an advancing ministerial career, being given to successful junior ministers and all Cabinet ministers who did not already have it. Thus Lane-Fox's heavy responsibilities as Minister for Mines during the long coal strike earned him his Privy Councillorship in 1926, with Salisbury observing that 'he most thoroughly deserves it by his abundant work and competence'.[33] Privy Councillorships were also given to the most respected long-serving backbenchers, in recognition to their standing in the House.

Whilst there was considerable common ground in social origin and education, and some obvious clustering in the occupational categories and age profile, Conservative MPs still had a wide variety of experiences, interests, and personalities. A number of MPs had notable sporting backgrounds: Lord Burghley (an MP from 1931 until 1943, later succeeding as 6th Marquess of Exeter in 1956) won the gold medal for the 400 metre hurdles at the 1928 Olympics; Harold Mitchell (Party Vice-chairman 1942–45) represented Great Britain at skiing in 1929, 1931, and 1933; Robert Bourne held a record as stroke oarsman in four university boat races (for Oxford, his later constituency); Charles Howard-Bury led the Mount Everest Reconnaissance Expedition of 1921, and William Wakefield was a former captain of England at rugby, whilst Party Chairman Stanley Jackson had captained England at cricket. The Marquess of Clydesdale, an MP from 1930 to 1940, was a noted amateur boxer and the Chief Pilot of the Mount Everest Flight Expedition of 1933; as Duke of Hamilton, he was the person whom Hitler's deputy, Rudolf Hess, aimed to contact when he flew to Scotland in May 1941. Even the appar-

---

[31] Headlam diary, 1 and 17 May 1933.
[32] This was not invariable, and ex-Cabinet ministers who received only a barony included Betterton, Colville, Guinness, Hilton Young, McNeill, and Sanders.
[33] Salisbury to Irwin, 16 July 1926, Halifax MSS, C152/17/1/67a.

ently staid might have unusual backgrounds or experiences, as can be illustrated by six men, five of whom have a common link of the sea: the Glasgow merchant Harold Moss began his working life as an apprentice on 'windjammers' sailing to Australia, a four-month voyage of hardship and danger; Burton Chadwick also spent a decade at sea and had been awarded a medal for life-saving; George Bowyer, Party Vice-Chairman for candidates 1930–35, on one occasion piloted the liner *Queen Mary* into dock; George Davies, a whip in the 1930s, was born at Honolulu and was Vice-Consul there before 1914; Admiral Sir William James, the Commander-in-Chief at Portsmouth in 1939–42 and then an MP for the city, was the grandson of the artist John Millais and the original model for his famous painting 'Bubbles'; whilst Lord Lymington was brought up on a ranch in Wyoming.

As with any large human company, there were stories of success and failure. Most of the former were accomplished in careers which had started before entering the Commons, such as the huge sales of John Buchan's adventure novels. Some prospered in business but others struggled, even before the slump of 1929; thus Cornelius Homan's seat was declared vacant when he was adjudicated a bankrupt in 1928. The shipping magnate Owen Phillips, chairman of the Royal Mail Steam Packet Company and the Union-Castle Line, was created Baron Kyslant in 1923, but five years later was sentenced to a year in prison for commercial fraud. On a lesser scale, the auctioneer Hugh Ferguson, briefly an MP in the 1923–24 parliament, was convicted ten years later of knowingly receiving stolen goods. Finally, some cases were clearly tragic, even if not always so perceived at the time. One such was Herbert Latham, an army officer who had a breakdown during wartime service in 1941; he resigned his seat whilst under arrest for disgraceful conduct and attempted suicide, was cashiered and sentenced to two years in prison, and was subsequently divorced by his wife.

THE WOMEN MPs

The almost-exclusively male composition of the parliamentary party reflected contemporary attitudes towards the appropriate roles for women. It was accepted that they now had the vote, but a full-time political career was felt by many of conservative temperament to be contrary to feminine nature. This was partly due to the combative nature of politics (especially the element of rowdiness involved in an election campaign), and partly to the neglect of family duties that it was assumed such a path must entail. Some of the resistance was based simply on prejudice, such as the feeling that women would be unable to master the procedures of the House or the factual expertise needed for debate, and would become emotional and shrill. There was certainly an element of misogyny on the part of many male MPs, who disliked the appearance of women in their sanctum and feared it would lose its clubbish character, and the first women MPs encountered a good deal of antagonism. This only partially diminished; the Chief Whip from 1941 to 1948, James Stuart, was particularly hostile, considering that the women MPs had 'failed to get satisfaction out of their normal lives'.[34] The view of their unsuitability for parliamentary life meant that any woman who sought election was by definition 'unnatural', and the fact that most of the women who were able to become MPs were either unmarried or childless reinforced this. Of course, for a woman to stand for parliament required an unusual degree of confidence and assertiveness, characteristics which male MPs found uncomfortable and unappealing. Thus, 'even the more feminine . . . become more like men and so worse and consequently less like women'.[35] The women MPs were generally dismissed as arid spinsters or 'blue-stocking' faddists, and the doubt that they might put loyalty to their gender first and espouse feminist positions meant that they were regarded as a potential fifth column.

These negative views of women as MPs were held not only by male MPs and not only by men, but also by many women, especially in the middle and upper classes. It must be remembered that most of the men in the House of Commons and those of both genders on constituency executives in the 1920s would be aged over forty, and thus brought up in late Victorian society. The crucial barrier was the reluctance of local associations to select a female candidate if there was any suitable male available, and so women were hardly ever chosen for safe seats or winnable marginals.[36] There was greater willingness, or perhaps necessity, to nominate a woman in the more hopeless prospects, and the landslide victory of 1931 dramatically boosted the number of female MPs, although this was a temporary effect and most of them were defeated at the next election. However, those who managed to hold their seats in 1935 remained in the House until 1945, benefiting from the wartime prolongation. With one exception, all of the women MPs then either vacated or lost their seats, although some—such as Irene Ward—had become well-known and were able to return later for safer constituencies. Even so, in the interwar period the overall position was one of few female candidates producing even fewer MPs, and of only a handful of women having parliamentary careers of any security or continuity.

Table 5.10. Conservative women candidates and MPs

	1918	1922	1923	1924	1929	1931	1935	1945
Candidates	1	5	7	12	10	16	19	14
MPs	–	1	3	3	3	13	6	1

Only four women sat as Conservative MPs in the period between 1918 and 1931, and they all entered the House for the constituency which their husband had previously represented. They were therefore already well-known to the local association and to the voters, and their abilities and popularity had been demonstrated. In each case, their husband had had no choice in relinquishing his seat, and his active support and local prestige were crucial in fostering the candidature.

---

[34] Stuart to Dugdale, 20 August 1941, CPA, Whips' Office MSS, 2/3; Cazalet-Keir, *From the Wings*, 126.
[35] Beamish diary notes, 29 March 1944, Beamish MSS, CAC, BEAM/3/5.
[36] Memo by Bowyer, 'Candidates', 19 July 1934, Baldwin MSS, 48/240–4.

In many ways this was the continuation of a connection by proxy, especially in the case of the three titled women, and was not different in nature from the recurrence of male candidates of the same family in other constituencies. However, whilst this may have opened the door at the outset, each of the women was a strong character who developed her own reputation and standing. The longest-serving and most famous was Nancy, Viscountess Astor, who became the first woman to sit in the House of Commons. Her husband's succession to a peerage caused a by-election at Plymouth Sutton in November 1919, and her adoption, campaign, and subsequent entry to the House aroused great press and public interest. She represented the seat until she retired in 1945 and throughout she was a focus of attention and a much-requested public speaker, especially by Conservative women's associations. However, she was too much of an individualist to be a likely prospect for office, and preferred to use her prominence to campaign for the causes she believed in—not all of which were in tune with traditional Conservative opinion, in particular her strong support for temperance. An American by birth and Christian Scientist by conviction, she was charismatic and could be charming but did not shirk confrontation and aroused considerable antipathy; she complained of being 'treated more like a poor relation than the only Unionist woman MP'.[37] In the later 1930s, the Astors were identified with support for appeasement, partly due to Lord Astor's ownership of *The Times* and support for its editor, Geoffrey Dawson, and partly to claims that their country estate at Cliveden was the social centre of a 'set' willing to seek peace at any price. Much of this was the invention of hostile journalists during the war; it was both hurtful and damaging, and contributed to Viscountess Astor's retirement in 1945. In fact, Astor had been one of the MPs whose abstention in the debate on the Norwegian campaign had caused Neville Chamberlain's downfall in May 1940.

The next to be elected was Mabel Philipson (née Russell), who was from a much humbler background than most Conservative MPs: her father was a commercial traveller who lived in Peckham. She became a leading actress between 1907 and 1917, retiring from the stage on her second marriage to Hilton Philipson (her first husband, a nephew of Cecil Rhodes, had been killed not long after their wedding in a car accident which left Mabel blind in one eye), and they had three children. Hilton was elected for Berwick in 1922; he stood as a National Liberal, but had Conservative support in a straight fight with the leading Asquithian Liberal, Walter Runciman. However, his agent had spent more than the legal maximum and the election was declared void; as he was barred from standing again, Mabel was adopted for the resulting by-election in May 1923. She stood as a Conservative candidate and won by a comfortable majority of over 6,000 against both Liberal and Labour opposition, retaining the seat with a reduced majority in the general election later that year. In March 1924, due to the conflict between her duties in the House and her family, she offered to retire in favour of her husband. This was agreed to, on condition that she assist him on the platform, but shortly afterwards

---

[37] Astor to Baird, 14 December 1923, Baldwin MSS, 35/129.

Hilton discovered that he was not eligible to stand.[38] Mabel was asked to resume the candidacy and she remained the MP until 1929, when she stood down despite requests to continue.[39] Her electoral style was similar to Nancy Astor's; both were extroverts who were energized by their interactions with crowds and adept at dealing with hecklers. However, Mabel Philipson did not enjoy speaking in the more austere atmosphere of the Commons and was relatively inactive, confining herself mainly to constituency interests and some 'women's issues', such as adoption and a bill of her own for the registration of nursing homes.

The third MP was less colourful but more effective, and she became the first Conservative woman to hold ministerial office. Katherine, Duchess of Atholl, was also of the highest social class, although by marriage rather than birth. She had been active in local government before her election in 1923 for Kinross & West Perthshire, the seat which her husband had represented until his succession as the 8th Duke in 1917. A serious-minded woman who had no children, she immersed herself in political and charitable work; in the 1924–29 government she was appointed as junior minister for education, which was seen as a suitable area of feminine concern as it dealt with the rearing of children. Her relations with her chief, Lord Eustace Percy, were difficult and he tended to ignore her, but this did not count against her as he was a prickly and aloof character to whom few warmed. During her first decade in the House, the Duchess was a model of orthodoxy and dullness who was effective through hard work rather than inspiration, and so her final five years as a rebel were a surprising contrast. In fact, her character and even her views had not changed, but rather the causes which she took up set her at variance with the party leadership and eventually—and disastrously—with her local association. The issues all stemmed from the sphere which Conservatives considered very suitable for women: charitable and humanitarian concern, especially the plight of women and children. In the early 1930s, this took her in a rightwards direction, as a campaign publicizing the slave labour camps in Russia gave her the appearance of a hammer of the Bolsheviks, and her fears for the position of the lowest castes in an India dominated by Hindu Brahmins led her to join the diehard opposition to the India Bill. Typically, 'she was so painstaking and hard working that her speeches were far too long'.[40]

By 1935, the Duchess was sufficiently alienated to be one of the five MPs who publicly resigned the National (but not the Conservative) whip in protest over India and other 'semi-Socialist' legislation. All this her constituency executive could accept, but the next phase took her into co-operation with the left and overstrained their tolerance. The issue was the Spanish Civil War, and concern over the plight of refugees led her, unlike most Conservatives, to support the Republican regime as legitimate and criticize Franco's Nationalists. As always, she threw herself into the cause, visiting Spain and writing a best-selling book on her return.[41] The

---

[38] Berwick & Alnwick CA, Exec., 12 January, 26 March, 14 June 1924.
[39] Berwick & Alnwick CA, Exec., 21 September 1928, Council, 19 November 1928.
[40] Peto's unpublished memoirs, Peto MSS.
[41] Duchess of Atholl, *Searchlight on Spain* (Harmondsworth, 1938).

campaign linked her to cross-party groups which included Communists, and her presence on the platform of a rally in Glasgow which was reported to have closed with the singing of the 'Internationale' created the image of the 'Red Duchess', which tarred her indelibly. She became a vocal critic of Neville Chamberlain's appeasement policy in general, and in 1938, after repeated infighting, she was repudiated by her constituency association. Typically, she decided to make no concessions and fight this straight on. Against Churchill's advice, not long after the Munich Agreement she resigned her seat and fought the resulting by-election as an Independent anti-appeaser. No Liberal or Labour candidates were nominated, and the contest became a straight fight with the official Conservative, a respected local farmer who defended Chamberlain's still-popular resolution of the Czech crisis. On a bitterly cold December day, she was defeated in a result which was considered surprising in a Highland region where feudal loyalty was still potent, but, although she had a band of staunch supporters, most of the gentry (some of whom, as Catholics, were pro-Franco) and farmers were against her. Chamberlain was 'overjoyed' at the vindication of his policy; although public opinion viewed matters differently within less than a year, the Duchess made no attempt to return to parliament.[42]

The fourth and last of the early women MPs was the most successful at working with the grain of Conservative politics. Gwendolen, Countess of Iveagh, was a daughter of the 4th Earl of Onslow who married into the wealthy Guinness family; in 1927 her husband succeeded as 2nd Earl of Iveagh and had to vacate the Southend-on-Sea constituency which he had represented since 1918. 'Gwenny' was popular without being abrasive, and noted for her good sense, calmness, and mediatory abilities. She had initial doubts—'When I first got into the House, I hated it'—but she became a successful speaker, in particular with a highly regarded contribution in the emotional theatre of the second Prayer Book debate in June 1928.[43] She was the most involved in the party organization, serving as Chairman of the National Union Women's Advisory Committee 1927–33 and as a member of the Executive Committee 1928–35—and as Chairman of the Central Council in 1930, she was praised for the tact and efficiency with which she presided effectively over the potentially fractious special conference of that year which revised the rules. She retired from the House at the 1935 general election, handing over the Southend seat to her son-in-law, Henry 'Chips' Channon.

The 1931 landslide swept ten new Conservative women MPs into the House to join the established trio of Astor, Atholl, and Iveagh. Ida Copeland (elected for Stoke), Marjorie Graves (who defeated Herbert Morrison in Hackney South), Norah Runge (Rotherhithe), Helen Shaw (Bothwell), and Sarah Ward (Cannock) were unexpected victors in safe Labour seats, and all were defeated in 1935; Mary Pickford sat for Hammersmith North until her death from pneumonia in March 1934. The other four newcomers held their seats in 1935, in the case of Mavis Tate by transferring from Willesden West (1931–35) to the Frome division of Somerset

---

[42] N. Chamberlain to Margesson, 23 December 1938, Margesson MSS, CAC, MRGN/1/3/23.
[43] Lady Iveagh to Irwin, 16 December 1927, Halifax MSS, C152/17/1/274c; Lane-Fox to Irwin, 14 June 1928, Halifax MSS, C152/18/1/69.

(1935–45). Tate was an example of almost bulldozing determination; she was a pioneer aviator in the 1920s and one of the first people to enter Buchenwald after its liberation in 1945, an experience which considerably affected her. After losing her seat in 1945, she suffered from painful illness and in June 1947 committed suicide by gas poisoning. Thelma Cazalet (Cazalet-Keir after her marriage in 1939), MP for Islington East 1931–45, succeeded by a combination of charm, cleverness, and good connections; her brother Victor was already an MP, and she was on friendly terms with Lloyd George (through his daughter, Megan), Baldwin, and Churchill. She was Parliamentary Private Secretary to the junior minister for Education in 1937–40, and was appointed to that office herself in the 'Caretaker' government of May–July 1945; on 28 March 1944 her motion for equal pay for male and female teachers led to the only defeat of the wartime coalition.[44]

Florence Horsbrugh won Dundee in 1931 and unexpectedly held it until 1945; she had the most successful ministerial career of all, serving as the junior minister for Health from 1939 to 1945 and, after returning to the House for a Manchester constituency in 1950, was Minister of Education from 1951 to 1954; in September 1953 she became the first Conservative woman member of the Cabinet. Irene Ward, who represented Wallsend in 1931–45, was another who returned for a safer seat in 1950; 'buxom, confident and able',[45] she was an influential backbencher for the next twenty-four years and was awarded a life peerage on her retirement in 1974; hers was the longest female Conservative parliamentary career, exceeding even Margaret Thatcher's thirty-three years. The last three arrivals returned to the pattern of the 1920s in succeeding to seats that had been vacated by their husbands. The most prominent was Joan 'Mimi' Davidson, wife of the former Party Chairman and herself a close friend of Baldwin; she had long been more popular than her husband in his Hemel Hempstead constituency and did much of the work there, and was invited to stand for the vacancy caused by his elevation to the peerage in Baldwin's resignation honours in 1937. This was a safe seat and she was the only woman Conservative elected in 1945; she sat until 1959, and was given a life peerage in 1964. In the case of the two wartime entrants, the vacancy was due to the death of their husband on active service: Beatrice Rathbone (Wright after remarriage in 1942) was MP for Bodmin from March 1941 until she retired at the 1945 election, and Lady Apsley was MP for Bristol Central from February 1943 until her defeat in 1945.

PARLIAMENTARY LIFE

Although a modest parliamentary salary of £400 had been introduced in 1912, this fell considerably short of the costs involved in being a Conservative MP. There were three aspects to this, the first of which was the expenses of the election

---

[44] Cazalet-Keir, *From the Wings*, 142–5.
[45] Beamish diary notes, 8 March 1944, Beamish MSS, CAC, BEAM/3/5.

campaign itself. Normally in the range of £700 to £1,000, in most cases these were found entirely by the candidate. However, candidates in the hopeless or uninviting prospects often received a grant from the central party funds, without which many of them would have been unwilling or unable to stand. During the 1930s, some associations began to share the burden: in England and Wales in the general election of 1935, twelve constituencies paid the whole of the expenses and forty-five others divided the cost with their candidate.[46] Of the rest, fifty-three were financed by combined contributions from the candidate, the local association, and the regional Area. This last was, by this time, the channel through which support from national party funds was disbursed, and in a further fifty-one cases the Area assisted the candidate with all or part of the costs, without any contribution from the constituency. Even so, 267 candidates (nearly two-thirds) were responsible for the entire amount themselves. Whether paying all or most of the election costs, the sum involved was no small item and the incidence of three general elections in twenty-four months in 1922–24 imposed strains on even the deeper pockets.[47] As Joynson-Hicks pointed out shortly before the 1923 dissolution, another contest so soon 'would be most unpopular with our party in the House. They have all paid one thousand pounds to get there, and they and their wives do not want to pay another thousand with a risk of being thrown out.'[48]

The second cost resulted from the expectation of constituency associations that the MP would be their largest subscriber, all the more so in the safer seats where several hundred pounds per annum was customary. In quite a few cases, the MP simply passed his entire parliamentary salary to the association, a pattern which was also partly an expression of disdain for the concept of gaining a financial reward for service in parliament, and partly an implicit affirmation of status and independence.[49] This subvention was a mixed blessing for constituency finances, with both safe and weak seats becoming over-dependent on their candidate. A related, but lesser, call on the MP's purse was the constant stream of small donations to various constituency charities and events which made manifest his interest and involvement in the community; as one candidate remarked, 'it is impossible to say no!'[50] Joynson-Hicks declared publicly in 1924 that, over a quarter of a century, his political career had cost him over £25,000, a very large sum in this period; only around one-third of this amount was accounted for by the cost of the seven elections that he had contested.[51] Even so, few spent on the scale of Thomas Cook, who estimated his political expenses during twelve years as candidate and MP for North Norfolk to total £19,250, which included the gift of four village halls,

---

[46] Special Finance Ctte., 'Election Expenses: How Provided', 1943, CPA, CCO/500/3/2. Six of the constituencies which paid the whole cost were in the West Midlands and five others were north of the River Trent; only one was in southern England, where most of the safest and wealthiest seats were located.

[47] Blake (chairman, West Wiltshire CA) to Long, 15 December 1923, Long MSS (WSA), 947/885.

[48] Joynson-Hicks to Baldwin, 20 October 1923, Baldwin MSS, 35/30–1.

[49] At least one MP also passed on the £200 salary increase enacted in 1937: Gravesend CA, Exec., 2 July 1937. For opposition to salaries, NU Conf., 1922.

[50] Perkins to Ashley, 20 November 1920, 6 July 1921, Ashley MSS, BR/71; see the extensive examples in the Locker-Lampson MSS, files OLL/2206–2438.

[51] *The Times*, 4 June 1924.

Christmas presents each year for every person in the local workhouses and hospitals, taking two groups of fifty to the war graves in France, and an annual outing to London for around a thousand constituents that included chartering special trains.[52]

The final cost was maintaining the necessary and expected standard of living whilst an MP, which for most involved accommodation in London and in the country, both probably employing domestic servants, and running a car (which often required a chauffeur as well). Political life entailed a good deal of travel; MPs' rail fares between Westminster and their constituency were paid by the state, but not those of their wives and secretaries, not if they travelled by car, and not if they were journeying to speak somewhere else. It was possible to combine membership of the Commons with an active career in the professions (especially law), the media, or business, and this was how most Conservative MPs bridged the yawning gap between their parliamentary salary and their expenditure. The need for substantial private income reinforced the social exclusivity of parliament, as the large majority of the population could not afford it. Whilst Central Office provided grants for the poorer constituencies, and frequently assisted with their candidates' expenses, it rarely subsidized the personal income of an MP. Where this did happen, the recipients were normally persons from the upper social strata who were attractive to impecunious constituencies because of their background and expertise or ability, but who did not have quite enough personal income to afford to stand. Headlam is an example here: the combination of his salary as editor of the *Army Quarterly*, some minor directorships, and the parliamentary salary made it possible for him to give up his clerkship in the House of Lords and become an MP, with Central Office covering the election expenses and, for the first few years, giving some direct subvention as well. One instance was due to political expediency: when the victor of the famous Newport by-election of 1922, Reginald Clarry, got into financial difficulties in the late 1920s, he was bailed out by Central Office, partly to avoid tarnishing the image of anti-Coalitionism and partly to avoid an awkward by-election.[53]

With the advent of democracy, MPs were obliged to adapt their conduct to the public's presumption that a Member's work was to speak in debate and vote in divisions. Absenteeism was criticized by the constituency grass roots, especially when the party was in opposition and opportunities to inflict defeats on the Labour government were lost, such as the December 1929 debate on the Coal Bill.[54] However, the work of the House was often routine and the legislation under consideration either obscure and dull or lost under a mass of detail and incomprehensible to all but a handful who had expert knowledge of the topic.[55] For almost all of the

---

[52] Young (Eastern Area CO Agent) to Davidson, 30 April 1936, Davidson MSS, DAV/226. This was certainly not unique: F. W. Astbury's local chairman estimated that he had spent £15,000 in Salford West between 1918 and 1933, Baldwin MSS, 58/202–4; Duckworth spent £2,600 in 1929–31, Shrewsbury CA, Central Ctte., 28 November 1931.

[53] Davidson to Evans, 2 February, Bottome to Davidson, 3 February 1927, Davidson MSS, DAV/180.

[54] Westminster St George's CA, Exec., 19 December 1929.

[55] Conway to his wife, 20 July 1925, Conway MSS, 7676/D/244.

interwar period, the Conservative Party was in government and its MPs were discouraged from pursuing their own initiatives and taking up parliamentary time; they were 'expected just to vote when they are told and are never able to express their own opinions'.[56] Moments of excitement were few and far between, and thus 'stormy scenes' were not unwelcome.[57] For similar reasons, wit and humour were highly prized, although its predominantly male and largely public-school-educated composition set the tone of 'the rather school-boy outlook of the House of Commons'.[58] It was also the case that each parliament had its own particular character and atmosphere, with a consequent rise and fall in reputations and effectiveness. Voting in as many divisions as possible was important, as a good division record impressed the voters and a poor one was vulnerable to attack. Nearly all divisions were on a party basis, and so MPs did not need to hear the debate in order to decide how to vote; they simply looked to the direction of their party's whips at the division lobby doors and entered the appropriate one. This meant that the ringing of the division bell would bring MPs not just from various parts of the Palace of Westminster, but also from the nearby clubs and ministerial offices in which bells had also been installed. Committee work was less visible to the public, but became an increasing part of MPs' activities in the interwar period, both in the official committees of parliament itself and the various party organizations discussed further later in this chapter. Service to the House in committee work led to its own path of promotion, leading from committee chairmen to the Chairman of Ways and Means and ultimately to the Speakership.

Whilst debates and votes were determined by party loyalty, the other identity which affected MPs was representing the interests of their constituency. Two consequences of the First World War led to increased constituency obligations for MPs in the interwar era: the enlarged electorate and the enlarged role of the state. MPs' postbags noticeably increased in the 1920s, and they became more engaged in acting as mediator between individual constituents and government departments. This involved letters to ministers even more than asking questions in the House, and it particularly revolved around pensions (especially for widows and war disabilities), unemployment benefit, and other social issues such as housing.[59] It was estimated that one Member, during twenty years' service, had assisted with the cases of nearly 8,000 constituents and had written 47,000 letters.[60] MPs also tended to have more frequent contact with their constituency than before the war, although this varied according to whether they were normally resident there when parliament was not sitting.[61] Living in the constituency was a mixed blessing, with

---

[56] Long to Wilson, 21 February 1923, Long MSS, Add.62427/151–5.
[57] Winterton to Irwin, 14 July 1926, Halifax MSS, C152/17/1/66.
[58] Winterton to Irwin, 12 July 1928, Halifax MSS, C152/18/1/89a.
[59] For a surviving example of such work, see Locker-Lampson MSS, files OLL/2001–2205; Sir Frank Sanderson estimated that he had written over 52,000 letters between the 1935 and 1945 general elections: Ealing CA, Council, 1 June 1945.
[60] Worcester CA, AGM, 21 April 1944; for an example of an active MP's day, Lady Peto diary, 20–21 May 1930.
[61] Ormsby-Gore to his mother, 15 November 1919, Ormsby-Gore MSS, PEC/10/1/11/15.

convenience balanced by being 'always at everybody's beck and call'.[62] If non-resident, then occasional but well-chosen and high-profile visits were the normal pattern; an annual speaking campaign often sufficed, together with an occasional presence at important events. Many MPs also undertook regular speaking engagements outside their own constituency; some of these were simply co-operation with neighbouring seats, but others could take them far afield, either at the invitation of a colleague or the behest of the party managers, especially for a by-election. In consequence, the more politically active MPs found themselves 'giving up business, home life, spending hours and days working and travelling for the cause', although there were many others who kept a lower profile.[63] Of course, it was not just in this era that an MP could feel 'if it only were not for one's damned constituency, what fun politics would be!'[64]

The daily life of an MP was, above all, a social life.[65] Some time might be occupied listening to debate in the chamber or in committee work, but much more was spent in conversation with colleagues in the lobbies, tea rooms, bars and library, or on the terrace. A favoured haunt of many Conservatives was the Smoking Room, which the female MPs entered only if invited.[66] It was a common practice to dine at the House, or to take lunch or dinner at one of the nearby clubs. Most MPs belonged to several, including, of course, the traditional base of Conservative MPs, the Carlton; other popular venues were the Constitutional, and non-political clubs such as the Travellers' (favoured by Baldwin), the Beefsteak, Pratt's (favoured by younger MPs), the Combined Universities, and so on. The effect of these interactions was the construction of many complex and interweaving social networks, in which most MPs were acquainted with many others on an informal basis, together with a more select number with whom they tended to dine, take refreshment, and sit in the chamber. These overlapping connections were the conduits along which rumour and gossip rapidly spread, creating the buzz of news and speculation that was much of the attraction of parliamentary life, with 'the excitement, the thrills, the atmosphere of ill-concealed nervousness, the self-interest, which comes over the House of Commons when there is a political crisis on, or rumours of a re-shuffle'.[67] The sense of being involved in great affairs, even if largely as a ringside spectator, counterbalanced the tedium of which many backbenchers complained. As Macmillan observed, 'politics is like drink—a very difficult habit to break'.[68]

Social contact took place mainly in the precincts of the Palace of Westminster and, to lesser extent, in the political 'zone' of nearby clubs and restaurants. MPs tended to be at the House if they were not engaged in other work; visiting each others' homes

---

[62] Lady Peto diary, 24 October 1922.
[63] Smithers to Baldwin, 1 March 1929, Baldwin MSS, 36/83–6; for an account of an average day, see Ganzoni's speech at Ipswich CA, AGM, 8 March 1929.
[64] McEwen to Emrys-Evans, 5 October 1937, Emrys-Evans MSS, Add.58248/38–9.
[65] For examples of MPs' daily routines, see the diaries of Headlam, Makins, Morrison-Bell, Southby, Winterton, and York.
[66] Memoir notes, n.d., Ward MSS, MSS.Eng.c.6959.
[67] Channon diary, 1 May 1940, 24 May 1937.
[68] Macmillan to Beamish, 7 August 1939, Beamish (Chelwood) MSS, CLW/2/1/18; Headlam diary, 2 December 1926, 23 February 1928.

was much less common and generally reserved for relatives and close friends, usually those known before becoming an MP. Social visiting was more a feature of the parliamentary recess, and the country house weekend enjoyed its golden autumn during these decades; such visits, however, were often linked with giving a speech or opening a fete somewhere in the vicinity. Many Conservative MPs were of the social class to be involved in the events of the London season, and all would be invited to the occasional formal party receptions which were held in the large London residences of the leading aristocrats, in particular Lords Londonderry, Derby, and Salisbury; Austen Chamberlain noted that 'these things count with Members and *Members' wives*'.[69] In addition, smaller groups of backbench MPs were invited in rotation to lunch or an afternoon 'at home' by the Party Leader or his wife; Mrs Baldwin did this regularly during the 1924–29 parliament, when there were many new Conservative MPs.

In this milieu of constant social contact, personality and reputation were of the greatest importance; together with ability in debate, they were the basis of influence and the route to prominence and promotion. New entrants were 'received almost in the same way as is a newcomer at...one of our public schools', and 'sized up as to whether he is a good fellow and at a later date whether he is a good House of Commons man'.[70] There was particular respect for the senior backbenchers who were not ambitious for office and 'who by long service and prestige in the House were in a position to make their influence felt'.[71] Such MPs were dependable, and yet possessed a certain independence, which was all the more significant because it was almost never exercised; in all parties, they tended to be regarded as the guardians of its core values. On the other hand, there were plenty of MPs whom their colleagues found unimpressive and uncongenial, as exemplified by Channon's verdict on Bower: 'a pompous ass, self-opinionated and narrow'.[72] There was dislike of those who did not adapt to the styles and conventions of the House. This could particularly hamper those who entered after substantial achievement in another career, as they were often regarded with some reserve and even resentment. It was a notable factor in relation to two groups: barristers who retained too much of the courtroom in their debating style, and bright young men who were too assured or impatient. A tendency to intrigue, ambition displayed too openly, or riding the coat-tails of powerful patrons were marks against a MP, and thus in 1924–29 Macmillan and Boothby were regarded with suspicion as on the make politically, too close to Churchill, and, even worse, inclined to stray into the orbit of Lloyd George.

Dubious conduct and unacceptable behaviour could be political, financial, or personal. One reason for the nickname of the 'Forty Thieves' given to the business element of the right wing was the inclusion in their number of some with unsavoury reputations, such as 'our drunken little Canadian financier' Grant Morden and Remer: 'ass and bankrupt, well known [to]...the House of Commons gener-

---

[69] A. Chamberlain to Baldwin, 9 November 1924, Baldwin MSS, 42/270–1 (emphasis in original).
[70] Memoir by Brittain, 'The House of Commons', n.d., Brittain MSS, 12; Macnamara, *The Whistle Blows*, 142.
[71] Winterton to Irwin, 14 July 1926, Halifax MSS, C152/17/1/66; Balfour, *Wings over Westminster*, 72–3.
[72] Channon diary, 4 April 1938.

ally as one of its greatest blemishes'.[73] Financial misconduct offended against the code that a gentleman's word was his bond, as well as appearing simply sordid and dishonest. Personal morality was more complicated, and in general a blind eye was turned to all but the most blatant breaches, if only on the prudent basis of those in glass houses not throwing stones. Drinking large amounts of alcohol was not regarded as a vice in itself, but there was disapproval of insobriety in public and especially in the chamber. However, accusing another Member of being drunk in the House was a serious matter, and if such an imputation seemed to be uncalled for it rebounded against the accuser. Members were certainly aware of who was overly fond of the bottle, such as J. H. 'Jimmy' Thomas, a Labour and then National Government Cabinet minister; significantly, his downfall came not from this but from disclosing a budget secret. However, repeated inebriation, especially in the case of someone unpopular for other reasons, went beyond tolerance; in the Earl of Birkenhead's case, Baldwin considered in early 1922 that it had made his future leadership of the party impossible: 'Our men simply will not have it.'[74]

As Butler and Channon noted, 'life in the House of Commons encourages infidelity in one's wife'.[75] Adultery was certainly not uncommon amongst the upper class, but was usually conducted discretely. Lady Dorothy Macmillan's long affair with Boothby was known to quite a few but otherwise ignored and never publicized; at most, it encouraged some sympathy for Macmillan and tolerance of his erratic trajectory, which was partly ascribed to his domestic strains, and it probably added to the caution with which Boothby was regarded. The position was not unique: another junior minister who had to adjust to his spouse conducting a lengthy liaison with a political colleague was Robert Hudson: in this case, his wife's lover was the National Labour minister, Earl De La Warr.[76] However, a case in the divorce courts was another matter and could end a promising career, even when not the guilty party.[77] Of the 1,143 persons who sat as Conservative MPs between 1918 and 1945, only six had been divorced before they were first elected. Interestingly, two of these were women—Mavis Tate and Nancy Astor. The latter had, in common with two of the four men, the fact that her divorce had been more than fifteen years before her entry into the House of Commons. A further sixteen men, and Tate for a second time, were divorced whilst sitting as MPs in the period up to 1945.[78] Of these, at the following general election, four retired and five were defeated (which, of course, might have happened anyway). One of the remainder was the Chief Whip, Margesson, who was divorced in 1940 after a long estrangement from his

---

[73] Lane-Fox to Irwin, 27 November 1929, Halifax MSS, C152/18/1/312.
[74] Baldwin to Fry, 11 February 1922, *BP*, 62.
[75] Channon diary, 13 May 1937.
[76] York diary, 17 October 1945. Hudson was ambitious; as with Macmillan, there was no divorce.
[77] Midleton (president, Guildford CA) to Baldwin, 30 December 1933, Baldwin MSS, 168/194–5; Wirral CA, Grace to Macdona (chairman), 16 July, Exec., 24 July and 2 October 1931.
[78] Calculated for all Conservative MPs who sat between 1918 and 1945, from the entries in Stenton and Lees, *Who's Who of British Members of Parliament*, vols 3 and 4. Additionally, ten of the 1918–45 MPs were divorced at some point after 1945, whilst still sitting in the House. Divorce remained a problematic issue in the 1950s and early 1960s: M. Rush, *The Selection of Parliamentary Candidates* (1969), 67.

wife; he was given a peerage in 1942 when he was sacked from the War Office, and so also did not stand again. Thus, only seven MPs continued uninterrupted in their political careers following a divorce; this included Davison, who had to face down a rebellion in his constituency association before he was able to do so. Divorce became more frequent and less remarked upon after 1945, but still in many cases it did not occur until after the Member had left the House (and often quite soon after, suggesting that it might have been linked to the retirement).

Most MPs were married and remained with that spouse, but 10.4 per cent of the Conservative MPs of the 1918–45 era appear to have been single throughout their lives.[79] Homosexuality was never referred to directly, although the social pretence that all male Conservative MPs—both married men and lifelong bachelors—were conventionally heterosexual can hardly have been the reality. Given the social pressures and legal penalties, there would have been much repression, accompanied by anxiety and unhappiness. However, total abstinence is scarcely credible, and homosexual or bisexual activity was, to some extent, known or suspected.[80] There were two definite cases: Harry Crookshank had a male lover, at least in his later years, whilst Sir Ian Horobin, an MP in 1931–35 and 1951–59, was sentenced to four years in prison in 1962 for sexual acts with teenage boys, which had taken place over many years.[81] However, homosexual liaisons and heterosexual extramarital affairs took place behind the scenes and were ignored by the press, and an MP was expected to conduct himself 'in public life as an honourable gentleman'.[82]

Day-to-day relations with MPs of other parties were moderated by the familiarity of sharing the same physical space, and the common grounds of having passed through similar experiences to get there and of doing the same job. Indeed, a marked feature of parliament's 'friendly camaraderie' and valuing of tradition was its inclusive effect even upon the fieriest of outsiders.[83] Convention and the rules of procedure usually prevented exchanges becoming too personal, and humour and politeness were great lubricants. There was partisanship but no general antagonism, and on the individual level there were frequently amicable interchanges across party boundaries, away from the floor of the House 'in such neutral places as the lavatory, the terrace and the smoking room'.[84] It was accepted that debate would be vigorous and feelings run high: 'bitterness and rancour are the usual concomitants of a big Parliamentary controversy,' Winterton commented after his

---

[79] In the biographical entries from *Dod's Parliamemtary Companion*, reproduced in Stenton and Lees, *Who's Who of British Members of Parliament*, vols 3 and 4, fifty-seven (4.98%) of the Conservative MPs of the 1918–45 era are specifically listed as 'unmarried', and for a further sixty-two (5.42%) no marriage is listed. A cross-check of other available sources for the latter group confirmed their unmarried status in nearly every case, except Edward Brotherton, who was married very briefly in 1882, twenty years before his first election.

[80] Balfour, *Wings over Westminster*, 80.

[81] S[imon] Ball, 'Harry Frederick Comfort Crookshank', *Oxford Dictionary of National Biography*; *The Times*, 6 and 19 June, 18 July 1962.

[82] Bryant, *Spirit of Conservatism*, 47–8.

[83] Memoir by Brittain, 'The House of Commons', n.d., Brittain MSS, 12.

[84] Lane-Fox to Irwin, 4 July 1926, Halifax MSS, C152/17/1/61; J. B. Cohen, *Count Your Blessings* (1956), 60.

first two decades as an MP.[85] However, there was anger if abuse was too sustained and especially where it seemed organized rather than spontaneous: after three weeks of bitter Labour attacks in late June and early July 1926 the parliamentary party 'was literally boiling with indignation', but remonstrations to the Speaker and the latter's rebuke of the opposition calmed the atmosphere.[86] Conservative MPs' views of the Labour Party were generally tolerant, and included respect for the class background, personal progress, and character of many of its working-class MPs. This was often tinged with some paternalism and a sense of superiority; in the 1920s the lack of parliamentary skill of Labour MPs was often noted, and their tendency to emotional rants and unruly behaviour commented upon in language which likened them to children. Winterton described the conduct of Labour MPs during the debates on the Trade Union Bill in 1927 'as 50 per cent disgraceful and 50 per cent merely childish and pathetic'.[87]

Many Conservative MPs were fond of some of Labour's working-class stalwarts and of 'characters' like Josiah Wedgwood, especially where these were seen as having some independence of mind. Parliamentary memoirs often take pride in these non-partisan relationships, particularly recounting anecdotes of James Maxton ('a favourite and now an institution'[88]), David Kirkwood, and other 'Clydesiders' of the left-wing Independent Labour Party (ILP).[89] There was general respect for most Labour leaders, who were seen as more constructive than their followers, and as trying to restrain outbursts and rein in the extremists. The best regarded were MacDonald, whose effectiveness in foreign policy was acknowledged, and Snowden, who was respected for his ability and incisiveness in debate. Neville Chamberlain, who was often admonished by Baldwin for showing too contemptuous an attitude to Labour in debate, wrote in 1927: 'I admire Snowden; he is a man of courage and he deserves success.'[90] The Labour MPs who were most disliked were mainly from middle- or upper-class backgrounds, where the element of 'class traitor' in the response was ironic from the party which explicitly rejected the centrality of class allegiance. Even so, it was stimulated primarily by their character and style in debate (and perhaps their effectiveness); thus Mosley was detested, but J. M. Kenworthy (heir of the 9th Baron Strabolgi) dismissed as an irritant or a joke. In the same way, in the 1930s there was little antagonism towards Attlee or even Cripps (who was regarded more as an eccentric, and so accorded greater tolerance), but much towards Hugh Dalton.

There was considerably more hostility towards the Liberals, especially as they were considered mainly responsible for the defeats of 1923 and 1929.[91] This antagonism was focused on a few of their leading figures, especially Lloyd George

---

[85] Winterton to Irwin, 14 July 1926, Halifax MSS, C152/17/1/66.
[86] Winterton to Irwin, 14 July 1926, Halifax MSS, C152/17/1/66.
[87] Winterton to Irwin, 6 June 1927, Halifax MSS, C152/17/1/226.
[88] Beamish diary notes, 6 May and 12 December 1941, Beamish MSS, CAC, BEAM/3/4.
[89] Balfour, *Wings over Westminster*, 75–6; H. J. Moss., *Windjammer to Westminster* (1941), 182–3; for a reciprocal example, see Tillett to Joynson-Hicks, 12 December 1926, Joynson-Hicks MSS, 3/3.
[90] N. Chamberlain to Irwin, 25 December 1927, Halifax MSS, C152/17/1/277a.
[91] Amery to Baldwin, 8 December 1923, Baldwin MSS, 35/169–72.

and Sir Herbert Samuel; Asquith was generally respected, as were some of his supporters such as Edward Grey, Donald Maclean, and Walter Runciman. After the fall of the Coalition in 1922, and perhaps well before that in some cases, the main target of venom was Lloyd George, as in the quip coined by an unknown backbencher in 1927: 'the Liberal Party has just a crook to lead it without a shepherd'.[92] Even so, Conservative MPs would fill the chamber when he rose to speak, as a 'star turn' who would provide entertainment and excitement, something to be savoured even if it was at the expense of their own leaders. This had no political meaning, for after 1922 very few MPs would consider active co-operation with the Liberals, even during the periods of minority Labour government. The distrust and hostility ran deep, with the Liberals considered 'ever ready to betray everyone in turn as is their wont'.[93] After the formation of the National Government this underlay the continuing suspicion of the Samuelite wing, and Basil Peto was far from alone amongst Conservative MPs in regarding Samuel's tactics during September 1931 as 'the dirtiest political game...that I have ever seen'.[94] However, antagonism abated quite swiftly in the case of Simon's followers, as they accepted tariffs and proved their reliability.

Although separate from the party institutions, many of the gentleman's clubs of London's West End were, in varying degrees, woven into the infrastructure of Conservatism. Some—such as the Travellers', St James's, and Pratt's, which were close enough to parliament to be used as dining venues by many MPs—had a purely social role, which helped to maintain cohesion and a sense of community. Others provided venues for meetings, and a few had specifically political roles as sources of prospective candidates and voluntary speakers, and sometimes of funds. Pre-eminent amongst these was the Carlton Club, linked to the Conservative Party since its early nineteenth-century foundation, and its later adjuncts, the Junior Carlton and the Ladies' Carlton. By the 1920s, the Carlton's role was largely decorative—its only function in the crisis of 1922 was to provide a suitable room for the party meeting.[95] The St Stephen's Club had also become less politically engaged, but remained popular with MPs because its proximity to the Palace of Westminster enabled division bells to be installed, and it had a subway beneath Bridge Street by which they could reach the lobbies in time to vote.[96] The other important club was the Constitutional, located in Northumberland Avenue, which was described as 'the stronghold of Conservatism'.[97] It was less exclusive and had a larger membership, and was more actively involved in campaigning; in the 1929 general election

---

[92] Davidson to Irwin, 17 August 1927, Halifax MSS, C152/17/1/249a.
[93] Ormsby-Gore to his mother, 30 March 1924, Ormsby-Gore MSS, PEC/10/1/12/23; Linlithgow to Salisbury, 24 July 1930, Salisbury MSS, S(4)136/75.
[94] Memo by Peto, Lady Peto diary, 30 September 1931; Samuel was 'odious and unctuous' and 'a detestable liar', Bridgeman to Salisbury, 9 October 1931, Salisbury MSS, S(4)141/112.
[95] This no longer exists as the building was destroyed by bomb damage in October 1940, the seventy members present and the staff escaping without casualties: Beamish diary notes, 16 October 1940, Beamish MSS, CAC, BEAM/3/4.
[96] Queenborough to Makins, 16 November 1922, Sherfield MSS, 223/10.
[97] Islington East CA, AR, 1943.

it contributed £2,400 to the party funds and organized 530 public meetings.[98] All of these clubs had a physical existence, but there were others which were associations of like-minded persons of particular generations: the Cecil Club (founded in 1882), the United Club (founded in 1887), the 1900 Club (founded in 1906), and the 1912 Club (which was mainly a City of London network). These were particularly a source of voluntary speakers for constituency and election meetings, although by the interwar period the first two groups were less active. There were also various dining clubs, including the cross-party 'Other Club', which had been created by Churchill and Birkenhead before the First World War, and the smaller and rather socially exclusive Conservative group which dined once a week at the House of Commons and was, for many years, 'more or less presided over' by the convivial backbench MP Herbert Spender-Clay; unusually, this continued in existence long after the latter's death in 1937.[99]

OPINIONS AND FACTIONS

The boredom and routine which characterized much of both Houses' proceedings led at best to a preoccupation with gossip and personalities, the 'little village' aspect of parliament.[100] It could also spill over into irritation and grumbling, which sometimes developed into alienation and dissidence; as a former Chief Whip commented, there was always 'a considerable number of Members who have a considerable number of growls'.[101] Trouble was most likely in the hot weather before the summer recess, or when matters were not going well and electoral prospects were diminishing, or when the leaders seemed tired and lacklustre. Unpopular measures affecting the leisure activities of the working class were, naturally, a particular cause of unrest, and so legislation on betting and the level of the beer tax ran into opposition from MPs in the 1920s and 1930s. However, although in 1932 the beer duty caused 'a really serious "angry" revolt movement in the House', which 'spread to many normally sound Members', spikes of concern over such limited and specific matters did not produce any lasting dissent or shake the position of leaders.[102] For most of the time, the spirit of party loyalty, the soothing ministrations of the whips, and electoral self-preservation combined to keep dissatisfaction from public view. As Hoare noted with relief in the fourth session of the 1924–29 parliament, 'considering that 99 out of 100 of them have nothing to do, the Party has been very patient and loyal in the House'.[103] Much of the nervous energy that was pent up, especially

---

[98] P. G. Cambray, *Club Days and Ways: The Story of the Constitutional Club* (1963), 74.
[99] Herbert to Wolmer, 1 February 1924, Wolmer MSS, MSS.Eng.hist.c.1012/144–5; York diary, 23 October 1945.
[100] See many entries in the Headlam diary, 1924–29, 1931–35, and 1940–45; Channon diary, 1 May 1940; Conway to his wife, 20 July 1925, 17 June 1931, Conway MSS, Add.7676/D/244, 330.
[101] Wilson to Wise, 7 December 1925, Wise MSS, C16.
[102] Lloyd to Davidson, 29 April 1932, Davidson MSS (Bodleian), MSS.Eng.hist.c.557/116–22.
[103] Hoare to Irwin, 30 March 1928, Halifax MSS, C152/18/1/33.

when the party was in office and there was less scope for backbenchers to speak, found release in the constant flow of speculation and rumour. This focused on two main aspects: personalities, especially who was likely to be promoted and who to be dropped; and election prospects, especially in the later stages of a parliament—'our minds are all centred in our individual seats,' wrote Ormsby-Gore in April 1929.[104] Parliamentary opinion was important, having an impact on general direction and momentum, rather than the alteration of bills once presented; thus the 'excited' state of opinion on the backbenches after the General Strike made changes in trade union law 'irresistible'.[105] The leadership were aware of such trends, and also that they reflected the party's public support—for the latter's 'general feeling', 'a good deal can be got, of course, from Members of Parliament by the Chief Whip'.[106]

However, detecting the precise balance of opinion in the House of Commons was not easy, and thus in early 1927 the Prime Minister believed 'that influence is veering towards the moderates in the party', whilst a member of his Cabinet thought 'that the drift is to the extreme right'.[107] The wings of the parliamentary party were never formally organized or even clearly delineated, but people understood their own position in the spectrum and its general size and shape. The right wing, or at least that part of it known as the 'diehards' and willing to rebel if necessary, was around 15–20 per cent of MPs; this is based on its approximate strength of forty in the 1929–31 parliament and the eighty MPs who voted against the India Bill in 1935. The right was the more continuous, cohesive, distinctive, and numerous section, whilst the left tended to ebb and flow in number; this was partly an effect of generational transitions and partly of the pattern of electoral success, as many of the centre-left and left sat for marginal constituencies. The left wing was certainly smaller: those clearly identified with it were often a dozen or less, and it was, at most, 5–10 per cent of MPs. The rest were shaded in-between, and did not always stay in the same place. Conservative MPs' attitudes tended to be issue-responsive rather than ideologically defined, and so their stance could vary from one question to the next. It could also be the case that an MP openly dissented on a single important issue but continued to support the party line on other matters; this was the case with most of the India rebels of 1933–35, and the anti-appeasers in 1937–39.

There were several factors which encouraged loyalty amongst Conservative MPs. The first two of these might be categorized as 'careerist': the hope of office or some other reward (which, in this era, motivated fewer than might be expected), and the need to maintain good relations with the constituency association in order to secure renomination. The latter was crucial for all who wished to remain in the House, because election without an official party endorsement was almost impossible—but, as local parties gave wide latitude and often supported dissidence in a rightwards direction, this was rarely an issue, and instances of deselection were rare. The other buttresses of loyalty were party spirit (an identification with the aims of the party and the wish to further them) and, reinforcing this, a desire to

[104] Ormsby-Gore to Irwin, 4 April 1929, Halifax MSS, C152/18/1/238.
[105] Hoare to Irwin, 18 June 1926, Halifax MSS, C152/17/1/55a.
[106] Steel-Maitland to Baldwin, 4 May 1925, Baldwin MSS, 160/160–2.
[107] Hoare to Irwin, 2 March 1927, Halifax MSS, C152/17/1/193.

achieve something of value during their time in parliament and thus gain a feeling of satisfaction from their career. External threats or hard times could also be a powerful force for unity; as one Conservative MP assured Baldwin, 'most of us are most anxious to give you all the support we can both at home and abroad as we realise the appalling character of the problems to be faced'.[108]

The forces which could pull the other way were generally much less powerful. The weakest of the three was loyalty to external economic or social interest groups, such as the residual connections of past or continuing involvement in a sector of business or a profession. Stronger than this were constituency problems and pressures, especially where one industry predominated. This particularly affected MPs for agricultural areas and those sitting for depressed industrial areas with high levels of unemployment, such as Macmillan's Stockton, whilst concern in the cotton district of Lancashire over markets and competition was a force against both tariffs in the 1920s and devolution in India in the 1930s. However, the single greatest cause of dissent and rebellion was personal views derived from principle or political judgement, and the fact that this was generally acknowledged was important in preventing the many cases of rebellion from leading to a splintering of the party itself. Only the most serious revolt did so, in 1922–23, and even then most on both sides made efforts to avoid worsening the rift (Birkenhead's blatant lack of care in this respect was a prime cause of his unpopularity). If an MP felt very strongly on an issue and cared little about continuing their career, as in the case of Viscount Lymington in 1933–34, they were almost entirely free to act. In most cases, censorship and conformity were the work not of the whips or the party machine, but of self-restraint due to sharing the fundamental values and ethos of the party.

The mainstream majority was the core of the party, and its essence was, in Sidney Herbert's phrase, 'the better sort of undistinguished Member'.[109] Many of these sat for the county constituencies, which provided 'a solid bloc…who are really the backbone of the Party'.[110] Mainstream MPs were, almost by definition, loyal in public, although Headlam's diaries show that this could conceal considerable private reservations about the quality of the leaders and the wisdom of their policies. The front bench was not always impressive on close acquaintance, and its occupants' performances could be disappointing as often as inspiring.[111] When the political situation did not look promising—which, despite the party's success between the wars, was very often the perception of its MPs—then doubt and criticism seethed beneath the surface. Under the greatest pressure, it would burst through; this is what happened on a large scale in October 1922, more limitedly in May 1940, and almost in September 1930. Many more Conservative MPs were anxious about the India reforms in 1931–35 than those who publicly dissented; even such a loyalist as Rhys, who had served as Baldwin's PPS in 1927–29, was doubtful and would have preferred a different policy.[112] Headlam was typical of this feeling, but without his diary his view would be invisible to the

---

[108] Burchall to Baldwin, 17 August 1923, Baldwin MSS, 159/8.
[109] Herbert to Baldwin, November 1924, Baldwin MSS, 42/281–3.
[110] Griffith-Boscawen to A. Chamberlain, 12 October 1922, AC, 33/2/49.
[111] Moss, *Windjammer to Westminster*, 171.
[112] Rhys, memorandum, 15 September 1932, Dynevor MSS.

historian, although it was probably known at the time to his friends, and perhaps expressed in casual conversation with colleagues in the lobbies and the clubs.[113] There was a certain inertia to the steady centre, and a sudden change of direction in policy could cause 'a state of acute discomfort', as with the Hoare–Laval Plan in December 1935.[114] On the latter occasion, one newly elected MP summed up the mainstream view: 'In common with many others, I do feel perfectly terrible over this Ethiopian matter, but I will not dream of voting against the government.'[115]

The goodwill of the majority could be eroded if their support was taken for granted in a flow of minor bills which ran counter to their preference for less government intervention and expenditure, and in November 1927 the Chief Whip warned that this was causing the loyalty of MPs to be 'highly and unnecessarily tested'.[116] However, even when they strained it, the leadership could normally count on the support of 'the quiet men in the House, who probably number seventy-five per cent of the whole'.[117] This habitual loyalty was what Austen Chamberlain was relying upon when he summoned the Carlton Club meeting, as 'it was thought that the great majority of those likely to attend would stand by the existing order'.[118] Whilst the rejections of the two Chamberlains in 1922 and 1940 were due to overly rigid and unresponsive leadership, between these dates problems more often arose due to drift and a lack of direction. As one whip noted during the uncertainty over the trade union political levy issue in February 1925: 'the vast majority . . . *would follow any definite lead*'.[119]

One reason for Baldwin's better party management and longer tenure than the other leaders was that 'I know the feelings of the silent men as well as of the vocal.'[120] This was the key, for it was the undemonstrative majority who were critical in determining the outcome of any dissent within the party, and shifts in their opinion were decisive. This was the reason for the impact on Bonar Law's attitude of the gathering organized by the respected senior backbenchers Hoare, Lane-Fox, and Pretyman, on the day before the Carlton Club meeting of 1922. They deliberately restricted the invitations to respected backbenchers, chosen 'for the impression they would make on the Conservative world'; it was the standing of the seventy-four who attended which 'greatly impressed' Bonar Law, who declared: 'These are very good names.'[121] He was already aware of the smaller meeting held a week earlier, organized by William Bull, which the retired leading figure Walter Long was asked to attend, and which, significantly, was composed 'of men representative in their character, of good position in the House of Commons, and who

---

[113] Headlam diary, 12 December 1934, 27 February 1935.
[114] Patrick to Hoare, 12 December 1935, Templewood MSS, VIII/1.
[115] The letter was signed 'yours in loyalty': Hannah to Baldwin, 11 December 1935, Baldwin MSS, 47/179.
[116] Eyres-Monsell to Baldwin, 10 November 1927, Baldwin MSS, 162/120–1.
[117] Fremantle to A. Chamberlain, 11 November 1921, AC, 31/3/17.
[118] Memo by Maclean of conversation with Baldwin, 25 July 1923, *BP*, 97.
[119] Note by Barnston, n.d. but *c.*20 February 1925, CPA, CRD/2/7/18, emphasis in original.
[120] Baldwin to Beaverbrook, 7 August 1918, *BP*, 38.
[121] Lord Templewood, *Empire of the Air* (1957), 24, 27; 'List of Members present at meeting at Cadogan Gardens', 18 October 1922, Templewood MSS, I/2.

had no sympathy whatever with the Diehard Party'.[122] It was crucial that both meetings, although reluctant to rebel and anxious for some compromise solution, were certain that the leadership's commitment to retaining Lloyd George as Prime Minister would break up the party.

The importance of weight rather than numbers was underlined by Austen Chamberlain's recognition that if he won a small majority at the Carlton Club meeting, but the minority contained many of 'the more substantial Conservatives', then he and his colleagues would have to resign.[123] It was not the attacks of the well-known minority of predictable, and therefore discountable, rebels who brought down the Leader in 1922 and 1940, but the erosion of support amongst mainstream MPs. Expressions of dissent from senior and normally steadfastly loyal backbenchers, men known to be unambitious for office, acted as a barometer of party opinion and always had considerable impact. Thus Duff Cooper, rather than rising himself, encouraged the senior mainstream backbencher Sir John Wardlaw-Milne to speak in the highly charged atmosphere of 2 September 1939; due to the latter's record of orthodox loyalty, his words 'carried great weight'.[124] As Neville Chamberlain acknowledged in October 1930, when loyal moderates like Edward Iliffe joined the critics, the position became much more serious.[125] For the same reason, although in this case one swallow did not make a summer, the former juinior minister J. T. C. Moore-Brabazon's abandonment of the task of defending Baldwin at the Westmininster St George's by-election in March 1931 set alarm bells ringing amongst the leadership. The Hoare–Laval Plan of 1935 became untenable when it was apparent that opposition to it was widespread amongst centrist MPs, whilst a striking example of draining confidence in the leadership in 1940 was the criticism of Sir Hugh O'Neill, Chairman of the 1922 Committee from December 1935 to September 1939, and a junior minister since then, who, on 1 May, 'in a mood of the deepest gloom', was contemplating resignation.[126]

On the other hand, equally decisive was when the mainstream did not shift their allegiance, however fierce the storm of external criticism and pressure. Their continuation of support for Baldwin after the 1923 defeat was a particularly important moment, and was the real basis of his power to resist coalitionist intrigues.[127] They accepted the seriousness of the August 1931 crisis and the necessity of the National Government, and remained committed to maintaining the alliance for the rest of the decade.[128] This was a significant factor in restraining mainstream MPs from moving

---

[122] Memo by Long, 'Memorandum of what took place on Tuesday, Wednesday and Thursday, the 10th, 11th and 12th October 1922', 13 October 1922, Long to Younger, 12 October 1922, Bonar Law MSS, BL/111/34/161.

[123] Derby to Lord Stanley, 18 October 1922, Derby MSS, 42/8; for a later comment on reputation mattering more than numbers, see Nicolson diary, 6 October 1938.

[124] Duff Cooper diary, 3 September 1939.

[125] N. Chamberlain to Bridgeman, 5 October 1930, Bridgeman MSS, 3386/98.

[126] Lord Zetland, *Essayez* (1957), 294–5.

[127] Long to Baldwin, 28 December 1923, Morrison-Bell to Baldwin, 11 December 1923, Baldwin MSS, 35/200–1, 186–7; Ormsby-Gore to his mother, 9 December 1923, Orsmby-Gore MSS, PEC/10/1/12/22; Rugby CA, Exec, 2 February 1924.

[128] See letter signed by 100 Conservative MPs, *The Times*, 14 June 1934.

towards the rebel group over India in 1933–35, despite their concerns and the attractive simplicity of the diehard outlook; it was also due to doubts about Churchill, the leading critic, and the lack of a credible alternative policy.[129] Nearly all mainstream MPs supported Chamberlain's strategy over appeasement as the most expedient and practical alternative to war. It was the damage done by the failure of the policy in 1939, and still more by the appearance of unwarranted complacency in the running of the war effort, which led to his loss of support in this key area. The crucial element in May 1940 was that the rebels (and especially the abstainers) extended far beyond the predictable 'glamour boys', with Chamberlain losing the confidence of such steady centrists as Sir Ralph Glyn.[130]

A general belief in the tariff reform programme had been a mainstream attitude since 1906, although it was sometimes latent and not always vigorously presented. However, whilst mainstream MPs accepted the need for caution and pragmatism in the 1922 and 1924 elections, they felt happier when advocating a 'constructive' policy; Spender-Clay during the 1923 campaign thanked Baldwin for 'the opportunity . . . of fighting for such a good cause'.[131] Anti-coalitionism was a powerful sentiment after 1922, and Baldwin was able to draw on this for over a decade—it played a key part in sustaining him after the 1923 defeat, and in restraining MPs from supporting Beaverbrook in 1929–31 and the India rebels at the key points in 1929, 1931, and 1933–35. Even the more level-headed mainstream figures such as George Lane-Fox tended to suspect the existence of coalitionist plots.[132] Antipathy to Lloyd George and a fear of returning to the unhappy and alarming politics of 1921–22, which had fostered the rapid advance of Labour, led to the bulk of the party ruling out any question of alliance with the Liberals, even in the hung parliaments of 1924 and 1929.[133] Ormsby-Gore spoke for many in telling Baldwin in January 1924 that 'I would far rather have a Labour government' than restore the dominance of Lloyd George or the coalitionist leaders.[134]

The party centre had some sympathy with the wings on either side, but regarded those on the left as naïve and inexperienced, and those on the right as sound in instinct but out of touch with reality. Neville Chamberlain expressed the general front-bench view of the right wing: 'I don't mind them, for they are loyal enough at bottom though very stupid.'[135] The attraction of fundamentalist attitudes was always counterbalanced by doubts about their simplicity and practicality, and reservations about the judgement and motivations of their proponents, who were categorized by Derby as 'men who are sore about something, or else supporters of lost causes'.[136] The right wing were generally known as the 'diehards', and could trace their lineage to the opponents of compromise over the Parliament Act of

---

[129] Speech of Roberts at Sheffield Ecclesall CA, Exec., 19 June 1933; Banks to Churchill, March 1933, Churchill MSS, CAC, CHAR/2/192/125–6.
[130] Abingdon CA, AGM, 10 May 1940.
[131] Spender-Clay to Baldwin, 6 December 1923, Baldwin MSS, 35/120–1.
[132] Lane-Fox to Irwin, 18 August 1926, Halifax MSS, C152/17/1/85.
[133] Tryon to Baldwin, 11 December 1923, Baldwin MSS, 35/188.
[134] Ormsby-Gore to Baldwin, 29 January 1924, Baldwin MSS, 42/182–7.
[135] N. Chamberlain to his wife, 24 July 1930, NC, 1/26/431.
[136] Derby to Woodhouse, 28 September 1922, Derby MSS, 16/12.

1911. The name was revived in 1920–22 for the group of about forty right-wing MPs who were the earliest critics of the Coalition, and who responded to the standard raised by Lords Selborne and Salisbury, particularly over the issue of restoring powers to the House of Lords. They had some overlapping membership with the 'Industrial Group' of the 1920s, which was organized around the British Commonwealth Union, and the amalgam was nicknamed the 'Forty Thieves' by younger left-wing MPs. The size of the diehard group was larger in the 1924–29 parliament than that label suggests, but not greatly so. Because they sat mainly for safe seats, few were defeated in 1929 and the right wing increased as a proportion of the reduced parliamentary ranks, particularly at the expense of the left and left-centre MPs who had lost in the marginals.

The core diehard group numbered around forty-six during the crisis over tariffs in 1930,[137] whilst in March 1931 it was suggested that 'thirty or forty' MPs were completely opposed to Baldwin's line on India.[138] The most extensive diehard campaign was that against the India Bill in 1933–35, although here the diehards were joined by some MPs who felt strongly on this issue alone and did not necessarily share the general views of the right on other matters. Even so, it was generally recognized that there were in the region of seventy or eighty diehards in the 1931–35 parliament. Although they included some younger MPs (especially in the India 'revolt' of 1933–35), such as Patrick Donner and Viscount Lymington, the general perception of the diehard MPs and their typical supporters in the constituencies was of older figures, often with a military background, who were characterized by simplistic views and a rigid caste of mind; this was the stereotype caricatured so effectively in cartoonist David Low's creation 'Colonel Blimp', and described by Davidson as the 'Club grousers'.[139]

The diehard MPs were informally organized and held group meetings when an issue required it; these usually resulted in a remonstrative petition or delegation to Baldwin.[140] The usual convenor of such meetings, and the figure generally regarded as the leader of the diehards insofar as they had such a thing, was the long-serving MP John Gretton.[141] He was personally liked and regarded as completely sincere by the party leadership, but was a notoriously inarticulate and ineffective speaker in the Commons and at party meetings. The other most prominent diehard was the energetic Henry Page Croft, best known for his passionate commitment to the 'whole-hog' protectionist agenda. His political career began in 1906 as a member of the tariff reform group known as the Confederates, which worked to eject free-trade Conservative MPs from their seats, and he entered the House in January 1910. He served in France in 1914–16, becoming a Brigadier-General, and then returned to politics in 1917, when the combination of his intense patri-

---

[137] Lady Peto diary, 28 October 1930.
[138] The figure was given by Lord Lloyd, quoted in Dawson to Irwin, 13 March 1931, Halifax MSS, C152/19/1/268.
[139] Davidson to Irwin, 24 January 1930, Halifax MSS, C152/19/1/8.
[140] Gretton to Baldwin, 19 December 1923, Baldwin MSS, 35/191–4.
[141] Gretton to Ashley, 18 November 1922, Ashley MSS, BR/71. Meetings were originally held at Gretton's house in Belgrave Square, and later at St Stephen's Club: Lady Peto diary, 23 and 29 January 1930.

otism and alienation from the compromises of coalition led to his temporarily leaving the Conservatives to form the 'National Party'. This was a short-lived venture and although technically it lasted until 1922, he was effectively back in the Conservative fold by 1920. Throughout his career he was supported by his constituency association in Bournemouth, although given the town's attraction as a place of retirement for army officers and imperial officials this was perhaps hardly surprising.

Page Croft was a tireless evangelist for protection, willing to speak wherever invited and possessed of confidence and good humour, which made him a success in impromptu street-corner meetings and in coping with hecklers in working-class districts, though he was less effective in the House of Commons.[142] He was a founder of the Empire Industries Association, a protectionist pressure group, and supported Beaverbrook's 'Empire Crusade' in 1929–30, though with some reservations and at a prudent distance. Like other protectionists, he was uneasy about the use of the press as a weapon of coercion, and particularly the personal animus against Baldwin that might be involved, and when the Party Leader adopted the 'free hand' position on tariffs in September 1930, Page Croft moved with alacrity to support him. After protection was achieved in 1932, he became a leading opponent of the India Bill, working closely with Churchill, but—like many other diehards—he was a strong supporter of Neville Chamberlain as Prime Minister and was disgusted at 'the depths of degradation and heights of ingratitude' displayed in the Norway debate of May 1940.[143] In Churchill's wartime coalition he served as a junior minister at the War Office from May 1940 to July 1945, and, in order to concentrate on the administrative work, he was relieved of both constituency and House of Commons duties by being raised to the peerage as Lord Croft. Despite their disagreements on policy, he was on friendly terms with the leading figures of the 1920s and 1930s, who regarded him as honest and genuine in his views. Indeed, in December 1927 both the Chief Whip and the President of the Board of Trade, Sir Philip Cunliffe-Lister, seriously suggested him for a vacant junior ministership in the latter's department; both emphasized that he was hard-working and 'a good debater', though Eyres-Monsell did not think him potential Cabinet material.[144]

Some of the diehards fitted the conventional stereotype in appearance, manner, and opinion, such as Frederick Banbury, long-serving MP for the City of London; Basil Peto, nicknamed 'Persistent Peto' by other MPs, a businessman who 'at heart was always a countryman';[145] and Guy Kindersley, the anti-Bolshevik crusader who was involved in the murky transactions that led to the publication of the 'Zinoviev letter' in 1924. However, there were considerable variations, such as Martin Conway: a cultured figure and an accomplished mountaineer, he was a strong sup-

---

[142] Headlam diary, 31 October 1930.
[143] Croft to N. Chamberlain, 12 May 1940, Croft MSS, CAC, CRFT/1/7/Ch66.
[144] Eyres-Monsell to Baldwin, 27 December 1927, Cunliffe-Lister to Baldwin, 24 December 1927, Baldwin MSS, 162/122–3, 162–3.
[145] *The Times*, 14 February 1945.

porter of the Coalition in 1922 and friendly with Churchill from the early 1920s, but was also a member of the Gretton group, which sought to oust Baldwin in 1930. The younger diehards, like any youth, could be both excessive and erratic, and Lord Lymington's rebellion over India in the early 1930s was accompanied by a semi-mystical idealization of ruralism and aristocracy. Edward Marjoribanks, the stepson of Lord Hailsham, was considered as brilliant by some of the other younger MPs, but made such a 'very queer speech' in opposition to Baldwin at the party meeting of October 1930 that the former Chief Whip, Lord Fitzalan, questioned his sanity.[146] Butler described Marjoribanks as 'raving like a madman', and in an ominous metaphor concluded that he had 'tied a halter around his political neck'— for it was an early sign of the instability which led to the young MP's suicide in April 1932.[147]

The diehard agenda revolved around a number of themes which were dear to Conservative hearts, and particularly linked to the empire and the maintenance of British prestige in the world. They were strongly for 'whole-hog' protectionism including food taxes, because the latter were essential to achieve the closer unity of the empire that had been the original purpose of tariff reform and the basis of its appeal to idealism; in addition, many sat for agricultural seats and favoured the defence of that sector from foreign competition. Thus, Gretton acclaimed Baldwin's tariff programme of 1923 as 'a policy which will save the country and we can fight for it with hope and confidence'.[148] They believed in a 'firm' imperial policy, which meant no political concessions to native populations and support for repressive policing where required; one of their grievances against the Coalition had been its treatment of General Dyer's actions at Amritsar, which they regarded as having been necessary in the circumstances to maintain law and order, and ultimately to preserve the British position in India.[149] Their opposition to devolution in India was based on the view that it was both unwise and unnecessary, as they regarded the Indian politicians campaigning for change as a tiny and unrepresentative minority who could easily be seen off by a government with backbone. The diehards' unremitting hostility to Bolshevik Russia incorporated an uncritical acceptance of anti-Soviet propaganda; they objected to Lloyd George's attempt at detente in 1920–22, and welcomed the breach of relations in 1927. Whilst they were generally concerned with maintaining strong defence forces, this was mitigated in the 1930s by concern over the economic costs and the desire to avoid another war, and thus most diehards supported the realism of Chamberlain's actively engaged form of appeasement and admired his decisiveness and resolution. Indeed, it was often their clearer and bleaker view of realities which led to such conclusions as 'we must make the peace before it is too late'.[150] However, one concession they firmly ruled out was any return of the former German colonies.

---

[146] Lord Long to Bull, 31 October 1930, Bull MSS, CAC, BULL/5/25.
[147] Butler to his parents, 4 November 1930, Butler MSS, D48/756a–62.
[148] Gretton to Baldwin, 31 October 1923, Baldwin MSS, 159/62–3.
[149] Speech by Foxcroft at Bath CA, AGM, 10 July 1922.
[150] A. Wilson to Hoare, 26 February 1936, Templewood MSS, VIII/6.

In domestic policy, their main demand was for the 'rigorous' and 'drastic' economy in expenditure which would produce a significant reduction in taxation. Even so, there were practical limits, and Gretton acknowledged privately in 1932 that further cuts in unemployment benefit 'would be folly' and likely to lead to widespread resentment and disorder, which might get out of hand.[151] The two other key diehard concerns were linked to the rise of Labour: the restoration of powers to the House of Lords so that it could act as a restraint if there should be a Socialist majority in the Commons, and the need to limit the political role of trade unionism by taking action to reform the political levy; both of these were constantly pressed for in the 1920s. In general, the diehards tended to support the orthodox views of the business sector, being suspicious of social reforms and government intervention, and hence their hostility to Neville Chamberlain's Factory Bill and Poor Law reforms in 1927–28. However, they were aware that the political environment had changed, and after the 1924 victory even Gretton urged that the government 'must in all things be . . . progressive or it will fail'.[152]

For most of the interwar period, the diehards were unable to achieve their aims and were marginalized, despite their visibility—for they 'always make their voices heard more than do the moderate men of the Party'.[153] Although the diehards included many long-serving backbenchers, their impact was reduced by their general obscurity; as Gretton admitted after one fiasco: 'the truth is we are not very strong in debate'.[154] In 1927, a junior minister on the centre right of the party considered the group antagonistic to Baldwin to be 'uninfluential' and—crucially—to have 'no leader of any kind whom the Party could follow'.[155] Collectively, the diehards fulfilled two functions in Conservative politics, of which the most important was that in times of crisis and uncertainty they could vocalize the party's deeper sentiments and amplify the concern of the mainstream centre; if their outlook was supported here, then the leadership would have to either bend (as Baldwin did in 1930) or break (as the Coalitionists did in 1922). Their second role, which operated throughout, was to hold the standard aloft of a 'pure' Conservatism, however impracticable or impolitic it might be to put this into practice. They could be admired as 'stalwarts of sheer prejudice and fixed tradition' with an 'admirable but unchanging code',[156] and in this sense they were 'the salt of the earth'.[157] The diehards made a number of interventions in the events of the period, some of which were more successful than others. Their greatest success was in rolling the first stones of what became the avalanche that swept away the Coalition in 1922.[158] However, when they began sniping in 1920 they had little support, and it was not until after the election scare of January 1922, and perhaps not even until

---

[151] Gretton to N. Chamberlain, 27 September 1932, Hailsham MSS, CAC, HAIL/1/2/1.
[152] Gretton to Baldwin, 1 November 1924, Baldwin MSS, 36/22–4.
[153] Pownall to A. Chamberlain, 11 November 1921, AC, 31/3/16.
[154] Gretton to Ashley, 6 November 1921, Ashley MSS, BR/71.
[155] Headlam diary, 22 December 1927.
[156] Feiling, *What Is Conservatism?*, 7.
[157] Unsigned memo, 'The Last Day of the Session', *c.*November. 1923, Davidson MSS, DAV/164.
[158] Gretton to Hewins, 14 December 1919, Hewins MSS, 75/228–30.

the honours scandal of summer 1922, that the centre adopted similar views.[159] The diehards played a relatively minor part at the end of the process, as the key actors in September and October 1922 were the junior ministers, the managers of Central Office, the mainstream backbenchers and the constituency associations which pressed or encouraged them, and, ultimately, Bonar Law. The diehards were unremittingly hostile to any hint of coalitionism for the rest of the 1920s, and a key force in supporting the Bonar Law and Baldwin ministry of 1922–24.[160] They encouraged the latter's shift to protectionism, with a petition organized by Gretton shortly before the summer recess in July 1923, which was signed by 103 MPs. After the 1923 debacle, they were a buttress of Baldwin's position and opposed any pacts with Liberals, even if it meant letting Labour into office.[161] For the rest of the decade, dislike of Baldwin's moderate course was balanced by personal regard and the belief that he was restoring standards of decency to public life.[162]

From 1925 to 1935 the diehards drifted apart from the leadership and became critical of its policies in several key areas. Their pressure for action on the political levy led to the private members' bill sponsored by F. A. Macquisten and Baldwin's famous speech in March 1925 appealing for its withdrawal, which was reluctantly accepted. The right wing were unhappy with the coal subsidy of 1925, although reassured by the defeat of the General Strike in the following year. There was understandably pressure for action after this, and satisfaction when the draft Trade Union Bill was published in April 1927; the diehards were described by one junior minister as 'slapping each other on the back over it, and saying "at last this bloody Government has shown some guts", etc., etc'.[163] They became even more concerned about the centrism of domestic policy during the remainder of the parliament, and were prominent in the pressure to extend safeguarding to iron and steel, which Baldwin explicitly ruled out in 1928. The defeat of the leadership's cautious 'Safety First' programme in 1929 opened the door not only to a return to protectionism but a general rejection of moderate policies. The diehards were also restive from early 1930 over 'the absence of policy or leadership', considering the party to be 'stagnant and distracted both in the House and the country'.[164] When Baldwin resisted advances towards a tariff policy in the summer of 1930, this provided 'a golden opportunity for our die-hards and right wing', which nearly ended his leadership.[165] However, in September, Baldwin shifted tariff policy to the 'free hand' that most MPs now favoured, and restored his position. He used a demand signed by forty-seven diehard MPs as the opportunity to call a party meeting on 30 October 1930; this became a public demonstration that the rest of the party supported Baldwin, and the diehards were once again isolated. Two days before the party meeting, the

---

[159] Salisbury to Bonar Law, 23 September 1922, Bonar Law MSS, BL/107/2/61.
[160] Gretton to Baldwin, 1 November 1924, Baldwin MSS, 36/22–4.
[161] Peto to Long, 14 December 1923, Long MSS (WSA), 947/850; Wolmer to Davidson, 8 December 1923, Wolmer MSS, MSS.Eng.hist.c.1012/121.
[162] Gwynne to Baldwin, 5 April 1929, Baldwin MSS, 36/11–15.
[163] Lane-Fox to Irwin, 13 April 1927, Halifax MSS, C152/17/1/208.
[164] Peto's memo of diehard group meeting, in Lady Peto diary, 23 January 1930.
[165] Ormsby-Gore to Irwin, 3 July 1930, Halifax MSS, C152/19/1/91a.

latters' position was embarrassingly undermined when a meeting of the group was leaked to the press; its appearance of disloyal plotting produced a critical backlash, made worse by the fact that several of the MPs listed as being present strenuously denied having had any involvement.[166] Sobered by this and by Baldwin's victory at the party meeting, the diehards affirmed that they 'would abide by the verdict and work for party unity', and the group took a lower profile.[167]

The diehards supported the decision to join the emergency National Government in August 1931, although they shared the mainstream concern of safeguarding the party's freedom of action on tariffs.[168] Their resistance to the India reforms derived mainly from 'an inward feeling that the Govt. were going too far and too fast'.[169] Most of the diehards opposed the proposals at every stage, 'losing their heads with childish vigour'.[170] Their activities were subsumed into the India Defence League, but they were uneasy about Churchill—who they never regarded as being their leader or in charge of the campaign—due to his past record in both imperial policy and general judgement.[171] They were severely embarrassed by the impulsive action of Churchill's son Randolph in contesting the Liverpool Wavertree by-election in early 1935, where his intervention against the official candidate split the Conservative vote and gave the seat to the Labour Party; this affair tarred all of the India rebels as 'the puppets of a Rothermere–Churchill stunt' and diminished their support at the grass roots. After this, Croft's conclusion was that 'the only sound course is to go on preaching the Conservative faith', which in practice amounted to 'more tariffs, more defence and a constructive empire policy'.[172] The diehards shared the widespread concerns in 1934–35 over maintaining the party's identity within the National Government, the role of the National Co-ordinating Committee, the share of offices in the Cabinet, and particularly what they saw as a range of interventionist policies of Socialist and Liberal origin.[173] However, only five of their number resigned the National Government whip (and not the Conservative one), which had a negligible impact. The diehards' hopes of holding the parliamentary balance following the next general election were dashed, as the National Government regained popularity and morale in the summer and autumn of 1935, and won a substantial majority. In the later 1930s, the diehards were a less distinct group and merged more into the mainstream, although with residual grumbling about what they saw as the neo-Socialism of some government policies.[174] This was also the case

---

[166] Renfrewshire West CA, AGM, 29 October 1930; Winchester CA, Council, 5 November 1930.
[167] Lady Peto diary, 28–31 October 1930.
[168] Croft to Baldwin, 25 August 1931, Croft MSS, CAC, CRFT/1/3/Ba9; Gretton to Salisbury, 17 September 1931, Salisbury MSS, S(4)141/77; see meeting of leading protectionists on 27 August in Steel-Maitland, 'Diary of events during crisis 1931', Steel-Maitland MSS, GD193/120/3/443–8.
[169] Moore to Baldwin, 9 February 1935, Baldwin MSS, 107/10.
[170] Butler to his parents, 4 March 1931, Butler MSS, D48/792–5.
[171] Knox to Sydenham, 24 June 1931, Indian Empire Society (Stuart) MSS, c.620/59.
[172] 'The policy of contesting by-elections', unsigned memo but by Croft, n.d. but c.Feb 1935, Wolmer MSS, MSS.Eng.hist.c.1012/71–2.
[173] Gretton to Baldwin, reporting the concerns raised by two meetings of MPs, n.d. but c.March 1935, Baldwin MSS, 48/245–50.
[174] Gretton to Croft, 12 May, and Gretton memo, 15 May 1936, Croft MSS, CAC, CRFT/1/12/Gr4–5.

during the Second World War when, like other Conservative MPs, they used the 1922 Committee as the means of raising these concerns.

The left wing was considerably fewer in number, but had at least equal impact due to their greater visibility and articulateness. It contained a few Members of experience and standing, such as Jack Hills, a founder of the pre-1914 Unionist Social Reform Committee, of which Baldwin had also been a member. A more maverick figure was the aristocrat Lord Henry Cavendish-Bentinck, half-brother of the 6th Duke of Portland and the bearer of a family name associated with the Disraelian age; indeed, Bentinck was almost of that era, having been first elected to the House at the age of twenty-three in 1886. His support for the tradition of 'Tory Democracy' was such that he opposed the Coal Mines (Eight Hours) Bill in 1926, and he was the only Conservative to vote against the Trade Disputes Bill in 1927. Hills too was unhappy about some of the latter's provisions, but followed the pattern of nearly all Conservative MPs in deciding: 'though I dislike some of it, I shall support it; in fact, to do anything else would be impossible'.[175]

Apart from the few such senior exceptions, the predominant tone and composition of the left was youth—quite often privileged youth, as it was money and connection which made it possible to be elected at an early age. This included scions of the aristocracy, such as the Earl of Derby's younger son, Oliver Stanley, elected aged twenty-eight in 1924 (although this was older than his elder brother, Lord Stanley, who was elected aged twenty-three in 1917); John de Vere Loder, elected aged twenty-nine in 1924; and Duff Cooper, who had a brief career in the Foreign Office before election in 1924 aged thirty-four. Later examples were Quintin Hogg (heir of 1st Viscount Hailsham), elected aged thirty-one in 1938, and Christopher York (of the long-established gentry family of that name of Long Marston, near York), elected aged thirty in 1939. A significant proportion of these young, articulate, and idealistic MPs progressed to office, as was shown by the 'Young Unionist Group' formed in 1919. A successor to the prewar Unionist Social Reform Committee, its members included Philip Cunliffe-Lister, Walter Guinness, Samuel Hoare, and Edward Wood, all of whom were Cabinet ministers in 1924–29, and Walter Elliot, William Ormsby-Gore, and Earl Winterton, who were Cabinet ministers in the 1930s.

Oliver Stanley, Duff Cooper, and Loder were members of a conspicuously active left-wing group of new MPs in 1924, together with Macmillan, Robert Boothby (who was twenty-four when first elected), and Noel Skelton (who had been an MP in 1922–23). This group was given the nickname of 'the YMCA' by the right-wing business element in retaliation for their label of the 'Forty Thieves'.[176] The name stuck because it encapsulated the rather earnest priggishness that was characteristic of all such social-reforming cliques of idealistic young men. They were certainly seen as bright and able, and possibly—once they became more experienced and less foolish—as the source of future leaders; in the meantime, however, they were regarded with tolerance more than respect, together with a little concern about

---

[175] Hills to Irwin, 28 April 1927, Halifax MSS, C152/17/1/213.
[176] Lane-Fox to Irwin, 30 June 1927, Halifax MSS, C152/17/1/237b.

where their notions might lead. The YMCA were certainly willing to consider a greater role for the state in economic affairs, and—again typically of such groups—set out their agenda in 1927 in a book, *Industry and the State*, authored by Boothby, Loder, Macmillan, and Oliver Stanley. Stanley spoke against the key contracting-in clause of the 1927 Trade Union Bill in a speech that was 'closely argued and evidently very carefully thought out, but the logic was ... very faulty', and, dangerously, 'he runs the risk of earning the reputation of being a crank'.[177] The YMCA were particularly vehement against Lord Cave's scheme for House of Lords reform in 1927; their reservations about this were shared by much of the mainstream, and the two elements combined to kill the proposals.

Several of the younger left-wing MPs lost their seats in 1929, but remained in close touch with their colleagues still in the House through a new group consisting of ten MPs and ten ex-MPs, in which many of the familiar faces were to be found.[178] The ambitions of the ousted to return were gratified through by-elections or in the 1931 landslide, but after this their cohesion was eroded by the ascent of many of them into office, which eventually left only Boothby and Macmillan to drift into increasingly dubious company and fractious criticism. In the 1930s, and partly under the influence of Lloyd George—a damning factor in the eyes of the leadership—several of the left wing were attracted to the idea of planning. They operated on the fringe of cross-party and non-party bodies such as the Next Five Years Group and Political and Economic Planning, and Macmillan published further books urging these novel theories.[179] In the 1929–31 parliament there was a conscious reaction against the YMCA on the part of a quartet of newly elected MPs, who, in deliberate contrast to their predecessors, called themselves the 'Boy's Brigade': R. A. Butler, Harold Balfour, Michael Beaumont, and Lord Lymington.[180] The group saw itself as right-of-centre but distinct from the diehards, although Lymington's evolution took him into that company, and he spoke against Baldwin's leadership at the party meeting of October 1930.[181] After 1931, the group fragmented: Beaumont became a PPS, whilst Lymington's vehement dissent over India put him on the opposite side to Butler, whose long ministerial career began with the junior post at the India Office in 1932—a career during which he was perceived as an impeccably Baldwinite centrist in the 1930s, and an almost 'pink' interventionist and social liberal after 1945.

The second important left-wing young men's movement was the Tory Reform Committee (TRC), founded in March 1943 by Lord Hinchingbrooke, York, Peter Thorneycroft (who had been elected aged thirty in a 1938 by-election), and Hugh Molson (who had won Doncaster at the age of twenty-eight in 1931, lost it in 1935, and then returned for the safe High Peak division of Derbyshire in October

---

[177] Lane-Fox to Irwin, 26 May 1927, Halifax MSS, C152/17/1/223.
[178] O'Connor draft letter, 11 July, O'Connor to Macmillan, 15 July 1929, Macmillan MSS, C.65/425, 428.
[179] H. Macmillan, *Reconstruction* (1933) and *The Middle Way*.
[180] Balfour, *Wings over Westminster*, 83; Earl of Portsmouth, *A Knot of Roots* (1965), 108–10.
[181] Butler to his parents, 4 November 1930, Butler MSS, D48/756a–62.

1939).[182] After differences in January 1944 between Thorneycroft and Hinchingbrooke over strategy and methods, the latter stepped down from the chairmanship and was succeeded by Hogg as a compromise candidate.[183] Like the YMCA, the TRC published its ideas, and followed up its initial manifesto, *Forward by the Right*, with a range of shorter pamphlets and slim books, taking stock—with some pride—in its activities and impact after the first twelve months with *One Year's Work* in 1944.[184] Like its 1920s predecessor again, the TRC advocated radical reconstruction with a greater role for planning, and generally made waves to the annoyance of older and established backbenchers.[185] It played a key part in the parliamentary storm in a teacup of 28 March 1944, when its amendment, moved by Thelma Cazalet-Keir, on equal pay for women teachers led to a government defeat—and Churchill's insistence on turning this into an issue of confidence and having it reversed the next day.[186]

In the case of both the YMCA and the TRC, the youthful reformers' sweeping enthusiasm for the new ideas of the moment, lack of practical experience, blithe confidence, self-absorbed cliquishness, desire for the limelight, open ambition, and the loose attitude to loyalty which often seemed to accompany it, did not render them attractive to the main body of older and staider backbenchers.[187] Acknowledgement of the young men's brilliance was often tempered by the feeling that they were too clever for their own good, by distaste for their antics, and by the suspicion that they were little more than soldiers of fortune. In the 1924–29 parliament, Boothby and Macmillan were seen to be patronized by Churchill, and, in consequence, 'both of them are rather mistrusted by the rank and file'.[188] In late 1930, when the turmoil of opposition and the impact of Mosley's breach with the Labour government focused press interest upon 'the movements among what are known as the young men', the Leader of the Conservative Party categorized them as 'those who are not so clever as they think they are, those who by leading a zig-zag course will never in future be trusted, and those [Baldwin] did not mention, who presumably follow the straight and narrow way'.[189] Indeed, despite their grumbles about their elders and their playing at drawing up prospective Cabinets of all the talents on the backs of dinner menus, most of the young MPs did not stray far

---

[182] York diary, 9 March 1943; the name 'Tory Reform Committee' was adopted in April: York diary, 14 April 1943.

[183] York diary, 19–27 January 1944. The York diary is a key source for the development of, and tensions within, the TRC; see also Hogg's diary, Hailsham (2nd Viscount) MSS, CAC, HLSM/1/6/1–6.

[184] Tory Reform Committee, *Forward by the Right* (1943); Viscount Hinchingbrooke, *Full Speed Ahead! Essays in Tory Reform* (1944); Tory Reform Committee, *One Year's Work* (1944); R. H. Innes, 'Conservative propaganda', *Ashridge Journal*, 112 (February 1945), 1.

[185] Headlam diary, 11 October 1944.

[186] York diary, 28–9 March 1944; Beamish diary notes, 29 March 1944, Beamish MSS, CAC, BEAM/3/5.

[187] Macmillan to Churchill, 10 April 1926, Churchill MSS, CAC, CHAR/2/147/73; Headlam diary, 6 May 1932, 29 November 1933, 18 January 1945.

[188] N. Chamberlain to Irwin, 12 August 1928, Halifax MSS, C152/18/1/114a.

[189] Summary of Baldwin's speech at the Constitutional Club, 17 December 1930, in Butler to his parents, 18 December 1930, Butler MSS, D48/770-2, full text in *The Times*, 18 December 1930; Emrys-Evans to Cranborne, 19 March 1928, Avon MSS, AP/14/1/739.

from the official orthodoxy; they supported Baldwin during the party crisis of 1930–31 and over India in 1933–35. Boothby warned Mosley in 1930 of 'the limitations of the existing young Conservatives', who 'are charming and sympathetic and intelligent at dinner' but 'there is not one of them who has either the character or the courage to do anything big'.[190] Some members of the YMCA (and later the TRC) were chosen for office due to their individual ability, but, in general, participation in groups was more of a drawback than an asset, as the Chief Whip sought to discourage 'groups that have a tendency to form caves and to be rather too superior (such as YMCA)'.[191] The most respected and influential of the younger figures were those on the cusp of the mainstream and the left wing, and who stood more by themselves than as part of a group, such as Walter Elliot, Noel Skelton, Anthony Eden, and Peter Thorneycroft.

Conservative MPs did not link up only on the basis of the similarity of their standpoint in the political spectrum from left to right; they also came together, sometimes in a more organized and significant way, through participation in regional or economic groups. Geographical community was an obvious common ground where collective action might either encourage or prevent government actions which could have a direct bearing upon the chances of re-election. The Scottish Unionist Members Committee generally met every two to three weeks during the parliamentary session in the 1930s, and more frequently during the wartime period. The various English groups tended to coalesce around an industrial region: thus in the 1930s there was a Merseyside Conservative Group and a Northern Group, the latter including non-Conservative supporters of the National Government.[192] These were gatherings of just MPs, but the Birmingham Club, which met at the House of Commons, comprised not only the city's Conservative MPs but also the editors of its two main newspapers and the principal officers of the city association.[193] The oldest-established private members' group derived from the economic interest which the party had been identified with for the longest time: agriculture. The Agricultural Committee was originally an unofficial body, and was a precursor and model of the party subject committees which were set up in 1924. There was also a more diffuse 'Industrial Group', organized around the British Commonwealth Union (BCU), which also promoted anti-Socialist propaganda in the country. Its Secretary and organizer was the long-serving Birmingham MP 'Paddy' Hannon, who was close to Rothermere and Beaverbrook, and was a keen supporter of protectionism and other diehard causes generally; he was not well-regarded in some quarters, but was on good terms with Neville Chamberlain and strongly supported appeasement. The Industrial Group's membership was drawn from those diehard and mainstream MPs who had strong business connections, and it could appear to be the defender of unbridled capitalism and the

---

[190] Boothby to Mosley, 18 May [1930], Boothby MSS, 677.
[191] Eyres-Monsell to Baldwin, 27 December 1927, Baldwin MSS, 162/122–3.
[192] Sandeman Allen to Baldwin, 11 February 1935, Baldwin MSS, 51/149–51; Headlam diary, 19 November 1931, 25 May 1932.
[193] A. Chamberlain to Baldwin, 9 December 1936, Baldwin MSS, 172/44.

employers' vested interests; the BCU was to evolve into the Federation of British Industries (and later the Confederation of British Industries).

Alongside these interest groups were pressure and policy groups of various kinds, often more ephemeral as issues came and went: one example of the many spontaneous initiatives which had a fairly short life, a low public profile, and relatively little impact, was the 'anti-planning' group founded in July 1935, with the rather dour figure of Herbert Williams as its chairman.[194] This and other such bodies often had parliamentary origins and a parliamentary leadership, but engaged in campaigning work outside Westminster. The largest and most significant policy-based pressure group was the Empire Industries Association (EIA), founded by Amery and Page Croft in April 1925. Its ostensible purpose was to campaign for the extension of the safeguarding legislation, in particular to iron and steel, but it was actually a vehicle for protectionism and imperial preference in all its forms. Conservative MPs who favoured the imposition of duties on manufactured imports (though not necessarily on food as well) joined its council, and by the time of the 1929 general election nearly half the parliamentary party were affiliated to it. After the heavy losses in the marginal seats, the proportion of the remaining MPs who were members of the EIA rose even higher. In April 1930, Page Croft declared that it represented 187 of the 260 MPs, and by December—when the party had officially adopted the 'free hand' on tariffs—the figure had become 90 per cent.[195] The EIA was most active from 1927 to 1930, when it was well-funded by industrialists, allowing it to offer speakers and literature to local constituencies without charge; as it was not evidently disloyal or disruptive, many were glad to accept this bounty. However, the EIA was forced to steer a careful course between Beaverbrook and Baldwin in 1930, and announced itself content with the latter's adoption of the 'free hand' policy in October.[196] It maintained a watching role on tariff policy into the mid-1930s, and a tenuous existence until the 1980s.

Before this, there had been the 'Conservative and Unionist Movement', initiated by Lords Salisbury and Selborne; its manifesto in the spring of 1922 was signed by forty-three peers and forty MPs. Essentially a diehard vehicle, it denounced the Coalition and called for House of Lords' reform and a return to 'Conservative principles'; not surprisingly, it had an impact in the safer seats, especially in southern England. The controversy over India was spearheaded by another mainly diehard body: originally founded as the Indian Empire Society in 1930, this was replaced by the India Defence League as the organization of MPs opposed to the government's policy; it claimed the adherence of eighty MPs in April 1935.[197] However, the counter-body guided and aided by Central Office—the Union of Britain and India—did not have a parliamentary dimension: its effective weapon was its membership of recent senior officials of the Indian civil service and provin-

---

[194] Duchess of Atholl to Todd and Nall, 30 August 1935, Atholl MSS, 23/3.
[195] Croft to Salisbury, 03 April 1930, Salisbury MSS, S(4)134/122–3; EIA, Parliamentary Council, 15 December 1930.
[196] EIA, Exec., 18 February, 11 March, Parliamentary Council, 5 June 1930.
[197] Duchess of Atholl to Salisbury, 26 April 1935, Atholl MSS, 95/2.

cial governors, whose speeches in support of the policy gave it validation and credibility. Concern over the increasing volume of legislation and regulations that were receiving little parliamentary scrutiny led to the forming of an 'Active Back Benchers' group in 1932; this suspended its self-appointed task at the start of the war, but resumed in 1942, when the number of orders under the Defence Regulations 'threatened to become an engulfing flood'.[198] Chaired by Herbert Williams, it had a membership of twenty-eight MPs, which was drawn from a mixture of the right and centre, but also included the leading TRC figure Hugh Molson. Finally, the left-leaning and pro-planning enthusiasm of the TRC provoked those who disagreed, especially those with strong individualist and free-market views, to form the Progress Trust to counter it in November 1943; unlike the TRC, this was deliberately a secretive body which avoided the limelight, but one known leading figure was Ralph Assheton, the Party Chairman at the end of the war.

There was one group of former MPs which, by definition, was entirely extra-parliamentary. This was the initiative led by a former junior minister, Moore-Brabazon, after the loss of his seat in 1929, to establish a Defeated Candidates' Association to represent the interests and views of the ex-MPs who sought to return.[199] Not surprisingly, the authorities were cautious about this, and resisted its pretensions to a permanent place in the party's organization. However, once Baldwin was assured of its loyal intentions, it was given a general endorsement under the amended name of Conservative Candidates' Association, 'provided it...looked to the future rather than the past'.[200] Even so, further delays followed, and formal approval was not given until six months after the election, by which time the latter was becoming a distant memory.[201] In the internal crisis of 1930, the group proved helpful as a moderating balance against the pressures from the diehards and protectionists to adopt potentially unpopular policies. However, it was already fading as a significant interest group when Moore-Brabazon's abandonment of defending Baldwin in the Westminster St George's by-election of March 1931 cast it into limbo. All of the former MPs who stood again recovered their seats in the 1931 landslide, following which the organization vanished like the mist after sunrise.[202]

REBELS AND REVOLTS

Conservative MPs were not expected to be slavish adherents of a party line, and there was a general belief in the Burkean principle that they were elected not as the

---

[198] *The Active Back Bench*, NU leaflet 44/2 (1944); Sir H. Williams, *Politics, Grave and Gay* (1949), 163–8.
[199] Minutes, memos, and correspondence, Moore-Brabazon MSS, Candidates' Association file; circular to ex-MPs, 11 July 1929, Steel-Maitland MSS, GD193/120/3/211; Moore-Brabazon to Baldwin, 19 and 23 July 1929, Baldwin MSS, 164/178–9.
[200] Report by Moore-Brabazon on interview with Baldwin, in minutes of inaugural meeting, 31 October 1929, Steel-Maitland MSS, GD193/120/3/519–20.
[201] Moore-Brabazon to Baldwin, 28 November, Baldwin to Moore-Brabazon, 5 December 1929, Moore-Brabazon MSS, Candidates' Association file.
[202] Moore-Brabazon to Ward, 31 October 1931, Ward MSS, MSS.Eng.c.6967.

tied delegates of their constituencies but as Members of the House with a duty to exercise their own judgement.[203] However, reservations were expected to be communicated through private channels if possible, and the acceptable parameters for dissent were that it be justifiable in terms of some important issue of principle and that it not be taken to the point of endangering the government when in office, or splitting the party and dividing its electoral base. This was the reason for the antagonism to Beaverbrook's 'Empire Crusade' in 1930–31 but, once their limited number was clear, the rather less concern over the India rebels and the anti-appeasers. Individual and occasional expressions of disagreement, when clearly based upon conviction, were tolerated and even respected, but too frequent recourse to this discretion provoked irritation and was a swift route to irrelevance. There was always suspicion of any combination of dissidents in a group, with questions arising as to their real motives and purposes, and the pull of party loyalty and unity were powerful inhibitors. The general presumption was that 'the proper role for loyal members of the Conservative Party is to convince our leaders if they can, but not to destroy them'.[204]

There were very few instances of the sanction of withdrawing the party whip being taken against dissident MPs, and the four which did occur related to individual and isolated acts.[205] One of these was a product of prolonged annoyance, culminating in an incident on a hot summer night in which tempers frayed, and it embarrassed the Chief Whip, Eyres-Monsell, almost more than the MP in question. This was the prominent diehard Sir Basil Peto, who had long been a thorn in the Chief Whip's side. The catalyst was minor indeed: one of Peto's interests was the charity for merchant seamen and, on their behalf, with typical obstinacy, he moved an amendment to a piece of routine legislation and insisted upon a division at a late hour on the humid night of 19 July 1928. This was an unpleasant surprise to Eyres-Monsell, who expected no further votes that evening and had allowed Conservative MPs to go home. Peto had already voted four times against the government over the unpopular Racecourse Betting Bill earlier in the evening, and 'was in a temper for some reason'; the junior minister in charge of the later measure was convinced that 'he did it to annoy'.[206] At the end of a long and difficult parliamentary year, and literally in the heat of the moment, the Chief Whip was furious and the division was followed by angry exchanges in the lobby and Eyres-Monsell's decision to withdraw the whip.[207] This was indeed a storm in a teacup, and lasted for the few weeks that it did mainly because neither party would back down. Peto had the complete support of his local association in Barnstaple, of which he had previously been chairman. After hearing his assertion that he had always sought to represent constituency interests and the Conservative cause, but could never be a

[203] Ripon CA, statement to the Exec. by Hills MP, 26 March 1938.
[204] Salisbury to Duchess of Atholl, 26 February 1935, Atholl MSS, 95/2.
[205] J. A. Cross, 'The withdrawal of the Conservative Party whip', *Parliamentary Affairs*, 21 (1967–68), 166–75; this does not discuss the case of Wayland.
[206] Headlam diary, 19–20 July 1928.
[207] Lady Peto diary, 27 July–31 October 1928; according to Peto's unpublished memoirs, he was not officially informed of either the withdrawal or the restoration of the whip, Peto MSS.

'completely subservient' MP, it passed a unanimous vote of confidence in him.[208] He also had a meeting with Baldwin which appeared to be friendly in tone, in which the Leader accepted that no disloyalty to himself personally had been intended. Tempers cooled after the end of the session, and on 28 August it was officially announced in the press that the whip would be restored when parliament reconvened.

The other three instances involved dissidence on more important political issues. The briefest of these was the case of Sir William Wayland, the only MP to endorse the press lords' anti-Baldwin candidate against the official Conservative nominee in the Westminster St George's by-election of March 1931. This was a public breach of party loyalty, and much more serious than Peto's offence; although he was similarly of some social standing in his constituency, Wayland's action was not in tune with Conservative sentiment in the spring of 1931 and he was in some danger of repudiation by his association in Canterbury.[209] The position was exacerbated by the fact that Wayland was one of the diehard group who had received negative publicity for organizing against Baldwin's leadership in October 1930, following which Wayland had given an explanation of his attitude and a promise to abide by the verdict of the party meeting.[210] His further dissidence and the consequent withholding of the whip was regarded by his constituency executive as creating a 'serious position', and it was only after Wayland gave a forty-five-minute apologia, including a promise of future loyal support to the party and to Baldwin, that the matter was allowed to rest.[211] The whip was restored shortly afterwards, and Wayland continued to sit as a Conservative MP until he retired in 1945. A similar situation arose in 1935, when a number of MPs opposed to the India policy spoke in support of Randolph Churchill's independent candidature and thus against the official nominee in the Wavertree by-election. However, although it was considered, it was decided not to withdraw the whip, partly because it was felt that some of the rebel MPs were acting unwillingly, and still more on the tactical grounds of not playing into the opposition's hands by making martyrs of them, and so arousing sympathy and consolidating their group.[212]

The two remaining cases where the whip was withdrawn did not return to the fold, although in the first of these it was a more reluctant parting of company. Sir Robert Newman, MP for Exeter since May 1918, was a prominent member of the Devon landed gentry whose support for free-trade and centrist views on domestic issues led to friction with his local association. They nearly chose an alternative nominee at the 1923 dissolution, but at the last moment lost their nerve.[213] However, relations deteriorated further, and in October 1927 the association decided to seek another candidate for the next election. This in itself would not have led to the

---

[208] *The Times*, 3 August 1928.
[209] Ball, *Baldwin and the Conservative Party*, 146.
[210] Canterbury CA, Council AGM, 15 November 1930.
[211] Canterbury CA, emergency meeting of Finance & Emergency Ctte, emergency meeting of Council, 28 March 1931; Stenton and Lees, *Who's Who of British Members of Parliament*, vol. 3, 371.
[212] N. to H. Chamberlain, 26 January 1935, *NCDL*; Cazalet diary, 28 January 1935.
[213] Headlam diary, 23–6 November 1923.

loss of the whip, and did not do so in other cases before or after; what made the difference was that Newman declared publicly that he would fight the seat as an independent. No official announcement of a withdrawal of the whip was made, but it seems that the whips regarded him as sitting as an independent and simply no longer sent it. Most unusually, Newman held his seat in the 1929 election, and was an extremely rare example of an independent surviving the challenge from an official candidate of his former party; he decided to retire shortly before the 1931 election, and received a peerage in the dissolution honours.

If Newman was an establishment figure of mildly unorthodox views, the fourth case turned himself into an one-man anti-establishment crusade of some public notoriety.[214] It did not start out that way, for Alec Cunningham-Reid was fairly unobtrusive as MP for the northern marginal of Warrington in 1922–23 and 1924–29; in the latter parliament he served as PPS to the Minister of Transport, Wilfrid Ashley, and married his daughter Ruth in 1927. He then returned to his home constituency, the safe seat of St Marylebone in the fashionable West End, where he proved to be a divisive figure. He was chosen as the candidate for a by-election in 1932, but this fractured the association in two, with an Independent Conservative candidate standing unsuccessfully against him. From time to time in the 1930s, he claimed an independence of mind and was critical of subservience to the whips and party machine, but this kind of rhetoric was far from unusual amongst backbenchers who did not seek or expect to get office. The breakdown occurred during the Second World War, in part due to its radicalizing effect, as Cunningham-Reid launched out in a populist and cross-party direction. His position was damaged by a protracted divorce, and in 1940 he was criticized for absence and repudiated by his association. However, this did not lead to the withdrawal of the whip, nor did further attacks on the 'whip system'—one of which, at the 1941 Conference, was ruled out of order by the Chairman. It was Cunningham-Reid's campaigning in support of W. J. Brown, the independent who defeated the official Conservative candidate at the Rugby by-election of April 1942, and his combining in the following month with Brown and another independent MP, Edgar Granville, to form a 'People's Movement', which finally overstepped the boundary—when the creation of the latter was announced, the Whips' Office informed the press that the whip had been withdrawn.[215] In 1943, Cunningham-Reid's former constituency association was disaffiliated by the National Union and its rival given recognition instead, and in the 1945 election the latter's official candidate won the seat, whilst Cunningham-Reid came third, with only 12 per cent of the poll.

Finally, there was another wartime case of quite different political complexion, but this was not so much the whip being withdrawn as becoming embarrassingly irrelevant. The virulent anti-Semitism of Captain Archibald Ramsay, MP for the Borders constituency of Peebles from 1931, fostered dangerous links with Nazi

---

[214] R. J. Ellis, *He Walks Alone: The Private and Public Life of Captain Cunningham-Reid, DFC, Member of Parliament 1922–1945* (n.d. [1946]).
[215] *The Times*, 15 May 1942; Cross, 'Withdrawal of the Conservative Party whip', 171–2.

Germany in the late 1930s. He believed that there was a secret Jewish conspiracy for world domination which sought war between Britain and Germany, and sincerely saw it as his patriotic duty to prevent this. This led him first to join the Nordic League, a racially based organization favourable to Nazism, and then in May 1939 to form a secret group called the Right Club. When war broke out, most of its members withdrew and took up war work, but Ramsay regarded it as a Jewish war and moved closer to Mosley and other neo-Fascists. He was under surveillance by MI5 and became implicated in the 'Tyler Kent affair', when a clerk at the American embassy in London smuggled out secret documents, including the telegrams between Churchill and Roosevelt.[216] This was the spur to action, but there was also mounting public concern over the activities of Mosley and fears of a 'fifth column' as France inexplicably collapsed under the German offensive. Ramsay was arrested under Defence Regulation 18B on 23 May 1940 along with Mosley, and, like him, was detained without trial in Brixton Prison; he was released in September 1944 and resumed his seat in the House, but was deselected by his constituency and did not attempt to contest the 1945 election.

There were also a number of instances when MPs resigned the whip of their own accord, in order to make a point. In May 1935, five Conservative MPs repudiated the National Government whip, although they made this distinct from any resignation of the party whip; the group consisted of three Lancashire MPs (F. W. Astbury, Sir Joseph Nall, and Linton Thorp), A. J. K. Todd, and the Duchess of Atholl.[217] Their reasons were partly their dissent over India and partly several domestic measures which they regarded as too close to Socialism.[218] In September 1935, the desire for unity during the Abyssinian crisis led them to resume taking the whip, and those of the five who stood again in the general election in November did so as official Conservative and National candidates. However, in April 1938 the Duchess again resigned the whip after a breach with her constituency association over her criticisms of the government's foreign policy. She sat as an independent until her decision after the Munich Agreement to fight a by-election, in which she was defeated in December 1938.[219] The other case was the future Party Leader, Macmillan, a critic of the National Government's economic policy, who was already to some extent 'semi-detached', although it was over the foreign policy issue of the dropping of sanctions against Italy that he resigned the whip in June 1936. He resumed taking the whip in July 1937, and a few years later warned the founding members of the Tory Reform Committee that 'he considered his polite rebellion in the Conservative Party was a failure'.[220] Macmillan became increasingly critical during the Czech crisis of 1938 and campaigned against the

---

[216] A. H. M. Ramsay, *The Nameless War* (1952); R. Griffiths, *Patriotism Perverted: Captain Ramsay, the Right Club and British Anti-Semitism 1939–1940* (1998).
[217] Duchess of Atholl to Butter, 14 August 1935, Atholl MSS, 23/3.
[218] Astbury, Duchess of Atholl, Nall, Todd, and Thorp to Baldwin, 1 and 21 May 1935, Baldwin MSS, 107/82–7, 94; Duchess of Atholl to Salisbury, 27 April 1935, Atholl MSS, 95/2.
[219] The causes of the breach and the by-election are discussed in S. Ball, 'The politics of appeasement'.
[220] York diary, 2 December 1942; H. Macmillan, *Winds of Change 1914–1939* (1966), 458–60.

official Conservative candidate at the crucial Oxford by-election in October, but the whip was not withdrawn either then or after his vote against the government on 29 March 1939; in the Norway debate of May 1940 he was, unsurprisingly, one of those who voted against Chamberlain.

It is striking that the only MP in the whole of this twenty-seven-year period to defect to another party whilst sitting in the House had never actually called himself a Conservative. This was W. E. D. Allen, Ulster Unionist MP for Belfast West, who joined the 'New Party' founded by Sir Oswald Mosley in March 1931.[221] Ulster Unionism essentially meant a Protestant identity which rejected rule from Dublin and saw its economy and culture as linked with that of mainland Britain; apart from that, it had always been a broad spectrum which included sometimes radical views on economic and social issues, and it combined a considerable measure of populism with an element of authoritarianism and discipline. Allen was an enterprising young member of an established family-run publishing firm, and had links to Harold Macmillan in particular and to other young MPs who were impatient with the 'old gang' of leaders, and whose thoughts were moving in channels parallel to Mosley on economic policy at least.[222] Whilst some of the mainland MPs were tempted but wisely took matters no further—not least due to personal distrust of Mosley himself—it was not surprising that Allen would be the one to feel most independent of the Conservative machine. However, the New Party was washed away in the flood tide of the economic crisis of August 1931 and the ensuing election, and Allen, who had run into strong criticism in Belfast and who was doubtful about Mosley's developing interest in Fascism, decided not to stand again; shortly after the election he resigned from the New Party, and after that concentrated upon his business career.

The common ground between the MPs who in various ways separated from, or were rejected by, the party is that they were maverick figures acting individually. They were not, of course, without friendships and connections with other MPs, but they were not operating as part of a group—they represented only themselves, and were not the visible peak of a bigger iceberg. When larger factions formed and revolts developed, they took place within the party and remained so. Those who lost accepted the verdict, or continued a form of sniping from within, or took up another issue, or retired from active politics. They may have been considerably alienated, but that did not lead to a change in their party allegiance.

The parliamentary party passed through several periods of unease and concern in the interwar era, and were more often in this mood than they were confident and contented—but such, perhaps, is human nature and the norm for elected politicians in a democracy. Approaching general elections were rarely regarded with much enthusiasm, especially as the party was usually in government and it was only too easy to see reasons why it might have disappointed its own supporters or become unpopular with the centrist voters essential for victory, or very possibly have managed both. These underlying tensions developed into serious unrest on

---

[221] Allen to Baldwin, 9 March 1931, Baldwin MSS, 166/2–4.
[222] Allen to Beaverbrook, 28 May 1930, Beaverbrook MSS, BBK/B123; P. Corthorn, 'W.E.D. Allen, Unionist politics and the New Party', *Contemporary British History*, 23/4 (2009), 509–25.

the part of a significant number of MPs over four matters: the continuation of the Coalition in 1921–22, protectionism in 1927–31, the India reforms in 1933–35, and appeasement in 1936–39. In the first three cases, the origins and core of the revolt were the well-known diehards on the right; in the case of anti-appeasement, it was a more heterogeneous collection ranging across the spectrum, but linked mainly to the left. It is important to remember that in each case the dissidents' primary aim was to persuade the majority of the parliamentary party of the validity of their case; dividing the party was never their purpose, and was something which they were generally driven to unwillingly, as a last resort. This also explains the responsiveness of critics to appeals for unity and moderation, and their reluctance to force open divisions. When Conservative MPs did rebel, they did so within the party, and it was almost unheard of—and counterproductive—to act in concert with any opposition party or to leave the ranks and join another party. As the long-serving left-wing MP Jack Hills advised from personal experience, 'Conservatives would weaken their case in Conservative circles if they could be taxed with joining an association consisting mainly or largely of members of the other side.'[223]

The impact and effectiveness of the critics depended upon whether their views came to be shared by a significant number of the mainstream majority. This did occur on a decisive scale with the fall of the Coalition, not at the time of the first diehard criticisms in 1920 or rebel votes in the House in 1921, but from the election scare of January 1922 onwards.[224] It did so in an unspectacular way, with no direct parliamentary manifestations until the showdown of the party meeting at the Carlton Club in October; this was perhaps why the seismic shift in sentiment was not registered by the Leader, Austen Chamberlain, although he was told of it, not least by his Chief Whip and Party Chairman.[225] The latter was particularly aware of the trend, as an important cause of the disaffection of many MPs sitting for safe seats was the growing hostility to the Coalition of their constituency associations and the resulting pressure to stand as a Conservative independent of it at the next election; by September 1922, 184 MPs and candidates had declared their intention to do so.[226] In the following month, there was opposition to continuing the coalition in its present form, with Lloyd George as Prime Minister, from an unprecedented range of elements in the parliamentary ranks. As well as the predictable diehards, there were many centrist MPs (including senior and respected backbenchers); some younger figures of the left offended by what they regarded as the cynical and unprincipled style of the Coalition leaders; a majority of the junior ministers; most of the party management, including the Deputy Chairman and Chairman of the Party, and the whips, led by their Chief; and two Cabinet ministers in the Commons who had long-standing backbench links (Baldwin and Griffith-Boscawen). The sentiments of them all were summed up by Hoare: 'the time has come for the Conservative Party to re-establish its unity and independence'; the Coalition had

---

[223] Hills to Duchess of Atholl, 4 October 1937, Atholl MSS, 45/2.
[224] Memo of Conservative MPs' views on an early dissolution, January 1922, AC, 32/2/79.
[225] Bayford diary, 21 August 1921.
[226] Wilson to A. Chamberlain, c.14 September 1922, AC, 33/2/26; Dutton, *Austen Chamberlain*, 193.

outlived its usefulness, and 'if...we do not bring it to an end now, we are destroying the Conservative Party for twenty years'.[227] It was symbolic of the shift in mainstream backbench opinion that Pretyman, the proposer of Chamberlain's election as Leader at the formal party meeting in March 1921, was also the mover of the resolution which ended his tenure in October 1922.

In this context, it is almost surprising that the majority against Chamberlain and the Coalition was not larger than the Carlton Club meeting result of 185 to eighty-eight. Whilst the ballot was secret at the time, the papers survive and show how each MP voted.[228] Those against continuing the Coalition were primarily MPs with safe or fairly safe seats, particularly in the southern half of England, whilst the pro-Coalition minority included many who sat for marginal seats, especially in Scotland and the northern industrial areas.[229] The latter were both more dependent upon the Liberal votes they had been given in 1918 and more immediately threatened by the rise of Labour, and so were most receptive to the Coalition case that the worst danger would be to separate the constitutional forces. The anti-Coalition MPs, on the other hand, saw the Coalition as having failed to stem the Socialist advance and likely in its style and conduct to further provoke it, whilst at the same time dividing the only really effective constitutional force, the Conservative Party.

Pressure for a more protectionist policy developed in the second half of the 1924–29 parliament, when it focused upon demands to extend the safeguarding legislation to the iron and steel industry. The core of the dissent was an overlapping combination of the diehards, who were unhappy with the centrism of the government across a range of issues, and the committed protectionists, who were marshalled by the Empire Industries Association. There was much grumbling when Baldwin made it clear in August 1928 that there would be no change in the official policy at the next election, but this held the line until his moderate strategy failed to bring victory in the 1929 election. The defeat reopened the issue in the context of a parliamentary party which had lost many of Baldwin's more moderate supporters—as they had sat for industrial marginals—and, as a result, the diehard wing was proportionately larger.

The most serious phases of the protectionist crisis occurred between the autumn of 1929 and the autumn of 1930, with a diminuendo lasting to March 1931. The pressure for the adoption of a tariff programme coincided with, and was both aided and hampered by, the extra-parliamentary campaign mounted by the press lords. The transformation of their 'Empire Crusade' agitation in February 1930 into a pressure group appealing for members to join its local branches and threatening to put up rival candidates sent waves of alarm through Conservative MPs, especially those from the southern strongholds where the press lords' newspapers had a large readership and support for tariffs had always been strong.[230] No sitting MP actually joined the Empire Crusade party, although Hannon and Page Croft worked closely with Beaverbrook, and many MPs sympathized with his aims whilst regretting his methods. Support for Baldwin's cautious position began to erode,

[227] Hoare to Long, 17 October 1922, Long MSS (WSA), 947/840.
[228] See the list in James, *Memoirs of a Conservative*, 129–33.
[229] Edinburgh North CA, Exec., 24 October 1922.
[230] Davidson to Tyrell, 9 March 1930, Davidson MSS, DAV/190.

especially after a compromise with Beaverbrook broke down in June 1930. By August there was 'a good deal of discontent among Conservatives who are certainly finding S.B'.s leadership rather uninspiring'.[231] The situation became most acute during the summer recess, with increasing signs of disaffection amongst MPs and their constituency associations.[232] However, before parliament met again, Baldwin made a swift and significant advance of policy in October which satisfied nearly all of the critics.

Baldwin was able to use MPs' dislike of coercion from the press lords to rally sentiment in his favour at two party meetings. The first, in June 1930, was in the nature of a holding operation, as MPs supported him on the issue of press dictation but with 'somewhat mixed feelings'.[233] However, the second, in October, was more decisive: after this approved Baldwin's new policy and his leadership by a large majority, almost all of the critics within the party accepted the verdict and fell into line. At both meetings leading diehard and protectionist MPs spoke against Baldwin: Gretton and Page Croft moved the resolution against his policy in June and both of them, as well as Kindersley, Lymington, and Marjoribanks, spoke against Baldwin's leadership in October. Unlike the Carlton Club meeting of 1922, these two gatherings included adopted candidates—who could vocalize opinion in the marginals and the north, which was much more favourable to Baldwin—and the October meeting included peers as well, though they were likely to be less in his favour. At the second meeting the vote on Baldwin's leadership was by secret ballot, and resulted in a convincing victory of 462 over the substantial minority of 116 against. However, the latter were dismissed by Austen Chamberlain as consisting of 'the group habitually described as the Forty Thieves, hangers-on of business, not of the best type' and 'a good many old and disgruntled peers'.[234] This marked the real end of the crisis, although Beaverbrook continued his campaign until his defeat in the Westminster St George's by-election in March 1931.

The opposition period of 1929–31 also saw the beginnings of the India revolt. It was apparent from the debate on the Irwin Declaration in November 1929 that there was a considerable gap between Baldwin's moderate bipartisan approach and the hostility of many MPs to any further devolution of power to the native population. Most Conservative MPs wanted no advance beyond the cautious proposals recommended by the Simon Commission in 1930, and were 'in a state of nervous suspicion' that this was being sidelined.[235] Baldwin's speech in the January 1931 debate after the first Indian Round Table conference considerably increased their anxiety, and it was heard with 'an ominous silence on our own benches'.[236] After a shaky few weeks in which diehard opinion came close to capturing the backbench India Committee, the Leader's moderate line was vindicated by the terms of the Irwin–Gandhi Pact in early March, which transformed the mood in the Smoking

[231] Lane-Fox to Irwin, 21 August 1930, Halifax MSS, C152/19/1/120.
[232] Ormsby-Gore to Salisbury, 5 October 1930, Salisbury MSS, S(4)137/44–5.
[233] Lady Peto diary, 25 June 1930.
[234] A. to I. Chamberlain, 2 November 1930, *ACDL*.
[235] Hoare to Irwin, 15 July 1930, Halifax MSS, C152/19/1/100.
[236] Lane-Fox to Irwin, 28 January 1931, Halifax MSS, C152/19/1/221.

Room.[237] This left the balance of opinion in the parliamentary party in a position which remained almost unchanged for the rest of the controversy, with the diehard group accounting for most of the minority who were vehemently opposed. Their criticisms had little apparent effect upon the centre and left-wing support for the leadership, although in many cases this was despite private doubts—as Rhys noted in 1932, 'no one of our party seems to be really easy in their minds'.[238]

The next two years were dominated by the economic slump and the introduction of tariffs, and the Indian issue did not return to the forefront until the government's proposals were announced in the White Paper of March 1933. Although there followed a long parliamentary battle until the final passage of the Government of India Act in June 1935, the policy of the leadership was never in serious danger. The landslide victory in the 1931 general election had created a parliamentary party with a huge preponderance of moderate MPs, many of whom were aware that the non-Conservative votes they had received as the 'National' candidate had been critical to their success. The India policy was a vital area of agreement within the National Government, and to reject it would inevitably mean the break-up of the combination. This was desired, if at all, only by a few diehards, and most of the rebels—including Churchill—were supporters of the National Government in other respects.[239] Nor was there any threat of the rebels combining with the official opposition, as the Labour Party had been reduced to fifty-two MPs and in any case advocated even greater reforms in India. With more than four-fifths of the 470 Conservative MPs accepting the government's policy (however unenthusiastically), the rebels could have no parliamentary impact; they had to hope instead that their resistance would arouse grass-roots Conservative opinion, and for that reason the struggle within the National Union was of much more significance.

However, although unsuccessful, the India 'revolt' saw some of the largest-ever votes by Conservative MPs against the official whip. The opposition to the bill was organized by the India Defence League, and around fifty MPs attended its inaugural meeting on 14 March 1933, three days before the publication of the White Paper; previously, forty-four MPs had voted for Churchill's motion against the India policy on 3 December 1931. The 'Black List' drawn up by the India Office in October 1934 of MPs believed to be 'uncompromisingly hostile' contained sixty names, although Churchill was not included, perhaps because his opposition was so well-known.[240] The highest level of dissent came when the eventual bill was debated, with seventy-seven MPs dividing against its first reading on 12 December 1934; this level was sustained to the high-water mark of eighty opposing the second reading on 11 February 1935. The foundation of the rebel group was the well-

---

[237] Spender-Clay to Irwin, 5 March 1931, Davidson to Irwin, 6 March 1931, Lane-Fox to Irwin, 4 and 5 March 1931, Halifax MSS, C152/19/1/251, 254, 246, 249; Eden diary, 4 and 5 March 1931, Avon MSS, AP/20/1/10.
[238] Rhys, memorandum, 15 September 1932, Dynevor MSS.
[239] S. Ball, 'Churchill and the Conservative Party', *Transactions of the Royal Historical Society*, 6th ser., 11 (2001), 317–18; Middleton & Prestwich CA, AGM, 3 March 1934.
[240] 'Black List', in Morley to Tweedy, 15 October 1934, Butler MSS, F73/66–7. Most of the names were the usual diehards, but it also included some outside that group, such as the future Chief Whip, James Stuart.

established diehards, many of whom had opposed the Coalition in 1922 and Baldwin's tariff policy and leadership in 1927–30.[241] Following the first reading vote, a disappointed Hoare typified the dissidents as mostly MPs 'sitting for safe Conservative seats, who take little part in the debates of the House and who can be moved by no arguments at all'.[242] This diehard core was augmented by some MPs influenced by constituency issues, principally from the cotton textile region of Lancashire, where there was much concern about its important export market in India. A further but smaller number, who overlapped with both the diehards and the constituency-based rebels, were motivated by their personal experience of India, although this was often not of the most recent vintage (Churchill falls into this category). Finally, there were a handful who had not joined the critics for any of these reasons, but who had become informed and deeply concerned about the issue—the Duchess of Atholl being a particular example.

In the case of the 'anti-appeasers', the popular mythology of the 1930s which was established after Dunkirk, and enshrined in the first volume of Churchill's war memoirs, depicts the heroic struggle of an earlier 'few' who fought against heavy odds to prevent national disaster and to whom also 'so much might be owed'. Although this simplistic scenario has been modified by historical reassessments since the 1960s, attention still tends to focus upon the famous names who are considered to have been the leaders around whom the others clustered—Churchill, Eden, and Amery. This makes the anti-appeasers too tidy and too disciplined, when in fact they were even more disconnected than had been the case in the other rebellions. They were a collection of individuals acting from the promptings of their own conscience, judgement, or past experience; there was often little by way of mutual consultation, and still less of conspiracy. The most distinctive circle was that of around twenty-five MPs which coalesced in early 1938 around Eden and the junior ministers who had resigned with him; this partly absorbed and partly overlapped with a less-defined 'group' of MPs linked to Amery.[243] Furthermore, until the spring of 1939, they sought to keep Churchill and his small band at arm's length, partly from lack of sympathy with his views on other issues and partly to avoid being tarnished by his reputation for ambition and poor judgement, which had been recently reaffirmed in the Abdication crisis of December 1936.[244] Despite their small size, the members of the various cliques were often unable to agree on policy or tactics, and their manoeuvres were frequently transparent and inept.[245]

Some common features were shared by a number of the critics, and this distinctive element in the group earned them the derogatory label from the whips of 'the glamour boys'. The first of these characteristics was comparative youthfulness, with

---

[241] List of the fifty-five India Defence League MPs who voted against the bill on 12 December 1934, Churchill MSS, CAC, CHAR/2/227/95.
[242] Hoare to Willingdon, 13 December 1934, Templewood MSS (BL), E240/4/1197–200.
[243] Astor to Eden, 27 July 1938, Avon MSS, AP/14/1/675; List of group members, Emrys-Evans to Amery, 23 June 1954, Emrys-Evans MSS, Add.58247/20–1; Nicolson to his wife, 9 November 1938, in Nicolson diary; R. Tree, *When the Moon Was High* (1975), 75–6.
[244] Crossley diary, 20 September 1938, *WSC*.
[245] Channon diary, 3–4 July 1939.

many of the critics drawn from the generation that had served as junior officers in the First World War (Eden and Macmillan) and those even younger (Adams, Boothby, Cartland, and Anthony Crossley). Several of the rebels were part of the intake of 1924, and others had entered the House in the second landslide of 1931. They tended to sit for marginals or constituencies which were usually Conservative, albeit not by large majorities, and had been chosen as candidates more for their personality, vigour, and platform ability than their wealth or local roots. These factors protected them to some extent from a backlash within their constituency associations, especially if they took some trouble to keep in touch with their chairman and executive and were careful in how far they took their dissent.[246] In some cases, such as Emrys-Evans, their connection with the wider membership was sufficient to balance or circumvent hostility from the local elite. They were keen to maintain the National coalition, and its broader electoral appeal was important in holding their seats. Most among this younger element were identified with the left or centre-left of the parliamentary party; this was a factor which increased the distrust of older and more mainstream MPs, and made it easier to contain the criticism. Several of the dissenters had a Foreign Office background, albeit at a junior level (Duff Cooper, Emrys-Evans, John McEwen, and the National Labour MP Harold Nicolson), and many were well-travelled and spoke foreign languages. The 'glamour boys' were metropolitan in tone and mostly professional in occupation, with connections to the worlds of journalism, literature, and history. They were also seen as preoccupied with their own political careers, and could be dismissed as motivated by ambition, the desire to be noticed, and pique at a lack of advancement.

However, not all of the anti-appeasers were from the 'glamour boy' mould; they included a few established businessmen or landed gentry—which was one reason for the greater impact of Sidney Herbert's speech in the Munich debate. Some MPs on the right wing disliked the policy for reasons of national pride or concerns about the security of the empire. However, relatively few of the diehards were involved and there was little continuity from the India revolt—the principal exceptions were Churchill, Wolmer, and the Duchess of Atholl. This last was one of the most prominent rebels, and her record of dissent over foreign policy in 1935–38 was more sustained than that of Churchill, Amery, Boothby, or even Macmillan. Criticism and doubts were expressed in speeches in the House, but rarely in votes. Churchill only abstained in the Munich debate—although that was a very public expression of dissent—and his first vote against the government did not come until a month later, on 17 November 1938, on the need to speed rearmament by establishing a Ministry of Supply. Whilst the strains had been evident since the Rhineland crisis in early 1936, and became much greater after Eden's resignation in February 1938, it was the Munich crisis and debate which brought matters into the open. Feeling on both sides—for Chamberlain had his ardent defenders, mainly from the right wing, such as Henry 'Chips' Channon—'ran high', and it was after

---

[246] Cranborne faced difficulties in his safe seat of Dorset South: Cranborne to Thomas, 8 October 1938, Cilcennin MSS, 47.

this that 'considerable bitterness' developed.[247] The rebels became increasingly alienated not just from the policy but from the party machine, distrusting the whips and believing (perhaps correctly) that their telephones were being tapped.[248]

The anti-appeasers were a small and often beleaguered group up to the spring of 1939, and it was not until after the outbreak of war that their criticism of the conduct of Chamberlain and his government came to be more widely shared amongst Conservative MPs. The Prime Minister's speech to the 1922 Committee in November 1939 raised doubts amongst even normally supportive MPs such as Nancy Astor and some junior Cabinet ministers such as Euan Wallace, and the feeling of ineffectiveness and drift during the first months of the war was a significant factor in undermining Chamberlain's position. Many of the younger Conservative MPs were military reservists who joined their units after the declaration of war; they were dismayed by the lack of preparedness which they found and the gap between reality and ministers' complacent public assurances.[249] One of the clearest examples of this was Quintin Hogg, who had been Chamberlain's champion in the Oxford by-election after the Munich settlement but who voted against him in May 1940. The failures of the Norwegian campaign and Chamberlain's misjudgements in the ensuing debate of 7 and 8 May 1940 brought these concerns to a head. The Prime Minister's speech sounded a narrowly partisan note which had a counterproductive effect amongst those MPs who had come to fear that he could not inspire the nation to make the necessary sacrifices, and that he lacked the imagination and initiative needed to drive the war effort. The first major setback in the war also gave new potency to the knowledge that Labour's refusal to serve under Chamberlain meant that he was a barrier to any genuine government of national unity, now that the need for one was more apparent and urgent.

These factors influenced the two groups who augmented the ranks of the usual critics to such significant effect: the MPs who attended the debate but deliberately abstained from the vote, and the MPs who had not previously been identified with the anti-appeasers but who voted against the government. The motivation of these MPs was not a retrospective change of mind about the merits of prewar appeasement, but an immediate judgement that the government was not performing effectively in its current structure, composition, and leadership.[250] In the Norway debate, those defending the government tended to concentrate on the details of the campaign, whilst its opponents dealt with it in more general terms as a reflection of wider tardiness and inadequacy. Thus Sir Roger Keyes, who attended in his full dress uniform as an Admiral of the Fleet, focused not upon the naval actions or the decisions of the Admiralty, but on the Cabinet and committee system.[251]

---

[247] Emrys-Evans memo after reading J. Wheeler-Bennett's book on Munich, n.d., and memo for Eden's memoirs, n.d. but c.1962, Emrys-Evans MSS, Add.58247.
[248] Ronald Tree stated in his memoirs that in a conversation during the war Joseph Ball admitted having arranged this: Tree, *When the Moon Was High*, 76.
[249] Cazalet diary, 7–9 May 1940; Nicolson diary, 20 September 1939; Ball, *The Guardsmen*, 212.
[250] Winterton to Hoare, 9 May 1940, Templewood MSS, XII/2; Channon diary, 8 May 1940.
[251] J. D. Fair, 'The Norwegian campaign and Winston Churchill's rise to power in 1940', *International History Review*, 9 (1987), 410–37.

Several groups sought to marshal anti-Chamberlain opinion behind the scenes, of which the most influential were the ostensibly neutral 'Watching Committee' of peers and MPs chaired by Lord Salisbury (whose members included Amery, Macmillan, and Emrys-Evans),[252] the 'Eden group' (which was continuing to meet under Amery, who had not been invited to join the government), and an 'All-Party' group of MPs organized by Clement Davies, a former Liberal National who was now sitting as an independent. The outcome was a decisive setback for Chamberlain, which made his resignation from the Premiership unavoidable, for although the government won the vote of confidence by 281 to 200, its formal majority of 220 had slumped to only eighty-one—a withdrawal of support which was too substantial to be overlooked. Forty-two National Government MPs had voted against; thirty-three of these were Conservatives, including several who had not previously been identified with the anti-appeasers. Eighty-eight government MPs did not vote, of whom a fair number were not able to attend; however, in most cases the reason for this was that they were on active service, and it is likely that quite a few these might have taken a critical line. Of more immediate importance, around thirty MPs who were present chose to abstain, in some cases ostentatiously remaining seated in the chamber during the division, and their number together with those who voted against had a cumulatively crucial impact. The proportion of younger MPs and those who were currently, or previously had been, in the armed services was higher amongst the dissidents than in the party as a whole, and whilst more service MPs voted with Chamberlain than against him, the sixteen uniformed officers who entered the opposition lobby made an indelible and damaging impression.

THE WHIPS IN THE HOUSE OF COMMONS

The most important role of the whips was to manage the day-to-day activity of parliament to the best advantage for their party. This could be a matter of either maintaining or curtailing discussion, which involved an awareness of who wished to speak on a subject, who had expertise upon it, and of the necessary scheduling of debates and divisions. The whips made arrangements about the order and timing of business, and they liaised on these matters with the whips of the other parties and the Speaker's office (this was known as 'behind the Chair' or 'the usual channels') to smooth the way; they would also intercede with the Speaker when problems arose. In government, it was their task to ensure that sufficient MPs were available to prevent the opposition from winning a snap division on some minor matter, and thereby gaining advantages in publicity and morale from the ministry's embarrassment.[253] This was actually a greater problem when the government had a

---

[252] Salisbury to Emrys-Evans, 31 March and 1 May 1940, Watching Ctte minute book, 4 April 1940–14 March 1944, Emrys-Evans MSS, Add.58245/1–2, 17, Add.58270; Salisbury to Stuart, 31 May 1941, CPA, Whips' Office MSS, 1/4.
[253] G. S. Harvie-Watt, *Most of My Life* (1980), 33; Moss, *Windjammer to Westminster*, 184.

large majority, as this led its supporters to be more casual in their attendance, especially in the later evening. To overcome this, in the 1924–29 parliament the Chief Whip divided the backbenchers into ten groups and issued a rotating schedule, under which seven of the groups were designated to attend each day.[254]

The whips' second role was to provide information and advice to MPs, not least in the most basic way by directing them into the correct lobby when they came pouring in at the sound of the division bell. The whips' relationship with the backbenchers was one of persuasion much more than of coercion, and they had little leverage against those MPs who were not seeking or expecting office, which was still the majority. Any MP who was sure of the backing of his or her constituency association had little to fear from the whips, as they had no power to require an association to deselect a candidate, even if the whip was withdrawn. It was no action of the whips but a blunt warning from his constituency chairman that he would not be nominated again which stopped Boothby from voting against the Munich Agreement in October 1938.[255] Cartland's bitter criticism in the adjournment debate of 2 August 1939, which outraged loyalist MPs, was responded to not by the withdrawal of the whip, but by Neville Chamberlain's vengeful resolve to stir up opposition against him in his constituency—which, as this was a Birmingham division, he was well-placed to do.[256] When Herbert Williams' sniping at the government in 1941 similarly became more than a nuisance, Churchill was advised not to withdraw the whip—as this might actually strengthen Williams' position and give him publicity—but to see if 'some steps could be taken by the Party organisation to bring influence to bear in his constituency to try and bring him to heel'.[257] The whips did not seek confrontation, and would rather persuade or cajole, using a combination of appeals to loyalty and party spirit on the one hand, and concessions, if necessary, on the other. These conversations could take forms that ranged from sympathetic understanding to bracing and even brutal frankness; on the day after the recently elected John Profumo had voted against the government in the Norway debate of May 1940, the Chief Whip scornfully told him: 'you utterly contemptible little shit...for the rest of your life you will be ashamed of what you did last night'.[258] The latter's successor as Chief Whip noted that being rude to backbenchers 'is harmless enough and spills no blood', and that 'Members, in return, can be rude to whips, which is fair enough.'[259] Being only human, there were times when a whip lost his temper, but these were exceptions to the general rule of patience and good fellowship. With most MPs—including critics whose stance was principled and understood—such spats were usually swiftly reconciled with a mutual

---

[254] Chief Whip's notice, 8 July 1927 and 12 June 1928, Bull MSS, CAC, BULL/5/19, 5/20.
[255] Boothby to Churchill, 10 October 1938, *WSC*.
[256] N. to I. Chamberlain, 5 August 1939, *NCDL*.
[257] Harvie-Watt report to Churchill, 14 November 1941, Harvie-Watt MSS, CAC, HARV/1/1.
[258] Recollections of Profumo in T. Renton, 'The total whip: David Margesson 1931–1940', in T. Renton, *Chief Whip: People, Power and Patronage in Westminster* (2004), 251–77, at 267.
[259] Lord Stuart of Findhorn, *Within the Fringe* (1967), 80.

apology, but there were a few *bêtes noires*, of whom one whip admitted: 'I prefer not to talk to them unless I have to.'[260]

Their third role was to be the eyes and ears of the leadership; as one MP noted during a crisis, 'the whips are buzzing about all over the place to find out our opinions'.[261] On an important issue, such as how to deal with Macquisten's bill on the trade union political levy in March 1925, there would be a systematic canvass of the backbenchers.[262] More usually, it would be a case of keeping a finger on the pulse and noting the issues which MPs raised themselves. At the least, the whips were a kind of political therapist; Robert Sanders was advised on his appointment as a whip in 1911: 'Always let a man talk. Even if nothing comes of it, it relieves his feelings.'[263] When concerns were widespread, the whips were a vital channel of communication to the leaders and, provided that they were effective at taking the temperature of the parliamentary ranks, they could warn of difficulties before they became unmanageable.[264] Three examples of this from the mid-1920s were the transmission of backbench concern about the proposed cuts in the naval programme in 1925, the report that the balance of parliamentary opinion was against immediate legislation to restrict the trade unions during General Strike of 1926, and the Chief Whip's warning to Baldwin in 1927 that over-legislation was stretching MPs' tolerance.[265] The whips could sometimes fail to detect a sudden squall, especially when the government had a secure majority, but these upsets were almost always on very minor matters and were more of an irritant and embarrassment than a real problem. This was particularly the case with the equal pay vote in March 1944, which was magnified out of all proportion by Churchill's furious overreaction.

There was an abiding impression that the whips were particularly drawn from the traditional elite of the landed aristocracy and country gentry, and this finds some substantiation in the five Chief Whips of the period. The first and last had aristocratic origins, Lord Edmund Talbot being a son of the 14th Duke of Norfolk and James Stuart of the 17th Earl of Moray. Of the other three, Bolton Eyres-Monsell came from the cadet branch of an Anglo-Irish gentry family, although his father's career was an urban one as Chief Constable of the Metropolitan Police from 1886 to 1910; David Margesson was the son of Sir Mortimer Margesson, who was private secretary to the Earl of Plymouth, whilst Leslie Wilson was from a middle-class background and had had a military career before entering the House. However, such a pattern is less clearly evident if the whips as a whole are examined for their

---

[260] Stuart to Emrys-Evans, 13 February 1940, Emrys-Evans MSS, Add.58248/75–6; Beamish diary notes, 29 March 1944, Beamish MSS, CAC, BEAM/3/5.
[261] Comment of Peto in Lady Peto diary, 22 September 1931; Wilson to A. Chamberlain, 9 November 1921, AC, 31/3/41.
[262] 'Trade Union Political Levy Bill', memo showing result of whips' canvass of MPs, and notes by Barnston, Hennessey, and Stanley, c.20 February 1925, CPA, CRD/2/7/18.
[263] Bayford diary, 23 March 1911.
[264] Bayford diary, 26 October 1919.
[265] Bridgeman diary, 22 July 1925, 1–12 May 1926; Eyres-Monsell to Baldwin, 10 November 1927, Baldwin MSS, 162/120–1.

educational background, which can be taken as an indicator of their family's social position. Despite the impression of being collectively 'a flutter of old school ties',[266] only thirty-five (68.6 per cent) of the fifty-one individuals who served as a whip at some point between January 1919 and May 1945 had attended an English public school. This was higher than the proportion in the parliamentary party as a whole (see Table 5.3), as was the number who had been at Eton (sixteen; 31.4 per cent), but in both cases not dramatically so; the number at Harrow (five; 9.8 per cent) was only slightly above the average. Of the remaining sixteen, one had been educated privately, five at Scottish academies, five at grammar schools, one at a local board school, three at sea in the Royal Navy or merchant navy, and there was one for whom no information could be found. The whips' pattern of further education was very much in line with the whole body of Conservative MPs, indeed slightly below it (see Table 5.4). Twenty-five (51 per cent) had attended university, of whom twelve (23.5 per cent) had been at Oxford and nine (17.6 per cent) at Cambridge. A noticeable feature amongst the remainder was an above-average incidence of military education: six whips were educated at Sandhurst and three at the Royal Military Academy in Woolwich, a total of 17.6 per cent. Even so, this was only a small proportion of the corps of whips as a whole, and any stereotype based upon it would be misleading; in fact, only three had followed the 'classic' progression of the governing elite, of education at Eton followed by Christ Church, Oxford.

The reality was that MPs were recruited to the Whips' Office not primarily due to their background, but because they possessed the personal characteristics that were desirable in the role—and the social profile of the whips was due to the greater prevalence of these amongst the more traditional elite. Even the well-known example of the appointment of Sanders as a junior whip because he had previously been Master of the Devon and Somerset Staghounds illustrates this, for to succeed in such a role involved hard work, responsibility, and remaining on good terms with a great many people. One Chief Whip observed that 'whips are picked because they have friends rather than enemies in their own party', and 'the ability to handle men and to get on with them'.[267] The ideal whip was steady, loyal, discreet, willing to work with little public recognition, clubbable and at ease with his fellow MPs, and authoritative without being overbearing; as Talbot admitted, these criteria effectively limited the selection to 'gentlemen' in the class sense.[268] Talbot himself 'added to his office the authority and manner which are still to be found in members of an ancient house'.[269] One other, perhaps obvious, factor inclined the recruitment of whips to the landowning class: the job required a lot of time to be spent at the House and was generally incompatible with a full-time career, and so sufficient private means were necessary. A safe seat was also almost essential, as the whips were

---

[266] Macnamara, *The Whistle Blows*, 145.
[267] Stuart, *Within the Fringe*, 80.
[268] Bayford diary, 17 April 1921.
[269] Memo by Pollock, 'The Fall of the Coalition in October 1922', n.d. but c.September 1931, Hanworth MSS, Eng.Hist.d.432/133–88.

less able to attend constituency events during the parliamentary session, but, unlike a minister, their work was not something that could be easily trumpeted or explained in public.

The whips were normally middle-aged, middle-ranking, and with solid parliamentary experience. The youngest whip appointed was Victor Warrender, at the age of twenty-eight; the oldest was William Boulton, who became an MP in 1931 at the age of fifty-eight and was sixty-six when he was appointed a whip in February 1940, in which capacity he served until the 1945 general election. This may have been partly a reflection of the absence of younger MPs on war service, and it certainly was a feature of both the First and Second World Wars that in their middle stages the Chief Whip summoned home experienced members of his team to help with the wartime workload.[270] Although just over half of the whips also served in ministerial posts, with a few reaching the Cabinet, becoming a whip was not regarded as a route to office or a career path for the ambitious: in 1924, Derby's son and heir, Lord Stanley, was acutely disappointed to be offered a position as a whip, and not as a junior minister.[271] It was rather a position for unobtrusive competence, and this was reflected in the characters and careers of those whips—generally the slightly younger—who moved on to periods of junior office; as the retiring Chief Whip commented in 1913, 'a whip must not desire to "get on"'.[272] Only six whips reached the Cabinet in the period 1919–45 (in chronological order: Robert Sanders, John Gilmour, Bolton Eyres-Monsell, Lord Stanley, Euan Wallace, and David Margesson), and three more did so after 1945 (James Stuart, Patrick Buchan-Hepburn, and Thomas Dugdale); significantly, four of these were former Chief Whips. One other whip reached what would normally be a Cabinet post: the unlucky J. J. Llewellin was President of the Board of Trade for just eighteen days in February 1942, before returning to junior offices.

A whip would have a good understanding of procedure, but did not need to be an expert—what mattered more was an understanding of the traditions of the House and a feel for its moods. It was not necessary to have been a particularly effective or frequent speaker, as during their service the whips did not take part in debates. Some were quite glad of this, but others found it 'often an irritating position' as 'I am always liable to be regarded as a "Yes-man" with no views or convictions of my own'.[273] Lack of personal ambition was an asset; it was almost unknown for a whip to have been, or later become, anything other than steadfastly loyal.[274] Talbot considered George Gibbs to be 'a most excellent whip' because he was 'always on the spot, reliable, willing and keen', and crucially 'I always know I can

---

[270] Bayford diary, 27 May 1917.
[271] Derby to Baldwin, 8 November, Lord Stanley to Derby, 12 November 1924, Derby MSS, 33, 42/8.
[272] Crawford to Bonar Law, 2 February 1913, Crawford diary.
[273] Stuart to Emrys-Evans, 13 February 1940, Emrys-Evans MSS, Add.58248/75–6.
[274] A rare exception was Patrick Ford, who had been briefly a whip for seven months in 1923; he was amongst the rebels against the India policy in 1933–35, but was by no means either extreme or prominent in that group.

Table 5.11. The Conservative whips in the House of Commons 1919–1945[275]

This table analyses all of the MPs who served as a whip (including assistant whips) between January 1919 and May 1945; the brief 'Caretaker' ministry of May to July 1945 is not included. The category of junior minister includes any Law Officers. Cabinet status is defined as all members of the Cabinet in the period 1919–40, as well as ministers in the Churchill Coalition of 1940–45 in offices which, in peacetime, were always of Cabinet rank. Titles already held before appointment include courtesy titles (see the definition in Table 5.9); titles acquired during or after appointment include titles inherited as well as those created. Each person is counted only once in each category, but if an individual had honours in more than one category, they will be counted once in each category (e.g. where a person with a knighthood or baronetcy became a peer, or a person with a courtesy title inherited a peerage).

Age profile	21–9	30–9	40–9	50–9	60 +
Whip only:					
age first elected an MP	5	7	11	2	–
age first appointed a whip	–	5	8	11	1
Whip and junior minister:					
age first elected an MP	4	8	4	–	–
age first appointed a whip	1	7	7	1	–
Whip and Cabinet rank:					
age first elected an MP	4	5	1	–	–
age first appointed a whip	–	8	2	–	–

Length of service (years and months)	less than 2 years	2.0 to 3.11	4.0 to 5.11	6.0 to 7.11	8.0 to 9.11	10 years & above
Whip only	5	3	8	3	2	4
Whip and junior minister	2	6	2	3	1	2
Whip and Cabinet rank	1	2	3	1	–	3

Honours	Title before first appointment	Becomes knight or baronet	Becomes peer
Whip only	4	13	9
Whip and junior minister	1	7	5
Whip and Cabinet rank	1	2	7

trust him.'[276] The whips felt a broad sense of duty to the party as a whole, rather than of fealty to an individual Leader. It was this which led Gibbs and Gilmour, who had supported the Coalition in October 1922, to overcome their initial reluctance and agree to continue in office in Bonar Law's undermanned ministry.[277] Indeed, Gilmour had already consented to carry on the duties of the Scottish Whip

---

[275] Calculated from the entries in Stenton and Lees, *Who's Who of British Members of Parliament*, vols 3 and 4; J. C. Sainty (ed.), 'Assistant Whips 1922–1964', *Parliamentary History*, 4 (1985), 201–4.
[276] Talbot to Long, 4 April 1920, Long MSS, Add.62425/13–14.
[277] Gibbs to A. Chamberlain, 30 October 1922, Long MSS, Add.62405/107; Gibbs also accepted partly due to pressures in his constituency, Gibbs to Pollock, 3 November 1922, Hanworth MSS, Eng. Hist.d.432/192–9.

as manager of the party organization in Scotland, 'in order to have as little disturbance as possible and obtain the greatest measure of unity'.[278]

The development of the party's subject committees in 1924 added further duties, as each whip was assigned to attend one or more of these.[279] The purpose was to monitor opinion and have early warning of dissatisfaction; in a similar way, a whip attended the weekly meeting of the general backbench 1922 Committee, where they also provided the useful informative function of giving MPs a briefing on the parliamentary business of the week ahead. Two of the regional whips had additional special roles of overseeing party organization outside parliament, in a remnant of the old model of party management. The Scottish Whip also acted as Party Chairman in Scotland, with his own headquarters in Edinburgh, which involved considerable extra work and responsibility. The London Whip acted in a similar but less elaborate role for the metropolis, where he was particularly involved in organizing elections to the London County Council. His work was closely integrated with Central Office, as his office was housed under the same roof.

The whips had an *esprit de corps* of their own, being 'a happy family' whose collegial working relationship was founded upon mutual confidence and team spirit.[280] They had a camaraderie of their own, and could relax in the Whips' Room, where the dominant tone of humour was rather blue and school-boyish.[281] The duties of the whips involved being constantly present around the Palace of Westminster, and they normally dined at the House. They would organize speakers so that debate was sustained through thin periods such as the dinner hour, and ensure that the House was not 'counted out' for lack of Members present when a government bill was being put through. Their role required knowing their flock, and this was both formalized and made more manageable by the introduction of a regional system in which each whip was responsible for the MPs from a particular area (which usually included his own seat). The whips were certainly not infallible, either in managing business (though there were no very significant upsets) or in familiarity with their charges: one despatched R. A. Butler, a year after he had entered the House, to speak at the Norfolk North by-election in the belief that he was the agricultural fertilizer manufacturer Clavering Fison.[282] As with any group of people, some were more capable and effective than others. Nevertheless, taken as a whole, the Conservative whips of the interwar period were both efficient and successful.

The Chief Whip was answerable to, and spent much time in contact with, the Party Leader; 'there is no relationship between men so close as that of a Prime Minister and his Chief Whip', Baldwin told Margesson in 1935.[283] The extent to which the Leader depended upon the Chief Whip meant that confidence, discretion, and loyalty were essential. Wilson's opposition to his Leader in October 1922

---

[278] Gilmour to Bonar Law, 25 October 1922, Bonar Law MSS, BL/108/1/16.
[279] List of Whips, n.d. but c.1925, Baldwin MSS, 48/28.
[280] Bayford diary, 24 March 1921; Crawford diary, 20 October 1922; Penny to Dugdale, c.June 1937, in Renton, *Chief Whip*, 261–2.
[281] Southby diary, 24 July 1941.
[282] Headlam diary, 2 April 1936; Butler to his parents, 14 July 1930, Butler MSS, D48/748–51.
[283] Baldwin to Margesson, 30 October 1935, Margesson MSS, CAC, MRGN/1/3/11.

would seem to be a flagrant breach of this code, but complete subordination could only have been expected if the occupant of the post was viewed as having no autonomy and being no more than the Leader's personal servant. Naturally enough, the Chief Whips themselves did not see it in such a menial light: they were appointed by the Leader and served at his pleasure, but in the same way as ministers in a Cabinet and with a similar right to form and present their own views. The duty they owed was of loyalty but not of subservience, and their office carried with it responsibilities to the party as well as to the Leader. These included the obligation to tell the latter the truth—however painful—and, ultimately, as Wilson found, to oppose him if the greater interests of the party were at stake. In fact, the breakdown of 1922 was an extraordinary exception to the normal state of harmony. Although Chief Whips sometimes felt ignored or insufficiently consulted, others often ascribed great influence to them; Margesson was later categorized by Hoare as Neville Chamberlain's 'evil genius'.[284] In government, the Chief Whip attended the Cabinet in his role as advisor on the legislative timetable, and he was also consulted over appointments to ministerial office—indeed, he was the main influence on who was chosen for the junior posts, as he was much more familiar with the backbenchers.[285] Thus, despite repeated pressure from Austen Chamberlain, Eyres-Monsell blocked the promotion of Oliver Locker-Lampson because it would be 'tantamount to confirming that rebellion (a mild term) is the best card in a politician's pack' and would undermine his efforts to encourage loyalty in the younger MPs.[286] In general elections, the Chief Whip worked with the Party Chairman in arranging the schedule of meetings for the leading figures.

Lord Edmund Talbot had fought his first parliamentary election in 1880, and was fifty-seven years old when he succeeded the capable Lord Balcarres as Chief Whip in 1913. He was generally very successful in containing the strains of the wartime years, first in the frustrating periods of 'patriotic opposition' in 1914–15 and the unproductive Asquith Coalition of 1915–16, and thereafter in stabilizing the Lloyd George Coalition's parliamentary foundations; throughout, he worked in a close and trusting partnership with Bonar Law.[287] One of Talbot's junior whips commented on his 'good sense and temper', and his standing with MPs was demonstrated by the rousing cheers that he was given at the close of the meeting which elected Austen Chamberlain as Leader in March 1921.[288] Shortly after, Talbot accepted the challenging role of Lord-Lieutenant of Ireland—in which, as a Roman Catholic, it was hoped that he could build bridges to moderate southern opinion—and was raised to the peerage as Viscount Fitzalan of Derwent. It seems that Lloyd George blocked the promotion of his deputy,

---

[284] Hoare's notes on April-May 1939, n.d. but c.1953, Templewood MSS, XII/3.
[285] Eyres-Monsell to Baldwin, 27 December 1927, Baldwin MSS, 162/122–3. Hacking noted that the Chief Whip was consulted on promotions, but the Party Chairman was not: Hacking to Derby, 5 June 1936, Derby MSS, 31/6.
[286] Eyres-Monsell to Baldwin, 6 November 1925, Baldwin MSS, 160/55.
[287] Long to Talbot, 22 March 1921, Long MSS, Add.62426/48–9.
[288] Bridgeman to Long, 21 March 1921, Long MSS, Add.62426/43–4.

Robert Sanders, and Talbot's successor was brought in from outside the Whips' Office. Leslie Wilson was a competent junior minister with no previous experience of whipping and did not particularly want the job, but the Prime Minister insisted upon him taking it on.[289] Wilson provided the desired combination of acquiescent effectiveness for the next twelve months, but, like many MPs, his concerns about the implications and consequences of his Leader's strategy grew steadily from the election scare of January 1922 onwards. By late September, Wilson found himself in an increasingly impossible position: Chamberlain was heedless of the warnings the Chief Whip was expressing ever more clearly, and then embarked suddenly on a course that seemed to be at variance with his previous intentions.[290] Wilson was in a position to know as a certainty that this would tear the party apart; in the resulting conflict of loyalties, he concluded that his duty to the institution was paramount over his obligations to his Leader.[291] Although Wilson had made his opinions clear in private,[292] Chamberlain felt shocked and bitterly betrayed when the Chief Whip spoke out against him at the Carlton Club meeting.[293] This was a lasting focus of grievance; when Wilson was considered as a possible Party Chairman in 1930, the difficulty was that 'the old Coalitioners hate him'.[294] A few weeks after Baldwin became Party Leader, Wilson accepted the position of Governor of Bombay; he served here until 1928, and then from 1932 to 1946 as Governor of Queensland in Australia (his wife was from New South Wales).

His replacement, Eyres-Monsell, a friend of Baldwin's who sat for an adjacent seat, was not only as capable in the arts of whipping as Talbot and his own successor, Margesson; he was also—unlike them—an important innovator. The subject committees founded in opposition in 1924, which have continued to this day as forums for backbenchers, were his idea, and he also took the fledgling 1922 Committee under his wing—without which it would have been as ephemeral as so many other unofficial cliques—and shaped it into a constructive and permanent body. He also formalized the arrangement by which each whip was responsible for MPs from a particular region, and developed the efficient rotational system to manage the large majority of 1924–29. When that government was in its mid-term doldrums, the lack of visible restiveness in the House of Commons was attributed by one old hand 'partly to the tact, urbanity and great popularity of Bobbie Monsell'.[295] He only rarely lost his temper, as in the incident of withdrawing the whip from Basil Peto, and was usually 'as mercurial and as charming as ever'; Winterton noted the Chief Whip was 'in the

---

[289] Bayford diary, 24 March 1921.
[290] Wilson to Sanders, 24 September 1922, Bayford diary.
[291] Wilson to A. Chamberlain, 22 September, 11 October, and 21 November 1922, AC, 33/2/24, 43, 94.
[292] Younger to Sanders, 25 September, Wilson to Sanders, 12 October 1922, Bayford diary.
[293] A. Chamberlain to Wilson, 22 November 1922, AC, 33/2/95; Amery diary, 19 October 1922.
[294] Bridgeman to Irwin, 15 June 1930, Halifax MSS, C152/19/1/79; A. to H. Chamberlain, 1 June 1930, *ACDL*.
[295] Winterton to Irwin, 6 June 1927, Halifax MSS, C152/17/1/226.

curious position of being very much liked and very much feared' by both the Labour and Liberal oppositions.[296] Eyres-Monsell was a loyal supporter of Baldwin during the internal dissensions of 1929–31, although the rumour heard by the wife of a diehard rebel at the height of the crisis in 1930, that the Chief Whip was 'getting a little weary of his leader', had disturbing overtones of 1922.[297] After eight years of exemplary service, Eyres-Monsell was rewarded with a Cabinet position after the general election of 1931, and there was a smooth transition to his deputy.

David Margesson, Chief Whip for the rest of the decade, is perhaps the most famous and probably the most controversial holder of that office. He has been variously depicted as a faceless power behind the scenes, a ruthless martinet, and the authoritarian imposer of an iron control that sustained in office the misguided appeasers and rendered impotent their small but heroic band of critics. However, most of these denunciations were subsequent to the change of public mood after 1940, and in one influential case came from an uninformed perspective outside of, and inimical to, the Conservative Party—the three left-wing journalists who wrote the denunciatory best-seller *Guilty Men*. Contemporary opinions were much more varied, and many of those who encountered or worked with Margesson described a handsome figure, 'probably the best dressed in the House', who was sociable, witty, and lively.[298] However, whilst far from being an autocrat, it was his task to maintain discipline, and to that end he could be rude and confrontational.[299] Like most whips, he was affronted by persistent dissent, and under provocation or stress could show his anger publicly.[300] To some extent, he naturally utilized and embellished his reputation for authority, for it was an effective tool considering that the whips had relatively few real sanctions at their disposal. In fact, Margesson did not use the weapon of withdrawing the whip from an MP once during his long term as Chief Whip, and Macmillan records that when he voted with the opposition on a censure motion on 23 June 1936, 'it was intimated to me that there would be no attempt to deprive me of the whip'.[301] Margesson was hard-working, and the breakdown of his marriage in 1930 enabled him to spend long hours at Westminster, especially when coping with the 'unwieldy majority' of 1931.[302] His role and conduct were important factors in making the 1931–35 National Government more stable and effective than the previous coalition of 1918–22 had been. He was loyal to the hypersensitive Ramsay MacDonald, and although he pressed for MacDonald's retirement during the latter's final year as Prime Minister, he was not alone in voicing concern that the Premier's waning health and capacity were endangering the government. Margesson worked in close liaison with Baldwin,

---

[296] Winterton to Irwin, 12 July 1928, Halifax MSS, C152/18/1/89a; Bayford diary, 14 July 1926.
[297] Lady Peto diary, 31 October 1930.
[298] Moss, *Windjammer to Westminster*, 183; Channon diary, 7 September 1937; Harvie-Watt, *Most of My Life*, 31; Renton, *Chief Whip*, 252, 258, 275–7.
[299] P. Donner, *Crusade* (1984), 80.
[300] Headlam diary, 20 December 1934; Nicolson diary, 20 September 1939.
[301] Macmillan, *Winds of Change*, 458; Stuart, *Within the Fringe*, 80.
[302] Margesson to Baldwin, 25 October 1935, Baldwin MSS, 47/136–8.

who was acting as Leader of the House in this period; the Conservative Leader was appreciative of the quality of support that he received, writing in 1935 that 'it has been a joy to work with you; you have never failed me'.[303] Margesson was aware that dissatisfaction with Chamberlain was growing in the spring of 1940,[304] but could do little to prevent the eventual crisis, which was a consequence of setbacks in the war and of his Leader's personal decisions, statements, and style.

Margesson was not a paragon, and had his share of setbacks and deficiencies. Some MPs felt that he favoured the established elite too much in his recommendations for junior office, although that was hardly unique or unusual.[305] There was certainly a feeling that the Chamberlain ministry contained an undue proportion of sycophants and lightweights, but that is often the perspective of those not chosen or on the margins, and Margesson was only following the pragmatic practice of other incumbents of his office in rewarding loyalty and repressing dissidence. One of his later junior whips described Margesson as 'a real dictator', but his methods were not just coercive: significantly, Macmillan, perhaps the most constant dissident of the 1930s, considered that the Chief Whip had used charm just as effectively, and 'always treated me with generous consideration'.[306] Although Margesson certainly corralled the anti-appeasers, the real reasons for their circumspection were the unwelcoming response of other backbench MPs, the mood of public opinion, and—most of all—the disapproval of their constituency associations. In fact, the Chief Whip's relations with the 'glamour boy' rebels were generally good: one of them, J. P. L. Thomas, 'always had the closest contact' with Margesson, who 'had always been particularly sympathetic and helpful so far as I myself was concerned'.[307] This was not just professional courtesy or expediency; at the nadir of the dissidents, in the wake of the Munich settlement, Boothby had 'a long and very friendly talk with the Chief Whip', and 'told him of my doubts and fears', of which 'I suspected him of being in sympathy with a good many'.[308] After becoming Party Leader in 1940, Churchill rebuffed the suggestion from an anti-appeasement backbencher that Margesson should be removed, giving as his reasons the fact that the Chief Whip had been guilty only of doing his job well and of loyalty to his Leader, that Churchill's personal relations with him had always been pleasant despite their differences, and that Margesson's executive and organizational abilities were an asset not to be discarded.[309] Indeed, it was the latter which led Churchill to move Margesson to the important post of Secretary for War in December 1940; he was later sacked after the fall of Singapore in February 1942, although in political circles it was recognized that this was a necessary sacrifice to public opinion rather than a judgement of the disaster being his fault.[310]

---

[303] Baldwin to Margesson, 30 October 1935, Margesson MSS, CAC, MRGN/1/3/11.
[304] Channon diary, 26 April, 3 May 1940.
[305] Headlam diary, 10 February 1941.
[306] Harvie-Watt, *Most of My Life*, 133; Macmillan, *Winds of Change*, 458, 447.
[307] Thomas, 'Account of events leading up to the resignation of A. E[den]', n.d., Cilcennin MSS, 50ff.11–12; Herbert to Margesson, 18 October 1935, in Renton, *Chief Whip*, 258.
[308] Boothby to Duff, 2 December 1938, Cilcennin MSS, 42.
[309] Churchill to Adams, 16 November 1940, Adams MSS, box 2.
[310] Renton, *Chief Whip*, 273–5.

Margesson was, in turn, succeeded by his deputy, James Stuart, who was surprised to be offered the post, as he had anticipated that Churchill would want to install one of his own retinue, both to secure his position and as the preliminary to a purge of Chamberlainite loyalists. In fact, Churchill was too prudent to try this, knowing that any such crude settling of scores would reap a whirlwind of fear and resentment, and still more was too busy with greater matters to waste effort on needless strife or to take the risk of appointing an inexperienced and unpopular person. Whilst they were never remotely as close as Talbot had been with Bonar Law, Eyres-Monsell with Baldwin, or even Margesson with Chamberlain, still Stuart managed to sustain an effective working relationship with Churchill, albeit with some abrasive moments.[311] He also faced the same problems as Talbot, Wilson, and Margesson, of being Chief Whip to a coalition, and especially of the former in doing so under the constraints and pressures of wartime. Whilst the Churchill Coalition worked well together at the ministerial level, it was a more difficult task in the House, where its parliamentary support was 'composed of elements as impossible to mix as "oil and water"'.[312] Serious challenges to Churchill's position never materialized, even with the military reverses of 1942, and the main problem was one of sniping and carping from a combination of the Labour left, such as Aneurin Bevan, discarded ministers, such as Leslie Hore-Belisha, and right-of-centre Conservatives suspicious of enlarging government controls and protective of the rights of the House, such as the pedantic Herbert Williams and the pompous Earl Winterton. However, Stuart's one upset originated from another discordant point on the political spectrum, the Tory Reformers: his reaction to the defeat on the equal pay amendment in March 1944 was just as uncompromising as Churchill's, and he wielded a sledgehammer to crush this particular nut with even less hesitation and compunction than Margesson would have done.[313]

PARLIAMENTARY ORGANIZATION

The development of specifically party organizations in parliament was a feature of the interwar era, with the establishment of structures that have continued since, in some cases becoming of more importance after 1945. There had been some previous unofficial bodies, mostly to meet a particular situation: the Unionist Social Reform Committee of 1911–14 sought to find a response to Liberal social policy, and the Unionist Business Committee and Unionist War Committee had aimed to express backbench concern for more vigorous prosecution of the war, especially, during the period of the Asquith Coalition, on the issue of conscription. The Unionist Business Committee (under the name Unionist Reconstruction Committee) continued in existence in the 1918–22 parliament as a protectionist pressure group, and eventually formed a basis for the Empire Industries Associ-

---

[311] Stuart, *Within the Fringe*, 91–3, 126, 138.
[312] Stuart to Glyn, 3 April 1944, Glyn MSS, D/EGL/C37/12.
[313] Stuart to Glyn, 3 April 1944, Glyn MSS, D/EGL/C37/12.

ation in the later 1920s.[314] The one longer-term group before 1914 was the Agricultural Committee, which was not restricted to Conservatives, and this also continued after 1918.[315] The two important innovations of the interwar period were founded almost simultaneously and became interlinked, but one of them was unofficial in origin, and the other the deliberate creation of the party leadership.

The latter was the establishment of a committee structure for Conservative MPs, organized on a subject basis. At the outset there were fifteen groups, each surveying the field of a particular government department or group of departments.[316] This organization was set up shortly after the party went into opposition in January 1924 for the purpose of preparing a new manifesto, and at first the committees were chaired by the appropriate former Cabinet minister, if he was an MP. The aim of the exercise was partly to produce a soundly based and well-supported programme, partly to make MPs better informed and equipped, and partly to keep them occupied under the supervision of a recognized chain of command and so avoid a vacuum in which factions and revolts might develop. The committees were the idea of Eyres-Monsell, and their productive work and useful function encouraged the crucial step. This was the decision to make them permanent, and so, after the party returned to office in November 1924, they were continued under elected backbench officers. The committees had been supported in opposition by the Policy Secretariat under Lancelot Storr, and when this was wound up they continued to have some liaison with Central Office. After the founding of the Conservative Research Department (CRD) in 1929 this was formalized and its staff provided clerical assistance; the records for some committees for periods in the 1930s are included in the CRD files.[317] When the party went into opposition in 1929, former cabinet ministers who were in the Commons resumed chairing the committees (although by election, rather than by direct appointment of the Leader, which had been the case in 1924).[318] However, they had a much lower profile, as no similar policy-making exercise was being undertaken. By early 1931, several of the committees were being chaired by senior backbenchers (including the important India Committee), and they all reverted to this form after the creation of the National Government. The subject committee system continued to work effectively during the rest of the period; by 1940 there were fourteen, as Education and the Home Office had merged.[319]

---

[314] Report of Unionist Reconstruction Ctte, Sub-ctte on dumping and key industries, 19 February 1920, Terrell to Bonar Law, 16 March 1920, Bonar Law MSS, BL/98/7/15, BL/98/8/9.

[315] D. H. Close, 'The growth of backbench organisations in the Conservative Party', *Parliamentary Affairs*, 27 (1974), 371–83.

[316] Diagram of committee structure in Wicks to Cecil, 5 April 1924, Cecil of Chelwood MSS, Add.51085/125; Minutes of Finance Ctte., 11 March, Army Ctte., 12 March, 26 March, 14 May, and of Commons Standing Conference (the overall co-ordinating body), 11 March–24 July 1924, Worthington-Evans MSS, MSS.Eng.hist.c.894/104–18, c.895/9–46.

[317] See also Agricultural Ctte, 'Report for the Session 1929–30', Heneage MSS, HNC/2/3; minutes of Foreign Affairs Ctte., December 1934–July 1935, Emrys-Evans MSS, Add.58246/95–119.

[318] Cunliffe-Lister to Steel-Maitland, 17 July 1929, Steel-Maitland MSS, GD193/120/3/193.

[319] 'Committees', February 1940, CPA, CCO/4/2/18.

The subject committees in their permanent form fulfilled a number of valuable roles. Unlike previous unofficial groups, there was no suggestion of conspiracy about them and no imputation of disloyalty when MPs expressed frank views at their meetings. Discussion was confidential as far as the public and press were concerned (though it sometimes leaked out, albeit mainly in general terms), but with a whip present it was in the open eyes of the leadership—indeed, much of the point was for it to be a channel of rapid and effective communication to those in authority.[320] The committees were both a safety valve and an informational forum, and the latter role was reinforced by the habit of having the responsible Cabinet or junior minister attend meetings from time to time, especially to explain forthcoming legislation.[321] A key feature of the subject committees was that attendance was open to all Conservative backbenchers. There was generally a small core who had particular interests in an area, but when it became a matter of greater concern the attendance level would inflate in response, and the subject committee could become almost an informal party meeting overnight. This made them a key arena on important and divisive issues, as happened particularly with the India Committee in January–March 1931, the Foreign Affairs Committee in 1935–39, and the Fuel and Power Committee over the coal industry in the Second World War. However, after 1924 they were not policy-making bodies, and resolutions were rarely passed for public release—indeed, the latter was a doubtful practice, as they had no authority to bypass the Leader.[322] It was more effective to transmit expressions of concern directly to the Leader; when more emphasis or speed was needed than was possible by leaving it to the whip to report back, the most effective tactic was to appoint a deputation to seek an interview.

The election of the committee officers was also open to all who chose to attend the first meeting of the parliamentary session, and, as with much else in the Conservative Party, it was usual for it to be unopposed, with rights of precedence and accumulated weight and experience being recognized. In only a few cases, where the committee was already something of a battleground, did it become contested or the whips seek to influence the choice. The retention of the loyalist Wardlaw-Milne as Chair of the India Committee in 1930–31 was valuable to the leadership, but it is not apparent that they took specific action to ensure this, although loyalist MPs would surely have been aware of the fact. In the late 1930s, however, the whips seem to have organized the ejection of anti-appeasers such as Emrys-Evans from the officerships of the Foreign Affairs Committee, and Channon was involved in packing a meeting 'with sound Chamberlain chaps' to elect Wardlaw-Milne as its Chairman in May 1939, confident that he would 'tolerate no nonsense' from the critics.[323] A subject committee Chairman did not have the status of an official

---

[320] Cunliffe-Lister to Baldwin, reporting discussion of Trade Ctte., 19 February 1925, Baldwin MSS, 11/989–9; Emrys-Evans to Margesson, 29 March 1935, Margesson to Emrys-Evans, 2 April 1935, 'Chapter V', draft memoirs, c. 1966, Emrys-Evans MSS, Add.58248/6–7, 58260/197–201.

[321] Memo by Cunliffe-Lister on discussion by the Trade Committee of the Maquisten's bill on the trade union political levy, 19 February 1925, CPA, CRD/2/7/18.

[322] Lane-Fox to Irwin, 4 March 1931, Halifax MSS, C152/19/1/246; Amery diary, 16 March 1931.

[323] Channon diary, 4 May 1939.

party spokesman, but those holding this visible position were expected to be careful and not launch initiatives that could embarrass other MPs, as George Courthope did whilst Chairman of the Agriculture Committee in 1927, in calling for the extension of safeguarding to agriculture—which would involve duties on food imports. The fact that in his position 'he could not play the free lance' was 'quite plainly explained to him in the Committee' and he offered to resign, 'which of course nobody wished to insist upon'.[324]

The unofficial group meanwhile, though founded first, took some time to develop. The general election of 1922 returned an unusually large number of new Conservative MPs, with 111 of the 345 Members not having sat before. During the first weeks of the parliamentary session, a number of the new MPs felt 'lost in the maze of Parliamentary procedure' and became concerned at their 'ineffectiveness and bewilderment'.[325] They held two meetings, on 18 and 23 April 1923, and at the second decided to form a group called 'the Conservative Private Members (1922) Committee', with the aim of 'mutual co-operation and assistance... in order to enable new Members to take a more active interest and part in parliamentary life'.[326] Several figures were involved in this, but the lead seems to have come from Gervais Rentoul and he was elected as Chairman. The date in the Committee's title thus refers to the election at which its founders entered the House, and not—as has since been often, but mistakenly, assumed—the overthrow of Lloyd George or the Carlton Club meeting, at which none of these MPs had been present.

There had been various groups of new Members before, but all had been ephemeral; what was different in this case was that this one survived, expanded, and became a permanent and increasingly official part of the party structure.[327] The whips generally regarded all such groups with reserve, suspicious that they might become factious, but at the outset the 1922 Committee sought the guidance of the Chief Whip, Leslie Wilson. The group's affirmation of loyalty to the Leader and whips at its founding meeting, its open activity, and its limited educational aims secured Wilson's approval. He addressed its next meeting on 30 April, giving 'some words of caution and advice' and offering the assistance of the whips.[328] Within a few weeks the whips were involving the Committee in some useful but mundane parliamentary tasks, and Wilson's positive attitude was continued by his successor in July 1923, Eyres-Monsell. From March 1924 the practice began of a junior whip attending the weekly meeting of the Committee 'to explain the legislation for the current week and to answer any questions'.[329] The whip could also report back the views of MPs, but the initial purpose was to give guidance rather than to be a channel of communication. However, by accident more than design, the 1922 Committee acquired a role as a sounding board, and this was one of the ways in

---

[324] Lane-Fox to Irwin, 9 June 1927, Halifax MSS, C152/17/1/229.
[325] G. Rentoul, *Sometimes I Think* (n.d. [1940]), 232.
[326] 1922 Ctte. minutes, 18 and 23 April 1923.
[327] For a fuller account, see S. Ball, 'The 1922 Committee: The formative years 1922–45', *Parliamentary History*, 9 (1990), 129–57.
[328] 1922 Ctte. minutes, 30 April 1923.
[329] 1922 Ctte. minutes, 3 March 1924.

which it became useful to both the backbenchers and the leadership. It also became an information nexus, as its meetings received unofficial reports from the meetings of the subject committees.[330]

The other crucial development was that membership of the Committee was rapidly widened; this was also a matter of chance—in this case the unexpected event of two further general elections in swift succession. The Committee had hardly taken definite shape when it was overtaken by the general election of December 1923, and at the start of the next parliament it decided to invite the new MPs to join. When another election followed in October 1924 and the landslide victory resulted in a further 112 new MPs, the doors were also opened to them, and by the end of the first session of this parliament membership had reached 185. MPs elected before 1922 were now a minority of the backbenchers, and the logical step was taken in February 1926, significantly after securing the approval of the Chief Whip, of widening the membership to embrace all Conservatives who were not in ministerial office.[331] The latter was the final important aspect of the Committee's utility and survival; whilst it was now broadly representative and by definition had a large majority of mainstream and loyal MPs, yet it also had a certain independence and its meetings were not dominated by the front-bench few who also had the lion's share of the limelight in the House.

Under the leadership of Rentoul and several of its original founders, the 1922 Committee was at its most active during the remainder of the 1924–29 parliament. As well as regular addresses from ministers, its Chairman noted in 1928 'the admitted usefulness of the Committee as a means of ascertaining and representing rank and file opinion'.[332] In this period controversial issues were discussed, votes taken, and resolutions passed, and there was sometimes vigorous debate between diehard MPs and those on the left wing. However, after the 1929 defeat a pattern developed of avoiding divisive topics, and the Committee took no part in the controversies over protectionism or India in 1929–31; significantly, in the latter case it was the official India Committee that became the important forum. The impact of the August 1931 crisis and the consequent sense of common purpose amongst Conservative MPs revived the 1922 Committee: attendance at the meetings immediately after the crisis more than doubled, and the average attendance for the 1931–32 session of 127 was considerably the highest of the interwar years.[333] However, it led the leaders of the Committee into disastrously overreaching themselves. In June 1932, Rentoul initiated what became an ambitious attempt to draw up proposals for 'drastic public economy on a scale not yet contemplated'.[334] During the summer recess five sub-committees took to this task with relish, and when the House reassembled in November their report proposed draconian cuts in all areas of expenditure, amounting to over £100 million. Despite a growing storm of pro-

---

[330] Reports by Heneage of meetings of the Transport Ctte, 1935, Heneage MSS, HNC/2/54.
[331] 1922 Ctte. minutes, 8 February 1926.
[332] Chairman's circular, 1922 Ctte. minutes, 7 June 1928.
[333] See the table of meetings and attendances in Ball, '1922 Committee', 157.
[334] 1922 Ctte. minutes, 13 June 1932.

test from the majority of MPs who had not been involved and now found themselves associated with a highly unpopular scheme, Rentoul published the report without securing approval, and then badly mishandled the heated meeting of the committee which followed.[335] A month later his position was challenged for the first time at the annual election of the Chairman, and he was defeated by the centrist W. S. Morrison by 117 votes to seventy-six; it was effectively the end of Rentoul's political career, and in late 1933 he left the House to become a Metropolitan Magistrate.

Under Morrison and his successor Sir Hugh O'Neill, a senior MP from Ulster, the 1922 Committee lapsed into quietude for the rest of the 1930s. It reverted to its earliest role as an information source, almost becoming a lecture club, and having an increasing proportion of outside guest speakers. The most important and divisive issues were generally avoided, and the Committee did not even meet when parliament reconvened after the Munich settlement in October 1938. Only a minority of MPs came to the weekly meetings, with average attendance slipping to fifty-six in the 1937–38 session. Lacking a clear role and with its leading figures either promoted to office or nearing the end of their parliamentary careers, it is likely that the Committee would have dwindled away if the outbreak of the war had not rescued it. In the wartime situation the Committee was useful as a means by which ministers could confidentially brief MPs, and during the first months of the war attendance rose to a peak of 200. However, the role was still informational, and the Committee itself played no part in the fall of Chamberlain in May 1940.

The creation of the wartime coalition was the crucial factor, as the 1922 Committee filled the need for a private forum in which Conservative MPs could express their concern over government policies without being disloyal or affecting public morale. This was due not so much to distrust of Churchill but of concern over his neglect of domestic issues and party matters, suspicion of some of his cronies and the 'anti-appeasers' appointed to office,[336] anxiety over the extent to which Labour ministers were dominant on the home front, and objections to certain of their proposals, especially when it was felt that they were using the wartime emergency to promote a Socialist agenda of 'nationalisation by stealth'.[337] At the same time, the Conservative MPs still attending the House felt frustrated, powerless, and distanced from the government, 'in a most unsettled state'[338] and 'very suspicious of their position under the coalition'.[339] With much of the rest of the party organization in suspense, the 1922 Committee took on the role of defender of the party's identity and watchdog of its interests; it still vocalized the mainstream view, but with more urgency and effect. James Stuart, the Chief Whip from January 1941, found the Committee useful as evidence and support when he had to express reservations to the Prime Minister, and its value as a touchstone was recognized by the

---

[335] Rentoul, *Sometimes I Think*, 241–5; 1922 Ctte. minutes, 14 November 1932.
[336] Elliot to his wife, 6 November 1940, Elliot MSS, 8/1.
[337] 1922 Ctte. minutes, 10 and 17 December 1941.
[338] Dugdale to Baldwin, 15 March 1941, Baldwin MSS, 175/60–2.
[339] Butler to Hoare, 6 March 1942, Butler MSS, G14/33–4.

regular presence of Churchill's Parliamentary Private Secretary, George Harvie-Watt.[340] In 1942, politically and strategically a critical year in the war, the average attendance for the first time exceeded one-third of those eligible to attend, and with many MPs absent on war service it was, in reality, higher still.[341] In the spring and summer of that year the Committee was active in resisting plans for coal rationing and objecting to Ernest Bevin's Catering Wages Bill, and in February 1943 its unenthusiastic response to the Beveridge Report represented the general Conservative view. The latter month also saw an important change in the Committee's composition, when, on Oliver Stanley's proposal, it was expanded to include Conservative MPs who were ministers, and its name was amended to simply 'the Conservative Members' Committee'.[342] This inclusion was a sign of the Committee's growing status and confidence, for it was intended to create a more direct means of influencing the leadership—not to become subservient to them. It was during the Second World War, and not before, that the 1922 Committee established its central role and importance in the Conservative Party, which was later confirmed in 1965 when it was given the trusteeship of the new system of electing the Party Leader.

THE HOUSE OF LORDS

It is symptomatic of the decline in political importance of the House of Lords that it only merits this short section in the examination of the Conservative Party in parliament between the wars. Although the peerage still retained much social prestige and owned a large portion of the national wealth, their legislative and governing authority had been diminished firstly by the pruning of the Upper House's powers in the 1911 Parliament Act and, secondly, and perhaps still more, by the advent of democracy in the 1918 Reform Act. These left a feeling of impotence and there was a sense that the life had gone out of the chamber, that it had become a shadow theatre only. This was exacerbated by the rise of the Labour Party to the position of alternative government, for the almost complete lack of Labour representation meant that there was little meaningful debate—indeed, the Conservative leaders in the Lords often had to be careful to deal gently with the handful of aged and sometimes incompetent representatives on the Labour front bench. This was still more the case in dealing with the legislation of the first and second Labour governments, as both Conservative leaders and ordinary peers feared provoking a popular reaction, and they would not risk again another 'peers versus people' con-

---

[340] See copies of his reports to Churchill, 1941–45, Harvie-Watt MSS, CAC, HARV/1/1–5/1.
[341] Ball, '1922 Committee', 157; unfortunately, later figures cannot be calculated as the minute book for 1943–50 appears to have been lost.
[342] 1922 Ctte. minutes, 3 February 1943. This plan had originated in November 1942: Harvie-Watt reports to Churchill, 20 and 27 November 1942, Stuart to Churchill, 14 December 1942, Churchill MSS, CAC, CHAR/2/450/64–7, 61–3, 55–8; Beamish diary notes, 14 July 1943, Beamish MSS, CAC, BEAM/3/5; after 1945, the Committee reverted to its previous pattern of being restricted to backbench MPs when the party was in office, and the former name returned to use.

frontation. Indeed, they were so paranoid in their concern that Labour might entrap them in this way that they kept an even lower profile in 1924 and most of 1929–31, which increased the sense of a lack of purpose and role. Only in 1931, with the Labour ministry tottering and clearly unwilling to face an election, was the Conservative predominance in the upper chamber used more assertively—but still only selectively, against measures which had little potential for popular appeal; there was no thought of using the House of Lords to force the government to a dissolution.

The political role of the Conservative peers was thus mainly one of grumbling inactivity, regardless of which party was in office. However, the Upper House was still a part of the legislative process, and, as the volume of legislation grew after 1918, so the peers also had much tedious material to get through, with government timetables often 'hurling Bills at their heads without leaving them any time to properly deal with them'.[343] The response of peers to the combination of workload and irrelevance included disillusion and absenteeism, frustration, and sometimes bitterness. Several were angry over their exclusion from Carlton Club meeting in October 1922: although, being the Leader in the House of Commons only, Austen Chamberlain technically lacked the authority to summon the peers, it was clear that the vital decision would be taken without them.[344] There were similar complaints that the policy committees formed when in opposition in 1924 were of MPs only, operating 'without any reference whatever to the opinion of the peers'.[345] Their sense of marginalization was fuelled by the dominance of ministerial office by MPs, which was resented and stated to be leading to the alienation of heirs to peerages.[346] In 1927, the party's Leader in the Lords, Lord Salisbury, deplored his own government's practice of 'forcing bills through the House of Lords . . . in the teeth of Conservative opinion'.[347] However, although the 'backwoodsmen' grumbled and could create difficulties, they were unwilling to wreck the measures of a Conservative or coalition government.

The upper chamber had been overwhelmingly dominated by the Conservative Party since the late nineteenth century; 483 members of the House of Lords took the Conservative Party whip in 1928, and 502 in 1937.[348] The large majority of these peers were not politically active, and their interests were focused elsewhere; they attended only infrequently, but nevertheless were a reserve army which the Conservative whips could call upon in a crisis. In practice, the House of Lords was the forum of a relatively small proportion of active and politically engaged peers; this had been the case even before 1911, and continued to be even more so after the First World War. Most of these were drawn from two elements, the first of which was the long-established great aristocratic families for whom governing was

---

[343] Salisbury to Balfour, 14 January 1927, Balfour MSS (Whittingehame), GD433/2/18/22.
[344] Curzon to A. Chamberlain, 18 October 1922, AC, 33/2/90; Lady Peto diary, 19 October 1922.
[345] Salisbury to Cecil, 8 April 1924, Cecil of Chelwood MSS, Add.51085/121–3.
[346] Midleton to Baldwin, 10 August 1928, Baldwin MSS, 59/211–6.
[347] Salisbury to Cave, 17 December 1927, Cave MSS, Add.62502/67–8; Midleton to Baldwin, 28 March 1925, Baldwin MSS, 160/105–6.
[348] Lists of Peers, 1928–30 and 1937, CPA, Whips' Office MSS, 2/5.

a duty ingrained by centuries of exercising regional and national power. These were particularly the Dukes of Devonshire, the Marquesses of Salisbury and Londonderry, the Earls of Derby, and holders of some of the Scottish dukedoms. In many cases, it was customary for the heir to the title to spend some time in the House of Commons as a young man, often until they succeeded to the title; all of the holders of the previously mentioned peerages in the interwar period did so, as did their sons after them. This political apprenticeship in the lower chamber was something which they had in common with the second element: the former MPs who were elevated to the peerage by the conferment of a new title. These consisted partly of former Cabinet ministers and partly of long-serving and respected backbenchers; most of those in both categories were drawn from the landed gentry or the relatives of peers, and so the social gulf was not as large as it might seem. As Balfour, himself an example of both categories as a former Prime Minister and the nephew of a Marquess, noted in 1927: 'a quite disproportionate number of the speakers are House of Commons men who have received peerages, or peers whose whole training has been in the House of Commons'.[349]

The largest element in the House of Lords was the hereditary peerage, and 'those who do not take a very keen interest . . . and who normally would be likely to support us' were the basis of Conservative predominance.[350] This element required some consideration, more by way of personnel than of policy, and inclusion of some of the old nobility in the ministry was worthwhile as a link and reassurance—hence the concern expressed by Hailsham at the dropping of Londonderry in the June 1935 reshuffle. Many of these were members of an important semi-detached body, the 'Unionist Independent Peers'. Their Chairman for most of the interwar period, the Earl of Midleton (a former Cabinet minister in the early 1900s), gave their membership as 160 in 1925.[351] The role of this body had some parallels with that of the 1922 Committee in the Lower House, as a means of communicating rank and file feeling to the Party Leaders both privately and effectively. One example of this was Midleton's expression of their preference for Salisbury as Leader in the Lords in succession to Curzon in 1925, and resistance of the claims of Birkenhead.[352] However, to be effective, the Unionist Independent Peers needed to maintain an active role, and sometimes they struggled to do so. As Midleton pointed out, if only forty or fifty troubled to vote on an important issue, they could not expect their views to be given particular consideration.[353] However, this absenteeism was partly a message in itself, as the aristocratic element was often critical of Baldwin's moderate policies in 1924–29, especially after the subsequent electoral defeat.[354]

---

[349] Balfour to Salisbury, 31 January 1927, Balfour MSS (Whittingehame), GD433/2/18/24.
[350] Hailsham to Baldwin, 28 May 1935, Hailsham MSS, CAC, HAIL/1/1/3.
[351] Midleton to Baldwin, 28 March 1925, Baldwin MSS, 160/105–6.
[352] Midleton to Duke of Atholl, 21 April 1925, Baldwin MSS, 160/3.
[353] Midleton to Salisbury, 19 April 1930, Salisbury MSS, S(4)134/164.
[354] Buccleuch to Salisbury, 2 June 1929, 8 February 1930, Malmesbury to Salisbury, 13 January 1930, Gisborough to Salisbury, 25 February 1930, Salisbury MSS, S(4)130/45–6, 133/100, 133/35–6, 133/175.

Two other categories of peers who were not formally organized also had a combination of partial independence and yet significant ties to the Conservative Party, by either present interest or past service. These were, firstly, the ennobled titans of industry: financiers, industrialists, and press magnates—the latter group including not only the aggressively assertive critics Northcliffe, Rothermere, and Beaverbrook, but also loyal supporters of Baldwin such as Lords Camrose, Kemsley, and Iliffe. The demands of their business empires meant that they attended rarely, but they could add a weighty element of 'expert' opinion to the debates; this group included Lords Nuffield, Weir, and Melchett—the latter being one of a number of former Liberals who moved across to the Conservative Party in the 1920s and were later ennobled. The second group were former imperial administrators, many of whom had been Conservative MPs, junior ministers, or whips before their appointments as colonial and Indian provincial governors or to the Governor-Generalships of the Dominions. Notable amongst these was George Lloyd, created Lord Lloyd of Dolobran after serving as Governor of Bombay in 1918–23 and before appointment as High Commissioner for Egypt and the Sudan in 1925, a post from which he was controversially dismissed by the incoming Labour government in 1929; before and briefly after his Indian post, he was a MP. Lloyd was a leading opponent—in some eyes, the leading figure—in the opposition to Baldwin's policy on India in 1931–35 and a critic of appeasement as well; Churchill made him Colonial Secretary and then Party Leader in the Lords in January 1941, but he died suddenly less than a month later. An abrasive and excitable figure, he was described by one MP in 1931 as 'the "Super-Diehard" and rightly or wrongly regarded in many quarters as a shit'.[355]

The Conservative Leader in the House of Lords was normally a scion of the grandest aristocratic families: in the five decades from 1881 to 1931, the office was held successively by the 3rd Marquess of Salisbury, the 8th Duke of Devonshire, the 5th Marquess of Lansdowne, the 1st Marquess Curzon, and the 4th Marquess of Salisbury. By the time the latter was appointed in 1925, it had become a subordinate position selected by the overall Leader of the Party, but it was necessary for its holder to be credible and respected, for Conservative peers were under no necessity to follow the lead given, and did so only from persuasion, solidarity, and loyalty.[356] Salisbury was the preferred choice of most of them, especially the hereditaries, as being 'a gentleman, with the best traditions of the House at his back', but also through his hard work and commitment, having attended 'more consistently and regularly than any other Lord, through fair weather and foul'.[357] Similarly, Midleton referred to Salisbury's 'unique' position and 'his intense application and readiness in debate'.[358] His departure in June 1931, ostensibly due to ill health, was a loss, although—with typical loyalty—the reason given disguised the main cause, which

---

[355] Boothby to Mosley, n.d. but 1931, Boothby MSS, 683.
[356] For the same reason, the whips in the House of Lords were mainly drawn from the old-established landed aristocracy.
[357] Duke of Atholl to Midleton, 23 April 1925, Baldwin MSS, 160/4.
[358] Midleton to Baldwin, 28 March 1925, Baldwin MSS, 160/105–6; Bridgeman diary, 'Lord Salisbury', November 1929.

was the widening rift over India that later led Salisbury to emerge in 1933–35 as the leading respectable opponent of the government's policy.[359] His successor, Lord Hailsham, was of different origins, having risen through the path of legal promotion to the Lord Chancellorship in 1928. Although personally popular, Hailsham was concerned that the hereditary peers of the feudal aristocracy would find it hard to accept his lead, and he was never able to be as firm with them as Salisbury had been. Hailsham held the leadership for exactly four years, and after the reshuffle of June 1935 it returned again to landed hereditaries (successively the 7th Marquess of Londonderry, the relatively parvenu 3rd Viscount Halifax, and the 7th Earl of Stanhope) until May 1940. The office returned full circle during the Second World War: in February 1942, the leadership of the party in the House of Lords reverted to the heir of the 4th Marquess of Salisbury, Viscount Cranborne, who was summoned to the Upper House during his father's lifetime in one of the family's lesser peerages. He remained the Leader for just over fifteen years; in outward appearance at least, the old order changed but slowly. However, underneath the shell of social prestige, sustained by customary deference, all significant power had evaporated, as Cranborne (by then the 5th Marquess of Salisbury) found when his resignation in March 1957 after clashing with Macmillan caused barely a ripple in the public consciousness.

In the period immediately before the First World War, Conservatives had been so passionately opposed to the Parliament Act of 1911 that they frequently spoke of the constitution being in suspense. This assertion was partly based on the preamble to the Act, which had stated that it was a temporary measure and that more considered reform would follow. Conservatives were not insincere in calling for this promise to be fulfilled, although their conception of any stabilizing solution involved strengthening the position of the Upper House, and so to a greater or lesser degree undoing their defeat. An over-powerful House of Commons was considered to be a danger to the balance of the constitution, reducing legislative scrutiny and the checks upon executive power. It was argued that the diminution of the House of Lords had given ultimate power to the House of Commons rather than to the electorate, and hence Lord Selborne's argument 'that the question at issue is not the privileges of peers but the rights of the electors'.[360] However, the real driving forces behind the demand for 'second chamber reform' were pragmatism and fear, as the increasing possibility of a Socialist overall majority in the House of Commons led many Conservative activists to place a high priority, indeed urgency, upon the need to make a bulwark of the House of Lords. As Selborne warned the Annual Conference in 1923, 'under the Parliament Act as it stood today, any revolution in our constitution was possible', his seconder adding that a Labour majority in the Lower House 'could abolish property, abolish the King if they liked, in open session of Parliament'.[361]

---

[359] Salisbury to Baldwin, draft letter of resignation, June 1931, Salisbury MSS, S(4)140/98–102.
[360] Selborne to Scott, 10 December 1925, Scott MSS, MSS.119/3/5/LO/6.
[361] NU Conf., 1923.

However, reform of the House of Lords was a political minefield. The first problem was the acute divergence between Conservative Party pressure on the one hand, and public disinterest or hostility on the other.[362] Secondly, in the post-1918 electoral system, there was great difficulty in presenting a strengthening of the Upper House as anything other than anti-democratic in tone, even if not intentionally. Here again arose the fear of giving the opposition an opening for 'a cry of Lords versus the people', on which 'we should be hopelessly beaten'.[363] This was the reason why the issue was customarily referred to as 'second chamber' reform, with the more emotive terms 'lords' and 'peers' being downplayed. Thirdly, it was impossible to arrive at a consensus even within Conservative ranks upon how to proceed. A few Conservatives openly (though no doubt most of them privately) desired to repeal the Parliament Act and restore the previous powers of the Lords. This at least had the virtue of simplicity, but was so overtly reactionary as to be self-defeating: it would alienate Liberal and moderate opinion, and so provoke the Labour Party that they would make the abolition of the Upper House a priority. However unsatisfactory, it was better to leave matters as they were than gift such a propaganda advantage to their opponents.[364] Any measure had, therefore, to be a reform, involving elements of give and take.

The main stumbling block was the link between the powers of the House of Lords and its composition, and over this balance it proved impossible to find sufficiently broad agreement. In 1927, when reform proposals were drafted by the Lord Chancellor, Lord Cave, it was agreed by the Chief Whip and Party Chairman 'that it was impossible to increase the power of the Lords, without altering its constitution'.[365] The proposal to introduce life peerages (which already existed for the Law Lords) on a wider scale had considerable support, but it did not address the thorny issue of the entitlements of the hereditary peers—some of whom were the upper chamber's most prominent debaters and assiduous attenders, but over two-thirds of whom were 'habitual absentees'.[366] Every plan foundered upon the dilemmas of who the upper chamber was to comprise, how they would be selected, and how any future clashes with the House of Commons were to be resolved. There was a fundamental conflict of interests between the two Houses: whilst Conservative MPs did not wish to see an unchecked lower chamber in the hands of a Socialist majority, still 'the House of Commons colleagues in their hearts do not want to give the Lords more power and the Lords colleagues will not agree to Lords reform on any other terms'.[367] This led a few young MPs on the left wing to conclude 'that the only practical alternative to the present House of Lords is an elected Senate'.[368]

---

[362] SUA Conf., 12 November 1926; Blair to Thomson (Scottish Whip), 30 June 1927, Baldwin MSS, 59/142–4; Wood Green CA, Palmers Green branch, Exec., 6 December 1929.

[363] Lord Stanley to Derby, 14 January 1922, Derby MSS, 39.

[364] Blair to Thomson (Scottish Whip), 30 June 1927, Baldwin MSS, 59/142–4; Crichton-Stuart to Davidson, 31 January 1928, Baldwin MSS, 59/185–6.

[365] Memo by Davidson, 24 January 1927, Davidson MSS, DAV/180.

[366] Onslow to Salisbury, 7 July 1929, Salisbury MSS, S(4)130/110; Winchester CA, Exec., 26 July 1927.

[367] Salisbury to Irwin, 24 April 1927, Halifax MSS, C152/17/1/209.

[368] Duff Cooper, dissenting minute to report of party committee, in Salisbury to N. Chamberlain, 31 July 1931, Salisbury MSS, S(4)141/60.

However, most MPs would not accept a purely elected chamber, not only as too radical a breach with the past and unlikely to command the necessary popular respect, but also as a potential rival which might lead to more constitutional conflict rather than less.[369]

For these reasons, second chamber reform became both counterproductive and divisive. At the time of the controversial proposals rather suddenly brought forward by Lord Cave, the Lord Chancellor, in 1927, Anthony Eden observed that 'there are as many views on this subject as there are Members of Parliament—probably more', although he delineated the largest gulf as that between 'the younger and also more progressive members of the party who would have been happier had the subject not been raised' and those who hoped that reforming the Lords would make it 'a more effective bulwark against the potential follies of a future Socialist government'.[370] Legislation along the lines of Cave's plan was likely to split the party, and was blocked by the combination of the vigorous hostility of the young left-wing MPs and those representing urban marginals (groups which overlapped, in the cases of Macmillan and Duff Cooper).[371] Influential peers such as Derby were also 'aghast' at what they considered would be 'political suicide'.[372] Proceeding with any substantial measure involved electoral risks which never seemed worthwhile, and the Party Chairman was far from alone in rejecting this: 'to fight an election on it would spell disaster'.[373] Thus, despite the general commitment to the idea of reform and the repeated passage by the National Union at regional and national meetings of resolutions demanding action, the timing never seemed to be right—whether it was early, middle, or late in a parliament. This was the reason for the repeated hedging and shelving which so infuriated the ardent champions of reform, with the Conservative governments of 1922–24 and 1924–29 proving just as reluctant to grasp the nettle as the Coalition had been in 1918–22. Such proposals as were generally acceptable were reduced to the lowest common denominator and amounted to mere tinkering, evoking little enthusiasm from anyone. In the end, although often reluctantly, most Conservatives came to the conclusion that 'it would be better to leave well alone'.[374] As Derby observed: 'it is quite true that the present position of the House of Lords is an illogical one, but much of our constitution is illogical and I am all for it remaining so'.[375]

---

[369] Memo by Davidson, 1 July 1927, Baldwin MSS, 59/138–41.
[370] Eden to A. Chamberlain, 2 July 1927, Avon MSS, AP/14/1/48.
[371] Stanley to Scott, n.d. but c.July 1927, Scott MSS, MSS.119/3/5/LO/19.
[372] Derby to Davidson, 29 June 1927, Davidson MSS, DAV/180.
[373] Davidson to Irwin, 17 August 1927, Halifax MSS, C152/17/1/249a.
[374] Memo by Davidson, 1 July 1927, Baldwin MSS, 59/138–41.
[375] Derby to Davidson, 29 June 1927, Davidson MSS, DAV/180.

6

Ministers

Juniors and Cabinet

GETTING INTO OFFICE

The route to ministerial office in British politics was through making a mark in parliament—in most cases, in the House of Commons, as ministers were now mainly drawn from the lower chamber. At the outset, this was always by effective speaking in debate, which was more important than having experience in the particular area; MPs were expected to have a general competence, whilst it was the function of civil servants to provide specialist advice.[1] In fact, there were reservations about appointing someone to a field with which they were already closely identified: their freedom of manoeuvre might be restricted by past statements and commitments, or they might approach the issues from a blinkered perspective—thus the National Farmers' Union objected to the possible appointment of Lord Bledisloe, a prominent agricultural reformer and a former chairman of the Central Chamber of Agriculture, as Minister of Agriculture in 1924.[2] Debating ability was the most valuable asset of all: for a junior ministerial vacancy in his department in 1927, the President of the Board of Trade placed a higher priority on getting a good parliamentary performer than someone with business experience.[3] In 1945, after four decades in the House, Winterton observed that 'debating skill...counts as much today as it ever did'.[4]

Effective speaking did not mean high flights of oratory, because what impressed fellow MPs more than the arts of the rhetorician were sincerity, clarity, and directness. Baldwin was told in 1920, when still a junior minister, that 'courage, honesty of purpose, and a thorough grip of your job have won for you the high esteem of the House'.[5] Whilst there was a necessary minimum of audibility and articulateness, it was character and content that earned respect—hence the success of apparently very ordinary speakers such as John Gilmour, whilst Walter Elliot rose in prominence in the early 1930s despite having 'a bad House of Commons manner' and 'a poor vocabulary'.[6] A conversational style worked much better than anything dramatic or hectoring: Lane-Fox described Lady Iveagh's speech in the second

---

[1] Crookshank diary, 17 June 1935.
[2] Pretyman to Baldwin, n.d. [November 1924], Baldwin MSS, 42/245–6.
[3] Cunliffe-Lister to Baldwin, 24 December 1927, Baldwin MSS, 162/162–3.
[4] Winterton to Harvie-Watt, 13 January 1945, Churchill MSS, CAC, CHAR/20/201/62.
[5] Chadwick to Baldwin, 7 June 1920, Baldwin MSS, 140/10.
[6] Somervell journal, 2 February and 21 April 1934, Somervell MSS, MSS.Eng.c.6565/18, 37; Winterton to Hoare, 20 November 1935, Templewood MSS, VIII/1; Headlam diary, 15 June 1932.

Prayer Book debate of June 1928 as 'really admirable' because it consisted of 'excellent phraseology and delivery, well-reasoned, definite points'.[7] Successful parliamentary speaking called for quite different skills from platform oratory; emotional tub-thumping did not work well in front of an informed and sceptical audience, and relying on passion rather than argument tended to fall flat in the sparsely attended chamber which most ordinary MPs addressed. A more forensic style was required, in which persuasion was by facts and logic, and rested upon knowledge. However, whilst it might seem that lawyers had a head start in acquiring these skills, anything that seemed too reminiscent of a courtroom manner was cordially disliked by most MPs. It was important not to 'show off', to seem too clever or too arrogant; tolerance and adaptability—without conceding points of importance—was the best approach, and thus Bridgeman effectively handled opposition to the Eight Hours Bill in 1926 through 'sheer good humour and absolute imperturbability'.[8] In a similar way, Douglas Hogg was successful as Attorney-General because 'he was a good hard hitter in plain and simple English, but his manner was so genial'.[9] However, there was no guarantee of continued success, as each parliament was a new arena with its own atmosphere and 'every man of position has to make good (or not!) in a new House'.[10]

A visible administrative competence came second, for it could only be demonstrated after achieving the first rung on the ladder of office. Responding to questions and seeing a bill through committee would demonstrate this, but a low profile was preferred—scoring points off the opposition might be entertaining, but it took up time and was likely to provoke them into more disruptive tactics. Baldwin commented: 'a Minister is in the House to get the business of his Office through', which often meant both the minister and government MPs saying as little as possible, and not rising to the bait of their opponents.[11] Diligence, steadiness, loyalty, and evidence of team spirit, rather than individual ambition, were the qualities looked for by the whips, whose opinions of the backbench MPs were relied upon by the Party Leader when forming a government or filling a vacancy. The 'usual method of advancement', observed Harold Balfour, was through 'attention to parliamentary duties, avoiding any form of criticism or embarrassment of the leaders, and constantly displaying what may be termed the cricket-field and public-school tradition'.[12] The Chief Whip's suggestion of promoting Herbert Williams, a middle-class engineer, and Duff Cooper, the ex-diplomat nephew of a duke, simultaneously to junior office in late 1927 was intended to 'show that it is immaterial out of which drawer recruits are drawn provided they show ability, industriousness and *loyalty*'.[13] Progression to the Cabinet was usually founded upon similar qualities;

---

[7] Lane-Fox to Irwin, 14 June 1928, Halifax MSS, C152/18/1/69.
[8] Lane-Fox to Irwin, 4 July 1926, Halifax MSS, C152/17/1/61.
[9] Memoir by Brittain, 'The House of Commons', n.d., Brittain MSS, 12.
[10] Baldwin to Reith, 31 January 1940, *BP*, 464.
[11] Baldwin to Reith, 31 January 1940, *BP*, 464.
[12] H. Balfour, *An Airman Marches* (1933), 253; Headlam diary, 16 June 1935.
[13] Eyres-Monsell to Baldwin, 27 December 1927, Baldwin MSS, 162/122–3, emphasis in original.

Henry King, who before his sudden death in 1930 was thought of by many as likely to enter the next Conservative Cabinet, 'was not a flier but one of those men who can always be relied on for loyalty and hard work', and 'very straight'.[14] After serving in two Cabinets, Bridgeman considered the qualifications for success at that level to be 'force of character, brains, experience & good judgement'.[15]

Most ministerial careers followed the conventional path of promotion. For younger MPs in particular, the first step was often an unpaid post as a junior or Cabinet minister's Parliamentary Private Secretary. Although usually in consultation with the whips, these selections were made by the minister himself, as it was necessary in such a close working relationship to have someone congenial in whom there was confidence; inevitably, the process was 'haphazard at the best of times and often dictated purely by personal favouritism or family connections'.[16] Backbenchers were also appointed directly to the next level, which consisted of the less-prestigious junior ministerial posts. Service in several departments at junior level was not unusual, and they were ranked in status in the same way as their Cabinet superiors. The junior positions at the Treasury, Foreign Office, and Home Office headed this list, together with the semi-autonomous appointments such as Minister for Mines, which was described by Baldwin as 'a Brigadier's job'.[17] The Party Chairman was usually recruited from the junior ministerial ranks, but this was a sideways move which could become a cul-de-sac. Promotion from the ranks of the junior ministers was normally either to one of the ministries outside the Cabinet, such as Pensions, Transport, Postmaster-General, or Chancellor of the Duchy of Lancaster, or directly to one of the lower or middle-ranking Cabinet offices. The latter was more likely to happen when a new government was being formed, especially if this followed a period in opposition or one of the periodic shifts in generations within the leadership, as in 1922 and 1931. In the former case, six juniors were advanced to the Cabinet, which was not an unusually large number; what was exceptional was that only four members of the outgoing Cabinet were continuing, with most other posts filled from those who had past experience of office, such as Cave, Derby, and, of course, Bonar Law himself (where the fall of the Lloyd George Coalition did open the door was to junior office, with nineteen of the twenty-five junior ministers being newcomers). After attaining Cabinet rank, a minister could, if both successful and fortunate, expect to move upwards to one of the most important offices, of which the plums were Foreign Secretary and Chancellor of the Exchequer; the tenure of one of these was normally necessary to be a credible candidate for the Premiership. In due course, an experienced Cabinet minister would reach 'elder statesman' status, and most likely occupy one of the non-departmental and therefore less onerous posts such as Lord President of the Council or Lord Privy Seal.

---

[14] N. to I. Chamberlain, 22 August 1930, *NCDL*.
[15] Bridgeman diary, 'December' 1929.
[16] Macnamara, *The Whistle Blows*, 147–50.
[17] Crookshank diary, 17 June 1935.

Table 6.1. The career pattern of Conservative junior ministers in the House of Commons 1919–1945[18]

This table analyses all of the Conservative MPs who served as junior ministers (excluding the Law Officers) between January 1919 and May 1945; the brief 'Caretaker' ministry of May to July 1945 is not included. For the Churchill Coalition of 1940–45, ministers in offices which in peacetime were always of Cabinet rank are considered to have been of Cabinet status and have been excluded from this table (they are included in Table 6.3). If an MP also served in junior office as a peer, this is included in the calculation of their length of service. Titles already held before appointment include courtesy titles (see the definition in Table 5.9); titles acquired during or after appointment include titles inherited as well as those created. Each person is counted only once in each category, but if an individual had honours in more than one category, they will be counted once in each category (e.g. where a person with a knighthood or baronetcy became a peer, or a person with a courtesy title inherited a peerage).

Age profile	21–9	30–9	40–9	50–9	60 +
Junior minister only:					
age first elected an MP	11	32	14	–	–
age first appointed a minister	–	13	27	16	1
Junior minister and Cabinet rank:					
age first elected an MP	15	19	10	1	–
age first appointed a minister	1	16	20	8	–

Length of service (years and months)	Less than 2 years	2.0 to 3.11	4.0 to 5.11	6.0 to 7.11	8.0 to 9.11	10 years & above
Junior minister only	14	13	14	9	4	3
Junior minister and Cabinet rank	8	9	7	11	7	3

Number of posts held	1	2	3	4	5	6	7
Junior minister only	24	14	15	4	–	–	–
Junior minister and Cabinet rank	8	12	10	9	4	1	1

Honours	Title before first appointment	Becomes knight or baronet	Becomes peer
Junior minister only	11	14	25
Junior minister and Cabinet rank	11	6	34

[18] Calculated from D. Butler and G. Butler (eds.), *Twentieth-Century British Political Facts* (2000), and Stenton and Lees, *Who's Who of British Members of Parliament*, vols 3 and 4.

The oldest appointee to junior office was a rather unusual case: Sir Edward Grigg had been a Liberal MP in 1922–25, before a successful term as Governor of Kenya from 1925 to 1930, and he re-entered the House as a Conservative supporter of the National Government in 1933. The youngest of all the ministerial appointments in this period was R. A. Butler, who was given office in September 1932 at the age of twenty-nine; this was also the fastest promotion amongst the younger MPs, as he had only entered the House three years and four months earlier, at the 1929 general election. Butler was to go on to the Cabinet, as did four of the other eight ministers who were appointed under the age of thirty-five. Three of this quartet were aged thirty-three when they were given office (Geoffrey Lloyd, Alan Lennox-Boyd, and Duncan Sandys), and the fourth—Anthony Eden—was thirty-four, although he had been the youngest of the group to become an MP, at the age of twenty-six. The ages at appointment were similar for the four who did not reach the Cabinet; in three cases, they might have done so, but their ministerial career ended abruptly in 1945. This was poignantly so with Rupert Brabner, appointed Under-Secretary for Air in November 1944, as he died when the aeroplane in which he was travelling vanished near the Azores in March 1945. Richard Pilkington had also been thirty-three when he became Civil Lord at the Admiralty in March 1942, holding the post until he lost his seat in the 1945 landslide; however, although he returned to the House in 1951–64, he was not given office again. Henry Scrymgeour-Wedderburn was thirty-four when he became Under-Secretary for Scotland in 1936, serving in that post until the outbreak of war and again from February 1941 to March 1942; he also returned to junior office much later in 1958–64, but this was in the House of Lords as the Earl of Dundee.

The last of the nine was already on the inside track before even becoming an MP: J. C. C. Davidson was private secretary to Bonar Law from 1915 until entering the Commons in 1920, after which he was immediately appointed as Bonar Law's Parliamentary Private Secretary. When the Party Leader initially retired in 1921, Davidson became Baldwin's PPS, but he returned to serve Bonar Law again in that role during the latter's short term as Prime Minister. Davidson was thirty-four when Baldwin appointed him to the non-departmental post of Chancellor of the Duchy of Lancaster in May 1923, and he spent nearly all of the rest of his career acting effectively as Baldwin's chief of staff, including a term as Party Chairman in 1926–30 and a return to the Duchy post from 1931 until Baldwin retired in 1937, whereupon Davidson was given a viscountcy, which was the usual reward for Cabinet rank. However, whilst there was no doubt that an early start was nearly as much of an advantage as having a safe seat (Headlam often bitterly regretted his lack of both), the four ministers who had become MPs at the very youngest of ages were not the fastest to rise. Earl Winterton entered the House at the age of twenty-one, but did not attain junior office until he was thirty-eight; William Ormsby-Gore was elected aged twenty-four, but had to wait nearly thirteen years for office until after the fall of the Lloyd George Coalition, and Arthur Griffith-Boscawen, first elected in 1892 at the age of twenty-six, did not become a minister until December 1916. The fourth case was slightly different: Lord Stanley was first elected aged twenty-two in 1917, but was not an MP in the 1918–22 parliament;

he became a whip in 1924 and served as Deputy Party Chairman in 1927–29, and then was appointed to junior office after the 1931 general election.

Alongside the political ladder of promotion, there was a legal one to which many of the lawyers in the party aspired, and this was certainly the reason why some of them became MPs; as James Clyde frankly declared, parliament was the 'door to the attainment of the highest professional ambition'.[19] The House of Commons was a frequent route to judicial office—to the Recorderships, which did not require the holder to give up his seat, or to appointments such as Metropolitan Magistrate, or County Court or High Court judge, which did require leaving the House. However, the biggest prizes lay within parliament: the Law Officers. The two Irish positions ceased to exist in 1921, after which there were four Law Officers: for the Scottish legal profession, there was the junior post of Solicitor-General for Scotland and the senior of Lord Advocate; for their English and Welsh colleagues, there was the junior office of Solicitor-General and the senior of Attorney-General, which led to the most glittering prize of all—the Lord Chancellorship. This route was taken by F. E. Smith (as Lord Birkenhead) in January 1919, and subsequently by Hogg (Lord Hailsham) and—less directly, and very briefly—by Inskip (Lord Caldecote) before 1945, and by Maxwell-Fyfe (Lord Kilmuir) in the 1950s. This quartet represented the lawyers who were nonetheless more interested in a political career than legal preferment; Hogg forever regretted his rushed acceptance after Cave's death of the Lord Chancellorship and the peerage which it entailed.

The longest-serving Law Officer was Donald Somervell, who was in post for eleven years and seven months from 1933 until May 1945, when he became Home Secretary in the Churchill 'Caretaker' ministry, until its defeat in July. Inskip served as a Law Officer for six months less than this, before entering the Cabinet, to some surprise and criticism, as the newly created Minister for Co-ordination of Defence in March 1936. The third longest tenure was James Reid as a Scottish Law Officer for just over nine years in 1936–45. However, this was unusual north of the border, where there was often a rapid turnover, as the Lord Advocate had an almost automatic entitlement to elevation whenever there was a vacancy among the Scottish Law Lords. During this period, nine of the eleven Scottish Law Officers became Law Lords in the Scottish legal system; of the two who did not, one died young and the other, Frederick Thomson, was only briefly a Law Officer during a lengthy career as a whip. The rewards were also substantial elsewhere: of the last handful of Irish Law Officers, Denis Henry became Lord Chief Justice of Northern Ireland when its courts were established in August 1921, and three others became High Court judges in Ulster. Of the English Law Officers, Inskip ended his career as Lord Chief Justice and Ernest Pollock was appointed Master of the Rolls, whilst two others became Law Lords and one a High Court judge. Honours were also liberally distributed, and not only the knighthoods, which were automatic upon appointment to either of the English posts: in addition to the judicial life peerages, seven of the Law Officers were also recipients of a hereditary peerage.

---

[19] Reply to question 6 of Wedgwood's survey for the History of Parliament, Wedgwood Questionnaire MSS.

Table 6.2. The career pattern of Conservative Law Officers in the House of Commons 1919–1945[20]

This table analyses all of the Conservative MPs who served as Law Officers between January 1919 and May 1945; the brief 'Caretaker' ministry of May to July 1945 is not included.

Age profile		21–9	30–9	40–9	50–9	60 +
Age first elected an MP		–	3	12	7	1
Age first appointed a Law Officer		–	–	12	10	1
Length of service (years and months)	Less than 2 years	2.0 to 3.11	4.0 to 5.11	6.0 to 7.11	8.0 to 9.11	10 years & above
Number of Law Officers	6	8	4	2	1	2

Finally, there was also a path of imperial preferment, as the whips and junior ministers were a common recruiting ground for the colonial and Indian provincial Governorships and the posts of High Commissioner to the self-governing Dominions. During this period, these provided seven governors of Indian provinces, one each of Ceylon and Burma, and one Governor-General and two provincial governors for Australia. The Viceroyalty of India was normally filled from Cabinet level or its near equivalents, as also on some occasions—especially in periods of crisis and war—were the ambassadorships to major friendly powers such as France (Lord Derby in 1917 and Duff Cooper in 1944) and the United States (Auckland Geddes in 1920 and Lord Halifax in 1940); in 1940, Hoare was despatched to the Madrid embassy, not just to remove him from the Cabinet but also because of Spain's strategic importance at that time.

The route to office could be slow and was often frustrating, and there were many potential cul-de-sacs. However, hope and ambition provided sustenance on the journey, and the prize of Cabinet eminence remained in tantalizing prospect, however much it might recede like the pot of gold at the end of the rainbow. As Winterton exclaimed after unexpectedly being offered a place: 'To be a Cabinet Minister... the fruition of thirty-three years of Parliamentary and political struggle!!'[21] There were alternative courses to the conventional progressions, but in all cases appointment depended upon the approval of those allocating the posts; it was difficult to coerce them or make oneself indispensable, certainly for any sustained period. Staid party orthodoxy, loyalty, and dependability were far surer and more frequent routes to the top than rebellious brilliance or principled independence. These were more often the symptoms of frustration rather than strategies of choice, and those who were passed over could gravitate to the 'awkward squad', as in the case of Macmillan in the 1930s and Williams during the Second World War. The pattern of promotion was also distorted by the effects of crises and electoral landslides (particularly defeats, which could open the way to a new generation), as

---

[20] Calculated from Butler and Butler, *Twentieth-Century British Political Facts*, and Stenton and Lees, *Who's Who of British Members of Parliament*, vols 3 and 4.

[21] Winterton diary, 19 February 1938, Winterton MSS, ellipsis and double exclamation mark in the original.

happened with the Conservatives in 1906, 1922, and 1945. The other unusual circumstance was wartime, in which persons with special skills or proven administrative competence could be brought in from outside parliament, in some cases directly to Cabinet posts. Thus Oliver Lyttelton, a successful City businessman in the metals trade, became first an official as Controller of Non-Ferrous Metals on the outbreak of war in 1939, and then a minister as President of the Board of Trade in October 1940, making his maiden speech from the front bench. For appointments like the latter, either the new minister was made a peer or a seat in the Commons had quickly to be provided—but there was usually a backbencher in a safe seat who could be persuaded to retire, often with a peerage as consolation.

JUNIOR MINISTERS

The junior ministers occupied a political half-world, in which they were neither privy to the decisions of the leadership (which they were expected to follow with unswerving loyalty) nor in the swim of backbenchers' concerns, gossip, and intrigues. As Butler observed after seven years in junior office: 'very often the Under-Secretary just has to do his job without quite knowing whether he fitted into the picture or not'.[22] Junior office was a difficult position to occupy well: much depended upon the personality of the senior minister and the scope which he permitted. He may not have had any say in the choice of his junior, or have become irritated with him—as Churchill did with Arthur Michael Samuel as Financial Secretary to the Treasury in 1927–29.[23] Quite apart from these matters of personal interaction, there was also the factor of the senior minster's competence and effectiveness, for this played the largest part in the reputation and perception of the department as a whole. Ironically, as Headlam found at the Ministry of Transport in 1932–34 when serving under first Percy Pybus and then Oliver Stanley, both the incompetent and the highly competent could mean that the junior minister had little chance to shine. Pybus had to be helped through his bills by the Attorney-General, whilst Stanley effortlessly fielded everything himself; in both cases, Headlam found himself marginalized and frustrated.

The experience for most of their holders was 'the dullness of subordinate Ministerial Office'.[24] However, some junior posts gave more opportunities to shine than others. There was most scope when the senior minister was in the House of Lords; this left the junior to handle departmental affairs in the lower chamber, and to do so effectively he had to be both more involved in the decision-making and permitted more discretion when responding to situations in the Commons. The other chance at the limelight was in a department with a heavy and politically significant legislative programme. It was the good fortune of R. A. Butler to benefit from each type of opportunity: the latter as junior to Hoare at the India Office during the

---

[22] Butler to Baldwin, 11 October 1938, Baldwin MSS, 174/13–14.
[23] N. Chamberlain to Irwin, 12 August 1928, Halifax MSS, C152/18/1/114a.
[24] Winterton to Irwin, 3 June 1926, Halifax MSS, C152/17/1/48.

struggle over reform in 1932–35, and the former as Under-Secretary at the Foreign Office under Lord Halifax in 1938–40; he made less impact in-between as junior at the Ministry of Labour in 1937–38. Another who made his name at an actively reforming department was Sir Howard Kingsley Wood, who earned Neville Chamberlain's admiration as his junior at the Ministry of Health in 1924–29: 'he is very quick, very industrious and painstaking, and moreover...he is the most loyal of officers'. Chamberlain was certain that 'Kingsley is marked out for promotion and will no doubt enter the next Cabinet'.[25] The temporary absence of a superior could also provide an opportunity, and thus Walter Elliot—already marked out as a rising star—had an unexpected share of the limelight during the 1932 budget debates due to the illness of the Chancellor of the Exchequer.

The junior positions at the great departments of state—Home Office, Foreign Office, and Treasury—carried the highest prestige. In particular, the Financial Secretaryship to the Treasury was regarded as the doyen of junior offices, and as an immediate stepping-stone to the Cabinet. There was a hierarchy of the junior posts further down, but the gradations were of fine distinction—and a move could be regarded as progress in itself, provided it did not clearly follow from a failure. When the expected order was flouted, resentment at the dashing of justified expectations could mount, as with Crookshank's series of junior offices in the 1930s and his bitter comments, when Financial Secretary to the Treasury, at being repeatedly passed over for promotion to the Cabinet.[26] A few of the junior offices carried specific responsibilities and gave greater prominence—one such post within the Board of Trade was the Minister of Mines, always a sensitive area in labour relations and exceptionally so during the 1920s. It was occupied with notable effectiveness first by Bridgeman and later by Lane-Fox; both were from gentry backgrounds, and both succeeded in coping with repeated attacks from Labour MPs by a combination of bluff good humour and a steady persistence with the task in hand. In 1926, Lane-Fox led for the government during the passage of the Eight Hours Bill, speaking several times in a crowded and contentious house and being congratulated by other MPs for 'having kept my end up without loss of temper'.[27]

Many holders of junior office hoped that it was the waiting-room for the arrival of the Cabinet express, but it could also be a limbo in which promising political careers ran out of momentum. Most promotions to junior office had resulted from the debating ability of the MP; this was certainly true of the appointments most widely expected in the 1924–29 parliament, such as Moore-Brabazon and Duff Cooper. However, once in office, the junior minister's contribution to debate could become almost nil: his voice would be heard only on the least contentious of matters, usually in an almost empty chamber; he would be given routine questions to answer and low-grade chores in committee stage; at best, he might be asked to speak in a few other debates, most of which were unlikely to be of much importance.

---

[25] N. Chamberlain to Irwin, 12 August 1928, Halifax MSS, C152/18/1/114a.
[26] Crookshank diary, 22 February and 24 November 1942.
[27] Lane-Fox to Irwin, 4 July 1926, Halifax MSS, C152/17/1/61.

Most junior ministers were not Privy Councillors, and did not enjoy the prestige or right of precedence in debate which that conferred. The majority of juniors stagnated in obscurity, the original reason for their advancement fading rapidly from the memory of the House. The very skill which had led to office was the least used whilst occupying it: eloquent disquisitions were not what the whips wanted from junior ministers, but rather sober brevity and the avoidance of controversy. Bridgeman observed that the junior cohort of the 1924–29 government 'did not appear very conspicuously deserving of rapid advance, possibly because few of them had much opportunity of showing their metal'.[28] The best that the juniors could do was to discharge their duties at Westminster competently, do the work asked of them in the anonymity of their department, and be the workhorses of Central Office for dull speeches in the provinces and as government spokesmen in by-elections—and even in the latter, the limelight would be taken by the Cabinet-rank big guns on their occasional forays. The departmental workload could be heavy and was often tedious,[29] and its ease and effectiveness depended upon the relationship with the senior civil servants, who were not always supportive as a new appointee tried to find his feet; in any case, their first loyalty and duty was to the minister in charge of the department. To add to all the other frustrations, junior ministers often found they had little influence within their department, and so were in the position of having to promote or defend cases with which they did not necessarily agree.

There was an element of the shuttlecock about junior office, and sideways changes of office became more frequent in the 1930s, and especially during the Second World War. The person who held the largest number of junior positions, J. J. Llewellin, had by no means the longest career. However, during eight years and one month, he occupied seven junior offices, most of them for around ten months. There was some element of progression in this, and, indeed, he had a brief taste of Cabinet rank—but not, in the war situation, of actual Cabinet membership—as President of the Board of Trade for eighteen days in February 1942; he later concluded his ministerial voyage of Ulysses as Minister of Food from November 1943 to July 1945. In a similar merry-go-round, Alan Lennox-Boyd passed through six junior positions in just six years and seven months. However, the most rapid turnover of all was that experienced by William Joynson-Hicks, with four posts during the eight months before he entered the Cabinet. He was junior minister at the Board of Trade from the fall of the Coalition in October 1922 to March 1923, when, in the stretched circumstances of the Bonar Law government, he was appointed to be simultaneously Postmaster-General and Paymaster-General; Baldwin made him Financial Secretary to the Treasury in May 1923, and from this expected jumping-off point he succeeded Neville Chamberlain when the latter moved from the Ministry of Health to be Chancellor of the Exchequer in August 1923.

---

[28] Bridgeman diary, 'July' 1929.
[29] For examples of the duties of junior ministers, see Crookshank diary, January 1935–September 1939, Headlam diary, January 1932–July 1934.

Not all of those appointed to junior office were being singled out as potential high-flyers: some appointments rewarded faithful service, such as those given to long-serving whips as the culmination of their careers. Some ministerial posts were well-known as political graveyards, and not only for the junior minister. This was especially true of the departments which did not have Cabinet status, or only intermittently, such as Pensions and Transport. The clearest example of becoming the ministerial equivalent of the 'Flying Dutchman' was George Tryon, who at seventeen years and nine months had by far the longest service at junior level. After five months as Under-Secretary for Air, he was junior minister at the Ministry of Pensions in 1920–22 and then the minister in the 1922–24, 1924–29, and 1931–35 governments, before a sideways move to become Postmaster-General from June 1935 to April 1940. He was then given a peerage and finally entered the safe harbour of the Cabinet as Chancellor of the Duchy of Lancaster—only to be cast out after forty days, following the formation of the Churchill Coalition. Tryon was transferred to another worthy backroom role as First Commissioner of Works until October 1940, when, in a grim example of political reincarnation, he became once again the junior minister at the Ministry of Pensions; perhaps not surprisingly, he dropped dead less than a month later. It was Headlam's misfortune to hold two of the most dismal junior posts in succession, at Pensions in 1931–32 and then at Transport in 1932–34, and he blamed this—to a large extent, correctly—for the ruin of his political ambitions. However, considering the number of likely candidates for junior office for whom room could not be found in the multi-party National Government, he was perhaps more fortunate than he appreciated to return to office at all, especially after having been out of the previous parliament.[30] Herbert Williams was amongst those who were not so lucky, and his career stalled in 1931, despite his success and competence in the 1924–29 parliament, when Winterton (who had been in the House since 1904) considered him 'the most successful man with facts and figures on trade and fiscal matters' since Bonar Law made his reputation in 1900–10.[31]

The junior ministers were not a cohesive body: they had common ground and might be of a similar age and intake, thus having friends and acquaintances amongst the other juniors, but they were also rivals for the chance to move upwards. However, they had a similarity of perspective and shared concerns, and in the course of their duties were in regular contact with each other in and around the Commons. Normally this resulted in nothing more than some grousing and gossip, and a perhaps valuable venting of frustrations in the privacy of the Smoking Room. On the rare occasions when they did act together, even if only as a network, it could have a considerable impact. When taking collective action they could act as, or appear to other MPs to be, the defenders of the mainstream position and of the party's core values and identity against a leadership that was neglecting or departing from them. This was reinforced by the fact that they were the level from which

---

[30] Baldwin to Wolmer, 11 November 1931, Wolmer MSS, MSS.Eng.hist.c.1013/59.
[31] Winterton to Irwin, 12 July 1928, N. Chamberlain to Irwin, 12 August 1928, Halifax MSS, C152/18/1/89a, 114a.

the party managers were drawn: the Chairman and Deputy Chairman of the Party, the senior whips and the Chief Whip. The close links between all of this 'middle tier' were demonstrated in the most famous example of collective action, the developing opposition in the summer of 1922 on the part of many Conservative junior ministers to continuing the Coalition under Lloyd George. This emerged after Younger's stand against an early election in January 1922, and they first began acting collectively during the concern over the Ulster boundary question in the following month.[32] It was cemented by the protest of Bridgeman, Winterton, and Wood over the honours list in June, which was echoed by some others; mainly on the initiative of Sanders, this developed into the holding of periodic unofficial meetings of junior ministers.[33] Some of them (including their senior figure, the Attorney-General, Ernest Pollock) still favoured continuing the Coalition, but the majority were becoming increasingly concerned about the position—especially by the swelling unrest in the constituencies. Sanders communicated this to Austen Chamberlain, and the Leader invited a number of the Law Officers, junior ministers, and whips 'to unburden ourselves candidly' in a meeting on 20 July with himself, a couple of less prominent Cabinet ministers, and the Chief Whip. The tone of the meeting was 'most pleasant and amicable', and there was no suggestion that the juniors' conduct was in any way improper or disloyal.[34] However, Chamberlain could give little reassurance, other than that matters should be left to him to discuss with his Cabinet colleagues.

The situation then drifted until the last days before the summer recess, with mounting concern on the part of the more restive junior ministers. The result was their request for a collective meeting with the party leaders, which Austen Chamberlain regarded as 'an unprecedented proceeding'.[35] When this was grudgingly held on 3 August, it made matters much worse. Chamberlain, who now seemed remote and unresponsive to the juniors' concerns, disastrously left most of the management of the meeting to Birkenhead. The latter was in his most overbearing and offensive form, his conduct such as to 'put presumptuous and wayward servants in their place'.[36] With Chamberlain failing to restrain or rebuke him, the result was that most of the juniors left the meeting 'spluttering in indignation', determined that Birkenhead should never lead the party, and alienated from the Coalition and the senior party leaders who supported it.[37] The hostility of the majority of the junior ministers was important in extending the parliamentary opposition beyond the predictable diehards, thus making it respectable and giving

[32] Bayford diary, 14 February 1922.
[33] Bridgeman diary, general entries '1922' and 'July 1922'.
[34] Pollock, 'Fall of the Coalition', Hanworth MSS, Eng.Hist.d.432/133–88; A. Chamberlain's notes, 'Conference with Under Secretaries of State', 20 July 1922, AC, 33/2/4; Bayford diary, 21 and 29 July 1922.
[35] E. Wood, 'Thoughts on some of the present discontents of the Conservative Party', not dated but marked 'early summer 1922', Halifax MSS (Borthwick), A4/410/9/1–13.
[36] Pollock, 'Fall of the Coalition', Hanworth MSS, Eng.Hist.d.432/133–88; Crawford diary, 3 and 12 August 1922.
[37] Amery diary, 3 August 1922; Bayford diary, 4 August 1922; Bridgeman diary, 'July 1922'; Wood to A. Chamberlain, draft letter, October 1922, Halifax MSS (Borthwick), A4/410/26/2.

it vital momentum in September and October 1922. However, the junior ministers did not resign their offices or move into open rebellion, and there were further meetings with Chamberlain and attempts to find a formula as late as 18 October.[38] The revolt only became a reality at the Carlton Club meeting the next day, in the votes which many of the juniors cast against their Leader's policy.[39]

Less well-known, and much more modest and circumspect, were the criticisms made by several junior ministers during Neville Chamberlain's government. There was a minor ripple of doubt at the time of Eden's resignation from Crookshank and Robert Bernays, a Liberal National, but they were readily soothed by a meeting with the Premier; later, the same pair's uncomfortableness about the Munich settlement was dealt with in a similar fashion.[40] The following months saw another stirring, purportedly of a larger group of juniors, although only Robert Hudson came into the open as their spokesman. The issue here was not Chamberlain's appeasement policy, for which they declared support, but the lack of drive in the rearmament programme. Under some pressure during meetings with the Prime Minister and the Chief Whip, Hudson named two peers, Lords Dufferin and Strathcona, as amongst the other juniors of like mind.[41] The complaint singled out several Cabinet ministers as ineffective, specifically Inskip, Winterton, Runciman, and Hore-Belisha (the first two were Conservatives, and the last two Liberal Nationals). However, whilst the leadership indicated some endorsement of these criticisms, only Winterton was dropped from the Cabinet—but not from the government, moving from Chancellor of the Duchy of Lancaster to Paymaster-General in January 1939. It is not clear how widespread or strong was this feeling amongst the juniors, and certainly those known to be involved backed down quite quickly. It was not so much a junior ministers' revolt as a complaint to the Leader intended to bypass the levels in-between. The desire to clear out ineffective ministers was not just confined to this instance, which had more in common with the widespread pressure in 1930–31 to drop the 'old gang' of long-serving frontbenchers than it did with the under-secretaries' revolt of 1922. At other times of crisis, junior ministers naturally congregated and gossiped with their existing friends; however, these gatherings were not politically significant, being a response to events rather than an attempt to mould them.[42]

---

[38] Amery diary, 16–18 October 1922; Bayford diary, 19 October 1922.

[39] Wilson to A. Chamberlain, 11 October, Wood to A. Chamberlain, 17 October, memo by A. Chamberlain, 18 October 1922, AC, 33/2/41–2, 84, 83. The meeting of 16 October was with Chamberlain, but he was not present at the following ones; that of 17 October was held in the Chief Whip's room, and Griffith-Boscawen was invited to attend. He was also present at a meeting of junior ministers on the morning of 18 October, whilst the final meeting at 10.00 p.m. that evening at Baldwin's house was more clearly of anti-Coalitionists, with Hoare and other senior backbenchers also present: memo by Griffith-Boscawen, 'The Break Up of the Coalition', n.d., Griffith-Boscawen MSS, c.396/121–2.

[40] Crookshank diary, 22–24 February, 30 September, 4–6 October 1938; Crookshank to N. Chamberlain, 23 February 1938, NC, 7/11/31/92; Headlam diary, 30 November 1938; Ball, *Guardsmen*, 190.

[41] Memo by Hudson, 12 December 1938, Halifax MSS (Borthwick), A4/410/22a; N. to H. Chamberlain, 11 December 1938, *NCDL*; Ball, *Guardsmen*, 193.

[42] Crookshank diary, 18–19 February 1942.

CABINET MINISTERS: SELECTION AND CONDUCT

The membership of the Cabinet was chosen by the incoming Prime Minister (normally the Party Leader), but with some advice. As the prospect of forming a government drew nearer, naturally the Party Leader began to consider possibilities. However, these often changed and had to be adapted to circumstances. Thus Baldwin's draft list of 31 October 1924 had Churchill down for the Board of Trade, Bridgeman or Hoare as Home Secretary, and Edward Wood as Minister of Labour; all of these went to other posts, whilst the eventual Minister of Labour, Steel-Maitland, was not on the list for any office.[43] When constructing the Cabinet a few days later, Baldwin asked Neville Chamberlain for his views on the selection of junior ministers and whips, and information on backbench opinion was gathered by Baldwin's PPS Sidney Herbert (though possibly on his own initiative).[44] It was customary and practical sense to consult the leader of the party in the Lords about appointments from that House, and Curzon told Baldwin that he had been consulted by Lloyd George and Bonar Law during their premierships.[45] The other crucial advisor was the Chief Whip, particularly about promotions to junior office and, of course, the choice of new whips. In the coalitions which were led by non-Conservatives, the Party Leader worked in close consultation with the Prime Minister; Bonar Law had considerable influence over appointments in 1916 and 1918, as did Baldwin in 1931 (when Austen Chamberlain succeeded Bonar Law in March 1921, the reshuffle was comparatively limited).

The constitutional theory was that the Prime Minister had an unfettered choice, but in practice this was subject to a number of restrictions. There was a need to construct a Cabinet which would carry authority in the view of the party and country, and this made the inclusion of most of the capable senior figures almost unavoidable—although one or two could be left out, especially if considered not quite reliable, such as Sir Robert Horne in 1924 or Amery in 1931.[46] Those who were appointed had to seem credible in their post from either experience or prestige, which was the problem when the Attorney-General, Sir Thomas Inskip, was made Minister for the Co-ordination of Defence in March 1936. There was also an expectation of balance, with different shades of opinion being represented, so that the decisions of the Cabinet would pull the party together rather than divide it. For this reason, only open and current rebellion, rejection of a major item in the manifesto on which the government was elected, or perhaps a known personal antagonism and incompatibility, were seen as valid reasons for excluding an otherwise weighty figure. Thus, there was no awkwardness about leaving Churchill out of the National Government in 1931, because he had quit the shadow cabinet and was known to be utterly opposed to the government's policy on India. Another

---

[43] Draft list of Cabinet appointments, 31 October 1924, Baldwin MSS, 42/192–6.
[44] N. Chamberlain to Baldwin, Herbert to Baldwin, 5 and [13] November 1924, Baldwin MSS, 42/243, 281–3.
[45] Curzon to Baldwin, 5 November 1924, Baldwin MSS, 42/239–42; Hailsham to Baldwin, 6 November 1931, Baldwin MSS, 45/205–6.
[46] Amery to Baldwin, 6 November 1931, Baldwin MSS, 45/201.

question of balance which was still considered was the representation of the most powerful regions, to avoid any of them feeling excluded and because Cabinet membership conferred additional prestige upon the party's leading figure in the area. After the formation of the 1924 Cabinet, Austen Chamberlain was 'a little anxious about Lancashire', as there was no Cabinet member from that region whilst there were four from Birmingham—a contrast that was particularly sensitive in relation to the long-standing difference of view between the two regions over protectionism.[47]

In the periods of coalition government, the most sensitive balance was that between their component parties. In both the Lloyd George (1918–22) and National (1931–40) governments, the Conservative share of places around the Cabinet table was notably smaller than their proportion of government MPs as a whole. This caused some resentment on the backbenches, which was often raised more by those who did not aspire to office than by those who did, and who might have felt their prospects diminished. However, the situation was maintained by the leadership, and, on the whole, accepted by their followers, in order to maintain the credibility of the smaller parties and thus the valuable electoral support which they could mobilize for all of the government's candidates. It was sometimes a problem that the minor parties lacked sufficient able and qualified ministers, and National Labour more or less faded away in 1935–37 for that reason. However, on becoming Prime Minister in 1937, Neville Chamberlain continued the policy of maintaining a balance of Cabinet representation between the component parties of the National Government, as its cross-party nature was still an electoral asset. The only time that resentment over the ministerial imbalance became serious was in the case of the Lloyd George Coalition in 1922, when the ministry had already lost much Conservative support for other reasons.

Churchill had limited room for manoeuvre in shaping his coalition Cabinet in 1940; he could sack the unpopular Hoare and get Simon out of the way by promoting him to the House of Lords as Lord Chancellor (summarily ejecting Inskip from the Woolsack in the process), whilst some minor figures had to be dropped to make room for the Labour entrants. However, only four 'anti-appeasers' were given ministerial posts, and Churchill had to include Chamberlain and Halifax as the other two Conservatives in his inner War Cabinet of five, together with two Labour leaders. At the outset in May 1940, the distribution of both War Cabinet and normal Cabinet-rank offices was in fairly close proportion to the number of Conservative MPs, but the party's position deteriorated from 1942 onwards. After the major reshuffle in February of that year, the seven members of the War Cabinet now comprised three Conservatives (Churchill, Eden, and Lyttelton), one non-party figure (Sir John Anderson), and three Labour figures. For the mainstream MPs on the Conservative benches, this slide in their party's numerical presence was compounded by the fact that none of the three Conservatives seemed to care for their views or represent their interests, and that all three in their various ways were mavericks, rebels, and interlopers.

---

[47] A. Chamberlain to Baldwin, 9 November 1924, Baldwin MSS, 42/270–1.

Table 6.3. Conservative Party share of Cabinet offices in coalition governments

This table analyses the position at the formation of coalitions and the major reshuffles afterwards. The calculation for 1940 and 1942 is not for the small War Cabinet, but for the twenty offices which were always of Cabinet rank in the peacetime governments. The figure for all government-supporting MPs in 1918 includes the fifty 'uncouponed' Conservatives and the two National Party MPs, and for 1931 and 1935 includes the two National Independent MPs. In 1940 and 1942, it is assumed that all MPs are nominally supporters of the government, with the sole exception of the one Communist MP in 1940.

	Con. MPs % of all govt. MPs	Con. % of Cabinet	Con. no. in Cabinet	Total no. in Cabinet	Prime Minister	Chanc. of Exch.	Foreign Secretary	Home Secretary
1919 January	73.1	55.0	11	20	L	Con	Con	L
1921 March	73.5	52.6	10	19	L	Con	Con	L
1931 August	78.8	40.0	4	10	Lab	Lab	L	L
1931 November	84.5	55.0	11	20	NLab	Con	LN	L
1932 September	84.5	68.4	13	19	NLab	Con	LN	Con
1935 November	89.8	68.2	15	22	Con	Con	Con	LN
1937 May	90.1	71.4	15	21	Con	LN	Con	Con
1940 May	61.1	55.0	11	(20)	Con	Con	Con	Nat
1942 February	61.0	45.0	9	(20)	Con	Con	Con	Lab

Party codes: Con = Conservative; L = Liberal; Lab = Labour; LN = Liberal National; NLab = National Labour; Nat = National.

The customary description of the Prime Minister as being 'first among equals' was more than misleading in its depiction of the status of the other Cabinet members, for this was anything but uniform. The most influence reposed with the traditional great offices of state: Chancellor of the Exchequer, Foreign Secretary, Home Secretary, Lord Chancellor, and Lord President of the Council. The middle tier consisted of the longer-established posts relating to the empire (Colonies and India) and the traditional armed services (Admiralty and War Office), the Board of Trade and the non-departmental office of Lord Privy Seal. The minor posts included the newer departments dealing with domestic affairs (Agriculture, Education, Health, and Labour), the infant armed service (Air), and the offices which were not automatically of Cabinet rank: Commissioner of Works, Chancellor of the Duchy of Lancaster, Minister of Transport, Postmaster-General. However, the economic and social domestic departments were more in the political limelight and gave greater opportunities—for both success and failure—to their ministers than many of the middle tier. Whilst the Admiralty and War Office had higher prestige, better salaries, and other benefits, in the interwar era of economies and disarmament, they were hardly exciting posts of opportunity. The non-departmental Cabinet posts were a useful means of including 'elder statesmen', not only for the prestige of their name but because they could make a valuable contribution in terms of experience, judgement, and skill in drafting statements or clauses—the latter was particularly a reason for appointing the elderly Balfour as Lord President of the Council in 1925, after the death of Curzon. In the case of selections for other offices, experience was not essential and moves from junior to Cabinet rank could involve a complete change of direction. The all-rounder and amateur traditions remained strong, and thus Bridgeman could be Home Secretary in one government and First Lord of the Admiralty in the next, or R. A. Butler take charge of education in 1941 after having spent almost the whole of the previous decade at the India and Foreign Offices.

One clear trend in Cabinet formation in the interwar period was the decline in the number of peers appointed, in comparison to their nearly half-share in the 1860s–70s and still significant role in the last prewar Conservative government of 1902–05. The proportion of peers in Bonar Law's Cabinet of 1922 was widely criticized as retrograde and out of tune with the new age of democracy. However, this was more a matter of perception than of reality: eight Conservative peers held Cabinet positions at some point in the 1922–24 government, which was only one more than the number who had done so during the life of the previous coalition ministry of 1918–22. On the other hand, fourteen Conservative MPs saw Cabinet service in 1922–24, whilst only ten had done so in 1918–22. Of course, in a coalition the Conservative Party's share of ministerial posts was inevitably restricted, but, nevertheless, no other interwar Cabinet had as high a proportion of peers amongst its Conservative members as did the Lloyd George Coalition of 1918–22. After the Conservative Party was reunited in 1924, the view of backbench MPs was 'that there should be as few peers as possible', and there were never again to be so many sitting at the Cabinet table at the same time.[48] Indeed, by the following year,

---

[48] Herbert to Baldwin, [13] November 1924, Baldwin MSS, 42/281–3.

a senior peer felt the pendulum had swung too far the other way, pointing out to Baldwin that only five out of the hundreds of hereditary peers were in a ministerial post of any rank.[49] In fact, during its longer life, ten peers were at some point members of the 1924–29 Cabinet, and the real reduction came after 1931. Only three Conservative peers held Cabinet office in the National Governments of August 1931 to June 1935; seven did so between the latter date and May 1940, but that was a government in which there was generally a greater turnover of posts—during the same period, there were also twenty-four Conservative MPs in Cabinet positions and forty-one in junior ministerial posts (including six Law Officers).

The oldest appointment of a Conservative Cabinet minister was Inskip, but this was only a week after his sixtieth birthday, and it followed eleven years of responsible service as a Law Officer. The other oldest entrants to the Cabinet room were Henry Betterton, aged fifty-nine, in 1931; Joynson-Hicks, aged fifty-eight, in 1923; and Bridgeman, aged fifty-seven, in 1922. The youngest by far was not a Conservative appointment at all: Churchill was promoted to Asquith's Cabinet in 1908 when he was only thirty-three, and then a member of the Liberal Party. The youngest Conservative appointed was Lord Eustace Percy, who became President of the Board of Education in 1924 at the age of thirty-seven, although he had only entered the House three years earlier. Four others became Cabinet ministers at thirty-eight: Cunliffe-Lister, Oliver Stanley, Eden, and (during the Second World War, in a post normally of Cabinet rank) Butler as education minister in 1941. Several of these early entrants also had some of the longest Cabinet careers: again, Churchill holds the record, with his combined service as a Liberal and a Conservative amounting to twenty-six years and eight months, including the two terms as Prime Minister. His near rival was Balfour, with twenty-five years and eight months, but after this there was a long gap to the other three who sat at the Cabinet table for more than fifteen years: Butler was a member for exactly seventeen years, Walter Long for sixteen years and two months, and Cunliffe-Lister for one month less, for part of which he was in the House of Lords.

Apart from Llewellin's fleeting occupancy of a post normally of Cabinet status in February 1942, the briefest actual Cabinet memberships were those of Tryon and Herwald Ramsbotham. They served alongside each other for only thirty-seven days, entering the Cabinet in Chamberlain's final reshuffle of 3 April 1940 and being dropped when Churchill constructed his small War Cabinet on 10 May, although Ramsbotham remained in his post as President of the Board of Education for a further fourteen months. The shortest peacetime Cabinet presence was that of Lord Stanley, who died only five months after his appointment as Dominions Secretary in May 1938. Political rather than physiological reasons were the cause of the brevity of five of the six other shortest tenures: Winterton was generally thought to be a weak link in an important post during his ten months in the Cabinet in 1938–39; Euan Wallace, a Chamberlainite who had held the minor post of Minister of Transport for thirteen months, was dropped in May 1940 to

---

[49] This included junior posts: Midleton to Baldwin, 28 March 1925, Baldwin MSS, 160/105–6.

Table 6.4. The career pattern of Conservative Cabinet ministers in
the House of Commons 1919–1945[50]

This table analyses all of the Conservative MPs who served as Cabinet ministers in the period 1919–45. For the Churchill Coalition of 1940–45, those included are all members of the War Cabinet and ministers in offices which in peacetime were always of Cabinet rank; the brief 'Caretaker' ministry of May to July 1945 is not included. If an MP also served in the Cabinet as a peer, this is included in the calculation of their length of service. Titles already held before appointment include courtesy titles (see the definition in Table 5.9); titles acquired during or after appointment include titles inherited as well as those created. Each person is counted only once in each category, but if an individual had honours in more than one category, they will be counted once in each category (e.g. where a person with a knighthood or baronetcy became a peer, or a person with a courtesy title inherited a peerage).

Age		21–9	30–9	40–9	50–9	60 +
Age first elected an MP		15	18	17	1	–
Age first appointed a junior minister		1	20	16	8	–
Age of attaining Cabinet rank		–	9	22	19	1

Length of service (years and months)	Less than 2 years	2.0 to 3.11	4.0 to 5.11	6.0 to 7.11	8.0 to 9.11	10.0 to 14.11	15 years & above
Cabinet ministers	11	9	9	5	3	9	5

Honours	Title before first appointment	Becomes knight or baronet	Becomes peer
Cabinet ministers	24	7	33

make room for the incoming Labour ministers; Margesson was sacked from the War Office in February 1942 after fourteen months, due to military setbacks and the need for another reshuffle; and Sanders and Montague Barlow were not considered successes during the fifteen-month duration of the 1922–24 government, and both lost their seats in the 1923 general election. The remaining case was Auckland Geddes, a businessman brought into the wartime government by Lloyd George. Whilst sitting as an MP, Geddes took the Conservative whip, but he was not a career politician; after a total of thirteen months in posts of Cabinet rank, he left parliament on appointment as Ambassador to the United States.

Despite the reduction of the peerage, the social background of Conservative Cabinet ministers tended to be even more reflective of the upper class than the parliamentary party as a whole; this can be seen from the analysis of their educational background, which can be taken as an indicator of their family's social position, in Table 6.5. However, this was not particularly due to snobbery—although an established family tradition of service to the state was certainly helpful—but to the fact that reaching the Cabinet was more likely for those who began their parliamentary careers relatively young and had the security of a safe seat; the prerequisites of these were personal or family wealth and social status, and probably both. An interruption to a parliamentary career could be damaging: Headlam, who

[50] Calculated from Butler and Butler, *Twentieth-Century British Political Facts*, and Stenton and Lees, *Who's Who of British Members of Parliament*, vols 3 and 4.

Table 6.5. The educational background of Conservative junior and Cabinet ministers[51]

SCHOOL	Eton	Harrow	Other public	Scots academy	Grammar school	At sea	Board school	Not known
Junior office only	16	6	23	3	5	1	1	2
Cabinet ministers	19	9	12	7	2	1	–	1

UNIVERSITY	Christ Church	Other Oxford	Trinity Camb.	Other Camb.	English univ.	Scottish univ.	Navy & military	Others
Junior office only	8	18	5	6	3	1	3	1
Cabinet ministers	6	14	8	5	–	4	4	2

might well have obtained a minor Cabinet post or a ministry outside the Cabinet if the Conservatives had won the 1929 election, always felt that his progress had suffered an irretrievable setback through being out of the 1929–31 parliament. When Sanders lost his seat in 1923, although he returned at the next election, he was no longer in the running for office—mainly because he had not shone in his previous post, but also partly because absence from the House had given him no opportunity to recover ground. It is difficult to estimate what proportion of the Cabinet were what might be termed 'career politicians' in the post-1945 sense of having no other career for most of their life and of being focused upon attaining high office. Many of those from aristocratic families with independent means and an early entrée to the House, such as Lord Burghley or the Marquess of Titchfield, did not have Cabinet careers. However, Viscounts Cranborne (later 5th Marquess of Salisbury) and Wolmer (later 3rd Earl of Selborne), whose fathers and grandfathers had been in the Cabinet, probably expected to follow in their footsteps. Others, not always from such exalted origins, were professional politicians in that politics was their foremost interest and the focus of their energies, such as Harold Macmillan, of the publishing firm, and Duff Cooper, who wrote books and kept up an extensive social life.

Drawing the leading figures from a restricted and homogeneous social elite brought certain advantages in empathy and co-operation. Winterton noted that the ministers in Bonar Law's government 'are nearly all personal friends and contemporaries at Eton, Oxford or Cambridge', with the result that 'the team work is better'; furthermore, Bridgeman considered that not having been at a public school or university had been 'a great drawback' for Worthington-Evans.[52] Over the whole interwar period, the atmosphere in Cabinet meetings and the personal relations between colleagues were generally good; there were frictions, of course, but these were usually veiled. Some were personal in basis, such as Derby's dislike of Curzon, and others the result of stress, frustration, or tiredness. Neville Chamberlain referred to 'the general raggedness of tempers that comes at the close of a very tiresome and

---

[51] Calculated from the entries in Stenton and Lees, *Who's Who of British Members of Parliament*, vols 3 and 4.
[52] Winterton to Lytton, 22 November 1922, Lytton MSS, F160/26/8–13; Bayford diary, 25 October 1922; Bridgeman diary, 'L. Worthington-Evans', November 1929.

weary session',[53] and of some meetings he told Baldwin (then visiting Canada) of 'hurried journeys to London to sudden Cabinets where resignations flew about like leaves in an autumn storm'.[54] However, this was not the norm, and should be seen in the context of Cabinets called in what should have been the relief of the holiday period after an exhausting year, which had included the General Strike. More frequent were the examples where working together in Cabinet improved relations and built respect, as in the case of the returned Coalitionists (especially Birkenhead) after 1924; when the latter retired in 1928, he considered the Cabinet had become 'a band of brothers'.[55] Similar feelings developed across party boundaries in the National Governments of 1931–40, such as Neville Chamberlain's respect for Walter Runciman. However, there was little such warmth for Coalition Liberal colleagues in 1918–22, apart perhaps for Hamar Greenwood, who occupied the unenviable post of Chief Secretary for Ireland from April 1920 to October 1922 (and who was to take Churchill's route as a 'Constitutionalist' into the Conservative ranks in 1924).

Members of the Cabinet were fully occupied with their ministerial duties, and Cabinet meetings were 'a scramble to get through an agenda', in which the focus was inevitably short term and departmentally oriented.[56] The usual role of the Cabinet was to support a minister in his decisions, rather than being asked to make them for him.[57] As Amery noted in 1928, 'most of us in the Cabinet have our own individual battles to fight and are reluctant to raise controversy on general issues'.[58] There was little time for looking ahead or thinking about wider strategies—it was the latter, as much as their departmental work, which distinguished both Churchill and Neville Chamberlain in 1924–29. Even such a capable and successful minister as Hoare noted that 'it is very difficult to get out of the rut of departmental and Cabinet business'.[59] Relatively minor measures could require a lot of attention and sometimes produced unexpected difficulties; for example, Cunliffe-Lister had 'a tough time' with the committee stage of the Films Bill in 1927.[60] During the latter part of the 1924–29 ministry, several of the Cabinet were exhausted and unwell; as one Cabinet minister observed in 1934, 'government is so complex and the pressures are such' that it 'wears down the strongest'.[61] Even in a period without a looming crisis, a Cabinet meeting could involve '4½ hours of strain'.[62] In addition,

[53] N. Chamberlain to Irwin, 25 August 1927, Halifax MSS, C152/17/1/249a.
[54] N. Chamberlain to Baldwin, 22 August 1927, Baldwin MSS, 162/65–6.
[55] Birkenhead to Baldwin, 16 October 1928, Birkenhead MSS, D703/44; on Austen Chamberlain, see Hailsham to Baldwin, 27 August 1928, Baldwin MSS, 163/142–3.
[56] Amery, *The Forward View*, 443.
[57] Balfour to Baldwin, 10 January 1927, Balfour MSS, Add.49694/6–8.
[58] Amery to Baldwin, 11 July 1928, Baldwin MSS, 30/66–70.
[59] Hoare to Irwin, 22 June 1927, Halifax MSS, C152/17/1/232b. For examples of workload, see Steel-Maitland, 'My Day's Work', *Home and Politics in Erdington*, August 1926, Steel-Maitland MSS, GD193/993; Joynson-Hicks memo, 'A Day in the Life of a Cabinet Minister', 25 July 1928; and Joynson-Hicks to Baldwin, 24 August 1928, Joynson-Hicks MSS, 1/1, 2/1.
[60] Winterton to Irwin, 26 August 1927, Halifax MSS, C152/17/1/249d.
[61] Ormsby-Gore to his mother, n.d. but in envelope postmarked 18 June 1934, Ormsby-Gore MSS, PEC/10/1/14/26; Bridgeman to Hoare, 4 September 1928, Templewood MSS, V/3. There were similar periods of illness in the 1930s, such as Neville Chamberlain's gout in July 1936.
[62] Ormsby-Gore to Eden, c.15 April 1935, Avon MSS, AP/14/1/491.

frontbenchers were regularly in demand as speakers at public meetings and party gatherings.[63] Their workload and responsibility separated the Cabinet ministers from ordinary MPs and even from the junior ministers, and was a contributory factor to the cohesion of the leadership in Cabinet. Team spirit and a sense of collegiality were, in fact, the normal condition, with well-informed junior ministers commenting that the 1924–29 Cabinet—which had been constructed from both sides of the coalition rift—was 'a happy family' and 'singularly free from serious internecine struggles and rivalries'.[64] This did not mean there was a lack of different perspectives or debate; as Neville Chamberlain noted in 1927: 'It is quite extraordinary how few subjects there are upon which we are unanimous and the divisions have sometimes been rather sharp.'[65] Cabinet discussion acted as a restraint upon the independence of ministers, as 'you cannot go further than your colleagues wish'; this might dampen initiative but it reinforced the most crucial element—unity.[66]

There was considerable continuity in office within a Cabinet, and, indeed, Baldwin prided himself on the lack of changes during the 1924–29 ministry. Once appointed, a Cabinet minister could expect to have security of tenure for the rest of the parliament or until the retirement of the Prime Minister. The latter was the main cause of Cabinet reshuffles, as in June 1935 and May 1937, whilst larger changes were needed in May 1940 to make room for Labour and Liberal ministers. Baldwin considered reshaping the Cabinet before the 1929 election, but in the end opted for the traditional course of waiting until afterwards (when defeat made such plans irrelevant). Otherwise, changes to more than an individual position were rare and usually the consequence of a vacant senior position causing a series of promotions, as was the case when Austen Chamberlain left the Treasury on becoming Party Leader in March 1921. There were several points at which there was such extensive or significant change in the Cabinet leadership as to amount to a change of generations. The first of these was the displacement of the Edwardian leadership in the fall of the Coalition in 1922, which capped the departures when Bonar Law first stood down in March 1921. Only four members of the Coalition Cabinet continued into Bonar Law's ministry: Curzon and Earl Peel (a recent appointment as India Secretary) in the Lords, and Baldwin and Griffith-Boscawen in the Commons.[67] Whilst several of the ousted figures returned to the Cabinet in 1924, neither they—nor Lord Curzon—carried the same weight again. The group which rose to prominence in 1922 departed the stage in three waves: the older figures between the elections of 1929 and 1931, some on Baldwin's retirement in 1937, and others when Chamberlain fell in 1940. The general election of 1945 also broke

---

[63] Steel-Maitland to Davidson, 20 February 1930, Steel-Maitland MSS, GD193/120/3/64.
[64] The first quote is from Lane-Fox to Irwin, 19 August 1926, and the second from Winterton to Irwin, 12 July 1928, Halifax MSS, C152/17/1/85, C152/18/1/89a.
[65] N. Chamberlain to Irwin, 25 August 1927, Halifax MSS, C152/17/1/249a.
[66] Hoare to Irwin, 17 November 1927, Halifax MSS, C152/17/1/249a.
[67] Bonar Law also sought to recruit two former prominent Cabinet ministers, Milner and McKenna, but the former declined on grounds of age and a suitable seat could not be found for the latter: Milner to Craven, 24 December 1922, Milner MSS, 50/252.

a swathe of careers; some were resumed quickly, like Macmillan and Richard Law, but others did not return, such as Amery and Henry Willink.

Progress up the Cabinet hierarchy was due to steady competence more than spectacular successes.[68] It depended less on making an impression on the public or even the House, and more upon impressing colleagues over a period of time; after a decade of Cabinet membership, it was Neville Chamberlain's view that 'it is by what a man is in Cabinet, rather than by what he is as a Departmental chief, that Ministers are ultimately weighed and assessed'.[69] For this reason, ministers who headed departments that were less in the public eye could rise in standing both by their general efficiency and the effectiveness of their contributions to discussion. Thus, whilst Douglas Hogg earned respect for his skilful handling of the Trade Union Bill in 1927, he also 'has become one of the most influential Members of the Cabinet by sheer force of character'.[70] Qualities of dependability and judgement could be more evident in Cabinet than on the floor of the House, and this explains the retention or promotion of some unimpressive parliamentary performers. Cunliffe-Lister's manner irritated MPs, but he was described by Neville Chamberlain as 'very quick and clever...one of our best administrators', and was chosen as one of the four Conservative members of the emergency National Cabinet in August 1931.[71] In 1924 the National Farmers' Union pressed for the retention of Sanders as Minister of Agriculture, even though he did not always succeed in debate, because 'they liked dealing with him as he is such a good chap and so straight and reliable'.[72] Acting with sensitivity—especially in dealing with important interest groups—when it was necessary to be negative was as important as originality or taking initiatives, for ministers have to say 'no' more often than 'yes'. An example of how to create difficulties was the friction between Walter Guinness as Minister of Agriculture and the National Farmers' Union in the late 1920s; as Hoare remarked 'if only...he could be a little less brutal in saying no to impracticable proposals, I believe that his course would be a good deal easier'.[73]

CABINET MINISTERS: SUCCESS AND FAILURE

The four individuals who rose to become Leader of the Party during this period of course had previously held important Cabinet positions: Austen Chamberlain, Baldwin, and Neville Chamberlain were serving as Chancellor of the Exchequer when they became Leader, and Churchill had held the same office, although he did not attain the leadership until over a decade afterwards. Discussion in this section

---

[68] N. Chamberlain to Irwin, 15 August 1926, Halifax MSS, C152/17/1/82a.
[69] N. Chamberlain to Duff Cooper, 23 November 1935, Duff Cooper MSS, CAC, DUFC/2/1.
[70] N. Chamberlain to Irwin, 25 August 1927, Halifax MSS, C152/17/1/249a.
[71] N. Chamberlain to Irwin, 25 December, 25 August 1927, Halifax MSS, C152/17/1/277a, 249a.
[72] Pretyman to Baldwin, n.d. [November 1924], Baldwin MSS, 42/245–6.
[73] Hoare to Irwin, 17 November 1927, Halifax MSS, C152/17/1/267c; Bridgeman diary, 'Walter Guinness', November 1929.

focuses upon the most prominent figures who did not become Leader (or who did so after 1945); it considers the most significant or controversial Cabinet ministers—both successes and failures—and is followed by an examination in greater depth of two of the most important examples: the Earl of Halifax and Sir Samuel Hoare.

Seven of the figures from the party's Edwardian leadership were still influential at the end of the First World War. As well as the Leader of the Party, Bonar Law, and his successor in March 1921, Austen Chamberlain, these were Walter Long, Birkenhead, Curzon, Derby, and the previous Leader and former Prime Minister, Balfour. Long came from old-established Wiltshire gentry and had a public image as the last hurrah of the traditional squire; in fact, although his appearance and sometimes choleric manner suggested such a caricature, he was an effective administrator, but was regarded by his colleagues as inconstant and inclined to intrigue. He had an important influence on Irish policy in 1919–20, but he suffered severe back pain which rendered him almost immobile, and he retired from the Cabinet a month before Bonar Law, in February 1921. A former Viceroy, Curzon became Foreign Secretary in 1919; his ability was acknowledged but the arrogance and pomposity of his manner offended many, including the Cabinet colleagues whom he rebuked if they strayed anywhere near to foreign affairs; the opposition in the Cabinet which effectively blocked him from becoming Prime Minister in May 1923 was mainly due to these personal frictions. Curzon never recovered from the bitter disappointment of being passed over, and his diplomatic reputation declined in 1923 during the Ruhr crisis. Baldwin was determined that he should not return to the Foreign Office in the 1924 government, and Curzon's position was now so weak that—despite his usual protests—he accepted a non-departmental office; however, he held this for only a few months, as he died in March 1925.[74]

Two of the most important voices against Curzon's accession were Balfour and Derby. The former's role after 1919 was that of an 'elder statesman', contributing judgement and experience to the Cabinet; he supported the Coalition in 1922, although in more moderate terms than Chamberlain or Birkenhead, and perhaps even more than them disliked the loss of standing in the party that resulted. In December 1923 he refused to support any intrigue against Baldwin, and rejoined the shadow cabinet with his colleagues in February 1924 at the age of seventy-six. His committee and drafting skills were still such that Baldwin invited him to become Lord President of the Council on Curzon's death in March 1925, and, although increasingly frail, he served until the 1929 election; he died in March 1930. The 17th Earl of Derby's importance was due mainly to his position as undisputed leader of the party in Lancashire, and he worked hard to maintain this.[75] Derby was inclined to be deferential to the Party Leader or Prime Minister, and was known for his malleability by more forceful personalities: from wartime experience, Field-Marshal Haig acutely observed that Derby 'like the feather pillow bears the mark of the last person who sat on him'.[76] The few occasions when Derby

---

[74] Baldwin to Curzon, 5 November 1924, Curzon MSS, F112/319/157–8.
[75] Derby to Beaverbrook, 5 November 1924, Derby MSS, 33.
[76] Lord Beaverbrook, *Men and Power 1917–1918* (1956), xvi.

was assertive were impelled by strong regional opinion in Lancashire, such as his advice to Baldwin in September 1930 to resign the leadership. More typical of his conduct was that after opposing an election in the Cabinet meeting of 13 November 1923; by the evening, he was writing a letter to Baldwin apologising for 'my little outburst' and giving assurances of 'support to the best of my ability when the time comes', and a similar pattern was repeated in 1930 and 1931.[77]

When the postwar Coalition Cabinet was formed in January 1919, the Attorney-General, F. E. Smith, was promoted to Lord Chancellor, taking the title of Baron Birkenhead (this was raised to a viscountcy in 1921, and an earldom in 1922). Together with his friend Churchill and the Prime Minister, he came to epitomize for many the worst aspects of the Coalition—cynical, unprincipled, ambitious, and operating in a moral vacuum and a constant atmosphere of intrigue. His outstanding abilities of destructive power in debate, analysis, and draftsmanship were universally acknowledged, but they were balanced by the hostility his manner provoked and the effects of his increasingly evident alcoholism, which made him 'a piteous figure...fuddled, reeling, dragging his dignity and his manhood into the dirt'.[78] Incidents of drunkenness had turned MPs against him before the Coalition fell, and in February 1922 Baldwin noted that because of it 'he has done for himself so far as his chances of the leadership go'.[79] Birkenhead's virulence after the fall of the Coalition confirmed this hostility, and wounding phrases such as the dismissal of Bonar Law's Cabinet as 'the second eleven' were deeply resented.[80] His unpopularity was compounded by his controversial Rectoral Address at Glasgow in 1923, which spoke of the 'glittering prizes' going to those with 'stout hearts and sharp swords' and produced a hostile reaction even from traditionalist Conservatives such as Ronald McNeill (who called it 'abominable') and Lord Bledisloe, who described it as 'the gospel of sordid, self-assertive greed (and contempt for the under-dog)'.[81] More importantly, it was considered that he was a liability with women voters, and in 1924 Lord Salisbury described him as 'disreputable', and criticized 'his crude attachment to the interests of wealth'.[82] He was readmitted to the shadow cabinet principally because Austen Chamberlain felt obligated to him and to make reunion complete, but relations improved as his new colleagues came to recognize his talents; Bridgeman noted that 'he would come to a morning meeting looking perfectly shattered, & suddenly produce the most lucid contribution of the day'.[83] Birkenhead served as India Secretary in Baldwin's second government, and declined the offer of the Lord Chancellorship on Cave's retirement in March 1928.[84] However, seven

[77] Derby to Baldwin, 13 November 1923, 29 April 1931, Baldwin MSS, 42/132, 166/116.
[78] Davidson memo of conversation with Birkenhead, n.d. but *c.*January 1927, Davidson MSS, DAV/180; Gibbs to Long, 18 March 1921, Long MSS, Add.62426/33–8.
[79] Baldwin to Fry, 11 February 1922, *BP*, 62.
[80] Derby to Younger, 13 November, to Salvidge, 17 November 1922, Derby MSS, 31/8, 8/8.
[81] McNeill to Baldwin, 12 November 1923, Baldwin MSS, 42/133–4; Bledisloe to Baldwin, 31 January 1924, Baldwin MSS, 159/183–4.
[82] Salisbury to Baldwin, 26 January 1924, Baldwin MSS, 159/258–61.
[83] Bridgeman diary, 'F.E. Smith, Earl of Birkenhead', November 1929.
[84] Birkenhead to Irwin, 29 March 1928, Halifax MSS, C152/4/12.

months later, in an amicable separation, he left the ministry in order to make money from journalism and in the City; this was despite the fact that the loss of his income from writing newspaper articles after taking office in 1924 had been compensated by a secret payment of £10,000 from party funds.[85] His wife commented 'he has expensive tastes'; drink remained a serious problem, and was the main cause of his death in September 1930 at the age of fifty-eight.[86]

One figure rose swiftly during the Coalition and fell with it: the Scottish businessman Sir Robert Horne was appointed Minister of Labour immediately after entering the Commons at the 1918 election, then became President of the Board of Trade, and, from April 1921 to the end of the Coalition, Chancellor of the Exchequer. He made a rapid impression, and was favoured by some MPs as the possible successor to Bonar Law in March 1921. Although a supporter of the Coalition, he was offered the Treasury by Baldwin in May 1923, but declined for personal and business reasons.[87] Derby, Jackson, and Younger thought of him as a possible replacement for Baldwin after the 1923 defeat.[88] Perhaps because of this, when the latter returned to power in 1924, it appeared that he did not want Horne in the Cabinet; Baldwin rather clumsily offered him the less attractive post of Minister of Labour, which was declined.[89] Horne remained in the Commons until 1937 and was respected by many MPs, especially those with business connections; he gave valuable support to Baldwin at the party meetings of 1930, and was one of his four potential successors in March 1931.

The fall of the Coalition brought into the Cabinet a group who dominated it until 1929, and in many cases until 1940. These included William Bridgeman, a particular ally of Baldwin's who persuaded him not to quit the leadership in March 1931; sometimes underrated at first by the quicker minds, they came to acknowledge that 'his judgement was very good and he could always be relied upon to get a common-sense view of the man in the street'.[90] He was an effective Home Secretary in 1922–24 and considered one of the successes of that ministry, and remained an influential voice in Baldwin's second government of 1924–29, holding the less prominent post of First Lord of the Admiralty. Another respected figure was the 4th Marquess of Salisbury, who was less abrasive and considered to have better judgement than his younger brothers Lord Robert and Lord Hugh Cecil. He had a strong position in the House of Lords, where he was Leader from 1925 until a combination of health and diverging views over India led him to step down quietly in 1931. Between 1933 and 1935 Salisbury emerged as the most significant and influential opponent of the India policy, although for several months he was

---

[85] Midland Bank to Jackson, 9 November 1926, Davidson MSS, DAV/179; J. Campbell, *F.E. Smith, 1st Earl of Birkenhead* (1983), 717–20, 804–6.
[86] N. Chamberlain to Irwin, 25 August 1927, Halifax MSS, C152/17/1/249c.
[87] Horne to Baldwin, 25 May 1923, Baldwin MSS, 42/29–30.
[88] Younger to Baldwin, 8 December 1923, Baldwin MSS, 35/179–82; Derby diary, 17 December 1923.
[89] Cazalet diary, 21 November 1924.
[90] Davidson memo of conversation with Birkenhead, n.d. but c.January 1927, Davidson MSS, DAV/180.

restrained by his membership of the Joint Select Committee, which was examining the bill. Salisbury was again influential in the crisis of May 1940, in which his 'Watching Committee' of elder statesmen played a part.

Salisbury's successor in 1931 as leader of the party in the House of Lords was Douglas Hogg, 1st Viscount Hailsham, who made his name as Attorney-General in the 1922–24 government; Bonar Law regarded him as 'a real discovery'.[91] Hogg returned to the same office in 1924, now as a member of the Cabinet, until—in a decision taken quickly, which he almost immediately regretted—he accepted the Lord Chancellorship in 1928.[92] His debating ability, personality, and centre-right views made him the most likely successor to Baldwin between 1927 and 1931; the latter thought Hailsham was 'first-rate and stuffed with character', whilst in Neville Chamberlain's view 'he has all the qualities of a great leader'.[93] By the summer of 1930, with Baldwin's position crumbling, it was widely accepted that Hailsham 'commands the confidence of the Party'.[94] He spoke very effectively in support of Baldwin on several critical occasions, in particular at the October 1930 party meeting and in the debate on India at the Central Council meeting of June 1933. However, their relationship cooled in the spring and summer of 1931, with Baldwin harbouring suspicions that Hailsham had been plotting against him in the March crisis, whilst in June, at a shadow cabinet meeting, Hailsham called rather pointedly for more assertive leadership.[95] The result was that he was not included in the August 1931 emergency Cabinet, although many assumed that Hailsham would be an automatic choice for one of the four Conservative places. The explanation offered in some quarters, including by Baldwin, was that MacDonald had blocked the appointment, but shortly afterwards the Prime Minister privately denied this and stated that Hailsham had not been put forward by the Conservative Leader.[96] As the former Labour Lord Chancellor, Lord Sankey, was continuing in office, when Hailsham was brought into the normal-sized Cabinet formed in October 1931, it was at the relatively unimportant War Office, where he remained until 1935. Although he was not a heavyweight figure in this Cabinet, Hailsham's presence in the National Government was a reassurance to the centre-right of the party—and, like them, he accepted its policy over India.[97] He served again as Lord Chancellor from 1935 until March 1938, moving from that office due to declining health, and retiring entirely from the Cabinet seven months later.

[91] Bonar Law to Curzon, 24 January 1923, Bonar Law MSS, BL/111/12/60: memoir by Brittain, 'The House of Commons', n.d., Brittain MSS, 12.
[92] N. Chamberlain diary, 28 March 1928, NC, 2/22.
[93] Baldwin to Irwin, 15 September 1927, N. Chamberlain to Irwin, 12 August 1928, Halifax MSS, C152/17/253f, C152/18/1/114a; Derby to N. Chamberlain, 25 February 1931, NC, 8/10/21.
[94] Peel to Baldwin, 22 August 1930, Taylor (chairman, Macclesfield CA) to Remer, 3 November 1930, Baldwin MSS, 104/42, 31/193–6.
[95] N. Chamberlain diary, 11 March 1931, NC, 2/22; Lockhart diary, 10 June 1931, K. Young (ed.), *The Diaries of Sir Robert Bruce Lockhart*, vol. 1: *1915–1938* (1973), 171; there was a suggestion that Baldwin was jealous and afraid of Hailsham as a potential rival: Amery diary, 30 August 1931.
[96] For the general view, see Hilton Young to his wife, 24 August 1931, Kennet MSS, 107/3; for MacDonald's denial, passed on by Beaverbrook, see N. Chamberlain diary, 3 September 1931, NC, 2/22.
[97] Stonehaven to Baldwin, 14 May 1933, Baldwin MSS, 106/75–7.

The efficient Philip Cunliffe-Lister (the surname was adopted in place of Lloyd-Greame in 1924, after a legacy) was a mainstay of the interwar governments and beyond, as President of the Board of Trade in 1922–24, 1924–29, and the first National Cabinet of 1931, Colonial Secretary in 1931–35, and then (after taking a peerage as Viscount Swinton) Air Minister. His position in the Lords made it hard to counter criticisms over the pace of rearmament and, lacking signs of support from Chamberlain, he resigned in May 1938. His 'unfortunate manner in the House' made him unpopular with the backbenchers, although his administrative competence was acknowledged.[98] He was always more respected by his Cabinet colleagues, and his career resumed under Churchill, who put him in charge of the Home Security Executive in May 1940 and then appointed him Minister Resident in West Africa in 1942–44, Minister of Civil Aviation in 1944–45, and, during his second premiership, Minister of Materials in 1951–52 and Commonwealth Secretary in 1952–55, making this the longest Cabinet career of any interwar Conservative. However, it was twice nearly nipped in the bud, firstly in 1925 when Cunliffe-Lister felt obliged to resign over a potential conflict of interest due to his wife's ownership of shares in coal mines, but was talked out of this by Baldwin and other colleagues, and secondly by serious illness whilst on an official visit to Kenya in 1934.[99]

Even more busy, though to less effect, was Leo Amery, who served as First Lord of the Admiralty in 1922–24, Colonial and Dominions Secretary in 1924–29, and later—after his own spell 'in the wilderness' during the 1930s—as India Secretary in Churchill's wartime coalition from 1940 to 1945. He was the most committed bearer of the torch of Joseph Chamberlain's ideals of tariff reform and imperial unity—certainly more vigorously and consistently than either of the latter's sons, Austen and Neville.[100] This was also part of the reason for his lack of success, as he was regarded as a faddist on this issue, and lacking in breadth of outlook. Amery was blind to this, bombarding Baldwin with lengthy letters urging protectionism (which led some, incorrectly, to blame him as the instigator of the 1923 tariff policy) and intervening frequently in Cabinet, to diminishing effect: 'in the Cabinet he is listened to with undisguised impatience and in the House he does not seem to carry much weight'.[101] His lack of height was sometimes mentioned as diminishing his impact, but his personality and approach played the larger part; as Neville Chamberlain observed, 'he has no sense of proportion and insists on little points with the same exasperating pertinacity as on big ones'.[102]

Three Conservatives held important positions in the 1931–35 National Government, but not thereafter. The most senior was John Gilmour, who became a whip in 1913 and entered the Cabinet as Scottish Secretary in 1924–29, where he was hard-working, capable, and 'won respect from all sides by straightforwardness

---

[98] Glyn, note on Cabinet ministers' reputations, n.d. but *c.*April–May 1934, Glyn MSS, D/EGL/O95/5.
[99] Hilton Young to his wife, 31 January 1934, Kennet MSS, 107/4.
[100] Amery to Baldwin, 22 March 1928, Baldwin MSS, 30/63.
[101] N. Chamberlain to Irwin, 15 August 1926, Halifax MSS, C152/17/1/82a.
[102] N. Chamberlain to Irwin, 15 August 1926, Halifax MSS, C152/17/1/82a.

in speech and conduct'.[103] Birkenhead, a shrewd judge of his Cabinet colleagues, rated him as 'surprisingly good' in 1927.[104] Appointed Minister of Agriculture in 1931, Gilmour became Home Secretary when the Samuelite Liberals withdrew from the National Government in September 1932. His success in the post surprised some MPs who did not know him, and his steadiness and courtesy saw him through difficult legislation such as the Betting Bill of 1934, where another might have run aground; he was one of the clearest interwar examples of that most desirable of Cabinet virtues, the safe pair of hands. In June 1935 he made way so that the Liberal National Leader, Sir John Simon, could be moved from the Foreign Secretaryship with minimal loss of face. However, Gilmour was later recalled to office as Minister of Shipping in 1939, and was in that post when he died suddenly in March 1940 at the age of sixty-three. The second of this trio was Henry Betterton, who had been junior minister at the Ministry of Labour in 1924–29 and held the Cabinet post from 1931 to 1934; he was thoroughly competent in his field and 'has the sincere respect of the whole House'.[105] He was considered the ideal person to chair the new Unemployment Assistance Board and retired from the House to do so in June 1934, receiving a peerage a few months later; the debacle which followed the Board's introduction of lower benefit rates in January 1935 was blamed mainly upon his successor, Oliver Stanley. The third figure was Edward Hilton Young, who, as Minister of Health in 1931–35, began the ambitious but controversial slum clearance programme. First elected as a Liberal MP in 1915 and serving as Chief Whip of the Lloyd George Liberals in 1922–23, he joined the Conservative Party immediately after the General Strike; he had served with distinction in the navy during the war, losing an arm, and in 1922 married the sculptress Kathleen Scott (the widow of Scott of the Antarctic), who was a friend and confidant of Baldwin. His record was more mixed: he was respected in Cabinet and considered an effective administrator of this key domestic department, but his 'failure to put anything across the footlights' meant that 'he has no appeal whatsoever to the House or to the general public', and he was dropped in the reshuffle of June 1935.[106]

The other Conservatives who advanced to prominence in the National Governments after 1931 had been marked out as the most promising new MPs and junior ministers of 1924–29. The highest rise was that of Anthony Eden, in a career entirely in foreign affairs. He had been Austen Chamberlain's PPS in 1926–29, then junior minister at the Foreign Office in the National Government to January 1934, when he became Lord Privy Seal with responsibility for League of Nations affairs—a role formally recognized when he entered the Cabinet in June 1935. Youthful and glamorous, he was the obvious choice to restore confidence

---

[103] Bridgeman diary, 'Sir J. Gilmour', November 1929.
[104] Davidson memo of conversation with Birkenhead, n.d. but c.January 1927, Davidson MSS, DAV/180.
[105] Glyn, note on Cabinet ministers' reputations; Somervell journal, 4 March 1934, Somervell MSS, MSS.Eng.c.6565/24.
[106] Glyn, note on Cabinet ministers' reputations; N. Chamberlain to Hilton Young, 9 June 1935, Kennet MSS, 16/12; Headlam diary, 25 July 1933.

after the Hoare–Laval Plan disaster, and he became Foreign Secretary in December 1935.[107] Disagreements with Neville Chamberlain led him to resign in February 1938, and, although he did not launch attacks on the government, this identified him as an 'anti-appeaser'—to his later great advantage. When Churchill became Party Leader in October 1940 it was already clear that Eden was the heir apparent, although he had a long and eventually frustrating wait for the inheritance until 1955; in-between he was again Foreign Secretary from December 1940 to July 1945 and during Churchill's second premiership in 1951–55, and also Leader of the House from November 1942 to the end of the war. However, the first of this group to make a significant mark in the 1930s was the Scottish doctor Walter Elliot, who, as Minister of Agriculture in 1932–36, introduced the marketing boards which began to improve the economic state of parts of the agricultural sector.[108] He was one of those often mentioned as a possible future Leader of the Party, but after service as Scottish Secretary in 1936–38 and Minister of Health from May 1938 to May 1940, his ministerial career ended with the fall of Chamberlain. Together with Duff Cooper and Oliver Stanley, he threatened to resign during the Czech crisis in September 1938, but—like Stanley—he vacillated and swallowed his doubts; as one Cabinet colleague noted, 'it was quite clear that he would agree to anything'.[109] By late July 1940, Elliot had realized that 'the nation is sore' and 'a very strong wind blows against the ex-Ministers…we may be out for a very long time'.[110]

The other rising star of the late 1920s and early 1930s almost shared the same fate, but had better connections and—probably more importantly—showed greater potential for making trouble. The younger son of the Earl of Derby, Oliver Stanley's privileged background gave him the great advantages of an early entry to parliament, a famous name and connections—on entering the House he at once became PPS to Lord Eustace Percy—but it was his evident ability that led to his advance. He was one of the 'YMCA' left-wing group in his first parliament of 1924–29, and whilst an effective debater his unorthodox views led to 'the risk of earning the reputation of being a crank'.[111] After serving as junior minister at the Home Office in 1931–33, he was a success as Minister of Transport and then entered the Cabinet as Minister of Labour in June 1934. In the early 1930s, he was considered by many to be a likely future Leader of the party.[112] However, his loss of nerve and mishandling of the crisis over unemployment benefit reductions in February 1935 raised doubts which were never really dispelled, and in June 1935 he was moved to a less exposed position as President of the Board of Education.[113] He advanced again to take charge

---

[107] Campbell to Baldwin, 16 November 1935, Baldwin MSS, 41/38.
[108] Newton to Baldwin, 15 November 1933, Baldwin MSS, 168/33.
[109] Inskip diary notes, 17 September 1938, Inskip MSS, CAC, INKP/1/1.
[110] Elliot to his wife, 20 July 1940, Elliot MSS, 7/1.
[111] Lane-Fox to Irwin, 26 May 1927, Halifax MSS, C152/17/1/223; Headlam diary, 8 February 1927.
[112] Headlam diary, 25 September 1930, 3 March, 11 July 1933.
[113] Crookshank diary, 28 January–11 February 1935; Elliot to his wife, 6 February 1935, Elliot MSS, 7/1; Headlam diary, 20 January, 6 and 8 February

of the Board of Trade when Chamberlain became Prime Minister, but the latter amazed many—and contributed substantially to the erosion of confidence in his judgement—when he switched Stanley to the War Office in January 1940. It was felt by some that 'it is his weakness which has been his chief recommendation in the eyes of the PM',[114] although a more charitable view was that 'the French would be pleased, and the Stanley tradition was popular with the Army'.[115] Stanley gave 'a shocking performance, luke-warm and ineffectual', when delivering the crucial winding-up speech for the government on the first day of the Norway debate in May 1940, and few can have been surprised when he was summarily removed upon Churchill becoming Prime Minister three days later.[116] However, when in November 1942 he began to make waves in the 1922 Committee at a difficult stage in the war, he was restored to office as Colonial Secretary, where he remained until the 1945 election defeat. In the postwar parliament, he was established as the third figure in the party after Churchill and Eden, and, but for his premature death from lung cancer in December 1950, he would almost certainly have become Chancellor of the Exchequer in Churchill's peacetime ministry.

The junior minister who was the most impressive in 1924–29, and was widely expected (together with Elliot) to be a certain entry into the next Conservative Cabinet, took a more circitituous route.[117] This was the leading London MP and prominent Methodist, Sir Howard Kingsley Wood, who served under Neville Chamberlain during the latter's ambitious term at the Ministry of Health, greatly impressing his superior as 'very quick, very industrious and painstaking'; the two formed an important alliance.[118] However, a coalition meant there were fewer offices for Conservatives and in 1931–35 Wood served as Postmaster-General, although he became a member of the Cabinet in December 1933. He returned to his area of expertise as Minister of Health in June 1935, and then in May 1938 replaced Swinton at the Air Ministry. In April 1940 his administrative skills led to a transfer to become Lord Privy Seal and Chairman of the important Home and Food Policy Committee. His turn against Chamberlain in May 1940 surprised many and was indicative of the Prime Minister's crumbling credibility with the party centre. Wood's ensuing appointment as Chancellor of the Exchequer has often but mistakenly been interpreted as a reward for switching sides, but Chamberlain would have fallen anyway; Churchill may have promoted Wood as a reassurance to the mainstream and a balance to the incoming 'glamour boys', but more probably the real reason was his uncharismatic efficiency, as simply the best man available for the job—which he carried out successfully, though the stress contributed to his sudden death in September 1943.

There were a number of Cabinet ministers who were merely dull or average, and whose careers advanced slowly if at all, and a slightly smaller number who were

---

[114] Emrys-Evans to Eden, 7 January 1940, Emrys-Evans MSS, Add.58242/20.
[115] Cazalet to Baldwin, 12 January 1940, Baldwin MSS, 234/19; Stanley's father had been Secretary for War from 1916 to 1918.
[116] Channon diary, 7 May 1940.
[117] Ormsby-Gore to Irwin, 4 April 1929, Halifax MSS, C152/18/1/238.
[118] N. Chamberlain to Irwin, 12 August 1928, Halifax MSS, C152/18/1/114a.

considered to be failures or liabilities. There were not as many of these in the 1922–24 government as the difficulty of forming it (and Birkenhead's scorn) might suggest—in fact, hardly more than average for any administration. Indeed, the greatest liability was the continuing Cabinet minister Griffith-Boscawen, who was 'very unpopular in the House' and 'has lost every seat he has ever held'; the continuation of the latter habit in two further by-elections was to end his career within a few months.[119] Two of the new ministers were thought not to have made the best of difficult and sensitive departments: Montague Barlow at Labour, and Sanders at Agriculture. These same offices were difficult berths in the next government, and Walter Guinness struggled at Agriculture from 1925 to 1929. The choice of Arthur Steel-Maitland, formerly the first Party Chairman in 1911–16, for the critical position of Minister of Labour surprised many in the leadership and was regarded as unwise from the outset. Steel-Maitland was unable to either delegate or cope with the mass of detail; he lost sight of the wider picture and became exhausted and, eventually, ill under the burden of office. By the end of 1927, Dawson, the editor of *The Times*, who knew him well, commented: 'he always tends to overwork himself… and is now all over the place'.[120] Steel-Maitland was also 'first and foremost a bore',[121] although in a less supercilious way than another minister who disappointed expectations, Lord Eustace Percy at Education. 'Somewhat of an intellectual snob', the latter dabbled with the fashionable concepts of planning during a brief return to the Cabinet in the mid-1930s, before leaving politics altogether to become Principal of the university college in Newcastle.[122]

The most erratic figure in the 1924–29 Cabinet was the Home Secretary, William Joynson-Hicks, whose conduct alternately amused and appalled his colleagues. Known to all as 'Jix', he was an exuberant exhibitionist with a taste for the limelight, and his diehard views were presented in a simplistic style that was 'undeniably popular in the constituencies'.[123] He had risen rapidly during the few months of Baldwin's 1923–24 ministry, but, even so, he staggered Derby by considering himself a possible Leader in January 1924—the latter noting that 'his self-confidence is something beyond belief'.[124] Although 'fond of speaking before he thinks' and 'always too impetuous', he was considered to have shown restraint and good judgement during the General Strike.[125] In this period, his nickname amongst the Cabinet was 'Mussolini Minor', which reflected his strutting self-promotion rather than any thought that he aspired to dictatorship.[126] His antics were transparent and could entertain his colleagues: 'no child ever took such pleasure in attracting notice as does our Jix,' observed Neville Chamberlain, and 'not the least part of the fun is

---

[119] Derby to Bonar Law, 29 November 1922, Derby MSS, 29/1.
[120] Dawson to Irwin, 29 December 1927, Halifax MSS, C152/17/1/282.
[121] N. Chamberlain to Irwin, 25 August 1927, Halifax MSS, C152/17/1/249c.
[122] Davidson memo of conversation with Birkenhead, n.d. but c.January 1927, Davidson MSS, DAV/180.
[123] Dawson to Irwin, 31 July 1927, Halifax MSS, C152/17/1/245a.
[124] Derby diary, 23 January 1924.
[125] Bridgeman diary, 'Sir W. Joynson Hicks', November 1929.
[126] Davidson to Irwin, 14 June 1926, Halifax MSS, C152/17/1/53a.

that to a great extent he "gets away with it"'.[127] Cabinet ministers had fits of laughter over his chosen manner of portrayal in a party propaganda film, in which his portion concluded with the caption 'Jix is the boy for work, Jix is the boy for play, Jix is the boy that means to keep the Alien far away!'[128] Less amusing was an imprudent statement in April 1927 which effectively pledged the government to equalize the franchise for both sexes at the age of twenty-one, placing his colleagues in a difficult position and upsetting party opinion. A month later he impulsively launched the raid on the offices of the Soviet trade delegation, ARCOS, but found little evidence to justify it, although it earned him 'great popularity from the "Clear out the Reds" section of the Conservative Party'.[129] His Protestant passions were aroused in the Prayer Book debate of December 1927, and he was acknowledged to have 'made the speech of his life' in denouncing in vivid terms its supposed Papist tendency.[130] This was accompanied by a moralistic crusade against the night clubs of London, which had a mixed reception, as it uneasily negotiated the narrow terrain between puritanical populism and farce. By the end of the government, further indiscretions, especially in relation to the unpopular restrictions still in place under the wartime Defence of the Realm Act, had led to his colleagues' patience wearing thin.[131] Jix had some heart problems and, despite apparently still seriously considering himself a candidate for the Leadership and Premiership, he retired at the election with a peerage as Viscount Brentford. In 1929–30, he flirted briefly with support for Beaverbrook's campaign, putting his loyalty under suspicion, but he was by then a marginal figure.

In the first years of the National Governments of 1931–40, Conservative grumbles about weak links in the Cabinet tended to focus on its Liberal and Labour members, including Ramsay MacDonald in the declining final year of his Premiership.[132] However, in the later 1930s Conservative ministers were also frequently criticized. Lord Londonderry as Air Minister was considered a lightweight, and there was always a suspicion that he had dined his way into the Cabinet through his role in hosting party receptions at his grand London residence and his—and still more his wife's—friendship with MacDonald. Inskip was considered unsuitable and ineffective as Minster for Co-ordination of Defence in 1936, although, in fact, the role required judicial skills as it involved mediating between the defence departments and not directing them. He was perhaps unlucky, and it is not clear that anyone else could have done much more in this ill-defined and ill-equipped post, but in January 1939 he was rather brutally removed by Chamberlain and replaced with the former First Sea Lord, Lord Chatfield. Duff Cooper's rise was

---

[127] N. Chamberlain to Irwin, 12 August 1928, Halifax MSS, C152/18/1/114a.
[128] N. Chamberlain to Irwin, 15 August 1926, Halifax MSS, C152/17/1/82a.
[129] Lane-Fox to Irwin, 26 May 1927, Halifax MSS, C152/17/1/223.
[130] N. Chamberlain to Irwin, 25 December 1927, Halifax MSS, C152/17/1/277a.
[131] Davidson to Baldwin, 27 February 1929, Davidson MSS, DAV/186; Headlam diary, 30 July 1928.
[132] Not all were so regarded: there was particular respect for Runciman in 1931–35, and later for the competence of Ernest Brown and MacDonald's son, Malcolm; Ormsby-Gore to Baldwin, 24 May 1935, Baldwin MSS, 47/56.

founded upon being 'an impressive front-bench speaker never using a note', but despite a solid performance as junior minister at the Treasury in 1934–35, he proved to be 'a very bad administrator' as a departmental chief.[133] He was thought lazy by his colleagues, and disappointed first Baldwin during his tenure of the War Office in 1935–37 and then Chamberlain at the Admiralty; his resignation over the Munich settlement in 1938 was considered a small loss. Like Eden, he made few waves—even ripples—in the months afterwards, assuring the Prime Minister in December: 'I have tried, since I left office, to say and write nothing that would make your heavy task more difficult and would be in any way offensive to you.'[134] Understandably, Chamberlain regarded such quiescence as an attempt to crawl back, which he had no intention, or need, of permitting.

There was a general feeling that Chamberlain's Cabinet of 1937–40 had too many lightweight or subservient ministers, and his Chief Whip considered that 'his was the only will that ever prevailed'.[135] Even one of Chamberlain's strongest supporters acknowledged that the Cabinet was 'composed of comparative nonentities' and the government 'almost a one man show'.[136] This was due to the combination of Chamberlain's driving self-confidence and the presence of quite a number of new and younger figures at the Cabinet table. However, if criticism of Chamberlain's Cabinet selection focused on anyone, it was the familiar face of 'Eddy' Winterton. Holder of an Irish peerage as the 6th Earl Winterton, he had become MP for the safe seat of Horsham in 1904 at the age of twenty-one. He was given office as Under-Secretary for India in the 1922–24 and 1924–29 governments, and was, at best, an average performer: his parliamentary style was described by a fellow junior minister as 'very pompous and rather aggressive'.[137] There was little surprise that he did not figure in the National Government in 1931 and he spent the next six years on the backbenches until, in a decision that puzzled observers, Neville Chamberlain made him Chancellor of the Duchy of Lancaster in May 1937. In March 1938, Winterton was brought into the Cabinet and given the new role of Deputy Secretary of State for Air and the task of defending the department in the Commons, but he was not a success and the post lapsed when Lord Swinton resigned as Secretary of State two months later. Despite the disregard of his colleagues,[138] Winterton remained a member of the Cabinet until January 1939, when he was switched to the post of Paymaster-General, which he held until November 1939. Swinton's fate illustrates another theme, that elevation or succession to a peerage often had the effect of ending a Cabinet career. This was immediate in the case of William Ormsby-Gore's succession as Lord Harlech in May 1938, whilst Eyres-Monsell (created Lord Monsell at the 1935 dissolution) and Cunliffe-Lister (created Lord Swinton at the same time) lasted seven months and two and a

---

[133] Unpublished memoir, n.d., James MSS, AJMS/3.
[134] Duff Cooper to N. Chamberlain, 23 December 1938, NC, 7/11/31/76.
[135] Memoir by Margesson, 'Chamberlain—A Candid Portrait', n.d., Margesson MSS, CAC, MRGN/1/5/1–5.
[136] Channon diary, 10 May 1939; N. to I. Chamberlain, 4 December 1938, *NCDL*.
[137] Lane-Fox to Irwin, 23 November 1927, Halifax MSS, C152/17/1/272.
[138] Inskip diary notes, 14 September 1938, Inskip MSS, CAC, INKP/1/1.

half years respectively after their elevations. However, Swinton was to return to office under Churchill both during the war and in his peacetime government in the early 1950s, thus completing one of the longest Cabinet careers of any interwar Conservative politician.

CABINET MINISTERS: TWO CASE STUDIES—HALIFAX AND HOARE

The career of Edward Wood, later 1st Earl of Halifax, was founded upon his personal character. He had a charm of manner, a gentlemanly style which was patrician but not superior, and a Christian sense of moral duty which never strayed into priggishness or dogmatism. Throughout his life, Wood was seen by his contemporaries as a man who could be implicitly trusted to do the right thing—which led to the corollary, that what he did must be the right thing, whether that was the declaration of future Dominion status for India in 1929 or supporting Chamberlain as his Foreign Secretary in 1938–39. It was this view of his character, likened by some colleagues without conscious hyperbole to political saintliness, rather than his more average administrative and perhaps below-average oratorical skills, which explains his role and importance. As Neville Chamberlain commented after Wood had left the Cabinet to become Viceroy of India, 'you are apt to leave a hole behind you which no one else can quite fill'.[139] He was not without the politician's arts: Channon noted admiringly of one meeting with the Foreign Affairs Committee that Halifax had 'cajoled them, led them up the garden path, played with them, impressed them with his charm, sincerity and high ideals. He fascinates and bamboozles everyone.'[140] Wood was the fourth son of the 2nd Viscount Halifax, but the deaths of his three older brothers made him heir to the title before he was nine years old; however, his father lived to the age of ninety-five and he did not inherit it until 1934. Wood was born with a withered left arm which he did not conceal, and which did not prevent him from becoming an accomplished rider and a great enthusiast of fox-hunting; in his first Cabinet post in 1922–24, one of his priorities was to ensure that he could still have two days free for hunting each week. His early interests were more academic than political, but in January 1910 he was elected for the safe Conservative seat of Ripon in his native Yorkshire. He served in the army for most of the war, and in the postwar parliament was one of a group of centre-left MPs that included future Cabinet members Hoare, Cunliffe-Lister, and Elliot. He was appointed Churchill's junior minister at the Colonial Office in the reshuffle of April 1921, but became increasingly disillusioned with Lloyd George's personal style and was a key figure in the group of Under-Secretaries who opposed the Coalition in 1922. Wood was typically concerned to avoid anything which might seem underhand, and so wrote to Austen Chamberlain setting out his reasoning at some length.[141]

---

[139] N. Chamberlain to Irwin, 15 August 1926, Halifax MSS, C152/17/1/82a.
[140] Channon diary, 16 February 1939.
[141] Wood to A. Chamberlain (draft), October 1922, Halifax MSS (Borthwick), A4/410/26/2.

As with the other anti-Coalition junior ministers, the sweeping away of most of those above opened his way to the Cabinet, and Bonar Law appointed Wood as President of the Board of Education. He made little mark here in the 1922–24 government, and not much more as Minister of Agriculture during the first year of the 1924–29 ministry; he had been one of the group in the Cabinet unhappy about the tariff policy in 1923, but played a valuable role as intermediary and interpreter between the more definite free traders and the Prime Minister, retaining the respect and confidence of both.[142] In respect of social policy, Wood's moderate outlook was very similar to Baldwin's, and they shared a strong sense of Christian motivation; he came to be seen by Baldwin as an example for others to emulate. Wood had never really mastered the Commons or enjoyed its combative style, and his only reservations before he accepted the Viceroyalty of India in 1925 were family ones—the age of his father, and the youth of his children. A peerage was conferred upon him, and he became Lord Irwin. As Viceroy he sought to adapt policy to a rapidly developing India, but misjudged the hostility of the native politicians' reaction to the Simon Commission being composed only of British parliamentarians. It was in order to recoup the initiative and create a more constructive atmosphere that he proposed a statement be made affirming that the aim was for India to evolve to Dominion status, which meant to become essentially self-governing but retain a link to the Crown and a place in the British Commonwealth; this became the Irwin Declaration of October 1929. The second Labour government had come into office a few months earlier, and Irwin worked readily with the India Secretary, Wedgwood Benn, and Prime Minister, Ramsay MacDonald, in what was a change not of policy but rather of pace and presentation. The Viceroy had secured Baldwin's support for his initiative when home on leave in the summer of 1929, but it produced a reaction of dismay and alarm from most of the Conservative Party. The Declaration sidelined the Simon Commission report, and led directly to the first Round Table conference in November 1930. However, the civil disobedience campaign led to Gandhi's arrest and in response the Congress Party boycotted the conference. Irwin's policy came under greatest fire from Conservatives in January 1931 when he released Gandhi and began a series of meetings with him, but their agreement in March—in which Gandhi made the key concessions of ending civil disobedience and agreeing to attend the next conference—was seen as a triumph and vindication.

This success came at the close of Irwin's five-year term, and after his return to Britain he spent a period away from politics. He declined office when the National Government was formed, but in June 1932 accepted, more from duty than enthusiasm, Baldwin's request to fill the vacancy at the Education ministry, caused by the death of the Liberal incumbent. It was a striking testimony to his almost above-party status and general respect that there seems to have been no serious objection to the resulting change in the balance of party representation in the Cabinet. In 1934 he succeeded his father as 3rd Viscount Halifax; he was later raised a step in

---

[142] Memo by Wood, 'Record of some events', October–November 1923, Baldwin MSS, 35/9–15.

the peerage in his own right, becoming 1st Earl of Halifax in 1944. After a few months at the War Office in 1935, Halifax was appointed by Baldwin and Chamberlain to the non-departmental posts of Lord Privy Seal and Lord President of the Council successively; he was also Leader of the Party in the House of Lords. In these posts he developed an increasing role in foreign policy, defending it in the upper chamber. However, an invitation from Göring to a hunting party in Germany, and the meeting with Hitler which followed, were more controversial and may have contributed to both sides misreading each other's intentions. When Eden's tensions with Chamberlain led him to resign in February 1938, Halifax had the weight and experience to replace him and steady the boat. As Foreign Secretary he became more sceptical of the dictators than Chamberlain, but, at first, was ineffective in moderating him. Halifax did not see his role as that of running a separate policy from the Prime Minister, and Chamberlain felt that he was being loyally and effectively supported at last. Halifax's opposition to the proposed terms to settle the Czech crisis that Chamberlain brought back from his second meeting with Hitler on 22–23 September 1938 was nevertheless crucial in the Cabinet's decision not to approve them, even at the risk of war. However, Halifax did support the slightly better terms obtained by Chamberlain at the Munich conference a week later.

By the winter of 1938–39, Halifax was being spoken of as the possible successor to Chamberlain; in many eyes he was 'the only alternative, as a large section of the Conservative Party would not have Sir Samuel Hoare and another section would not have Sir John Simon'.[143] He took a firmer line in policy towards both Italy and Germany, and his junior minister's PPS noted that the issuing of the guarantees to Poland and other eastern European countries after the German occupation of Bohemia in March 1939 was his particular scheme.[144] Although 'veering away from the Prime Minister' in the following months,[145] he supported Chamberlain in the difficult days after the German attack on Poland in September, as he was aware of the French desire to hold back from declaring war for a few days in order to be better prepared. Halifax did not attract similar hostility to the other members of the 'inner cabinet' group of appeasers, Hoare and Simon, and his moderate position and good relations with the Labour Party meant that he was not only the alternative to Churchill as Prime Minister in May 1940, but probably the preferred choice of the Labour leaders and of the King.[146] However, Halifax himself recognized that the position would be unworkable, for as a member of the upper chamber he would have to give most of the direction of the war to the leader in the Commons—who would have to be Churchill. When Churchill's silence at the crucial meeting with Chamberlain on 9 May 1940 indicated unwillingness to subordinate himself to Halifax, the latter moved quickly to withdraw his claim. He remained at the Foreign Office in the new coalition, and in late May 1940 was the leading figure in suggesting

---

[143] Memo by Hudson, 12 December 1938, Halifax MSS (Borthwick), A4/410/22a; it is revealing that Hudson ensured that he had a copy of this.
[144] Channon diary, 25 August 1939.
[145] Channon diary, 5 and 13 April 1939.
[146] Butler to Halifax, 9 May 1940, Halifax MSS (Borthwick), A4/410/16.

not that German peace terms should be accepted but rather that they should at least be looked into. Halifax had an important role during the rest of 1940, but his authority was weakened by public criticism of the appeasers and the retirement and death of Chamberlain. The vacancy as Ambassador to the United States due to the sudden death of Lord Lothian in December 1940 gave Churchill the opportunity to move Halifax from the Foreign Office (to which Eden returned), and his reluctance to take the embassy was overcome by pressure on the grounds of duty. This was effectively the end of his political career and influence; he remained at Washington, with considerable success, until May 1946, during his final year once again working amicably with a Labour government.

Sir Samuel Hoare's rise to prominence was based upon competence, caution, and carefully cultivated connections. The first of the latter was his acquaintance with Bonar Law, and the meeting of respected backbench MPs organized by Hoare before the Carlton Club meeting played a significant role in persuading Bonar Law to come out of retirement. Hoare was rewarded with a ministry in the new government in 1922, albeit a minor one outside the Cabinet. As Air Minister in 1922–24 and 1924–29 he demonstrated administrative ability, joining the Cabinet when Baldwin became Prime Minister in May 1923 and being marked for further promotion at the time of the 1929 defeat.[147] By then, he had made his most important and enduring connection: his friendship with Neville Chamberlain, which was particularly strengthened by their close working relationship in opposition during 1929–31.[148] This partnership was not quite one of equals—Chamberlain was the leading figure in both standing and initiative—but Hoare was far from being overshadowed. They held similar views (or Hoare was careful to express similar views) on the problems facing the party, especially protection. Hoare had another useful connection in the latter case: he was also friendly with Beaverbrook and played an important role as a go-between in the early stages of the Empire Crusade, arranging the crucial dinner meetings which led to the temporary truce in the spring of 1930. He also worked closely with Chamberlain after the latter's appointment as Party Chairman in June 1930; earlier in 1930, he had been appointed Treasurer of the Party.

Hoare's other important connections were with Lord Irwin, his former frontbench colleague who was now crucially placed as Viceroy of India, and with Baldwin. Indeed, Irwin had recommended Hoare as a possible Party Chairman in 1926, describing him as 'a person of clear ideas and far from a fool' and 'ingenious at getting round brick walls'.[149] From late 1929 onwards Hoare was signalling his interest in going to the India Office and his support for Irwin's policy, as 'someone who was looking to the future rather than to the past'.[150] Baldwin's view that he 'represents the left centre',[151] together with his caution and competence, made him

---

[147] Draft Cabinet list, in Baldwin's hand, n.d. but marked '? 1929', Baldwin MSS, 42/205.
[148] N. Chamberlain diary, 8 December 1929, NC, 2/22.
[149] Irwin to Baldwin, 10 October 1926, Baldwin MSS, 102/88–91.
[150] Hoare to Irwin, 24 December and 13 November 1929, Halifax MSS, C152/18/1/339, 298.
[151] Baldwin to Salisbury, 2 August 1930, Salisbury MSS, S(4)198/29.

an obvious choice as one of the four Conservative representatives at the first Indian Round Table conference in 1930. The delegation was ostensibly led by the former India Secretary, Earl Peel, but Hoare's tactical skill exerted growing influence on its strategy. He was able to keep in step with mainstream Conservative opinion and manage the difficult manoeuvre of avoiding commitment to any specific reform proposals, without breaching the bipartisan line or offending the Indian delegations. At the same time, he was 'quite justifiably keeping his eye on the position which he is creating for himself'.[152] By August 1931, Hoare's standing had advanced to the point that he was the logical choice, as well as Chamberlain's preferred colleague, to accompany the latter in the bilateral meetings with Labour leaders, which paved the way towards the formation of the National Government. He was one of the four Conservatives in the original Cabinet of ten, and entrusted with the key and sensitive post of Secretary of State for India.

The tenure of the India Office from 1931 to 1935 was the crucial stage in Hoare's career. He saw the reform proposals which had originated with the Irwin Declaration of 1929 through to the statute book as the Government of India Act of 1935, despite much concern and opposition from within the party. The government's huge majority made this much easier, but it was never a foregone conclusion—especially as far as constituency opinion was concerned. It was achieved in part by care and caution, and by steering a moderate course that held true to the principles and aims of the reforms, but provided sufficient reassurance to most anxious Conservatives.[153] It is wrong to view Hoare as a 'radical' over India: in the spectrum of Conservative opinion, he was in fact a centrist moderate, following the most expedient course.[154] The latter led him close to the wind on occasion, especially in the influencing of the Manchester Chamber of Commerce's evidence to the Joint Select Committee. There was certainly some fire to this smoke; if Churchill's charges of a breach of parliamentary privileges had been better targeted, Hoare would have been in considerable trouble—as it was, with some relief, he escaped.[155] Hoare always sought to keep his options open, and had something of a tendency to show different faces in different directions—never so much as to be accused of trickery, but it was more apparent than with most politicians and enough to earn him the nicknames of 'Slippery Sam' and 'Soapy Sam'.[156] Despite his competence, his 'manner is so prim and his voice so affected' that he did not greatly appeal to younger MPs or have any personal following. At the time of the privileges case, one junior minister noted in his diary: 'Poor Hoare, childless and unbending. His career means everything to him.'[157] Those who worked more closely with him, especially during this period, respected him as 'the really

---

[152] Hailey to Irwin, 6 January 1931, Halifax MSS, C152/19/1/201.
[153] Stopford to Peel, 26 August, to Zetland, 16 September 1931, Stopford MSS, E346/7.
[154] Butler to his parents, 14 July 1930, Butler MSS, D48/748–51; NU Conf., 1932, speech by Hoare; Amery diary, 6 October 1933.
[155] Butler to Brabourne, 15 May 1934, Brabourne MSS, F.97/20b/169–74.
[156] Hilton Young to his wife, 29 July 1932, Kennet MSS, 107/4.
[157] Bernays diary, 20 June 1934.

sound, courageous and intelligent fellow he is', whilst also finding him cold, impersonal, and self-absorbed.[158]

Hoare perceived where the realities of power lay, and his ambitious progress was founded upon this.[159] However, when success at the India Office led to his promotion to Foreign Secretary in June 1935, it was also his undoing. His attempt to resolve the Abyssinian crisis by a practical deal in the Hoare–Laval Plan (framed jointly with the French Foreign Minister) became public knowledge in December 1935, provoking a storm of criticism. The gulf between its apparent cynicism and the endorsement of the League of Nations given a few weeks previously by the government in the general election, and by Hoare in person at the League's Assembly in Geneva, was too great to be sustainable. Amidst fears that the government might fall, the Cabinet hastily back-pedalled, leaving Hoare in an exposed position and with no alternative but to resign.[160] He was not disgraced: there was private sympathy for the realism of his policy, the friendship with Chamberlain remained intact, and even the relationship with Baldwin was not broken.[161] Indeed, there was a recognition that Hoare had been, to some extent, a sacrifice and that there were obligations to him, so that the question was not whether he should return to office but rather how soon this could decently be done.[162] However, Hoare's impatience led him into a misjudgement which further damaged his reputation, when a speech in March 1936 shocked the House with its open flattery of Baldwin.[163] Three months later he was appointed to the Admiralty, and his return to the inner circle was confirmed by promotion to Home Secretary when Chamberlain formed his Cabinet in May 1937.

Hoare's prominence as one of the Prime Minister's closest colleagues marked him indelibly as an architect of the appeasement policy and a 'man of Munich', and his reputation fell even more than Chamberlain's during the 'phoney war' period of 1939–40. However, the Prime Minister refused to sacrifice his increasingly unpopular colleague, and the unwise decision to return him to the Air Ministry in April 1940 was an important factor in Chamberlain's own downfall. Hoare was amongst the ministers Churchill was determined to exclude, and this time there was no likely prospect of return. A few days after Chamberlain's resignation, Hoare accepted the post of Ambassador to Spain—which had crucial strategic importance after the fall of France—and served there effectively, but out of sight, until the end of the war; in 1944 he was raised to the peerage as Viscount Templewood. Hoare had administrative ability and considerable political skills but he was never able to inspire complete trust or much in the way of affection, and so, despite his prominence, he was rarely considered likely to reach the highest post of all.

---

[158] Glyn, note on Cabinet ministers' reputations; Butler to his parents, 17 June 1931, Butler MSS, D48/835–9.
[159] Lane-Fox to Irwin, 26 December 1927, Halifax MSS, C152/17/1/277b.
[160] N. to H. Chamberlain, 15 December 1935, *NCDL*.
[161] Hoare to Baldwin, 22 and 29 December 1935, Baldwin MSS, 123/250–1.
[162] Baldwin to Hoare, 13 March and 9 April 1936, Templewood MSS, VIII/6.
[163] N. to I. Chamberlain, 14 March 1936, *NCDL*.

DIVISIONS IN THE CABINET

The membership of the Cabinet included individuals with strong views and the confidence and ability to argue their case, and so debate within this confidential forum could often be vigorous. Of course, some ministers had more authority than others by virtue of their office, standing, or personality; some stayed more in the background whilst others could irritate or bore their colleagues through overly frequent or dogmatic interventions. In most Cabinets there were ministers who tended to figure regularly on the same side in discussions, but this was rarely seen as factional and they could often disagree about other issues—an example of this was Churchill and Birkenhead in the 1924–29 Cabinet. Thus it was not a matter for concern that a Cabinet minister would describe the discussion over whether to break off relations with Soviet Russia after the General Strike in 1926 as 'a set battle',[164] or that there were frequent references to a 'row' in Cabinet. In many cases the disputants were expressing their departments' competing agendas, as in the conflict between Bridgeman at the Admiralty and Churchill at the Treasury over the naval construction budget in 1925. The Prime Minister—particularly in the cases of Bonar Law and Baldwin—would generally let the arguments be well-ventilated before adopting a summarizing role or delivering his own opinion, and the silent majority around the Cabinet table would usually be most influenced by this and swing behind it. Votes were sometimes taken in Cabinet; they marked the resolution of discussion rather than being a prologue to division, and so were a positive feature. Disagreement taken to the point of resignation from the Cabinet was very rare; threats of resignation as a tactic were less uncommon, but it was a device that could not be resorted to very frequently without becoming threadbare and an irritant to colleagues. Some such threats were clearly hot air even at the time, such as Amery's spat with Churchill over funds for the Empire Marketing Board, shortly before the summer recess in August 1927, which led to a hasty and bad-tempered resignation threat at end of a tiring year; two or three meetings later, both Churchill and Joynson-Hicks threatened to depart over a relatively minor point in the disarmament negotiations, which Bridgeman was overseeing at Geneva.[165] Others were more significant, such as Baldwin's offer to resign from the Cabinet in July 1922 due to Lloyd George's reluctance to support him over the implementation of the Safeguarding of Industries Act, and, three years later, Bridgeman's determination to go if the Cabinet reduced the naval construction programme below the Admiralty's minimum requirement.[166]

Between 1918 and 1939, only seven resignations by Conservative Cabinet ministers were attributed to differences over policy, and all of them related to issues of foreign affairs.[167] In the first three cases, this was a final straw rather than the main

---

[164] Hoare to Irwin, 18 June 1926, Halifax MSS, C152/17/1/55a.
[165] N. Chamberlain to Irwin, 25 August 1927, Halifax MSS, C152/17/1/249c.
[166] Memo by Maclean, 25 July 1923, *BP*, 96–7; Bridgeman diary, 22 July, to his son, 2 July 1925.
[167] The resignation of Lord Eustace Percy as Minister without Portfolio in March 1936 may have been influenced by a lack of sympathy from senior Cabinet members for his growing enthusiasm for forms of 'planning', but this was not stated publicly or even privately. He told a Cabinet colleague that

factor, as they took place during the fall of the Coalition in 1922, for which Lloyd George's Turkish policy and handling of the Chanak crisis was the precipitating event. The first two of these resignations occurred in tandem, when two relatively junior members of the Cabinet—Baldwin and Griffith-Boscawen—indicated that they could no longer support the continuation of the Coalition with Lloyd George as Prime Minister.[168] This fact was clearly communicated to the Prime Minister and the Conservative Leader some days before the latter summoned the party meeting at the Carlton Club, and thus the two ministers had effectively resigned, although it is unclear whether this was put formally in writing. The third 'resignation' in October 1922 was very much motivated by the conduct of foreign policy: this was the relatively late decision of the aggrieved Foreign Secretary, Lord Curzon, to join the dissidents.[169]

The remaining four departures are more clear-cut, as they were all individual actions during the life of a government rather than at its demise. The first was Lord Robert Cecil, who was created Viscount Cecil of Chelwood in 1923. Since 1918 he had become passionately committed to the League of Nations, to an extent which led him to be sympathetic to Liberal and Labour views of foreign policy and to become detached from Conservative opinion. He was persuaded by Baldwin to join the 1924 Cabinet to assist with League of Nations affairs, taking the non-departmental office of Chancellor of the Duchy of Lancaster but effectively being an additional foreign affairs Cabinet minister. This was a situation both he and the Foreign Secretary, Austen Chamberlain, found awkward and suspected would be unworkable—and so it proved. After Baldwin had persuaded him out of resigning in the previous year, the divergence between the government's policy in the Geneva disarmament negotiations and his own view of what was needed led to his resignation in August 1927. By this time his colleagues were aware of the wide difference in outlook, and he had exhausted their patience with a combination of erratic and pedantic behaviour; at the end, he failed to make clear to them (or perhaps they were no longer listening) what the precise issue was, so they regarded his action as unfair. Hoare considered that 'Bob's resignation was completely unjustifiable', and Neville Chamberlain commented: 'I never could clearly make out what he was after.'[170] Baldwin was more upset than anyone else at this rift in the unity of his team, but far from doing the government any damage Cecil's departure 'was on the whole popular with the Conservatives'.[171]

---

there was 'one reason only for his resignation, and that was that "the British Constitution abhors sinecures"': Zetland to Linlithgow, 17 April 1936, Zetland MSS, D609/7.

[168] Griffith-Boscawen's position was more ambiguous than Baldwin's, although on 10 October he had determined to resign after the Cabinet rejected his agriculture policy: 'The Break Up of the Coalition', Griffith-Boscawen MSS, c.396/119–21.

[169] Curzon had been acting jointly with Griffith-Boscawen and Baldwin since 11 October, but his intention to resign was not made clear to the leading Coalitionists until his meeting with Bonar Law late in the evening of the day before the Carlton Club meeting: 'The Break Up of the Coalition', Griffith-Boscawen MSS, c.396/120; Salvidge, *Salvidge of Liverpool*, 238–9.

[170] Hoare to Irwin, 17 November 1927, Halifax MSS, C152/17/1/267c; N. Chamberlain to Irwin, 25 December 1927, Halifax MSS, C152/17/1/277a.

[171] Hoare to Irwin, 17 November 1927, Halifax MSS, C152/17/1/267c.

The other three resignations all concerned different aspects of the appeasement policy in the 1930s. The first could be said to be more of a dismissal than a resignation, for in December 1935 when the Cabinet refused to endorse the proposals of the leaked Hoare–Laval Plan—and took the face-saving line that Hoare had exceeded his mandate in negotiating it—the Foreign Secretary had no option but to depart. Although deeply resentful of being made a sacrifice in this way, he was persuaded, by promises of a return in due course, to moderate his words in his resignation speech, and thereby did the government, though hardly himself, no further harm. The second departure was also of a Foreign Secretary, in this case Hoare's successor Anthony Eden in February 1938, after increasing divergence from the Prime Minister's views of foreign policy priorities and mounting exasperation at the latter's encroachment upon the Foreign Secretary's freedom of manoeuvre. As with Cecil in 1927, other members of the Cabinet had seen this coming, but this time with rather more sympathy for the resigner—although nearly all of the Cabinet thought Chamberlain's policy to be sounder than Eden's, and accepted that, ultimately, the decision of the Prime Minister must hold sway. There were several attempts by other Cabinet ministers to mediate or persuade Eden to remain, but to no avail. However, the confidentiality of diplomatic exchanges with other powers meant that Eden could not fully explain his reasons to the House of Commons, and his resignation speech left the government benches more confused than alarmed. Neither then nor during the remaining months of peace did Eden seek to bring down the Prime Minister or the government, and indeed his strategy was to be as unfactious as possible, whilst still maintaining a separate position on foreign policy. His resignation was unique amongst the seven in that his junior minister (Viscount Cranborne) and his Parliamentary Private Secretary (J. P. L. Thomas) also resigned with him; they linked up with the existing dissident group that loosely revolved around Amery, so that it became known as the Eden Group—or, to the whips and Chamberlain's supporters, the 'glamour boys'.

The final resignation was Duff Cooper, the First Lord of the Admiralty, in the sole departure over the Munich Agreement in October 1938. His decision was hesitant and not very convincing to his colleagues, and, with Chamberlain's popularity at its height, was more of a quixotic gesture than a threatening one; Duff Cooper wrote to a colleague that he had not wished to damage the government.[172] He had also not been a particularly successful minister and there were some doubts about his future; the loss was therefore viewed as that of a dispensable lightweight. Duff Cooper seemed to regret his resignation almost immediately, even to hint that he wished to withdraw it, and during the following year kept so low a profile as to earn the contempt rather than the gratitude of the Prime Minister and the whips; notably, he was not taken back into office along with Churchill and Eden when war broke out, and had to wait until Churchill became Prime Minister. Several other members of the Cabinet had wobbled considerably during the Czech

---

[172] Duff Cooper to Winterton, 6 October 1938, Winterton MSS, 64; Duff Cooper diary, 30 September 1938.

crisis and had talked of possible resignation, including Walter Elliot and Oliver Stanley, but none of them did so; this shilly-shallying gained them little respect, and they were amongst those dropped by Churchill in 1940—indeed, Elliot never held office again.

Whilst individual issues could be vigorously debated, anything in the nature of a wider Cabinet crisis was very infrequent. Even in the case of the most serious rift in Conservative politics between the wars, over the Lloyd George Coalition in 1922, only a minority of the Cabinet took up a position of intransigence; the crisis was much more one between leaders and followers than it was within the leading cadre. The fall of the Coalition elevated the rebel junior ministers to the Cabinet, but its lasting impact was due to more than just a changing of the guard. The rejection of coalition had profound consequences for the outlook and ethos of the Conservative Party and its positioning in British politics. The opponents of the Coalition saw the decision of October 1922 as vital to the survival and integrity of the party, and any hint of reversing it produced a disproportionate reaction. For nearly two years the wisdom of the course set by the Carlton Club meeting was open to question, and although the ousted Coalitionists fairly quickly accepted that a joint government with Lloyd George was no longer feasible (not least because of his move to the left), the suspicion that they could be easily tempted into old habits remained strong long after their return to the fold in 1924. For these reasons, the distinction between Coalitionists and anti-Coalitionists continued to be the most significant fault-line in Conservative politics for almost a decade after 1922.[173] Disagreements in the reunited leadership after 1924 were viewed by many through the lens of 1922, and assumed by the anti-Coalitionists to relate to a hidden agenda. Many pro-Coalitionists, even of minor standing, remained subject to suspicion and hostility up to the early 1930s, as was shown by the Chief Whip's attitude to honours or office for Oliver Locker-Lampson and Leslie Scott.[174] The effect was not crudely universal, and there was a much swifter and easier return to the mainstream for some more orthodox figures, whose support of Chamberlain was clearly a matter of duty and honour rather than political agreement—particularly amongst the whips, such as Gilmour and Gibbs.

There were several reasons why the issue of coalitionism remained so important after 1922. The first of these was the continuing active role of Lloyd George and the fact that he retained (or was believed by the anti-Coalitionists to retain) an attraction for the leading pro-Coalitionists.[175] The second factor was the reluctance of the latter to accept their situation. At first, they expected their successors of the 'second eleven' to collapse due to weakness and inexperience. This was not entirely wishful thinking: the Cabinet nearly broke up over the American debt in early 1923, and did lose office after Baldwin led it into an election defeat at the end of that year. The former ministers therefore had little incentive to humble themselves

---

[173] For a fuller discussion, see S. Ball, 'The legacy of Coalition: Fear and loathing in Conservative politics 1922–1931', *Contemporary British History*, 25/1 (2011), 65–82.
[174] Eyres-Monsell to Baldwin, 25 May 1928, Baldwin MSS, 163/201.
[175] Bridgeman diary, 'Baldwin', November 1929.

and, even if not expecting a complete restoration of the pre-Carlton Club position, they preferred to stand aloof and spurn the sometimes awkward overtures made towards them. At his interview with Baldwin on 12 November 1923, Austen Chamberlain made it clear that he and Birkenhead would only rejoin 'in positions which would show clearly that we returned to the counsels of the party on the same footing of influence and authority as we had previously held'—a pretension that was both unwarranted and dangerous, and to which Baldwin could hardly accede.[176] By the time they returned to office in Baldwin's next Cabinet a year later, they may have been politically reconciled to the new dispensation but they did not conduct themselves as if they were emotionally reconciled. They still tended to underestimate or belittle their former juniors, and this whiff of superiority inevitably seeped from their private comments into common knowledge. This, in turn, fed the paranoia of the anti-Coalitionists, especially amongst the more junior figures such as J. C. C. Davidson, who was prone to see plots being hatched in every corner. The fact that the ex-Coalitionists often adopted a similar position in Cabinet and shadow cabinet debates was viewed with much suspicion. They were considered to be inveterate intriguers, and it was assumed that much more was going on behind the scenes than was apparent.[177]

A classic example of this syndrome was the crisis over the cruiser programme in the naval budget of 1925, which was viewed as a step towards a Coalitionist coup simply because the protagonist ministers, Churchill and Bridgeman, had been prominent on opposite sides in 1922. In fact, this was no more than a typical clash between an economizing Chancellor of the Exchequer and a big spending department, exactly as Churchill had experienced himself, although the other way around, when he was at the Admiralty in 1914. Propinquity diminished the doubts at Cabinet level, where frictions were eased by the collegiality of common service, but suspicion remained strong lower down the ranks and on the back benches. This was not just a view held by diehards; it was equally axiomatic amongst the Baldwinite centre, ranging from Ormsby-Gore to Smithers. Rumours of Coalitionist plots and the belief that the Coalition's former supporters were pursuing a hidden agenda were significant factors in determining MPs' responses at several key points when the party was in opposition in 1929–31, most particularly over the Irwin Declaration in November 1929. Winterton was far from alone in giving credence to the 'circumstantial rumours' that, as he revealingly phrased it, 'some nominal members of our Party' were intriguing with Rothermere and Lloyd George to achieve the dual aim of Baldwin's downfall and 'a new Coalition'.[178] Concern was greater during this period because being out of office diminished Baldwin's authority, weakened the ties of loyalty to him of former Cabinet ministers, and, in general, gave more temptation and scope for individual stratagems. At the same time

---

[176] A. Chamberlain's note of meeting with Baldwin on 12 November 1923, AC, 35/3/21b; A. to H. Chamberlain, 14 November 1923, *ACDL*.

[177] For examples of this suspicion, see: Dawson to Irwin, 31 October 1929, Halifax MSS, C152/18/1/288; A. Lane-Fox to Irwin, 17 June 1930, Halifax MSS (Borthwick), A2/278/6/2.

[178] Winterton to Irwin, 11 November 1929, Halifax MSS, C152/18/1/295.

Lloyd George, who now held the parliamentary balance, seemed to be giving hints that he would be willing to come to an arrangement, not with Baldwin but perhaps with the pro-Coalitionists. The result was prickly sensitivity amongst the parliamentary party, and a rally to Baldwin whenever he seemed under attack, despite considerable reservations about some of his decisions and the quality of his opposition leadership.

The other reason why the issue of coalitionism would not go away before October 1931 was the perennial problem of the electoral arithmetic facing the Conservatives. There was a need to attract as many former Liberal voters as possible, and a question of how to respond tactically in parliament to a minority Labour government. Naturally enough, the ex-Coalitionists were more inclined to think of pacts with the Liberals, and to take a less robust view of the dangers involved in letting the Labour Party hold office. This explains their manoeuvres in the period from December 1923 to February 1924, and their immediate response to defeat in June 1929, all of which provided evidence to reinforce the assumptions of the anti-Coalitionists. The issue only receded when the leading Coalitionists faded from the scene in the early 1930s, as a result of the deaths of Balfour, Birkenhead, and Worthington-Evans in 1930–31, the departure of Churchill from the shadow Cabinet in January 1931, and the translation of Austen Chamberlain and—less officially—Horne to the role of elder statesmen once the National Government was firmly established in October 1931.

The immediate problem caused by the overthrow of the Coalition in 1922 was a public split in the Conservative Cabinet-level leadership of a kind not seen since the tariff reform rift of 1903—which, ominously, had been the precursor to the landslide defeat of 1906. Conservatives were also very aware of the parallel with the more recent Liberal split of 1916, and the subsequent decline of that party. However, there were crucial differences between the latter and the Conservative disunity of 1922. Firstly, the party was not split into roughly equal groupings which might each claim legitimacy: the Coalitionist wing had many chiefs, but few indians in the House of Commons and still less support at constituency level. This stabilized the situation, restraining the ousted leaders (apart from Birkenhead) and reassuring the surprised victors so that they did not need to take further hostile steps to secure their position. Partly for this reason, and still more due to the ethos within Conservatism of maintaining unity, the argument was not carried into the constituencies in the 1922 election; unlike the Liberals, constituency associations did not splinter and there were no opposing candidatures splitting the vote. Workable personal relations were maintained between the leading figures in both camps, and, despite some frostiness, the channels of communication were kept open. In reality, whatever their feelings, the former Coalitionists had no alternative but to give Bonar Law's government a chance. A refusal to accept the verdict of the party meeting and of the voters would only further demonstrate the arrogance and unrepresentativeness which had been their downfall, and they could not afford the appearance of an irreconcilable faction. Any undermining of the first Conservative government since 1905 would provoke a backlash from the rank and file, and even the fairly harmless gesture of the dinner to Austen Chamberlain on 23 October

1922 was viewed unfavourably. The Coalitionist ex-ministers could only stand aloof, which left them in a sterile position, appearing rigid and out of touch. They were mistaken in thinking that time was on their side; in fact their position steadily eroded as the new Cabinet became more used to office and better-known, in most cases gaining experience and status. One Cabinet minister considered by May 1923 that 'the Party has pulled itself together' and 'has been playing as a team'.[179] However, because they focused upon every hesitancy and stumble, the Coalitionists failed to perceive this and continued to overrate their value and to ask too high a price for their return.

At the same time, it was incumbent upon the new leadership to respond to the party's desire for unity and seek to heal the rift, although not at the price of conceding the key issues of party independence and strategy towards the Liberals. The rapid rise of Labour meant that the Conservatives could not afford the luxury of division, and so the anti-Coalitionists needed to extend an olive branch whenever the opportunity arose. It was certainly Bonar Law's aim to secure reunion as soon as possible, and he might have been willing to drop some of the Cabinet to do so. Baldwin was less determined, or at least more willing to let time take its course: he wanted reunion but on his terms, and would only pay a limited price for it. In particular, there must be no rejection of the victors of 1922 or alienation of any wing of the party. When he became Prime Minister in May 1923, and later when he launched his protectionist policy in November, the invitations to reunion which Baldwin made were conditional upon accepting the existing management and direction. Any influence upon policy would be after readmittance and not before, and, of course, could then be contained by the remaining anti-Coalition majority in the Cabinet. It was a crucial part of Baldwin's strategy that he refused to treat the Coalitionists as a group, which would effectively recognize their legitimacy as a party within the party. He made individual offers only, which was important in relation to Austen Chamberlain's feeling of personal commitment to Birkenhead and refusal to return without him. Baldwin's invitation in May 1923 was tentative—so much so that it offended Chamberlain, and he turned it down. Whether this was misjudgement or intention on Baldwin's part will never be known, but having publicly made a gesture and having it declined was almost certainly the best outcome for him. His position as Prime Minister was far from secure (especially given Curzon's disappointment at being passed over), and reunion at this point would not have aided stability. There was a danger of provoking resignations from the existing Cabinet, and a complete return of the Coalitionists would have looked too much like a takeover; in any case, hostility to Birkenhead was too strong to include him, even as the price of gaining Austen Chamberlain. The one return was also a tactical success: the cohesion of the Coalitionist group was broken by Worthington-Evans' acceptance of a post, whilst his eager swallowing of so small a fly as the office of Postmaster-General permanently damaged his reputation with both sides.

The next attempt at reunion in November 1923 was driven by different tactical considerations, as Baldwin was interested in balancing the free-trade group within

---

[179] Lloyd-Greame to Curzon, 21 May 1923, Curzon MSS, F112/320/78.

the Cabinet and deterring them from resigning. The possible inclusion of the Coalitionists was a reminder that Baldwin could replace the free-trade ministers, and had access to other sources of support; it also gave them an incentive to remain and balance any shift in a protectionist direction—and especially to block the return of Birkenhead. Baldwin's other motive for reunion at this point was the pressure from Derby, who was essential for the reassurance of traditionally anti-tariff Lancashire and who was to lead the fight in this key electoral battlefield. However, he would not agree to promote a policy which he disliked if he was to be sniped at by Birkenhead, who still had influence in Lancashire. It was therefore the gain of the active support of the Coalitionists in the election campaign which was important for Baldwin, and admission to the Cabinet was only the means to that end. When, in fact, he was able to secure this anyway, it mattered less whether they were in or out of the Cabinet, and the blocking of reunion mainly by the Cecilian free-trade group was not a critical matter. Indeed, Baldwin had again achieved the desired effect without causing a split or resignations amongst his core support of anti-Coalitionists, and without appearing to be bending a knee or buying Coalitionist support with office. By February 1924, when reunion was eventually accomplished, it was no longer controversial within the party. The Liberal vote to put the Conservatives out of office and Labour in had closed the door to any revival of coalition, whilst the election defeat led to a new consensus on dropping the full tariff programme for the limited version of safeguarding. Since November, the two wings had been effectively working together, and formal reunion simply recognized this fact. In any case, a return to the shadow cabinet was not as prestigious as ministerial office, and it also avoided the previous problem of which—or whose—posts the prodigals were to be given. There was thus no valid reason to object even to the return of Birkenhead when Baldwin announced that he, Chamberlain, Balfour, and Lord Crawford would attend the first meeting of the shadow cabinet on 7 February.[180]

The opposition of the group of free-trade Cabinet ministers to Baldwin's protectionist initiative in November 1923 was the only occasion when a group of ministers held meetings outside the Cabinet in order to resist the policy of the Prime Minister. This did not begin immediately upon Baldwin's unveiling of his intentions to the Cabinet on 23 October 1923, and was more a response to the gathering pace of the crisis and the increasing likelihood of an immediate general election—which would remove the ability of doubting ministers to sit on the fence and neither publicly endorse the policy or resign. The first meeting, at Lord Salisbury's house in Arlington Street on 7 November, was composed of five ministers: Devonshire, Novar, Cecil, Wood, and their host. Their concern was as much about the way in which the new policy was being brought forward as the policy itself, and as events moved towards an election by 12 November Wood, at least, 'was very much disposed to resign'.[181] When Baldwin announced the dissolution at the Cab-

---

[180] Salisbury to Baldwin, 26 January 1924, R. Cecil to Baldwin, 1 February 1924, Baldwin MSS, 159/258–61, 35/203–7; N. to H. Chamberlain, 24 January 1924, to I. Chamberlain, 30 January 1924, *NCDL*.
[181] Memo by Wood, 'Record of some events', October–November 1923, Baldwin MSS, 35/9–15.

inet next day, Wood lunched with the other four at Arlington Street and found them all in favour of resigning, partly over the policy but also because 'they were convinced that the P.M. wanted to get rid of them to make room for Austen Chamberlain and Birkenhead'.[182] Wood now adopted a moderating and mediating position, urging his fellow free traders to wait, and advising Baldwin to conciliate them. Taking heed of the warning, Baldwin soothed their concerns with a long and friendly letter to Salisbury on the evening of 13 November, and three meetings with him in the following two days. This formulated a written agreement in which the free traders accepted that the country would be asked for 'an unconditional deletion' of Bonar Law's pledge of 1922 against protection, and in return they obtained 'an unequivocal statement' of no 'further taxes on the essential food of the people', with a list of the latter which Baldwin accepted, with the sole deletion of potatoes.[183] After this was considered by a further meeting of the group, Salisbury wrote to Baldwin accepting his answers and informing him that 'we have therefore abandoned the idea of resignation'—the fleeting crisis was over.[184]

There were divisions between pro-tariff Cabinet ministers (mainly Amery and Joynson-Hicks) and those doubtful or opposed (principally Churchill and Salisbury) in 1928–29, but they never amounted to a serious rift and the protectionists were too weak in standing and number to press the matter, despite their support amongst MPs. The differences over tariff issues in the Cabinet of the National Government in 1931–32 were not within the Conservative Party but between parties; after the general election they were just with the Samuelite wing of the Liberal Party, as the Simonite wing and the National Labour key figures of MacDonald and Thomas had all come round to accepting protectionist measures. It was striking that there was no apparent dissension within the Cabinet over India in 1931–35, despite the opposition and doubts within the parliamentary party and the constituencies; in fact, the issue was common ground between the key components of the government—especially between MacDonald and Baldwin—and so was one of the main sources of its stability and continuance, the need for which was, to most Conservatives, of overriding necessity. In a similar way, Cabinet endorsement of the appeasement policy in 1936–39 was almost complete, Eden's resignation in February 1938 being a lone act which his colleagues did not really understand. Thereafter, the 'inner cabinet' of Chamberlain, Halifax, Hoare, and Simon held sway, and the only period before the outbreak of war when there was 'a serious risk of a split in the Cabinet' was during the Czech crisis in September 1938, when several ministers contemplated resignation and met together to discuss issues and strategy.[185] However, Chamberlain's decisive action in flying to meet Hitler in Munich, the more acceptable terms he brought back, the promise of peace, the horror of war, and the lack of a convincing alternative, led all of the waverers except Duff Cooper to remain with the Cabinet ark.

---
[182] Memo by Wood, 'Record of some events', October–November 1923, Baldwin MSS, 35/9–15.
[183] Salisbury to Baldwin, 14 November 1923, Baldwin MSS, 35/16–18.
[184] Salisbury to Baldwin, 15 November 1923, Baldwin MSS, 42/135–6.
[185] Zetland to Brabourne, 25 September 1938, Zetland MSS, D609/10; Duff Cooper diary, 23 September 1938; Winterton diary, 25–30 September 1938, Winterton MSS.

Finally, in the interwar period there were two unusual but crucial examples of the Cabinet differing from the views of the Prime Minister on an important matter of policy, and requiring that he not resign but change course and accept the majority opinion. The first of these was Bonar Law's opposition in January 1923 to the settlement of the American debt, which Baldwin had negotiated. All but one of the other Cabinet ministers took Baldwin's view that better terms could not be obtained, and there was resentment that Bonar Law's obdurate and 'unreasonable' stance 'practically meant that there was not a Cabinet but a Dictator'—which, of course, had been a key complaint against Lloyd George.[186] However, Bonar Law's resignation so soon after the fall of the Coalition would have broken up not just the government but also possibly the party—and it was by means of an appeal to his duty to the party that the Prime Minister was persuaded to swallow his opposition and remain. The other occasion was in 1939, when the delay in declaring war after the German invasion of Poland was seen by the majority of the Cabinet as inexplicable and damaging to Britain's prestige in the form of keeping its word—a very sensitive spot for any upper-class Englishman. On the evening of 2 September, a group of twelve Cabinet ministers met in the Chancellor of the Exchequer's room at the House of Commons and sent two of their number to see Chamberlain and insist upon an immediate ultimatum to Germany, which was then agreed by a hastily summoned Cabinet just before midnight.[187]

There were also two significant episodes of confusion and manoeuvre amongst the Conservative front bench whilst the party was in opposition. The intrigues after the 1923 election defeat resulted from some within the leadership giving the greatest priority to preventing a Labour government. The only way to do so was to form an anti-Socialist alliance with the Liberals under some mutually acceptable figure, such as Balfour or Derby; it could not be Baldwin because of his identification with the tariff policy, and thus his departure was a necessary first step. However, the element favouring this included the two most prominent ex-Coalitionists, Austen Chamberlain and Birkenhead, and their intentions were viewed with widespread suspicion. The events before and during the election seemed to Chamberlain and Birkenhead to demonstrate everything they had thought about the inadequacy of the government, the incompetence of Baldwin, and the folly of dividing the forces of constitutionalism and letting in Labour. The logic of their position involved reversing the verdict of 1922, although their aim was an agreement with Asquith, as Leader of the Liberal Party, rather than Lloyd George.[188] There was a brief window of opportunity immediately after the election results, when a despondent Baldwin was known to be considering resignation. The next five days saw a burst of feverish activity, with the pace being set by the former Coalitionists but also involving some members of the existing Cabinet who were manoeuvring in

---

[186] Derby diary, 30 January 1923.
[187] Wallace diary, 2 September 1939, Wallace MSS; Channon diary, 2 September 1939; Duff Cooper diary, 3 September 1939; N. to I. Chamberlain, 10 September 1939, *NCDL*.
[188] A. Chamberlain to Long, Long to A. Chamberlain, 11 December 1923, Long MSS (WSA), 947/826.

anticipation of Baldwin's departure. The plot was compromised by the devious and inept tactics of Birkenhead, who 'absolutely misled' Derby about Balfour's position.[189] In fact, Balfour's judgement was that Baldwin had established his position with the public during the campaign and had become the party's strongest electoral asset, that he should remain in place despite being defeated, and that, constitutionally, the government should not resign but meet parliament.[190]

However, whether or not Asquith was willing to consider a pact, the intrigue foundered on the immovable rock of the hostility of the large majority of the Conservative Party to any revival of Coalition.[191] Whatever the causes of the defeat and the resulting circumstances, it was clear that they had not changed their minds about the rejection of coalition and that they would rather accept a Labour government—especially one boxed in by its minority status—than go cap in hand to Asquith and Lloyd George.[192] Baldwin recovered confidence over the weekend after the poll, and once he had decided to stay in office as Prime Minister and meet parliament, the party fell into line behind him. Support for the plot evaporated—with Derby half-hearted as always—whilst the rumour of the intrigue produced a rally of support for Baldwin amongst MPs; added to this, the attacks from Beaverbrook and Rothermere 'caused a complete revulsion in his favour'.[193] Baldwin remained the most acceptable leader, and his continued presence was seen by the majority as a guarantee of the party's independence and integrity.[194] Lord Hugh Cecil, who was a lifelong opponent of protectionism and sharply critical of the 'very blameable' mistakes which had led to the defeat, nevertheless told the Chief Whip that 'as things are, the continuance of Baldwin's leadership is important to the Party'.[195] As Amery told Baldwin, 'you embody and personify the decision of the Party to live its own life'.[196]

When the Cabinet met for the first time after the poll, on 11 December 1923, it unanimously endorsed Baldwin's strategy. This ruled out any deal to prevent a Labour government and accepted it as the logical outcome; most importantly, it forced the Liberal Party to take responsibility for putting the Socialists into office. On 18 December Asquith publicly announced that the Liberals would vote with Labour against the government, and this duly occurred when the new House of Commons met on 17 January 1924. These events marked the real end of coalitionism as a viable strategy, a reality which was recognized by the Conservative

---

[189] Derby diary, 10–11 December 1923; Devonshire diary, 11 December 1923, Devonshire MSS.
[190] Memo by Balfour of conversation with the King on 9 December 1923, written on 10 December 1923, Balfour MSS (Whittingehame), GD433/2/1/1.
[191] Balfour to Birkenhead, 11 December 1923, Balfour MSS (Whittingehame), GD433/2/1/2.
[192] Ormsby-Gore to Baldwin, 29 January 1924, Baldwin MSS, 42/182–7; Malcolm to Baldwin, 7 December 1923, Baldwin MSS, 35/168.
[193] Derby diary, 17 December 1923; Derby to Birkenhead, 11 December 1923 (first of two letters not sent), Derby MSS, 29/1; Norton-Griffiths to Davidson, 12 December 1923, Ormsby-Gore to Davidson, 9 December 1923, Jackson to Davidson, 9 December 1923, Davidson MSS, DAV/168.
[194] Bridgeman to Baldwin, 8 December 1923, Baldwin MSS, 35/173–4; Wakefield CA, Council, 11 February 1924.
[195] H. Cecil to Eyres-Monsell, 7 February 1924, CPA, Whips' Office MSS, 2/5.
[196] Amery to Baldwin, 8 December 1923, Baldwin MSS, 35/169–72.

ex-coalition leaders. Furthermore, with the advent of a Labour government any perpetuation of internal divisions would have been deeply unpopular with Conservative MPs and the grass roots, who would have blamed it upon the Coalitionists. They had no choice but to return to the fold under Baldwin's leadership and without any special concessions. This enabled Baldwin to achieve what had eluded him at the start of the election: a reunion which was genuinely effective, without losing any of his existing Cabinet.[197] On 7 February the first meeting of the shadow cabinet was attended by Austen Chamberlain, Balfour, Birkenhead, and Lord Crawford; from this point onwards—despite recurring suspicions of coalitionist leanings—the Conservative leadership avoided public division.

The second episode was in February and March 1931, at the end of the disputes over policy which had begun after the defeat of 1929. Until this point there had been expressions of dissatisfaction with Baldwin's policy and leadership from some MPs and constituencies, but—despite some restiveness under pressure—no significant breakdown of confidence within the front-bench leadership. Signs that this was fraying in early 1931 were not, however, principally due to the attacks from Beaverbrook and Rothermere, as the press lords had lost most of their support within the Conservative ranks after Baldwin's victory at the party meeting of October 1930. More serious was the concern amongst MPs over the bipartisan policy on India and Baldwin's overemphatic support for the outcome of the Round Table conference when it was debated in January—the speech which had precipitated Churchill's resignation from the shadow cabinet. The most important factor was the series of poor parliamentary performances by Baldwin during the winter months, which eroded his authority and credibility. The combination of all three problems led some of the shadow cabinet to fear that Baldwin's position had deteriorated beyond recovery, and to consider what should be done.[198]

As Party Chairman, Neville Chamberlain was particularly aware of the way in which the tide of opinion in the party was flowing away from Baldwin, and, on 25 February, this was confirmed in a formal memorandum drawn up by the Principal Agent. Topping's view was definite: dissatisfaction had reached critical levels and Baldwin was 'not strong enough to carry the Party to victory'.[199] Chamberlain was in a sensitive position: he was one of the most likely successors if there should be a vacancy, and he did not want and could not afford any appearance of using his office to push Baldwin out. Rather than taking immediate action, during the next three days he consulted several front-bench colleagues. All of them—including the Chief Whip, Eyres-Monsell, and Bridgeman, Baldwin's closest friend in the shadow cabinet—were agreed that the memo should be shown to the Leader. The final impetus was given by an extraneous event: the announcement on 28 February that the expected Conservative candidate in the Westminster St George's by-election,

---

[197] Salisbury to Baldwin, 26 January 1924, R. Cecil to Baldwin, 1 February 1924, Baldwin MSS, 159/258–61, 35/203–7.
[198] A. to I. Chamberlain, 28 February 1931, *ACDL*; Amery diary, 22 and 24 February, 6 March 1931; Bayford diary, 22 March 1931.
[199] Topping to N. Chamberlain, 25 February 1931, Baldwin MSS 166/50–3.

Moore-Brabazon, had withdrawn because he felt unable to defend Baldwin's leadership against an independent challenger put up by Beaverbrook and Rothermere. In this circumstance, Chamberlain felt he could delay no longer, and so, on the morning of Sunday 1 March, he had Topping's memo delivered to Baldwin at his home.[200] The covering note was careful not to imply that Baldwin should retire, and there was no pressure in that direction from any of the frontbenchers. Although strained, the loyalty of the shadow cabinet was still intact and there was no evidence of a conspiracy; there was deepening concern about party morale and Baldwin's effectiveness, but no plot to remove him.

Baldwin's conclusion after reading Topping's depressing review that the time had come to go was, therefore, his own decision, and in the afternoon he told Neville Chamberlain of his intention to resign. In fact, Chamberlain had not expected this to be the immediate response, as he thought the press lords' challenge at Westminster St George's would make it too difficult for Baldwin to withdraw.[201] Baldwin's reaction was due to his low spirits at this moment rather than a real collapse of his position, and in the evening—after the arguments in favour of staying on were vigorously put to him by Bridgeman and Davidson—he changed his mind and resolved to fight. However, for the next three weeks it was unclear whether he would be able to recover enough ground and restore his authority. As in 1923, the manoeuvring was not about getting Baldwin to vacate the leadership but about what would happen if he should do so; it was focused upon the possible succession rather than the existing Leader. When Chamberlain realized that Baldwin might be on the verge of stepping down, he moved swiftly to seize the tactical initiative and consulted Hailsham, and on 5 March they agreed that if a vacancy came they would stand together and let it be known that each was willing to serve under the other if he was chosen.

This deal proved to be unnecessary: Baldwin's position was stronger than it had seemed, and once he had decided to stay his tactics were vigorous and successful. An effective candidate for Westminster St George's was found in Duff Cooper, and he headed the poll on 19 March. More importantly, Baldwin restored confidence in both his India policy and his skills of parliamentary leadership with an outstanding speech in the House of Commons on 12 March. The final element in resolving this crisis was a clearing of the air within the shadow cabinet. Baldwin had misinterpreted the motives and actions of some of his colleagues—in particular Neville Chamberlain and Hailsham—and his suspicion and resentment became known. This caused further affront, especially to Chamberlain, who indicated that he wished to be relieved of the Party Chairmanship. Baldwin listened to Chamberlain's grievances on 24 March and a similar venting of frustrations by the shadow cabinet the following day, and his conciliatory and apologetic response had a soothing effect.[202] Chamberlain held to his request to leave Central Office, but his

---

[200] N. Chamberlain to Baldwin, 1 March 1931, NC, 8/10/24.
[201] N. to I. Chamberlain, 7 March 1931, *NCDL*.
[202] N. Chamberlain diary, 25 March 1931, NC, 2/22; Amery diary, 25 and 26 March 1931.

position there had always been intended to be temporary and he was needed on the front bench to lead the opposition to the Labour government's budget. More significantly, the two meetings closed the rifts that had opened up between Baldwin and his immediate colleagues, restoring the normal atmosphere of mutual trust and confidence within the party leadership.

THE MAKING OF POLICY

The programme of the Conservative Party was pronounced by its Leader, and no one else had the authority to do so. He was responsible for the key decisions about the overall strategy to be adopted, the priorities to be highlighted, and the line to be taken on the most vital issues of the day.[203] However, the Leader rarely took a major decision without some form of consultation with front-bench colleagues. When he did not do so, or appeared to have consulted only in a partial and selective way, it could cause serious strains, as with the protectionist programme in 1923, the Irwin Declaration in 1929, the flight to Munich in 1938, and the tone adopted by Churchill in the 1945 election. The usual method of presenting key policies was in a public speech, and these declarations were generally delivered to mass meetings of party supporters in the major urban centres (and often the referred to as 'the Sheffield programme', and so on). Apart from the Royal Address setting out the government's intentions at the start of each session, the House of Commons had become the place for explaining the detailed aspects of legislation and making any modifications to it, rather than setting out the broad context. Baldwin observed in 1933 that he would 'never' make a policy declaration during a parliamentary debate: 'I should make it to the Party.'[204] For this reason, he had created a precedent in 1929 by inviting members of the Central Council to the meeting at which the platform for the general election campaign was unveiled.[205] On more specific points, or when it was a matter of urgency, policy could be made public by a statement or an exchange of letters in the press. Baldwin used such methods to reject extending safeguarding to iron and steel in 1928 and to announce his adoption of the 'free hand' policy on tariffs in October 1930, in letters to the Chief Whip and the Party Chairman respectively.

The election manifesto was the formal summary of the party's position, and the authority of the Leader was underlined by the fact that it was issued as a personal statement rather than a corporate one. In the 1920s and 1930s, it still took the form of being the Leader's election address to his own constituency, which was then reissued nationally, but by 1945 it had become *Mr Churchill's Statement to the Electors* as a whole. Nevertheless, even at the start of this period, it was not written by the Leader alone; the text was composed by an inner circle

---

[203] Croft to Baldwin, 27 July 1928, Croft MSS, CAC, CRFT/1/3/Ba3.
[204] Davidson to Winterton, 28 November 1933, Davidson MSS (Bodleian), MSS.Eng.hist. c.560/149.
[205] NU Exec., 12 March 1929.

of Cabinet colleagues and advisers, although their contribution lay in presentation and detail, and not in determining the main strategy. Thus, whilst Amery was responsible for the basic drafts of the 1922, 1923, and 1924 manifestos, the position adopted on the crucial issue of tariffs and imperial preference was decided by Bonar Law and Baldwin respectively.[206] Skill at draftsmanship was more important than political viewpoint; hence the regular involvement of legal figures, and also of Amery: despite colleagues' doubts about his general judgement, he was recognized as being gifted in this respect. The manifesto for the 1929 election had a much longer gestation, with a Cabinet 'Policy Committee' formed in September 1927.[207] Despite this, 'the election manifesto itself was left until the last minute', and Baldwin delegated the task of integrating the various departmental positions to a group of half a dozen Cabinet ministers presided over by Hailsham, the Lord Chancellor.[208]

In 1922, Bonar Law observed: 'there can be no really definite policy to put forward except to endeavour to restore confidence and that you could really put in one sentence'.[209] For most general elections, the manifesto was not a very lengthy document and it was not necessary for it to cover everything, but in later years it grew more expansive. Even so, most of the points were general statements of aims; the purpose of the manifesto was to obtain a mandate for action rather than to set out a blueprint of methods which might tie the hands of government—that is, to provide coherence without giving hostages to fortune. When the party was in an alliance, there was also, necessarily, a stage of negotiation between the coalition partners. In 1918, Bonar Law and Lloyd George already had a good working relationship and agreement was arrived at quickly and fairly easily, with some concessions on each side (principally, that the Conservatives would not press for tariffs and Lloyd George would not close the door against them, and that Ulster would be safeguarded whilst Home Rule was granted to the rest of Ireland). In 1931, the lack of agreement between the parties over tariffs led to the issuing of separate manifestos, under the umbrella of seeking a 'doctor's mandate' to apply whatever remedies seemed necessary. Not only was the National Government more united and better co-ordinated in 1935, but there was nothing then in Conservative objectives which conflicted in vital principle with their partners, and a representative cross-party Cabinet committee had little difficulty in drawing up a unified programme. To a large extent, this drew on proposals developed by the Conservative Research Department, under the direction of Neville Chamberlain, in a series of meetings of a Cabinet Conservative Committee of leading ministers at the department's offices, which began in 1934.[210]

---

[206] Amery diary, 24–25 October 1922, 16 November 1923, 10 October 1924.
[207] Worthington-Evans to Cabinet ministers, 13 September 1927, Policy Ctte minutes, 16 July 1928, Worthington-Evans MSS, MSS.Eng.hist.c.895/61–2, c.896/27–32.
[208] Memo by Hoare, 'The resignation of the Second Baldwin Government', June 1929, Templewood MSS, V/4; Amery diary, 2–3 May 1929.
[209] Derby diary, 25 October 1922.
[210] N. to I. Chamberlain, 3 March, to H. Chamberlain, 28 July 1934, *NCDL*.

Policy decisions were discussed in the Cabinet and shadow cabinet (which was known as the Leader's Conference in 1924 and the Business Committee in 1929–31[211]), but these forums tended to focus on short-term tactics rather than long-term strategy. A more constant flow of advice came from the Leader's aides, cronies, and sometimes family members. The Chief Whip reported on parliamentary views, and played a key part in deciding priorities and timing in the parliamentary order of business.[212] These figures on the front bench and in the Leader's entourage had the vital access which enabled them to put across their point of view or give warnings, though these could still be ignored. Other MPs could only do so intermittently or indirectly, by means of requesting an interview, being part of a deputation, using the subject committees and 1922 Committee, or simply talking to the whips. When the subject committees were first created, under the direction of the former Cabinet ministers, their backbench members played a part in the most elaborate formal policy exercise conducted during this period. This was the reshaping of policy in opposition in 1924, when there was a need to distance the party from the 1923 tariff policy and find a broader positive public appeal—what became Baldwin's 'New Conservatism' of principled moderation, as stated in very general terms in the pamphlet *Looking Ahead*.

The other person in frequent consultation with the Leader was the Party Chairman. He could act as a channel for constituency views, particularly up to 1930 when he was also ex officio chairman of the National Union's Executive Committee. The latter could forward resolutions to the Leader, a procedure which was formalized following the rule changes of 1930, whilst on matters of particular importance it could send a deputation. Constituency opinion also influenced decision-making through being transmitted to, and vocalized by, members of parliament. The latter also had their own sense of public opinion, and passed on through the whips their views as to what would be acceptable or popular. One of the roles of Central Office and its network of Area Offices was to gather impressions of public opinion, as well as that of the party membership.

The principal influence upon policy-making from outside the party was the press, which claimed both to represent and to shape public opinion. Several of the editors of respectable pro-Conservative national and regional newspapers had access to the Party Leader or other senior frontbenchers, and these discussions were used by the leadership as a source of information, a sounding board and a means of influence. These channels were all clearly and conventionally 'political', and their participation in shaping the direction of government was expected and accepted. However, groups acting for particular interests or promoting a specific issue were less welcome and had less impact than might be expected. Any element of coercion was resented, and the favouring of a sectional interest ran counter to

---

[211] The term 'shadow cabinet' is used for convenience here and elsewhere; however, according to Bridgeman, during this period there was no established regular meeting. Baldwin summoned 'such of his old colleagues, singly or in batches, and other advisers, according to the subject under consideration', and there had only been one gathering of all members of the former Cabinet: Bridgeman to Croft, 11 October 1930, Croft MSS, CAC, CRFT/1/5/Br5.

[212] Eyres-Monsell to Baldwin, 10 November 1927, Baldwin MSS, 162/120–1.

the Conservative values of social unity and fair play. The party was not in the pocket of its donors, and, at the national level, the various employers' organizations and, locally, the Chambers of Commerce had limited direct contact. Single-issue pressure groups were seen as lacking in balance and an understanding of the wider context, and to be the preserve of cranks and faddists. Of course, there was one other powerful determinant of strategic choices: the need to respond to the programmes of the opposition parties. In this sense, the parties were participants in a dynamic dialogue, reacting to each other's moves.

In the decade after 1918, the wider sphere of government activity and the greater expectations of the democratic electorate made it necessary to formulate policy in more detail. This was not a problem when the party was in office, as the researching and drafting of proposals was done by civil servants. However, the 'governing mentality', which resulted from long spells in power, could have a dulling effect on ministers' political awareness, with the result being something of an uneasy compromise. Davidson's phrasing was revealing when he proposed that a Cabinet committee begin framing the programme for the 1929 election: the aim was to 'determine how far the political interests and desires of the Party can be translated into policy acceptable to Ministers in the light of their departmental experience'.[213] When the party was in opposition, the leaders were cut off from the resources of the civil service at the very point when a reappraisal of policy was most needed. The library and information services at Central Office were inadequate to the task and had many other calls on their time, and this led to the development of other bodies to provide the decision-makers with support and expert advice. During the opposition period in 1924, a Policy Secretariat was created to service the committees which were working towards a new programme, but this was disbanded when the party returned to office after the 1924 general election.[214] The early impetus towards creating a permanent research staff came from the university MP and famous novelist John Buchan, who, in January 1928, proposed a scheme in two parts: 'adult education', which was already under way, and 'political research work…which badly needs undertaking'.[215] He was appointed chairman of a committee which considered the whole field of the party's educational work, but with the general election on the horizon this focused mainly on the educational work (which led to the establishment of Ashridge), and little progress was made regarding a research staff.[216]

However, after the 1929 defeat, the return to opposition and the loss of access to the civil service made the deficiency more apparent and urgent, and this led to the establishment of the Conservative Research Department (CRD). To emphasize its different functions of analysis and the development of long-term strategy, it was housed in separate premises from Central Office, although not very far away, at 24

---

[213] Davidson to Baldwin, 13 June 1927, Baldwin MSS, 36/65–70.
[214] Amery diary, 23 and 25 January, 14 November 1924; for the staffing and work of the Policy Secretariat, see Lloyd, oral history interview in Cohen, 'Disraeli's Child', 578, Cohen MSS.
[215] Buchan to Baldwin, 5 January 1928, Baldwin MSS, 53/76–7.
[216] Ball to Waterhouse, 10 January 1928, Baldwin MSS, 53/97.

Old Queen Street, which was shared with the Party Leader and his staff. The CRD was not under the control of the Party Chairman; it had its own Chairman and its own funds, which were overseen by its own Treasurer.[217] Joseph Ball, who had been head of the Publicity Department at Central Office since 1927, vacated that post to become the senior official of the CRD, with the title of Director. Neville Chamberlain became its Chairman in March 1930 (whilst he was overseas in the winter of 1929–30, Lord Eustace Percy acted as an initial caretaker, but he was not the department's founder). Chamberlain was greatly interested in the potential of the new body, through which he expected 'I shall have my finger on the springs of policy.'[218] After ceasing to be Party Chairman in 1931, he made a point of retaining the chairmanship of the CRD, which he held until his death in November 1940. However, in June 1940, with the German breakthrough in France, Chamberlain had agreed to Ball's suggestion that the CRD's remaining staff of four should seek 'active war work of some kind or another', and its operations were then suspended for the duration of the conflict.[219]

During the opposition period in 1930–31, the CRD produced a number of reports which provided the detailed basis of policy developments on key areas such as agriculture, iron and steel, imperial trade, the mechanics of introducing a tariff system, and the reform of unemployment insurance.[220] Chamberlain's prominence in the leadership and his active interest in the work of the CRD combined to establish the new institution in a secure but subordinate role, finding information and working out the details of party policy. He worked closely with Ball (who served as Director until 1945); they shared the hobby of trout fishing, and Chamberlain came to rely upon Ball's loyalty and discretion.[221] As a result, especially after Chamberlain became Party Leader, Ball was entrusted with a number of confidential tasks which drew on his previous career in the intelligence services. These included the manipulation of the press and, according to the later account of the anti-appeasement MP Ronald Tree, the tapping of the telephones of the critics.[222] However, these activities were personal and quite separate from the work of the CRD, which did not directly intervene in public or party affairs. Its role was advisory rather than executive: 'its function is to explore avenues', but 'the CRD has nothing to do with the determination of policy'.[223] It worked to the brief decided upon at a higher level, and added quality and effectiveness—but mostly at the level of detail. Its twin functions remained as Chamberlain had initially defined them:

---

[217] Baldwin to Luke, 27 January 1932, Baldwin MSS, 167/179–80.
[218] N. to I. Chamberlain, 22 March 1930, *NCDL*; Lord Percy of Newcastle, *Some Memories* (1958), 149.
[219] Ball to N. Chamberlain, 5 June, N. Chamberlain to Ball, 6 June 1940, NC, 8/21/13–14; N. Chamberlain to Churchill, 19 October 1940, Churchill MSS, CAC, CHAR/2/402/28.
[220] Copies of these early reports are in AC, 49/1/1–8. For the staffing and work of the CRD, see Brooke, oral history interview in Cohen, 'Disraeli's Child', 575–6, Cohen MSS; J. Ramsden, *The Making of Conservative Party Policy: The Conservative Research Department since 1929* (1980), 39–60.
[221] Ball to N. Chamberlain, 21 February, 6 June 1938, NC, 7/11/31/9–10.
[222] Tree, *When the Moon Was High*, 76; R. B. Cockett, 'Ball, Chamberlain and "Truth"', *Historical Journal*, 33 (1990), 131–42.
[223] Wolmer to N. Chamberlain, 24 March 1930, Wolmer MSS, MSS.Eng.hist.c.997/13–15.

'at once an Information Bureau providing data and briefs for leaders, and a long range Research Body'.[224] The work which the CRD provided was valuable, but its importance should not be overestimated: control of the selection and announcement of policy remained where it always had been, with the front-bench parliamentary leadership and—where a critical decision had to be taken—with the Leader of the Party alone.

[224] N. to I. Chamberlain, 22 March 1930, *NCDL*.

7

Leaders

Authority and Crises

The traditional basis on which the Conservative Party was organized was of a Leader in the House of Commons and a Leader in the House of Lords. In government, whichever of these was Prime Minister was recognized as the Leader of the whole party and exercised that authority, which in the nineteenth and early twentieth centuries made the selection 'really the act of the Sovereign'.[1] When the party went into opposition, the former Prime Minister retained this status until he chose to retire, as in the case of Balfour from 1905 to 1911. Although there was then formally a reversion to the previous system of parallel leadership, the importance of public opinion and the declining significance of the Lords—especially after the Parliament Act of 1911—meant that, in practice, his successor as Leader in the Commons, Bonar Law, was generally regarded as being the Party Leader. Even so, as far as the shadow cabinet was concerned, it was the existing Leader in the Lords 'who holds the position of seniority, would issue the summons and take the chair'.[2] When Bonar Law retired for the first time in 1921, there was a reversion to the previous practice, whereby Austen Chamberlain became only the Leader in the Commons. In one sense, as Curzon had been leading the Lords since 1916, Chamberlain was the junior of the tandem, but in reality he exercised overall control and acted as the Party Leader, and he was referred to as such by the Chairman of the Party.[3] However, it was because Chamberlain's formal position was only that of Leader in the Commons that the meeting which he summoned at the Carlton Club in October 1922 was restricted to being a gathering of MPs (the only peers who were present attended as Cabinet ministers and party leaders—not as members of the upper chamber—and they had no vote). When the Lloyd George Coalition fell, Bonar Law's need to establish his authority and rally the divided party led to an innovation, as he declined to accept the royal commission to form a government until he had been appointed as Leader of the whole party by a hastily organized representative meeting. This created, for the first time, a recognized

---

[1] Talbot to Long, 24 March 1921, Long MSS, Add.62426/54–7; A. to H. Chamberlain, 20 March 1921, *ACDL*.
[2] Memo by Balcarres (Chief Whip), 'The organisation of the Shadow Cabinet', 28 November 1911, Bonar Law MSS, BL/41/I/1a.
[3] NU Labour Ctte., 10 July 1922; Younger certainly acted in this way, reporting to and taking instructions from Chamberlain alone. However, when the breach came over continuing the Coalition government, he receded from this in private correspondence, stating 'after all he is only Leader in the House of Commons': Younger to Sanders, 25 September 1922, Bayford diary.

office of 'Leader of the Conservative Party', which thereafter was handed on in continuous succession. From October 1922 onwards, Conservative peers participated in the formal meeting at which a new Party Leader was enthroned, and the leadership of the Lords became a subordinate office; since then its holder has been appointed and dismissed by the Leader of the Party, although with regard to the sentiments of Conservative peers.[4] This chapter examines two related areas: firstly, the selection of the party leaders, their role, and the reasons for their decline; secondly, the crises of leadership and policy which were a repeated feature of the interwar period.

THE SELECTION OF LEADERS

There was no set of rules for selecting the Party Leader, and even to senior figures it was not clear who was responsible for overseeing the process and had the authority to decide upon the method and timetable.[5] In practice, it was accepted that the choice of Leader in the House of Commons was a matter for all the MPs who were in receipt of the party whip. It was assumed that if there was a contest, it would be decided by a meeting and a vote; this would have occurred in 1911, but for the withdrawal of the other candidates in favour of Bonar Law. In 1921, Bonar Law intimated his resignation by writing to the Chief Whip; Talbot 'thought better under the circumstances to regard it as a Whips' business to decide what initial action should be taken', and he presided at the meeting of MPs held on 21 March.[6] The effects of the 1911 Parliament Act and the 1918 Reform Act shaped the assumption, which had become general by the early 1920s, that the person chosen by Conservative MPs was effectively the overall Leader. Thus, Chamberlain's defeat at the Carlton Club meeting not only ended his leadership of the Commons but also created a vacancy in the overall leadership, which did not simply revert to Curzon as Leader in the Lords. After 1911, it was clear that the overall Party Leader had to have the support of the party in the House of Commons—although this did not mean he had to be an MP, as Lord Hailsham in 1929–31 and Lord Halifax in 1938–40 were generally regarded as the most likely choice if a vacancy should occur.

From October 1922 onwards, however his selection had come about, a new Party Leader was confirmed in his post by formal election at a party meeting, which was chaired by the Leader in the House of Lords. In 1922 and 1923, those present consisted of the MPs and peers in receipt of the party whip, and prospective candidates who had been officially adopted. From the next such meeting, fourteen years later, the Executive Committee of the National Union was also invited to attend; whilst the party outside parliament had no direct influence upon the selection of the Leader, the presence of the representatives of the rank and file at the

---

[4] Hailsham to Salisbury, 2 April 1931, Salisbury MSS, S(4)140/58–61.
[5] Long to Talbot, 22 March 1921, Long MSS, Add.62426/48–52.
[6] Talbot to Long, 24 March 1921, Long MSS, Add.62426/54–7.

formal confirmatory meetings implied a kind of consultation with—and consent by—the constituencies. The resolution to elect the new Leader was usually proposed by his principal rival (Chamberlain and Long in 1911, Curzon in 1923, and Halifax in 1940), whilst Churchill, the largest loose cannon on the deck, was the seconder in 1937.[7] This coronation ceremony was important as a demonstration of unity, and it marked the fact that any debate about the leadership was now closed.[8] It also gave the appearance of a democratic process in which the party voted its Leader into office, albeit unopposed. To the extent that this implied choice, it was misleading—but symbolically it was true: the Leader held his place by virtue of having the confidence of Conservative MPs and (less crucially) peers, who could withdraw it.

This was the reason for the careful distinction made by Baldwin when summoning a party meeting in June 1930, when his position was under rising threat: it was restricted to MPs and prospective candidates—'those who are actively engaged in the constituencies'—and so was not 'a party meeting in the accepted sense of the term' as 'the question of leadership, according to ancient practice, is as I understand it a matter for Lords and Commons alone'.[9] This rather hair-splitting distinction served its immediate purpose, but ignored the reality of what had happened in 1922. In any case, it is hard to see how Baldwin could have remained as Leader if he had lost the vote at this gathering, which everyone, in fact, termed a 'party meeting'. It also illustrates how malleable the supposed conventions actually were, for less than a year earlier Baldwin had assured the embryonic Defeated Candidates' Association that 'to any party meeting in the commonly accepted sense of the words I would certainly summon the defeated candidates of 1929', whereas in fact the decision to invite them to the June meeting was taken only at the eleventh hour.[10] Significantly, when his tactical position was much stronger in October 1930, Baldwin had no hesitation about summoning a meeting which had the necessary composition and authority, in order to secure a vote of confidence in his leadership as well as his policy. This gathering was of peers and MPs, although at a late stage, as extra insurance, the mostly moderate and loyalist prospective candidates (many of them former MPs seeking to recover the marginals) were summoned to attend as well.[11] However, the idea of the Leader securing a vote of confidence by resigning and submitting himself for re-election was criticized as

---

[7] Churchill's role was the result of his own suggestion: 'Memo on Party Meeting', May 1937, CPA, Whips' Office MSS, 2/5; Austen Chamberlain indicated that he would be willing to propose Baldwin's re-election as Leader at the party meeting in February 1924, but in the event this was not necessary: Derby diary, 23 January 1924.
[8] Davidson to Bonar Law, 24 March 1921, Bonar Law MSS, BL/107/1/4.
[9] Baldwin to Salisbury, 23 June 1930, Salisbury MSS, S(4)135/184; Salisbury to Baldwin, 23 June 1930, Baldwin MSS, 165/301.
[10] Baldwin to Moore-Brabazon, 26 July 1929, Moore-Brabazon MSS; N. Chamberlain to Davidson, 23 June 1930, Conservative Research Department, CPA, CRD/1/24/1.
[11] Headlam diary, 25–9 October 1930; Castle Stuart to Baldwin, 24 October 1930, Baldwin MSS, 31/178. The chair for the debate on the leadership was taken by the Party Leader in the House of Lords, Lord Salisbury.

'undignified and farcical' when Baldwin considered such a tactic in February 1924, and he abandoned the idea.[12]

All of the leadership selections between the wars occurred whilst the party was in government, and were therefore directly linked with ministerial office—in nearly every case, the Premiership. Baldwin in 1923 and Neville Chamberlain in 1937 became Prime Minister within an existing government, and succeeded to the party leadership in consequence. Chamberlain offered to vacate the leadership after Churchill became Prime Minister in May 1940, but at this point the latter was more concerned about emphasizing national unity and establishing his position above parties, and he asked Chamberlain to carry on.[13] However, when terminal illness forced the latter to stand down in October 1940, Churchill decided—against his wife's strong advice—that it would be unsafe to allow the position to be taken by someone else, and so the leadership was reunited with the Premiership after a temporary divergence. The reverse situation applied in the situation after the fall of the Coalition in 1922, when Bonar Law insisted upon being elected Party Leader before he considered himself able to form a government. In fact this had symbolic rather than real importance, as the victorious anti-Coalitionists had no other credible candidate for either position. Finally, although the Premiership was not vacant, in 1921 when Austen Chamberlain succeeded Bonar Law as Party Leader in the House of Commons, he also inherited his predecessor's role as the second figure in the Coalition government.

The choice of a Prime Minister is, in theory, the selection of the Crown, but in constitutional practice the monarch is required to act upon advice. This meant that the choice of both Premiers and Party Leaders was mainly determined by the opinions of the front bench, although they would take into account their awareness of feelings in the parliamentary party. The selection was therefore made by those in the closest proximity to the candidates, who were best able to assess them and most likely to be aware of any drawbacks. The objections to Curzon in 1923 from members of the Cabinet (and former Prime Minister Balfour outside it) were based on more than simply irritation with a difficult colleague: his conduct had reduced confidence in his judgement and raised concerns about the manner in which he would lead the Cabinet and the party. Cunliffe-Lister later recalled: 'we thought Curzon was autocratic without being strong, and intellectually arrogant and unwilling to consider other men's views'.[14] The opinions of front-bench colleagues were formed over time, and usually settled well before a vacancy occurred. For this reason, it was often the case that consensus had developed that one particular person was the clear 'heir apparent'. Where that was well-known and widely accepted, it obviated the need for any canvass of opinion by the Crown—and so the exercise which chose Baldwin in 1923 was not needed when he retired in 1937. In all cases, there was a desire to move swiftly: this reduced the period of uncertainty in which factions might form, and so aided in the preservation of stability and continuity.

---

[12] A. Chamberlain, memo of meeting with Baldwin, 7 February 1924, AC, 35/4/35, also in *BP*, 144; some held the same view when John Major did this in 1995.

[13] Churchill to N. Chamberlain, 16 May 1940, Churchill MSS, CAC, CHAR/2/402/1.

[14] Lord Swinton, *Sixty Years of Power* (1966), 76.

Four of the five selections of leaders during this period occurred when there was a pre-eminent candidate, and were uncontested. In 1921 and 1937, a clear successor had been established for a long period and enjoyed general confidence and approval, and there was no serious rival.[15] In 1940, the period of the successor's pre-eminence had been only a few months, but the extraordinary circumstances under which Churchill had established his authority—even more than the fact that he was Prime Minister already—ensured that no other choice could be contemplated. Those MPs who had doubts about his judgement (especially in domestic politics) and who did not welcome the change nevertheless accepted Churchill's succession as inevitable when illness unexpectedly forced Neville Chamberlain to resign. The fall of the latter's half-brother Austen in 1922 was also unexpected, but in the vacuum created by the displacement of the other senior figures in the leadership, and with his status as a successful previous Leader who had had a decade's experience in the post, Bonar Law had the clearest field of all. His standing was such that the legitimacy of his occupancy of the leadership was accepted even by the ousted ministers, which helped to minimize the damage caused by the split, while the tentative explorations of reconciliation in the following months took it for granted that any reunion would be under his leadership.[16]

The only point during this period when there was any real element of choice was in 1923, and even here it was only between two alternatives: the glittering and greatly experienced Lord Curzon, former Viceroy of India and Foreign Secretary since 1919, and the almost unknown Stanley Baldwin, whose position as one of the two Commons Cabinet ministers to oppose the Coalition had led to his unexpected promotion to Chancellor of the Exchequer in 1922 (though not before Bonar Law had approached some other candidates first). The leadership selection in May 1923 had several unusual features. The first of these was that the vacancy occurred so soon after the installation of the previous Leader, as the interval of seven months was not long enough for a single definite successor to have become established. The second matter was the unhealed rift in the front-bench leadership, which removed the former Coalitionists from consideration. Linked to this, the question of which potential Leader could best achieve reunion assumed particular importance as a criterion. The final complication was Bonar Law's refusal to recommend to the King which of the two candidates should succeed him as Prime Minister. His advice would almost certainly have been acted upon, and the person invited to form a government would then have succeeded him as Party Leader as well. Bonar Law's silence made the confusion greater still, adding the problem of how the decision should be made to the question of what it should be. Without his endorsement, the burden of determining the succession to both posts was left with the King by default—not because it lay within his normal powers, but because the politicians failed to exercise theirs.

---

[15] Long to Bull, 18 March 1921, Long MSS, Add.62426/27–32.
[16] Although Austen Chamberlain would not serve under Bonar Law, this was a personal feeling due to the latter's failure to give any intimation of his intention to oppose Chamberlain at the Carlton Club meeting: he did not seek to discourage or prevent other ex-Coalitionists from accepting office: A. to I. Chamberlain, 18 November 1922, *ACDL*; A. Chamberlain to Worthington-Evans, 24 May 1923, AC, 35/2/6.

In this situation, and in his preferred role as a kind of constitutional umpire, George V took steps to consult the party opinion that mattered, which was that of its most authoritative leading figures apart from the departing Leader and the two candidates who might succeed him. The King's aim was not to choose whom he preferred, but whom the party leadership would rally behind, so that the government could continue with as little disruption as possible. Balfour was consulted as a former Prime Minister and the previous Party Leader to Bonar Law, and not as one of the exiled Coalitionists. The others whose views were sought by the King were those of weight and judgement, such as Lord Salisbury. There were several attempts to push advice on the King (through his private secretary and emissary in these consultations, Lord Stamfordham) by Cabinet ministers supportive of Baldwin such as Amery and Bridgeman; a still more controversial matter was the pro-Baldwin memorandum written by Bonar Law's PPS, J. C. C. Davidson, but delivered to Stamfordham by the Prime Minister's private secretary, Ronald Waterhouse, with the comment that it 'practically reflected' the views of the otherwise silent departing Premier.[17] The latter particularly has been the source of much debate, but in fact it seems that the King was not much influenced by any of these initiatives, although they may have confirmed his developing view that Baldwin had a much wider basis of support.

Baldwin's only drawback was inexperience, but in every other respect he was the stronger candidate. He was more acceptable to the Coalitionists and therefore the more unifying figure; his open and honest opposition to the Coalition in 1922 caused much less resentment than Curzon's last-minute change of sides.[18] He had not alienated crucial colleagues—in particular, Derby would serve under Baldwin but not Curzon—and Cabinet ministers were lining up to support him, whilst no one indicated so for Curzon. Baldwin's presentational style and image of the 'plain man' was also much more appropriate to the needs of the new democratic age than Curzon's aristocratic hauteur. The latter point was crucial: the King's view was determined by his concept of the national interest, and what weighed most with him was the need to avoid a provocative class-war gesture. The Labour Party had almost no representation in the House of Lords, and to place the Prime Minister where the principal opposition party could not challenge him would only make matters worse. It was thus Curzon's position in the Lords which became both a decisive point and the presentable justification for preferring Baldwin, and the insuperable barrier of the personality issue and his consequent rejection by the Cabinet was thereby disguised. Curzon was summoned from his country house in Somerset and seen first by the King with the intention of breaking the news to him gently, but Curzon had assumed from being invited to attend on the monarch first that the long-coveted post was his, and his disappointment was all the more bitter. Receiving the royal commission later that day, Baldwin had no trouble in securing

---

[17] Davidson memo, and copy with Stamfordham's annotation, 20 May 1923, Davidson MSS, DAV/143.
[18] Derby diary, 23 November 1922.

Cabinet support or, in view of this, in persuading the chagrined Curzon to continue as Foreign Secretary.[19]

The only occasion when there was the prospect of choosing a Leader whilst in opposition was the near-vacancy in early March 1931, when, for a brief period, it seemed that Baldwin might depart. Four names were generally spoken of as possible successors, two of whom were in the group loosely referred to as the 'shadow cabinet' whilst the other two were, in different ways, detached from it. Of the latter, the one considered least likely to be supported by Conservative MPs was Churchill, partly because of the long-standing distrust of his ambitions and judgement, and partly because he was identified with opposition to tariffs, although he had—with reluctance—accepted the 'free hand' protectionist policy adopted in the previous autumn.[20] However, the parliamentary opposition to Baldwin's line on India seemed so strong in February 1931 that it was thought possible that Churchill's diehard stance might win him new support and sweep him into the leadership. Even so, the more likely outside contender was Sir Robert Horne, who was seen as sufficiently strong on protection that he would be able secure the cessation of the press lords' attacks; he was on good terms with Beaverbrook, without having been involved in his campaign. Horne had distanced himself from his Coalitionist past, as for most of the period since 1924 he had concentrated upon business affairs, in which field he had a substantial reputation. However, he was not keen to return to full-time politics, and would, at best, have been a reluctant candidate.

The most probable successors were the two within the current front-bench leadership, as they could retain the loyalty of Baldwin's supporters whilst hoping to reconcile some of his critics. Neville Chamberlain had even more firmly established his position in the front rank since 1929, especially in filling the difficult post of Party Chairman since June 1930. His drive, vigour in debate, and command of policy were admired but he was seen by some as narrow and an administrator rather than a statesman, 'more at home in the frozen regions of politics'.[21] Chamberlain himself considered that the party was more likely to choose Lord Hailsham, who was at this time the acting-Leader in the House of Lords.[22] Before his elevation to the Lord Chancellorship in 1928, he had been a highly effective pilot of legislation through the Commons as Attorney-General, and he was regarded with favour by the right wing of the party. Both Hailsham and Chamberlain wished to block the outside contenders and prevent any radical change of direction, and at the latter's suggestion they made a pact to stand together, with each willing to serve under the other if he was the party's choice.[23] There is little doubt that this combination would have secured overwhelming support from MPs and peers, principally because it offered continuity with greater stability and effectiveness. However, the situation

---

[19] Baldwin to Curzon, 22 May 1923, Curzon MSS, F112/320/107.
[20] Ormsby-Gore to his mother, 9 March 1931, Ormsby-Gore MSS, PEC/10/1/14/5.
[21] Hannon to Beaverbrook, 15 August and 7 October 1930, Beaverbrook MSS, C154, Hannon MSS, HNN/17/1.
[22] N. to I. Chamberlain, 21 February, to H. Chamberlain, 1 March 1931, *NCDL*.
[23] N. Chamberlain diary, 8 March 1931, NC, 2/22.

did not arise, as Baldwin recovered his authority and continued as Leader for a further six years. Hailsham lost ground during the spring and summer of 1931, whilst Neville Chamberlain established a position as sole heir apparent which was reinforced by his appointment as Chancellor of the Exchequer in October 1931;[24] he continued in both roles for the remainder of Baldwin's leadership, and was his automatic and undisputed successor in May 1937.

The party's desire for unity was the most important factor in leadership selection, whilst contests might cause polarization. The party meeting of March 1921 'got into a very good frame of mind, with the note of loyalty as the dominant idea', and so the few supporters of Birkenhead who had intended to call for delay remained silent.[25] Candidates who would open or widen rifts were rejected, even if they were more impressive—such as Curzon in 1923. On the other hand, of the four possible candidates in March 1931, Hailsham and Neville Chamberlain were the unity candidates, and so when they acted together the combination swept the board. To gain the leadership, it was necessary not to be seen chafing for the crown or trying to snatch it from its present wearer, but instead to be presented with it and to accept it almost reluctantly. This was in tune with accepted forms of gentlemanly behaviour, which deprecated open shows of ambition or of triumphant conduct in a competitive environment, and cherished a belief in the moral superiority of amateurism as principled and disinterested with regard to personal gain.[26]

At any point, there were only a very limited number of credible candidates for the leadership. There were no outsiders: all of those talked about as possible future leaders came into consideration because of their effectiveness in the parliamentary arena and had leading front-bench roles. This was the reason for Horne being considered by some MPs in the aftershock of Bonar Law's sudden resignation in March 1921, but, significantly, one of the whips recorded 'there is a strong feeling that he has been here such a short time'.[27] The opportunity for backbench MPs and even for most of the Cabinet to shape the succession lay not at the point when there was a vacancy but during the process from which potential candidates emerged. It was often in the early stages of a Cabinet career that a minister showed the characteristics which marked him as likely to rise to the top; thus W. S. Morrison had been in the Cabinet for less than eighteen months when Baldwin described him as 'certainly to his mind a future Prime Minister'.[28] To be a contender for the leadership, it was necessary to be in the forefront, to be respected and to have support amongst MPs. Potential leaders usually held, or had held, one of the great offices of state. Churchill was already Prime Minister when he became Party Leader; Austen Chamberlain, Baldwin, Neville Chamberlain, Churchill, and Horne had been Chancellor of the Exchequer; Curzon, Halifax, and Eden had been Foreign Secre-

---

[24] N. to H. Chamberlain, 25 May 1931, *NCDL*.
[25] Bridgeman to Long, 21 March 1921, Long MSS, Add.62426/43–4; Bayford diary, 24 March 1921.
[26] Headlam diary, 29 June 1933.
[27] Gibbs to Long, 18 March 1921, Long MSS, Add.62426/33–8.
[28] Robertson Scott memo, 28 January 1938, *BP*, 447.

tary, and Hailsham had been Lord Chancellor. The exception was Bonar Law in 1911, but this was after the party had been out of office for six years, and he was not the only member of the front bench who had not served in the last Cabinet. He was also an unexpected candidate in a confused situation where there was strong opposition to the most likely choice, Austen Chamberlain, who had been the most recent Conservative Chancellor of the Exchequer, in 1903–05.

A credible contender needed to be regarded as fully part of the party, and more or less in its mainstream. In 1911, this was the case with Bonar Law, a moderate tariff reformer after his backing of the referendum policy in the December 1910 election, but not with the Liberal Unionist and tariff 'whole-hogger' Austen Chamberlain; however, it was the case with the latter by 1921, when he did become Leader. It was not the case with Churchill as Chancellor of the Exchequer in 1924–29 due to his free-trade views, and certainly not the case when he was a backbench rebel in the 1930s. It was for this reason that Baldwin refused to anoint the prodigal a second time, telling Hoare in 1936 that 'on no account would he contemplate' giving Churchill a post, 'chiefly for the risk that would be involved by having him in the Cabinet when the question of his successor became imminent'.[29]

There were several other factors involved in determining who was and who was not a possible contender for the leadership. Some of these were practical: the person had to be in the suitable age range, which was usually somewhere between fifty and sixty (although both Neville Chamberlain and Churchill were older, at sixty-eight and sixty-five respectively), and to have no significant health problems. Confidence in the potential Leader's dependability and judgement was essential; in early 1922, when Birkenhead was still at the height of his influence, the Deputy Party Chairman was sure he would never become Leader: the party 'would want someone more stable if less brilliant'.[30] More important than just possessing drive and energy was the ability to provide the party with a sense of direction and purpose. It was also necessary not to be carrying negative baggage, whether of personal temperament, responsibility for unpopular or unsuccessful policies, or too close an identification with a particular section. In 1923, Curzon's methods of relating to his Cabinet colleagues had alienated too many of them, including crucial figures such as Derby. Neville Chamberlain's prospects in 1930–31 were hampered not so much by his position as Party Chairman and defender of Baldwin, but by the view that he was 'rather cold and detached and has not been a good "mixer" with the rank and file'.[31] By 1937, it was not only the weight of his authority and experience but also some lessening in this distance from his followers which overcame reservations in most quarters.

There were few credible leadership candidates from the right, partly because the diehards were mainly backbenchers and partly because the right-wing programme was considered by most MPs to be impracticable and unappealing to the mass of

---

[29] Hoare to N. Chamberlain, 23 February 1936, Templewood MSS, VIII/6.
[30] Bayford diary, 10 March 1921.
[31] Hannon to Beaverbrook, 18 September 1930, Beaverbrook MSS, BBK/C154.

voters. The contender furthest to the right was Hailsham, but, although he was popular with that wing, it is an oversimplification to see him as a diehard. His views inclined more to the right than some of the Cabinet on some issues, but in most respects he was a pragmatist committed to party unity, and it was his vigour and ability as an advocate that gave his views greater impact. The only other putative Leader with support principally on the right was Joynson-Hicks, Home Secretary in 1924–29, and, in reality, few apart from himself took his chances seriously. Churchill's path to the leadership was more complex, and his identification with the diehards in opposition to the India Bill in 1931–35 (as well as his own conduct) rendered him less credible and attractive as a Leader, whilst from 1935 to 1939 his criticism of appeasement linked him more with the youthful left—to their discomfort.

Baldwin remarked that 'you want a left-winger to lead the Party; you will want your right wing but do not let them get control'.[32] It is true that several leadership contenders emerged from the left of the Conservative spectrum, in particular Eden, Elliot, and Oliver Stanley, and—after 1945—Butler and Macmillan. However, most of the potential leaders were seen as centrist moderates: this was the case with Bonar Law by 1918, Baldwin in 1923 (he became more identified with the left after 1925), Horne in 1931, Neville Chamberlain in 1931 and 1937, Halifax in 1940, and others sometimes spoken of, such as Inskip, Morrison, and Kingsley Wood.[33] From this position, they had the best prospect of delivering the two things which were most desired: an electoral appeal to the mass of uncommitted voters, and unity in the party. The latter was perhaps the most important factor of all, as the rejection of Austen Chamberlain and return of Bonar Law in 1922 demonstrated. If there had been a recent period of disunity especially, the party desired a Leader who was above faction and who could turn attention forwards and outwards rather than inwards and backwards. For all these reasons, it was not unusual for the potential choice to narrow to just one individual, and for that candidate to acquire the momentum of inevitability. However, if that situation remained static over a long period its very predictability could produce a counter-reaction and encourage speculation—although it was usually no more than that—about candidates from the next generation. Thus, Neville Chamberlain's long wait from 1931 to 1937 led to talk of Inskip leapfrogging over him to succeed Baldwin directly.[34] Certainly, no succession was ever truly guaranteed, and so not even the clearest heirs apparent could be sure that they would inherit.

THE ROLE AND DUTIES OF LEADERS

The position of Leader of the Conservative Party was, in theory, immensely powerful, conferring unchecked authority over appointments to the front bench, the

---

[32] Rhys, note of conversation with Baldwin, 8 December 1932, Dynevor MSS.
[33] Channon diary, 12 September 1937, 2 June 1938, 20 September 1939; Headlam diary, 1 April 1936, 23 January 1938, 6 April, 22 June 1943.
[34] Crookshank diary, 14 March 1936; Elliot was also favoured by many in the mid-1930s: Somervell journal, 2 February and 4 March 1934, Somervell MSS, MSS.Eng.c.6565/18, 24.

Whips' Office, and the central party organization, and possessing the sole right to choose and announce the party's policies. In practice, the Leader's position had considerable defensive strengths, but was often less effective in a creative role: the latter could only be accomplished on a broader front and involved the participation of—and therefore a dialogue with—colleagues and subordinates. Baldwin commented after retiring from the leadership: 'I was very far from being a dictator!'[35] This was even truer as far as the backbench MPs and the constituency grass roots were concerned; the Leader had no powers or sanctions with which to impose control, and therefore had to show the way by exhortation and example. The visible outcome can easily be misinterpreted: if everyone is marching down the same road, the man at the front may be leading but this does not mean that he has caused those behind to follow. To employ another metaphor, the Leader should be seen not as a solo performer but as the conductor of an orchestra. However, provided he retained at least the tacit support of his most respected colleagues and acted with some sensitivity and prudence, the Leader could carry the party some way in a direction that was not the preference of many, or even most, of the rank and file. In 1930, Baldwin and Salisbury, the Leader in the Lords, had 'no doubt that they can really control their Party' in its response to the outcome of the India Round Table conference, and so it proved.[36] Younger was aware that 'the leaders can lead [the party] if they are courageous and tactful, but they cannot drive them'.[37] The fate of the Coalition in 1922 demonstrated both sides of this, for the leadership were able to keep the party committed to it for months after the January election scare had revealed that it had ceased to have much attraction for many MPs and constituencies, whilst the final collapse was mainly due to errors and imprudence on the part of the Leaders. Instead of recognizing that in times of difficulty 'our leaders owe a somewhat special consideration to their followers', they treated constituency and backbench opinion with aloof disregard.[38]

The foremost role of the Party Leader was to decide its aims and direction at the strategic level. Of course, these normally unfolded gradually and from a context of consultation and deliberation, not least so that there should not be too many shocks and strains for the Leader's followers. This was a particular cause of complaint after the sudden unveiling of the protectionist programme at the 1923 Annual Conference, although the fact that it led to an unwelcome election and defeat added considerably to the objections; the Leader of the Party in Leeds, Sir Charles Wilson, declared that it had 'savoured too much of the act of a Dictator'.[39] As Hoare observed in his letter to *The Times* three days before the Carlton Club meeting in 1922, and as Austen Chamberlain's fate there demonstrated, the Leader could not simply 'impose from above'.[40] In Baldwin's view, 'the responsibility of

[35] Note by Mrs Burges, 24 April 1940, *BP*, 470.
[36] Hailey to Irwin, 9 December 1930, Halifax MSS, C152/19/1/184.
[37] Younger to Long, 27 March 1922, Long MSS, Add.62427/31–2.
[38] Long to A. Chamberlain, 27 March 1922, Long MSS, Add. 62405/96–9.
[39] Wilson to Wood, 12 December 1923, Baldwin MSS, 42/145–6.
[40] *The Times*, 16 October 1922; Long thought this expressed the opinions of 'an immense majority in the Conservative Party', Long to Hoare, 16 October 1922, Templewood MSS, I/2.

the Leader is to form an opinion on the facts before him and to put it before his party'.[41] The Leader was therefore expected to take the initiative and set an agenda, and to be something more than just a mouthpiece for his followers.[42] It was clear where the ultimate responsibility lay and, in Baldwin's words, the Leader 'must rely largely—certainly finally—on his own judgement by which ultimately he must stand or fall'.[43] The party understood that—especially in a crisis—the Leader had to take decisions, and that these might be based, at least partly, upon knowledge which was not available to his followers. The Leader must be allowed discretion in his judgement, whilst others should not rush to form their judgement; to a large extent, this was what was meant by loyalty to the Leader. Thus, in September 1931, the Chairman of a Provincial Area 'asked everyone present to give the Leader loyal support in whatever decision he came to in this crisis'.[44]

Two clear examples of this role can be found in the middle period of Baldwin's leadership, of which the first was his initial approval in October 1929 of the Irwin Declaration before consulting his colleagues. Although he told the following meeting of the shadow cabinet that 'he had only approved of it in his personal capacity and not as Leader carrying the Party with him', in practice this was an almost meaningless distinction.[45] Repudiation of Baldwin's personal pledge would have made his continued leadership impossible, which none of his colleagues seriously desired at this point—for whilst the party had lost the general election a few months before, this had established even more clearly that he was its greatest electoral asset. There were expressions of unhappiness, but the result was that, despite some short-term damage to Baldwin's standing, the party was effectively committed to continuing his preferred bipartisan policy and supporting his chosen Viceroy, Lord Irwin, despite a significant forward move, without either front-bench resignations or a backbench revolt. On the second occasion, Baldwin had less freedom of initiative, for his agreement on 23 August 1931 to join an all-party emergency Cabinet and serve under MacDonald was neither his preferred outcome from the economic crisis nor the one he had expected only hours before.[46] However, the point is that he attended the meeting at Buckingham Palace with the authority to commit his party, and none of his front-bench colleagues questioned that right; the party meeting called a few days later at the Kingsway Hall was summoned more to inform it about the decision than to seek its sanction, although the meeting did pass a resolution of support for the action that had been taken. In the opinion of Somervell, Solicitor-General in 1933–36, Baldwin's strengths were 'complete single-mindedness in his main policy and line'; once this was chosen, he was 'a very astute advocate' who understood his audiences.[47]

[41] Baldwin's address to the Women's Annual Conference, *The Times*, 13 May 1933.
[42] Gwynne to Baldwin, 1 February 1931, Gwynne MSS, 15.
[43] Baldwin to Lytton, 26 October 1927, *BP*, 203.
[44] East Midlands Area, Exec., 22 September 1931.
[45] Hoare to Irwin, 28 October 1929, Halifax MSS, C152/18/1/287.
[46] Butler to his parents, 28 August 1931, Butler MSS, D48/873.
[47] Somervell journal, 17 February 1934, Somervell MSS, MSS.Eng.c.6565/22.

The second role of the Leader was to provide a focal point of authority. This involved being seen to take decisions and give a lead, and included responsibility for choosing tactics and making appointments. Baldwin once commented that 'a Tory leader has to be "quick on the draw" or the rival gang gets him',[48] although, ironically, he was often criticized by colleagues and backbenchers for being slow and cautious. Neville Chamberlain's stubborn determination and intolerance of opposition were the very qualities which led many MPs to see him as a strong, clear-sighted, and capable leader. On the other hand, nothing undermined confidence in a Leader so much as lack of clarity (the problem with Austen Chamberlain's intentions about a general election and the rebalancing of the Coalition in 1922) or lack of decision (a particular criticism of Baldwin in opposition from autumn 1929 to autumn 1930, and a major factor in the erosion of his position). Developing from this, the third role of the Leader was to ensure that the party had a coherent programme and a clear set of priorities. Balfour expressed the traditional patrician view in 1922: there were issues which 'ought not to be decided by the hazard of a vote of the Party', as 'they were matters for the statesmanship of leaders'.[49] Baldwin did not dissent from this, but defined 'the responsibility—and it is a great responsibility—that rests with a leader' as seeking to 'adapt the policy according to the deep-laid foundations of the Party principles to meet whatever may come in this world'.[50] The task of the Leader was therefore concerned less with the detail of policy—which could be delegated to front-bench colleagues—and more with its co-ordination and management, with the aim of keeping the collective movement of the party as cohesive, harmonious, and effective as possible. This would lead to a sense of purpose, which was normally linked with the prospect of electoral success: if in office, of a reasonable prospect of continuing to be so; if in opposition, of soon returning to power.

The fourth role was an essential precondition for this: to preserve the unity of the party. This was always the most fundamental duty of any Conservative Leader,[51] but he could call upon the reciprocal duty of his followers to support with loyalty; the consequent effect was that normally the Leader led from the centre, or the centre formed where the Leader was. The fifth role of the Leader also contributed significantly to maintaining unity, which was the obligation upon the Leader to be aware of party feeling: to be responsive and respectful towards opinions from below, and to take them into account in the decisions which it was his prerogative to make. Baldwin was particularly noted for the time and effort which he devoted to managing parliamentary opinion. In his own words, he 'seldom went home for dinner. Stayed around the buildings all the time; not always in the House but continually in touch with members', in this way 'gaining their confidence'.[52] Backbench and constituency support for

---

[48] Baldwin to Stanhope, 2 September 1934, Stanhope MSS, U1590/C658.
[49] Pollock, 'Fall of the Coalition', Hanworth MSS, Eng.Hist.d.432/133–88.
[50] *Looking Ahead*, speech by Baldwin.
[51] Younger to Sanders, 25 September 1922, Bayford diary.
[52] MacKenzie King diary, 17–18 April 1939, *BP*, 463. In early 1932, he made a particular effort to meet the many newly elected MPs: Lloyd to Davidson, 4 March 1932, Davidson MSS (Bodleian), MSS.Eng.hist.c.557/42–6.

the Leader was habitual but not unconditional, and one of its prerequisites was that the Leader did not ride at fences which his followers were unwilling to jump; this was Austen Chamberlain's fatal miscalculation in 1922 and it caused the unravelling of the normal bonds of loyalty, not just of the rank and file but also of the junior ministers and the party management in the whips' room and at Central Office.[53]

The addition of the Premiership to the party leadership added a further layer of responsibility, as 'being PM is different from anything else. One is in the front and has to lead, guide and decide all the time.'[54] The Premiership gave increased authority over immediate colleagues and the wider party but also a sense of distance, and Baldwin wrote to a former Premier of 'the essential and ultimate loneliness of that position'.[55] When Prime Minister, the Party Leader's relations with his colleagues were through the cabinet system, and his concerns were focused upon the management of the government much more than the affairs of the party. The Prime Minister's role was primarily that of a nexus: providing advice and support to Cabinet ministers in the management of their departmental business, ironing out difficulties and frictions, arranging the priorities of the legislative programme, and keeping a sense of the larger picture. Most business was conducted face to face rather than on paper, and matters were dealt with by individual discussion or at meetings: as Baldwin described it, 'one is in constant conference from after breakfast to dinner'.[56] In a situation where the leading figures came into constant contact with each other, these methods were more direct, practical, and effective, especially in reaching a consensus or probing where the problems really lay. However, the Prime Minister or Party Leader was on a unique level of responsibility and had to be cautious in what he said to colleagues—it was easy to give offence, or to be misunderstood in the extent of a commitment made or (more dangerously) assumed to have been made. To a non-politician, Baldwin talked of the 'fearful strain' involved in continuously seeing people whilst 'having to be at your best and guarding every word', for 'every smallest word is liable to burst into flame'.[57] In Baldwin's case in particular, this meant that, with political colleagues, he often listened more than he spoke, and remained reticent or vague about his views and intentions—which could give the impression of not having understood their arguments, of inaction, and even of laziness; in fact he preferred 'making the other fellow talk' whilst giving away much less of his own mind.[58] All this involved a great deal of time and work; a little over a month after assuming both the party leadership and the Premiership, Baldwin described his week as being 'at the beck and call of everyone for 14 hours a day for four days and for eight hours on the fifth day'.[59]

---

[53] Bridgeman to his son, 13 October 1922, Bridgeman MSS.
[54] Baldwin to Louisa Baldwin, 27 October 1923, *BP*, 125.
[55] Baldwin to Asquith, 23 October 1926, Baldwin MSS, 161/196–7.
[56] Baldwin to Louisa Baldwin, 27 October 1923, *BP*, 125; Baldwin to Bridgeman, 19 January 1926, Bridgeman MSS, 3389/17.
[57] P. Lubbock (ed.), *The Diary of A.C. Benson* (1926), 302–3; also in *BP*, 5.
[58] Lubbock, *Diary of A.C. Benson* 302–3; also in *BP*, 5 Hoare to Eden, 24 September 1935, Avon MSS, AP/14/1/450d.
[59] Baldwin to Louisa Baldwin, 9 July 1923, *BP*, 96.

The practical duties of the Leader were to speak in debate on the most important occasions in parliament and to deliver an increasing number of major public speeches between general elections and, more intensively, during them. If Prime Minister, he chaired the Cabinet and had the extensive work of co-ordination and responsibility involved in leading a government. In opposition, the load was lighter, but there were still meetings of the ex-ministers (normally weekly) and many other consultations with front-bench colleagues. In office, there was often little time to spare for matters of party organization, but in opposition—when there was usually a feeling that the organization needed to be revived—there was more liaison with the Party Chairman and Central Office. In carrying out his duties, the Leader had the support of a personal staff of several private secretaries. These were usually young men in their twenties or thirties, and, during Baldwin's leadership, often from aristocratic backgrounds. Their service in this role was a form of political apprenticeship and many went on to parliamentary careers. The one who went furthest was Geoffrey Lloyd, who was President of the Union at Cambridge University in 1924, then private secretary to Hoare in 1926–29 and Baldwin in 1929–31, at which point he became an MP and continued to serve Baldwin as his PPS from 1931 to 1935; this was followed by a decade of junior ministerships to 1945, and Cabinet office from 1951 to 1959. In contrast, Geoffrey Fry remained as Baldwin's principal private secretary for a long period. The Leader's private office was paid for out of party funds, and was separate from the civil service assistance which he received when in office as Prime Minister—though the lines could become blurred, particularly with the role of Tom Jones, the Deputy Secretary of the Cabinet, in drafting speeches for Baldwin. During the two periods in opposition, the Leader's secretariat was housed in its own premises not far from Central Office and the Palace of Westminster. The private secretaries were part of a network of their own, as is natural with people whose work brings them into frequent contact in a context which is generally co-operative rather than competitive, and information and rumour were often transmitted by this route.

What were the decisions of the Party Leader and leadership that really mattered during this period, when a different policy was possible and would have made a significant difference? Because the party was in office for so much of this time, in some cases it is difficult to separate the decisions which could be described as political from those which were more purely governmental (that is, actions which almost certainly would have been taken by any British government under the same circumstances, such as the granting of the vote to women at age twenty-one in 1928, trying to maintain the gold standard in 1931, and accepting the remilitarization of the Rhineland in 1936). The list of key political decisions is not that long: to continue the wartime Coalition in late 1918; not to press for fusion of parties in 1920; to propose continuing the Coalition with Lloyd George as Prime Minister in 1922; to prefer Baldwin to Curzon in May 1923; to go to the country on a tariff programme in late 1923; not to resign after the election defeat but to meet parliament in January 1924; to oppose the Macquisten Bill on the political levy in 1925; to give a subsidy to the coal industry in the same year; to rule out the safeguarding of iron and steel from the next manifesto in 1928; to support the Irwin

Declaration on Dominion status for India in November 1929; to endorse the outcome of the Round Table conference and the Irwin–Gandhi Pact in early 1931; to agree to serve under MacDonald in the emergency National Government in August 1931; not to intervene to direct labour or capital in the rearmament programmes of 1935–39;[60] to seek face-to-face negotiations with Hitler to resolve the Czech crisis in September 1938; not to construct an all-party government on the outbreak of war in 1939; to be lukewarm and cautious about the proposals of the Beveridge Report in 1942; and to adopt a highly partisan tone in the election campaign in 1945. This list shows that there were only seventeen significant points of decision in twenty-seven years, and it is striking that twelve of them are in the first half of the period, and only five in 1932–45—with a particular gap in the early to mid-1930s. This last is due to the party's relative submergence in the National Government, caused by the combined effects of the pressures of the economic crisis, the Party Leader not being Prime Minister, and the need to hold the National Government together and accept certain compromise positions. Similar factors of the distraction of crises threatening the nation and the coalition nature of the government also affected the periods 1935–40 and especially 1940–45, so that in between 1931 and 1945 there were less distinctively *Conservative* political decisions taken by the Conservative Party Leader.

STYLES OF LEADERSHIP

Every Leader of the Conservative Party from 1918 to 1997 also served as Prime Minister, with the single exception of Austen Chamberlain—and he was at the centre of government, and effectively deputy Prime Minister, during his brief leadership. For Eden, Macmillan, and John Major, their entire tenure of the party leadership coincided with being Prime Minister, and that was also almost the case with Neville Chamberlain. It is therefore difficult to separate specific styles of party leadership from more general styles of government, and there is inevitably a good deal of overlap between the two. With this in mind, it can be suggested that three broad types of public persona were projected by Conservative leaders during these eight decades. The first might be termed the 'honest and modest', and encompasses Bonar Law, Baldwin, Douglas-Home, and Major. The second is the 'decisive and dominant', which comprises Neville Chamberlain, Edward Heath, and Margaret Thatcher. The third is the 'charismatic hero', and accounts for Churchill, Eden, and Macmillan. Some leaders bracket more than one category—Thatcher clearly also belongs in the charismatic and heroic group, and Heath in the honest (if not the modest). Austen Chamberlain is hardest to place, with elements of the honest (but combined with aloofness) and the decisive (but without the accompanying dominance); the way in which he falls between categories perhaps illuminates aspects of his difficulties and downfall. No categories are perfect, and these qualities are not

---

[60] R. P. Shay, *British Rearmament in the 1930s: Politics or Profits* (Princeton, 1977), 125–33.

exclusive—they are a matter of predominant image and methods, which relate to the fundamental character of the individual.

In their mode of operation, the five Party Leaders of the 1918–45 period exhibited two main approaches to the leadership. The Chamberlain brothers were the more authoritarian; adopting specific strategies and expecting obedience, they tended to tow the party behind them, which was satisfactory enough if there was agreement upon the destination and the road to it was not too bumpy. On the other hand, Bonar Law, Baldwin, and even Churchill were more cautious, and in some ways more collegial (although Austen Chamberlain's inflexibility in 1922 was partly due to his certainty that the other significant leading figures shared his view). They were less personally affronted by dissent and more prepared to persuade their followers or make adjustments to smooth the path—although they were not necessarily any more willing to concede on matters which they regarded as crucial.

As the office of Party Leader was so influential and set the tone for the party as a whole, the character and temperament of its various holders was of crucial importance. Bonar Law remains the least appreciated and the least understood, partly because he has been written about less than any of his three successors who held the Premiership, and partly because his tenure of the party leadership, although lengthy in total, is obscured by the war, the coalitions, and, finally, the brevity of his term as Prime Minister.[61] Bonar Law saw the party through very difficult times during his first long spell as Leader in 1911–21, and there was undoubtedly a substantial reserve of gratitude and goodwill that resulted from his role, all the more for his modesty and reticence.[62] Bonar Law's personal character was significant in both creating and reinforcing this, and he had the lasting affection and support of a wide range of figures in the party, including those as disparate in style and temperament as Baldwin and Beaverbrook, Davidson and Younger.[63] Walter Long, who lost his chance of becoming Leader due to Bonar Law's intervention in 1911, nevertheless testified to 'the wonderful lovable character of the man', which was appreciated by those who worked closely with him—as indeed it was by Lloyd George, who found Austen Chamberlain to be lacking by comparison.[64] Bonar Law's personal manner of mildness, patience, and reflection was never mistaken by anyone for the malleability shown by Derby, or indeed the hesitation in arriving at a decision for which Baldwin was regularly criticized. Moreover, Bonar Law's generally collegial style overlay 'an uncompromising attitude' on any matter upon which he was certain about his own view and its importance.[65] This was shown more than once during his brief Premiership, not only over the American debt settlement, in which his stubborn resistance gave way only to the united pressure of his whole Cabinet and the vital need, for the party's sake (always his crucial consideration), that the new

---

[61] This remains the case despite Robert Blake's pioneering study, *The Unknown Prime Minister: The Life and Times of Andrew Bonar Law* (1955), and an excellent recent biography: Adams, *Bonar Law*.
[62] Speeches of Pretyman, Curzon, and Derby at the party meeting of 28 May 1923, *The Times*, 29 May 1923.
[63] Younger to Blumenfeld, 30 October 1923, Blumenfeld MSS, BLU/1/YOU/3.
[64] Long to Talbot, 22 March 1921, Long MSS, Add.62426/48–9; Derby diary, 28 August 1921.
[65] Devonshire to Hoare, 30 March 1923, Templewood MSS, V/1.

government should not collapse, but also over policy in the Middle East. Bonar Law's final months during his first period as Party Leader, which led up to his initial retirement in March 1921, and his short second term from October 1922 to May 1923, were overshadowed by his problems of health. These were exacerbated by both workload and temperament: Long considered that in the year up to March 1921, 'he took things too greatly to heart, and his share of the work was most excessive'.[66] As Prime Minister, Bonar Law's government drifted without positive direction, partly due to his pragmatic electoral pledge of 1922 to make no move towards a tariff policy, and partly due to his refusal to embark on a substantial legislative programme. The latter was consistent with the aims and style of his leadership: the period of 'tranquillity' was intended to restore business confidence and create stability in the economy, and thus reduce the level of unemployment. However, the final collapse of his health in May 1923 left the latter problem in the hands of Baldwin, who soon came to feel impossibly circumscribed by Bonar Law's pledge.

Austen Chamberlain falls into the category of Conservative leaders whose long apprenticeships as heir apparent were matched only by the disappointments and failures of their performance when they finally reached the top of the greasy pole, a company which includes his half-brother Neville, Balfour, and Eden. Chamberlain was a consistently capable debater in the Commons, certainly more so than either Baldwin or Churchill, but was rarely remarkable and never inspiring in the way that either of them could be. In the later phase of his career, after his brief leadership, he was categorized by one backbencher as a 'heavy type of Parliamentarian, possessing some charm and a grand manner, but clearly a kind heart and not a great deal of backbone. He inclines to talk one down and evade in this way unpleasant queries and thrusts.'[67] From long and close acquaintance, Lord Robert Cecil described Austen Chamberlain as having 'that kind of sobriety of political judgement which often comes from long familiarity with politics', although another Cabinet colleague more critically considered that he was 'no judge at all of men or their motives'.[68] Any politician who reaches the very front rank must have both determination and self-belief, but both of the Chamberlain brothers possessed these qualities in a 'rigid and unbending' way which was crucially different from Bonar Law or Baldwin, or even Churchill.[69] In Austen's case, this narrowness was even more apparent than in Neville's, although it was the flaw that led to both their downfalls: in both cases, certainty became inflexibility, and they exhibited a dangerous disregard for constructive opinion and advice.

As Leader in 1921–22, Austen Chamberlain's unresponsiveness to moderate and well-disposed concerns eventually alienated key figures who would otherwise have supported him, such as the Chief Whip, Party Chairman, and Principal Agent. Six weeks before the smash at the Carlton Club meeting, Long, who, unlike Chamberlain, had a

---

[66] Long to Bull, 18 March 1921, Long MSS, Add.62426/27–32.
[67] Beamish memo, 'The naval mutiny of September 1931', n.d. but *c.*September 1931, Beamish MSS, CAC, BEAM/3/3.
[68] R. Cecil to Baldwin, 1 February 1924, Baldwin MSS, 35/203–7; Bridgeman diary, 'Austen Chamberlain', November 1929.
[69] Crawford diary, 18 October 1922.

lifelong experience of the Conservative Party and a sure sense of its inner nature, observed simply: 'this is not the way to keep a party together'.[70] During the final months of the Lloyd George Coalition, Chamberlain certainly felt under increasing pressure, and by early October he was 'very disturbed', declaring that he was 'between the devil and the deep sea'.[71] However, the consequence was that his conduct became 'needlessly stiff and uncompromising',[72] and in the last days he presented a 'completely wooden' face to all mediatory overtures.[73] Even from someone who remained on Chamberlain's side when the split came, there was resentment of his aloof and prickly conduct, and unbending expectation of unquestioning loyalty.[74] Within the Conservative Party as much as—and perhaps even more than—in any organization founded mainly on voluntary co-operation, command has to be exercised with discretion and smoothed with some unction, and applied with sensitivity to the needs and perceptions of those below; in all such skills, Chamberlain showed himself to be utterly lacking.

All of Baldwin's colleagues appreciated the moral qualities of his character, as well as his almost unique ability to project these to the general public. Neville Chamberlain, so often frustrated by Baldwin's cautious appreciation of a wider range of nuances and his sensitivity to atmosphere, valued most of all the fact that 'one can have absolute confidence in his straight-forwardness'.[75] Lord Salisbury, who served as Leader in the House of Lords from 1925 to 1931, wrote of 'the qualities of the man—modesty, idealism, cultivation of mind, immense influence', although, significantly, he added: 'but though I admire and follow, I cannot understand his methods...sometimes at the critical moment he seems to be almost impotent'.[76] The latter tendency was observed by sympathetic senior backbenchers as well: 'S.B. is very far from being an ideal Party Leader,' commented Spender-Clay during the internal crisis of March 1931; 'he sees the pros and cons of every question too nearly balanced.'[77]

Baldwin's sense of public opinion and sureness of touch was his first great strength; there was 'a certain simple shrewdness about him which seems to provide him with an instinctive knowledge of the mind of the common man'.[78] This was matched by a felicity with words used in oratory which was only equalled or surpassed by Churchill, a fellow academic underachiever in early life. Baldwin's second, less consistent strength, was his command of the House of Commons, derived from the ability when it really mattered to move his audience and raise the level of debate; although not alone, four such instances stand out: the Macquisten Bill in 1925, the Irwin Declaration in 1929, the India debate of March 1931, and the Abdication crisis in 1936. Baldwin's third strength was his escapology; he was willing to retreat when tactically advisable, as after the 1923 election defeat over

[70] Long to Younger, 4 September 1922, Long MSS (WSA), 947/859.
[71] Wilson to Younger, copied to Sanders, 5 October 1922, Bayford diary.
[72] Memo by Curzon on the break-up of the Coalition, October 1922, Curzon MSS, F/112/319.
[73] Memo by Hoare, 'The fall of the Coalition', Templewood MSS, XX/5; Templewood, *Empire of the Air*, 27.
[74] Pollock, 'Fall of the Coalition', Hanworth MSS, Eng.Hist.d.432/133–88.
[75] N. Chamberlain to Irwin, 25 December 1927, Halifax MSS, C152/17/1/277a; Bridgeman diary, 'Baldwin', November 1929; Derby to Blumenfeld, 29 March 1930, Blumenfeld MSS, BLU/1/DER/48.
[76] Salisbury to Irwin, 16 July 1926, Halifax MSS, C152/17/1/67a.
[77] Spender-Clay to Irwin, 5 March 1931, Halifax MSS, C152/19/1/251.
[78] N. Chamberlain to Irwin, 12 August 1928, Halifax MSS, C152/18/1/114a.

both policy and the personnel of his shadow Cabinet, in the truce with Beaverbrook in March 1930, and over the Hoare–Laval Plan in 1935. He was willing to compromise 'if he felt that compromise would assist a larger issue', and able to admit an error candidly in the House of Commons, thereby escaping most of the blame and minimizing the political damage.[79]

However, Baldwin's 'natural diffidence' was, as with Bonar Law, 'by no means inconsistent with a streak of obstinacy'.[80] The comment of Baldwin's long-serving aide and confidant, Davidson, after the General Strike of 1926 could be applied to the whole of Baldwin's leadership: once sure of his purpose, he was 'calm, crisp and unwavering on the great issue'.[81] Baldwin shared with Bonar Law and Churchill, albeit in slightly different forms, a collegial approach to the party leadership, in which there was no doubt of his ultimate authority and willingness to exercise it, but in which there was a freedom of discussion and a sense of collective endeavour. These leaders led, but not from too far ahead and not without looking shrewdly back over their shoulder—and they did not drive. This made all three of them successful Party Leaders within coalition governments, in the cases of Bonar Law and Baldwin willingly in the secondary position. In fact, Baldwin's trustworthiness and moderation made the existence of the National Government both possible and credible, and his conciliation and understanding of the needs of its other components enabled it to continue.

Neville Chamberlain was Prime Minister for the all but the last few months of his party leadership; his relations with his colleagues were therefore through the Cabinet system, and his concerns were focused upon the management of the government much more than the party, and even more so after the declaration of war. Before then, this was especially the case with foreign affairs, where he assumed that his policy would be given uncritical support. He was a more purposeful Cabinet Chairman than Baldwin: he had always mastered the papers and, whilst allowing debate, he 'intervened with his own view at the right time, when others had had their say but before the discussion became desultory. He was always ready to take a decision.'[82] Thus, the Cabinet were 'told, not consulted' about the plan to negotiate directly with Hitler in September 1938, a bold strategy which made the apparent success triumphantly Chamberlain's own after the Munich Agreement, but also left him solely exposed when the latter was repudiated by the German seizure of Bohemia six months later.[83] Chamberlain had an unshakeable confidence in the superiority of his own clarity of thought and strength of purpose—abilities which he assumed were of paramount importance for political success. This self-belief led to the betraying touches of arrogance and contempt which he exhibited, towards not only his opponents in other parties and in his own, but even some of his ministers. Chamberlain's imperviousness to criticism enabled him to remain

---

[79] Draft memoirs, Somervell MSS, MSS.Eng.c.6565/247.
[80] Irwin to N. Chamberlain, 15 September 1926, Halifax MSS, C152/17/2/108.
[81] Davidson to Irwin, 14 June 1926, Halifax MSS, C152/17/1/53a.
[82] Draft memoirs, Somervell MSS, MSS.Eng.c.6565/246.
[83] Duff Cooper diary, 14 September 1938.

resolute and single-minded in pursuit of his goals; when things were going well, this made his authority paramount and his position almost impregnable, especially with the constituency grass roots. His defects were similar to those of Austen; as with his older half-brother, they became more apparent when he encountered setbacks and resistance.

Neville Chamberlain's leadership lasted longer than his brother's, for several reasons. Firstly, he inherited a far sounder and more stable position than had Austen, being in a government climbing out of the trough of economic depression rather than one falling into it. Secondly, in the late 1930s, the Conservative Party machine at both Westminster and in the country was far stronger, sounder, and smooth-running than it had been in 1921–22, in the wake of the wartime cessation and disruption. Thirdly, Neville Chamberlain held the office of Prime Minister, with all of its powers and prestige, rather than being in second place to another. Finally, far from any of his colleagues overshadowing him (as, in their different ways, Birkenhead, Balfour, Curzon, Churchill, and even Horne had done with Austen in 1921–22), none of Neville Chamberlain's Cabinet ministers came anywhere near to him in stature, not even his two Foreign Secretaries, Eden and Halifax. In fact, this was so marked that it became a problem and source of weakness, critically so in May 1940. Even in peacetime, there was a widespread feeling that the Cabinet was overly subordinate to the Prime Minister, and Chamberlain was seen as preferring weak or compliant ministers in key positions. On a personal level, he had 'a rather close habit of reserve', which gave many an impression of coldness; this was due to an upbringing and early life which had fostered self-containment, and a form of shyness which was its consequence.[84] In fact, Neville Chamberlain was not the unemotional personality that he was often perceived to be: he was a passionate politician with strong views, and he was not easily discouraged or distracted from his chosen path. In a judgement that could have applied exactly to his half-brother Austen and on some occasions to Bonar Law, but never to Baldwin or Churchill, Neville Chamberlain was assessed by a backbench MP who had supported his policy of appeasement as 'extremely obstinate…[he] should have been more elastic and constructive'.[85] In addition, Chamberlain's parliamentary performances in the first months of the war were 'most discouraging'; he seemed to be 'obviously tired and depressed', and unsuited to the role of a war leader.[86] The fall of Neville Chamberlain in May 1940 was thus a personal rather than a party one; it was of his own making, as it followed from decisions before and during the war which were clearly his own, and from his personal and political style.

It is only relevant here to discuss Churchill's period as Party Leader from 1940 to the general election of 1945, although, of course, his most extensive focus on this role was from 1945 to his second Premiership of 1951–55.[87] Even more so than with Chamberlain, Churchill's party leadership in the wartime period cannot be divorced

---

[84] Bridgeman diary, 'Neville Chamberlain', November 1929.
[85] Beamish diary notes, 13 November 1940, Beamish MSS, CAC, BEAM/3/4.
[86] Nicolson diary, 20 and 26 September 1939; Channon diary, 26 September 1939.
[87] This has been discussed elsewhere: S. Ball, 'Churchill and the Conservative Party', 323–9.

from his occupancy of the Premiership. This was partly because it was entirely in the context of a war which strained every resource of the nation, even when the desperate perils of 1940–41 had eased. It was also due to Churchill's 'wilderness' years of the 1930s and the way in which he had become Prime Minister in 1940: more than any other Leader of the Conservative Party, even Disraeli, Bonar Law, or Thatcher, he had been the outsider, distant from the party managers and in tension with the strategies which their predecessors had been committed to. This accounted for the nervousness with which Churchill's accession was regarded in the autumn of 1940, although his conduct and contribution during the five months since he had become Prime Minister in May made a huge difference; certainly, there was no thought of resistance, and no sideways glances towards potential alternatives, not even Halifax. However, even with the acceptance that Churchill was the one essential figure in the government, and that he must be maintained and worked with, whatever the difficulties of so doing, there were many moments of tension—with some ministers, with the whips, with the 1922 Committee, and with the mainstream backbenchers.

In character, Churchill's egotism was open, enthusiastic, and unashamed: it was linked with great vitality and a profusion of ideas—some good, some bad, but none of them commonplace. This egotism was neither arrogant nor chilling, as was the case with some other leading politicians, but instead had a childlike quality of charm and innocence. Many colleagues up to 1940 responded to Churchill on this level, and language or anecdotes depicting him in a pre-adult way were a recurring feature throughout his career—'cherubic' for his appearance, 'tempests' and 'tantrums' for his behaviour, and so on. Churchill commanded the House of Commons, in part due to the value of unmatchable experience. An MP noted of one debate during the Battle of Britain that 'the Prime Minister played upon the House like a skilled musician on an instrument and everybody seemed content to give him complete power'.[88] Churchill was particularly effective in debate during the middle period of the war, after the turn of the tide in late 1942, with speeches and interventions in debate giving a youthful backbencher a 'supreme lesson in the art of speaking and in parliamentary practice'.[89] The richness and power of language which Churchill could employ was appreciated and admired, yet with reservations: after his memorial encomium on the death of Chamberlain, an MP noted in his diary: 'no wonder some men distrust the P.M. for his capacity for cajolery and fervent persuasive English'.[90] The setbacks of the middle period of the war, which could less easily be blamed on the unpreparedness of the prewar governments, gave occasional moments of parliamentary disturbance, but made little impact upon Churchill's standing in the country.[91] After this, as the war turned in favour of the Allies, there were no further threats to his position, for 'with better times, things have become quieter politically'.[92]

---

[88] Beamish diary notes, 16 September 1940, Beamish MSS, CAC, BEAM/3/4.
[89] York diary, 13 October 1943, 10 December 1942.
[90] Beamish diary notes, 13 November 1940, Beamish MSS, CAC, BEAM/3/4.
[91] Cranborne to Ormsby-Gore, 23 May 1942, Ormsby-Gore MSS, PEC/11/2/32.
[92] Emrys-Evans to Cross, 11 January 1943, Emrys-Evans MSS, Add.58243/158–9.

What remained, and surfaced over issues such as coal rationing, the influence of Labour Party ministers on the home front, and plans for postwar reconstruction, was an undercurrent of doubt amongst the mainstream Conservative MPs. There was some alienation, and a fear of a loss of the party's identity in the wartime Coalition, which coincided with the sense that Churchill did not hold the party in high regard and was unwilling to look after its interests. An experienced MP who was also Chairman of a Provincial Area complained in 1944: 'never was a party so leaderless as is the Conservative Party today', and concluded that it was 'drifting to its doom'.[93] It was evident that Churchill had little time for his party role during most of his wartime Premiership, and he did not read the reports of the Post-War Problems Committee before they were published.[94] His priorities were summed up in his response to the initial manifesto of the Tory Reform Committee: 'I dread distraction of minds from the war effort.'[95] However, Assheton (Party Chairman in 1944–46) testified that in the final months before the 1945 general election, 'Churchill took an intense personal interest in every phase...I saw him perhaps more than some of my predecessors had seen their Leader.'[96] Ironically, when he publicly adopted the mantle of Party Leader in the election campaign, his actions were so counterproductive that many might have wished that he had remained in Olympian detachment instead. However, Churchill's reliance in party management for most of the wartime period upon stalwarts of the previous regime—Stuart as Chief Whip, Hacking and Dugdale as Party Chairmen—and his generally consensual approach as opposition leader in 1945–51, places him much closer to Baldwin and Bonar Law in style, and perhaps closest of all to the latter.

THE REMOVAL OF LEADERS

There were a number of factors which could undermine the position of the Leader and, if strongly present, bring a leadership to an end, either by the Leader deciding to withdraw or by direct removal. Electoral defeat was not the most serious of these—it was damaging, but on its own was not critical. No Leader of the Conservative Party during this period (or, indeed, prior to 1997) departed directly because he had presided over a defeat. Balfour in 1906, Baldwin in 1923 and 1929, and Churchill in 1945 remained the Leader for several years afterwards—and these reverses included two of the worst in the party's history. The two further election defeats in January and December 1910 certainly contributed to Balfour's departure several months later, but his handling of the Parliament Act crisis in 1911 was the more immediate cause. It is true that Baldwin's position was shaky immediately after the 1923 defeat—but it was his own uncertainty about continuing, rather than loss of support or attacks upon him, which might have led to his resignation.

---

[93] Headlam diary, 3 October 1944.
[94] Stuart to Churchill, 1 October 1943, Churchill MSS, CAC, CHAR/2/480/11.
[95] Churchill to Hinchingbrooke, 28 March 1943, Churchill MSS, CAC, CHAR/2/480/10.
[96] Assheton, oral history interview in Cohen, 'Disraeli's Child', 567, Cohen MSS, CPA, CRD/731.

As in March 1931, when he also doubted before the dawn, once Baldwin resolved to continue and face any criticism, this was revealed to be lacking in bite and much of the party rallied round him—if for their own sake, as much as for his.[97] Much more corrosive than electoral defeat was a loss of confidence in the ability of the Leader to manage the situation effectively, and to carry out the roles—or, at least, most of the roles—discussed above. This ebbing of confidence could result from poor performances and lack of impact in parliament, doubts about decisions taken and policies chosen, or disapproval of appointments made. None of these would be critical in a single instance, and they were only corrosive if repeated over a length of time and without any counterbalancing successes. It was such a combination that eroded Baldwin's position from the Irwin Declaration in November 1929 to the late summer of 1930, and resulted in his leadership hanging by a precarious thread. Similarly, Neville Chamberlain's downfall was mostly of his own making, as it resulted from decisions taken before and during the war which were clearly his own, and from his personal and political style. The swiftest cause of any Leader's downfall was failure to maintain the unity of the party, especially if his decisions had contributed to the divisions, and still more if he came to be seen as endangering its continued existence or identity—this was the road which led to the Carlton Club meeting in 1922.

The authority of the Leader depended upon retaining the support of the majority of the parliamentary party and the confidence of the Cabinet or shadow cabinet. These two normally went together, and it was unlikely that any significant number of front-bench figures would desert a Leader who was the preferred choice of the majority of MPs. However, what was more possible was that the Leader and most of his front-bench colleagues would drift away from the parliamentary party, which is what happened in 1922 and 1940, and looked as if it was occurring in 1930. Small groups of dissatisfied and rebel MPs could be discounted; there were always such, and as long as they remained a minority fringe they could make a distracting noise but do little damage. Indeed, an attack from a hostile wing, especially if the latter was not clearly within the ambit of the party, could make others rally in support, as happened with the press lords' attacks on Baldwin in 1930–31.[98] What was critical was an erosion of confidence in the mainstream, and recognition of this led to R. T. McKenzie's famous dictum, oft-quoted since its publication in 1955: 'in the Conservative Party...the Leader leads and the Party follows, except when the Party decides not to follow—then the Leader ceases to be Leader'.[99] However, this begs the question of how exactly this would be made apparent, and what mechanism operated to curtail a leadership involuntarily.

The simplest and least damaging method might seem to be for the Leader's front-bench colleagues to intimate that he had lost their confidence, but that was

---

[97] Gretton to Croft, 4 February 1924, Croft MSS, CAC, CRFT/1/12/Gr1.
[98] Eden diary, 18 October 1930, Avon MSS, AP/20/1/10.
[99] R. T. McKenzie, *British Political Parties* (1955), 145. A former junior minister put it more succinctly: 'When they had once elected a leader they must back him or sack him', NU Conf., 1929, speech by Williams; his remark was followed by cheers.

much easier said than done. Firstly, sufficient unanimity was by no means certain, as every Leader naturally had some strong partisans or personal friends sitting in his council. There would also probably be some others who preferred the present Leader to his obvious successor, or were unconvinced of the need to act, or feared that the removal process would do more damage than was worth the risk, or, for reasons of their junior status or personal ambition, preferred not to be involved. Unless there was an overwhelming and evident majority acting in concord, it would seem the work of a clique or faction; it could be tarred with the brush of self-seeking, and add to the party's troubles and divisions rather than resolve them. Even so, at two key points during the 1929–31 crisis, some of Baldwin's colleagues at least considered presenting him with such an intimation. However, when Austen and Neville Chamberlain tentatively discussed this, at the very height of the crisis in early October 1930, the more they considered it, the less practicable they found it. The essential preliminary would be a secret meeting of the front bench without the Leader present, and, as Austen realized, any such proceeding 'would lend itself to every form of misconception'.[100] Meanwhile, Neville had consulted Hoare, who raised objections to the plan 'which I considered good', and so he 'concluded that there is nothing which [Baldwin's] colleagues can usefully do at this juncture; and that, if any move is made, it should really come from the House of Commons—the body which makes, and can presumably unmake, leaders'.[101] In March 1931, when the shadow cabinet had again lost confidence in Baldwin, they were equally indecisive and ineffective. On both occasions, Baldwin rode out the storm and recovered his position, although in 1931 this involved—after the crisis was safely past—allowing his colleagues to express their frustrations.

Thus, the only certain method takes us back to the appointing of leaders, for the party meetings which formalized this were the basis of the Leader's authority, and rejection by a properly constituted meeting would terminate a leadership, as happened in 1922. Perhaps for this reason, party meetings were not often called: apart from those held to confirm the selection of a Leader, there were only six during the interwar period. These were over continuing the Coalition after the war and endorsing the programme agreed by Bonar Law and Lloyd George in November 1918; over continuing the Coalition in October 1922; over the shelving of the tariff policy in February 1924; over the referendum policy on tariffs and the attacks of the press lords in June 1930; over the adoption of the 'free hand' tariff policy and Baldwin's leadership in October 1930; and over the decision to join the emergency National Government in August 1931. Whilst Baldwin's leadership was explicitly debated and voted upon at the October 1930 meeting, it was also the unwritten issue on the agenda of the February 1924 and June 1930 meetings. This was not the case in August 1931; as there had been almost no criticism of his decision to join the National Government, the confirmatory meeting was 'very dull and purely formal'.[102]

---

[100] A. to N. Chamberlain, 9 October 1930, AC, 39/2/40.
[101] N. to A. Chamberlain, 8 and 10 October 1930, AC, 39/2/39, 58/75.
[102] Conway diary, 28 August 1931, Conway MSS, Add.7676/Y/63; Duff Cooper to his wife, 28 August 1931, Duff Cooper MSS, CAC, DUFC/1/8/8.

Party meetings were called entirely at the discretion of the Leader, and MPs had no power to compel this.[103] On several occasions, diehard MPs gathered signatures to press for one, but the mode was always to 'respectfully request' that a meeting be called; there was no basis for public protest, and few repercussions, when the Leader turned such petitions down.[104] The party meetings were a tool of the leadership, and their timing and composition was chosen to the Leader's maximum advantage. This was the case with the Carlton Club meeting of 1922: it excluded the peers (more of whom had diehard leanings) and was held at a time when the expected failure of the independent Conservative candidate at the Newport by-election would be known. It was particularly the context of the two party meetings of 1930, both of which were timed to catch the press lords at maximum disadvantage and capitalize on a rally to the Leader. Indeed, so confident were the leadership of the strength of their position before the October 1930 meeting that they allowed the inclusion of peers (although this was later balanced by a last-minute invitation to prospective candidates), and ensured that the critics would have no grounds for complaint by allowing them to select their motion and speakers and by conceding a secret ballot.[105] The holding of the 1924 and, still more, the 1918 and 1931 party meetings was dictated more by immediate events, but, even so, in February 1924 there was deliberate method in holding the meeting of MPs—who were more moderate and pro-Baldwin—on the day before the National Union Central Council, thus leaving the latter no scope other than to endorse the decision of the party meeting.

It is most likely that at all of the party meetings, the majority of those who attended had already made up their minds on the issues—even if only in the previous few hours or days. This certainly seems to have been the case at the Carlton Club meeting in 1922, which is the only one for which we have the record of how each person voted, whilst the negative votes at the two 1930 meetings were a fair match for the proportion of the party known to be dissatisfied with the policy and Leader. The result was, therefore, not primarily due to what was said at the meeting, as this could only affect the votes of the undecided minority. However, in each case the effectiveness of the speeches made reinforced the existing flow of opinion. All the accounts of the Carlton Club meeting agree that the pro-Coalition speakers were ineffective, and at best—as in Balfour's case—listened to with polite impatience. The impact of Baldwin's speech, well-worded though it was, has been overrated due to his later prominence, but Bonar Law's speech—or indeed just his presence—was crucial in offering an alternative direction under a credible leader. At the February 1924 and October 1930 meetings, Baldwin took much of the steam out of the feeling against him by changing policy in the direction which the major-

---

[103] A. Chamberlain to Chaplin, 2 March 1922, AC, 33/1/35; N. to H. Chamberlain, 21 June 1930, *NCDL*.
[104] Gretton to Heneage, enclosing text of petition, 19 July 1929, Heneage MSS, HNC/1/G; Baldwin to Gretton, 26 July 1929, Baldwin MSS, 164/68; Gretton to N. Chamberlain, enclosing petition, 21 October 1930, CPA, Whips' Office MSS, 2/5.
[105] N. Chamberlain to Bridgeman, 1 November 1930, Bridgeman MSS, 3389/105; N. Chamberlain diary, 6 November 1930, NC, 2/22.

ity desired, and then by making an effective speech before any vote was taken. In June 1930, he caused some strain by sticking with the referendum policy when many Conservative MPs would have preferred to move on from it, but the passages of his speech attacking the press lords were highly effective and attracted the support of most MPs due to a mixture of self-respect and outrage: 'people resented bitterly the insolent patronage of newspaper-owners', and Baldwin 'got them into quite a white heat of indignation'.[106] At both the 1930 meetings, the speeches made against Baldwin were either of poor quality or completely predictable in content, whilst he had very effective support, particularly from Horne at the June meeting and Hailsham at the October one.[107] In February 1924, Baldwin had similarly been bolstered when Balfour (the only living former Conservative premier) proposed the vote of confidence, and Austen Chamberlain spoke unequivocally in its favour. There was no real dissenting comment at the February 1924 meeting, whilst the remaining two party meetings of 1918 and 1931 were essentially affirmatory.

It was the Leader's decision to summon a party meeting, but thereafter the arrangements were in the hands of the Chief Whip in the House of Commons. He was understood to be acting in an essentially neutral way, governed by his responsibility to the party as a whole rather than to the current incumbent, but in reality his position naturally made him an upholder of the status quo—this was the reason why Wilson's dissent at the Carlton Club so shocked and infuriated the Coalitionists. There were no formal rules governing either the procedure or the composition of these party meetings, and, indeed, only a few days before that of February 1924, the Chief Whip was still undecided about the inclusion of defeated candidates and of all Conservative peers.[108] It is notable that four of the party meetings—all those after 1922—took place when the party was in opposition (this was effectively the case in August 1931; although the Conservatives had returned to office a few days previously, the meeting concerned the reasons for doing so). The other two (or three, if 1931 is included here as well) were held in a coalition situation under a non-Conservative Prime Minister. This pattern is not coincidental: when the party was in office, the votes which could become ones of confidence were the support of MPs in the division lobbies for the key measures and decisions of the government, and this obviated the need to summon a meeting. The repudiation of the leadership, or the withdrawal of support by abstention, of a large enough number of MPs on a critical issue would terminate the Leader's position. For this to happen, the loss of support would have to be considerable—the rebel votes against the India Bill in 1933–35 were clearly those of a diehard minority and not a threat in this way, but the fall in the government's majority in the Norway division on 8 May 1940 was too large to be ignored.

---

[106] Lane-Fox to Irwin, 25 June 1930, Halifax MSS, C152/19/1/87.
[107] 'Party Meeting, 30 October 1930', verbatim record, CPA, Whips' Office MSS, 2/5; Headlam diary, 30 October 1930; Lane-Fox to Baldwin, 30 October 1930, Baldwin MSS, 165/201.
[108] Derby diary, 23 January 1924.

CRISES OF LEADERSHIP AND POLICY: THE FOUR MAJOR CRISES

The two distinctive features of the Conservative Party between the wars were its record of electoral success and the series of internal dissensions which ran through most of the period. Whilst these varied in intensity, the periods of tranquillity were few and far between. There were four significant crises during which internal disputes within the party were publicly exhibited: over the Coalition from 1921 to reunion in 1924 (at its peak in 1922), over tariffs from 1927 to 1931 (at its peak in 1930–31), over India from 1931 to 1935 (at its peak in 1933–35), and over appeasement from 1936 to 1940 (at its peak in 1938–39). Because control over policy rested with the Party Leader, these crises inevitably became challenges of leadership as well as differences over issues. Of the five party leaders of the period, Austen Chamberlain and Neville Chamberlain were overthrown in 1922 and 1940 respectively, Baldwin was under serious threat after the 1923 defeat and in 1930–31, Bonar Law had experienced strong criticism in 1912–13 and 1916, and many thought it would be for the best if Churchill retired with dignity after the 1945 defeat. This part of the chapter assesses the nature and outcome of each crisis in turn, which leads into the final section of thematic and comparative analysis. The aim of both parts is to explain the varying impact of each crisis and to illuminate the relationships within the party, the power of the Leader, and the constraints upon that power.

The most famous, the most extensive, and the most successful revolt was that against the continuation of the Coalition with Lloyd George in 1922. It began in a minor way with sniping from the diehards in 1921, but they were a relatively small group of around forty MPs and, at first, they had little impact.[109] As always, they were not a danger on their own, but blunders by the leadership could convince others of the merits of their case and lead to a snowball effect, and this was what occurred from the autumn of 1921 to the fall of the government in October 1922. Setbacks and failures occurred on a wide range of issues, including several of emotive importance to Conservatives such as the Union with Ireland, the future of the second chamber, and the honours scandal.[110] By-election results and other indications of declining public support, such as the increasing hostility of the popular press, suggested that serious electoral difficulties lay ahead. Although in government, the party lacked confidence in its control over policy due to the apparent acquiescence of its leaders to the directions of a non-Conservative Prime Minister with a dominant political style. The sense of distance from the decision-making process was considerably beyond the normal for the backbenchers of a governing party. To some extent, this was due to the coalition situation, but it became more apparent after Austen Chamberlain became Leader in March 1921. This was partly because political problems accumulated during that time, and partly because his relationship with Lloyd George was perceived to be much less equal and effective

---

[109] E. Wood, 'Thoughts on some of the present discontents of the Conservative Party', not dated but marked 'early summer 1922', Halifax MSS (Borthwick), A4/410/9/1–13.

[110] Pollock, 'Fall of the Coalition', Hanworth MSS, Eng.Hist.d.432/133–88; Derby to A. Chamberlain, 11 September 1922, AC, 33/2/15.

than Bonar Law's had been. The nature of the Coalition limited Chamberlain's scope for establishing a strong personal position when he became Leader, and so he had 'only a slender following in the H[ouse] of C[ommons], while in the country he really counts for nothing'.[111] As early as August 1921, Lloyd George was agreeing with Lord Derby that 'with all his good qualities [Chamberlain] was a poor substitute for Bonar Law'.[112] Already by the end of 1921, 'a very marked Conservative reaction' was gathering support, based upon 'a reaction from a policy of adventure' and 'a longing for stability'.[113] When the pressures mounted in 1922, the future direction of the Coalition was far from clear and this uncertainty became, in itself, a destabilizing factor. With this range of problems, it is not surprising that the crisis was the most serious of the interwar period, and had the most spectacular results.

The Coalition government had two fundamental problems: policies which were unsuccessful or unpopular with Conservatives, and the personal style of the Prime Minister. The difficulties of policy emerged first, in some cases as early as 1920, and mounted steadily as the government progressed. They were the basis of the increasing dissatisfaction with Lloyd George, but his conduct exacerbated it.[114] Some of these matters were minor and yet symbolic: when the Prime Minister summoned the Cabinet to the north of Scotland for his own convenience, Winterton was far from alone in finding it 'intolerable that he should assume this American Presidential attitude'.[115] As Austen Chamberlain acknowledged in April 1922, many Conservatives 'dislike his methods and are kept in a perpetual state of uncertainty as to what he will do next'.[116] The problems of policy became so serious because they extended over almost all the areas of government responsibility, including many which were of particular concern to Conservatives.[117] One of these was foreign policy, especially the deterioration in relations with France, the moves hinting at recognition of Soviet Russia, and the failure of Lloyd George's approach to European diplomacy at the Genoa conference in April 1922. There were continuing problems over the situation in Ireland, whilst the government's policies in India and the Middle East demonstrated a lack of grip and decision which worried not just the diehards but a good many more moderate Conservatives, as did Lloyd George's reckless support for Greek adventurism in Asia Minor.[118]

At home, the failure to achieve sufficient reductions in expenditure to make a noticeable easing of the burden upon taxpayers was a constant source of complaint, to which was added the alarm of Conservative MPs in the safer southern seats at the possibility that an Anti-Waste candidate might be put up against them. The economic depression since 1920 affected the government's popularity with all

---

[111] Long to Younger, 4 September 1922, Long MSS (WSA), 947/859.
[112] Derby diary, 28 August 1921.
[113] Salisbury to Steel-Maitland, 25 December 1921, Steel-Maitland MSS, GD193/275/9.
[114] Bull to Long, 16 April 1921, Long MSS, Add.62426/72–8; Salisbury to Bonar Law, 23 September 1922, Bonar Law MSS, BL/107/2/61.
[115] Winterton to Hoare, 5 October 1921, Templewood MSS, I/2.
[116] A. Chamberlain to Long, 27 April 1922, Long MSS, Add.62405/100–1; Crawford diary, 16 October 1922.
[117] Long to A. Chamberlain, 19 February 1933, Long MSS, Add.62405/89–92.
[118] Derby to Blumenfeld, 29 March 1930, Blumenfeld MSS, BLU/1/DER/48.

classes, and the rise in unemployment contributed to the Labour Party's successes in by-elections and its advance in local government. It was the fear of Labour sweeping to power which fuelled the demands from the Conservative grass roots for action on the trade union political levy and—still more—the strengthening of the powers of the House of Lords. The apparent reneging by the government on its pledges to deal with the latter was the main cause of Younger's objection to an early general election in January 1922 and of the alienation of the National Union. By the autumn of 1922, it was hard to find an area where the government had anything positive to show. Many of the failures were directly attributable to the Prime Minister, because they were either his chosen policies or were linked to his character and methods. This eroded the desire to continue the Coalition under his leadership; as one of the dissatisfied junior ministers noted, 'what commonly passes as Anti-Coalition feeling, is principally personal mistrust of and antagonism to Mr Lloyd George'.[119] Whilst most Conservatives were willing to continue some form of anti-Socialist pact with the Coalition Liberals, they wanted the balance in the next Cabinet to reflect the strengths of the two parties and the Prime Minister to be a Conservative.[120] However, this view was not shared by the Conservative leaders in the Cabinet; here, due to feelings of obligation to Lloyd George and a pragmatic belief in the need to work together, most ministers were 'v[ery] anxious to maintain the alliance and to work under his leadership'. The resulting dilemma was encapsulated by one member of the Cabinet: 'the problem of our party is to shed Lloyd George, the problem of ministers, how to keep him'.[121]

The significant shift in parliamentary opinion took place during 1922. Before this there had certainly been concerns and strains, particularly over the Irish treaty in late 1921, the decline in relations with France, and the need to reduce government spending. However, the most serious political damage was caused by the election scare of January 1922, which suggested that an attempt to secure a renewed term for the Coalition on its present basis might be rushed into without warning or consultation. The outrage this provoked in the National Union was expressed by Younger as Chairman of its Executive Committee, and the public rebukes which he received from leading Coalitionists only made the atmosphere worse. From this point onwards many constituency associations, especially in southern England and safer seats elsewhere, were pressing their Members to commit themselves to standing at the next election simply as Conservatives with no coalition prefix.[122] This was often pressure applied to an open door, and it is sometimes unclear whether

---

[119] E. Wood, 'Thoughts on some of the present discontents of the Conservative Party', not dated but marked 'early summer 1922', Halifax MSS (Borthwick), A4/410/9/1–13; Malcolm to Curzon, 3 March 1922, Curzon MSS, F112/226A.

[120] Derby to A. Chamberlain, 1 September, 9 and 12 October 1922, Derby MSS, 33; Lord Hemingford, *Backbencher and Chairman* (1946), 41–2.

[121] Crawford diary, 10 October 1922.

[122] Younger to A. Chamberlain, 30 January 1922, AC, 32/3/4; Hemel Hempstead CA, Council, 7 January 1922, Exec., 30 September 1922; Sevenoaks CA, AGM, 18 February, Exec., 1 April 1922; Reigate CA, Exec., 15 September and 18 October 1922; Lane-Fox to Bonar Law, 14 October 1922, Bonar Law MSS, BL/107/2/68.

the association or the Member took the lead, a fact which underlines the collective purpose with which Conservative opinion was moving away from the existing form of coalition.[123] During the spring and early summer, in many Conservative seats there was growing conviction that 'a prolongation of the present state of things will result in disaster to our Party'.[124] The final stage was the summer recess, partly for its effect of putting MPs in closer touch with constituency opinion (especially if they were making speeches), and partly due to the lingering impact of the honours list of June 1922 (which was a reminder of the worst features of Lloyd George). Many anti-Coalition MPs had made up their minds before September, but for some of those still wavering the Turkish crisis proved the last straw, with the prospect of a breach with the Dominions and a needless conflict, and of being cynically bounced into an election in a manufactured 'war scare' atmosphere.

Austen Chamberlain's insensitivity and lack of tactical skill were major factors in the fall of the Coalition and the end of his own leadership. He was overly conscious of the dignity of his position, and possessed the fatal combination of lacking imagination and being 'as obstinate as a mule'.[125] For Chamberlain, the essential point was that his strategy was supported by the other Conservative mandarins in the Cabinet; the assumed role for MPs and the rank and file was that of followers, not doubters or critics—for 'how a party which rejects the advice of all its leaders is to succeed passes my comprehension'.[126] In consequence, he remained aloof from his subordinates and appeared to be too rigidly committed to continuing the Coalition unaltered.[127] This seemed to be due not only to his sense of honour and loyalty to the Prime Minister and his Cabinet colleagues but also, and more dangerously, to the hypnotic sway that Conservatives outside the Cabinet believed Lloyd George was exerting over the political and moral sense of the Conservative leaders. Bridgeman considered that Chamberlain 'has been very stupid in not listening to good advice which has been given him, and he seems infatuated with Ll.G'.[128] Whilst Chamberlain was the most trusted and respected figure amongst the senior leaders, he did not appear to stand up to Lloyd George as Bonar Law had done, and this unbalanced the vital relationship which preserved the party's tolerance for the Coalition. Constrained by his conviction that to separate from Lloyd George and his Liberal followers would be 'to engage the constitutional forces in a fratricidal struggle', Chamberlain was unwilling to assert a clearly Conservative identity and unable to reassure those who feared that the party was losing its independence.[129] He was

[123] Terrell to Bonar Law, 18 September 1922, Bonar Law MSS, BL/107/2/60; Rye CA, 5 March, 23 July 1921, 29 July 1922; Cirencester & Tewkesbury CA, Exec., 18 March 1922.
[124] Long to A. Chamberlain, 27 March 1922, Long MSS, Add.62405/96–9.
[125] Younger to Strachey, 20 November 1922, Strachey MSS, STR/19/4/26b; Amery diary, 16 and 17 October 1922.
[126] A. Chamberlain to Steel-Maitland, 23 March 1922, A. Chamberlain to Derby, 7 September 1922, AC, 33/1/49, 33/2/13.
[127] A. Chamberlain to Lloyd George, 18 March 1922, Wilson to A. Chamberlain, 21 November 1922, AC, 33/1/66, 33/2/94; Dutton, *Austen Chamberlain*, 188–99.
[128] Bridgeman to his son, 13 October 1922, Bridgeman diary.
[129] A. Chamberlain to Leith, 7 March 1922, AC, 33/1/24; NU Conf., 1921; NU Central Council, 21 February 1922; Younger to Long, 27 March 1922, Long MSS, Add.62427/31–2; Lane-Fox to Bonar Law, 14 October 1922, Bonar Law MSS, BL/107/2/68.

aware that the Coalition was becoming more unpopular, but attributed this to the unavoidable problems of postwar dislocation and high taxation, and drew the conclusion that 'the shoulders of the Coalition are broader than the shoulders of the Party'.[130] It remained his belief up to the Carlton Club meeting that 'those who think that the Conservative or Unionist Party, standing as such and disavowing its Liberal allies, could return with a working majority are living in a fool's paradise'.[131] However, the majority of MPs shared the view expressed by Bonar Law, that 'to give the electorate no alternative but a Coalition which they distrusted' was 'the one way to ensure a Labour government sooner or later'.[132]

The mounting disaffection in the constituencies was evident to the senior figures at Central Office: Younger, the Party Chairman; Sanders, the Deputy Chairman; and Fraser, the Principal Agent. Younger's position was particularly difficult, for whilst his role was to carry out the instructions of the Party Leader, it was also his duty, as Chairman of the National Union Executive Committee, to represent their views to the Leader—and during 1922 these became increasingly divergent. From January to September 1922, Younger sought to keep the situation manageable, to follow Chamberlain's strategy as he understood it, and to warn the Leader about the dangers ahead. However, by late August it had become clear to the Party Chairman that entering an election with Lloyd George as the prospective Prime Minister 'would be fatal and it would complete the disintegration of the Party'.[133] At the same time, the majority of the junior ministers were in almost open revolt, and the Chief Whip was delivering ever-blunter warnings that MPs would not follow Chamberlain any further along his present path.[134] Even worse was the developing intention of the leading Conservative Cabinet ministers not to consult the party at large and to avoid the approaching Annual Conference; the Chief Whip feared that such 'tricky' methods 'would break our party in fragments'.[135]

Despairing of Chamberlain's rigidity and lack of responsiveness, the key party managers of Chief Whip, Party Chairman, Deputy Chairman, and Principal Agent became opponents of their Leader. Their awareness of parliamentary and constituency opinion led to the inescapable conclusion that Chamberlain's strategy 'must inevitably lead to such a split in our party as would take years to heal, if it ever were healed', and, accordingly, they sought to avoid this disaster by

---

[130] A. Chamberlain to Long, 27 April 1922, Long MSS, Add.62405/100–1; hence Chamberlain's assumption that the Independent Conservative candidate at the Newport by-election would lose: A. Chamberlain to Fraser, 6 October 1922, AC, 33/2/32.

[131] A. Chamberlain to Parker Smith, 11 October 1922, to Long, 20 October 1922, AC, 33/2/38, 104; his view was partly based upon Central Office's forecast, A. Chamberlain to Gilmour, 7 October 1922, Gilmour MSS, GD383/17/11–12.

[132] Account of the Carlton Club meeting by Curzon's private secretary (who attended as his observer), 19 October 1922, Curzon MSS, F112/319; Ormsby-Gore to Bonar Law, 17 October 1922, Bonar Law MSS, BL/111/19/92.

[133] Younger to Long, 29 August and 9 September 1922, Long MSS (WSA), 947/859.

[134] Wilson to A. Chamberlain, c.14 September, 27 September, 11 October, 21 November 1922, AC, 33/2/26, 27, 43, 94; Salisbury to Selborne, 13 October 1922, Selborne (2nd Earl) MSS, MS. Selborne/7.

[135] Wilson to Gilmour, 12 October 1922, Gilmour MSS, GD383/17/13–14; 'The Break Up of the Coalition', Griffith-Boscawen MSS, c.396/119.

whatever means possible.[136] This 'middle management' of the party provided the respectability and momentum which the diehards on their own lacked, and they were reinforced by the views of the senior backbenchers at the gathering convened by Hoare a few days before the Carlton Club meeting. Knowledge of Baldwin's resignation from the Cabinet was confirmation that the soundest elements of the party were in the same camp, but the crucial factor was that the rebels needed a credible alternative Leader with clean hands—and this made the key question whether Bonar Law could be persuaded to emerge from retirement and oppose his former colleagues and his successor.[137] He was understandably reluctant for a range of reasons from his health to the potential charge of dishonourable conduct, but he became convinced by the weight and strength of party feeling against the Coalition that a rupture was unavoidable and would be less damaging if he acted than if he stood aside—whereupon it became his duty to intervene to save the party.[138]

Austen Chamberlain summoned the meeting of Conservative MPs at the Carlton Club on 19 October 1922 for two reasons.[139] Firstly, it was a way of pre-empting the party Conference, which was almost certain to pass resolutions hostile to the Coalition. Of course, these had no power to bind the Leader, but, in practice, they would make his position almost impossible. This part of Chamberlain's strategy failed immediately, for on 18 October the Executive of the National Union decided to summon an emergency conference, to be held even if an election took place. Their resolution was given to the press, and so at the Carlton Club meeting the next day MPs were well aware that backing Chamberlain would result in a major rift in the party, potentially as damaging as that suffered by the Liberals since 1916. Secondly, the meeting was a final means of asserting control, and Chamberlain expected to succeed in this and to isolate his opponents as a minority. Secure in the position that all of the prominent Conservatives in the Cabinet supported continuing the Coalition, he intended to confront the parliamentary party and 'tell them bluntly that they must either follow our advice or do without us'; mistakenly, he believed they would be cowed by this threat, recognizing that 'they would be in a d—d fix!'[140] Instead, his strategy forced MPs to take sides, and most of them—although reluctantly—decided against their Leader's analysis of the situation. The rebels had a slightly clearer sense of the balance of forces but were far from

---

[136] Wilson to Younger, copied to Sanders, 5 October 1922, Bayford diary.

[137] 'The Break Up of the Coalition', Griffith-Boscawen MSS, c.396/121–2.

[138] Younger to Long, 9 September 1922, Long MSS (WSA), 947/859; Amery diary, 13 October 1922; memo by Curzon, 'Notes on events attending break-up of Ll.G. Govt', c.25 October 1922, Curzon MSS, F112/319/36–62. This argument was put strongly by influential figures such as the editor of *The Times* (Steed to Bonar Law, 17 October 1922, Bonar Law MSS, BL/117/2/1) and senior backbenchers (E. Cecil to Bonar Law, 18 October 1922, Bonar Law MSS, BL/107/2/69).

[139] A month later, he also claimed that he had not waited for the Conference because this would have seen a public fight, with the losers seceding from party, and that 'the result would be a complete break up, whereas in the Carlton it was quite possible to have an adverse vote and still for all to remain friends': Derby diary, 23 November 1922. However, there is no sign of this having been a consideration before the Carlton Club meeting.

[140] A. Chamberlain to Birkenhead, 12 October 1922, to Wilson, 12 October 1922, AC, 33/2/52, 43a.

confident; they expected to make a stand on principle rather than to take over the leadership in a coup. When Baldwin entered the building, he 'had not the slightest idea of the ultimate result' and was expecting to be in the minority.[141] Chamberlain handled the meeting in a clumsy and confrontational style: his speech was 'dictatorial in tone', and delivered with an 'uncompromising and somewhat aggressive attitude', which confirmed his opponents in their view and alienated some of the waverers.[142] Baldwin's short and pithy speech made the point that Lloyd George might split the Conservatives as he had the Liberals, but all accounts agree that Bonar Law's intervention was the decisive factor.[143] One passage in his speech contained the heart of the matter: after appealing for the postponement of any decision until after the party Conference, to which Chamberlain 'shook his head decisively', Bonar Law declared 'I do personally attach more importance to keeping our Party a united body, than to winning the next election'[144]—a statement which 'was received with more applause than any other part of his or anyone else's speeches'.[145] At the end, the secret ballot rejected Chamberlain's leadership by 185 to eighty-eight, a majority so substantial that it acted as a stabilizing force. The fact that the bulk of the MPs and even more of the constituency associations were of the same view made the verdict conclusive, although it was to take some time for the former Coalition leaders to see the reality of the position.

Whilst there was 'great chaos and confusion' in the immediate aftermath of the Carlton Club meeting,[146] key elements of the party management (including the Chief Whip, Party Chairman, and Leader in the Lords) remained in place, and, with Bonar Law's assumption of the party leadership and the Premiership, stability rapidly returned. By 24 October, Walter Long, whose diary had simply recorded the reaction 'disastrous' on hearing the news of the Carlton Club vote, was noting 'all apparently going well politically'.[147] The months which followed the overthrow of the Coalition were marked by a remarkable degree of restraint on the part of MPs, with the deliberate aim of not making the split any worse.[148] This worked with the grain of Conservative attitudes towards unity and was encouraged by the leaders of both sides; in addition, Conservative MPs had the state of the Liberal Party as a sobering example of what to avoid. The problem was largely circumvented by acting

---

[141] Baldwin's remarks in memo by Maclean, 25 July 1923, *BP*, 97; memo by Scott, 12 November 1924, Scott MSS, MSS.119/3/P/BA/1/2.

[142] L. S. Amery, *My Political Life*, vol. 2: *War and Peace 1914–1929* (1953), 238–9; Hemingford, *Backbencher and Chairman*, 42.

[143] Bridgeman diary, 'October 1922'; Amery diary, 19 October 1922; memo by Curzon, 'Notes on events attending break-up of Ll.G. Govt', c.25 October 1922, Curzon MSS, F112/319/36–62; Derby to Lord Stanley, 20 October 1922, Derby MSS, 42/8; 'The Break Up of the Coalition', Griffith-Boscawen MSS, c.396/122.

[144] Transcript of the Carlton Club meeting, 19 October 1922, CPA, PUB/207/2; this full record differs slightly from other accounts, and is assumed to be the most accurate.

[145] Account of the Carlton Club meeting by Curzon's private secretary, 19 October 1922, Curzon MSS, F112/319.

[146] Long diary, 19 October 1922, Long MSS (WSA), 947/1888.

[147] Long diary, 19 and 24 October 1922, Long MSS (WSA), 947/1888.

[148] The exception to this was Birkenhead, e.g. his letter to Scott, 31 October 1922, Scott MSS, MSS.119/3/5/L1/11.

as much as possible as if it did not exist, and the fact that a Conservative ministry had won a mandate and was in office helped considerably. The former Coalition leaders expected Bonar Law's Cabinet to collapse through lack of ability, and did not want to take any of the blame for this; Austen Chamberlain's punctiliousness in encouraging his followers to support the government was not just an expression of his characteristic emphasis on being honourable but also the best tactical option. There was some turmoil in the parliamentary party after the 1923 election defeat, although, of course, many of the most upset were no longer MPs. Because the poll was immediately followed by the Christmas recess, there was no opportunity for any collective view of MPs to be expressed in the vital days of early December. By the time they did reconvene, the issues of both leadership and strategy had effectively been settled, and in the direction which most MPs and local associations preferred—no return to coalition, and no change of Party Leader to an ex-Coalitionist (and therefore, though partly indirectly, the continuation of Baldwin).[149] On that basis, the reunion of the party symbolized by the return of Austen Chamberlain to the shadow cabinet was welcome, and the end of the period of internal tension a relief. Conservative MPs therefore entered the period of opposition to the first Labour government in a remarkably positive frame of mind, took some enjoyment from the opportunities of opposition which were novel to many of them, and were more than satisfied with the substantial victory that followed in the 1924 election.

The next crisis in order of magnitude was that during the period of opposition to the second Labour government of 1929–31. The authority of the leadership was diminished by defeat in the 1929 election on the cautious platform which they had imposed against the wishes of a vocal minority of protectionists. Dissatisfaction over this key area of domestic and imperial policy was exacerbated by poor performances by Baldwin in parliament and his apparent unwillingness to adapt his style or strategy to changed circumstances. There was also resistance to Baldwin's bipartisan approach to the India question, although, fortunately for him, this peaked before and after the greatest danger from the protectionist campaign. The hung parliament added to the tension and uncertainty, as it seemed that an election might occur at any time. For most of the period this was a cause of anxiety rather than an opportunity to be sought; the hostility of the mass circulation Conservative newspapers to Baldwin's leadership was an impediment which worried many candidates, and by-elections did not show signs of a Conservative revival until mid-1931. The pressure for a more protectionist policy came from the safe seats, which provided most of the MPs who had survived the defeat. In these regions, and especially in south-east and eastern England, the temperature was raised by the campaign for a full tariff programme, including food taxes and imperial preference, which was launched by the press magnates, Beaverbrook and Rothermere, under the slogan of 'Empire Free Trade'.[150] Their onslaught was dangerous not because of their ownership of popular

---

[149] Horne to Balfour, 27 December 1923, Balfour MSS, Add.49868; Flintshire CA, Exec, 5 January 1924; Yorkshire Area, Council, 2 May 1924.
[150] Chelmsford CA, Exec., 13 June, 26 September 1930; Lewisham West CA, Exec., 27 February, Council, 6 October 1930.

newspapers, but because they were vocalizing the demands of the rank and file in the Conservative strongholds; as Lady Peto noted, 'it is merely a question of their putting a match to the fire already laid'.[151]

The fundamental cause of the party crisis was that, between October 1929 and October 1930, Baldwin resisted moving towards a tariff policy. He did so for sound political reasons, the first of which was electoral pragmatism. The party could only return to power by recovering marginal seats in the Midlands and north, and in these mainly urban and industrial districts concern about the effect of tariffs on the cost of living made the policy unpopular.[152] As the minority Labour government might be defeated or resign, and an election occur with little warning, it was essential that the party should not adopt a programme which would be an electoral liability in these key seats, whatever the enthusiasm for it in the Conservative bastions. This tension led to the second reason for caution about any advance: that protectionism was divisive in Conservative politics, with differing views held in the shadow cabinet and between grass-roots opinion in the north and the south.[153] Baldwin was primarily concerned to maintain unity and his approach was cautious and moderate; as he explained to a diehard backbencher, 'I must try to keep as many of my people with me as I can!'[154] These reasons explain the support of the shadow cabinet for Baldwin's strategy, as it was balanced between the dislike of tariffs of Salisbury and Churchill and the desire to take steps in the protectionist direction of Amery and Neville Chamberlain. However, this left a dangerously widening gap between the leaders and many of their followers, as 'there has been a general swing to the right throughout the Tory Party, not merely in a protectionist direction, but all along the line'.[155]

Problems in Baldwin's style and conduct of the leadership in opposition added fuel to these flames. The appearance of delay and indecision was the most damaging, and in May 1930 Hoare complained of 'the leaderless state of our party'.[156] Other problems included Baldwin's adherence to Davidson as Party Chairman in the spring of 1930 when unpopularity had made the latter a liability, his overemphasis on negativism and caution in his speeches on policy (particularly in the spring and summer of 1930 when the pressure was greatest), and his deep hostility to the press lords, which made any accommodation difficult—although there was a precarious truce with Beaverbrook from March to May 1930. Baldwin scored a victory in the party meeting held on 24 June 1930, but this brought only short-term relief as it did not resolve the growing pressure from below for a full tariff

---

[151] Lady Peto diary, 22 February 1930; Gwynne to Beaverbrook, 22 February 1930, Beaverbrook MSS, C149; Croft to N. Chamberlain, 4 October 1930, Croft MSS, 1/7/Ch34.

[152] Gwynne to Beaverbrook, 5 February, Baldwin to Gwynne, 28 July 1930, Gwynne MSS, 14, 15; N. Chamberlain to Scott, 17 July 1930, Scott MSS, MSS.119/3/P/CH/3; Bradford CA, Central Ctte., 26 March 1930; Wakefield CA, Exec., 18 June 1930.

[153] Croft to Beaverbrook, 26 June 1930, Beaverbrook MSS, C101.

[154] Baldwin's comment to Peto, Lady Peto diary, 5 February 1930.

[155] Ormsby-Gore to Irwin, 3 July 1930, Halifax MSS, C152/19/1/91a.

[156] Hoare to Irwin, 31 May 1930, Halifax MSS, C152/19/1/71; Winterton diary, 20 February 1930, Winterton MSS.

policy.[157] Stirred up by the intervention of the press lords in by-elections in Norfolk North, Bromley, and Paddington South, the disaffection of the grass roots mounted to serious levels during the summer recess. In July, just two weeks after taking over the Party Chairmanship, Neville Chamberlain admitted in a private talk with a group of young backbenchers that 'a terrible demoralisation in the Party was resulting from the present guerrilla warfare'.[158] In early October 1930, the Party Chairman reported that all those who came to see him at Central Office told the same tale: 'that the rank and file as well as the officers of Associations have lost all confidence in the Leader and declare that we can never win under him'.[159] 'Baldwin was never in a more dangerous plight,' a former junior minister warned the Party Leader in the House of Lords in early October 1930: 'the Party is simply rotting before our eyes'.[160] It appeared to many in the party—including some of the shadow cabinet—that the situation was sliding dangerously out of control, and Hoare warned that 'things are moving so fast that unless something happens quickly, everything and everybody will collapse like a pack of cards'.[161] For the first time, the criticism of the southern and agricultural seats was being echoed in the Midlands and north—this both made the situation acute, and gave Baldwin his opportunity.[162]

The change was the result of the impact of the depression in the industrial areas, which at last was moving public opinion in the protectionist direction.[163] Baldwin could now safely give his followers what they wanted, whilst increasing the party's electoral appeal rather than diminishing it. At the crucial point, as his position was crumbling in October 1930, an offer of preferential tariffs by the Canadian Prime Minister, R. B. Bennett, at the Imperial Conference in London provided 'a Heaven-sent opportunity' for adopting a full protectionist policy, without this appearing to be a surrender to the press lords.[164] The adoption of the 'free hand' policy was enough to satisfy even the ardent protectionists; it took the wind of grass-roots support out of Beaverbrook's sails and detached almost all of his significant Conservative supporters.[165] As there was now hardly any difference of policy, his continued campaign was seen as based upon personality rather than principle and

[157] St. Albans CA, Exec., 25 July 1930.
[158] Butler to his parents, 14 July 1930, Butler MSS, D48/748–51.
[159] N. Chamberlain to Bridgeman, 5 October 1930, Bridgeman MSS, 3389/98; Bridgeman diary, 'September' 1930; Campbell to Bowyer, 15 September 1930, Baldwin MSS, 51/13–15; Dawson diary, 6 October 1930, Dawson MSS.
[160] Ormsby-Gore to Salisbury, 5 October 1930, Salisbury MSS, S(4)137/44–5.
[161] Hoare to N. Chamberlain, 8 October 1930, NC, 8/10/8; Croft to N. Chamberlain, 4 September and 4 October 1930, Croft MSS, CAC, CRFT/1/7/Ch33–4; Ormsby-Gore to Salisbury, 5 October 1930, Salisbury MSS, S(4)137/44–5.
[162] Hannon to Beaverbrook, 18 September 1930, Beaverbrook MSS, BBK/C154; North West Area, Council, 4 October 1930; Renfrewshire West CA, Council, 6 October 1930; Derby to N. Chamberlain, 10 October 1930, Derby MSS, 33.
[163] Bolton CA, Womens Exec., 29 July 1930; Newport CA, Exec., 26 September 1930; Darlington CA, Exec., 29 September 1930; Aberdeen South CA, Chairman's Ctte., 3 October 1930.
[164] N. Chamberlain to Bridgeman, 10 October 1930, Bridgeman MSS, 3389/100.
[165] N. Chamberlain to Bridgeman, 15 October 1930, Bridgeman MSS, 3389/102; Elibank to Baldwin, 30 October 1930, Baldwin MSS, 165/130; Lewes CA, Exec., 27 October 1930; Lewisham West CA, special general meeting, 27 October 1930.

he became isolated. Baldwin's coup was reinforced by securing a large majority (462 to 116 against, in a secret ballot) at a second party meeting held on 30 October, and his position never again came under such serious and widespread criticism. Immediately after the meeting, the diehard critics in the parliamentary ranks announced that they accepted its verdict and would loyally support Baldwin, which removed the danger of a corrosive guerrilla campaign. However, the party crisis was not over, for it had been fuelled by Baldwin's poor performances in the House of Commons in a number of important debates.[166] This continued to be a problem after the resolution of the tariff issue in October 1930 and, together with the anxiety provoked by his support for the Labour government's policy on India, was the cause of the further erosion of his position in the winter months which led to the last phase of the crisis in February and March 1931.

The most visible, but least important, element in this final flurry was the last by-election assaults of the Empire Crusade at Islington East and Westminster St George's, which proved to be counterproductive, and forced the leading figures in the party to rally behind the Leader.[167] More significant was the alarm in the party machine over growing grass-roots hostility to Baldwin's stance on India, with Central Office 'in a condition bordering on despair' and its mandarins 'in a real funk as to what may happen'.[168] This produced the famous memorandum from the Principal Agent, Topping, to Neville Chamberlain as Party Chairman, although its warning that Baldwin's position had deteriorated irretrievably was unduly pessimistic.[169] This crisis was principally a matter of crumbling morale and confidence in the parliamentary party, which in turn affected the front-bench leadership; even so, the Leader still retained substantial support amongst MPs.[170] It was resolved when Baldwin, who for a few hours on 1 March had contemplated resignation after reading Topping's memo, instead launched a vigorous recovery.[171] He was able to rally the party, and his more reluctant front-bench colleagues, behind him by focusing upon the issue of dictation from the press lords.[172] This was more of a holding tactic, and it enabled Baldwin to give crucial reassurance over his line on India by further emphasizing the safeguards to be included in any reforms; to restore his parliamentary reputation with a triumphant success in the key debate on India on 12 March; and to clear the air within the leadership by listening to a

---

[166] Smithers to Fry, 1 January 1931, Baldwin MSS, 166/275–8.
[167] N. Chamberlain to Derby, 4 March 1931, NC, 8/10/23; N. to H. Chamberlain, 1 March 1931, *NCDL*.
[168] Conversation with Bowyer (Deputy Party Chairman) recounted in Hannon to Beaverbrook, 4 February 1931, Beaverbrook MSS, BBK/C155.
[169] Ball, *Baldwin and the Conservative Party*, 137–8, 141–2; N. Chamberlain diary, 1 March 1931, NC, 2/22; N. Chamberlain to Baldwin, 1 March 1931, enclosing memo by Topping, 25 February 1931, Baldwin MSS, 166/47–53.
[170] Inskip to Baldwin, 4 March 1931, Baldwin MSS, 166/41, referring to 'scores of people in the House on our side who would beg you not to go'.
[171] Dawson diary, 1–3 March 1931, Dawson MSS; Bridgeman diary, 1 and 28 March 1931; Jones diary, 11 March 1931, in T. Jones, *A Diary with Letters 1931–1950* (1954), 4–5.
[172] Baldwin's public letter to Duff Cooper, 12 March 1931, Duff Cooper MSS, CAC, DUFC/2/8; Lady Smithers diary, 19 March 1931, Smithers MSS.

frank expression of the shadow cabinet's concerns later in the month.[173] His success was capped by Beaverbrook's decision, following his candidate's defeat in the acrimonious Westminster St George's by-election, to abandon his campaign and conclude an agreement with Neville Chamberlain, who was still serving as Party Chairman. From this point onwards, as the economic depression eroded Labour support, the signs of improvement in Conservative fortunes led to stability and unity in the party, and to concentration upon opposing the weakening government and securing its removal from office. This seemed increasingly likely, and the by-election results of the summer of 1931 gave every reason to expect a Conservative victory in an autumn general election on a similar scale to that of 1924—but, this time, with a mandate to introduce protection.

Although many of Baldwin's problems were of his own making, he emerged victorious from the party crisis by exploiting the strengths of his position and the weaknesses of his opponents, in particular the press lords. The latter were only strong when they provided a channel for the pent-up frustration of the party rank and file, and even here they had a limited regional base—primarily southern England (especially the Home Counties), East Anglia, and some of the arable farming areas.[174] The press lords were unable to persuade any senior Conservative figures to lead or support the Empire Crusade, which left them exposed. Their campaign appeared to have too much of the personal vendetta about it, and here Beaverbrook's alliance with Rothermere was a source of weakness rather than strength.[175] The latter in particular gave Baldwin an easy target to attack, and the Conservative Leader was able to raise the debate to the higher level of constitutional principle. Ironically, it was to Baldwin's advantage when the press lords switched the issue from policy to leadership in June 1930, for by doing so they lost much of their support within the party and Baldwin was able to raise the cry of press domination and outside attempts to dictate the party's Leader. The press lords' tactics were also sometimes counterproductive: not only their use of their newspapers, which aroused sympathy for Baldwin on grounds of fair play, but also their launch of a separate political organization in February 1930.[176] The appeal which this made for members and subscriptions, and the threat to put up its own candidates, alarmed Conservative constituency committees and MPs in the regions where the Empire Crusade programme had an appeal. However, whilst it led to anxiety on the back benches and pressure within the party organization, the intrusion of this interloper also provoked resentment and hostility. There was an even stronger backlash when the running of rival candidates split the Conservative vote to the benefit of the opposition. The negative reaction when this led to a Labour victory in the Islington East by-election of February 1931 was a key factor in both

---

[173] N. Chamberlain to Cunliffe-Lister, 26 March 1931, Swinton MSS, I(174)/2/1/8; Hailsham to Salisbury, 27 March 1931, Salisbury MSS, S(4)140/47–8.
[174] SUA, EDC, Exec., 26 February 1930.
[175] Gwynne to Beaverbrook, 22 February 1930, Gwynne MSS, 14; Croft to Beaverbrook, 28 June 1930, Beaverbrook MSS, C101; Birmingham Handsworth CA, AGM, 6 March 1931.
[176] Middleton & Prestwich CA, AGM, 1 March 1930.

the failure of the anti-Baldwin candidate in the following Westminster St George's by-election and Beaverbrook's decision after that to give up the fight.

Baldwin survived this lowest point of his leadership for several reasons. Although he sometimes frustrated his front-bench colleagues with an apparent complacency, despite some grumbling he retained their loyalty. This was partly due to respect for his character and 'absolute confidence in his straightforwardness',[177] and partly to recognition of his standing with the public and the fact that he remained an important electoral asset. It was also the case that the attacks from the non-respectable quarter of the press lords gave them no option but to rally in support of the Leader, especially when he raised the standard of constitutional principle. Baldwin maintained his position by a combination of shrewd tactics and careful timing, both in changes of policy and in the summoning of the party meetings of June and October 1930, and by producing an oratorical success when it was most crucial to do so. In October 1930, a hostile diehard peer 'thought his speech today was above all praise as a leader's speech', whilst in March 1931, 'the great thing was that he undeniably spoke as a leader'.[178] The problem, of course, was the extended troughs between these peaks. However, Baldwin's position was further sustained by the absence of any more attractive replacement. He remained the least divisive figure: as Bridgeman noted shortly before the first party meeting, 'everyone knows that there is no possible leader who could get anything like the amount of support that Baldwin commands'.[179] There was particular resistance to any alternative who had a Coalitionist past or inclinations, but even Hailsham or Neville Chamberlain were not seen as having the same breadth of appeal to the public or party as Baldwin, whatever his immediate deficiencies. Chamberlain remained close to Baldwin until the very last stage of the crisis in March 1931; even then, he was not yet sufficiently established or popular to be the party's most likely choice and did not directly seek the leadership, although he was aware that it might fall to him should Baldwin decide to throw in his hand. Instead, Baldwin's prestige and authority were restored by the improvement in the party's fortunes during the next few months, as a Conservative election landslide in the autumn seemed increasingly probable.

Although they lasted longer, the other two rebellions were on a more limited front and thus easier to contain. Dissension over India first appeared after Baldwin's endorsement of the Irwin Declaration in November 1929, was renewed in January to March 1931 after the first Round Table conference, and became a running battle from the publication of the White Paper in 1933 to the passage of the India Act in 1935. The period in early 1931 was in many ways the most critical, as the party was out of power and the Leader's position had already been weakened by the battles over tariff policy in the previous year. However, at that point the reform proposals were still at a formative stage, and their critics did not launch a direct

---

[177] N. Chamberlain to Irwin, 25 December 1927, Halifax MSS, C152/17/1/277a.
[178] Halsbury to Salisbury, 30 October 1930, Salisbury MSS, S(4)137/94; Stonehaven to Irwin, 17 March 1931, Halifax MSS, C152/19/1/271.
[179] Bridgeman to Irwin, 15 June 1930, Halifax MSS, C152/19/1/79; Ipswich CA, Exec., 13 March 1931.

challenge to the leadership or seek to mobilize grass-roots opposition. When the revolt reached this stage in 1933–35, the political situation was very different. By this time, the party generally had confidence in the effectiveness of the National Government and—especially after the departure of the Samuelite Liberals in 1932—the harmonious relations of its leaders. Its majority was so large that even the more surprising by-election defeats, such as Fulham East in 1933, caused only transitory concern. The political problems which did exist were primarily domestic; the focus of public concern in the spring of 1935 was the Unemployment Assistance Board's reduction of benefit levels, not the passage of the Government of India Act. Indeed, many Conservatives stifled their doubts about the India policy to avoid disrupting the National Government, and one of the most effective charges against Churchill and the rebels was that they sought its destruction.[180] The other issues, such as disarmament, agriculture, and housing, tended to encourage cohesion in the government's parliamentary support. Whilst there might have been grumbles in the lobbies, only five right-wing Conservative MPs repudiated the Coalition over a range of issues—a proportion almost vanishingly small compared to the rebellion of 1922. Almost all of the MPs who opposed the India policy confined their dissent to that issue alone and were not prepared to make it the starting point of a wider rebellion, and this was also true of the criticism at constituency level. So long as this was the case, it was relatively simple to contain the disruption, and the position of the leaders was safe. There was also less pressure applied from outside: whilst Lord Rothermere's *Daily Mail* supported the India revolt, there was no attempt to organize an electoral pressure group as there had been over tariffs in 1929–31, and the rest of the Conservative press were either neutral or supported the government.

In the case of the 'India revolt', too much attention has been focused on the group of visible rebels: Churchill, Lloyd, Page Croft, and the eighty diehard MPs who voted against the key stages of the bill. Given the unprecedented size of the government's majority in 1931–35, this group was too small to do anything more than protest and agitate—they were a nuisance and a delay, but almost never a real threat. That would only happen if events made the moderate centre of the parliamentary party more receptive to the diehard case, which was something that would be determined by external factors rather than the effectiveness of the rebels. A crucial element in the credibility and persuasiveness of the government's policy was its endorsement by nearly all of the most recently serving 'men on the spot', particularly the provincial Governors (many of whom had been respected middle-ranking Conservative MPs, generally junior ministers or whips, before their appointment).[181] Despite the strains caused within the party, Baldwin's support for the

---

[180] Wolmer to Lloyd, 10 November 1933, Wolmer MSS, MS.Eng.hist.c.1013/118; Davidson to Sykes, 21 March 1933, Davidson MSS (Bodleian), MSS.Eng.hist.c.559/50–3; SUA, EDC, 26 April 1933. Churchill's conduct in 1934–35 led to criticism from branches in his constituency, and although a resolution of confidence was carried at the AGM, there were twenty-five votes against: Essex West CA, AGM, 28 March 1935.

[181] It was also crucial that some who had reservations remained silent: Jackson to Croft, 23 October 1933, Croft MSS, CAC, CRFT/1/15/Ja1.

reform proposals was strengthened 'by the fact that every experienced person coming from India, including even soldiers (who were in the ordinary way of a Tory and no-surrender disposition) told him that we must persevere with the White Paper policy'.[182] During the whole period from the Irwin Declaration promising 'dominion status' in October 1929 to the passage of the Government of India Act in June 1935, the moments of doubt amongst the majority of Conservative MPs were not due to the critique of the dissident minority, but to signs that the official policy was not working or fears that too much was being conceded too feebly. The vital aspects were, therefore, the support of the Indian Princes for a more conservative federal constitution and the credibility of the 'safeguards' which were to be incorporated into the bill; if both of these were maintained, dissent would not spread beyond an irreconcilable few. However, the leadership could take nothing for granted, as the support given by MPs and much of the grass roots was unenthusiastic and reluctant, and the large majority were strongly inclined to caution.[183]

The second factor shaping opinion was whether the situation in India appeared to be under control. This involved the maintenance of law and order, and of the morale of the Indian civil service, police, and army—hence the sensitivity of Churchill's claims of political manipulation of civil service promotions. The barometer of parliamentary concern rose and fell in accordance with the political atmosphere in India, for the mood in the lobbies responded to this much more than to the attacks of the diehards. This explains the variable effectiveness of the appeals made by the critics to party opinion not only at the national Conference and Central Council, but also at Area and local level. The lowest points of credibility for the policy supported by Baldwin came following his speech after the first Round Table conference in January 1931, which was too moderate for most of his followers, and with the meetings between Gandhi and the Viceroy in March 1931, which made the diehards 'see red'.[184] The spectacle provoked Churchill to his famous denunciation of the humiliation of the 'half-naked fakir' ascending the steps of the Viceregal Palace to be received as if an equal, and the stress and concerns which it caused were evident in the restiveness of the parliamentary party's India Committee.[185] Baldwin's leadership seemed on the brink of collapse, and, ironically, it was the intrusion of Beaverbrook's final challenge in the Westminster St George's by-election which forced his colleagues to rally in support. Most importantly, the success of the Irwin–Gandhi talks pacified the situation in India and vindicated Baldwin's support of the Viceroy whom he had appointed; when the news broke on 5 March, he was 'scarcely able to restrain his joy'.[186] This was capped by a public speech at Newton Abbot placing greater emphasis on the safeguards,

---

[182] Notes by Crozier, interview with Baldwin, 12 June 1934, *BP*, 320; Cazalet to Baldwin (reporting official opinion in India), 30 January 1934, Baldwin MSS, 106/201–5.
[183] Duke of Atholl to Butter, 18 April 1933, Atholl MSS, 9/1.
[184] Lady Peto diary, 6 March 1931; Eden diary, 4 March 1931, Avon MSS, AP/20/1/10; Baldwin to Macdonald, 2 March, Lloyd to Baldwin, 5 March 1931, Baldwin MSS, 104/216, 226–7.
[185] Butler to his parents, 4 March 1931, Butler MSS, D48/792–5.
[186] Eden diary, 5 March 1931, Avon MSS, AP/20/1/10.

and an assertive and effective Commons speech a few days later, which 'seems to have made all the difference to our own Party'.[187] Although there were recurrences of agitation and unrest in India after this, the firm 'law and order' policy of Lord Willingdon as Viceroy from 1931 to 1936 provided vital reassurance to Conservative opinion in Britain, and the situation did not again seem in danger of slipping out of control.

The third factor which disinclined moderate MPs to join the rebels was the lack of widespread public concern over the proposed reforms in India. Even in Lancashire, where the implications for the export markets of the cotton industry caused anxiety, concern was generally expressed in a cautious and muted way. The final and crucial factor was that far from undermining the government, the bipartisan policy over India was an important factor in making it workable—and the preservation of the stability provided by the National combination was a high priority for almost all Conservatives in the continuing economic difficulties of the early 1930s. Together with the focus upon disarmament and support of the League of Nations in its foreign policy, the 'Round Table' programme of reform in India was evidence of its genuinely cross-party outlook, whatever the balance between its parliamentary components. Indeed, co-operation over India since the Irwin Declaration in 1929 was an important factor in MacDonald's feeling of confidence that he could work with Baldwin and his willingness to continue as Prime Minister in August 1931. Of course, the centrism of the India policy meant that the Conservative leaders had a fine line to follow: they must not be too 'Tory' and put the bonds holding the Coalition together under strain, but, equally, they must not seem too 'pink' and risk alienating the main body of Conservatives. One reassurance for the latter was that the Secretary of State for India, Sir Samuel Hoare, was a Conservative, and he demonstrated skill, sensitivity, and patience when taking the legislation through its many stages, from the White Paper of 1933 to successful passage in 1935. The result was that, far from the Leaders' policy steering the party towards the electoral rocks—as had seemed clearly the case in 1922, and as it had already done in 1929—it was the rebels who posed a danger by dividing the vote at the Wavertree and Norwood by-elections in 1935.[188] By that point, only a few were still responsive to their charges: confidence in Baldwin and the reassurances which he had given at party gatherings, Hoare's adeptness in the House of Commons, the emphasis upon the safeguards, the relative passivity in India, and the importance of continuing the National Government kept the majority of the party, in both parliament and the constituencies, behind the leadership. These were the determining factors in the containment of the India revolt, and they were more significant than such matters as the leadership, tactics, organization, and even the arguments of the rebels.

The final rebellion, over the policy of appeasement between 1936 and 1940, was the least dangerous of the four. It was more episodic, generally more restrained in

---

[187] Fremantle to Salisbury, 14 March 1931, Salisbury MSS, S(4)140/20–1.
[188] Rawson to Baldwin, 28 January 1935, Baldwin MSS, 107/10; SUA, EDC, 13 March 1935.

the terms of its criticism, and much more limited in numbers. It had two distinctive features—the rebellious MPs were drawn more from the left wing than the right, and they had almost no support in the constituencies. It was always the case that dissidence in a rightwards—or apparently more Conservative—direction was more likely to gain sympathy at the grass roots than rebellions on the left, which seemed to favour the policies and benefit the fortunes of the opposition parties. Apart from the shaky moment over the Hoare–Laval Pact in December 1935, which was largely due to the government appearing to have contradicted its own public position, parliamentary support for its foreign and defence policies was never seriously in doubt. The erosion of Baldwin's command in 1936 was due to his state of health, and not to any dissent in the ranks. From May 1937 onwards, Neville Chamberlain was firmly in control of the National Government, the Conservative Party, and the political situation generally. Victory had been achieved in the 1935 election by a comfortable margin, by-elections were giving few grounds for anxiety, the Labour opposition in the House of Commons was making little impact, and the prospects for victory in a late 1939 or 1940 election were very good. The other dissensions of 1936–40 were short-lived and rarely on vital points of domestic policy. Slum clearance, the Coal Bill, and the National Defence Contribution all provoked opposition, but with a combination of flexibility and firmness the government easily weathered these squalls. In the case of the most important underlying anxiety—the high levels of taxation needed to finance rearmament—appeasement offered the best hope of ameliorating this; the dissidents could only demand more expenditure, and their stance seemed more likely to cause a war. The Conservative press were more solidly behind the Party Leader and his policy than had ever been the case before, and public opinion was generally favourable, especially during the Czech crisis in 1938. The anti-appeasers therefore had an extremely difficult uphill struggle, with the weight of party, press, and public opinion against them. In such circumstances, it is not surprising that they were not cohesive, consistent, persistent, or effective—until the failure of appeasement, and still more the setbacks in the war, appeared to validate their criticisms and began to turn sentiment in their direction in the spring of 1940.

After succeeding to the Premiership in May 1937, Neville Chamberlain was vigorous in seeking a lasting basis of peace through the conciliation of the dictators ruling Italy and Germany, and his pursuit of 'appeasement' was a bold and ambitious policy. However, whilst most Conservatives supported it—many with a fervent enthusiasm founded on a mixture of fear and hope—a minority disagreed. Their effect was diminished by the fact that they often did so at different times and on different issues; thus Churchill focused upon policy towards Germany, whilst the cause of Eden's resignation in February 1938 was concessions to Italy. Criticism was focused upon the wisdom of Chamberlain's methods rather than their morality (which was emphasized later, with the benefit of hindsight). It was not so much objection to appeasement in principle, but disagreement over which of the pressing dangers facing the empire should be appeased and which resisted, and how far it was safe to go in either direction. However, despite its strong appeal, appeasement did run counter to some Conservative sentiments, and patriotic pride as well as practicality motivated many of the

Conservative critics.[189] They were 'shocked by Munich as the worst humiliation we had suffered up to that time', but also feared 'that as long as the policy continued, there would be more in the future'.[190] Their problem was to find a constructive alternative that did not seem more likely to lead to war, and without this they seemed to be merely negative and carping. It was felt that their belligerent tone and confrontational strategy would worsen the situation, and they were open to the charge of irresponsibility and the unreality of armchair strategists, and even of having 'a lust for war'.[191]

Chamberlain's settlement of the Czech crisis with the Munich Agreement of September 1938 was the high point of his prestige and popularity with both the public and the Conservative Party. Until this began to unravel in the early months of 1939, the opponents of appeasement were a beleaguered and disregarded handful, often operating as individuals or fragmentary groups—there was never the degree of co-operation and organization which had marked the India revolt. One reason for this was that the foreign policy crises of 1935–39 were episodic and varied in nature, and there was not the continuity and coherence that opposing a piece of legislation provided. The critics based their position on the core Conservative values of patriotism, self-respect, insularity, and defence of the empire; they considered the Munich settlement to be a shameful humiliation and 'a sheer surrender to violence'.[192] However, they were again handicapped by the lack of a convincing alternative to the government's line. As with the India revolt, the course advocated by the dissidents seemed, to most Conservative MPs, more likely to provoke conflict than the policy of the leadership; they might have doubts about the wisdom of the latter, but they had much greater reservations about the judgement of the rebels. In this instance, the critics' case was rendered even more unattractive because (alone of the four crises) it deviated to the left of the official line, making common cause with Liberal, Socialist, and even—under the 'United Front' banner—Communist opponents of the government. Most importantly, until early 1939 there were grounds for believing that the government's policy might be successful, and there was strong evidence of its popularity. Unlike the position in 1921–22 and 1933–35, the Coalition was led by a Conservative Prime Minister of undisputed authority; unlike in late 1922 and to some extent in early 1935, there was general confidence in the government's prospects at the next election. Once again, the rebel position seemed to imply the disruption of the National Government, and by the late 1930s most of the Conservative Party had nothing to gain from this—which left the suspicion that it was only the malcontents' personal ambitions which would do so.

The position of the anti-appeasers was considerably weaker than that of previous rebel groups. They were disunited and lacked leadership: Churchill was discredited,

---

[189] Duchess of Atholl to Duke of Atholl, 22 September 1938, Atholl MSS, 54/12; Rose to Adams, 2 October 1938, Adams MSS, box 10.
[190] Emrys-Evans to Salisbury, 21 July 1943, to Doncaster, 22 September 1938, Emrys-Evans MSS, Add.58247/4, Add.58249/14.
[191] Mickel to Duchess of Atholl, 9 and 12 May 1938, Atholl MSS, 22/24.
[192] Amery to Hannon, 21 September 1938, Hannon MSS, HNN/17/1; Nicolson diary, 4 October 1938; Duff Cooper diary, 17 September 1938.

Eden and Duff Cooper kept a low profile, and Amery alone was not weighty enough. They were constrained by the usual pressures for conformity exerted by the leaders, the whips, and—most of all—the local associations, where the strength of support for appeasement placed its handful of parliamentary opponents in an uncomfortable position. The polarizing event was the Czech crisis, which took Britain to the brink of war in September 1938. The terms which Chamberlain agreed at Munich pushed the critical MPs into more open opposition, whilst the wave of popular relief at the avoidance of war and gratitude for Chamberlain's bold initiative of flying to meet Hitler reduced grass-roots tolerance of parliamentary dissent.[193] In the months immediately after the Munich settlement, several of the critics, including Churchill, faced moves within their constituencies to deselect them as candidates, and had to tread warily.[194] Due to the seriousness of the issue of peace or war, these pressures were stronger than in any of the previous party crises. In a time of national peril, Conservatives placed great importance upon closing ranks against an external threat. At such a time, 'unity was essential'[195] and open disagreement was almost an unpatriotic self-indulgence: 'the present moment was not the one for any Member to embarrass the Prime Minister with advice or persuasion publicly given'.[196] Indeed, the critics were distrusted for the arrogance and egotism involved in claiming wisdom superior to the diplomatic establishment and the government, despite lacking access to their sources of information.[197] So long as the policy of appeasement had credibility, its opponents would remain a marginal irritation rather than a serious threat.

For this reason, the German occupation of Bohemia in March 1939 was a turning point, as Hitler effectively repudiated the Munich Agreement and shattered the hopes which had been built upon it.[198] However, it took some time for confidence in the purposeful Prime Minister to diminish and for the belief that he could still snatch peace from the jaws of war to erode; consequently, the response to Hitler's coup was a wave of constituency resolutions as fervently supportive of Chamberlain as those of the previous autumn.[199] Nevertheless, from this point onwards, events seemed to lend more substance to the critics' case and to undermine the leadership, making them appear gullible, lacking in judgement, and—particularly after the outbreak of war—dangerously complacent.[200] Two key statements by Chamberlain were especially damaging in hindsight: the claim of having secured 'peace in our time' on his return from Munich in October 1938, and the assertion that Hitler had

---

[193] Doncaster (chairman, Derbyshire South CA) to Emrys-Evans, 20 October 1938, Emrys-Evans MSS, Add.58249/32–4.
[194] See correspondence in the Cilcennin MSS, Churchill MSS, Emrys-Evans MSS, and Wolmer MSS.
[195] Aldershot CA, Council, 22 October 1938.
[196] Shrewsbury CA, Exec., 5 April 1939, in discussion of its MP's support, subsequently withdrawn, for a motion tabled by the Eden group.
[197] Aldrich-Blake to Thomas, 14 December 1938, Cilcennin MSS, 34.
[198] Rother Valley CA, AGM, 20 March 1939; Chelmsford CA, AGM, 20 March 1939.
[199] Bury CA, AGM, 3 April 1939; Halifax CA, AGM, 3 April 1939; Gravesend CA, Exec., 14 April 1939; Dundee CA, Exec., 20 April 1939.
[200] Harborough CA, AGM, 29 April 1939; Emrys-Evans, diary, 23 April 1940, Emrys-Evans MSS, Add.58246/123–9.

'missed the bus' on 4 April 1940, shortly before the German seizure of Denmark and Norway. Between March and September 1939, parliamentary support for the official policy was given with growing pessimism and in the unhappy knowledge that little else could be done in the immediate circumstances, as the ebbing of confidence in the leadership was not matched by any rising tide of conviction that the critics' alternatives were practicable or better. In that respect, the case was, at least, not proven, and there was no visible swelling of the rebel ranks; as late as 1 August 1939, in Hoare's opinion at least, 'the Winston opposition is going very thin'.[201]

The events surrounding the declaration of war, with the Prime Minister apparently making another attempt at appeasement, shook confidence further; Chamberlain's statement on 2 September 'left the House aghast' and 'a puff would have brought the Govt. down'.[202] However, the commencement of hostilities smothered any potential rebellion under the greater pressures of patriotism and unity. During the first months of the war, several uninspiring speeches from Chamberlain further eroded his position, but the common expectation of a major assault—particularly from the air—and the absence on military service of many younger MPs militated against the expression of open criticism. It was, therefore, during the period from December 1939 to April 1940 that disillusion with the leadership began to spread. The issue of the prewar policy of appeasement inevitably merged with concerns about the readiness of the armed forces and the conduct of the war.[203] The resulting erosion of confidence was not initially expressed as dissatisfaction with the Prime Minister, but as criticism of the inner circle of Cabinet ministers most identified with appeasement, particularly Hoare and Simon.[204] However, Chamberlain's refusal to drop any of them and his unwise reshuffle of April 1940—which moved Hoare to the Air Ministry, and seemed to close the door to more substantial revision—meant that, as in 1922, the Prime Minister became the impediment which would have to be removed in order to address the flaws of the government. The other similarity to the fall of Lloyd George was that the political and personal dominance of the Prime Minister was such that failures were disproportionately damaging to his personal standing. By April 1940, the cumulative effect of the failure of prewar appeasement, the slowness of gearing up for war production, and concern over a leadership style which seemed too routine in its methods and complacent in its outlook had sapped the confidence of a significant number of National Government MPs.[205] Crucially, the view of a prewar critic, that 'the Prime Minister has no gift for inspiring anybody', came to be shared by a growing proportion of the mainstream MPs, not least due to the evident contrast with the determination and focused aggression displayed by Churchill after his return to office at the Admiralty.[206]

---

[201] Hoare to Astor, 1 August 1939, Templewood MSS, X/4.
[202] Crookshank diary, 2 September 1939; Wallace diary, 2 September 1939, Wallace MSS; Lady Smithers diary, 2 September 1939, Smithers MSS.
[203] Inskip diary notes, 16 December 1939, INKP/1/2.
[204] Hannon to N. Chamberlain, 9 May 1940, Hannon MSS, HNN/17/3.
[205] Keyes to Churchill, 28 April 1940, Keyes MSS, Add. 82379; Crookshank diary, 2 May 1940; Channon diary, 2–4 May 1940.
[206] Nicolson diary, 26 September 1939.

The Norway debate was the first opportunity to express these feelings, now further stoked by dismay at the inadequacies of the British response to the Nazi blitzkrieg. Although the government was on the defensive, the hostility of the known group of 'glamour boys' could be taken for granted and dismissed as a serious threat. The key factor in the fall of Chamberlain was the withdrawal of support by an unexpectedly large number of previously loyal MPs, either by voting with the rebels or by abstaining. Some of these came to the debate with their minds already made up, but their number was augmented by the failure of the government speakers in the debate—most of all, and critically, of the Prime Minister himself, who 'was poor and [made] the House uncomfortable'.[207] The content and tone of Chamberlain's speech added fuel to the driving force of the revolt, which was the growing concern over the government's ability to conduct the war with competence, judgement, and energy. He failed to answer the case of the critics in terms that reassured the doubtful; an appeal to loyalty, especially when phrased awkwardly and in a combative style, was no longer enough.[208] The other important concern in the Norway debate was the issue of national unity, and the extent to which Conservatives feared the effects of domestic division in wartime should not be underestimated. Whatever their views of the conduct or abilities of the Labour opposition, it was apparent that the Prime Minister and his immediate circle were the impediment to co-operation, and there was nothing in the debate to suggest that Chamberlain regarded this as a matter of necessity that required compromise or concession. The crucial factor was that the Labour Party would not join a government led by Chamberlain; on 9 May, Dalton confirmed to Butler, for transmission to Halifax, that 'the Labour Party had too many grudges against Neville'.[209] In these circumstances, Chamberlain had no alternative but to resign as Prime Minister, which he did on 10 May.

CRISES OF LEADERSHIP AND POLICY: THEMES AND ISSUES

The final section of this chapter is a comparative analysis of the nature of the four party crises, which builds upon the discussion above and the examination of Conservative attitudes, constituency opinion, and parliamentary dissidence in previous chapters. The dangers posed by the four major crises varied according to a number of factors. One of the most important of these was the number of sources of discontent. The leadership was able to contain challenges more easily when they derived from a single issue, even when this was of critical importance to national security, as was the case over the future of India and the responses to the European dictators in the 1930s. The most serious crises were in 1921–22 and 1929–31, when there were

---

[207] Emrys-Evans diary, 7 and 8 May 1940, Emrys-Evans MSS, Add.58246/123–9, copy in Cilcennin MSS, 12.
[208] Amery diary, 8 May 1940.
[209] Comments of Dalton and Morrison, reported in Butler to Halifax, 9 May 1940, Halifax MSS (Borthwick), A4/410/16; Margesson to Baldwin, 4 March 1941, MRGN/1/4/3–5.

several areas of criticism and the position of the Leader was already weaker than normal. The fulcrum in all of the crises was the relationship between the small group of committed rebels, who were motivated by the conviction that the leadership's strategy was fatally flawed, and the mainstream of the parliamentary party, a proportion of whom were, at the least, uneasy. The latter were the crucial element, and their movement on any scale would change the balance of opinion and impart significant momentum and credibility to the critics.[210] However, despite their doubts, the majority of MPs tended to trust their leaders, especially if they were united and—as in the case of India and appeasement—supported by the 'men on the spot' or other recognized authorities and experts. The steady central bulk of the parliamentary party disliked open dissidence, and was often repelled by the characters, methods, or aims of the critics. This gulf was very difficult for the rebels to bridge, for the harder they fought, the more they alienated the group whom it was essential to win over. If the party seemed threatened with a split, it was much more likely that the rebels would be seen as the cause of the problem rather than its result, and pressures for unity would always encourage a rally around the official 'flag', the Party Leader. Only in 1922, when 'a great mass of moderate Conservative opinion' turned against the Coalition, and, to a much lesser extent, in 1940, did the centre of political gravity in the parliamentary party shift away from the Leader, causing his downfall.[211] However, in 1940 the scale of this repudiation was still limited and selective, and only the particular circumstances of wartime compelled Neville Chamberlain's resignation. A similar crumbling of support was beginning in September 1930, but Baldwin's change of course in the following month restored his position before the damage became critical.

Support for the Party Leader and his policy would hold steady, provided certain criteria were met. The first of these was simple enough: that his approach appear fitted to the circumstances and show some signs of working. The leadership would enjoy considerable benefit of the doubt and, especially if they could put up a convincing case, it would take more than one failure of policy before a significant proportion of the centre would lose faith in it and them. Their strategy was not expected to be an unqualified success, as Conservative MPs by temperament lived in a realistic and imperfect world; it just had to seem better than the probable consequences of the rebels' alternatives. This was the case with the electoral liability of the protectionists' food taxes (until this changed in late 1930), the reactionary remedies offered by the India rebels, the dangerous path of apparent bellicosity and provocation proposed by the anti-appeasers, and the collapse of Wardlaw-Milne's potentially damaging criticisms in 1942 when he proposed that a Royal Duke become Commander-in-Chief. On the other hand, a dwindling of faith had corrosive effects; in March 1922, a pro-Coalition MP noted the grass-roots feeling

---

[210] Amery diary, 10 and 31 May 1922; Salisbury to Bonar Law, 23 September 1922, Bonar Law MSS, BL/107/2/61; Croft to N. Chamberlain, 4 October 1930, NC, 8/10/7; Hoare to Willingdon, 13 February 1935, Templewood MSS (BL), E240/4/1238–41.
[211] Fraser to Sanders, 7 October 1922, Bayford diary.

that the party leaders 'were making the speeches of weak men, who were not clear themselves as to where they were going'.[212] Support could ebb quickly even in a key area: in March 1935, when the government was also embroiled in a domestic crisis, rumours that the Indian Princes were backing away from the federal plan led Cabinet members and MPs to consider abandoning the India Bill, and Hoare to liken the government's position to 'walking on a volcano'.[213] The second criterion was equally obvious and fundamental: that the policy was not provoking a hostile public reaction, which might translate into electoral defeat. Examples of this were the danger of 'food taxes' and the fear in the 1931 crisis that 'economy', if rigorously applied, would alienate the masses. This was not the same thing as press criticism, especially after it became clear that Rothermere and Beaverbrook were personally antagonistic to Baldwin, and their attacks became both predictable and discounted. However, a wider circle of press criticism would certainly make MPs uncomfortable, especially if it was voiced by influential regional newspapers such as the *Yorkshire Post* or *The Scotsman*.

The strongest force inhibiting dissent was the fear of splitting the party, and thereby enabling the opposition to gain power and make significant social and economic changes, probably of an irreversible nature. That danger was the leadership's strongest card, producing in times of crisis the impulse to close ranks around them and a corresponding pressure on the critics to fall into line. This was particularly effective whenever the actions of the rebels appeared to be dividing the Conservative vote and letting Labour in, as was the case with the press lords at Islington East in February 1931 and the India rebels at Liverpool Wavertree four years later.[214] However, the Newport by-election of October 1922 (which the leaders believed would operate in this way,[215] hence their timing of the Carlton Club meeting after its result) had the opposite effect, as the 'rebel' candidate won the seat whilst the official Coalitionist could not mount a credible resistance to the Socialist. The events surrounding the fall of the Coalition were also different in nature from the other three internal party crises in these aspects of unity and loyalty to the leadership. In the first place, the leader provoking criticism was not that of the Conservative Party but Lloyd George, who was due much less of the customary deference which the party would give to a Conservative Prime Minister. Secondly, and unlike the weak and declining Ramsay MacDonald in 1933–35, Lloyd George was the dominant figure in the government. The criticism in 1922 was focused upon the Prime Minister and his closest clique of Cabinet supporters—principally Birkenhead and Churchill—and the Conservative Party Leader was only under fire indirectly due his misguided but honourable support of them. One of the reasons why the revolt against the Coalition succeeded was that it was

---

[212] Cockerill's comments in Grigg to Balfour, 3 March 1922, Balfour MSS (Whittingehame), GD433/2/1/23.
[213] Hoare to Willingdon, 15, 1, and 8 March 1935, Templewood MSS (BL), E240/4/1261–3, 1247–55.
[214] *Home and Empire*, March 1935.
[215] Chamberlain considered it 'a beautiful illustration of the results of a split', and expected 'to be in a position to point the moral when the election is over and the seat is lost': A. Chamberlain to Fraser, 6 October 1922, AC, 33/2/32.

possible to regard the Conservative leaders as the hypnotized prisoners of Lloyd George, and to believe that forcing a breach would bring them to their senses and restore their proper sense of duty. Hoare's letter in *The Times* three days before the Carlton Club meeting was revealing in its priorities: 'the vital need is not so much to form a government as to keep the Party united'.[216]

The leadership could only exploit the instinct for unity and the habit of loyalty when their conduct appeared to be legitimate; support was conditional upon this, and not absolute in all circumstances. Whilst economic problems and policy failures contributed to the fall of the Lloyd George Coalition, many backbench and grass-roots Conservatives were alienated as much 'because they act without principle or judgement and their course on any question that affects votes...is determined by opportunism'.[217] In the spring of 1922, the government's repeated failure to fulfil pledges on House of Lords reform was pointedly declared by the Executive of the National Union to be 'a breach of the understanding upon which the allegiance of the Party to its leaders depends'.[218] The Leader was always given the benefit of the doubt, and often for a long period—but that asset could waste away, as happened with Austen Chamberlain in autumn 1922, Baldwin in late summer 1930, and Neville Chamberlain in spring 1940. When the Leader appeared to disregard the party's values or be careless of its wider interests, and especially when his conduct might result in it becoming split, then he became the problem.[219] The growing alienation of the rank and file during 1922 was the product of their perception of 'the absolute neglect of the interests of the Conservative Party, as a party, by the very men who ought to have guarded those interests'.[220] If the peril to the party's identity and independence was great enough, rebellion was justified and acceptable, even though it involved the danger of division. When the leadership decided at the Chequers meeting of 17 September 1922 to have an immediate election and avoid consulting the National Union, it led to 'a stormy interview' in which the Party Chairman told Austen Chamberlain: 'It is a question of either breaking the Party or breaking you, and I intend to do the latter.'[221] The loyalty which was customarily expressed as support for the Leader was in fact loyalty to the understood values and ethos of the party, which had a higher call than any personal loyalty; hence Winterton's conclusion that Younger and Wilson 'performed a plain and simple duty by acting as they did' in opposing their Leader in 1922.[222]

---

[216] *The Times*, 16 October 1922, and draft copy, Templewood MSS, I/2.
[217] Steel-Maitland to Salisbury, 22 December 1921, Steel-Maitland MSS, GD193/275/14–21.
[218] NU Exec., 9 May 1922.
[219] Younger to Sanders, 25 September 1922, Bayford diary; memo by Griffith-Boscawen, 'The Break Up of the Coalition', n.d., Griffith-Boscawen MSS, c.396/120–1; Devizes CA, Central Ctte., 20 May 1922.
[220] Notes by Leith, enclosed with Fraser to A. Chamberlain, 31 December 1921, AC, 32/4/18; this was written less than two months before Leith took office as Chairman of the NU Central Council.
[221] Winterton to Lytton, 22 November 1922, Lytton MSS, F160/26/8–13; this sentiment is confirmed in Younger to Strachey, 20 November 1922, Strachey MSS, STR/19/4/26b. See also Younger to Gilmour, 22 and 27 September 1922, Gilmour MSS, GD383/17/8–10; Younger to A. Chamberlain, 22 September 1922, AC, 33/2/21.
[222] Earl Winterton, *Orders of the Day* (1953), 117.

Conservatives were at least as much inclined as anyone else to grumble about the shortcomings of their leaders; indeed, perhaps more so, being already, by temperament, dissatisfied with developments in the world around them. Such rumblings of discontent, for which the diehard wing was both exemplar and mouthpiece, were endemic but very difficult to harness into an effective challenge to the leadership (although they could be more readily mobilized against a particular bill or policy). In this respect, the grousing was genuinely aimless, and even the most discontented reacted with suspicion to anyone who tried to exploit such feeling as a weapon against the leaders. Conservatives tended to resent the interference of outsiders, however ostensibly friendly the motive or manner of their advice. Thus, whilst there were many constraints inhibiting revolts within the party, it was equally difficult to intervene in its affairs from outside. The failure of the Empire Crusade, and, to some extent, of the India revolt, demonstrate this. As Amery warned Beaverbrook after the launch of the United Empire Party in February 1930, a direct challenge would result in a rally around the Leader, as 'our ranks close instinctively'.[223] Whether of external or internal origin, attacks which were personal in nature tended to be counterproductive. Lord Derby, who had steered a vacillating course through many leadership crises, observed that 'it makes it very difficult if a man is personally attacked to leave him, even if you are all for his giving up the leadership'.[224] Instead, it was necessary for critics to maintain a façade of public unity, whatever their private misgivings and manoeuvrings; as Derby noted of Baldwin after the election debacle of 1923, 'we must be thoroughly loyal to him as long as he is leader of our Party'.[225]

There were two forms of unrest which, if not ameliorated or contained, could lead to a crisis. The first was a swelling of dissatisfaction from the constituency rank and file, either through or together with the backbench MPs; this was often not clearly vocalized, and did not manifest in any organized form. The second was the visible dissent of a section of the parliamentary party, with some support or at least tolerance in the constituencies, and frequently aided by outside forces in the press or business community; this was public and specific in its criticism, and often given focus by meetings or an organized pressure group. There is an assumption that the first form, being inchoate—even incoherent—and lacking a credible leadership contender at its head, was the less dangerous, and that the second and more visible form was the more serious threat. In fact, the reverse is the case, for generalized grievance is much harder to appease or contain. It cannot be accused of disloyalty in any very effective way, nor of being motivated by personal ambition. It can only be dealt with by addressing the issue or concern which gives it impetus, and if this is not done or is not possible, it may spread and eventually gain a critical mass. As a leading diehard observed, 'anxious mutterings below [are] much more

---

[223] Amery to Beaverbrook, 28 February 1930, Beaverbrook MSS, C5; N. Chamberlain to Bridgeman, 18 October 1930, Bridgeman MSS, 3389/104; Cornwall North CA, AGM, 13 March 1931.
[224] Derby to Beaverbrook, 21 October 1930, Horne to Beaverbrook, 24 January 1931, Beaverbrook MSS, C113, C178.
[225] Derby to Salvidge, 25 February 1924, Derby MSS, 8/9.

significant than organised protests'.[226] The second form of dissent, by definition, began as a minority viewpoint, and could always be pointed to as the instigator of disruption. Unless it conducted itself in a most cautious way—in which case, of course, it would probably be ineffective—and had leaders of unimpeachable respectability and record—which was unlikely—it could be represented as unreasonable and doctrinaire in its views, and led or manipulated by ambitious scoundrels. These difficulties explain the tentative actions of the anti-appeasers in 1937–39, their desire to avoid identification with Churchill, and Eden's reluctance to seem dissident at all. They also explain the effectiveness of Lord Salisbury's discrete Watching Committee in 1940, and the failure of the more public attacks of the diehard movement on the Coalition in 1920–21, even when associated with such respected figures as Salisbury and Selborne.

The habit of deference to the position of authority occupied by the Leader gave him great advantages in countering any open attack. Unity was always easier to maintain when there was a clear threat that factionalism might damage the health and prospects of the party. This facilitated the isolation of the rebels and encouraged the mainstream of the party to rally in support of the Leader. This pattern recurred several times during the press lords' Empire Crusade campaign in 1929–31; although the majority of the party sympathized with the tariff policy which they were pressing, when Baldwin turned the issue into one of attempted dictation to the Leader he was assured of support—as demonstrated in the party meeting of June 1930, which was held before he made any significant change of policy.[227] As soon as dissent became open in the parliamentary ranks, it could be quantified and pressurized. Once it was evident that the rebels were a minority, the pull of party sentiment would act to draw them back to the main body—and the smaller the disaffected group, the greater that tug of gravity would be. It was for this reason that dissident MPs tended to organize, as this balanced the wider loyalty with links amongst themselves. There was a threshold beyond which a group was sufficiently large to resist or at least mitigate the pressure for unity, especially after its members had had the experience of acting together on several occasions. As this was a psychological factor there was no precise figure for the necessary size; it was a matter of proportion, and was affected by the firmness and frequency of any action. However, any group which had the consistent involvement of 10 per cent or more of the parliamentary party was likely to have sufficient ballast to be able to ride out the buffets of disapproval from fellow MPs, the whips, and the leaders. This was the case with the forty or so in the diehard group of 1920–22 and 1929–31 and the approximately seventy India rebels of 1933–35, and contributed to the vicissitudes of the much smaller number of anti-appeasers in 1937–39. If the balance of opinion was very heavily tilted against the dissenters, it appeared that they were ignoring the democratic will of the party. They could then seem idiosyncratic and

---

[226] Gretton to Baldwin, 1 November 1934, Baldwin MSS, 169/122.
[227] Lady Peto diary, 24 and 25 June 1930; Dixey to Baldwin, 8 September, Forster to Baldwin, 29 October 1930, Baldwin MSS, 165/104–6, 138.

eccentric; their cause would lose credibility and their conduct legitimacy, and the tolerance of their colleagues would soon run out.

The spread of a less visible but broader-based alienation was the key factor in the two occasions upon which a Leader was removed by discontent from below, in 1922 and 1940. This was clearly the case with the erosion of support for the Coalition from January 1922 onwards and is much of the explanation of the fall of Chamberlain in May 1940. In both instances there was an immediate trigger (the Chanak crisis in 1922 and the failure in Norway in 1940), but this acted as the final spark—and the reason why the conflagration spread so quickly was that the ground was already parched and bare. As early as February 1922, the Deputy Party Chairman noted in his diary: 'our leaders do not realise and cannot apparently be made to realise how very fast the main body of the Tory Party is slipping away from them'.[228] The loss of support for Neville Chamberlain in May 1940 was not the belated triumph of the anti-appeasers, even though many rationalized it in that way. Their prewar criticisms now appeared to have some validity and this did diminish Chamberlain's stature, but the real reason for his fall was a more widespread and growing unhappiness with the prosecution of the war. There was, especially, a feeling that the government was undeservedly complacent, which was crystallized by Chamberlain's two oratorical blunders—his premature assertion that Hitler had 'missed the bus', made shortly before the blitzkrieg on Denmark and Norway, and the style and phrasing of his speech in the Norway debate (which Fitzalan, a former Chief Whip, considered 'deplorable'[229])—and by the ministerial reshuffle in April 1940 (or rather, the lack of any real restructuring). The concern had grown particularly amongst MPs from the mainstream of the party who had joined their reserve units and encountered the lack of military preparation by personal experience; because this took place away from Westminster, the whips largely failed to detect it.[230] They and the leaders were so conditioned to think in terms of a challenge from the known critics that they did not see the ebbing of support from former loyalists, who acted as they did from no sense of community with the contemptuously labelled 'glamour boys'. The truth was, as Davidson told Baldwin, 'there were too many factors that weighed against Neville'.[231]

The presence of an alternative Leader amongst a group of critics did not make a revolt more dangerous, but actually weakened it. At once, it clouded the issue with personalities, and made it an easy matter to portray the prominent dissident as motivated by ambition for office, bitterness at being passed over, or suffering from an excess of egotism. In the cases of Beaverbrook in 1929–31 and Churchill over India, the leading rebel was only too vulnerable to such charges, and this discouraged the respectable and influential amongst the backbenchers from openly associating with them. When there was an apparent challenger in the field—even if that

---

[228] Bayford diary, 8 February 1922.
[229] Watching Ctte minutes, 8 May 1940, Emrys-Evans MSS, Add.58270/12–13.
[230] Emrys-Evans, 'Diary, 23 April–14 May 1940', n.d. but c.15 May 1940, Emrys-Evans MSS, Add.58246/123–9, copy in Cilcennin MSS, 12.
[231] Davidson to Baldwin, 12 May 1940, Baldwin MSS, 174/273–4.

person insisted that they had no such aim—the Party Leader was normally secure in the knowledge that he was unlikely to be deposed in order that a rival might reign in his place. One reason for this was exhibited during the troughs of Baldwin's leadership in September 1930 and March 1931: that whatever the superior merits of the alternative Leader might be, the advantage gained would be more than outweighed by the damage which a forced transition would cause—deepening the existing rifts within the party perhaps to the point of fissure, and replacing the hostility of the dissident minority with the resentment of the loyal majority. There was also, of course, the recognition that any such deposition would establish a precedent which would weaken the position of all future Leaders, and thereby the cohesion of the party as a whole.

It was striking that the revolt against the Coalition during most of 1922 differed from the other three crises in this key respect, for it lacked heavyweight leadership. By the autumn the roles of Salisbury and Selborne had become peripheral, partly because they were peers and partly because of their limited political agenda,[232] whilst Baldwin and Griffith-Boscawen were junior members of the Cabinet and only emerged from the confines of collective responsibility at a relatively late stage;[233] none of these figures were credible leadership contenders. The role of Bonar Law was crucial in the very final act, but his position was enigmatic and unpredictable until the moment that he arrived at the Carlton Club meeting.[234] Since February 1922, he had given repeated warnings privately to Lloyd George 'that in the present mood of the Party it was impossible that things should go on as they were',[235] but he stood apart from the critics; they could not be attacked through him, nor he smeared by their actions. Bonar Law's detached position was not a source of weakness with regard to the revolt, as is often supposed. He was untainted by any appearance of faction, although there was some discourtesy in his not warning Austen Chamberlain of his intention to attend the meeting and oppose him.[236] Bonar Law could, therefore, be the figure to whom the party could turn in its hour of need, and who could—allowing for an inevitable degree of resentment on the part of the ousted ministers—most quickly and effectively heal the rifts.

---

[232] Long to Cockerill, 14 August 1922, Long MSS (WSA), 947/827.

[233] In early August, Griffith-Boscawen had unequivocally affirmed his loyalty to Lloyd George, declaring 'I could never be a party to any movement against him': Griffith-Boscawen to Pollock, 4 August 1922, Hanworth MSS, Eng.Hist.d.432/75b. However, he was alienated by the 'bellicose' attitude of senior Cabinet ministers in the Chanak crisis, and decided to resign following the Cabinet's rejection of his agriculture policy on 10 October; his final letter opposed an immediate election as 'it would be regarded as a trick to avoid the conference' and 'do much more harm than good': Griffith-Boscawen to A. Chamberlain, 2, 9, 10, and 12 October 1922, AC, 33/2/28, 46, 47, 49.

[234] Late on the previous evening, Baldwin had told the meeting of junior ministers and other dissidents held at his house that Bonar Law 'had decided to attend the meeting, but that he had not quite settled what line he would take' as he was anxious to avoid a split: 'The Break Up of the Coalition', Griffith-Boscawen MSS, c.396/122.

[235] Balfour memo of conversation with Bonar Law, 22 December 1922, Balfour MSS, Add.49693/300–5; Derby diary, 21 November 1922.

[236] Pollock, 'Fall of the Coalition', Hanworth MSS, Eng.Hist.d.432/133–88.

Of the other crises, it is significant that the next most dangerous was the case which was most similar to 1922 in the lack of participation from Cabinet-status parliamentarians. Beaverbrook so dominated the Empire Crusade of 1929–31 that senior figures were unwilling to associate too closely with him, partly for fear of appearing as his puppets and partly due to recognizing that they could not control his actions and would be in constant danger of being compromised by them. Several former Cabinet members resisted his blandishments, and the executive committee unveiled when the Crusade was launched in February 1930 contained only minor names. However, Beaverbrook's well-known personal animus enabled Baldwin to present the campaign as an attempt to change the Leader, even if it was unclear who his replacement would be. In the last phase of the crisis in March 1931, Horne was seen as a possible alternative Leader who was on good terms with, and acceptable to, Beaverbrook, and it was to block this possibility that two other potential successors, Neville Chamberlain and Hailsham, agreed to serve under each other. The India campaign of 1933–35 was bedevilled by Churchill's high-profile presence, a fact which some of the dissidents realized and lamented. There was a similar problem with anti-appeasement, although Churchill was looking less and less like a possible Leader as the years passed; after his resignation as Foreign Secretary in February 1938, Eden was careful to avoid actions which might suggest he had his eyes on the leadership. Finally, Churchill stood apart from the revolt in the spring of 1940, even more clearly than Bonar Law had done in 1922. Not only did Churchill give no discernible encouragement to the critics, but he went out of his way to take a share of the blame and to support the Prime Minister during the Norway debate. Thus, on the two occasions during this period when the Conservative Party discarded its Leader, it did so when the revolt was most diffuse and most genuinely the work of backbench MPs.

Most damaging, because of their apparent sincerity, were rebels who had little prospect of gaining anything personally from their stance and who were motivated by some issue of principle. It was the very fact that Baldwin and Griffith-Boscawen were so junior in the Cabinet, as well as being respected by backbench MPs as party stalwarts who had not 'gone native' in the way that their superiors appeared to have done, which made their disavowal of the Coalition so damaging in October 1922. It was evident that Baldwin in particular felt obliged to quit the Cabinet for reasons of principle and integrity, and expected his action to be the end of his political career. Whilst Curzon's prestige was of value to Bonar Law in forming the post-Coalition Cabinet, it is a sign of the lack of understanding on the part of Lloyd George and his principal lieutenants that they were more dismayed by the Foreign Secretary's last-minute switch than they had been by the loss of figures who were in tune and close contact with the junior ministers and senior backbenchers. It was therefore a strength of the anti-Coalitionists that their leading lights were figures such as Salisbury, Selborne, Gretton, and Baldwin—none of them political 'stars', and all of them proven stalwarts of the party. In 1940, it was the previously loyal MPs serving in the armed forces and motivated by their personal experiences of disorganization, unpreparedness, and complacency who made the most impression.[237] In both cases, these were reluctant and principled rebels, to whom charges of personal ambition did not readily stick.

The final months of Neville Chamberlain's leadership had several parallels with the last period of his half-brother Austen's in 1922, with similar hallmarks of rigidity, apparent hauteur, strategic incomprehension, tactical maladroitness, and misplaced loyalty to unpopular Cabinet colleagues. In 1940 as in 1922, the Leader refused to bend to what he dismissed as an inconsequential breeze, and, as a result, turned it into a gale. That Austen and Neville Chamberlain were the only two leaders of the period to be overthrown by their followers may owe something to their family relationship in terms of temperament, and owes almost everything to their methods and styles of leadership. They were the two most authoritarian and least flexible of the Leaders—a style which, as also discovered later by Edward Heath and Margaret Thatcher, pays great dividends when it delivers success and rapidly exhausts the tolerance of MPs when it has every prospect of bringing defeat. Bonar Law, Baldwin, and (in many ways) Churchill were far more consensual and cautious as leaders, and had a much more subtle understanding of their interaction with the party that they led.

[237] N. to I. Chamberlain, 11 May 1940, *NCDL*; Cazalet diary, 7 and 8 May 1940.

Conclusion
Effectiveness and Nature

THE SUCCESS OF THE CONSERVATIVE PARTY BETWEEN THE WARS

This was the second of the four periods of success and dominance that the Conservative Party enjoyed between the late nineteenth century and the close of the twentieth—the others being from 1886 to 1905 (with a brief Liberal interlude in 1892–95), from 1951 to 1964, and from 1979 to 1997. Together with the interwar years, this record justifies the description of twentieth-century British politics as the 'Conservative century'.[1] The party's success in the interwar period is particularly striking. It was the largest single party in the House of Commons for over 90 per cent of the twenty-seven years between the general elections of 1918 and 1945. Furthermore, in the one parliament where it was in second place (1929–31), it had received the largest total vote in the preceding general election, with 8.65 million votes to Labour's 8.38 million. The Conservatives not only won most of the elections of the interwar years, with five victories to two defeats, they also won with massive majorities: in all five of the successes, they had a margin of more than 200 MPs over the next largest party. Some of the foundations of Conservative success had been laid in the age of Disraeli and Salisbury, and since the 1860s it had seemed that Conservative fortunes improved as the franchise was extended. However, the party had experienced strife, defeat, and frustration in the decade before the outbreak of the First World War, and it approached the new democracy created in 1918 with trepidation rather than confidence. In the interwar era, Conservative leaders and MPs were rarely optimistic about their electoral prospects, even shortly before their greatest triumphs. Ironically, the three general elections when the Leader or Central Office particularly anticipated victory—in 1923, 1929, and 1945—were also the party's only defeats.

The factors which contributed to the Conservative Party's electoral success between the wars can be divided into two categories, the first of which is the underlying and long-term elements. The foundation was created by the appeal of the Conservatives' values, image, and programme to a substantial block of social support which was deep-rooted, cohesive, and enduring. Of course, there was some variation in the scale of support and the vigour of its commitment according to economic and political circumstances, the most important of which were

---

[1] The term was coined in the title of a previous project: Seldon and Ball (eds.), *Conservative Century*.

perceptions of the performance of the government (whichever party was in office), pressure from economic depression and the level of taxation, apprehension of domestic unrest, and concern over external threats. The next element was the ability of the Conservative Party to mobilize its core support and reach beyond this to voters who were uncommitted or potentially detachable from another allegiance. This had three aspects: the resonance of its stance on the immediate issues of the day, the appeal of its leadership, and the effectiveness of its organization. The first of these aspects developed from the party's fundamental attitudes and outlook, and the extent to which the resulting policies meshed with the needs of voters determined whether they encouraged or discouraged support. The other aspects of leadership and organization were important in communicating the party's message, but could not, on their own, determine its fortunes; in particular, organizational strength was a product of the extent of support more than a cause of it. The preponderance of support for the Conservative Party in the upper and upper-middle classes provided it with extensive resources in the munitions of political warfare—not only money, but also local candidates and leaders who possessed the confidence and cachet of their superior social status. The dividend from this was an organization that was stronger and more sophisticated, innovative, and effective than its rivals at both the national and local levels.[2]

Another underlying element was the developments in the electoral system at the end of the First World War. These brought more advantages than disadvantages, and even the change which Conservative politicians at the time viewed with most concern was far from being entirely negative. In reality, the new male voters were not entirely working class: the previous suffrage had been based on the head of household and ratepayer, and this excluded many younger middle- and upper-class men who had not yet established their own separate domiciles. The women enfranchised were in all social classes, and the age limitation at thirty tilted the female suffrage towards the more conservative, if not the more Conservative. The party already had considerable and positive experience of organizing women in the Primrose League, and it was more effective than its rivals in shaping and presenting an image that appealed to the housewife and mother. Other aspects of the 1918 Reform Act benefited the Conservatives in varying degrees. One of the most important was, in truth, the rectification of an imbalance, as by 1914 the movement of population had led to some Conservative seats—particularly around the edges of London—having much larger electorates than the norm. When the boundaries were revised these seats became several, all of which returned Conservative MPs; at the same time, the smaller seats which were abolished or merged were mostly Liberal, particularly in Scotland. It has been estimated that the net effect of the redistribution alone was a gain of thirty-four seats for the Conservative Party.[3] Three minor aspects of the nature of the franchise were also in the party's favour: the retention of

---

[2] However, in purely financial terms, the Labour Party was able to spend almost as much at constituency level in general elections: M. Pinto-Duschinsky, *British Political Finance 1830–1980* (Washington, 1982), 72–7.

[3] Kinnear, *The British Voter*, 70–2.

the university seats and the vote for business premises, and the rejection of proportional representation, which would have been of more help to the other two parties. The 'first past the post' system had the effect of squeezing the vote of the party in third place, and this was almost never the Conservative Party.

A political change which immediately followed the First World War also helped the Conservatives: the disappearance from the House of Commons of the block of around eighty-five seats from the Catholic-populated regions of Ireland, which from 1886 to 1914 had given constant support to the Liberal Party as a result of the Home Rule issue. The sweeping away of the Irish Nationalist Party in the 1918 general election by Sinn Fein, who refused to take their seats, was the first part of the process, which was made permanent in the Anglo-Irish Treaty of 1921. The remaining seats from Northern Ireland were almost all Unionist, and during this period the Ulster Unionists were an integral part of the Conservative Party, taking its whip and, in a few cases, serving in office. The consequence was that instead of being a major hindrance to the Conservatives' prospects of securing a majority in the House of Commons, Ireland was now a minor help.

These structural changes assisted the Conservative Party in establishing itself as the natural majority party, which in itself brought advantages in terms of self-confidence and public expectations. A further significant factor was the consolidation of the upper and middle classes behind the Conservative Party, a process stimulated by the rise of the Labour Party and the decline of the Liberals, and which further contributed to the latter. However, as discussed in Chapter 2, neither middle-class votes nor rural constituencies existed in sufficient numbers to deliver a parliamentary majority, and the crucial factor was the securing of substantial working-class support as well. This was more variable in scale than the middle-class support, and its relative volatility probably accounts for most of the rise and fall in the Conservative vote between different general elections. The Conservatives were able to appear to a significant section of working-class voters as the best choice for their vote: the reasons for this included, in different combinations, the image of the party, its Leader, and its policies; the circumstances and temperament of the voter; the long-term effects of local or family tradition; and the short-term impact of the current economic and political situation. The result was a large block of safe seats, the core of which were the suburban, the mixed urban/rural, and the predominantly rural constituencies, of around 200 in number (as shown by Table 2.12, and the holding of 210 seats in 1945). In addition, there were between 100 and 150 constituencies which were more urbanized and industrial, and with a higher proportion of working-class voters, which were often winnable. As the House of Commons consisted of 615 MPs from 1922 to 1945, this meant that the bare majority of 308 was very much within the Conservative grasp.

These developments made the general context more favourable to the Conservatives than had been the case in the Edwardian era, but on their own did not guarantee victory. Electoral success resulted from the combination of these systemic factors with other more immediate issues and realignments. Several of these were consequences of the First World War; as one of the party's leading figures observed in 1920, 'in the storm of war many of the old political questions have disappeared'.[4] The war had an immediate impact in raising the importance of patriotism and discrediting the Liberal government that had been in office when it began, and it led to the decline in significance of old (mainly Liberal) issues such as temperance, disestablishment, and land reform. The rise of the Labour Party appeared to be a challenge to capitalism and property, bringing with it a fear of revolution. This both energized support for the Conservatives and gave them an easy target to attack. Britain had prospered during the previous century, and although there was certainly poverty and hardship, for the most part the economic system remained stable in the interwar era. There were, therefore, certain advantages in being a capitalist party defending a capitalist system, and its opponents had the much more difficult task of demonstrating that their hypothetical alternative would be better. Provided that there was no economic collapse (which was a worry in 1920–21 and still more in 1931), it was likely that most voters would stay with the system that they knew—once again, 'natural' conservatism was a powerful recruiter for the party's cause.

For this to be effective, a vital part of the equation was that the Conservatives did not respond to the fears of their core support in the middle and upper classes by adopting positions which the rest of the electorate would have perceived as reactionary and hard-hearted. In this, the personal appeal of Baldwin played an important part, especially in reaching across normal party boundaries. His projection of a Conservatism based upon shared traditions and values, and which emphasized community, trust, honesty, and Christian morality, was reassuring to the middle and upper classes, whilst also appealing—or, at the least, appearing unthreatening—to the working class. It had a particular attraction for that section of former Liberal support, mainly in the middle class and self-employed skilled working class, that was linked to Nonconformity in religion, and the washing away of the ecclesiastical division in the middle class as a matter of political significance did much to enable those previously non-Conservative to vote for—and even work for—the Conservative Party without too much reluctance or blame.

The most fruitful situation for Conservative candidates was a straight fight with only one opposition party, preferably Labour. There were several reasons why it was to the advantage of the Conservatives that the Liberal Party should disappear, for the intervention of a Liberal candidate often drew away enough support for the Conservative to be defeated, very often by Labour. It was no coincidence that the election defeats of 1923 and 1929 were the two occasions between the wars when the Liberal Party was at its most united, invigorated, coherent in programme, and well-funded. On the other hand, disunity in the Liberal Party assisted the Conservatives, as in 1922 and 1924, and still more so when this was institutionalized in an electoral pact or coalition, as in 1918, 1931, and 1935. The latter had the effect of removing most of the competing Liberal candidates, and those which remained (Asquithian in 1918 and Samuelite in 1935) were largely discredited, lacked any clear political identity or programme, and were relatively few in number.

---

[4] Selborne to Younger, 27 February 1920, Selborne (2nd Earl) MSS, MS.Selborne/87.

There is no doubt that the Conservative Party was fortunate in one piece of unpredictable timing: that the onset of the slump in 1930–31 occurred whilst they were in opposition, and the political damage was sustained by the second Labour government, ultimately with shattering effects. In fact, the Conservatives were in the process of securing an electoral pact with the Simonite half of the Liberal Party before the August 1931 crisis, and if it had not occurred it is almost certain the government would have been ousted early in the new session of parliament and that the following general election would have been a Conservative victory on a similar scale to 1924. One effect of the pact with the Simonites was that it brought the support of most of the Liberal MPs in Scotland, where the Conservatives were comparatively weak, and this remained with the National Government for the rest of the 1930s. Indeed, the withdrawal of the Samuelite section of the Liberal Party from the National Government in 1932 did it very little damage, either electorally or even in its 'national' credibility. Unlike the Lloyd George Coalition, a combination of different circumstances and better political management made the National Government the most effective of all the peacetime coalitions in modern British history. It was heading for almost certain victory in a 1940 general election when the Second World War intervened, and it was only after May 1940 that it came to be condemned at the bar of public opinion.

The final short-term element to be considered is the role of the programme that the Conservatives presented, and, in particular, the effects of any reappraisal of policy. In fact, specific policies were, in nearly every instance, a relatively minor factor in the party's electoral success. The events and legacy of the previous government (whether Conservative or of their opponents) were more significant than hypothetical prospects for the next one, and where the latter was a factor it was in the broad sense of stability—continued or restored—rather than any particular proposal in the manifesto. Two of the five election victories between the wars were the product of having played the major role in a coalition which had steered the nation through a dangerous crisis. In 1918 and 1935 the party's appeal was based upon results which vindicated its previous conduct, the assurance of stability by continuing the existing arrangement, and, lastly, the general prospect that better and easier times lay ahead. Two of the other successes owed more to a pointed lack of policy than its presence—of one policy in particular, protectionism. Bonar Law's victory in 1922 was based upon the general appeal of 'tranquillity' and moderation, and of two negatives—ruling out tariffs and dropping the alliance with Lloyd George. The reappraisal of policy undertaken in opposition in 1924 was valuable in distancing the party from the 1923 tariff debacle and in restoring its morale; at the ballot box, the retreat from food taxes to the strictly limited defensive protectionism of 'safeguarding', and the appeal of Baldwin due to the values which he personified, were more important than the vague statements published in *Looking Ahead*.

Only in 1931 can it be said that the policies which the Conservatives put in the forefront of their programme had a specific appeal which significantly extended beyond their habitual supporters. For the first time, the severe economic depression undermined the resistance of the urban working-class electorate to the tariff policy, although what was just as important was the emphasis on economy in expenditure and balancing the budget. The self-evident truth that governments could not operate beyond their means for long, any more than businesses or individuals could do so, was embedded in the popular consciousness many decades before Margaret Thatcher's espousal of 'housewife economics' in the 1970s. Although policy was only one ingredient in the recipe for Conservative success—and frequently more of a flavouring than the substance—it can, on the other hand, be said that the policy presented was a substantial contributor to the two defeats. This was unarguably the case in 1923, with the sudden adoption of tariffs, while much of the 1929 reverse was due to the choices made about the presentation of the party's appeal and the standard-bearer legislation set in its forefront—de-rating was worthy, but it was difficult to explain it and demonstrate its worth, and impossible to become inspired about it. To sum up, as far as the immediate political situation was concerned, the best combination was a weak or divided Liberal party, a credible threat from Labour, a united Conservative Party with a moderate image, and some sense of crisis or national danger. This produced the major victories of 1918, 1924, 1931, and—to a lesser extent—1935.

THE ANATOMY OF THE CONSERVATIVE PARTY BETWEEN THE WARS

The Conservative Party was far from being a monolithic structure, and the diversity of its various parts becomes more apparent the closer they are inspected. There were three distinct elements which, in different ways, were the repository of the Conservative identity. They normally worked together effectively and in reasonable harmony, recognizing and respecting each others' roles, rights, and responsibilities. This should not be taken for granted, as they were unalike in composition, form, instinct, outlook, and—most of all—experience. The first of these elements was the leadership, which was the group most readily identified by the general public as being the Conservative 'party'; the second was the parliamentary party; and the third was the local membership—acknowledged by one senior figure as 'the backbone' of the party.[5] The widest gulf, physically and psychologically, separated the first and second elements from the third. This was the divide between those whose lives were in politics, and those in whose lives politics played a part. It was the function of the organizational structure—itself an amalgam of the professional and the voluntary—to connect these three disparate elements and to ensure communication between them.[6] However, the formal links were actually few, and, to a large extent, each element inhabited its own world. The rank and file only impacted upon the parliamentarians through the individual contact which each candidate or MP had with their own local officials and workers, and on certain infrequent occasions at the regional and national levels of the National Union—in the latter case, further attenuated due to its dominance by the social elite. The parliamentary

---

[5] Selborne to Salisbury, 13 June 1921, Selborne (2nd Earl) MSS, MS.Selborne/7.
[6] East Midlands Area, Council, inaugural meeting, 15 January 1931.

party received a mass of varied impressions from outside, which it processed and passed on through the whips and the committees; most of this was a matter of individuals talking to individuals. However, whilst the backbench MPs and party leadership might both frequent the Palace of Westminster, their relationship was often distant. Ministers were fully occupied in their departmental work and public engagements; when they were in the House, it was for specific business, and they were rarely casually accessible in the lobby or Smoking Room. One of a group of MPs attending a private dinner with Neville Chamberlain in 1930 commented that after eight years in parliament 'it was his first contact with an authoritative head of the Party'.[7]

The authority of the party leadership was subject to consent, and their freedom of manoeuvre was limited by what was acceptable; frequently they were swayed by the claims of wider 'national' cares and responsibilities, or hamstrung by the tension between what was practicable and what their followers believed could and should be done. However, the right and role of the Leader to define party policy was almost never disputed: Kingsley Wood was citing established fact when he told the National Union Executive that 'it was perfectly clear that all questions of policy have to be formulated by the Leader of the Party'.[8] The voluntary membership did not normally seek to infringe upon this, and even after electoral defeat 'they did not want to lead the Leader'.[9] Thus, a resolution from Lowestoft after the 1929 election that 'important questions of policy, before embodiment in the party programme, shall be submitted to the consideration of constituency Associations', was explicitly not supported by the National Union Executive, which noted that it 'would mean taking all responsibility out of the hands of the Leader of the Party, which was not a practicable proposition'.[10] A similar suggestion made tentatively at the 1928 Conference was likened by the Party Chairman to the Soviet system of government by party committees, and was overwhelmingly defeated.[11] The rank and file accepted that those in high office bore a heavy burden of duty and responsibility, and based their decisions upon greater experience and knowledge than the backbench MP or ordinary citizen.[12] Thus, a northern industrial constituency concluded on three separate occasions during the controversy over India in 1933–35 that 'the question can safely be left in the hands of our leaders'.[13] As one MP told his constituency association: 'unless they set themselves up as super-men or super-women, their first duty was to give their ungrudging loyalty to those who were serving them in these difficult and trying times'.[14] For this reason, far more than any social deference, the leadership were able to count upon a presumption of loyalty which was probably greater and more enduring amongst the crucial

---

[7] Butler to his parents, 14 July 1930, Butler MSS, D48/748–51; Balfour, *Wings over Westminster*, 76.
[8] NU Exec., 29 June 1931, 12 July 1927.
[9] NU Conf., 1929, speech by Campbell.
[10] NU Exec., 22 October 1929; NU Central Council, 25 November 1930.
[11] NU Conf., 1928, speeches by Saunders and Davidson.
[12] NU Conf., 1923, speech by McNeill.
[13] Sowerby CA, Exec., 29 June, 25 October 1933, 31 May 1934.
[14] Harwich CA, AGM, 11 March 1922; NU Labour Ctte., 6 April 1925.

managerial figures in the rank and file—the local constituency and regional Area chairmen—than was the case with the parliamentary party.[15] This was summed up by Sir Alexander Leith, Chairman of the Northern Area and a long-serving stalwart of the National Union Executive, as follows:[16]

> During 30 years of political servitude I have endeavoured to make it a rule to protest once only to my Leader, and then only when I considered the subject to be of grave importance. I have always considered that a Conservative P.M. and Cabinet must have good reasons, unknown to me, that have induced them to act contrary to my ideas. That appears to me to be political loyalty.

Of course, Leith's conduct as Chairman of the Central Council in 1922 was also proof that this loyalty could be overstrained and had its limits. The leaders had to carry their followers with them; coercion was impossible and ambush, as Austen Chamberlain appeared to be attempting in October 1922, would only provoke a counter-reaction. The pro-Coalitionists' aims, and still more methods, in the weeks leading up to the Carlton Club meeting were such as to corrode the normal chains of loyalty to unprecedented effect, as seen in the side taken by the Chief Whip, Party Chairman, and Principal Agent in October 1922. Their actions were based upon a greater loyalty to the party as a concept and a whole, rather than to any particular leading figures.[17] 'I care for nothing but the interests of the Party,' Younger wrote; 'I have given the greater part of my life to it, and I fear that it is in critical danger.'[18] Although not as severe, there were complaints from the constituencies after the 1923 defeat about the lack of consultation in the adoption of the tariff programme and the timing of the election, and after the 1929 defeat over the failure to prioritize the policies which the rank and file wanted. The events of the party crisis of 1929–30 demonstrated that the Leader was far from untrammelled and had to pay attention to the strongest concerns of the rank and file. The lesson of 1922 was clear enough: the party could always find new leaders, but the leaders could not find a new party.

The relationship between the leaders and the party membership was not a simple polarity of authority and deference; it was more complex and intimately reciprocal than was admitted by either contemporary critics or later commentators. The focus has been too exclusively limited to the loyalty which the leadership could call upon from those below, for equally, as a constituency delegate observed at the 1927 Annual Conference, 'there was such a thing as loyalty of leaders to their followers'.[19] The party's long-serving senior official in Scotland had no doubts 'that one of the main functions of the Unionist organisation was to transmit to the party leaders the views of their followers'.[20] The concerns of the grass roots were listened to, and

---

[15] NU Conf., 1921, speech by Salvidge; Moray & Nairn CA, Council, 31 October 1922.
[16] Leith to Davidson, 27 January 1929, Baldwin MSS, 12/531–2.
[17] Leith to A. Chamberlain, 4 March 1922, AC, 33/1/22; Younger to A. Chamberlain, 30 January 1922, AC, 32/3/4.
[18] Younger to Long, 9 September 1922, Long MSS (WSA), 947/859.
[19] NU Conf., 1927, speech by Maconachie.
[20] SUA, EDC, Exec., 24 May 1933.

the passing of resolutions—even repeatedly on the same issues—was not a pointless exercise, even if they sometimes grumbled that 'the opinions of constituency associations do not receive the consideration they deserve'.[21] At the least, they provided the backdrop against which the party leaders had to set out their stall. The National Union could not be taken for granted or disregarded, and it was concern over the consequences of trying do this which motivated the rebellion of the core of the party—the whips, the Central Office, the junior ministers, and the mainstream backbenchers—against the leaders in October 1922. The danger was real: circumventing the National Union in such a way 'would have meant the complete break-up of the Tory Party and the end of its usefulness, at any rate for a generation'.[22]

There was a link between the concerns of the constituencies and the agenda of the Cabinet, although not necessarily a direct and immediate one. This can be seen in the four issues about which the rank and file felt passionately, but which aroused public resistance as much as support: tariffs, economy, the House of Lords, and the trade union political levy. In each case, Conservative ministers tried to find a policy which would attain the desired ends, but not at the cost of alienating working-class voters.[23] It was also the case that constituency concerns would set off reverberations elsewhere. The classic instance of this was the pressure upon MPs and candidates to disavow the Coalition in 1922; the Chief Whip acknowledged in the month before the Carlton Club meeting that 'the influence of their Associations' would be critical in the refusal of many MPs to follow the Party Leader's strategy of continuing the present Coalition.[24] In a similar way, grass-roots antagonism to the 'flapper vote' in 1927 had such an effect that a well-placed junior minister would write that 'the Central Office is proportionately disturbed' and Baldwin was 'having a rough time'.[25] However, usually the rank and file preferred to wait for the leadership to set out the policy, even on issues where they felt strongly.[26] As one local figure noted, 'for Conservatives it is not easy to vote against the Leader'.[27]

The purpose of Central Office was not to control the party in the country, but to assist it to electoral victory. After more than three years in post as Party Chairman, Stonehaven was unequivocal in declaring 'that there was no substance in the bogey of dictation by Central Office. "It is merely a bogey, as anyone with my job is well aware."'[28] The limits of Central Office influence were very clearly shown by the failure to develop the trade unionist section of the party organization—even with the repeated lip service paid to the idea by the voluntary membership at regional and national gatherings. In practice, the structure, roles, and hierarchical relation-

---

[21] Lewisham West CA, Council, 11 October 1929; this sentiment was particularly voiced following the 1929 defeat.
[22] Winterton to Lytton, 22 November 1922, Lytton MSS, F160/26/8–13.
[23] NU Labour Ctte., 9 May 1921.
[24] Wilson to A. Chamberlain, n.d. but September 1922, AC, 33/2/26.
[25] Lane-Fox to Irwin, 28 April 1927, Halifax MSS, C152/17/1/212.
[26] SUA, WDC, 1 April 1925; Northwich CA, Exec., 18 February 1927.
[27] Blair to Hoare, 5 December 1934, Templewood MSS, VII/3.
[28] NU Conf., 1935.

ship of the different elements in the party were broadly acceptable nearly all of the time. The outgoing Chairman of the National Union Executive reminded its members in 1937: 'although the National Union was not a part of the Central Office but was the mouth-piece of the Party, it must, in order to be really useful, work in close co-operation with it'.[29] Central Office was looked to for guidance by most constituencies,[30] just as most MPs looked to the whips for advice and assistance. However, the willingness to co-operate could not be forced where the association and MP were not critically dependent upon national party funds or the MP was not ambitious for office—which, in both cases, was the position of the majority. As Neville Chamberlain observed when serving as Party Chairman: 'we circulate literature which gives the policy but we cannot edit the speeches of individuals'.[31]

The diversification of structures and functions within the Conservative Party organization may not have seemed the most efficient model on paper, but its 'stratified geographical formation' had significant advantages.[32] This prevented the dominance of the machine by any one opinion, region, group, or individual; the sectionalism and parochialism which could flourish was a drawback, but, in combination with the entrenched defence of local autonomy, it ensured that there was 'no room for a party dictator'.[33] Even the apparently all-powerful Leader was quite limited in the extent to which he could directly control the movement that he headed. The growth of specialist sections could foster the tendency not to see the wood for the trees, but it meant that particular groups were known and understood by professional staff who had continuity of devoted service, often over many years. Most of all, however haphazardly and pragmatically it had evolved, the organization was generally effective at every level, and probably had a more complete national reach than any other voluntary body of any kind. Of course, the Conservative Party shared the same weaknesses as other large organizations—of not attracting certain sections of the population, of having a particular kind of popular image, and of suffering from the tensions inevitable in any numerous collective endeavour. Many of its strengths also carried with them a compensating disadvantage, and thus its social and temperamental cohesion meant that it was 'too deferential to wealth, too patient of old men, too closed to the young, and too unwelcoming of brain'.[34] Nevertheless, in the words of Lord Woolton, who inherited the interwar organizational structure on becoming Party Chairman in 1946, 'it is a design that is fit for its purpose'.[35]

Both followers and leaders agreed that 'the foundation of Conservative strength is the constituency'.[36] Local autonomy was a real and prized factor in Conservative

[29] NU Exec., 14 April 1937.
[30] Memo by Thornton (Area Agent, South East), 'Central Office Agents and their work', *c.* October 1930, Templewood MSS, VI/3.
[31] N. to H. Chamberlain, 14 December 1930, *NCDL*.
[32] Butler to Hoare, 6 March 1942, Butler MSS, G14/33–4.
[33] Woolton, *Memoirs*, 332.
[34] Feiling, *What is Conservatism?*, 7.
[35] Woolton, oral history interview in Cohen, 'Disraeli's Child', 568, Cohen MSS, CPA, CRD/731.
[36] Special Finance Ctte. Report, 16 March 1944, 3, CPA, CCO/500/3/1.

politics, and it placed crucial limits upon the leadership and the professional machine in the vital areas of the selection of parliamentary candidates and the disciplining of rebellious MPs. It is significant that it was accepted as a reality, and not just a convenient excuse, by the minor partners in the National Government Coalition.[37] Thus, in 1932 Baldwin could only promise the Simonite Liberals that he and Central Office 'will exercise all the influence and authority we possess' to ensure they would not be opposed in their seats.[38] In fact, what accounted for the different grass-roots response to the Samuelite and Simonite Liberals in the National Government in 1931 was the Simonites' acceptance of tariffs and the lack of friction with them over other policies. Ultimately, power rested with the mass party, although it was almost never exerted. The National Union's rules allowed for the summoning of a special conference from below, and, whilst this never actually happened, it was threatened or at least genuinely considered during the three most stressful internal crises: in the waning of the Coalition in 1922, during the Empire Crusade campaign of 1930 (urged by Beaverbrook), and in the final phase of the India revolt in 1934–35. If the Annual Conference had rejected the policy of the leadership on an issue of vital importance, such as the Irish negotiations in 1921, the continuance of the Coalition in 1922 (if that Conference had taken place), or India in 1933 and 1934, the Leader would have been 'in an impossible position' and have had no option but to resign.[39]

The parliamentary party was the essential link between the party's basis of support and its decision-making leadership, and thus exerted importance influence in two directions.[40] The first of these was upwards to the Cabinet and Party Leader, by routes which were swift, discreet, and effective. The channels of communication were improved in the interwar period, with the introduction of the backbench subject committees in 1924 and the development of the 1922 Committee as a general forum. The other direction of influence is less frequently noted, but most constituency associations looked to their MP for guidance, especially on complicated or controversial issues. At the very least, there was a reluctance to pass a resolution to which the Member was strongly opposed or which would embarrass him.[41] Even when grass-roots feeling was strong, if the MP was loyal to the leadership and the line followed was within the acceptable parameters of Conservatism, it was unlikely that the association would go beyond a coded expression of doubt or opposition. For this reason, Baldwin believed that 'a big debate in the House…[can] steady opinion in the Tory Party'.[42] Addressing an issue and showing that parliamentary opinion wholly or mainly supported the leadership had a reassuring effect on the grass roots, and reduced the likelihood that they would become assertive. This was demonstrated by the party meetings held in February 1924 and October

---

[37] De La Warr to MacDonald, 15 November 1934, Baldwin MSS, 46/110–13.
[38] Baldwin to Simon (public letter), 26 October 1932, Baldwin MSS 167/254–5.
[39] Wilson to Younger, copied to Sanders, 5 October 1922, Bayford diary; Bridgeman to his son, 13 October 1922, Bridgeman diary.
[40] Chelmsford CA, Exec., 25 September 1925.
[41] Abingdon CA, Council, 27 April 1922.
[42] Notes by Crozier, interview with Baldwin, 12 June 1934, *BP*, 321.

1930, and after the formation of the National Government in August 1931. The parliamentary party was also the nexus of Conservative politics in another sense, for 'it is on the back benches that the true and fundamental character of a party can be assessed'.[43] This was true most of all of the mainstream Conservative MPs who accounted for the majority, and who normally could be relied upon to support the leadership, whatever their private doubts. The self-promotion of the bright and ambitious young men on the left wing and the disgruntlement of the diehard right, memorably captured in the forthright stupidity of David Low's cartoon character 'Colonel Blimp', might both have greater visibility, but what really mattered were 'the silent useful Members of whom nobody ever hears'.[44] If they should turn or fracture, then seismic change would indeed follow, as in 1922.

In conclusion, the strengths of the Conservative Party in this period can be categorized under eight headings. The first of these was a basic *consensus on principles*, which was fostered and facilitated by an acceptance of diversity in their definition and expression. The party enjoyed the benefits of a broad identification with patriotism and with continuity in both national institutions and culture, but was never too closely bound to a particular interest or a single issue. Conservative attitudes and beliefs were a force with elasticity and yet the strength to bind; as Lord Salisbury told the Annual Conference in 1920, 'the principles of Conservatism survived whatever the questions were'.[45] Their durability rested upon two foundations, the first of which was provided by the complementary nature of unconscious and conscious Conservatism:[46]

> For those who do not think, Toryism is a habit of mind; for those who do think, Toryism is a moral code harnessed to an objective and empirical study of human nature in politics.

The second foundation was the underlying Conservative temperament, defined by Duff Cooper as 'a happy faith' with the hallmarks of 'lack of malice, disinclination to quarrel, inability to hate'; though to more critical observers its characteristic might seem rather to have been a stolid complacency.[47] Where there were differences, they were very rarely of principle, sometimes of policy (as over tariffs, India, or appeasement), and, more usually, of personality; as Marjorie Maxse noted of one long-running regional friction, 'money, prestige and parochial outlook are at the bottom of all this trouble'.[48] More heated debate could arise over whether spiked shoes should be allowed in the tug-of-war competition at the constituency Junior Imperial League's sports day than the merits of different schemes to reform the House of Lords or the best way to tackle the trade union political levy; this should not be mocked, for the first question was more directly relevant to the lives of the people involved. Of course, there were issues that mattered; some of them

---

[43] Memoir notes, n.d., Ward MSS, MSS.Eng.c.6959.
[44] Nicolson to his wife, 17 May 1938, Nicolson diary.
[45] NU Conf., 1920.
[46] Crichton, *Tory Oxford*, 38.
[47] Duff Cooper speech notes, 'Toryism', n.d., Duff Cooper MSS, CAC, DUFC/8/1/17.
[48] Maxse to General-Director, 'Provincial Area Organisation', 12 July 1946, CPA, CCO/4/2/5.

were of a 'bread and butter' nature, such as high taxation, shelter for struggling industries, assistance to depressed agriculture, and the demolition of housing without adequate compensation, whilst others touched on national security and pride: the unity of the empire, the development of India, the strength of the armed services. It was not that the Conservative Party lacked internal debate and uncertainty on a day-to-day basis, rather that it did not doubt that it was a collective force which should hold together, and that it was one founded upon shared values and principles, so deeply embedded in its ethos and identity that they rarely needed explicit articulation. This was the basis of the second strength: an *underlying self-confidence* in the party's relevance and long-term role in national life. As an ex-Cabinet minister observed in late 1929, the party was 'in the trough, but it has a way of coming again, of which I have no doubt'.[49]

The third strength was the *flexibility and pragmatism of methods* which rested upon these foundations, and the consequent approach of focusing upon the immediate and attainable prospect and not a distant destination. The party was noted for its adaptability, and its response to setbacks was not rigidity or reaction but a reappraisal of policies and organization and, almost invariably, the setting of a course towards the political centre and the recovery of those less-committed supporters who had been lost. Thus, the Conservative 'clings to his Conservative principles, but leaves himself entirely free to advocate any sound methods which are likely to secure his aim'.[50] These included a willingness to work with other parties and groups, although in domestic politics this had to be justified by their movement towards Conservative positions and was within clear limiting parameters. This pragmatism extended to foreign affairs as well: it was the basis of support for the active appeasement initiatives of Neville Chamberlain, and it was shown in the Second World War when, despite years of fearful denunciations of the evils of Communism, following the German invasion of Russia the conclusion of an alliance with the Soviet state 'has not created apprehension in the Party'.[51] The other facet of Conservative flexibility was seen in the party's organization and tactics, especially in responding to changes in society and exploiting developments in technology. In both respects, as Baldwin stated, Conservatism demonstrated that it was 'capable of continuous adaptation to the ever-changing facts of social life'.[52]

The next pair of strengths were social and economic in origin. The fourth factor derived from the extent of the party's active support in both numbers and wealth, which provided substantial *organizational resources*. This was the product of the rallying of the overwhelming majority of the upper and middle classes behind the Conservative standard, together with the continuing expansion and general prosperity of the middle class in the interwar period, and it provided what one Party Chairman described as 'the great framework of officers and workers in the local

---

[49] Worthington-Evans to Chetwode, 25 October 1929, Worthington-Evans MSS, MSS. Enghist.c.897/99–101.
[50] Stelling, *Why I Am a Conservative*, 14.
[51] 'Digest' of Central Office Agents' reports, Topping to Stuart, 24 November 1941, CPA, CCO/4/2/162.
[52] Baldwin's preface in Elliot, *Toryism*, ix.

constituency associations'.[53] The fifth strength, the *social and cultural cohesion* of the Conservative Party, built upon the same foundation's support. The cultural values of Conservatives, in parliament and amongst the leading figures in the constituencies, were imbued with ethos of the boys' public school; this valued tradition rather than innovation, conformity rather than novelty, unity rather than dissent, team spirit rather than solo virtuosity, good fellowship in adversity, and the avoidance of arrogance in success.[54] Women were exhorted to similar values; the party's senior female official of the interwar period affirmed that 'One should think of Party first and not self-prominence or adulation. One should work in the spirit of a regiment.'[55] Thus, the culture of the parliamentary party emphasized loyalty and was antipathetic to ambition and factionalism; as one MP concluded after the party meeting of March 1921, 'we were still a party of gentlemen'.[56] Significantly, at the greatest confrontation in Conservative politics between the wars, the Carlton Club meeting of October 1922, 'everyone was very restrained and very sad at having to ventilate our differences with our leader';[57] there were 'no harsh or excited words', and instead the mood was 'extraordinarily restrained' and 'all most gentlemanly'.[58] These modes of conduct were reinforced by the conventional behaviour of the middle class, who made up most of the party membership: in the mass, quiet people who were deferential to traditional forms of authority and customary methods of procedure, and who disliked confrontation and preferred civility. Thus, at the party Conference in 1921 there was no bitterness in the speeches on Ireland, and the crucial debate on India in 1933 was 'all polite and good-tempered'.[59] After the deep divisions on that issue, 'the very warm and loyal tribute' to Baldwin in speeches by the leading rebels at the 1935 Annual Conference went down well with the rank and file.[60] Personal relationships were often maintained effectively despite sharp disagreements on issues, as Churchill affirmed of his contacts with the Chief Whip during the 1930s.[61]

This was closely linked to the sixth strength: the pull exerted by the habitual *instinct for unity*. Despite many pressures, internal disagreements, and even open revolts, the Conservative Party never divided in the damaging way in which the Liberals did over Irish Home Rule in the 1880s, the Boer War at the turn of the century, and during and after the First World War, or in which the Labour Party

[53] Davidson to Baldwin, 26 February 1930, Davidson MSS, DAV/190.
[54] Bonar Law's conduct in failing to forewarn Austen Chamberlain of his intention to attend the Carlton Club meeting was ascribed by one junior minister to Bonar Law's lack of a public school education: Pollock, 'Fall of the Coalition', Hanworth MSS, Eng.Hist.d.432/133–88.
[55] Marjorie Maxse address to East Midlands Area Women Organisers, meeting, 7 September 1927.
[56] Bridgeman to Long, 21 March 1921, Long MSS, Add.62426/43–4; Bayford diary, 24 March 1921; Courtauld to Baldwin, 14 December 1934, Baldwin MSS, 106/368.
[57] Bridgeman diary, letter to his son, 22 October 1922; account of the Carlton Club meeting by Curzon's private secretary, 19 October 1922, Curzon MSS, F112/319.
[58] Bayford diary, 19 October 1922.
[59] Bayford diary, 9 October 1933, 27 November 1921; NU Conf., 1933, speech by Croft; York diary, 20 April 1944.
[60] Norfolk North CA, Exec., 23 September 1935; Lewes CA, Women's Advisory Ctte., 7 October 1935; SUA, EDC, 9 October 1935.
[61] Churchill to Adams, 16 November 1940, Adams MSS, box 2.

did in 1931, 1952–55, and in the early 1980s. This was partly a matter of tribalism and sentiment; Page Croft described the party's members as 'curious people' whose 'loyalties are very deep-seated'.[62] These had not only a vertical vector, but also even more constant horizontal bonds—within the Cabinet team, amongst the parliamentary ranks, and, most of all, at the grass roots, where 'constituency loyalty is the glory of the Conservative Party'.[63] As the former Attorney-General observed, when looking back on the fall of the Lloyd George Coalition, 'there is a natural and proper horror of making a split in the Party where, side by side, so many battles against our opponents have been fought, and wherein so many sincere and valued friendships have been made'.[64] The emphasis on unity was also based upon hard-headed electoral pragmatism, 'that a strong feeling exists against any division of the party in the face of the enemy',[65] and a wider concern not to weaken the forces which were maintaining the constitution and all that depended upon it. The argument that 'those who did not trust their leaders played into the hands of the enemy' carried much weight.[66] There were certainly grumbles and grievances, but these were expressed in private and normally suppressed in public, or at least couched in respectful language.[67] Direct attacks, whether from without or within, generally had a consolidating rather than a fragmenting effect; as Beaverbrook was privately warned after the party meeting of June 1930, 'the Conservative Party is an obstinate creature which cannot be beaten over the head too much'.[68] Instead, 'there is only one way that can lead to success, and that is the way of united effort and good tempered collaboration'.[69] A summation of Conservative attitudes can be found in the response of the pro-Coalition whip, George Gibbs, immediately after the fall of the Coalition in 1922: 'I feel that it is essential to preserve unity.'[70]

The seventh strength was the clear chain of command within the party and the sole *focus of authority in the Leader*. The party had a firmly delineated hierarchical structure, in which the different parts were generally comfortable with their roles and their mutual relationships. This accommodated most strains and meant that disputes within the party very rarely did any lasting damage, which was true even of the split of 1922. Indeed, it is significant that the events of the fall of the Coalition, which came closest to an overthrowing of accepted authority and methods, was due to the failure of the leading elements within the party properly to fulfil their responsibilities. The eighth and final strength was that throughout this period

[62] Croft to Churchill, 21 November 1934, *WSC*.
[63] Special Finance Ctte. Report, 16 March 1944, 13, CPA, CCO/500/3/1.
[64] Pollock, 'Fall of the Coalition', Hanworth MSS, Eng.Hist.d.432/133–88; Bayford diary, 19 March 1922.
[65] Doncaster (chairman, Derbyshire South CA) to Emrys-Evans, 12 April 1938, Emrys-Evans MSS, Add.58249/6–7; Birmingham CA, Management Ctte., 14 December 1923.
[66] Edinburgh South CA, Exec., 28 February 1927.
[67] Glasgow CA, General Ctte., 28 February 1927, 30 April 1928; St Albans CA, Exec., 15 February 1929.
[68] Amery to Beaverbrook, 28 June 1930, Beaverbrook MSS, BBK/C5.
[69] Bridgeman to Beaverbrook, 11 September 1930, Bridgeman diary.
[70] Gibbs to Bull, 2 November 1922, Bull MSS, CAC, BULL/5/6; Bird to Gilmour, 22 October 1922, text of telegram in Wolverhampton West CA, Management Ctte., 22 October 1922.

the Conservatives were led on the basis of a *moderate and centrist strategy*. This was as much the case with Bonar Law as Prime Minister in 1922–23 and Neville Chamberlain in both his foreign and domestic policies in 1937–39, as it was with Baldwin in between them.[71] It was also true of Churchill's management of his wartime Coalition, although unfortunately not of his strategy in the 1945 election, with such misjudgements as the harsh dissonance of the 'Gestapo' speech. It is yet again the later period of the 1918–22 Lloyd George Coalition which provides the exception to prove the general rule, but even the Coalition was continued into peacetime in 1918 precisely because it was the most centrist of the strategies available. However, its methods, its failures, and, still more, the consequent alarming advance of Socialism meant that, by 1922, perpetuating it in its present form had become the most provocative option: by this time, most Conservative MPs had concluded that to do so was more likely to lead to a Labour majority in the House of Commons than was the case if the party separated from Lloyd George. To this last, general strength can be added a supplementary factor: the attractive style of leadership projected by Baldwin, over and above the content and direction of his programme, was of acknowledged benefit to the Conservatives at the ballot box. They would probably have done nearly as well if they had followed the same course under some other personality, but Baldwin's ability to turn the spotlight on the most widely appealing and resonant elements in Conservatism, and to relegate to the shadows—even to confront and repudiate—the less pleasant ones, was an asset which aided the dominance enjoyed by the Conservative Party in the era between the two world wars.

Many of these eight strengths continued into the first postwar era of 1945–75, and help to explain the party's relatively swift and smooth recovery from the 1945 defeat and its further long term in power from 1951 to 1964. Several were set aside during the Thatcher era, particularly during its high noon of 1983–89; at first this seemed not to matter, but then it turned out to do so after all, and the Conservatives struggled for two decades, from 1990 to 2010, both in and out of office, to regain their former unity and breadth of appeal; it is not yet clear to what extent they have done so, or for how long it may last. Even so, looking back over the long history of the party since the early nineteenth century, many would agree with the confident assertion of the MP, Lord Burghley, at the 1934 Annual Conference, that 'the Conservative Party, like the Phoenix, was immortal'.

---

[71] Headlam diary, 24 January 1929.

APPENDIX 1

Conservative Party Office-Holders 1918–1945

The dates are those of the formal election or appointment; the public announcement normally appeared in the press on the following day. On some occasions, a short interval elapsed between the resignation or death of one occupant and the formal appointment of a successor.

Leader of the Party	Date appointed
Andrew Bonar Law (Leader in the House of Commons only)	13 November 1911
Austen Chamberlain (Leader in the House of Commons only)	21 March 1921
Andrew Bonar Law	23 October 1922
Stanley Baldwin	28 May 1923
Neville Chamberlain	31 May 1937
Winston Churchill	9 October 1940

Leader of the Party in the House of Lords	Date appointed
1st Earl Curzon (elevated to 1st Marquess, 1921)	10 December 1916
4th Marquess of Salisbury	27 April 1925
1st Viscount Hailsham	17 June 1931
7th Marquess of Londonderry	7 June 1935
3rd Viscount Halifax	22 November 1935
7th Earl Stanhope	9 March 1938
1st Viscount Caldecote	14 May 1940
3rd Viscount Halifax	3 October 1940
1st Baron Lloyd	10 January 1941
1st Baron Moyne	8 February 1941
Viscount Cranborne (courtesy title, summoned to the Lords in 1942)	22 February 1942

Chief Whip in the House of Commons	Date appointed
Lord Edmund Talbot (courtesy title, son of the Duke of Norfolk)	4 February 1913
Leslie Wilson	1 April 1921
Bolton Eyres-Monsell (knighted, 1929)	25 July 1923
David Margesson	10 November 1931
James Stuart	14 January 1941

Chairman of the Party Organization	Date appointed

*The dates below are those from which the appointments took effect. Normally this was the same day as the public announcement, but in a few instances an interval of more than a week elapsed and this is indicated by an * after the date upon which the new Chairman took up his duties.*

Sir George Younger	1 January 1917 *
[Francis] Stanley Jackson	13 March 1923
John Colin Campbell Davidson	4 November 1926
Neville Chamberlain	23 June 1930
1st Baron Stonehaven	14 April 1931 *
Douglas Hacking (created baronet, 1938)	2 March 1936
Thomas Dugdale	6 March 1942 *
Ralph Assheton	29 October 1944

Deputy Chairmen of the Party Organization	Period of office
Robert Sanders (created baronet, 1920)	Feb. 1918–Oct. 1922
2nd Marquess of Linlithgow	May 1924–Jan. 1926
3rd Baron Strathcona and Mount Royal	Oct. 1927–Nov. 1927
Lord Stanley (courtesy title, heir of the Earl of Derby)	Nov. 1927–Jul. 1929
Sir George Bowyer	Mar. 1930–{1931}
Countess of Iveagh (appointment announced, but unable to take up post)	–
Lady Falmouth (*acting*, in place of the Countess of Iveagh)	Mar. 1930–{1931}

Although no formal announcement of a change can be traced, from mid-1931 Bowyer and Falmouth were listed on Central Office notepaper not as Deputy- but as Vice-Chairmen, and they were so described when a third Vice-Chairman was appointed in December 1931.

Principal Agent		Date appointed
John Boraston (knighted, 1916)	{Joint June 1915–April 1920}	May 1912
William Jenkins	{Joint June 1915–April 1920}	June 1915
Sir Malcolm Fraser (baronet, 1921)	Honorary (unsalaried)	December 1920
Sir Reginald Hall		March 1923
Herbert Blain (knighted, 1925)		March 1924
Sir T. J. Leigh Maclachlan		January 1927
H. Robert Topping (knighted, 1934)	(General Director, from February 1931)	February 1928
Stephen Pierssene	(General Director)	October 1945

Treasurer	Period of office
1st Earl Farquhar	August 1911–March 1923
1st Viscount Younger of Leckie	March 1923–April 1929
Sir Samuel Hoare	January 1930–July 1931
1st Baron Ebbisham	July 1931–November 1933
1st Viscount Greenwood	November 1933–June 1938
1st Viscount Marchwood	June 1938–February 1947

Chairman of the Conservative Private Members' '1922' Committee	Date elected
Gervais Rentoul (knighted, 1929)	23 April 1923
William S. Morrison	5 December 1932
Sir Hugh O'Neill	16 December 1935
Sir Annesley Somerville (Acting Chairman)	20 September 1939
William Spens	6 December 1939
Alexander Erskine-Hill	11 December 1940
John McEwen	12 December 1944

National Union, Chairman of the Executive Committee	Period of office

Until the revised rules of the National Union came into effect in October 1930, this post was occupied ex officio by the Chairman of the Party Organization; thereafter it was elected by the Executive Committee.

Sir Howard Kingsley Wood	October 1930–March 1932
George Herbert	March 1932–April 1937
Sir George Stanley	April 1937–April 1938
Sir Eugene Ramsden	April 1938–April 1943
Richard George Proby	April 1943–April 1946

APPENDIX 2

The Economic and Social Analysis of Conservative Electoral Support

THE BASIS OF THE ANALYSIS

The analysis of Conservative electoral support in Chapter 2 is derived from a database which correlates the voting pattern in the constituencies with their economic and social composition, based upon data in the published reports of the census of 1931. The methodology and the sources of information which have been used are explained here, together with a number of complexities and limitations, which are mainly a consequence of the nature of the census data.

The first element in the database is the voting figures for every candidate (including all minor parties and independents) in each constituency for the general elections from 1918 to 1945. This information was taken from the authoritative reference source compiled by F. W. S. Craig, *British Parliamentary Election Results 1918–1949* (2nd edn, 1977). The party identification codes used follow those given by Craig, except that: (a) for most analyses, the Conservative candidates in the 1918 general election who did not receive endorsement as an official Coalition nominee have been taken together with the Conservative candidates who did receive the 'coupon' letter; (b) except in Table 2.1, the twelve candidates in 1924 who described themselves as 'Constitutionalists' and who, as the result of an electoral pact, were supported by their local Conservative Associations, have been regarded as being the Conservative candidate, as has G. W. S Jarrett at Dartford in 1922 and 1923. Apart from these cases, all candidates of all other parties (including those in any coalition with the Conservative Party) and all independents (including any described as Independent Conservative) have been regarded as separate, and their votes are not included in the analysis of the electoral support of the Conservative Party. For the other parties, the Liberal followers of Lloyd George and of Asquith have been treated separately in 1918, but taken together as Liberals in 1922; throughout, Co-operative Party candidates have been counted as Labour candidates, but Independent Labour Party candidates have been regarded as separate. In the database, the constituencies have been allocated to regions on a county basis, as described in Appendix 3.

The second element in the database is statistics from the published reports for England and Wales of the 1931 census. The main part of this is the detailed figures for occupational categories in *Census of England and Wales, 1931: Occupation Tables* (1934), which are given in Table 16 (pp. 154–425), for 'County Boroughs and other Urban Areas with Populations exceeding 50,000', and Table 17 (pp. 426–583), for 'Urban Areas with Populations not exceeding 50,000 and Rural Districts'. This is a vast array of many thousands of individual figures, and it would have been an impossible task to input this manually for this project. Fortunately, in the late 1990s, an inter-university project of historical geographers, funded by the Economic and Social Research Council and the Leverhulme Trust, entered all of the data in the published *Occupation Tables* into a database. This was subsequently reorganized and rechecked for errors by Professor Humphrey Southall of Portsmouth University in 2000–01, and then deposited as text files at the UK Data Archive, from where (with grateful acknowledgement to all concerned) a copy of the data was obtained.[1]

The third, and original, element in the database is the linkage of the census data with the individual parliamentary constituencies, as they were constituted at the time of the 1931 census (see Part I, Table 8, in the county volumes). This is essential for accurate analysis, as there had been changes in the boundaries of a considerable number of local government areas since the constituencies were originally drawn up in the 1918 Reform Act. However, the linkage is a highly complex matter, as constituencies do not map straightforwardly on to the local government districts used by the census. The analyses in this book are derived from an intricate system for the correlation of the two, which is still in development in the School of Historical Studies at the University of Leicester. My colleague Graham Smith, whose project that is, plans to publish details of his methodology in due course and then to offer the linkage system itself for deposit in the UK Data Archive. His work draws on parish-level population statistics that Humphrey Southall and his team have also deposited in the UK Data Archive, for which we make further grateful acknowledgement.[2]

LIMITATIONS DUE TO THE NATURE OF THE CENSUS DATA

The largest exclusion is Scotland, for which the published census information is much more limited: whereas there are ninety-two published volumes for England and Wales, consisting of both county and overall subject volumes, there are only four volumes for Scotland. The main problem is that in *Census of Scotland, 1931*, vol. 3: *Occupations and Industries* (Edinburgh, 1934), the data in Table 2 (pp. 42–137) on occupations is provided only as an overall figure for the four cities (Aberdeen, Dundee, Edinburgh, and Glasgow), the thirty-three counties, and twenty of the towns. These geographical units can only be matched to specific constituencies in a relatively small number of cases, principally in the rural Highland and Border regions where some constituencies consisted of a whole county or a combination of whole counties. The resulting sample would be too limited and too unrepresentative of Scotland as a whole, and therefore the analysis has been restricted to England and Wales.

There are some similar limitations in analysing the information given for the cities in England and Wales, as these are treated in the census as being a single county borough, for which only an overall figure is given for each census category. These are quite detailed in occupational terms, and thus it is possible to know how many basket-makers there were in the city of Birmingham, but not how they were distributed amongst its twelve parliamentary constituencies. It is therefore only possible to analyse the towns and cities which consisted of two or more separate single-Member constituencies by aggregating the voting figures for the separate divisions and comparing this to the overall census data. This can produce reasonably precise results in towns and cities which consisted of two, three, and,

---

[1] H. R. Southall, D. Dorling, E. M. Garrett, P. Ell, D. A. Gatley, D. R. Gilbert, C. Lee, A. Reid, and M. Woollard, *Great Britain Historical Database: Census Data: Occupational Statistics, 1841–1991* [computer file], Colchester, Essex: UK Data Archive [distributor], August 2004, SN: 4559. <http://dx.doi.org/10.5255/UKDA-SN-4559-1>.

[2] H. R. Southall, I. Gregory, P. Ell, and D.A. Gatley, *Great Britain Historical Database: Census Data: Parish-Level Population Statistics, 1801–1951* [computer file], Colchester, Essex: UK Data Archive [distributor], August 2004, SN: 4560, http://dx.doi.org/10.5255/UKDA-SN-4560-1.

perhaps, four parliamentary divisions, but obviously becomes a much cruder exercise when applied to the largest cities, in particular Birmingham, Liverpool, and Manchester. The situation regarding London is better, for here the census data are provided at the level of the London boroughs, of which ten were a single constituency (including the double-Member City of London), and eleven were divided into only two constituencies; of the remainder, four had three seats, three had four seats, and one had five seats (see Table 2.6).

The census provides occupation data at three levels of detail, according to the size of the place:

(a) the highest level is the thirty-two Orders, identified by roman numerals, which consist of broad occupational categories related to the nature of the work and the materials being used;

(b) fourteen of the Orders are initially divided into between two and seven Sub-Orders;

(c) all of the Orders and Sub-Orders are divided into a large number of Groups, each of which is allocated a three-figure code number.

In the *Occupation Tables* volume, the full range of these categories is used in Table 16, which gives the statistics for the urban areas with a population above 50,000; however, Table 17, which deals with towns of up to 50,000 and with all of the rural areas, uses a much more restricted range. Furthermore, it does so differently for males and females. For the occupations of males, a separate total is given for almost all of the Orders (orders XX and XXI are combined together), for most of the Sub-Orders, and for a very few of the most significant Groups. For females, there is information for only a limited number of the Orders and a small number of Groups, although these are the categories in which women were significantly represented, and they include Group 850 for Domestic Servants. It has therefore been necessary in the analyses which cover all parts of the country to use only the occupational categories which are present in both Table 16 and Table 17, as listed below. However, it is possible in analyses which focus only upon the larger towns and cities to make use of the more detailed breakdowns given in Table 16, and so for these places to identify certain 'upper-middle class' occupations within the broader middle-class range (see below). All of the analyses have to use the census categories as their building blocks, and are therefore limited by the nature and scope of these; detailed definitions of the various categories are given in the separate volume: *Census, 1931: Classification of Occupations* (1934).

THE SAMPLE OF CONSTITUENCIES WITH 'THREE-PARTY' CONTESTS IN THE 1929 GENERAL ELECTION

For consistency of comparison, the general analyses of Conservative electoral support use only the votes from those constituencies in England and Wales which (a) can be matched to the geographical units used in the census, and (b) in the general election of 1929 were contested by candidates from all three of the main parties (Conservative, Labour, and Liberal); these are defined as 'three-party contests', irrespective of whether there were other candidates standing as well. This category includes any divided borough in which there were 'three-party contests' in all of its constituencies, and double-Member boroughs where at least one candidate was present from each main party (in the latter, where two Conservative candidates stood, the party's share of the vote is calculated from their combined total). The sample thus consists of the following:

286	individual single-Member borough and county constituencies (286 parliamentary seats)
10	individual double-Member borough constituencies (20 parliamentary seats)
5	London divided boroughs of two constituencies (10 parliamentary seats)
4	London divided boroughs of three constituencies (12 parliamentary seats)
2	London divided boroughs of four constituencies (8 parliamentary seats)
12	English & Welsh divided boroughs of two constituencies (24 parliamentary seats)
5	English & Welsh divided boroughs of three constituencies (15 parliamentary seats)
2	English & Welsh divided boroughs of four constituencies (8 parliamentary seats)

This makes a total of 373 constituencies which, due to the ten double-Member boroughs, returned 383 MPs. However, analysis of the voting in other elections is not limited to the constituencies with 'three-party contests' in 1929, and can use a wider range of constituencies which match the census areas or be more specifically targeted upon groups of seats, such as those won or lost.

THE REVISION OF CONSTITUENCY BOUNDARIES BEFORE THE 1945 GENERAL ELECTION

A revision of boundaries, which took place before the general election of 1945, affected a number of constituencies in which the size of the electorate had become very large, and this poses an obvious problem of continuity for those analyses that compare constituency results across the whole period from 1918 to 1945. The thirty-one constituencies with minor changes and the nine which continued in existence but with substantial alteration (Birmingham Moseley, Chislehurst, Epping, Epsom, Essex South-East, Nuneaton, St Albans, Uxbridge, and Wycombe) have been treated as being the same seat as previously. However, thirteen constituencies were completely abolished, whilst thirty-eight new ones were created (the net effect increasing the size of the House of Commons from 615 to 640 MPs); in four cases, a large county division was abolished and a smaller borough seat created around its main town, with the same name as the previous constituency. To enable comparison across the period, each of the abolished constituencies has been linked with the most appropriate of its successors, as its designated 'continuation seat'. Where possible, this has been determined by the best geographical match, but in the cases of Blackpool, Coventry, Ealing, Harrow, and Ilford—where the former seat was divided in half—the choice has been determined by which constituency the sitting MP chose to contest in 1945. In the case of Hendon, where the sitting Conservative MP retired in 1945, Hendon South has been selected as the 'continuation seat' because this was won by a Conservative candidate, whereas Hendon North was won by Labour.

1935 constituency		1945 'continuation seat'	
Name	Type	Name	Type
Altrincham	county	Altrincham & Sale	borough
Blackpool	borough	Blackpool South	borough
Coventry	borough	Coventry West	borough
Dartford	county	Dartford	borough
Ealing	borough	Ealing East	borough
Harrow	county	Harrow West	borough
Hendon	county	Hendon South	borough
Horsham & Worthing	county	Horsham	county
Ilford	borough	Ilford North	borough
Mitcham	county	Mitcham	borough
Romford	county	Romford	borough
Tamworth	county	Sutton Coldfield	county
Twickenham	county	Twickenham	borough

DEFINITIONS OF THE CONSTITUENCY PROFILE CATEGORIES USED IN THE TABLES IN CHAPTER 2

In most of the census-based tables, the occupation data are arranged in ten main categories on the basis of the overall Orders. These categories are applicable to all constituencies and have the advantage of each representing a substantial part of the working population, although not all the census Orders are included.

Main category	Census Orders	Workers
Agriculture	II	1,172,256
Mining	III	968,771
Metal Industries	VII	1,445,894
Construction	V + XVIII + XIX	1,087,628
Light Industries	VIII + IX + X + XV + XVI + XVII + XX + XXI	1,214,097
Textiles & Clothing	XII + XIII	1,695,193
Service & Leisure	XXVI + XXVII	2,503,936
Commerce & Finance	XXIII	2,071,420
Clerical	XXVIII	1,375,431
Professional	XXV	746,085

Figures for 'shopkeepers' are also provided in the census for areas with population of up to 50,000 as well as those above, and this category has been used in Table 2.5:

Shopkeepers	XXIII Groups 670–85	569,137

Appendix 2

Five of the above main categories, together with further categories derived from the more specific data available only for towns with population above 50,000, have been used in the analysis of large town and cities in Table 2.8. These sixteen categories are defined in the list below, which for all categories gives *only* the number of workers in the towns with a population of above 50,000.

Large towns category	Census Orders, Sub-Orders, and Groups	Workers
Docks & Shipping	XXII Sub-order 3	197,687
Railways	XXII Sub-order 1	147,404
Metal Industries	VII	892,504
Construction	V + XVIII + XIX	569,174
Chemicals	VI	24,611
Electrical	IX	137,215
Textiles & Clothing	XII + XIII	957,423
Paper & Printing	XVI + XVII	202,926
Food, Drink, & Tobacco	XIV	146,369
Retail	XXIII Groups 670–85 + Groups 700–16	767,209
Wholesale & Finance	XXIII *minus* Retail category (as above)	446,194
Entertainment & Catering	XXVI + XXVII Groups 861–2, 864–9, 871	332,197
Domestic Servants	XXVII Group 850	646,350
Government & Defence	XXIV	132,764
Clerical	XXVIII	912,256
Professional	XXV	376,113

In Table 2.6, which uses only the data for towns with population above 50,000, a category of 'Core middle class' has been created by the combination of the Professional, Clerical, and Shopkeepers categories (Order XXV, Order XXVIII, and Groups 670–85 of Order XXIII), which amount in these places to 1,590,938 persons. A separate 'Upper-middle class' category has also been constructed from selected individual census Groups, as shown below, totalling 243,413 persons.

Order	Groups	Definition
III	040. 050, 060	owners, agents, & managers
IV–XXI	Groups defined as	employers & managers
XXII	610	owners, managers, & superintendents
	630	owners, managers, brokers, & agents
	650	employers & managers
XXIII	730	company directors
	731	bank officials (heads of departments, managers)
XXIV	740	civil service: administrative & executive
	750	police: inspectors & above
	760, 762, 764	navy, army, & air force: commissioned officers

(*continued*)

(continued)

Order	Groups	Definition
XXV	770	Anglican clergy
	780	judges
	781	solicitors
	790	doctors
	791	dentists
	813	architects
	814	ship designers
	815	chartered accountants
XXVI	832	film producers
XXVIII	880	secretaries & registrars of companies & institutions

The *Occupation Tables* also provide data from which the level of unemployment can be calculated: as the number of persons aged fourteen and over who were classified as 'out of work' expressed as a percentage of the number who were classified as 'occupied'. Other tables in the census reports provide data on a parliamentary constituency basis for the number of male and female voters, and for the number of voters with 'other qualifications'; that is, who possessed an additional vote due to the ownership of business premises in a constituency different from the one in which they resided. There is also information on population density per acre and per room, which respectively indicate the rural nature of constituencies and the concentration of population in the slum districts of towns and cities.

APPENDIX 3

The Regional Analysis of Conservative Electoral Support

For the investigation of the pattern of voting in Chapter 2, mainland Britain has been divided into a number of regions; in some cases, these have been further divided into sub-regions for particular analyses. These regions are not identical with the Provincial Areas which the Conservative Party used for its own regional organization, although some are the same and others are broadly similar. They are based upon two criteria: (a) those areas which are commonly accepted as having a particular regional cohesion and identity, and (b) the economic nature of the region. These generally have congruence, but the second criterion has led to some variations from the 'standard' geographical regions—for example, in the allocation of Lincolnshire, where the agricultural pattern is similar to East Anglia—to an East England region, and not to the East Midlands, as might be customary. The regions are organized on a county basis, as follows.

SOUTHERN ENGLAND		
South-East:	London:	London
	Home Counties North:	Buckinghamshire, Essex, Hertfordshire, Middlesex
	Home Counties South:	Kent, Surrey, Sussex
South Central:	Berkshire, Gloucestershire (including Bristol), Hampshire, Isle of Wight, Oxfordshire, Wiltshire	
South-West:	Cornwall, Devon, Dorset, Somerset	

MIDLAND & EAST ENGLAND	
East:	Bedfordshire, Cambridgeshire, Huntingdonshire, Isle of Ely, Lincolnshire (including Rutland), Norfolk, Suffolk
East Midlands:	Derbyshire, Leicestershire, Northamptonshire, Nottinghamshire
West Midlands:	Herefordshire, Shropshire, Staffordshire, Warwickshire, Worcestershire

NORTHERN ENGLAND		
North-East:	Yorkshire:	Yorkshire (including Cleveland)
	Tyneside:	Durham, Northumberland
North-West:	Cheshire, Cumberland, Lancashire, Westmorland	

(continued)

(*continued*)

WALES	
Wales Industrial:	Glamorgan, Monmouthshire
Wales Rural:	Anglesey, Brecon, Caernarvonshire, Cardiganshire, Carmarthenshire, Denbighshire, Flintshire, Merionethshire, Montgomeryshire, Pembrokeshire
SCOTLAND	
South Scotland:	Ayrshire, Berwickshire, Dumfriesshire, Dunbartonshire, Galloway, East Lothian, Fife, Kirkcudbrightshire, Lanarkshire, Linlithgowshire, Midlothian, Peeblesshire, Renfrewshire, Roxburghshire, Selkirkshire, Stirlingshire
North Scotland:	Aberdeenshire, Argyllshire, Banffshire, Caithness, Forfarshire, Invernesshire, Morayshire, Orkney & Shetland, Perthshire (including Kinross), Ros-shire

APPENDIX 4

Conservative Party National Expenditure 1925–1945

Detailed accounts for each calendar year have survived from 1925 onwards (for 1925–29, Davidson MSS, 175–6; for 1930–45, CPA, FIN/2–9 & Accn/2004/28), consisting, for each year, of audited balance sheets and supplementary schedules. However, both the departmental structure of Central Office and the presentation of information in the accounts changed at various times; in order to provide data for the whole period on a consistent basis, in some cases the figures are the sum of selected sub-headings within departments, and therefore vary from the departmental total shown in the balance sheet for that year.

	1925	1926	1927	1928	1929	1930
Organizing sections[a]	31,870	31,247	30,842	27,528	22,765	19,388
Area Agents[b]	24,642	25,729	27,393	28,238	27,799	30,827
London Whip[c]	7,000	8,000	11,100	12,000	10,200	6,000
Scottish Whip's Office[d]	1,906	1,890	1,881	1,943	1,911	1,933
Junior Imperial League	3,804	3,879	6,658	7,950	5,460	7,732
Young Britons[e]	76	177	164	1,271	2,573	2,459
National Union Secretary's Office	2,569	2,772	2,917	2,611	3,827	2,768
Publicity Department	30,756	23,796	28,300	27,196	29,674	38,686
Cinema vans/Films Association[f]	779	1,600	3,173	8,284	17,898	9,233
Publications free to MPs & speakers	110	1,988	2,579	3,250	3,421	3,629
Party Leader's Secretariat	–	–	–	–	–	3,841
House of Commons Whips' Office	138	157	128	129	1,287	2,343
Research Department[g]	692	1,008	200	–	2,331	11,500
Administrative & clerical staff[h]	8,987	8,938	9,931	16,111	14,117	16,178
By-elections & public meetings[i]	9,722	16,494	10,988	16,279	12,460	7,681
Special campaigns[j]	4,633	2,289	10,694	1,383	–	541
Grants to constituencies[k]	27,613	22,131	34,611	40,425	27,520	19,490
Grants to related organizations[l]	675	1,024	877	1,909	1,226	974
Grants to educational institutions[m]	1,180	–	1,109	5,305	3,491	1,489
Private & special payments	2,651	5,440	3,222	3,143	2,698	2,415
Pensions paid directly	3,135	3,184	4,575	5,888	6,168	5,634
Insurance and superannuation[n]	2,168	1,661	3,233	3,294	2,237	2,231
Premises rent, rates, & maintenance[o]	7,848	7,935	10,243	10,692	11,468	12,042
Lighting, heating, & housekeeping	1,433	1,488	1,843	1,872	2,347	2,418
Postage, telephone, & telegrams	3,128	2,634	3,263	3,299	3,522	4,249
Stationery & general printing[p]	3,982	1,944	2,578	2,495	1,734	2,023
Legal, accounting, & bank charges	1,171	1,111	1,159	1,468	1,136	2,269
Exceptional expenditure[q]	100	–	–	973	9,291	918
Miscellaneous other expenditure	4,023	1,597	1,808	3,492	6,314	4,925
TOTAL	186,791	180,113	215,469	238,428	234,875	225,816

Appendix 4

	1931	1932	1933	1934	1935
Organizing sections[a]	15,310	9,135	6,675	6,868	7,544
Area Agents[b]	27,022	24,997	23,906	24,586	24,027
London Whip[c]	5,300	-1,757	–	–	–
Scottish Whip's Office[d]	1,912	1,737	2,000	2,000	2,000
Junior Imperial League	5,243	5,557	3,155	3,259	3,370
Young Britons	1,917	1,142	1,166	1,114	1,165
National Union Secretary's Office	1,934	2,086	3,048	3,171	3,086
Publicity Department	23,209	15,895	12,898	12,318	13,460
Cinema vans/Films Association[f]	15,750	4,033	3,564	12,034	7,761
Publications free to MPs & speakers	4,391	2,383	1,005	832	859
Party Leader's Secretariat	4,304	2,501	2,209	1,450	1,296
House of Commons Whips' Office	1,637	224	210	225	250
Research Department	10,000	6,500	5,500	4,500	5,750
Administrative & clerical staff[h]	15,960	14,849	14,073	14,519	15,191
By-elections & public meetings[i]	8,846	1,612	1,746	2,511	1,137
Special campaigns[j]	–	–	–	6,770	–
Grants to constituencies[k]	11,391	5,093	2,351	1,198	5,418
Grants to related organizations[l]	1,196	982	963	975	899
Grants to educational institutions[m]	–	–	–	–	–
Private & special payments	3,818	4,646	2,865	1,520	2,379
Pensions paid directly	7,864	9,109	7,933	8,943	8,100
Insurance and superannuation[n]	2,096	1,854	1,806	2,084	2,220
Premises rent, rates, & maintenance[o]	10,690	10,081	8,581	8,069	7,801
Lighting, heating, & housekeeping	2,229	1,912	1,593	1,632	1,615
Postage, telephone, & telegrams	3,047	2,297	2,339	2,445	2,548
Stationery & general printing[p]	1,673	959	859	712	1,041
Legal, accounting, & bank charges	2,635	1,363	1,501	2,056	1,404
Exceptional expenditure[q]	777	3,226	1,000	–	–
Miscellaneous other expenditure	3,386	2,040	1,396	1,891	1,195
TOTAL	193,537	134,456	114,342	127,682	121,516

538   *Portrait of a Party*

	1936	1937	1938	1939	1940
Organizing sections[a]	6,592	7,129	7,342	6,612	3,845
Area Agents[b]	23,769	23,881	24,420	25,887	12,731
London Whip[c]	–	–	–	–	–
Scottish Whip's Office[d]	2,000	2,000	2,000	2,000	2,000
Junior Imperial League	3,260	3,348	3,858	4,490	273
Young Britons	1,205	1,073	1,127	3,157	–
National Union Secretary's Office	2,936	2,610	2,833	2,389	1,038
Publicity Department	12,845	12,316	13,080	16,752	6,593
Cinema vans/Films Association[f]	4,171	4,579	4,630	4,007	1,833
Publications free to MPs & speakers	807	1,374	1,892	850	–
Party Leader's Secretariat	1,025	872	1,656	1,374	1,500
House of Commons Whips' Office	280	311	323	322	59
Research Department	6,000	6,500	5,000	1,250	–
Administrative & clerical staff[h]	14,851	15,299	16,132	14,192	6,974
By-elections & public meetings[i]	1,635	2,867	2,770	2,679	124
Special campaigns[j]	–	–	–	–	1,423
Grants to constituencies[k]	2,872	6,046	8,119	7,026	1,454
Grants to related organizations[l]	953	1,022	1,196	1,140	607
Grants to educational institutions[m]	–	–	–	–	–
Private & special payments	637	1,503	1,724	2,980	1,496
Pensions paid directly	10,214	8,714	6,938	8,080	7,291
Insurance and superannuation[n]	2,103	2,051	2,095	2,034	1,516
Premises rent, rates, & maintenance[o]	7,695	7,630	7,921	8,494	7,047
Lighting, heating, & housekeeping	1,604	1,604	1,619	1,386	775
Postage, telephone, & telegrams	2,595	2,768	2,294	2,072	1,119
Stationery & general printing[p]	1,018	1,248	1,711	1,171	104
Legal, accounting, & bank charges	831	1,124	796	872	472
Exceptional expenditure[q]	14,000	–	–	3,227	–
Miscellaneous other expenditure	1,330	778	750	702	47
TOTAL	127,228	118,647	122,226	125,145	60,321

Appendix 4

	1941	1942	1943	1944	1945
Organizing sections[a]	2,480	3,014	4,294	6,543	12,765
Area Agents[b]	11,690	11,049	11,232	12,406	19,624
London Whip[c]	–	–	–	–	–
Scottish Whip's Office[d]	2,000	2,000	2,000	2,000	2,000
Junior Imperial League	72	–	–	–	1,986
Young Britons	–	–	–	–	–
National Union Secretary's Office	867	940	1,056	850	2,065
Publicity Department	4,962	4,891	5,437	10,401	16,424
Cinema vans/Films Association[f]	–	–	–	–	–
Publications free to MPs & speakers	–	–	–	–	–
Party Leader's Secretariat	1,559	620	–	–	914
House of Commons Whips' Office	63	64	69	69	870
Research Department	–	–	–	–	959
Administrative & clerical staff[h]	5,108	5,766	6,565	8,017	15,270
By-elections & public meetings[i]	584	745	2,055	1,052	5,082
Special campaigns[j]	–	–	–	–	–
Grants to constituencies[k]	1,471	696	295	421	5,533
Grants to related organizations[l]	565	154	73	58	242
Grants to educational institutions[m]	–	–	–	–	–
Private & special payments	2,216	725	387	515	2,494
Pensions paid directly	7,199	6,870	5,357	5,995	5,161
Insurance and superannuation[n]	1,628	1,333	1,438	1,742	1,757
Premises rent, rates, & maintenance[o]	6,659	6,584	4,692	6,047	8,273
Lighting, heating, & housekeeping	767	771	584	756	1,385
Postage, telephone, & telegrams	631	789	1,061	1,208	2,138
Stationery & general printing[p]	115	384	403	829	1,307
Legal, accounting, & bank charges	291	755	370	349	678
Exceptional expenditure[q]	–	3,310	–	–	–
Miscellaneous other expenditure	702	839	804	1,039	2,167
TOTAL	51,629	52,299	48,172	60,297	109,094

ᵃ Defined as Chairman's office, Principal Agent/General Director and section, Speakers' section, Labour section, Women's section (to 1932), Organizing section (from 1933); also includes costs of speakers' training classes, 1925–28.

ᵇ Salaries and expenses of the Area Agents and Deputy Area Agents in the twelve regional offices in England and Wales, including the London Department to 1932. The figures do not include their clerical staff, who were not separately identified and were included in the general list of Central Office clerical staff.

ᶜ The block grant given to the London Whip; no breakdown exists of how this was disbursed. The other expenditure of the London Department is included in the figures for Area Agents and grants to constituencies. The last block grant was given in 1932, and the last London Department salaries and expenses are listed in the accounts for 1933.

ᵈ Salaries and expenses of the Scottish Whip's Office, not including grants to constituencies; from 1933 only a block grant figure is given, with no breakdown of costs.

ᵉ In 1925–27, the Young Britons salary costs were not separately identified within the Women's section, and the figure shown is for expenses only.

ᶠ The figures are the total of the operating costs and the allowance for depreciation, which was shown as a charge on the accounts in 1928–30 and 1937–40; the figure for 1930 is only to 30 September. The operation of the cinema vans was transferred to the Films Association from October 1930, and the figures for 1931–36 are the block grant to the Films Association, for which no breakdown of costs was given; the figure for 1936 is only to 30 September and the figure for 1937 is for 1 October 1936 to 31 December 1937.

ᵍ The figures for 1925–27, and £331 of the 1929 figure, are costs of the Policy Department.

ʰ These were included in the Principal Agent/General Director's Department up to 1932, after which they formed a separate Establishment Department.

ⁱ Nearly all of this was expenditure on by-elections, but in some years there was also an amount for the costs of Cabinet ministers' public meetings.

ʲ The annual summer Seaside Campaigns, 1925–28; the Trade Union Bill campaign, 1927 (£8,373); the Home and Empire campaign, 1930; the National Government propaganda campaign, 1934; and the 'special canvassers and observers campaigns', 1940.

ᵏ Includes grants to constituencies in Scotland up to 1933; thereafter the figure is for England and Wales only.

ˡ Includes grants to the Association of Conservative Clubs (1925–39, £550 p.a.; 1940, £450; 1941, £412; 1942–45, nil); to the National Conservative Musical Union (1927–39, varying amounts, generally in the range £200–325, apart from £521 in 1931; 1940, £25; 1941–45, £4–5); to the Northern Area Women's Advisory Council (1928, £750), and to the Young Conservatives Union (1928, £175; 1929, £300).

ᵐ Grants to the Philip Stott College (also known as the 'Conservative & Unionist Educational Institute'), 1925 and 1927–29 (two separate grants in 1928), and to the Bonar Law Memorial College (Ashridge), 1929–30.

ⁿ The cost of buildings insurance and National Insurance employer contributions are not shown separately in the balance sheets; the totals in this row also include employer contributions to the Agents' and Women Organisers' superannuation schemes for staff employed by Central Office, and in 1925–27 an amount granted to some staff in relief of income tax.

ᵒ Rent, rates, repairs and alterations, furniture and fittings (including an allowance for depreciation).

ᵖ The printing, carriage, and postage costs of publications is included in the Publicity Department figure.

ᵠ Grants to unspecified newspapers (1925, £100; 1928, £410); grants to the Norfolk Press syndicate (1928, £563; 1929, £770; 1930, £918; 1931, £777; 1932, £3,226); the Plymouth election petition (1929, £8,521); grants paid in 1933 to the Liberal National Council (£600) and the National Labour Committee (£400), in relation to the 1931 general election; National Tours Limited (1936, £14,000, amount written off described as 'special expenditure incurred by the company in the past'; 1939, amount written off, £3,227); dilapidation allowance for Palace Chambers (1942, £2,100); and wartime removal expenses and cost of blackout curtains (1942, £1,210).

ʳ This is shown as a credit amount of £1,757, as the block grant of £1,000 given in 1932 was more than offset by the receipt of £2,757 following the closure of the London Fund in June 1932.

Bibliography

The locations given for primary sources are where they were consulted; if a collection is known subsequently to have been deposited elsewhere, this is indicated afterwards in parentheses. Unless otherwise stated, books and pamphlets were published in London.

I PRIMARY SOURCES

1. Conservative Party records: national

National Union, Rules	CPA, Bodleian Library
National Union, Annual Conference	CPA, Bodleian Library
National Union, Central Council reports to Conference	CPA, Bodleian Library
National Union, Central Council	CPA, Bodleian Library
National Union, Executive Committee reports to Central Council	CPA, Bodleian Library
National Union, Executive Committee	CPA, Bodleian Library
National Union, General Purposes Committee	CPA, Bodleian Library
National Union, Central Women's National Advisory Council	CPA, Bodleian Library
National Union, Labour Committee	CPA, Bodleian Library
National Union, Standing Advisory Committee on Candidates	CPA, Bodleian Library
National Union, Annual Statements of Accounts	CPA, Bodleian Library
Conservative Central Office	CPA, Bodleian Library
Conservative Research Department	CPA, Bodleian Library
Treasurer's Department	CPA, Bodleian Library
Junior Imperial League	CPA, Bodleian Library
Young Britons	CPA, Bodleian Library
Bonar Law Memorial College (Ashridge)	CPA, Bodleian Library
Conservative Whips' Office	CPA, Bodleian Library
Conservative Private Members' '1922' Committee	CPA, Bodleian Library

2. Conservative Party records: regional

East Midlands Area	East Midlands Area (CPA, Bodleian Library)
Eastern Area	CPA, Bodleian Library
Essex & Middlesex Area	CPA, Bodleian Library
Metropolitan Area	CPA, Bodleian Library
North West Area	CPA, Bodleian Library
Northern Area	Northumberland RO
South East Area	CPA, Bodleian Library
Wales & Monmouthshire Area	Clwyd RO, Ruthin Branch
Wessex Area	CPA, Bodleian Library
West Midlands Area	West Midlands Area (CPA, Bodleian Library)
West Midlands Area (CRL)	Cadbury Research Library, University of Birmingham
Western Area	CPA, Bodleian Library
Yorkshire Area	Yorkshire Area (Leeds Archives)
Scottish Unionist Association	Scottish Central Office (NL of Scotland)

SUA, Eastern Division   Scottish Central Office (NL of Scotland)
SUA, Western Division   Scottish Central Office (NL of Scotland)
Scottish Unionist MPs' Committee   CPA, Bodleian Library
Cheshire Provincial Division   CPA, Bodleian Library
Cornwall Provincial Division   CPA, Bodleian Library
Durham Provincial Division   Durham RO
Glamorgan Provincial Division   NL of Wales
Lancashire Provincial Division   CPA, Bodleian Library
North Staffordshire Federation   CPA, Bodleian Library
Somerset Provincial Division   CPA, Bodleian Library
Sussex Provincial Division   East Grinstead CA

3. Conservative Party records: local
Details of constituency records can be found in S. Ball, *A Summary List of the Regional and Local Records of the Conservative Party 1867–1945*, which is available at the Conservative Party Archive, Bodleian Library, or on application to the author.

(a) City associations
Birmingham CA   Birmingham Central Library
Bradford CA   West Yorkshire Archive Service, Bradford
Bristol CA   Bristol RO
Glasgow CA   Scottish Central Office (NL of Scotland)
Leeds CA   West Yorkshire Archive Service, Leeds
Liverpool CA   Liverpool RO
Sheffield CA   Sheffield Central Library

(b) Constituency associations: southern England
Abingdon CA   at CA
Aldershot CA   at CA (Hampshire RO)
Ashford CA   at CA
Aylesbury   at CA
Bath CA   Bath & NE Somerset RO (1918–37) and at CA (1938–45)
Berkshire South CA   Berkshire RO
Bristol East CA   Bristol RO
Bristol South CA   Bristol RO
Bristol West CA   Bristol RO
Brixton CA   London School of Economics & Political Science Library
Camberwell North CA Southwark Local History Library
Camborne CA   Cornwall RO
Canterbury CA   at CA (later partially destroyed by fire in 1992)
Chelmsford CA   Essex RO
Chichester CA   West Sussex RO
Chippenham CA   at CA (Wiltshire & Swindon Archives)
City of London CA   Westminster City Library
Clapham CA   London School of Economics & Political Science Library
Cornwall North CA   Cornwall RO
Cornwall South-East CA Cornwall RO
Devizes CA   Wiltshire & Swindon Archives
Dorset East CA   Poole CA

Bibliography

Dorset West CA	Dorset RO
Ealing CA	London Metropolitan Archives
East Grinstead CA	at CA
Epsom CA	at CA (Surrey History Centre)
Essex West CA	Essex RO
Finchley CA	at CA (Barnet Archives)
Gravesend CA	Kent History & Library Centre
Guildford CA	Surrey History Centre
Hackney North CA	North East London Conservative Group
Hampshire East CA	Petersfield CA (Hampshire RO)
Hampshire North-West CA	CPA, Bodleian Library
Hampstead	at CA
Hastings & St Leonards CA	Hastings Museum
Hemel Hempstead CA	at CA
Hendon CA	CPA, Bodleian Library
Hertford CA	Hertfordshire Archives
Hitchin CA	at CA
Ilford CA	Redbridge Local Studies & Archives and at CA
Islington East CA	North East London Conservative Group
Kennington CA	London School of Economics & Political Science Library
Kensington South CA	at CA
Lewes CA	at CA
Lewisham West CA	at CA
Maidstone CA	Kent History & Library Centre
Norwood CA	Lambeth Archives
Oxford CA	at CA (Oxfordshire RO)
Oxfordshire North CA	Oxfordshire RO
Oxfordshire South CA	Oxfordshire RO
Penryn & Falmouth CA	Cornwall RO
Plymouth Drake CA	West Devon RO
Plymouth Sutton CA	West Devon RO
Putney CA	Wandsworth CA
Reigate CA	Surrey History Centre
Rochester & Chatham CA	at CA
Rye CA	at CA (East Sussex RO)
Salisbury CA	Wiltshire & Swindon Archives
Sevenoaks CA	at CA
Southampton CA	Southampton RO
St Albans CA	at CA (Hertfordshire Archives)
Streatham CA	Lambeth Archives
Surrey East CA	CPA, Bodleian Library
Torquay CA	at CA
Twickenham CA	at CA
Uxbridge CA	at CA
Watford CA	Hertfordshire Archives
Wells CA	at CA
Westminster St George's CA	Westminster City Library
Wiltshire West CA	Wiltshire & Swindon Archives
Wimbledon CA	Wandsworth CA

Winchester CA	Hampshire RO; branch records at Southampton RO
Wood Green CA	London Metropolitan Archives
Woolwich West CA	Greenwich Heritage Centre

(c) Constituency associations: Midlands & East Anglia

Bedford CA	Bedfordshire RO
Bewdley CA	Worcestershire RO
Birmingham Aston CA	Birmingham Central Library
Birmingham Edgbaston CA	Birmingham Central Library
Birmingham Erdington CA	Birmingham Central Library
Birmingham Handsworth CA	at CA
Birmingham Ladywood CA	Birmingham Central Library
Bosworth CA	Leicestershire RO
Burton CA	East Staffordshire CA
Cambridge CA	Cambridgeshire Archives
Cambridgeshire CA	South Cambridgeshire CA
Cannock CA	at CA
Cheltenham CA	Gloucestershire Archives
Cirencester & Tewkesbury CA	at CA (Gloucestershire Archives)
Derby CA	Derbyshire RO
Derbyshire South CA	Derbyshire RO
Derbyshire West CA	Derbyshire RO
Forest of Dean CA	Gloucestershire Archives
Gloucester CA	Gloucestershire Archives
Harborough CA	Leicestershire RO
Harwich CA	at CA
Herefordshire North CA	Herefordshire RO
Horncastle CA	Lincolnshire RO
Ilkeston CA	Derbyshire RO
Ipswich CA	Suffolk RO, Ipswich
King's Lynn CA	North West Norfolk CA
Leek CA	Staffordshire RO
Lincoln CA	at CA (Lincolnshire RO)*
Loughborough CA	Leicestershire RO
Louth CA	Lincolnshire RO
Ludlow CA	Shropshire RO
Melton CA	at CA
Mid-Bedfordshire CA	Bedfordshire RO
Newark CA	at CA
Norfolk East CA	Norfolk RO
Norfolk North CA	at CA (Norfolk RO)
Northampton CA	Northamptonshire RO
Norwich CA	at CA (Norfolk RO)
Nottingham South CA	Nottinghamshire RO
Oswestry CA	at CA
Peterborough CA	at CA
Rugby CA	at CA
Rushcliffe CA	Nottinghamshire RO
Rutland & Stamford CA	at CA

Shrewsbury CA	at CA
Stafford CA	Staffordshire RO
Stone CA	Staffordshire RO
Stroud CA	Gloucestershire Archives
Tamworth CA	Warwickshire RO
Walsall CA	at CA (Walsall Local History Centre)
Warwick & Leamington CA	Warwickshire RO
Wolverhampton Bilston CA	Wolverhampton Archives
Wolverhampton West CA	Wolverhampton Archives
Worcester CA	at CA (Worcestershire RO)

* The records for 1939–42, seen at the CA, were not included in the deposit at Lincolnshire RO.

(d) Constituency associations: northern England

Accrington CA	Manchester University Library
Barkston Ash CA	West Yorkshire Archive Service, Leeds
Berwick & Alnwick CA	Northumberland RO
Blackpool CA	Lancashire RO
Bolton CA	at CA (Bolton Archives)
Bradford Central CA	West Yorkshire Archive Service, Bradford
Bradford East CA	West Yorkshire Archive Service, Bradford
Bradford North CA	West Yorkshire Archive Service, Bradford
Bradford South CA	West Yorkshire Archive Service, Bradford
Bury CA	Bury Archives Service
Clitheroe CA	Lancashire RO
Darlington CA	at CA
Darwen CA	Lancashire RO
Fylde CA	Lancashire RO
Halifax CA	at CA
Hartlepool CA	Durham RO
Hexham CA	at CA
Holderness CA	Beverley CA
Howdenshire CA	Beverley CA
Keighley CA	West Yorkshire Archive Service, Bradford
Knutsford CA	Tatton CA
Lancaster CA	at CA
Leeds West CA	West Yorkshire Archive Service, Leeds
Lonsdale CA	at CA (Cumbria RO)
Middlesbrough CA	Teeside Thornaby CA
Middleton & Prestwich CA	Lancashire RO
Newcastle West CA	Tyne & Wear RO
Northwich CA	Cheshire RO
Penistone CA	at CA
Ripon CA	Harrogate CA
Rochdale CA	at CA
Rother Valley CA	South Yorkshire Conservative Federation
Rotherham CA	South Yorkshire Conservative Federation
Rothwell CA	Wakefield CA
Sheffield Brightside CA	Sheffield Central Library

Sheffield Central CA	Sheffield Central Library
Sheffield Ecclesall CA	Sheffield Central Library
Sheffield Park CA	Sheffield Central Library
Skipton CA	at CA
Southport CA	at CA
Sowerby CA	at CA (West Yorkshire Archive Service, Calderdale)
Stockton CA	Durham RO
Thirsk & Malton CA	at CA
Tynemouth CA	Local Studies Centre, North Shields
Wakefield CA	at CA
Wansbeck CA	Tyne & Wear RO
Waterloo CA	Lancashire RO
Wirral CA	at CA
York CA	York City Archives

(e) Constituency associations: Wales & Monmouthshire

Brecon & Radnor CA	at CA
Cardiff Central CA	NL of Wales
Cardiff South CA	NL of Wales
Denbighshire CA	Clwyd RO, Ruthin Branch
Flintshire CA	Clwyd RO, Hawarden Branch
Llandaff & Barry CA	NL of Wales
Merionethshire CA	Gwynedd Archives, Dolgellau Branch
Monmouthshire CA	NL of Wales
Newport & Monmouth CA	NL of Wales
Pembrokeshire CA	Pembrokeshire RO
Wrexham CA	NL of Wales

(f) Constituency associations: Scotland

Aberdeen South CA	at CA
Argyll CA	at CA
Ayr Burghs CA	at CA (Ayrshire Archives)
Ayrshire South CA	Ayrshire Archives
Berwickshire & East Lothian CA	East Lothian CA
Bute & North Ayrshire CA	at CA (Ayrshire Archives)
Dumfriesshire CA	at CA
Dunbartonshire CA	NL of Scotland
Dundee CA	Dundee University Archives
Edinburgh East CA	Edinburgh South CA
Edinburgh North CA	at CA (Edinburgh Archives)
Edinburgh South CA	NL of Scotland
Edinburgh West CA	at CA
Glasgow Bridgeton CA	Scottish Central Office*
Glasgow Maryhill CA	Scottish Central Office (NL of Scotland)
Glasgow Pollok CA	Scottish Central Office*
Inverness CA	at CA
Kilmarnock CA	North Cunninghame CA & NL of Scotland
Kincardine & West Aberdeenshire CA	Kincardine & Deeside CA

Bibliography

Kinross & West Perthshire CA	Tayside North CA (Perth & Kinross Archives)
Kirkcaldy Burghs CA	St Andrews University Library
Moray & Nairn CA	Moray & West Banff CA
Perth CA	Perth & Kinross Archives at CA
Renfrewshire West CA	
Scottish Universities CA	Glasgow University Library
Stirling & Falkirk Burghs CA	Falkirk CA (Falkirk Archives)
Stirlingshire West CA	Stirling CA

* These records, seen in 1983, were not included in the deposit at the NL of Scotland.

4. Conservative Party records: ancillary organizations

East Midlands Area Agents	Derbyshire RO (in Derbyshire West CA)
East Midlands Area Women Organisers	CPA, Bodleian Library
Kent Conservative Agents' Union	Canterbury CA
Metropolitan Area Agents (1918–24, 1938–45)	London School of Economics & Political Science Library
Metropolitan Area Agents (1925–37)	CPA, Bodleian Library
National Association of Women Organisers	CPA, Bodleian Library
National Society of Conservative Agents	Westminster City Library
North West Area Women Organisers	CPA, Bodleian Library
South East Area Agents	Surrey History Centre (in Reigate CA)
SUA Organising Secretaries South West Area	Ayr Burghs CA
Wales & Monmouthshire Area Women Organisers	CPA, Bodleian Library
Wessex Area Agents	CPA, Bodleian Library
Wessex Area Women Organisers	CPA, Bodleian Library
West Midlands Area Women Organisers	CPA, Bodleian Library

5. Conservative Party records: publications

National Union, pamphlets and leaflets	CPA, Bodleian Library
Ashridge Journal	Conservative Central Office (CPA, Bodleian Library)
Conservative Agents' Journal	Conservative Central Office (CPA, Bodleian Library)
Conservative & Unionist Pocket Book	British Library
Daily Notes (during general elections)	CPA, Bodleian Library
Election Notes (1929, 1931, 1935)	CPA, Bodleian Library
Gleanings and Memoranda	Conservative Central Office (CPA, Bodleian Library)
Handbook for Juvenile Organisations (1925)	CPA, Bodleian Library
Handbook for Organisers and Workers (1925)	CPA, Bodleian Library
Handbook for Organisers and Workers (n.d. [1933])	CPA, Bodleian Library
Handbook for Women Organisers and Workers (1925)	CPA, Bodleian Library
Handbook for Women Organisers and Workers (1928)	CPA, Bodleian Library
Handbook for Young Britons: Officers and Helpers (1936)	CPA, Bodleian Library
Handbook on Constituency Organisation (1925)	CPA, Bodleian Library
Handbook on Constituency Organisation (1933)	CPA, Bodleian Library
Handbook on Young Britons (1931)	CPA, Bodleian Library

Hints for Speakers	Conservative Central Office (CPA, Bodleian Library)
Home and Empire	Conservative Central Office
Home and Politics	CPA, Bodleian Library
Junior Imperial League Gazette	CPA, Bodleian Library
Model Rules for Associations, Branches and Sections (1933)	CPA, Bodleian Library
Notes for Conservative Canvassers & Workers	CPA, Bodleian Library
Notes for Speakers and Workers	Conservative Central Office (CPA, Bodleian Library)
Politics in Review	CPA, Bodleian Library
The Campaign Guide (1922)	British Library
The Elector	CPA, Bodleian Library; also at British Library
The Imp	CPA, Bodleian Library
The Man in the Street	Conservative Central Office (CPA, Bodleian Library)
The Onlooker	British Library
The Popular View	Conservative Central Office (CPA, Bodleian Library)
Torchbearer	CPA, Bodleian Library
Unionist Central Office Parliamentary Election Manual (1921)	CPA, Bodleian Library
Young Britons' Organisers Manual (c.1937)	Bolton CA (Bolton Archives)

6. Private papers: Conservative Leaders, Cabinet ministers, and Party Chairmen

Amery MSS	J. Amery, London (Churchill College, Cambridge)
Ashley MSS	Southampton University Library
Austen Chamberlain MSS	Cadbury Research Library, University of Birmingham
Avon MSS	Cadbury Research Library, University of Birmingham
Baldwin MSS	Cambridge University Library
Baldwin MSS (Worcs RO)	Worcestershire Record Office
Balfour MSS	Western MSS Collections, British Library
Balfour MSS (Whittingehame)	National Records of Scotland
Bayford MSS	Conservative Central Office (Bodleian Library)
Birkenhead MSS	Asia, Pacific & Africa Collections, British Library
Bonar Law MSS	Parliamentary Archives
Butler MSS	Trinity College, Cambridge
Butler MSS (CPA)	CPA, Bodleian Library
Cave MSS	Western MSS Collections, British Library
Cecil of Chelwood MSS	Western MSS Collections, British Library
Churchill MSS	Churchill College, Cambridge
Curzon MSS	Asia, Pacific & Africa Collections, British Library
Davidson MSS	Parliamentary Archives
Davidson MSS (Bodleian)	Bodleian Library
Derby MSS	Liverpool RO
Devonshire MSS	Chatsworth House, Derbyshire
Duff Cooper MSS	Churchill College, Cambridge
Elliot MSS	NL of Scotland
Gilmour MSS	National Records of Scotland
Griffith-Boscawen MSS	Bodleian Library

Hailsham (1st Viscount) MSS	Churchill College, Cambridge
Halifax MSS	Asia, Pacific & Africa Collections, British Library
Halifax MSS (Borthwick)	Borthwick Institute, York
Inskip MSS	Churchill College, Cambridge
Joynson-Hicks MSS	East Sussex RO
Kennet MSS	Cambridge University Library
Lee of Fareham MSS	Courtauld Institute of Art
Lloyd of Dolobran MSS	Churchill College, Cambridge
Londonderry MSS	Durham RO
Long MSS	Western MSS Collections, British Library
Long MSS (WSA)	Wiltshire & Swindon Archives
Macmillan MSS	Bodleian Library
Margesson MSS	Churchill College, Cambridge
Milner MSS	Bodleian Library
Neville Chamberlain MSS	Cadbury Research Library, University of Birmingham
Ormsby-Gore (Brogyntyn) MSS	NL of Wales
Peel MSS	Asia, Pacific & Africa Collections, British Library
Salisbury MSS	Hatfield House, Hatfield
Stanhope MSS	Kent History & Library Centre
Steel-Maitland MSS	National Records of Scotland
Stonehaven MSS	NL of Australia
Swinton MSS	Churchill College, Cambridge
Templewood MSS	Cambridge University Library
Templewood MSS (BL)	Asia, Pacific & Africa Collections, British Library
Wallace MSS	Bodleian Library
Willink MSS	Churchill College, Cambridge
Winterton MSS	Bodleian Library
Worthington-Evans MSS	Bodleian Library
Zetland MSS	Asia, Pacific & Africa Collections, British Library

7. Private papers: Conservative junior ministers, backbench MPs, and peers

Adams MSS	London School of Economics & Political Science Library
Astor MSS	Reading University Library
Atholl MSS	Blair Atholl
Balfour of Inchrye MSS	Parliamentary Archives
Beamish (Chelwood) MSS	East Sussex RO
Beamish MSS	Churchill College, Cambridge
Boothby MSS	NL of Scotland
Bower MSS	Churchill College, Cambridge
Brabourne MSS	Asia, Pacific & Africa Collections, British Library
Brittain MSS	London School of Economics & Political Science Library
Buchan MSS	NL of Scotland
Bull MSS	Churchill College, Cambridge
Bull MSS (PA)	Parliamentary Archives
Cilcennin MSS	Carmarthenshire Archive Service
Coates MSS	Parliamentary Archives
Conway MSS	Cambridge University Library
Croft MSS	Churchill College, Cambridge
Crookshank MSS	Bodleian Library

Dynevor (8th Baron) MSS	NL of Wales
Elibank (2nd Viscount) MSS	National Records of Scotland
Emrys-Evans MSS	Western MSS Collections, British Library
Glyn MSS	Berkshire RO
Gower MSS	Tunbridge Wells Library
Hailes MSS	Churchill College, Cambridge
Hailsham (2nd Viscount) MSS	Churchill College, Cambridge
Hall MSS	Churchill College, Cambridge
Hammersley MSS	Manchester Central Library
Hannon MSS	Parliamentary Archives
Hanworth MSS	Bodleian Library
Harvie-Watt MSS	Churchill College, Cambridge
Haslam MSS	Lincoln RO
Headlam MSS	Durham RO
Heneage MSS	Lincoln RO
Horsbrugh MSS	Churchill College, Cambridge
James MSS	Churchill College, Cambridge
Kerr MSS	Glasgow University Archives
Keyes MSS	Western MSS Collections, British Library
Kilmuir MSS	Churchill College, Cambridge
Lennox-Boyd MSS	Bodleian Library
Locker-Lampson MSS	Norfolk RO
Lytton MSS	Asia, Pacific & Africa Collections, British Library
Mancroft MSS	Churchill College, Cambridge
Marriott MSS	York RO
Moore-Brabazon MSS	Royal Air Force Museum, Hendon
Morrison-Bell MSS	Parliamentary Archives
Paget MSS	Leicestershire RO
Peto MSS	J. Peto, Bealings House, Woodbridge, Suffolk
Scott MSS	Warwick University Library
Selborne (2nd Earl) MSS	Bodleian Library
Selborne (2nd Earl) MSS (HRO)	Hampshire RO
Sherfield (Makins) MSS	Bodleian Library
Smithers MSS	Sir D. Smithers, Ringfield, Knockholt, Kent
Somervell MSS	Bodleian Library
Southby MSS	Bodleian Library
Spears MSS	Churchill College, Cambridge
Wakehurst MSS	Parliamentary Archives
Ward MSS	Bodleian Library
Williams MSS	Bodleian Library
Wise MSS	London School of Economics & Political Science Library
Wolmer (3rd Earl Selborne) MSS	Bodleian Library
York MSS	E. York, Hutton Wandesley Hall, Long Marston, Yorkshire

8. Private papers: Conservative Party officials and office-holders
Ball MSS	Bodleian Library
Cohen MSS	Conservative Central Office (CPA, Bodleian Library)

Cranna MSS	NL of Scotland
Emmet MSS	Bodleian Library
Fraser MSS	Bodleian Library
Fraser MSS (PA)	Parliamentary Archives

9. Private papers: other collections

Beaverbrook MSS	Parliamentary Archives
Blumenfeld MSS	Parliamentary Archives
Dawson MSS	Bodleian Library
Dawson MSS (Times)	Times Newspapers Archives
Empire Industries Association MSS	Warwick University Library
Gwynne MSS	Bodleian Library
Hewins MSS	Sheffield University Library
Indian Empire Society (Stuart) MSS	Bodleian Library
Lockhart MSS	Parliamentary Archives
MacDonald MSS	Public Records Office
Mann MSS	Bodleian Library
Samuel MSS	Parliamentary Archives
Simon MSS	Bodleian Library
Stopford MSS	Asia, Pacific & Africa Collections, British Library
Strachey MSS	Parliamentary Archives
Thompson (UBI) MSS	Asia, Pacific & Africa Collections, British Library
Wedgwood Questionnaire MSS	History of Parliament
Wrench MSS	Western MSS Collections, British Library

10. Editions of contemporary sources

Ball, S. [Stuart] (ed.), *Parliament and Politics in the Age of Baldwin and MacDonald: The Headlam Diaries 1923–1935* (1992).

Ball, S. (ed.), *Parliament and Politics in the Age of Churchill and Attlee: The Headlam Diaries 1935–1951* (Cambridge, 1999).

Barnes, J. and Nicholson, D. (eds.), *The Leo Amery Diaries*, vol. 1: *1899–1929* (1980).

Barnes, J. and Nicholson, D. (eds.), *The Empire at Bay—The Leo Amery Diaries*, vol. 2: *1929–1945* (1988).

Boyce, D. G. (ed.), *The Crisis of British Unionism: The Domestic Political Papers of the 2nd Earl of Selborne 1885–1922* (1987).

Clark, A. (ed.), *A Good Innings: The Private Papers of Viscount Lee of Fareham* (1974).

Cockett, R. B. (ed.), *My Dear Max: The Letters of Brendan Bracken to Lord Beaverbrook 1925–1958* (1990).

Colville, J. (ed.), *The Fringes of Power: Downing Street Diaries 1939–1955* (1985).

Gilbert, M. (ed.), *Winston S. Churchill*, vol. 5: *Companion Documents, Part 1 (1924–1929)* (1979).

Gilbert, M. (ed.), *Winston S. Churchill*, vol. 5: *Companion Documents, Part 2 (1929–1935)* (1981).

Gilbert, M. (ed.), *Winston S. Churchill*, vol. 5: *Companion Documents, Part 3 (1935–1939)* (1982).

Gilbert, M. (ed.), *The Churchill War Papers*, vol. 1: *At the Admiralty, September 1939–May 1940* (1993).

Gilbert, M. (ed.), *The Churchill War Papers*, vol. 2: *Never Surrender, May–December 1940* (1995).

Gilbert, M. (ed.), *The Churchill War Papers*, vol. 3: *The Ever-Widening War, 1941* (2000).
Hart-Davis, D. (ed.), *In Royal Service: The Letters and Journals of Sir Alan Lascelles*, vol. 2: *1920–1936* (1989).
Hart-Davis, D. (ed.), *King's Counsellor: Abdication and War—The Diaries of Sir Alan Lascelles* (2006).
James, R. R. (ed.), *Chips: The Diaries of Sir Henry Channon* (1967).
James, R. R. (ed.), *Memoirs of a Conservative: J.C.C. Davidson's Memoirs and Papers 1910–1937* (1969).
Jones, T., *A Diary with Letters 1931–1950* (1954).
Mitchell, A. (ed.), *Election '45: Reflections on the Revolution in Britain* (1995).
Nicolson, N. (ed.), *Harold Nicolson: Diaries and Letters 1930–1939* (1966).
Nicolson, N. (ed.), *Harold Nicolson: Diaries and Letters 1939–1945* (1967).
Norwich, J. J. (ed.), *The Duff Cooper Diaries 1915–1951* (2005).
Ramsden, J. (ed.), *Real Old Tory Politics: The Political Diaries of Sir Robert Sanders, Lord Bayford: 1910–1935* (1984).
Self, R. (ed.), *The Austen Chamberlain Diary Letters* (Cambridge, 1995).
Self, R. (ed.), *The Neville Chamberlain Diary Letters*, vol. 1: *The Making of a Politician 1915–1920* (Aldershot, 2000).
Self, R. (ed.), *The Neville Chamberlain Diary Letters*, vol. 2: *The Reform Years 1921–1927* (Aldershot, 2000).
Self, R. (ed.), *The Neville Chamberlain Diary Letters*, vol. 3: *The Heir Apparent 1928–1933* (Aldershot, 2002).
Self, R. (ed.), *The Neville Chamberlain Diary Letters*, vol. 4: *The Downing Street Years 1934–1940* (Aldershot, 2005).
Smart, N. (ed.), *The Diaries and Letters of Robert Bernays 1932–1939* (Lampeter, 1996).
Stuart, C., (ed.), *The Reith Diaries* (1975).
Vincent, J. (ed.), *The Crawford Papers* (Manchester, 1984).
Williamson, P. (ed.), *The Modernisation of Conservative Politics: The Diaries and Letters of William Bridgeman 1904–1935* (1988).
Williamson, P. and Baldwin, E. (eds.), *Baldwin Papers: A Conservative Statesman 1908–1947* (Cambridge, 2004).
Young, K. (ed.), *The Diaries of Sir Robert Bruce Lockhart*, vol. 1: *1915–1938* (1973).
Young, K. (ed.), *The Diaries of Sir Robert Bruce Lockhart*, vol. 2: *1939–1965* (1980).

11. Contemporary publications
'A Gentleman with a Duster' [H. Begbie, pseud.], *The Conservative Mind* (1925).
'A Modern Conservative' [C. Alport, pseud.], *A National Faith* (1938).
Adam, H. M., *The Fallacies of Socialism* (1926).
Amery, L. S., *The Forward View* (1935).
Baldwin, S., *Looking Ahead: A Restatement of Unionist Principles and Aims* (1924).
Baldwin, S., *On England* (1926).
Baldwin, S., *Our Inheritance* (1928).
Baldwin, S., *This Torch of Freedom* (1935).
Baldwin, S., *Service of our Lives* (1937).
Baldwin, S., *An Interpreter of England* (1939).
Banks, Sir R. M., *The Conservative Outlook* (1929).
Beaverbrook, Lord, *My Case for Empire Free Trade* (1930).
Bentinck, H., *Tory Democracy* (1918).

Boothby, R., Loder, G., Macmillan, H., and Stanley, O., *Industry and the State: A Conservative View* (1927).
Braine, B., *Conservatism and Youth: As a Young Man Sees It* (1939).
Bryant, A., *The Spirit of Conservatism* (1929).
Bryant, A., *The National Character* (1934).
Bryant, A., *Humanity in Politics* (1938).
Cartland, R., *The Common Problem* (1943).
Cecil, Lord H., *Conservatism* (1912).
Cecil, Lord H., *Conservative Ideals* (1923).
Cook, E. T. (ed.), *Conservatism and the Future* (1935).
Cooper, A. D., *The Conservative Point of View* (1926).
Crichton, D. M. (ed.), *Tory Oxford: Essays in University Conservatism* (1935).
Crisp, D. (ed.), *The Rebirth of Conservatism* (1931).
Drucker, P. F., *The Future of Industrial Man: A Conservative Approach* (1943).
Elliot, W., *Toryism and the Twentieth Century* (1927).
Feiling, K., *Toryism: A Political Dialogue* (1913).
Feiling, K., *What is Conservatism?* (1930).
'Haxey, S.' [pseud.], *Tory M.P.* (1939).
Hearnshaw, F. J. C., *Conservatism in England* (1933).
Hinchingbrooke, Viscount, *Full Speed Ahead! Essays in Tory Reform* (1944).
Hogg, Q., *The Times We Live In* (1944).
Hogg, Q., *The Left is Never Right* (1945).
Hollis, C., *Quality or Equality?* (1944).
Jenner, R. V., *Will Conservatism Survive?* (1944).
Jones, A., *Right and Left* (1944).
Lloyd, Sir G. and Wood, E., *The Great Opportunity* (1918).
Loftus, P., *The Creed of a Tory* (1926).
Ludovici, A. M., *A Defence of Conservatism* (1926).
Lymington, Viscount, *Ich Dien: The Tory Path* (1931).
Macmillan, H., *The Middle Way* (1938).
Northam, R., *Conservatism: The Only Way* (1939).
Parker, A. R., Cooke, R. G., and Green, F. (eds.), *A Declaration of Tory Principles* (Cambridge, 1929).
Percy, Lord E., *Democracy on Trial* (1931).
Pickthorn, K., *Principles and Prejudices* (1943).
Riley, E. S., *Our Cause: A Handbook of Conservatism* (Derby and London, 1939).
Salisbury, Marquess of, *Post-War Conservative Policy* (1942).
Scottish Unionist Whip's Office, *The Choice: Unionist Principles versus Socialism* (Edinburgh, 1936).
Sellon, H., *Whither, England? The Letters of a Conservative* (1932).
Skelton, N., *Constructive Conservatism* (1924).
Smithers, W., *Conservative Principles* (Sidcup, 1933).
Smithers, W., *Socialism Offers Slavery* (1945).
Stelling, D., *Why I Am a Conservative* (1943).
Tory Reform Committee, *Forward by the Right* (1943).
Tory Reform Committee, *What is a Tory?* (1945).
Wolfe, A. B., *Conservatism, Radicalism and Scientific Method* (New York, 1923).
Wood, E., *Conservative Beliefs* (1924).

12. Memoirs: Conservative Leaders, Cabinet ministers, and Chief Whips
Amery, L. S., *My Political Life*, vol. 2: *War and Peace 1914–1929* (1953).
Amery, L. S., *My Political Life*, vol. 3: *The Unforgiving Years 1929–1940* (1955).
Avon, Earl of, *The Eden Memoirs*, vol. 1: *Facing the Dictators* (1962).
Butler, Lord, *The Art of the Possible* (1971).
Cecil of Chelwood, Lord, *All the Way* (1949).
Chamberlain, Sir A., *Down the Years* (1935).
Churchill, W. S., *The Second World War*, vol. 1: *The Gathering Storm* (1948).
Churchill, W. S., *The Second World War*, vol. 2: *Their Finest Hour* (1949).
Cooper, A. D., *Old Men Forget* (1953).
Geddes, Lord, *The Forging of a Family* (1952).
Griffith-Boscawen, Sir A., *Memories* (1925).
Halifax, Earl of, *Fulness of Days* (1957).
Londonderry, Lady, *Retrospect* (1938).
Londonderry, Lord, *Wings of Destiny* (1943).
Long, Lord, *Memories* (1923).
Lyttleton, O., *The Memoirs of Lord Chandos* (1962).
Macmillan, H., *Winds of Change 1914–1939* (1966).
Macmillan, H., *The Blast of War 1939–1945* (1967).
Midleton, Earl of, *Records and Reactions 1856–1939* (1939).
Onslow, Earl of, *Sixty-Three Years* (1944).
Percy of Newcastle, Lord, *Some Memories* (1958).
Stuart of Findhorn, Lord, *Within the Fringe* (1967).
Swinton, Lord, *I Remember* (n.d. [1948]).
Swinton, Lord, *Sixty Years of Power* (1966).
Templewood, Viscount, *Nine Troubled Years* (1954).
Templewood, Viscount, *Empire of the Air* (1957).
Winterton, Earl, *Orders of the Day* (1953).
Zetland, Lord, *Essayez* (1957).

13. Memoirs: Conservative junior ministers and backbench MPs
Agg-Gardner, Sir J., *Some Parliamentary Recollections* (1927).
Balfour, H., *An Airman Marches* (1933).
Balfour, H., *Wings over Westminster* (1973).
Boothby, R., *I Fight to Live* (1947).
Brittain, Sir H., *Happy Pilgrimage* (1949).
Buchan, J., *Memory Hold-the-Door* (1940).
Cazalet-Keir, T., *From the Wings: An Autobiography* (1967).
Cockerill, G. K., *What Fools We Were* (1944).
Cohen, J. B., *Count Your Blessings* (1956).
Conway, Sir M., *Episodes in a Varied Life* (1932).
Critchley, A. C., *Critch! The Memoirs of Brigadier-General A. C. Critchley* (1961).
Croft, Lord, *My Life of Strife* (1949).
De Chair, S., *Morning Glory* (1989).
De Chair, S., *Buried Pleasure* (1995).
Donner, P., *Crusade* (1984).
Elibank, Lord, *A Man's Life* (1934).
Gaunt, Sir G., *The Yield of the Years* (1940).

Hailsham, Lord, *The Door Wherein I Went* (1975).
Hailsham, Lord, *A Sparrow's Flight* (1990).
Hales, H. K., *The Road to Westminster and My Impressions of Parliament* (n.d. [1936]).
Harvie-Watt, G. S., *Most of My Life* (1980).
Hemingford, Lord, *Backbencher and Chairman* (1946).
Home, Lord, *The Way the Wind Blows* (1976).
Hopkinson, Sir A., *Penultima* (1930).
Hume-Williams, Sir E., *The World, the House, and the Bar* (1930).
Hurst, Sir G. B., *Closed Chapters* (Manchester, 1942).
Kilmuir, Earl of, *Political Adventure: The Memoirs of the Earl of Kilmuir* (1964).
Macnamara, J. R. J., *The Whistle Blows* (1938).
Marriott, Sir J. A. R., *Memories of Four Score Years* (1946).
Mitchell, Sir H. P., *In My Stride* (1951).
Mitchell, Sir H. P., *The Spice of Life* (1974).
Moore-Brabazon, J. T. C., *The Brabazon Story* (1956).
Moss, H. J., *Windjammer to Westminster* (1941).
Mott-Radclyffe, Sir C., *Foreign Body in the Eye* (1975).
Murchison, Sir K., *Family Notes and Reminiscences* (1940).
Oman, Sir C., *Things I Have Seen* (1933).
Ponsonby, C., *Ponsonby Remembers* (Oxford, 1965).
Portsmouth, Earl of, *A Knot of Roots* (1965).
Rentoul, Sir G., *Sometimes I Think* (n.d. [1940]).
Rentoul, Sir G., *This is My Case* (1944).
Richardson, Sir P., *It Happened to Me* (1952).
Sassoon, Sir P., *The Third Route* (1929).
Smyth, Sir J., *Only Enemy* (1959).
Smyth, Sir J., *Milestones* (1979).
Stewart, G., *Letters of a Back Bencher to His Son 1908–1923* (Liverpool, 1923).
Sykes, Sir F., *From Many Angles* (1942).
Thornton-Kemsley, C., *Through Winds and Tides* (Montrose, 1974).
Tree, R., *When the Moon was High* (1975).
Williams, Sir H., *Politics, Grave and Gay* (1949).
Wilson, Sir A., *Walks and Talks: The Diary of a Member of Parliament in 1933–1934* (1934).
Wilson, Sir A., *Walks and Talks Abroad: The Diary of a Member of Parliament in 1934–1936* (1936).

13. Memoirs: others
Beaverbrook, Lord, *Men and Power 1917–1918* (1956).
Bull, P., *Bulls in the Meadows* (1957).
Johnston, J., *A Hundred Commoners* (1931).
Leggett [previously Margesson], F., *Late and Soon: The Transatlantic Story of a Marriage* (Boston, 1968).
Profumo, D., *Bringing the House Down: A Family Memoir* (2006).
Shakespeare, Sir G., *Let Candles be Brought In* (1949).
Simon, Viscount, *Retrospect* (1952).
'Watchman' [V. Adams, pseud.], *Right Honourable Gentlemen* (1939).
Woolton, Lord, *The Memoirs of the Rt. Hon. the Earl of Woolton* (1959).

14. Reference

Butler, D. and Butler, G. (eds.), *Twentieth-Century British Political Facts* (2000).
Catholic Directory.
Craig, F. W. S. (ed.), *British Parliamentary Election Results 1918–1949* (2nd edn, 1977).
Crowson, N. J. (ed.), *The Longman Companion to the Conservative Party since 1830* (2001).
Davies, S. and Morley, B. (eds.), *County Borough Elections in England and Wales 1919–1938* (3 vols, 1999, 2000, 2006).
Dictionary of National Biography.
Gallup, G. (ed.), *The Gallup International Public Opinion Polls: Great Britain, 1937–1975*, vol. 1: *1937–1964* (New York, 1976).
Incorporated Society of British Advertisers, *The Readership of Newspapers and Periodicals in Great Britain 1936* (1937).
Kinnear, M., *The British Voter: An Atlas and Survey since 1885* (2nd edn, 1981).
Oxford Dictionary of National Biography.
Stenton, M. and Lees, S. (eds.), *Who's Who of British Members of Parliament*, vols 3 and 4 (Brighton, 1979 and 1981).
The Times Guide to the House of Commons.
Walding, T. (ed.), *Who's Who in the New Parliament* (1922).
Who was Who.

II SECONDARY SOURCES

1. The Conservative Party and Conservatism

Aughey, A., Jones, G., and Riches, W. T. M., *The Conservative Political Tradition in Britain and the United States* (1992).
Ball, S. [Stuart], 'The Conservative Party and the formation of the National Government: August 1931', *Historical Journal*, 29 (1986), 159–82.
Ball, S., 'Failure of an opposition? The Conservative Party in parliament 1929–1931', *Parliamentary History*, 5 (1986), 83–98.
Ball, S., *Baldwin and the Conservative Party: The Crisis of 1929–1931* (New Haven and London, 1988).
Ball, S., 'The 1922 Committee: The formative years 1922–1945', *Parliamentary History*, 9 (1990), 129–57.
Ball, S., *The Conservative Party and British Politics 1902–1951* (Harlow, 1995).
Ball, S., 'National politics and local history: The regional and local archives of the Conservative Party 1867–1945', *Archives*, 22/94 (1996), 27–59.
Ball, S., 'The Conservatives in opposition, 1906–1979: A comparative analysis', in M. Garnett and P. Lynch (eds.), *The Conservatives in Crisis* (Manchester, 2003), 7–28.
Ball, S., 'The Conservative Party, the role of the state and the politics of protection, c.1918–1932', *History*, 96/323 (2011), 280–303.
Ball, S., *Dole Queues and Demons: British Election Posters from the Conservative Party Archive* (Oxford, 2011).
Ball, S., 'The legacy of Coalition: Fear and loathing in Conservative politics 1922–1931', *Contemporary British History*, 25/1 (2011), 65–82.
Ball, S. and Holliday, I. (eds.), *Mass Conservatism: The Conservatives and the Public since the 1880s* (2002).

Ball, S. and Seldon, A. (eds.), *Recovering Power: The Conservatives in Opposition since 1867* (Basingstoke, 2005).

Beichman, A., 'Hugger-mugger in Old Queen Street: The origins of the Conservative Research Department', *Journal of Contemporary History*, 13 (1978), 671–88.

Bennett, R., 'The Conservative tradition of thought', in N. Nugent and R. King (eds.), *The British Right: Conservative and Right Wing Politics in Britain* (Farnborough, 1977), 11–25.

Bentley, M., 'Liberal Toryism in the twentieth century', *Royal Historical Society, Transactions*, 6th ser., 4 (1994), 177–201.

Berthezène, C., 'Creating Conservative Fabians: The Conservative Party, political education and the founding of Ashridge College', *Past & Present*, 182 (2004), 211–40.

Berthezène, C., 'Ashridge College, 1929–1954: A glimpse at the archive of a Conservative intellectual project', *Contemporary British History*, 19/1 (2005), 79–93.

Blake, R., *A Century of Achievement: An Illustrated Record of the National Union of Conservative and Unionist Associations 1867–1967* (1967).

Blake, R., *The Conservative Party from Peel to Churchill* (1970).

Bridge, C., 'Conservatism and Indian reform 1929–1939', *Journal of Imperial and Commonwealth History*, 4 (1975–76), 176–93.

Bridge, C., *Holding India to the Empire: The British Conservative Party and the 1935 Constitution* (New Delhi, 1986).

Butler, D. and Pinto-Duschinsky, M., 'The Conservative elite 1918–1978: Does un-representativeness matter?', in Z. Layton-Henry (ed.), *Conservative Party Politics* (1980), 186–209.

Butler, Lord (ed.), *The Conservatives: A History from their Origins to 1965* (1977).

Campbell, B., *The Iron Ladies: Why Do Women Vote Tory?* (1987).

Carr, R., 'Veterans of the First World War and Conservative anti-appeasement', *20th Century British History*, 22/1 (2011), 28–51.

Charmley, J., *A History of Conservative Politics 1900–1996* (Basingstoke, 1996).

Clark, A., *The Tories: Conservatives and the Nation State 1922–1997* (1998).

Close, D. H., 'Conservatives and Coalition after the First World War', *Journal of Modern History*, 45 (1973), 240–60.

Close, D. H., 'The growth of backbench organisations in the Conservative Party', *Parliamentary Affairs*, 27 (1974), 371–83.

Close, D. H., 'The collapse of resistance to democracy: Conservatives, adult suffrage, and Second Chamber reform 1911–1928', *Historical Journal*, 20 (1977), 893–918.

Coleman, B., 'The Conservative Party and the frustration of the extreme right', in A. Thorpe (ed.), *The Failure of Political Extremism in Inter-war Britain* (Exeter, 1989), 49–66.

Cooke, A. (ed.), *Tory Policy-Making: The Conservative Research Department 1929–2009* (Eastbourne, 2009).

Cooke, A., *A Gift from the Churchills: The Primrose League 1883–2004* (2010).

Cragoe, M., 'Conservatives, "Englishness" and "civic nationalism" between the wars', in D. Tanner (ed.), *Debating Nationhood and Government in Britain 1885–1939* (Manchester, 2006), 192–210.

Cross, J. A., 'The withdrawal of the Conservative Party whip', *Parliamentary Affairs*, 21 (1967–68), 166–75.

Crowson, N. J., 'The British Conservative Party and the Jews in the late 1930s', *Patterns of Prejudice*, 29/2–3 (1995), 15–32.

Crowson, N. J., 'Conservative parliamentary dissent over foreign policy during the premiership of Neville Chamberlain: Myth or reality?', *Parliamentary History*, 14/3 (1995), 315–36.

Crowson, N. J., 'The Conservative Party and the call for national service 1937–1939: Compulsion versus voluntarism', *Contemporary Record*, 9/3 (1995), 507–28.

Crowson, N. J., *Facing Fascism: The Conservative Party and the European Dictators 1935–1940* (1997).

Crowson, N. J., 'Citizen defence: The Conservative Party and its attitude to national service 1937–1957', in A. Beech and R. Weight (eds.), *The Right to Belong: Citizenship and National Identity in Britain 1920–1960* (1998), 205–22.

Cunningham, H., 'The Conservative Party and patriotism', in R. Colls and P. Dodd (eds.), *Englishness: Politics and Culture 1880–1920* (1986), 283–307.

Cuthbert, D. D., 'Lloyd George and the Conservative Central Office 1918–1922', in A. J. P. Taylor (ed.), *Lloyd George: Twelve Essays* (1971), 167–87.

Davies, A. J., *We, the Nation: The Conservative Party and the Pursuit of Power* (1995).

Dean, D. W., 'Problems of the Conservative Sub-committee on Education 1941–1945', *Journal of Educational Administration and History*, 3 (1970), 26–37.

Dean, D. W., 'Conservatism and the national education system 1922–1940', *Journal of Contemporary History*, 6 (1971), 150–65.

Defries, H., *Conservative Party Attitudes to Jews 1900–1950* (2001).

Dorey, P., *The Conservative Party and the Trade Unions* (1995).

Dorey, P., *British Conservatism: The Politics and Philosophy of Inequality* (2011).

Dutton, D., 'Power brokers or just "glamour boys"? The Eden group, September 1939–May 1940', *English Historical Review*, 118/476 (2003), 412–24.

Eccleshall, R. (ed.), *English Conservatism since the Restoration: An Introduction and Anthology* (1990).

Evans, B. and Taylor, A., *From Salisbury to Major: Continuity and Change in Conservative Politics* (Manchester, 1996).

Evans, S., 'The Conservatives and the redefinition of Unionism 1912–1921', *20th Century British History*, 9/1 (1998), 1–27.

Fair, J. D., 'The Conservative basis for the formation of the National Government of 1931', *Journal of British Studies*, 19 (1980), 142–64.

Fair, J. D. and Hutcheson, J. A., 'British Conservatism in the twentieth century: an emerging ideological tradition', *Albion*, 19/4 (1987), 549–78.

Fawcett, A., *Conservative Agent: A Study of the National Society of Conservative and Unionist Agents and its Members* (1967).

Ferris, J. and Bar-Joseph, U., 'Getting Marlowe to hold his tongue: The Conservative Party, the Intelligence Services, and the Zinoviev letter', *Intelligence and National Security*, 8 (1993), 100–37.

Fisher, N., *The Tory Leaders* (1977).

Francis, M. and Zweiniger-Bargielowska, I. (eds.), *The Conservatives and British Society 1880–1990* (Cardiff, 1996).

Gamble, A., *The Conservative Nation* (1974).

Ghosh, S. C., 'Decision-making and power in the British Conservative Party: A case study of the Indian problem 1929–1934', *Political Studies*, 13 (1965), 198–212.

Glickman, H., 'The Toryness of English Conservatism', *Journal of British Studies*, 1/1 (1961), 111–43.

Goodhart, P. and Branston, U., *The 1922: The Story of the Conservative Backbenchers' Parliamentary Committee* (1973).

Grayson, R. S., 'Imperialism in Conservative defence and foreign policy: Leo Amery and the Chamberlains 1903–1932', *Journal of Imperial and Commonwealth History*, 34/4 (2006), 505–27.

Grayson, R. S., 'The historiography of inter-war politics: Competing Conservative world views in high politics, 1924–1929', in W. Mulligan and B. Simms (eds.), *The Primacy of Foreign Policy in British History 1660–2000* (Basingstoke, 2011), 277–90.

Green, E. H. H., *Ideologies of Conservatism: Conservative Political Ideas in the Twentieth Century* (Oxford, 2002).

Green, E. H. H., 'The Conservatives and the City', in R. C. Michie and P. Williamson (eds.), *The British Government and the City of London in the Twentieth Century* (Cambridge, 2004), 153–73.

Green, E. H. H, 'The Conservative Party and Keynes', in E. H. H. Green and D. Tanner (eds.), *The Strange Survival of Liberal England* (Cambridge, 2007), 186–211.

Greenwood, J., *The Conservative Party and the Working Classes: The Organisational Response* (Warwick, 1974).

Harbour, W., *The Foundations of Conservative Thought: An Anglo-American Tradition in Perspective* (Notre Dame, 1982).

Hazlehurst, C., 'The Baldwinite conspiracy', *Historical Studies*, 16 (1974–75), 167–91.

Hicks, G., '"Appeasement" or consistent Conservatism? British foreign policy, party politics and the guarantees of 1867 and 1939', *Historical Research*, 84/225 (2011), 513–34.

Hicks, G. (ed.), *Conservatism and British Foreign Policy 1820–1920: The Derbys and their World* (Farnham, 2011).

Hollins, T. J., 'The Conservative Party and film propaganda between the wars', *English Historical Review*, 96 (1981), 359–69.

Hutchinson, I. G. C., 'Scottish Unionism between the two World Wars', in C. Macdonald (ed.), *Unionist Scotland 1800–1997* (Edinburgh, 1998), 73–99.

Jackson, A., '"Tame Tory hacks"? The Ulster Party at Westminster 1922–1972', *Historical Journal*, 54/2 (2011), 453–75.

Jarvis, D., 'Mrs Maggs and Betty: The Conservative appeal to women voters in the 1920s', *20th Century British History*, 5/2 (1994), 129–52.

Jarvis, D., 'British Conservatism and class politics in the 1920s', *English Historical Review*, 111/440 (1996), 59–84.

Jarvis, D., 'The shaping of the Conservative electoral hegemony 1918–1939', in J. Lawrence, and M. Taylor (eds.), *Party, State and Society: Electoral Behaviour in Britain since 1820* (Aldershot, 1997), 131–52.

Jarvis, D., '"Behind every great party": Women and Conservatism in twentieth-century Britain', in A. Vickery (ed.), *Women, Privilege and Power* (Stanford, 2001), 289–314.

Jeffries, A., 'British Conservatism: Individualism and gender', *Journal of Political Ideologies*, 1/1 (1996), 33–52.

Johnston, R. J., Pattie, C., Dorling, D., and Rossiter, D.,'The Conservative century? Geography and Conservative electoral success during the twentieth century', in D. Gilbert, D. Matless, and B. Short (eds.), *Geographies of British Modernity* (Oxford, 2003), 54–79.

Kandiah, M. D., 'The Conservative Party and the 1945 election', *Contemporary Record*, 9/1 (1995), 22–47.

Keohane, N., *The Party of Patriotism: The Conservative Party and the First World War* (Farnham, 2010).

Krishtalka, A., 'Loyalty in wartime: The old Tories and British war policy 1939–1940', in B. P. Farrell (ed.), *Leadership and Responsibility in the Second World War: Essays in Honour of Robert Vogel* (Montreal, 2004), 39–66.

Kumarasingham, H., '"For the good of the party": An analysis of the fall of British Conservative Party Prime Ministers from Chamberlain to Thatcher', *Political Science*, 58/2 (Wellington, New Zealand, 2006), 43–62.

Lindsay, T. F. and Harrington, M., *The Conservative Party 1918–1979* (1979).

Lynch, P., *The Politics of Nationhood: Sovereignty, Britishness and Conservative Politics* (Basingstoke, 1999).

McCrillis, N. R., 'Taming democracy? The Conservative Party and House of Lords' reform 1916–1929', *Parliamentary History*, 12/3 (1993), 259–80.

McCrillis, N. R., *The British Conservative Party in the Age of Universal Suffrage: Popular Conservatism 1918–1929* (Columbus, Ohio, 1998).

McEwen, J. M., 'The coupon election of 1918 and Unionist members of parliament', *Journal of Modern History*, 34 (1962), 294–306.

Macintyre, C., 'Policy reform and the politics of housing in the British Conservative Party 1924–1929', *Australian Journal of Politics & History*, 45/3 (1999), 408–21.

McKibbin, R., 'Class and conventional wisdom: the Conservative Party and the "public" in inter-war Britain', in R. McKibbin, *The Ideologies of Class* (Oxford, 1990), 259–93.

Maguire, G. E., *Conservative Women: A History of Women and the Conservative Party 1874–1997* (Basingstoke, 1998).

Moore, S., *The Conservative Party: The First 150 Years* (1980).

Moore, S., 'The agrarian Conservative Party in Parliament 1920–1929', *Parliamentary History*, 10 (1991), 342–62.

Norton, P. (ed.), *The Conservative Party* (Hemel Hempstead, 1996).

Norton, P. and Aughey, A., *Conservatives and Conservatism* (1981).

O'Gorman, F. (ed.), *British Conservatism: Conservative Thought from Burke to Thatcher* (1986).

Peele, G. and Cook, C. (eds.), *The Politics of Reappraisal 1918–1939* (1975).

Pugh, M., *The Tories and the People 1880–1935* (Oxford, 1985).

Pugh, M., 'Popular Conservatism in Britain: Continuity and change 1880–1987', *Journal of British Studies*, 27 (1988), 254–82.

Pugh, M., 'Lancashire, cotton, and Indian reform: Conservative controversies in the 1930s', *20th Century British History*, 15/2 (2004), 143–51.

Ramsden, J., *The Age of Balfour and Baldwin 1902–1940* (1978).

Ramsden, J., *The Making of Conservative Party Policy: The Conservative Research Department since 1929* (1980).

Ramsden, J., *The Age of Churchill and Eden 1940–1957* (1995).

Ramsden, J., *An Appetite for Power: A History of the Conservative Party since 1830* (1998).

Rasmussen, J. S., 'Government and intra-party opposition: Dissent within the Conservative Parliamentary Party in the 1930s', *Political Studies*, 19/2 (1971), 172–83.

Rodner, W. S., 'Conservatism, resistance and Lord Hugh Cecil', *History of Political Thought*, 9 (1988), 529–51.

Rose, I., *Conservatism and Foreign Policy during the Lloyd George Coalition* (1999).

Schinness, R., 'An early pilgrimage to Soviet Russia: Four Conservative MPs challenge Tory Party policy', *Historical Journal*, 18 (1975), 623–31.

Schinness, R., 'The Conservative Party and Anglo-Soviet relations 1925–1927', *European Studies Review*, 7 (1977), 393–407.

Schwarz, B., 'The language of constitutionalism: Baldwinite Conservatism', in ['Formations collective'], *Formations of Nation and People* (1984), 1–18.

Schwarz, B., 'Ancestral citizens: Reflections on British Conservatism', *New Formations*, 28 (1996), 101–20.

Self, R., *Tories and Tariffs: The Conservative Party and the Politics of Tariff Reform 1922–1932* (New York and London, 1986).
Self, R., 'Conservative reunion and the general election of 1923: A reassessment', *20th Century British History*, 3/3 (1992), 249–73.
Seldon, A. (ed.), *How Tory Governments Fall: The Tory Party in Power since 1783* (1996).
Seldon, A. and Ball, S. (eds.), *Conservative Century: The Conservative Party since 1900* (Oxford, 1994).
Shepherd, R., *The Power Brokers: The Tory Party and its Leaders* (1991).
Smith, J., '"Ever reliable friends"? The Conservative Party and Ulster Unionism in the twentieth century', *English Historical Review*, 121/490 (2006), 70–103.
Southgate, D. (ed.), *The Conservative Leadership 1832–1932* (1974).
Stevenson, J., 'Conservatism and the failure of Fascism in inter-war Britain', in M. Blinkhorn (ed.), *Fascists and Conservatives* (1990), 264–82.
Stewart, G., *Burying Caesar: Churchill, Chamberlain and the Battle for the Tory Party* (1999).
Thackeray, D., 'The crisis of the Tariff Reform League and the division of "Radical Conservatism", c.1913–1922', *History*, 91/301 (2006), 45–61.
Thackeray, D., 'Home and politics: Women and Conservative activism in early twentieth-century Britain', *Journal of British Studies*, 49/4 (2010), 826–48.
Thompson, N., *The Anti-Appeasers: Conservative Opposition to Appeasement in the 1930s* (Oxford, 1971).
Thorpe, A., 'Conservative Party Agents in Second World War Britain', *20th Century British History*, 18/3 (2007), 334–64.
Thorpe, A., 'Reconstructing Conservative Party membership in World War II Britain', *Parliamentary Affairs*, 62/2 (2009), 227–41.
Vincent, A., 'British Conservatism and the problem of ideology', *Political Studies*, 42 (1994), 204–27.
Webber, G. C., 'Intolerance and discretion: Conservatives and British Fascism 1918–1926', in T. Kushner and K. Lunn (eds.), *Traditions of Intolerance* (Manchester, 1989), 155–72.
Whiteley, P., Seyd, P., and Richardson, J., *True Blues: The Politics of Conservative Party Membership* (Oxford, 1994).
Williamson, P., '"Safety First": Baldwin, the Conservative Party, and the 1929 general election', *Historical Journal*, 25 (1982), 385–409.
Williamson, P., 'The Conservative Party 1900–1939: From crisis to ascendancy', in C. Wrigley (ed.), *A Companion to Early Twentieth-Century Britain* (Oxford, 2002), 3–22.
Williamson, P., 'The Conservative Party, Fascism and anti-Fascism 1918–1939', in N. Copsey and A. Olechnowicz (eds.), *Varieties of Anti-Fascism: Britain in the Inter-War Period* (Basingstoke, 2010), 73–97.
Young, K., *Local Politics and the Rise of Party: The London Municipal Society and the Conservative Intervention in Local Elections 1894–1963* (Leicester, 1975).

2. Biography
Adam, C. F., *Life of Lord Lloyd* (1948).
Adams, R. J. Q., *Bonar Law* (1999).
Adams, R. J. Q., *Balfour: The Last Grandee* (2007).
Addison, P., 'The political beliefs of Winston Churchill', *Royal Historical Society, Transactions*, 5th ser., 30 (1980), 23–47.
Addison, P., *Churchill on the Home Front 1900–1955* (1992).
Addison, P., *Churchill: The Unexpected Hero* (Oxford, 2005).
Adelson, R., *Mark Sykes* (1975).

Aster, S., *Anthony Eden* (1976).
Ayerst, D., *Garvin of the Observer* (1985).
Baldwin, A. W., *My Father: The True Story* (1955).
Ball, S. [Simon], *The Guardsmen: Harold Macmillan, Three Friends and the World They Made* (2004).
Ball, S., 'Mosley and the Tories in 1930: The problem of generations', *Contemporary British History*, 23/4 (2009), 445–59.
Ball, S. [Stuart], 'Stanley Baldwin', in R. Kelly and J. Cantrell (eds.), *Modern British Statesmen 1867–1945* (Manchester, 1997), 161–78.
Ball, S., 'Churchill and the Conservative Party', *Royal Historical Society, Transactions*, 6th ser., 11 (2001), 307–30.
Ball, S., *Winston Churchill* (2003).
Ball, S., 'Stanley Baldwin', *Oxford Dictionary of National Biography*, vol. 3 (Oxford, 2004), 460–77.
Bennett, G. H. and Gibson, M., *The Later Life of Lord Curzon of Kedleston* (Lampeter, 2000).
Best, A. and Sandwich, J. (eds.), *Hinch: A Celebration of Viscount Hinchingbrooke MP 1906–1995* (Dorset, 1997).
Best, G., *Churchill: A Study in Greatness* (2001).
Birkenhead, Earl of, *F.E: Life of F.E. Smith, First Earl of Birkenhead* (1959).
Birkenhead, Lord, *Halifax: The life of Lord Halifax* (1965).
Blake, R., *The Unknown Prime Minister: The Life and Times of Andrew Bonar Law* (1955).
Blake, R., 'Baldwin and the right', in J. T. Raymond (ed.), *The Baldwin Age* (1960), 25–65.
Blake, R. and Louis, W. R. (eds.), *Churchill* (Oxford, 1993).
Bolitho, H., *Alfred Mond, First Lord Melchett* (1932).
Boyle, A., *Poor, Dear Brendan: The Quest for Brendan Bracken* (1974).
Bridge, C., 'Churchill, Hoare, Derby, and the Committee of Privileges: April to June 1934', *Historical Journal*, 22 (1979), 215–27.
Brodrick, A. H., *Near to Greatness: Life of the 6th Earl Winterton* (1965).
Campbell, J., *F.E. Smith, 1st Earl of Birkenhead* (1983).
Cannadine, D., 'Politics, propaganda and art: The case of two "Worcestershire lads"', *Midland History*, 4 (1977), 97–122.
Carlton, D., *Anthony Eden* (1981).
Cartland, B., *Ronald Cartland* (1942).
Cesarani, D., 'Joynson-Hicks and the Radical Right in England after the First World War', in T. Kushner and K. Lunn (eds.), *Traditions of Intolerance* (Manchester, 1989), 118–39.
Charmley, J., *Duff Cooper* (1986).
Charmley, J., *Lord Lloyd and the Decline of the British Empire* (1987).
Charmley, J., *Chamberlain and the Lost Peace* (1989).
Charmley, J., *Churchill: The End of Glory* (1993).
Chisholm, A. and Davie, M., *Beaverbrook* (1992).
Churchill, R., *Lord Derby: 'King of Lancashire'* (1959).
Clarke, P. F., *A Question of Leadership: Gladstone to Thatcher* (1991).
Cockett, R. B., 'Ball, Chamberlain and "Truth"', *Historical Journal*, 33 (1990), 131–42.
Collis, M., *Nancy Astor* (1960).
Cooke, A., *Tory Heroine: Dorothy Brant and the Rise of Conservative Women* (Eastbourne, 2008).

Cooper, C., 'Heir not apparent: Douglas Hailsham, the role of the House of Lords, and the succession to the Conservative Leadership, 1928–1931', *Parliamentary History*, 31/2 (2012), 206–29.
Coote, C., *A Companion of Honour: The Story of Walter Elliot* (1965).
Corthorn, P., 'W.E.D. Allen, Unionist politics and the New Party', *Contemporary British History*, 23/4 (2009), 509–25.
Crankshaw, E., *The Forsaken Idea: A Study of Viscount Milner* (1952).
Crooks, S., *Peter Thorneycroft* (Winchester, 2007).
Cross, J. A., *Sir Samuel Hoare* (1977).
Cross, J. A., *Lord Swinton* (Oxford, 1982).
Crowson, N. J., 'Much ado about nothing? Macmillan and appeasement', in R. Aldous and S. Lee (eds.), *Harold Macmillan: Aspects of a Political Life* (Basingstoke, 2000), 59–74.
Cullen, T., *Maundy Gregory: Purveyor of Honours* (1974).
Davenport-Hines, R., *The Macmillans* (1992).
De Courcy, A., *Circe: The Life of Edith, Marchioness of Londonderry* (1992).
Dilks, D., 'The twilight war and the fall of France: Chamberlain and Churchill in 1940', in D. Dilks (ed.), *Retreat From Power*, vol. 2: *After 1939* (Basingstoke, 1981), 36–65.
Dilks, D., *Neville Chamberlain*, vol. 1: *1869–1929* (Cambridge, 1984).
Driberg, T., *Beaverbrook: A Study in Power and Frustration* (1956).
Dugdale, B., *Arthur James Balfour* (2 vols, 1936).
Dutton, D., *Austen Chamberlain* (Bolton, 1985).
Dutton, D., *Simon: A Political Biography of Sir John Simon* (1992).
Dutton, D., *Anthony Eden: A Life and Reputation* (1997).
Dutton, D., 'Sir Austen Chamberlain and British foreign policy 1931–1937', *Diplomacy and Statecraft*, 16/2 (2005), 281–95.
Egremont, M., *Balfour* (1980).
Egremont, M., *Under Two Flags: The Life of Major-General Sir Edward Spears* (1997).
Ellis, R. J., *He Walks Alone: The Private and Public Life of Captain Cunningham-Reid, DFC, Member of Parliament 1922–1945* (n.d. [1946]).
Faber, D., *Speaking for England: Leo, Julian and John Amery—The Tragedy of a Political Family* (2005).
Feiling, K., *The Life of Neville Chamberlain* (1946).
Fisher, N., *Harold Macmillan* (1982).
Fleming, N. C., *The Marquess of Londonderry: Aristocracy, Power and Politics in Britain and Ireland* (2005).
Fuchser, L. W., *Neville Chamberlain and Appeasement* (1982).
Gilbert, M., *Winston S. Churchill*, vol. 5: *1922–1939* (1976).
Gilbert, M., *Winston S. Churchill*, vol. 6: *Finest Hour 1939–1941* (1983).
Gilbert, M., *Winston S. Churchill*, vol. 7: *Road to Victory 1941–1945* (1986).
Gilbert, M., *Churchill: A Life* (1991).
Gilmour, D., *Curzon* (1994).
Griffiths, R., *Patriotism Perverted: Captain Ramsay, the Right Book Club and British Anti-Semitism 1939–1940* (1998).
Grigg, J., *Nancy Astor: Portrait of a Pioneer* (1980).
Hartwell, Lord, *William Camrose: Giant of Fleet Street* (1992).
Hetherington, S., *Katharine Atholl 1874–1960: Against the Tide* (Aberdeen, 1989).
Heuston, R. F. V., *Lives of the Lord Chancellors 1885–1940* (Oxford, 1964).
Heuston, R. F. V., *Lives of the Lord Chancellors 1940–1970* (Oxford, 1987).
Horne, A., *Macmillan*, vol. 1: *1894–1956* (1988).

Howard, A., *Rab: The Life of R.A. Butler* (1987).
Hyde, H. M., *Baldwin* (1973).
Hyde, H. M., *Neville Chamberlain* (1976).
James, R. R., *Churchill: A Study in Failure 1900–1939* (1970).
James, R. R., *Victor Cazalet* (1976).
James, R. R., *Anthony Eden* (1986).
James, R. R., *Bob Boothby: A Portrait* (1991).
Jenkins, R., *Baldwin* (1987).
Jenkins, R., *Churchill: A Biography* (2001).
Kershaw, I., *Making Friends with Hitler: Lord Londonderry and the Roots of Appeasement* (2004).
Lewis, G., *Lord Hailsham* (1997).
Lewis, T. L., *Prisms of British Appeasement: Revisionist Reputations of John Simon, Samuel Hoare, Anthony Eden, Lord Halifax and Alfred Duff Cooper* (Brighton, 2010).
Louis, W. R., *In the Name of God, Go! Leo Amery and the British Empire in the Age of Churchill* (1992).
Lysaght, C. E., *Brendan Bracken* (1979).
Lytton, Earl of, *Antony, Viscount Knebworth: A Record of Youth* (1935).
Mackay, R. F., *Balfour: Intellectual Statesman* (Oxford, 1985).
Mackintosh, J. P. (ed.), *British Prime Ministers in the Twentieth Century*, vol. 1 (1977).
Macleod, I., *Neville Chamberlain* (1961).
Mallet, Sir C., *Lord Cave: A Memoir* (1931).
Marlowe, J., *Milner: Apostle of Empire* (1976).
Marquand, D., *Ramsay MacDonald* (1977).
Masters, A., *Nancy Astor* (1981).
Middlemas, K. and Barnes, J., *Baldwin—A Biography* (1969).
Morris, M., '"Et l'honneur?" Politics and principles—a case study of Austen Chamberlain', in C. Wrigley (ed.), *Warfare, Diplomacy and Politics* (1986), 80–92.
Mosley, L., *Curzon* (1960).
Nott, J. J., '"The plague spots of London": William Joynson-Hicks, the Conservative Party and the campaign against London's nightclubs 1924–1929', in C. V. J. Griffiths, J. J. Nott, and W. W. Whyte (eds.), *Classes, Cultures and Politics* (Oxford, 2011), 227–46.
O'Brien, T., *Milner* (1979).
Parker, R. A. C., *Churchill and Appeasement* (2000).
Parry, J. P., 'From the Thirty-Nine Articles to the Thirty-Nine Steps: Reflections on the thought of John Buchan', in M. Bentley (ed.), *Public and Private Doctrine* (Cambridge, 1993), 209–35.
Pelling, H., *Winston Churchill* (1974).
Petrie, Sir C., *Walter Long and His Times* (1936).
Petrie, Sir C., *The Chamberlain Tradition* (1938).
Petrie, Sir C., *The Life and Letters of the Rt. Hon. Sir Austen Chamberlain* (2 vols, 1939 and 1940).
Petrie, Sir C., *The Powers behind the Prime Ministers* (1958).
Ramsden, J., 'Baldwin and film', in N. Pronay and D. W. Spring (eds.), *Politics, Propaganda and Film 1918–1945* (Basingstoke, 1982), 126–43.
Ramsden, J., 'Winston Churchill and the leadership of the Conservative Party', *Contemporary Record*, 9/1 (1995), 99–119.
Renton, T., 'The total whip: David Margesson 1931–1940', in T. Renton, *Chief Whip: People, Power and Patronage in Westminster* (2004), 251–77.

Robbins, K., *Churchill* (Harlow, 1992).
Roberts, A., *The Holy Fox: A Biography of Lord Halifax* (1991).
Rock, W., *Neville Chamberlain* (New York, 1969).
Rose, K., *Curzon: A Most Superior Person* (1969).
Rose, K., *The Later Cecils* (1975).
Rose, N., *Churchill: An Unruly Life* (1994).
Rothwell, V., *Anthony Eden: A Political Biography 1931–1957* (Manchester, 1992).
Rubinstein, W. D., 'Henry Page Croft and the National Party 1917–1922', *Journal of Contemporary History*, 9 (1974), 129–48.
Salvidge, S., *Salvidge of Liverpool: Behind the Political Scene 1890–1928* (1934).
Self, R., *Neville Chamberlain* (Aldershot, 2006).
Smart, N., *Neville Chamberlain* (2009).
Smith, J. A., *John Buchan* (1965).
Somervell, D. C., *Stanley Baldwin* (1953).
Sykes, C., *Nancy: The Life of Lady Astor* (1972).
Taylor, A. J. P., *Beaverbrook* (1972).
Taylor, H. A., *Jix, Viscount Brentford* (1933).
Thorpe, D. R., *The Uncrowned Prime Ministers* (1980).
Thorpe, D. R., *Alec Douglas-Home: The Under-Rated Prime Minister* (1996).
Thorpe, D. R., *Eden: The Life and Times of Anthony Eden, First Earl of Avon, 1897–1977* (2003).
Thorpe, D. R., *Supermac: The Life of Harold Macmillan* (2010).
Toye, R., 'Winston Churchill's "crazy broadcast": Party, nation, and the 1945 Gestapo speech', *Journal of British Studies*, 49/3 (2010), 655–80.
Turner, J., *Macmillan* (1994).
Ward-Smith, G., 'Baldwin and Scotland: More than Englishness', *Contemporary British History*, 15/1 (2001), 61–82.
Williamson, P., 'The doctrinal politics of Stanley Baldwin', in M. Bentley (ed.), *Public and Private Doctrine* (Cambridge, 1993), 181–208.
Williamson, P., *Stanley Baldwin: Conservative Leadership and National Values* (Cambridge, 1999).
Witherell, L. L., 'Sir Henry Page Croft and Conservative backbench campaigns for empire 1903–32', *Parliamentary History*, 25/3 (2006), 357–81.
Wrench, J. E., *Geoffrey Dawson and Our Times* (1955).
Wrench, J. E., *Alfred, Lord Milner: The Man of No Illusions* (1958).
Young, G. M., *Baldwin* (1952).
Young, K., *Arthur James Balfour* (1963).
Young, K., *Churchill and Beaverbrook* (1966).
Young, K., *Sir Alec Douglas-Home* (1970).
Zebel, S. H., *Balfour* (Cambridge, 1973).

3. Select list of other works
Addison, P., *The Road to 1945: British Politics and the Second World War* (1975).
Alderman, G., *The Jewish Vote in Great Britain since 1945* (Glasgow, 1980).
Antcliffe, J., 'Politics of the airwaves: Party political broadcasts in the 1920s and 1930s', *History Today*, 34/1 (1984), 4–10.
August, A., *The British Working Class 1832–1940* (Harlow, 2007).
Baines, P., 'Josiah Wedgwood and his contemporaries: The History of Parliament Survey 1936–1940', *Parliamentary History*, 26/3 (2007), 411–13.

Ball, S. [Stuart], 'Asquith's decline and the general election of 1918', *Scottish Historical Review*, 61 (1982), 44–61.
Ball, S., 'The politics of appeasement: The fall of the Duchess of Atholl and the Kinross & West Perth by-election, December 1938', *Scottish Historical Review*, 69 (1990), 49–83.
Ball, S., 'Parliament and politics in Britain 1900–1951', *Parliamentary History*, 10/2 (1991), 243–76.
Ball, S., Thorpe, A., and Worley, M., 'Researching the grass roots: The records of constituency level political parties in five British counties, 1918–1940', *Archives*, 29/110 (2004), 1–23.
Ball, S., Thorpe, A., and Worley, M., 'Elections, leaflets and whist drives: Constituency party members in Britain between the wars', in M. Worley (ed.), *Labour's Grass Roots* (Aldershot, 2005), 7–32.
Bennett, G. H., 'The wartime political truce and hopes for postwar coalition: The West Derbyshire by-election, 1944', *Midland History*, 17 (1992), 118–35.
Bennett, G. H., '"Part of the puzzle": Northampton and other Midlands by-election defeats for the Conservatives 1927–1929', *Midland History*, 20 (1995), 151–73.
Berkeley, H., *The Myth that Will Not Die: The Formation of the National Government 1931* (1978).
Bingham, A., '"Stop the Flapper Vote folly": Lord Rothermere, the *Daily Mail*, and the equalization of the franchise 1927–1928', *20th Century British History*, 13/1 (2002), 17–37.
Blondel, J., *Voters, Parties and Leaders: The Social Fabric of British Politics* (1963).
Bowley, R. and Stamp, J., *The National Income, 1924* (1927).
Bromhead, P. A., *The House of Lords and Contemporary Politics 1911–1957* (1958).
Brookes, P., *Women at Westminster: An account of Women in the British Parliament 1918–1966* (1967).
Butler, D., *The Electoral System in Britain since 1918* (2nd edn, Oxford, 1963).
Butler, D. (ed.), *Coalitions in British Politics* (1978).
Butler, D. and Stokes, D., *Political Change in Britain* (1969).
Cambray, P. G., *The Game of Politics* (1932).
Cambray, P. G., *Club Days and Ways: The Story of the Constitutional Club* (1963).
Capie, F., 'The pressure for tariff protection in Britain 1916–1931', *Journal of European Economic History*, 9/2 (1980), 431–48.
Carr-Saunders, A. M. and Caradog Jones, D., *A Survey of the Social Structure of England and Wales as Illustrated by Statistics* (2nd edn, Oxford, 1937).
Close, D. H., 'The realignment of the British electorate in 1931', *History*, 67 (1982), 393–404.
Cockett, R., *Twilight of Truth: Chamberlain, Appeasement, and the Manipulation of the Press* (1989).
Collins, M., 'The fall of the English gentleman: The national character in decline, *c.*1918–1970', *Historical Research*, 75/187 (2002), 90–111.
Cook, C., *The Age of Alignment: Electoral Politics in Britain 1922–1929* (1975).
Cook, C. and Ramsden, J. (eds.), *By-Elections in British Politics* (1973).
Cooper, A., *British Agricultural Policy 1912–1936: A Study in Conservative Politics* (Manchester, 1989).
Cowling, M., *The Impact of Labour 1920–24* (Cambridge, 1971).
Cowling, M., *The Impact of Hitler: British Politics and British Policies 1933–1940* (Cambridge, 1975).

Dawson, M., 'Money and the real impact of the Fourth Reform Act', *Historical Journal*, 35 (1992), 369–81.
Dean, K. J., *Town and Westminster: A Political History of Walsall* (Walsall, 1972).
Fair, J. D., 'The Norwegian campaign and Winston Churchill's rise to power in 1940', *International History Review*, 9 (1987), 410–37.
Fielding, S., 'What did "the people" want? The meaning of the 1945 general election', *Historical Journal*, 35 (1992), 623–39.
Fry, G., 'A reconsideration of the British general election of 1935 and the electoral revolution of 1945', *History*, 76 (1991), 43–55.
Fry, G., *The Politics of Crisis: An Interpretation of British Politics 1931–1945* (2001).
Harris, J. P., 'The "Sandys storm": The politics of British air defence in 1938', *Historical Research*, 62 (1989), 318–36.
Harrison, B., *The Transformation of British Politics 1860–1995* (Oxford, 1996).
Heathorn, S. and Greenspoon, D., 'Organising youth for partisan politics in Britain 1918–1932', *The Historian*, 68/1 (2006), 89–119.
Hinton, J., *Women, Social Leadership and the Second World War* (Oxford, 2002).
Garside, W. R., 'Party politics, political economy and British protectionism 1919–1932', *History*, 83/269 (1998), 47–65.
Good, K., '"Quit ye like men": Platform manliness and electioneering 1895–1939', in M. McCormack (ed.), *Public Men: Masculinity and Politics in Modern Britain* (Basingstoke, 2007), 143–64.
Grainger, J. H., *Character and Style in English Politics* (Cambridge, 1969).
Grainger, J. H., *Patriotisms: Britain 1900–1939* (1986).
Greenleaf, W. H., *The British Political Tradition*, vol. 2: *The Ideological Heritage* (1987).
Guttsman, W. L., *The British Political Elite* (1963).
Jackson, A., *The Middle Classes 1900–1950* (Nairn, 1991).
Jeffery, T., 'The suburban nation: Politics and class in Lewisham', in D. Feldman and G. S. Jones (eds.), *Metropolis London* (1989), 189–216.
Jeffery, T. and McClelland, K., 'A world fit to live in: The *Daily Mail* and the middle classes 1918–1939', in J. Curran, A. Smith, and P. Wingate (eds.), *Impacts and Influences: Essays on Media Power in the Twentieth Century* (1987), 27–52.
Jefferys, K., *The Churchill Coalition and Wartime Politics 1940–1945* (Manchester, 1991).
Jefferys, K., 'May 1940: The downfall of Neville Chamberlain', *Parliamentary History*, 10 (1991), 363–78.
Jefferys, K., *Politics and the People: A History of British Democracy since 1918* (2007).
Jessop, R. D., 'Civility and traditionalism in British political culture', *British Journal of Political Science*, 1/1 (1971), 1–24.
Jones, G. W., *Borough Politics: A Study of the Wolverhampton Town Council 1888–1964* (1969).
Jones, H., *Women in British Public Life 1914–1950* (Harlow, 2000).
Kinnear, M., *The Fall of Lloyd George* (1973).
Koss, S., *The Rise and Fall of the Political Press in Britain*, vol. 2: *The Twentieth Century* (1984).
Lawrence, J., 'Forging a peaceable kingdom: War, violence and the fear of brutalisation in post-First World War Britain', *Journal of Modern History*, 75/3 (2003), 557–89.
Lawrence, J., 'The transformation of British public politics after the First World War', *Past & Present*, 190 (2006), 185–215.
Lawrence, J., *Electing our Masters: The Hustings in British Politics from Hogarth to Blair* (Oxford, 2009).

Leonard, S., *A Century of Premiers: Salisbury to Blair* (2004).
Lee, J. M., *The Churchill Coalition* (1980).
Light, A., *Forever England: Femininity, Literature and Conservatism between the Wars* (1991).
Lowe, R., *Adjusting to Democracy: The Role of the Ministry of Labour in British Politics 1916–1939* (Oxford, 1986).
McCallum, R. and Readman, A., *The British General Election of 1945*.
McCarthy, H., 'Parties, voluntary associations, and democratic politics in interwar Britain', *Historical Journal*, 50/4 (2007), 891–912.
McKenzie, R. T., *British Political Parties* (1955).
McKenzie, R. T. and Silver, A., *Angels in Marble: Working Class Conservatives in Urban England* (1968).
McKibbin, R., *Classes and Cultures: England 1918–1951* (Oxford, 1998).
McKibbin, R., *Parties and People: England 1914–1951* (Oxford, 2010).
Mandler, P., *The English National Character: The History of an Idea from Edmund Burke to Tony Blair* (New Haven and London, 2006).
Maor, M., *Political Parties and Party Systems: Comparative Approaches and the British Experience* (1997).
Marrison, A. J., 'Businessmen, industries, and tariff reform in Great Britain 1903–1930', *Business History*, 28 (1983), 148–78.
Marrison, A., *British Business and Protection 1903–1932* (Oxford, 1996).
Masterman, C. F. G., *England after the War* (1922).
Middlemas, K., *Politics in Industrial Society* (1979).
Miller, F. M., 'The unemployment policy of the National Government 1931–1936', *Historical Journal*, 19 (1976), 453–76.
Miller, F. M., 'The British unemployment assistance crisis of 1935', *Journal of Contemporary History*, 14 (1979), 329–52.
Milne, R. S. and Mackenzie, H. C., *Straight Fight: A Study of Voting Behaviour in the Constituency of Bristol North-East at the General Election of 1951* (1954).
Morgan, K., *Consensus and Disunity: The Lloyd George Coalition Government 1918–1922* (Oxford, 1979).
Muldoon, A., '"An unholy row in Lancashire": The textile lobby, Conservative politics, and Indian policy, 1931–1935', *20th Century British History*, 14/2 (2003), 93–111.
Muldoon, A., *Empire, Politics and the Creation of the 1935 India Act* (Farnham, 2009).
Nicolson, H., *King George V* (1952).
Petrie, Sir C. and Cooke, A., *The Carlton Club* (2nd edn, 2007).
Phelps, B., *Power and the Party: A History of the Carlton Club 1832–1982* (Basingstoke, 1983).
Pinto-Duschinsky, M., *British Political Finance 1830–1980* (Washington, 1982).
Rasmussen, J. S., 'Party discipline in wartime: The downfall of the Chamberlain government', *Journal of Politics*, 32 (1970), 379–406.
Reimann, A., 'Popular culture and the reconstruction of British identity', in H. Berghoff and R. von Friedeburg (eds.), *Change and Inertia: Britain under the Impact of the Great War* (Bodenheim, 1998), 99–120.
Rose, K., *King George V* (1983).
Rowe, E. A., 'Broadcasting and the 1929 general election', *Renaissance and Modern Studies*, 12 (1968), 108–19.
Rubinstein, W. D., 'Britain's elites in the inter-war period', *Contemporary British History*, 12/1 (1998), 1–18.
Rush, M., *The Selection of Parliamentary Candidates* (1969).

Sainty, J. C. (ed.), 'Assistant Whips 1922–1964', *Parliamentary History*, 4 (1985), 201–4.
Sampson, A., *The Anatomy of Britain* (1962).
Shay, R. P., *British Rearmament in the 1930s: Politics or Profits* (Princeton, 1977).
Sibley, R., 'The swing to Labour during the Second World War: When and why?', *Labour History Review*, 55/1 (1990), 23–34.
Smart, N., 'Constituency politics and the 1931 election', *Southern History*, 16 (1994), 122–51.
Smart, N., 'Baldwin's blunder: The general election of 1923', *20th Century British History*, 7/1 (1996), 110–39.
Smart, N., 'Four days in May: The Norway debates and the downfall of Neville Chamberlain', *Parliamentary History*, 17/2 (1998), 215–43.
Smart, N., *The National Government 1931–1940* (Basingstoke, 1999).
Smyth, J. J., 'Resisting Labour: Unionists, Liberals, and Moderates in Glasgow between the wars', *Historical Journal*, 46/2 (2003), 375–401.
Soffer, R. N., 'The Conservative historical imagination in the twentieth century', *Albion*, 28/1 (1996), 1–17.
Soffer, R. N., *History, Historians and Conservatism in Britain and America: From the Great War to Thatcher and Reagan* (Oxford, 2009).
Stacey, M., *Tradition and Change: A Study of Banbury* (1960).
Stannage, T., *Baldwin Thwarts the Opposition: The British General Election of 1935* (1980).
Stevens, C., 'The electoral sociology of modern Britain reconsidered', *Contemporary British History*, 13/1 (1999), 62–94.
Stevenson, J. and Cook, C., *The Slump: Society and Politics during the Depression* (1977).
Stone, D., 'The English Mistery, the BUF, and the dilemmas of British Fascism', *Journal of Modern History*, 75/2 (2003), 336–58.
Studdert-Kennedy, G., 'The Christian imperialism of the diehard defenders of the Raj 1926–1935', *Journal of Imperial and Commonwealth History*, 18 (1990), 342–62.
Thompson, F. M. L., 'English landed society in the twentieth century: IV—prestige without power?', *Royal Historical Society, Transactions*, 6th ser., 3 (1993), 1–22.
Thorpe, A., *The British General Election of 1931* (Oxford, 1991).
Thorpe, A., *Parties at War: Political Organisation in Second World War Britain* (Oxford, 2009).
Turner, J., *British Politics and the Great War: Coalition and Conflict 1915–1918* (New Haven and London, 1992).
Waller, P. J., *Democracy and Sectarianism: A Political and Social History of Liverpool 1868–1939* (Liverpool, 1981).
Ward, R., *City-State and Nation: Birmingham's Political History 1830–1940* (Chichester, 2005).
Wasson, E. A., 'The House of Commons 1660–1945: Parliamentary families and the political elite', *English Historical Review*, 106/420 (1991), 635–51.
Webber, G. C., *The Ideology of the British Right 1918–1939* (1986).
Whetham, E. H., 'The Agriculture Act (1920) and its repeal: "the great betrayal"', *Agricultural History Review*, 22/1 (1974), 36–49.
Wiener, M. J., *English Culture and the Decline of the Industrial Spirit 1850–1980* (Cambridge, 1981).
Williams, A. S., *Ladies of Influence: Women of the Elite in Interwar Britain* (2000).
Williamson, P., *National Crisis and National Government: British Politics, the Economy and Empire 1926–1932* (Cambridge, 1992).
Williamson, P., 'Christian Conservatives and the totalitarian challenge', *English Historical Review*, 105/462 (2000), 607–42.

Willson, F. M. G., 'The routes of entry of new members of the British cabinet 1868–1958', *Political Studies*, 7/3 (1959), 222–32.

Wilson, G., *The Psychology of Conservatism* (1973).

Wilson, K. M., 'A venture in "the caverns of intrigue": The conspiracy against Lord Curzon and his foreign policy 1922–1923', *Historical Research*, 70/173 (1997), 213–336.

Wrench, D. J., 'Cashing in: The parties and the National Government, August 1931–September 1932', *Journal of British Studies*, 23/2 (1984), 135–53.

Wrench, D. J., '"The needs of the time": The National Government and the agreement to differ, 1932', *Parliamentary History*, 23/2 (2004), 249–64.

4. Unpublished Theses

Bates, J. W. B., 'The Conservative Party in the [West Midland] Constituencies 1918–1939', DPhil. thesis, University of Oxford (1994).

Carr, R., 'The Phoenix Generation at Westminster: Great War Veterans turned Tory MPs, Democratic Political Culture, and the Path of British Conservatism from the Armistice to the Welfare State', PhD thesis, University of East Anglia (2010).

Dean, D. W., 'The Contrasting Attitudes of the Conservative and Labour Parties to Problems of Empire 1922–36', PhD thesis, University of London (1974).

Greenwood, J. R., 'Central Control and Constituency Autonomy in the Conservative Party: The Organisation of "Labour" and Trade Unionist Support 1918–1970', PhD thesis, University of Reading (1981).

Herzog, R. D., 'The Conservative Party and Protectionist Politics 1918–1932', PhD thesis, University of Sheffield (1984).

Jarvis, D., 'Stanley Baldwin and the Ideology of the Conservative Response to Socialism, 1918–1931', PhD thesis, University of Lancaster (1991).

Keohane, N., 'The Unionist Party and the First World War', PhD thesis, University of London (2004).

McEwen, J. M., 'The Unionist and Conservative Members of Parliament 1914–1939', PhD thesis, University of London (1959).

Moore, S., 'Reactions to Agricultural Depression: The Agrarian Conservative Party in England and Wales, 1920–1929', DPhil thesis, University of Oxford (1988).

Ramsden, J. A., 'The Organisation of the Conservative and Unionist Party in Britain 1910–1930', DPhil thesis, University of Oxford (1975).

Thomas, G., 'Conservatives and the Culture of "National" Government between the Wars', PhD thesis, University of Cambridge (2010).

Williams, T. W., 'The Conservative Party in North-East Wales, 1906–1924', PhD thesis, University of Liverpool (2009).

Index

Abdication crisis (1936) 217, 301, 364, 468
Abingdon 199–200
Accrington 208
Acland-Troyte, G. 309
Active Back Benchers' Group 354
Acton 150
Adair, T. 310
Adams, V. 316, 365
Agg-Gardner, J. 319
Agricultural Committee 352, 379
agriculture:
  and Conservative voting 113, 132
  depression of 223, 303, 311, 420
  grass-roots opinion and 194, 229, 232, 233, 258
  images from 43, 70, 87,
  MPs and 200, 309, 315, 352
  significance of 71
Aldershot 216
Aliens Act (1905) 44
Allen, W. E. D. 359
All-Party Group (1940) 367
Amery, L. S.:
  anti-appeasement 364, 365, 367, 433, 495
  and Baldwin 441, 455
  and Cabinet discussion 411, 431
  career 418
  drafting of party manifestos 445
  education 313
  and Empire Industries Association 353
  and Liberal Party 67
  and party opinion 253, 258
  and party unity 501
  need for a positive policy 62
  and protectionism 439, 485
  on propaganda 90, 99
  and Zionism 65
  mentioned 11, 41, 404
Amritsar massacre (1919) 226, 345
Anderson, J. 405
Anglo-Irish Treaty (1921) 80, 479, 509
anti-Semitism 65–6
Anti-Waste League 194, 206, 224, 478
Apsley, Lady 327
Apsley, Lord 315
ARCOS raid (1927) 229, 423
Argyll 184, 189
Armstrong, H. 250
Ashley, W. 357
Asquith, H. 63, 128, 336, 440–1
Assheton, R. 31, 273, 274, 280, 354, 472
Association of Conservative Clubs 160

Ashford 152, 167
Astbury, F. W. 358
Aston 151
Astor, Lady 324–5, 326, 333, 366
Atholl, Duchess of:
  breach with constituency association 214, 216–17, 238
  career 325–6, 365
  and India 364
  resigns National Government whip 358
Atholl, Duke of 49, 51
Attlee, C. 63, 92, 335
Austin, H. 308
Ayr Boroughs 187
Ayrshire South 191

Baillie-Hamilton, C. 213–14
Baldwin, L. 99, 332
Baldwin, S.:
  attitudes and opinions:
    anti-coalitionism (after 1922) 342
    attitude to the Labour Party 51
    on Conservatism 10, 19, 20, 24, 32, 35, 50, 51, 70, 74, 446, 519
    on democracy 54
    on England 43, 44, 76, 87
    on leadership 460–1, 462
    on parliamentary speaking 391, 392
    on party 72
    on Premiership 463
    speeches 55–6, 190
    on young MPs 351
  career and events:
    and Ashridge 295
    cabinet formation 404
    at Carlton Club meeting (1922) 475
    Earldom 321
    and fall of Coalition (1922) 360, 432, 482, 483, 504, 505
    General Strike 50
    and India 439, 442, 490–1
    and Irwin Declaration (1929) 461
    in 1920–2: 431
    in 1923–4: 228, 244, 435, 437–9, 440–2, 453, 472–3, 475
    in 1924–9: 361, 412, 432
    in 1929–31: 41, 223, 231–2, 244, 272, 275, 281, 361–2, 435–6, 452, 462, 473, 476, 484–9, 500
    in 1935–37: 493
    becomes Leader 454
    Macquisten Bill speech 347

572

Index

Baldwin, S.: (*cont.*)
  March 1931 crisis 442–4, 487–8
  and National Government 75–6,
    101, 376–7
  policy-making 444–5
  become Prime Minister (1923) 454–6
  and press dictation 97, 487, 488, 502
  electoral appeal of 133, 510, 511
    broadcasting 100–1
    public appeal 85, 93, 522
  style of leadership 340, 461, 462, 465, 466,
    468–9, 470, 506, 522
Balfour, A. J.:
  appointment of Party Chairman 272
  career 319, 321, 407, 408, 414, 467
  at Carlton Club meeting (1922) 475
  death 436
  on House of Lords 386
  in 1923–4: 438, 440, 441, 442, 476
  on role of leadership 462
  and succession to Bonar Law 453, 455
  and Zionism 65
  mentioned 242, 450, 467, 470, 472
Balfour, G. 308
Balfour, H. 310, 350, 392
Ball, J. 279, 284, 286, 293, 448
Balniel, Lord 316
Banbury, F. 80, 344
Barkston Ash 149
Barlow, M. 409, 422
Barnard Castle 127
Bath 167, 213, 219, 221
Battersea South 178, 180
Baxter, B. 309
Bayford, Lord, *see* Sanders, R.
Beale, A. 172
Beaton, A. 204
Beamish, T. 202, 309
Beaumont, M. 350
Beaverbrook, Lord:
  criticism of Baldwin 441, 442, 499, 505
  and Empire Crusade 223, 230, 423, 488,
    505, 517
  and Empire Free Trade policy 484
  and Conservative grass roots 231, 486
  financial donation (1923) 300
  in March 1931: 297, 362, 442–3, 488,
    489, 491
  as newspaper owner 97, 98
  on 1929 election 109
  truce with Baldwin (March–June 1930) 252,
    275, 362, 428, 469, 485
  mentioned 290, 342, 352, 353, 355, 361,
    387, 456, 466, 501, 503, 521
beer duty 337
Belper 178
Benn, W. 426
Bennett, A. 214, 306
Bennett, R. B. 486

Bennett, T. 309
Benson, S. H. 100, 294
Bentinck, Lord H. 216, 315, 349
Berkshire South 168, 189
Bernays, R. 403
Berwick 175
Betterton, H. 408, 419
betting 337, 419
Bevan, A. 62, 378
Beveridge report (1942) 31, 239, 465
Bevin, E. 384
Bewdley 184, 197
Bird, A. 318
Bird, R. 308
Birkenhead, Earl of:
  alcoholism 333, 415
  in Cabinet 411, 431
  career 415–16, 458
  death 436
  and fall of the Coalition (1922) 402,
    414, 499
  on Gilmour 419
  and House of Lords 386
  Lord Chancellor 396
  in 1922–4: 339, 422, 435, 436, 437, 438,
    439, 440–3
  peerage 321
  rectoral address 29, 415
  mentioned 337, 457, 458, 470
Birmingham 20, 28, 41, 74, 114, 151, 193
Birmingham Club 352
Birmingham Post 95
Blackpool 189
Blain, H. 175, 249, 254, 264, 278
Blair, P. 248
Bledisloe, Lord 19, 391, 415
Blitz, the 47
Blundell, F. 312, 314
Bolton 181
Bonar Law, A.:
  at Carlton Club meeting (1922) 75, 475,
    481, 483, 504
  and fall of the Coalition (1922) 340,
    347, 482
  first retirement 227, 451, 467
  as Leader 404, 450, 454, 458, 459, 465,
    466–7, 470, 478, 506
  as Prime Minister 437, 440, 445, 453
  succession after resignation as Prime
    Minister 454
  mentioned 49, 76, 205, 221, 252, 267, 273,
    295, 393, 395, 401, 414, 417, 426,
    469, 471, 474, 480, 522
Boothby, R.:
  affair with Dorothy Macmillan 333
  anti-appeasement 365
  and Chief Whip 377
  and limits of dissent 210, 368
  and Mosley 352

Index

regarded with suspicion 332, 351
and 'YMCA' group 349–50
mentioned 316
Boulton, W. 371
Bourne, Lady H. 276
Bourne, R. 321
Bournemouth 175, 344
Bower, R. 211, 332
Bowyer, G. 276–7, 322
'Boys Brigade' group 350
Brabner, R. 395
Bradford 110, 196
Bramham Park 190
Bridgeman, C. 250, 268, 289
Bridgeman, W.:
  on Baldwin 489
  on Birkenhead 415
  on Cabinet ministers 393
  career 408, 416
  and cruiser crisis (1925) 431, 435
  and fall of the Coalition (1922) 228, 402, 480
  in the House of Commons 392
  on junior ministers 400
  in March 1931 crisis 442, 443
  Minister for Mines 399
  on role of Party Chairman 275
  peerage 321
  mentioned 66, 312, 404, 407, 410, 435, 455
Briscoe, D. 215
Bristol 110, 174
British Broadcasting Corporation 100, 101, 239
British Commonwealth Union 343, 352–3
British Union of Fascists 24
Brooksbank, E. 149
Broughton, U. 295
Brown, W. J. 357
Brunel Cohen, J. 316
Bryant, A. 21, 43, 295
Buccleuch, Duke of 312
Buchan, J. 35, 36, 294, 309, 322
  and policy research 447
Buchan-Hepburn, P. 371
Buckley, A. 215
Bull, W. 309, 340
Bunyan, J. 45
Burghley, Lord 73, 155, 321, 410, 522
Burke, E. 11, 37, 207
Bury 213
Bury St Edmunds 175
Bute, Earl of 314
Bute and North Ayrshire 167
Butler, R. A.:
  and 'Boys Brigade' group 350
  career 350, 395, 398–9, 407, 408
  on junior ministers 398
  on Marjoribanks 345
  memoirs 23

possible future Leader 459
on rural tradition 42
mentioned 316, 333, 373, 497
Butt, A. 309
by-elections:
  Bosworth (1927) 311
  Bromley (1930) 486
  Fulham East (1933) 490
  Hammersmith North (1926) 66
  Hammersmith North (1934) 193
  Islington East (1931) 487, 488–9, 499
  Newport (1922) 329, 475, 499
  Norfolk North (1930) 373, 486
  Norwood (1935) 285, 492
  Nottingham Central (1930) 290
  Oxford (1938) 359, 366
  Paddington South (1930) 486
  Rugby (1942) 357
  Twickenham (1929) 290
  Wavertree (1935) 348, 356, 492, 499
  Westminster St George's (1931) 341, 354, 356, 362, 442–3, 487–8, 491

Camrose, Lord 96, 303
Canterbury 183–4, 356
Cardiff South 212
Cardiganshire 137
Carlton Club 331, 336
Carlton Club meeting (1922), see CONSERVATIVE PARTY, III – party meetings
Cartland, R. 318, 365, 368
Catering Wages Bill (1942) 384
Cave, Lord 350, 389, 390, 393, 415
Cavendish-Bentinck, Lord H., see Bentinck, Lord H.
Cayzer, H. 308
Cazalet, V. 318, 327
Cazalet-Keir, T. 327, 351
Cecil, E. 312
Cecil, Lord H.:
  on Conservatism 11, 12, 34
  on government 25
  on 'natural conservatism' 35, 82
  support of Baldwin 441
  on taxation 27
  mentioned 416
Cecil, Lord R. 416, 432, 438, 467
Chadwick, B. 322
Chamberlain, A.:
  and Bonar Law 504
  conduct as Leader 260, 268, 462, 463, 465, 466, 467–8, 470, 477–8
  comparison to Neville Chamberlain 470
  and fall of the Coalition (1922) 227, 360–1, 454, 460, 478, 480–3, 500, 506
  Foreign Secretary 432
  formal position as Leader 385, 450, 453
  and junior ministers in 1922: 402–3

Chamberlain, A.: (cont.)
  in 1922–4: 9–80, 435, 436–8, 440, 442, 476, 484
  in 1929–31: 474
  strategy before Carlton Club meeting (1922) 340, 341, 482–3, 514
  and Younger 274, 500
Chamberlain, J. 418
Chamberlain, N.:
  and anti-appeasers 368
  appeasement policy 493–4, 519
  on Baldwin 468
  attitude to Labour Party 56
  and Conservative Research Department 448
  death 428
  and Eden 420, 433
  and Halifax 427
  as Leader 267, 462, 465, 466, 467, 469–70, 522
  leadership prospects in 1931: 442, 505
  and Munich Agreement (1938) 237, 494
  in 1924–9: 411, 421
  in 1929–31: 442–4, 456–7, 474, 485, 486, 487, 488, 489
  in 1939–40: 342, 366, 405, 421, 430, 470, 473, 495–6, 498, 500, 503, 506
  as Party Chairman 272, 273, 275, 279, 281–2, 291, 297, 443–4, 516
  as Prime Minister 405, 424, 440, 469, 493
  resignation as Party Leader 454
  rise to the Leadership 458, 467
  speech in Norway debate (May 1940) 366, 497
Chambers of Commerce 447
Channon, H. 65, 332, 333, 365, 380, 425
Chatfield, Lord 423
Chaucer, G. 45
Chelmsford 178, 191
Cheltenham 163, 206
Chichester 167
Chippenham 190
Chorlton, A. 213
Christianity 12, 16, 33, 40, 44, 510
Church of England 21, 26
Churchill, Lord R. 19
Churchill, R. 206, 348, 356
Churchill, W.S.:
  anti-appeasememt 326, 364, 365, 493, 494
  becomes Leader 413, 453, 454, 458, 459, 471
  cabinet formation 421
  career before 1914: 408
  and Chief Whip 377–8, 520
  distrust of 342, 348, 490–1, 503, 505
  and equal pay vote (1944) 351
  financial problems of 303
  'Gestapo' broadcast (1945) 30, 522
  in 1924–9: 431, 435, 439
  in 1929–31: 436, 456, 485
  and India 32, 210, 235, 244, 253, 363, 429
  as Leader 253, 267, 465, 466, 470–2, 506, 533
  length of service as MP 319
  and National Governments 363, 404
  in Norway debate (May 1940): 505
  relations with constituency 210, 216, 240, 495
  resignation from shadow Cabinet (1931) 442
  return to the Conservative Party (1924) 133, 404, 411
  in wartime government 496
cinema 101
Cirencester and Tewkesbury 175, 219–20
Clapham 188
Clarry, R. 329
Clavering, A. 293–4
Cleveland 211
clubs, in London west end 330, 331, 336–7
Clyde, J. 396
Clydesdale, Marquess of 321
Coal Bill:
  (1929) 329
  (1936–7) 27, 233, 493
coalitionism 67, 336 434–8, 440–1
coal subsidy (1925) 347
Cohen, P. 284
Colchester 214
Colman, N. 243
'Colonel Blimp', 343, 518
Communist Party of Great Britain 57, 61
Conservatism:
  difference from Fascism 14, 24, 42, 51, 57–8, 65, 80
  fears 52–67
    class politics 20
    Communism 52, 56, 57–8
    democracy 53–4, 507
    Labour Party 56, 61, 63, 90–2, 335
    national decline 52–3
    social change 36
    Socialism 37–8, 39, 58, 62–3, 388, 479, 510
    view of the working class 54–6, 61, 88
  hostility to:
    anti-modernism 36, 53
    bureaucracy 60, 92
    intellectuals 13, 63, 70, 91
    the left 23, 46
    laissez-faire 29
    Liberal Party 66–7, 90
    Liberalism 28, 33, 58, 61
    middle and upper class Socialists 64
    Socialism 17, 28, 33, 55, 58–63, 82, 91–2
    Socialist state 27
    view of the Jews 65–6
  importance of 4–5, 518
  nature of 9–11, 23, 27, 34–5, 67–8
  principles of 12–35
    adaptation 22, 77
    authority 13, 14, 18, 25, 27

Index

bureaucracy 13
capitalism 28–9, 59
change 15, 22–3, 82
civilization 14
class 15–16, 45–6, 52, 74, 87–8
  the common law 21, 24, 26
  the constitution 21, 24–6, 43, 388
  democracy 20, 25, 33
  dictatorship 24, 25, 49
  the empire 32–4, 45, 62, 84, 494
  the family 13, 27
  freedom 24–25
  government 26,28
  human nature 12–14, 16, 20, 59
  the individual 13, 26–7
  inequality 16, 18, 24
  inheritance 17
  justice 16, 40, 41
  lessons of the past 21–22
  morality of 16, 40
  private enterprise 28
  property 16–18, 27, 107
  reason 13–15, 59
  rights of man 14
  religion and 12, 20–1, 70
  role of the state 26–30
  social reform 30–1
  social unity 18, 19
  society 12, 15–15, 17
  stability 16, 21, 22
  trust in the people 19, 20, 37, 88, 145
sources for 11–12
temperament of 10, 35–52, 501, 518
  amateurism 50
  aristocracy 48–9
  character 17, 49–51
  common sense 38, 45, 50
  deference 48
  duty 39–40, 53, 73, 500
  Englishness 42, 44, 47, 84, 87
  fairness 40–1, 47, 447, 488
  history 21, 44–5
  honesty 19, 36, 50
  middle class attitudes 51–2, 83, 88
  moderation 85
  national identity 42–4, 70–1
  national unity 46–7, 61, 83
  'natural conservatism' 35–6, 82–3, 112, 518
  order 48, 49
  paternalism 49
  patriotism 32, 45–6, 53, 84, 493–4, 495
  pessimism 36, 52, 93
  populism 18–19
  pragmatism 9, 28, 35, 38, 77, 519
  quality 20, 22, 48, 60
  race 33, 44
  realism 31, 37–8, 498
  ruralism 42, 43–4, 47
  scepticism 36–8

  service 24, 38–9
  toleration 43, 44, 51, 85
  tradition 41–2
CONSERVATIVE PARTY, I – general:
composition of 512–3
distribution of power within 516–18
electoral success 1, 102–3, 145, 507
historiography of 6–8
identity of 67–81, 512
  cohesion 76, 80–1, 518, 519–20
  diehards and 79, 346
  independence 75–6, 434, 472, 480, 501
  junior ministers and 401–2
  language of 69–71, 87–8, 218, 389
  loyalty 73, 76–7, 355, 375, 392, 462–3, 500–1, 514, 515
  metaphors of 50, 70, 76, 87
  resonance with national character 44
  role of party 71–4, 76, 232
  self-image 74–5
  senior backbench MPs and 332
  symbols of 46
  and two-party system 72
  unity 10, 78–80, 81, 436–7, 457, 459, 501, 502, 520–1
  view of politics 51, 63
  view of society 77, 78
lines of communication within 209–10, 228, 244, 257–8, 262, 267, 269, 338, 369, 380, 446, 512–13, 514
name of 46, 68–9
nature of 9, 25, 72, 78, 86–7, 121, 146, 199, 346, 468, 500, 507–8, 515–16, 517–21
periods of disunity 477
policies and issues 518–9
  agriculture 71
  appeasement 32, 84–5
  defence 31
  expenditure 108, 223–4, 346, 499
  foreign policy 31–2, 73
  House of Lords reform 194, 267, 343, 346, 350, 353, 388–90, 479, 500
  housing 28
  India 489–92, 499
  political levy 55–6, 71, 229, 340, 346, 479
  poor relief 41
  protectionism 29, 70, 86, 131, 342, 345, 484–5, 499, 511, 512
  safeguarding 229, 255, 256, 258, 347, 361, 438
  social reform 30–1, 90
  taxation 27, 108
policy-making 444–9
primary sources for 1–6, 165, 265–6, 379
role of organization within 241, 512
social outlook of 51–2
strengths of 11, 74–5, 76–8, 195–6, 301, 518–22

CONSERVATIVE PARTY, II – Leadership:
  formal position of 385, 450–1, 459–60
  Leader in the House of Lords 387–8, 404, 427, 450–1
  secretarial support for 464
  selection of Party Leaders 451–9
    in 1923: 454–5
    possible succession in 1931: 456–7
    potential Leaders 443, 457–9
    role of front bench in 453
    role of grass roots in 262
    role of monarch in 453
    rise to Leadership 413, 457
    undisputed successions 454
  removal of Party Leaders 472–6
    forms of unrest 501–2
    methods and procedure 473–4
    role of National Union 517
    role of party meetings 475–6
  role of Party Leaders 459–65, 521
    attendance at National Union Central Council 252–3
    attendance at National Union Executive Committee 267
    address to Annual Conference 256
    conduct of 466–72, 480, 500, 514–15
    danger of rigidity 340
    flexibility of 64
    in general elections 85
    in Cabinet formation 404
    in policy-making 444–5
    key decisions of 464–5
    powers of 459–61, 513, 516
    relationship with Premiership 453, 463
    relationship with rank and file 500
    styles of leadership 465–6, 469, 506
CONSERVATIVE PARTY, III – party meetings:
  composition of 268, 362, 452, 475
  role of 474
  meeting of October 1922 (Carlton Club) 432, 434, 451, 460, 473, 475, 483, 504, 514, 520
    composition of 450
    reason for calling 482
    timing of 499
  meeting of February 1924 (Hotel Cecil) 474–6, 517
  meeting of June 1930 (Caxton Hall) 362, 416, 452, 474–6, 485, 489, 502
  meeting of October 1930 (Caxton Hall) 347, 362, 416, 417, 442, 452, 474–6, 487, 489, 517–8
  meeting of August 1931 (Kingsway Hall) 461, 474, 476, 518
  meetings to confirm a selected leader 451–2
  meeting of MPs of March 1921: 374, 457, 520
  summoning of party meetings 475, 476

CONSERVATIVE PARTY, IV – ministers:
  Cabinet ministers:
    ages of 408
    career patterns of 408–9, 412–30
    change of generations 412–13
    composition of coalition Cabinets 405–6
    conduct of Cabinets 410–12, 431, 440
    election policy committee 445
    free trade group (1923) 438–9
    peers in 407–8
    promotion to 393, 407
    receipt of peerages 321
    resignations 431–3
    resignation threats 411, 420, 431, 438–9
    social basis of 409–10
    selection of 404–5
    shadow Cabinet 438, 442–3, 446, 456, 474, 484, 487–8
    status within the Cabinet 407
    views of right wing 342
  junior ministers:
    appointment of 393–5
    criticisms of 1938: 403
    fall of Coalition (1922) and 402–3, 434, 481
    hierarchy of offices 399
    Law Officers 396–7
    nature of junior office 398–9, 400–1
  party managers 402, 481–2, 483, 514, 515
  path of promotion 391–8
    administrative ability 392–3
    imperial appointments 397
    junior offices 393
    membership of groups 352
    Parliamentary Private Secretaries 393
    speaking ability 391–2, 399
CONSERVATIVE PARTY, V – parliamentary party:
  composition of 307–16, 321–7
    ages of 316
    aristocracy 312
    deaths in Second World War 318
    education 312–14
    landowners 311
    local connections 315–16
    occupations 308–11, 329
    political spectrum of 338
    religion 314–15
    war veterans 310, 316
    women 322–7
    working class 311
  career patterns of 317–21
    career politicians 311
    continuity 318–9
    costs and finances 327–9
    departures 317–18
    divorce 212–13, 333–4, 357
    receipt of honours 319–21, 396
    turnover 317
    young MPs 332, 367, 518

Chief Whip 228, 368, 369, 444, 481
  and anti-appeasers 366
  and groups 352
  and honours 304, 320, 434
  and loyalty 70, 374, 375, 392
  and party meetings
  and promotions 392, 393, 404
  role of 272, 338, 340, 373–4
constituency work 330–1
  relations with local association 207–17, 338
  deselection 212–14
culture of 70, 308, 314, 330, 337–9, 392, 498, 518, 520
  attitudes to women MPs 322–3
  clubs 331, 336–7
  and election campaigns 193
  formative influences upon 37
  homosexuality 334
  lack of defections to other parties 72
  loyalty 338–9, 340
  reputation and conduct 332–4
  social relations of 331–2, 334–6
  standing of senior backbench MPs 340–1
  views of young MPs 351
dissent 215–16, 339, 341, 349, 354–5, 359–60, 365, 473, 493, 501–2
  defections 359
  independent and unofficial candidates 206
  periods of revolt 360–7,
  resignation of the whip 348, 358–9, 490
  withdrawal of the whip 355–8, 368, 376
left wing 349–52
mainstream centre 339–42, 360, 473, 498, 518
  opposition to continuing Coalition (1922) 342
  in Second World War 472, 505–6
  support for appeasement 342, 344, 494
1922 Committee:
  chairmen 341
  development of 375, 381–2
  role of whip 373, 381–2
  in Second World War 349, 421, 471
  work of 382–4
parliamentary subject committees:
  development of 375, 379, 446, 517
  India Committee
  role of the whips 373
  work of 380–1
regional and interest groups 352–4
right wing, or 'diehards':
  and appeasement 345
  and Coalition 477
  composition of 342–9
  'Forty Theives' 332, 343, 349, 362
  and India 348, 490
  number of 343, 363, 502
  organization of 343
  views of 345–6, 364
  mentioned 11, 57, 79, 362, 475, 487, 501

whips 367–78, 401; *see also* Chief Whip
  composition of 369–71
  and junior ministers 373–4
  London Whip 247, 373
  outlook of 371–3
  relations with MPs 368–9
  roles of 330, 367–9, 373
  Scottish Whip 130, 248, 372–3
CONSERVATIVE PARTY, VI – Central Office:
  Chairman of the Party Organisation:
    appointment 274, 393
    Deputy Chairman 276
    and honours 304
    as National Union Executive Committee chairman 263, 275, 481
    payment of 273–4
    post established 242
    role of 275–6, 280, 374, 444, 446, 464
    special fund of 305
    status 272–4
    tour of Areas after 1931 crisis 245
    Vice-Chairmen 271, 276–7, 291
  Central Office, general:
    and coalitions 147, 191, 204, 228, 285–6
    cost 282
    foundation 242
    in general elections 128, 141, 285
    premises 280
    relations with Areas 245, 246
    relations with constituencies 183, 187, 204–5, 219, 221, 287, 289–91
    role of 280, 285–7, 446, 447, 515–6
    structure of 279, 281–2
    staff 282–4
    in Second World War 239, 284, 298
  Central Office, Organisation Department:
    financial subsidies 164, 185, 195, 300
    labour department 289
    London department 247, 298
    missioners 98, 188
    and parliamentary candidates 200, 202, 204–5, 287–8
    services to constituencies 287–9
    training of agents 176, 288, 295
    women's department 288
  Central Office, Publicity Department:
    Director of 281
    cinema vans 101–2, 293–4
    functions of 291–2
    Lobby Press Service 95, 292
    political education 294–6
    publicity and propaganda 88–92, 98–102, 195, 291–3
    role of 291
  Conservative Research Department:
    origins 447–8
    role of 448–9
  educational institutions:

CONSERVATIVE PARTY, VI – Central Office: (*cont.*)
  Bonar Law Memorial College (Ashridge) 21, 270, 295–6, 303, 447
  Stott College 21, 295
  organizational inquiries:
    Chamberlain Committee (1930–1) 245, 282
    Fraser Committee (1937) 156, 288
    Monsell Committee (1937) 282
    Palmer Committee (1943) 156
    Special Finance Committee (1942–4) 306
    Stanley Committee (1927–28) 281
    Unionist Organisation Committee (1911) 242, 272
  Policy Secretariat (1924) 379, 447
  Principal Agent (later General Director) 242, 277–80, 282
  publications:
    Ashridge Journal 296
    Conservative Agents' Journal 175, 183
    Constitutional Yearbook 291
    The Elector 293
    Gleanings & Memoranda 95, 291
    Hints for Speakers 95, 291
    Home and Empire 293
    Home and Politics 87, 187, 292–3
    The Man in the Street 292, 293
    The Onlooker 293
    Popular View 292

CONSERVATIVE PARTY, VII – finances:
  administration of 305–6
    accountants 305
    National Conservative Board of Finance 306
    Treasurer of the Party 275, 305–06
    Treasurer's Department 306
  expenditure 297–9
    candidates' expenses 328, 329
    in general elections 300
    reductions 298
  income 299, 301–6
    donations 302–3
    relationship with honours 303–4
    social basis of 301–2, 519
  investments and reserves 304–5
  trusts 304

CONSERVATIVE PARTY, VIII – National Union:
  general:
    foundation 69, 241–2
    officers 250
    powers 205
    role 262, 514, 515, 516
    rules 259, 263, 268, 517
    Secretary, 250
  Annual Conference 253–62
    agenda 255–6, 259
    chairman 250, 256, 259
    composition 254–5, 257
    Leader's address at 256
    political discussion 259–62
    proceedings of 256–7, 259
    role 253–4, 257–9, 268, 482, 517
    specific conferences:
      (1920) 518
      (1921) 72, 258, 259–60, 520
      (1922) 76
      (1923) 388
      (1926) 258, 261
      (1927) 76, 514
      (1928) 19, 258, 513
      (1929) 263
      (1932) 68, 261
      (1933) 65, 261, 520
      (1934) 29, 163, 258, 271, 522
      (1935) 75, 271, 520
      (1941) 357
  Central Council 248–53
    chairmanship 243
    composition 248–50
    functions 250–1, 444
    political discussion 251–3
    special meeting (December 1934) 253
    mentioned 34, 176, 200, 222, 417, 491
  Executive Committee 263–8
    chairmanship 243, 263–4, 268
    composition 264–5
    and conference agenda 255
    and fall of the Coalition (1922) 260–1, 479, 481, 482, 500
    and party meetings 451–2
    role of 265–8, 446
  Sub-committees:
    Central Women's National Advisory Council 268–9
    deputations sub-committee 267
    education sub-committee 270
    General Purposes committee 243, 255, 264, 271–2
    junior advisory committee
    Labour sub-committee 269, 289
    Post-War Problems sub-committee 31, 472
    propaganda sub-committee 270
    Standing Advisory Committee on Candidates 205, 270, 290

CONSERVATIVE PARTY, IX – specialist and ancilliary organizations:
  Conservative Films Association 294
  Junior Imperial League 154–7, 174, 194, 197, 199, 276, 295
    regional organizers 246, 288
    publications 293
  National Association of Conservative & Unionist Women Organizers 181
  National Society of Conservative Agents 175–6, 180, 288

National Tours 288
Teachers' Circles 270
trade unionist 515
  Unionist Labour Movement 269–70
women, annual conference 262, 268
Young Britons 40, 194, 157, 288–9, 293
Young Conservatives 155, 156, 199
CONSERVATIVE PARTY, X – regional organization:
  Central Office Areas:
    Area Agents 242, 244, 245–6
    relations with constituencies 204, 246, 290
    relationship with Central Office 245
    role 245–7, 286, 446
    staff salaries 246
  National Union Provincial Areas:
    Area Chairman 243, 244, 514
    Area Councils 243, 244
    Area President 243–4
    development of 242–3
    and election expenses 328
    and fund-raising 306
    and political education 296
    role of 244–5, 283
    women's organization 245
    specific areas:
      Eastern Area 168, 242, 255, 266–7
      Essex and Middlesex Area 243, 244
      Metropolitan Area 171, 243, 247
      Northern Area 206, 243, 514
      North West Area 243–4, 266
      South East Area 168
      Surrey Provincial Division 159
      Sussex Provincial Division 289–90
      Wales and Monmouthshire Area 255
      Wessex Area 242, 296
      Western Area 243
      Yorkshire Area 243
  Scottish Unionist Association 247–8, 251, 255
CONSERVATIVE PARTY, XI – constituency organization:
  agent:
    dismissals 177–80
    duties 173–4, 181, 192
    number of 196
    role of 149, 150, 171–3, 209–10
    salaries 176–7, 186
    in Second World War 181–3
    social class 174–5
    transport 190
    women organizers 180–1
  candidate selection 198–205
    autonomy in 204–5, 271
    and Central Office 287–8
    local candidates 198
    finance and 184–6, 201–2, 203
    social status 199–200, 203

  and women 200–1, 323
  working class 200, 271
culture 170–1, 179
  divisions and splits 205–6
  local autonomy 146–7, 186, 204–5, 289–90, 516–17
  social activities, 64, 188–90, 197
  social attitudes 51–2, 86, 88, 219, 520, 521
finance 183–7
  branches and 153
  and coalitions 185
  expenditure 190
  following defeat 177
  frauds 179–80
  fund-raising 187–8
  MPs' contributions 183, 184–6, 190
  overdrafts 191
  property 181
  in Second World War 182, 185
membership:
  activism 155, 161–2, 170, 192
  apathy 193–4
  estimated numbers 163–8
  gender balance 167
  social basis 104, 107, 150, 162–4, 184, 222, 508, 519–20
  working class 163
  women 98, 151, 154, 168–71, 186, 188, 189, 193, 197
political activities 94
  canvassing 98, 157, 191
  in elections 99–100, 174, 192–3
political opinions, general:
  and coalitions 191, 222, 229, 285–6
  criticism of legislation 27
  forms of 217–19
  general outlook 69, 71, 93, 96, 194, 202
  influences upon 221–4
  issues causing concern 221–4
  means of expressing 265–6
  relationship with leaders 514–5, 521
  'round robin' resolutions 219–20
  significance of 17
  view of Labour Party 56
  view of leaders 23, 49, 75, 78, 218, 230, 235–6, 513–4
  view of opponents 64
political opinions, specific issues:
  appeasement 236–9, 495
  and Empire Crusade (1930–1) 81, 230, 488
  fall of Coalition (1922) 125, 170, 227–8, 479–80
  House of Lords reform 222, 229
  housing 234
  and India 216, 218–19, 232, 234–6, 244, 487, 513
  Irish settlement (1921) 80, 226–7

CONSERVATIVE PARTY, XI – constituency
      organization: (cont.)
   and 1924–9 government 229–30
   and 1929–31 crisis 230–2, 485, 486
   and National Government 142, 185, 216,
      232–4, 236
   national service 238
   protectionism 222, 228–9
   Russia 229
   relations with MP 149, 185, 207–17, 329,
      338, 517
      deselection 212–14
      influence of constituency upon 209–10
         228, 446, 515
      financial relations 214, 328–9
      limits of dissent 215–17, 368
   structure:
      Annual General Meeting 149, 208, 217
      branches 152–3
      chairman 148–9, 209–11,
         218, 514
      city associations 151–2, 176
      clubs 160–1
      effectiveness of 194–6
      executive committee 149, 150–1, 208,
         209, 234
      president 147–8
      rules 150
      in Second World War 196–8
      sub-committees 150, 158, 194, 195, 222,
         248, 289
      treasurer 149
      vice-presidents 150, 183
      women's committee 152, 153–4
      youth 154–7
CONSERVATIVE PARTY, XII – internal
      dissent and divisions:
   divisions of party leadership 434–44
   divisions over coalitionism 434–6
   divisions of 1920–2: 69, 75, 343, 477–83,
      503, 504
      constituency pressure in 207, 210, 515
      election scare of January 1922: 479
      honours scandal (1922) 480
      intention of leaders to continue the
         Coalition 479
      fall of the Coalition (September-October
         1922) 360–1, 468, 521
      meetings of backbench MPs 340–1
      National Union and 260–1, 500
      parliamentary party and 360–1
      revolt of junior ministers 402–3, 425
      revolt of party managers 374, 375,
         481–2, 515
      unpopularity of the Coalition 125, 346–7,
         353, 360, 460, 479–80, 522
   divisions of 1922–4: 75, 339 434–5, 436–9,
      440–2, 483–4
      diehards and 347

   nature of 436
   support for Baldwin after 1923
      defeat 341, 441
divisions of 1929–31: 41, 69, 484–9, 504
   and coalitionism 435–6
   constituency unrest 207, 230–1, 485, 486
   crisis of March 1931: 341, 442–4,
      456–7, 474
   crisis of summer 1930: 347, 415,
      417, 486
   leadership divisions 442–4, 474
   parliamentary party and 361–2
   policy advance 362, 486–7
   support for Baldwin against press
      attacks 231–2, 344
divisions of 1931–5 over India 253, 290,
   348, 353, 476, 489–92
   constituency opinion 234–6, 429, 488
   doubts of mainstream MPs 339–40, 442
   failure of revolt 501
   parliamentary party and 362–4, 442
   political context 490
   unity of leadership 439, 490
divisions of 1935–40 over appeasement
   492–7, 503
   anti-appeasement group 211, 216–17,
      355, 380, 433, 494–5503
   choice of Prime Minister in May
      1940: 427
   constituency pressures 238–9, 495
   decline of confidence in Chamberlain 342,
      377, 470, 495–6, 503, 506
   parliamentary party and 364–7
   problem of Churchill 502
   nature of group 365, 377, 493
   Norway debate (May 1940) 359, 366–7,
      368, 421, 476, 497, 503, 505
   unity of leadership 439
periods of division compared 339, 477,
   497–506
CONSERVATIVE PARTY, XIII – electoral
      support:
   appeal to the public:
      anti-Socialism 82, 510
      avoidance of reaction 93, 510
      centrist strategy 522
      communication of 93–102, 508
      election manifestos 444–5
      language of 87–8
      leadership style and 465–6
      nature of 82–7, 90, 124, 508, 509–11
      programme 511–12
      propaganda and publicity 54, 88–92,
         98–102
      style and methods of 88–93
      tranquility 83, 511
      to women 82, 83–4, 119
   electoral record 102–3, 113, 507
      in the cities 110–11, 114–15

effect of coalitions 102–3, 510, 511
in the university seats 104–5
economic and social factors:
  domestic servants 110–11, 117
  gender gap 84, 118
  generations 120–1
  middle class 104, 106–11, 113
  nature of 144–5, 507–8, 509
  nonconformity 130–1
  profile of 112–14
  regional basis 121–2
  women 89–90, 117–19, 133, 508
  working class 89, 112, 116–17, 123, 509, 515
political factors:
  constituencies not contested 103–4
  electoral pacts 129
  electoral prospects in late 1930s 142
  expectation of success 507
  franchise and electoral system 104–6, 508–9
  governing party 125
  Liberal voters 124–5, 136, 137, 436
  marginal seats 125–6
  safe seats 122–3, 509
  splitting of Conservative vote 206
  straight fights 126–7, 133, 510
  three-way contests 127
  unopposed returns 122, 124
Conservative and Unionist Movement 353
Constitutional Club, 331, 336–7
Conway, M. 344
Cook, A. J. 63
Cook, T. 328–9
Cooper, A. Duff:
  anti-appeasement 495
  background 312, 349, 365
  career 392, 397, 399, 410, 423–4
  on Conservatism 37, 46, 518
  resignation 433, 439
  on revolutions 56
  Westminster St George's by-election 443
  and 'YMCA' group 349
  mentioned 11, 216, 261, 341, 390, 420
Cooper, Lady D. 48, 99, 312
co-operative societies 222–3
Copeland, I. 326
Cornwall 137
Cornwall North 197
Country Landowners' Association 309
Courthope, G. 39, 309, 312, 381
Cranborne, Lord, see Salisbury, 5th Marquess of
Crawford, Earl of 438, 442
Crichel Down affair (1954) 273
Crichton-Stuart, Lord C. 314
Cripps, S. 62, 216, 335
Crisp, D. 38
Critchley, A. 308, 318
Croft, H. Page:

on annual conference 253
career 343–4
on diehard strategy 348
and Empire Crusade 361
and Empire Industries Association 353
and India 235, 490
and June 1930 party meeting 362
and National Party 72
on party loyalty 521
and protectionism 255, 343, 344
and wartime politics 73, 81,
mentioned 265, 348
Crookshank, H. 310, 316, 334, 399, 403
Crossley, A. 365
Culverwell, C. T. 213
Cunliffe-Lister, P.:
  career 349, 418, 424–5
  resignation 424
  mentioned 344, 408, 411, 413, 453
Cunningham-Reid, A. 205, 357
Curzon, Lord 247
Curzon, Marquess:
  career 412, 414
  death 407
  and fall of the Coalition (1922) 410, 432, 455, 505
  Leader in the House of Lords 387, 404, 450, 451
  succession to Bonar Law (1923) 453, 454–6, 458
  mentioned 386, 437, 452, 457, 464, 470

Daily Express 96, 97, 309
Daily Herald 97
Daily Mail 96, 97, 224, 490
Daily Mirror 97
Daily Telegraph 96
Dalton, H. 335, 497
Darwen 141
Davidson, J. 327
Davidson, J. C. C.:
  anti-coalitionism 435
  Ashridge 295
  career of 395
  criticism of 244, 267, 485
  and honours 303–4
  in March 1931 crisis 443
  National Union Executive Committee chairmanship 263
  Party Chairman 102, 175, 255, 272, 273, 274–5, 276, 278–9, 281, 285, 288, 294, 297
  and party funds 304, 305
  papers of 2–3
  and policy-making 447
  and succession to Bonar Law (1923) 455
  and youth movement 155
  mentioned 84, 253, 343, 466, 469, 503

Davies, C. 367
Davies, G. 322
Davies, T. 175
Davison, W. 205, 212, 334
Dawson, G. 96, 422
Dawson, P. 208
Defeated Candidates' Association 354, 452
Defence of the Realm Act (1914) 221, 423
De Frece, W. 309
De La Warr, Earl 333
Denbighshire 137
Derby 174
Derby, Earl of:
  career 393, 397, 414–5
  character 414, 466
  on the diehards 342
  dislike of Curzon 410, 455, 458
  on House of Lords reform 390
  on loyalty to the Leader 501
  at 1921 annual conference 258, 260
  in 1923–24: 440–1
  position in Lancashire 48, 303,
  and protectionism 243–4,
  mentioned 312, 332, 386, 416, 422, 438, 478
Derbyshire 137
Derbyshire South 211
Derbyshire West 152
Devizes 186
Devonshire, Duke of 312, 386, 387, 438
Disraeli, B.:
  and empire 32
  definition of Conservative principles 34
  as founder of Conservatism 11, 19, 37, 66
  and party organization 242
  and social reform 30
  'Tory democracy' 19
  and 'two nations' 46
  mentioned 471, 507
Doncaster 350
Doncaster, R. 211
Donner, P. 343
Doran, E. 65
Dorset West 190, 231
Douglas-Home, A., see Dunglass, Lord
Drudge, H. A. 175
Duckworth, G. 212
Du Cros, A. 308
Dufferin & Ava, Marquess of, 403
Dugdale, T. 273, 319, 371, 472
Dunbartonshire 167
Dundee 327
Dunglass, Lord 154–5, 316, 465
Dunkirk 142, 364
Dyer, R. 226, 345

East Ham North 205
Ebbisham, Lord 306
Eddisbury 137

Eden, A.:
  anti-appeasement 364
  career 352, 365, 395, 405, 408, 419–20, 428
  and Conservatism 17, 19
  on House of Lords reform 390
  resignation 433, 439, 493
  after resignation 495, 502, 505
  mentioned 421, 427, 457, 459, 465, 467, 470
Eden Group 367, 433
Ednam, Viscount 315
Eight Hours Bill (1926), 349, 392
election campaigning 192–3
  canvassing 98
  election address 99–100
  leafleting 98–100
  posters 100
  public meetings 94–5
  in working-class districts 95
Elliot, W.:
  background 309, 316
  career 349, 420, 459
  on Conservatism 21–2
  on the countryside 71
  on democracy 54
  in Munich crisis (1938) 434
  rise to office 352, 391, 399, 421
  mentioned 11, 425
Empire Crusade:
  by-election candidacies of 206, 487
  fears of disunity 355
  grass roots attracted to 81, 194, 223, 230–1, 488
  Croft and 344, 361
  and press dictation 502
  pressure upon MPs 207, 361
  mentioned 4, 203, 252, 428, 501, 505
Empire Free Trade 484
Empire Industries Association 221, 344, 353, 361, 378–9
Empire Marketing Board 431
Emrys-Evans, P. 207, 211, 365, 367, 380
Entwistle, C. 308
Epsom 167, 208
equal pay vote (1944) 214, 351, 369, 378
Essex West 210
Evans, A. 212, 214, 215
Evans, R. 250, 261
Everard, W. 308
Exeter 206, 356–7
Exeter, Marquess of 321
Eyres-Monsell, B.:
  background 369
  as Chief Whip 374, 375–6, 378
  and Monsell Committee 282
  and 1922 Committee 381, 382
  and subject committees 379
  withdrawal of the whip 355
  and Topping memorandum (1931) 442
  mentioned 344, 371, 424

Factory Acts 29, 346
Falmouth, Lady 245, 268, 276, 281–2
Farquhar, Lord 305
Federation of British Industries 353
Feiling, K. 11, 21, 37
Ferguson, H. 322
Fielden, E. B. 319
Fife East 128
Films Bill (1927) 411
Findlay, J. 309
First World War:
 changes in political system 330, 508, 509
 military service in 174, 310, 311, 316
 political effects of 26, 46, 73, 84, 194, 237
 popular support for 19
 and rise of Labour 52, 55
 mentioned 99
fishing 114
Fison, C. 321, 373
Fitzalan, Lord, *see* Talbot, Lord E.
'flapper vote' 53, 119, 229–30, 515
Flintshire 269
franchise, equalisation of (1928) 109, 120, 423
Fraser, I. 316
Fraser, M. 277, 280, 304, 306, 481
Fry, G. 464
Fyfe, C. 250

Gainsborough 202
Galloway 206
Gallup opinion poll 142
Garvin, J. L. 96
Gates, E. 214–15
Geddes, A. 397, 409
Gee, R. 311
George V, King 455
general elections:
 (1918) 127–8, 145
 (1922) 129–30, 305, 445
 (1923) 131–4
 (1924) 133–6
 (1929) 67, 78, 98, 100, 104, 108–9, 136–8, 336–7
 (1931) 139–41, 336, 363, 445, 511–12
 (1935) 142–3, 445
 (1945) 143–4, 472
General Strike (1926):
 Baldwin and 49–50, 217, 229, 469
 causes of failure 19
 consequences of 56, 338
 Joynson-Hicks and 422
 nature of public response 47, 55, 64
 revolutionaries and 57, 229
 mentioned 18, 25, 26, 221, 301, 347, 369, 411, 419, 431
Genoa conference (1922) 478
Germany 41
Gibbs, G. 371–2, 434, 521

Gilmour, J.:
 career 371, 372, 391, 418–19
 on role of government 29
 as Scottish Whip 372–3
 support of Coalition (1922) 434
 trustee of party funds 304
Glasgow 28, 117, 151
Glasgow Herald 95
Gloucester 174, 189
Glyn, R. 342
Godwin, G. 250, 284
Goring, H. 427
Government of India Act (1935) 363, 429, 489, 490, 491
governments:
 (1918–22):
  composition 405
  Conservative oposition to 23, 55, 405
  decision to continue in 1918: 128, 522
  failure of policies 478–9
  proportion of peers in 407
  support for in Scotland 130
 (1922–4) 70, 125, 415, 467, 484
  American debt crisis 434, 440
  composition 410, 422
  dissolution 438–9, 440–1
  proportion of peers in 407
 (1924–9) 23, 31, 412, 439
 (1931–5):
  formation 26, 73, 341, 348, 361
  India policy 363, 490, 492
  Liberals and 107, 511
  relations in 285–6, 376–7, 405, 439, 465, 469
  support for continuing 216, 232–4, 236, 363, 439
  views of 75, 77–8, 185, 348
 (1935–40) 90, 493, 494
  appeasement 74
  composition under Chamberlain 377, 405, 408, 424
  declaration of war 440, 496
  in wartime 496
 (1940–5) 383, 405, 471–2
Gower, P. 279, 284, 293
Grace, J. 312
Graham, A. 213
Grantham 198
Granville, E. 357
Grattan-Doyle, N. 186
Graves, M. 326
Greenwood, H., *see* Greenwood, Lord
Greenwood, Lord 306, 411
Gregory, 'Maundy' 303
Gretton, J.:
 background 308
 career 319, 343
 diehard group, 345, 346
 on economies (1932) 346
 at June 1930 party meeting 362

Gretton, J.: (cont.)
  and National Union 263, 265
  at 1921 annual conference 259
  and 1923 election 345, 347
  opposition to Coalition (1922) 219, 505
  importance of principles 72
Grey, E. 336
Griffith-Boscawen, A. 360, 395, 412, 422, 432, 504, 505
Grigg, E. 395
Grimsby 114
Gritten, H. 212
Guildford 159, 212
Guilty Men (1940) 239, 376
Guinness, W., 349, 413, 422
Gwynne, H. A. 96

Hacking, D. 238, 273, 274, 280, 472
Haggard, H. Rider 45
Haig, D. 414
Hailsham, 1st Viscount, *see* Hogg, D.
Halifax, Earl of, *see* Wood, E.
Hall, R. 277–8
Halliley, E. 175
Hambro, A. 309
Hamilton, Duke of, *see* Clydesdale, Marquess of
Hampshire North-West 211
Hampstead 185–6
Hand, A. 160
Hankow 43
Hannon, P. 352, 361
Harborough 152
Harmsworth, E. 309
Hartland, G. 213
Harvie-Watt, G. 384
Harwich 137
Hastings 214
Hawkey, J. 210
Hayek, F. A. 61
Headlam, C.:
  and Barnard Castle 127
  baronetcy 320–1
  career 319, 395, 409–10
  finances of 309, 329
  on the Junior Imperial League 154
  as junior minister 398, 401
  and National Conservative League 160
  and National Union Executive Committee chairmanship 264
  and Newcastle North 186, 205, 206
  and north-east region politics 164
  political views 339–40
Heath, E. 465, 506
Hemel Hempstead 183, 327
Henderson, V. 117
Heneage, A. 312
Hennessy, G. 276, 314
Henry, D. 396
Herbert, G. 263, 273

Herbert, S. 339, 365, 404
Herefordshire North 212
Hertford 102
Hess, R. 321
High Peak 350
High Wycombe 182
Hillingdon, Lady 250, 268
Hills, J. 349, 360
Hinchingbrooke, Lord 350–1
Hitchin 215
Hitler, A. 427, 439, 465, 469, 495
Hoare, S.:
  and Beaverbrook, 428
  career 428–30
  and fall of the Coalition (1922) 340–1, 360–1, 428, 460, 482, 500
  Foreign Secretary 430, 433
  and India 234, 261, 364, 428–9, 492, 499
  and Neville Chamberlain 428, 474
  in 1939–40: 496
  Party Treasurer 306, 428
  possible Leader 427
  and Young Unionist Group 349
  mentioned 142, 257, 275, 309, 337, 349, 374, 398, 404, 405, 411, 413, 425, 432, 439, 485, 486
Hoare-Laval Plan (1935):
  parliamentary reaction to 340, 341, 493
  and promotion of Eden 420
  and resignation of Hoare 430, 433
  mentioned 32, 207, 469
Hogg, D.:
  in Cabinet 413
  career 396, 417, 459
  as Leader in the House of Lords 386, 388
  at October 1930 party meeting 476
  and parliamentary speaking 392
  peerage 321
  as possible Leader 50, 417, 443, 451, 456–7, 458, 459, 489, 505
  mentioned 345, 445
Hogg, Q. 201, 349, 351, 366
Homan, C. 322
honours scandal (1922) 347
Hopkinson, E. 309
Hore-Belisha, L. 378, 403
Hornby, F. 308
Honcastle 184
Horne, R.:
  career 416, 436
  at June 1930 party meeting 476
  omitted from 1924 Cabinet 404
  as possible Leader 456, 457, 459, 505
  mentioned 470
Horobin, I. 334
Horsbrugh, F. 327
Hoskins, R. 295

House of Commons:
  Smoking Room 331, 334, 401, 513
  social relations in 331–2, 334–6
  speaking in 391–2
  work of 329–30, 337–8, 444
House of Lords 384–90
  composition 385–7
  leadership 387–8
  life peerages 389
  marginalization of 384–5
  reform of 55, 388–90
Housing Act (1934) 234
Howard-Bury, C. 321
Hudson, R. 308, 333
Hughes, C. 281
Hull 151
Hunter-Weston, A. 37, 309
Hurd, P. 309
Hutchinson, W. 309

Ilford 205
Iliffe, E. 341, 387
Imbert-Terry, H. 154, 155
Independent Labour Party 335
India Defence League 211, 221, 348, 363
Indian Empire Society 353
Indian Statutory Commission, *see* Simon Commission
India Round Table Conference (1930–1) 362, 426, 442, 489
India White Paper (1933) 363, 489, 492
Industrial Group 343, 352
Inskip, J. H. 261
Inskip, T.:
  career 396, 405, 408, 459
  criticism of 403, 404, 423
  on the General Strike (1926) 47, 49–50
Irwin Declaration (1929):
  Baldwin and 444, 461, 468, 492
  coalitionism and 435
  parliamentary debate on 362
  reasons for 425
  mentioned 232, 429, 464–5, 473, 489, 491
Irwin-Gandhi Pact (1931) 232, 362, 426, 465, 491
Irwin, Lady 48
Irwin, Lord, *see* Wood, E.
Isle of Wight 175
Iveagh, Lady:
  career 326
  Chairman of National Union 250, 255
  and Deputy Party Chairmanship 276
  and parliamentary speaking 391–2
  and Women's Advisory Committee 268, 269

Jackson, S.:
  Blain and 278
  career 273,
  departure from Party Chairmanship 274,

increase in expenditure 297
  and fund-raising 305
  as Party Chairman 275
  mentioned 277, 285, 305, 321, 416
James, W. 322
Jarvis, D. 88
Jenkins, W. 277
Jessel, H. 66, 247
Jews 41, 44, 65–6
jingoism 46
Joint Select Committee on India (1933–4) 261, 417, 429
Jones, T. 464
Joynson-Hicks, W. 212, 321, 328
  career 400, 408, 422–3, 431, 439, 459
Junior Imperial League, *see* CONSERVATIVE PARTY, IX – specialist and ancilliary organizations

Kellett, E. 318
Kemsley, Lord 96, 387
Kennedy, E. 182
Kensington South 205, 212
Kenworthy, J. M. 335
Keyes, R. 309, 366
Kindersley, G. 344, 362
King, H. 318, 393
Kinross and West Perthshire 216, 238
Kipling, R. 45
Kirkcaldy Burghs 204
Kirkwood, D. 335
Knebworth, Viscount 318
Kristallnacht (1938) 65
Kyslant, Lord 265, 322

Labour Party
  electoral support of 104, 130
  in House of Lords 384, 455
  middle class and 117
  nature of 83
  after 1931: 236, 363
  rise of 116, 301, 437, 479, 509, 510
  in Second World War 239, 366
  and trade unions 55, 72, 302
Ladies' Carlton Club 297
Lancashire 121, 159, 303, 317, 405, 415
  Conservative trade unionists 269, 289
  and India 218–9, 235, 236, 339, 364, 492
  Labour advance in 130
  and protectionism 244, 339, 438
Lane-Fox, G.:
  and coalitionist plots 342
  and fall of the Coalition (1922) 340
  on the General Strike 55
  on the 'flapper vote' 229
  on India policy 234
  Minister for Mines 321, 399
  on parliamentary speaking 391–2
Latham, H. 322

Law, R. 413
League of Nations 31, 237, 430, 432
League of Nations Union 221
Lee, A. 321
Leech, J. 309
Leeds 28, 189, 196
Leicester 108
Leith, A. 252, 268, 514
Lennox-Boyd, A. 395, 400
Lewes 202
Lewis, O. 308
Lewisham West 208
Liberal National Party 139, 140, 141, 142, 511, 517
Liberal Party:
  disunity of 72
  electoral support of 104, 127, 133, 510
  hostility to 66–7, 336
  and middle class 106–7, 302
  after 1923 election 441
  in 1931–2: 39, 141–2, 439
  and nonconformity 130–1
  revival in 1927–9: 136–7
Liberal Unionist Party 241, 264
Linlithgow, Marquess of 274, 276, 289
Lipson, D. 206
Liverpool 110, 114, 117, 139, 151, 176, 183, 196
Llewellin, J. J. 371, 400, 408
Lloyd, B. 213
Lloyd, G., 395, 464
Lloyd George, D.
  attitude to the press 97
  on Austen Chamberlain 466, 478, 480
  and Coalition 360, 474, 477, 522
  fund of 67
  honours scandal 303–4
  hostility to 62, 67, 335–6, 342, 350, 499
  and 1918 election 128
  in 1922–4: 434, 440
  in 1929–31 435–6
  opposition to in 1922: 360, 478–9, 500
  revival of Liberal Party (1927–9) 136
  and young Conservative MPs 332
  mentioned 75, 102, 104, 345, 374, 434, 496, 505
Lloyd of Dolobran, Lord 387, 490
Locker-Lampson, O. 65, 91, 374, 434
Lockwood, J. H. 206
Loder, J. 349, 350
London 113
London, City of 106
Londonderry, Lady 244
Londonderry, Marquess of 386, 388, 423
Long, W.:
  on Bonar Law 466, 467
  and fall of the Coalition (1922) 340, 467–8, 483
  career 408, 414
  mentioned 309, 452

Lothian, Marquess of 428
Louth 172
Low, D. 343, 518
Lowestoft 114, 513
Lucas-Tooth, H. 316
Lumley, R. 315
Lymington, Lord 312, 332, 343, 345, 350, 362
Lyttelton, O. 22, 309, 398, 405

Macaulay, Lord 37
MacDonald, J. Ramsay:
  and appointment of Hailsham (1931) 417
  and India 426, 492
  Margesson and 376
  formation of National Government 125, 139, 461, 465
  in the National Government 141, 142, 233, 286, 423, 439, 499
  and National Labour 104
  and 1929 election 90, 136,
  in 1931 election 101
  mentioned 63, 125, 311, 335, 426
McEwen, J. 365
McKenzie, R. T. 473
McKibbin, R. 83
McKie, J. 206
Mackinder, H. 309
Maclachlan, L. 191, 278–9
Maclean, D. 336
Macmillan, H.:
  anti-appeasement 365, 367
  anti-intellectualism 63
  background 308, 410
  dissent of 358–9, 376, 397
  on Margesson 377
  marriage 312, 333
  member of Watching Committee 367
  as Party Leader 465
  political views 11, 215,
  on politics 331
  on role of the state 29, 350
  suspicion of 332, 350, 351
  war service 310, 365
  and 'YMCA' group 349
  mentioned 80, 316, 339, 359, 388, 390, 413, 459
Macmillan, Lady D. 48, 99, 333
McNeill, R. 415
Macquisten, F. A. 55, 212
Macquisten Bill (1925) 218, 222, 347, 369, 464, 468
Maidstone 168, 207
Major, J. 465
Manchester 80, 118, 151, 154
Manchester Guardian 95
Mann, A. 95
Marchwood, Lord 306
Margesson, D.:
  anti-coalitionism 72

background 369
  as Chief Whip 373, 374, 376–7
  and Churchill 377
  dismissal from War Office (1942) 409
  divorce 333–4
  mentioned 371
Marjoribanks, E. 345, 362
Marlborough, Duke of 312
Marriott, J. 309
Marston, C. 263
Marxism 20, 58, 59
Mass-Observation 142
Masterman, C. 107
Mathams, R. 269
Maxse, M. 178, 280, 281, 282, 284, 518
Maxton, J. 335
Maxwell-Fyfe, D. 76, 396
Maxwell Hicks & Company 305
Melchett, Lord 65, 387
Merseyside Conservative Group 352
middle class 85–6, 88, 106–8
Middle Class Union 80
Midleton, Earl of 162, 260, 386, 387
Millais, J. 322
Milton, J. 45
Mines, Minister for 321, 393, 399
Mitchell, A. E. 284
Mitchell, H. 276, 321
Molson, H. 350, 354
monarchy 25, 453
Mond, A., *see* Melchett, Lord
Moore, N. 309
Moore-Brabazon, J. 341, 354, 399, 443
Morden, G. 332
Morning Post 96
Morrison, W. S. 190, 383, 457, 459
Mosley, O. 80, 335, 351, 352, 358, 359
Moss, H. 322
Muirhead, M. 284
Munich Agreement (1938):
  Boothby and 368
  Churchill and 210
  Duchess of Atholl and 326, 358
  Duff Cooper and 433
  Neville Chamberlain and 469, 494
  repudiation of 211, 495

Nall, J. 358
National Conservative League 159–60
National Co-ordinating Committee 75, 286, 348
National Defence Contribution (1937) 238, 493
National Democratic Party 128
National Farmers' Union 202, 223, 391, 413
National Labour Party 104, 139
National Party 72, 81, 344
National Publicity Bureau 233, 292, 294, 298, 309

Nazism 21
Newcastle 110
Newcastle North 186, 198–9, 205, 206, 211
Newcastle West 168
Newman, R. 206, 356–7
New Party 359
Newport 189; *see also* by-elections
Next Five Years Group 350
Nicolson, H. 365
Nield, B. 309
Nightingale, F. 45
nonconformity 26, 127, 130–1, 510
Nordic League 358
Norfolk, Duke of 314
Norfolk, North 173; *see also* by-elections
Norfolk, South 205
Northampton 197
Northcliffe, Lord 96, 387
Northern Group 352
Northumberland, Duke of 212
Norwich 213
Nottingham 189
Novar, Lord 41, 438
Nuffield, Lord 387

Observer, 96, 97
Oldham 216
O'Neill, H. 341, 383
Ormsby-Gore, W.:
  anti-coalitionism 342, 435
  career 349, 395, 424
  on summer 1930 crisis 231
  mentioned 338
Oxford Union debate (1933) 39
Oxfordshire South 200

Pacifism 62, 64
Paisley 228
Palmer, G. 308
Parliament, *see* House of Commons; House of Lords
Parliament Act (1911) 343, 384, 388, 450, 451, 472
Peat, C. 308
Peel, Earl 412, 429
Penryn and Falmouth 178
Percy, Lord E. 11, 25, 408, 420, 422
  and Conservative Research Department 448
Perth 218
Peto, B. 37, 215, 320, 336, 344
  withdrawal of the whip 355–6, 375
Philipson, H. 324–5
Philipson, M. 324–5
Pickford, M. 326
Pilkington, R. 395
Plays for Patriots 64
Plymouth, Earl of 265
Political and Economic Planning 350
Pollock, E. 396, 402

588   Index

Poor Law 346
Porritt, R. 318
Portland, Duke of 349
Prayer Book debate (1927) 423
press:
  and appeasement 493
  influence on policy 446
  national 95–8, 484–5
  power of 97–8, 231–2
  regional 85
Pretyman, E. 309, 340, 361
Priestley, J. B. 101, 239
Prime Minister 404, 407, 453, 463
Primrose League 120, 153–4, 194, 508
Proby, R. 264
Profumo, J. 368
Progress Trust 354
psychoanalysis 14
public opinion 71, 93–4
Putney 167, 184, 189
Pybus, P. 398
Pym, L. 312

Racecourse Betting Bill (1928) 355
radio broadcasts 100–1
Ramsay, A. M. 357–8
Ramsbotham, H. 408
Rathbone, B. 327
Ramsden, E. 243, 264
Reading, Marquess of 65
Rees, J. 318
referendum 231
Reform Act (1918) 53, 104, 118
  boundary revision 508
  business vote 105–6
  effects of 20, 89, 174, 451, 508–9
Reid, J. 396
Reigate 189
Reith, J. 101
Remer, J. R. 314, 332–3
Rentoul, G. 309, 381, 382–3
Rhys, C. 212, 339, 363
Right Club 358
Riley, E. S. 174
Rivers, A. T. 284
Rothermere, Lord:
  and Anti-Waste League 224
  attacks on Baldwin 441, 442, 443, 499
  and Empire Crusade 230, 488
  and Empire Free Trade 484
  and India 235, 348, 490
  and Irwin Declaration 435
  as newspaper owner 97, 387
  and 1929 election 98
  and March 1931 crisis 442–3
  mentioned 352
Rother Valley 197
Rowlands, G. 269, 271, 311
Royden, T. 308

Runciman, W. 324, 336, 403, 411
Rugby 191, 219; *see also* by-elections
Runge, N. 326
Rushcliffe 183
Russia 56, 345, 431, 478
Rutland, Duke of 312
Rye 191

Safeguarding of Industries Act (1921) 431
St Ives 114
St Marylebone 205, 357
Salford 152
Salisbury, 3rd Marquess of 30, 387, 507
Salisbury, 4th Marquess of:
  on Baldwin 468
  on Birkenhead 415
  career 265, 416–17
  on Conservative principles 518
  and fall of Coalition (1922) 219, 343, 353, 502, 504, 505
  and India 388,
  on Lane-Fox 321
  Leader in the House of Lords 460, 385, 386, 387
  and protectionist policy 438–9, 485
  and succession to Bonar Law (1923) 455
  and Watching Committee 367, 417, 502
  mentioned 235, 322
Salisbury, 5th Marquess of 30, 388, 410, 433
Salmon, I. 29, 308
Salvidge, A. 151, 260
Samuel, A. M. 398
Samuel, H. 65, 104, 139, 141, 285, 336
Samuel, S. 184
Sanders, Lady 268
Sanders, R.:
  career 371, 409, 410
  Deputy Party Chairman 276, 277
  and junior ministers' meetings (1922) 402
  Minister of Agriculture 273, 413, 422
  and National Union Executive Committee 265
  and party funds 304
  on unpopularity of the Coalition 125, 227, 481
  as whip 369, 370, 375
Sandys, D. 395
Sankey, Lord 417
Scotland 84
Scotsman 95, 309, 499
Scott, K. 419
Scott, L. 434
Scott, W. 45
Scottish Unionist Members' Committee 352
Scrymgeour-Wedderburn, H. 395
Second World War 22, 25, 30
Selborne, Earl of 265, 343, 353, 388, 502, 504, 505
Selborne, Lady 268

Sevenoaks
Shaftesbury, Lord 19, 30
Shakespeare, W. 45
Shaw, H. 326
Shedden, L. 248
Sheffield 28, 151, 187
Shipley 206
Shipwright, D. 77
Shrewsbury 168, 186, 212, 213
Simon Commission (1928–30) 234, 362, 426
Simon, J.:
   and India Statutory Commission 147
   in National Government 141, 419, 439
   negotiates electoral pact (1931) 107, 139
   in 1931 election 101, 104
   unpopularity (1938–40) 405, 427, 496
SinnFein, 509
Skelton, A. N.:
   on 1923 defeat 75
   on ownership of property 17
   on Socialism 60
   and young left-wing MPs 11, 349, 352
Skipton 178
Smithers, W. 52, 435
Snowden, P. 125, 335
Socialist Sunday School movement 157
Somervell, D. 396, 461
Southby, A. 208
South Shields 154
Sowerby 187
Spanish civil war, responses to 325
Speaker of the House of Commons 330, 335, 367
Spencer, D. 284
Spender-Clay, H. 337, 342, 468
Spen Valley 147
Sprot, A. 128
Stafford 196
Stamfordham, Lord 455
Stanhope, Earl 388
Stanley, G. 264
Stanley, Lord:
   career 273, 276, 349, 371, 395–6
   death 408
   and Junior Imperial League 155, 276
   Stanley Committee (1927) 281
Stanley, O.:
   career 349, 408, 420–1
   in Czech crisis (1938) 420, 434
   Minister of Labour 419
   Minister of Transport 398
   and 1922 Committee 384
   possible leader 459
   and 'YMCA' group 349–50
Steel-Maitland, A.:
   and National Union Executive Committee 265
   Party Chairman 272
   and party funds 304
   as Cabinet minister 273, 404, 422

Stelling, D. 34, 42, 51
Stirling and Falkirk Burghs 167
Stockton 168, 215, 339
Stonehaven, Lord
   on local autonomy 289, 515
   and National Government 75–6
   as Party Chairman 243, 245, 274, 276, 280, 282
   and status of Party Chairman 272, 273
   reduction of expenditure 297
Storr, L. 379
Stott, P. 294
Strathcona and Mount Royal, Lord 276, 403
Stuart, J. 279, 312, 322, 369, 383
   as Chief Whip 378, 472
Swinton, Earl of, *see* Cunliffe-Lister, P.

Talbot, Lady E. 268
Talbot, Lord E.:
   background 345, 369
   as Chief Whip 370, 374, 378
   and leadership succession (1921) 451
   Roman Catholicism 314
   on selection of whips 370, 371
   mentioned 345, 375
Tamworth 183
Tariff Reform League 194
Tate, M. 326–7, 333
taxation 108
Thatcher, M. 327, 465, 471, 506, 512, 522
Thomas, J. H. 333, 439
Thomas, J. P. L. 377, 433
Thomson, F. 396
Thorneycroft, P. 350–1, 352
Thorp, L. 358
Tilley, V. 309
Times, The 96, 97
Titchfield, Marquess of 410
Todd, A. J. 175, 358
Topping Memorandum (1931) 279–80, 286, 442–3, 487
Topping, R. 279–80, 284, 442
Torquay 173, 218
Tory Reform Committee 30, 79, 215, 354, 358, 378, 472
   assessed 350–2
Tottenham South 172
Trade Disputes Act (1927) 56, 215, 270, 287, 301, 349, 350, 413
trade unions 55–6, 82
Trades Union Congress 72
Tree, R. 448
Tryon, G. 274, 319, 401, 408
Turton, R. 319
Tyler Kent affair (1940) 358
Tynemouth 194

Ulster Unionism 359, 509
Unemployment Assistance Board 419, 490

Union of Britain and India 221, 290, 353–4
Unionist Business Committee 378
Unionist Independent Peers 162, 386
Unionist Social Reform Committee 349, 378
Unionist War Committee 378
United Empire Party 72, 81, 501
university seats 104–5

Vickers, D. 308

Wakefield, W. 321
Wales 84
Walker, G. E. M. 284
Wallace, E. 366, 371, 408
Wansbeck 205
Ward, I. 323, 327
Ward, S. 326
Wardlaw-Milne, J. 341, 380, 498
Warrender, V. 371
Warwick and Leamington 168
Watching Committee 367, 417, 502
Waterhouse, R. 455
Waterloo 215
Wayland, W. 215, 356
Wedgwood, J. 335
Weir, Lord 387
Wells, R. 308
Westminster St George's 186, 214; see also by-elections
Weston, W. 308
Whiteley, J. 318
Whitstable 231
Whittaker, J. 269
Williams, H.:
  and Active Back Benchers' Group 354
  and 'anti-planning' group 353
  career 309, 392, 401
  during Second World War 368, 378, 397
  mentioned 378
Willingdon, Marquess of 492
Willink, H. 413
Wilson, A. 318
Wilson, C. 460
Wilson, L. 278, 304, 369, 373, 374, 500
  as Chief Whip 375, 476
  and 1922 Committee 381
Wimbledon 186
Winchester 167, 168, 204
Windlesham, Lord, see Hennessy, G.
Winterton, Earl:
  on Bonar Law's Cabinet 410
  career 319, 395, 397, 403, 408, 424
  on the Conservative Party 76
  criticism of Lloyd George 478
  on Eyres-Monsell 375–6
  and fall of the Coalition (1922) 402, 500
  on the Labour Party 335
  on parliamentary debate 334–5, 391
  during Second World War 378

suspicion of coalitionism 435
  on Williams 401
  and Young Unionist Group 349
Wirral 168, 186
Withington 151
Wolmer, Lord 80, 216, 365, 410
women
  Conservative appeal to 82, 83–4, 86, 89–90
  opportunities for in Conservative Party 284
  voters 53, 117–19, 133, 230
Women's Tariff Reform League 153
Wood, E.:
  career 397, 404, 405, 425–8
  on conduct of government 41
  and fall of the Coalition (1922) 210, 402
  Foreign Secretary 439, 470
  Leader in the House of Lords 388
  as possible Party Leader 451, 457, 471
  and protectionist policy (1923) 438–9
  on social unity 18
  and Young Unionist Group 349
  mentioned 49, 399, 452, 461, 497
Wood, H. K.:
  on authority of the Party Leader 513
  on Beveridge Report 31
  career 399, 421, 459
  chairman of National Union Executive Committee 263, 265
Woolton, Lord 273, 516
Worcester 170
working class:
  Conservative appeal to 62, 85, 92, 93, 99, 510, 513
  Conservative attitudes to 19, 30, 48, 64, 71, 88–9, 90
  Conservative fears of 38, 54–5, 61, 62
  electoral support from 111–13, 116–17, 121, 509
  in General Strike 47, 64
  and Labour Party 56, 123, 130
  and need for stability 56
  as part of the nation 15, 83
  and parliamentary candidates 200, 271, 311
  and party membership 157–8, 163–4, 296
  and party organization 249, 265, 269–70, 289
  and property 17
  and protectionism 139, 511
  and role of the state 53
  and Socialism 62
  and 'Tory Democracy' 19
  women 119
Working Mens' Clubs 120
Worthington-Evans, L. 214, 410, 436, 437

'YMCA' group 349–50, 351, 420
York, C. 79, 349, 350
Yorkshire Post 95, 499

Young Britons, *see* CONSERVATIVE PARTY, IX – specialist and ancilliary organizations
Young, E. H. 419
Young Unionist Group 349
Younger, G.:
 background 308
 care for the party 514
 on Conservative principles 15
 and fall of the Coalition (1922) 479, 481–2
 and January 1922 election scare 222, 286–7
 on leadership 460
 and National Union Executive Committee 263, 267
 on nature of Party Chairmanship 275
 on the political levy 221
 Party Chairman 273, 274, 280, 281
 and party funds 300, 304, 305
 and party organization 279, 285
 mentioned 230, 277, 278, 416, 466, 500

Zinoviev letter, 61, 91, 108–9, 133, 344
Zionism 65